PSYCHOLOGY THIRD EDITION

Don and Sandra Hockenbury

Take a guided tour of the Psychology, Third Edition, media and supplements—you will be nothing short of amazed! Following are just a few highlights from the updated media and supplements at your disposal on adopting Don and Sandra Hockenbury's innovative and market-leading text.

Unique Assessment Tools

PRINTED TEST BANK

Written by text authors Don and Sandra Hockenbury, this revised and significantly enhanced printed test bank includes over 5,000 multiple-choice, true-false, and short-answer essay questions, plus Learning Objectives for each chapter that correspond to those in the *Instructor's Resource Manual*. Each question is page-referenced to the textbook, identified as a factual/definitional or conceptual/analytical question, and rated for level of difficulty.

⇨ NEW! **The revision of this test bank includes ready-to-use "Quick Tests" for each chapter and a comprehensive final examination.**

⇨ NEW! **The authors have added many easy-level questions.**

Worth is also pleased to offer a Brownstone Computerized Test Bank CD-ROM (Windows and Macintosh compatible). This CD-ROM allows you to add, edit, and scramble questions from the printed test bank, format tests, and import pictures, equations, or media links. The CD-ROM is also the access point for secure online testing. A multifunctional gradebook allows you to track student progress on both printed and online tests. **To learn more, visit www.brownstone.net**

ONLINE QUIZZING at www.worthpublishers.com/hockenbury

Now you can securely quiz students online using prewritten multiple-choice questions for each text chapter. Students receive instant feedback and can take the quizzes multiple times. An online gradebook allows you to view results by quiz, student, or question, or by weekly e-mail reports.

New Video Resources

⇨NEW! **Worth Digital Media Archive CD-ROM**

Dual Platform CD-ROM

This Instructor's Presentation CD-ROM contains a rich collection of more than 30 digitized video clips of classic experiments and research. **Footage includes Albert Bandura's Bobo doll experiment, Harold Takoshian's bystander studies, Piaget's conservation experiment, electrical brain stimulation footage, Harlow's monkey experiments, Milgram's obedience experiments, and Ulric Neisser's selective attention studies.** The Digital Media Archive clips are available in MPEG format and are compatible with Microsoft PowerPoint® software.

⇨NEW! *Psychology: The Human Experience* **Video Teaching Modules**

Available in VHS or DVD-ROM formats

This new series includes more than **three hours of footage** from the new introductory psychology telecourse, *Psychology: The Human Experience*, produced by Coast Learning Systems in collaboration with Worth Publishers. Tied specifically to the Hockenbury text, these brief clips are ideal for lecture openers. Footage contains noted scholars, the latest research, and beautiful animations.

Worth is also pleased to offer the following video series in both **VHS and DVD formats:**
Scientific American Frontiers Video Collection, **Second Edition**
The Mind Video Teaching Modules, **Second Edition**
The Brain Video Teaching Modules, **Second Edition**

New Presentation Resources

OVERHEAD TRANSPARENCY SET

The set includes more than 200 full-color illustrations from the text, including artwork, tables, and full-size photographs of historical figures in psychology, such as William James, Sigmund Freud, and Karen Horney.

IMAGE AND LECTURE GALLERY at www.worthpublishers.com/ILG

Using the Image and Lecture Gallery, you can browse, search, and download all chapter art, illustrations, outlines, and prebuilt PowerPoint presentation files for all Worth titles. Users can also create personal folders for easy organization of the materials.

more ⇨

INSTRUCTOR PRESENTATION CD-ROM FOR *PSYCHOLOGY*, Third Edition
Using the Instructor's Presentation CD-ROM, you can build your classroom presentations around a variety of still and moving images—from the text, from your own sources, even from the Web. The CD-ROM also includes the PowerPoint slide sets described below, which are also available on the Web site.

▷**NEW! CUSTOMIZED PowerPoint® SLIDES FOR *PSYCHOLOGY*, Third Edition**
by Marian Gibney, Phoenix College, at www.worthpublishers.com/hockenbury
Developed by a longtime adopter of the Hockenburys' text, these slides focus on key terms and themes from *Psychology*, Third Edition, and feature tables, graphs, and figures from the text.

▷**NEW! PowerPoint® SLIDES FOR *PSYCHOLOGY*, Third Edition at www.worthpublishers.com/hockenbury**
These customizable PowerPoint slide sets offer two prebuilt versions for each chapter—one featuring chapter text, the other featuring all chapter art and illustrations.

▷**NEW! TOPICS-BASED PowerPoint® SLIDES by Harvey Shulman, Ohio State University,**
at www.worthpublishers.com/hockenbury
Created around a traditional set of lecture topics for any introductory psychology course, these topics-based slides feature PowerPoint-designed tables, text, figures, and photographs. The slides can easily be used as is or integrated with the *Psychology*, Third Edition, PowerPoint slide set.

New Approaches to Online Learning
Companion Web site at http://www.worthpublishers.com/hockenbury
Free to adopters and students
The *Psychology*, Third Edition, Companion Site provides your students with a virtual study guide twenty-four hours a day, seven days a week. **Best of all, these resources are free and do not require any special access codes or passwords.** The tools within the site include

•**Learning Objectives**
•**Interactive Crossword Puzzles**, written by the Hockenburys and tied to chapter key concepts (solutions provided)
•**"Thinking Critically" Exercises**
•**Glosario/Glossary:** An online English-Spanish glossary, tied to each of the textbook chapters, enables students for whom Spanish is their native language to read and understand the content of the text with greater ease. Each glossary entry includes the English term and the Spanish term followed by a definition in Spanish (plus page references). Terms and definitions from the glossary are also available in flashcard format so students can quiz themselves on key terminology in their native language. The **Glosario/Glossary is also available as a book that can be packaged with the text!**
•**Over 150 Annotated Web Links**
•**Online Quizzes**
•**Interactive Animations, Simulations, Demonstrations, and Flashcards**
•**Online Versions of PsychQuest and PsychSim (both authored by Thomas Ludwig, Hope College)**

The *Psychology*, Third Edition, Web site also includes a password-protected Instructor Site that offers a full array of teaching tools, such as text-specific PowerPoint® Slides, an online quiz gradebook, and links to various resources (including WebCT, Blackboard, and the Worth Image and Lecture Gallery).

PsychOnline
Tom Ludwig, Hope College
PsychOnline provides a complete Web-based learning environment for introductory psychology courses incorporating tutorials, interactive activities, simulated lab experiences, lecture demonstrations, reference and core assessment tools. The first course of its kind, PsychOnline was written and edited for online delivery by award-winning media author Thomas Ludwig and is based on the latest research in online learning theory. To learn more or to view a demonstration of PsychOnline, contact your Worth sales representative.

Online Course Materials (WebCT, Blackboard)
As a service for adopters using WebCT or Blackboard course management systems, Worth will provide the electronic instructor and student resources for *Psychology*, Third Edition, in the appropriate format for their system. The files will be organized and prebuilt to match specific software and can be easily downloaded (via the WebCT or Blackboard content showcases) directly onto the department server and can be used to create entire online courses, to provide supplemental materials for existing courses, or for distance learning purposes. Course outlines, prebuilt quizzes, links, activities, and a whole array of materials are included, eliminating hours of work.

PSYCHOLOGY

High Life (collage, 40" x 30", detail)

The stunning artwork that appears on the cover and chapter-opening pages of *Psychology* was created by Phoebe Beasley, an award-winning artist and lithographer. Ms. Beasley's luminous oil paint and tissue paper collages capture the unique, yet universal, life experiences of all kinds of people. Similarly, psychologists study a wide range of human experiences—creativity, love, memory, dreaming, sexuality, growing up and growing old—looking for the general patterns underlying the expression of human individuality. The personal narratives portrayed in Beasley's work, like those in Don and Sandy Hockenbury's chapter Prologues, help us understand and appreciate human behavior.

PSYCHOLOGY THIRD EDITION

Don H. Hockenbury
Tulsa Community College

Sandra E. Hockenbury

WORTH PUBLISHERS

Psychology
Third Edition

Copyright © 2003 by Worth Publishers
All rights reserved.
Printed in the United States of America.
ISBN: 0-7167-5129-1
First printing, 2002

Publisher: Catherine Woods
Senior Development Editor: Sharon Balbos
Executive Marketing Manager: Renée Altier
Associate Managing Editor: Tracey Kuehn
Production Manager: Sarah Segal
Art Director/Cover Design: Barbara Reingold
Text Designer: Lissi Sigillo
Design/Layout: Lee Ann Mahler
Photo Editor: Vikii Wong
Photo Researcher: June L. Whitworth
Illustration Coordinator: Shawn Churchman
Line Art: J/B Woolsey Associates
Composition: Compset Inc.
Printing and Binding: R.R. Donnelley and Sons
Cover Art: Phoebe Beasley

Illustration credits and permissions start on page IC-0 and constitute an extension of the copyright page.

Library of Congress Control Number: 2002104484

Worth Publishers
41 Madison Avenue
New York, New York 10010
www.worthpublishers.com

to TOM

About the Authors

Don and Sandy Hockenbury are the authors of *Psychology* and *Discovering Psychology.* As an author team, they bring their unique talents and abilities to the teaching of introductory psychology.

Don H. Hockenbury is an Assistant Professor of Psychology at Tulsa Community College. Don received his B.S. in psychology and his M.A. in clinical psychology from the University of Tulsa. Before he began his teaching career, Don worked in psychiatric facilities and in private practice. With over 20 years of experience in teaching introductory psychology, Don appreciates the challenges of engaging the diverse students of today's college classrooms and of showing them the scientific nature and the personal relevance of psychology. Before co-authoring *Psychology* and *Discovering Psychology,* Don served as a reviewer and supplements author for several psychology textbooks. Don is an associate member of the American Psychological Association and a member of the American Psychological Society and the American Association for the Advancement of Science.

Sandra E. Hockenbury is a science writer who specializes in psychology. Sandy received her B.A. from Shimer College and her M.A. from the University of Chicago, where she was also a Research Associate at the Institute of Social and Behavioral Pathology. Prior to co-authoring *Psychology* and *Discovering Psychology,* Sandy worked for several years as a psychology editor in both academic and college textbook publishing. Sandy's particular areas of interest are cross-cultural psychology, comparative cognition, and nonconscious processes. Sandy has also taught as an adjunct faculty member at Tulsa Community College. She is a member of the American Psychological Society and the American Association for the Advancement of Science.

Don and Sandy have a 12-year-old daughter named Laura. They also share their home in the woods outside of Tulsa, Oklahoma, with a calorically challenged tailless cat named Nubbin. They are still happily married, despite having co-written two books and numerous other publications.

brief contents

contents

chapter 1
Introduction and Research Methods

CULTURE AND HUMAN BEHAVIOR 1.1: What Is Cross-Cultural
Psychology? 12 ▪ **CRITICAL THINKING 1.2:** What Is Critical
Thinking? 17 ▪ **SCIENCE VERSUS PSEUDOSCIENCE 1.3:** What Is a
Pseudoscience? 34 ▪ **IN FOCUS 1.4:** Questions About the Use of
Animals in Psychological Research 36

chapter 2
Neuroscience and Behavior

chapter 3
Sensation and Perception

chapter 4
Consciousness and Its Variations

chapter 5
Learning

chapter 6
Memory

chapter 7
Thinking, Language, and Intelligence

chapter 8
Motivation and Emotion

chapter 9
Lifespan Development

chapter 10
Gender and Sexuality

chapter 11
Personality

chapter 12
Social Psychology

chapter 13
Stress, Health, and Coping

chapter 14
Psychological Disorders

chapter 15
Therapies

appendix A
Statistics: Understanding Data

Marie D. Thomas   California State University, San Marcos

appendix B
Industrial/Organizational Psychology

Marie Waung   University of Michigan, Dearborn

Welcome to the third edition of Hockenbury & Hockenbury *Psychology*! For those of you who are using Hockenbury & Hockenbury *Psychology* for the first time, this faculty preface will help orient you to the many features of our text, its supplements, and its media package. If you want to get the most out of our teaching package, reading this preface will be well worth your time.

To those of you who used a previous edition of Hockenbury & Hockenbury *Psychology,* thank you for helping make our text a success! Rest assured that we've taken several steps to help make your transition to the new edition as smooth as possible. A complete list of changes in the new edition is available in the Instructor's Section of the *Psychology, Third Edition* companion Web site.

We've been gratified by the enthusiastic response to the two previous editions of *Psychology*. We've especially enjoyed the many e-mails and letters we've received from students who felt that the book was speaking directly to them. Students and faculty alike told us how much they appreciated *Psychology*'s distinctive voice, its inviting learning environment, and the clarity of explanations on every page—qualities we've steadfastly maintained in the third edition.

Like the two previous editions, the third edition reflects our heartfelt belief that psychology is the most exciting science that exists. More so than any other science, psychology speaks to students' lives. Psychology provides a wealth of meaningful and practical insights about behavior and mental processes. Our desire to communicate the excitement and relevance of our scientific discipline to students is one of the main reasons we've spent the last 12 years of our lives researching and writing the first three editions of *Psychology*.

This edition of *Psychology* continues to reflect our commitment to the goals that have guided us as teachers and authors. Once again, we invite you to explore every page of the new edition of *Psychology* so that you can see firsthand how we:

- Communicate both the scientific rigor and personal relevance of psychology
- Show how classic psychological studies help set the stage for today's research
- Clearly explain psychological concepts and how they are linked
- Create a warm, personal learning environment
- Encourage and model critical and scientific thinking
- Expand student awareness of cultural and gender influences
- Actively engage diverse students, including adult learners
- Provide an effective pedagogical system that helps students test for retention and develop more effective learning strategies

What's New in the Third Edition

Almost immediately after the publication of the second edition of *Psychology,* we began the revision process for the third edition. Along with the thoughtful feedback and recommendations we received from our reviewers and colleagues, we also had face-to-face dialogues with approximately 800 students at four different colleges. We are very proud of the fact that student feedback continues to play an important role in shaping our text. The students not only provided constructive—and sometimes creative—suggestions concerning the text and learning aids, but they also reviewed the third edition book design at two different stages of its development. We continue to be impressed by how conscientiously most students approach the task of improving *Psychology* for future students.

After we carefully evaluated the feedback from faculty and students, our vision for the third edition of *Psychology* came into clear focus. Here's what's new in *Psychology*:

New topics and revised discussions to reflect contemporary psychological research

Without sacrificing coverage of classic research and theories that provide the foundations of psychological knowledge, we've taken a fresh look at classic topics in psychology and added a wealth of new topics. Our text now includes a greater emphasis on neuroscience, evolutionary theory, and other emerging trends in psychology. For example, the discussion of the evolutionary perspective in Chapter 1 has been expanded. Chapter 2 has been retitled "Neuroscience and Behavior." Chapter 8, "Motivation and Emotion," has been completely reconceptualized, with evolutionary theory as a guiding theme to unite its diverse topics.

More than 800 new research citations, over half published in 2000, 2001, and 2002

Faculty have told us how much they appreciate our efforts to present interesting *and* current psychology research to students. Keeping up with our incredibly diverse and productive discipline is an ongoing process for us. Just so you know, we personally subscribe to 22 print and 3 electronic psychology journals, and we regularly monitor numerous psychology and science Web sites. The result of our research efforts? There are over 800 new references in the third edition of *Psychology,* more than half of which are 2000, 2001, and 2002 references. Interested faculty are welcome to download a complete list of the new references in *Psychology,* which can be found in the Instructor's Section of our companion Web site. The new citations reflect the many new and updated topics and discussions in the third edition. Here's a sampling:

- Effects of media portrayals of violence and violent video games on aggressive behavior
- Use of subliminal advertising in the 2000 presidential campaign
- How human pheromones influence emotions
- Cultural differences in our earliest memories
- Emotion in nonhuman animals
- The effects of stereotype threat on performance
- Cigarette smoking as a causal factor in mental disorders
- The validity of eye movement desensitization therapy (EMDR)
- The use of "implementation intentions" to help you achieve your goals
- Interpersonal therapy and cognitive-behavioral therapy
- The effects and mechanisms of "club drugs," including ecstasy and ketamine

- The use of the ganzfield procedure in ESP research
- The "tend-and-befriend" stress response
- The sociocultural explanation of gender differences in mate preferences

NEW Focus on Neuroscience feature

The new Focus on Neuroscience feature is the most visible example of our expanded neuroscience coverage throughout the third edition of *Psychology*. As brain-imaging technology has moved into the mainstream of psychology research, it has yielded fascinating insights into the relationship among the brain, behavior, and mental processes. Modern neuroscience techniques have also shed light on some of the classic problems and controversies in psychology. Among these are such questions as: Is hypnosis a distinct brain state? How does meditation differ from simple rest? How do placebos work? Does psychotherapy affect the brain? How do mental images compare to visual images? Why do we enjoy looking at attractive people, and why is falling in love such an intoxicating experience?

In expanding our neuroscience coverage, we stayed keenly attuned to the goal of presenting these findings in language that would be accessible to students. We also felt that it was very important to present neuroscience findings in the context of established psychological knowledge about a particular behavior. Thus, you'll find the new Focus on Neuroscience features positioned close to the broader psychological discussion of a particular topic. A complete listing of the new Focus on Neuroscience features is contained later in this preface.

NEW "Motivation and Emotion" chapter

The topic of motivation, and especially the subtopic of hunger and eating behavior, is an area in which research findings have changed dramatically in the last few years. Similarly, the field of emotion research has changed considerably due to the influence of the evolutionary perspective and new neuroscience findings. After surveying the research, we decided a complete overhaul of the "Motivation and Emotion" chapter was in order. We wanted to present students not only with the latest findings but also with some fascinating psychological issues, such as emotions in nonhuman animals and the kinds of evolutionary forces that might push humans in food-abundant societies to overeat. If you don't normally teach the "Motivation and Emotion" chapter, we encourage you to take a close look at our completely revamped chapter.

Revised and expanded "Learning" chapter

Truth be told, the "Learning" chapter is one of our personal favorites. With each edition we've gone through the "Learning" chapter with a fine-tooth comb looking for ways to make it more interesting, relevant, and understandable to students. In this edition we added more examples, two new sections, a new Critical Thinking box, and expanded coverage of Thorndike's pioneering studies. Of particular note is the new section titled "Classical Conditioning and Drug Use," which addresses the role of classical conditioning in drug tolerance, drug withdrawal, and drug relapse.

Enhanced pedagogical system

If you're new to Hockenbury & Hockenbury *Psychology,* take a look at the Advance Organizers, one of our main pedagogical features. Many students struggle with trying to determine what's important to learn in a particular section. As a pedagogical technique, the Advance Organizer helps direct the student toward the most important ideas, concepts, and information in the section. Each Advance Organizer mentally primes the student for the important information that follows in a way that encourages active learning.

In providing feedback on the second edition, students told us that they wanted the function of the Advance Organizers to be more obvious. They also wanted the Advance Organizers to stand out more so they would be less likely to skip over them as they read. In response to that feedback, we revamped the Advance Organizers so that both the Key Theme and the Key Questions of the section are clearly identified.

You'll find another improvement at the end of each chapter, in the newly designed Chapter Review section. The end-of-chapter review materials are now easier to use and an even more effective tool for students. In response to feedback from instructors, key terms are now boldfaced in the Chapter Review. A Web link for the *Psychology* companion Web site is highlighted in multiple chapters.

NEW photos, illustrations, summary tables, cartoons, and Prologues

It should be obvious that we don't subscribe to the "slap-a-new-cover-on-it-and-call-it-a-new-edition" philosophy of updating textbooks. As you look through our new edition, you'll find that there are many changes, big and small. In response to student feedback, there are more summary tables and cartoons. There are several new illustrations as well as several updated illustrations. There are also a variety of new photos to help illustrate concepts and ideas. And, there are new Prologues in three chapters.

Enhanced Test Bank with NEW QuickTest feature

As the authors of the test bank, we appreciate how important it is for you to have a wide selection of high-quality multiple-choice, true–false, and short-answer essay test questions. In this edition we've added close to 1,000 new test items and developed the new **QuickTest** feature.

Whether you want to test for extensive knowledge of the chapter, ensure that core information is being understood, or simply quiz your students, the QuickTest feature can help you quickly accomplish those goals. The key word in that last sentence is quickly. We've preselected test questions to create QuickTests for you in three ready-to-use configurations: a 50-question multiple-choice test, a 25-question multiple-choice test, and a 25-question true–false quiz. If you're pressed for time, you should find the QuickTest feature to be helpful. Additional information about the new QuickTest feature can be found in the test bank.

Expanded Resources for Instructors

Along with revising and updating, the authors of our Instructor's Resource Manual— Beverly Drinnin, Des Moines Area Community College, and Nancy Melucci, Los Angeles Community College—have added 60 new activities for classroom use. Features that faculty have found useful in previous editions, such as the detailed chapter outlines, continue to be part of the Instructor's Resource Manual. And as we'll describe in "The Supplements" section, we have some significant new additions to our video and CD resources for the third edition.

Features of *Psychology*

For all that is new in the third edition, we were careful to maintain the unique elements that have been so well received in the previous editions. Every feature and element in our text was carefully developed and serves a specific purpose. From comprehensive surveys, reviewers, and our many discussions with faculty and students, we learned what elements people wanted in a text and why they thought those features were important tools that enhanced the learning process. We also surveyed the research literature on text comprehension, student learning, and memory. In the process, we acquired many valuable insights from the work of cognitive and educational psychologists. Described below are the main features of *Psychology* and how those features enhance the learning process.

The Narrative Approach

As you'll quickly discover, our book has a very distinctive voice. From the very first page of this text, the reader comes to know us as people and teachers through carefully selected stories and anecdotes. Some of our friends and relatives also graciously allowed us to tell stories about their lives. The stories are quite varied—some are funny, others are dramatic, and some are deeply personal. All of them are true.

The stories we tell reflect one of the most effective teaching methods—the *narrative approach*. In addition to engaging the reader, each story serves as a pedagogical springboard to illustrate important concepts and ideas. Every story is used to connect new ideas, terms, and ways of looking at behavior to information with which the student is already familiar.

Prologues

As part of the narrative approach, every chapter begins with a **Prologue,** a true story about ordinary people with whom students can readily identify. Each Prologue effectively introduces the chapter's themes and lays the groundwork for explaining why the topics treated by the chapter are important. The Prologue establishes a link between familiar experiences and new information—a key ingredient in facilitating learning. Later in the chapter, we return to the people and stories introduced in the Prologue, further reinforcing the link between familiar experiences and new ways of conceptualizing them.

Logical Organization, Continuity, and Clarity

As you read the chapters in *Psychology,* you'll see that each chapter tells the story of a major topic in psychology in a logical way that flows continuously from beginning to end. Themes are clearly established in the first pages of the chapter. Throughout the chapter, we come back to those themes as we present subtopics and specific research studies. Chapters are very thoughtfully organized so that students can easily see how ideas are connected. The writing is carefully paced to maximize student interest and comprehension. Rather than simply mentioning terms and findings, we explain concepts clearly. And we use concrete analogies and everyday examples, rather than vague or flowery metaphors, to help students grasp abstract concepts and ideas.

Paradoxically, one of the ways that we maintain narrative continuity throughout each chapter is through the use of in-text boxes. The boxes provide an opportunity to explore a particular topic in depth without losing the narrative thread of the chapter.

The **In Focus boxes** do just that—they focus on interesting topics in more depth than the chapter's organization would allow. These boxes highlight interesting research, answer questions that students commonly ask, or show students how psychological research can be applied in their own lives. The third edition of *Psychology* includes the following In Focus boxes:

- Questions About the Use of Animals in Psychological Research (p. 36)
- Phineas Gage, Then and Now (p. 74)
- The Puzzle of the Left-Hander (p. 79)
- Do Pheromones Influence Human Behavior? (p. 109)
- What You *Really* Want to Know About Sleep (p. 145)

---

*A*ssociate the new with the old in some natural and telling way, so that the interest, being shed along from point to point, finally suffuses the entire system of objects. . . . Anecdotes and reminiscences [should] abound in [your] talk; and the shuttle of interest will shoot backward and forward, weaving the new and the old together in a lively and entertaining way.

William James, *Talks to Teachers* (1899)

- What You *Really* Want to Know About Dreams (p. 157)
- Watson, Classical Conditioning, and Advertising (p. 195)
- Biological Preparedness and Conditioned Fears: What Gives You the Creeps? (p. 203)
- Changing the Behavior of Others: Alternatives to Punishment (p. 213)
- Does a High IQ Score Predict Success in Life? (p. 299)
- Detecting Lies: From Polygraphs to the P300 (p. 349)
- Everything You Wanted to Know About Sexual Fantasies (p. 438)
- Explaining Those Amazing Identical-Twin Similarities (p. 483)
- Stress and the Common Cold (p. 552)
- Gender Differences in Responding to Stress: "Tend-and-Befriend" or "Fight-or-Flight?" (p. 562)
- Minimizing the Physical Effects of Stress (p. 564)
- Mary Cover Jones: The First Behavior Therapist (p. 630)
- Using Virtual Reality to Conquer Phobias (p. 632)
- Self-Help Groups: Helping Yourself by Helping Others (p. 642)
- What Every Employee Should Know (p. B-4)
- Differences Between Male and Female Managers (p. B-10)

Scientific Emphasis

Many first-time psychology students walk into the classroom operating on the assumption that psychology is nothing more than common sense or a collection of personal opinions. Clearly, students need to come away from an introductory psychology course with a solid understanding of the scientific nature of the discipline. To help you achieve that goal, in every chapter we show students how the scientific method has been applied to help answer different kinds of questions about behavior and mental processes.

Because we carefully guide students through the details of specific experiments and studies, students develop a solid understanding of how scientific evidence is gathered and the interplay between theory and research. And because we rely on original rather than secondary sources, students get an accurate presentation of both classic and contemporary psychological studies.

One unique way that we highlight the scientific method in *Psychology* is with our trademark **Science Versus Pseudoscience boxes.** In these boxes, students see the importance of subjecting various claims to the standards of scientific evidence. These boxes promote and encourage scientific thinking by focusing on topics that students frequently ask about in class. The third edition of *Psychology* includes the following Science Versus Pseudoscience boxes:

- What Is a Pseudoscience? (p. 34)
- Phrenology: The Bumpy Road to Scientific Progress (p. 64)
- Subliminal Perception (p. 93)
- Iridology (p. 96)
- Biorhythms Versus Circadian Rhythms (p. 141)
- Remembering Past Lives (p. 257)
- Subliminal Self-Help Tapes: Effortless Motivation? (p. 342)
- Is Your Personality Written in the Stars? (p. 485)
- Graphology: The "Write" Way to Assess Personality? (p. 487)
- EMDR: Can You Wave Your Fears Away? (pp. 646–647)

Critical Thinking Emphasis

Another important goal of *Psychology* is to encourage the development of critical thinking skills. To that end, we do not present psychology as a series of terms, definitions, and facts to be skimmed and memorized. Rather, we try to give students an understanding of how particular topics evolved. In doing so, we also demonstrate the process of challenging preconceptions, evaluating evidence, and revising theories based on new evidence. In short, every chapter shows the process of psychological research—and the important role played by critical thinking in that enterprise.

Because we do not shrink from discussing the implications of psychological findings, students come to understand that many important issues in contemporary psychology are far from being settled. Even when research results are consistent, how to interpret those results can sometimes be the subject of considerable debate. As the authors of the text, we very deliberately try to be evenhanded and fair in presenting both side of controversial issues. In encouraging students to join these debates, we often challenge them to be aware of how their own preconceptions and opinions can shape their evaluation of the evidence.

Beyond discussions in the text proper, every chapter includes one or more **Critical Thinking boxes.** These boxes are carefully designed to encourage students to think about the broader implications of psychological research—to strengthen and refine their critical thinking skills by developing their own position on questions and issues that don't always have simple answers. Each Critical Thinking box ends with two or three questions that you can use as a written assignment or for classroom discussions. The third edition of *Psychology* includes the following Critical Thinking boxes:

- What Is Critical Thinking? (p. 17)
- ESP: Can Perception Occur Without Sensation? (pp. 114–115)
- Is Hypnosis a Special State of Consciousness? (pp. 164–165)
- Is Human Freedom Just an Illusion? (pp. 214–215)
- Does "Reel" Violence *Cause* Aggressive Behavior? (pp. 228–229)
- Recovering "Repressed" Memories of Childhood Sexual Abuse (p. 264)
- The Persistence of Unwarranted Beliefs (p. 290)
- Has Evolution Programmed Us to Overeat? (p. 333)
- Emotion in Nonhuman Animals: Laughing Rats, Silly Elephants, and Smiling Dolphins? (pp. 354–355)
- The Effects of Child Care on Attachment and Development (p. 379)
- Are Women *Really* More Emotional Than Men? (p. 415)
- "His" and "Her" Brains? (pp. 416–417)
- Freud Versus Rogers on Human Nature (p. 471)
- Freud Versus Bandura on Human Aggression (p. 476)
- Were Milgram's Obedience Experiments Ethical? (p. 523)
- Do Personality Factors *Cause* Disease? (p. 558)
- Are People with a Mental Illness as Violent as the Media Portrays Them? (p. 574)
- Does Smoking Cause Depression and Other Psychological Disorders? (pp. 592–593)
- Is DID a Real Psychological Disorder? (p. 601)

Cultural Coverage

As you can see in Table 1, we weave cultural coverage throughout many discussions in the text. But because students are usually unfamiliar with cross-cultural psychology, we also highlight specific topics in **Culture and Human Behavior boxes.** These boxes increase student awareness of the importance of culture in many areas of human experience. They are unique in that they go beyond simply describing cultural differences in behavior. Instead, they show students how cultural influences shape behavior and attitudes, including the student's *own* behavior and attitudes. The third edition of *Psychology* includes the following Culture and Human Behavior boxes:

- What Is Cross-Cultural Psychology? (pp. 12–13)
- Culture and the Müller-Lyer Illusion: The Carpentered-World Hypothesis (p. 128)
- Siestas and Naps (p. 148)
- Cultural Differences in Earliest Memories (p. 247)
- Do Cultural Beliefs Affect Memory in Old Age (p. 274)
- The Effect of Language on Perception (p. 294)
- Stereotype Threat: Performing When There's a "Threat in the Air" (p. 311)
- Where Does the Baby Sleep? (p. 377)
- Conflict Between Adolescents and Their Parents (p. 390)
- Evolution and Mate Preferences (p. 426)
- Explaining Failure and Murder: Culture and Attributional Biases (p. 504)
- The Stress of Adapting to a New Culture (p. 545)
- Travel Advisory: The Jerusalem and Florence Syndromes (p. 604)
- Cultural Values and Psychotherapy (p. 649)

Table | 1

Integrated Cultural Coverage

Page(s)	Topic	Page(s)	Topic
In addition to the topics covered in the Culture and Human Behavior boxes, cultural influences are addressed in the following discussions:		155	Cross-cultural study on environmental influences on dream content in Finnish and Palestinian children
11–12	Cross-cultural perspective in contemporary psychology	155–156	Dream themes in different cultures
22	Cross-cultural study of "pace of life" as example of naturalistic observation	166	Meditation in different cultures
		169	Use of psychoactive drugs in different cultures
32–33	Chronic noise and stress in German elementary schoolchildren	170	Racial and ethnic differences in drug metabolism rate
54	Effect of traditional Chinese acupuncture on endorphins	170–171	Cultural norms and patterns of drug use
102	Racial differences in color blindness	170–171	Differences in alcohol use by U.S. ethnic groups
108	Cross-cultural evidence of gender differences in olfactory sensitivity	175	Tobacco and caffeine use in different cultures
		177	Peyote use in religious ceremonies in other cultures
112	Use of acupuncture in traditional Chinese medicine for pain relief	214–215	Clash of B. F. Skinner's philosophy with American cultural ideals and individualistic orientation
112	Pain experience affected by cultural learning experiences	243	Seven-item limit of short-term memory in non-Western cultures

Table continues

Table **1**_{continued}

Integrated Cultural Coverage

Gender Coverage

Along with a specific chapter devoted to gender and sexuality, gender influences and gender differences are also discussed in other chapters. Table 2 shows the integrated coverage of gender-related issues and topics in *Psychology*. To help identify the contributions made by female researchers, the full names of researchers are provided in the References section at the end of the text. When researchers are identified using initials instead of first names (as APA style recommends), many students automatically assume that the researchers are male.

Table 2

Integrated Gender Coverage

Page(s)	Topic	Page(s)	Topic
6	Contributions of Mary Whiton Calkins to psychology	399	Gender and patterns of career development and parenting responsibilities
7	Contributions of Margaret Floy Washburn to psychology	411	Definitions of gender, gender role, and gender identity
20	Declining gender differences in spatial ability—example of meta-analysis	412	Gender stereotypes and gender roles
22–23	Gender and childhood bullying—example of naturalistic observation	413–414	Gender differences and similarities in personality and cognitive abilities
59–61	Endocrine system and effects of sex hormones	415	Gender differences in emotional expression
102	Gender differences in incidence of color blindness	416–417	Sex differences in brain structure
108	Gender differences in olfactory function across cultures	416–417	Gender differences in sexual attitudes and behaviors
114	Gender differences in responses to human chemosignals (pheromones)	418–420	Development of gender identity and gender roles
151	Gender difference in stress-related insomnia following terrorist attacks	420–422	Theories of gender-role development
151–152	Gender differences in incidence of some sleep disorders	423–424	Sex differences in the pattern of human sexual response
156	Gender differences in dream content	424–425	Sexual motivation and sexual behavior
169	Gender influence on drug effects	426	Gender differences in mate preferences
172	Gender and rate of metabolism of alcohol	427–430	Sexual orientation
174	Gender differences in rate of inhalant abuse	432–434	Sex differences in the onset of secondary sex characteristics and sexual behavior
178	Gender differences in effects of MDMA (ecstasy) on the brain	434	Gender stereotypes
293	Language, gender stereotypes, and gender bias	432–439	Gender differences and similarities in sexual attitudes and behavior
331	Gender and dieting behavior	438	Gender and sexual fantasies and paraphilias
331	Gender differences in rates of overweight and obesity	440	Sex differences in the prevalence of sexual problems
332	Sex differences in metabolism rate	440–441	Sex differences in sexual dysfunctions
334	Gender differences in activity level	441–442	Gender identity disorder
335	Gender and sex differences in rate of eating disorders	446–447	Overcoming gender differences during interpersonal conflict
346	Gender similarities and differences in experience and expression of emotion	462–463	Gender in Freud's theory of psychosexual development
354–355	Gender differences in cultural display rules and emotional expression	465	Sexual archetypes (anima, animus) in Jung's personality theory
371–372	Sex differences in genetic transmission of recessive characteristics	466	Horney's critique of Freud's view of female psychosexual development
394–395	Gilligan's research on gender and moral development	468–469	Critique of sexism in Freud's theory
397	Gender differences in friendship patterns and age of first marriage	521	Gender similarities in results of Milgram's obedience studies
		529	Gender and social loafing

Table continues

Table 2 *continued*

Integrated Gender Coverage

Page(s)	Topic	Page(s)	Topic
542–543	Gender differences in frequency, impact, and source of daily hassles	591	Lack of gender differences in prevalence of bipolar disorder
560	Gender differences in social support and effects of social support	596	Gender differences in incidence of paranoid personality disorder
562	Gender differences in responding to stress—the "tend-and-befriend" response	597	Gender differences in incidence of antisocial personality disorder
576	Gender differences in the prevalence of psychological disorders	597–598	Gender differences in incidence of borderline personality disorder
580	Gender differences in prevalence of phobias	608	Paternal age and incidence of schizophrenia
581	Gender differences in prevalence of social phobia	613	Gender differences in number of suicide attempts and in numbers of suicide deaths
583	Gender differences in prevalence of posttraumatic stress disorder	629–630	Contributions of Mary Cover Jones to behavioral therapy
589	Gender differences in prevalence of major depression	632	Sex differences in incidence of enuresis (bedwetting)
589	Gender differences in prevalence of seasonal affective disorder	B10	Gender differences in management style

Neuroscience Coverage

Psychology and neuroscience have become intricately intertwined. Especially in the last decade, the scientific understanding of the brain and its relation to human behavior has grown dramatically. The imaging techniques of brain science—PET scans, MRIs, and functional MRIs—have become familiar terminology to many students, even if they don't completely understand the differences between them. To reflect that growing trend, we have increased our neuroscience coverage to show students how understanding the brain can help explain the complete range of human behavior, from the ordinary to the severely disturbed. Although neuroscience coverage has always been integrated throughout *Psychology*, the third edition marks the introduction of our new **Focus on Neuroscience** feature. Starting with Chapter 2, each chapter contains one or more Focus on Neuroscience features that are designed to complement the broader chapter discussion. Here is a complete list of the new Focus on Neuroscience features in *Psychology:*

- Einstein's Brain: A Case Study (p. 63)
- Understanding Brain-Imaging Techniques (pp. 66–67)
- Watching the Brain Watch Objects (p. 100)
- Imaging the Brain During Peak Meditation Experiences (p. 167)
- Reinforcement and Punishment in the Brain (p. 211)
- Assembling Memories: Echoes and Reflections of Perception (p. 268)
- Seeing Faces and Places in the Mind's Eye (p. 282)
- Dopamine Receptors and Obesity: Eating to Stimulate Brain Reward? (p. 335)
- Do Different Emotions Activate Different Brain Areas? (p. 351)
- Brain Changes During Childhood: Pruning Synaptic Connections (p. 388)
- Romantic Love and the Brain (p. 435)

- Personality Traits and Patterns of Brain Activity (p. 480)
- Brain Reward When Making Eye Contact with Attractive People (p. 502)
- Mind, Body, and the Mysterious Placebo Effect (p. 548)
- The Hallucinating Brain (p. 603)
- Chromosomal Regions Linked to Schizophrenia and Bipolar Disorder (p. 607)
- Schizophrenia: A Wildfire in the Brain (p. 610)
- Comparing Psychotherapy and Antidepressant Medication (p. 656)

Chapter Applications

Among all the sciences, psychology is unique in the degree to which it speaks to our daily lives and applies to everyday problems and concerns. The **Application** at the end of each chapter provides an opportunity to present the findings from psychological research that address a wide variety of problems and concerns. In every Application, we present research-based information in a form that students can use to enhance everyday functioning. As you can see in the following list, topics range from improving self-control to overcoming gender differences in handling interpersonal conflict:

- Evaluating Mass Media Reports About Psychology (pp. 37–38)
- Pumping Neurons: Maximizing Your Brain's Potential (pp. 84–85)
- Strategies to Control Pain (p. 130)
- Improving Sleep and Mental Alertness (p. 180)
- Using Learning Principles to Improve Self-Control (p. 232)
- How to Make Those Memories Last (p. 275)
- A Workshop on Creativity (pp. 313–314)
- Turning Your Goals Into Reality (pp. 361–362)
- Raising Psychologically Healthy Children (pp. 403–405)
- Men, Women, and Conflict: Bridging the Gender Gap (pp. 446–447)
- Possible Selves: Imagine the Possibilities (pp. 491–492)
- The Persuasion Game (pp. 532–533)
- Providing Effective Social Support (p. 567)
- Understanding and Helping to Prevent Suicide (pp. 613–614)
- What to Expect in Psychotherapy (pp. 659–660)

The Pedagogical System

The pedagogical system in *Psychology* was carefully designed to help students identify important information, test for retention, and learn how to learn. It is easily adaptable to an SQ3R approach, for those instructors who have had success with that technique.

As described below, the different elements of this text form a pedagogical system that is very student-friendly, straightforward, and effective. We've found that it appeals to diverse students with varying academic and study skills, enhancing the learning process without being gimmicky or condescending. A special student preface titled **To the Student** on pages xxxvii to xl immediately before Chapter 1 describes the complete pedagogical system and how students can make the most of it.

The pedagogical system has four main components: (1) Advance Organizers, (2) Concept Reviews, (3) Chapter Review, and (4) the *Psychology* third edition Web companion site. Major sections are introduced by an **Advance Organizer** that identifies the section's *Key Theme* followed by a bulleted list of *Key Questions*. Each Advance Organizer mentally primes the student for the important information that is to follow and does so in a way that encourages active learning. Students often struggle with trying to determine what's important to learn in a particular section or chapter. As a pedagogical technique, the Advance Organizer provides a guide that directs the reader toward the most important ideas, concepts, and information in the section. It helps students identify main ideas and distinguish them from supporting evidence and examples.

The **Concept Reviews** encourage students to review and check their learning at appropriate points in the chapter. As you look through the text, you'll see that the Concept Reviews vary in format. They include multiple-choice, matching, short-answer, and true–false questions. Many of the Concept Reviews are interactive exercises that help students transfer their learning to new situations or examples.

Several other in-chapter pedagogical aids support the Advance Organizers and Concept Reviews. A clearly identified **Chapter Outline** provides an overview of topics and organization. Within the chapter, **Key Terms** are set in boldface type and defined in the margin. *Pronunciation guides* are included for difficult or unfamiliar words. Because students often have trouble identifying the most important theorists and researchers, names of **Key People** are set in boldface type within the chapter.

The **Chapter Review** at the end of each chapter contains several elements to help students review for exams. The chapter's **Key Points** are summarized and bulleted under each major section heading. This is followed by a page-referenced list of **Key Terms.** We also provide a page-referenced brief biography of **Key People** at the end of each chapter, mentioning again why each person is important. And the **Concept Review Answers** can be found on the last page of the chapter.

Beyond the learning aids contained in the text, the ***Psychology* Web Companion** contains multiple review activities. At the Web companion site, each chapter has a 15-question *self-scoring practice quiz, flashcards* to rehearse key terms, and *two interactive crossword puzzles.* The *Psychology* companion Web site also contains several other great features, including Thomas Ludwig's award-winning **PsychSIM 4** computer simulations and **PsychQuest** interactive experiments and simulations. The Web companion can be accessed at: **www.worthpublishers.com/hockenbury**

The *Psychology* Teaching Package: Print Supplements

The comprehensive teaching package that accompanies *Psychology* is designed to help you save time and teach more effectively. Many elements of the supplements package will be particularly helpful to the adjunct or part-time instructor. This superb teaching package, expanded in the third edition, includes the following elements:

▪ **Study Guide for *Psychology*,** written by Cornelius Rea, Douglas College, New Westminster, British Columbia, Canada. The Study Guide is carefully designed to help students understand text information and prepare for exams. For every chapter, the study guide includes a Preview and "At a Glance" sections (both provide an overview of and objectives for the chapter). Each major topic includes a progress test, comprised of multiple-choice, matching, and/or true–false questions. The Guide also contains "Graphic Organizers," which encourage students to complete graphs, charts, and flow diagrams that ultimately provide a visual synopsis of text material. End-of-chapter material includes "Something To Think About" sections, which contain thought-provoking questions designed to encourage critical thinking and application of the material.

- **NEW! Glosario/Glossary,** an English-Spanish glossary, is tied to each of the textbook chapters. The Glosario/Glossary will help students whose native language is Spanish read and understand the text contents. Each glossary entry includes the English term and the Spanish term followed by the definition in Spanish plus text page references. **The Glosario/Glossary can be packaged with the text and is also available online.**

- **NEW!** *Psychology: The Human Experience* **Telecourse Study Guide,** written by Ken Hutchins, Orange Coast College, Costa Mesa, California. The new Emmy-award–winning Coast Learning Systems telecourse titled *Psychology: The Human Experience* is based on Hockenbury & Hockenbury *Psychology,* the sole designated text to accompany the telecourse. Ken Hutchins, Don Hockenbury, and Sandra Hockenbury were members of the Faculty Advisory Committee and were closely involved in the development of the telecourse. The Telecourse Study Guide by Ken Hutchins draws clear connections between the text and the telecourse, helping students to get the most out of the learning experience.

- **Instructor's Resources and Binder,** prepared by Beverly Drinnin, Des Moines Area Community College, Wayne Hall, San Jacinto College-Central Campus, and Nancy Melucci, Los Angeles Community College District. The Instructor's Resources include an abundance of materials to aid instructors in planning their courses, including chapter learning objectives, detailed chapter outlines, lecture guides, classroom demonstrations and activities, student exercises, advice on teaching the nontraditional student, and "Psychology in the News" topics. Also included are two **Video Guides,** both written by Don and Sandy Hockenbury. These video guides tie the *Scientific American Teaching Modules* and *The Brain Teaching Modules* directly to the text. Last but not least, the Instructor's Resources include **Crossword Puzzles,** also prepared by Don and Sandy Hockenbury. There are two crossword puzzles for each text chapter and one puzzle for each Appendix. The crossword puzzles are also available as interactive puzzles on the student section of the companion Web site.

- **Test Bank, written by Don and Sandra Hockenbury.** This revised and enhanced printed test bank includes over 5,000 multiple-choice, true–false, and short answer essay questions, plus Learning Objectives for each chapter that correspond to those in the Instructor's Resources. Each question is page-referenced to the textbook, identified as a factual/definitional or conceptual/ analytical question, and keyed to the learning objective. The revision of this test bank has been significantly enhanced to include new ready-to-use "**Quick-Tests**" for each chapter and a comprehensive final examination. The revision also includes a significant number of new easy-level questions.

- **Brownstone's Diploma Computerized Test Bank, Online Testing, and Gradebook** This versatile test-generating software allows instructors to edit, add, or scramble questions; format tests; and administer exams over a local area network or online. The Gradebook software allows you to track student progress and generate grade reports.

- **Full-color transparencies** with more than 200 images, charts, and photos from the text, including archival photographs of famous psychologists.

- The *Scientific American* **Psychology Reader** is a collection of nine articles selected by Don and Sandra Hockenbury from recent issues of *Scientific American* magazine. The Hockenburys have written an introduction and preview of each article, as well as a series of thoughtful discussion questions to encourage classroom discussions.

- **NEW!** *Making Sense of Psychology on the Web* **with CD-ROM** by Connie K. Varnhagen, University of Alberta, is a brief booklet that helps students become discriminating Web users, locate reliable information, evaluate sites, and organize research. The guide includes a CD-ROM containing Research Assistant HyperFolio, intuitive software that enables students to clip bits and pieces of Web sites and other electronic resources (snippets of text, illustrations, video clips, audio clips, and more) and compile them into worksheets and an easily-accessible electronic filing cabinet.

- **NEW!** *The Critical Thinking Companion,* **Second Edition,** by Jane Halonen, James Madison University, and Cynthia Gray, Alverno College. Tied to the main topics in introductory psychology, this engaging handbook includes six categories of critical thinking exercises: pattern recognition, practical problem solving, creative problem solving, scientific critical thinking, psychological reasoning, and perspective taking. The Second Edition has been updated to include six activities per chapter.

- **NEW!** *Scientific American Presents: The Hidden Mind*   In this special edition of *Scientific American* magazine, *The Hidden Mind* updates reports from some of the most notable neuroscientists studying the human brain, including Michael Gazzaniga, Antonio Damasio, Joseph LeDoux, Ursala Bellugi, and Doreen Kimura.

The *Psychology* Teaching Package: Media Supplements

- **NEW!** **Worth Digital Media Archive CD-ROM**   This dual-platform Instructor's Presentation CD-ROM contains a rich collection of more than 40 digitized video clips of classic experiments and research. Footage includes Albert Bandura's Bobo doll experiment, Harold Takoshian's bystander studies, Piaget's conservation experiment, electrical brain stimulation footage, Harlow's monkey experiments, Milgram's obedience study, and Ulric Neisser's selective attention studies. The Digital Media Archive clips are compressed in MPEG format and are compatible with Microsoft PowerPoint software.

- **NEW!** *Psychology: The Human Experience* **Teaching Modules. Available in VHS or DVD formats**   This new Emmy-award–winning series includes more than three hours of footage from the new Introductory Psychology telecourse, *Psychology: The Human Experience,* produced by Coast Learning Systems in collaboration with Worth Publishers. Tied specifically to the Hockenbury text, these brief clips are ideal for lecture. Footage contains noted scholars, the latest research, and beautiful animations.

- *Scientific American Frontiers* **Teaching Modules, Second Edition. Available in VHS or DVD formats**   This updated collection of more than 30 video segments is adapted from the award-winning television series *Scientific American Frontiers.* Hosted by Alan Alda, these 8- to-12 minute teaching modules take your students behind the scenes to see how psychology research is actually conducted. The series features the work of such notable researchers as Daniel Schacter, Michael Gazzaniga, Steven Pinker, Benjamin Beck, Steve Sumi, Renée Baillargeon, Barry Beyerstein, Ray Hyman, Carl Rosengren, Laura Pettito, Barbara Rothbaum, Robert Stickgold, and Irene Pepperberg. The **Faculty Guide** written by Don and Sandra Hockenbury links the modules to specific topics in *Psychology*. These video modules are an excellent resource to stimulate class discussion and interest on a variety of topics.

- *The Brain* **Teaching Modules, Second Edition. Available in VHS or DVD formats**　Along with new modules from the acclaimed PBS series, the second edition of *The Brain Teaching Modules* includes a **Faculty Guide** written by Don and Sandra Hockenbury that links the modules to specific topics in the third edition of *Psychology*. The second edition contains 10 new and 13 revised modules using added material, new audio, and new graphics. Individual segments range from 4 to 12 minutes in length, providing flexibility in highlighting specific topics.

- *The Mind* **Teaching Modules, Second Edition. Available in VHS or DVD formats**　This revised and rich collection of 35 short clips dramatically enhances and illustrates key topics in the lectures and the text. The second edition contains updated segments on language processing, infant cognitive development, genetic factors in alcoholism, and living without memory (featuring a dramatic new interview with Clive Wearing).

- **Presentation Manager Pro to Accompany** *Psychology,* **Third Edition.** This easy-to-operate CD-ROM is compatible with most commercially available presentation software, such as PowerPoint. With Presentation Manager Pro, you can build your classroom presentations around a variety of still and moving images—from *Psychology,* Third Edition, from your own sources, even from the Web. The Instructor's Presentation CD-ROM also includes PowerPoint slides.

- **PowerPoint Slides** are available in four different formats and can be customized to fit your needs. Chapter art and text outlines make up two presentation formats. The third set, developed by longtime Hockenbury adopter Marian Gibney, Phoenix College, focuses on key terms and themes from the text and feature tables, graphs, and figures from the text. The fourth set is developed around a traditional set of lecture topics in any introductory psychology course. These topic-based slides feature PowerPoint–designed tables, figures, and graphs and were created by Harvey Shulman, Ohio State University.

- **PsychInquiry for** *Psychology,* **Third Edition.** Developed by leading multimedia author Thomas Ludwig (author of PsychOnline, PsychSim, and PsychQuest), this new CD-ROM contains dozens of highly interactive activities designed to help students learn about psychological research and to improve their critical thinking. These activities enable students to work hands-on with descriptive, correlational, and experimental research (using observation, surveys, case studies, and experiments) to help them hone the critical thinking mindset required for psychological research. PsychInquiry activities are complete with animations, video, fresh illustrations, and self-assessment instruments that draw students into the discipline and introductory course. In addition to the coverage of core research concepts, PsychInquiry also offers a handful of more extensive research activities for use as classroom projects or lab assignments. Tied specifically to *Psychology,* Third Edition, the CD-ROM includes text-specific chapter quizzes, crossword puzzles, and flashcards (also available on the companion Web site).

- **Hockenbury** *Psychology* **Web Companion at www.worthpublishers.com/ hockenbury** provides students with an online study guide, twenty-four hours a day, seven days a week. Features include Learning Objectives, interactive Crossword Puzzles, Thinking Critically Web activities, annotated Web Links, Online Quizzes, and online versions of **PsychSim** and **PsychQuest** by Thomas Ludwig, Hope College. Instructors can download PowerPoint slides and access the Worth Image and Lecture Gallery.

- **Worth Image and Lecture Gallery at www.worthpublishers.com/ILG** Using the Image and Lecture Gallery, you can browse, search and download all chapter art, illustrations, and pre-built PowerPoint presentation files for all Worth titles. Users can also create personal folders for easy organization of materials.

- **Glosario/Glossary,** an online English–Spanish glossary, is tied to each of the textbook chapters. The Glosario/Glossary will help students whose native language is Spanish read and understand the text contents. Each glossary entry includes the English term and the Spanish term followed by the definition in Spanish plus text page references. Terms and definitions from the glossary will also be available in flashcard format so students can quiz themselves on key terminology in their native language. **The Glosario/Glossary is also available in printed form and can be packaged with the text.**

- **PsychOnline,** by Tom Ludwig, Hope College. *PsychOnline* provides a complete Web-based learning environment for introductory psychology courses incorporating tutorials, interactive activities, simulated lab experiences, lecture demonstrations, reference and core assessment tools. The first course of its kind, *PsychOnline* was written and edited for online delivery by award winning media author, Thomas Ludwig, and is based on the latest research in online learning theory. For those instructors involved in distance education, *PsychOnline* offers an easily accessible, comprehensive content resource available 24 hours a day anywhere in the world. It provides guidance through the content, hands-on activities, and methods of evaluating student progress and understanding. To review *PsychOnline,* visit

  http://cshowcase.webct. com/ [WebCT],
  http://showcase.blackboard.com [Blackboard], or
  http://www.metatext.com

- **Online Course Materials** As a service for adopters using WebCT or Blackboard course management systems, Worth Publishers will provide the electronic instructor and student resources for this text in the appropriate format for their system. The files will be organized and prebuilt to match the specific software and can be easily downloaded (via the WebCT or Blackboard content showcases) directly onto the department server; they can be used to create entire online courses, to provide supplemental materials for existing courses, or for distance learning purposes. Course outlines, prebuilt quizzes, links, activities, and a whole array of materials are included, eliminating hours of work for instructors. For more information please visit www.bfwpub.com/mediaroom.

These print and media supplements are available to all qualified adopters of Hockenbury & Hockenbury *Psychology.* For more information about these supplements, contact your regional Worth/Freeman sales representative or call Faculty Services at 1-800-446-8923.

Acknowledgments

Many talented people contributed to this project. First, we would like to acknowledge the efforts of our supplements team. Our thanks to:

- **Cornelius Rea** at Douglas College in British Columbia, Canada, for once again writing a very effective Student Study Guide.

- **Ken Hutchins** at Orange Coast College, Costa Mesa, California, for writing a thorough telecourse study guide that helps students get the most out of the new Coast Learning Systems Telecourse "Psychology: The Human Experience" and Hockenbury & Hockenbury *Psychology,* the text on which the telecourse is based.

- **Beverly Drinnin** of Des Moines Area Community College, and **Nancy Melucci** of Los Angeles Community College District, for preparing a comprehensive Instructor's Resource Manual with some 60 new activities. Thanks also to **Wayne Hall** of San Jacinto College for his contributions to this supplement.

- **Marian Gibney** at Phoenix College for updating the robust Web Companion.

- **Marie Waung** at the University of Michigan at Dearborn for revising and updating her exceptional appendix on industrial/organizational psychology.

- **Marie D. Thomas** at California State University, San Marcos, for providing a student-friendly statistics appendix.

- **Angela Ruiz Daudet**, translator of the English/Spanish Glosario/Glossary supplement to this text.

As colleagues who care as much as we do about teaching, they have our gratitude for their hard work and commitment to excellence.

We are indebted to our colleagues who acted as reviewers throughout the development of the third edition of *Psychology.* Their thoughtful suggestions and advice helped us refine and strengthen the third edition. To each and every reviewer, thank you for generously sharing your time and candid thoughts with us:

Tricia Alexander, Long Beach City College
Roy F. Baumeister, Case Western Reserve University
Tamara M. Beauboeuf, University of Houston–Downtown
Connie Bosworth, El Paso Community College
Mike Chase, Quincy University
Edward L. Deci, University of Rochester
Robin DesJardin, John Tyler Community College
Harvey R. Schiffman, Rutgers University
N. Clayton Silver, University of Nevada, Las Vegas
Kendra Gilds, Lane Community College
Harvey Ginsburg, Southwest Texas State University
Sally Hill, Bakersfield College
Bryan Hoyt, Fort Hays State University

Louise Katz, Columbia State Community College
Beverly R. King, South Dakota State University
Laura Madson, New Mexico State University
Kam Majer, Glendale Community College
Brent Mallinckrodt, University of Missouri
Doug Mook, University of Virginia
Joel Morgovsky, Brookdale Community College
Denise M. Sloan, Temple University
Richard W. Townsend, Miami–Dade Community College
Marie Waung, University of Michigan at Dearborn
Marcia Wehr, Santa Fe Community College
Cecelia K. Yoder, Oklahoma City Community College

In developing the third edition of *Psychology,* we began by reviewing the comments, suggestions, and ideas from the reviewers who helped shape the second edition of our text. We would like to thank these reviewers for their lasting contributions:

Harry Avis, Sierra College

J. Michael Bailey, Northwestern University

Marie Banich, University of Illinois

Rebecca S. Bigler, University of Wisconsin

Connie Bosworth, El Paso Community College

Robert T. Brown, University of North Caroline/Wilmington

Ann N. Dapice, Rogers University

B. David Das, Elgin Community College

Ernest Dzendolet, University of Massachusetts

David Eckerman, University of North Carolina

Robert Fisher, University of Texas

Peter Flynn, Northern Essex Community College

Elizabeth L. Glisky, University of Arizona

Frank Hagar, Allegany College

Diane F. Halpern, California State University

Richard Harland, West Texas A&M University

Jean Hill, New Mexico Highlands University

Dean Hinshaw, Shasta College

Edassery V. James, Purdue University–Calumet

Jon H. Kaas, Vanderbilt University

Mark Kelland, Lansing Community College

James E. King, University of Arizona

Alfred D. Kornfeld, Eastern Connecticut State University

Ilona Kovacs, Rutgers University

Linda Lawrence, University of New Mexico/Valencia

Richard L. Mascolo, El Camino College

Nancy J. Melucci, El Camino College

Akira Miyake, University of Colorado at Boulder

Carolyn L. Morgan, University of Wisconsin/Whitewater

Hajime Otani, Central Michigan University

W. Gerrod Parrott, Georgetown University

Joan Piroch, Coastal Carolina University

Kathleen Pope, Dixie College

Jack Powell, University of Hartford

James S. Previte, Victor Valley College

Debra Rowe, Oakland Community College

Brett Silverstein, City College of New York

Nancy Simpson, Trident Technical College

Gregory Snodgrass, Southwest Texas State University

Patricia Stephenson, Miami–Dade Community College

Mark Stewart, American River College

Ivonne Tjoe Fat, Rochester Community College

Peter Urcuioli, Purdue University

David G. Webster, Georgia Southern University

Eugene Winograd, Emory University

Brian W. Young, University of Nevada, Las Vegas

Michael J. Zeller, Mankato State University

We are also thankful for the help we received on many other fronts. We are grateful for the support that Don has received from Tulsa Community College. **Dr. Dean VanTrease,** the President of Tulsa Community College, is strongly committed to academic excellence in serving the needs of our diverse student population. He has enthusiastically supported Don's research and writing efforts as well as his presentations at psychology conferences.

Our colleagues and fellow TCC psychology faculty—especially **Phoebe Baker, Cathy Furlong, John Hensley, Cheryl Hyland, Susan Kamphaus, Fern Marrs, Chrystie Meziere, Camille Quinn, and Krena White**—continue to inspire us with their dedication to excellence in teaching. We greatly appreciate their constructive feedback and suggestions. A special note of thanks also goes to **Doug Price,** Associate Dean of Liberal Arts at the Northeast Campus.

The remarkable people who make up **Worth Publishers** have a reputation for producing college textbooks of the highest quality. From the earliest stages of the editorial process to the last stages of the production process, their attention to every detail of this project never wavered. Each one of them played a critical role in helping us produce the best book possible.

At the helm of Hockenbury & Hockenbury *Psychology* is publisher **Catherine Woods.** Through every phase of the project, Catherine has been a reliable source of insight, encouragement, and advice. She embraces the challenge of managing a complicated project, a breakneck schedule, and a pair of sometimes unruly authors with their own ideas about making books. Incredibly, Catherine never loses her sense of humor! (Well, *almost* never.) Catherine is truly a remarkable person, both professionally and personally. It is a privilege to call her our friend.

The soft-spoken demeanor of our developmental editor **Sharon Balbos** (a.k.a. "the velvet glove") disguises her passionate commitment to excellence and uncompromising determination to get all the details right. Sharon's wealth of creative ideas, perceptive suggestions, and organizational skills have all immeasurably improved the third edition of *Psychology* and its supplements. Sharon, you are a pleasure to work with!

The beautiful new design of this second edition owes much of its effectiveness to the creative talents of art director **Barbara Reingold,** who patiently reworked numerous elements until they were just right. We enjoyed the opportunity to work closely with designer **Lee Mahler,** who achieved the extraordinary interaction of text, graphics, boxes, and features that you see on the pages of *Psychology.*

The wonderful photographs throughout this text are due to the hard work and admirable eye of **June Lundborg Whitworth,** who we were delighted to have again as our photo researcher, and of **Vikii Wong,** photo editor. The innovative illustrations by **John Woolsey** and his colleagues at J/B Woolsey Associates help teach psychological concepts better than any art we have seen in a college textbook. And we thank award-winning artist **Phoebe Beasley** for embracing the goals of our book and, once again, graciously allowing us to use her stunning collages for our cover and chapter opening images.

Working diligently behind the scenes, associate managing editor **Tracey Kuehn** never lost her cool (or anything else) throughout the sometimes nerve-wracking production schedule. Tracey's expertise, creativity, and delightful sense of humor were invaluable as she tackled and resolved the inevitable problems that accompany a project of this complexity. Copyeditor **Karen Osborne,** proofreaders **Andrew Roney** and **Michele Kornegay,** and bibliographer **Beverly Wehrli** chased down the gremlins that seem to haunt publishing companies at night and managed to catch just about every one of them.

Up until the very last minute, production manager **Sarah Segal** performed one miracle after another to bring the book to press on schedule. Put simply, Sarah is amazing. In coordinating a bewildering array of technical details, Sarah maintained quality right up until the last page came off the press.

Supplements editors **Graig Donini, Eve Moeller, Stacey Alexander,** and **Betty Probert** brought a new level of expertise, reliability, and dedication to the development and production of a complex supplements package. With conscientious attention to the multitude of details, they expertly coordinated an integrated program of print, video, computer, and Internet supplements. Many thanks, too, to assistant editor **Andrea Musick** for all of her contributions.

The help of **Renée Altier,** executive marketing manager for psychology, was invaluable. With creativity and endless energy, Renée met challenges on numerous fronts to make the third edition of *Psychology* accessible to the widest possible range of instructors and students. The dedication and enthusiasm of marketing coordinator **Caroline Shahbazian** contributed mightily to this effort. We also appreciate the support and leadership of **Tom Scotty,** national sales manager. Special thanks to our longtime friend and adopted family member, **Steve Patrick,** southwest regional manager. You're an inspiration, Steve!

Without question, the success of Hockenbury & Hockenbury *Psychology* has benefited from the help of several very talented people who are no longer with Worth Publishers. Included here are **Thomas Gay, Suzanne Thibodeau, Rochelle Diogenes, Susan Driscoll,** and **Henry Staat.** Collectively, these are some of the most talented people in college publishing, and it has been our privilege to work with and learn from them.

Finally, a few personal acknowledgments are in order. Several friends and family members kindly allowed us to share their stories with you. Sandy's parents, Fern and Erv, who recently celebrated their 53rd wedding anniversary, deserve particular thanks for their constant support and never-ending supply of funny stories. Fern and Erv, we hope that our respect, love, and appreciation comes through every time we tell another funny story about the two of you! We also thank Janeen and Marty, Terry and Jean, Judy, and all the other members of our extended family for their support and encouragement. We are grateful to our niece Katie and to our good friends Asha and Paul, Marcia, Nina and Mike, and Warren for allowing us to tell their stories in our book. Had Richard lived to see *Psychology,* we know he would have been proud to be part of its pages. Special thanks to our good friend Tom Gay, who challenged us to write this book 12 years ago and then guided us along the way. We continue to value Tom's wisdom, sage advice, and delightful sense of humor.

Last but not least, our daughter Laura has lived with this project since its inception and her own conception, as the two events very nearly coincided. Over the years, Laura has become accustomed to postponing many simple pleasures of childhood "until the chapter is done." Now 12 years old, Laura is a high-spirited seventh-grader, aspiring neurosurgeon/comedian/scientist/ oceanographer/photographer, and dedicated pianist. We are blessed to have a daughter who has been a constant source of joy and happiness, laughter and love throughout the writing process. More so than anyone else, Laura's life has been affected by our writing this book.

An Invitation

We hope that you will let us know how you and your students like the third edition of *Psychology.* And as always, we welcome your thoughts, comments, and suggestions! You can write to us in care of Worth Publishers, 41 Madison Avenue, 36th Floor, New York, NY 10010, or contact us via e-mail at:

Psychology3e@cox.net

Above all, we hope that your semester is an enjoyable and successful one as you introduce your students to the most fascinating and personally relevant science that exists.

With best wishes,

Learning from *Psychology*

Welcome to psychology! Our names are Don and Sandy Hockenbury, and we're the authors of your textbook. Every semester we teach several sections of introductory psychology. We wrote this text to help you succeed in the class you are taking. Every aspect of this book has been carefully designed to help you get the most out of your introductory psychology course. Before you begin reading, you will find it well worth your time to take a few minutes to familiarize yourself with the special features and learning aids in this book.

Learning Aids in the Text

Key Theme
- You can enhance your chances for success in psychology by using the learning aids that have been built into this textbook.

Key Questions
- What are the functions of the Prologue, Advance Organizers, Key Terms, Key People, and Concept Reviews?
- What are the functions of the different types of boxes in this text, and why should you read them?
- Where can you go to access a virtual study guide at any time of the day or night, and what study aids are provided?

First, take a look at the **Chapter Outline** at the beginning of each chapter. The Chapter Outline shows you the progression of topics and subtopics that will be covered in the chapter. You might also want to flip through the chapter and browse a bit so you have an idea of what's to come.

Next, read the chapter **Prologue**. The Prologue is a true story about real people. Some of the stories are humorous, some dramatic. We think you will enjoy this special feature, but it will also help you to understand the material in the chapter and why the topics are important. The Prologue will help you relate the new information in this book to experiences that are already familiar to you. In each chapter, we return to the people and stories introduced in the Prologue to help illustrate important concepts and ideas.

As you begin reading the chapter, you will notice several special elements. **Major Sections** are easy to identify because the title uses red-colored type. The beginning of each major section also includes an **Advance Organizer**—a short section preview that looks like the one above.

The **Key Theme** provides you with a brief preview of the material in the section to come. The **Key Questions** will help you focus on the most important material in the section. Keep the questions in mind as you read the section. They will help you identify the most important points in the chapter material. After you finish reading each section, look again at the Advance Organizer. Make sure that you can comfortably answer each question before you go on to the next section. If you want to maximize your understanding of the material, you should write out the answer to each question. You can also use the questions in the Advance Organizer to aid you in taking notes or outlining chapter sections.

Notice that some terms in the chapter are printed in **boldface,** or darker, type. Some of these **Key Terms** may already be familiar to you, but most will be new. The dark type signals that the term has a specialized meaning in psychology. Each Key Term is formally defined within a sentence or two of being introduced. The Key Terms are also defined in the margins, usually on the page upon which they appear. Some Key Terms include a **pronunciation guide** to help you say the word correctly. Occasionally, we also print words in *italic type* to signal either that they are boldfaced terms in another chapter or that they are specialized terms in psychology.

Certain names also appear in boldface type. These are the **Key People**—the researchers or theorists who are especially important within a given area of psychological study. Typically, Key People are the psychologists or other researchers whose names your instructor will expect you to know.

A **Concept Review** appears several times in every chapter. The Concept Reviews contain exercises that allow you to check to make certain that you understand and remember important information. Write down your answers to the questions by filling in the blanks or by circling one of the multiple choices. Then check your work against the correct answers provided at the end of each chapter.

Reviewing for Examinations

The **Chapter Review** at the end of each chapter includes several elements to help you review what you have learned. The **Key Points** section provides a concise summary of the main ideas of the chapter. Because the Key Terms are boldfaced within the summary, you can see them again in the context in which they were introduced and used. All of the chapter's **Key Terms** are listed, along with the pages on which they appear and are defined. You can check your knowledge of the Key Terms by going down the list and defining each term in your own words, then comparing it to information on the page where it is discussed. Brief biographical sketches of the chapter's **Key People** appear at the end of each chapter, along with the page number on which the person was discussed. These brief biographical sketches will help you remember why each scientist is important. The **Concept Review Answers** appear at the very end of the Chapter Review.

Special Features in the Text

Each chapter in *Psychology* has several boxes that focus on different kinds of topics. Take the time to read the boxes, because they are an integral part of each chapter. They also present important information that you may be expected to know for class discussion or tests. There are four types of boxes:

- **Critical Thinking boxes** ask you to stretch your mind a bit, by presenting issues that are provocative or controversial. They will help you actively question the implications of the material that you are learning.

- **Science Versus Pseudoscience boxes** examine the evidence for various popular pseudosciences—from astrology to subliminal motivation tapes. In addition to being interesting in themselves, these boxes will help teach you how to critically evaluate claims and think scientifically.

- **Culture and Human Behavior boxes** are a special feature of this text. Many students are unaware of the importance of cross-cultural research in contemporary psychology. These boxes highlight cultural differences in thinking and behavior, and they will also sensitize you to the ways in which people's behavior, including your own, has been influenced by cultural factors.

- **In Focus boxes** present interesting information or research. Think of them as sidebar discussions. They deal with topics as diverse as sexual fantasies, human pheromones, whether animals dream, and why snakes give so many people the creeps.

There is also a special feature called **Focus on Neuroscience.** The Focus on Neuroscience sections provide clear explanations of intriguing studies that use brain-imaging techniques or genetic analysis to study psychological processes. Among the topics that are highlighted: Einstein's brain, schizophrenic hallucinations, mental images, the placebo effect, and romantic love and the brain.

We think you'll find the **Application** section at the end of each chapter particularly helpful. Each Application provides concrete suggestions to help you deal with a real-life problem or issue. These suggestions are based on psychological research, rather than opinions, anecdotes, or self-help philosophies. The Applications show you how psychology can be applied to a wide variety of everyday concerns. We hope that the Applications make a difference in your life. Because the Applications for Chapters 5, 6, and 8 deal with motivation, study skills, and enhancing memory, you may want to skip ahead and read them right after you finish this student preface.

There are two special appendices at the back of the text. The **Statistics: Understanding Data** appendix discusses how psychologists use statistics to summarize and draw conclusions from the data they have gathered. The **Industrial/Organizational Psychology** appendix describes the branch of psychology that studies human behavior in the workplace. Your instructor may assign one or both of these appendices, or you may want to read them on your own.

Also at the back of this text is a **Glossary** containing the definitions for all Key Terms in the book and the page on which they are discussed in more detail. You can use the **Subject Index** to locate discussions of particular topics and the **Name Index** to locate particular researchers.

The Hockenbury *Psychology* Companion Web Site

The Hockenbury *Psychology* companion Web site provides you with a free virtual study guide, available 24 hours a day, seven days a week. The companion Web site has a wealth of helpful study aids for each chapter in this book. You can take a **Self-Scoring Quiz** or use the **Flashcards** feature to test yourself on the Key Terms. **Drag and Drop Figures** give you an opportunity to match Key Terms to the appropriate parts of a diagram or other graphic. The **Interactive Crossword Puzzles** are a fun way to test your knowledge of Key Terms and ideas. There are two puzzles for each chapter and one for each appendix. **Critical Thinking Exercises** are linked to more than 100 other Web sites, and additional **Annotated Web Links** will allow you to explore psychology on the Internet.

You can visit the Hockenbury companion Web site at the following Internet address:

www.worthpublishers.com/hockenbury

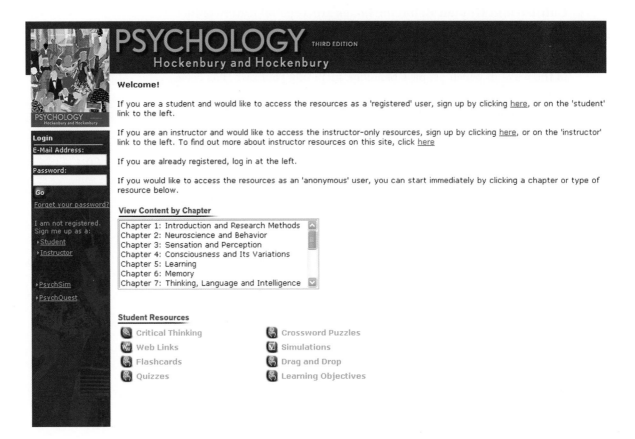

The Study Guide

Beyond the learning aids contained in each chapter and at the *Psychology* home page, we also highly recommend the excellent **Study Guide** that accompanies this text. The Study Guide was written by our colleague, Cornelius Rea, at Douglas College in New Westminster, British Columbia, Canada. Your bookstore should have copies available or will be happy to order it. The ISBN number for the Study Guide is 0716751259. You can also order the Study Guide from one of the online book sellers.

That's it! We hope you enjoy reading and learning from the third edition of *Psychology.* If you want to share your thoughts or suggestions for the fourth edition of this book, you can write to us at the following address:

Don & Sandy Hockenbury
c/o Worth Publishers
41 Madison Avenue, 36th Floor
New York, NY 10010

Or you can contact us at our e-mail address:

Psychology3e@cox.net

Have a great semester!

PSYCHOLOGY

Second Circle Dance

Introduction and Research Methods

chapter **1**

Prologue

Just a Game?

Walking into our 9:30 class on the Monday after Thanksgiving break, we could hear our students already engaged in a lively debate. Stacking our notebooks on the table at the front of the class, we started setting up the overhead projector. We were half-listening to the students talking and arguing when several words seemed to suddenly punctuate the air: *Columbine. Massacre. Plot. Guns. Jocks and preppies. Outcasts.*

We glanced at each other. *Another Columbine?*

"I remember how I felt in high school," Tanisha was saying. "It seemed like every other day was just another chance to get picked on. But I can't imagine wanting to kill everybody at school."

"Jared, what are you guys talking about?" Don asked as he fiddled with the focus on the overhead projector.

"There was this thing on the news this morning about the police arresting five high school students in Massachusetts who were supposedly planning a massacre like the one at Columbine," Jared explained.

"Did anyone get hurt?" Sandy asked.

"Nobody got hurt," Nicole answered. "This one girl warned her favorite teacher not to go to the high school because these other students were planning the attack."

"I was telling them that I heard this military psychologist talk at Holland Hall," Carla added. "He claimed that playing violent video games was involved in the school shootings at Columbine, Jonesboro, and that place in Kentucky."

"Was that the presentation by Dave Grossman?" Sandy asked.

"That was him!" Carla responded. "He had all these graphs showing how violent video games teach kids how to kill and make them think that shooting people is cool."

"I went to his talk," Don said. "Grossman made some interesting points."

"Man, that is so *not* true!" Kyle interjected. "I play *Quake III* and *Doom* all the time. They're fun! They're just shoot-'em-up video games!"

Kyle was one of those students who had stood out in class from the first day. Eighteen years old, six-foot-four, almost always wearing a red OU baseball cap and a "Students for Christ" T-shirt or sweatshirt, a professed Scooby-Doo addict, *and* the top scoring student in all of his classes. Not the kind of young man that you'd expect to be spending his free time racking up kills on a video game.

"It may not affect you, Kyle, but I won't let either of my boys play those kinds of games," Kim said. "I think those boys at Columbine were addicted to those violent video games."

"I don't think the video games had anything to do with it," Kyle insisted. "Those kids had other problems, serious psychological problems."

What Do Psychologists Study? Flirting and friendship, attraction and relationships. Public behavior, private thoughts. Happiness and hope, stress and pessimism. These are just a few of the wide range of topics studied in psychology, which is defined as the science of behavior and mental processes. But whether psychologists study the behavior of a single brain cell or the behavior of a crowd in a football stadium, they rely on the scientific method to guide their investigations.

"Maybe so," Sandy said. "Still, it's an interesting question. I think there's quite a bit of research on that topic."

"Let's talk about this," Don said. "How could you test the claim that violent video games make people more aggressive?" As the discussion continued, we volunteered to look up some of the original research studies on the effects of video games and bring them to the next class. Later in the chapter, you'll see what we uncovered.

As this spontaneous class discussion demonstrated, psychology is a science that speaks to our lives in very real and meaningful ways. Indeed, many of the topics we cover strike a responsive chord in our students. As teachers, we've found that building on the many links between psychological knowledge and our students' personal experiences is a very effective way to learn about psychology.

Throughout this text, you'll see that we frequently relate new information to familiar experiences or use personal examples to illustrate abstract concepts. In linking familiar information to new information, our goal is to build a conceptual bridge between your existing knowledge and the new material that you need to learn. A key component of this approach is the Prologue that opens every chapter. Each Prologue is a true story about real people and events. The Prologue lays the groundwork for the chapter by introducing some of its major themes, and it shows you how those themes are linked to everyday life and familiar situations.

In this introductory chapter, we'll establish the foundation for the rest of the text. We'll build a bridge to the past as you learn about some of the key players who helped establish psychology as a science. One was the famous American psychologist William James. James was a master teacher who understood that information that is personally meaningful is better comprehended and remembered. We'll also establish a bridge to the present as we look at how psychologists investigate questions about behavior and mental processes—including whether playing violent video games can make people more aggressive. We hope that you, like our students, will see how psychological findings can make a difference in your own life.

Welcome to psychology!

The Origins of Psychology

Key Theme

- Today, psychology is defined as the science of behavior and mental processes, a definition that reflects psychology's origins and history.

Key Questions

- How did philosophy and psychology affect the emergence of psychology as a science?
- What roles did Wundt and James play in establishing psychology?
- What were the early schools and approaches in psychology, and how did their views differ?

We begin this introductory chapter by stepping backward in time to answer several important questions: How did psychology begin? When did psychology begin? Who founded psychology as a science?

It's important to consider these historical issues for several reasons. First, students are often surprised at the wide range of topics studied by contemporary psychologists. Those topics can range from the behavior of a single brain cell to the behavior of people in groups, from prenatal development to old age, and from normal behavior and mental processes to severely maladaptive behavior and mental processes. As you become familiar with how psychology began and developed, you'll have a better appreciation for how it has come to encompass such diverse subjects.

Second, you need to understand how the definition of **psychology** has evolved over the past century to what it is today—*the science of behavior and mental processes*. Indeed, the history of psychology is the history of a field struggling to define itself as a separate and unique scientific discipline. The early psychologists struggled with such fundamental issues as:

- How should psychology be defined?
- What is the proper subject matter of psychology?
- Which areas of human experience should be studied?
- What methods should be used to investigate psychological issues?
- Should psychology include the study of nonhuman animal behavior?
- Should psychological findings be used to change or to enhance human behavior?

These debates helped set the tone of the new science, define its scope, and set its limits. Over the past century, the shifting focus of these debates has influenced the topics studied, the emphasis given to particular areas, and the research methods used.

Yet long before these debates began, the seeds for the themes and methods that would eventually evolve into psychology were being planted. As you'll see in the next section, the beginnings of psychology can be traced back for centuries to the writings of the great philosophers.

The Influence of Philosophy

Throughout history, many great philosophers have been concerned with issues that are still important in psychology. Philosophers have tried to explain many psychological processes, such as consciousness, perception, and motivation. For example, more than 2,000 years ago, the Greek philosopher Aristotle (384–323 B.C.) wrote extensively about such topics as sleep, dreaming, the senses, memory, and learning. He also described the traits and dispositions of different types of animals (Robinson, 1997).

Many of Aristotle's ideas remained influential until the beginnings of modern science in the sixteenth and seventeenth centuries. In the early 1600s, French philosopher and mathematician René Descartes (1596–1650) actively speculated about the nature of consciousness. Descartes promoted a doctrine called *interactive dualism*—the idea that mind and body are separate entities that interact to produce sensations, emotions, and other conscious experiences. Today, psychologists continue to debate the relationship between mind and brain.

The great philosophers also laid the groundwork for another issue that would become central to psychology—the *nature–nurture issue*. For centuries, philosophers debated which was more important: the inborn *nature* of the individual or the impact of environmental influences that *nurture* the individual. Psychologists continue to focus on this question, which today is usually framed in terms of *heredity* (nature) versus *environment* (nurture). You'll encounter discussions of this issue in our treatment of many topics in this text, including intelligence (Chapter 7), human development (Chapter 9), gender and sexuality (Chapter 10), personality (Chapter 11), and psychological disorders (Chapter 14).

psychology
The scientific study of behavior and mental processes.

Nature or Nurture? Both mother and daughter are clearly enjoying the experience of painting together. Is the child's interest in painting an expression of her natural tendencies, or is it the result of her mother's encouragement and teaching? Parental influence is just one of many environmental factors that can nurture the developing child's talents, interests, and motives. Are such environmental factors more important than the child's inborn abilities? Originally posed by philosophers hundreds of years ago, such questions continue to interest psychologists today.

Although such issues continue to be discussed in contemporary psychology, there is a key difference between the philosophical debates of centuries ago and the scientific debates of today. The philosophers relied largely on logical reasoning and intuition to arrive at their conclusions. In contrast, modern psychologists base their conclusions on the systematic gathering of evidence to test and support ideas.

As recently as 200 years ago, many influential scientists doubted that human behavior and mental processes could be studied scientifically. Thus, the emergence of psychology as a new and separate science hinged on advances in already established sciences.

The Influence of Physiology

The established science most responsible for the emergence of psychology as a scientific discipline was physiology. *Physiology* is a branch of biology that studies the functions and parts of living organisms, including humans. Beginning in the 1600s, physiologists were becoming increasingly interested in the human brain and its relation to behavior. By the mid-1600s, major brain structures were accurately depicted in anatomical drawings. By the early 1700s, it was discovered that damage to one side of the brain produced a loss of function in the opposite side of the body. And by the early 1800s, scientists were vigorously debating the idea that different brain areas were related to different behavioral functions. We'll discuss this debate more fully in Chapter 2.

Physiologists were also beginning to develop scientific explanations for the functioning of the senses, such as vision and hearing. For example, in the mid-1800s, German physiologist Hermann von Helmholtz developed an explanation for color vision. Collectively, the scientific discoveries made by physiologists were establishing the foundation for an idea that was to prove critical to the emergence of psychology—namely, that scientific methods could be applied to understanding human behavior and mental processes.

Wilhelm Wundt
The Founder of Psychology

By the second half of the 1800s, the stage had been set for the emergence of psychology as a distinct scientific discipline. The leading proponent of this idea was a German physiologist named **Wilhelm Wundt,** who had been an assistant in Helmholtz's laboratory. Like Helmholtz, Wundt applied experimental methods to studying fundamental psychological processes, such as mental reaction times in response to visual or auditory stimuli. For example, Wundt tried to measure precisely how long it took a person to consciously detect the sight and sound of a bell being struck.

A major turning point in psychology occurred in 1874, when Wundt published his landmark text, *Principles of Physiological Psychology.* In this book, Wundt outlined the connections between physiology and psychology. He also promoted his belief that psychology should be established as a separate scientific discipline that would use experimental methods to study mental processes (Fancher, 1996). A few years later, in 1879, Wundt realized that goal when he opened the first psychology research laboratory at the University of Leipzig. Many regard this event as marking the formal beginning of psychology as an experimental science (Bringmann & others, 1997).

Wundt defined psychology as the study of consciousness and emphasized the use of experimental methods to study and measure consciousness. Until he died in 1920, Wundt exerted a strong influence on the development of psychology as a science. Two hundred students from around the world, including many from the United States, traveled to Leipzig to earn doctorates in experimental psychology

Wilhelm Wundt (1832–1920) German physiologist Wilhelm Wundt is generally credited as being the founder of psychology as an experimental science. In 1879, he established the first psychology research laboratory in Leipzig, Germany. By the early 1900s, many American students had come to study at Wundt's facilities, which now occupied several floors at the university. By that time, Wundt's research had expanded to include such topics as cultural psychology and developmental psychology.

under Wundt's direction (Benjamin, 1997). And over the years, some 17,000 students attended Wundt's afternoon lectures on general psychology, which often included demonstrations of devices he had developed to measure mental processes (Blumenthal, 1998).

structuralism
Early school of psychology that emphasized studying the most basic components, or structures, of conscious experiences.

Edward B. Titchener
Structuralism

One of Wundt's most devoted students was a young Englishman named **Edward B. Titchener.** After earning his psychology doctorate in Wundt's laboratory in 1892, Titchener accepted a position at Cornell University in Ithaca, New York. There he established a psychology laboratory that ultimately spanned 26 rooms.

Titchener eventually departed from Wundt's position and developed his own ideas on the nature of psychology. Titchener's approach, called structuralism, became the first major school of thought in psychology. **Structuralism** held that even our most complex conscious experiences could be broken down into elemental *structures,* or component parts, of sensations and feelings. To identify these structures of conscious thought, Titchener trained subjects in a procedure called *introspection.* The subjects would view a simple stimulus, such as a book, and then try to reconstruct their sensations and feelings immediately after viewing it. They might first report on the colors they saw, then the smells, and so on, in the attempt to create a total description of their conscious experience (Tweney, 1997).

In addition to being distinguished as the first school of thought in early psychology, Titchener's structuralism holds the dubious distinction of being the first school to disappear. With Titchener's death in 1927, structuralism as an influential school of thought in psychology essentially ended. But even before Titchener's death, structuralism was often criticized for relying too heavily on the method of introspection.

As noted repeatedly by Wundt and others, introspection had significant limitations (Blumenthal, 1998). First, introspection was an unreliable method of investigation. Different subjects often provided very different introspective reports about the same stimulus. Even subjects well trained in introspection varied in their responses to the same stimulus from trial to trial.

Second, introspection could not be used to study children or animals. Third, complex topics, such as learning, development, mental disorders, and personality, could not be investigated using introspection. In the end, the methods and goals of structuralism were simply too limited to accommodate the rapidly expanding interests of the field of psychology.

Edward B. Titchener (1867–1927) Born in England, Titchener studied with Wundt in Germany and then became a psychology professor at Cornell University in 1892. In contrast to the psychology programs at Harvard and Columbia University at the time, Titchener welcomed women into his graduate program at Cornell. In fact, more women completed their psychology doctorates under Titchener's direction than with any other male psychologist of his generation (Evans, 1991).

William James
Functionalism

By the time Titchener arrived at Cornell University, psychology was already well established in the United States. The main proponent of American psychology was one of Harvard's most outstanding teachers—**William James.** James had first become intrigued by the emerging science of psychology after reading one of Wundt's articles, entitled "Recent Advances in the Field of Physiological Psychology," in the late 1860s.

In the early 1870s, James began teaching a physiology and anatomy class at Harvard University. An intense, enthusiastic teacher, James was prone to changing the subject matter of his classes as his own interests changed (B. Ross, 1991). Gradually, his lectures came to focus more on psychology than on physiology. By the late 1870s, James was teaching classes devoted exclusively to the topic of psychology.

At about the same time, James began writing a comprehensive textbook of psychology, a task that would take him more than a decade. James's *Principles of Psychology* was finally published in two volumes in 1890. Despite its length of more

William James (1842–1910) Harvard professor William James was instrumental in establishing psychology in the United States. In 1890, James published a highly influential text, *Principles of Psychology.* James's ideas became the basis of another early school of psychology, called functionalism, which stressed studying the adaptive and practical functions of human behavior.

functionalism
Early school of psychology that emphasized studying the purpose, or function, of behavior and mental experiences.

psychoanalysis
Personality theory and form of psychotherapy that emphasizes the role of unconscious factors in personality and behavior.

G. Stanley Hall (1844–1924) G. Stanley Hall helped organize psychology in the United States. Among his many achievements, Hall established the first psychology research laboratory in the United States and founded the American Psychological Association. In 1888, Hall became the first president of Clark University in Worcester, Massachusetts.

Mary Whiton Calkins (1863–1930) Under the direction of William James, Mary Whiton Calkins completed all the requirements for a Ph.D. in psychology. Calkins had a distinguished professional career, establishing a psychology laboratory at Wellesley College and becoming the first woman president of the American Psychological Association.

than 1,400 pages, *Principles of Psychology* quickly became the leading psychology textbook. In it, James discussed such diverse topics as brain function, habit, memory, sensation, perception, and emotion. James's dynamic views had an enormous impact on the development of psychology in the United States (Bjork, 1997b).

James's ideas became the basis for a new school of psychology, called functionalism. **Functionalism** stressed the importance of how behavior *functions* to allow people and animals to adapt to their environments. Unlike structuralists, functionalists did not limit their methods to introspection. They expanded the scope of psychology research to include direct observation of living creatures in natural settings. They also examined how psychology could be applied to areas such as education, child rearing, and the work environment.

Both the structuralists and the functionalists thought that psychology should focus on the study of conscious experiences. But the functionalists had very different ideas about the nature of consciousness and how it should be studied. Rather than trying to identify the essential structures of consciousness at a given moment, James saw consciousness as an ongoing stream of mental activity that shifts and changes. As James wrote in *Talks to Teachers* (1899):

> Now the *immediate* fact which psychology, the science of mind, has to study is also the most general fact. It is the fact that in each of us, when awake (and often when asleep) *some kind of consciousness, is always going on.* There is a stream, a succession of states, or waves, or fields (or whatever you please to call them), of knowledge, of feeling, of desire, of deliberation, etc., that constantly pass the repass, and that constitute our inner life. The existence of this is the primal fact, [and] the nature and origin of it form the essential problem, of our science.

Like structuralism, functionalism no longer exists as a distinct school of thought in contemporary psychology. Nevertheless, functionalism's twin themes of the importance of the adaptive role of behavior and the application of psychology to enhance human behavior continue to be evident in modern psychology (D. N. Robinson, 1993).

William James and His Students

Like Wundt, James profoundly influenced psychology through his students, many of whom became prominent American psychologists. Two of James's most notable students were G. Stanley Hall and Mary Whiton Calkins.

In 1878, **G. Stanley Hall** received the first Ph.D. in psychology awarded in the United States. Hall founded the first psychology research laboratory in the United States at Johns Hopkins University in 1883. He also began publishing the *American Journal of Psychology,* the first U.S. journal devoted to psychology. Most important, in 1892, Hall founded the American Psychological Association and was elected its first president (Early & others, 1997). Today, the American Psychological Association (APA) is the world's largest professional organization of psychologists, with more than 150,000 members.

In 1890, **Mary Whiton Calkins** was assigned the task of teaching experimental psychology at a new women's college—Wellesley College. Calkins studied with James at nearby Harvard University. She completed all the requirements for a Ph.D. in psychology. However, Harvard refused to grant her the Ph.D. degree because she was a woman and at the time Harvard was not a coeducational institution.

Although never awarded the degree she had earned, Calkins made several notable contributions to psychology (Stevens & Gardner, 1982). She conducted research in many areas, including dreams, memory, and personality. In 1891 she established a psychological laboratory at Wellesley College. At the turn of the century, she wrote a well-received textbook, titled *Introduction to Psychology*. In 1905, Calkins was elected president of the American Psychological Association— the first woman, but not the last, to hold that position.

Just for the record, the first American woman to earn an official Ph.D. in psychology was **Margaret Floy Washburn.** Washburn was Edward Titchener's first doctoral student at Cornell University. Like Calkins, Washburn made many contributions to psychology despite the discrimination against women that was widespread in higher education at the turn of the twentieth century. Washburn strongly advocated the scientific study of the mental processes of different animal species. In 1908, she published an influential text, titled *The Animal Mind.* Her book summarized research on sensation, perception, learning, and other "inner experiences" of different animal species. In 1921, Washburn became the second woman elected president of the American Psychological Association (Carpenter, 1997).

Sigmund Freud
Psychoanalysis

Wundt, James, and other early psychologists emphasized the study of conscious experiences. But at the turn of the century, new approaches challenged the principles of both structuralism and functionalism.

In Austria, a physician named **Sigmund Freud** was developing an intriguing theory of personality based on uncovering causes of behavior that were *unconscious,* or hidden from the person's conscious awareness. Freud's school of psychological thought, called **psychoanalysis,** emphasized the role of unconscious conflicts in determining behavior and personality. At the invitation of G. Stanley Hall, Freud and some of his colleagues visited the United States in 1909 to lecture on his theory at Clark University.

Freud's psychoanalytic theory of personality and behavior was based largely on his work with his patients and on insights derived from self-analysis. Freud believed that human behavior was motivated by unconscious conflicts that were almost always sexual or aggressive in nature. Past experiences, especially childhood experiences, were thought to be critical in the formation of adult personality and behavior. According to Freud (1904), glimpses of these unconscious impulses are revealed in everyday life in dreams, memory blocks, slips of the tongue, and spontaneous humor. Freud believed that when unconscious conflicts became extreme, psychological disorders could result.

Margaret Floy Washburn (1871–1939) After becoming the first American woman to earn an official Ph.D. in psychology, Washburn went on to a distinguished career. Among her accomplishments, Washburn was the second woman to be elected president of the American Psychological Association.

Sigmund Freud (1856–1939) In 1909, Freud (*front left*) and several other psychoanalysts were invited by G. Stanley Hall (*front center*) to participate at Clark University's 20th anniversary celebration in Worcester, Massachusetts. Freud delivered five lectures on psychoanalysis. Listening in the audience was William James, who later wrote to a friend that Freud struck him as "a man obsessed with fixed ideas" (Rosenzweig, 1997). Carl Jung, who later developed his own theory of personality, is on Hall's right. Ernest Jones, Freud's biographer and translator, is standing behind Hall.

behaviorism
School of psychology and theoretical viewpoint that emphasize the study of observable behaviors, especially as they pertain to the process of learning.

humanistic psychology
School of psychology and theoretical viewpoint that emphasize each person's unique potential for psychological growth and self-direction.

Along with constituting a theory of personality, Freud's psychoanalysis represented a distinct form of psychotherapy. Many of the basic ideas of psychoanalysis continue to influence psychologists and other professionals in the mental health field. In Chapter 11, on personality, and Chapter 15, on psychotherapy, we'll explore Freud's ideas in more detail.

John B. Watson
Behaviorism

The course of psychology changed dramatically in the early 1900s when another approach, called **behaviorism,** emerged as a dominating force. Behaviorism rejected the emphasis on consciousness promoted by structuralism and functionalism. It also flatly rejected Freudian notions about unconscious influences. Instead, behaviorism contended that psychology should focus its scientific investigations strictly on *overt behavior*—observable behaviors that could be objectively measured and verified.

Behaviorism is yet another example of the influence of physiology on psychology. Behaviorism grew out of the pioneering work of a Russian physiologist named **Ivan Pavlov.** Pavlov demonstrated that dogs could learn to associate a neutral stimulus, such as the sound of a bell, with an automatic behavior, such as reflexively salivating to food. Once an association between the sound of the bell and the food was formed, the sound of the bell alone would trigger the salivation reflex in the dog. Pavlov enthusiastically believed he had discovered the mechanism by which all behaviors were learned.

In the United States, a young, dynamic psychologist named **John B. Watson** shared Pavlov's enthusiasm. Watson (1913) championed behaviorism as a new school of psychology. Structuralism was still an influential perspective, but Watson flatly rejected both its method of introspection and its focus on conscious mental processes. As Watson (1924) wrote in his classic book, *Behaviorism:*

Ivan Pavlov

> Behaviorism, on the contrary, holds that the subject matter of human psychology *is the behavior of the human being.* Behaviorism claims that consciousness is neither a definite nor a usable concept. The behaviorist, who has been trained always as an experimentalist, holds, further, that belief in the existence of consciousness goes back to the ancient days of superstition and magic.

The influence of behaviorism on American psychology was enormous. The goal of the behaviorists was to discover the fundamental principles of *learning*—how behavior is acquired and modified in response to environmental influences. For the most part, the behaviorists studied animal behavior under carefully controlled laboratory conditions.

Although Watson left academic psychology in the early 1920s, behaviorism was later championed by an equally forceful proponent—the famous American psychologist **B. F. Skinner.** Like Watson, Skinner believed that psychology should restrict itself to studying outwardly observable behaviors that could be measured and verified. In compelling experimental demonstrations, Skinner systematically used reinforcement or punishment to shape the behavior of rats and pigeons (Bjork, 1997a).

Between Watson and Skinner, behaviorism dominated American psychology for almost half a century (R. Evans, 1999a). During that time, the study of conscious experiences was largely ignored as a topic in psychology (Hilgard, 1992). In Chapter 5, on learning, we'll look at the lives and contributions of Pavlov, Watson, and Skinner in greater detail.

John B. Watson

Three Key People in the Development of Behaviorism Based on the pioneering research of Russian physiologist Ivan Pavlov (1849–1936), American psychologist John B. Watson (1878–1958) founded the school of behaviorism. Behaviorism advocated that psychology should study observable behaviors, not mental processes. Following Watson, B. F. Skinner (1904–1990) continued to champion the ideas of behaviorism. Skinner became one of the most influential psychologists of the twentieth century. Like Watson, he strongly advocated the study of observable behaviors rather than mental processes.

B. F. Skinner

Carl Rogers
Humanistic Psychology

For several decades, behaviorism and psychoanalysis were the perspectives that most influenced the thinking of American psychologists. In the 1950s, a new school of thought emerged, called **humanistic psychology.** Because humanistic psychology was distinctly different from both psychoanalysis and behaviorism, it was sometimes referred to as the "third force" in American psychology (Cain, 2002).

Humanistic psychology was largely founded by American psychologist **Carl Rogers.** Like Freud, Rogers was influenced by his experiences with his psychotherapy clients. However, rather than emphasizing unconscious conflicts, Rogers emphasized the *conscious* experiences of his patients, including each person's unique potential for psychological growth and self-direction. In contrast to the behaviorists, who saw human behavior as being shaped and maintained by environmental causes, Rogers emphasized self-determination, free will, and the importance of choice in human behavior (Bozarth & others, 2002).

Abraham Maslow was another advocate of humanistic psychology. Maslow developed a theory of motivation that emphasized psychological growth, which we discuss in Chapter 8. Like psychoanalysis, humanistic psychology included both influential theories of personality and a form of psychotherapy, which we'll discuss in later chapters.

By briefly stepping backward in time, you've seen how the debates among the key thinkers in psychology's history shaped the development of psychology as a whole. Each of the schools that we've described had an impact on the topics and methods of psychological research. As you'll see throughout this textbook, that impact has been a lasting one.

From the founding of Wundt's laboratory in 1879, psychology has evolved to its current status as a vigorous, dynamic, and diverse science. In the next section, we'll touch on some of the more recent developments in psychology's evolution. We'll also explore the diversity that characterizes contemporary psychology.

Carl Rogers (1902–1987)   Abraham Maslow (1908–1970)

Two Key People in the Development of Humanistic Psychology Carl Rogers and Abraham Maslow were key figures in establishing humanistic psychology. Humanistic psychology emphasized the importance of self-determination, free will, and human potential. The ideas of Carl Rogers have been particularly influential in modern psychotherapy. Abraham Maslow's theory of motivation emphasized the importance of psychological growth.

1.1 R·E·V·I·E·W*

C·O·N·C·E·P·T

Major Schools in Psychology

Identify the school or approach *and* the founder associated with each of the following statements.

1. Psychology should study how behavior and mental processes allow organisms to adapt to their environments.

   School/Approach _____

   Founder _____

2. Psychology should emphasize each person's unique potential for psychological growth and self-directedness.

   School/Approach _____

   Founder _____

3. Psychology should focus on the elements of conscious experiences, using the method of introspection.

   School/Approach _____

   Founder _____

4. Human behavior is strongly influenced by unconscious sexual and aggressive conflicts.

   School/Approach _____

   Founder _____

5. Psychology should scientifically investigate observable behaviors that can be measured objectively and should not study consciousness or mental processes.

   School/Approach _____

   Founder _____

*Note: Answers to Concept Review questions appear on the final page of this and every chapter.

Contemporary Psychology

Key Theme
- As psychology has developed as a discipline, the topics it investigates have become progressively more diverse.

Key Questions
- How do the seven perspectives in psychology differ in emphasis and approach?
- What are psychology's major specialty areas?

Since the 1960s, the range of topics in psychology has become progressively more diverse. And, as psychology's knowledge base has increased, psychology itself has become more specialized (Bower, 1993). Rather than being dominated by a particular approach or school of thought, today's psychologists tend to identify themselves according to (1) the *perspective* they emphasize in investigating psychological topics and (2) the *specialty area* in which they have been trained and practice.

Major Perspectives in Psychology

Any given topic in contemporary psychology can be approached from a variety of perspectives. Each perspective discussed here represents a different emphasis or point of view that can be taken in studying a particular behavior, topic, or issue. As you'll see in this section, the influence of the early schools of psychology is apparent in the first four perspectives that characterize contemporary psychology.

The Biological Perspective

As we've already noted, physiology has played an important role in psychology since it was founded. Today, that influence continues, as is shown by the many psychologists who take the biological perspective. The *biological perspective* emphasizes studying the physical bases of human and animal behavior, including the nervous system, endocrine system, immune system, and genetics.

Interest in the biological perspective has grown in the last few decades, partly because of advances in technology and medicine. For example, in the late 1950s and early 1960s, medications were developed that helped control the symptoms of serious psychological disorders, such as schizophrenia and depression. The relative success of these new drugs sparked new questions about the interaction among biological factors and human behavior, emotions, and thought processes.

Equally important were technological advances that have allowed psychologists and other researchers to explore the human brain as never before. The development of the PET scan, MRI scan, and functional MRI (fMRI) scan allowed scientists to study the structure and activity of the intact brain. These and other advances have produced new insights into the biological bases of memory, learning, mental disorders, and other behaviors. In Chapter 2, we'll explore the biological foundations of behavior in detail.

The Psychodynamic Perspective

The key ideas and themes of Freud's landmark theory of psychoanalysis continue to be important among many psychologists, especially those working in the mental health field. As you'll see in the chapters on personality and therapies, many of Freud's ideas have

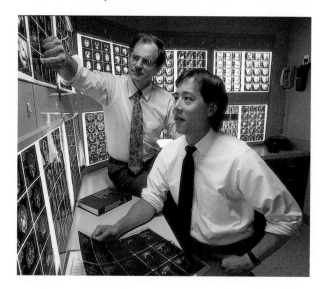

The Biological Perspective Biological psychologists study the physical aspects of behavior and mental processes. Biological psychologists who specialize in the study of the brain and the rest of the nervous system are often called *neuroscientists.* Here, two neuroscientists are conducting a study using brain imaging techniques, which we will discuss further in Chapter 2.

been expanded or modified by his followers. Today, psychologists who take the *psychodynamic perspective* emphasize the importance of unconscious influences, early life experiences, and interpersonal relationships in explaining the underlying dynamics of behavior or in treating people with psychological problems.

The Behavioral Perspective

Watson and Skinner's contention that psychology should focus on observable behaviors and the fundamental laws of learning is evident today in the *behavioral perspective*. Contemporary psychologists who take the behavioral perspective continue to study how behavior is acquired or modified by environmental causes. Many psychologists who work in the area of mental health also emphasize the behavioral perspective in explaining and treating psychological disorders. In Chapter 5, on learning, and Chapter 15, on therapies, we'll discuss different applications of the behavioral perspective.

The Humanistic Perspective

The influence of the work of Carl Rogers and Abraham Maslow continues to be seen among contemporary psychologists who take the humanistic perspective. The *humanistic perspective* focuses on the motivation of people to grow psychologically, the influence of interpersonal relationships on a person's self-concept, and the importance of choice and self-direction in striving to reach one's potential. Like the psychodynamic perspective, the humanistic perspective is often emphasized among psychologists working in the mental health field. You'll encounter the humanistic perspective in the chapters on motivation, personality, and therapies.

The Cognitive Perspective

During the 1960s, psychology experienced a return to the study of how mental processes influence behavior (Evans, 1999c). This movement was called "the cognitive revolution" because it represented a break from traditional behaviorism. Cognitive psychology focused once again on the important role of mental processes in how people process information, develop language, solve problems, and think.

The development of the first computers in the 1950s was a contributing factor to the cognitive revolution. Computers gave psychologists a new model for conceptualizing human mental processes—human thinking, memory, and perception could be understood in terms of an information-processing model. We'll consider the cognitive perspective in several chapters, including Chapter 7, on thinking, language, and intelligence.

The Cross-Cultural Perspective

More recently, psychologists have taken a closer look at how cultural factors influence patterns of behavior—the essence of the *cross-cultural perspective*. By the late 1980s, *cross-cultural psychology* had emerged in full force as large numbers of psychologists began studying the diversity of human behavior in different cultural settings and countries (Segall & others, 1998; Triandis, 1996). In the process, psychologists discovered that some well-established psychological findings that had been thought to be universal were not.

Studying Behavior from Different Psychological Perspectives Psychologists can study a particular behavior, topic, or issue from different perspectives. For example, consider people who risk their lives to help other people in crisis situations, such as immediately following the attacks on the World Trade Center and the Pentagon. Taking the biological perspective, a psychologist might ask whether there were biological differences between rescue workers and other people, such as a genetic predisposition to be risk-takers. In contrast, a psychologist taking the behavioral perspective might study the ways in which risk-taking behaviors are learned through training and rewarded by social recognition, parental approval, and so forth.

Psychology is the one discipline that uniquely encompasses the complex interplay between intrapersonal, biological, interpersonal, and sociostructural determinants of human functioning.

Albert Bandura (2001)

CULTURE AND HUMAN BEHAVIOR 1.1

What Is Cross-Cultural Psychology?

All cultures are simultaneously very similar and very different.

Harry Triandis (1994)

Culture is a broad term that refers to the attitudes, values, beliefs, and behaviors shared by a group of people and communicated from one generation to another (Matsumoto, 2000). A person's sense of cultural identity is influenced by such factors as ethnic background, nationality, race, religion, and language. When this broad definition is applied to people throughout the world, about 4,000 different cultures can be said to exist. Studying the differences among those cultures and the influences of culture on behav-ior are the fundamental goals of **cross-cultural psychology** (Betancourt & López, 1993; Segall & others, 1998).

People around the globe share many attributes: We all eat, sleep, form families, seek happiness, and mourn losses. Yet the way in which we express our human qualities can vary considerably among cultures. *What* we eat, *where* we sleep, and *how* we form families, define happiness, and express sadness can take very different forms in different cultures. That's why cross-cultural psychologist

Harry Triandis (1994) observed, "All cultures are simultaneously very similar and very different."

As we grow up within a given culture, we learn our culture's *norms,* or rules of behavior. Once those cultural norms are understood and internalized, we tend to act in accordance with them without too much thought. For example, according to the dominant cultural norms in the United States, infants, toddlers, and small children are not supposed to routinely sleep in the same bed as their parents. In many other cultures around the world, however, it's taken for granted that children *will* sleep in the same bed as their parents or other adult relatives (Morelli & others, 1992). Members of these other cultures are often surprised and even shocked at the U.S. practice of separating infants and small children from their parents at night. (In Culture and Human Behavior Box 9.1 on page 377, we discuss this topic at greater length.)

Whether considering sleeping habits or hairstyles, most people share a natural tendency to accept their own cultural rules as defining what's "normal." This tendency to use your own culture as the standard for judging other cultures

is called **ethnocentrism** (Triandis, 1994). Although it may be a natural tendency, ethnocentrism can lead to the inability to separate ourselves from our own cultural backgrounds and biases so that we can understand the behaviors of others (Matsumoto, 2000). Ethnocentrism may also prevent us from being aware of how our behavior has been shaped by our own culture.

Some degree of ethnocentrism is probably inevitable, but extreme ethnocentrism can lead to intolerance for other cultures. If we believe that our way of seeing things or behaving is the only proper one, other ways of behaving and thinking may seem not only foreign, but ridiculous, inferior, wrong, or immoral.

In addition to influencing how we behave, culture affects how we define our sense of self (Kitayama & others, 1997; Markus & Kitayama, 1991, 1998). For the most part, the dominant cultures of the United States, Canada, Australia, New Zealand, and Europe can be described as individualistic cultures. **Individualistic cultures** emphasize the needs and goals of the individual over the needs and goals of the group

---

culture
The attitudes, values, beliefs, and behaviors shared by a group of people and communicated from one generation to another.

cross-cultural psychology
Branch of psychology that studies the effects of culture on behavior and mental processes.

ethnocentrism
The belief that one's own culture or ethnic group is superior to all others, and the related tendency to use one's own culture as a standard by which to judge other cultures.

For example, one well-established psychological finding was that people exert more effort on a task when working alone than when working as part of a group, a phenomenon called *social loafing.* First demonstrated in the 1970s, social loafing has been a common finding in many psychological studies conducted with American and European subjects. But when similar studies were conducted with Chinese participants during the 1980s, the opposite was found to be true (see Moghaddam & others, 1993). Chinese participants worked harder on a task when they were part of a group than when they were working alone.

These findings were just the tip of the iceberg. Today, psychologists are keenly attuned to the influence of cultural and ethnic factors on behavior (Matsumoto, 2001). We have included Culture and Human Behavior boxes throughout this textbook to help sensitize you to the influence of culture on behavior—including your own. We describe cross-cultural psychology in more detail in Culture and Human Behavior Box 1.1: What Is Cross-Cultural Psychology?

The Evolutionary Perspective

The newest psychological perspective to gain prominence is that of evolutionary psychology. **Evolutionary psychology** refers to the application of the principles of evolution to explain psychological processes and phenomena (Buss, 1999). The evolutionary perspective has grown out of a renewed interest in the work of En-

(Triandis, 1996). In individualistic societies, social behavior is more strongly influenced by individual preferences and attitudes than by cultural norms and values. In such cultures, the self is seen as *independent,* autonomous, and distinctive. Personal identity is defined by individual achievements, abilities, and accomplishments.

In contrast, **collectivistic cultures** emphasize the needs and goals of the group over the needs and goals of the individual. Social behavior is more heavily influenced by cultural norms than by individual preferences and attitudes. In a collectivistic culture, the self is seen as being much more *interdependent* with others (Simon & others, 1995). Relationships with others and identification with a larger group, such as the family or tribe, are key components of personal identity. The cultures of Asia, Africa, and Central and South America tend to be collectivistic. According to Triandis (1995), about two-thirds of the world's population live in collectivistic cultures.

Cultural Differences in Subway Norms Like thousands of commuters in the United States, many commuters in Tokyo take the subway to work each day. In Japan, however, commuters line up politely behind white lines on the subway platform and patiently wait their turn to board the train. White-gloved conductors obligingly "assist" passengers in boarding by shoving them in from behind, cramming as many people into the subway car as possible. Clearly, the norms that govern subway-riding behavior are very different in American and Japanese cultures.

The distinction between individualistic and collectivistic societies is useful in cross-cultural psychology. Nevertheless, psychologists are careful not to assume that these generalizations are true of *every* member or *every* aspect of a given culture. Many cultures are neither completely individualistic nor completely collectivistic, but fall somewhere between the two extremes (Kagitçibasi, 1997). Equally important, psychologists recognize that there is a great deal of individual variation among the members of every culture (Gudykunst & Bond, 1997). It's important to keep that qualification in mind when cross-cultural findings are discussed, as they will be throughout this book.

The Culture and Human Behavior boxes that we have included in this book will help you learn about human behavior in other cultures. They will also help you understand how culture affects *your* behavior, beliefs, attitudes, and values as well. We hope you will find this feature both interesting and enlightening!

glish naturalist **Charles Darwin.** Darwin's first book on evolution, *On the Origin of Species by Means of Natural Selection,* was published in 1859.

The theory of evolution proposes that the individual members of a species compete for survival. Because of inherited differences, some members of a species are better adapted to their environment than are others. Organisms that inherit characteristics that increase their chances of survival in their particular habitat are more likely to survive, reproduce, and pass on their characteristics to their offspring. Conversely, individuals that inherit less useful characteristics are less likely to survive, reproduce, and pass on their characteristics. This process reflects the principle of *natural selection:* The most adaptive characteristics are "selected" and perpetuated to the next generation.

How is evolutionary theory applied to psychology? Basically, psychologists who take the evolutionary perspective assume that psychological processes are also subject to the principle of natural selection. As David Buss (1995a) writes, a given psychological process exists in the form it does because it "solved a specific problem of individual survival or reproduction recurring over human evolutionary history." That is, those psychological processes that helped individuals adapt to their environments also helped them survive, reproduce, and pass those abilities on to their offspring.

As you consider the role of evolution in shaping modern psychological processes, keep a couple of things in mind. We tend to take the trappings of civilization—governments, transportation systems, factories and manufacturing,

individualistic cultures
Cultures that emphasize the needs and goals of the individual over the needs and goals of the group.

evolutionary psychology
The application of principles of evolution, including natural selection, to explain psychological processes and phenomena.

collectivistic cultures
Cultures that emphasize the needs and goals of the group over the needs and goals of the individual.

The Evolutionary Perspective The evolutionary perspective analyzes behavior in terms of how it increases a species' chances to survive and reproduce. Comparing behaviors across species can often lead to new insights about the adaptive function of a particular behavior. For example, humans, monkeys, and apes are all members of the primate family. Close bonds with caregivers are essential to the primate infant's survival—whether that infant is a golden monkey at a wildlife preserve in northern China or a human infant at a family picnic in Norway.

education and organized medicine—for granted. But these aspects of everyday life developed only recently in the evolutionary history of *Homo sapiens*. What we think of as human history has existed for less than 10,000 years, since the earliest appearance of agriculture.

In contrast, our evolutionary ancestors spent *2 million years* as primitive hunter-gatherers. Our lives as humans living in agricultural, industrial, and postindustrial societies make up less than 1 percent of the time that humans spent as hunter-gatherers. The important point here is that a few thousand years is not long enough for sweeping evolutionary changes to take place. Psychological processes that were adaptations to a prehistoric way of life may continue to exist in the behavioral repertoire of people today. However, some of those processes may not necessarily be adaptive in our modern world (Cosmides & others, 1992).

A revealing example of the usefulness of the evolutionary perspective applied to a problem in modern psychology can be seen in one explanation for phobias. A *phobia* is an extreme fear of a particular object or situation. Even though your average city-dweller is unlikely to be menaced by a snake or a spider, snakes and spiders are two of the most common objects of phobias. Why?

Evolutionary psychologists think they have an answer. To our prehistoric hunter-gatherer ancestors, poisonous snakes and spiders were common—and potentially deadly—threats. Over hundreds of thousands of years, humans who inherited a predisposition to fear and avoid snakes and spiders were more likely to survive and reproduce than humans who did not (Buss, 1999). As you'll see in later chapters, the evolutionary perspective has been applied to many different areas of psychology, including human relationships, mate selection, eating behavior, and emotional responses (Caporael, 2001).

Specialty Areas in Psychology

The following list describes some of the important specialty areas in contemporary psychology, which reflect the enormous diversity of psychology today. Figure 1.1 shows the approximate percentage of American psychologists working in the different specialty areas.

FIGURE 1.1 **Specialty Areas and Employment Settings** The pie chart on the left shows the specialty areas of psychologists who recently received their doctorates. Although many psychologists work in more than one setting, the pie chart on the right shows their primary place of employment.

SOURCES: APA Research Office (2001), National Opinion Research Office (2001), National Science Foundation (2000).

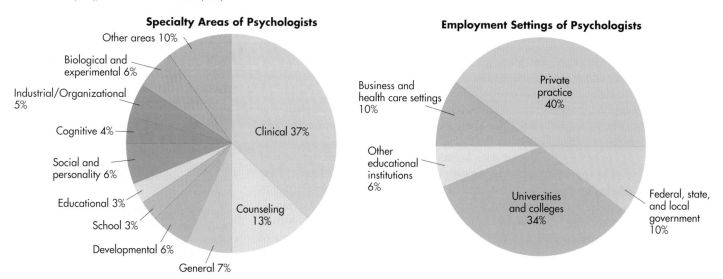

Specialty Areas of Psychologists

Other areas 10%
Biological and experimental 6%
Industrial/Organizational 5%
Cognitive 4%
Social and personality 6%
Educational 3%
School 3%
Developmental 6%
General 7%
Counseling 13%
Clinical 37%

Employment Settings of Psychologists

Business and health care settings 10%
Other educational institutions 6%
Universities and colleges 34%
Private practice 40%
Federal, state, and local government 10%

Biological psychology focuses on the relationship between behavior and the body's physical systems, including the brain and the rest of the nervous system, the endocrine system, the immune system, and genetics.

Cognitive psychology investigates mental processes, including reasoning and thinking, problem solving, memory, perception, mental imagery, and language.

Experimental psychology is the term traditionally used to describe research focused on such basic topics as sensory processes, principles of learning, emotion, and motivation. However, note that experiments are used by psychologists in every area of psychology.

Developmental psychology studies the physical, social, and psychological changes that occur at different ages and stages over the lifespan, from conception to old age.

Social psychology explores how people are affected by their social environments, including how people think about and influence others. Topics as varied as conformity, obedience, persuasion, interpersonal attraction, helping behavior, prejudice, aggression, and social beliefs are studied by social psychologists.

Personality psychology examines individual differences and the characteristics that make each person unique, including how those characteristics originated and developed.

Health psychology focuses on the role of psychological factors in the development, prevention, and treatment of illness. Health psychology includes such areas as stress and coping, the relationship between psychological factors and health, patient–doctor relationships, and ways of promoting health-enhancing behaviors.

Educational psychology studies how people of all ages learn. Educational psychologists help develop the instructional methods and materials used to train people in both educational and work settings. A related field, *school psychology*, focuses on designing programs that promote the intellectual, social, and emotional development of children, including children with special needs.

Industrial/organizational psychology is concerned with the relationship between people and work. This specialty includes such topics as worker productivity and job satisfaction, personnel selection and training, consumer reactions to a company's products or services, and the interaction between people and equipment. Industrial/ organizational psychology is discussed in Appendix B.

Clinical psychology studies the causes, treatment, and prevention of different types of psychological disorders, such as debilitating anxiety or depression, eating disorders, and chronic substance abuse. A related specialty area is *counseling psychology*, which aims to improve everyday functioning by helping people cope more effectively with challenging situations and solve problems in daily living.

Like clinical psychologists, psychiatrists also study the causes, treatment, and prevention of psychological disorders. How are clinical psychologists and psychiatrists

School Psychology There are about 25,000 school psychologists in the United States who provide a variety of psychological services to children, adolescents, and families in public and private schools. School psychologists help teachers, school administrators, and parents understand how children learn and develop. Some of the activities that school psychologists perform include assessing and counseling students with special needs, consulting with parents and school staff, and working with outside agencies to promote learning and development.

Clinical Psychologists Working in private practice, hospitals, or community mental health centers, clinical psychologists have extensive training in psychological disorders, psychotherapy techniques, and psychological testing. Along with conducting psychotherapy with individuals, clinical psychologists also work with married couples, families, and groups of unrelated people.

Rx Privileges for Psychologists? In 2002, New Mexico became the first state to enact legislation authorizing properly trained psychologists to prescribe medications for psychological symptoms. To qualify for prescription privileges, New Mexico psychologists must complete additional coursework and a practicum supervised by a physician. Similar legislation is pending in other states. In areas underserved by mental health professionals, allowing trained psychologists to prescribe medications may help many people who have been unable to gain access to mental health care.

scientific method
A set of assumptions, attitudes, and procedures that guide researchers in creating questions to investigate, in generating evidence, and in drawing conclusions.

critical thinking
The active process of trying to minimize the influence of preconceptions and biases while rationally evaluating evidence, determining what conclusions can be drawn from the evidence, and considering alternative explanations.

different? A *clinical psychologist* typically has a doctorate in psychology, which includes intensive training in treating people with psychological disorders. In contrast, a *psychiatrist* has a medical degree plus years of specialized training in the treatment of psychological disorders. Both clinical psychologists and psychiatrists can treat patients with psychological disorders. However, only psychiatrists can order medical procedures like electroshock treatments. In most of the United States, psychiatrists and some other medical professionals, but not psychologists, can prescribe medications, but that is starting to change. Finally, a *psychoanalyst* is a clinical psychologist, psychiatrist, or other mental health professional with extensive training in Freud's psychoanalytic method of psychotherapy. In Chapter 15 we'll describe other workers in the mental health field, such as clinical social workers, licensed professional counselors, and marriage and family therapists.

In Figure 1.1, you can see the settings in which psychologists work. Despite the diversity of their work settings and interests, psychologists share common methods of investigating facets of human behavior and mental processes. In the next section, we'll look at how psychologists are guided by the scientific method in their efforts to understand behavior and mental processes.

The Scientific Method

Key Theme

■ The scientific method is a set of assumptions, attitudes, and procedures that guide all scientists, including psychologists, in conducting research.

Key Questions

■ What are the four goals of psychology?
■ What assumptions and attitudes are held by psychologists?
■ What characterizes each step of the scientific method?

The four basic goals of psychology are to (1) describe, (2) explain, (3) predict, and (4) control or influence behavior and mental processes. To achieve these goals, psychologists rely on the scientific method. The **scientific method** refers to a set of assumptions, attitudes, and procedures that guide researchers in creating questions to investigate, in generating evidence, and in drawing conclusions.

Like all scientists, psychologists are guided by the basic scientific assumption that *events are lawful* (Rutherford & Ahlgren, 1991). When this scientific assumption is applied to psychology, it means that *psychologists assume that behavior and mental processes follow consistent patterns*. Psychologists are also guided by the assumption that *events are explainable*. Thus, *psychologists assume that behavior and mental processes have a cause or causes that can be understood through careful, systematic study*.

In striving to discover and understand consistent patterns of behavior, psychologists are *open-minded*. They are willing to consider new or alternative explanations of behavior and mental processes. However, their open-minded attitude is tempered by a healthy sense of *scientific skepticism*. That is, psychologists *critically evaluate the evidence* for new findings, especially those that seem contrary to established knowledge. And, in promoting new ideas and findings, psychologists are *cautious* in the claims they make.

Collectively, the assumptions and attitudes that psychologists assume reflect critical thinking. Ideally, you should assume the same set of attitudes as you approach the study of psychology. To learn how to be a better critical thinker, see Critical Thinking Box 1.2: What Is Critical Thinking?

What Is Critical Thinking?

As you'll see throughout this text, many issues in contemporary psychology are far from being settled. And although research findings may have been arrived at in a very objective manner, the *interpretation* of what findings mean and how they should be applied can be a matter of considerable debate. In short, there is a subjective side to *any* science, but subjectivity is especially prominent in discussions of psychological research because psychology tackles topics and issues that concern people from all walks of life.

As you look at the evidence that psychology has to offer on many topics, we want to encourage you to engage in critical thinking. In general, *critical thinking* refers to *actively questioning* statements rather than blindly accepting them. More precisely, we define **critical thinking** as the active process of:

- Trying to minimize the influence of preconceptions and biases while rationally evaluating evidence.

- Determining the conclusions that can be drawn from the evidence.

- Considering alternative explanations.

In the following list we summarize some of the key attitudes and mental skills that characterize critical thinking. You may already use many of these skills in everyday life to make decisions and form opinions.

1. The critical thinker can assume other perspectives.

Critical thinkers are not imprisoned by their own points of view. Nor are they limited in their capacity to imagine life experiences and perspectives that are fundamentally different from their own. Rather, the critical thinker strives to understand and evaluate issues from many different angles. This aspect of critical thinking can be particularly challenging when the issue is emotionally charged and you have strong personal feelings about the topic.

2. The critical thinker is aware of biases and assumptions.

In evaluating evidence and ideas, critical thinkers strive to identify the biases and assumptions that are inherent in

BIZARRO   By DAN PIRARO

CAPRICORN: TODAY IS A GOOD DAY TO MAKE IMPORTANT DECISIONS ABOUT YOUR LIFE BASED ON ARBITRARY NONSENSE WRITTEN BY AN ANONYMOUS STRANGER IN A NEWSPAPER.

any argument. Critical thinkers also try to identify and minimize the influence of their *own* biases. It's difficult to apply this critical thinking skill when you are attempting to rationally evaluate ideas that contradict your own biases.

3. The critical thinker is flexible yet maintains an attitude of healthy skepticism.

Critical thinkers are open to new information, ideas, and claims. They genuinely consider alternative explanations and possibilities. However, this open-mindedness is tempered by a healthy sense of skepticism, as the critical thinker consistently asks, "What evidence supports that claim?" It's especially challenging to critically evaluate new claims that you *hope* are true, such as "Learn while you sleep!" or "Shed pounds effortlessly!"

4. The critical thinker engages in reflective thinking.

Critical thinkers avoid knee-jerk responses. Instead, critical thinkers are *reflective*. Most complex issues are unlikely to have a simple resolution. Therefore, critical thinkers resist the temptation to sidestep complexity by boiling an issue down to an either/or, yes/no kind of proposition. Instead, the critical thinker *expects* and *accepts* complexity (Halpern, 1998). It's not always easy to think reflectively and ac-

cept complexity when what you really want is a simple or instant answer.

5. The critical thinker scrutinizes the evidence before drawing conclusions.

Critical thinkers strive to weigh all the available evidence *before* arriving at conclusions. And, in evaluating evidence, critical thinkers distinguish between *empirical evidence* and *opinions* based on feelings or personal experience. It can be particularly difficult to scrutinize the evidence when the opinions and feelings that are used to bolster an argument happen to be the same as your own private opinions and feelings.

As you can see, critical thinking is not a single skill, but rather a *set* of attitudes and thinking skills. As is true with any set of skills, you can get better at these skills with practice. That's one reason we've included Critical Thinking boxes in many chapters of this text.

You'll discover that these Critical Thinking boxes do not follow a rigid formula but are very diverse. Some will challenge your preconceptions about certain topics. Others will invite you to take sides in the debates of some of the most important contributors to modern psychology. For example, in Chapter 5, you'll have the opportunity to debate the issue of free will with one of the most influential psychologists of the twentieth century, B. F. Skinner. Other Critical Thinking boxes will help you identify and critically evaluate the evidence for various phenomena—from the effects of media violence to animal emotions. In every case, our goal is to encourage you to actively use your critical thinking skills.

We hope you enjoy this feature!

Critical Thinking Questions

- Why would other people want to discourage you from thinking critically?

- In what situations is it probably most important for you to exercise critical thinking skills?

The Steps in the Scientific Method
Seeking Answers

Like any science, psychology is based on **empirical evidence**—evidence that is the result of objective observation, measurement, and experimentation. As part of the overall process of producing empirical evidence, psychologists follow the four basic steps of the scientific method. In a nutshell, these steps are:

- Formulate a specific question that can be tested.
- Design a study to collect relevant data.
- Analyze the data to arrive at conclusions.
- Report the results.

Following the basic guidelines of the scientific method does not guarantee that valid conclusions will be reached. However, these steps do help guard against bias and minimize the chance for error and faulty conclusions. Let's look at some of the key concepts associated with each step of the scientific method.

Step 1. Formulate a Hypothesis That Can Be Tested Empirically

Once a researcher has identified a question or an issue to investigate, he or she must formulate a hypothesis that can be tested empirically. Formally, a **hypothesis** is a tentative statement that describes the relationship between two or more variables. A hypothesis is often stated as a specific prediction that can be empirically tested, such as "psychological stress increases the likelihood of physical illness."

The **variables** contained in any given hypothesis are simply the factors that can vary, or change. These changes must be capable of being observed, measured, and verified. The psychologist must provide an operational definition of each variable to be investigated. An **operational definition** defines the variable in terms of how it is to be measured, manipulated, or changed.

Operational definitions are important because many of the concepts that psychologists investigate—such as memory, happiness, or stress—can be measured in more than one way. In providing operational definitions of the variables in the study, the researcher spells out in very concrete and precise terms how the variables will be manipulated or measured. Thus, other researchers can understand exactly how the variables were measured or manipulated in a particular study.

For example, consider the hypothesis that negativity reduces marital stability (see Karney & Bradbury, 1995). To test this hypothesis, you would need to formulate an operational definition of each variable. How could you operationally define "negativity" and "marital stability"? What could you measure?

You could operationally define negativity in many different ways. For example, you might operationally define negativity as the number of arguments the couple has per month or as the number of critical comments each partner made about the other in a one-hour interview. In a similar way, you would have to devise an operational definition for marital stability, such as the number of times the couple has separated.

Although operational definitions may sometimes sound

Formulating a Hypothesis: Is It Dangerous to Talk on a Cell Phone While Driving? Hypotheses are often generated from everyday observations. For example, many people believe that talking on a cell phone while you're driving increases the likelihood that you'll get into a traffic accident. How could a psychologist investigate this question? What kinds of variables would need to be operationally defined?

completely arbitrary, they usually are not. As research develops on a particular topic in psychology, whether that topic is happiness, creativity, or loneliness, methods of measuring the variable in question become established. For example, a standard measure of loneliness is the 20-item *UCLA Loneliness Scale*. The scale produces a loneliness score between 20 (very low loneliness) and 80 (very high loneliness). Thus, a widely accepted operational definition of loneliness is a person's score on the UCLA Loneliness Scale (Gambrill, 1995a).

Step 2. Design the Study and Collect the Data

This step involves deciding which research method to use for collecting data. There are two basic categories of research methods—*descriptive* and *experimental*. Each research method answers different kinds of questions and provides different kinds of evidence.

Descriptive methods are research strategies for *observing* and *describing* behavior, including identifying the factors that seem to be associated with a particular phenomenon. Descriptive methods answer the who, what, where, and when kinds of questions about behavior. Who engages in a particular behavior? What factors or events seem to be associated with the behavior? Where does the behavior occur? When does the behavior occur? How often? In the next section, we'll discuss commonly used descriptive methods, including *naturalistic observation, surveys, case studies,* and *correlational studies.*

In contrast, the *experimental method* is used to show that one variable causes change in a second variable. In an experiment, the researcher deliberately varies one factor, then measures the changes produced in a second factor. Ideally, all experimental conditions are kept as constant as possible except for the factor that the researcher systematically varies. Then, if changes occur in the second factor, those changes can be attributed to the variations in the first factor.

For example, suppose a psychologist wished to study the effect of temperature on aggressive behavior. The researcher might systematically vary the temperature in a room and then measure how the frequency of aggressive behaviors was affected by the change in the temperature. As you'll see shortly, there are numerous issues involved in designing a good experiment.

Step 3. Analyze the Data and Draw Conclusions

Once observations have been made and measurements have been collected, the raw data need to be summarized and analyzed. Researchers use the methods of a branch of mathematics known as **statistics** to summarize, analyze, and draw conclusions about the data they have collected.

Researchers rely on statistics to determine whether their results support their hypotheses. They also use statistics to determine whether their findings are statistically significant. If a finding is **statistically significant,** it means that the results are not very likely to have occurred by chance. As a rule, statistically significant results confirm the hypothesis. Appendix A provides a more detailed discussion of the use of statistics in psychology research.

Keep in mind that statistical significance and practical significance are not necessarily the same thing. If a study involves a large number of participants, even small differences among groups of subjects may result in a statistically significant finding. But the actual average differences may be so small as to have little practical significance or importance. For example, a recent study tried to identify risk factors for people who attempt suicide (Mann & others, 1999). One statistically significant finding was that suicide attempters had fewer years of education (12.7 years) as compared to nonattempters (14 years). In practical

empirical evidence
Evidence that is based upon objective observation, measurement, and/or experimentation.

hypothesis
(high-POTH-eh-sis) A tentative statement about the relationship between two or more variables.

variable
A factor that can vary, or change, in ways that can be observed, measured, and verified.

operational definition
A precise description of how the variables in a study will be manipulated or measured.

statistics
A branch of mathematics used by researchers to summarize data and draw conclusions based on the data.

statistically significant
A mathematical indication that research results are not very likely to have occurred by chance.

terms, however, the difference was not substantial enough to be clinically meaningful in trying to help identify people who pose a suicide risk. So remember that a statistically significant result is simply one that is not very likely to have occurred by chance. Whether the finding is significant in the everyday sense of being important is another matter altogether.

A statistical technique called **meta-analysis** is increasingly being used in psychology to analyze the results of many research studies on a specific topic. Basically, meta-analysis involves pooling the results of several studies into a single analysis. By creating one large pool of data to be analyzed, meta-analysis can sometimes reveal overall trends that may not be evident in individual studies. Meta-analysis is especially useful when a particular issue has generated a large number of studies, some of which have produced weak or contradictory results.

For example, suppose you wanted to pool research done on gender differences in spatial abilities, such as the ability to mentally rotate an image (see Figure 1.2). Researchers Daniel Voyer, Susan Voyer, and M. P. Bryden (1995) used meta-analysis to combine the results of 286 separate studies investigating gender differences in spatial abilities. The meta-analysis revealed that males tend to do better than do females on some, but not all, tests of spatial ability. The meta-analysis also showed that gender differences in spatial ability have decreased in recent years. One possible explanation for this decrease is that changing educational practices have helped narrow the gap between males and females on spatial abilities.

Circle the figures on the right that can be rotated (without being lifted off the page) to exactly match the one on the left.

FIGURE 1.2 Example of a Spatial Ability Test Item *Spatial abilities* are involved in tasks that require the actual or mental manipulation of objects in space, such as mentally rotating objects or reading maps. Shown here is an example from one test of spatial ability, the Card Rotations Test. A meta-analysis conducted by Daniel Voyer, Susan Voyer, and M. P. Bryden (1995) found that males tend to do better than females on this type of spatial ability test.

SOURCE: Plomin & DeFries (1998).

Step 4. Report the Findings

For advances to be made in any scientific discipline, researchers must publish or share their findings with other scientists. In addition to reporting their results, psychologists provide a detailed description of the study itself, including the following:

- Who participated in the study
- How participants were selected
- How variables were operationally defined
- What procedures or methods were used
- How the data were analyzed
- What the results seem to suggest

Describing the precise details of the study makes it possible for other investigators to **replicate,** or repeat, the study. Replication is an important part of the scientific process. When a study is replicated and the same basic results are obtained again, scientific *confidence* that the results are accurate is increased. Conversely, if the replication of a study fails to produce the same basic findings, confidence in the original findings is reduced.

One way in which psychologists report their findings is by formally presenting their research at a professional conference. For example, thousands of psychologists gather every year at the annual meetings of the *American Psychological Association (APA)* and the *American Psychological Society (APS)* to share and discuss new research findings.

A researcher can also write a paper summarizing the study and submit it to one of the many psychology journals for publication. Before accepting papers for publication, most psychology journals send them to other psychologists to review. The reviewers critically evaluate different aspects of a study, including how the results were analyzed. If the study conforms to the principles of sound scientific

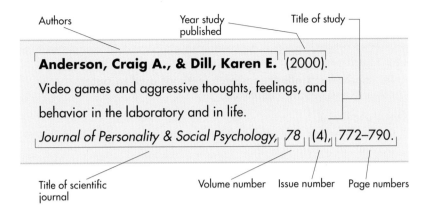

Authors — Year study published — Title of study

Anderson, Craig A., & Dill, Karen E. (2000).
Video games and aggressive thoughts, feelings, and
behavior in the laboratory and in life.
Journal of Personality & Social Psychology, 78, (4), 772–790.

Title of scientific journal — Volume number — Issue number — Page numbers

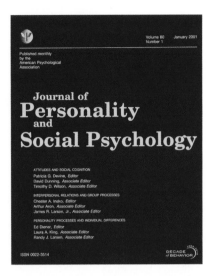

research and contributes to the existing knowledge base, the paper is accepted for publication.

Some of the leading psychology journals include the *Journal of Personality and Social Psychology, Developmental Psychology,* and the *Journal of Abnormal Psychology.* These journals represent forums for presenting research in different specialty areas of psychology. Other important psychology journals, such as *Psychological Science, American Psychologist, Psychological Bulletin,* and *Psychological Review,* cover a broad spectrum of topics.

Throughout this text, you'll see citations that look like the following: (Anderson & Dill, 2000). These citations identify the sources of the research and ideas that are being discussed. The citation tells you the author or authors (Anderson & Dill) of the published study and the year (2000) in which the study was published. Using this information, you can find the complete reference in the alphabetized References section at the back of this text. The complete reference lists the authors' full names, the article title, and the journal or book in which the article was published. Figure 1.3 shows you how to interpret the different parts of a typical journal reference.

FIGURE 1.3 How to Read a Journal Reference Using the References section at the back of this text, you can find the complete source for each citation that appears in a chapter. This figure shows the different components of a typical journal reference. In the chapter itself, the citation for this particular reference would read "(Anderson & Dill, 2000)."

Building Theories: Integrating the Findings

As research findings accumulate from individual studies, eventually theories develop. A **theory,** or *model,* is a tentative explanation that tries to account for diverse findings on the same topic. Note that theories are *not* the same as hypotheses. A hypothesis is a specific question or prediction to be tested. In contrast, a theory integrates and summarizes a large number of findings and observations. Along with explaining existing results, a good theory often generates predictions and new hypotheses that can be tested by further research.

As you encounter different theories, try to remember that theories are *tools* for explaining behavior and mental processes, not statements of absolute fact. Like any tool, the value of a theory is determined by its usefulness. A useful theory is one that furthers the understanding of behavior, allows testable predictions to be made, and stimulates new research. Often, more than one theory proves to be useful in explaining a particular area of behavior or mental processes, such as the development of personality or the experience of emotion.

It's also important to remember that theories often reflect the *self-correcting nature of the scientific enterprise.* In other words, when new research findings challenge established ways of thinking about a phenomenon, theories are expanded, modified, and even replaced. Thus, as the knowledge base of psychology evolves and changes, theories evolve and change to produce more accurate and useful explanations of behavior and mental processes.

meta-analysis
A statistical technique that involves combining and analyzing the results of many research studies on a specific topic in order to identify overall trends.

replicate
To repeat or duplicate a scientific study in order to increase confidence in the validity of the original findings.

theory
A tentative explanation that tries to integrate and account for the relationship of various findings and observations.

Descriptive Methods

Key Theme
- Descriptive methods are research methods used to systematically observe and describe behavior.

Key Questions
- What are naturalistic observation and case study research, and why and how are they conducted?
- What are surveys, and why is random selection important in survey research?
- What are the advantages and disadvantages of each descriptive method?

Descriptive methods are research strategies for observing and describing behavior. Using descriptive methods, researchers can answer important questions, such as when certain behaviors take place, how often they occur, and whether they are related to other factors, such as a person's age, ethnic group, or educational level. As you'll see in this section, descriptive methods can provide a wealth of information about behavior, especially behaviors that would be difficult or impossible to study experimentally.

Naturalistic Observation
The Science of People- and Animal-Watching

When psychologists systematically observe and record behaviors as they occur in their natural settings, they are using the descriptive method called **naturalistic observation.** Usually, researchers engaged in naturalistic observation try to avoid being detected by their subjects, whether people or nonhuman animals. The basic goal of naturalistic observation is to detect the behavior patterns that exist naturally—patterns that might not be apparent in a laboratory or if the subjects knew they were being watched.

As you might expect, psychologists very carefully define the behaviors that they will observe and measure before they begin their research. For example, social psychologist Robert Levine (1997) set out to compare the "pace of life" in 31 different countries. How could you operationally define the "pace of life"? One measure that Levine adopted was "the amount of time it took a pedestrian to walk a distance of 60 feet on a downtown city street." To collect the data, observers unobtrusively timed at least 35 male and 35 female pedestrians in each country (Levine & Norenzayan, 1999).

The results? The fastest walkers were clocked in Ireland, and the slowest in Brazil. When the 31 countries were ranked from fastest to slowest, the United States came in 6th and Canada ranked 11th.

Often, to increase the accuracy of the observations, two or more observers are used. In some studies, observations are videotaped or audiotaped so that the researchers can carefully analyze the details of the behaviors being studied.

One advantage of naturalistic observation is that it allows researchers to study human behaviors that cannot ethically be manipulated in an experiment. For example, suppose that a psychologist wants to study bullying behavior in children. It would not be ethical to deliberately create a situation in which one child is aggressively bullied by another child. However, it would be ethical to study bullying by observing aggressive behavior in children on a crowded school playground.

Psychologists Debra Pepler and Wendy Craig (1995) did just that. From their vantage point on the second floor of a school, they used a camcorder with a telephoto lens and small, wireless microphones to observe the spontaneous interactions of schoolchildren. Using this naturalistic observation strategy, they discovered that physical and verbal aggressive incidents are far from rare. Even

Naturalistic Observation Here, Chinese scientists study a 14-month-old giant panda cub. The goal of naturalistic observation is to study behavior patterns in their natural environment with as little interference as possible. Observers often take special precautions to avoid being detected by the animals under study. Naturalistic observation is also used to investigate human behavior.

among children whom teachers regarded as nonaggressive, instances of physical aggression occurred about once every 11 minutes, verbal aggression about once every 5 minutes. And, contrary to what many people assume, Pepler and Craig found that girls bully other children at the same rate as do boys.

As a research tool, naturalistic observation can be used wherever patterns of behavior can be openly observed—from the rain forests of the Amazon to fast-food restaurants, shopping malls, and singles' bars. Because the observations occur in the natural setting, the results of naturalistic observation studies can often be generalized more confidently to real-life situations than can the results of studies using artificially manipulated or staged situations (see Pepler & Craig, 1995).

Case Studies

Details, Details, Details

A **case study** is an intensive, in-depth investigation of an individual. Case studies involve compiling a great deal of information, often from a variety of different sources, to construct a detailed picture of a single subject. The subject may be intensively interviewed, and his or her friends, family, and co-workers may be interviewed as well. Psychological records, medical records, and even school records may be examined. Other sources of information can include extensive psychological testing and observations of the person's behavior. Clinical psychologists and other mental health specialists routinely use case studies to develop a complete profile of a psychotherapy client.

Case studies are also used to investigate rare, unusual, or extreme conditions. Yet case studies often provide psychologists with information that can be used to help understand normal behavior (Adler, 1993). For example, in Chapters 2 and 6, you'll see how case studies of people with brain damage have contributed to our understanding of such normal psychological functions as language, emotional control, and memory.

The case study method can be applied to more than one individual. In a *multiple case study,* a small group of individuals is intensively studied (Schneider, K., 1998). Psychologists may also combine information from several case studies that focus on the same type of behavior, a strategy that is called *case study research.* In both types of research, psychologists look for characteristics or patterns of behavior that are consistent across the individual cases.

Surveys

(A) Always (B) Sometimes (C) You've Got to Be Kidding!

A direct way to find out about the behavior, attitudes, and opinions of people is simply to ask them. In a **survey,** people respond to a structured set of questions about their experiences, beliefs, behaviors, or attitudes. One key advantage offered by survey research is that information can be gathered from a much larger group of people than is possible with other research methods.

descriptive methods
Scientific procedures that involve systematically observing behavior in order to describe the relationship among behaviors and events.

naturalistic observation
The systematic observation and recording of behaviors as they occur in their natural setting.

case study
A highly detailed description of a single individual or event.

survey
A questionnaire or interview designed to investigate the opinions, behaviors, or characteristics of a particular group.

Calvin and Hobbes　　　　　　　by Bill Watterson

Table | **1.1**

Comparing the NHSLS Sample and the U.S. Population

	NHSLS Sample	U.S. Population
Gender		
Men	44.6%	49.7%
Women	55.4	50.3
	100 %	100 %
Age		
18–24	15.9%	18.2%
25–29	14.5	14.3
30–39	31.3	29.5
40–49	22.9	22.7
50–59	15.3	15.3
	100 %	100 %
Education		
Less than high school	13.9%	15.8%
High school or equivalent	62.2	64.0
Any college	16.6	13.9
Advanced	7.3	6.3
	100 %	100 %
Marital Status		
Never married	28.2%	27.7%
Currently married	53.3	58.3
Divorced, separated	16.2	12.4
Widowed	2.3	1.6
	100 %	100 %
Race/Ethnicity		
White	76.5%	75.9%
Black	12.7	11.7
Hispanic	7.5	9.0
Other	3.3	3.3
	100 %	100 %

SOURCE: Michael & others (1994).

Using random selection, approximately 3,000 people were chosen for the sample used in the National Health and Social Life Survey (NHSLS). In this table, you can see that the overall characteristics of those in the NHSLS sample were very representative of the U.S. population as a whole.

Typically, surveys involve a carefully designed questionnaire in a paper-and-pencil format that is mailed or otherwise distributed to a select group of people. Surveys can also be conducted over the telephone or in person, with the interviewer recording the person's responses. As with paper-and-pencil surveys, the interviewer usually asks a structured set of questions in a predetermined order. Such interview-based surveys are typically more expensive and time-consuming than questionnaire-based surveys.

Surveys are seldom administered to everyone within the particular group or population under investigation. Instead, researchers usually select a **sample**—a segment of the larger group or population. Selecting a sample that is representative of the larger group is the key to getting accurate survey results. A **representative sample** very closely parallels, or matches, the larger group on relevant characteristics, such as age, sex, race, marital status, and educational level.

How do researchers select the participants for the sample so that they end up with a sample that is representative of the larger group? The most common strategy is to randomly select the sample participants. **Random selection** means that every member of the larger group has an equal chance of being selected for inclusion in the sample.

To illustrate how random selection works, let's look at how the sample was created for the *National Health and Social Life Survey* (abbreviated *NHSLS*). Conducted by researcher Robert T. Michael and his colleagues (1994) at the University of Chicago, the NHSLS focused on the sexual practices of American adults between the ages of 18 and 59. Here is Michael's description of how his team used random selection to choose the survey participants:

> Essentially, we chose at random geographic areas of the country, using the statistical equivalent of a coin toss to select them. Within these geographic regions, we randomly selected cities, towns, and rural areas. Within those cities and towns we randomly select neighborhoods. Within those neighborhoods, we randomly select households. . . . If there were two people living in a household who were in our age range, we flipped a coin to select which one to interview. If there were three people in the household, we did the equivalent of flipping a three-sided coin to select one of them to interview.

Notice that the participants who were interviewed in the NHSLS did *not* volunteer to participate in the survey. A specific individual was randomly selected through the process described. If that person refused to participate, someone else in the household could *not* substitute for that person. Using this random selection process, more than 3,000 people were interviewed for the National Health and Social Life Survey.

How closely did the NHSLS sample match important characteristics of the U.S. population? You can see for yourself by comparing the two columns in Table 1.1. Clearly, the random selection process used in the NHSLS study resulted in a sample that very closely approximated the characteristics of the U.S. population as a whole.

In constructing the random sample for the National Health and Social Life Survey, the goal was to emulate the entire U.S. adult population. However, some surveys are designed to sample the experiences, behaviors, or opinions of a specific group of people. For example, researchers Craig Anderson and Karen Dill (2000) were interested in how much time young people spend playing video games, especially violent video games. They surveyed 227 college students taking introductory psychology classes at a large midwestern university. The students also completed some personality measures and a questionnaire on past delinquent behaviors.

Figure 1.4 shows some of the survey results. In general, the amount of time spent playing video games decreased as the participants advanced in their level of education. But even at the college level, 88 percent of the female students and 97 percent of the male students reported being regular video game players. *Super Mario Brothers, Tetris,* and *Mortal Kombat* were the most popular games.

Although Anderson and Dill's data are interesting, it's important to stress that their survey was not based on a random sample of American youth. Consequently, all you can really conclude from this survey is what it indicated about the characteristics of the college students who participated. To make broader generalizations about the video game habits and preferences of American youth, a survey based on a true random sample of American youth would be needed.

One potential problem with surveys and questionnaires is that people do not always answer honestly. Subjects can misrepresent their personal characteristics or lie in their responses. These problems can be addressed in a well-designed survey. One strategy is to rephrase and ask the same basic question at different points in the survey or during the interview. The researchers can then compare the responses to make sure that the participant is responding honestly and consistently.

If you're wondering just what the National Health and Social Life Survey did reveal about the sexual practices of Americans, stay tuned. In Chapter 10, on gender and sexuality, we'll look at what the NHSLS revealed about the sexual practices and preferences of American adults.

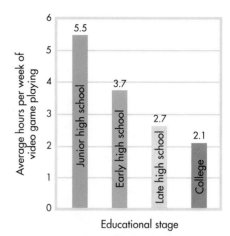

FIGURE 1.4 Time Spent Playing Video Games Anderson and Dill's (2000) survey of 227 college students revealed that the amount of time they spent playing video games decreased as they attained higher levels of education. Notice that even at the college level, students reported playing video games for more than two hours per week on the average.

SOURCE: Adapted from data reported in Anderson & Dill (2000).

Correlational Studies
Looking at Relationships and Making Predictions

Key Theme
- Correlational studies show how strongly two factors are related.

Key Questions
- What is a correlation coefficient?
- What is the difference between a positive correlation and a negative correlation?
- Why can't correlational studies be used to demonstrate cause-and-effect relationships?

Along with answering who, what, where, and when, the data gathered by descriptive research techniques can be analyzed to show how various factors are related. A **correlational study** examines how strongly two variables are related to, or associated with, each other. Probably the best way to develop an appreciation of correlational studies—and of their limitations—is to look at a simple example.

Many people believe that there is a relationship between stress and susceptibility to colds—the more stress you're under, the more likely you are to catch a cold. How could we investigate this relationship? First, we could survey people about the number of stressful events they've experienced in the last six months—financial troubles, relationship problems, job-related pressures, and so on. Then, we could ask them how many colds and respiratory infections they've had during the same time period.

With these data in hand, we could use a statistical procedure to calculate a figure called a correlation coefficient. A **correlation coefficient** is a numerical indicator of how strongly related two factors seem to be. A correlation coefficient always falls in the range from −1.00 to +1.00. The correlation coefficient has two parts—the number and the sign. The number indicates the *strength* of the relationship, and the sign indicates the *direction* of the relationship between the two variables.

More specifically, the closer a correlation coefficient is to 1.00, whether it is positive or negative, the stronger the correlation or association between two factors. Hence, a correlation coefficient of +.80 or −.80 would represent a strong association, whereas a correlation coefficient of +.10 or −.10 would represent a weak correlation. (Correlation coefficients are discussed in greater detail in Appendix A.)

sample
A selected segment of the population used to represent the group that is being studied.

representative sample
A selected segment that very closely parallels the larger population being studied on relevant characteristics.

random selection
Process in which subjects are selected randomly from a larger group such that every group member has an equal chance of being included in the study.

correlational study
A research strategy that allows the precise calculation of how strongly related two factors are to one another.

correlation coefficient
A numerical indication of the magnitude and direction of the relationship (the correlation) between two variables.

Jazzing Up Your Love Life with Correlation Coefficients Using data from the University of Chicago's ongoing General Social Survey, researchers John Robinson and Geoffrey Godbey (1998) discovered that adult sexual behavior was positively correlated with certain musical preferences. After controlling for age and race, the researchers found that people who have a strong preference for jazz are 30 percent more sexually active than the average American. Liking other types of music, such as rock or rap, was unrelated to sexual activity. Does this mean that listening to jazz *causes* an increase in sexual activity? Not necessarily. Remember, a correlation between two factors does not necessarily indicate causality—only that the two factors co-vary in a systematic way.

Notice that correlation coefficients do not function like the algebraic number line. A correlation of −.80 represents a stronger relationship than does a correlation of +.10. The plus or minus sign in a correlation coefficient simply tells you the direction of the relationship between the two variables. A **positive correlation,** say, +.80, is one in which the two factors vary in the *same* direction. That is, the two factors increase or decrease together. For example, there is a positive correlation between years of education and average annual earnings: As years of education increase, average yearly earnings increase.

In contrast, a **negative correlation** is one in which the two variables move in *opposite* directions: As one factor increases, the other factor decreases. For example, a negative correlation exists between marital satisfaction and rate of divorce. As reported marital satisfaction *increases,* the rate of divorce *decreases* (Karney & Bradbury, 1995). Thus, when two factors are negatively correlated, they vary in opposite directions.

Given the basics of correlation coefficients, let's go back to our example of investigating the relationship between stress and colds. After crunching the data, let's assume that we found a very strong positive correlation of +.90 between the number of stressful events people experienced and the number of colds people had. That is, people who experienced a high number of stressful events had a higher number of colds than did people who experienced a lower number of stressful events. Now here's the critical question: Based on this evidence, can we conclude that stress *causes* susceptibility to colds?

Not necessarily. Even if stressful life events and colds are very strongly correlated, it's completely possible that some other factor is involved. For example, it may be that people who are under a great deal of stress have more contact with other people and thus are more frequently exposed to cold germs. Or it could be that people who are under a great deal of stress engage in more unhealthy behaviors, such as smoking, eating a poor diet, or getting inadequate sleep. Rather than stress, it may be that unhealthy behaviors increase vulnerability to colds.

The critical point here is that even if two factors are very strongly correlated, *correlation does not necessarily indicate causality*. A correlation tells you only that two factors seem to be related or co-vary in a systematic way. Although two factors may be very strongly correlated, correlational evidence cannot demonstrate a true cause-and-effect relationship. As you'll see in the next section, the experimental method is the strategy that can demonstrate a cause-and-effect relationship between two variables.

Even though you can't draw conclusions about causality with correlational research, correlational research is still very valuable for two reasons. First, correlational research can be used to rule out some factors and identify others that merit more intensive study. For example, earlier we mentioned the survey that Craig Anderson and Karen Dill (2000) conducted with college students about their video game–playing habits. The same students also completed a personality scale measuring aggressiveness and a questionnaire on past delinquent behaviors, such as purposely damaging or destroying public property. When the data were analyzed, there was a moderately strong correla-

A Perfect Positive Correlation: The Clock and the Bell Tower If a +1.00 correlation occurred between two variables, it would be termed a *perfect positive correlation*. This means that every time Factor A occurred, Factor B would also occur. This might seem to suggest that Factor A is causing Factor B to occur, but that's not necessarily the case. For example, every time the big hand on the clock tower gets to 12, two miles away the bell starts ringing. The two events are perfectly correlated yet, in this case, one does not cause the other.

tion of +.46 between playing violent video games and aggressive delinquent behaviors. And there was a positive correlation of +.22 between exposure to video game violence and aggressive personality characteristics. Anderson and Dill believe that both of these correlations point to the potentially negative consequences of long-term exposure to violent video games.

Second, the results of correlational research can allow you to make meaningful predictions. As you'll see in Chapter 13, on stress, health, and coping, there is compelling evidence that demonstrates a strong positive correlation between stress and susceptibility to colds and infections (Cohen & others, 1993, 1998). Thus, the amount of stress you are under *is* a good predictor of your susceptibility to colds and infections.

Each of the descriptive methods we've looked at in this section can provide information about when behavior happens, how often it happens, and whether other factors or events are related to the behavior being studied. Next, we'll look at the method that provides the most compelling evidence of a cause-and-effect relationship between two variables—the experimental method.

1.2 R·E·V·I·E·W

C·O·N·C·E·P·T

Descriptive Methods

Fill in each blank with one of these terms: naturalistic observation, the case study method, correlational research, positive correlation, negative correlation.

1. A psychologist discovers that as negative life events increase, episodes of depression also increase. The psychologist concludes that there is a _____ between negative life events and episodes of depression.

2. A psychologist is interested in what hospital staff members say about their patients in public. His research assistants spend four hours riding elevators in various hospitals and unobtrusively recording the public conversations. This psychologist is using _____.

3. A psychologist is using police reports and weather reports to determine whether there is any relationship between the frequency of arrests for aggressive behavior and the temperature. She is using _____ to study this relationship.

4. Researchers have found that the more credit cards people have, the less money they tend to have in their savings accounts. These researchers have discovered a _____ between the number of credit cards and the amount of savings.

5. Dr. Romano conducts in-depth interviews and gives extensive psychological tests to individuals who claim to have been abducted by aliens. Dr. Romano is using _____ in these investigations.

The Experimental Method

Key Theme

■ The experimental method is used to demonstrate a cause-and-effect relationship between two variables.

Key Questions

■ What was the hypothesis, independent variable, and dependent variable in the Anderson and Dill video game experiment?

■ What are the roles of random assignment, the experimental group, and the control group?

■ What are some important variations in experimental design, and what are the limitations of experiments?

positive correlation
A finding that two factors vary systematically in the same direction, increasing or decreasing together.

negative correlation
A finding that two factors vary systematically in opposite directions, one increasing as the other decreases.

experimental method
A method of investigation used to demonstrate cause-and-effect relationships by purposely manipulating a factor thought to produce change in a second factor.

The **experimental method** is a research method used to demonstrate a cause-and-effect relationship between changes in one variable and the effect that is produced on another variable. Conducting an experiment involves deliberately varying one factor, which is called the **independent variable.** The researcher then measures the changes, if any, that are produced in a second factor, called the **dependent variable.** The dependent variable is so named because changes in it *depend* on variations in the independent variable.

To the greatest degree possible, all other conditions in the experiment are held constant. Thus, when the data are analyzed, any changes that occur in the dependent variable can be attributed to the deliberate variations of the independent variable. In this way an experiment can demonstrate a cause-and-effect relationship between the independent and dependent variables.

Do Violent Video Games Increase Aggressive Behavior?

Remember the chapter Prologue and our students' questions about the influence of video games on aggressive behavior? To help you understand the experimental method, let's look at part of an experiment conducted by psychologists Craig Anderson and Karen Dill.

Anderson and Dill (2000) wanted to study the effects of playing violent video games on behavior, especially aggressive behavior. In the previous section, we noted that Anderson and Dill conducted a correlational study based on questionnaires and personality measures that were administered to a large number of college students. Analysis of the data indicated that playing violent video games was strongly and positively correlated with two factors: aggressive delinquent behavior in real life and, to a lesser degree, aggressive personality characteristics. However, as Anderson and Dill noted, such correlational evidence *cannot* be used to draw conclusions about cause-and-effect relationships. Experimental evidence is needed to show that a causal relationship exists between two variables—in this case, between playing violent video games and exhibiting real-life aggression.

The Hypothesis, Participants, and Random Assignment

Anderson and Dill set out to experimentally test the hypothesis that playing violent video games would increase aggressive behavior. The participants in their study were 210 undergraduate students—104 females and 106 males—taking an introductory psychology class. All students received partial credit in the class for voluntarily participating in the experiment. An alternate activity was available for class credit for students who did not want to participate in the study.

The researchers used a process called *random assignment* to assign participants to the different experimental groups. **Random assignment** means that all participants in the study have an equal chance of being assigned to any of the groups in the experiment. Random assignment is an important element of good experimental design, because it helps ensure that potential differences among the subjects are spread out across all experimental conditions. And, because the same criteria are used to assign all participants to the different groups in the experiment, random assignment helps make certain that the assignment of participants is done in an unbiased manner.

The Experimental and Control Groups

In this experiment, the *independent variable,* which is also sometimes referred to as the *treatment of interest,* was playing a violent video game. Those participants who were randomly assigned to play the violent video game constituted the **experimental group,** or the **experimental condition.** Subjects in the experimental group go through all the different phases of the experiment and are exposed to the independent variable or treatment of interest.

independent variable
The purposely manipulated factor thought to produce change in an experiment; also referred to as the *treatment of interest.*

dependent variable
The factor that is observed and measured for change in an experiment; thought to be influenced by the independent variable.

random assignment
Assigning participants to experimental conditions in such a way that all participants have an equal chance of being assigned to any of the conditions or groups in the study.

experimental group or **experimental condition**
In an experiment, the group of participants who are exposed to all experimental conditions, including the independent variable or treatment of interest.

control group or **control condition**
In an experiment, the group of participants who are exposed to all experimental conditions, except the independent variable or treatment of interest; the group against which the experimental group is compared.

In any well-designed experiment, there is at least one **control group,** or **control condition.** In Anderson and Dill's experiment, the control group consisted of the participants who were assigned to play a *nonviolent* video game. In a typical experiment, the participants assigned to the control group go through all the experimental phases but are *not* exposed to the independent variable (the treatment of interest). Thus, the control group serves as a baseline against which changes in the experimental group can be compared.

How were the violent and nonviolent video games chosen? Anderson and Dill selected them based on a previous study they had done in which participants rated several video games. That study had indicated that two video games were essentially the same in terms of difficulty, enjoyment, and frustration, but differed in the amount of violence. Those two video games were *Wolfenstein 3D* and *Myst.*

Here's the basic storyline of *Wolfenstein 3D:* It's World War II. You, the hero, have been imprisoned by the Nazis in the dungeon of Castle Wolfenstein. You escape (of course) and gain access to an arsenal of weapons, including a machine gun, a revolver, a knife, and a flame thrower. Your goal? Kill the Nazi guards as you make your way through the maze of tunnels and halls that wind through Castle Wolfenstein, progressively advancing in game levels so that you can kill the most nefarious Nazi of all—Adolf Hitler.

In contrast, *Myst* is an engaging, interactive game set on a mysterious island. Lush scenery, background music, and three-dimensional effects enhance the game, which was deliberately designed to be nonviolent. To play the game, you explore the island, uncover secrets, collect clues, and solve a variety of puzzles with logic and the information you've gathered.

Violent Video Games and Aggressive Behavior As you can see in this screen shot from a bestselling video game, *Grand Theft Auto 3,* graphic violence is a core theme of many popular computer games. Using realistic sounds and sophisticated 3-D visual effects, the player typically assumes the role of the main character, firing a variety of weapons and racking up points for killing and mutilating opponents or even innocent bystanders. Are such games harmless fun? Or do they encourage real-life aggressive behavior?

The Dependent Variable: Aggressive Behavior

The hypothesis predicted that playing violent video games (the independent variable) would increase aggressive behavior (the dependent variable). How did Anderson and Dill operationally define "aggressive behavior"? Ethically, of course, the researchers could not create an experimental situation in which participants could actually attack or harm one another, either physically or otherwise. Instead, they used a standard measure of aggressive behavior called the *Competitive Reaction Time Task.*

Here's how the Competitive Reaction Time Task works. Two research participants are situated in different rooms, each wearing headphones and sitting in front of a computer screen. As soon as the participants hear a signal tone, each tries to push the mouse button faster than his opponent in the other room. Whichever participant loses the race gets blasted with noise through the headphones. There are a total of 25 reaction time races.

How does the Competitive Reaction Time Task provide a measure of aggressive begavior? Before each race, each participant sets the noise level and duration that will be delivered to his opponent if his opponent loses. Participants can choose a sound blast level that ranges from Level 1, which corresponds to 50 decibels, to a high of Level 10, which corresponds to a very loud 100 decibels. On their computer screens, the participants can see the penalty for losing that has been set by their opponents.

Because the players determine the penalty that will be delivered to the loser of the game, the Competitive Reaction Time Task allows researchers to precisely measure the level of aggression that a research participant is willing to mete out to another participant. In this experiment, then, Anderson and Dill operationally defined aggressive behavior as "the intensity and duration of noise blasts the participant chooses to deliver to the opponent."

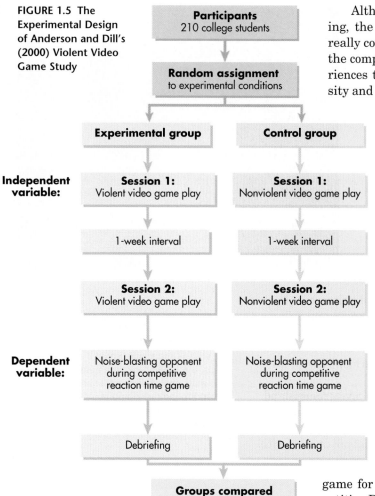

FIGURE 1.5 The Experimental Design of Anderson and Dill's (2000) Violent Video Game Study

Although the Competitive Reaction Time Task appears convincing, the game is actually rigged. The research participant is not really competing against another person in a different room. Instead, the computer is programmed so that each research participant experiences the exact same outcome—13 wins and 12 losses. The intensity and duration of the noise blasts that they receive when they lose are also predetermined, and they are the same for all participants.

The Experimental Procedure

To give participants ample playing experience with the assigned video game, the researchers had them come to the laboratory for two separate sessions approximately one week apart. When participants first arrived at the laboratory, they were told they were taking part in a study to investigate how people learn and develop skills at motor tasks such as those involved in playing video games and how these skills affect other mental and motor tasks. They were also told that they would be recorded in order to carefully analyze their motor skill development. To help make this believable, a VCR was set up and running near their computer, complete with bogus wires connecting the VCR and the computer.

During the first laboratory session, each participant was instructed on how to play the assigned video game. Then they played either *Wolfenstein 3D* or *Myst* for 30 minutes, depending on whether they were part of the experimental or control group. At the second laboratory session a week later, participants played their assigned video game for another 15-minute period. This was followed by the Competitive Reaction Time Task in which they had multiple opportunities to blast their opponent with noise. Given the opportunity to behave aggressively against an invisible opponent, would those who had just played *Wolfenstein 3D* (the violent game) behave more aggressively than those who had just played *Myst* (the nonviolent game)?

At the conclusion of the second experimental session, each participant received a debriefing statement that explained the study's actual hypotheses and procedures and debunked the cover story. The research assistant also answered any questions about the experiment. Figure 1.5 outlines the basic steps in Anderson and Dill's study.

The Results and Discussion

What did Anderson and Dill find? Let's look at the experimental results. As Figure 1.6 shows, there was a statistically significant difference between the experimental and control conditions. Students who had played *Wolfenstein 3D,* the violent game, scored higher on one measure of aggressive behavior than students who had played *Myst,* the nonviolent video game. On average, they delivered longer blasts of noise to their opponents. This result confirmed that participants who had played a violent video game were more aggressive than people who had played a nonviolent video game.

However, remember that Anderson and Dill (2000) operationally defined aggressive behavior "as the intensity and duration of noise blasts the participant chooses to deliver to the opponent." Although there were statistically significant differences between the two groups on the *duration* of the noise blasts, the two groups did not differ significantly on *intensity* of the sound setting. In other words, playing the violent versus the nonviolent video game had no effect on how loudly the research participants blasted their opponents. The researchers were surprised by the lack of significant group differences on intensity of the noise blasts.

Nonetheless, combining these experimental results with Anderson and Dill's correlational study that we described earlier provides converging lines of real-world and laboratory evidence. As Anderson and Dill (2000) explain:

> In the laboratory, college students who played a violent video game behaved more aggressively toward an opponent than did students who had played a nonviolent video game. Outside the laboratory, students who reported playing more violent video games over a period of years also engaged in more aggressive behavior in their own lives. This convergence of findings across such disparate methods lends considerable strength to the main hypothesis that exposure to violent video games can increase aggressive behavior.

Reporting the Findings

On April 23, 2000, the headline of the American Psychological Association's news release read:

Violent Video Games Can Increase Aggression:
May Be More Harmful Than Violent Television and Movies
Because of the Interactive Nature of the Games

The news release was issued on the day that Anderson and Dill's study was published in the *Journal of Personality and Social Psychology*, one of psychology's premier scientific journals. Because of the amount of public interest in the study, the American Psychological Association made the full text of the study available on the Internet at http://www.apa.org/journals/psp/psp784772.html.

Needless to say, the study attracted considerable attention—and provoked considerable debate—in the mass media when it was published. Adding fuel to that debate was the fact that shortly before the study was published, Anderson had testified before the U.S. Senate Commerce Committee in a hearing on "The Impact of Interactive Violence on Children." You can read a transcript of Anderson's testimony at http://psych-server.iastate.edu/faculty/caa/abstracts/2000-2004/00Senate.html.

At the Senate hearing and in the published study, Anderson and Dill argued that playing violent video games may be more harmful than watching violent television and movies. Why? One reason is that playing violent video games involves the player taking on the role of and identifying with the aggressor. Another reason is that violent video games are interactive, requiring the player to actively choose to act aggressively.

And how did our students in the 9:30 class react to the Anderson and Dill study? Kim was even more determined to keep her boys away from violent computer games. Kyle, however, remained unconvinced. "Maybe some people get frustrated when they play those kinds of games," he argued. "But still, there's a big difference between playing some make-believe video game and killing real people." Tanisha had another idea: "Not everyone is as self-disciplined as you, Kyle. Maybe the effects aren't the same for everybody. Maybe some kids are very easily influenced by playing violent video games and we need to identify those kids."

"A new hypothesis!" Sandy exclaimed.

Variations in Experimental Design

The design of any particular experiment depends on the issues being investigated. In this section, we'll look at two specific variations in experimental designs—the use of a placebo control group and natural experiments. We'll also describe some additional elements that are often used to safeguard against bias.

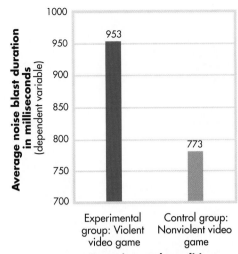

FIGURE 1.6 Results of the Violent Video Game Experiment In the graph you can see that briefly playing a violent video game increased aggressive behavior. As compared to those who played a nonviolent video game, the participants who played the violent video game blasted their opponents with longer noise bursts in the Competitive Reaction Time Task. The difference between the two groups was statistically significant.

SOURCE: Data adapted from Anderson & Dill (2000).

Psychologist Craig Anderson Testifying before the U.S. Senate Commerce Committee, Anderson said, "Of course, most people who consume high levels of violent media, adults or youth, do not end up in prison for violent crimes. The more relevant question is whether many (or most) people become more angry, aggressive, and violent as a result of being exposed to high levels of media violence. Are they more likely to slap a child or spouse when provoked? Are they more likely to drive aggressively and display 'road rage'? Are they more likely to assault co-workers? The answer is a clear 'yes.'"

Placebos in Space Because astronauts sometimes sleep poorly in space, a study was designed to see whether they could be helped by taking *melatonin,* a hormone that helps induce sleep. During the study aboard the space shuttle *Columbia,* half of the astronauts took a pill containing melatonin, and the other half took a pill that appeared identical but was a placebo. None of the astronauts knew whether they were taking the placebo or melatonin. Shown here is an astronaut wearing sensors that monitored his brain activity, breathing, heart rate, and other physical functions during sleep.

Placebo Control Group

Some experiments are designed to assess the effectiveness of a therapeutic treatment, such as a particular medication or a type of psychotherapy. In this kind of experiment, participants assigned to the experimental group receive the treatment of interest—the actual drug or therapy. Other participants are assigned to a **placebo control group** and receive a placebo. Definitions vary, but essentially a *placebo* is an inert substance or a treatment that has no known effects (Straus & von Ammon Cavanaugh, 1996). In a typical therapeutic effectiveness study, participants are told the purpose of the study and that they have a 50–50 chance of receiving the actual versus the placebo treatment.

Why is a placebo control group an important element in such studies? A placebo control group helps check for **expectancy effects,** which are changes that may occur simply because subjects expect change to occur. Expectancy effects are also sometimes referred to as *placebo effects.* Using this method, researchers can compare the effects of the actual treatment versus the expectancy effects, if any, that are demonstrated by the placebo control group.

In therapeutic effectiveness studies, researchers often use a double-blind technique. A **double-blind study** is one in which neither the participants nor the researcher who interacts with the participants is aware of the treatment or condition to which the participants have been assigned. For example, in a study with a placebo control group, researchers who interact with the subjects would not know which were receiving the placebo and which the actual treatment. The researchers who *do* know which participants have been assigned to each group do not interact with or evaluate the participants. In contrast, a *single-blind study* is one in which the researchers, but not the subjects, are aware of critical information.

The purpose of the double-blind technique is to guard against the possibility that the researcher will inadvertently display **demand characteristics,** which are subtle cues or signals that communicate what is expected of certain subjects (Kihlstrom, 1995). A behavior as subtle as smiling when dealing with some participants, but not when dealing with others, could bias the outcome of a study.

Natural Experiments

Psychologists often want to study phenomena that would be impossible or unethical to duplicate in a controlled laboratory setting. For example, a psychologist might want to know whether prolonged exposure to a noisy urban environment creates psychological and physical stress in young children. Obviously, it would be unethical to subject children to loud noise for a prolonged (or even a short) period of time.

Sometimes researchers are able to study such phenomena by taking advantage of naturally occurring events. In a *natural experiment,* researchers carefully observe and measure the impact of a naturally occurring event on their study participants. Gary Evans and his colleagues (1998) used this strategy to study the effects of exposure to chronic noise on children. They compared stress levels in elementary school children before and after a large international airport was built in their once-quiet community near Munich, Germany. The researchers measured both physical and psychological indicators of stress, such as blood pressure, levels of stress hormones, and perceptions of the daily quality of life. They also measured the same indicators over the same period of time in a matched control group of children who lived in a community that remained quiet.

What were the results of this natural experiment? The children who were exposed to chronic noise (the independent variable) showed increased psychological and physical stress (the dependent variable). In contrast, the control-group children, who were not exposed to constant noise, showed little change in stress. Evans and his colleagues (1998) concluded that chronic noise does cause a significant increase in psychological stress in children.

Limitations of Experiments

The strength of a well-designed experiment is that it can provide convincing evidence of a cause-and-effect relationship between the independent and dependent variables. Experiments do have limitations, however. Because experiments are often conducted in highly controlled laboratory situations, they are frequently criticized for having little to do with actual behavior. That is, the artificial conditions of some experiments may produce results that do not *generalize* well, meaning that the results cannot be applied to real situations or to a more general population beyond the participants in the study. In order to make experimental conditions less artificial, experiments are sometimes conducted in a natural setting rather than in a laboratory.

Another limitation of the experimental method is that even when it is possible to create the conditions that the researchers want to study, it may be unethical to do so. In the final section of this chapter, we'll look at the kinds of ethical considerations that psychologists must take into account in conducting any kind of research. While the conclusions of psychology rest on empirical evidence gathered using the scientific method, the same is not true of *pseudoscientific* claims. As you'll read in Science Versus Pseudoscience Box 1.3: What Is a Pseudoscience on page 34, pseudosciences often violate the basic rules of science.

placebo control group
(pluh-SEE-bo) In an experiment, a control group in which the participants are exposed to a fake independent variable, or placebo, the effects of which are compared to a group receiving the actual independent variable, or treatment of interest.

expectancy effects
Changes in a subject's behavior produced by the subject's belief that change should happen; also called *placebo effects*.

double-blind study
Experimental technique in which neither the participants nor the researcher interacting with the participants is aware of the group or condition to which the participants have been assigned.

demand characteristics
In a research study, subtle cues or signals expressed by the researcher that communicate the kind of response or behavior that is expected from the participant.

1.3 R·E·V·I·E·W

CONCEPT

The Experimental Method

Identify each component of the video game and aggression experiment conducted by Anderson and Dill (2000). Choose from the following terms:

- a. independent variable
- b. control group
- c. dependent variable
- d. experimental group
- e. hypothesis
- f. random assignment
- g. operational definition

_____ 1. The measured duration and intensity of the noise blast delivered to opponents in the Competitive Reaction Time Task.

_____ 2. The prediction that aggressive behavior increases after violent video game play.

_____ 3. "Aggressive behavior" is measured by a participant's choice of level and length of noise delivered to his or her opponent after winning in the Competitive Reaction Time Task.

_____ 4. Group of participants who played the video game *Myst*.

_____ 5. Group of participants who played the video game *Wolfenstein 3D*.

_____ 6. Participants had an equal chance of being assigned to either the experimental or control group.

_____ 7. Playing a violent video game.

SCIENCE VERSUS PSEUDOSCIENCE 1.3

What Is a Pseudoscience?

What do astrology, numerology, graphology, palmistry, aura reading, and crystal therapy have in common? All of these are examples of *pseudosciences*. The word *pseudo* means "fake" or "phony," so a pseudoscience is a *fake science*. More specifically, a **pseudoscience** is a theory, method, or practice that promotes claims in a way that appears to be scientific and plausible even though supporting empirical evidence is lacking or nonexistent (Lilienfeld & others, 2001; Shermer, 1997).

Some claims of paranormal phenomena also fall under the category of pseudoscience. **Paranormal phenomena** are alleged abilities or events that fall outside the range of normal experience and established scientific explanations. Examples of paranormal phenomena include *extrasensory perception* (ESP), such as mental telepathy, psychic predictions, and channeling (in which a spirit entity supposedly speaks through a human medium).

Many pseudoscientific claims violate a basic rule of science, called the **rule of falsifiability:** In order for a claim to be proved true, you must be able to identify some type of evidence that would refute the claim or prove that it is *false*. If there is no conceivable evidence that could disprove a claim, the claim is irrefutable—and examining evidence is pointless. *Irrefutable claims* often take the form of broad or vague statements that are essentially meaningless.

For instance, take the claim that "Wearing a quartz crystal will align your aura and balance your spiritual energy." How could such a statement be tested? Is there any kind of evidence that would *disprove* such a claim?

Pseudosciences often use anecdotes or testimonials as evidence to support their claims (Hines, 1988). For example, "My sister wore a quartz crystal for a month and she lost 15 pounds!" Although such testimonials may sound convincing, they are *not* acceptable scientific evidence because they lack the basic controls used in experimental research. Many different factors

could account for the apparent success of the claim, some of which we'll describe in future chapters. These include simple coincidence, expectancy or placebo effects, misremembering, and illusory correlation. An **illusory correlation** is the mistaken belief that two factors or events are related when they are not—like the person's sister wearing a crystal and losing weight.

Mixing established scientific facts with unfounded claims is another common pseudoscience strategy. For example, astrology claims that the gravitational forces of distant planets influence human personality and behavior on earth (Dean & others, 1996). But pseudosciences typically apply scientific principles in ways that are *not* substantiated by empirical evidence and are actually *contradicted* by scientific explanations. In the case of astrology, the gravitational effects of even the closest planets are far too weak to have any impact on earth-bound humans (Hines, 1988).

Many pseudosciences claim to enhance human behavior or abilities. To bolster the credibility of their claims, pseudosciences typically use lots of scientific jargon. Vague references to "leading researchers," "controlled psychological studies," "technological breakthroughs," and so forth may be cited without any documentation or specific sources.

One of our goals as the authors of your text is to help you develop the ability to think scientifically. This includes using scientific thinking to evaluate claims about behavior or mental processes that seem farfetched. To help you understand how the scientific method could be used to test any claim, we created the **Is It TRUE?** model (Hockenbury & Hockenbury, 1999). Each letter of the word *TRUE* refers to a different step in the evaluation process, as follows:

T = *Is It Testable?* Can the claim be stated as a testable hypothesis? If the procedure to test the claim is an experiment, what are the independent and dependent variables? What are the operational definitions of the variables? What controls are needed for the test? If the claim is not testable, is there physical evidence to support the claim?

R = *Is It Reliable?* How many times was the claim tested? Has evidence for the claim been replicated? If the test was repeated by others, were the same results obtained?

U = *Is It Unusual?* Are the results significantly different from what you would expect if nothing more than chance or guessing were operating during the test? Do the results appear to support or undermine the claim?

E = *Is It Explainable?* How would a reasonable person explain the outcome? Are there other possible explanations for the outcome? If the results fail to provide support, how do proponents of the claim account for the results? Why would people be motivated to believe in the claim despite a lack of evidence supporting it?

Using the "Is It TRUE?" model can help you evaluate evidence and help keep you from being duped by pseudoscientific and paranormal claims. In the coming chapters, you'll see how a variety of pseudoscience claims have stood up to scientific testing. We hope you enjoy the Science Versus Pseudoscience feature boxes throughout this text!

Ethics in Psychological Research

Key Theme

- Psychological research conducted in the United States is subject to ethical guidelines developed by the American Psychological Association.

Key Questions

- What are five key provisions of the APA for research involving humans?
- Why do psychologists sometimes conduct research with nonhuman animals?

pseudoscience
A fake or false science that makes claims based on little or no scientific evidence.

paranormal phenomena
Alleged abilities or events that fall outside the range of normal experience and established scientific explanations.

rule of falsifiability
In order for a claim to be scientifically tested and proved true, there must be identifiable evidence that could prove the claim false.

illusory correlation
The mistaken belief that two factors or events are related when they are not.

What might happen if you were to volunteer to participate in a psychology experiment or study? Are psychologists allowed to manipulate or control you without your knowledge or consent? Could a psychologist force you to reveal your innermost secrets? Could he or she administer electric shocks? Trick you into doing something embarrassing against your will?

The answer to all these questions is "no." The American Psychological Association (APA) has developed a strict code of ethics for conducting research with both human and animal subjects. This code is contained in a document called *Ethical Principles of Psychologists and Code of Conduct* (APA, 1992a). You can access the complete guidelines at http://www.apa.org/ethics/code.html.

In general, psychologists must respect the dignity and welfare of participants. Psychologists cannot expose research participants to dangerous or harmful conditions that might cause either physical or emotional harm. And any psychological research using human or animal subjects must be approved by an ethics panel at the institution where the study is to be conducted.

Not surprisingly, the ethical guidelines for research with human and animal subjects are somewhat different. However, the use of animals in psychological research is also governed by specific ethical guidelines (APA, 1992b). These guidelines, as well as other issues, are discussed in In Focus Box 1.4: Questions About the Use of Animals in Psychological Research on page 36.

Here are five of the key provisions in the most recent version of the APA ethical guidelines regulating research with human participants:

- **Informed consent and voluntary participation.** In reasonably understandable language, the psychologist must inform the participants of the nature of the research, including significant factors that might influence a person's willingness to participate in the study, such as physical risks, discomfort, or unpleasant emotional experiences. The psychologist must also explain to the participants that they are free to decline to participate or to withdraw from the research at any time.

- **Students as research participants.** When research participation is a course requirement or an opportunity for extra credit, the student must be given the choice of an alternative activity to fulfill the course requirement or earn extra credit.

- **The use of deception.** Psychologists can use deceptive techniques as part of the study only when two conditions have been met: (1) It is not feasible to use alternatives that do not involve deception, and (2) the potential findings justify the use of deception because of their scientific, educational, or applied value.

- **Confidentiality of records.** Psychologists may not publicly disclose personally identifiable information about research participants.

- **Information about the study and debriefing.** All participants must be provided with the opportunity to obtain information about the nature, results, and conclusions of the research. Psychologists are also obligated to *debrief* the participants and to correct any misconceptions that participants may have had about the research.

Questions About the Use of Animals in Psychological Research

The use of nonhuman animal subjects in psychological and other research is based on the premise that human life is intrinsically more valuable than animal life (Morrison, 2001). Not everyone agrees with this position (see Mukerjee, 1997; Plous, 1996; Rowan, 1997).

The American Psychological Association (1992b) condones the use of animals in psychological research, but only under certain conditions. First, research using animal subjects must have an *acceptable scientific purpose.* Second, there must be a reasonable expectation that the research will (a) increase knowledge about behavior, (b) increase understanding of the species under study, or (c) produce results that benefit the health or welfare of humans or other animals.

What standards must psychologists meet in using animal subjects?

The American Psychological Association (1992b) publishes the *Guidelines for Ethical Conduct in the Care and Use of Animals,* which you can read at http://www.apa.org/science/anguide. html. The APA Guidelines for animal care have been praised as being the most comprehensive set of guidelines of their kind (Fisher, 1986). In addition, federal and state laws govern the care and use of research animals (Overmier & Carroll, 2001).

How many animal subjects are used in psychological research?

The majority of psychological research involves human subjects, not animals. Animals are used in only about 7 to 8 percent of psychological studies conducted in a given year. Most psychological research with animal subjects does *not* involve pain, suffering, or deprivation (APA, 1995; Shapiro, 1991).

In a survey conducted by the APA, the total number of animals used by psychology departments throughout the United States was about 200,000. Of these, about 170,000 were rats, mice, or other rodents. Approximately 1,200 were primates, 800 dogs, and 600 cats. The rest

of the total comprised a variety of creatures, from bats to sea snails (APA, 1986). In comparison, more than *5 million* dogs and cats are destroyed in pounds every year.

Why are animals used in psychological research?

Here are a few of the key reasons that psychologists might use animal subjects rather than human subjects in research:

1. Many psychologists are interested in the study of animal behavior for its own sake.

The branch of psychology that focuses on the study of the behavior of different species is called *comparative psychology.* Some psychologists also do research in the area called *animal cognition,* which is the study of animal learning, memory, thinking, and language (Boysen & Hines, 1999).

Animal research is also pursued for its potential benefit to animals themselves. For example, psychological research on animal behavior has been used to improve the quality of life of animals in zoos and to increase the likelihood of survival of endangered species in the wild.

2. Animal subjects are sometimes used for research that could not feasibly be conducted on human subjects.

There are many similarities between human and animal behavior, but animal behavior tends to be less complex. Thus, it is sometimes easier to identify basic principles of behavior by studying

animals. Psychologists can also observe some animals throughout their entire lifespan, from the prenatal stage to old age. To track such changes in humans would take many decades of research. Finally, psychologists can exercise much greater control over animal subjects than over human subjects. If necessary, researchers can control every aspect of the animals' environment and even their genetic background.

In what areas of psychology has research using animals produced valuable information?

Psychological research with animal subjects has made essential contributions to virtually every area of psychology (Domjan & Purdy, 1995; Overmier & Carroll, 2001). Along with contributing to knowledge of the workings of the human brain, animal research has contributed to psychological knowledge in the areas of learning, memory, cognition, psychological disorders, therapies, and stress. Research with animals has produced significant gains in the treatment of many conditions, including substance abuse, spinal cord injury, hypertension, and sleep disorders (see Carroll & Overmier, 2001). Significant gains have also been made in helping animals, including the successful breeding and preservation of endangered species, improvements in the care of zoo animals, and the prevention of animal diseases (APA, 1995; Miller, 1985).

Psychologists Helping Animals Psychologist Benjamin Beck directs a program that has successfully reintroduced over 250 golden lion tamarins, an endangered species, to the wild (Ruiz-Miranda & others, 1999). The tamarin is a small, tree-dwelling monkey that inhabits a small area of Brazilian rain forest. As associate director of the National Zoo in Washington, D.C., Beck is also actively involved in developing enrichment activities for the zoo's residents—from orangutans to dung beetles (Cohn, 2002).

Who makes sure that these ethical guidelines are followed? First, all institutions where psychological research is conducted have ethics committees that must review and approve all research proposals. Second, the APA has established the Committee on Scientific and Professional Ethics, which investigates all complaints it receives. Any psychologist who is found to be in violation of the ethics code may be suspended or expelled from the APA.

Summing Up
Introduction and Research Methods

In this chapter we've laid the foundation for exploring a wide range of topics in psychology. Throughout this textbook, you'll see how psychologists have applied the tools of science, sometimes very ingeniously, to understand why we humans do what we do. Whether it is dealing with the common experiences of everyday life or with more extreme events, psychology can provide many insights into human behavior and mental processes. As you'll discover, psychology has much to teach you, not only about other people, but about yourself as well. It's a fascinating journey and one that we look forward to sharing with you.

APPLICATION | Evaluating Mass Media Reports About Psychology

Psychologists and psychological findings are often featured in the media. Sometimes it's a researcher, such as Craig Anderson, who is being interviewed about the published results of a study that has caught the interest of the popular press. Or it may be a psychologist who is appearing on a television or radio talk show to discuss a particular topic, such as the degree to which parents influence a child's personality.

How can you evaluate the information about psychology and psychology-related topics reported in the mass media? The following guidelines will help you critically evaluate what you see and hear in the news.

1. Be especially skeptical of sensationalistic claims or findings.

News headlines proclaiming "discoveries" or "breakthroughs" in psychological research are designed to grab your attention. Almost always, if you listen or read further, you'll encounter a much more cautious tone in the statements of the psychologists themselves. As scientists, psychologists tend to be conserva-

tive in stating their research results so as not to mislead the public. Reporters, in contrast, are sometimes more interested in attracting readers or viewers than in accurately portraying scientific results (Connor-Greene, 1993). As media psychologist Rhea Farberman (1999) explains:

> What the researcher sees in his or her research results—one piece of the overall research puzzle that can be applied within the limits of this particular study—is different from what the reporter wants to find in a research study—the all-encompassing headline. The challenge for the psychologist is how to translate the research into a meaningful sound bite.

Given the difficulty of compressing complicated information into a 10-second sound bite, it's common for researchers to be quoted out of context or for important qualifying statements to be left out by a reporter or producer (Broder, 1999). A 60-minute interview may be edited down to just 30 seconds of air time.

2. Anecdotes are the essence of talk shows, not scientific evidence.

Because psychology investigates the entire range of human experience, psychology-related topics are standard fare on news and talk shows. Although such programs often feature psychologists with research experience and expertise in a particular area, the shows tend to quickly abandon discussions of scientific evidence in favor of anecdotal evidence.

Anecdotal evidence consists of personal stories told to confirm or support a particular claim. The personal stories are often dramatic, funny, or heartrending, making them subjectively very compelling. However, an anecdote by definition is one person's experience. There's no way to know if the person's experience is representative of other peoples—or if it is exceptional or unusual. In contrast, descriptive and experimental research typically involves large groups of carefully selected subjects. When the number of participants in a study is small, researchers usually take that limitation into account when they draw conclusions from their findings.

3. Remember that the goal of "shock" radio and television is ratings.

Let's face it. The mass media are not educational institutions. They are a profit-driven industry, and the size of the audience is crucial to realizing those profits. So what draws viewers and listeners? Shock value is a big draw. Consider the popular radio personality "Dr." Laura Schlessinger, who is neither a psychologist nor a psychiatrist. Her blunt and caustic style makes money for the radio stations that carry her show. Because of the "shock" trend, qualified psychologists are often reluctant to appear on radio programs (DeAngelis, 1997). As media psychologist Michael Broder (1999) explains, "It's not how nice, professional, smart, loyal, helpful, or thorough you are, but how well you attract numbers of people."

4. Look for the original source of professional publication.

When the mass media report on a study that has been conducted by a reputable researcher, the original source of professional publication is almost always noted in the news report. Usually, psychological research is published in a professional psychology journal before it is shared with the general public. For example, it was only *after* Craig Anderson and Karen Dill (2000) published their findings about playing violent video games in the *Journal of Personality and Social Psychology* that they discussed their findings with reporters. Even so, reporters don't always read the research report or understand the research issues under discussion. And they may add their own interpretations to those of the researchers, thereby distorting or misrepresenting the actual findings (Farberman, 1999; McCall, 1988).

There's another reason why it's important to look for the original source of professional publication. The research published in most of the professional psychology journals is reviewed by peers. Before the research is accepted for publication, psychologists with expert knowledge in research methods and statistics review the study. In doing so, they verify that all aspects of the study were carefully designed to guard against erroneous conclusions. Thus, peer review helps ensure that psychological research adheres to the rigorous standards of scientific evidence.

5. Separate opinions from data.

Testimonials, isolated cases, and conjecture are *not* the same as scientifically gathered data. The essence of psychology as a science is objective data gathering that either supports or refutes the idea being tested. It's difficult for individuals to be objective about events with which they are directly connected. Emotions, attitudes, past history, and culture can all play a part in the misinterpretation of events.

6. Consider how the research was funded.

It costs money to conduct research. Research published in professional journals usually notes the funding sources in a footnote or endnote. Given that, would you be wary of research that was funded by a company or agency whose motive is to convince you to buy some product or service? Such situations do not necessarily invalidate the research, but they do raise concerns about conflicts of interest.

7. Consider the methods and operational definitions used.

At this point you should understand the importance of such elements as control groups in experiments, operational definitions of variables, the use of multiple observers in descriptive research, random assignment of subjects to experimental conditions, and the use of a sample that is representative of the population being studied. Look for these elements in the description of the study to increase your confidence in the research findings.

8. Remember the distinction between correlation and causality.

Remember the correlation we mentioned between higher levels of sexual activity and a preference for jazz? Many research results reported in the mass media are correlational studies, yet the news reports imply that a cause-and-effect relationship has been discovered (Connor-Greene, 1993). From our earlier discussion, you now understand that two factors may be correlated, but one does not necessarily cause the other. It is entirely possible that a third factor is responsible for the behavior in question. As a general rule, whenever the words *link, tie, connection, association,* or *relationship* are used in headlines describing psychological findings, the research being described is correlational.

9. Skepticism is the rule, not the exception, in science.

It seems as if it is basic to human nature to look for easy answers to life's dilemmas—whether that involves increasing your motivation and self-discipline, improving your memory, combating stress, or enhancing relationships. As you'll see in these Application sections at the end of each chapter, psychological research has much to say about these and other practical topics. But achieving these goals is rarely as easy as the popular press portrays it. Therefore, remember one final axiom in evaluating research claims reported in the mass media: If it sounds too good to be true, it probably is!

Chapter Review
Introduction and Research Methods

Key Points

Introduction: The Origins of Psychology

■ **Psychology** is now defined as the science of behavior and mental processes. However, the definition of psychology has evolved over time.

■ Early philosophers, such as Aristotle and Descartes, used logic and intuition to understand psychological topics. Later, the discoveries of physiologists demonstrated that scientific methods could be applied to psychological topics.

■ Wilhelm Wundt, a German physiologist, is credited with founding psychology as an experimental science. Wundt's student Edward B. Titchener established **structuralism,** the first school of psychology. The structuralists used introspection to try to identify the structures of conscious experiences.

■ William James founded and promoted psychology in the United States. James established **functionalism,** a school of psychology that emphasized the adaptive role of behavior. James's students G. Stanley Hall and Mary Whiton Calkins were two important figures in early American psychology.

■ Sigmund Freud established **psychoanalysis** as a theory of personality and form of psychotherapy. Psychoanalysis emphasized the role of unconscious conflicts in determining behavior and personality.

■ **Behaviorism** emerged in the early 1900s, based on Ivan Pavlov's research. Behaviorism was first championed by John Watson and further developed by B. F. Skinner. Behaviorism rejected the study of mental processes and emphasized the study of observable behavior, especially the principles of learning.

■ Carl Rogers and Abraham Maslow promoted **humanistic psychology,** which emphasized psychological growth and the importance of choice in human behavior.

Contemporary Psychology

■ Psychology today is a diverse field. Topics can be approached from different perspectives, which include the biological, psychodynamic, behavioral, humanistic, cognitive, cross-cultural, and **evolutionary** perspectives.

■ Important specialty areas of psychology include biological psychology, cognitive psychology, experimental psychology, developmental psychology, social psychology, personality psychology, health psychology, educational psychology, industrial/organizational psychology, and clinical psychology.

The Scientific Method

■ The four goals of psychology are to describe, explain, predict, and influence human behavior and mental processes. Psychology is based on **empirical evidence.**

■ Psychologists are trained in the **scientific method,** which has four steps: (1) generate a **hypothesis** that can be tested empirically, (2) design the study and collect the data, (3) analyze the data and draw conclusions, and (4) report the findings. **Variables** must be **operationally defined.**

■ Research methods include descriptive methods and the experimental method. **Statistics** are used to analyze the data and to determine whether findings are **statistically significant. Meta-analysis** can be used to combine and analyze multiple studies on a single topic. Reporting the results of a study allows other researchers to **replicate** the study.

■ As research findings accumulate from individual studies, **theories** or models develop to explain the different findings on a related topic. Theories are tools for understanding and explaining behavior and mental processes. Theories evolve and change as new evidence emerges.

Descriptive Methods

■ **Descriptive methods** are research strategies used to observe and describe behavior. The goal of **naturalistic observation** is to detect behavior patterns as they exist in their natural settings. The **case study** method involves intensive study of a single subject or a small group of subjects.

■ **Surveys,** questionnaires, and interviews are administered to a **sample** of the larger group to be investigated. For results to be generalizable to the larger population, the sample must be a **representative sample.** Participants are usually chosen through **random selection.**

■ **Correlational studies** investigate how strongly two factors are related to each other. The relationship is expressed in terms of a **correlation coefficient.** A **positive correlation** indicates that two factors vary in the same direction, whereas a **negative correlation** indicates that two factors vary in opposite directions.

■ Even when two factors are strongly related, conclusions cannot be drawn about causality because a third factor may actually be responsible for the association. However, correlational evidence can be used to identify important relationships and to make meaningful predictions.

The Experimental Method

■ The **experimental method** can demonstrate a cause-and-effect relationship between one variable and another. Experiments involve manipulating the **independent variable** and measuring the effects of the manipulation on the **dependent variable.**

■ An experiment testing the effects of playing violent video games on aggressive behavior was used to help illustrate **random assignment** of subjects to experimental conditions, **experimental groups** compared to a **control group,** systematic manipulation of the independent variable, and objective measurement of the dependent variable.

■ There are many variations in experimental design. A **placebo control group** is used to check for **expectancy effects.** The use of a **double-blind study** helps guard against **demand characteristics.** Natural experiments involve measuring the impact of a naturally occurring event on subjects. Although experiments can provide evidence of causality, they are sometimes criticized for creating artificial conditions. Not all questions can be studied experimentally.

Ethics in Psychological Research

■ All psychological research is subject to regulations contained in an ethical code developed by the American Psychological Association. For research with human subjects, the ethical code requires that informed consent and voluntary participation must be ensured, student subjects must be given alternatives to participating in research, deceptive techniques can be used only under specific conditions, records are kept confidential, and participants are to be debriefed and given the opportunity to learn more about the study.

■ Research with animal subjects is also governed by an ethical code developed by the American Psychological Association.

Key Terms

psychology, p. 3

structuralism, p. 5

functionalism, p. 6

psychoanalysis, p. 7

behaviorism, p. 8

humanistic psychology, p. 9

culture, p. 12

cross-cultural psychology, p. 12

ethnocentrism, p. 12

individualistic cultures, p. 12

evolutionary psychology, p. 12

collectivistic cultures, p. 13

scientific method, p. 16

critical thinking, p. 17

empirical evidence, p. 18

hypothesis, p. 18

variable, p. 18

operational definition, p. 18

statistics, p. 19

statistically significant, p. 19

meta-analysis, p. 20

replicate, p. 20

theory, p. 21

descriptive methods, p. 22

naturalistic observation, p. 22

case study, p. 23

survey, p. 23

sample, p. 24

representative sample, p. 24

random selection, p. 24

correlational study, p. 25

correlation coefficient, p. 25

positive correlation, p. 26

negative correlation, p. 26

experimental method, p. 27

independent variable, p. 28

dependent variable, p. 28

random assignment, p. 28

experimental group (experimental condition), p. 28

control group (control condition), p. 29

placebo control group, p. 32

expectancy effects, p. 32

double-blind study, p. 32

demand characteristics, p. 32

pseudoscience, p. 34

paranormal phenomena, p. 34

rule of falsifiability, p. 34

illusory correlation, p. 34

Key People

Mary Whiton Calkins (1863–1930) American psychologist who conducted research on memory, personality, and dreams; established one of the first U.S. psychology research laboratories; first woman president of the American Psychological Association. (p. 6)

Charles Darwin (1809–1882) English naturalist and scientist whose theory of evolution through natural selection was first published in *On the Origin of Species* in 1859. (p. 13)

Sigmund Freud (1856–1939) Austrian physician and founder of psychoanalysis. (p. 7)

G. Stanley Hall (1844–1924) American psychologist who established the first psychology research laboratory in the United States; founded the American Psychological Association. (p. 6)

William James (1842–1910) American philosopher and psychologist who founded psychology in the United States and established the psychological school called functionalism. (p. 5)

Abraham Maslow (1908–1970) American humanistic psychologist who developed a theory of motivation. (p. 9)

Ivan Pavlov (1849–1936) Russian physiologist whose pioneering research on learning contributed to the development of behaviorism; discovered the basic learning process that is now called classical conditioning. (p. 8)

Carl Rogers (1902–1987)   American psychologist who founded the school of humanistic psychology. (p. 9)

B. F. Skinner (1904–1990)   American psychologist and leading proponent of behaviorism; developed a model of learning called operant conditioning; emphasized studying the relationship between environmental factors and observable behavior. (p. 8)

Edward B. Titchener (1867–1927)   British-born American psychologist who founded structuralism, the first school of psychology. (p. 5)

Margaret Floy Washburn (1871–1939)   American psychologist who was the first woman to earn a doctorate in psychology in the United States; published research on mental processes in animals. (p. 7)

John B. Watson (1878–1958)   American psychologist who founded behaviorism, emphasizing the study of observable behavior and rejecting the study of mental processes. (p. 8)

Wilhelm Wundt (1832–1920)   German physiologist who founded psychology as a formal science; opened first psychology research laboratory in 1879. (p. 4)

Concept Review Answers

1.1   page 9

1. functionalism; William James
2. humanistic psychology; Carl Rogers
3. structuralism; Edward Titchener
4. psychoanalysis; Sigmund Freud
5. behaviorism; John Watson

1.2   page 27

1. positive correlation
2. naturalistic observation
3. correlational research
4. negative correlation
5. the case study method

1.3   page 33

1. c   *2.* e   *3.* g   *4.* b   *5.* d   *6.* f   *7.* a

Web Companion   Review Activities

You can find additional review activities at **www.worthpublishers.com/hockenbury**
The Psychology 3e Web Companion has a self-scoring practice quiz, flashcards, two interactive crossword puzzles, and other activities to help you master the material in this chapter.

Pathfinders

Neuroscience and Behavior

Prologue

Asha's Story

The headaches began without warning. A pounding, intense pain just over Asha's left temple. Asha just couldn't seem to shake it—the pain was unrelenting. She was uncharacteristically tired, too.

But our friend Asha, a 32-year-old university professor, chalked up her constant headache and fatigue to stress and exhaustion. After all, the end of her demanding first semester of teaching and research was drawing near. Still, Asha had always been very healthy and usually tolerated stress well. She didn't drink or smoke. And no matter how late she stayed up working on her lectures and research proposals, she still got up at 5:30 every morning to work out at the university gym.

There were other, more subtle signs that something was wrong. Asha's husband Paul noticed that she had been behaving rather oddly in recent weeks. For example, at Thanksgiving dinner, Asha had picked up a knife by the wrong end and tried to cut her turkey with the handle instead of the blade. A few hours later, Asha had made the same mistake trying to use scissors: She held the blades and tried to cut with the handle.

Asha laughed these incidents off, and for that matter, so did Paul. They both thought she was simply under too much stress. And when Asha occasionally got her words mixed up, neither Paul nor anyone else was terribly surprised. Asha was born in India, and her first language was Tulu. Although Asha was extremely fluent in English, she often got English phrases slightly wrong—like the time she said that Paul was a "straight dart" instead of a "straight arrow." Or when she said that it was "storming cats and birds" instead of "raining cats and dogs."

There were other odd lapses in language. "I would say something thinking it was correct," Asha recalled, "and people would say to me, 'What are you saying?' I wouldn't realize I was saying something wrong. I would open my mouth and just nonsense would come out. But it made perfect sense to me. At other times, the word was on the tip of my tongue—I knew I knew the word, but I couldn't find it. I would fumble for the word, but it would come out wrong. Sometimes I would slur words, like I'd try to say 'Saturday,' only it would come out 'salad-day.' "

On Christmas morning, Paul and Asha were with Paul's family, opening presents. Asha walked over to Paul's father to look at the pool cue he had received as a gift. As she bent down, she fell forward onto her father-in-law. At first, everyone thought Asha was just joking around. But then she fell to the floor, her body stiff. Seconds later, it was apparent that Asha had lost consciousness and was having a seizure.

43

Asha remembers nothing of the seizure or of being taken by ambulance to the hospital intensive care unit. She floated in and out of consciousness for the first day and night. A CAT scan showed some sort of blockage in Asha's brain. An MRI scan revealed a large white spot on the left side of her brain. At only 32 years of age, Asha had suffered a stroke—brain damage caused by a disruption of the blood flow to the brain.

She remained in the hospital for 12 days. It was only after Asha was transferred out of intensive care that both she and Paul began to realize just how serious the repercussions of the stroke were. Asha couldn't read or write and had difficulty comprehending what was being said. Although she could speak, she couldn't name even simple objects, such as a tree, a clock, or her doctor's tie. In this chapter, you will discover why the damage to Asha's brain impaired her ability to perform simple behaviors, like naming common objects.

Introduction
Neuroscience and Behavior

As Asha's story demonstrates, even simple behaviors and psychological processes are intimately connected to the workings of the brain. If we showed you a picture of a bicycle, you would not find it difficult to verbally identify it. If we handed you today's newspaper, you could read the headlines back to us and explain what they meant. If you watched a TV talk show, you could easily follow the rapid exchange of dialogue between two riled-up guests. But for months after her stroke, Asha found it impossible to perform any of these simple tasks.

In this chapter, you will discover why Asha's brain damage impaired her ability to perform simple behaviors such as those just described. You'll also gain a better understanding of the biological bases of your own behavior.

As we discussed in Chapter 1, **biological psychology** is the scientific study of the biological bases of behavior and mental processes. This area of research is also called *biopsychology*. Both terms emphasize the idea of a biological approach to the study of psychological processes. Biological psychology is one of the scientific disciplines that makes important contributions to **neuroscience**—the scientific study of the nervous system. As *neuroscientists*, biopsychologists bring their expertise in behavior and behavioral research to this scientific endeavor. Some of the other scientific disciplines that contribute to neuroscience include *physiology, pharmacology, biology,* and *neurology.*

Neuroscience and biological psychology are not limited to the study of the brain and the nervous system. Throughout this textbook, you'll encounter questions that have been studied by neuroscientists. Here are some examples:

- How do we tell the difference between red and blue, cold and hot, loud and soft? (Chapter 3)

- What happens in the brain when we sleep, dream, or meditate? (Chapter 4)

- What exactly is a memory, and how are memories stored in the brain? (Chapter 6)

- Why do we get hungry? How do emotions occur? (Chapter 8)

- How do emotions and attitudes affect our vulnerability to infection and disease? (Chapter 13)

- How does heredity influence our development? What role does genetics play in personality traits? (Chapters 9, 11, and 14)

- What role does abnormal brain chemistry play in psychological disorders? How do medications alleviate the symptoms of serious psychological disorders? (Chapters 14 and 15)

Neuroscience and Behavior Maintaining your balance on a bicycle, smiling, talking with a friend—all your behaviors involve the complex integration of many physical processes working in harmony. For that matter, so does your ability to perceive and recognize the image in this photograph. What kinds of questions might neuroscientists ask about the common behaviors shown here?

This chapter will lay an important foundation for the rest of this book by helping you develop a broad appreciation of the *nervous system*—the body's primary communication network. We'll start by looking at *neurons,* the basic cells of the nervous system. We'll also consider the organization of the nervous system and a closely linked communication network, the *endocrine system.* We'll then move on to a guided tour of the brain. We'll look at how certain brain areas are specialized to handle different functions, such as language, vision, and touch. In the Application, we'll discuss how the brain responds to environmental stimulation by literally altering its structure. And at several points, we'll return to Asha's story and tell you how she fared after her stroke.

biological psychology
Specialized branch of psychology that studies the relationship between behavior and bodily processes and systems; also called *biopsychology.*

neuroscience
The study of the nervous system, especially the brain.

neuron
Highly specialized cell that communicates information in electrical and chemical form; a nerve cell.

glial cells
(GLEE-ull) Support cells that assist neurons by providing structural support, nutrition, and removal of cell wastes; manufacture myelin.

The Neuron
The Basic Unit of Communication

Key Theme

- Information in the nervous system is transmitted by specialized cells, called neurons.

Key Questions

- What are the basic components of the neuron, and what are their functions?
- What are glial cells, and what is their role in the nervous system?
- What is an action potential, and how is it produced?

Communication throughout the nervous system takes place via **neurons**—cells that are highly specialized to receive and transmit information from one part of the body to another. The number of neurons in the nervous system is astronomical. The human brain is estimated to have 100 billion neurons. To help put this in perspective, if you could count neurons at the rate of one per second, it would take more than 3,000 years to count the neurons in a human brain!

Most neurons, especially those in the brain, are extremely small. A bit of brain tissue no larger than a grain of rice contains about 10,000 neurons! Special magnifying equipment, such as an electron microscope, is usually used to study neurons.

Fortunately for neuroscientists, there are often striking similarities between the workings of the human nervous system and those of the nervous systems of many other creatures in the animal kingdom. Very simple creatures, such as sea snails and squid, tend to have larger neurons and simpler nervous systems than do humans. Neuroscientists have been able to observe the actions and reactions of a single neuron by studying the nervous systems of such simple animals.

Along with neurons, the human nervous system is made up of other types of specialized cells, called **glial cells** (see Figure 2.1). Glial cells outnumber neurons by about 10 to 1, but are much smaller. Unlike neurons, glial cells do not send or receive information. Rather, they are cast in supporting roles to the major player, the neuron. *Glia* is Greek for "glue," and at one time it was believed that glial cells were the glue that held the neurons of the brain together. Although they don't actually glue neurons together, glial cells do provide structural support for neurons. Glial cells also provide nutrition, enhance the speed of communication between neurons, and remove waste products, including dead or damaged neurons (Lees, 1993).

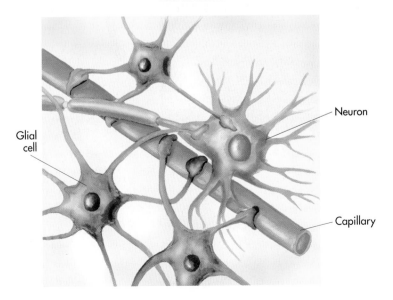

FIGURE 2.1 Glial Cells Glial cells vastly outnumber neurons in the brain. They provide support and nutrition for the neuron. One type of glial cell, shown here, provides a connection between neurons and blood vessels in the brain. Another type of glial cell produces the myelin sheath that surrounds some neuron axons.

Neuron

Glial cell

Capillary

Neurons vary greatly in size and shape, reflecting their specialized functions. There are three basic types of neurons, each communicating different kinds of information. **Sensory neurons** convey information about the environment, such as light or sound, from specialized receptor cells in the sense organs to the brain. Sensory neurons also carry information from the skin and internal organs to the brain. **Motor neurons** communicate information to the muscles and glands of the body. Simply blinking your eyes activates thousands of motor neurons. Finally, **interneurons** communicate information *between* neurons. By far, most of the neurons in the human nervous system are interneurons, and many interneurons connect to other interneurons.

Characteristics of the Neuron

Most neurons have three basic components: a *cell body, dendrites,* and an *axon* (see Figure 2.2). The **cell body** contains the nucleus, which provides energy for the neuron to carry out its functions. The cell body also contains genetic material and other structures that are found in virtually all the cells in the body.

Extending out from the cell body are many short, branching fibers, called **dendrites.** The term *dendrite* comes from a Greek word meaning "tree," and the

FIGURE 2.2 The Parts of a Typical Neuron The drawing shows the location and function of key parts of a neuron. The photograph, made with the aid of an electron microscope, reveals actual cell bodies, dendrites, and axons in a cluster of neurons. The green coloring was added to provide contrast in the photograph to make the neurons more visible.

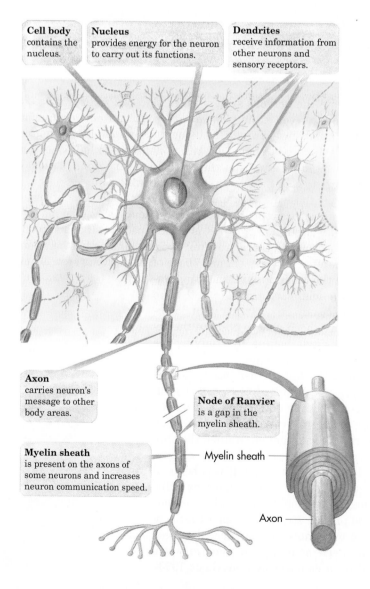

Cell body contains the nucleus.

Nucleus provides energy for the neuron to carry out its functions.

Dendrites receive information from other neurons and sensory receptors.

Axon carries neuron's message to other body areas.

Node of Ranvier is a gap in the myelin sheath.

Myelin sheath is present on the axons of some neurons and increases neuron communication speed.

Myelin sheath

Axon

intricate branching of the dendrites do often resemble the branches of a tree or bush. Dendrites *receive* messages from other neurons or specialized cells (Johnston & others, 1996). Dendrites with many branches have a greater surface area, which increases the amount of information the neuron can receive. Some neurons have thousands of dendrites.

The **axon** is a single, elongated tube that extends from the cell body in most, though not all, neurons. (Some neurons do not have axons.) Axons carry information *from* the neuron *to* other cells in the body, including other neurons, glands, and muscles. In contrast to the potentially large number of dendrites, a neuron has no more than one axon exiting from the cell body. However, many axons have branches near their tips that allow the neuron to communicate information to more than one target.

Axons can vary enormously in length. Most axons are very small; some are no more than a few thousandths of an inch long. Other axons are quite long. For example, the longest axon in your body is that of the motor neuron that controls your big toe. This neuron extends from the base of your spine into your foot. If you happen to be a seven-foot-tall basketball player, this axon could be four feet long! For most of us, of course, this axon is closer to three feet long.

The axons of many, though not all, neurons are surrounded by the **myelin sheath.** The myelin sheath is a white, fatty covering manufactured by special glial cells. In much the same way that you can bundle together electrical wires if they are insulated with plastic, myelin helps insulate one axon from the axons of other neurons. Rather than forming a continuous coating of the axon, the myelin sheath occurs in segments that are separated by small gaps where there is no myelin. The small gaps are called the *nodes of Ranvier,* or simply *nodes* (see Figure 2.2). Neurons wrapped in myelin communicate their messages up to 20 times faster than do unmyelinated neurons (Noseworthy, 1999).

The importance of myelin becomes readily apparent when it is damaged. For example, *multiple sclerosis* is a disease that involves the degeneration of patches of the myelin sheath. This degeneration causes the transmission of neural messages to be slowed or interrupted, resulting in disturbances in sensation and movement. Muscular weakness, loss of coordination, and speech and visual disturbances are some of the symptoms that characterize multiple sclerosis.

sensory neuron
Type of neuron that conveys information to the brain from specialized receptor cells in sense organs and internal organs.

motor neuron
Type of neuron that signals muscles to relax or contract.

interneuron
Type of neuron that communicates information from one neuron to the next.

cell body
The part of a neuron that contains the nucleus.

dendrites
Multiple short fibers that extend from the neuron's cell body and receive information from other neurons or from sensory receptor cells.

axon
The long, fluid-filled tube that carries a neuron's messages to other body areas.

myelin sheath
(MY-eh-lin) A white, fatty covering wrapped around the axons of some neurons that increases their communication speed.

action potential
A brief electrical impulse by which information is transmitted along the axon of a neuron.

stimulus threshold
The minimum level of stimulation required to activate a particular neuron.

Communication Within the Neuron

The All-or-None Action Potential

Essentially, the function of neurons is to transmit information throughout the nervous system. But exactly *how* do neurons transmit information? What form does this information take? In this section, we'll consider the nature of communication *within* a neuron, and in the following section we'll describe communication *between* neurons. As you'll see, communication in and between neurons is an electrochemical process.

In general, messages are gathered by the dendrites and cell body and then transmitted along the axon in the form of a brief electrical impulse called an **action potential.** The action potential is produced by the movement of electrically charged particles, called *ions,* across the membrane of the axon. Some ions are negatively charged, others positively charged.

Think of the axon membrane as a gatekeeper that carefully controls the balance of positive and negative ions on the interior and exterior of the axon. As the gatekeeper, the axon membrane opens and closes *ion channels* that allow ions to flow into and out of the axon.

Each neuron requires a minimum level of stimulation from other neurons or sensory receptors to activate it. This minimum level of stimulation is called the neuron's **stimulus threshold.** While waiting for sufficient stimulation to activate

resting potential
State in which a neuron is prepared to activate and communicate its message if it receives sufficient stimulation.

all-or-none law
The principle that either a neuron is sufficiently stimulated and an action potential occurs or a neuron is not sufficiently stimulated and an action potential does not occur.

it, the neuron is said to be *polarized.* In this state the axon's interior is more negatively charged than is the exterior fluid surrounding the axon.

Just in case you're wondering, scientists have measured the negative electrical charge of the neuron's interior, using giant squid neurons to do so. And how much electricity are we discussing? About −70 millivolts (thousandths of a volt) (See Figure 2.3a). The −70 millivolts is referred to as the neuron's **resting potential.**

This polarized, negative-inside/positive-outside condition is primarily due to the different concentrations of two particular ions: sodium and potassium. While the neuron is in resting potential, the fluid surrounding the axon contains a larger concentration of sodium ions than does the fluid within the axon. The fluid within the axon contains a larger concentration of potassium ions than is found in the fluid outside the axon.

When sufficiently stimulated by other neurons or sensory receptors, the neuron *depolarizes,* beginning the action potential. At each successive axon segment, sodium ion channels open for a mere thousandth of a second. The sodium ions rush to the axon interior from the surrounding fluid, and then the sodium ion channels close. Less than a thousandth of a second later, the potassium ion channels open, allowing potassium to rush out of the axon and into the fluid surrounding it. Then the potassium ion channels close (see Figure 2.3b). This sequence of depolarization and ion movement continues in a self-sustaining fashion down the entire length of the axon.

As sodium ions penetrate the axon membrane and potassium ions exit, the electrical charge on the inside of the axon momentarily changes to a positive electrical charge of about +30 millivolts. The result is a brief positive electrical impulse that progressively occurs at each segment down the axon—the *action potential.*

FIGURE 2.3a Electrical Changes During an Action Potential This graph shows the changing electrical charge of the neuron during an action potential. When the neuron depolarizes and ions cross the axon membrane, the result is a positive electrical impulse of +30 millivolts—the action potential. During the refractory period, the neuron reestablishes the resting potential negative charge of −70 millivolts and then is ready to activate again.

Although it's tempting to think of the action potential as being conducted much as electricity is conducted through a wire, that's *not* what takes place in the neuron. The axon is actually a poor conductor of electricity. At each successive segment of the axon, the action potential is *regenerated* in the same way in which it was generated in the previous segment—by depolarization and the movement of ions.

Once the action potential is started, it is self-sustaining and continues to the end of the axon. In other words, there is no such thing as a partial action potential. Either the neuron is sufficiently stimulated and an action potential occurs, or the neuron is not sufficiently stimulated and an action potential does not occur. This principle is referred to as the **all-or-none law.**

Following the action potential, a *refractory period* occurs during which the neuron is unable to fire. This period lasts for a mere thousandth of a second or less. During the refractory period, the neuron *repolarizes* and reestablishes the negative-inside/positive-outside condition. Like depolarization, repolarization occurs progressively at each segment down the axon. This process of pumping sodium ions out and drawing potassium ions back in reestablishes the *resting potential* conditions so that the neuron is capable of firing again. The graph in Figure 2.3a depicts the complete sequence from resting potential to action potential and back to resting potential.

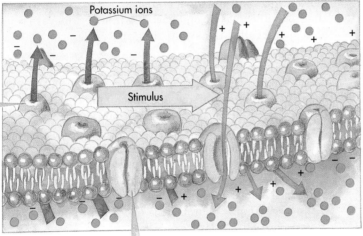

Sodium ions

Stimulus arrives

Sodium channels open and sodium ions rush in.

Sodium ions

Potassium ions

Potassium channels open and potassium ions rush out of the axon.

Stimulus

The first sodium channels have closed, but those farther down the axon open, carrying the movement of depolarization along.

FIGURE 2.3b Communication Within the Neuron: The Action Potential When sufficiently stimulated, a neuron depolarizes and an action potential begins. At each progressive segment of the axon's membrane, sodium ion channels open and sodium ions rush into the interior of the axon. A split second later, the sodium ion channels close and potassium channels open, allowing potassium ions to rush out of the axon. As this sequence occurs, the electrical charge on the interior of the axon changes from negative to positive. Once started, an action potential is self-sustaining and continues to the end of the axon.

For clarity, we've simplified some of the details involved in the action potential, but this is basically how information is communicated *within* a neuron. Remember, action potentials are generated in mere thousandths of a second. Thus, a single neuron can potentially generate hundreds of neural impulses per second. Given these minute increments of time, just how fast do neural impulses zip around the body?

The fastest neurons in your body communicate at speeds of up to 270 miles per hour. In the slowest neurons, messages creep along at about 2 miles per hour. This variation in communication speed is due to two factors: the axon diameter and the myelin sheath. The greater the axon's diameter, the faster the axon conducts action potentials. And, as we said earlier, myelinated neurons communicate faster than unmyelinated neurons. In myelinated neurons, the sodium ion channels are concentrated at each of the nodes of Ranvier where the myelin is missing. So, in myelinated neurons the action potential jumps from node to node rather than progressing down the entire length of the axon.

The Brain Capturing a Thought In the brain, as in the rest of the nervous system, information is transmitted by electrical impulses (red area) that speed from one neuron to the next.

synapse
(SIN-aps) The point of communication between two neurons.

synaptic gap
(sin-AP-tick) The tiny space between the axon terminal of one neuron and the dendrite of an adjoining neuron.

axon terminals
Branches at the end of the axon that contain tiny pouches, or sacs, called synaptic vesicles.

synaptic vesicles
(sin-AP-tick VESS-ick-ulls) Tiny pouches or sacs in the axon terminals that contain chemicals called neurotransmitters.

neurotransmitters
Chemical messengers manufactured by a neuron.

synaptic transmission
(sin-AP-tick) The process through which neurotransmitters are released by one neuron, cross the synaptic gap, and affect adjoining neurons.

reuptake
The process by which neurotransmitter molecules detach from a postsynaptic neuron and are reabsorbed by a presynaptic neuron so they can be recycled and used again.

Communication Between Neurons
Bridging the Gap

Key Theme
■ Communication between neurons takes place at the synapse, the junction between two adjoining neurons.

Key Questions
■ How is information communicated at the synapse?
■ What is a neurotransmitter, and what is its role in synaptic transmission?
■ What are five important neurotransmitters, and how do psychoactive drugs affect synaptic transmission?

The primary function of a neuron is to communicate information to other cells, most notably other neurons. The point of communication between two neurons is called the **synapse.** At this communication junction, the message-*sending* neuron is referred to as the *presynaptic neuron.* The message-*receiving* neuron is called the *postsynaptic neuron.* For cells that are specialized to communicate information, neurons have a surprising characteristic: They don't touch each other. The presynaptic and postsynaptic neurons are separated by a tiny, fluid-filled space, called the **synaptic gap,** which is only about *five-millionths* of an inch wide.

The transmission of information between two neurons occurs in one of two ways: electrically or chemically. When communication is electrical, the synaptic gap is extremely narrow, and special ion channels serve as a bridge between the neurons. Electrical communication between the two neurons is virtually instantaneous.

Although some neurons in the human nervous system communicate electrically, over 99 percent of the synapses in the brain use chemical transmission (Greengard, 2001). Chemical communication occurs when the presynaptic neuron creates a chemical substance that diffuses across the synaptic gap and is detected by the postsynaptic neuron. This one-way communication process has many important implications for human behavior.

Here's how chemical communication takes place between neurons. When the presynaptic neuron is activated, it generates an action potential that travels to the end of the axon. At the end of the axon are several small branches called **axon terminals.** Floating in the interior fluid of the axon terminals are tiny sacs called **synaptic vesicles** (see Figure 2.4). The synaptic vesicles hold special chemical messengers manufactured by the neuron, called **neurotransmitters.**

When the action potential reaches the axon terminals, some of the synaptic vesicles "dock" on the axon terminal membrane, then release their neurotransmitters into the synaptic gap. These chemical messengers cross the synaptic gap and attach to *receptor sites* on the dendrites of the surrounding neurons. This journey across the synaptic gap takes less than ten-millionths of a second. The entire process of transmitting information at the synapse is called **synaptic transmission.**

What happens to the neurotransmitter molecules after they've attached to the receptor sites of the postsynaptic neuron? Most often, they detach from the receptor and are reabsorbed by the presynaptic neuron so they can be recycled and used again. This process is called **reuptake.** Reuptake also occurs with many of the neurotransmitters that failed to attach to a receptor and are left floating in the synaptic gap. Neurotransmitter molecules that are not reabsorbed or that remain attached to the receptor site are broken down or destroyed by enzymes. As you'll see in the next section, certain drugs can interfere with both of these processes, prolonging the presence of the neurotransmitter in the synaptic gap.

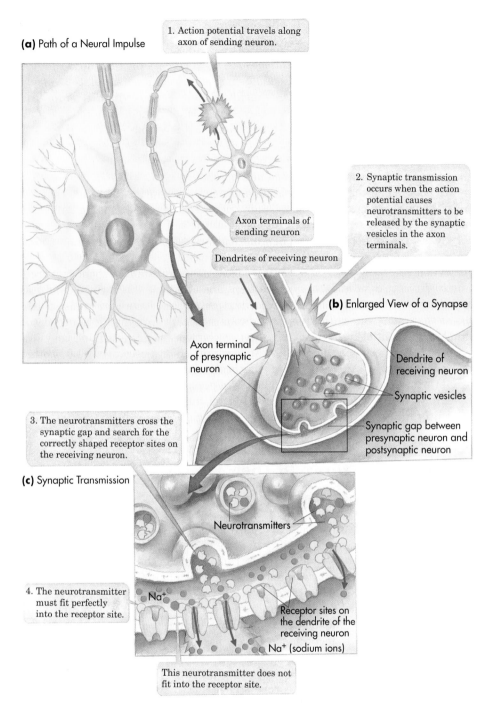

(a) Path of a Neural Impulse

1. Action potential travels along axon of sending neuron.

2. Synaptic transmission occurs when the action potential causes neurotransmitters to be released by the synaptic vesicles in the axon terminals.

Axon terminals of sending neuron

Dendrites of receiving neuron

(b) Enlarged View of a Synapse

Axon terminal of presynaptic neuron

Dendrite of receiving neuron

Synaptic vesicles

3. The neurotransmitters cross the synaptic gap and search for the correctly shaped receptor sites on the receiving neuron.

Synaptic gap between presynaptic neuron and postsynaptic neuron

(c) Synaptic Transmission

Neurotransmitters

4. The neurotransmitter must fit perfectly into the receptor site.

Na+

Receptor sites on the dendrite of the receiving neuron

Na+ (sodium ions)

This neurotransmitter does not fit into the receptor site.

FIGURE 2.4 Communication Between Neurons: The Process of Synaptic Transmission

The number of neurotransmitters that a neuron can manufacture varies. Some neurons produce only one type of neurotransmitter, whereas others manufacture three or more. Although estimates vary, scientists have thus far identified more than 100 different compounds that function as neurotransmitters in the brain (Greengard, 2001).

Each type of neurotransmitter has a chemically distinct, different shape. When released by the presynaptic neuron, neurotransmitters search for the correctly shaped receptor sites on the dendrites of the postsynaptic neurons. Like a key in a lock, a neurotransmitter's shape must precisely match that of a receptor site on the postsynaptic neuron's dendrites for the neurotransmitter to affect that neuron. Keep in mind that the postsynaptic neuron can have many differently shaped receptor sites on its dendrites and thus may accommodate several different neurotransmitters (see Figure 2.5).

FIGURE 2.5 Neurotransmitter and Receptor Site Shapes Each neurotransmitter has a chemically distinct shape. Like a key in a lock, a neurotransmitter must perfectly fit the receptor site on the receiving neuron for its message to be communicated. In this figure, NE is the abbreviation for the neurotransmitter norepinephrine and ACh is the abbreviation for acetylcholine.

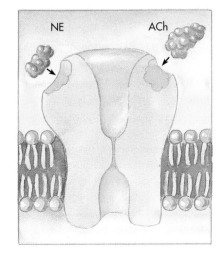

NE   ACh

acetylcholine
(uh-*seet*-ull-KO-leen) Neurotransmitter that causes muscle contraction and is involved in memory function.

dopamine
(DOPE-uh-meen) Neurotransmitter involved in the regulation of bodily movement, thought processes, and rewarding sensations.

serotonin
(ser-ah-TONE-in) Neurotransmitter involved in sleep and emotions.

norepinephrine
(nor-ep-in-EF-rin) Neurotransmitter involved in learning and memory; also a hormone manufactured by adrenal glands.

GABA (gamma-aminobutyric acid)
Neurotransmitter that usually communicates an inhibitory message.

Excitatory and Inhibitory Messages

A neurotransmitter communicates either an excitatory or an inhibitory message to a postsynaptic neuron. An *excitatory message* increases the likelihood that the postsynaptic neuron will activate and generate an action potential. Conversely, an *inhibitory message* decreases the likelihood that the postsynaptic neuron will activate. If a postsynaptic neuron receives an excitatory and an inhibitory message simultaneously, the two messages cancel each other out.

It's important to note that the effect of any particular neurotransmitter depends on the particular *receptor* to which it binds. So, the same neurotransmitter can have an inhibitory effect on one neuron and an excitatory effect on another.

Depending on the number and kind of neurotransmitter chemicals that are taken up by the dendrites of the adjoining neurons, the postsynaptic neurons are more or less likely to activate. If the net result is a sufficient number of excitatory messages, the postsynaptic neuron depolarizes, generates an action potential, and releases its own neurotransmitters.

When released by a presynaptic neuron, neurotransmitter chemicals cross hundreds, even thousands, of synaptic gaps and affect the intertwined dendrites of adjacent neurons. Because the receiving neuron can have thousands of dendrites that intertwine with the axon terminals of many presynaptic neurons, the number of potential synaptic interconnections between neurons is mind-boggling. On the average, each neuron in the brain communicates directly with 1,000 other neurons (Greengard, 2001). Thus, in your brain alone, there are up to 100 *trillion* synaptic interconnections. To help put this in perspective, look up at the sky on a clear, dark night. There are nearly a thousand times more synaptic connections in your brain than there are stars in our entire galaxy.

Neurotransmitters and Their Effects

Neurotransmitters play a crucial role in communication between neurons. The activation of most neurons is determined by the messages delivered by neurotransmitters. Thus, neurotransmitters have profound effects on our physical and psychological functioning. Our ability to perceive, feel, think, move, act, and react depends on the delicate balance of neurotransmitters in the nervous system. Too much or too little of a given neurotransmitter can have devastating effects.

Yet neurotransmitters are present in only minuscule amounts in the human body. If you imagine trying to detect a pinch of salt dissolved in an Olympic-sized swimming pool, you will have some idea of the infinitesimal amounts of neurotransmitters present in brain tissue.

Researchers have linked abnormal levels of specific neurotransmitters to various physical and behavioral problems. Nevertheless, it's important to remember that any connection between a particular neurotransmitter and a particular effect is not a simple one-to-one relationship. Many behaviors are the result of the complex interaction of different neurotransmitters. Further, neurotransmitters sometimes have different effects in different areas of the brain. Despite this complexity, some generalizations about the action of particular neurotransmitters can be made. In this section, we'll look at the behavioral effects of some of the most important neurotransmitters, including acetylcholine, serotonin, dopamine, GABA, and the endorphins. A summary of this information can be found in Table 2.1.

Table **2.1**

Summary of Important Neurotransmitters		
Neurotransmitter	**Primary Roles**	**Associated Disorders**
Acetylcholine	Learning, memory	Alzheimer's disease
	Muscle contractions	
Dopamine	Movement	Parkinson's disease
	Thought processes	Schizophrenia
	Rewarding sensations	Drug addiction
Serotonin	Emotional states	Depression
	Sleep	
Norepinephrine	Physical arousal	Depression, stress
	Learning	
	Memory	
GABA	Inhibition of brain activity	Anxiety disorders
Endorphins	Pain perception	Opiate addiction
	Positive emotions	

Important Neurotransmitters

Acetylcholine, the first neurotransmitter discovered, is found in all motor neurons. It stimulates muscles to contract, including the heart and stomach muscles. Whether it is as simple as the flick of an eyelash or as complex as a back flip, all movement involves acetylcholine.

Acetylcholine is also found in many neurons in the brain, and it is important in memory, learning, and general intellectual functioning. People with *Alzheimer's disease,* which is characterized by progressive loss of memory and deterioration of intellectual functioning, have a severe depletion of several neurotransmitters in the brain, most notably acetylcholine.

The neurotransmitter **dopamine** is involved in movement, attention, learning, and pleasurable or rewarding sensations (Nader & others, 1997; Schultz & others, 1997). Evidence suggests that the addictiveness of many drugs, including cocaine and nicotine, is related to their dopamine-increasing properties (Greengard, 2001; Volkow & others, 2001a).

The degeneration of the neurons that produce dopamine in one brain area causes *Parkinson's disease,* which is characterized by rigidity, muscle tremors, poor balance, and difficulty in initiating movements. Symptoms can be alleviated by a drug called *L-dopa,* which converts to dopamine in the brain (Youdim & Riederer, 1997).

Excessive brain levels of dopamine are sometimes involved in the hallucinations and perceptual distortions that characterize the severe mental disorder called *schizophrenia.* Some antipsychotic drugs that relieve schizophrenic symptoms work by blocking dopamine receptors and reducing dopamine activity in the brain. Unfortunately, these antipsychotic drugs can also produce undesirable side effects. Because the drugs reduce dopamine in several different areas of the brain, long-term use sometimes produces symptoms that are very similar to those of Parkinson's disease. In the chapters on psychological disorders (Chapter 14) and therapies (Chapter 15), we'll discuss schizophrenia, dopamine, and antipsychotic drugs in more detail.

The neurotransmitters **serotonin** and **norepinephrine** are found in many different brain areas. Serotonin is involved in sleep, moods, and emotional states, including depression. Antidepressant drugs such as *Prozac* increase the availability of serotonin in certain brain regions. Norepinephrine is implicated in the activation of neurons throughout the brain and helps the body gear up in the face of danger or threat. Norepinephrine also seems to be a key player in learning and memory retrieval. Like serotonin and dopamine, norepinephrine dysfunction is implicated in some mental disorders, especially depression (Nemeroff, 1998).

GABA is the abbreviation for **gamma-aminobutyric acid,** a neurotransmitter found primarily in the brain. GABA usually communicates an inhibitory message to other neurons, helping to balance and offset excitatory messages. Alcohol makes people feel relaxed and less inhibited partly by increasing GABA activity, which reduces brain activity. Antianxiety medications, such as Valium and Xanax, also work by increasing GABA activity, which inhibits action potentials and slows brain activity.

Interestingly, GABA seems to play a dual role in the brain area that regulates daily sleep–wake cycles. During the day, GABA communicates an excitatory message to other neurons in this brain area. At night, however, GABA communicates an inhibitory message to these same neurons (Wagner & others, 1997).

Nerve Gas and Acetylcholine By filtering the air, the gas mask protects this soldier against chemical weapons, like nerve gas. Nerve gas kills by causing acetylcholine to be continuously released by the motor neurons. Excessive acetylcholine builds up in the synaptic gap, causing muscle spasms that are so severe the victim is unable to breathe and quickly suffocates. Atropine, a drug that was carried by U.S. troops in the Persian Gulf War, is an effective antidote for nerve gas. When injected, atropine counteracts the effects of nerve gas by blocking acetylcholine receptor sites.

Michael J. Fox and Parkinson's Disease Actor Michael J. Fox was diagnosed with Parkinson's disease in 1990 at the age of 30. As the disease has progressed, Fox has experienced trembling, muscle stiffness, and difficulty initiating movements and speech. To help control the symptoms, he takes a medication containing L-dopa, which increases brain levels of the neurotransmitter dopamine. As Fox (1998) said in an interview, "The ugly truth is that I am flesh and blood and I am a bunch of neurotransmitters that may or may not work." Fox is keenly aware that the disease is progressive and, thus far, incurable. Fox left his hit TV series, *Spin City,* to devote himself to fundraising and increasing public awareness of Parkinson's disease. Among the estimated 1 million Americans who are afflicted with Parkinson's disease are former U.S. Attorney General Janet Reno, singer Johnny Cash, and the Reverend Billy Graham.

endorphins
(en-DORF-ins) Neurotransmitters that regulate pain perceptions.

nervous system
The primary internal communication network of the body; divided into the central nervous system and the peripheral nervous system.

nerves
Bundles of neuron axons that carry information in the peripheral nervous system.

Endorphins: The Brain's Natural High

In 1973, researchers Candace Pert and Solomon Snyder of Johns Hopkins University made the startling discovery that the brain contains receptor sites that are specific for the group of painkilling drugs called *opiates* (Pert & Snyder, 1973). Opiates include morphine, heroin, and codeine, all derived from the opium poppy. In addition to alleviating pain, opiates often produce a state of euphoria. Why would the brain have neurotransmitter receptor sites for specific drugs like morphine? Pert, Snyder, and other researchers concluded that the brain must manufacture its own painkillers, morphinelike chemicals that act as neurotransmitters.

Within a few years, researchers identified a number of such chemicals manufactured by the brain (Snyder, 1984). Collectively, they are called **endorphins,** a term derived from the phrase "endogenous morphines." (The word *endogenous* means "produced internally in the body.") Although chemically similar to morphine, endorphins are 100 times more potent. Today, it is known that endorphins are released in response to stress or trauma and that they reduce the perception of pain.

Researchers have found that endorphins are implicated in the pain-reducing effects of *acupuncture,* an ancient Chinese medical technique that involves inserting needles at various locations in the body (Chao & others, 1999). Endorphins are also associated with positive mood. For example, the "runner's high" associated with aerobic exercise has been attributed to endorphins. In marathon runners, endorphin levels have been found to increase up to four times over their normal levels (Mahler & others, 1989).

How Drugs Affect Synaptic Transmission

Much of what is known about different neurotransmitters has been learned from observing the effects of drugs and other substances. Many drugs, especially those that affect moods or behavior, work by interfering with the normal functioning of neurotransmitters in the synapse.

As Figure 2.6 illustrates, some drugs increase or decrease the amount of neurotransmitter released by neurons. For example, the venom of a black widow spider bite causes acetylcholine to be released continuously by motor neurons, causing severe muscle spasms. Drugs may also affect the length of time the neurotransmitter remains in the synaptic gap, either increasing or decreasing the amount available to the postsynaptic receptor.

One way in which drugs can prolong the effects of the neurotransmitter is by blocking the reuptake of the neurotransmitter by the sending neuron. For example, Prozac inhibits the reuptake of serotonin, increasing the availability of serotonin in the brain. The illegal drug cocaine produces its exhilarating rush by interfering with the reuptake of dopamine (Volkow & others, 1997).

Drugs can also mimic specific neurotransmitters. When a drug is chemically similar to a specific neurotransmitter, it may produce the same effect as that neurotransmitter. It is partly through this mechanism that nicotine works as a stimulant. Nicotine is chemically similar to acetylcholine and can occupy acetylcholine receptor sites, stimulating skeletal muscles and causing the heart to beat more rapidly.

Alternatively, a drug can mimic and block the effect of a neurotransmitter by fitting into receptor sites and preventing the neurotransmitter from acting. For example, the drug *curare* mimics acetylcholine and blocks acetyl-

FIGURE 2.6 How Drugs Affect Synaptic Transmission Drugs affect brain activity by interfering with neurotransmitter functioning in the synapse. Drugs may also affect synaptic transmission by increasing or decreasing the amount of a particular neurotransmitter that is produced.

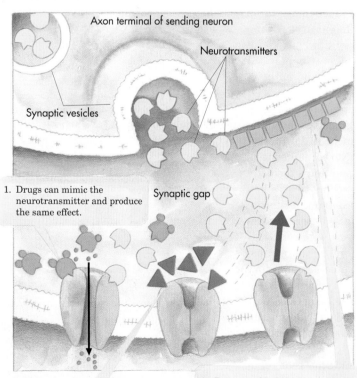

Axon terminal of sending neuron

Neurotransmitters

Synaptic vesicles

1. Drugs can mimic the neurotransmitter and produce the same effect.

Synaptic gap

2. Drugs can block the receptor site on the receiving neuron and prevent the effect of the neurotransmitter.

3. Drugs can block the reuptake of the neurotransmitter, increasing the effects of the neurotransmitter.

choline receptor sites, causing almost instantaneous paralysis. The brain sends signals to the motor neurons, but the muscles can't respond because the motor neuron receptor sites are blocked by the curare. Similarly, a drug called *naloxone* eliminates the effects of both endorphins and opiates by blocking opiate receptor sites.

2.1 R·E·V·I·E·W*

C·O·N·C·E·P·T

The Neuron

Match the part of the neuron in the list with its function in neural communication.

    a. action potential   d. myelin sheath
    b. axon   e. neurotransmitters
    c. synapse   f. dendrite

1. A fluid-filled tube that carries information to other neurons, glands, and muscles

2. Receives information from other neurons

3. Brief electrical charge that communicates information within the neuron

4. Fluid-filled space between sending and receiving neurons

5. Chemical messengers manufactured by a neuron

6. White, fatty covering surrounding an axon that increases speed of neural communication

*Note: Answers to Concept Review questions appear on the final page of this and every chapter.

FIGURE 2.7 The Nervous System The nervous system is a complex, organized communication network that is divided into two main divisions: the central nervous system (shown in yellow) and the peripheral nervous system (shown in blue).

The Nervous System and the Endocrine System
Communication Throughout the Body

Key Theme
■ Two major communication systems in the body are the nervous system and the endocrine system.

Key Questions
■ What are the divisions of the nervous system and their functions?
■ How is information transmitted in the endocrine system, and what are its major structures?
■ How do the nervous and endocrine systems interact to produce the fight-or-flight response?

Specialized for communication, up to 1 *trillion* neurons are linked throughout your body in a complex, organized communication network called the **nervous system.** The human nervous system is divided into two main divisions: the *central nervous system* and the *peripheral nervous system* (see Figure 2.7). In order for even simple behaviors to occur, such as curling your toes or scratching your nose, these two divisions must function as a single, integrated unit. Yet each of these divisions is highly specialized and performs different tasks.

    The neuron is the most important transmitter of messages in the central nervous system. In the peripheral nervous system, communication occurs along **nerves.** Nerves and neurons are not the same thing (see Figure 2.8). Nerves are made up of large bundles of neuron axons. Unlike neurons, many nerves are large enough to be seen easily with the unaided eye.

FIGURE 2.8 Nerves and Neurons Are Not the Same A cross section of a peripheral nerve is shown in this electron micrograph. You can see that a nerve is actually composed of bundles of neuron axons.

central nervous system
Division of the nervous system that consists of the brain and spinal cord.

spinal reflexes
Simple, automatic behaviors that are processed in the spinal cord.

The Central Nervous System

The **central nervous system** includes the brain and the spinal cord. The central nervous system is so critical to your ability to function that it is entirely protected by bone—the brain by your skull and the spinal cord by your spinal column. As an added measure of protection, the brain and spinal cord are suspended in *cerebrospinal fluid* to protect them from being jarred.

The central nervous system is aptly named. It is central to all your behaviors and mental processes. And it is the central processing center—every action, thought, feeling, and sensation you experience is processed through the central nervous system. The most important element of the central nervous system is, of course, the brain, which acts as the command center. We'll take a tour of the human brain in a later section.

Think of the spinal cord as an old-fashioned but very busy telephone switchboard, handling both incoming and outgoing messages. Sensory receptors send messages along sensory nerves to the spinal cord, then up to the brain. To activate muscles, the brain sends signals down the spinal cord, which are relayed out along motor nerves to the muscles.

Most behaviors are controlled by your brain. However, the spinal cord can produce **spinal reflexes**—simple, automatic behaviors that occur without any brain involvement. One of the simplest spinal reflexes involves a three-neuron loop of rapid communication—a *sensory neuron* that communicates sensation to the spinal cord, an *interneuron* that relays information within the spinal cord, and a *motor neuron* leading from the spinal cord that signals muscles to react.

The spinal reflex shown in Figure 2.9 illustrates one of your authors' recent attempt to rescue his English muffin, trapped in a life-or-death struggle with an obstinate toaster. Half awake, Don poked his coffee spoon into the toaster to pry out the smoking muffin. The resulting electrical shock, detected by sensory re-

FIGURE 2.9 A Spinal Reflex Arc A spinal reflex is a simple, involuntary behavior that is processed in the spinal cord without brain involvement. As you follow the sequence, you can see that the withdrawal reflex occurs before the brain processes the conscious perception of pain.

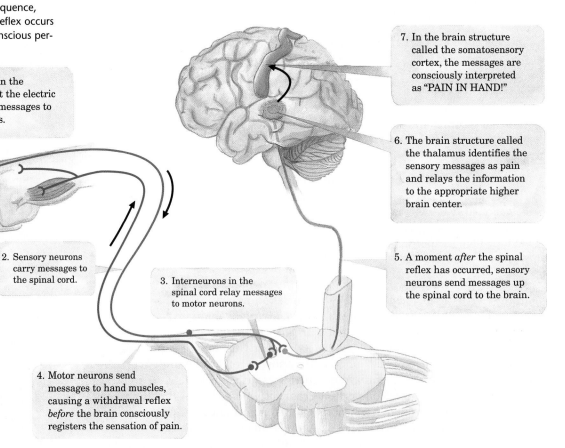

1. Skin receptors in the fingertips detect the electric shock, sending messages to sensory neurons.

2. Sensory neurons carry messages to the spinal cord.

3. Interneurons in the spinal cord relay messages to motor neurons.

4. Motor neurons send messages to hand muscles, causing a withdrawal reflex *before* the brain consciously registers the sensation of pain.

5. A moment *after* the spinal reflex has occurred, sensory neurons send messages up the spinal cord to the brain.

6. The brain structure called the thalamus identifies the sensory messages as pain and relays the information to the appropriate higher brain center.

7. In the brain structure called the somatosensory cortex, the messages are consciously interpreted as "PAIN IN HAND!"

ceptors in his hand, sent a barrage of neural impulses along his sensory neurons to his spinal cord. Interneurons relayed the information within his spinal cord, and motor neurons leading from his spinal cord signaled his muscles to jerk back.

The result? Don reflexively pulled his hand away *before* becoming consciously aware of either the sensation or his own movement. This spinal reflex occurred in just a fraction of a second, without involving your author's brain (which was obviously not fully functioning anyway). A moment later, the stimulus was interpreted by his brain (PAIN IN HAND!) as he danced around the kitchen, shaking his tingling hand (*"Yow!* that #%!* toaster attacked me!"*).

Spinal reflexes are crucial to your survival. The additional few seconds that it would take you to consciously process sensations and decide how to react could result in serious injury. Spinal reflexes are also important as indicators that the neural pathways in your spinal cord are working correctly. That's why physicians test spinal reflexes during neurological examinations by tapping just below your kneecap for the knee-jerk spinal reflex or scratching the sole of your foot for the toe-curl spinal reflex.

The Peripheral Nervous System

The **peripheral nervous system** is the other major division of your nervous system. The word *peripheral* means "lying at the outer edges." Thus, the peripheral nervous system comprises all the nerves outside the central nervous system that extend to the outermost borders of your body, including your skin. The communication functions of the peripheral nervous system are handled by its two subdivisions: the *somatic nervous system* and the *autonomic nervous system.*

The **somatic nervous system** takes its name from the Greek word *soma,* which means "body." It plays a key role in communication throughout the entire body. First, the somatic nervous system communicates sensory information received by sensory receptors along sensory nerves *to* the central nervous system. Second, it carries messages *from* the central nervous system along motor nerves to perform voluntary muscle movements. All the different sensations that you're experiencing right now are being communicated by your somatic nervous system to your spinal cord and on to your brain. When you perform a voluntary action, such as turning a page of this book, messages from the brain are communicated down the spinal cord, then out to the muscles via the somatic nervous system.

The other subdivision of the peripheral nervous system is the **autonomic nervous system.** The word *autonomic* means "self-governing." Thus, the autonomic nervous system regulates *involuntary* functions, such as heartbeat, blood pressure, breathing, and digestion. These processes occur with little or no conscious involvement. This is fortunate, because if you had to mentally command your heart to beat or your stomach to digest the pizza you had for lunch, it would be difficult to focus your attention on anything else.

However, the autonomic nervous system is not completely self-regulating. By engaging in physical activity or purposely tensing or relaxing your muscles, you can increase or decrease autonomic activity. Emotions and mental imagery also influence your autonomic nervous system. Vividly imagining a situation that makes you feel angry, frightened, or even sexually aroused can dramatically increase your heart rate and blood pressure. A peaceful mental image can lower many autonomic functions.

The involuntary functions regulated by the autonomic nervous system are controlled by two different branches: the *sympathetic* and *parasympathetic nervous systems.* These two systems control many of the same organs in your body but cause them to respond in opposite ways (see Figure 2.10 on page 58). In general, the sympathetic nervous system arouses the body to expend energy, and the parasympathetic nervous system helps the body conserve energy.

Activating the Sympathetic Nervous System The sympathetic branch of the autonomic nervous system gears the body up in response to perceived threats. This arousal of the body's systems prepares organisms to flee from danger or confront it head-on—the essence of the *fight-or-flight syndrome.* When the sympathetic nervous system activates in humans, tiny muscles in the skin contract, which elevates your hair follicles, producing the familiar sensation of "goose bumps" and making your hair stand on end. A similar process takes place in many mammals, making the fur or hair bristle, with rather spectacular results in this long-haired cat.

peripheral nervous system
(per-IF-er-ull) Division of the nervous system that includes all the nerves lying outside the central nervous system.

somatic nervous system
Subdivision of the peripheral nervous system that communicates sensory information to the central nervous system and carries motor messages from the central nervous system to the muscles.

autonomic nervous system
(aw-toe-NOM-ick) Subdivision of the peripheral nervous system that regulates involuntary functions.

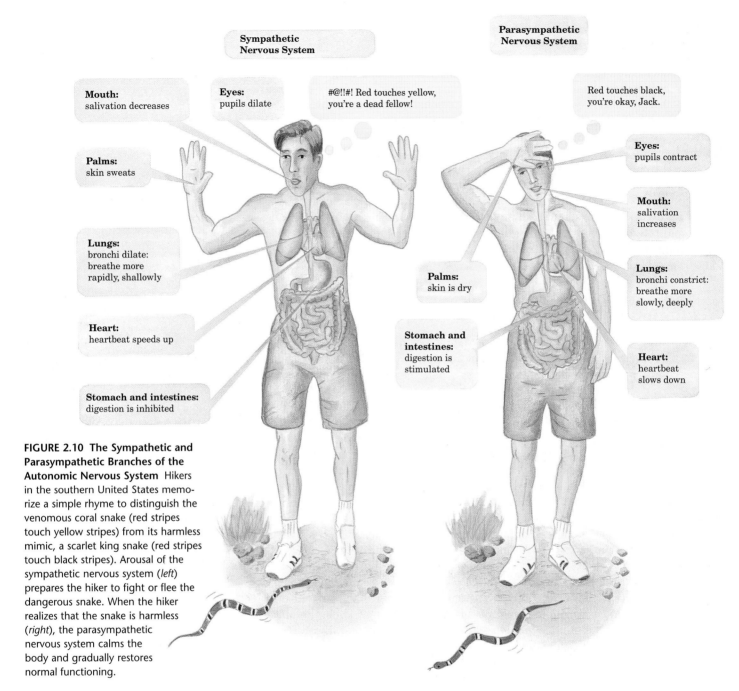

Sympathetic Nervous System

Parasympathetic Nervous System

Mouth: salivation decreases

Eyes: pupils dilate

#@!!#! Red touches yellow, you're a dead fellow!

Red touches black, you're okay, Jack.

Palms: skin sweats

Eyes: pupils contract

Mouth: salivation increases

Lungs: bronchi dilate: breathe more rapidly, shallowly

Palms: skin is dry

Lungs: bronchi constrict: breathe more slowly, deeply

Heart: heartbeat speeds up

Stomach and intestines: digestion is stimulated

Heart: heartbeat slows down

Stomach and intestines: digestion is inhibited

FIGURE 2.10 The Sympathetic and Parasympathetic Branches of the Autonomic Nervous System Hikers in the southern United States memorize a simple rhyme to distinguish the venomous coral snake (red stripes touch yellow stripes) from its harmless mimic, a scarlet king snake (red stripes touch black stripes). Arousal of the sympathetic nervous system (*left*) prepares the hiker to fight or flee the dangerous snake. When the hiker realizes that the snake is harmless (*right*), the parasympathetic nervous system calms the body and gradually restores normal functioning.

The **sympathetic nervous system** is the body's emergency system, rapidly activating bodily systems to meet threats or emergencies. When you are frightened, your breathing accelerates, your heart beats faster, digestion stops, and the bronchial tubes in your lungs expand. All these physiological responses increase the amount of oxygen available to your brain and muscles. Your pupils dilate to increase your field of vision, and your mouth becomes dry, because salivation stops. You begin to sweat in response to your body's expenditure of greater energy and heat. These bodily changes collectively represent the *fight-or-flight response*—they physically prepare you to fight or flee from a perceived danger (Cannon, 1932).

As a short-term response, the fight-or-flight response helps you cope with an emergency situation. However, if this heightened physiological arousal continues, such as during times of prolonged stress, you can suffer from mental and physical deterioration or exhaustion (Stein & Miller, 1993). We'll discuss the fight-or-flight response in greater detail in later chapters on emotion (Chapter 8) and stress (Chapter 13).

Other types of emotional arousal also involve your sympathetic nervous system. The anxiety you feel when you have to make an important presentation, the anger you experience during a heated argument with a loved one, and the acute discomfort you feel when your boss chews you out—all these unpleasant emotions involve physical arousal resulting from the activation of your sympathetic nervous system.

Heightened arousal of the sympathetic nervous system can sometimes work against you. For example, have you ever found yourself "choking" while taking an important exam? Your hands begin to sweat, your mouth becomes dry, your heart pounds, and, of course, your mind goes blank. These are all symptoms of your sympathetic nervous system going into high gear.

Whereas the sympathetic nervous system mobilizes your body's physical resources, the **parasympathetic nervous system** conserves and maintains your physical resources. It calms you down after an emergency. Acting much more slowly than the sympathetic nervous system, the parasympathetic nervous system gradually returns your body's systems to normal. Heart rate, breathing, and blood pressure level out. Pupils constrict back to their normal size. Saliva returns, and the digestive system begins operating again.

Although the sympathetic and parasympathetic nervous systems produce opposite effects, they act together, keeping the nervous system in balance (see Figure 2.11). Each division handles different functions, yet the whole nervous system works in unison so that both automatic and voluntary behaviors are carried out smoothly.

FIGURE 2.11 Organization of the Nervous System

The Endocrine System

The **endocrine system** is made up of glands that are located throughout the body (see Figure 2.12 on page 60). Like the nervous system, the endocrine system involves the use of chemical messengers to transmit information from one part of the body to another. Although the endocrine system is not part of the nervous system, it interacts with the nervous system in some important ways, as you'll see in this section.

Endocrine glands communicate information from one part of the body to another by secreting messenger chemicals called **hormones** into the bloodstream. The hormones circulate throughout the bloodstream until they reach specific hormone receptors on target organs or tissue. By interacting with the nervous system and affecting internal organs and body tissues, hormones regulate physical processes and influence behavior in a variety of ways. Metabolism, growth rate, digestion, blood pressure, and sexual development and reproduction are just some of the processes that are regulated by the endocrine hormones. Hormones are also involved in emotional response and your response to stress.

Endocrine hormones are closely linked to the workings of the nervous system. For example, the release of hormones may be stimulated or inhibited by certain parts of the nervous system. In turn, hormones can promote or inhibit the generation of nerve impulses. Finally, some hormones and neurotransmitters are chemically identical. The same molecule can act as a hormone in the endocrine system and as a neurotransmitter in the nervous system.

In contrast to the rapid speed of information transmission in the nervous system, communication in the endocrine system takes place much more slowly. Hormones rely on the circulation of the blood to deliver their chemical messages to target organs, so it may take a few seconds or longer for the hormone to reach its target organ after it has been secreted by the originating gland.

sympathetic nervous system
Branch of the autonomic nervous system that produces rapid physical arousal in response to perceived emergencies or threats.

parasympathetic nervous system
Branch of the autonomic nervous system that maintains normal bodily functions and conserves the body's physical resources.

endocrine system
(EN-doe-krin) System of glands located throughout the body that secrete hormones into the bloodstream.

hormones
Chemical messengers secreted into the bloodstream by endocrine glands.

FIGURE 2.12 The Endocrine System The endocrine system and the nervous system are directly linked by the hypothalamus in the brain, which controls the pituitary gland. In turn, the pituitary releases hormones that affect the hormone production of several other endocrine glands. In the male and female figures shown here, you can see the location and main functions of several important endocrine glands.

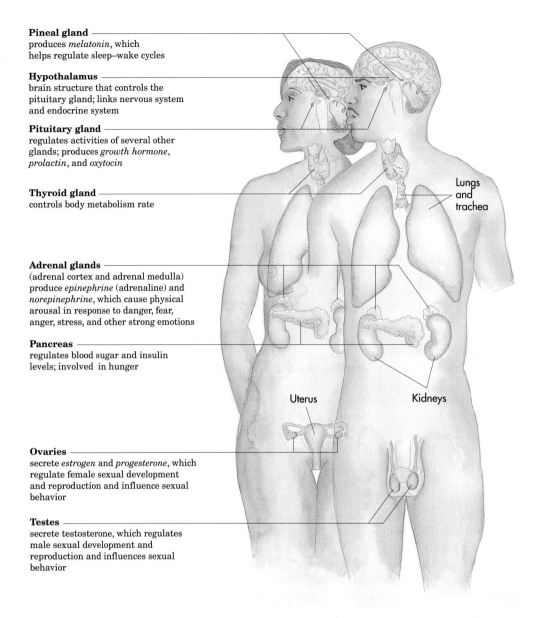

Pineal gland
produces *melatonin*, which helps regulate sleep–wake cycles

Hypothalamus
brain structure that controls the pituitary gland; links nervous system and endocrine system

Pituitary gland
regulates activities of several other glands; produces *growth hormone*, *prolactin*, and *oxytocin*

Thyroid gland
controls body metabolism rate

Adrenal glands
(adrenal cortex and adrenal medulla) produce *epinephrine* (adrenaline) and *norepinephrine*, which cause physical arousal in response to danger, fear, anger, stress, and other strong emotions

Pancreas
regulates blood sugar and insulin levels; involved in hunger

Ovaries
secrete *estrogen* and *progesterone*, which regulate female sexual development and reproduction and influence sexual behavior

Testes
secrete testosterone, which regulates male sexual development and reproduction and influences sexual behavior

Lungs and trachea

Uterus

Kidneys

The signals that trigger the secretion of hormones are regulated by the brain, primarily by a brain structure called the *hypothalamus*. (You'll learn more about the hypothalamus later in the chapter.) The hypothalamus serves as the main link between the endocrine system and the nervous system. The hypothalamus directly regulates the release of hormones by the **pituitary gland,** a pea-sized gland just under the brain. The pituitary's hormones, in turn, regulate the production of other hormones by many of the glands in the endocrine system. Thus, under the direction of the hypothalamus, the pituitary gland directly controls hormone production in other endocrine glands.

The pituitary gland also produces some hormones that act directly. For example, the pituitary produces *growth hormone,* which stimulates normal skeletal growth during childhood. In nursing mothers, the pituitary produces both *prolactin,* the hormone that stimulates milk production, and *oxytocin,* the hormone that produces the let-down reflex, in which stored milk is "let down" into the nipple.

Breast-feeding is a good example of the complex interaction among the nervous system, the endocrine system, and behavior. When an infant nurses at the breast, a message is sent by the hypothalamus to the pituitary to produce oxytocin, leading to the let-down of milk (see Figure 2.13). In a nursing mother, a baby's cry, the sight of her infant, or just the thought of her infant can stimulate this complex chain of internal events and lead to milk production even in the absence of physical stimulation of the nipple.

Another set of glands, called the **adrenal glands,** is of particular interest to psychologists. The adrenal glands consist of the **adrenal cortex,** which is the outer gland, and the **adrenal medulla,** which is the inner gland. Both the adrenal cortex and the adrenal medulla produce hormones that are involved in the human stress response. As you'll see in Chapter 13, on stress, hormones secreted by the adrenal cortex also interact with the *immune system,* the body's defense against invading viruses or bacteria.

The adrenal medulla plays a key role in the fight-or-flight response, described earlier. When aroused, the sympathetic nervous system stimulates the adrenal medulla. In turn, the adrenal medulla produces *epinephrine* and *norepinephrine.* (You may be more familiar with the word *adrenaline,* which is another name for epinephrine.)

As they circulate through the bloodstream to the heart and other target organs, epinephrine and norepinephrine complement and enhance the effects of the sympathetic nervous system. These hormones also act as neurotransmitters, stimulating activity at the synapses in the sympathetic nervous system. The action of epinephrine and norepinephrine is a good illustration of the long-lasting effects of hormones. If you've noticed that it takes a while for you to calm down after a particularly upsetting or stressful experience, it's because of the lingering effects of epinephrine and norepinephrine in your body.

Also important are the **gonads,** or sex organs—the *ovaries* in women and the *testes* in men. The pituitary gland secrets hormones called *gonadotrophins,* which regulate the secretions of sex hormones by the gonads. In men, the testes secrete the hormone *testosterone.* In women, the ovaries secrete the hormones *estrogen* and *progesterone.* These sex hormones have profound effects on sexual development, reproduction, and sexual behavior. For example, the sexual development of the fetus is determined by the prenatal activity of testosterone or estrogen. The development of secondary sexual characteristics at puberty is caused by increased levels of sex hormones. And the cyclical release of estrogen and progesterone, directed by the pituitary, produces the menstrual cycle in women.

Other important endocrine glands include the *thyroid,* which controls metabolism, and the *pancreas,* which regulates blood sugar levels and plays a key role in hunger and eating. Finally, the tiny *pineal gland,* located in the center of the brain, produces the hormone *melatonin.* Melatonin is involved in the regulation of sleep and wakefulness. We'll discuss the pineal gland in more detail in Chapter 4.

The endocrine system plays an important role in regulating many functions and behaviors. And, as noted, some of the hormones secreted by endocrine glands can even function as neurotransmitters that influence the communication of the nervous system. Thus the nervous system, the endocrine system, and behavior form a highly interdependent network.

Hypothalamus

Nerve impulses to hypothalamus

Posterior pituitary

Release of oxytocin

FIGURE 2.13 Interacting Systems Breastfeeding is an example of the complex interaction among the nervous system, the endocrine system, and behavior. Nerve impulses from sensory receptors in the mother's skin are sent to the brain. The hypothalamus signals the production of oxytocin by the pituitary gland, which causes the mother's milk to let down and begin flowing.

pituitary gland
(pi-TOO-ih-tare-ee) Endocrine gland attached to the base of the brain that secretes hormones that affect the function of other glands as well as hormones that act directly on physical processes.

adrenal glands
Pair of endocrine glands that are involved in the human stress response.

adrenal cortex
The outer portion of the adrenal glands.

adrenal medulla
The inner portion of the adrenal glands; secretes epinephrine and norepinephrine.

gonads
The endocrine glands that secrete hormones that regulate sexual characteristics and reproductive processes; ovaries in females and testes in males.

2.2 R·E·V·I·E·W

C·O·N·C·E·P·T

The Nervous System and the Endocrine System

Circle the letter of the item that correctly completes each statement.

1. While watching a suspenseful video late at night, you hear a sudden crash in another room. You leap out of your chair in fear, then realize that your dog has knocked over the trash again. Your fear reaction involved the activation of the _____ of the nervous system. Calming down involved the _____ of the nervous system.
   a. hypothalamus; endocrine branch
   b. somatic branch; sympathetic division
   c. sympathetic division; parasympathetic division
   d. parasympathetic division; sympathetic division

2. The part of the nervous system that controls voluntary movement is the _____.
   a. parasympathetic nervous system
   b. somatic nervous system
   c. autonomic nervous system
   d. fight-or-flight response

3. The glands of the endocrine system communicate via _____.
   a. electrically charged ion channels
   b. neural impulses along the axon
   c. spinal reflexes
   d. messenger chemicals called hormones

4. The main link between the nervous system and the endocrine system occurs at the _____.
   a. adrenal glands
   b. pineal gland
   c. somatic nervous system
   d. hypothalamus

5. In response to stress, epinephrine is pumped into the bloodstream by the _____.
   a. adrenal glands
   b. pineal gland
   c. thyroid gland
   d. pituitary gland

A Guided Tour of the Brain

Key Theme
- The brain is a highly complex, integrated, and organized system of neurons.

Key Questions
- What methods have been used to study the human brain, and how has each contributed to knowledge of the brain?
- What are neural pathways?
- How does the brain develop, and what is neurogenesis?

The Human Brain Weighing roughly three pounds, the human brain is about the size of a small cauliflower. Although your brain makes up only about 2 percent of your total body weight, it uses some 20 percent of the oxygen your body needs while at rest. The oxygen is used in breaking down glucose to supply the brain with energy.

Forget all the hype about the Internet. The *real* information superhighway is the human brain. In fact, the most complex mass of matter known to exist sits right between your two ears: your brain.

Neuroscientists have made enormous advances in the past decades in understanding the brain structures and neural pathways involved in behavior. New discoveries are made so frequently that even experts find it hard to keep up with the explosion of research on the brain. All the same, a great deal remains to be explained about how the brain processes information and translates neural impulses into complex behavior (Albright & others, 2000).

In this section, we'll take you on a guided tour of the human brain. As your tour guides, our goal here is not to tell you everything that is known or suspected about the human brain. Such an endeavor would take stacks of books rather than a single chapter in a college textbook. Instead, our first goal is to familiarize you with the basic organization and structures of the brain. In later chapters, we'll add to your knowledge of the brain as we discuss the brain's involvement in specific psychological processes in more detail. Our second goal is to give you a general sense of *how* the brain works.

At the beginning of this tour, it's important to note that the brain generally does not lend itself to simple explanations. As we describe the different areas of the brain, we'll identify important centers where particular functions seem to be localized. Nevertheless, bear in mind that specific functions seldom correspond neatly to a single, specific brain site. Many psychological processes, particularly complex ones, involve multiple brain structures and regions. Even simple tasks—such as watching TV, carrying on a conversation, or walking down the street—involve the smoothly coordinated synthesis of information among many different areas of your brain.

How is information communicated and shared among these multiple brain regions? Many brain functions involve the activation of *neural pathways* that link different brain structures. Neural pathways are formed by groups of neuron cell bodies in one area of the brain that project their axons to other brain areas. These neural pathways form communication networks and circuits that link different brain areas. As a result, damage to one area of the brain may disrupt many neural pathways and affect many different functions. Thus, even though we'll talk about brain centers and structures that are involved in different aspects of behavior, the best way to think of the brain is as an *integrated system.*

Before we begin our tour, we'll provide a brief overview of the methods that have been used to study the human brain.

Studying the Brain
The Toughest Case to Crack

Imagine how difficult it would be to try to figure out how something works without being able to open it, take it apart, or watch it operate. Such has long been the challenge faced by scientists investigating the workings of the human brain. Because the brain is encased entirely by bone, it has been impossible to directly observe a normal, living brain in action. One early approach to mapping brain functions involved examining the bumps on a person's skull. As you can see in Science Versus Pseudoscience Box 2.1, this approach was not very successful.

Another obstacle is the complexity of the brain itself—complex not only in its enormous number of interconnected neurons, but also in the intricate structures, regions, and pathways formed by those neurons. But scientists are not an easily discouraged lot.

Some of the oldest methods of studying the brain are still commonly used. In the *case study,* researchers systematically observe and record the behavior of people whose brains have been damaged by illness or injury. Case studies of individuals with brain damage have provided valuable insights into behavior in such areas as memory, speech, emotion, movement, and personality. As you'll see later, the knowledge gained from such observations allowed scientists to begin mapping the functions of the brain.

However, generalizing results from a case study must be done cautiously. By their very nature, case studies usually focus on unusual situations or behaviors—in this case, brain disease or injury. Because these behaviors or situations are out of the ordinary, they may not reflect typical behavior.

Another potential limitation to using case studies in brain research is that injuries to the brain are rarely limited to specific, localized areas or contained within well-defined anatomical boundaries. It's often difficult to be sure exactly which brain area is responsible for specific behavioral problems. In addition, many brain areas are linked to other brain areas, and damage in one area may disrupt functioning in another, otherwise normal area.

A related research method involves producing *lesions*—surgically altering, removing, or destroying specific portions of the brain—and observing subsequent behavior. In humans, lesions are sometimes produced for medical reasons, such as when part of the brain is surgically altered or removed to relieve

SCIENCE VERSUS PSEUDOSCIENCE 2.1

Phrenology: The Bumpy Road to Scientific Progress

Are people with large foreheads smarter than people with small foreheads? Does the shape of your head provide clues to your abilities, character, and personality characteristics? Such notions were at the core of **phrenology,** a popular pseudoscience founded by Franz Gall, a German physician and brain anatomist.

In the early 1800s, Gall made several important contributions to the understanding of brain anatomy. He correctly noted, for example, that the cortex of animals was smaller and less developed than the cortex of intellectually superior humans. Eventually, he became convinced that the size and shape of the cortex were reflected in the size and shape of the skull. Taking this notion a step further, he suspected that variations in the size and shape of the human skull might reflect individual differences in abilities, character, and personality.

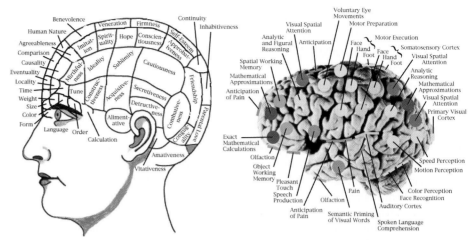

Cortical Localization: Then and Now As the 19th century phrenology map at left indicates, bumps on the skull supposedly revealed the underlying brain areas responsible for a variety of psychological "faculties," such as secretiveness and mirthfulness. On the right, you can see the collective results of hundreds of PET and functional MRI studies showing areas of increased brain activity and cerebral blood flow corresponding to various cognitive and perceptual functions (Nichols & Newsome, 1999).

The Psycograph Henry Lavery invented the psycograph in the early 1900s to improve the accuracy of phrenology measurements. More than 30 probes in the helmetlike headpiece made contact with the skull. The machines stamped out brief summaries of the different "faculties" measured, such as: "You are fairly secretive but can improve. You tell things to your friends. Don't do it." Forty of the machines were built, and they were popular attractions in department stores and theater lobbies throughout the United States (McCoy, 1996).

To gather evidence, Gall went to hospitals, prisons, asylums, and schools to examine people with oddly shaped heads. Gall noted the association between a particular person's characteristics and any distinctive bulges and bumps on the person's skull. On the basis of these observations, he identified 27 personality characteristics, or "faculties," that he believed could be diagnosed by examining specific areas of the head. Gall devised elaborate maps showing the skull location of various personality characteristics and abilities. For instance, Gall believed that a thick neck was associated with increased sexual motivation and that a prominent forehead was associated with greater intellectual ability (McCoy, 1996).

Gall's methods of testing his theory were both careless and highly subjective. When confronted with evidence that seemed to contradict his theory, Gall merely dismissed it (Fancher, 1996). And when his theory of phrenology was ridiculed by other scientists for lack of adequate evidence, Gall took his ideas to the general public by presenting lectures and demonstrations. He lectured widely and gave "readings" in which he provided a personality description based on measuring the bumps on a person's head. Phrenology continued to be popular with the general public well into the 1900s.

Is phrenology merely a historical curiosity? Actually, phrenology played a significant role in advancing the scientific study of the human brain (Zola-Morgan, 1995). As it became popular in the early 1800s,

phrenology triggered scientific interest in the possibility of **cortical localization,** or *localization of function*—the idea that specific psychological and mental functions are located (or localized) in specific brain areas (Nichols & Newsome, 1999; van Wyhe, 2000). Although phrenology was eventually dismissed as pseudoscience, scientists began debating the more general notion of cortical localization. By the mid-1800s, solid scientific evidence for cortical localization began to emerge (Damasio & others, 1994). Later in the chapter, we'll look at how the work of Broca and Wernicke provided that initial evidence.

Today, sophisticated imaging techniques that reveal the brain's activity, such as PET and functional MRI scans, are providing numerous insights about the cortical localization of cognitive and perceptual abilities (Nichols & Newsome, 1999). So although Franz Gall and the phrenologists were wrong about the significance of bumps on the skull, they were on target about the idea that different psychological functions are localized in different brain areas (Sabbatini, 1997).

uncontrollable seizures. Following such medical treatment, researchers can study the behavioral effects of the lesions (e.g., F. Friedrich, & others, 1998). Lesions are sometimes produced in animals to systematically investigate the behavioral effects of damage in specific brain areas.

Researchers have also studied the behavioral effects of electrically stimulating specific brain areas (e.g., Mangina & Beuzeron-Mangina, 1996). This procedure usually involves implanting tiny electrified disks or wires, called *bipolar electrodes,* into a specific brain area. Electrical stimulation causes activation of the neurons in the area around the tip of the electrode and usually produces the opposite behavioral effect of a lesion in the same brain area.

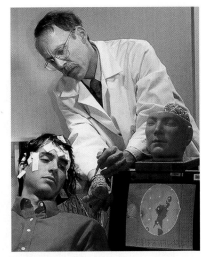

Electroencephalograph

The invention of the **electroencephalograph** allowed scientists to record the brain's electrical activity through the use of large, disk-shaped electrodes placed harmlessly on a person's scalp. The graphic record of the brain's electrical activity that this instrument produces is called an *electroencephalogram,* abbreviated as *EEG.* Modern electroencephalographs provide sophisticated computerized analyses of the brain's electrical activity, recording the electrical activity of the brain from millisecond to millisecond.

As technology has become more advanced, so have the tools used to study the brain. In the Focus on Neuroscience on page 66, we take a look at the new imaging techniques that allow neuroscientists to see the human brain at work.

The Developing Brain
New Neurons Throughout Life?

Our guided tour will follow the same general sequence that the brain follows in its development before birth. The human brain begins as a fluid-filled neural tube that forms about two weeks after conception. Gradually, the neural tube expands and develops into separate, fluid-filled cavities, called *ventricles,* which are at the core of the fully developed brain. *Cerebrospinal fluid* is manufactured in the ventricles by special glial cells. We noted previously that cerebrospinal fluid acts as a shock absorber for the central nervous system and cushions the brain.

As the human fetus develops, brain cells multiply, differentiate, and migrate to their final locations. By the fourth week of prenatal development, new neurons are being generated at the rate of 500,000 per minute. By 24 weeks of prenatal age, the brain has nearly its full complement of neurons. These neurons will continue to function for decades throughout the person's lifespan.

The fetal brain is constantly changing, forming as many as 2 million synaptic connections per second. Connections that are used are strengthened, while unused connections are pruned (Rakic, 1995). Progressively, the three major regions of the brain develop: the *hindbrain,* the *midbrain,* and the *forebrain.* Over the course of fetal development, the forebrain structures eventually come to

Human Embryo at Six Weeks Though the embryo is less than an inch long, the prominent structures of the hindbrain and the beginnings of the forebrain can clearly be seen at this early stage of prenatal development.

phrenology
(freh-NOL-uh-gee) A discredited pseudoscientific theory of the brain that claimed that personality characteristics, moral character, and intelligence could be determined by examining the bumps on a person's skull.

cortical localization
The notion that different functions are located or localized in different areas of the brain; also referred to as *localization of function.*

electroencephalograph
An instrument that produces a graphic record of the brain's electrical activity by using electrodes placed on the scalp.

focus on **Neuroscience**
Understanding Brain Imaging Techniques

Positron emission tomography, or a PET scan, generates images of the brain's activity by tracking the brain's use of a radioactively tagged compound, such as glucose, oxygen, or a particular drug. An invasive procedure, PET involves injecting participants with a radioactive substance before the scan. The PET scan then measures the amount of the radioactively tagged substance used in thousands of brain areas while the person engages in some type of mental activity. Over the course of several minutes, the information is collected, analyzed, and averaged by computer. In the resulting color-coded images, the areas of greatest brain activity are indicated by red and yellow colors.

Magnetic resonance imaging, or MRI, is a noninvasive procedure that provides highly detailed images of the body's internal structures, including the brain. MRI is very versatile, producing thin "slice" images of body tissue from virtually any angle. As the person lies motionless in a long magnetic tube, powerful but harmless magnetic fields bombard the brain or other body area. In response to these magnetic fields, the molecules of the body generate electromagnetic signals, which are analyzed by computer to create the highly detailed images. Tissues with high concentrations of water, such as fat, appear lighter in color, while bone and other tissues with less water appear darker.

Functional magnetic resonance imaging, or fMRI, provides moment-by-moment images of the brain's changing activity. Using the same scanning hardware as an MRI, fMRI also tracks changes in the brain's blood flow and oxygen levels. Compared to PET scans, fMRI produces a much sharper picture and can detail much smaller brain structures. Another advantage of fMRI is that it provides a picture of brain activity averaged over seconds rather than the several minutes required by PET scans. Because fMRI is a noninvasive procedure, researchers can repeatedly scan a single subject. In an fMRI image, the areas of greatest brain activity are indicated by red and orange colors.

Commonly Used Brain Imaging Techniques

Brain scan images have become so commonplace in news articles and popular magazines that it's easy to forget just how revolutionary brain imaging technology has been to the field of neuroscience (Posner & DiGirolamo, 2000). Shown above are the three types of brain imaging techniques most commonly used in psychological research—**PET scans, MRI,** and **functional MRI,** which is abbreviated **fMRI.** The descriptions explain how each brain imaging technique works and the kind of information it provides.

How Psychologists Use Brain Imaging Technology

Like other scientific data gathering methods described in Chapter 1, brain imaging is used for both descriptive and experimental research. A descriptive study utilizing brain scans might compare the brain structure or functioning of one carefully defined group of people with another. For example, MRI scans were used to compare London taxi drivers, who are required to have an encyclopedic knowledge of the city streets to pass their licensing exam, with matched participants who were not London taxi drivers (Maguire & others, 2000). The MRI scans showed that part of a brain structure involved in spatial memory, the *hippocampus,* was significantly larger in the experienced taxi drivers than in the control subjects. The size of the hippocampus was also positively correlated with the length of time the participants had been driving taxis in London. One implica-

tion of this study is that structures in the adult human brain can change in response to learning and environmental demands—an important topic that we'll explore later in the chapter.

Brain imaging technology is also used in experimental research, especially in an important new field called cognitive neuroscience. Integrating contributions from psychology, neuroscience, and computer science, **cognitive neuroscience** is the study of the neural basis of cognitive processes.

How is brain imaging used in cognitive neuroscience research? In a typical experiment, a brain scan is taken during a control task or condition, such as lying down with eyes closed. In the top row of PET scans in the image on page 67, the control condition is shown in the middle PET scan. In that particular study, the control condition consisted of resting while staring at a fixed point.

The control scan is compared to brain scans taken while the participant is exposed to the experimental treatment or performing the experimental task. In the top row of PET scans, the first PET scan is the treatment task, which is labeled "Stimulation." More specifically, the treatment task in that study was looking at a flickering checkerboard pattern. The difference between the PET scans is calculated to determine the brain activity that can be attributed to the experimental condition (Gusnard & Raichle, 2001). In the chapters to come, you'll see several examples of experimental research that use brain-imaging techniques.

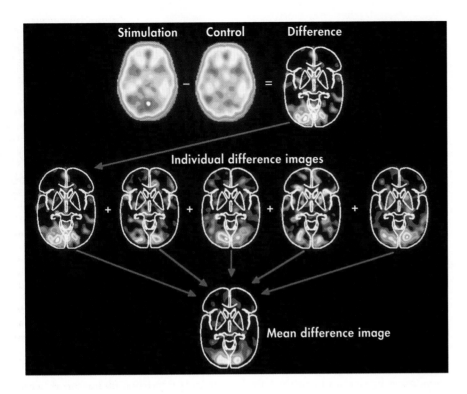

Stimulation   Control   Difference

Individual difference images

Mean difference image

Cognitive neuroscience research often follows the procedure shown on the left. In this particular study, the researchers used positron emission tomography to track changes in the participant's brain activity. In the *Control* condition, the participant's brain is scanned while looking at a fixed point on a blank screen. In the *Stimulation* (experimental) condition, the participant is scanned while engaged in the treatment task. In this study, the treatment task was looking at a flickering checkerboard pattern. After the control scan is "subtracted" from the experimental condition scan, the *Difference* image reveals the brain activity that is assumed to be uniquely attributable to the experimental task. In the next phase of the research (center row), difference images from the individual subjects are *combined and averaged*. This step helps minimize any idiosyncratic responses among the participants. It also provides a composite PET image identifying the brain regions selectively activated by the experimental task.

Potential Limitations of Brain Imaging Studies

As technological advances occur, brain imaging technology continues to improve, offering increasingly detailed pictures of the intact living brain. Nevertheless, brain imaging research has some limitations. When you consider the results of brain imaging studies, including those presented in this textbook, keep the following points in mind:

1. *Most brain imaging studies involve small groups of subjects.*
   Because of the limited availability of sophisticated equipment and the high cost of brain-imaging technology, brain-scan research tends to involve small groups of subjects, often as few as few as a dozen or less. As is true with any research that involves a small number of participants, caution must be exercised in generalizing results to a wider population.

2. *Most brain imaging studies involve simple aspects of behavior.*
   Human behavior is extraordinarily complex, and even seemingly simple tasks involve the smooth coordination of multiple brain regions. Reading this paragraph, for example, activates visual, language, memory, and auditory centers in your brain. As psychologist William Uttal (2001) observes, "The more complex the psychological process, the less likely it is that a narrowly circumscribed [brain] region uniquely associated with that process will be found."

3. *Knowing what brain area is involved may tell us little about the psychological process being investigated.*
   Knowing the brain location of a psychological process does not necessarily translate into an understanding of that process. For example, identifying a particular brain structure as being involved in fear does little to explain our psychological experience of fear (Miller & Keller, 2000). Snapshots of brain activity can only be interpreted within the context of psychological knowledge about the behavior being studied.

Looking at Brain Scan Images

What should you notice when you look at a brain scan image? First, read the text description carefully, so that you understand the task or condition that is being measured. Second, when a control condition brain scan is shown, carefully compare the control scan with the treatment scan, noting how the two scans differ. Third, keep the limitations of brain scan technology in mind, remembering that human experience is much more complex than can be captured by a single snapshot of brain activity.

Although brain imaging research has its limitations, the advent of sophisticated imaging technology has revolutionized our understanding of the human brain. But brain-imaging technology has also revealed just how much remains to be discovered about the most complex piece of matter known to exist in the universe—the human brain.

magnetic resonance imaging (MRI)
An imaging technique that provides three-dimensional, highly detailed images of the brain using electrical signals generated by the brain in response to magnetic fields.

positron emission tomography (PET scan)
An imaging technique that provides color-coded images of brain activity by measuring the amount of a radioactive compound, glucose, or oxygen used in different brain regions.

functional magnetic resonance imaging (fMRI)
An imaging technique that uses magnetic fields to map brain activity by measuring changes in the brain's blood supply during different mental activities.

cognitive neuroscience
The study of the neural basis of cognitive process that integrates contributions from psychology, neuroscience, and computer science.

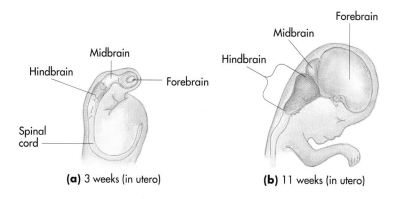

(a) 3 weeks (in utero)

(b) 11 weeks (in utero)

(c) At birth

FIGURE 2.14 The Sequence of Fetal Brain Development The human brain begins its development as a fluid-filled neural tube at about two weeks after conception. The hindbrain structures are the first to develop, followed by midbrain structures. The forebrain structures develop last, eventually coming to surround and envelop the hindbrain and midbrain structures.

surround and envelop the hindbrain and midbrain structures (See Figure 2.14).

At birth, the infant's brain weighs less than a pound and is only about one-fourth the size of an adult brain. After birth, the neurons grow in size and continue to develop new dendrites (Johnston & others, 1996). Myelin forms on neuron axons in key areas of the brain, such as those involved in motor control. Axons also grow longer, and the branching at the ends of axons becomes more dense (Shatz, 1992). By adulthood, the fully mature human brain weighs about three pounds.

For many years, scientists believed that people and most animals did not experience **neurogenesis**—the development of new neurons—after birth. With the exception of birds, tree shrews, and some rodents, it was thought that the mature brain could lose neurons but could not grow new ones. But new studies offered compelling evidence that persuaded most neuroscientists to abandon that dogma (Gross, 2000).

First, research by psychologist Elizabeth Gould and her colleagues (1998) showed that adult marmoset monkeys were generating a significant number of new neurons every day in the *hippocampus,* a brain structure that plays a critical role in the ability to form new memories. Gould's groundbreaking research provided the first demonstration that new neurons could develop in an adult primate brain. Could it be that the human brain also has the capacity to generate new neurons in adulthood?

Researchers Peter Eriksson, Fred Gage, and their colleagues (1998) provided evidence that it does. The subjects were five adult cancer patients, whose ages ranged from the late fifties to the early seventies. These patients were all being treated with a drug used in cancer treatments to determine whether tumor cells are multiplying. The drug is incorporated into newly dividing cells and colors the cells. Using fluorescent lights, this chemical tracer can be detected in the newly created cells. The reasoning was that if new neurons were being generated, the drug would be present in their genetic material.

Within hours after each patient died, an autopsy was performed and the hippocampus was removed and examined. The results were unequivocal. In each patient, *hundreds* of new neurons had been generated since the drug had been administered, even though all the patients were over 50 years old (see accompanying photo). The conclusion? Contrary to the traditional scientific view, the hippocampus has the capacity to generate new neurons throughout the lifespan (Eriksson & others, 1998; Kempermann & Gage, 1999).

Neurogenesis in the Adult Human Brain
Using laser microscopes to examine sections of the adult hippocampus, researchers Peter Eriksson and Fred Gage (1998) documented the presence of new neurons, shown in green, amid already established neurons, shown in red. In the area of the hippocampus studied, each cubic centimeter of brain tissue contained from 100 to 300 new neurons. New research on adult mice has shown that the newly generated neurons develop into fully functional neurons that form synaptic connections with existing cells in the hippocampus (van Praag & others, 2002).

Is the capacity to generate new neurons limited to just the hippocampus? Not according to later research by Gould and her colleagues (1999b), which showed that adult macaque monkeys continually develop new neurons that migrate to *multiple* brain locations. These brain areas are involved in sophisticated cognitive abilities, including memory, learning, and decision making.

In the next section, we'll continue our guided tour of the brain. Following the general sequence of the brain's development, we'll start with the structures at the base of the brain and work our way up to the higher brain regions, which are responsible for complex mental activity.

neurogenesis
The development of new neurons.

brainstem
A region of the brain made up of the hindbrain and the midbrain.

The Brainstem
Hindbrain and Midbrain Structures

Key Theme

◾ The brainstem includes the hindbrain and midbrain, located at the base of the brain.

Key Questions

◾ Why does damage to one side of the brain affect the opposite side of the body?

◾ What are the key structures of the hindbrain and midbrain, and what are their functions?

The major regions of the brain are illustrated in Figure 2.15, which can serve as a map to keep you oriented during our tour. At the base of the brain lie the hindbrain and, directly above it, the midbrain. Combined, the structures of the hindbrain and midbrain make up the brain region that is also called the **brainstem.**

Forebrain
Uppermost and largest brain region composed of several structures, the most prominent being the cerebral cortex

Corpus callosum
Thick band of axons connecting the two hemispheres of the cerebral cortex

Cerebral cortex
Divided into two hemispheres and responsible for sophisticated mental functions

Hindbrain
Region at base of brain that connects the brain to the spinal cord

Pons
Helps coordinate movements on left and right sides of body

Cerebellum
Coordinates movement, balance, and posture

Midbrain
Middle region of brain; involved in processing visual and auditory information

Reticular formation
Helps regulate attention and alertness

Medulla
Controls breathing, heartbeat, and other vital life functions

FIGURE 2.15 Major Regions of the Brain This cross section of the human brain shows the primary structures that make up the hindbrain region (yellow labels), the midbrain region (blue label), and the forebrain region (pink labels). The hindbrain and midbrain regulate many of the most basic life functions, and the forebrain is involved in more sophisticated behaviors and higher mental processes.

The Hindbrain

The **hindbrain** connects the spinal cord with the rest of the brain. Sensory and motor pathways pass through the hindbrain to and from regions that are situated higher up in the brain. Sensory information coming in from one side of the body crosses over at the hindbrain level, projecting to the opposite side of the brain. And outgoing motor messages from one side of the brain also cross over at the hindbrain level, controlling movement and other motor functions on the opposite side of the body.

This crossover accounts for why people who suffer strokes on one side of their brain experience muscle weakness or paralysis on the opposite side of their body. Our friend Asha, for example, suffered only minor damage to motor control areas in her brain. However, because the stroke occurred on the *left* side of her brain, what muscle weakness she did experience was localized on the *right* side of her body, primarily in her right hand.

Three structures make up the hindbrain—the medulla, the pons, and the cerebellum. The **medulla** lies directly above the spinal cord and contains centers active in the control of such vital autonomic functions as breathing, heart rate, and digestion. Because the medulla is involved in such critical life functions, damage to it can result in death. The medulla also controls a number of vital reflexes, such as swallowing, coughing, vomiting, and sneezing.

Above the medulla is a swelling of tissue called the **pons,** which represents the uppermost level of the hindbrain. Bulging out behind the pons is the large **cerebellum.** On each side of the pons, a large bundle of axons connects it to the cerebellum. The word *pons* means "bridge," and the pons is a bridge of sorts: Information from various other brain regions located higher up in the brain is relayed to the cerebellum via the pons.

The cerebellum functions in the control of balance, muscle tone, and coordinated muscle movements. It is also involved in the learning of habitual or automatic movements and motor skills, such as typing, writing, or gracefully backhanding a tennis ball.

Jerky, uncoordinated movements can result from damage to the cerebellum. Simple movements, such as walking or standing upright, may become difficult or impossible. The cerebellum is also one of the brain areas affected by alcohol consumption, which is why a person who is intoxicated may stagger and have difficulty walking a straight line or standing on one foot. (This is also why a police officer will ask a suspected drunk driver to execute these normally effortless movements.)

At the core of the medulla and the pons is a network of neurons called the **reticular formation,** or the *reticular activating system.* The reticular formation is composed of many groups of specialized neurons that project up to higher brain regions and down to the spinal cord. The reticular formation plays an important role in regulating attention and sleep.

The Midbrain

The **midbrain** is an important relay station that contains centers important to the processing of auditory and visual sensory information. Auditory sensations from the left and right ears are processed through the midbrain, helping you orient toward the direction of a sound. The midbrain is also involved in processing visual information, including eye movements, helping you visually locate objects and track their movements. After passing through the midbrain level, auditory and visual information is relayed to sensory processing centers farther up in the forebrain region, which will be discussed shortly.

A midbrain area called the **substantia nigra** is involved in motor control and contains a large concentration of dopamine-producing neurons. *Substantia nigra* means "dark substance," and as the name suggests, this area is darkly pigmented. The substantia nigra is part of a larger neural pathway that helps

hindbrain
A region at the base of the brain that contains several structures that regulate basic life functions.

medulla
(meh-DOOL-uh) A hindbrain structure that controls vital life functions such as breathing and circulation.

pons
A hindbrain structure that connects the medulla to the two sides of the cerebellum; helps coordinate and integrate movements on each side of the body.

cerebellum
(sare-uh-BELL-um) A large, two-sided hindbrain structure at the back of the brain responsible for muscle coordination and maintaining posture and equilibrium.

reticular formation
(reh-TICK-you-ler) A network of nerve fibers located in the center of the medulla that helps regulate attention, arousal, and sleep; also called the *reticular activating system.*

midbrain
The middle and smallest brain region, involved in processing auditory and visual sensory information.

substantia nigra
(sub-STAN-she-uh NYE-gruh) An area of the midbrain that is involved in motor control and contains a large concentration of dopamine-producing neurons.

forebrain
The largest and most complex brain region, which contains centers for complex behaviors and mental processes; also called the *cerebrum.*

cerebral cortex
(suh-REE-brull or SARE-uh-brull) The wrinkled outer portion of the forebrain, which contains the most sophisticated brain centers.

cerebral hemispheres
The nearly symmetrical left and right halves of the cerebral cortex.

corpus callosum
A thick band of nerve fibers that connects the two cerebral hemispheres and acts as a communication link between them.

prepare other brain regions to initiate organized movements or actions. In the section on neurotransmitters, we noted that Parkinson's disease involves symptoms of abnormal movement, including difficulty initiating or starting a particular movement. Many of those movement-related symptoms are associated with the degeneration of dopamine-producing neurons in the substantia nigra.

The Forebrain

Key Theme
- The forebrain includes the cerebral cortex and the limbic system structures.

Key Questions
- What are the four lobes of the cerebral cortex and their functions?
- What is the limbic system?
- What functions are associated with the thalamus, hypothalamus, hippocampus, and amygdala?

Situated above the midbrain is the largest region of the brain: the **forebrain.** In humans, the forebrain, also called the *cerebrum,* represents about 90 percent of the brain. In Figure 2.16, you can see how the size of the forebrain has increased during evolution, although the general structure of the human brain is similar to that of other species (Clark & others, 2001). Many important structures are found in the forebrain region, but we'll begin by describing the most prominent—the cerebral cortex.

FIGURE 2.16 Evolution and the Cerebral Cortex The brains of these different animal species have many structures in common, including a cerebellum and cortex. However, the proportion devoted to the cortex is much higher in mammals than in species that evolved earlier, such as fish and amphibians. The relative size of the different structures reflects their functional importance (Kaas & Collins, 2001). The cross-section of the human brain shows how the cerebral cortex has developed around and above more primitive brain structures

Fish

Frog

Bird

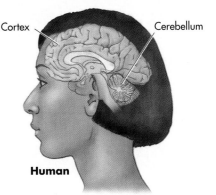
Human

The Cerebral Cortex

The outer portion of the forebrain, the **cerebral cortex,** is divided into two **cerebral hemispheres.** The word *cortex* means "bark," and much like the bark of a tree, the cerebral cortex is the outer covering of the forebrain. A thick bundle of axons, called the **corpus callosum,** connects the two cerebral hemispheres, as shown in Figure 2.17. The corpus callosum serves as the primary communication link between the left and right cerebral hemispheres (Hoptman & Davidson, 1994).

The cerebral cortex is only about a quarter of an inch thick. It is mainly composed of glial cells and neuron cell

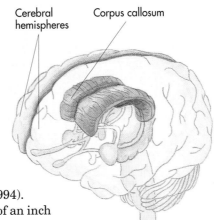

FIGURE 2.17 The Cerebral Hemispheres and the Corpus Callosum This transparent view of the brain shows the corpus callosum, the C-shaped bundle of axons that links the left and right hemispheres of the cerebral cortex.

temporal lobe
An area on each hemisphere of the cerebral cortex near the temples that is the primary receiving area for auditory information.

occipital lobe
(ock-SIP-it-ull) An area at the back of each cerebral hemisphere that is the primary receiving area for visual information.

parietal lobe
(puh-RYE-et-ull) An area on each hemisphere of the cerebral cortex located above the temporal lobe that processes somatic sensations.

FIGURE 2.18 Lobes of the Cerebral Cortex Each hemisphere of the cerebral cortex can be divided into four regions, or *lobes.* Each lobe is associated with distinct functions. The association areas, shaded in purple, make up most of the cerebral cortex.

bodies and axons, giving it a grayish appearance—which is why the cerebral cortex is sometimes described as being composed of *gray matter.* Extending inward from the cerebral cortex are white myelinated axons that are sometimes referred to as *white matter.* These myelinated axons connect the cerebral cortex to other brain regions.

Numerous folds, grooves, and bulges characterize the human cerebral cortex. The purpose of these ridges and valleys is easy to illustrate. Imagine a flat, three-foot by three-foot piece of paper. You can compact the surface area of this piece of paper by scrunching it up into a wad. In much the same way, the grooves and bulges of the cerebral cortex allow about three square feet of surface area to be packed into the small space of the human skull.

Look again at Figure 2.16. The drawing of the human brain is cut through the center to show how the cerebral cortex has folded above and around the rest of the brain. In contrast to the numerous folds and wrinkles of the human cerebral cortex, notice the smooth appearance of the cortex in fish, amphibians, and birds. Mammals with large brains—such as cats, dogs, and nonhuman primates—also have wrinkles and folds in the cerebral cortex, but to a lesser extent than humans (Allman, 1999).

Each cerebral hemisphere can be roughly divided into four regions, or *lobes:* the *temporal, occipital, parietal,* and *frontal* lobes (see Figure 2.18). Each lobe is associated with distinct functions. Located near your temples, the **temporal lobe** contains the *primary auditory cortex,* which receives auditory information. At the very back of the brain is the **occipital lobe.** The occipital lobe includes the *primary visual cortex,* where visual information is received.

The **parietal lobe** is involved in processing bodily, or *somatosensory,* information, including touch, temperature, pressure, and information from receptors in the muscles and joints. A band of tissue on the parietal lobe, called the *somatosensory cortex,* receives information from touch receptors in different parts of the body.

Each part of the body is represented on the somatosensory cortex, but this representation is not equally distributed. Instead, body parts are represented in proportion to their sensitivity to somatic sensations. For example, your hands and face, which are very responsive to touch, have much greater representation on the somatosensory cortex than do the backs of your legs, which are far less sensitive to touch. If body areas were actually proportional to the amount of representation on the somatosensory cortex, humans would resemble the misshapen character on the right side of Figure 2.19.

Parietal lobe

Frontal lobe

Occipital lobe

Temporal lobe

Primary motor cortex
(on frontal lobe)
controls voluntary movement

Somatosensory cortex
(on parietal lobe)
receives information about body sensations

Association areas
(on all four lobes)
combine sensory and motor information; coordinate interaction among different brain areas

Primary visual cortex
(on occipital lobe)
processes visual information

Primary auditory cortex
(on temporal lobe)
processes auditory information

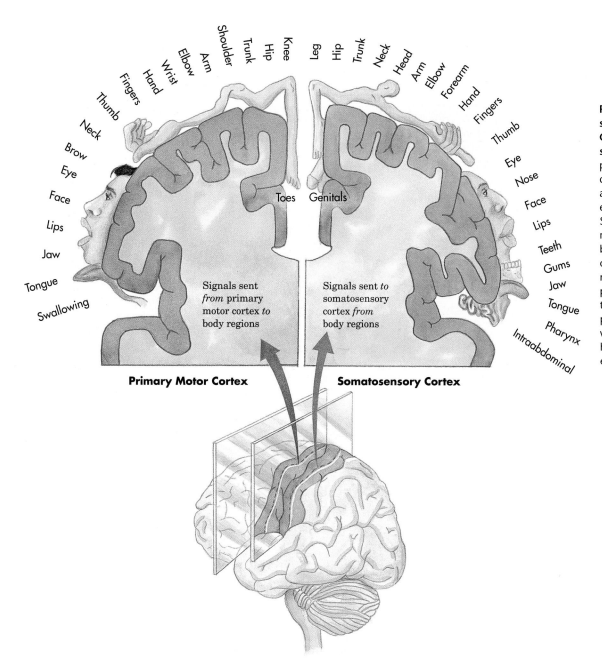

FIGURE 2.19 The Body's Representation on the Primary Motor Cortex and on the Somatosensory Cortex Touch, temperature, pressure, and pain sensations for different areas of the body occur at distinct locations on the parietal lobe's somatosensory cortex. Similarly, the initiation of movement for different parts of the body occurs at distinct locations on the frontal lobe's primary motor cortex. If body parts were proportional to their representation on the somatosensory and primary motor cortex, they would look like the misshapen human figures on the outer edges of the drawing.

The largest lobe of the cerebral cortex, the **frontal lobe,** is involved in planning, initiating, and executing voluntary movements. In the nineteenth century, a railroad worker named Phineas Gage suffered a devastating injury to part of his frontal lobe when an iron spike accidentally blasted through his brain. Gage survived, but a section of his frontal lobe was seriously damaged, producing dramatic changes in his personality (Macmillan, 2000). The fascinating story of how Phineas Gage has contributed to the understanding of the frontal lobe, both then and now, is told in In Focus Box 2.2: Phineas Gage, Then and Now on page 74.

Just as sensory information is received by the somatosensory cortex on the parietal lobe, the movements of different body parts are represented in a band of tissue on the frontal lobe called the *primary motor cortex.* The degree of representation on the primary motor cortex for a particular body part reflects the diversity and precision of its potential movements, as shown on the left side of Figure 2.19. Thus, it's not surprising that almost one-third of the primary motor cortex is devoted to the hands and another third is devoted to facial muscles. The disproportionate representation of these two body areas on the primary motor cortex is reflected in the human capacity to produce an extremely wide range of hand movements and facial expressions.

frontal lobe
The largest lobe of each cerebral hemisphere; processes voluntary muscle movements and is involved in thinking, planning, and emotional control.

Phineas Gage, Then and Now

On September 13, 1848, a freak accident occurred—an event that was to become a landmark in our understanding of the brain's role in behavior (Macmillan, 2000). Phineas Gage, 25 years old, was the foreman of a railroad crew that was blasting rock near Cavendish, Vermont. The crew would drill a hole in the rock, fill it with gunpowder, and cover the gunpowder with a layer of sand. Then, using a fine-pointed, three-and-a-half-foot-long iron rod, Gage would pack the sand and gunpowder down into the hole. The sand kept sparks from igniting the gunpowder when Gage tamped it down with the iron rod.

On this particular day, Gage and a crew member were momentarily distracted while filling the hole. When Gage turned back to his task, he thought his assistant had already poured the sand into the hole, but this was not the case. Gage thrust the iron rod into the hole. A spark caused by the rod's scraping the rock ignited the gunpowder.

The iron rod blew out like a javelin, striking Gage just below his left eye. The rod went completely through his skull, tore a hole in the top of his head, and landed some 50 feet away. The crew stared in horror at Gage lying on the ground, thinking he must surely be dead.

But after a few minutes, Gage began to speak. His crew, astonished that he was still alive, rushed Gage to the town of Cavendish. The town's doctors, John Harlow and Edward Williams, helped Gage walk up three flights of stairs to an attic room, where they cleaned his wounds (Harlow, 1848).

Miraculously, Phineas Gage survived. In many respects, his recovery was near complete. Movement, speech, memory, and the ability to learn new information were not impaired. Gage appeared to be as intelligent as he had been before the accident.

But the accident produced a profound change in Gage's personality. The previously friendly, competent, responsible

A Model of Gage's Injury Computer-simulated reconstruction of Gage's skull by Damasio and her colleagues (1994) suggests that Gage's left and right frontal lobes were both damaged.

foreman became stubborn, ill tempered, profane, and unreasonable. He also became incapable of carrying out plans and could no longer hold down a job. As Dr. Harlow (1868) later wrote, "His mind was radically changed, so decidedly that his friends and acquaintances said he was 'no longer Gage.'"

Gage survived for more than 12 years following the accident. After Gage's death in 1861, Harlow persuaded Gage's family to have the body exhumed so that the skull could be recovered and kept as a medical record. The tamping iron, which had been buried with Gage, was also recovered.

In 1868, Harlow presented a paper to the Massachusetts Medical Society detailing the accident. He suggested that the changes in Gage's behavior and cognitive functioning were the result of damage to Gage's frontal lobes. In effect, Harlow proposed that the frontal lobes were involved in social and emotional behavior, reasoning, the ability to think and plan, and decision making.

At the time, Harlow's ideas about the frontal lobes were dismissed. Why?

One reason was that Harlow had not performed an autopsy. Without anatomical evidence, critics discounted Harlow's suggestions. However, phrenology also played a role in the rejection of Harlow's ideas (see Science Versus Pseudoscience Box 2.1). Claims for brain specialization were viewed with great skepticism by scientists because of their rejection of the pseudoscientific claims of phrenology (Fancher, 1996). Harlow's ideas were too close to Gall's notion of "faculties" that could be determined from the bumps on a skull (Damasio & others, 1994).

Harlow's suspicions were finally confirmed almost 125 years after Gage's death. In 1994, Drs. Hanna and Antonio Damasio, of the Department of Neurology at the University of Iowa, reexamined Phineas Gage's skull. Using X-rays and sophisticated computerized brain-modeling techniques, they created a three-dimensional model of the injury to Gage's brain (see photograph). In effect, the Damasios simulated the autopsy that was never performed on Phineas Gage.

The Damasios found that the specific brain damage sustained by Gage and the subsequent behavioral changes fit the same pattern found in other individuals with similar frontal-lobe damage (Damasio & others, 1994). Damage to this area of the frontal lobes is associated with an impaired ability to make rational decisions in personal and social matters and also compromises the processing of emotions (Robin & Holyoak, 1995).

Although Harlow's ideas about the role of the frontal lobe in behavior and emotions were initially rejected, more than a hundred years later the Damasios confirmed the accuracy of Harlow's proposal. As Hanna Damasio and her colleagues (1994) wrote, "The mysteries of frontal lobe functioning are slowly being solved, and it is only fair to establish, on a more substantial footing, the roles that Gage and Harlow played in the solution."

The primary sensory and motor areas found on the different lobes represent just a small portion of the cerebral cortex. The remaining bulk of the cerebral cortex consists mostly of three large *association areas.* These areas are generally thought to be involved in processing and integrating sensory and motor information. For example, the *prefrontal association cortex,* situated in front of the primary motor cortex, is involved in the planning of voluntary movements. Another association area includes parts of the temporal, parietal, and occipital lobes. This association area is involved in the formation of perceptions and in the integration of perceptions and memories.

The Limbic System

Beneath the cerebral cortex are several other important forebrain structures, which are components of the **limbic system.** The word *limbic* means "border," and as you can see in Figure 2.20, the structures that make up the limbic system form a border of sorts around the brainstem. In various combinations, the limbic system structures form complex neural circuits that play critical roles in learning, memory, and emotional control (Squire & Knowlton, 1995).

One interesting aspect of the limbic system is its involvement in pleasurable or rewarding sensations. In the 1950s, neuropsychologist James Olds (1958, 1962) discovered that rats could be trained to perform a task, such as pressing a bar, in order to receive electrical stimulation to certain regions in the limbic system. In their early work, Olds and other researchers found that rats seemed to prefer brain stimulation to food, even when the rats were extremely hungry.

This finding led researchers to speculate that there might be some sort of "pleasure center" located in the limbic system. Since the initial discovery, the existence of such pleasure centers has been demonstrated in other animals, including rabbits, cats, dogs, monkeys, and even goldfish.

Today it's known that electrical stimulation of *many* different parts of the brain can produce similar effects (Olds & Fobes, 1981). Exactly how electrical stimulation can produce rewarding sensations is still not completely understood, but neural pathways involving the neurotransmitter dopamine seem to play a prominent role (Schultz & others, 1997; Wise, 1996).

Let's briefly consider some of the key limbic system structures and the roles they play in behavior.

The Hippocampus

The **hippocampus** is a large structure embedded in the temporal lobe in each cerebral hemisphere (see Figure 2.20). The word *hippocampus* comes from a Latin word meaning "sea horse." If you have a vivid imagination, the hippocampus does look a bit like the curved tail of a sea horse. The hippocampus plays an important role in the ability to form new memories of events and information (Gabrieli, 1998). As noted earlier, neurogenesis takes place in the adult hippocampus. The possible role of new neurons in memory formation is an active area of neuroscience research (Gross, 2000; Shors & others, 2001). In Chapter 6, we'll take a closer look at the role of the hippocampus and other brain structures in memory.

Hypothalamus
Peanut-sized structure that maintains homeostasis, links endocrine system to brain, and is involved in motivation and emotional drives

Thalamus
Processes and integrates information from all the senses except smell, and relays information to appropriate higher brain centers

Amygdala
Almond-shaped structure involved in emotion and memory

Hippocampus
Wishbone-shaped structure involved in forming new memories

FIGURE 2.20 Key Structures of the Forebrain and Limbic System In the cross-sectional view shown here, you can see the locations and functions of four important subcortical brain structures. In combination, these structures make up the *limbic system,* which regulates emotional control, learning, and memory.

limbic system
A group of forebrain structures that form a border around the brainstem and are involved in emotion, motivation, learning, and memory.

hippocampus
A curved forebrain structure that is part of the limbic system and is involved in learning and forming new memories.

FIGURE 2.21 The Thalamus Almost all sensory and motor information going to and from the cerebral cortex is processed through the thalamus. This figure depicts some of the neural pathways from different regions of the thalamus to specific lobes of the cerebral cortex.

The Thalamus

The word *thalamus* comes from a Greek word meaning "inner chamber." And indeed, the **thalamus** is a rounded mass of cell bodies located within each cerebral hemisphere. The thalamus processes and distributes motor information and sensory information (except for smell) going to and from the cerebral cortex. Figure 2.21 depicts some of the neural pathways going from the thalamus to the different lobes of the cerebral cortex. However, the thalamus is more than just a sensory relay station. The thalamus is also thought to be involved in regulating levels of awareness, attention, motivation, and emotional aspects of sensations.

The Hypothalamus

Hypo means "beneath" or "below." As its name implies, the **hypothalamus** is located below the thalamus. Although it is only about the size of a peanut, the hypothalamus contains many neural connections. These neural pathways ascend to other forebrain areas and descend to the midbrain, hindbrain, and spinal cord.

The hypothalamus regulates both divisions of the autonomic nervous system, increasing and decreasing such functions as heart rate and blood pressure. It also helps regulate a variety of behaviors related to survival, such as eating, drinking, frequency of sexual activity, fear, and aggression. One area of the hypothalamus, called the *suprachiasmatic nucleus* (SCN), plays a key role in regulating daily sleep–wake cycles and other rhythms of the body. We'll take a closer look at the SCN in Chapter 4.

The hypothalamus exerts considerable control over the secretion of endocrine hormones by directly influencing the pituitary gland. The *pituitary gland* is situated just below the hypothalamus and is attached to it by a short stalk. The hypothalamus produces both neurotransmitters and hormones that directly affect the pituitary gland. As we noted in the section on the endocrine system, the pituitary gland releases hormones that influence the activity of other glands.

The Amygdala

The **amygdala** is an almond-shaped clump of neuron cell bodies at the base of the temporal lobe. The amygdala is involved in a variety of emotional response patterns, including fear, anger, and disgust (Aggleton, 1992). Studies with animals have shown that electrical stimulation of the amygdala can produce these emotions. In contrast, destruction of the amygdala reduces or disrupts behaviors that are linked to fear and rage. For example, when their amygdala is destroyed, monkeys lose their fear of natural predators, such as snakes. In humans, electrical stimulation of the amygdala produces feelings of fear and apprehension. The amygdala is also involved in learning and forming memories, especially those with a strong emotional component (Le Doux, 2000; Morris & others, 1998). In Chapter 8, we'll take a closer look at the amygdala's role in emotion.

thalamus
(THAL-uh-muss) A forebrain structure that processes sensory information for all senses, except smell, and relays it to the cerebral cortex.

hypothalamus
(hi-poe-THAL-uh-muss) A peanut-sized forebrain structure that is part of the limbic system and regulates behaviors related to survival, such as eating, drinking, and sexual activity.

amygdala
(uh-MIG-dull-uh) An almond-shaped forebrain structure that is part of the limbic system and is involved in emotion and memory.

The Brain as an Integrated System

In our brief guided tour, we've covered the major brain structures from the hindbrain to the forebrain. In doing so, we've described how different brain areas are involved in and control different functions. But it's important to remind you that even simple behaviors, such as waving at a friend or turning your head in the direction of a sound, involve the seamless interaction of multiple neural pathways and brain regions.

In the final section of this chapter, we will look at one of the most intriguing examples of specialization in the brain: the different functions of the left and right cerebral hemispheres. As you'll see, the functioning of the two cerebral hemispheres is another example of the twin themes of specialization and integration in the human brain.

Specialization in the Cerebral Hemispheres

Key Theme

- The two hemispheres of the cerebral cortex are specialized for different tasks, although they share many functions in common.

Key Questions

- How did Broca, Wernicke, and Sperry contribute to our knowledge of the brain?
- What is the corpus callosum, and what happens when it is cut?
- How do the functions of the right and left cerebral hemispheres differ?

If you were to hold a human brain in your hand, the two cerebral hemispheres would appear to be symmetrical. Although the left and right hemispheres are very similar in appearance, they are not identical. Anatomically, one hemisphere may be slightly larger than the other. There are also subtle differences in the sizes of particular structures; in the distribution of gray matter and white matter; and in the patterns of folds, bulges, and grooves that make up the surface of the cerebral cortex.

What about differences in the functions of the two hemispheres? In many cases, the functioning of the left and right hemispheres is symmetrical, meaning that the same functions are located in roughly the same places on each hemisphere. Examples of such functional symmetry include the primary motor cortex and the somatosensory cortex, which we discussed in the previous section. With regard to other important processes, however, the left and right cerebral hemispheres do differ—each cerebral hemisphere is specialized for particular abilities.

Here's a rough analogy. Imagine two computers that are linked through a network. One computer is optimized for handling word processing, the other for handling graphic design. Although specialized for different functions, the two computers actively share information and can communicate with each other across the network. In this analogy, the two computers correspond to the left and right cerebral hemispheres, and the network that links them is the corpus callosum.

As you'll see in this section, the first discoveries about the differing abilities of the two brain hemispheres were made more than a hundred years ago by two important pioneers in brain research, Pierre Broca and Karl Wernicke.

The Corpus Callosum Brain tissue from the top of the brain has been cut away to expose the thick fibers of the corpus callosum, the structure that connects the left and right hemispheres of the brain. As you'll read in this section, cutting the corpus callosum eliminates the transfer of information between the two hemispheres, with some surprising consequences.

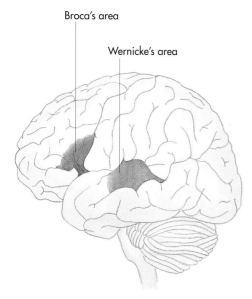

Broca's area

Wernicke's area

FIGURE 2.22 Broca's and Wernicke's Areas of the Cerebral Cortex Broca's area, located in the lower frontal lobe, is involved in the production of speech. Wernicke's area, found in the temporal lobe, is important in the comprehension of written or spoken language. Damage to either of these areas will produce different types of speech disturbances, or aphasia. In most people, both areas are found on the left hemisphere.

cortical localization
The notion that different functions are located or localized in different areas of the brain.

lateralization of function
The notion that specific psychological or cognitive functions are processed primarily on one side of the brain.

aphasia
(uh-FAZE-yuh) The partial or complete inability to articulate ideas or understand spoken or written language because of brain injury or damage.

Language and the Left Hemisphere
The Early Work of Broca and Wernicke

By the end of the 1700s it had already been well established that injury to one side of the brain could produce muscle paralysis or loss of sensation on the opposite side of the body (Fancher, 1996). By the early 1800s, animal experiments had shown that specific functions would be lost if particular brain areas were destroyed. And, as discussed in Box 2.1 on phrenology and Box 2.2 on Phineas Gage, scientists were beginning to debate the notion of **cortical localization**—the idea that particular areas of the human brain are associated with particular functions.

In the 1860s, more conclusive evidence for cortical localization was gathered by a French surgeon and neuroanatomist named **Pierre Paul Broca.** Broca treated a series of patients who had great difficulty speaking but could comprehend written or spoken language. Subsequent autopsies of these patients revealed a consistent finding—brain damage to an area on the *lower left frontal lobe.* Today, this area on the left hemisphere is referred to as *Broca's area,* and it is known to play a crucial role in speech production (see Figure 2.22).

About a decade after Broca's discovery, a young German neurologist named **Karl Wernicke** discovered another area in the left hemisphere that, when damaged, produced a different type of language disturbance. Unlike Broca's patients, Wernicke's patients had great difficulty understanding spoken or written communications. They could speak quickly and easily, but their speech sometimes made no sense. They sometimes used meaningless words or even nonsense syllables, though their sentences seemed to be grammatical (Fancher, 1996). In response to the question "How are you feeling?" a patient might say something like, "Don't glow glover. Yes, uh, ummm, bick, bo chipickers the dallydoe mick more work mittle." Autopsies of these patients' brains revealed consistent damage to an area on the *left temporal lobe* that today is called *Wernicke's area* (see Figure 2.22).

The discoveries of Broca and Wernicke provided the first compelling clinical evidence that language and speech functions are performed primarily by the left cerebral hemisphere. If similar brain damage occurs in the exact same locations on the *right* hemisphere, these severe disruptions in language and speech are usually *not* seen.

The notion that one hemisphere exerts more control over or is more involved in the processing of a particular psychological function is termed **lateralization of function.** Speech and language functions are *lateralized* on the left hemisphere. Generally, the left hemisphere exerts greater control over speech and language abilities in virtually all right-handed and the majority of left-handed people (Damasio & Damasio, 1992). What about the left-handed people who don't fit this pattern? For more insights on hand preference and brain organization, see In Focus Box 2.3: The Puzzle of the Left-Hander.

The language disruptions demonstrated by Broca's and Wernicke's patients represent different types of aphasia. **Aphasia** refers to the partial or complete inability to articulate ideas or understand spoken or written language because of brain injury or damage. There are many different types of aphasia. People with *Broca's aphasia* find it difficult or impossible to produce speech, but their comprehension of verbal or written words is relatively unaffected. People with *Wernicke's aphasia* can speak, but they often have trouble finding the correct words and have great difficulty comprehending written or spoken communication. In more severe cases of Wernicke's aphasia, speech can be characterized by nonsensical, meaningless, incoherent words, as in the example given earlier.

At the beginning of this chapter, we described the symptoms experienced by our friend Asha in the weeks before and the months following her stroke. Asha, who is right-handed, experienced the stroke in her left hemisphere. About three days after her stroke, an MRI brain scan showed where the damage had occurred: the left temporal lobe.

IN FOCUS 2.3

The Puzzle of the Left-Hander

Anatomically, our left and right hands are mirror images. Nevertheless, the vast majority of people use their right hand exclusively for tasks requiring dexterity. Only about 8 percent of the population are left-handed. Remarkably, this percentage has been consistent for more than 50 centuries. Even Stone Age cave drawings and tools indicate that our prehistoric ancestors were predominantly right-handed (Coren, 1992).

Like humans, nonhuman primates also show a strong tendency to be right-handed on a variety of tasks (Westergaard & others, 1998). In one study by William Hopkins (1995), chimpanzees were given a 12-inch opaque tube with peanut butter in the middle. About two-thirds of the adult and adolescent chimpanzees used the index finger of their right hand to extract the peanut butter.

Almost all right-handed people display left-hemisphere dominance for speech and language functions. However, neurosurgeons have discovered a surprising pattern of differences in brain organization among left-handers.

Before brain surgery, each hemisphere can be separately anesthetized, allowing the hemisphere that controls speech functions to be identified. Using this technique, Theodore Rasmussen and Brenda Milner (1977) found that about 70 percent of left-handers show the same pattern as right-handers, with the left hemisphere dominant for language. About 15 percent of left-handed individuals show the opposite pattern, with language functions localized in the right hemisphere. The remaining 15 percent of left-handed individuals process language in both hemispheres. Other researchers, using fMRI, have found similar results (Pujol & others, 1999).

Scientists have also discovered that the corpus callosum in left-handed and ambidextrous individuals is about 11 percent larger than that in right-handed individuals (Habib & others, 1991; Witelson, 1985). This finding suggests that left-handers may experience more efficient communication between the two hemispheres and less hemispheric specialization. It might also help explain why some left-handed people process speech and language in both hemispheres.

The variability in brain organization among left-handed people may also account for the differences in degree of hand preference. Right-handed people consistently perform virtually all tasks requiring dexterity with their right hands. But many left-handers show a pattern of mixed-handedness, preferring to use their right hand for some tasks (Springer & Deutsch, 1998). Your author Don, for example, writes and holds a fork with his left hand. But he uses his right hand to swing a hammer, move the computer mouse, throw a ball, and play tennis.

What causes hand preference? Many theories have been proposed, but no one theory has succeeded in mustering unequivocal evidence. Some evidence suggests that genetics may be involved in determining handedness (Corballis, 1997). If both parents are right-handed, the odds of their having a left-handed child are about 1 in 10. If one parent is left-handed and the other right-handed, the odds of their having a left-handed child are about 1 in 5. If both parents are left-handed, the odds of their having a left-handed child are approximately 1 in 4 (McManus & Bryden, 1992). And the incidence of left-handedness is higher among identical and fraternal twins than among singletons (Coren, 1994; Davis & Annett, 1994).

Adding some support to the idea of genetic determination, hand preference has been demonstrated before birth. Psychologist Peter G. Hepper and his colleagues (1990) used ultrasound to observe more than 200 developing fetuses. Approximately 95 percent preferred sucking their right thumb, and 5 percent preferred their left thumb. These figures correspond very closely to the number of left- and right-handed people in the population.

Despite considerable research, the bottom line is that psychologists still don't know what causes left-handedness. Nonetheless, these discoveries about the differences in handedness and cerebral organization underscore the human brain's tremendous flexibility and adaptability.

HAGAR

Asha experienced many symptoms of Wernicke's aphasia. Talking was difficult, not because Asha couldn't speak, but because she had to stop frequently to search for the right words. Asha was unable to name even simple objects, like the cup on her hospital dinner tray or her doctor's necktie. She recognized the objects but was unable to say what they were. She had great difficulty following a normal conversation and understanding speech, both in English and in her native language, Tulu.

Asha also discovered that she had lost the ability to read. She could see the words on the page, but they seemed to have no meaning. Paul brought some of their Christmas cards to the hospital. Asha recalls, "When I realized I couldn't

Roger Sperry (1913–1994) For his pioneering research using split-brain patients to investigate the relationship between brain and behavior, Sperry received the 1981 Nobel Prize in Physiology or Medicine.

read the Christmas cards, I thought my life was over. I just lost it. I remember crying and telling the nurse, 'I have a doctorate and I can't read, write, or talk!' "

When we visited Asha in the hospital, we brought her a Christmas present: a portable cassette tape player with headphones and some tapes of relaxing instrumental music. Little did we realize how helpful the music would be for her. One tape was a recording of Native American flute music called *Sky of Dreams*. The music was beautiful and rather unusual, with intricate melodies and unexpected, complex harmonies. Although it was very difficult for Asha to follow normal speech, listening to *Sky of Dreams* was an entirely different experience. As Asha explained:

> I tried cranking up the music very high and it soothed me. I could sleep. At the time, the flute music seemed to be just perfectly timed with the way my brain was working. It was tuning out all the other noises so I could focus on just one thing and sleep. So I would play the music over and over again at a very high level. I did that for a long time because my mind was so active and jumbled that I couldn't think.

Asha's language functions were severely disrupted, yet she was able to listen to and appreciate instrumental music—even very complex music. Why? At the end of the next section, we'll offer a possible explanation for what seems to have been a disparity in Asha's cognitive abilities following her stroke.

Cutting the Corpus Callosum
The Split Brain

Since the discoveries by Broca and Wernicke, the most dramatic evidence illustrating the independent functions of the two cerebral hemispheres has come from a surgical procedure called the **split-brain operation.** This operation is used to stop or reduce recurring seizures in severe cases of epilepsy that can't be treated in any other fashion. The procedure involves surgically cutting the corpus callosum, the thick band of axons that connects the two hemispheres.

What was the logic behind cutting the corpus callosum? An epileptic seizure typically occurs when neurons begin firing in a disorganized fashion in one region of the brain. The disorganized neuronal firing quickly spreads from one hemisphere to the other via the corpus callosum. If the corpus callosum is cut, seizures should be contained in just one hemisphere, reducing their severity or eliminating them altogether. This is exactly what happened when the split-brain operation was first tried in this country in the 1940s (Springer & Deutsch, 1998).

Surprisingly, cutting the corpus callosum initially seemed to produce no noticeable effect on the patients, other than reducing their epileptic seizures. Their ability to engage in routine conversations and tasks seemed to be unaffected. On the basis of these early observations, some brain researchers speculated that the corpus callosum served no function whatsoever (see Gazzaniga, 1995). One famous psychologist, Karl Lashley, joked that its primary function seemed to be to keep the two hemispheres from sagging (Hoptman & Davidson, 1994).

In the 1960s, however, psychologist and neuroscientist **Roger Sperry** and his colleagues began unraveling the puzzle of the left and right hemispheres. Sperry and his colleagues used the apparatus shown in Figure 2.23 to test the abilities of split-brain patients. They would direct a split-brain subject to focus on a point in the middle of a screen, while briefly flashing a word or picture to the left or right of the midpoint.

In this procedure, visual information to the right of the midpoint is projected to the person's *left* hemisphere, and visual information to the left of the midpoint is projected to the *right* hemisphere. Behind the screen were several objects that were hidden from the split-brain subjects. The split-brain subject could reach under a partition below the screen to pick up the concealed objects but could not see them (Sperry, 1982).

Specialization in the Left and Right Hemispheres The red arrow at the top of each PET scan points to the front of the brain. The red and yellow colors indicate the areas of greatest brain activity. Listening to speech involves a greater degree of activation of the language areas of the left hemisphere. Listening to music involves more activation in right-hemisphere areas. Notice, however, that there is some degree of activity in both hemispheres during these tasks.

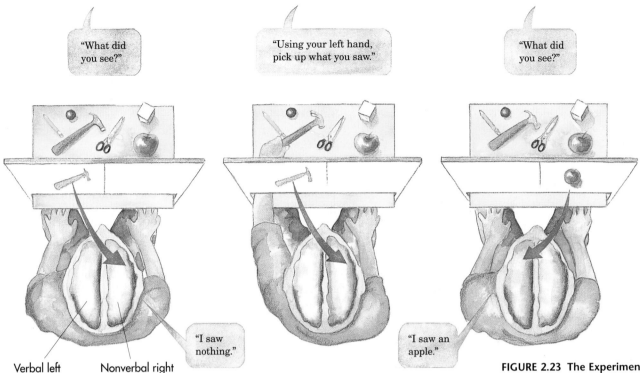

"What did you see?"

"Using your left hand, pick up what you saw."

"What did you see?"

"I saw nothing."

"I saw an apple."

Verbal left hemisphere

Nonverbal right hemisphere

FIGURE 2.23 The Experimental Setup in Split-Brain Research In a typical split-brain experiment, as shown here, the participant focuses his attention on the midpoint of the screen. Notice that he is unable to verbally identify the picture that is flashed to the nonverbal right hemisphere, but he is able to grasp the hammer with his left hand. In contrast, when the image of the apple is flashed to his verbal left hemisphere, he can easily name it.

In a typical experiment, Sperry projected the image of an object concealed behind the screen, such as a hammer, to the left of the midpoint. Thus, the image of the hammer was sent to the right, nonverbal hemisphere. If a split-brain subject was asked to *verbally* identify the image flashed on the screen, he could not do so and often denied that anything had appeared on the screen. Why? Because his verbal left hemisphere had no way of knowing the information that had been sent to his right hemisphere. However, if a split-brain subject was asked to use his left hand to reach under the partition for the object that had been displayed, he would correctly pick up the hammer. This was because his left hand was controlled by the same right hemisphere that saw the image of the hammer.

Sperry's experiments reconfirmed the specialized language abilities of the left hemisphere that Broca and Wernicke had discovered more than a hundred years earlier. But notice, even though the split-brain subject's right hemisphere could not express itself verbally, it still processed information and expressed itself *nonverbally:* The subject was able to pick up the correct object.

Over the last four decades, researchers have gained numerous insights about the brain's lateralization of functions by studying split-brain patients, using brain-imaging techniques with normal subjects, and other techniques (Gazzaniga, 1998). On the basis of this evidence, researchers have concluded that—in most people— the left hemisphere is superior in language abilities, speech, reading, and writing.

In contrast, the right hemisphere is more involved in nonverbal emotional expression and visual-spatial tasks (Corballis & others, 2002). Deciphering complex visual cues, such as completing a puzzle or manipulating blocks to match a particular design, also relies on right-hemisphere processing (Gazzaniga, 1995). And the right hemisphere excels in recognizing faces and emotional facial cues, reading maps, copying designs, and drawing (Heller & others, 1998; Reuter-Lorenz & Miller, 1998). Finally, the right hemisphere shows a higher degree of specialization for musical appreciation or responsiveness—but not necessarily for musical ability, which involves the use of the left hemisphere as well (Springer & Deutsch, 1998).

Figure 2.24 on page 82 summarizes the research findings for the different specialized abilities of the two hemispheres for right-handed people. As you look at the figure, it's important to keep two points in mind. First, the differences between the left and right hemispheres are almost always relative differences, *not* absolute differences. In other words, *both* hemispheres of your brain are activated

split-brain operation
A surgical procedure that involves cutting the corpus callosum.

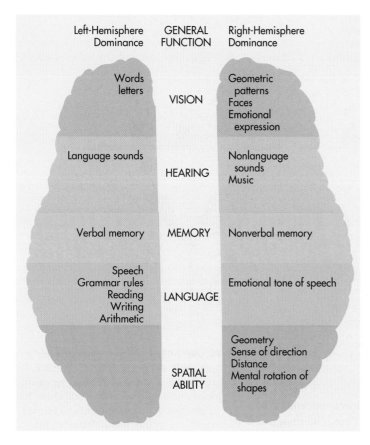

Left-Hemisphere Dominance	GENERAL FUNCTION	Right-Hemisphere Dominance
Words letters	VISION	Geometric patterns Faces Emotional expression
Language sounds	HEARING	Nonlanguage sounds Music
Verbal memory	MEMORY	Nonverbal memory
Speech Grammar rules Reading Writing Arithmetic	LANGUAGE	Emotional tone of speech
	SPATIAL ABILITY	Geometry Sense of direction Distance Mental rotation of shapes

FIGURE 2.24 Specialized Abilities of the Two Hemispheres

to some extent as you perform virtually any task (Beeman & Chiarello, 1998; Chabris & Kosslyn, 1998). In the normal brain, the left and right hemispheres function in an integrated fashion, constantly exchanging information (Banich, 1998). Thus, Figure 2.24 indicates the hemisphere that typically displays greater activation or exerts greater control over a particular function. Second, many functions of the cerebral hemispheres, such as those involving the primary sensory and motor areas, *are* symmetrical. They are located in the same place and are performed in the same way on both the left and the right hemisphere.

Given the basic findings on the laterality of different functions in the two hemispheres, can you speculate about why Asha was unable to read or follow a simple conversation but could easily concentrate on a complex piece of music? Why were her language abilities so disrupted, while her ability to focus on and appreciate music remained intact after her stroke?

A plausible explanation has to do with the location of the stroke's damage on Asha's left temporal lobe. Because language functions are usually localized on the left hemisphere, the stroke produced serious disruptions in Asha's language abilities. However, her *right* cerebral hemisphere sustained no detectable damage. Because one of the right hemisphere's abilities is the appreciation of musical sounds, Asha retained the ability to concentrate on and appreciate music.

2.3   R·E·V·I·E·W

C·O·N·C·E·P·T

The Brain

Fill in the blanks in the following statements.

1. The three major regions of the brain are the _____, _____, and _____.

2. Coordinated muscle movements and balance are regulated by the _____.

3. Auditory information is processed in the _____ lobe.

4. The signals for voluntary movements originate in the _____, which is located on the _____ lobe.

5. The _____ plays a critical role in the formation of new memories.

6. The hypothalamus, hippocampus, amygdala, and parts of the thalamus and frontal cortex make up the _____.

7. Damage to _____ on the brain's left hemisphere disrupts the ability to speak but not the ability to understand spoken or written communication.

8. The _____ is surgically cut in the split-brain operation.

9. About _____ percent of left-handed people are left-hemisphere dominant for language functions.

Summing Up
Neuroscience and Behavior

In our exploration of the biological foundations of behavior, we've traveled from the activities of individual neurons to the complex interaction of the billions of neurons that make up the human nervous system, including the brain. Crucial to the development of a scientific understanding of brain functioning were two areas—localization and lateralization.

Phrenology's incorrect interpretation of bumps on the head and the tragic accident of Phineas Gage helped focus scientific debate on the notion of *localization*—that different functions are localized in different brain areas. The early clinical evidence provided by Broca and Wernicke, and the later split-brain evidence provided by Sperry and his colleagues, confirmed the idea of *lateralization*—that some functions are performed primarily by one cerebral hemisphere.

The ideas of localization and lateralization are complemented by another theme evident in this chapter—*integration*. Despite the high degree of specialization in the human nervous system, the smooth functioning of the nervous system demands an equally high degree of integration and harmony. Your ability to process new information and experiences, your memories of previous experiences, your sense of who you are and what you know, your actions and reactions—all are products of the brain working in harmony with the rest of the nervous system.

Asha's Recovery After leaving the hospital, Asha began retraining her brain with speech therapy. Asha's husband Paul and her mother Nalini helped her with the speech drills. Day after day, Asha repeatedly paired words with objects or identified numbers, weekdays, or months. As Asha recalls, "My mom was a Montessori teacher for many years and she was incredibly patient with me, like she was with her own students and with us as children." As Asha gradually made progress, Nalini began taking her to stores. "She'd tell the clerk I was from India and that my English wasn't very good and ask them to please be patient with me. She basically forced me to talk to the sales clerks." Today, more than three years after the stroke, Asha has completely recovered and resumed teaching.

The story of Asha's stroke illustrated what can happen when this harmony is disrupted. Your physical survival and conscious experience are mediated by the delicate balance of chemicals and the complex, intricate connections in your nervous system. Asha survived her stroke, but many people who suffer strokes do not. Of those who do survive a stroke, about one-third are left with severe impairments in their ability to function.

What happened to Asha? Fortunately, Asha's story has a happy ending. She was luckier than many stroke victims—she was young, strong, and otherwise healthy. Asha's recovery was also aided by her high level of motivation, willingness to work hard, and sheer will to recover. After being discharged from the hospital, Asha began months of intensive speech therapy. Her speech therapist assigned a great deal of homework that consisted of repeatedly pairing pictures with words, objects with words, and words with objects.

Asha set a very high goal for herself: to return to teaching at the university by the fall semester. With the help of her husband Paul and her mother Nalini, who traveled from India to stay with her for four months, Asha made significant gains.

With remarkable determination, Asha reached the goal she had set for herself. She returned to her teaching and research at the university the following fall semester. Today, more than three years after her stroke, you would be unable to detect any signs of impairment indicating that Asha had sustained significant brain damage.

Asha's story also illustrates the brain's incredible ability to shift functions from damaged to undamaged areas, a phenomenon called *functional plasticity*. Even more astonishing, the uninjured brain has the ability to change and grow throughout life. As researchers have discovered, the brain can literally change its structure in response to the quality of environmental stimulation. In the chapter Application, we'll take a look at how researchers have documented the remarkable *structural plasticity* of which the brain is capable. And you'll learn how you can use the research findings on brain plasticity to enhance your own dendritic potential!

structural plasticity
A phenomenon in which brain structures physically change in response to environmental influences.

Researchers once believed that by early adulthood the brain's physical structure was *hardwired,* or fixed for life. It's now known that the brain's physical structure is sculpted by experience. This phenomenon, called **structural plasticity,** was first demonstrated in the early 1960s in studies with rats (Rosenzweig, 1996).

In these studies, rats were systematically exposed to either an enriched or an impoverished environment at different ages and for varying lengths of time. The enriched environment is spacious, houses several rats, and has assorted wheels, ladders, tunnels, and objects to explore. The environment is also regularly changed for further variety. In the impoverished environment, a solitary rat lives in a small, bare laboratory cage with only a water bottle and food tray to keep it company.

Using this basic design, researchers found that enrichment increases the number and length of dendrites, enlarges the size of neurons, and increases the number of potential connections with other neurons (Johnston & others, 1996). Enrichment also increases the number of glial cells, which manufacture the myelin sheath that increases communication speed between neurons.

Enrichment produces *more synaptic connections* between brain neurons, whereas impoverishment decreases synaptic connections. In young rats, enrichment increases the number of synapses in the cortex by as much as 20 percent (Kolb &

Rats in an Enriched Environment Compared with solitary rats raised in bare laboratory cages, rats raised in groups in an enriched environment, like the one shown here, show significant increases in brain growth and number of synaptic interconnections.

Whishaw, 1998). With more synapses, the brain has a greater capacity to integrate and process information and to do so more quickly. Collectively, these changes result in increased processing and communication capacity in the brain.

The cerebral cortex, where sophisticated mental functions occur, is the area most strongly affected by enrichment or impoverishment. Structures below the cerebral cortex, such as those in the limbic system, apparently change very little in response to environmental enrichment or impoverishment.

Even the aged brain can change in response to environmental stimulation. Researchers investigated this issue by raising rats in impoverished environments until an age equivalent to that of 75 years in humans. (Ten days of rat life is roughly equivalent to one year of the human lifespan.) The rats were then placed in enriched environments until they reached the equivalent of 90 human years of age.

The result? Despite the normal decline expected in the aged brain, the senior-citizen rats showed significant increases in brain growth and synaptic interconnections (Diamond, 1988). In fact, no matter what the age of the rats studied, environmental enrichment or impoverishment has had a significant impact on brain structure (Kempermann & others, 1998).

From Animal Studies to Humans

Enrichment studies have been carried out with many other species, including monkeys, cats, birds, honeybees, and even fruit flies (Kolb & Whishaw, 1998). In all cases, enriched environments are associated with striking changes in the brain, however primitive. As psychologists Bryan Kolb and Ian Whishaw (1998) observed, "There is little doubt . . . that experience is a major force in shaping the nervous system of all animals."

Can the conclusions drawn from studies on rats, monkeys, and other animals be applied to human brains? Obviously, researchers cannot directly study the effects of enriched or impoverished environments on human brain tissue as they can with rats. However, psychologists and other researchers have amassed an impressive array of correlational evidence showing that the human brain also seems to benefit from enriched, stimulating environments (Rosenzweig, 1996).

For example, autopsy studies have compared the brains of university graduates with those of high school dropouts. The brains of university graduates had up to 40 percent more synaptic connections than those of high school dropouts (Jacobs & others, 1993). According to UCLA neuroscientist Bob Jacobs (1993), "This is the human equivalent of the animals exposed to enriched environments having smarter brains. As you go up the educational ladder there is a dramatic increase in dendritic material."

Of course, it's possible that people with more synapses are also more likely to attend college than are people with fewer synaptic connections. However, the key is not just getting a higher education. University graduates who led mentally unstimulating lives had fewer dendritic connections than did those who remained mentally active throughout their lives.

Another line of evidence comes from studies comparing symptoms of Alzheimer's disease in elderly individuals with different levels of education (Katzman, 1993; Stern & others, 1992, 1994). Autopsies showed that the more educated individuals had just as much damage to their brain cells as did the poorly educated individuals. However, because the better-educated people had more synaptic connections, their symptoms were much less severe than those experienced by the less-educated people.

Research has shown the importance of a stimulating lifestyle throughout the lifespan. For example, neurologist Robert Friedland and his colleagues (2001) discovered that people who had developed the symptoms of Alzheimer's disease by the age of 70 were much less active, both physically and intellectually, in early and middle adulthood—long before they developed symptoms of the disease—than healthy seniors who were free of Alzheimer's symptoms.

Analyzing the life histories of the Alzheimer's patients and the matched control group of healthy seniors, the researchers discovered that the healthy seniors had spent less time in passive pursuits than the Alzheimer's patients had. The *best* protection against developing Alzheimer's? Engaging in intellectually stimulating hobbies, such as reading or playing a musical instrument, or taking up creative hobbies, such as woodworking

Never Too Old to Learn At 102 years of age, Gemisto Villani returned to school to complete his education. A steep decline in intellectual and cognitive functioning is not an inevitable consequence of aging, especially if your environment is mentally challenging (Schaie, 1994).

or knitting. Solving puzzles and playing mind-challenging games like chess or board games were other intellectual activities that predicted a cognitively healthy old age. But there was *one* activity that the Alzheimer's patients had engaged in more than their healthy counterparts had: The Alzheimer's patients had spent a lot more time watching television.

The results of this study echo earlier research on intellectual enrichment: A mentally stimulating, intellectually challenging environment is associated with enhanced cognitive functioning. Just as physical activity strengthens the heart and muscles, mental activity strengthens the brain. Even in late adulthood, remaining mentally active can help prevent or lessen mental decline (Inouye & others, 1993; White & others, 1994).

More generally, the results of the enrichment research have fundamentally changed our understanding of the brain. As Bryan Kolb and Ian Whishaw (1998) conclude, "Experience alters the synaptic organization of the brain in species as diverse as fruit flies and humans."

Pumping Neurons: Exercising Your Brain

So, here's the critical question: Are you a mental athlete—or a cerebral couch potato? Whatever your age, there seems to be a simple prescription for keeping your brain fit. According to neuroscientist Arnold Scheibel (1994), "The important thing is to be actively involved in areas unfamiliar to you. Anything that's intellectually challenging can probably serve as a kind of stimulus for dendritic

growth, which means it adds to the computational reserves in your brain." In short, you must actively exercise your brain cells. Try the new and unfamiliar. Here are just a few suggestions:

- If you are a "number" or "word" person, sign up for an art class.
- If you are a "math" or "spatial" person, start a personal journal or take a creative writing class.
- Unplug your television set for two weeks—or longer.
- Go to the library and browse until you find at least three books that spark your interest. Check them out and read them.
- Try all kinds of puzzles—word, visual, matching, and maze puzzles.
- Attend a play, an art exhibit, or a performance of classical or jazz music.
- Go to a museum.
- Read or reread a classic work of fiction or poetry.
- Pick a topic that interests you, log onto the Internet, and follow the links to other Web sites.
- Sign up for a class on a subject that you want to know more about.

Better yet, take a few minutes and generate your own list of mind-expanding opportunities!

Chapter Review
Neuroscience and Behavior

Key Points

Introduction: Neuroscience and Behavior

- Psychological and biological processes are closely linked. **Biological psychologists** investigate the physical processes that underlie psychological experience and behavior. **Neuroscience** is the study of the nervous system, especially the brain.

The Neuron: *The Basic Unit of Communication*

- Information in the nervous system is transmitted via cells specialized for communication, called **neurons. Glial cells** help neurons by providing nutrition, removing waste products, and producing the **myelin sheath.** There are three basic types of neurons: **sensory neurons, motor neurons,** and **interneurons.**

- Most neurons have three basic components: a **cell body, dendrites,** and an **axon.** The axons of some neurons are wrapped in a myelin sheath, which speeds the rate at which neural messages are sent.

- Within the neuron, information is communicated in the form of brief electrical messages called **action potentials.**

The minimum level of stimulation required to activate a neuron is called the **stimulus threshold.** A neuron's **resting potential** is the state in which it is ready to activate and communicate its message, if sufficiently stimulated. According to the **all-or-none law,** either a neuron is sufficiently stimulated resulting in an action potential, or it isn't sufficiently stimulated and an action potential doesn't occur.

■ The point of communication between two neurons is called the **synapse.** Neurons communicate information to other neurons either electrically or chemically. In chemical communication, **neurotransmitters** cross the **synaptic gap** and affect neighboring neurons. These neurotransmitters are held within **synaptic vesicles,** which float in **axon terminals.** The entire process of transmitting information at the synapse is called **synaptic transmission. Reuptake** is the process in which neurotransmitter molecules detach from the receptor and are reabsorbed and recycled. There are many different kinds of neurotransmitters, which send either excitatory or inhibitory messages to the receiving neuron. Some drugs influence behavior and mental processes by influencing neurotransmitter activity. Important neurotransmitters include **acetylcholine, dopamine, serotonin, norepinephrine, GABA,** and **endorphins.**

The Nervous System and the Endocrine System: *Communication Throughout the Body*

■ The **nervous system** is divided into two main divisions: the **central nervous system** and the **peripheral nervous system.** The central nervous system is composed of the brain and the spinal cord. The spinal cord can produce **spinal reflexes.**

■ The peripheral nervous system consists of all the **nerves** outside the central nervous system. The two main subdivisions of the peripheral nervous system are the **somatic nervous system** and the **autonomic nervous system.** The autonomic nervous system is divided into the **sympathetic nervous system** and the **parasympathetic nervous system.**

■ The **endocrine system** is composed of glands that secrete **hormones** into the bloodstream, regulating many body functions, including physical growth, stress response, and sexual development. The endocrine system itself is regulated by the hypothalamus in the brain. Under the direction of the hypothalamus, the **pituitary gland** directly controls hormone production in other endocrine glands as well as hormones that act on physical processes. Another set of glands, called the **adrenal glands,** which include the **adrenal cortex** and the **adrenal medulla,** produce hormones that are involved in the human stress response. The **gonads** are endocrine glands that secrete hormones that regulate sexual characteristics and reproductive processes.

A Guided Tour of the Brain

■ Most psychological processes involve the integrated processing of information via neural pathways in multiple brain structures and regions.

■ Case studies of individuals with brain damage or injury have provided information about the brain's function. Researchers have also observed the behavioral effects of surgically altering or electrically stimulating a specific area of the brain. The **electroencephalograph** records the brain's electrical activity. **MRI** scanners use magnetic signals to produce highly detailed images of the brain's structures. **PET** scans use radioactive substances to produce color-coded images of the brain's activity. **Functional MRI** scans track the brain's activity by measuring changes in blood flow in brain areas.

■ During prenatal development, the human brain begins as a fluid-filled neural tube, which ultimately forms the three key brain regions: the hindbrain, midbrain, and forebrain. Evidence now suggests that new neurons can develop in the adult brain, a process called **neurogenesis.**

■ Combined, the hindbrain and midbrain structures constitute the **brainstem.** Sensory and motor pathways cross over in the **hindbrain.** The key structures of the hindbrain are the **medulla,** the **cerebellum,** and the **pons.** The **reticular formation** is located in the core of the medulla and the pons.

■ Auditory and visual information is integrated and coordinated in the **midbrain.** The **substantia nigra** is involved in motor control and contains a concentration of neurons that produce dopamine.

■ The outer portion of the **forebrain** is called the **cerebral cortex.** The cerebral cortex is divided into the left and right **cerebral hemispheres,** with the **corpus callosum** serving as the main communication link between them. Each hemisphere is divided into four lobes. The **temporal lobe** contains the primary auditory cortex. The **occipital lobe** contains the primary visual cortex. The **parietal lobe** contains the somatosensory cortex. The **frontal lobe** contains the primary motor cortex. The remainder of the cerebral cortex is composed of association areas.

■ The **limbic system** structures are found beneath the cerebral cortex and form neural circuits that play critical roles in learning, memory, and emotional control. The limbic system includes part of the frontal cortex and the **hippocampus, thalamus, hypothalamus,** and **amygdala.**

Specialization in the Cerebral Hemispheres

■ The notion that particular areas of the brain are associated with particular functions is called **cortical localization.** In the mid-1800s, it was discovered that damage to the left hemisphere produced disruptions in speech and language called aphasia. Different forms of **aphasia** include Broca's aphasia and Wernicke's aphasia. Damage to the same areas of the right hemisphere did not produce aphasia. The notion that specific psychological or cognitive functions are processed primarily on one side of the brain is called **lateralization of function.**

■ More evidence for the specialized abilities of the two hemispheres has resulted from the **split-brain operation,** in which the corpus callosum connecting the two hemispheres is cut. Roger Sperry and his colleagues demonstrated the different strengths of each hemisphere in split-brain patients. The left hemisphere is specialized for language tasks, and the right hemisphere is specialized for visual-spatial tasks.

Key Terms

biological psychology, p. 44

neuroscience, p. 44

neuron, p. 45

glial cells, p. 45

sensory neuron, p. 46

motor neuron, p. 46

interneuron, p. 46

cell body, p. 46

dendrites, p. 46

axon, p. 47

myelin sheath, p. 47

action potential, p. 47

stimulus threshold, p. 47

resting potential, p. 48

all-or-none law, p. 48

synapse, p. 50

synaptic gap, p. 50

axon terminals, p. 50

synaptic vesicles, p. 50

neurotransmitters, p. 50

synaptic transmission, p. 50

reuptake, p. 50

acetylcholine, p. 53

dopamine, p. 53

serotonin, p. 53

norepinephrine, p. 53

GABA (gamma-aminobutyric acid), p. 53

endorphins, p. 54

nervous system, p. 55

nerves, p. 55

central nervous system, p. 56

spinal reflexes, p. 56

peripheral nervous system, p. 57

somatic nervous system, p. 57

autonomic nervous system, p. 57

sympathetic nervous system, p. 58

parasympathetic nervous system, p. 59

endocrine system, p. 59

hormones, p. 59

pituitary gland, p. 60

adrenal glands, p. 61

adrenal cortex, p. 61

adrenal medulla, p. 61

gonads, p. 61

phrenology, p. 64

cortical localization, pp. 64, 78

electroencephalograph, p. 65

positron emission tomography (PET scan), p. 66

magnetic resonance imaging (MRI), p. 66

functional magnetic resonance imaging (fMRI), p. 66

cognitive neuroscience, p. 66

neurogenesis, p. 68

brainstem, p. 69

hindbrain, p. 70

medulla, p. 70

pons, p. 70

cerebellum, p. 70

reticular formation, p. 70

midbrain, p. 70

substantia nigra, p. 70

forebrain, p. 71

cerebral cortex, p. 71

cerebral hemispheres, p. 71

corpus callosum, p. 71

temporal lobe, p. 72

occipital lobe, p. 72

parietal lobe, p. 72

frontal lobe, p. 73

limbic system, p. 75

hippocampus, p. 75

thalamus, p. 76

hypothalamus, p. 76

amygdala, p. 76

lateralization of function, p. 78

aphasia, p. 78

split-brain operation, p. 80

structural plasticity, p. 84

Key People

Pierre Paul Broca (1824–1880) French surgeon and neuroanatomist who in 1861 discovered an area on the lower left frontal lobe of the cerebral cortex that, when damaged, produces speech disturbances but no loss of comprehension. (p. 78)

Roger Sperry (1913–1994) American psychologist who received the Nobel Prize in 1981 for his pioneering research on brain specialization in split-brain patients. (p. 80)

Karl Wernicke (1848–1905) German neurologist who in 1874 discovered an area on the left temporal lobe of the cerebral cortex that, when damaged, produces meaningless or nonsensical speech and difficulties in verbal or written comprehension. (p. 78)

Concept Review Answers

2.1   page 55

1. b   *2.* f   *3.* a   *4.* c   *5.* e   *6.* d

2.2   page 62

1. c   *2.* b   *3.* d   *4.* d   *5.* a

2.3   page 82

1. hindbrain; midbrain; forebrain
2. cerebellum
3. temporal
4. primary motor cortex; frontal
5. hippocampus
6. limbic system
7. Broca's area
8. corpus callosum
9. 70

Sculling at Sunset

Sensation and Perception

Chapter Outline

Prologue

Don't Ask These Guys to Stop and Smell the Roses

We have two good friends, quite dissimilar in most ways, who share one common characteristic—they have no sense of smell. Paul is an electrical engineer in his early thirties. Warren is a well-known professor of psychology some 20 years older. Although you might expect this condition to be extremely rare, the inability to smell, called *anosmia,* is relatively common, occurring in about 1 in 500 people (Doty, 2001).

Paul was born without a sense of smell. But he was completely unaware that he lacked this ability until he was about 10 years old. Paul's mother asked him to smell an arrangement of freshly cut flowers, but the puzzled child couldn't detect a thing. Because Paul has never experienced smell, it's impossible for him to imagine what a smell smells like. Friends have tried to describe the aroma of garlic, flowers, burning leaves, and so forth. But it's almost impossible to describe one smell without relating it to another. Try it, and you'll see what we mean. How would you describe the smell of steaks barbecuing? A new car? A locker room? Sour milk?

As you'll discover in this chapter, the senses of taste and smell are closely related, and the flavor of a food is strongly tied to its aroma. That's part of the reason that food often tastes bland, or cardboardy, when you have a bad head cold. What does food taste like for Paul? Paul is married to Asha, whom you met in Chapter 2. Asha cooks some wonderfully spicy Indian meals. Asha has discovered that Paul bases many of his food preferences on the *texture* of foods rather than on their flavor. For example, Paul dislikes noodles because their texture seems "slimy" to him. He also dislikes the sensation of certain textures combined, such as nuts in ice cream or brownies. Other foods, like chocolate, have no taste at all.

Unlike Paul, Warren knows what he's missing. Warren was born with a normal sense of smell. Then, as a young man, he underwent major surgery to repair an artery at the front of his brain. To get to the artery, the surgeon cut through the neural tract for smell, destroying Warren's sense of smell.

For several days following the surgery, Warren's eyes were swollen shut. Deprived of both visual and odor cues, he was unable to identify many of the foods he was fed. For example, he couldn't tell the difference among strawberry, chocolate, and vanilla pudding—they all tasted the same to him. And, like Paul, Warren found that the texture of different foods became much more significant. For example, peanut butter now tasted like "oily sand" to Warren.

The experience of taste was very different for Warren following the surgery. He experimented with familiar as well as new and unusual foods to see how they would taste. As time went on, Warren learned to compensate for the missing sense of smell—at least for its role in taste. Now, many years later, Warren has become accustomed to the way foods taste in the absence of aromas.

In this chapter, we'll explore how we sense the world around us and how the brain integrates and interprets those sensory signals to form meaningful perceptions. We'll also tell you more about our friends Paul and Warren.

Introduction

What Are Sensation and Perception?

Glance around you. Notice the incredible variety of colors, shades, shadows, and images. Listen carefully to the diversity of sounds, loud and soft, near and far. Focus on everything that's touching you—your clothes, your shoes, the chair you're sitting on. Now, inhale deeply through your nose and identify the aromas in the air.

With these simple observations you have exercised four of your senses: vision, hearing, touch, and smell. As we saw in Chapter 2, the primary function of the nervous system is communication—the transmission of information from one part of the body to the other. Where does that information come from? Put simply, your senses are the gateway through which your brain receives all its information about the environment. It's a process that is so natural and automatic that we typically take it for granted until it is disrupted by illness or injury. Nevertheless, as the stories of Paul and Warren demonstrate, people with one nonfunctional sense are amazingly adaptive. Often, they learn to compensate for the missing environmental information by relying on their other senses.

In this chapter, we will explore the overlapping processes of *sensation* and *perception*. **Sensation** refers to the detection and basic sensory experience of environmental stimuli, such as sounds, objects, and odors. **Perception** occurs when we integrate, organize, and interpret sensory information in a way that is meaningful. Here's a simple example to contrast the two terms. Your eyes' physical response to light, splotches of color, and lines reflects *sensation*. Integrating and organizing those sensations so that you interpret the light, splotches of color, and lines as a painting, a flag, or some other object reflects *perception*.

Where does the process of sensation leave off and the process of perception begin? There is no clear boundary line between the two processes as we actually experience them. In fact, many researchers in this area of psychology regard sensation and perception as a single process.

Although the two processes overlap, in this chapter we will present sensation and perception as separate discussions. In the first half of the chapter, we'll discuss the basics of *sensation*—how our sensory receptors respond to stimulation and transmit that information in usable form to the brain. In the second half of the chapter, we'll explore *perception*—how the brain actively organizes and interprets the signals sent from our sensory receptors.

Experiencing the World Through Our Senses Imagine biting into a crisp, red apple. All your senses are involved in your experience—vision, smell, taste, hearing, and touch. Although we're accustomed to thinking of our different senses as being quite distinct, all forms of sensation involve the stimulation of specialized cells called sensory receptors.

Basic Principles of Sensation

Key Theme

- Sensation is the result of neural impulses transmitted to the brain from sensory receptors that have been stimulated by physical energy from the external environment.

Key Questions

- What is the process of transduction?
- What is a sensory threshold, and what are two main types of sensory threshold?
- How do sensory adaptation and Weber's law demonstrate that sensation is relative rather than absolute?

sensation
The process of detecting a physical stimulus, such as light, sound, heat, or pressure.

perception
The process of integrating, organizing, and interpreting sensations.

sensory receptors
Specialized cells unique to each sense organ that respond to a particular form of sensory stimulation.

transduction
The process by which a form of physical energy is converted into a coded neural signal that can be processed by the nervous system.

We're accustomed to thinking of the senses as being quite different from one another. However, all our senses involve some common processes. All sensation is a result of the stimulation of specialized cells, called **sensory receptors,** by some form of *energy.*

Imagine biting into a crisp, red apple. Your experience of hearing the apple crunch is a response to the physical energy of vibrations in the air, or *sound waves.* The sweet taste of the apple is a response to the physical energy of *dissolvable chemicals* in your mouth, just as the distinctive sharp aroma of the apple is a response to *airborne chemical molecules* that you inhale through your nose. The smooth feel of the apple's skin is a response to the *pressure* of the apple against your hand. And the mellow red color of the apple is a response to the physical energy of *light waves* reflecting from the irregularly shaped object you've just bitten into.

Sensory receptors convert these different forms of physical energy into electrical impulses that are transmitted via neurons to the brain. The process by which a form of physical energy is converted into a coded neural signal that can be processed by the nervous system is called **transduction.** These neural signals are sent to the brain, where the perceptual processes of organizing and interpreting the coded messages occur. In Figure 3.1, you can see the basic steps involved in sensation and perception.

We are constantly being bombarded by many different forms of energy. For instance, at this very moment radio and television waves are bouncing around the atmosphere and passing through your body. However, sensory receptors are

Sensation		Perception
Energy from an environmental stimulus activates specialized receptor cells in the sense organ.	Coded neural messages are sent along a specific sensory pathway to the brain.	These neural messages are decoded and interpreted in the brain as a meaningful perception.

FIGURE 3.1 **The Basic Steps of Sensation and Perception**

absolute threshold
The smallest possible strength of a stimulus that can be detected half the time.

difference threshold
The smallest possible difference between two stimuli that can be detected half the time; also called *just noticeable difference.*

Weber's law
A principle of sensation that holds that the size of the just noticeable difference will vary depending on its relation to the strength of the original stimulus.

sensory adaptation
The decline in sensitivity to a constant stimulus.

subliminal perception
The perception of stimuli that are below the threshold of conscious awareness.

Table | **3.1**

Absolute Thresholds

Sense	Absolute Threshold
Vision	A candle flame seen from 30 miles away on a clear, dark night
Hearing	The tick of a watch at 20 feet
Taste	One teaspoon of sugar in two gallons of water
Smell	One drop of perfume throughout a three-room apartment
Touch	A bee's wing falling on your cheek from a height of about half an inch

Psychologist Eugene Galanter (1962) provided these classic examples of the absolute thresholds for our senses. In each case, people are able to sense these faint stimuli at least half the time.

so highly specialized that they are sensitive only to very specific types of energy (which is lucky, or you might be seeing *I Love Lucy* reruns in your brain right now). So, for any type of stimulation to be sensed, the stimulus energy must first be in a form that can be detected by our sensory receptor cells. Otherwise, transduction cannot occur.

Sensory Thresholds

Along with being specialized as to the types of energy that can be detected, our senses are specialized in other ways as well. We do not have an infinite capacity to detect all levels of energy. To be sensed, a stimulus must first be strong enough to be detected—loud enough to be heard, concentrated enough to be smelled, bright enough to be seen. The point at which a stimulus is strong enough to be detected because it activates a sensory receptor cell is called a *threshold*. There are two general kinds of sensory thresholds for each sense—the absolute threshold and the difference threshold.

The **absolute threshold** refers to the smallest possible strength of a stimulus that can be detected half the time. Why just half the time? Because the minimum level of stimulation that can be detected varies from person to person and from trial to trial. Because of this human variability, researchers have arbitrarily set the limit as the minimum level of stimulation that can be detected half the time. Under ideal conditions (which rarely occur in normal daily life), our sensory abilities are far more sensitive than you might think (see Table 3.1). Can stimuli that are below the absolute threshold affect us? We discuss this question in Science versus Pseudoscience Box 3.1, "Subliminal Perception."

The other important threshold involves detecting the *difference* between two stimuli. The **difference threshold** is the smallest possible difference between two stimuli that can be detected half the time. Another term for difference threshold is *just noticeable difference,* which is abbreviated *jnd.*

The just noticeable difference will *vary* depending on its relation to the original stimulus. This principle of sensation is called *Weber's law.* **Weber's law** holds that for each sense, the size of a just noticeable difference is a constant proportion of the size of the initial stimulus. So, whether we can detect a change in the strength of a stimulus depends on the intensity of the *original* stimulus. For example, if you are holding a pebble (the original stimulus), you will notice an increase in weight if a second pebble is placed in your hand. But if you start off holding a very heavy rock (the original stimulus), you probably won't detect an increase in weight when the same pebble is balanced on it.

What Weber's law underscores is that our psychological experience of sensation is *relative.* There is no simple, one-to-one correspondence between the objective characteristics of a physical stimulus, such as the weight of a pebble, and our psychological experience of it.

Sensory Adaptation

Suppose your best friend has invited you over for a spaghetti dinner. As you walk in the front door, you're almost overwhelmed by the odor of onions and garlic cooking on the stove. However, after just a few moments, you no longer notice the smell. Why? Because your sensory receptor cells become less responsive to a constant stimulus. This gradual decline in sensitivity to a constant stimulus is called **sensory adaptation.** Once again, we see that our experience of sensation is relative—in this case, relative to the *duration of exposure.*

Because of sensory adaptation, we become accustomed to constant stimuli, which allows us to quickly notice new or changing stimuli. This makes sense. If we were continually aware of all incoming stimuli, we'd be so overwhelmed with sensory information that we wouldn't be able to focus our attention. So, for example, once you manage to land your posterior on the sofa, you don't need to be constantly reminded that the sofa is beneath you.

Subliminal Perception

The U.S. presidential election campaign of 2000 was unusual in many respects, but certainly one of the odder controversies that surfaced had to do with a particular television commercial. During the campaign, one political party (let's call them the "Democrats") accused the other political party (let's call them the "Republicans") of using subliminal techniques in a political ad. When the ad was played at slower-than-normal speed, the word "RATS" appeared in large white letters while the announcer criticized candidate Al Gore's prescription drug plan as one in which "bureaucrats decide." Democrats accused the Republicans of embedding a subliminal message in their ad, Republicans denied the accusation, and the firm that created the advertisement claimed that it was just a coincidence. Predictably, the resulting flap kept political commentators and headline writers busy for days.

What are subliminal messages? Can they be used to persuade people to change their attitudes or buy products? **Subliminal perception** refers to the perception of stimuli that are below the threshold of conscious perception or awareness. (The word *limen* is Latin for "threshold.") Subliminal stimuli could be sounds presented too faintly for a person to consciously hear or visual images presented too rapidly for a person to consciously recognize.

Psychologists have studied subliminal perception for more than 60 years (e.g., Collier, 1940; A. C. Williams, 1938). But the idea that people's behavior could be manipulated by subliminal messages first attracted public attention in 1957. James Vicary, a marketing executive, claimed to have increased popcorn and Coca-Cola sales at a New Jersey movie theater by subliminally flashing the words "Eat popcorn" and "Drink Coke" during the movie.

Not surprisingly, Vicary's claim sparked a public uproar. People feared that advertisers could use subliminal persuasion to coerce consumers to buy their products or that government agencies might use subliminal techniques to brainwash citizens. Controlled tests, however, failed to replicate Vicary's claims (Bornstein, 1989). Vicary later admitted that his boast was a hoax to drum up customers for his failing marketing business (Pratkanis & Aronson, 1992). Nevertheless, many people still believe that subliminal messages can exert a powerful and irresistible influence.

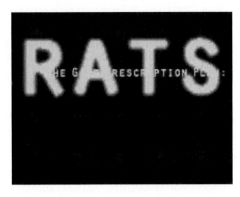

Subliminal Advertising in Politics In the original campaign ad, the words "RATS" appeared in large white letters, superimposed over the words "The Gore Prescription Plan." In a fraction of a second, "RATS" disappeared and the words "BUREAUCRATS DECIDE" appeared in smaller letters. If you were aware of the word's presence, you might have been able to spot it when the ad played at normal speed, but most viewers wouldn't detect it.

Can your behavior be profoundly influenced by subliminal self-help tapes? By backward soundtracks on music albums? Or by vague sexual images or words embedded in advertisements? In a word, no. Numerous studies have shown that subliminal self-help tapes do *not* produce the changes they claim to produce (e.g., Greenwald & others, 1991; Mitchell, 1995; Moore, 1988). Studies of backward soundtracks show that they have *no* effect (Begg & others, 1993; Swart & Morgan, 1992; Vokey & Read, 1985). And numerous studies on subliminal messages in advertising have shown that they also are *ineffective* in influencing consumer decisions (Trappey, 1996).

Consider this study by Kirk Smith and Martha Rogers (1994). Subjects watched television commercials with the words "Choose this" presented either subliminally or overtly. The commercials with the subliminal messages were not only *less* likely to be remembered than the commercials with overt messages, but they were also disliked more. In neither case were the subjects more likely to choose the product shown.

So, do subliminal stimuli have *any* effect? Surprisingly, the answer is a qualified yes (Epley & others, 1999). The effects of subliminally presented stimuli are well documented in psychological research (Bargh & Churchland, 1999). For example, in a 1959 study, Morris Eagle flashed subliminal images of a boy either angrily throwing a birthday cake or pleasantly presenting a birthday cake. When subjects were shown a picture of the same boy in a neutral posture, those who had been exposed to the angry image evaluated the boy's personality in much more negative terms than did those who had seen the pleasant image of the same boy. A more recent experiment showed that subliminally presenting subjects with a pleasant scene (cute kittens) or with an unpleasant scene (a skull) can influence how people judge a person shown in a neutral context (Krosnick & others, 1992).

Another area of research in subliminal perception involves a phenomenon called the mere exposure effect. The *mere exposure effect* refers to the fact that when people are repeatedly exposed to a novel stimulus, like a shape or a Chinese ideograph, their liking for that particular stimulus will increase (Zajonc, 1998). The mere exposure effect also holds true for subliminal exposure to stimuli (Bornstein, 1993; Murphy & others, 1995). For example, when people are exposed to a subliminal image of a geometric shape and later asked to pick the shape they prefer from a group of geometric shapes, they are more likely to choose the subliminally presented shape.

Today it is known that a wide variety of methods can be used to present information outside conscious awareness that influences emotions, thoughts, and attitudes (Merikle & Daneman, 1998; Katkin & others, 2001). However, note that there is a difference between subliminal *perception* and subliminal *persuasion* (Epley & others, 1999). To date, there is *no* evidence that subliminally presented stimuli can change behavior or personality in any long-lasting or significant way.

Rather, psychologists have found that the effects of subliminal stimuli tend to be weak and short lived, usually lasting only seconds or minutes (Greenwald, 1992; Kihlstrom & others, 1992). Further, effectiveness is limited to very simple stimuli, such as a single word or image. When more complex messages are subliminally presented, no effect is seen (Kihlstrom, 1993). And, finally, the effects of subliminal stimuli are best demonstrated under carefully controlled laboratory conditions.

wavelength
The distance from one wave peak to another.

cornea
(CORE-nee-uh) A clear membrane covering the visible part of the eye that helps gather and direct incoming light.

pupil
The opening in the middle of the iris that changes size to let in different amounts of light.

iris
(EYE-riss) The colored part of the eye, which is the muscle that controls the size of the pupil.

Vision
From Light to Sight

Key Theme
■ The receptor cells for vision respond to the physical energy of light waves and are located in the retina of the eye.

Key Questions
■ What is the visible spectrum?
■ What are the key structures of the eye and their functions?
■ What are rods and cones, and how do their functions differ?

A lone caterpillar on the screen door, the pile of dirty laundry in the closet corner, a spectacular autumn sunset, the intricate play of color, light, and texture in a painting by Monet. The sense organ for vision is the eye, which contains receptor cells that are sensitive to the physical energy of *light*. But before we can talk about how the eye functions, we need to briefly discuss some characteristics of light as the visual stimulus.

What We See
The Nature of Light

Light is just one of many different kinds of electromagnetic energy that travel in the form of waves. Other forms of electromagnetic energy include X-rays, the microwaves you use to bake a potato, and the ultraviolet rays that give you a sunburn. The various types of electromagnetic energy differ in **wavelength,** which is the distance from one wave peak to another. Figure 3.2 shows the spectrum of different forms of electromagnetic energy.

Humans are capable of visually detecting only a minuscule portion of the electromagnetic energy range. In Figure 3.2, notice that the visible portion of the electromagnetic energy spectrum can be further divided into different wavelengths. As we'll discuss in more detail later, the different wavelengths of visible light correspond to our psychological perception of different colors.

FIGURE 3.2 The Electromagnetic Spectrum We are surrounded by different kinds of electromagnetic energy waves, yet we are able to see only a tiny portion of the entire spectrum of electromagnetic energy. Some electronic instruments, like radio and television, are specialized receivers that detect a specific wavelength range. Similarly, the human eye is sensitive to a specific and very narrow range of wavelengths.

How We See

The Human Visual System

Suppose you're watching your neighbor's yellow and white tabby cat sunning himself on the front steps. How do you see the cat? Simply seeing a yellow tabby cat involves a complex chain of events. We'll describe the process of vision from the object to the brain. You can trace the path of light waves through the eye in Figure 3.3.

First, light waves reflected from the cat enter your eye, passing through the *cornea, pupil,* and *lens.* The **cornea,** a clear membrane that covers the front of the eye, helps gather and direct incoming light. The *sclera,* or white portion of the eye, is a tough, fibrous tissue that covers the eyeball except for the cornea. The **pupil** is the black opening in the middle of the eye. The pupil is surrounded by the **iris,** the colored structure that we refer to when we say that someone has brown or blue eyes. The iris is actually a ring of muscles that contract or expand to precisely control the size of the pupil and thus the amount of light entering the eye. In dim light, the iris widens the pupil to let light in; in bright light, the iris narrows the pupil. Some people, calling themselves *iridologists,* claim that they can diagnose health problems

How a Pit Viper Sees a Mouse at Night Does the world look different to other species? In many cases, yes. Each species has evolved a unique set of sensory capabilities. Pit vipers see infrared light, which we sense only as warmth. The mouse here has been photographed through an infrared viewer. The image shows how a pit viper uses its infrared "vision" to detect warm-blooded prey at night (Gould & Gould, 1994). Similarly, many insect and bird species can detect ultraviolet light, which is invisible to humans.

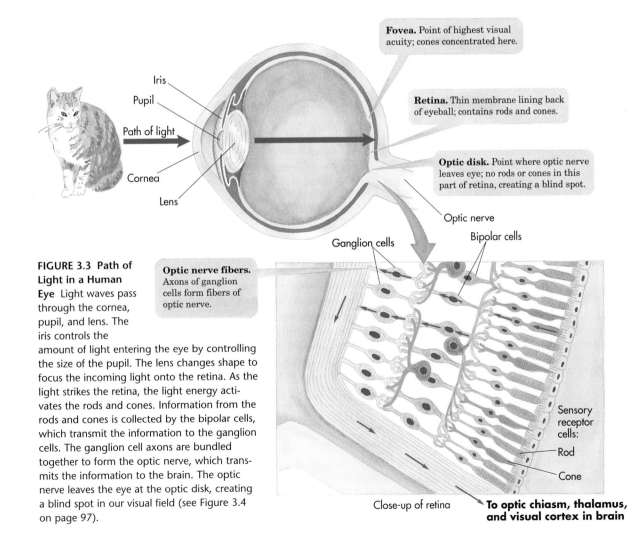

FIGURE 3.3 Path of Light in a Human Eye Light waves pass through the cornea, pupil, and lens. The iris controls the amount of light entering the eye by controlling the size of the pupil. The lens changes shape to focus the incoming light onto the retina. As the light strikes the retina, the light energy activates the rods and cones. Information from the rods and cones is collected by the bipolar cells, which transmit the information to the ganglion cells. The ganglion cell axons are bundled together to form the optic nerve, which transmits the information to the brain. The optic nerve leaves the eye at the optic disk, creating a blind spot in our visual field (see Figure 3.4 on page 97).

Fovea. Point of highest visual acuity; cones concentrated here.

Retina. Thin membrane lining back of eyeball; contains rods and cones.

Optic disk. Point where optic nerve leaves eye; no rods or cones in this part of retina, creating a blind spot.

Optic nerve fibers. Axons of ganglion cells form fibers of optic nerve.

Iris

Pupil

Path of light

Cornea

Lens

Optic nerve

Ganglion cells

Bipolar cells

Sensory receptor cells:

Rod

Cone

Close-up of retina

To optic chiasm, thalamus, and visual cortex in brain

SCIENCE VERSUS PSEUDOSCIENCE 3.2

Iridology

Iridology is a popular pseudoscience based on the unproven notion that physical and psychological functioning are reflected in the iris (Barrett, 1996). Iridologists claim that simply examining the color and markings of your iris with a magnifying glass can reveal a wealth of information about you. Supposedly, a skilled iridologist can determine your level of mental stress, personality characteristics, genetic tendencies, nutritional deficiencies, and past diseases and injuries (Bamer, 1996; Jackson, 1995). Iridologists use highly detailed charts, such as the one shown here, to "diagnose" such characteristics. They also recommend that you have your eyes "read" about once a year to detect any significant changes.

How have the notions of iridology stood up to scientific investigation? In one study, iridologists were asked to evaluate photographs of irises taken before and after people had developed an acute disease (see Worrall, 1986). The iridologists were to state whether a change in the iris had occurred and which organ was affected. They found that one before-and-after set of photographs indicated clear-cut changes. Unfortunately for the iridologists, those two photographs of the same individual

An Iridologist's Map of the Eye According to proponents of iridology, specific areas of the iris correspond to areas of the body and psychological functions. Using elaborate maps of the iris, such as the one shown here, iridologists evaluate physical and mental health based on the iris's color patterns.

had been taken only two minutes apart and were part of the control conditions for the experiment.

In another study, three iridologists and three ophthalmologists (physicians with specialized training in diseases of the eye) were asked to judge photographs of the irises of 143 people. Of these people, 48 had kidney disease, which can supposedly be detected quite easily using iridology. The ophthalmologists acted as an expert control group in the study. Ophthalmologists do not normally claim to be able to diagnose kidney disease by examining the eye, but in this case they were instructed to try to judge kidney function with "whatever methods they could best do so" (Simon & others, 1979).

The iridologists correctly predicted whether subjects had kidney disease 49 percent of the time. The ophthalmologists were equally impressive, correctly identifying the subjects with kidney disease 53 percent of the time. In other words, both groups were about as accurate as they would have been had they simply flipped a coin.

Such controlled scientific studies have failed to confirm the claims of iridology. In fact, since iridology was founded over a hundred years ago, advocates of iridology have failed to publish even one well-documented study to support their claims (Worrall, 1986).

---

iridology
(ear-ruh-DOLL-uh-jee) A pseudoscience based on the unproven notion that the physical and psychological functioning of an individual is represented in the markings of the iris.

lens
A transparent structure located behind the pupil that actively focuses, or bends, light as it enters the eye.

accommodation
The process by which the lens changes shape to focus incoming light so that it falls on the retina.

by studying the distinctive patterns of the iris. Can they? We take a critical look at iridology in Science versus Pseudoscience Box 3.2, Iridology.

Behind the pupil is the **lens,** another transparent structure. In a process called **accommodation,** the lens thins or thickens to bend or focus the incoming light so that the light falls on the retina. If the eyeball is abnormally shaped, the lens may not properly focus the incoming light on the retina. The result is a visual disorder, such as *nearsightedness, farsightedness,* or *astigmatism.* In nearsightedness, or *myopia,* light from a distant object is focused in front of the retina. In farsightedness, or *hyperopia,* light from an object or image close by is focused behind the retina (Figure 3.4). During middle age, another form of farsightedness often occurs, called *presbyopia.* Presbyopia is caused when the lens becomes brittle and inflexible. In *astigmatism,* an abnormally curved eyeball results in blurry vision for lines in a particular direction. Corrective glasses remedy these conditions by intercepting and bending the light so that the image falls properly on the retina.

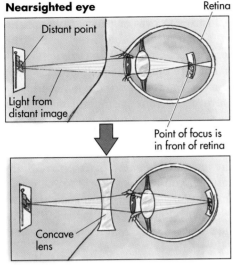

Nearsighted eye

Distant point

Retina

Light from distant image

Point of focus is in front of retina

Concave lens

Farsighted eye

Near point

Retina

Light from nearby image

Point of focus is behind retina

Convex lens

FIGURE 3.4 Common Visual Disorders: Nearsightedness and Farsightedness Nearsightedness and farsightedness, common visual disorders, are both caused by an abnormally shaped eyeball. In each case, the lens does not properly focus the incoming light onto the retina. Corrective lenses intercept and bend the light before it reaches the eye, so that the image falls properly on the retina. The thickness and curvature of the corrective lens determines where the image falls.

The Retina

Rods and Cones

The **retina** is a thin, light-sensitive membrane that lies at the back of the eye, covering most of its inner surface (see Figure 3.3). The retina contains the two kinds of sensory receptors for light: **rods** and **cones.** When exposed to light, rods and cones undergo a chemical reaction that results in a neural signal.

Rods and cones differ in many ways. First, as their names imply, rods and cones are shaped differently. Rods are long and thin, with blunt ends. Cones are shorter and fatter, with one end that tapers to a point. The eye contains far more rods than cones. It is estimated that each eye contains about 7 million cones and about 125 million rods!

Cones   Rods

Slim Rods and Fat Cones The rods and cones in the retina are the sensory receptors for vision. They convert light into electrical impulses that are ultimately transmitted to the brain. This photograph shows the rods and cones magnified about 45,000 times. The rods are long and thin; the cones are shorter, fatter, and tapered at one end. As you can see, the rods and cones are densely packed in the retina, with many rods surrounding a single cone or pair of cones.

Rods and cones are also specialized for different visual functions. Although both are light receptors, rods are much more sensitive to light than are cones. Once the rods are fully adapted to the dark, they are about a thousand times better than cones at detecting weak visual stimuli (Masland, 2001). We therefore rely primarily on rods for our vision in dim light and at night.

Rods and cones also react differently to *changes* in the amount of light. Rods adapt relatively slowly, reaching maximum sensitivity to light in about 30 minutes. In contrast, cones adapt quickly to bright light, reaching maximum sensitivity in about 5 minutes. That's why it takes several minutes for your eyes to adapt to the dim light of a darkened room, but only a few moments to adapt to the brightness when you switch on the lights.

You may have noticed that it is difficult or impossible to distinguish colors in very dim light. This difficulty occurs because only the cones are sensitive to the different wavelengths that produce the sensation of color, and cones require much more light than rods do to function effectively. Cones are also specialized for seeing fine details and for vision in bright light.

Most of the cones are concentrated in the **fovea,** which is a region in the very center of the retina. Cones are scattered throughout the rest of the retina, but they become progressively less common toward the periphery of the retina.

retina
(RET-in-uh) A thin, light-sensitive membrane located at the back of the eye that contains the sensory receptors for vision.

rods
The long, thin, blunt sensory receptors of the eye that are highly sensitive to light, but not to color, and that are primarily responsible for peripheral vision and night vision.

cones
The short, thick, pointed sensory receptors of the eye that detect color and are responsible for color vision and visual acuity.

fovea
A small area in the center of the retina, composed entirely of cones, where visual information is most sharply focused.

There are no rods in the fovea. Images that do not fall on the fovea tend to be perceived as blurry or indistinct. For example, focus your eyes on the word *For* at the beginning of this sentence. In contrast to the sharpness of the letters in *For,* the words to the left and right are somewhat blurry. The image of the outlying words is striking the peripheral areas of the retina, where cones are much less common.

Rods are most prevalent in the periphery of the retina. When you see something out of the corner of your eye, you are using your peripheral vision and relying primarily on your rods. However, because there are a few cones in the peripheral areas of the retina, the world doesn't suddenly become black and white on the edges of your visual field.

Because rods are more sensitive to light than are cones, at night or in a dimly lit room you will actually be able to see better if you use peripheral vision (relying on your rods) than if you look directly in front of you (using your cones). If you want to view a particular object in dim light, look slightly above, below, or to the side of it. Try this when looking at a star at night—a trick that astronomers and sailors have known for hundreds of years.

The Blind Spot

One part of the retina lacks rods and cones altogether. This area, called the **optic disk,** is the point at which the fibers that make up the optic nerve leave the back of the eye and project to the brain. Because there are no photoreceptors in the optic disk, we have a tiny hole, or **blind spot,** in our field of vision. To experience the blind spot, try the demonstration in Figure 3.5.

Why don't we notice this hole in our visual field? Some researchers have suggested that we simply don't notice that any information is missing because the blind spot is located in an area that has few receptors. Other researchers have suggested that the left eye compensates for the missing information in the right eye and vice versa. A more compelling explanation is that the brain actually fills in the missing background information (Ramachandran, 1992a, 1992b). In effect, the brain "paves over" the blind spot with the color and pattern of the surrounding visual information.

Processing Visual Information

Key Theme
- Signals from the rods and cones undergo preliminary processing in the retina before they are transmitted to the brain.

Key Questions
- What are the bipolar and ganglion cells, and how do their functions differ?
- How is visual information transmitted from the retina to the brain?
- What properties of light correspond to color perceptions, and how is color vision explained?

Visual information is processed primarily in the brain. However, before visual information is sent to the brain, it undergoes some preliminary processing in the retina by specialized neurons called **ganglion cells.** This preliminary processing of visual data in the cells of the retina is possible because the retina actually developed from a bit of brain tissue that "migrated" to the eye during fetal development (see Hubel, 1995).

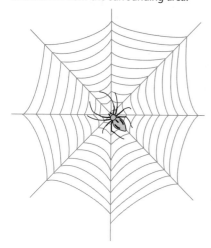

FIGURE 3.5 Demonstration of the Blind Spot Hold the book a few feet in front of you. Close your right eye and stare at the insect spray can with your left eye. Slowly bring the book toward your face. At some point the spider will disappear, because you have focused it onto the part of your retina where the blind spot is located. Notice, however, that you still perceive the spider web. That's because your brain has filled in information from the surrounding area.

optic disk
Area of the retina without rods or cones, where the optic nerve exits the back of the eye.

blind spot
The point at which the optic nerve leaves the eye, producing a small gap in the field of vision.

ganglion cells
In the retina, the specialized neurons that connect to the bipolar cells; the bundled axons of the ganglion cells form the optic nerve.

When the numbers of rods and cones are combined, there are over 130 million receptor cells in each retina. However, there are only about 1 million ganglion cells. How do just 1 million ganglion cells transmit messages from 130 million visual receptor cells?

Visual Processing in the Retina

Information from the sensory receptors, the rods and cones, is first collected by specialized neurons, called **bipolar cells** (see lower part of Figure 3.3 on page 95). The bipolar cells then funnel the collection of raw data on to the ganglion cells. Each ganglion cell receives information from photoreceptors in its *receptive field,* a particular area of the retina. In this early stage of visual processing, each ganglion cell combines, analyzes, and encodes the information from the photoreceptors in its receptive field before transmitting the information to the brain (Masland, 2001).

Signals from rods and signals from cones are processed differently in the ganglion cells. For the most part, a single ganglion cell receives information from only one or two cones, but might well receive information from a hundred or more rods. The messages from these many different rods are combined in the retina before they are sent to the brain. Thus, the brain receives less specific visual information from the rods and messages of much greater visual detail from the cones.

Imagine listening to a hundred people trying to talk at once over the same telephone line. You would hear the sound of many people talking, but individual voices would be blurred. This is analogous to how rod information is processed. Now, imagine listening to the voice of a single individual being transmitted across the same telephone line. Every syllable and sound would be clear and distinct. In much the same way, cones use the ganglion cells to provide the brain with more specific visual information than is received from rods.

Because of this difference in how information is processed, cones are especially important in *visual acuity*—the ability to see fine details. Visual acuity is strongest when images are focused on the fovea, because of the high concentration of cones there.

From Eye to Brain

How is information transmitted from the ganglion cells of the retina to the brain? The 1 million axons of the ganglion cells are bundled together to form the **optic nerve,** a thick nerve that exits from the back of the eye at the optic disk and extends to the brain (see Figure 3.6). The optic nerve has about the same diameter as a pencil. After exiting the eyes, the left and right optic nerves meet and converge at the **optic chiasm.**

If you think of visual information moving along the left and right optic nerves in terms of cars moving along the interstate, the optic chiasm would represent a major interchange, where highways merge and then branch out again. After merging at the optic chiasm, the fibers of the left and right optic nerves split in two. One set of axons crosses over and projects to the opposite side of the brain. The other set of axons forms a pathway that continues along the same side of the brain (see Figure 3.6).

From the optic chiasm, most of the optic nerve axons project to the brain structure called the

bipolar cells
In the retina, the specialized neurons that connect the rods and cones with the ganglion cells.

optic nerve
The thick nerve that exits from the back of the eye and carries visual information to the visual cortex in the brain.

optic chiasm
(KI-az-em) Point in the brain where the optic nerve fibers from each eye meet and partly cross over to the opposite side of the brain.

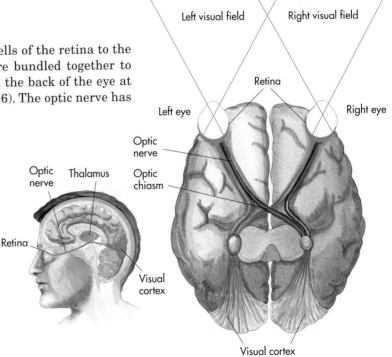

FIGURE 3.6 Neural Pathways from Eye to Brain The bundled axons of the ganglion cells form the optic nerve, which exits the retina at the optic disk. The optic nerves from the left and right eyes meet at the optic chiasm, then split apart. One set of nerve fibers crosses over and projects to the opposite side of the brain, and another set of nerve fibers continues along the same side of the brain. Most of the nerve fibers travel to the thalamus and then on to the visual cortex of the occipital lobe.

color
The perceptual experience of different wavelengths of light, involving hue, saturation (purity), and brightness (intensity).

hue
The property of wavelengths of light known as color; different wavelengths correspond to our subjective experience of different colors.

saturation
The property of color that corresponds to the purity of the light wave.

brightness
The perceived intensity of a color, which corresponds to the amplitude of the light wave.

thalamus. This primary pathway seems to be responsible for processing information about form, color, brightness, and depth. A smaller number of axons follow a detour to areas in the *midbrain* before they make their way to the thalamus. This secondary pathway seems to be involved in processing information about the location of an object. Neuroscientists now know that there are several distinct neural pathways in the visual system, each responsible for handling a different aspect of vision (Zeki, 2001). Although specialized, the separate pathways are highly interconnected.

From the thalamus, the signals are sent to the *visual cortex,* where they are decoded and interpreted. Most of the receiving neurons in the visual cortex of the brain are highly specialized (Logothetis & Sheinberg, 1996). Each responds to a particular type of visual stimulation, such as angles, edges, lines, and other forms, and even to the movement and distance of objects (Hubel, 1995; Livingstone & Hubel, 1988). These neurons are sometimes called *feature detectors,* because they detect, or respond to, particular features or aspects of more complex visual stimuli. Reassembling the features into a recognizable image or object involves additional levels of processing in the visual cortex and other regions of the brain, including the *frontal lobes* (Lumer & others, 1998).

Understanding exactly how neural responses of individual feature detection cells become integrated into the visual perceptions of faces and objects is a major goal in contemporary neuroscience (Cohen & Tong, 2001). In the Focus on Neuroscience, we present a look at how such integration takes place in the brain's visual system.

focus on Neuroscience

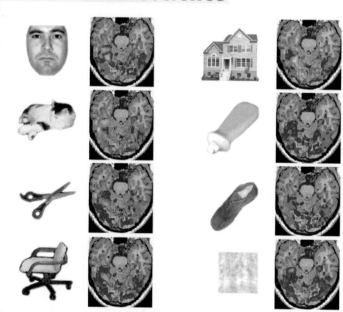

Watching the Brain Watch Objects Neuroscientists still can't read your mind, but they're getting closer—a lot closer. In a recent study, neuroscientist James Haxby and his colleagues (2001) were able to look at brain scans and correctly identify the objects that research participants were viewing. The neuroscientists used functional magnetic resonance imaging (fMRI) to measure brain response patterns in six people while they looked at pictures of faces, cats, and five other types of objects: houses, chairs, scissors,

shoes, and bottles. Shown at the left are the fMRI scans of one individual. Remember that red and yellow areas indicate higher levels of brain activity.

As you study the scans, notice that all of the objects triggered brain activity in roughly the same brain region—a visual processing area of the brain called the *extrastriate cortex*. However, you should also note that each category of object evoked a unique activity pattern. By looking at the activation pattern, the researchers were able to predict which object the person was viewing at the time the scan was made. Overall, the researchers were 96 percent accurate in predicting the object being viewed. When it came to predicting faces or houses, their accuracy rate was 100 percent.

One important finding in Haxby's study was that multiple brain areas were activated when people viewed each category of objects. In contrast, other researchers, like psychologist Paul Downing, have found that very specific cortical areas respond selectively to particular categories of information. One such area, dubbed the *extrastriate body area* by Downing and his colleagues (2001), responds selectively to images of the human body, including body parts, faces, and even stick figures. Such evidence suggests that very discrete brain areas, or "modules," are specialized to respond to specific kinds of information.

The debate over whether the brain organizes information in discrete "modules" or distributes it across overlapping brain areas has been going on for some time. Interestingly, the historical roots of this debate can be traced back to the nineteenth-century pseudoscience called *phrenology,* which we discussed in Chapter 2. While no single experiment is likely to settle this controversy, the fMRI study presented here emphasizes that even simple visual processes rely on the integrated interaction of multiple brain areas (Cohen & Tong, 2001).

Color Vision

We see images of an apple, a banana, and an orange because these objects reflect light waves. But why do we perceive that the apple is red and the banana yellow? What makes an orange orange?

The Experience of Color

What Makes an Orange Orange?

To explain the nature of color, we must go back to the visual stimulus—light. Our experience of **color** involves three properties of the light wave. First, what we usually refer to as color is a property more accurately termed **hue.** Hue varies with the wavelength of light. Look again at Figure 3.2 on page 94. *Different wavelengths correspond to our subjective experience of different colors.* Wavelengths of about 400 nanometers are perceived as violet. Wavelengths of about 700 nanometers are perceived as red. In between are orange, yellow, green, and blue.

Second, the **saturation,** or *purity,* of the color corresponds to the purity of the light wave. Pure red, for example, produced by a single wavelength, is more *saturated* than pink, which is produced by a combination of wavelengths (red plus white light). In everyday language, saturation refers to the richness of a color. A highly saturated color is vivid and rich, whereas a less saturated color is faded and washed out.

The third property of color is **brightness,** or perceived intensity. Brightness corresponds to the amplitude of the light wave: the higher the amplitude, the greater the degree of brightness.

These three properties of color—hue, saturation, and brightness—are responsible for the amazing range of colors we experience. A person with normal color vision can discriminate from 120 to 150 color differences based on differences in hue, or wavelength, alone. When saturation and brightness are also factored in, we can potentially perceive millions of different colors (Bornstein & Marks, 1982).

Many people mistakenly believe that white light contains no color. White light actually contains all wavelengths, and thus all colors, of the visible part of the electromagnetic spectrum. A glass prism placed in sunlight creates a rainbow because it separates sunlight into all the colors of the visible light spectrum.

So we're back to the question: Why is an orange orange? Common sense tells us that the color of any object is an inseparable property of the object (unless we paint it, dye it, or spill spaghetti sauce on it). But, actually, *the color of an object is determined by the wavelength of light that the object reflects.* If your T-shirt is red, it's red because the cloth is *reflecting* only the wavelength of light that corresponds to the red portion of the spectrum. The T-shirt is *absorbing* the wavelengths that correspond to all other colors. An object appears white because it *reflects* all the wavelengths of visible light and absorbs none. An object appears black when it *absorbs* all the wavelengths of visible light and reflects none.

How We See Color

Color vision has interested scientists for hundreds of years. The first scientific theory of color vision, proposed by Hermann von Helmholtz (1821–1894) in the mid-1800s, was called the *trichromatic theory.* A rival theory, the *opponent-process theory,* was proposed in the late 1800s. Each theory was capable of explaining some aspects of color vision, but neither theory could explain all aspects of color vision. Technological advances in the last few decades have allowed researchers to gather direct physiological evidence to test both theories. The resulting evidence indicates that *both* theories of color vision are accurate. Each simply describes color vision at a different stage of visual processing (Hubel, 1995).

When Red + Blue + Green = White When light waves of different wavelengths are combined, the wavelengths are added together, producing the perception of a different color. Thus, when green light is combined with red light, yellow light is produced. When the wavelengths of red, green, and blue light are added together, we perceive the blended light as white.

The Most Common Form of Color Blindness To someone with red–green color blindness, these two photographs look almost exactly the same. People with this form of color blindness have normal blue-sensitive cones, but their other cones are sensitive to either red *or* green.

trichromatic theory of color vision
The theory that the sensation of color results because cones in the retina are especially sensitive to either red light (long wavelengths), green light (medium wavelengths), or blue light (short wavelengths).

color blindness
One of several inherited forms of color deficiency or weakness in which an individual cannot distinguish between certain colors.

afterimage
A visual experience that occurs after the original source of stimulation is no longer present.

opponent-process theory of color vision
The theory that color vision is the product of opposing pairs of color receptors, red/green, blue/yellow, and black/white; when one member of a color pair is stimulated, the other member is inhibited.

The Trichromatic Theory   As you'll recall, only the cones are involved in color vision. According to the **trichromatic theory of color vision,** there are three varieties of cones. Each type of cone is especially sensitive to certain wavelengths—red light (long wavelengths), green light (medium wavelengths), and blue light (short wavelengths). For the sake of simplicity, we will refer to red-sensitive, green-sensitive, and blue-sensitive cones, but keep in mind that there is some overlap in the wavelengths to which a cone is sensitive (Abramov & Gordon, 1994). A given cone will be *very* sensitive to one of the three colors and only slightly responsive to the other two.

When a color other than red, green, or blue strikes the retina, it stimulates a *combination* of cones. For example, if yellow light strikes the retina, both the red-sensitive and green-sensitive cones are stimulated; purple light evokes strong reactions from red-sensitive and blue-sensitive cones.

The trichromatic theory of color vision received compelling research support in 1964, when George Wald showed that different cones were indeed activated by red, blue, and green light. The trichromatic theory provides a good explanation for the most common form of **color blindness:** red–green color blindness. People with red–green color blindness cannot discriminate between red and green. That's because they have normal blue-sensitive cones, but their other cones are *either* red-sensitive or green-sensitive. Thus, red and green look the same to them.

What we commonly refer to as color blindness is really misnamed. People who are completely color-blind and see the world only in shades of gray are extremely rare. Roughly one in a million people have this condition (Hurvich, 1981). Most instances of color blindness would more accurately be described as *color deficiency.*

Red–green color blindness is a genetically transmitted disorder. Because of the way in which it is inherited, red–green color blindness is relatively common in males but extremely rare in females. Less than one-half of 1 percent of women are color-blind. However, approximately 8 percent of white men and a slightly lower percentage of Asian, black, and Native American men have some form of color deficiency. Because red–green color blindness is so common, stoplights are designed so that the location of the light as well as its color provides the information. In vertical stoplights the red light is always on top, and in horizontal stoplights the red light is always on the far left.

The Opponent-Process Theory   The trichromatic theory cannot account for all aspects of color vision. One important phenomenon that the theory does not explain is the afterimage. An **afterimage** is a visual experience that occurs after the original source of stimulation is no longer present. To experience an afterimage firsthand, follow the instructions in Figure 3.7. What do you see?

Afterimages can be explained by the opponent-process theory of color vision, which proposes a different mechanism of color detection from the one set forth in the trichromatic theory. According to the **opponent-process theory of color vision,** there are four basic colors, which are divided into two pairs of color-sensitive neurons: red–green and blue–yellow. The members of each pair *oppose* each other. If red is stimulated, green is inhibited; if green is stimulated, red is inhibited. Green and red cannot both be stimulated simultaneously. The same is true for the blue–yellow pair. In addition, black and white act as an opposing pair. Color, then, is sensed and encoded in terms of its proportion of red OR green, and blue OR yellow.

For example, red light evokes a response of RED-YES–GREEN-NO in the red–green opponent pair. Yellow light evokes a response of BLUE-NO–YELLOW-YES. Colors other than red, green, blue, and yellow activate one mem-

FIGURE 3.7 Demonstration of Afterimage Stare at the white dot in the center of this oddly colored flag for about 30 seconds, and then look at a white wall or white sheet of paper. What do you see?

ber of each of these pairs to differing degrees. Purple stimulates the *red* of the red–green pair plus the *blue* of the blue–yellow pair. Orange activates *red* in the red–green pair and *yellow* in the blue–yellow pair.

Afterimages can be explained when the opponent-process theory is combined with the general principle of sensory adaptation (Jameson & Hurvich, 1989). If you stare continuously at one color, sensory adaptation eventually occurs and your visual receptors become less sensitive to that color. What happens when you subsequently stare at a white surface?

If you remember that white light is made up of the wavelengths for *all* colors, you may be able to predict the result. The receptors for the original color have adapted to the constant stimulation and are temporarily "off duty." Thus they do not respond to that color. Instead, only the receptors for the opposing color will be activated, and you perceive the wavelength of only the *opposing* color. For example, if you stare at a patch of green, your green receptors eventually become "tired." The wavelengths for both green and red light are reflected by the white surface, but since the green receptors are "off," only the red receptors are activated. Staring at the green, black, and yellow flag in Figure 3.7 should have produced an afterimage of opposing colors: a red, white, and blue American flag.

An Integrated Explanation of Color Vision   At the beginning of this section we said that current research has shown that *both* the trichromatic theory and the opponent-process theory of color vision are accurate. How can both theories be right? It turns out that each theory correctly describes color vision at a *different level* of visual processing.

As described by the *trichromatic theory,* the cones of the retina do indeed respond to and encode color in terms of red, green, and blue. But recall that signals from the cones and rods are partially processed in the ganglion cells before being transmitted along the optic nerve to the brain. Researchers now believe that an additional level of color processing takes place in the ganglion cells.

As described by the *opponent-process theory,* the ganglion cells respond to and encode color in terms of opposing pairs (DeValois & DeValois, 1975). In the brain, the thalamus and visual cortex also encode color in terms of opponent pairs (Boynton, 1988; Engel, 1999). Consequently, both theories contribute to our understanding of the process of color vision. Each theory simply describes color vision at a different stage of visual processing (Hubel, 1995).

3.1   R·E·V·I·E·W

C·O·N·C·E·P·T

Principles of Sensation and Vision

Fill in the missing words to complete each statement.

1. Sensory receptors convert different forms of physical energy into neural signals through the process of _____.

2. The sensory receptors for vision are contained in the

   _____.

3. Complete the sequence of visual information transmission: rods and cones, _____ cells, _____ cells, optic nerve, _____, thalamus, _____.

4. According to the _____ theory of color vision, the person with red–green color blindness has normal blue-sensitive cones.

5. When people stare at a yellow circle and then shift their eyes to a white surface, the afterimage of the circle appears _____. This phenomenon can best be explained by the _____ theory of color vision.

audition
The technical term for the sense of hearing.

loudness
The intensity (or amplitude) of a sound wave, measured in decibels.

amplitude
The intensity or amount of energy of a wave, reflected in the height of the wave; the amplitude of a sound wave determines a sound's loudness.

decibel
(DESS-uh-bell) The unit of measurement for loudness.

pitch
The relative highness or lowness of a sound, determined by the frequency of a sound wave.

frequency
The rate of vibration, or the number of sound waves per second.

timbre
(TIM-ber) The distinctive quality of a sound, determined by the complexity of the sound wave.

Hearing
From Vibration to Sound

Key Theme
- Auditory sensation results from sound waves, which are collected in the outer ear, amplified in the middle ear, and converted to neural messages in the inner ear.

Key Questions
- How do sound waves produce different auditory sensations?
- What are the key structures of the ear and their functions?
- How do place theory and frequency theory explain pitch perception?

We have hiked in a desert area that was so quiet we could hear the whir of a single grasshopper's wings in the distance. And we have waited on a subway platform where the screech of metal against metal forced us to cover our ears. The sense of hearing, or **audition,** is capable of responding to a wide range of sounds, from very soft to very loud, simple to complex, harmonious to discordant. The ability to sense and perceive very subtle differences in sound is important to physical survival, social interactions, and language development. Most of the time, all of us are bathed in sound—so much so that moments of near-silence, like our experience in the desert, can seem almost eerie.

What We Hear
The Nature of Sound

Whether it's the ear-splitting screech of metal on metal or the subtle whir of a grasshopper's wings, *sound waves* are the physical stimuli that produce our sensory experience of sound. Usually, sound waves are produced by the rhythmic vibration of air molecules, but sound waves can be transmitted through other media, too, such as water. Our perception of sound is directly related to the physical properties of sound waves (see Figure 3.8).

One of the first things that we notice about a sound is how loud it is. **Loudness** is determined by the intensity, or **amplitude,** of a sound wave and is measured in units called **decibels.** Zero decibels represents the loudness of the softest sound that humans can hear, or the absolute threshold for hearing. As decibels increase, perceived loudness increases.

Pitch refers to the relative "highness" or "lowness" of a sound. Pitch is determined by the frequency of a sound wave. **Frequency** refers to the rate of vibration, or number of waves per second, and is measured in units called *hertz.* Hertz simply refers to the number of wave peaks per second. The faster the vibration, the higher the frequency, the closer together the waves are—and the higher the tone produced. If you pluck the high E and the low E strings on a guitar, you'll notice that the low E vibrates far fewer times per second than does the high E.

Most of the sounds we experience do not consist of a single frequency but are *complex,* consisting of several sound-wave frequencies. This combination of frequencies produces the distinctive quality, or **timbre,** of a sound, which enables us to distinguish easily between the same note played on a saxophone or a piano. Every human voice has its own distinctive timbre, which is why you can immediately identify a friend's voice on the telephone from just a few words, even if you haven't talked to each other for years.

FIGURE 3.8 Characteristics of Sound Waves The length of a wave, its height, and its complexity determine the loudness, pitch, and timbre that we hear. In **(a)** the sound would be high-pitched and loud. In **(b)** the sound would be soft and low. The sound in **(c)** is complex, like the sounds we usually experience in the natural world.

High-pitched, loud (high frequency, high amplitude)

Low-pitched, soft (low frequency, low amplitude)

Complex (high and low frequency, high and low amplitude)

How We Hear

The Path of Sound

The ear is made up of the outer ear, the middle ear, and the inner ear. Sound waves are *collected* in the outer ear, *amplified* in the middle ear, and *transduced, or transformed into neural messages,* in the inner ear (see Figure 3.9).

The **outer ear** includes the *pinna,* the *ear canal,* and the *eardrum.* The pinna is that oddly shaped flap of skin and cartilage that's attached to each side of your head. The pinna helps us pinpoint the location of a sound. But the pinna's primary role is to catch sound waves and funnel them into the ear canal. The sound wave travels down the ear canal, then bounces into the **eardrum,** a tightly stretched membrane. When sound waves hit the eardrum, it vibrates, matching the vibrations of the sound wave in both intensity and frequency.

The eardrum separates the outer ear from the **middle ear.** The eardrum's vibration is transferred to three tiny bones in the middle ear—the *hammer,* the *anvil,* and the *stirrup.* Each bone sets the next bone in motion. The joint action of these three bones almost doubles the amplification of the sound. The innermost bone, the stirrup, transmits the amplified vibration to the *oval window.* If the tiny bones of the middle ear are damaged or become brittle, as they sometimes do in old age, *conduction deafness* may result. Conduction deafness can be helped by a hearing aid, which amplifies sounds.

outer ear
The part of the ear that collects sound waves; consists of the pinna, the ear canal, and the eardrum.

eardrum
A tightly stretched membrane at the end of the ear canal that vibrates when hit by sound waves.

middle ear
The part of the ear that amplifies sound waves; consists of three small bones, the hammer, the anvil, and the stirrup.

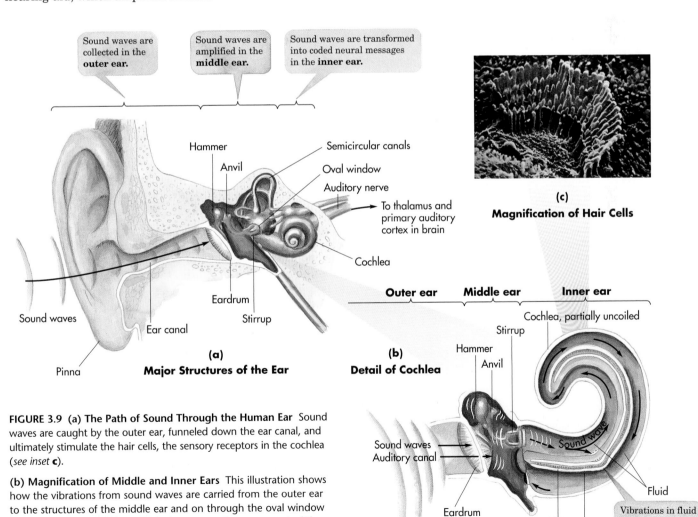

Sound waves are collected in the **outer ear.**

Sound waves are amplified in the **middle ear.**

Sound waves are transformed into coded neural messages in the **inner ear.**

(c)
Magnification of Hair Cells

(a)
Major Structures of the Ear

(b)
Detail of Cochlea

Vibrations in fluid cause the basilar membrane to wave up and down.

FIGURE 3.9 (a) The Path of Sound Through the Human Ear Sound waves are caught by the outer ear, funneled down the ear canal, and ultimately stimulate the hair cells, the sensory receptors in the cochlea (*see inset* **c**).

(b) Magnification of Middle and Inner Ears This illustration shows how the vibrations from sound waves are carried from the outer ear to the structures of the middle ear and on through the oval window to the fluid in the cochlea, which then causes the movement of the basilar membrane. As the basilar membrane ripples, the hair cells bend (again, see inset **c**). The hair cells stimulate the auditory nerve, which transmits the neural messages to the auditory cortex of the brain.

Table | **3.2**

Decibel Level of Some Common Noises		
Decibels	**Examples**	**Exposure Danger**
180	Rocket launching pad	Hearing loss inevitable
140	Shotgun blast, jet plane	Any exposure is dangerous
120	Speakers at rock concert, sandblasting, thunderclap	Immediate danger
100	Chain saw, pneumatic drill	2 hours
90	Truck traffic, noisy home appliances, lawn mower	Less than 8 hours
80	Subway, heavy city traffic, alarm clock at 2 feet	More than 8 hours
70	Busy traffic, noisy restaurant	Critical level begins with constant exposure
60	Air conditioner at 20 feet, conversation, sewing machine	
50	Light traffic at a distance, refrigerator	
40	Quiet office, living room	
30	Quiet library, soft whisper	
0	Lowest sound audible to human ear	

inner ear
The part of the ear where sound is transduced into neural impulses; consists of the cochlea and semicircular canals.

cochlea
(COCK-lee-uh) The coiled, fluid-filled inner-ear structure that contains the sensory receptors for sound.

basilar membrane
(BAS-uh-ler) The membrane within the cochlea of the ear that contains the hair cells.

hair cells
The hairlike sensory receptors for sound, found in the basilar membrane of the cochlea.

frequency theory
The view that the basilar membrane vibrates at the same frequency as the sound wave.

place theory
The view that different frequencies cause larger vibrations at different locations along the basilar membrane.

Like the eardrum, the oval window is a membrane, but it is many times smaller than the eardrum. The oval window separates the middle ear from the **inner ear.** As the oval window vibrates, the vibration is next relayed to an inner structure called the **cochlea,** a fluid-filled tube that's coiled in a spiral. The word *cochlea* comes from the Greek word for "snail," and the spiral shape of the cochlea does resemble a snail's shell. Although the cochlea is a very complex structure, it is quite tiny—no larger than a pea.

As the fluid in the cochlea ripples, the vibration in turn is transmitted to the **basilar membrane,** which runs the length of the coiled cochlea. Embedded in the basilar membrane are the sensory receptors for sound, called **hair cells,** which have tiny, projecting fibers that look like hairs. Damage to the hair cells or auditory nerve can result in *nerve deafness,* which cannot be helped by a hearing aid. Exposure to loud noise can cause nerve deafness (see Table 3.2).

The hair cells bend as the basilar membrane ripples. It is here that transduction finally takes place: The physical vibration of the sound wave is converted into neural impulses. As the hair cells bend, they stimulate the cells of the auditory nerve, which carries the neural information to the thalamus and the auditory cortex in the brain.

Distinguishing Pitch

How do we distinguish between the low-pitched throb of a bass guitar and the high-pitched tones of a flute? Remember, pitch is determined by the *frequency* of a sound wave. The basilar membrane is a key structure involved in our discrimination of pitch. Two complementary theories describe the role of the basilar membrane in the transmission of differently pitched sounds.

According to **frequency theory,** the basilar membrane vibrates at the *same* frequency as the sound wave. Thus, a sound wave of about 100 hertz would excite each hair cell along the basilar membrane to vibrate 100 times per second, and neural impulses would be sent to the brain at the same rate. However, there's a limit to how fast neurons can fire. Individual neurons cannot fire faster than about 1,000 times per second. But we can sense sounds with frequencies that are many times higher than 1,000 hertz. A child, for example, can typically hear pitches ranging from about 20 to 20,000 hertz. Frequency theory explains how low-frequency sounds are transmitted to the brain, but it cannot explain the transmission of higher-frequency sounds.

So, how do we distinguish higher-pitched sounds? According to **place theory,** different frequencies cause larger vibrations at different *locations* along the basilar membrane. High-frequency sounds, for example, cause maximum vibration near the stirrup end of the basilar membrane. Lower-frequency sounds cause maximum vibration at the opposite end. Thus, different pitches excite different hair cells along the basilar membrane. Higher-pitched sounds are interpreted according to the place where the hair cells are most active.

Both frequency theory and place theory are involved in explaining our discrimination of pitch. Frequency theory helps explain our discrimination of frequencies lower than 500 hertz. Place theory helps explain our discrimination of higher-pitched sounds. For intermediate frequencies or midrange pitches, both place and frequency are involved.

The Chemical and Body Senses
Smell, Taste, Touch, and Position

olfaction
Technical name for the sense of smell.

gustation
Technical name for the sense of taste.

Key Theme
- Chemical stimuli produce the sensations of smell and taste, while pressure and other stimuli are involved in touch, pain, position, and balance sensations.

Key Questions
- How do airborne molecules result in the sensation of an odor?
- What are the primary tastes, and how does the sensation of taste arise?
- What is the gate-control theory of pain, and how do body sensations of movement, position, and balance arise?

Remember Paul and Warren, who both lack a sense of smell? As Paul and Warren are well aware, the senses of smell and taste are closely linked. If you've ever temporarily lost your sense of smell because of a bad cold, you've probably noticed that your sense of taste was also disrupted. Even a hot fudge sundae tastes bland.

Smell and taste are linked in other ways, too. Unlike vision and hearing, which involve sensitivity to different forms of energy, the sensory receptors for taste and smell are specialized to respond to different types of *chemical* substances. That's why smell, or **olfaction,** and taste, or **gustation,** are sometimes called the "chemical senses" (Bartoshuk & Beauchamp, 1994).

As the cases of Paul and Warren illustrate, people can get along quite well without a sense of smell. A surprisingly large number of people are unable to smell specific odors or lack a sense of smell completely, a condition called *anosmia.* Fortunately, humans gather most of their information about the world through vision and hearing. However, many animal species depend on chemical signals as their primary source of information (Agosta, 1992).

Even for humans, smell and taste can provide important information about the environment. Tastes help us determine whether a particular substance is to be savored or spit out. Smells, such as the odor of a smoldering fire, leaking gas, or spoiled food, alert us to potential dangers. For example, shortly after Paul and Asha built a new house, Paul noticed water seeping up into the lawn and called the builder to complain about the leaking undergound sprinkler system. When the builder came to check on it, he quickly informed Paul that it wasn't the sprinkler system that was leaking—it was the *septic* system. Paul, of course, could not smell the distinctive odor of sewage. Had it been the gas line rather than the septic tank that was leaking, Paul's inability to smell could have had serious consequences.

The Chemical Senses: Smell and Taste Andrea Immer is one of only ten women in the world to hold the title of Master Sommelier, and is the Dean of Wine Studies at the world-famous French Culinary Institute in New York City. Why does she sniff the wine before tasting it? Professional (and amateur) wine-tasters are keenly aware of the fact that senses of smell and taste are closely intertwined. Specialized receptors in the nasal passages are able to detect the subtle aromas that differentiate among fine wines, and a wine expert relies as much on her sense of smell as she does her sense of taste to evaluate the wine's overall quality.

How We Smell (Don't Answer That!)

The sensory stimuli that produce our sensation of an odor are *molecules in the air.* These airborne molecules are emitted by the substance we are smelling. We inhale them through the nose and through the opening in the palate at the back of the throat. In the nose, the molecules encounter millions of *olfactory receptor cells* located high in the nasal cavity.

Unlike the sensory receptors for hearing and vision, the olfactory receptors are constantly being replaced. Each cell lasts for only about 30 to 60 days. In 1991, neuroscientists Linda Buck and Richard Axel identified the odor receptors that are present on the hairlike fibers of the olfactory neurons. Like synaptic receptors, each odor receptor seems to be specialized to respond to molecules of a different chemical structure. When these olfactory receptor cells are stimulated by the airborne molecules, the stimulation is converted into neural messages that pass along their axons, bundles of which make up the *olfactory nerves.*

(a)

FIGURE 3.10 (a) The Olfactory System
Inhaled through the nose or the mouth, airborne molecules travel to the top of the nasal cavity and stimulate the olfactory receptors. When stimulated, these receptor cells communicate neural messages to the olfactory bulb, which is part of the olfactory cortex of the brain, where the sense of smell is registered.

(b) The Olfactory Receptor Cells More than 5 million olfactory neurons make up the moist, mucus-bathed tissue at the back of the nose. Projecting from the olfactory neurons are the fiberlike olfactory hairs, which can be clearly seen in this photograph. Olfactory neurons are replaced every month or two.

olfactory bulb
(ole-FACK-toe-ree) The enlarged ending of the olfactory cortex at the front of the brain where the sensation of smell is registered.

pheromones
Chemical signals released by an animal that communicate information and affect the behavior of other animals of the same species.

So far, hundreds of different odor receptors have been identified (Mombaerts, 1999). We probably don't have a separate receptor for each of the estimated 10,000 different odors that we can identify, however. Rather, each receptor is like a letter in an olfactory alphabet. A particular odor activates a specific *combination* of different receptors (Malnic & others, 1999). Specific odors are identified by the brain as it interprets the pattern of receptors that are stimulated (Buck, 2000).

As shown in Figure 3.10, the olfactory nerves directly connect to the **olfactory bulb** in the brain, which is actually the enlarged ending of the *olfactory cortex* at the front of the brain. Warren lost his sense of smell because the surgeon cut through the nerve fibers leading to his olfactory bulb. Axons from the olfactory bulb form the *olfactory tract*. These neural pathways project to different brain areas, including the temporal lobe and structures in the limbic system (Angier, 1995). The projections to the *temporal lobe* are thought to be part of the neural pathway involved in our conscious recognition of smells. The projections to the *limbic system* are thought to regulate our emotional response to odors.

The direct connection of olfactory receptor cells to areas of the cortex and limbic system is unique to our sense of smell. As discussed in Chapter 2, all other bodily sensations are first processed in the thalamus before being relayed to the higher brain centers in the cortex. Olfactory neurons are unique in another way, too. They are the only neurons that *directly* link the brain and the outside world (Axel, 1995). The axons of the sensory neurons that are located in your nose extend directly into your brain!

Odor Sensitivity and Recognition

Human sensitivity to odors varies widely (Doty, 2001). Across different cultures, women have a much better sense of smell than men. Although women tend to retain a keen sense of smell longer than men, olfactory function does tend to decline with age. About half of those aged 65 to 80 have a significant loss of olfactory function, a number that increases to three-quarters of people aged 80 and above. At any age, air pollution, smoking, and exposure to some industrial chemicals can decrease the ability to smell. Loss of olfactory function is also associated with several diseases—including Parkinson's disease, schizophrenia, and multiple sclerosis—and may be an early marker of Alzheimer's disease (Devenand & others, 2000).

Although humans are highly sensitive to odors, many animals display even greater sensitivity (Agosta, 1992). Dogs, for example, have about 200 million olfactory receptor cells, compared with the approximately 10 million receptors that humans have.

IN FOCUS 3.3

Do Pheromones Influence Human Behavior?

Many animals communicate by releasing **pheromones,** chemical signals that affect the behavior of other animals of the same species. Pheromones may mark territories and serve as warning signals to other members of the same species (Agosta, 1992). Ants use pheromones to mark trails for other ants, as do snakes and snails (Dusenberry, 1992). Pheromones are also extremely important in regulating sexual attraction, mating, and reproductive behavior in many animals (Lerner & others, 1990; Rutowski, 1998). A lusty male cabbage moth, for example, can detect pheromones released from a sexually receptive female cabbage moth that is several miles away.

Do humans produce pheromones as other animals do? The best evidence for the existence of human pheromones comes from studies of the female menstrual cycle by University of Chicago biopsychologist Martha McClintock (1992). While still a college student, McClintock (1971) set out to scientifically investigate the folk notion that women who live in the same dorm eventually develop synchronized menstrual periods. McClintock was able to show that the more time women spent together, the more likely their cycles were to be in sync. She also discovered that women who spent more time with men had shorter and more regular menstrual cycles.

Later research showed that smelling an unknown chemical substance in underarm sweat from female donors seemed to be responsible for synchronized menstrual cycles (Preti & others, 1986).

Later research by McClintock and her colleague Kathleen Stern has demonstrated the existence of two human pheromones in women. Stern and McClintock (1998) collected perspiration samples from female donors who had normal menstrual cycles. They mixed the perspiration with isopropyl alcohol to disguise any odor and dabbed the blend under the noses of female subjects two to four days before the women were due to ovulate. Control-group subjects were dabbed with alcohol only.

When subjects smelled perspiration samples from donors who were in the

The Scent of Attraction Some perfume manufacturers claim that their products contain human pheromones that will make you "irresistible" to members of the opposite sex. But is there any evidence that pheromones affect human sexual attraction?

early stages of their menstrual cycles, the subjects' menstrual cycles were shortened. When subjects smelled perspiration samples from donors who were in the later stages of their menstrual cycles, the subjects' menstrual cycles were lengthened. The control subjects, who were not exposed to any perspiration sample, experienced no changes in their menstrual cycles.

Since this finding, McClintock and her co-researchers have made a number of discoveries in their quest to discover human pheromones, which they prefer to call *human chemosignals*. Their search has narrowed to chemicals found in steroid compounds that are naturally produced by the human body and found in sweat, armpit hair, blood, and semen. In one study, Suma Jacob and McClintock (2000) tested men and women's responses to minute amounts of male and female steroids swabbed under their nostrils. Each volunteer then spent two tedious hours filling out a questionnaire, a task designed to be frustrating. Jacob and McClintock found that exposure to either the male or the female steroid helped women maintain a positive mood. Men, however, had a totally

different response. Their moods tended to deteriorate after exposure to either steroid.

In another experiment, Jacob and her colleagues (2001) used PET scans to track brain changes in women after they were exposed to the same male steroid. Comparing the PET images to scans made before exposure, the researchers discovered that exposure to the steroid increased activity in several key brain regions involved in emotion and attention, including the prefrontal cortex, amygdala, and cerebellum. Interestingly, olfactory regions in the brain were also activated, despite the fact that the women could not consciously detect the odor of the steroid, another example of the effects of unconscious or subliminal perception.

Notice, however, that the human chemosignals did *not* function as a sexual signal in any of the studies we've reviewed. Rather than producing sexual attraction, McClintock (2001) believes, it's more likely that human chemosignals affect mood and emotional states. It may be that these subliminal chemical signals can affect social interactions and relationships in ways that we just can't consciously recognize. Rather than simply triggering specific behaviors, including sexual behavior, human chemosignals may be social signals, affecting how people react and work together in groups.

Given the increasing evidence that chemical signals can affect reproductive functions, moods, and brain activity, what can we say about the notion that sexual attraction might also be influenced by some sort of pheromone or chemical signal? At this point, such evidence does not exist. So far, no one has found evidence for chemical signals that affect sexual attraction in humans. The human sexual response is much more complex than that of other animals, and it's unlikely that pheromones alone could be the powerful stimulus that they are elsewhere in the animal kingdom. So, despite what you might have seen in those sexy cologne ads, there is no evidence for the existence of human sex pheromones that will make you irresistible to members of the preferred sex.

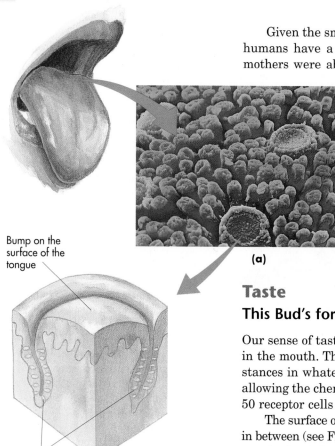

(a)

Bump on the
surface of the
tongue

Taste buds

(b)

FIGURE 3.11 Taste Buds (a) The photograph shows the surface of the tongue magnified hundreds of times. Taste buds are located in the grooves of the bumps on the surface of the tongue. (b) Embedded in the surface of the tongue are thousands of taste buds, the sensory receptor organs for taste. Each taste bud contains an average of 50 taste receptor cells. When activated, the taste receptor cells send messages to adjoining sensory neurons, which relay the information to the brain. Taste buds, like the olfactory neurons, are constantly being replaced. The life expectancy of a particular taste bud is only about 10 days.

Given the small number of smell receptors we have relative to other animals, humans have a remarkable ability to recognize familiar smells. In one study, mothers were able to distinguish the T-shirt that had been worn by their own children from that worn by unrelated children with close to 95 percent accuracy. In another test, parents were highly accurate in distinguishing between their children solely on the basis of smell (Porter & Moore, 1981).

As with the other senses, we experience sensory adaptation to odors when exposed to them for a period of time. In general, we reach maximum adaptation to an odor in less than a minute. We continue to smell the odor, but we have become about 70 percent less sensitive to it.

Taste
This Bud's for You!

Our sense of taste, or *gustation,* results from the stimulation of special receptors in the mouth. The stimuli that produce the sensation of taste are chemical substances in whatever you eat or drink. These substances are dissolved by saliva, allowing the chemicals to activate the **taste buds.** Each taste bud contains about 50 receptor cells that are specialized for taste.

The surface of the tongue is covered with thousands of little bumps with grooves in between (see Figure 3.11). These grooves are lined with the taste buds. Taste buds are also located on the insides of your cheeks, on the roof of your mouth, and in your throat (Oakley, 1986). When activated, special receptor cells in the taste buds send neural messages along pathways to the thalamus in the brain. In turn, the thalamus directs the information to several regions in the cortex (O'Doherty & others, 2001b).

There were long thought to be four basic taste categories: sweet, salty, sour, and bitter. Recently, the receptor cells for a fifth basic taste, *umami,* were identified (Chaudhari & others, 2000). Loosely translated, *umami* means "yummy" or "delicious" in Japanese. *Umami* is the distinctive taste of monosodium glutamate and is associated with protein-rich foods and the savory flavor of Parmesan and other aged cheeses, mushrooms, seaweed, and meat.

Each taste bud shows maximum sensitivity to one particular taste, and lesser sensitivity to other tastes. Most tastes are complex and result from the activation of different combinations of basic taste receptors. Taste is just one aspect of *flavor,* which involves several sensations, including the aroma, temperature, texture, and appearance of food.

The specialized sensitivity of taste buds is easy to demonstrate. Brush your teeth, then drink some orange juice. Why does the orange juice taste so bitter right after you've brushed your teeth? The culprit is a chemical that is present in most brands of toothpaste. It intensifies bitter tastes while disrupting the binding of sweet-tasting substances to the sweetness receptors (Schiffman, 1983). Because the sweetness receptors are temporarily blocked, you can taste only the bitter chemical substances that are present in the orange juice.

The Skin and Body Senses

While vision, hearing, smell, and taste provide you with important information about your environment, another group of senses provides you with information that comes from a source much closer to home: your own body. In this section, we'll first consider the *skin senses,* which provide essential information about your physical status and your physical interaction with objects in your environment. We'll next consider the *body senses,* which keep you informed as to your position and orientation in space.

Touch and Temperature

We usually don't think of our skin as a sense organ. But the skin is in fact the largest and heaviest sense organ. The skin of an average adult covers about 20 square feet of surface area and weighs about six pounds.

There are many different kinds of sensory receptors in the skin. Some of these sensory receptors are specialized to respond to just one kind of stimulus, such as pressure, warmth, or cold. Other skin receptors respond to more than one type of stimulus.

One important receptor involved with the sense of touch, called the *Pacinian corpuscle,* is located beneath the skin. When stimulated by pressure, the Pacinian corpuscle converts the stimulation into a neural message that is relayed to the brain. If a pressure is constant, sensory adaptation takes place. The Pacinian corpuscle either reduces the number of signals sent or quits responding altogether (which is fortunate, or you'd be unable to forget the fact that you're wearing underwear).

Speaking of underwear, have you ever wondered exactly what was responsible for the "itch" sensation caused by scratchy underclothes, mosquito bites, and hives? Neuroscientists have. For almost a century, neuroscientists have tried to explain the precise cause of an itch, some arguing that the itch sensation was merely a milder version of a pain sensation (Schmelz, 2001). But pain researchers David Andrew and Andrew "Bud" Craig (2001) recently isolated the sensory receptors responsible for that itchy feeling. It turns out that there are specific "itch-sensitive" neurons. Unresponsive to pressure or temperature, these cells react strongly to histamines like those the immune system produces in an allergic reaction or in response to an insect bite.

Sensory receptors are distributed unevenly among different areas of the body, which is why sensitivity to touch and temperature varies from one area of the body to another. Your hands, face, and lips, for example, are much more sensitive to touch than are your back, arms, and legs. That's because your hands, face, and lips are much more densely packed with sensory receptors.

How do we sense temperature? A given section of skin is like a patchwork of small but specific spots that, when stimulated, produce *either* cold or warm sensations, but not both. Cold spots can actually be activated by either a *cold* (around 50°F) or a *hot* stimulus (around 125°F). When a cold spot is stimulated with *either* a cold or a hot stimulus, it produces the sensation of cold. But warm spots only seem to respond to warm stimuli, reaching peak sensitivity at around 105 degrees Fahrenheit.

How do we experience hot sensations? The sensation of hot occurs when warm and cold spots are *simultaneously* stimulated (see Figure 3.12). A cold spot will activate in response to either a cold or a hot stimulus, but a warm spot can be activated only by a stimulus that is warm. Thus, if both warm and cold receptors are simultaneously activated, the brain makes the most logical interpretation of the pattern of stimulation: the stimulus must be hot.

Pain

Pain is important to our survival. It provides us with important information about our body, telling us to pay attention, to stop what we are doing, or to pull away from some object or stimulus that is injuring us.

A wide variety of stimuli can produce **pain**—the sensation of discomfort or suffering. Virtually any external stimulus that can produce tissue damage can cause pain, including certain chemicals, electric shock, and extreme heat, cold, pressure, or noise. Pain can also be caused by internal stimuli, such as disease, infection, or deterioration of bodily functions. Some areas of the body are more sensitive to pain than are other areas (see Table 3.3).

taste buds
The specialized sensory receptors for taste that are located on the tongue and inside the mouth and throat.

pain
The unpleasant sensation of physical discomfort or suffering that can occur in varying degrees of intensity.

Cold   Warm
water   water

FIGURE 3.12 The Sensation of Hot The sensation of hot occurs when warm and cold spots on the skin are simultaneously stimulated. This phenomenon can be demonstrated using two intertwined metal pipes, one containing cold water and the other containing warm water. A person who grasps both pipes will immediately react as though he's touched a very hot surface, quickly yanking his hand away.

Table | **3.3**

Sensitivity of Different Body Areas to Pain	
Most Sensitive	**Least Sensitive**
Back of the knee	Tip of the nose
Neck region	Sole of the foot
Bend of the elbow	Ball of the thumb

SOURCE: Geldard (1972)

Pain Relief Through Acupuncture
Acupuncture is a pain-relieving technique that has been used in traditional Chinese medicine for thousands of years. Acupuncture involves inserting tiny needles at specific points in the body. The needles are then twirled, heated, or, as shown here, stimulated with a mild electrical current. Although it is not yet understood exactly how acupuncture interrupts the transmission of pain signals, it is known that acupuncture stimulates the release of endorphins (Chao & others, 1999).

The most influential theory of pain is the **gate-control theory,** developed by psychologist Ronald Melzack and anatomist Patrick Wall (1965, 1996). The gate-control theory suggests that the sensation of pain is controlled by a series of "gates" that open and close in the spinal cord. If the spinal gates are open, pain is experienced. If the spinal gates are closed, no pain is experienced.

Pain begins when an intense stimulus activates small-diameter sensory fibers, called *free nerve endings,* in the skin, muscles, or internal organs. The free nerve endings carry their messages to the spinal cord, releasing a neurotransmitter called **substance P.** In the spinal cord, substance P causes other neurons to become activated, sending their messages through open spinal gates to the thalamus in the brain (Turk & Nash, 1993). Other areas of the brain involved in the experience of pain are the somatosensory cortex and areas in the frontal lobes and limbic system that are involved in emotion (Hunt & Mantyh, 2001; Rainville & others, 1997).

When the sensory pain signals reach the brain, the sensory information is integrated with psychological information. Depending on how the brain interprets the pain experience, it regulates pain by sending signals down the spinal cord that either open or close the gates. If, because of psychological factors, the brain signals the gates to open, pain is experienced or intensified. If the brain signals the gates to close, pain is reduced.

Anxiety, fear, and a sense of helplessness are some of the psychological factors that can intensify the experience of pain. Positive emotions, laughter, distraction, and a sense of control can reduce the perception of pain. The experience of pain is also influenced by social and cultural learning experiences about the meaning of pain and how people should react to pain (Turk, 1994; Turk & Rudy, 1992).

Psychological factors also influence the release of *endorphins,* the body's natural painkillers that are produced in many parts of the brain and the body (see Chapter 2). Endorphins are released as part of the brain's overall response to physical pain or stress. In the brain, endorphins can inhibit the transmission of pain signals. In the spinal cord, endorphins inhibit the release of substance P.

Finally, a person's mental or emotional state can influence other bodily processes that affect the experience of pain. Muscle tension, psychological arousal, and rapid heart rate can all produce or intensify pain (Turk & Nash, 1993). Today, a variety of techniques and procedures can effectively eliminate or reduce pain. These techniques are explored in the chapter Application, Strategies to Control Pain, on page 130.

Movement, Position, and Balance

The phone rings. Without looking up from your textbook, you reach for the receiver, pick it up, and guide it to the side of your head. You have just demonstrated your **kinesthetic sense**—the sense that involves the location and position of body parts in relation to one another. (The word *kinesthetics* literally means "feelings of motion.") The kinesthetic sense involves specialized sensory neurons, called **proprioceptors,** which are located in the muscles and joints. The proprioceptors constantly communicate information to the brain about changes in body position and muscle tension.

Closely related to the kinesthetic sense is the **vestibular sense,** which provides a sense of balance, or equilibrium, by responding to changes in gravity, motion, and body position. The two sources of vestibular sensory information, the *semicircular canals* and the *vestibular sacs,* are both located in the ear (see Figure 3.13). These structures are filled with fluid and lined with hairlike receptor cells that shift in response to motion, changes in body position, or changes in gravity.

Semicircular canals

Vestibular sacs

FIGURE 3.13 The Vestibular Sense The vestibular sense provides our sense of balance, or equilibrium. Shown here are the two sources of vestibular sensory information, both located in the ear: the semicircular canals and the vestibular sacs. Both structures are filled with fluids that shift in response to changes in body position, gravity, or motion.

Table | 3.4

Summary Table of the Senses

Sense	Stimulus	Sense Organ	Sensory Receptor Cells
Hearing (audition)	Sound waves	Ear	Hair cells in cochlea
Vision	Light waves	Eye	Rods and cones in retina
Color vision	Different wavelengths of light	Eye	Cones in retina
Smell (olfaction)	Airborne odor molecules	Nose	Hairlike receptor cells at top of nasal cavity
Taste (gustation)	Chemicals dissolved in saliva	Mouth	Taste buds
Touch	Pressure	Skin	Pacinian corpuscle
Temperature	Warmth, cold	Skin	Warm and cold "spots" on skin
Pain	Tissue injury or damage; varied	Skin, organs, and other body sites	No single specific receptor; pattern of messages from many kinds of receptors
Movement (kinesthetic sense)	Movement of the body	None; muscle and joint tissue	Proprioceptors in muscle and joint tissue
Balance (vestibular sense)	Changes in position, gravity	Semicircular canals and vestibular sacs	Hairlike receptor cells in semicircular canals and vestibular sacs

When you experience environmental motion, like the rocking of a boat in choppy water, the fluids in the semicircular canals and the vestibular sacs are affected. Changes in your body's position, such as falling backward in a heroic attempt to return a volleyball serve, also affect the fluids. Your vestibular sense supplies the critical information that allows you to compensate for such changes and quickly reestablish your sense of balance.

Maintaining equilibrium also involves information from other senses, particularly vision. Under normal circumstances, this works to our advantage. However, when information from the eyes conflicts with information from the vestibular system, the result can be dizziness, disorientation, and nausea. These are the symptoms commonly experienced in motion sickness, the bane of many travelers in cars, on planes, on boats, and even in space. One strategy that can be used to combat motion sickness is to minimize sensory conflicts by focusing on a distant point or an object that is fixed, such as the horizon.

3.2 R·E·V·I·E·W

C·O·N·C·E·P·T

The Nonvisual Senses

Fill in the blanks with the correct term.

1. The sensory receptors for hearing are embedded in the _____ membrane in the _____.

2. The _____ theory of hearing best explains how we hear the low-frequency sound of thunder rumbling.

3. The bundled axons of the olfactory receptors project to a brain structure called the _____.

4. Hearing loss caused by damage to the bones of the middle ear is called _____.

5. The neurotransmitter called _____ plays an important role in the processing of pain signals.

6. Because of your _____ sense, you can touch your chin with your index finger even when your eyes are closed.

gate-control theory
The theory that pain is a product of both physiological and psychological factors that cause spinal gates to open and relay patterns of intense stimulation to the brain, which perceives them as pain.

substance P
A neurotransmitter that is involved in the transmission of pain messages to the brain.

kinesthetic sense
(kin-ess-THET-ick) The technical name for the sense of location and position of body parts in relation to one another.

proprioceptors
(pro-pree-oh-SEP-ters) Sensory receptors, located in the muscles and joints, that provide information about body position and movement.

vestibular sense
(vess-TIB-you-ler) The technical name for the sense of balance, or equilibrium.

ESP: Can Perception Occur Without Sensation?

Do you believe in ESP? If you do, you're not alone. A Gallup poll found that almost half of American adults believed in ESP and another quarter thought ESP might exist (Gallup & Newport, 1991). In fact, Americans spend over $600 million a year calling psychic hotlines (Nisbet, 1998).

ESP, or **extrasensory perception,** means detecting information in some way other than through the normal processes of sensation. Forms of ESP include:

- *Telepathy*—direct communication between the minds of two individuals
- *Clairvoyance*—the perception of a remote object or event, such as sensing that a friend has been injured in a car accident
- *Psychokinesis*—the ability to influence a physical object, process, or event, such as bending a key or stopping a clock, without touching it
- *Precognition*—the ability to predict future events

The general term for such unusual abilities is *paranormal phenomena. Paranormal* means "outside the range of normal experience." Thus, these phenomena cannot be explained by known laws of science and nature. **Parapsychology** refers to the scientific investigation of claims of various paranormal phenomena. Only a small percentage of psychologists are parapsychologists.

Have you ever felt as if you had just experienced ESP? Consider the following two examples:

- Your sister was supposed to stop by around 7:00. It's now 7:15, and you "sense" that something has happened to her. Shortly after 8:00 she calls, informing you that she's been involved in a fender bender. Did you experience clairvoyance?
- Sandy had a vivid dream that our cat Nubbin got lost. The next morning, Nubbin sneaked out the back door, went for an unauthorized stroll in the woods, and was gone for three days. Did Sandy have a precognitive dream?

Such common experiences may be used to "prove" that ESP exists. However, two less extraordinary concepts can explain both occurrences: coincidence and the fallacy of positive instances.

Coincidence describes an event that occurs simply by chance. For example, you have over a thousand dreams per year, most of which are about familiar people and situations. By mere chance, *some* aspect of *some* dream will occasionally correspond with reality.

The *fallacy of positive instances* is the tendency to remember coincidental events that seem to confirm our belief about unusual phenomena and to forget all the instances that do not. For example, think of the number of times you've

thought something happened to someone but nothing did. Such situations are far more common than their opposites, but we quickly forget about the hunches that are not confirmed.

Why do people attribute chance events to ESP? Research has shown that believers in ESP are less likely to accurately estimate the probability of an event occurring by chance alone. Nonbelievers tend to be more realistic about the probability of events being the result of simple coincidence or chance (Blackmore, 1985).

Parapsychologists attempt to study ESP in the laboratory under controlled conditions. Many initially convincing demonstrations of ESP are later shown to be the result of research design problems or of the researcher's unintentional cuing of the subject. Occasionally, outright fraud is involved on the part of either the subject or experimenter (Randi, 1980, 1982).

Another problem involves *replication.* To be considered valid, experimental results must be able to be replicated, or repeated, by other scientists under identical laboratory conditions. To date, no parapsychology experiment claiming to show evidence of the existence of ESP has been successfully replicated (Hyman, 1994; Milton & Wiseman, 2001).

One active area of parapsychological research is the study of clairvoyance using an experimental procedure called the *ganzfield procedure.* (*Ganzfield* is a German word that means "total field.") In

Perception

Key Theme
- Perception refers to the process of integrating, organizing, and interpreting sensory information into meaningful representations.

Key Questions
- What are bottom-up and top-down processing, and how do they differ?
- What is Gestalt psychology?
- What Gestalt principles determine our perceptions of objects and their relationship to their surroundings?

ESP (extrasensory perception)
Perception of information by some means other than through the normal processes of sensation.

parapsychology
The scientific investigation of claims of paranormal phenomena and abilities.

As we've seen, our senses are constantly registering a diverse range of stimuli from the environment and transmitting that information to the brain. But to make use of this raw sensory data, we must organize, interpret, and relate the data to existing knowledge.

Dilbert   Scott Adams

a ganzfield study, a "sender" in one room attempts to communicate the content of pictures or short video clips to a receiver in a separate room. Isolated from all contact and wearing goggles and headphones to block external sensory stimuli, the "receiver" attempts to detect the image that is being sent. One set of carefully controlled ganzfield studies showed a "hit" rate that was well above chance, implying that some sort of transfer of information had taken place between sender and receiver (Bem & Honorton, 1994). These results, published in a well-respected psychology journal, *Psychological Bulletin,* led some psychologists to speculate that there might be something to extrasensory perception after all—and that the ganzfield procedure might be the way to detect it. But other psychologists, like Ray Hyman (1994), argued that the study did *not* offer conclusive proof that ESP had been demonstrated.

In the past decade, many ganzfield studies have been published, some show-ing positive results, some negative. Psychologists have used meta-analysis to try to determine whether the so-called ganzfield effect has been successfully replicated. The verdict? British psychologists Julie Milton and Richard Wiseman (1999, 2001) concluded that the ganzfield effect has *not* produced replicable evidence of an ESP effect in the laboratory. Other psychologists, however, dispute *that* conclusion with their own meta-analyses (Storm & Ertel, 2001). Most psychologists agree with Milton and Wiseman's (2001) bottom line: "The final verdict on [ESP] depends upon replication of an effect across experimenters under methodologically stringent conditions." To date, that bottom-line requirement has not been met.

Of course, the history of science is filled with examples of phenomena that were initially scoffed at and later found to be real. For example, the pain-relieving effects of acupuncture were initially dismissed by Western scientists as mere superstition or the power of suggestion. However, controlled studies have shown that acupuncture does effectively relieve pain and may be helpful in treating other conditions (J. B. Murray, 1995; Ulett & others, 1998).

So keep an open mind about ESP, but also maintain a healthy sense of scientific skepticism. It is entirely possible that someday convincing experimental evidence will demonstrate the existence of ESP abilities (see Bem & Honorton, 1994; Milton & Wiseman, 2001; Storm & Ertel, 2001). In the final analysis, all psychologists, including those who accept the possibility of ESP, recognize the need for evidence that meets the requirements of the scientific method.

Critical Thinking Questions

- Why do you think that people who believe in ESP are less likely to attribute events to chance than people who don't think ESP is a real phenomenon?

- Can you think of any reasons why replication might be particularly elusive in research on extrasensory perception?

- Why is replication important in all psychological research, but particularly so in studies attempting to prove extraordinary claims, like the existence of ESP?

Psychologists sometimes refer to this flow of sensory data from the sensory receptors to the brain as **bottom-up processing.** Also called *data-driven processing,* bottom-up processing is often at work when we're confronted with an ambiguous stimulus. For example, imagine trying to assemble a jigsaw puzzle one piece at a time, without knowing what the final picture will be. To accomplish this task, you would work with the individual puzzle pieces to build the image from the "bottom up," that is, from its constituent parts.

But as we interact with our environment, many of our perceptions are shaped by **top-down processing,** which is also referred to as *conceptually driven processing*. Top-down processing occurs when we draw on our knowledge, experiences, expectations, and other cognitive processes to arrive at meaningful perceptions, such as people or objects in a particular context.

Both top-down and bottom-up processing are involved in our everyday perceptions. As a simple illustration, look at the photograph on page 116, which sits on Don's desk. Top-down processing was involved as you reached a number of perceptual conclusions about the image. You quickly perceived a little girl holding a black cat—our daughter Laura holding her cat, Nubbin. You also perceived a child as a

bottom-up processing
Information processing that emphasizes the importance of the sensory receptors in detecting the basic features of a stimulus in the process of recognizing a whole pattern; analysis that moves from the parts to the whole; also called *data-driven processing.*

top-down processing
Information processing that emphasizes the importance of the observer's knowledge, expectations, and other cognitive processes in arriving at meaningful perceptions; analysis that moves from the whole to the parts; also called *conceptually driven processing.*

Organizing Sensations into Meaningful Perceptions With virtually no conscious effort, the psychological process of perception allows you to integrate, organize, and interpret the lines, colors, and contours in this image as meaningful objects—a laughing child holding a panicky black cat in front of a Christmas tree. How did you reach those perceptual conclusions?

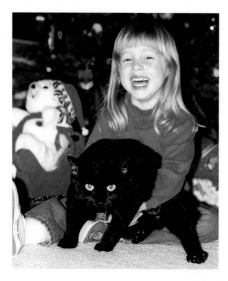

whole object even though the cat is actually blocking a good portion of the view of Laura.

But now look at the background in the photograph, which is more ambiguous. Deciphering these images involves both bottom-up and top-down processing. Bottom-up processes help you determine that behind the little girl looms a large, irregularly shaped, dark green object with brightly colored splotches on it. But what is it?

To identify the mysterious object, you must interpret the meaning of the sensory data. Top-down processes help you identify the large green blotch as a Christmas tree—a conclusion that you probably would *not* reach if you had no familiarity with the way many Americans celebrate the Christmas holiday. The Christmas tree branches, ornaments, lights, and packages are really just fuzzy images at best, but other images work as clues—a happy child, a stuffed bear with a red-and-white stocking cap, brightly colored packages. Our learning experiences create a conceptual knowledge base from which we can identify and interpret many objects, including kids, cats, and Christmas trees.

Clearly, bottom-up and top-down processing are both necessary to explain how we arrive at perceptual conclusions. But whether we are using bottom-up or top-down processing, a useful way to think about perception is to consider the basic perceptual questions we must answer in order to survive. We exist in an ever-changing environment that is filled with objects that may be standing still or moving, just like ourselves. Whether it's a bulldozer or a bowling ball, we need to be able to identify objects, locate objects in space, and, if they are moving, track their motion. Thus, our perceptual processes must help us organize our sensations to answer three basic, important questions: (1) What is it? (2) How far away is it? and (3) Where is it going?

In the next few sections, we will look at what psychologists have learned about the principles we use to answer these perceptual questions. Much of our discussion reflects the work of an early school of psychology called **Gestalt psychology,** which was founded by German psychologist **Max Wertheimer** in the early 1900s. The Gestalt psychologists emphasized that we perceive whole objects or figures (*gestalts*) rather than isolated bits and pieces of sensory information. Roughly translated, the German word *Gestalt* means a unified whole, form, or shape. Although the Gestalt school of psychology no longer formally exists, the pioneering work of the Gestalt psychologists established many basic perceptual principles.

Max Wertheimer (1880–1943) Arguing that the whole is always greater than the sum of its parts, Wertheimer founded Gestalt psychology. Wertheimer and other Gestalt psychologists began by studying the principles of perception but later extended their approach to other areas of psychology.

Gestalt psychology
(geh-SHTALT) A school of psychology founded in Germany in the early 1900s that maintained that our sensations are actively processed according to consistent perceptual rules that result in meaningful whole perceptions, or *gestalts.*

figure–ground relationship
A Gestalt principle of perceptual organization that states that we automatically separate the elements of a perception into the feature that clearly stands out (the figure) and its less distinct background (the ground).

The Perception of Shape
What Is It?

When you look around your world, you don't see random edges, curves, colors, or splotches of light and dark. Rather, you see countless distinct objects against a variety of backgrounds. Although to some degree we rely on size, color, and texture to determine what an object might be, we rely primarily on an object's *shape* to identify it. This tendency is evident at a very early age and becomes even more pronounced as we get older.

A clever series of experiments demonstrated the importance of shape in object identification (Landau, 1994; Landau & Jackendoff, 1993). Three-year-olds were shown a blue, wooden object, like the one depicted in Figure 3.14a. The experimenter told the children that the object was a "dax." Then the children were shown a variety of other objects, like those depicted in Figure 3.14b, c, and d. Some objects had the same shape as the dax, but were made of different materials or were a different color or size. Other objects were identical to the original dax in every way except that they were shaped a little differently. The experimenter asked the children which of these objects was a dax. It turned out that as long as the object had the same *shape* as the original dax, the children identified it as a dax.

FIGURE 3.14 The Dax Experiment
SOURCE: Landan & Jackendoff (1993). Reprinted with permission of Cambridge University Press.

(a) Original dax

(b) (c) Objects also identified as a dax

(d) Rejected

Figure–Ground Relationship

Whether we focus on a dax, a duck, or some other object, how do we organize our perceptions so that we see the object as separate from other objects? The early Gestalt psychologists identified an important perceptual principle called the **figure–ground relationship,** which describes how this works. When we view a scene, we automatically separate the elements of that scene into the *figure,* which is the main element of the scene, and the *ground,* which is its background.

You can experience the figure–ground relationship by looking at a coffee cup on a table. The coffee cup is the figure, and the table is the ground. Notice that usually the figure has a definite shape, tends to stand out clearly, and is perceptually meaningful in some way. In contrast, the ground tends to be less clearly defined, even fuzzy, and usually appears to be behind and farther away than the figure.

The early Gestalt psychologists noted that figure and ground have vastly different perceptual qualities (N. Rubin, 2001). As Gestalt psychologist Edgar Rubin (1921) observed, "In a certain sense, the ground has no shape." We notice the shape of the figure but *not* the shape of the background, even when that ground is used as a well-defined frame (see Figure 3.15). It turns out that the neurons of the brain also respond differently to a stimulus that is perceived as a figure versus a stimulus that is part of the ground. Particular neurons in the cortex that responded to a specific shape when it was the shape of the figure did *not* respond when the same shape was presented as part of the background (Baylis & Driver, 2001).

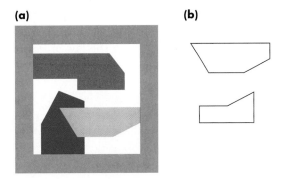

(a) (b)

FIGURE 3.15 Figures Have Shape, but Ground Doesn't Which shape in (b) can also be found in (a)? The answer is that *both* shapes are in (a). It's easy to spot the top shape, because it corresponds to one of the shapes perceived as a figure in (a). The bottom shape is harder to find because it is part of the ground or background of the total scene. Because we place more importance on figures, we're more likely to notice their shape while ignoring the shape of background regions.
SOURCE: Rubin (2001).

The separation of a scene into figure and ground is not a property of the actual elements of the scene you're looking at. Rather, your ability to separate a scene into figure and ground is a psychological accomplishment. To illustrate, look at the classic example shown in Figure 3.16. This perception of a single image in two different ways is called a *figure–ground reversal*. Figure–ground reversals underscore that perception of figure and ground is a psychological phenomenon. Artist M. C. Escher used the principle of figure–ground reversal to illustrate the dynamic tension between figure and ground, as *Winged Lion* on the next page shows.

In nature, ambiguous figure–ground relationships are quite common. Many

FIGURE 3.16 A Classic Example of Figure–Ground Reversal Figure–ground reversals illustrate the psychological nature of our ability to perceptually sort a scene into the main element and the background. If you perceive the white area as the figure and the dark area as the ground, you'll perceive a vase. If you perceive the dark area as the figure, you'll perceive two faces.

Figure–Ground Reversal in Art The Dutch artist M. C. Escher (1898–1972) is perhaps best known for creating complex visual puzzles. In *Winged Lion*, Escher uses figure–ground reversal to create a compelling image. Even if you look carefully at the picture, it is difficult to perceive the black lions and the gold lions simultaneously. Escher was fascinated by the "psychological tension" created by such images (Schattschneider, 1990).

insects and animals have markings that act as natural camouflage and prevent their detection by predators. When an animal blends in with its background, a predator cannot distinguish the animal (the *figure*) from the natural background (the *ground*). In much the same way, military personnel and equipment are often concealed from enemy forces by clothing or tarps that are designed to blend in with the terrain, whether it be jungle or desert.

Perceptual Grouping

Many of the forms we perceive are composed of a number of different elements that seem to go together (Prinzmetal, 1995). It would be more accurate to say that we actively organize the elements to try to produce the stable perception of well-defined, whole objects. This is what perceptual psychologists refer to as "the urge to organize." What sort of principles do we follow when we try to organize visual elements?

The Gestalt psychologists studied how the perception of visual elements becomes organized into patterns, shapes, and forms. They identified several laws, or principles, that we tend to follow in grouping elements together to arrive at the perception of forms, shapes, and figures. These principles include *similarity, closure, good continuation,* and *proximity.* Examples and descriptions of these perceptual laws are shown in Figure 3.17.

The Perceptual Urge to Organize As you scan this image, you'll experience firsthand the strong psychological tendency to organize visual elements to arrive at the perception of whole figures, forms, and shapes. Notice that as you shift your gaze across the pattern, you momentarily perceive circles, squares, and other geometric forms.

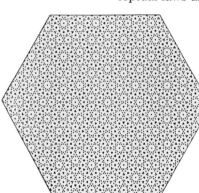

The Gestalt psychologists also formulated a general principle called the *law of Prägnanz,* or the *law of simplicity.* This law states that when several perceptual organizations of an assortment of visual elements are possible, the perceptual interpretation that occurs will be the one that produces the "best, simplest, and most stable shape" (Koffka, 1935). To illustrate, look at Figure 3.18. Do you perceive the image as two six-sided objects and one four-sided object? If you are following the law of Prägnanz, you don't. Instead, you perceptually

FIGURE 3.17 The Gestalt Principles of Organization The Gestalt psychologists formulated several basic principles of perceptual organization, which are illustrated here. We tend to follow these principles in grouping elements together to arrive at the perception of shapes, forms, and figures. **(a)** The *law of similarity* is the tendency to perceive objects of similar size, shape, or color as a unit or a figure. Thus, you perceive four horizontal rows of holiday cookies rather than six vertical columns of cookies. **(b)** The *law of closure* is the tendency to fill in the gaps or contours in an incomplete image. Thus, you perceive the two circles on the face of the clock as smooth, continuous circles, even though the curved lines are actually interrupted by the hands of the clock, the hands of the person, and the edges of the photograph. **(c)** The *law of good continuation* is the tendency to group elements that appear to follow in the same direction as a single unit or figure. In this image, good continuation is reflected in the strong tendency to identify the straight sections of highway as continuous units and the curved sections of highway as continuous units. **(d)** The *law of proximity* is the tendency to perceive objects that are close to one another as a unit or a figure. Thus, you perceive these six people as two groups of three.

(a) The Law of Similarity

(b) The Law of Closure

(c) The Law of Good Continuation

(d) The Law of Proximity

organize the elements in the most cognitively efficient and simple way, perceiving them as three overlapping squares.

According to the Gestalt psychologists, the law of Prägnanz encompasses all the other Gestalt principles, including the figure–ground relationship. The implication of the law of Prägnanz is that our perceptual system works in an economical way to promote the interpretation of stable and consistent forms (van der Helm, 2000). The ability to efficiently organize elements into stable objects helps us perceive the world accurately. In effect, we actively and automatically construct a perception that reveals "the essence of something," which is roughly what the German word *Prägnanz* means.

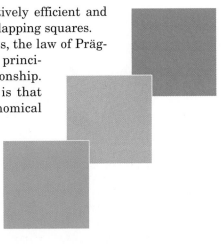

FIGURE 3.18 What Do You See? The law of simplicity refers to our tendency to efficiently organize the visual elements of a scene in a way that produces the simplest and most stable forms or objects. You probably perceived this image as that of three overlapping squares rather than as two six-sided objects and one four-sided object.

Depth Perception
How Far Away Is It?

Key Theme
- Perception of distance and motion help us gauge the position of stationary objects and the likely path of moving objects.

Key Questions
- What are the monocular and binocular cues, and how does binocular disparity explain our ability to see three-dimensional forms in two-dimensional images?
- What visual and auditory cues help us perceive motion, distance, and direction?
- Why do we perceive the size, shape, and brightness of objects as unchanging despite changes in sensory input?

Being able to perceive the distance of an object has obvious survival value, especially regarding potential threats, such as snarling dogs or oncoming trains. But simply walking through your house or apartment also requires that you accurately judge the distance of furniture, walls, other people, and so forth. Otherwise, you'd be constantly bumping into doors, walls, and tables. The ability to perceive the distance of an object as well as the three-dimensional characteristics of an object is called **depth perception.**

Monocular Cues

We use a variety of different cues to judge the distance of objects. The following cues require the use of only one eye. Hence, they are called **monocular cues** (*mono* means "one"). After familiarizing yourself with these cues, look at the photographs on the next page. Try to identify the monocular cues you used to determine the distance of the objects in each photograph.

1. *Relative size.* If two or more objects are assumed to be similar in size, the object that appears larger is perceived as being closer.

2. *Overlap.* When one object partially blocks or obscures the view of another object, the partially blocked object is perceived as being farther away.

depth perception
The use of visual cues to perceive the distance or three-dimensional characteristics of objects.

monocular cues
(moe-NOCK-you-ler) Distance or depth cues that can be processed by either eye alone.

Texture Gradient, Overlap, and Aerial Perspective When you look at a photograph, you rely on monocular cues to gauge the distance of the objects depicted. Here, the details of the tall grass are crisp in the foreground and fuzzy in the background, an example of texture gradient. The bushes are perceived as being closer than the house they overlap. Finally, the haze of the low-hanging cloud blurs the foothills, contributing to the perception of even greater distance. Linear perspective is also evident in the parallel wheel tracks in the grass that seem to converge.

Relative Size, Linear Perspective, and Aerial Perspective Several monocular depth cues are operating in this photograph. Relative size is particularly influential: The very small image of the jogger and the decreasing size of the street lamps contribute to the perception of distance. Linear perspective is evident in the apparent convergence of the walkway railings. Aerial perspective contributes to the perception of depth from the hazy background.

Motion Parallax This photograph of waiters in India passing a tray from one train car to the next captures the visual flavor of motion parallax. Objects that whiz by faster are perceptually judged as being closer, as in the case here of the blurred ground and bushes. Objects that pass by more slowly are judged as being farther away, as conveyed by the clearer details of buildings and more distant objects.

3. *Aerial perspective.* Faraway objects often appear hazy or slightly blurred by the atmosphere.

4. *Texture gradient.* As a surface with a distinct texture extends into the distance, the details of the surface texture gradually become less clearly defined. The texture of the surface seems to undergo a gradient, or continuous pattern of change, from crisp and distinct when close to fuzzy and blended when farther away.

5. *Linear perspective.* Parallel lines seem to meet in the distance. For example, if you stand in the middle of a railroad track and look down the rails, you'll notice that the parallel rails seem to meet in the distance. The closer together the lines appear to be, the greater the perception of distance.

6. *Motion parallax.* When you are moving, you use the speed of passing objects to estimate the distance of the objects. Nearby objects seem to zip by faster than do distant objects. When riding on a commuter train, for example, houses and parked cars along the tracks seem to whiz by, while the distant downtown skyline seems to move very slowly.

When mononuclear cues are used by artists to create the perception of distance or depth in paintings, they are referred to as *pictorial cues*. If you look at the cover of this book, you can see how artist Phoebe Beasley used pictorial cues, including overlap and relative size, to create the perception of depth in her artwork.

Another monocular cue is *accommodation*. Unlike pictorial cues, accommodation utilizes information about changes in the shape of the lens of the eye to help us estimate distance. When you focus on a distant object, the lens is flat, but focusing on a nearby object causes the lens to thicken. Thus, to some degree, we use information provided by the muscles controlling the shape of the lens to judge depth. In general, however, we rely more on pictorial cues than on accommodation for depth perception.

Binocular Cues

Binocular cues for distance or depth perception require information from both eyes. One binocular cue is *convergence*—the degree to which muscles rotate your eyes to focus on an object. The more the eyes converge, or rotate inward, to focus on an object, the greater the strength of the muscle signals and the closer the object is perceived to be. For example, if you hold a dime about six inches in front of your nose, you'll notice the slight strain on your eye muscles as your eyes converge to focus on the coin. If you hold the dime at arm's length, less convergence is needed. Perceptually, the information provided by these signals from your eye muscles is used to judge the distance of an object.

Another binocular distance cue is *binocular disparity*. Because our eyes are set a couple of inches apart, a slightly different image of an object is cast on the retina of each eye. When the two retinal images are very different, we interpret the object as being close by. When the two retinal images are more nearly identical, the object is perceived as being farther away.

Here's a simple example that illustrates how you use binocular disparity to perceive distance. Hold a pencil just in front of your nose. Close your left eye, then your right. These images are quite different—that is, there is a great deal of binocular disparity between them. Thus you perceive the pencil as being very close. Now focus on another object across the room and look at it first with one eye closed, then the other. These images are much more similar. Because there is less binocular disparity between the two images, the object is perceived as being farther away. Finally, notice that with both eyes open, the two images are fused into one.

A *stereogram* is a picture that uses the principle of binocular disparity to create the perception of a three-dimensional image (Kunoh & Takaoki, 1994). Look at the stereogram shown here. When you first look at it, you perceive a two-dimensional picture of leaves. Although the pictorial cues of overlap and texture gradient provide some sense of depth to the image, the elements in the picture appear to be roughly the same distance from you.

However, a stereogram is actually composed of repeating columns of carefully arranged visual information. If you focus as if you are looking at some object that is farther away than the stereogram, the repeating columns of information will present a slightly different image to each eye. This disparate visual information then fuses into a single image, enabling you to perceive a three-dimensional image—three rabbits! To see the rabbits, follow the directions in the caption.

binocular cues
(by-NOCK-you-ler) Distance or depth cues that require the use of both eyes.

Binocular Disparity and the Perception of Depth in Stereograms This stereogram, *Rustling Hares,* was created by artist Hiroshi Kunoh (Kunoh & Takaoki, 1994). To see the three-dimensional images, first hold the picture close to your face. Focus your eyes as though you are looking at an object that is beyond the book and farther away. Without changing your focus, slowly extend your arms and move the picture away from you. The image of the leaves will initially be blurry, then details will come into focus and you should see three rabbits. The three-dimensional images that can be perceived in stereograms occur because of binocular disparity—each eye is presented with slightly different visual information.

C·O·N·C·E·P·T

3.3 R·E·V·I·E·W

Depth Perception

Several monocular depth cues are evident in this photograph of the Ginza, a major shopping and entertainment district of Tokyo, Japan. After studying the photograph, identify examples of the following monocular depth cues:

1. Relative size   *3.* Aerial perspective   *5.* Linear perspective

2. Overlap   *4.* Texture gradient

The Perception of Motion

Where Is It Going?

In addition to the ability to perceive the distance of stationary objects, we need the ability to gauge the path of moving objects, whether it's a baseball whizzing through the air, a falling tree branch, or an egg about to roll off the kitchen counter. How do we perceive movement?

As we follow a moving object with our gaze, the image of the object moves across the retina. Our eye muscles make microfine movements to keep the object in focus. We also compare the moving object to the background, which is usually stationary. When the retinal image of an object expands, we perceive the object as moving toward us. And our perception of the speed of the object's approach is based on our estimate of the object's rate of expansion (Schrater & others, 2001). Neural pathways in the brain combine information about eye-muscle activity, the changing retinal image, and the contrast of the moving object with its stationary background (Wallach, 1987). The end result? We perceive the object as moving.

Neuroscientists do not completely understand how the brain's visual system processes movement. It's known that some neurons are highly specialized to detect motion in one direction but not in the opposite direction. Other neurons are specialized to detect motion at one particular speed. Research also shows that different neural pathways in the cerebral cortex process information about the depth of objects, movement, form, and color (Livingstone & Hubel, 1988; Zeki, 2001).

Psychologically, we tend to make certain assumptions when we perceive movement. For example, we typically assume that the *object,* or figure, moves while the background, or frame, remains stationary (Rock, 1995). Thus, as you visually follow a bowling ball down the alley, you perceive the bowling ball as moving and not the alley, which serves as the background.

Motion Perception As this center fielder dives for a fly ball, his brain is rapidly calculating information about the location, speed, and trajectory of the baseball. Psychologists still don't completely understand how the visual system perceives and predicts the motion of objects. Most of the time, we accomplish this complex feat with remarkable accuracy. But in this case, center fielder Jason Neilsen missed the ball!

Stroboscopic Motion and Movies The perception of smooth movements in a motion picture is due to stroboscopic motion. Much like this series of still photographs of a gymnast performing a back flip, a motion picture is actually a series of static photographs that are projected onto the screen at the rate of 24 frames per second, producing the illusion of smooth motion.

Induced Motion

Because we have a strong tendency to assume that the background is stationary, we sometimes experience an illusion of motion called *induced motion*. Induced motion was first studied by Gestalt psychologist **Karl Duncker** in the 1920s (King & others, 1998). Duncker (1929) had subjects sit in a darkened room and look at a luminous dot that was surrounded by a larger luminous rectangular frame. When the *frame* slowly moved to the right, the subjects perceived the *dot* as moving to the left.

Why did subjects perceive the dot as moving? Part of the explanation has to do with top-down processing. Perceptually, Duncker's subjects *expected* to see the smaller dot move within the larger rectangular frame, not the other way around. If you've ever looked up at a full moon on a windy night when the clouds were moving quickly across its face, you've probably experienced the induced motion effect. The combination of these environmental elements makes the moon appear to be racing across the sky.

Or perhaps you've had an experience like the one Sandy had recently. She pulled into a parking space and stopped her car just as the van parked next to her began to back up slowly. Because of the phenomenon of induced motion, Sandy perceived her *own* car, rather than the van, to be moving—and hit the brakes!

Stroboscopic Motion

Another illusion of apparent motion is called *stroboscopic motion*. First studied by Gestalt psychologist Max Wertheimer in the early 1900s, stroboscopic motion creates an illusion of movement with two carefully timed flashing lights (Wertheimer, 1912). A light briefly flashes at one location, followed about a tenth of a second later by another light briefly flashing at a second location. If the time interval and distance between the two flashing lights are just right, a very compelling illusion of movement is created.

What causes the perception of stroboscopic motion? Although different theories have been proposed, researchers aren't completely sure. The perception of motion typically involves the movement of an image across the retina. However, during stroboscopic motion the image does *not* move across the surface of the retina. Rather, the two different flashing lights are detected at two different points on the surface of the retina. Somehow the brain's visual system combines this rapid sequence of visual information to arrive at the perceptual conclusion of motion, even though no movement has occurred. The perception of smooth motion in a movie is also due to stroboscopic motion.

Auditory Cues

We use *auditory* information to judge distance and direction as well. Just as we can use information from one or both eyes to perceive the distance of an object, we can use information from one or both ears to detect the distance of a sound. Using only one ear, the louder the sound, the closer we perceive it to be.

Using both ears allows us to more accurately locate the direction as well as the distance of a sound (Konishi, 1993). For example, when a sound is directly to your left, the sound wave reaches your left ear a few thousandths of a second before it reaches your right ear. Because your left ear is closer to the source, the sound it detects is also slightly louder. Your brain calculates these differences in time lag and loudness, and you quickly perceive that the source of the sound is to your left (Phillips & Brugge, 1985). Notice that when you are trying to determine the direction from which a sound is coming, such as an ambulance siren a few blocks away, you instinctively tilt your head to one side. Doing so adds to the contrast between the information received by your two ears and helps you perceive the distance and direction of the sound.

Perceptual Constancies

Consider this scenario. As you're driving on a flat stretch of highway, a red van zips past you and speeds far ahead. As the distance between you and the van grows, its image becomes progressively smaller until the van is no more than a dot on the horizon. Yet, even though the image of the van on your retinas has become progressively smaller, you don't perceive the van as shrinking. Instead, you perceive its shape, size, and brightness as unchanged.

This tendency to perceive objects, especially familiar objects, as constant and unchanging despite changes in sensory input is called **perceptual constancy.** Without this perceptual ability, our perception of reality would be in a continual state of flux. If we simply responded to retinal images, our perceptions of objects would change as lighting, viewing angle, and distance from the object changed from one moment to the next. Instead, the various forms of perceptual constancy promote a stable view of the world.

Size Constancy

Size constancy is the perception that an object remains the same size despite its changing image on the retina. When our distance from an object changes, the image of the object that is cast on the retinas of our eyes also changes, yet we still perceive it to be the same size. The example of the red van illustrates the perception of size constancy. As the distance between you and the red van increased, you could eventually block out the retinal image of the van with your hand, but you don't believe that your hand has suddenly become larger than the van. Instead, your brain automatically adjusts your perception of the van's size by combining information about retinal image size and distance.

An important aspect of size constancy is that if the retinal image of an object does *not* change but the perception of its distance *increases,* the object is perceived as larger. To illustrate, try this: Stare at a 75-watt light bulb for about 10 seconds. Then focus on a bright, distant wall. You should see an afterimage of the light bulb on the wall that will look several times larger than the original light bulb. Why? When you looked at the wall, the lingering afterimage of the light bulb on your retina remained constant, but your perception of distance increased. When your brain combined and interpreted this information, your perception of the light bulb's size increased. Remember this demonstration. We'll mention it again when we explain how some perceptual illusions occur.

Shape and Brightness Constancy

Shape constancy is the tendency to perceive familiar objects as having a fixed shape regardless of the image they cast on our retinas. Try looking at a familiar object, such as a door, from different angles, as in the accompanying photograph. Your perception of the door's rectangular shape remains constant despite changes in its retinal image.

Shape constancy has a greater influence on your perceptions than you probably realize. Look at Figure 3.19, count the right angles, and write the number in

The Doors of Perception Each door in the photograph is positioned at a different angle and thus produces a differently shaped image on your retinas. Nevertheless, because of the perceptual principle of shape constancy, you easily identify all five objects as rectangular doors.

FIGURE 3.19 How Many Right Angles Do You See?

the margin. If you're like most people, you probably counted 12 right angles in the drawing of the slightly tilted cube. Now look at it again, this time more carefully. There are *no* right angles in the drawing. Because of shape constancy, you perceived an image of a cube with right angles despite the lack of sensory information to support that perception.

Another kind of perceptual constancy is **brightness constancy,** in which the perceived brightness of an object seems to stay the same even though the lighting conditions change. The white sheet on a bed is perceived as equally bright whether seen in full sunlight or in the dim light of a night-light. A black outdoor grill or crow is perceived as equally dark during the day or at night. The perception of brightness constancy occurs because objects always reflect the same *proportion* of available light, even if the lighting conditions change dramatically (Zeki, 2001).

Perceptual Illusions

Key Theme

▦ Perceptual illusions underscore the idea that we actively construct our perceptual representations of the world according to psychological principles.

Key Questions

▦ How can the Müller-Lyer and moon illusions be explained?

▦ What do perceptual illusions and impossible figures reveal about perceptual processes?

▦ What roles do perceptual sets, learning experiences, and culture play in perception?

Our perceptual processes are largely automatic and unconscious. On the one hand, this arrangement is mentally efficient. With a minimum of cognitive effort, we decipher our surroundings, answering important perceptual questions and making sense of the environment. On the other hand, because perceptual processing is largely automatic, we can inadvertently arrive at the wrong perceptual conclusion. When we misperceive the true characteristics of an object or an image, we experience a **perceptual illusion.**

During the last century, well over 200 perceptual illusions have been discovered. The perceptual contradictions of illusions are not only fascinating, but can also shed light on how the normal processes of perception guide us to perceptual conclusions. Given the basics of perception that we've covered thus far, you're in a good position to understand how and why some famous illusions seem to occur. In this section, we'll consider two of the best-known perceptual illusions: the Müller-Lyer illusion and the moon illusion. Then we'll look at the perceptual puzzles posed by impossible figures. At the end of this section, we'll return to the issue of what perceptual illusions and impossible figures tell us about the process of perception.

The Müller-Lyer Illusion

Look at the center line in each of the two photographs in Figure 3.20 on the next page. Which line is longer? If you said the one in the bottom photo, then you've just experienced the **Müller-Lyer illusion.** In fact, the two center lines are the same length, even though they *appear* to have different lengths. You can confirm that they are the same length by measuring them. The same illusion occurs when you look at a simple drawing of the Müller-Lyer illusion, which is also shown in Figure 3.20.

perceptual constancy
The tendency to perceive objects, especially familiar objects, as constant and unchanging despite changes in sensory input.

size constancy
The perception of an object as maintaining the same size despite changing images on the retina.

shape constancy
The perception of a familiar object as maintaining the same shape regardless of the image produced on the retina.

brightness constancy
The perception that the brightness of an object remains the same even though the lighting conditions change.

perceptual illusion
The misperception of the true characteristics of an object or an image.

Müller-Lyer illusion
A famous visual illusion involving the misperception of the identical length of two lines, one with arrows pointed inward, one with arrows pointed outward.

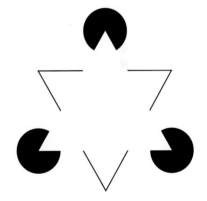

Illusory Contours The Gestalt principles of perceptual organization contribute to the illusion of triangular contours of this image. The second you look at this ambiguous image, you instantly reverse figure and ground so that the black circular regions become the ground, while the white region is visually flavored as the figure. In organizing these visual fragments, which are lined up very precisely, the Gestalt principles of closure and good continuation contribute to the perceptual construction of a solid white triangle covering three black disks and an inverted triangle. An intriguing second illusion is also occurring—the pure white illusory triangle seems brighter than the surrounding white paper.

FIGURE 3.20 The Müller-Lyer Illusion Compare the two photographs. Which corner line is longer? Now compare the two line drawings. Which center line is longer? In reality, the center lines in the photographs and the line drawings are all exactly the same length, which you can prove to yourself with a ruler.

FIGURE 3.21 The Moon Illusion Dispelled The *moon illusion* is subjectively very compelling. When viewed on the horizon, the moon appears to be much larger than when it is viewed higher in the sky. But as this time-lapse sequence of the moon rising over the Seattle skyline shows, the size of the moon remains the same as it ascends in the sky.

The Müller-Lyer illusion is caused in part by visual depth cues that promote the perception that the bottom line is *farther* from you (Gregory, 1968; Rock, 1995). When you look at the photograph on the right, the center line is that of a wall jutting away from you. When you look at the drawing of the Müller-Lyer illusion on the right, the outward-pointing arrows create much the same visual effect—a corner jutting away from you. In the left photograph and line drawing, visual depth cues promote the perception of *lesser* distance—a corner that is jutting toward you.

Size constancy also seems to play an important role in the Müller-Lyer illusion. Because they are the same length, the two center lines in the photographs and the line drawings produce retinal images that are the same size. However, we noted in our earlier discussion of size constancy that if the retinal size of an object stays the same but the perception of its distance increases, we will perceive the object as being larger. Previously, we demonstrated this with the afterimage of a light bulb that seemed much larger when viewed against a distant wall.

The same basic principle seems to occur with the Müller-Lyer illusion. Although the two corner lines produce retinal images that are the same size, the bottom corner line is embedded in visual depth cues that make you perceive it as farther away. Hence, you perceive the bottom corner line as being longer, just as you perceived the afterimage of the light bulb as being larger when viewed on a distant wall.

Keep in mind that the arrows pointing inward or outward are responsible for creating the illusion in the Müller-Lyer illusion. Take away those potent depth cues and the Müller-Lyer illusion evaporates. You perceive the two lines just as they are—the same length.

The Moon Illusion

Another famous illusion is one you've probably experienced firsthand—the **moon illusion,** shown in Figure 3.21. When a full moon is rising on a clear, dark night, it appears much larger when viewed on the horizon against buildings and trees than it does when viewed in the clear sky overhead. But the moon, of course, doesn't shrink as it rises. In fact, *the retinal size of the full moon is the same in all positions.* Still, if you've ever watched the moon rise from the horizon to the night sky, it does *appear* to shrink in size. What causes this illusion?

Part of the explanation has to do with our perception of the distance of objects at different locations in the sky (Kaufman & Kaufman, 2000; Rock, 1995). Researchers have found that people perceive objects on the horizon as farther away than objects that are directly overhead in the sky. The horizon contains many familiar distance cues, such as buildings, trees, and the smoothing of the texture of the landscape as it fades into the distance. The moon on the horizon is perceived as being *behind* these depth cues, so the depth perception cue of overlap adds to the perception that the moon on the horizon is farther away.

The moon illusion also involves the misapplication of the principle of size constancy. Like the afterimage of the glowing light bulb, which looked larger on a distant wall, the moon looks larger when the perception of its distance increases. Remember, the retinal image of the moon is the *same* in all locations, as was the afterimage of the light bulb. Thus, even though the retinal image of the moon remains constant, we perceive the moon as being larger because it seems farther away on the horizon (Kaufman & Kaufman, 2000).

If you could somehow remove the additional distance cues that the horizon seems to contain, would the moon appear to be the same size in all locations? Here's one way to find out. Look at a full moon on the horizon through a cardboard tube or through your cupped hands. Either strategy will effectively remove the distance cues provided by trees, faraway buildings, and other objects on the horizon that the moon appears to be behind. When you do this, the size of the moon on the horizon will rapidly shrink—and look the same size as it does when directly overhead.

Impossible Figures

Artists have created a variety of "impossible figures." Though not illusions in the true sense, these figures baffle our natural tendency to perceptually organize a scene. The person most famous for creating elaborate impossible figures was Dutch artist M. C. Escher (1898–1972). Escher's work entitled *Waterfall* is shown here. When you look at the image, you try to sort and integrate the different visual elements to arrive at a stable, well-organized, whole image. However, this is not possible with impossible figures. As you study one area of the picture and try to integrate it with other parts of the picture, perceptual contradictions arise—such as the conclusion that water is running uphill. In effect, impossible figures are visual riddles that capitalize on our urge to organize visual elements into a meaningful whole.

Perceptual illusions such as the Müller-Lyer illusion underscore the fact that what we see is *not* merely a simple reflection of the world, but our subjective perceptual interpretation of it. And although seeing is said to be believing, in the case of illusions, believing can lead to seeing something that isn't really there. Impossible figures remind us that we actively construct perceptual conclusions about the information detected through our senses. Our conclusions are guided by well-established perceptual principles, such as depth and distance cues.

Like any psychological process, perception can be influenced by many factors, including our expectations (Bruner, 1992). In the final section of this chapter, we'll consider how our prior experiences and cultural factors can influence our perceptions of reality.

The Effects of Experience on Perceptual Interpretations

Our educational, cultural, and life experiences shape what we perceive. As a simple example, consider airplane cockpits. If your knowledge of the instruments contained in an airplane cockpit is limited, as is the case with your author Sandy, an airplane cockpit looks like a confusing, meaningless jumble of dials. But your author Don, who is a pilot, has a very different perception of an airplane cockpit. Rather than a blur of dials, he sees altimeters, VORs, airspeed and RPM indicators, and other instruments, each with a specific function. Our different perceptions of an airplane cockpit are shaped by our prior learning experiences.

moon illusion
A visual illusion involving the misperception that the moon is larger when it is on the horizon than when it is directly overhead.

Artist M. C. Escher's Lithograph *Waterfall* **(1961)** Misleading depth cues in this lithograph by Escher trick the viewer into perceiving the water as flowing uphill.

Doric Dilemma At first glance, the image in this drawing by psychologist Roger Shepard (1990) seems to be simple enough. However, if you look at the columns carefully, you'll see that figure and ground are constantly shifting. Hence, it is impossible to arrive at a stable perception of the image.

Culture and the Müller-Lyer Illusion: The Carpentered-World Hypothesis

The Gestalt psychologists believed that perceptual processes are inborn, a viewpoint called the *nativist position*. According to this position, people everywhere, whatever their background, see the world in the same way because they share the same perceptual rules. Other psychologists have advocated the *empiricist position,* believing that people actively construct their perceptions by drawing on their prior learning experiences, including cultural experiences.

The Müller-Lyer illusion has played a key role in the debate on this issue. Since the early 1900s, it has been known that people in industrialized societies are far more susceptible to the Müller-Lyer illusion than are people in some nonindustrialized societies (see Matsumoto, 1994). How can this difference be explained?

Cross-cultural psychologist Marshall Segall and his colleagues (1963, 1966) proposed the *carpentered-world hypothesis.* They suggested that people living in urban, industrialized environments have a great deal of perceptual experience in judging lines, corners, edges, and other rectangular, manufactured objects. Thus, people in carpentered cultures would be more susceptible to the Müller-Lyer illusion, which involves arrows mimicking a corner that is jutting toward or away from the perceiver.

In contrast, people who live in noncarpentered cultures more frequently encounter natural objects. In these cultures, perceptual experiences with straight lines and right angles are relatively rare. Segall predicted that people from these cultures would be less susceptible to the Müller-Lyer illusion.

To test this idea, Segall and his colleagues (1963, 1966) compared the re-

A Noncarpentered Environment People who live in urban, industrialized environments have a great deal of perceptual experience with straight lines, edges, and right angles. In contrast, people who live in a noncarpentered environment, like the village shown here, have little experience with right angles and perfectly straight lines. Are people who grow up in a noncarpentered environment equally susceptible to the Müller-Lyer illusion?

sponses of people living in carpentered societies, such as Evanston, Illinois, with those of people living in noncarpentered societies, such as remote areas of Africa. The results confirmed their hypothesis. The Müller-Lyer illusion was stronger for those living in carpentered societies. The findings provided strong support for the idea that culture could influence perception.

However, nativists were quick to suggest that Segall's results might be due to racial rather than cultural differences. After all, they pointed out, the non-Western subjects in Segall's research were mostly Africans, and racial

differences in eye pigmentation had been shown to affect the ability to visually detect contours (see Segall, 1994). Could the difference in illusion susceptibility be due to some sort of physiological difference rather than a cultural difference?

To address this issue, psychologist V. M. Stewart (1973) compared groups of white and African-American schoolchildren living in the carpentered society of Evanston, Illinois. Stewart found that the Evanston children, regardless of race, were equally susceptible to the Müller-Lyer illusion. She then compared groups of black African children in five different areas of Zambia—ranging from the very carpentered capital city of Lusaka to rural, noncarpentered areas of the country.

The results of this second comparison? The African children living in the carpentered society of Lusaka were just as susceptible to the illusion as were the white and African-American children living in Evanston. And the children living in the rural, noncarpentered countryside were far less susceptible. In other words, the children's race made no difference at all. What mattered was the children's experience, or lack of experience, with a carpentered environment.

Clearly, differences in susceptibility to the Müller-Lyer illusion underscore the important role that cultural experiences can play in shaping our perceptions. Segall (1994) summarized the empiricist view: "Every perception is the result of an interaction between a stimulus and a perceiver shaped by prior experience." Thus, people from very different cultural backgrounds might well perceive aspects of the world differently.

Learning experiences can vary not just from person to person but also from culture to culture. In Culture and Human Behavior Box 3.5, we discuss the important role experiences unique to a particular culture can play in the perception of illusions.

Past experience often predisposes us to perceive a situation in a particular way, even though other perceptions are possible. Consider this experience, which one of our students shared in class. As he was driving home late at night, he stopped at a convenience store to buy a pack of cigarettes. Standing at the counter and rummaging through his wallet for some cash, he requested "a pack of Nows." When he looked up, the young female clerk had put a copy of *Penthouse* on the counter. Obviously, the clerk perceived what she had expected to hear.

This example illustrates the notion of **perceptual set**—the expectancies and predispositions that the observer brings to a perceptual situation. We're often mentally primed to interpret a particular perception in a particular way. Our perceptual sets are, of course, influenced by our prior learning experiences. To use an example discussed in an earlier section, an oddly shaped piece of wood might be a dax to one child and simply an oddly shaped piece of wood to another. One person's mystery dial is another person's altimeter.

Perceptual sets can exert a strong influence on the perceptual conclusions we reach. Our perceptual sets usually lead us to reasonably accurate conclusions. If they didn't, we would develop new perceptual sets that were more accurate. But sometimes a perceptual set can lead us astray. For example, when the partially decomposed body of a large, hairy creature was discovered in upstate New York, it generated much excitement because the remains were perceived by several people as proof of the existence of "Bigfoot" (Hines, 1988). Scientists operating with a different perceptual set examined the dead creature and duly proclaimed it for what it was—the remains of a brown bear.

Similar examples of erroneous perceptual sets have occurred with supposed sightings of UFOs, the Loch Ness monster, mermaids, and ghosts. In each case, observers interpreted ambiguous stimuli in terms of the perceptual set they held in that situation and saw what their expectations led them to see.

Evidence of Extra-Terrestrial Civilations?

Visitors from Another Planet? Perceptual set may lead the avid believer in UFOs to see this photograph of unusual cloud formations as evidence for the existence of flying saucers.

The Face on Mars Was it built by ancient astronauts, time-traveling astronauts from Earth's future, or perhaps the artisans of an ancient Martian civilization? Perceptual set led many people to see a "face" in this dimly lit rock formation (left), photographed by NASA's *Viking 1* expedition. Higher-resolution photos taken at a later date (right) revealed the mile-long "face" to be nothing more than one of many similar features sculpted into the planet's rocky surface by wind.

3.4 R·E·V·I·E·W

C·O·N·C·E·P·T

Perceptual Principles

Fill in the blanks using the correct term.

1. When Jenny was flying to the South Pacific, she saw several lush green islands that stood out in a sea of bright blue. In this example, the islands are the _____ and the sea is the _____.

2. As the football is hurtling toward you, it creates a progressively larger image on your retina, and the angle of the ball is constantly changing. Despite these drastic changes in sensory output, the phenomena of _____ and _____ enable you to continue to perceive the object as a football.

3. •••• •••• •••• If you followed the law of _____, you perceived this arrangement as three groups of four dots.

4. ○○○○••••○○○○•••• If you followed the law of _____, you perceived this arrangement as two groups of four circles and two groups of four dots.

5. Hundreds of people flocked to an Indiana town when it was reported that the face of a religious figure had appeared in a rust stain on the side of a water tower. This perception was probably an example of _____.

perceptual set
The influence of prior assumptions and expectations on perceptual interpretations.

Summing Up
Sensation and Perception

In this chapter, we've seen the interaction of biological, behavioral, and psychological factors. As Paul's and Warren's stories illustrated, our experience of the world is highly dependent on our physiology, specifically, our sense organs. Paul and Warren both live in a world without odor or aroma—olfactory cues that are important to many people, and as essential as sight to many other species.

The process of sensation results in the transmission of neural messages to the brain, where the psychological process of perception occurs. We actively construct perceptual conclusions about this sensory information. In arriving at those perceptual conclusions, we are guided by well-established perceptual principles, such as the cues that typically indicate distance, movement, form, and so forth. But our perceptual conclusions can also be influenced by a variety of psychological factors, including our expectations, learning experiences, and experiences that are unique to our culture.

APPLICATION   Strategies to Control Pain

There are several strategies for controlling pain. Each of the following simple self-administered techniques can be useful for dealing with the everyday pain of a headache, an injury, or a trip to the dentist. Of course, the techniques described here are not a substitute for seeking appropriate medical attention, especially when pain is severe, recurring, or of unknown origin.

1. Distraction.

By actively focusing your attention on some nonpainful stimulus, you can often reduce pain (Fernandez, 1986; Turk & Nash, 1993). For example, you can mentally count backward by 7s from 901; multiply pairs of two-digit numbers; draw different geometric figures in your head; or count ceiling tiles. You can also stare at the details of a picture or other object or intently listen to music.

2. Imagery.

One form of distraction is imagery. Creating a vivid mental image can help control pain (Rossman, 1993). Usually people create a pleasant and progressive scenario, such as walking along the beach or hiking in the mountains. Aggressive imagery can also be useful, such as imagining fighting an enemy or driving a race car (Lyles & others, 1982). Whatever scenario you use, try to imagine all the different sensations involved, including the sights, sounds, aromas, touches, and tastes. The goal is to become so absorbed in your fantasy that you distract yourself from sensations of pain.

3. Positive self-talk.

This strategy involves making positive coping statements, either silently or out loud, during a painful episode or procedure (Cioffi & Holloway, 1993; Fernandez, 1986). Examples of positive self-talk include statements such as "It hurts, but I'm okay, I'm in control"; "I'm uncomfortable, but I can handle it"; and "The pain is uncomfortable but not unbearable."

Such self-talk can also include redefining the pain. By using realistic and constructive thoughts about the pain experience in place of threatening or harmful thoughts, you can minimize pain (McCaul & Malott, 1984). For example, an athlete in training might say, "The pain means my muscles are getting stronger." Someone wearing orthodontic braces might tell himself that the pain means that his teeth are moving into place.

4. Counterirritation.

The technique of counterirritation has been used for centuries. Counterirritation decreases pain by creating a strong, competing sensation that's mildly stimulating or irritating. People often do this naturally, as when they vigorously rub an injury or bite their lip during an injection. How does rubbing the area where an injury has occurred reduce pain? The intense sensations of pain and the normal sensations of touch are processed through different nerve fibers going to the spinal cord. Increasing normal sensations of touch interferes with the transmission of high-intensity pain signals.

While undergoing a painful procedure, you can create and control a competing discomfort by pressing your thumbnail into your index finger. Focusing your attention on the competing discomfort may lessen your overall experience of pain.

5. Relaxation.

Deep relaxation can be a very effective strategy for deterring pain sensations (Benson, 1993; Turk & Nash, 1993). Relaxation procedures can be used in a particular situation or can be practiced repeatedly during prolonged pain. One simple strategy to achieve relaxation is deep breathing: Inhale deeply, then exhale very slowly and completely, releasing tension throughout your body. As you exhale, consciously note the feelings of relaxation and warmth you've produced in your body.

Beyond these self-administered strategies, pain specialists use a variety of techniques to control pain, including painkilling drugs and hypnosis. Both of these topics will be discussed in the next chapter. Another strategy is biofeedback. *Biofeedback* is a process of learning voluntary control over largely automatic body functions, such as heart rate, blood pressure, and muscle tension. Using sensitive equipment that signals subtle changes in a specific bodily function, people can learn to become more aware of their body's signals and exercise conscious control over a particular bodily process. For example, an individual who experiences chronic tension headaches might use biofeedback to learn to relax shoulder, neck, and facial muscles. Biofeedback has proven effective in helping many people who experience tension headaches, migraine headaches, jaw pain, and back pain (M. S. Schwartz & N. M. Schwartz, 1993).

Chapter Review
Sensation and Perception

Key Points

Introduction: What Are Sensation and Perception?

■ **Sensation** refers to the response of sensory receptors in the sense organs to stimulation and the transmission of that information to the brain. **Perception** refers to the process through which the brain organizes and interprets sensory information.

■ When **sensory receptors** are stimulated by an appropriate form of energy, **transduction** converts the energy into neural impulses, which are transmitted to the brain.

■ Each sense is specialized in terms of the type and level of energy to which it will respond. Sensory thresholds include the **absolute threshold** and the **difference threshold.** **Weber's law** states that the just noticeable difference will vary depending on the strength of the original stimulus. **Sensory adaptation** takes place when the sensory receptor cells gradually decline in sensitivity to a constant stimulus.

Vision: *From Light to Sight*

■ The sensory receptors for vision respond to light waves. The human eye is sensitive to a very narrow, specific range of **wavelengths** in the electromagnetic energy spectrum.

■ Light waves enter the eye and pass through the **cornea** and the **pupil.** The **iris** controls how much light is allowed in. Behind the pupil is the **lens,** which focuses light on the **retina** through **accommodation.** The retina contains the sensory receptors for vision, the rods and cones.

■ **Rods** are used for vision in dim light and for peripheral vision. **Cones** are used for color vision, for vision in bright light, and for seeing fine details. Cones are concentrated in the **fovea,** whereas rods are more prevalent in the periphery of the retina. There are no rods or cones in the **optic disk,** which creates a **blind spot** in the visual field.

■ Rods and cones send information to the **bipolar** and **ganglion cells.** The ratio of cones to ganglion cells is much smaller than the ratio of rods to ganglion cells. The **optic nerve** fibers exit the back of each retina at the optic disk and meet at the **optic chiasm,** where some of the fibers cross over to the opposite side of the brain and then transmit information from the thalamus to the visual cortex. Feature detectors are highly specialized neurons in the visual cortex.

■ **Color** is the psychological experience of different wavelengths of light and involves **hue, brightness,** and **saturation.** The color of an object is determined by the light wave it reflects. In combination, the **trichromatic theory** and the **opponent-process theory** explain color vision. The trichromatic theory explains red–green **color blindness** and color processing in the retina. The opponent-process theory explains **afterimages** and color processing in the ganglion cells and the brain.

Hearing: *From Vibration to Sound*

■ The sense of hearing is called **audition.** The **loudness, pitch,** and **timbre** of a sound are determined by the **amplitude, frequency,** and complexity of a sound wave. Loudness is measured in **decibels.**

■ Sound waves are collected in the **outer ear,** amplified by the **eardrum** in the **middle ear,** and transduced in the **inner ear.** The sensory receptors for hearing are the **hair cells,** which are located on the **basilar membrane** in the **cochlea.** The auditory nerve carries information to the thalamus and auditory cortex in the brain. **Frequency theory** and **place theory** explain the sensation of pitch.

The Chemical and Body Senses: *Smell, Taste, Touch, and Position*

■ The sensory receptors for smell (**olfaction**) and taste (**gustation**) are specialized to respond to chemical substances. The sensation of smell is caused by airborne molecules stimulating odor receptors on the olfactory receptor cells in the nasal lining. Olfactory information travels via the axons of the receptor cells to the **olfactory bulb** and is transmitted along the olfactory tract to different brain areas, including the temporal lobe and limbic system.

■ Taste results from the stimulation of sensory receptors in the **taste buds,** which are located on the tongue and the inside of the mouth. When activated by chemical substances dissolved in saliva, the taste buds send neural messages to the thalamus in the brain. There are five primary tastes: sweet, salty, sour, bitter, and umami.

■ The skin includes several kinds of sensory receptors, which are unevenly distributed among the parts of the body. The Pacinian corpuscle is the skin receptor that is sensitive to pressure. Skin receptors for temperature include cold spots and warm spots.

■ **Pain** sensation is partly explained by the **gate-control theory.** Pain sensations result from the release of a neurotransmitter called **substance P.** The transmission of pain signals is inhibited by the release of endorphins. Psychological factors mediate the experience of pain.

■ The **kinesthetic sense** involves the location and position of body parts in relation to one another, which is detected by specialized neurons called **proprioceptors.** The **vestibular sense** provides information about balance, equilibrium, and orientation.

Perception

■ Both **bottom-up** and **top-down processing** are involved in everyday perception. The **Gestalt** psychologists emphasized the perception of *gestalts,* or whole forms.

■ We rely primarily on shape to identify an object. **Figure-ground relationships** are important in distinguishing an object from its background. The Gestalt psychologists noted perceptual principles of organization including proximity, similarity, closure, good continuation, and the law of Prägnanz.

- **Depth perception** involves both monocular and binocular cues. **Monocular depth cues** include relative size, overlap, aerial perspective, texture gradient, linear perspective, motion parallax, and accommodation. **Binocular depth cues** include convergence and binocular disparity.

- The perception of movement involves integrating information from the eye muscles, the retina, and the environment. The illusion of induced motion is a result of our assumption that the background is stationary. The perception of stroboscopic motion results from images being rapidly registered on the retina. Auditory cues help us judge the distance and direction of an object.

- Objects are perceived as stable despite changes in sensory input and retinal image, a concept called **perceptual con-**

stancy. Size constancy, shape constancy, and **brightness constancy** are three important forms of perceptual constancy.

Perceptual Illusions

- **Perceptual illusions** and impossible figures are used to study perceptual principles. The **Müller-Lyer illusion** involves the principles of depth cues and size constancy. The **moon illusion** results from the principles of overlap and size constancy.

The Effects of Experience on Perceptual Interpretations

- Perceptual interpretations can be influenced by learning experiences, culture, and expectations. **Perceptual set** often determines the interpretation of an ambiguous stimulus.

Key Terms

sensation, p. 90

perception, p. 90

sensory receptors, p. 91

transduction, p. 91

absolute threshold, p. 92

difference threshold, p. 92

Weber's law, p. 92

sensory adaptation, p. 92

subliminal perception, p. 93

wavelength, p. 94

cornea, p. 95

pupil, p. 95

iris, p. 95

iridology, p. 96

lens, p. 96

accommodation, p. 96

retina, p. 97

rods, p. 97

cones, p. 97

fovea, p. 97

optic disk, p. 98

blind spot, p. 98

ganglion cells, p. 98

bipolar cells, p. 99

optic nerve, p. 99

optic chiasm, p. 99

color, p. 101

hue, p. 101

saturation, p. 101

brightness, p. 101

trichromatic theory of color vision, p. 102

color blindness, p. 102

afterimage, p. 102

opponent-process theory of color vision, p. 102

audition, p. 104

loudness, p. 104

amplitude, p. 104

decibel, p. 104

pitch, p. 104

frequency, p. 104

timbre, p. 104

outer ear, p. 105

eardrum, p. 105

middle ear, p. 105

inner ear, p. 106

cochlea, p. 106

basilar membrane, p. 106

hair cells, p. 106

frequency theory, p. 106

place theory, p. 106

olfaction, p. 107

gustation, p. 107

olfactory bulb, p. 108

pheromones, p. 109

taste buds, p. 110

pain, p. 111

gate-control theory, p. 112

substance P, p. 112

kinesthetic sense, p. 112

proprioceptors, p. 112

vestibular sense, p. 112

ESP (extrasensory perception), p. 114

parapsychology, p. 114

bottom-up processing, p. 115

top-down processing, p. 115

Gestalt psychology, p. 116

figure–ground relationship, p. 117

depth perception, p. 119

monocular cues, p. 119

binocular cues, p. 121

perceptual constancy, p. 124

size constancy, p. 124

shape constancy, p. 124

brightness constancy, p. 125

perceptual illusion, p. 125

Müller-Lyer illusion, p. 125

moon illusion, p. 126

perceptual set, p. 129

Key People

Karl Duncker (1903–1940) German Gestalt psychologist who is best known for his studies on the perception of motion; also studied the perception of pain and the effects of past experience on perception; immigrated to the United States in 1938. (p. 123)

Max Wertheimer (1880–1943) German psychologist who founded Gestalt psychology in the early 1900s, immigrated to the United States in 1933, studied the optical illusion of apparent movement, and described principles of perception. (p. 116)

Concept Review Answers

3.1   page 103

1. transduction
2. retina
3. bipolar; ganglion; optic chiasm; visual cortex
4. trichromatic
5. blue; opponent-process

3.2   page 113

1. basilar; cochlea
2. frequency
3. olfactory bulb
4. conduction deafness
5. substance P
6. kinesthetic

3.3   page 122

1. *Relative size.* The cars, people, street posts, and banners at the bottom of the photo seem closer because they are larger than those toward the top of the photo.
2. *Overlap.* Many objects in the photograph are partially obscured by other objects—such as the signs, people, and vehicles. In each case, the object that is not obscured is perceived as being closer.
3. *Aerial perspective.* The buildings in the upper middle of the photograph are fuzzy and slightly blurred, and thus are perceived as being farther away.
4. *Texture gradient.* Details of the sidewalk, street, and cars are crisp in the foreground but become progressively more blurred as you move toward the top of the photograph.
5. *Linear perspective.* The parallel boundaries of the street, the lines of yellow and orange banners, and the lines of parked cars seem to converge at the top of the photo, creating a sense of greater distance.

3.4   page 129

1. figure; ground
2. size constancy; shape constancy
3. proximity
4. similarity
5. perceptual set

Web Companion   Review Activities

You can find additional review activities at **www.worthpublishers.com/hockenbury**
The Psychology 3e Web Companion has a self-scoring practice quiz, flashcards, two interactive crossword puzzles, and other activities to help you master the material in this chapter.

Shaded Lives

Consciousness and Its Variations

Prologue

A Scream in the Night

Our friends Mike and Nina had only been married for four months, but they already had their nighttime routine down. Both of them needed to get up early in the morning—Nina worked the 7 A.M. to 3 P.M. shift as a neurology nurse, and Mike had to open the gift shop he managed at a large downtown hotel by 7:30 A.M. A confirmed night person, Nina had worked the 3-to-11 shift ever since she became a registered nurse. She had recently switched to the day shift so her schedule would mesh better with Mike's schedule. But even after a couple of weeks, she was still having difficulty adjusting to the early morning schedule. "My brain feels foggy until about noon," she complained to Mike.

One night, Nina and Mike crawled into bed, both exhausted. As they drifted off to sleep, Mike kept thinking about his job. His new boss had hinted that he really didn't like the way Mike was running the store. Mike closed his eyes and waited for his thoughts to slow down. As he relaxed, he thought about the shipment of greeting cards that was supposed to arrive early the next morning and imagined himself sorting through boxes at work. Just as he felt himself gently drifting off . . . "Ouch! Nina, stop kicking me!" he cried.

"I was sound asleep," Nina replied sleepily. "How could I have kicked you? You're imagining things, Michael. Just go to sleep."

Mike closed his eyes. A few moments later, he felt Nina's leg twitching and jerking against his, her breathing rhythmical as she snored lightly. He sighed and rolled over.

A few hours later, Mike was having a vivid dream about his new boss. His boss was standing at the top of a giant staircase, and Mike was at the bottom looking up. The dream scene switched quickly. Now Mike was at the top of a very tall escalator that wound around downward in a tight spiral in empty space, the escalator steps moving faster and faster. Terrified, he grabbed the edge of the escalator and held on, falling away, then struggling to swim back through midair. Suddenly, a blood-curdling scream cut through his dream.

Heart pounding, Mike jolted awake. *Am I dreaming?*

In the darkness, Nina screamed again.

Oh my God, there's someone in the apartment!

Mike leaped out of bed and fumbled for the baseball bat he kept underneath the bed. Shaking, he switched on the light. Nina was sitting up in bed, her eyes wide open, hands clasping her throat. Staring straight ahead, she screamed a third time, kicking at the blankets.

"Nina! What's wrong?!" Mike quickly scanned the bedroom. He ran out into the living room and turned on the lights. The front door was still securely locked and bolted from the inside. Baseball bat in hand, he ran into the kitchen. The back door was locked, the chain latch undisturbed. Completely baffled, he took a deep breath and walked back to the bedroom. "Nina, why did you scream?"

Nina didn't answer. She was slumped back down in bed, her eyes closed, sound asleep. She was the picture of blissful slumber. His heart still pounding, Mike stood in the doorway for another minute or so, watching Nina sleep. Nina sighed deeply and rolled over, snuggling toward Mike's side of the bed.

Finally, Mike shut off the lights and climbed into bed, his mind racing as he mentally replayed the incident. Now, every creak of the floor and rattle of the windows seemed to signal an intruder or some other danger. He glanced at the clock—12:47 A.M. Another 15 minutes passed before he got out of bed and padded into the kitchen. Reaching into the freezer for some ice cubes, he fixed himself a vodka and tonic. Toby, the cat, rounded the corner and joined him in the kitchen. As Toby rubbed up against his leg, Mike lit a cigarette and stared out the kitchen window into the darkness. *Why did Nina scream?*

In this chapter, we'll answer that question and tell you more about Nina's history of sleep disturbances. As you'll learn, this was not the first time—nor the last—that Nina screamed in her sleep for no apparent reason.

Sleep and dreaming are among the topics that we'll cover in this chapter as we look at consciousness and how it changes over the course of each day. Psychologists have learned a great deal about the daily fluctuations of consciousness as well as about the different ways that alterations in consciousness can be induced, such as through the use of hypnosis, meditation, or psychoactive drugs.

Consciousness

Experiencing the "Private I"

Key Theme

■ Consciousness refers to your immediate awareness of internal and external stimuli.

Key Questions

■ What did William James mean by the phrase *stream of consciousness*?
■ How has research on consciousness evolved over the past century?

Your immediate awareness of thoughts, sensations, memories, and the world around you represents the experience of **consciousness** (Hobson, 1999). That the experience of consciousness can vary enormously from moment to moment is easy to illustrate. Imagine that we could videotape three one-minute segments of your conscious activities at different times while your psychology instructor lectures in class. What might those three one-minute segments of consciousness reveal? Here are just a few of the possibilities:

■ Focused concentration on your instructor's words and gestures

■ Drifting from one fleeting thought, memory, or image to another

■ Awareness of physical sensations, such as the beginnings of a headache or the sharp sting of a paper cut

consciousness
Personal awareness of mental activities, internal sensations, and the external environment.

- Replaying an emotionally charged conversation and thinking about what you wish you had said
- Active mental problem solving, as you try to think of a topic for your humanities term paper
- Sexual fantasies
- Mentally rehearsing what you'll say and how you'll act when you meet a friend later in the day
- Wishful, grandiose daydreams about the future

Most likely, the three video clips would reveal very different scenes, dialogues, and content as your consciousness changed from one minute to the next. Yet even though your conscious experience is constantly changing, you don't experience your personal consciousness as disjointed (Tononi & Edelman, 1998). Rather, the subjective experience of consciousness has a sense of continuity. One stream of conscious mental activity seems to blend into another, effortlessly and seamlessly.

This characteristic of consciousness led the influential American psychologist **William James** (1892) to describe consciousness as a "stream" or "river." Although always changing, consciousness is perceived as unified and unbroken, much like a stream. Despite the changing focus of our awareness, our experience of consciousness as unbroken helps provide us with a sense of personal identity that has continuity from one day to the next.

The nature of human consciousness was one of the first topics to be tackled by the fledgling science of psychology in the late 1800s (Schneider, 1993). In Chapter 1, we discussed how the first psychologists tried to determine the nature of the human mind through *introspection*—verbal self-reports that tried to capture the "structure" of conscious experiences. But because such self-reports were not objectively verifiable, many of the leading psychologists at the turn of the twentieth century rejected the study of consciousness. Instead, they emphasized the scientific study of *overt behavior*, which could be directly observed, measured, and verified.

Beginning in the late 1950s, many psychologists once again turned their attention to the study of consciousness (Hilgard, 1992; Schacter, 1995a). This shift occurred for two main reasons. First, it was becoming clear that a complete understanding of behavior would *not* be possible unless psychologists considered the role of conscious mental processes in behavior.

Second, although the experience of consciousness is personal and subjective, psychologists had devised more objective ways to study conscious experiences. For example, psychologists could often *infer* the conscious experience that seemed to be occurring by carefully observing behavior. Technological advances in studying brain activity were also producing intriguing correlations between brain activity and different states of consciousness (Damasio, 1999a).

Today, the scientific study of consciousness is incredibly diverse. Working from a variety of perspectives, psychologists and other neuroscientists are piecing together a picture of consciousness that takes into account the role of psychological, physiological, social, and cultural influences (Farber & Churchland, 1995; Horgan, 1994; Thompson, 1997).

Consciousness, then, does not appear to itself chopped up in bits. . . . It is nothing jointed; it flows. A "river" or a "stream" are the metaphors by which it is most naturally described. In talking of it hereafter, let us call it the stream of thought, or consciousness, of subjective life.

William James (1892)

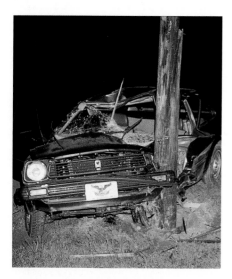

Circadian Rhythms, Mental Alertness, and Traffic Accidents We experience two dips in mental alertness each day, at about 3:00 P.M. and 3:00 A.M. It's not surprising, then, that traffic accidents are more likely when mental alertness is low. When more than 6,000 fatigue-related traffic accidents were analyzed, it was found that the highest number of accidents occurred at 3:00 A.M. During the daytime, traffic accidents peaked at around 3:00 P.M. (Mitler, 1994).

Biological and Environmental "Clocks" That Regulate Consciousness

Key Theme
- Many body functions, including mental alertness, are regulated by circadian rhythms, which systematically vary over a 24-hour period.

Key Questions
- How do sunlight, the suprachiasmatic nucleus, and melatonin regulate the sleep–wake cycle?
- How do free-running conditions affect circadian rhythms?
- What is jet lag, and how is it produced?

Throughout the course of the day, there is a natural ebb and flow to consciousness. The most obvious variation of consciousness that we experience is the daily sleep–wake cycle. But conscious states also change in more subtle ways.

For example, you've probably noticed that your mental alertness varies throughout the day in a relatively consistent way. Most people experience two distinct peaks of mental alertness: one in the morning, usually around 9:00 or 10:00 A.M., and one in the evening, around 8:00 or 9:00 P.M. In between these two peaks, you'll probably experience a slump in mental alertness at about 3:00 P.M. And, should you manage to stay awake, your mental alertness will probably reach its lowest point at about 3:00 A.M. One practical implication of this consistent daily pattern is the increase in the number of traffic accidents at the times when mental alertness is at its lowest points.

Mental alertness and the sleep–wake cycle are just two examples of the daily highs and lows you experience in a wide variety of bodily processes. These daily cycles are called **circadian rhythms.** The word *circadian* combines the Latin words for "about" and "day." So, the term *circadian rhythms* refers to biological processes that systematically vary over a period of about 24 hours.

You actually experience many different circadian rhythms that ebb and flow over the course of any given 24-hour period (see Table 4.1). Researchers have discovered over 100 bodily processes that rhythmically peak and dip each day, includ-

circadian rhythm
(ser-KADE-ee-en) A cycle or rhythm that is roughly 24 hours long; the cyclical daily fluctuations in biological and psychological processes.

suprachiasmatic nucleus (SCN)
(soup-rah-*kye*-az-MAT-ick) A cluster of neurons in the hypothalamus in the brain that governs the timing of circadian rhythms.

melatonin
(mel-ah-TONE-in) A hormone manufactured by the pineal gland that produces sleepiness.

Table **4.1**

Examples of Human Circadian Rhythms

Function	Typical Circadian Rhythm
Peak mental alertness and memory functions	Two daily peaks: around 9:00 A.M. and 9:00 P.M.
Lowest body temperature	About 97°F around 4:00 A.M.
Highest body temperature	About 99°F around 4:00 P.M.
Peak physical strength	Two daily peaks: around 11:00 A.M. and 7:00 P.M.
Peak hearing, visual, taste, and smell sensitivity	Two daily peaks: around 3:00 A.M. and 6:00 P.M.
Lowest sensitivity to pain	Around 4:00 P.M.
Peak sensitivity to pain	Around 4:00 A.M.
Peak degree of sleepiness	Two daily peaks: around 3:00 A.M. and 3:00 P.M.
Peak melatonin hormone in blood	Between 1:00 A.M. and 3:00 A.M.
Peak allergic sensitivity to pollen and dust	Between 11:00 P.M. and 1:00 A.M.

SOURCES: Campbell (1997); Czeisler & Dijk (2001); Refinetti (2000);, M. Young (2000).

ing blood pressure, the secretion of different hormones, and pain sensitivity. Normally, your circadian rhythms are closely synchronized with one another. For example, the circadian rhythm for the release of growth hormone is synchronized with the sleep–wake circadian rhythm so that growth hormone is released only during sleep.

The Suprachiasmatic Nucleus

The Body's Clock

Your many circadian rhythms are controlled by a master biological clock—a tiny cluster of neurons in the *hypothalamus* in the brain. As shown in Figure 4.1, this cluster of neurons is called the **suprachiasmatic nucleus,** abbreviated **SCN.** The SCN is the internal pacemaker that governs the timing of circadian rhythms, including the sleep–wake cycle and the mental alertness cycle (Weaver, 1998).

Keeping the circadian rhythms synchronized to one another and on a 24-hour schedule also involves environmental time cues. The most important of these cues is bright light, especially sunlight. In people, light detected by special photoreceptors in the eye is communicated via the visual system to the SCN in the hypothalamus (Brainard & others, 2001a, 2001b). However, an intriguing study by psychologists Scott Campbell and Patricia Murphy (1998) tentatively suggests that we may also have photoreceptors in the skin (see the nearby photograph).

How does sunlight help regulate the sleep–wake cycle and other circadian rhythms? As the sun sets each day, the decrease in available light is detected by the SCN through its connections with the visual system. In turn, the SCN triggers an increase in the production of a hormone called **melatonin.** Melatonin is manufactured by the *pineal gland,* an endocrine gland located in the brain (Turek & Czeisler, 1999).

Increased blood levels of melatonin make you sleepy and reduce activity levels. At night, blood levels of melatonin rise, peaking between 1:00 and 3:00 A.M. Shortly before sunrise, the pineal gland all but stops producing melatonin, and you soon wake up. As the sun rises, exposure to sunlight and other bright light suppresses melatonin levels, and they remain very low throughout the day. In this way, sunlight *entrains,* or sets, the SCN so that it keeps circadian cycles synchronized and operating on a 24-hour schedule (Czeisler & Wright, 1999; Lavie, 2001).

Photoreceptors in the Skin? Psychologists Scott Campbell and Patricia Murphy (1998) discovered that light applied to the skin at the back of the knees could reset the body's clock for melatonin and body temperature. A pad equipped with more than 2000 fiber-optic cables was wrapped around the knee, as shown in the photograph above, and worn for up to three hours. Bright light applied in this way was just as effective as light detected by the eyes in resetting melatonin and body temperature levels.

Pineal gland
Melatonin
First thing in the morning

Shortly after light exposure

Later in the day

Pineal gland
Suprachiasmatic nucleus
Optic nerve

FIGURE 4.1 The Biological Clock Special photoreceptors in the retina regulate the effects of light on the body's circadian rhythms (Brainard & others, 2001a). In response to morning light, signals from these special photoreceptors are relayed via the optic nerve to the suprachiasmatic nucleus. In turn, the suprachiasmatic nucleus causes the pineal gland to reduce the production of melatonin, a hormone that causes sleepiness. As blood levels of melatonin decrease, mental alertness increases. Daily exposure to bright light, especially sunlight, helps keep the body's circadian rhythms synchronized and operating on a 24-hour schedule.

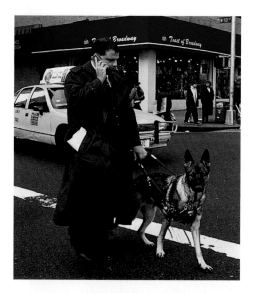

Circadian Rhythms and the Blind Many blind people have free-running circadian cycles because they are unable to detect the light that normally sets the SCN. Like people deprived of environmental time cues, blind people can experience free-running melatonin, body temperature, and sleep–wake circadian cycles (Czeisler & others, 1995; Klerman & others, 1998). Consequently, many blind people suffer from recurring bouts of insomnia and other sleep problems (Leger & others, 1999; Sack & others, 1992).

Jet Lag and the Direction of Travel Most people find it easier to adjust to the time changes when flying westward than eastward. Why? Flying westward adds hours to a traveler's day, which corresponds with the natural tendency of your internal body clock to drift toward longer days. As a general rule, it takes considerably longer to resynchronize your circadian rhythms to a new time zone when you fly eastward, which shortens your day.

Life Without a Sundial
Free-Running Circadian Rhythms

Given that sunlight is responsible for setting your internal clock, what would happen to the timing of your circadian rhythms if they were allowed to "run free" in the absence of environmental time cues like sunlight and clocks? To create *free-running conditions,* researchers typically use underground isolation units. In some studies, they have even constructed rooms in caves. Volunteers live in these underground bunkers for weeks or months at a time, deprived of all environmental time cues (Webb, 1994).

Under free-running conditions, two distinct effects occur (Kronauer, 1994; Lewy & Sack, 1987). First, in the absence of normal light, darkness, and other time cues, people tend to drift to the natural rhythm of the suprachiasmatic nucleus—roughly a 25-hour day, not a 24-hour day. Thus, people in a free-running condition go to sleep about an hour later each day. Exactly why the human sleep–wake cycle gravitates toward a 25-hour cycle—and under what conditions—is an issue that continues to be actively researched and debated (S. Campbell, 2000; Czeisler & others, 2000; Wright & others, 2001).

Second, under free-running conditions, circadian rhythms lose their normal synchronization with one another (Aschoff, 1993, 1994). All circadian rhythms become longer, but to different degrees. For example, normally the sleep–wake cycle, body temperature, and the melatonin cycle are closely coordinated. At about 3:00 A.M., your body temperature dips to its lowest point, just as melatonin is reaching its highest level and you are at your sleepiest. But in the absence of environmental cues, the sleep–wake, body temperature, and melatonin–circadian rhythms become desynchronized, so that they are no longer properly coordinated with one another.

What happens when people leave the free-running condition and are once again exposed to normal daylight and darkness cues? Within days, sunlight resets the biological clock. Circadian rhythms become synchronized again and resume operating on a 24-hour rather than a 25-hour cycle (Lewy & Sack, 1987).

Circadian Rhythms and Sunlight
Some Practical Implications

The close tie between your internal biological clock and environmental time cues has some very important practical applications. For example, imagine that you leave Denver at 2:00 P.M. on a 10-hour flight to London. When you arrive in London, it's 7:00 A.M. and the sun is shining. However, your body is still on Denver time. As far as your internal biological clock is concerned, it's midnight.

The result? Your circadian rhythms are drastically out of synchronization with daylight and darkness cues. The psychological and physiological effects of this disruption in circadian rhythms can be severe. Thinking, concentration, and memory get fuzzy. You experience physical and mental fatigue, depression or irritability, and disrupted sleep (Zammit, 1997). Collectively, these symptoms are called *jet lag.*

Although numerous physiological variables are involved in jet lag, the circadian cycle of the hormone melatonin plays a key role. When it's 10:00 A.M. in London, it's 3:00 A.M. in Denver. Since your body is still operating on Denver time, your melatonin production is peaking. Rather than feeling awake, you feel very sleepy, sluggish, and groggy. For many people, it can take a week or longer to adjust to such an extreme time change (Moore-Ede, 1993).

You don't need to travel across multiple time zones to experience symptoms of jet lag. People who work night shifts or rotating shifts often suffer from jet lag symptoms because their circadian rhythms are out of sync with daylight and darkness time cues (Monk, 1997). Like Nina in the Prologue, nurses, doctors, and other medical personnel often have to work night shifts or rotating shifts. So do people working in law enforcement

SCIENCE VERSUS PSEUDOSCIENCE 4.1

Biorhythms Versus Circadian Rhythms

Biorhythms is a pseudoscience based on the unproven notion that from birth onward, three rigidly fixed "natural biorhythms" reflect high, low, and critical periods of a person's physical, emotional, and intellectual functioning. The timing of these biorhythms is presumably determined by your date of birth. Physical functioning supposedly follows a 23-day cycle; emotional, a 28-day cycle; and intellectual, a 33-day cycle (Crawley, 1996).

As in other pseudosciences, biorhythms practitioners use scientific-looking charts, like the one shown here, to plot an individual's three cycles. If a particular cycle is above the horizontal midline on a given day, it's a good day to engage in behaviors related to that particular cycle; below the midline is a bad indicator. "Critical days" supposedly occur when a cycle crosses the midpoint (Lester, 1990).

To underscore the seriousness of critical days, biorhythms proponents cite examples of airplane crashes, athletic losses, deaths of famous people, space-travel mishaps, industrial accidents, and so forth (Hines, 1996). Along with causing disasters, biorhythm cycles also purportedly influence mental health, marital compatibility, the day on which a woman gives birth, and the sex of her newborn!

Although "biorhythms" and "biological rhythms" *sound* very similar, they have about as much in common as mold and gold. The legitimate scientific study of *biological rhythms* examines the consistent but potentially varying cycles of living organisms over time, including plants, animals, insects, and humans. Circadian rhythms are an example of scientifically verified biological rhythms. These rhythms tend to be consistent but are not rigidly fixed like the supposed 23-, 28-, and 33-day cycles of biorhythms. To avoid confusion between the science and the pseudoscience, many scientists use the term *chronobiology* to refer to the scientific study of biological rhythms over time.

Scientific investigations of biorhythms are certainly not in short supply. Psychologist Terence M. Hines (1998) published a comprehensive review of 134 studies examining the validity of biorhythm theory. These studies evaluated the effects of biorhythms on such variables as:

- Automobile, aircraft, and industrial accidents
- Sports, academic, and intelligence-test performance
- Day of birth, death, or suicide
- Sex of newborns

Ninety-nine studies arrived at the same conclusion: *No* relationship exists between a person's biorhythms and any of these events. So what about the 35 studies that found support for biorhythm theory? In examining each of these studies, Hines (1998) found that the scientific or statistical methods used were flawed. According to Hines (1998), "This often led to serious errors that caused several authors to think that they had found evidence for biorhythm theory when, in fact, they had not."

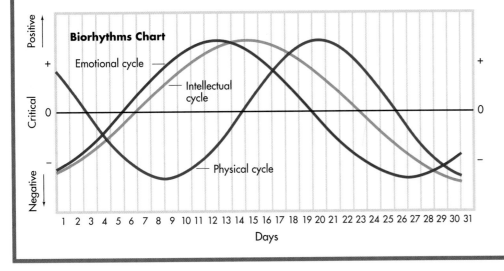

A Sample Biorhythms Chart The blue line represents the 23-day physical cycle, the purple line represents the 28-day emotional cycle, and the red line represents the 33-day intellectual cycle. Performance is presumably better than average on positive days and worse than average on negative days. Performance is supposed to be particularly poor on "critical days," when the cycle crosses the midline. Biorhythms proponents predict that accidents and other mishaps are especially likely on critical days. Are such predictions accurate?

and the military, broadcasting and weather services, and other businesses that operate around the clock.

For night workers, the problem of being out of sync with the environmental clock is compounded every morning when they return home in the bright morning light. Exposure to bright morning light is a potent stimulus that can reset the body clock to a day schedule (Shanahan & Czeisler, 1991). Even traces of sunlight through curtains can prevent a person's body clock from staying in sync with the night work schedule. Because sunlight time cues exert such a powerful influence on circadian rhythms, many night-shift workers never fully adjust to a nighttime work schedule.

Although there are several practical implications of the research on circadian rhythms, we should point out that circadian rhythms have *no* connection to biorhythms, a pseudoscience discussed in Science Versus Pseudoscience Box 4.1.

electroencephalograph
(e-lec-tro-en-SEFF-uh-low-graph) An instrument that uses electrodes placed on the scalp to measure and record the brain's electrical activity.

EEG (electroencephalogram)
The graphic record of brain activity produced by an electroencephalograph.

REM sleep
Type of sleep during which rapid eye movements and dreaming usually occur and voluntary muscle activity is suppressed; also called *active sleep* or *paradoxical sleep.*

NREM sleep
Quiet, typically dreamless sleep in which rapid eye movements are absent; divided into four stages; also called *quiet sleep.*

beta brain waves
Brain-wave pattern associated with alert wakefulness.

alpha brain waves
Brain-wave pattern associated with relaxed wakefulness and drowsiness.

hypnagogic hallucinations
(hip-na-GAH-jick) Vivid sensory phenomena that occur during the onset of sleep.

Monitoring Sleep Using electrodes that are attached harmlessly to the face and scalp, the electroencephalograph records the brain's electrical activity throughout the night. Although the equipment may look cumbersome and uncomfortable, people generally sleep just fine with all the wires attached.

Sleep

Key Theme
- Modern sleep research began with the invention of the EEG and the discovery that sleep was a state marked by distinct physiological processes and stages.

Key Questions
- What are REM sleep and NREM sleep?
- What characterizes sleep onset, each of the NREM sleep stages, and REM sleep?
- What is the typical progression of sleep cycles, and how do sleep patterns change over the lifespan?

Birds do it. Giraffes do it. Cats do it a lot, mostly during the day. Dolphins do it, too, but only one brain hemisphere at a time. And, of course, you do it and we do it, but not as much as we'd like to. Sleep, that is. In fact, if you live a long life, you'll spend approximately 22 years of your life sleeping.

From Aristotle to Shakespeare to Freud, history is filled with examples of scholars, writers, and scientists who have been fascinated by sleep and dreams. But prior to the twentieth century, there was no objective way to study the internal processes that might be occurring during sleep. Instead, sleep was largely viewed as a period of restful inactivity in which dreams sometimes occurred.

The Dawn of Modern Sleep Research

The invention of the **electroencephalograph** by German psychiatrist Hans Berger in the 1920s gave sleep researchers an important tool for measuring the rhythmic electrical activity of the brain (Stern, 2001). These rhythmical patterns of electrical activity are referred to as *brain waves.* The electroencephalograph produces a graphic record called an **EEG,** or *electroencephalogram.* By studying EEGs, sleep researchers have firmly established that brain-wave activity systematically changes throughout sleep.

Along with brain activity, today's sleep researchers monitor a variety of other physical functions during sleep. Eye movements, muscle movements, breathing rate, airflow, pulse, blood pressure, amount of exhaled carbon dioxide, body temperature, and breathing sounds are just some of the body's functions that are measured in contemporary sleep research (Ancoli-Israel, 1997; Cooper & Bradbury, 1994).

The next milestone in sleep research occurred in the early 1950s. Eugene Aserinsky, a graduate student at the University of Chicago, was working in the laboratory of renowned sleep researcher Nathaniel Kleitman. Using his eight-year-old son as a subject, Aserinsky discovered that particular EEG patterns during sleep were often associated with rapid movements of the sleeper's eyes (Alvarez, 1995). Moreover, these periods of rapid eye movement were highly correlated with the subject's reports of dreaming. In 1953, Aserinsky and Kleitman published their findings, heralding the discovery of *rapid-eye-movement sleep,* usually abbreviated *REM sleep.*

Today, sleep researchers distinguish between two basic types of sleep. **REM sleep** is often called *active sleep* or *paradoxical sleep* because it is associated with heightened body and brain activity during which dreaming consistently occurs. **NREM sleep,** or *non-rapid-eye-movement sleep,* is often referred to as *quiet sleep* because the body's physiological functions and brain activity slow down during this period of slumber. NREM sleep is further divided into four stages, as we'll describe shortly.

The Onset of Sleep and Hypnagogic Hallucinations

Awake and reasonably alert as you prepare for bed, your brain generates small, fast brain waves, called **beta brain waves.** After your head hits the pillow and you close your eyes, your muscles relax. Your brain's electrical activity gradually gears down, generating slightly larger and slower **alpha brain waves.** As drowsiness sets in, your thoughts may wander and become less logical.

Garfield

During this drowsy, presleep phase, you may experience odd but vividly realistic sensations. You may hear your name called or a loud crash, feel as if you're falling or floating, smell something burning, or see kaleidoscopic patterns or an unfolding landscape. These vivid sensory phenomena that occasionally occur during the transition from wakefulness to light sleep are called **hypnagogic hallucinations** (Mavromatis, 1987). Some hypnagogic hallucinations can be so vivid or startling that they cause a sudden awakening.

Probably the most common hypnagogic hallucination is the vivid sensation of falling. The sensation of falling is often accompanied by a *myoclonic jerk*—an involuntary muscle spasm of the whole body that jolts the person completely awake (Cooper, 1994). Also known as *sleep starts,* these experiences can seem really weird (or embarrassing) when they occur. But, you can rest assured, they are not abnormal. Almost all of our students have reported occasionally experiencing the hypnagogic hallucination of falling combined with a myoclonic jerk.

The First 90 Minutes of Sleep and Beyond

The course of a normal night's sleep follows a relatively consistent cyclical pattern. As you drift off to sleep, you enter NREM sleep and begin a progression through the four NREM sleep stages (see Figure 4.2). Each progressive NREM sleep stage is characterized by corresponding decreases in brain and body activity. On average, the progression through the first four stages of NREM sleep occupies the first 50 to 70 minutes of sleep (Cooper, 1994).

FIGURE 4.2 The First 90 Minutes of Sleep From wakefulness to the deepest sleep of stage 4 NREM, the brain's activity, measured by EEG recordings, progressively diminishes, as demonstrated by larger and slower brain waves. The four NREM stages occupy the first 50 to 70 minutes of sleep. Then, in a matter of minutes, the brain cycles back to smaller, faster brain waves, and the sleeper experiences the night's first episode of dreaming REM sleep, which lasts 5 to 15 minutes. During the rest of the night, the sleeper continues to experience 90-minute cycles of alternating NREM and REM sleep.

SOURCE: Based on Hobson (1995).

sleep spindles

Short bursts of brain activity that characterize stage 2 NREM sleep.

K complex

Single but large high-voltage spike of brain activity that characterizes stage 2 NREM sleep.

Stage 1 NREM

As the alpha brain waves of drowsiness are replaced by even slower *theta brain waves,* you enter the first stage of sleep. Lasting only a few minutes, stage 1 is a transitional stage during which you gradually disengage from the sensations of the surrounding world. Familiar sounds, such as the hum of the refrigerator or the sound of traffic, gradually fade from conscious awareness. During stage 1 NREM, you can quickly regain conscious alertness if the phone rings or your three-year-old wanders into your bedroom to ask if Big Bird likes Fruit Loops.

Although hypnagogic experiences can also occur in stage 1, less vivid mental imagery is common, such as imagining yourself engaged in some everyday activity, such as Mike imagined himself unpacking boxes at work. Although dreamlike, these images lack the unfolding, sometimes bizarre details of a true dream.

Stage 2 NREM

Stage 2 represents the onset of true sleep. Stage 2 sleep is defined by the appearance of **sleep spindles,** brief bursts of brain activity that last a second or two, and **K complexes,** single but large high-voltage spikes of brain activity that periodically occur (see Figure 4.2). Other than these occasional sleep spindles, brain activity continues to slow down considerably. Breathing becomes rhythmical. Slight muscle twitches may occur. Theta waves are predominant in stage 2, but large, slow brain waves, called *delta brain waves,* also begin to emerge. During the 15 to 20 minutes initially spent in stage 2, delta brain-wave-activity gradually increases.

Stage 3 and Stage 4 NREM

Stages 3 and 4 of NREM are physiologically very similar. Both stages are defined by the amount of delta-brain-wave activity. In combination, stages 3 and 4 are sometimes referred to as *slow-wave sleep.* When delta brain waves represent more than 20 percent of total brain activity, the sleeper is said to be in stage 3 NREM. When delta brain waves exceed 50 percent of total brain activity, the sleeper is said to be in stage 4 NREM (Cooper, 1994).

During the 20 to 40 minutes spent in the night's first episode of stage 4 NREM, delta waves eventually come to represent 100 percent of brain activity. At that point, heart rate, blood pressure, and breathing rate drop to their lowest levels. Not surprisingly, the sleeper in stage 4 NREM is virtually oblivious to the world. Noises as loud as 90 decibels may fail to wake him (Empson, 1993). However, his muscles are still capable of movement. For example, if sleepwalking occurs, it typically happens during stage 4 NREM sleep (see In Focus Box 4.2).

It can easily take 15 minutes or longer to regain full waking consciousness from stage 4. It's even possible to answer a ringing phone, carry on a conversation for several minutes, and hang up without ever leaving stage 4 sleep—and without remembering the conversation the next day. When people are briefly awakened by

Synchronized Sleepers As these time-lapse photographs show, couples who regularly sleep in the same bed tend to have synchronized sleep cycles. Since bed partners fall asleep at about the same time, they are likely to have similarly timed NREM–REM sleep cycles. The movements of this couple are also synchronized. Both sleepers shift position just before and after episodes of REM sleep.

What You Really Want to Know About Sleep

How do "morning larks" and "night owls" differ?

Compared with people who are morning larks, the circadian rhythms of people who are night owls are delayed. Morning people reach peak mental alertness during the morning hours, while evening people reach peak mental alertness in the late afternoon. Age differences also exist. Adolescents and young adults tend to be evening types. Middle-aged and older adults tend to be morning types. Work schedules seem to play a key role in the gravitation toward morningness as people get older.

Why do I yawn? Is yawning contagious?

Research has contradicted the popular notion that too little oxygen or too much carbon dioxide causes yawning. Rather, yawning regulates and increases your level of arousal. Yawning is typically followed by an *increase* in activity level. Hence, you frequently yawn after waking up in the morning or while attempting to stay awake in the late evening. When dealing with repetitive, uninteresting stimuli, yawning is one way your body maintains mental and physical arousal.

If you think or read about yawning, it can trigger the behavior. (Have you yawned yet?) However, the idea that watching other people yawn causes yawning has little research support. For example, students in a lecture class often yawn, but the instructor doesn't, despite seeing the students yawning.

Why do I get sleepy?

Most people erroneously believe that boredom makes people sleepy, even if they have had enough sleep. Contrary to this popular belief, boredom does *not* make you sleepy. Rather, boredom unmasks underlying sleepiness.

Research suggests that a naturally occurring compound in the body called *adenosine* may be the culprit. In studies with cats, prolonged wakefulness results in a sharp increase in adenosine levels, which reflect energy used for brain and body activity. As adenosine levels shoot up, so does the need for sleep. Slow-wave NREM sleep reduces adenosine levels. In humans, the common stimulant drug caffeine blocks adenosine receptors, promoting wakefulness.

Sometimes in the morning when I first wake up, I can't move. I'm literally paralyzed! Is this normal?

REM sleep is characterized by paralysis of the voluntary muscles, which keeps you from acting out your dreams. In a relatively common phenomenon called *sleep paralysis,* the paralysis of REM sleep carries over to the waking state for up to 10 minutes. If preceded by an unpleasant dream or hypnagogic experience, this sensation can be frightening. Sleep paralysis can also occur as you're falling asleep. In either case, the sleep paralysis lasts for only a few minutes. So, if this happens to you, relax—voluntary muscle control will soon return.

If I tape-record my chemistry class notes and play them while I sleep, can I learn the material without studying?

Not a chance. Although some perceptual processing can occur during sleep, the ability to learn and recall information requires wakefulness.

Do deaf people who use sign language sometimes "sleep sign" during sleep?

Yes.

Do the things people say when they talk in their sleep make any sense?

Sleeptalking typically occurs during NREM stages 3 and 4. There are many anecdotes of spouses who have supposedly engaged their sleeptalking mates in extended conversations, but sleep researchers have been unsuccessful in having extended dialogues with people who chronically talk in their sleep. As far as the truthfulness of the sleeptalker's utterances go, they're reasonably accurate insofar as they reflect whatever the person is responding to while asleep. By the way, not only do people talk in their sleep, but they can also sing in their sleep. In one case we know of, a little boy sleepsang "Frosty the Snowman."

Is it dangerous to wake a sleepwalker?

It's not dangerous to wake a sleepwalker, it's just difficult, because sleepwalkers are in deep sleep. However, as sleepwalkers usually respond to verbal suggestions, it's relatively easy to guide them back to bed.

Sleepwalking may be genetically determined. Identical twins are much more likely to share this characteristic than are nontwin siblings. One college student confided to sleep researcher Jacob Empson (1993) that her whole family sleepwalked. She reported that on one occasion, her entire family woke up in the early-morning hours seated around the kitchen table, where they had all gathered in their sleep!

SOURCES: Arkin (1981); Baenninger (1997); Empson (1993); National Sleep Foundation (2002); Ozbayrak & Berlin (1995); Porkka-Heiskanen & others (1997); Portas & others (1997); Rothenberg (1997); Spanos & others (1995a); Tankova & others (1994).

---

sleep researchers during stage 4 NREM and asked to perform some simple task, they often don't remember it the next morning (Dinges, 1990; Goodenough, 1991).

Thus far in our description, the sleeper is approximately 70 minutes into a typical night's sleep and immersed in deeply relaxed stage 4 NREM sleep. At this point, the sequence reverses. In a matter of minutes, the sleeper cycles back from stage 4 to stage 3 to stage 2 and enters a dramatic new phase: the night's first episode of REM sleep.

FIGURE 4.3 The 90-Minute Cycles of Sleep During a typical night, you experience five 90-minute cycles of alternating NREM and REM sleep. The deepest stages of NREM sleep, stages 3 and 4, occur during the first two 90-minute cycles. Dreaming REM sleep episodes become progressively longer as the night goes on. Sleep position shifts, indicated by the dots, usually occur immediately before and after REM episodes.

SOURCE: Based on Hobson (1995).

REM Sleep

During REM sleep, the brain becomes more active, generating smaller and faster brain waves. Visual and motor neurons in the brain fire repeatedly, just as they do during wakefulness. Dreams usually occur during REM sleep. Although the brain is very active, voluntary muscle activity is suppressed, which prevents the dreaming sleeper from acting out those dreams (Hirshkowitz & others, 1997).

REM sleep is accompanied by considerable physiological arousal. The sleeper's eyes dart back and forth behind closed eyelids—the rapid eye movements. Heart rate, blood pressure, and respirations can fluctuate up and down, sometimes extremely. Muscle twitches occur. In both sexes, sexual arousal may occur, which is not necessarily related to dream content.

This first REM episode tends to be brief, about 5 to 15 minutes. From the beginning of stage 1 NREM sleep through the completion of the first episode of REM sleep, about 90 minutes have elapsed.

Beyond the First 90 Minutes

Throughout the rest of the night, the sleeper cycles between NREM and REM sleep. Each cycle lasts about 90 minutes on average, but the duration of cycles may vary from 70 to 120 minutes. Usually, four more 90-minute cycles of NREM and REM sleep occur during the night. Just before and after REM periods, the sleeper typically shifts position (Hobson, 1995).

The progression of a typical night's sleep cycles is depicted in Figure 4.3. Stages 3 and 4 NREM, slow-wave sleep usually occur only during the first two 90-minute cycles. As the night progresses, REM sleep episodes become increasingly longer and less time is spent in NREM. During the last two 90-minute sleep cycles before awakening, NREM sleep is composed primarily of stage 2 sleep and periods of REM sleep can last as long as 40 minutes. In a later section, we'll look at dreaming and REM sleep in more detail.

Changes in Sleep Patterns over the Lifespan

Over the course of our lives, the quantity and quality of our sleep change considerably (see Figure 4.4). REM sleep begins long before birth, as scientists have discovered by using ultrasound to document fetal eye movements and by studying the sleep of premature infants. Four months before birth, REM sleep seems to constitute virtually all of fetal life. By one month before birth, the fetus demonstrates distinct sleep–wake cycles, spending around 12 hours each day in REM sleep (Mindell, 1997).

A newborn sleeps about 16 hours a day, about 50 percent of which is REM sleep. By the end of the first year of life, total sleep time drops to around 13 hours a day, about one-third of which is REM sleep.

In general, from birth onward, the average amount of time spent sleeping each day gradually decreases (see Figure 4.4). The amount of time devoted to REM sleep and slow-wave NREM sleep each night also gradually decreases over the

REM rebound
A phenomenon in which a person who is deprived of REM sleep greatly increases the amount of time spent in REM sleep at the first opportunity to sleep uninterrupted.

lifespan (Bliwise, 1997). Young children can easily spend two hours or more each night in the deep sleep of stages 3 and 4 NREM. By early adulthood, about an hour is spent in deep sleep each night. And by late adulthood, only about 20 minutes of a night's sleep is spent in stages 3 and 4 NREM sleep (Williams & others, 1994).

As the amount of deep sleep and REM sleep decreases throughout adulthood, more time is spent in lighter, stage 2 NREM sleep. Consequently, sleep becomes more fitful as people get older. Beginning in their forties, people wake up more frequently during the night and sleep may feel less satisfying. People tend to wake up feeling less rested and find it harder to regain alertness and get their brains in gear each morning (Williams & others, 1994). By the time people reach their sixties, total sleep time averages about six hours per night and the quality of sleep is much more shallow.

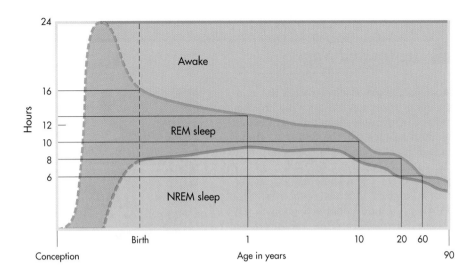

FIGURE 4.4 Changes in REM and NREM Sleep Both the quality and quantity of sleep change over the lifespan. Even before birth, the cycles of REM and NREM sleep are evident. A newborn infant sleeps about 16 hours per day, with about 50 percent of sleep time devoted to REM. From birth onward, total sleep time, REM sleep, and NREM sleep slowly decrease. Time spent in stages 3 and 4, the deepest stages of NREM, also decreases over the lifespan.

SOURCE: Based on Hobson (1995).

Why Do We Sleep?

Key Theme

▪ Sleep deprivation studies demonstrate that we have a biological need for sleep, but the functions of sleep are not completely understood.

Key Questions

▪ What are REM and NREM rebound, and what insights do they provide into the function of sleep?
▪ How do the restorative and adaptive theories of sleep explain the function of sleep?

That we have a biological need for sleep is clearly demonstrated by *sleep deprivation studies.* After as little as one night's sleep deprivation, research subjects develop *microsleeps,* which are episodes of sleep lasting only a few seconds that occur during wakefulness. People who go without sleep for a day or more also experience disruptions in mood, mental abilities, reaction time, perceptual skills, and complex motor skills (Gökcebay & others, 1994).

Getting *less* sleep than you need (as many adults do) can also have negative effects. In one study, young men whose sleep was restricted to four hours a night for as few as six consecutive nights experienced harmful changes in metabolic and endocrine functioning (Spiegel & others, 1999). As sleep researcher Eve Van Cauter (1999) explained, "After only one week of sleep restriction, young, healthy males had glucose levels that were no longer normal. That's a rapid deterioration of the body's functions."

Sleep researchers have also selectively deprived people of different components of normal sleep. For example, to study the effects of *REM deprivation,* researchers wake sleepers whenever the monitoring instruments indicate that they are entering REM sleep. After several nights of being selectively deprived of REM sleep, the subjects are allowed to sleep uninterrupted. What happens? The first time subjects are allowed to sleep without interruption, they experience **REM rebound**—the amount of time spent in REM sleep increases by as much as 50 percent (Ellman & others, 1991). Similarly, when people are selectively deprived of NREM stages 3 and 4, they experience *NREM rebound,* spending more time in NREM sleep.

The Beginnings of REM Sleep By using ultrasound to create images of the developing fetus in the uterus, researchers have documented the beginnings of REM sleep and rapid eye movements months before birth.

Siestas and Naps

Most people get sleepy around the middle of the afternoon. Eating a big lunch or getting inadequate sleep the night before is often blamed for the 3:00 P.M. slump in our mental alertness, but neither of these factors is the culprit. Instead, as we discussed earlier in the chapter, our circadian rhythm dictates reduced mental alertness around midafternoon each day (Moore-Ede, 1993). This midafternoon sleepiness seems to occur regardless of how much food we've consumed or how much sleep we've had the night before (Broughton, 1989; Lavie, 1989). In other words, the human brain seems to be programmed for an afternoon siesta (Campbell, 1997).

In some Latin American, Mediterranean, Middle Eastern, and Spanish cultures, as well as in Israel, society as a whole has adapted to this midafternoon slump in mental alertness. For about two hours in the afternoon, which is also the hottest part of the day in tropical climates, the traditional siesta occurs.

During the siesta period, shops, banks, government offices, and restaurants may close for a few hours. Evening events, such as the nighttime meal, tend to occur later than they do in nonsiesta cultures. It's common for people to eat their last meal of the day at about 10:00 P.M., go to bed very late, and get up early in the morning (Webb & Dinges, 1989). Businesses may be closed from 2:00 until 4:00 P.M., but they remain open during the evening

Power Nap, Anyone? Some U.S. companies have recognized the benefits of an afternoon siesta. Employees at an architectural firm in Kansas City are encouraged to take advantage of these "spent tents" to recharge their batteries in the middle of a workday. Each brightly colored tent is equipped with blankets, pillows, and an alarm clock.

hours. So, in some cities, it's impossible to buy a postage stamp at 3:00 P.M., but you can go to the bank at 11:00 P.M.!

Even siesta cultures are subject to change, however. In some developing countries, the incidence of afternoon naps

has declined as the countries have become more urban and more industrialized.

In most industrialized cultures, including American culture, afternoon naps are discouraged. The emphasis on productivity has created a 24-hour society, with people working around the clock (Moore-Ede, 1993). It's not surprising, then, that a high percentage of Americans report getting less sleep than they need. One survey found that more than a third of Americans reported that daytime sleepiness had interfered with their daily activities (National Sleep Foundation, 2002).

Even though a strategically timed nap might improve overall productivity, naps are simply not acceptable in most American workplaces. A few U.S. companies, mindful of the research showing that midafternoon naps improve mood, productivity, and alertness, have added napping facilities to their office suites (Mulrine, 1998). Many sleep researchers applaud this trend, noting that naps reduce fatigue and sleepiness (Gillberg & others, 1996).

A regular afternoon nap can also reduce the amount of sleep needed at night. And, contrary to popular belief, taking an afternoon's nap does not make it more difficult to fall asleep at night (Dinges, 1989). The tendency to take an afternoon nap is a normal, even beneficial, aspect of our daily sleep–wake circadian rhythm. Just don't do it while driving, interviewing for a job, or attending psychology class!

The phenomena of REM rebound and NREM rebound seem to indicate that the brain needs to make up for missing components of sleep. Clearly, we need both to sleep and to experience the full range of sleep stages. But what particular functions does sleep serve?

The Restorative Theory of Sleep

restorative theory of sleep
The view that sleep and dreaming are essential to normal physical and mental functioning.

adaptive theory of sleep
The view that the unique sleep patterns of different animals evolved over time to help promote survival and environmental adaptation; also referred to as the *evolutionary theory of sleep*.

The **restorative theory of sleep** suggests that sleep promotes physiological processes that restore and rejuvenate the body and the mind (Gökcebay & others, 1994). According to this theory, NREM and REM sleep serve different purposes. NREM sleep is thought to be important for restoring the body, whereas REM sleep is thought to restore mental and brain functions (Maquet, 2001; Stickgold & others, 2001).

Evidence supporting the role of NREM sleep in restoring the body comes from studies that have demonstrated increased deep sleep following sleep deprivation, starvation, and strenuous athletic activity. The secretion of growth hormone, testosterone, prolactin, and other hormones increases during NREM sleep (Hirshkowitz & others, 1997).

The importance of REM sleep in mental and brain functions is suggested by the abundance of REM sleep in the developing fetus, in infants, and in young children and its subsequent decrease throughout adulthood (see Figure 4.4). Tentatively, this suggests that REM sleep plays some role in the high rate of brain development that occurs in the early stages of the lifespan. The abundant amounts of REM sleep experienced by the developing fetus, infants, and young children may provide needed stimulation for this brain development.

Question: When Does an 800-Pound Predator Sleep? Answer: Any time it wants to! According to the adaptive theory of sleep, animals that have few predators, such as lions and polar bears, have the luxury of sleeping out in the open during daylight hours. Animals that are vulnerable to predators, such as giraffes and mice, sleep only fitfully or in well-protected nests.

The Adaptive Theory of Sleep

As its name implies, the **adaptive theory of sleep** suggests that the sleep patterns exhibited by different animals, including humans, are the result of evolutionary adaptation (Webb, 1975). Also called the *evolutionary theory of sleep,* the basic idea is that different sleep patterns evolved as a way of preventing a particular species from interacting with the environment when doing so is most hazardous. Animals with few natural predators, such as gorillas and lions, sleep as much as 15 hours a day. In contrast, grazing animals, such as cattle and horses, tend to sleep in short bursts that total only about 4 hours per day. Hibernation patterns of animals such as bears and gophers also coincide with periods during which environmental conditions pose the greatest threat to survival.

Although there is evidence to support both the restorative and the adaptive theories of sleep, many questions remain. The bottom line is that researchers still aren't sure exactly what physiological functions are served by sleep (Maquet, 2001). Sleep may well fulfill multiple purposes (Gökcebay & others, 1994).

4.1 R·E·V·I·E·W

C·O·N·C·E·P·T

Circadian Rhythms and Stages of Sleep

Fill in the blanks with the missing terms.

1. Sheila works the night shift. Despite getting adequate sleep before going to work, Sheila feels extremely tired and sleepy at about 3:00 A.M. Her fatigue at 3:00 A.M. is probably due to increased levels of _____.

2. As a research volunteer, Keith agreed to live in an underground bunker for two months without a clock or other time cues. Over the first few weeks, his _____ will naturally drift to a _____-hour cycle, and his circadian rhythms may become desynchronized.

3. Within days after leaving the underground bunker, Keith's exposure to _____ resets his circadian rhythms so that they become synchronized and operate on a _____-hour cycle.

4. You have been asleep for about 10 minutes and are experiencing brief bursts of brain activity, called sleep spindles. It is likely that you are in _____ sleep.

5. Marsha has been asleep for well over an hour. Her eyes start to dart back and forth beneath her closed eyelids. Her heart rate and blood pressure fluctuate up and down, yet her voluntary muscle activity is suppressed. Marsha is experiencing _____ sleep, and _____ is occurring.

6. During your first night in a sleep research lab, a lab assistant wakes you up and asks you to recite the alphabet. You do so, but you remember nothing about this incident the next morning. You were probably awakened during _____ sleep.

sleep disorders
Serious disturbances in the normal sleep pattern that interfere with daytime functioning and cause subjective distress.

insomnia
A condition in which a person regularly experiences an inability to fall asleep, to stay asleep, or to feel adequately rested by sleep.

restless legs syndrome (RLS)
A condition in which unpleasant sensations in the lower legs are accompanied by an irresistible urge to move the legs, temporarily relieving the unpleasant sensation but disrupting sleep.

sleep apnea
(APP-nee-uh) A sleep disorder in which the person repeatedly stops breathing during sleep.

sleepwalking
A sleep disturbance characterized by an episode of walking or performing other actions during stage 3 or stage 4 NREM sleep; also called *somnambulism*.

Sleep Disorders: Troubled Sleep

Key Theme
- Sleep disorders take many different forms and are surprisingly common.

Key Questions
- How is insomnia defined, and how common is it?
- What are most important parasomnias?
- What is narcolepsy?

Sleep disorders are serious disturbances in the normal sleep pattern that interfere with daytime functioning and cause subjective distress (American Psychiatric Association, 2000a). Virtually everyone is seriously troubled by the quality or quantity of their sleep at some point. And, if you happen to be someone who regularly experiences sleep-related problems, you're not alone. According to the 2002 Sleep in America Poll, seven out of ten American adults report frequent sleep problems, including inadequate amounts of sleep. Other highlights from the National Sleep Foundation's survey are presented in Table 4.2.

Insomnia

By far the most common sleep complaint among adults is insomnia (Dement & Pelayo, 1997). According to the 2002 National Sleep Foundation survey, 58 percent of adults are affected a few nights or more each week by at least one symptom of insomnia, such as waking up and being unable to go back to sleep.

Insomnia is not defined solely on the basis of the amount of time a person sleeps, because people vary in how much sleep they need to feel refreshed. Rather, people are said to experience **insomnia** when they repeatedly complain about the quality or duration of their sleep, have difficulty going to sleep or staying asleep, or wake before it is time to get up.

For an estimated 12 million Americans, complaints of insomnia are related to a condition called **restless legs syndrome,** abbreviated **RLS.** People with RLS complain of unpleasant creeping, crawling, tingling, itching, or prickling sensations deep inside their lower legs accompanied by an irresistible urge to move (National Institute of Neurological Disorders and Stroke, 2001). These sensations are most prominent in the evening and at night, especially when the individual lies down or sits still for any length of time (Rothenberg, 1997). Moving the legs temporarily reduces the unpleasant sensations but also interferes with the person's ability to fall asleep or stay asleep.

Table | **4.2**

The National Sleep Foundation Survey: Asleep at the Wheel?

Key findings from the 2002 Sleep in America Poll, a national survey of randomly selected American adults:

- 37% reported being so sleepy during the day that it interfered with their daily activities.
- 40% compensated for sleep lost during the week by sleeping an extra hour or more on the weekends.
- 43% use caffeine to help them stay awake during the day.
- 51% have driven when drowsy during the past year.
- 17% have actually fallen asleep at the wheel in the past year.
- 1% have had a traffic accident due to being drowsy or falling asleep at the wheel.

SOURCE: National Sleep Foundation (2002).

Adding to the disruptive effects on sleep, approximately 80 percent of the people with RLS also have *periodic limb movement disorder,* which involves sudden jerks of the legs, ankle flexing, or flexing of the knees and hips during sleep (Restless Legs Syndrome Foundation, 2001). These brief movements typically occur every 20 to 40 seconds on and off throughout the night, although the number of such movements can vary from night to night.

More commonly, insomnia can often be traced to stressful life events, such as job or school difficulties, troubled relationships, the death of a loved one, or financial problems. Concerns about sleeping can add to whatever waking anxieties the person may already be experiencing. This can create a *vicious circle—* worrying about the inability to sleep makes troubled sleep even more likely, further intensifying anxiety.

Numerous studies have shown that behavior therapy and different medications are effective in the short-term treatment of insomnia (M. T. Smith & others, 2002). Behavioral techniques often help people develop better sleep habits. For example, a treatment called *stimulus control* conditions the person to associate the bed only with sleepiness and sleep, rather than with watching television, talking on the phone, or other nonsleep activities. Relaxation training and meditation, which we will discuss later in the chapter, are also used to treat insomnia (Murtagh & Greenwood, 1995).

Educating people on sleep hygiene is often part of the successful treatment of insomnia. For example, many people troubled by the inability to sleep use alcohol or over-the-counter sleep medications to induce sleep. In the Prologue to this chapter, you saw how Mike resorted to a stiff drink to help him relax and go back to sleep. Although such remedies may temporarily help people fall asleep, both sleeping pills and alcohol disrupt normal sleep cycles, including REM sleep. Even the sleep-inducing medications sometimes prescribed by physicians to treat insomnia must be carefully managed to avoid drug dependence (Bootzin & Rider, 1997; Dement, 1992).

Sleep Apnea

The second most common sleep disorder, sleep apnea, affects some 20 million Americans (Carskadon & Taylor, 1997). In **sleep apnea,** the sleeper repeatedly stops breathing during the night. Carbon dioxide builds up in the blood, causing a momentary awakening, during which the sleeper snorts or gulps in air. Breathing may stop for as little as 10 seconds or for so long that the sleeper's skin turns blue before he or she wakes up. During a single night, more than 300 sleep apnea attacks can occur. Often the person has no recollection of the repeated awakenings but feels sleepy throughout the following day (Orr, 1997).

Sleep apnea is more common in men over the age of 50, especially those with a weight problem. Special mouthpieces, weight loss, and surgical intervention have been effective in treating sleep apnea. For people who suffer from sleep apnea only when they sleep on their backs, treatment is sometimes as simple as sewing a tennis ball to the back of their pajama tops, which forces them to sleep on their sides (Saskin, 1997).

Sleepwalking and Night Terrors

Unlike insomnia, sleepwalking and night terrors are much more common in children than in adults (Lask, 1995; Mindell, 1993). These sleep disturbances occur during the deepest stages of NREM sleep, stages 3 and 4. As noted previously, young children spend considerably more time each night in deep sleep than do adolescents or adults (Whyte & Schaefer, 1995). Not surprisingly, most instances of bedwetting, or *nocturnal enuresis,* also tend to occur when the child is in deep sleep (Barclay & Houts, 1995a).

About 25 percent of all children have at least one episode of **sleepwalking,** also known as *somnambulism.* Sleepwalking typically occurs during the first

Insomnia Following the September 11th Attacks A surge in the number of Americans experiencing symptoms of insomnia occurred in the weeks and months following the attacks on the Pentagon and the World Trade Center on September 11, 2001. According to a survey conducted by the National Sleep Foundation (2002), seven out of ten Americans experienced one or more symptoms of insomnia, such as having trouble falling asleep at night or frequent awakenings during the night. The psychological toll of the terrorist attacks was more pronounced in women. Females were more likely than males (78% vs. 59%) to report that they had experienced symptoms of insomnia during the weeks immediately following the attacks.

Terror in the Night This print by French artist Jean Ignace Gérard is titled *The Nightmare*. However, the image of a monster lowering a weight on the sleeper's chest suggests instead the frightening experience of a night terror. Night terrors occur during NREM sleep and are almost always accompanied by a sensation of being crushed or smothered.

three hours after the child has gone to sleep. The child gets out of bed and moves about in a slow, poorly coordinated, automatic manner, usually with a blank, staring look on his face. Surprisingly, the sleepwalking child is usually able to navigate around objects without much difficulty. However, the child's general lack of awareness of his surroundings is evident. The sleepwalker may try to dress, eat, or go to the bathroom in the wrong location (Ozbayrak & Berlin, 1995).

Night terrors, or *sleep terrors,* also typically occur during stage 3 or 4 NREM sleep in the first few hours of sleep. Physiologically, a night terror is much more intense than a run-of-the-mill nightmare. The first sign of a night terror is sharply increased physiological arousal—restlessness, sweating, and a racing heart. Typically, the child experiencing night terrors abruptly sits up in bed and lets out a panic-stricken scream or cry for help as she thrashes about in bed or even sleepwalks. Terrified and disoriented, the child may struggle with a parent who tries to calm her down (Lask, 1995).

Night terrors tend to be brief, usually lasting only a matter of seconds. Amazingly, the child almost immediately goes back to quiet sleep and wakes in the morning with no recollection of the incident. Unlike the unfolding dream story of a nightmare, night terrors are usually accompanied by a single but terrifying sensation, such as being crushed or falling. Often, the child imagines that she is choking or that a frightening figure is present, such as a threatening animal or monster (Kahn & others, 1991). Though dramatic, night terrors are not regarded as a true sleep disorder or psychological problem unless they occur frequently. For the vast majority of children who often experience night terrors, the problem usually resolves itself by early adolescence (Lask, 1995).

Our friend Nina, whom we described in the Prologue, is among the small percentage of people whose night terrors continue into adulthood. Just as when she was a child, Nina doesn't remember her sleep terror episodes the next morning. However, her husband Mike has found that she seems most likely to experience a sleep terror episode when she is very tired or under stress.

Nina's parents have reported that both Nina and her sister were sleepwalkers until their teenage years. As a child, Nina also experienced *sleep bruxism*—she would grind her teeth loudly in her sleep. Collectively, night terrors, sleepwalking, and sleep bruxism are referred to as parasomnias. The **parasomnias** are a general category of sleep disorders that involve arousal or activation during sleep or sleep transitions.

REM Sleep Behavior Disorder

Another, more serious parasomnia is **REM sleep behavior disorder** (Mahowald & Schenck, 1990). REM sleep behavior disorder typically affects men over the age of 60 and is characterized by the brain's failure to suppress voluntary muscle movements during REM sleep. Consequently, the dreamer acts out his dreams, sometimes leaping out of bed, lashing out at imagined intruders, or tackling a chest of drawers. Such behavior might seem comical if the potential for serious injury to the sleeper or the sleeper's bed partner weren't so great. Evidence suggests that the cause of REM sleep behavior disorder is deterioration or damage in the lower brain centers that control physical and mental arousal during sleep (Zoltoski & Gillin, 1994).

night terrors
A sleep disturbance characterized by an episode of increased physiological arousal, intense fear and panic, frightening hallucinations, and no recall of the episode the next morning; typically occurs during stage 3 or stage 4 NREM sleep; also called *sleep terrors.*

parasomnias
(pare-uh-SOM-nee-uz) A category of sleep disorders characterized by arousal or activation during sleep or sleep transitions; includes *sleepwalking, night terrors, sleep bruxism,* and *REM sleep behavior disorder.*

REM sleep behavior disorder
A sleep disorder in which the sleeper acts out his or her dreams.

Narcolepsy

Unlike the sleep disorders discussed so far, the symptoms of **narcolepsy** are experienced during the day. The most common symptom of narcolepsy is excessive daytime sleepiness and brief lapses into sleep throughout the day, usually lasting an hour or less. Some people with narcolepsy experience dramatic, sudden daytime "sleep attacks" that last up to several minutes. Laughter, anger, surprise, and other forms of arousal, including sexual arousal, can trigger the sleep attacks. During sleep attacks, narcoleptics instantly enter REM sleep and experience sleep paralysis—their muscles go limp and they collapse. Vivid and sometimes terrifying hypnagogic hallucinations are common during sleep attacks (Siegel, 2000).

Approximately 250,000 Americans have narcolepsy (Carskadon & Taylor, 1997). The onset of narcolepsy typically occurs during adolescence, and it is considered a chronic, lifelong condition. Genetics seems to play an important role, as the disorder tends to run in families (Gibbons & Kotagal, 1995). Adding to the genetic evidence, scientists have recently identified the genes that produce narcoleptic symptoms in mice and dogs (Chemelli & others, 1999; Lin & others, 1999). Many sleep researchers are hopeful that such discoveries will lead to a new understanding of narcolepsy in humans and, ultimately, to new treatments for this debilitating sleep disorder (Siegel, 2000; Takahashi, 1999). Although narcolepsy cannot be cured, a new drug, called *modafinil*, reduces daytime sleepiness in people with narcolepsy (Schwartz & others, 2000). Scheduled naps and stimulant drugs can also help minimize narcoleptic symptoms.

An Episode of Cataplexy in Narcolepsy In this sequence of images, a man with narcolepsy experiences one of its most dramatic symptoms – cataplexy. Cataplexy involves the sudden and complete loss of muscle tone, and is typically triggered by laughter, embarrassment, or some other type of emotional arousal. Although he is unable to move, the person remains conscious and aware of what is going on around him.

Dreams and Mental Activity During Sleep

Key Theme

- A dream is an unfolding episode of vivid mental images that occurs during sleep.

Key Questions

- What patterns of brain activity are associated with dreaming sleep?
- How are dreams thought to aid memory consolidation?
- What do people dream about, and why don't we remember our dreams?

Dreams have fascinated people since the beginning of time. On average, about 25 percent of a night's sleep, or almost two hours every night, is spent dreaming. So, assuming you live to a ripe old age, you'll devote more than 50,000 hours, or about six years of your life, to dreaming.

Although dreams may be the most spectacular brain productions during sleep, they are *not* the most common. More prevalent is **sleep thinking,** which takes place during NREM sleep and consists of vague, uncreative, bland, and thought-like ruminations about real-life events (Hobson & Stickgold, 1995; Schatzman & Fenwick, 1994). For example, just before an important exam, students may review terms and concepts during NREM sleep.

narcolepsy
(NAR-ko-lep-see) A sleep disorder characterized by excessive daytime sleepiness and brief lapses into sleep throughout the day.

sleep thinking
Repetitive, bland, and uncreative ruminations about real-life events during sleep.

Dream Images Although people tend to emphasize visual imagery when they describe their dreams, sounds and physical sensations are also commonly present. Sensations of falling, flying, spinning, or trying to run may be experienced. We tend to dream of familiar people and places, but the juxtapositions of characters, objects, and events are typically illogical, even bizarre. Nevertheless, the dreamer rarely questions the dream details—until he or she wakes up!

In contrast to sleep thinking, a **dream** is an unfolding episode of mental images that is storylike, involving characters and events. According to sleep researcher J. Allan Hobson (1988), dreams have five basic characteristics:

- Emotions can be intense.
- Content and organization are usually illogical.
- Sensations are sometimes bizarre.
- Even bizarre details are uncritically accepted.
- Dream images are difficult to remember.

Many people believe that dreams occur only during REM sleep, but this is not the case. Dreams occur during both NREM and REM sleep (Rosenlicht & Feinberg, 1997). However, dreams during REM sleep are more frequent and of longer duration than are dreams during NREM sleep (Foulkes, 1997). When people are awakened during REM sleep, they will report a dream up to 90 percent of the time—even people who claim that they never dream.

People usually have four or five episodes of dreaming each night. Early morning dreams, which can last as long as 40 minutes, are the dreams people are most likely to remember. Contrary to popular belief, dreams happen in real time, not in split seconds. In fact, dreamers tend to be quite accurate in estimating how long they've been dreaming (Empson, 1993).

FIGURE 4.5 The Brain During REM Sleep
The dreaming brain is highly active, but the dreamer is cut off from both the reality-testing functions of the frontal lobes and visual input from the external environment. The PET images show the difference between REM sleep and wakefulness (left) and between REM sleep and slow-wave-sleep (right). The PET scans are color-coded such that bluish-purple indicates a decrease in blood flow and yellow-red indicates an increase. As compared to wakefulness, REM sleep involves a decrease in activity in the frontal lobes and the primary visual cortex, but an increase in visual areas associated with mental imagery (red). As compared to slow-wave-sleep, REM sleep involves a sharp increase in activity in limbic system areas associated with emotion, motivation, and memory (red), and an increase in areas associated with visual imagery.

The Brain During REM Sleep

What happens in the brain during REM sleep? Earlier in the chapter, we noted that EEG measurements show that the brain is highly active during REM sleep. In a recent series of PET scans of sleeping subjects, neuroscientist Allen Braun and his colleagues (1998) showed that the brain's activity during REM sleep is distinctly different from its activity during either wakefulness or slow-wave (NREM) sleep.

Braun found that both the primary visual cortex and the frontal lobes are essentially shut down during REM sleep. As we discussed in Chapter 2, the *primary visual cortex* is the area at the back of the brain that first registers visual information transmitted by the retinas of the eye. The *frontal lobes* are the brain areas responsible for higher-level cognitive processes, including reasoning, planning, and integrating perceptual information. Thus, during REM sleep, the sleeper is cut off from information about the external world *and* from the brain centers most involved in rational thought (see Figure 4.5).

Other brain areas, however, are highly active during REM sleep. Activated areas include the *amygdala* and the *hippocampus,* structures of the limbic system that are involved in emotion and memory (see Figure 2.19 on page 73). Also highly active are other parts of the brain's visual system that are involved in generating visual images.

These results suggest that the dreamer's uncritical acceptance of bizarre and chaotic dream images and narrative can be explained in terms of the inactivity of the frontal lobes—the very areas of the brain that are normally most active in analyzing and interpreting new information. In the absence of meaningful stimuli from the outside world, emotions and stored memories provide the raw data for the vivid visual images conjured up by the sleeping brain.

REM and Memory Consolidation

As you'll see in Chapter 6, *memory consolidation* refers to the gradual process of converting new memories into a long-term, relatively permanent form. Research suggests that REM sleep helps consolidate memories, especially *procedural memories* (Stickgold & others, 2001). Procedural memories are essentially memories for *how* to perform sequences of behaviors. For example, when you play basketball, the video game Tetris, or the piano, you're drawing on your procedural memories.

Both animal and human studies have shown that REM sleep increases after learning a novel task and that deprivation of REM sleep following training disrupts learning (Maquet, 2001). The importance of REM sleep was demonstrated in one study in which volunteers were trained on a simple but challenging perceptual task before going to sleep (Karni & others, 1994). Half the participants were repeatedly awakened during NREM sleep stages, while the other half were repeatedly awakened during REM sleep. The volunteers who enjoyed uninterrupted REM (dreaming) sleep improved their performance on the test the next day, but the participants whose REM sleep was disrupted did not.

While REM sleep appears to play an important role in memory consolidation, exactly how it does so is still unknown (Maquet, 2001). Recent studies have shown that brain areas activated during training on a particular task are actually *reactivated* during REM sleep (Louie & Wilson, 2001; Maquet & others, 2000). Thus, REM sleep may help stabilize the neural connections acquired through recent experience.

What Do We Dream About?

Although nearly everyone can remember an unusually bizarre dream, most dreams are a reflection of everyday life, including people we know and familiar settings (Domhoff, 1999; Weinstein & others, 1991). Recall Mike's nightmare about his new boss, which was described in the Prologue. The giant staircase and spiral escalators were exaggerated versions of real architectural features of the atrium-style lobby of the hotel where he works.

Dream researcher Calvin Hall collected and analyzed over 10,000 dreams from hundreds of people. He found that a dream's themes often reflect the daily concerns of the dreamer (Hall & Van de Castle, 1966). Worries about exams, money, health, troubled relationships, or jobs are all likely to be reflected in our dreams—as was Mike's anxiety about his new boss.

The role of environmental influences on dream content was demonstrated in a recent study that compared the dreams of three groups of children: Palestinian children living in the Gaza Strip during a time of violent military confrontations; Palestinian children living in a peaceful area of Israel; and children in Finland (Punamäki & Joustie, 1998). The Palestinian children in Gaza were much more likely to dream about acts of violence, aggression, and persecution than were the Palestinian children living in a peaceful area or the Finnish children.

Certain themes, such as falling, being chased, or being attacked, are surprisingly common across cultures. As you can see in Table 4.3, although thousands of miles apart and immersed in two very different cultures, American and Japanese college students share many dream themes. Surveys of dream content in many cultures have shown that dreamers around the world report more instances of negative events than of positive events

dream
A storylike episode of unfolding mental imagery during sleep.

Table | **4.3**

Common Dream Themes Across Cultures

	Percentage of Students Saying Yes	
Have you ever dreamed of . . . ?	**American**	**Japanese**
1. being attacked or pursued	77	91
2. falling	83	74
3. trying again and again to do something	71	87
4. school, teachers, studying	71	86
5. being frozen with fright	58	87
6. sexual experiences	66	68
7. arriving too late (e.g., missing train)	64	49
8. dead people as though alive	46	57
9. loved person being dead	57	42
10. being on the verge of falling	47	45
11. failing an examination	39	41
12. flying or soaring through air	34	46
13. being smothered, unable to breathe	44	33
14. seeing self as dead	33	35
15. being nude	43	17

SOURCE: Adapted from data reported in Empson (1993).

(Domhoff, 1996). Instances of aggression are more common than are instances of friendliness, and dreamers are more likely to be victims of aggression than aggressors in their dreams. There is more aggression in men's dreams than in women's dreams, but women are more likely to dream that they are the victims of physical aggression.

Environmental cues *during* dreaming can also influence dream content. In sleep labs, researchers have played recordings of a rooster crowing, a bugle playing reveille, and a dog barking. Researchers have even sprayed water on sleeping subjects. Depending on the stimulus, up to half the dreamers incorporated the external stimulation into their dream content (Arkin & Antrobus, 1991).

Why Don't We Remember Our Dreams?

Even the best dream recallers forget the vast majority of their dreams—at least 95 percent by one estimate (Hobson, 1995). Why are dreams so much more difficult to remember than waking experiences? Several theories have been proposed, each with at least some evidence to support it.

As we'll discuss in more detail in Chapter 6, memory requires information to be processed and stored in such a way that it can be retrieved at a later time. One theory is that the fundamental changes in brain chemistry and functioning that occur during sleep fail to support such information processing and storage. For example, frontal lobe areas are involved in the formation of new memories, and PET scans of sleeping volunteers have shown that the frontal lobes are inactive during REM sleep (Braun & others, 1998). Research has also shown that the neurotransmitters needed to acquire new memories—including serotonin, norepinephrine, and dopamine—are greatly reduced during REM sleep (J. A. Hobson & others, 1998; Siegel, 2001).

"Off with his head! Off with his head!"

Some dreams are remembered, however, and several factors have been found to influence dream recall. First, you're much more likely to recall a dream if you wake up during it (Schredl & Montasser, 1997). When people are intentionally awakened during REM sleep, they usually recall the dream content. There are also individual differences in dream recall. Some people, like Sandy, frequently remember their dreams in vivid detail. Other people, like Don, hardly ever remember their dreams. Research has shown that people who are better at remembering visual details while awake are also better at recalling their dreams (Schredl & others, 1995).

Second, the more vivid, bizarre, or emotionally intense a dream is, the more likely it is to be recalled the following morning. Vivid dreams are also more likely to be remembered days or weeks after the dream has occurred (Goodenough, 1991). In many respects, this is very similar to waking experiences. Whether you're awake or asleep, mundane and routine experiences are most likely to be forgotten.

Third, distractions on awakening interfere with our ability to recall dreams, as noted by psychologist Mary Calkins (1893) over a century ago:

> To recall a dream requires usually extreme and immediate attention to the content of the dream. Sometimes the slight movement of reaching for paper and pencil or of lighting one's candle seems to dissipate the dream-memory, and one is left with the tantalizing consciousness of having lived through an interesting dream-experience of which one has not the faintest memory.

Finally, it's difficult to remember *any* experience that occurs during sleep, not just dreams. Sleep researchers have found that people who are briefly awakened during the night to give reports or perform simple tasks frequently do not remember the incident the next morning (Goodenough, 1991). It seems clear, then, that the brain is largely programmed to forget not only the vast majority of dream experiences but also other experiences that happen during sleep.

What You Really Want to Know About Dreams

If I fall off a cliff in my dreams and don't wake up before I hit the bottom, will I die?

The first obvious problem with this bit of folklore is that if you did die before you woke up, how would anyone know what you'd been dreaming about? Beyond this basic contradiction, studies have shown that about a third of dreamers can recall a dream in which they died or were killed. Dream sensations such as falling, soaring through the air, and being paralyzed seem to be universal.

Do animals dream?

Virtually all mammals experience sleep cycles in which REM sleep alternates with slow-wave NREM sleep. Animals clearly demonstrate perception and memory. They also communicate using vocalizations, facial expressions, posture, and gestures to show territoriality and sexual receptiveness. Thus, it's quite reasonable to conclude that the brain and other physiological changes that occur during animal REM sleep are coupled with mental images. One bit of anecdotal evidence supporting this idea involved a gorilla that had been taught sign language to communicate. The gorilla signed "sleep pictures," presumably referring to REM dream activity while it slept.

What do blind people "see" when they dream?

People who become totally blind before the age of five typically do not have visual dreams as adults. Even so, their dreams are just as complex and vivid as sighted people's dreams; they just involve other sensations—of sound, taste, smell, and touch.

Is it possible to control your dreams?

Yes, if you have lucid dreams. A *lucid dream* is one in which you become aware that you are dreaming while you are still asleep. About half of all people can recall at least one lucid dream, and some people frequently have lucid dreams. The dreamer can often consciously guide the course of a lucid dream, including backing it up and making it go in a different direction.

Can you predict the future with your dreams?

History is filled with stories of dream prophecies. Over the course of your life, you will have over 100,000 dreams. Simply by chance, it's not surprising that every now and then a dream contains elements that coincide with future events.

Are dreams in color or black and white?

Up to 80 percent of our dreams contain color. When dreamers are awakened and asked to match dream colors to standard color charts, soft pastel colors are frequently chosen.

SOURCES: Anch & others (1988); Blackmore (1998); Empson (1993); Halliday (1995); Hobson (1995); Hurovitz & others (1999); Schatzman & Fenwick (1994); Weinstein & others (1991).

Nightmares

An unpleasant anxiety dream that occurs during REM sleep is called a **nightmare.** Nightmares often produce spontaneous awakenings, during which the vivid and frightening dream content is immediately recalled. The general theme of nightmares is of being helpless or powerless in the face of great danger or destruction.

Nightmares are especially common in young children (Halliday, 1995). For example, when our daughter Laura was four years old, she told us about this vivid nightmare:

> There was a big monster chasing me and Nubbin the Cat! And we jumped on a golden horse but the monster kept chasing us! Then Nubbin jumped off and started to eat the monster. And then Mommy came and saved me! And then Daddy took a sword and killed the monster! And then me and Mommy and Nubbin rode the horse into the clouds.

Like Laura, young children often have nightmares in which they are attacked by an animal or monster. In dealing with a child who has experienced a nightmare, simple reassurance is a good first step, followed by an attempt to help the child understand the difference between an imaginary dream and a real waking experience. In adults, an occasional nightmare is a natural and relatively common experience (Wood & Bootzin, 1990). Nightmares are not considered indicative of a psychological or sleep disorder unless they frequently cause personal distress.

nightmare
A frightening or unpleasant anxiety dream that occurs during REM sleep.

manifest content
In Freud's psychoanalytic theory, the elements of a dream that are consciously experienced and remembered by the dreamer.

latent content
In Freud's psychoanalytic theory, the unconscious wishes, thoughts, and urges that are concealed in the manifest content of a dream.

activation–synthesis model of dreaming
The theory that brain activity during sleep produces dream images (*activation*), which are combined by the brain into a dream story (*synthesis*).

Dream Researcher J. Allan Hobson
Neuroscientist J. Allan Hobson developed the activation–synthesis model of dreams with his colleague Robert McCarley. Although Hobson believes that dreams are the by-products of physiological processes in the brain, he does not believe that dreams are meaningless. Hobson (1999) observed, "Dreaming may be our most creative conscious state, one in which the chaotic, spontaneous recombination of cognitive elements produces novel configurations of information: new ideas. While many or even most of these ideas may be nonsensical, if even a few of its fanciful products are truly useful, our dream time will not have been wasted."

The Significance of Dreams

Key Theme

- Theoretical approaches vary greatly in their explanations of the meaning of dreams.

Key Questions

- How did Freud explain dreams?
- How does the activation-synthesis model explain dreams?
- What general conclusions can be drawn about the nature of dreams?

For thousands of years and throughout many cultures, dreams have been thought to contain highly significant, cryptic messages. Do dreams mean anything? Do they contain symbolic messages? In this final section on dreaming, we will look at two theories that try to account for the purpose of dreaming, starting with the most famous one.

Sigmund Freud: Dreams as Fulfilled Wishes

In the chapters on personality and psychotherapy (Chapters 11 and 15), we'll look in detail at the ideas of **Sigmund Freud,** the founder of psychoanalysis. As we discussed in Chapter 1, Freud believed that sexual and aggressive instincts are the motivating forces that dictate human behavior. Because these instinctual urges are so consciously unacceptable, sexual and aggressive thoughts, feelings, and wishes are pushed into the unconscious, or *repressed*. However, Freud believed that these repressed urges and wishes could surface in dreams.

In his landmark work, *The Interpretation of Dreams* (1900), Freud wrote that dreams are the "disguised fulfillments of repressed wishes" and provide "the royal road to a knowledge of the unconscious mind." Freud believed that dreams function as a sort of psychological "safety valve" for the release of unconscious and unacceptable urges.

Freud (1904) believed that dreams have two components: the **manifest content,** or the dream images themselves, and the **latent content,** the disguised psychological meaning of the dream. For example, Freud (1911) believed that dream images of sticks, swords, and other elongated objects were phallic symbols, representing the penis. Dream images of cupboards, boxes, and ovens supposedly symbolized the vagina.

In many types of psychotherapy today, especially those that follow Freud's ideas, dreams are still seen as an important source of information about psychological conflicts. However, Freud's belief that dreams represent the fulfillment of repressed wishes has not been substantiated by psychological research (Fisher & Greenberg, 1996; Schatzman & Fenwick, 1994). Furthermore, research does not support Freud's belief that the dream images themselves—the manifest content of dreams—are symbols that disguise the dream's true psychological meaning (Domhoff, 1996).

The Activation–Synthesis Model of Dreaming

Armed with an array of evidence that dreaming involves the activation of different brain areas during REM sleep, researcher **J. Allan Hobson** and his colleague Robert McCarley first proposed a new model of dreaming in 1977. Called the **activation–synthesis model of dreaming,** this model maintains that dreaming is our subjective awareness of the brain's internally generated signals during sleep (Hobson, 1995; Hobson & Stickgold, 1995). Since it was first proposed, the model has evolved as new findings have been reported (Hobson & others, 1998; Stickgold & others, 2001).

Specifically, the activation–synthesis model maintains that the experience of dreaming sleep is due to the automatic activation of brainstem circuits at the base of the brain (see Figure 4.6). These circuits arouse more sophisticated brain areas, including visual and auditory pathways. As noted earlier, limbic system structures involved in emotion, such as the amygdala and hippocampus, are also activated during REM sleep. When we're awake, these pathways and brain structures are involved in registering stimuli from the external world. But rather than responding to stimulation from the external environment, the dreaming brain is responding to its own internally generated signals.

In the absence of external sensory input, the activated brain combines, or synthesizes, these internally generated sensory signals and imposes meaning on them. The dream story itself is derived from a hodge-podge of memories, emotions, and sensations that are triggered by the brain's activation and chemical changes during sleep. According to this model, then, dreaming is essentially the brain's synthesizing and integrating memory fragments, emotions, and sensations that are internally triggered (Hobson & others, 1998).

The activation–synthesis theory does *not* state that dreams are completely meaningless, however (Hobson & Stickgold, 1995). As Hobson (1995) observed, "For all their nonsense, dreams have a clear import and a deeply personal one." But if there is a meaning to dreams, that meaning lies in the deeply personal way in which the images are organized, or synthesized. In other words, the meaning is to be found not by decoding the dream symbols, but by analyzing the way the dreamer makes sense of the progression of chaotic dream images.

Some Observations About the Meaning of Dreams

Subjectively, it seems obvious that at least some of our dreams mirror our real-life concerns, frustrations, anxieties, and desires. Less subjectively, this observation is consistent with sleep research on the content of dreams (Weinstein & others, 1991). Large-scale analyses of dream reports demonstrate that dreams reflect the waking concerns and preoccupations of the dreamer (Domhoff, 1993, 1996). Thus, the topics you think about during the day are most likely to influence the topics you dream about at night (Nikles & others, 1998). Some dream researchers believe that most dreams, however chaotic or disorganized, are meaningfully related to the dreamers' current concerns, problems, and waking lives (Domhoff, 1998).

It may well be that the more bizarre aspects of dream sequences—the sudden scene changes, intense emotions, and vivid, unrealistic images—are due to physiological changes in the brain during REM and NREM sleep. Dream researcher David Foulkes (1993, 1997) argues that dreaming consciousness is no different from waking consciousness in its attempt to make sense of the information that is available to it. What differs is the *source* of the information. When we're awake, we monitor the external environment, making sense of the stimuli that impinge upon us from the environment as well as our own thoughts, feelings, and fantasies. During sleep, we try—as best we can—to make sense of the less orderly stimuli produced by the brain itself.

If nothing else, remember that the interpretation of dreams occurs when we're awake. It seems reasonable, then, to suggest that conscious speculations about the meaning of these elusive nightly productions might reveal more about the psychological characteristics of the interpreter than about the dream itself (Cartwright & Kaszniak, 1991).

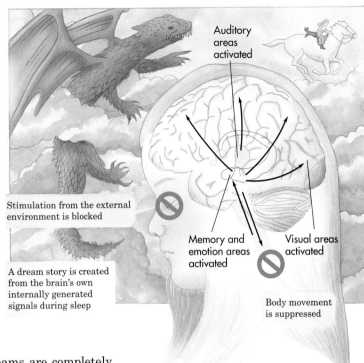

Auditory areas activated

Stimulation from the external environment is blocked

A dream story is created from the brain's own internally generated signals during sleep

Memory and emotion areas activated

Visual areas activated

Body movement is suppressed

FIGURE 4.6 The Activation–Synthesis Model of Dreaming: Laura's Dream According to the activation–synthesis model, dreaming is caused by the activation of brainstem circuits that arouse other brain areas involved in sensations, emotions, and memories. The results of these internally generated signals are the dream images and sensations that the activated brain synthesizes, or combines. The dreaming person imposes a personal meaning on the dream story (Hobson, 1995; Hobson & others, 1998).

4.2 R·E·V·I·E·W

Sleep Disorders and Dreams

1. Lisa is having a very frightening dream in which she is being chased by a large dog with big fangs. Lisa is probably in _____ sleep and experiencing a _____.
   a. stage 4 NREM; night terror
   b. stage 1 NREM; hypnagogic hallucination
   c. REM; nightmare
   d. REM; night terror

2. Mrs. Johnson complains that she is unable to sleep because her husband snores loudly and snorts as though he is gulping for air throughout the night, especially when he sleeps on his back. During the day, Mr. Johnson is constantly tired. Mr. Johnson is probably experiencing _____.
   a. insomnia
   b. REM sleep behavior disorder
   c. narcolepsy
   d. sleep apnea

3. The night before an important job interview, Marjorie doesn't sleep well. Each time she briefly awakens, the vague, thoughtlike imagery filling her mind is that of rehearsing details she wants to remember to say during the interview. These ruminations during sleep represent _____.

   a. dreams
   b. nightmares
   c. parasomnias
   d. sleep thinking

4. During psychotherapy sessions, Jake's therapist asks him to describe his dreams in detail so that the therapist can help him uncover the hidden meaning of the dream images. Jake is describing the _____ content of his dreams. The therapist is trying to decipher the _____ content of Jake's dreams.
   a. lucid; circadian
   b. manifest; latent
   c. activated; synthesized
   d. restorative; adaptive

5. According to the activation–synthesis model, dreams are _____.
   a. meaningless
   b. symbolic representations of repressed wishes
   c. the subjective awareness of the brain's internally generated signals during sleep
   d. produced by newly consolidated memories

Hypnosis

Key Theme

- During hypnosis, people respond to suggestions with changes in perception, memory, and behavior.

Key Questions

- What characteristics are associated with responsiveness to hypnotic suggestions?
- What are some important effects of hypnosis?
- How has hypnosis been explained?

Although its use can be traced back to the late 1700s, serious scientific investigations of hypnosis began about 75 years ago (Gauld, 1995). Since then, thousands of studies have answered many questions about hypnosis, but researchers continue to debate its exact nature.

What is hypnosis? Definitions vary, but **hypnosis** can be defined as a cooperative social interaction in which the hypnotic participant responds to suggestions made by the hypnotist. These suggestions for imaginative experiences can produce changes in perception, memory, thoughts, and behavior (American Psychological Association, [APA] 2001).

For many people the word *hypnosis* conjures up the classic but sinister image of a hypnotist inducing hypnosis by slowly swinging a pocket watch back and forth. Actually, the induction procedure can be as simple as having the person concentrate on a tack or a Post-It note on the wall while the hypnotist speaks in

hypnosis
(hip-NO-sis) A cooperative social interaction in which the hypnotized person responds to the hypnotist's suggestions with changes in perception, memory, and behavior.

a soothing, monotonous voice suggesting that the person relax, experience feelings of heaviness, and close his eyes. But contrary to popular belief, as psychologist John Kihlstrom (2001) explains, "The hypnotist does not hypnotize the individual. Rather, the hypnotist serves as a sort of coach or tutor whose job is to help the person become hypnotized." After experiencing hypnosis, some people are able to self-induce hypnosis.

The word *hypnosis* is derived from the Greek *hypnos,* meaning "sleep." The idea that the hypnotized person is in a sleep-like trance is still very popular among the general public. However, the phrase *hypnotic trance* is misleading and rarely used by researchers today (Wagstaff, 1999). When hypnotized, people do *not* lose control of their behavior. Instead, they typically remain aware of where they are, who they are, and what is transpiring.

More accurately, hypnosis is characterized by highly focused attention, increased responsiveness to suggestions, vivid images and fantasies, and a willingness to accept distortions of logic or reality. During hypnosis, the person temporarily suspends her sense of initiative and voluntarily accepts and follows the hypnotist's instructions (Hilgard, 1986a).

People vary in their responsiveness to hypnotic suggestions. During an induction procedure, the person's responsiveness is often determined using standardized tasks, such as those on the *Stanford Hypnotic Susceptibility Scale* or the *Harvard Group Scale of Hypnotic Susceptibility* (Council, 1999). For example, the person might be asked to extend his arm and imagine a heavy object pushing his arm down. Or he might be asked to imagine that he can hear an annoying fly buzzing about his head. If his arm moves downward in response to the imaginary weight or if he swats at the imagined fly buzzing about his head, then the person has passed these tasks. The more tasks passed, the greater the person's degree of hypnotizability.

Most adults are moderately hypnotizable. About 15 percent of adults are highly susceptible to hypnosis, and 10 percent are difficult or impossible to hypnotize (Hilgard, 1982; Register & Kihlstrom, 1986). Children tend to be more responsive to hypnosis than are adults, and children as young as five years old can be hypnotized (Kohen & Olness, 1993). Evidence suggests that the degree of susceptibility to hypnosis tends to run in families. And, identical twins are more likely than fraternal twins to have similar scores on the *Stanford Hypnotic Susceptibility Scale* (Nash, 2001).

The best candidates for hypnosis are individuals who approach the experience with positive, receptive attitudes. The expectation that you will be responsive to hypnosis also plays an important role (Kirsch & others, 1995; Spanos & others, 1993). People who are highly susceptible to hypnosis have the ability to become deeply absorbed in fantasy and imaginary experience. For instance, they easily become absorbed in reading fiction, watching movies, and listening to music (Barnier & McConkey, 1999; Kihlstrom, 2001).

How Is The Hypnotic State Produced? In a willing volunteer, hypnosis can be induced in a variety of ways, but swinging a pocket watch is usually not one of them. Instead, as psychologist Michael Nash demonstrates, hypnosis is more commonly induced by speaking in a calm, monotonous voice, suggesting that the person is becoming drowsy, sleepy, and progressively more relaxed. To help the volunteer focus her attention, the hypnotist may also ask her to concentrate on a simple visual stimulus, such as a spot on the wall.

Effects of Hypnosis

Deeply hypnotized subjects sometimes experience profound changes in their subjective experience of consciousness. They may report feelings of detachment from their bodies, profound relaxation, or sensations of timelessness. More commonly, hypnotized people converse normally and remain fully aware of their surroundings. Often, they will later report that carrying out the hypnotist's suggestions seemed to happen by itself. The action seems to take place outside the hypnotized person's will or volition.

Sensory and Perceptual Changes

Some of the most dramatic effects that can be produced with hypnosis are alterations in sensation and perception. Sensory changes that can be induced through hypnosis include temporary blindness, deafness, or a complete loss of sensation in some part of the body (Hilgard, 1986a). For example, when the suggestion is

Hypnotic Suppression of Pain In this classic photo taken at the Stanford Laboratory of Hypnosis Research, psychologist Ernest Hilgard (1904–2001) instructs this hypnotized young woman that she will feel no pain in her arm. Her arm is then immersed in circulating ice water for several minutes, and she reports that she does not experience any pain. In contrast, a nonhypnotized subject perceives the same experience as extremely painful and can keep his arm in the ice water for no more than a few seconds.

made to a highly responsive subject that her arm is numb and cannot feel pain, she will not consciously experience the pain of a pinprick or of having her arm immersed in ice water. This property of hypnosis has led to its use as a technique in pain control (Montgomery & others, 2000). Painful dental and medical procedures, including surgery, have been successfully performed with hypnosis as the only anesthesia (Hilgard & others, 1994).

People can experience hallucinations under hypnosis. If a highly responsive hypnotic subject is told that a close friend is sitting in a chair on the other side of the room, she will not only report seeing the friend in vivid detail but will walk over and "touch" the other person. Under hypnosis, people can also *not* perceive something that *is* there. For example, if the suggestion is made that a jar of rotten eggs has no smell, a highly suggestible person will not consciously perceive any odor.

Hypnosis can also influence behavior *outside* the hypnotic state. When a **posthypnotic suggestion** is given, the person will carry out that specific suggestion after the hypnotic session is over. For example, under hypnosis, a student was given the posthypnotic suggestion that the number 5 no longer existed. He was brought out of hypnosis and then asked to count his fingers. He counted 11 fingers! Counting again, the baffled young man was at a loss to explain his results.

Some posthypnotic suggestions have been reported to last for months, but most last only a few hours or days (Barnier & McConkey, 1998). So, even if the hypnotist does not include some posthypnotic signal to cancel the posthypnotic suggestion, the suggestion will eventually wear off.

Hypnosis and Memory

Memory can be significantly affected by hypnosis. In **posthypnotic amnesia,** a subject is unable to recall specific information or events that occurred before or during hypnosis. Posthypnotic amnesia is produced by a hypnotic suggestion that suppresses the memory of specific information, such as the subject's street address. The effects of posthypnotic amnesia are usually temporary, disappearing either spontaneously or when a posthypnotic signal is suggested by the hypnotist. When the signal is given, the information floods back into the subject's mind.

The opposite effect is called **hypermnesia,** which is enhancement of memory for past events through hypnotic suggestion. Police investigators sometimes use hypnosis in an attempt to enhance the memories of crime victims and witnesses. Despite the common belief that you can "zoom in" on briefly seen crime details under hypnosis, such claims are extremely exaggerated (Smith, 1983). Compared with regular police interview methods, hypnosis does *not* significantly enhance memory or improve the accuracy of memories (Nash, 2001; Register & Kihlstrom, 1987).

Many studies have shown that efforts to enhance memories hypnotically can lead to distortions and inaccuracies (Burgess & Kirsch, 1999). In fact, hypnosis can greatly increase confidence in memories that are actually incorrect (Kihlstrom & Barnhardt, 1993). False memories, also called *pseudomemories,* can be inadvertently created when hypnosis is used to aid recall (Lynn & Nash, 1994; Yapko, 1994a).

For example, in one study it was suggested to hypnotized subjects that they had been awakened one night during the previous week by loud noises (Laurence & Perry, 1983). Following the hypnotic session, almost half the subjects claimed that loud noises had disturbed their sleep during the previous week. Even *after* the subjects were told the loud noises had been hypnotically suggested, several subjects persisted in the belief that the disturbance had actually taken place.

The problem of inaccurate, distorted, or contrived memories also frequently occurs in *age regression*—the use of hypnosis to recall or reexperience an earlier developmental period (J. Green, 1999b). When hypnotized people are taken through age regression, they confidently "relive" experiences from early childhood and display childlike behaviors and abilities. However, when attempts are made to objectively verify specific details from the experience, the details are generally inaccurate. So are the adult subject's depictions of how a small child thinks or

Hypnosis and Memory Many people believe that hypnosis can be used to enhance recall, particularly of upsetting or traumatic events. However, research has shown that hypnosis is no more effective than other types of memory-enhancing methods. Simply looking at a family photograph album can provide potent cues to help retrieve memories thought to be forgotten.

behaves (Spanos, 1987–1988). Just as deafness or blindness is not actually produced by hypnotic suggestion, neither is the return to childhood. Instead, subjects combine fragments of actual memories with fantasies and information about how they think children at a particular age will behave.

The Limits of Hypnosis

Although the effects of hypnosis can be dramatic, there are limits to the behaviors that can be influenced by hypnosis. First, contrary to popular belief, you cannot be hypnotized against your will. Second, hypnosis cannot make you perform behaviors that are contrary to your morals and values. Thus, you're very unlikely to commit criminal or immoral acts under the influence of hypnosis—unless, of course, you find such actions acceptable (Hilgard, 1986b).

Third, hypnosis cannot make you stronger than your physical capabilities or bestow new talents. However, hypnosis *can* enhance physical skills or athletic ability by increasing motivation and concentration (Morgan, 1993). Table 4.4 provides additional examples of how hypnosis can be used to help people.

Can hypnosis be used to help you lose weight, stop smoking, or stop biting your nails? The effectiveness of hypnosis in modifying habitual behaviors varies. For example, research provides little evidence to support the notion that hypnosis is more effective than other methods in controlling smoking behavior (Green & Lynn, 2000). In study after study, hypnosis has failed to produce long-term changes in the cessation of smoking behavior (Spanos & others, 1995b). In contrast, hypnosis coupled with cognitive-behavior therapy enhances the effectiveness of weight-loss programs (J. Green, 1999a; Kirsch, 1996). In Chapter 15, on therapies, we'll explore cognitive and behavior therapy techniques in detail.

Explaining Hypnosis
Consciousness Divided?

How can hypnosis be explained? Psychologist **Ernest Hilgard** (1986a, 1991, 1992) believed that the hypnotized person experiences **dissociation**—the splitting of consciousness into two or more simultaneous streams of mental activity. According to Hilgard's **neodissociation theory of hypnosis,** a hypnotized person consciously experiences one stream of mental activity that is responding to the hypnotist's suggestions. But a second, dissociated stream of mental activity is also operating, processing information that is unavailable to the consciousness of the hypnotized subject. Hilgard (1986a, 1992) referred to this second, dissociated stream of mental activity as the **hidden observer.** (The phrase *hidden observer* does *not* mean that the hypnotized person has multiple personalities.)

Hilgard accidentally discovered the "hidden observer" while conducting a classroom demonstration. Hilgard hypnotized a student and induced hypnotic deafness. The student was completely unresponsive to very loud, sudden sounds, such as the sound of a starter pistol firing or of wooden blocks being banged together.

Another student, observing the demonstration, asked Hilgard if "some part" of the hypnotized person was actually aware of the sounds. Hilgard instructed the hypnotized student to raise his right index finger if some part of him could still hear. To Hilgard's surprise, the hypnotized student's right index finger rose! When brought out of hypnosis, the student had no recall of any sounds during the hypnotically induced deafness, *including* Hilgard's suggestion to raise his index finger. Hypnosis, it seems, had produced a split in consciousness. A conscious segment complied with the hypnotic suggestion of deafness, but a separate, dissociated segment unavailable to consciousness continued to process information—the hidden observer.

Not all psychologists agree that hypnotic phenomena are due to dissociation, divided consciousness, or a hidden observer. In Critical Thinking Box 4.5, we examine this controversy more fully.

Table | 4.4

Help Through Hypnosis

Research has demonstrated that hypnosis can effectively:

- Reduce pain and discomfort associated with cancer, rheumatoid arthritis, burn wounds, and other chronic conditions
- Reduce pain and discomfort associated with childbirth
- Reduce the use of narcotics to relieve postoperative pain
- Improve the concentration, motivation, and performance of athletes
- Lessen the severity and frequency of asthma attacks
- Eliminate recurring nightmares
- Enhance the effectiveness of psychotherapy in the treatment of obesity, hypertension, and anxiety
- Remove warts
- Eliminate or reduce stuttering
- Suppress the gag reflex during dental procedures

---

posthypnotic suggestion
A suggestion made during hypnosis that the person should carry out a specific instruction following the hypnotic session.

posthypnotic amnesia
The inability to recall specific information because of a hypnotic suggestion.

hypermnesia
(high-perm-NEE-zha) The supposed enhancement of a person's memory for past events through a hypnotic suggestion.

dissociation
The splitting of consciousness into two or more simultaneous streams of mental activity.

neodissociation theory of hypnosis
Theory proposed by Ernest Hilgard that explains hypnotic effects as being due to the splitting of consciousness into two simultaneous streams of mental activity, only one of which the hypnotic participant is consciously aware of during hypnosis.

hidden observer
Hilgard's term for the hidden, or dissociated, stream of mental activity during hypnosis.

Is Hypnosis a Special State of Consciousness?

One of the great debates in modern psychology comes down to this question: Are the changes in perception, thinking, and behavior that occur during hypnosis the result of a "special" or "altered" state of consciousness? Here, we'll briefly touch on some of the evidence for three competing points of view on this issue.

The State View: Hypnosis Involves a Special or Altered State of Consciousness

Considered the traditional viewpoint, the "state" explanation contends that hypnosis is a unique state of consciousness, distinctly different from our normal waking consciousness (Kosslyn & others, 2000). The state view is advocated by the research of numerous psychologists, including David Spiegel (1998a, 1998b), Michael Nash (1997, 2001), and Kenneth S. Bowers (1992, 1995).

The state view is perhaps best represented by the late Ernest Hilgard's *neodissociation theory of hypnosis.* According to Hilgard (1986a, 1994), the sometimes dramatic effects seen during hypnosis occur because consciousness is split into two simultaneous streams of mental activity. In this special state of consciousness, one stream of mental activity remains conscious. But a second stream of mental activity—the one responding to the hypnotist's suggestions—is "dissociated" from awareness. So according to the neodissociation explanation, the hypnotized young woman shown on page 162, whose hand is immersed in circulating ice water, reported no pain because the painful sensations were dissociated from awareness.

The Non-State View: Ordinary Social Psychological Processes Can Explain Hypnosis

Some psychologists—most notably the late Nicholas Spanos (1986, 1989, 1996), Theodore Sarbin (1999), and British psychologist Graham Wagstaff (1996, 1999)—have sharply challenged Hilgard's neodissociation theory. They fundamentally reject the notion that hypnotically induced changes involve a "special" state of consciousness. Instead,

they contend that the same effects can be produced *without* hypnosis if the individuals are appropriately instructed and motivated.

According to the *social-cognitive view of hypnosis,* hypnotic subjects are responding to the *social demands* of the hypnosis situation. That is, they are motivated to be "good" subjects and to cooperate with the hypnotic suggestions. They act the way they think good hypnotic subjects are supposed to act, conforming to the expectations of the hypnotist, their own expectations, and situational cues. Either consciously or unconsciously, hypnotic subjects are playing a socially prescribed role—the role of good hypnotic subject. According to the social-cognitive view, the "hypnotized" young woman on page 162 reported no

pain because that's what she expected to happen during the hypnosis session.

To back up the social-cognitive theory of hypnosis, Nicholas Spanos (1991, 1994) and his colleagues have amassed an impressive array of evidence showing that highly motivated people often perform just as well as hypnotized subjects in demonstrating pain reduction, amnesia, age regression, and hallucinations. Studies of people who simply *pretended* to be hypnotized have shown similar results. Based on such findings, non-state theorists contend that hypnosis can be explained in terms of rather ordinary psychological processes, including imagination, situational expectations, role enactment, compliance, and conformity. As Graham Wagstaff (1999) summarizes, "Non-state theorists see hypnosis as a

Brain Activation During Hypnosis While hypnotized or un-hypnotized, participants viewed the two rectangles above in four ways: the color image as it appeared or as an imagined gray-scale image, and the gray-scale image as it appeared or as an imagined color image. PET scans revealed that, when hypnotized, color areas of the left and right hemisphere were activated when participants were asked to perceive color, whether they were looking at the color or the gray-scale image. While not hypnotized, only the color areas in the right hemisphere were activated, regardless of which image was being viewed (Kosslyn & others, 2001).

Left hemisphere color areas activated only while hypnotized

Right hemisphere color area activated whether hypnotized or not strategic role enactment. In other words, 'susceptible' hypnotic subjects enact the role of a 'hypnotized' person as defined by cultural expectations and cues provided by the immediate situation."

Do "Real" and "Role-Playing" Hypnotic Participants Act the Same?

Not according to a classic study by Frederick Evans and Martin Orne, dubbed the "disappearing hypnotist" experiment. Evans and Orne (1971) compared the behavior of research participants who pretended to be hypnotized with highly hypnotizable participants. After each group went through a standard hypnotic induction procedure, a bogus power failure occurred and the experimenter left the room. When they thought they were not being observed, the role-playing participants immediately dropped their act. The hypnotized participants, however, did not.

Similar results were found in a more recent study by Eve Perugini and her colleagues (1998). Participants who were instructed to fake hypnotic-like responses stopped their behavior when they thought they were not being observed by the experimenter. But the participants who were hypnotized did not, even when they thought they were alone. These results seem to undermine the notion that behavior during hypnosis is motivated solely by compliance.

PET Scans During Hypnosis: A Neural Basis for Hypnosis?

In trying to settle the state versus nonstate explanations of hypnosis, researchers have turned to brain-imaging studies. Of particular interest is a recent PET scan study by psychologist Stephen Kosslyn and his colleagues (2000) that directly tested the role-playing explanation of hypnosis. In the study, highly hypnotizable volunteers viewed two images of rectangles, one in color and one in shades of gray, while lying in a PET scanner (see photos on page 164). While hypnotized, participants were asked to see both images as they were. Participants were also instructed to mentally "drain" each color

image so that it appeared in gray-scale. And, participants were instructed to see the gray-scale image as if it were in color. These last two suggested tasks were essentially hypnosis-induced hallucinations—draining color from a colored image or adding color to the gray-scale image. The participants also attempted the same visual tasks while they were not hypnotized. The PET scans revealed three important findings:

1. Activity *increased* in the left and right hemisphere color areas when the hypnotized participants were told to perceive *colored* rectangles, regardless of whether they were looking at the colored or gray-scale image.

2. Activity *decreased* in the left and right hemisphere color areas when the hypnotized participants were told to see *gray* rectangles, regardless of whether they were looking at the colored or gray-scale image.

3. Finally, when the participants were *not* hypnotized and attempted the same perceptual tasks, *only* the right hemisphere color areas activated.

So what does this mean? According to Kosslyn (2001), "Hypnosis is not simply 'role playing,' but does in fact reflect the existence of a distinct mental brain state." Adding support to that claim is other brain-imaging research also showing distinct neural differences during hypnosis (see Maquet & others, 1999; Rainville & others, 1997, 1999). But lest you think the debate is settled, read on.

The Imaginative Suggestibility View: Some People Are Highly Suggestible

University of Connecticut psychologists Irving Kirsch and Wayne Braffman (2001) dismiss the idea that hypnotic subjects are merely putting on an act to appease an observer. And although brain-imaging studies support the idea that hypnotic suggestions can radically alter behavior and experiences, they contend that those studies don't necessarily prove that hypnosis is a unique or distinct state. Rather, Kirsch and Braffman maintain that such studies emphasize individual differences in *imaginative*

suggestibility—the degree to which a person is able to experience an imaginary state of affairs as if it were real.

In previous research, Braffman and Kirsch (1999) found that many participants were just as responsive to suggestions when they had *not* been hypnotized as when they were hypnotized. These are people who have a high degree of imaginative suggestibility, whether hypnotized or not. So, according to their view, the effects of hypnosis are due neither to a unique psychological state nor to role-playing. "Hypnotic responses reveal an astounding capacity that some people have to alter their experience in profound ways," Kirsch and Braffman (2001) write. "Hypnosis is only one of the ways in which this capacity is revealed. It can also be evoked—and almost to the same extent—without inducing hypnosis."

Psychologists continue to debate the essential nature of hypnosis and the best explanation of hypnotic effects (Kihlstrom, 2001). Yet despite the sometimes intense controversy over how best to explain hypnotic effects, psychologists do agree on one point: Hypnosis can be a highly effective therapeutic technique (Kirsch & others, 1995; Montgomery & others, 2000). Indeed, if the effects of hypnosis were less striking, the debate among psychologists would undoubtedly be much less spirited.

Critical Thinking Questions

- Does the fact that highly motivated subjects can "fake" hypnotic effects invalidate the notion of hypnosis as a unique state of consciousness?

- Do individual differences in "imaginative suggestibility" provide a more parsimonious explanation than "dissociation" in explaining responsiveness to hypnotic suggestions?

- What kinds of evidence could prove or disprove the notion that hypnosis is a unique state of consciousness?

meditation
Any one of a number of sustained concentration techniques that focus attention and heighten awareness.

Meditation

Key Theme

- Meditation involves using one of various techniques to deliberately change conscious experience, inducing a state of focused attention and awareness.

Key Questions

- What are two general types of meditation?
- What are the effects of meditation?

Meditation refers to a group of techniques that induce an altered state of focused attention and heightened awareness. Meditation takes many forms and has been used for thousands of years as part of religious practices throughout the world. Virtually every major religion—Hindu, Taoist, Buddhist, Jewish, Christian, and Muslim—has a rich tradition of meditative practices (Nelson, 2001). However, many people practice meditation independently of any religious tradition or spiritual context. Some forms of psychotherapy also include meditative practice as a component of the overall therapy (Epstein, 1995; Snaith, 1998).

Common to all forms of meditation is the goal of controlling or retraining attention. Although meditation techniques vary a great deal, they can be divided into two general categories. *Concentration techniques* involve focusing awareness on a visual image, your breathing, a word, or a phrase. When a sound is used, it is typically a short word or a religious phrase, called a *mantra,* that is repeated mentally. *Opening-up techniques* involve a present-centered awareness of the passing moment, without mental judgment (Tart, 1994). Rather than concentrating on an object, sound, or activity, the meditator engages in quiet awareness of the "here and now" without distracting thoughts. The *zazen,* or "just sitting," technique of Zen Buddhism is a form of opening-up meditation (Austin, 1998).

Effects of Meditation

One meditation technique that has been widely used in research is called *transcendental meditation,* or *TM.* TM is a form of concentrative meditation that can be quickly mastered, follows a simple format, and does not require any changes in lifestyle or beliefs. Meditators sit quietly with eyes closed and mentally repeat the mantra they have been given. Rather than struggling to clear the mind of thoughts, meditators are taught to allow distracting thoughts to simply "fall away" while they focus their attention on their mantra.

Numerous studies have shown that even beginning meditators practicing TM experience a state of lowered physiological arousal, including a decrease in heart rate, lowered blood pressure, and changes in brain waves (Dillbeck & Orme-Johnson, 1987). Advocates of TM claim that such physical changes produce a unique state of consciousness with a wide variety of benefits, including stress reduction.

Meditation in Different Cultures Meditation is an important part of many cultures. A Buddhist monk (below left), wearing a traditional saffron robe, practices meditation at a temple in Thailand. Below right, people practice tai chi in a park in Hong Kong. Tai chi is a form of meditation that involves a structured series of slow, smooth movements. Throughout China, many people begin their day with tai chi, often meeting in parks and other public places.

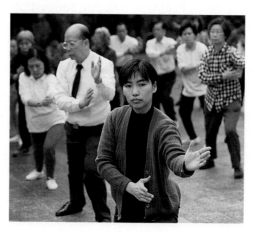

focus on **Neuroscience**

SPECT Images at Baseline and During Meditation

Imaging the Brain During Peak Meditation Experiences Meditative practices have been a part of every major world religion for centuries. But independent of religious affiliation, experienced meditators have described their peak spiritual experiences during meditation in very similar terms. Experienced meditators frequently report a heightened sense of concentration and attention, a sense of timelessness and infinity, and a profound sense of connectedness to everyone and everything in existence (Newberg & d'Aquili, 2000).

How is brain functioning different during these intense meditation experiences? One challenge in answering this question is that PET scans and fMRI scans are noisy, which is not conducive to maintaining a deep meditative state. That's why researcher Andrew Newberg and his colleagues (2001) at the University of Pennsylvania Medical Center opted to use an imaging technique called SPECT, which stands for *single photon emission computed tomography.* SPECT detects a radioactive tracer that is injected into the bloodstream. Once injected, the radioactive tracer almost immediately locks into brain cells, reflecting the brain's blood-flow patterns and utilization at that particular moment. Because the tracer remains locked in position for hours, the actual SPECT scan can be performed long after the injection.

Eight highly experienced Tibetan Buddhist meditators—four men and four women—participated in this study. A baseline SPECT scan was performed on each person, and then the person meditated until he or she had achieved the "peak" moment of the meditation. The meditator signaled this moment by tugging a string. In the next room, the researchers injected the radioactive tracer into a long intravenous tube connected to a vein in the meditator's arm. When the meditation ended approximately 15

minutes later, the meditator was taken to another room and then scanned with the SPECT camera.

In the above SPECT images, increased blood flow is indicated by red and yellow colors, which correspond with heightened brain activity. If you look closely at the SPECT images, two distinct changes are evident during the meditation: (1) increased blood flow to both *frontal lobes* and (2) decreased blood flow to the left *parietal lobe.*

According to Newberg and his colleagues (2001), both of these brain changes during peak meditation experiences make sense. Why? Because the frontal lobes are involved in attention-focusing tasks, which is heightened during meditation. Other studies have also reported increased frontal lobe activity during meditation (e.g., Lazar & others, 2000).

In contrast, the parietal lobes are involved in visual-spatial tasks, such as helping us stay oriented in physical space, judging distances, and gauging time. During meditation experiences, the usual sense of time and space is altered and the meditator often experiences a profound sense of timelessness and connectedness to the world. Hence, Newberg and his colleagues (2001a) predicted that activity in the parietal lobe would be decreased.

So what do these findings mean? Newberg and his colleagues have been studying the relationship between religious practices and brain functioning for several years (Newberg & others 2001). "Spiritual experience, at its very root, is intimately interwoven with human biology," contends Newberg. "In the study with the Buddhist meditators, we believe that we were seeing colorful evidence on the SPECT's computer screen of the brain's capacity to make spiritual experience real."

Like other forms of meditation, TM has diverse effects. Meditators show EEG patterns that are dominated by alpha-brain-wave activity, which is similar to the state of drowsiness that precedes stage 1 sleep (Fenwick, 1987). However, experienced meditators tend to describe meditation in very different subjective terms than they use to describe drowsiness (Pekala, 1987). Often, meditation is described as producing both relaxation and a state of wakeful alertness. In contrast, people who practice mental relaxation with their eyes closed often describe the experience as relaxing but boring.

Table | 4.5

How to Meditate

Here is a simple but effective meditation technique developed by British psychologist and meditation researcher Michael A. West. Practice the technique for 15 to 20 minutes twice a day for at least two weeks.

1. Sit quietly in an upright position in a room where you are not likely to be disturbed.
2. Close your eyes and relax your body. Sit quietly for about half a minute.
3. Begin to repeat the word *one* easily and silently to yourself, or choose some other simple word, such as *peace* or *calm.*
4. Don't concentrate too hard on the sound. The word need only be a faint idea at times—you don't have to keep repeating it clearly.
5. Think the word easily. It may change by getting louder or softer, longer or shorter, or it may not change at all. In every case, just take it as it comes.

6. Remember, the word has no special meaning or special significance. It is a simple device that helps in meditation.
7. Continue the meditation in this way for about 15 minutes. Don't worry about achieving a deep level of meditation or about whether you are concentrating on the sound.
8. Don't try to control thoughts. If thoughts come during meditation, don't worry about it. When you become aware that you have slipped into a train of thought, just go very easily back to the sound. Don't make great efforts to exclude thoughts—just favor the sound.
9. If you become aware of outside noises or other distracting sounds, go easily back to the word; don't fight to exclude those distractions. Do the same as you would with thoughts. Accept them, but favor the sound.
10. Above all, you are meant to enjoy the meditation, so don't try too hard; just take it easily as it comes.

SOURCE: West (1987).

Many studies have shown that regular meditation can enhance physical and psychological functioning beyond that provided by relaxation alone (C. N. Alexander & others, 1994; Andresen, 2000; Austin, 1998). If you would like to try a simple meditative technique, follow the instructions in Table 4.5.

Meditation and hypnosis are similar in that both involve the deliberate use of mental techniques to change the experience of consciousness. In the final section of this chapter, we'll consider one of the oldest strategies for deliberately altering conscious awareness—psychoactive drugs.

4.3 R·E·V·I·E·W

C·O·N·C·E·P·T

Hypnosis and Meditation

1. Jill is very responsive to hypnotic suggestions. Jill probably _____.
   a. has a very vivid imagination and a rich fantasy life
   b. has a very negative attitude toward hypnosis
   c. is easily distracted
   d. can be easily hypnotized against her will

2. While Marshall is under hypnosis, the hypnotist tells him that he remembers being lost in a shopping mall as a young child. After being brought out of hypnosis, Marshall is completely convinced that the event occurred and describes it in detail. The hypnotist has successfully created _____.
   a. an age regression
   b. posthypnotic amnesia
   c. hypermnesia
   d. a pseudomemory

3. Dr. Kildare used hypnosis instead of an anesthetic when setting a patient's broken toe. The patient insisted that she felt no pain, but when instructed to raise her right index finger if some part of her felt pain, she raised her finger. This example best illustrates the notion of _____.
   a. age regression
   b. posthypnotic suggestion
   c. the hidden observer
   d. transcendental meditation

4. To help deal with the stress of his busy schedule, Erik meditates for about 15 minutes on the commuter train as he is going to and from work. His meditation consists of focusing his awareness on mentally repeating the word *peace.* Erik is using a(n) _____ technique of meditation.
   a. concentration
   b. relaxation
   c. opening-up
   d. self-hypnosis

Psychoactive Drugs

Key Theme
- Psychoactive drugs alter consciousness by changing arousal, mood, thinking, sensations, and perceptions.

Key Questions
- What are four broad categories of psychoactive drugs?
- What are some common properties of psychoactive drugs?
- What factors influence the effects, use, and abuse of drugs?

Psychoactive Drugs As they take a break in a Sarajevo cafe, these young Bosnian soldiers talk and relax—with the help of beer, coffee, and cigarettes. Alcohol, caffeine, and nicotine are three of the most widely used psychoactive substances in the world.

Do you start your day with a cup of coffee? We do. (To be honest, we tend to start our mornings with a *pot* of coffee.) Most Americans sip (or gulp) coffee to help them wake up in the morning and stay alert throughout the day. Many people drink a beer or a glass of wine to help them relax and unwind in the evening.

Caffeine and alcohol are two of the most widely used psychoactive drugs. **Psychoactive drugs** are chemical substances that can alter arousal, mood, thinking, sensation, and perception. In this section, we will look at the characteristics of four broad categories of psychoactive drugs:

1. *Depressants*—drugs that depress, or inhibit, brain activity

2. *Opiates*—drugs that are chemically similar to morphine and that relieve pain and produce euphoria

3. *Stimulants*—drugs that stimulate, or excite, brain activity

4. *Psychedelic drugs*—drugs that distort sensory perceptions

Common Properties of Psychoactive Drugs

Addiction is a broad term that refers to a condition in which a person feels psychologically and physically compelled to take a specific drug (Leshner, 1997). People experience **physical dependence** when their body and brain chemistry have physically adapted to a drug (Berridge & Robinson, 1995). Many physically addictive drugs gradually produce **drug tolerance**, which means that increasing amounts of the drug are needed to gain the original, desired effect.

For people who are physically dependent on a drug, abstaining from the drug produces withdrawal symptoms. **Withdrawal symptoms** are unpleasant physical reactions to the lack of the drug, plus an intense craving for it. Withdrawal symptoms are alleviated by taking the drug again. Often, the withdrawal symptoms are opposite to the drug's action, a phenomenon called the **drug rebound effect.** For example, withdrawing from stimulating drugs, like the caffeine in coffee, may produce depression and fatigue. Withdrawal from depressant drugs, such as alcohol, may produce excitability.

Biological Effects of Drugs

Each psychoactive drug has a distinct biological effect. Psychoactive drugs may influence many different bodily systems, but their consciousness-altering effects are primarily due to their effect on the brain. Typically, these drugs influence brain activity by altering synaptic transmission among neurons. As we discussed in Chapter 2, drugs affect synaptic transmission by increasing or decreasing neurotransmitter amounts, or by blocking, mimicking, or influencing a particular neurotransmitter's effects (see page 54).

The biological effects of a given drug vary somewhat from one person to another. The person's weight, gender, and age may influence the intensity of the

psychoactive drug
A drug that alters consciousness, perception, mood, and behavior.

physical dependence
A condition in which a person has physically adapted to a drug so that he or she must take the drug regularly in order to avoid withdrawal symptoms.

drug tolerance
A condition in which increasing amounts of a physically addictive drug are needed to produce the original, desired effect.

withdrawal symptoms
Unpleasant physical reactions, combined with intense drug cravings, that occur when a person abstains from a drug on which he or she is physically dependent.

drug rebound effect
Withdrawal symptoms that are the opposite of a physically addictive drug's action.

drug's effects. Whether the drug is taken on a full or empty stomach or in combination with other drugs also plays a role. Racial and ethnic differences may affect how a drug is metabolized. For example, African-Americans seem to absorb more nicotine from cigarettes than do European-Americans or Mexican-Americans, and they metabolize the nicotine more slowly (Caraballo & others, 1998; Pérez-Stable & others, 1998).

Psychological and Environmental Influences

Psychological and environmental factors can also influence the effects of a drug. The response to a drug can be significantly affected by personality characteristics, mood, expectations, and experience with the drug, as well as by the setting in which the drug is taken (Marlatt & others, 1988; Stacy & others, 1990). For example, what effect do you think three drinks would have on each of the following individuals?

- A college student at an end-of-semester bash the night final exams are over
- A father toasting his youngest daughter at her bat mitzvah
- A man involved in an angry, escalating argument with his wife on a hot summer night

Even though the physiological effect of alcohol is essentially the same for each individual, the behavioral and psychological responses would clearly be different. One drinker feels joyously uninhibited; another is feeling sentimental and proud; and the third may be feeling dangerously aggressive. Alcohol provides a familiar example, but individual responses to other psychoactive drugs are also subject to psychological and environmental influences.

Why Do People Abuse Drugs?

There is no easy answer to the question of why people abuse drugs. First, it's difficult to draw a hard-and-fast line between drug *use* and drug *abuse,* especially when the drug in question is legal, such as alcohol. Most people would not consider having a cold beer at a summer picnic an instance of drug abuse. Downing a six-pack, however, falls into a different category altogether.

In contrast to drug use, **drug abuse** refers to recurrent drug use that results in disruptions in academic, social, or occupational functioning, or in legal or psychological problems (American Psychiatric Association, 1994). Some authorities widen the definition of drug abuse to refer to *any* form of drug taking that results in harmful effects.

Many factors influence drug-taking behavior. Listed here are some of the most important factors that have been found to be involved in drug abuse (Hawkins & others, 1992; Petraitis & others, 1995):

- Social and cultural norms that are favorable toward drug taking
- Availability and cost of the drug
- Drug-taking behavior of role models and family members
- Occupational, social, and academic problems
- Association with drug-using peers
- Rebelliousness or alienation from society as a whole

Cultural norms also have a strong influence on drug use and abuse. For example, determining what level of alcohol constitutes "abuse" varies from one culture to another (Tanaka-Matsumi & Draguns, 1997). Even in the United States, different ethnic groups have very different norms regarding the use of alcohol. Jewish-, Italian-, Greek-, and Chinese-Americans have a tradition of moderate

Dangerous Drugs, Tragic Deaths Comedian Chris Farley was only 33 when he died of an accidental drug overdose. His death was caused by a lethal mixture of morphine (an opiate) and cocaine (a stimulant). Farley was also known to be a heavy drinker.

drinking. Drinking alcohol may be restricted to particular social occasions, such as weddings and other formal celebrations. Some U.S. religious groups, such as the Mormons, Amish, and Muslims, forbid drinking alcohol under any circumstances. On the other hand, Irish-Americans tend to be more tolerant of heavy drinking (Trimble, 1994).

In the United States, the media stereotype is that drug abuse occurs largely among members of minorities. However, national surveys have consistently shown that a much higher percentage of white teenagers than African-American or other minority teenagers use illegal drugs (Substance Abuse and Mental Health Services Administration, 1994).

drug abuse
Recurrent drug use that results in disruptions in academic, social, or occupational functioning or in legal or psychological problems.

depressants
A category of psychoactive drugs that depress or inhibit brain activity.

The Depressants
Alcohol, Barbiturates, and Inhalants

Key Theme
■ Depressants inhibit central nervous system activity, while opiates are addictive drugs that relieve pain and produce euphoria.

Key Questions
■ What are the physical and psychological effects of alcohol?
■ How do barbiturates, tranquilizers, and inhalants affect the body?
■ What are the effects of opiates, and how do they affect the brain?

The **depressants** are a class of drugs that depress or inhibit central nervous system activity. In general, depressants produce drowsiness, sedation, or sleep. Depressants also relieve anxiety and lower inhibitions. All depressant drugs are potentially physically addictive. Further, the effects of depressant drugs are *additive,* meaning that the sedative effects are increased when depressants are combined.

Alcohol

A staple of the human diet for thousands of years, alcoholic beverages provide a good example of the potential for a psychoactive drug to be misused (Vallee, 1998). Used in small amounts, alcohol reduces tension and anxiety. Evidence exists that light drinking reduces the risk of heart disease, probably because of its beneficial effects on cholesterol levels (Rimm & others, 1991). Weddings, parties, and other social gatherings often include alcohol, a tribute to its relaxing and social lubricating properties.

But even though alcohol is a legal and readily available drug for adults, it's also a dangerous drug with a high potential for abuse. Consider these facts:

■ Many drug experts believe that alcohol abuse has the highest social cost of all drug addictions.

■ Every year, alcohol is implicated in over 25,000 fatal automobile accidents and 12,000 murders in the United States.

■ Approximately two-thirds of all cases of spousal abuse and violent child abuse involves alcohol use (Steele & Josephs, 1990).

■ Drinking by pregnant women is the third leading cause of birth defects that result in mental retardation—and the only preventable one.

More than two-thirds of the Americans who are old enough to drink do so at least occasionally. Of those, an estimated 14 million have serious alcohol problems. These people may drink excessively on a regular basis and suffer social, occupational, and health problems as a result of drinking (Rosenberg, 1993). About half of this group, some 7 million people, are considered *alcoholic*—they are physically addicted to alcohol.

How Does Alcohol Affect the Body? Generally, it takes about one hour to metabolize the alcohol in one drink, which is defined as 1 ounce of 80-proof whiskey, 4 ounces of wine, or 12 ounces of beer. All three drinks contain the same amount of alcohol; the alcohol is simply more diluted in beer than in hard liquor.

Factors such as body weight, gender, food consumption, and the rate of alcohol consumption also affect blood alcohol levels. A slender person who quickly consumes three drinks on an empty stomach will become more than twice as intoxicated as a heavier person who consumes three drinks with food. Women metabolize alcohol more slowly than do men. If a man and a woman of equal weight consume the same number of drinks, the woman will become more intoxicated.

Alcohol depresses the activity of neurons throughout the brain. Alcohol impairs cognitive abilities, such as concentration, memory, and speech, and physical abilities, such as muscle coordination and balance. As blood levels of alcohol rise, more brain activity is impaired, until the person loses consciousness. If blood alcohol levels continue to rise, death can occur, because the brain's respiratory center can no longer function. For this reason, drinking contests are potentially lethal.

Binge drinking is a particularly risky practice. *Binge drinking* is defined as five or more drinks in a row for men, or four or more drinks in a row for women. Every year, several college students die of alcohol poisoning after ingesting large amounts of liquor in a short amount of time. Less well publicized are the other negative effects associated with binge drinking, including aggressive behavior, sexual assault, accidents, and property damage (Hingson & others, 2002; Wechsler & others, 2002).

A national survey of college students at 119 colleges found that close to 50 percent of all male students and 40 percent of all female students were binge drinkers (Wechsler & others, 2002). White students were most likely to binge-drink, while African-American students were least likely. While close to half of dormitory residents binged at least occasionally, more than 75 percent of fraternity and sorority house residents were binge drinkers. Table 4.6 shows the behavioral and physical effects of blood alcohol levels.

Because alcohol is physically addictive, the person with alcoholism who stops drinking may suffer from physical withdrawal symptoms. Alcohol withdrawal causes rebound hyperexcitability in the brain. The severity of the withdrawal symptoms depends on the level of physical dependence (Schuckit & others, 1998). With a low level of dependence, withdrawal may involve disrupted sleep, anxiety, and mild tremors ("the shakes"). At higher levels of physical dependence on alcohol, withdrawal may involve confusion, hallucinations, and severe tremors or seizures. Collectively, these severe symptoms are sometimes called *delirium tremens,* or the *DTs.* In cases of extreme physical dependence, withdrawal can cause seizures, convulsions, and even death in the absence of medical supervision (O'Brien, 1997).

What Are Alcohol's Psychological Effects? People are often surprised that alcohol is classified as a depressant. Initially, alcohol produces a mild euphoria, talkativeness, and feelings of good humor and friendliness, leading many people to think of alcohol as a stimulant. But these subjective experiences occur because alcohol *lessens inhibitions* by depressing the brain centers responsible for judgment and self-control. Reduced inhibitions and self-control contribute to the aggressive and violent behavior sometimes associated with alcohol abuse (Steele & Josephs, 1990). But the loss of inhibitions affects individuals differently, depending on their environment and expectations regarding alcohol's effects (Bushman, 1993).

The Dangers of Driving Under the Influence As the crumpled wreckage of her car attests, even Britain's Princess Diana was not immune to the devastation caused by drunk driving. According to blood tests by the police in Paris, where the fatal accident occurred, the driver of her Mercedes had drunk the equivalent of nine shots of whiskey before taking the wheel of the car. His blood alcohol level was three times the French legal limit. An intoxicated driver has impaired perceptual ability and psychomotor functions, delayed reaction time, and poor coordination. He or she is also likely to display impaired judgment, poor impulse control, and an inflated self-image.

Table 4.6

Behavioral Effects of Blood Alcohol Levels

Blood Alcohol Level	Behavioral Effects
0.05%	Lowered alertness; release of inhibitions; impaired judgment
0.10%	Slowed reaction times; impaired motor function; less caution
0.15%	Large, consistent increases in reaction time
0.20%	Marked depression in sensory and motor capability; decidedly intoxicated
0.25%	Severe motor disturbance; staggering; sensory perceptions greatly impaired
0.30%	Stuporous but conscious; no comprehension of the world around them
0.35%	Surgical anesthesia; minimal level causing death
0.40%	About half of those at this level die

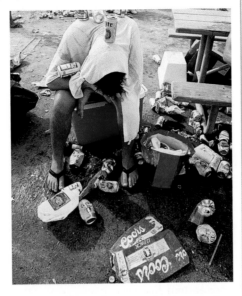

This Is Fun? According to a national survey of college students, more than half "drank to get drunk" in the previous year (Wechsler & others, 2002). Approximately 75 percent of students who are members of fraternities and sororities admit to binge drinking. Despite the deaths from alcohol poisoning of several college students each year, binge drinking and public drunkenness remain common at spring break celebrations.

Barbiturates and Tranquilizers

Barbiturates are powerful depressant drugs that reduce anxiety and promote sleep, which is why they are sometimes called "downers." Barbiturates depress activity in the brain centers that control arousal, wakefulness, and alertness. They also depress the brain's respiratory centers.

Like alcohol, barbiturates at low doses cause relaxation, mild euphoria, and reduced inhibitions. Larger doses produce a loss of coordination, impaired mental functioning, and depression. High doses can produce unconsciousness, coma, and death. Barbiturates produce a very deep but abnormal sleep; REM sleep is greatly reduced. Because of the additive effect of depressants, barbiturates combined with alcohol are particularly dangerous.

Common barbiturates include the prescription sedatives *Seconal* and *Nembutal*. The illegal drug *methaqualone* (street name *quaalude*) is almost identical chemically to barbiturates and has similar effects.

Barbiturates produce both physical and psychological dependence. Withdrawal from low doses of barbiturates produces irritability and REM rebound nightmares. Withdrawal from high doses of barbiturates can produce hallucinations, disorientation, restlessness, and life-threatening convulsions.

Tranquilizers are depressants that relieve anxiety. Commonly prescribed tranquilizers include *Xanax, Valium, Librium,* and *Ativan.* Chemically different from barbiturates, tranquilizers produce similar, although less powerful, effects. We will discuss these drugs in more detail in Chapter 15, on therapies.

barbiturates
(barb-ITCH-yer-ets) A category of depressant drugs that reduce anxiety and produce sleepiness.

tranquilizers
Depressant drugs that relieve anxiety.

inhalants
Chemical substances that are inhaled to produce an alteration in consciousness.

opiates
(OH-pee-ets) A category of psychoactive drugs that are chemically similar to morphine and have strong pain-relieving properties.

stimulants
A category of psychoactive drugs that increase brain activity, arouse behavior, and increase mental alertness.

Heroin Cough Syrup Opium and its derivatives, including heroin, morphine, and codeine, were legal in the United States until 1914. In the late nineteenth and early twentieth centuries, opiates were commonly used in over-the-counter medications for a variety of ailments, from sleeplessness to "female problems" (Musto, 1991). This ad for "Glyco-Heroin" cough syrup appeared in 1904. Codeine is still used in some prescription cough syrups.

Inhalants

Inhalants are chemical substances that are inhaled to produce an alteration in consciousness. Paint solvents, model airplane glue, gasoline, nitrous oxide, and certain aerosol sprays are just a few of the substances that are abused in this way.

Although psychoactive inhalants do not have a common chemical structure, they generally act as central nervous system depressants. At low doses, they may cause relaxation, giddiness, and reduced inhibition. At higher doses, inhalants can lead to hallucinations and a loss of consciousness.

Inhalants are also quite dangerous. Suffocation is one hazard, but many inhaled substances are also toxic to the liver and other organs. Inhalants are inexpensive and readily available, and inhalant abuse is most prevalent among adolescent and young adult males.

The Opiates
From Poppies to Demerol

Often called *narcotics,* the **opiates** are a group of addictive drugs that relieve pain and produce feelings of euphoria. Natural opiates include *opium,* which is derived from the opium poppy; *morphine,* the active ingredient in opium; and *codeine,* which can be derived from either opium or morphine. Synthetic and semisynthetic opiates include *heroin, methadone,* and the prescription painkillers *Percodan* and *Demerol.*

Opiates produce their powerful effects by mimicking the brain's own natural painkillers, called *endorphins.* Opiates occupy endorphin receptor sites in the brain. As you may recall from Chapter 2, the word *endorphin* literally means "the morphine within."

When used medically, opiates alter an individual's reaction to pain, not by acting at the pain site but by reducing the brain's perception of pain. Many people recovering from surgery experience a wave of pain relief after receiving narcotics such as morphine, Demerol, or Percodan. People who take opiates in such circumstances rarely develop drug tolerance or dependence (Jacox & others, 1994).

The most frequently used opiate is heroin. When injected into a vein, heroin reaches the brain in seconds, creating an intense rush of euphoria that is followed by feelings of contentment, peacefulness, and warmth. Withdrawing from heroin is not life-threatening, but it does produce unpleasant drug rebound symptoms (O'Brien, 1997). Withdrawal symptoms include an intense craving for heroin, fever, chills, muscle cramps, and gastrointestinal problems.

The Stimulants
Caffeine, Nicotine, Amphetamines, and Cocaine

Key Theme
- Stimulant drugs increase brain activity, while the psychedelic drugs create perceptual distortions, alter mood, and affect thinking.

Key Questions
- What are the general effects of stimulants and the specific effects of caffeine, nicotine, amphetamines, and cocaine?
- What are the effects of mescaline, LSD, and marijuana?
- What are the "club drugs," and what are their effects?

Stimulants vary in the strength of their effects, legal status, and the manner in which they are taken. All stimulant drugs, however, are at least mildly addicting, and all tend to increase brain activity. We'll first look at the most widely used and legal stimulants, caffeine and nicotine. Then we'll examine much more potent stimulants, cocaine and the amphetamines.

Caffeine and Nicotine

Caffeine is found in coffee, tea, cola drinks, chocolate, and many over-the-counter medications (see Table 4.7). Most Americans consume caffeine in some form every day (DeAngelis, 1994b). In fact, caffeine is the most widely used psychoactive drug in the world.

Caffeine stimulates the cerebral cortex in the brain, resulting in an increase in mental alertness and wakefulness. Even a single cup of coffee has a noticeable effect on the cerebral cortex.

Yes, coffee drinkers, caffeine *is* physically addictive. Regular coffee, tea, or cola drinkers will experience withdrawal symptoms if they abruptly stop their caffeine intake. Headaches, irritability, drowsiness, and fatigue may last up to a week. Even just a few hours of caffeine deprivation can produce noticeable withdrawal symptoms of sleepiness and fatigue (Phillips-Bute & Lane, 1997). At high doses, caffeine can produce anxiety, restlessness, insomnia, and increased heart rate—symptoms that are collectively called "coffee nerves."

When Mike lit up a cigarette, he did so under the mistaken impression that smoking would help him relax and fall asleep. But cigarettes contain **nicotine,** an extremely addictive stimulant. Nicotine is found in all tobacco products, including pipe tobacco, cigars, cigarettes, and smokeless tobacco. About 25 percent of American adults use tobacco regularly. The proportion of smokers is much higher in Japan, many European countries, and developing countries (Bartecchi & others, 1995).

Like coffee, nicotine increases mental alertness and reduces fatigue or drowsiness. Functional MRI scans show that nicotine increases neural activity in many areas of the brain, including the frontal lobes, thalamus, hippocampus, an(dala (Stein & others, 1998). Thus, it's not surprising that smokers report that tobacco enhances mood, attention, arousal, and vigilance.

When cigarette smoke is inhaled, nicotine reaches the brain in seconds. But within 30 minutes or so, nicotine has left the brain. Thus, the addicted pack-a-day smoker will light a cigarette every 30 to 40 minutes to maintain a relatively constant nicotine level in the brain. Over the course of a year, that averages out to 70,000 "hits" of nicotine. Nicotine is highly addictive, both physically and psychologically. People who start smoking for nicotine's stimulating properties often continue smoking to avoid the withdrawal symptoms. Along with an intense craving for cigarettes, withdrawal symptoms include jumpiness, irritability, tremors, headaches, drowsiness, "brain fog," and lightheadedness (Shiffman & others, 1995).

Amphetamines and Cocaine

Like caffeine and nicotine, amphetamines and cocaine are addictive substances that stimulate brain activity, increasing mental alertness and reducing fatigue. However, amphetamines and cocaine also elevate mood and produce a sense of euphoria (Snyder, 1986). When abused, both drugs can produce severe psychological and physical problems.

Sometimes called "speed" or "uppers," **amphetamines** suppress appetite and were once widely prescribed as diet pills. Tolerance to the appetite-suppressant effects occurs quickly, so progressive increases in amphetamine dosage are required to maintain the effect. Consequently, amphetamines are rarely prescribed today for weight control.

Using any type of amphetamines for an extended period of time is followed by "crashing"—withdrawal symptoms of fatigue, deep sleep, intense mental depression, and increased appetite.

caffeine
(kaff-EEN) A stimulant drug found in coffee, tea, cola drinks, chocolate, and many over-the-counter medications.

nicotine
A stimulant drug found in tobacco products.

amphetamines
(am-FET-uh-meens) A class of stimulant drugs that arouse the central nervous system and suppress appetite.

Caffeine and Conversation Caffeine is the most widely used psychoactive drug in the world and is commonly consumed in social settings. These French college students are enjoying a cup of espresso at an outdoor café.

Table | **4.7**

Common Sources of Caffeine

Item	Caffeine Content (average, in milligrams)
Coffee (5 ounces)	100
Tea (5 ounces)	50
Cocoa (5 ounces)	5
Chocolate (semisweet, baking; 1 ounce)	25
Chocolate milk (1 ounce)	5
Cola drink (12 ounces)	40
Water Joe (16 ounces)	60
Over-the-counter stimulants (No Doz, Vivarin)	100+
Over-the-counter analgesics (Anacin, Midol)	33
Over-the-counter cold remedies (Triaminicin)	30
Over-the-counter diuretics (Aqua-ban)	100

SOURCE: Julien (2001)

Cocaine Toothache Drops? Prior to 1914, cocaine was legal in the United States and, like the opiates, was widely used as an ingredient in over-the-counter medicines (Jonnes, 1999). From this 1885 advertisement for Cocaine Toothache Drops, it's clear that cocaine was used to treat children as well as adults. Cocaine derivatives, such as novocaine and lidocaine, are still used medically as anesthetics. Cocaine was also part of Coca-Cola's original formula in 1888. It was replaced in 1903 with another stimulant, caffeine. Coca leaves, with the cocaine extracted for medical purposes, are still used for flavoring cola drinks.

FIGURE 4.7 The Damaging Effects of Methamphetamine on the Brain Methamphetamine not only is highly addictive but also causes long-term damage to brain structures and functioning. The red and yellow areas on these PET scans show the concentration of dopamine transporters in a normal brain *(left)* and in the brain of a former methamphetamine abuser *(right)*. Damage to the brain's dopamine system was associated with memory and motor skill defects.

Control Subject   METH Abuser

This is another example of a drug rebound effect. Users also become psychologically dependent on the drug for the euphoric state, or "rush," that it produces, especially when injected.

Benzedrine and *dexedrine* are prescription amphetamines. *Methamphetamine,* also known as *meth,* is an illegal drug that can be easily manufactured in home or street laboratories. Providing an intense high that is longer-lasting and less expensive than cocaine, meth usage has spread from the western United States to the rest of the country, including small towns in the rural Midwest and South.

As the popularity of methamphetamine has increased, so have concerns about the drug's long-term effects. PET scans of former methamphetamine users have shown abnormalities in brain structure and functioning (Volkow & others, 2001a, 2001b, 2001c). Even after several months of abstinence, the brains of former meth users showed a significant reduction in the number of dopamine receptors and transporters (see Figure 4.7). Dopamine transporters help transport "used" dopamine back into the neurons that produce it. Some former methamphetamine users had lost up to 24 percent of the normal level of dopamine transporters. Memory and motor skill problems were common in the former abusers and were most severe in those with the greatest loss of dopamine transporters.

Cocaine is an illegal stimulant derived from the leaves of the coca tree, which is found in South America. (The coca plant is not the source of cocoa or chocolate, which is made from the beans of the *cacao* plant.) When inhaled, or "snorted," in purified, powdered form, cocaine reaches the brain within a few minutes. Inhaling cocaine produces intense euphoria, mental alertness, and self-confidence, which lasts for several minutes. A more concentrated form of cocaine, called *crack,* is smoked rather than inhaled.

Prolonged use of amphetamines or cocaine can result in **stimulant-induced psychosis,** also called *amphetamine psychosis* or *cocaine psychosis* (Snyder, 1986). Schizophrenia-like symptoms develop, including auditory hallucinations of voices and bizarrely paranoid ideas. "Cocaine bugs" refers to an unusual tactile hallucination that occurs in stimulant-induced psychosis but not in schizophrenia: People itch and tingle, claiming that insects or small animals are crawling on or under their skin.

Psychedelic Drugs
Mescaline, LSD, and Marijuana

The term **psychedelic drug** was coined in the 1950s to describe a group of drugs that create profound perceptual distortions, alter mood, and affect thinking. *Psychedelic* literally means "mind manifesting" (Tart, 1990).

Mescaline and LSD

Naturally occurring psychedelic drugs have been used for thousands of years. **Mescaline,** which is derived from the peyote cactus, has been used for centuries in the religious ceremonies of Mexican Indians. Another psychedelic drug, called *psilocybin,* is derived from *Psilocybe* mushrooms, sometimes called magic mushrooms. Psilocybin has been used since 500 B.C. in religious rites in Mexico and Central America (Snyder, 1986).

In contrast to these naturally occurring psychedelics, **LSD** (*lysergic acid diethylamide*) is a powerful psychedelic drug that was first synthesized in the late 1930s. LSD is far more potent than mescaline or psilocybin. Just 25 micrograms, or one-millionth of an ounce, of LSD can produce profound psychological effects with relatively few physiological changes.

LSD and psilocybin are very similar chemically to the neurotransmitter *serotonin,* which is involved in regulating moods and sensations (see Chapter 2). LSD and psilocybin mimic serotonin in the brain, stimulating serotonin receptor sites (Aghajanian, 1994).

The effects of a psychedelic experience vary greatly, depending on an individual's personality, current emotional state, surroundings, and the other people present. A "bad trip" can produce extreme anxiety, panic, and even psychotic episodes. Tolerance to psychedelic drugs may occur after heavy use. However, even heavy users of LSD do not develop physical dependence nor do they experience withdrawal symptoms if the drug is not taken.

Adverse reactions to LSD include flashbacks (recurrences of the drug's effects), depression, long-term psychological instability, and prolonged psychotic reactions (Smith & Seymour, 1994). In a psychologically unstable or susceptible person, even a single dose of LSD can precipitate a severe psychotic reaction.

Marijuana

The common hemp plant, *Cannibis sativa,* is used to make rope and cloth. But when its leaves, stems, flowers, and seeds are dried and crushed, the mixture is called **marijuana,** one of the most widely used illegal drugs. Marijuana's active ingredient is the chemical *tetrahydrocannabinol,* abbreviated *THC.* When marijuana is smoked, THC reaches the brain in less than 30 seconds. One potent form of marijuana, *hashish,* is made from the resin of the hemp plant. Hashish is sometimes eaten.

To lump marijuana with the highly psychedelic drugs mescaline and LSD is somewhat misleading. At high doses, marijuana can sometimes produce sensory distortions that resemble a mild psychedelic experience. Low-to-moderate doses of THC typically produce a sense of well-being, mild euphoria, and a dreamy state of relaxation. Senses become more focused and sensations more vivid. Taste, touch, and smell may be enhanced; time perception may be altered.

A little more than a decade ago, researchers discovered receptor sites in the brain that are specific for THC (Herkenham, 1992; Matsuda & others, 1990). They've also discovered a naturally occurring brain chemical, called *anandamide,* that is structurally similar to THC and that binds to the THC receptors in the brain (Devane & others, 1992). Anandamide appears to be involved in regulating the transmission of pain signals and may reduce painful sensations (Calignano & others, 1998; Walker & others, 1999). Researchers also suspect that anandamide may be involved in mood and memory.

There are very few THC receptors in the brainstem, the part of the brain that controls such life support functions as breathing and heartbeat. Thus, high doses of THC do not interfere with respiratory and cardiac functions as depressants and opiates do.

Most marijuana users do not develop tolerance or physical dependence. Chronic users of extremely high doses can develop some tolerance to THC and may experience withdrawal symptoms when its use is discontinued (de Fonseca & others, 1997). Such symptoms include irritability, restlessness, insomnia, tremors, and decreased appetite.

Peyote-Inspired Visions The Huichol Indians of Mexico have used peyote in religious ceremonies for hundreds of years. Huichol yarn paintings, like the one shown here, are flat pieces of wood inlaid with designs made with colored yarn. The yarn paintings often depict imagery and scenes inspired by traditional peyote visions, which resemble the geometric shapes and radiating patterns of hallucinations induced by psychedelic drugs. Today, peyote continues to be used as a sacrament in the religious ceremonies of the Native American Church, a religion with more than 600,000 members (Swan & Big Bow, 1995).

cocaine
A stimulant drug derived from the coca tree.

stimulant-induced psychosis
Schizophrenia-like symptoms that can occur as the result of prolonged amphetamine or cocaine use; also called *amphetamine psychosis* or *cocaine psychosis.*

psychedelic drugs
A category of psychoactive drugs that create sensory and perceptual distortions, alter mood, and affect judgment.

mescaline
A psychedelic drug derived from the peyote cactus.

LSD
A synthetic psychedelic drug.

marijuana
A psychoactive drug derived from the hemp plant.

MDMA or ecstasy
Synthetic club drug that combines stimulant and mild psychedelic effects.

dissociative anesthetics
Class of drugs that reduce sensitivity to pain and produce feelings of detachment and dissociation; includes the club drugs phencyclidine (PCP) and ketamine.

(a) Control, Non-use

(b) Moderate MDMA use

(c) Heavy MDMA use

FIGURE 4.8 Effects of Ecstasy on the Brain
The "ecstasy" of an MDMA trip takes a heavy toll on the brain, especially in women. These brain-scan images show serotonin activity (red) in the brains of **(a)** a normal female volunteer who had never taken ecstasy, **(b)** a moderate ecstasy user, and **(c)** a heavy ecstasy user. The study by Dutch scientist Liesbeth Reneman and her colleagues (2001a) included both male and female participants, but the female participants were more susceptible to brain damage from ecstasy use than men were.

Marijuana and its active ingredient, THC, have been shown to be helpful in the treatment of pain, epilepsy, hypertension, nausea, glaucoma, and asthma (Snyder, 1990). In cancer patients, THC can prevent the nausea and vomiting caused by chemotherapy. However, the medical use of marijuana is limited and politically controversial.

On the negative side, marijuana interferes with muscle coordination and perception and may impair driving ability. When marijuana and alcohol use are combined, marijuana's effects are intensified—a dangerous combination for drivers. Marijuana has also been shown to interfere with learning, memory, and cognitive functioning (Pope & others, 2001).

Designer "Club" Drugs
Ecstasy and the Dissociative Anesthetic Drugs

Some drugs don't fit into neat categories. The "club drugs" are a loose collection of psychoactive drugs that are popular at dance clubs, parties, and the all-night dance parties called "raves." Many of these drugs are *designer drugs,* meaning that they were synthesized in a laboratory rather than derived from naturally occurring compounds. In this section, we'll take a look at three of the most popular club drugs—*ecstasy, ketamine,* and *PCP.*

The initials **MDMA** stand for the long chemical name of the quintessential club drug better known as **ecstasy.** Other street names are *X, XTC, Adam,* and the "love drug". Ecstasy was developed by a German pharmaceutical company in 1912 for use as a possible appetite suppressant, but it was not tested on humans until the 1970s. Structurally similar to both mescaline and amphetamine, MDMA has stimulant and psychedelic effects. While the use of other illegal drugs has remained stable or declined over the past decade, the use of ecstasy has sharply increased in Western Europe and the United States (Zickler, 2001).

At low doses, MDMA acts as a stimulant, but at high doses it has mild psychedelic effects. Its popularity, however, results from its emotional effects: Feelings of euphoria and increased well-being are common. People who have taken ecstasy also say that the drug makes them feel loving, open, and closer to others—effects that led to its use in psychotherapy for a brief time until its adverse effects became apparent (Braun, 2001). Ecstasy's side effects hint at the problems that can be associated with its use: dehydration, rapid heartbeat, tremors, muscle tension and involuntary teeth-clenching, and hyperthermia (abnormally high body temperature). Rave party-goers who take MDMA in crowded, hot surroundings are particularly at risk for collapse or death from dehydration and hyperthermia.

The "love drug" effects of ecstasy may result from its unique effect on serotonin in the brain. Along with causing neurons to release serotonin, MDMA also blocks serotonin reuptake, amplifying and prolonging serotonin effects (Braun, 2001). While flooding the brain with serotonin may temporarily enhance feelings of emotional well-being, there are adverse trade-offs. First, the "high" of ecstasy is often followed by depression when the drug wears off. More ominously, animal studies have shown that moderate or heavy use of ecstasy can lead to long-term, potentially irreversible damage to serotonin nerve endings in the brain (Ricaurte & others, 1998). Several studies have shown similar damage to serotonin neurons in the human brain (Croft & others, 2001; Reneman & others, 2001a). Female users may be more susceptible to brain damage than male users (see Figure 4.8). Other studies have shown that serotonin levels become severely depleted after long-term use, possibly causing the depression that follows when the drug wears off (Kuhn & Wilson, 2001). Equally troubling are cognitive effects: In one study, memory and verbal reasoning problems persisted up to a year after the last dose was taken (Reneman & others, 2001b).

Another class of drugs that make their appearance at dance clubs and raves are the **dissociative anesthetics,** including phencyclidine, better known as *PCP* or *angel dust,* and *ketamine* (street name *Special K*). Originally developed to serve as general anesthetics for surgery in the late 1950s, both PCP and ketamine deaden pain and, at high doses, can induce a stupor or coma. Because of their psychological effects, these drugs were largely abandoned for general surgical use in humans.

Rather than producing actual hallucinations, PCP and ketamine produce marked feelings of dissociation and depersonalization. Feelings of detachment from reality—including distortions of space, time, and body image—are common. Generally, the effects of PCP are more intense and of a longer duration than those of ketamine.

PCP can be eaten, snorted, or injected, but it is most often smoked or sprinkled on tobacco or marijuana. The effects are unpredictable, and a PCP trip can last for several days. Some users of PCP report feelings of invulnerability and exaggerated strength. PCP users can become severely disoriented, violent, aggressive, or suicidal. High doses of PCP can cause hyperthermia, convulsions, and death. PCP affects levels of the neurotransmitter *glutamate,* indirectly stimulating the release of dopamine in the brain. Thus, PCP is highly addictive. Memory problems and depression are common effects of long-term use.

Summing Up

Consciousness and Its Variations

In this chapter, we've taken a close look at the rather elusive topic of consciousness. We've described many possible variations in conscious experience, both those that occur naturally and those that are artificially induced. We also looked at the body rhythms and processes that regulate these naturally occurring cycles of consciousness.

In the Prologue, you read about the experiences of Mike and Nina. Some aspects of their nighttime experience are universal—all humans experience similar stages of wakefulness, drowsiness, deep sleep, and dreaming sleep. Other experiences, like Nina's night terrors and Mike's insomnia, represent disruptions in the daily cycle of sleep and wakefulness.

We hope that you have gained some insight into your own daily changes in consciousness and some understanding of how conscious experience can be influenced. In the chapter Application, we'll suggest some ways in which you can use the findings of psychological research to improve the quality of *your* consciousness.

4.4 R·E·V·I·E·W

C·O·N·C·E·P·T

Psychoactive Drugs

For each of the following descriptions, name the drug class, and give two (or more) examples.

	Drug Class	Examples
1. Drugs that create perceptual distortions, alter mood, and affect thinking	_____	_____
2. Drugs that inhibit central nervous system activity; produce drowsiness, sedation, or sleep; and may reduce anxiety and lower inhibitions	_____	_____
3. Addictive drugs that mimic endorphins and relieve pain and produce euphoria	_____	_____
4. Addictive drugs that increase brain activity and mental alertness	_____	_____

In this section we'll give you some research-based, practical suggestions to help you wake up in the morning, improve the quality of your sleep, and minimize the mental and physical disruptions that can occur when your body clock is out of sync with environmental time cues.

Dealing with Morning Brain Fog

There is surprisingly little research on how to deal with **sleep inertia**—sleepiness on awakening that interferes with your ability to perform mental or physical tasks. For some people, "morning brain fog" can last an hour or more before they feel fully alert (Jewett & others, 1999).

People who have trouble getting up in the morning tend to stay in bed until the last possible moment. This strategy, of course, only intensifies their disorientation, because they are forced to hustle out the door before they are fully awake.

The simplest antidote for sleep inertia seems to be the passage of time. So if you suffer from sleep inertia, try setting your alarm clock (and possibly a second one in the next room) to wake you 15 minutes *earlier* than usual. Resolve to hit the floor when the alarm goes off. The extra 15 minutes will help give your mind time to clear.

During that 15 minutes, sip a cup of coffee or tea, which promotes wakefulness. It takes approximately half an hour to feel the full effects of the caffeine. If the sun is up, sit near a window. If it's not, turn on the lights. Bright light, especially sunlight, helps brain fog dissipate by reducing blood levels of the hormone melatonin (Brown, 1994). To help engage your brain, glance at the newspaper or start a list of what you want to accomplish for the day. Though simple, these suggestions really do help, as your night-owl authors, neither of whom exactly greets the morning with enthusiasm, have discovered.

Improving the Quality of Your Sleep

Sleep researchers have identified many ways to improve the quality of your sleep:

- Timing is more important than you probably realize. In the early-evening hours, usually between 8:00 and 10:00 P.M., we normally experience a period of increased wakefulness that occurs prior to sleepiness. Sleep researchers call this presleep burst of wakefulness the "forbidden zone for sleep" (Lavie, 1989). So to avoid suddenly feeling wide awake in bed, you should go to bed after the forbidden zone, when your brain has begun to gear down to sleepiness.

- Monitor your caffeine intake, and don't drink caffeine-containing beverages or eat chocolate for at least three or four hours before going to bed. Look again at Table 4.7 on page 175, which lists some common sources of caffeine. Many over-the-counter medications include caffeine. Check the label if you take such medications before bedtime.

- Going to bed very hungry or very full will disrupt sleep, but a light snack will help reduce nighttime restlessness and increase total sleep time.

- Moderate exercise during the day seems to promote deep sleep, but exercise in the evening or shortly before going to bed may keep you awake.

- Soaking in a very warm bath shortly before retiring promotes deep sleep by raising your core body temperature.

- A consistent bedtime routine and familiar surroundings enhance the quality of sleep. Try to go to bed about the same time each night and get up at approximately the same time every morning so that you stay in sync with your own pattern of circadian rhythms.

- Depressant drugs, such as alcohol and barbiturates, may produce drowsiness, but they also reduce REM sleep, disrupting the quality of your sleep. Hence, they should be avoided.

Finally, you may be pleased to discover that sex promotes sleep. For example, rabbits tend to sleep very little—with the exception of quickly nodding off into REM sleep after some amorous activity in the old rabbit hutch. The same phenomenon also seems to occur in humans, which is why sleep so often follows sexual interaction. As sleep researcher J. Allan Hobson (1995) put it, sex "not only leads to muscle relaxation, but also clears the cerebral circuits of tedious humdrum."

Almost everyone occasionally has trouble falling asleep or staying asleep.

Often this occurs because we're mentally ruminating about some problem or conflict. One strategy to help psychologically let go of the problem for the night is to write down your concerns and what you plan to do about them the next day. Another strategy is to redirect your thoughts. Try vividly imagining yourself exploring a tranquil landscape or walking along a familiar route. A third strategy is to use the meditation technique described in Table 4.5 on page 168.

If you still can't fall asleep or stay asleep, don't overreact. Instead, get up and read in a comfortable chair until you feel drowsy, and then return to bed. If your sleeping problems persist for a week or more, ask your family doctor for advice or a referral to a sleep specialist.

Coping with the Night Shift

People vary in the ease with which they develop tolerance for working the night shift or rotating shifts (Monk, 1997). Here are some suggestions for minimizing the negative effects of night work:

- If you have a choice in your work schedule, the longer you can stay with one shift, the better. Frequent shift changes increase jet lag symptoms (Wilkinson, 1992).

- If you work rotating shifts, try to make your schedule changes more compatible with circadian rhythms. Because of our natural tendency to drift toward longer days, it is easier to lengthen our days than to shorten them. Therefore, try to arrange your shift changes to progress from the morning to evening to night shifts (Gallo & Eastman, 1993).

- If you work the midnight shift, bright lights in the workplace, especially during the early part of the shift, will help your circadian cycles adjust to the night schedule (Czeisler & others, 1990; Dawson & Campbell, 1991).

- To promote sleep during the daytime, ask your doctor about taking melatonin. Melatonin supplements can help induce daytime sleep, improving mental alertness during night shifts (Dawson, 1995; Folkard & others, 1993).

Chapter Review
Consciousness and Its Variations

Introduction: Consciousness: *Experiencing the "Private I"*

■ **Consciousness** refers to the immediate awareness of internal and external stimuli. Most psychologists today consider consciousness an important area of research, as did early psychologists.

Biological and Environmental "Clocks" That Regulate Consciousness

■ **Circadian rhythms** are regulated by the **suprachiasmatic nucleus (SCN)**, the "master clock" located in the hypothalamus of the brain. In response to light detected by special photoreceptors, the SCN reduces the production of **melatonin** by the pineal gland. Increased melatonin makes you sleepy.

■ Under free-running conditions, human circadian rhythms drift toward a 25-hour day. Circadian rhythms become disrupted when environmental time cues are out of sync with the body clock. Symptoms of jet lag can be produced by travel across time zones or by rotating shift work.

Sleep

■ The invention of the **electroencephalograph,** which produces an **EEG** or **electroencephalogram,** and the discovery of rapid eye movements (REM) changed scientific views about sleep. The two basic types of sleep are **REM sleep** and **NREM sleep.**

■ When we are awake and alert, the brain generates **beta brain waves.** As brain activity gears down and drowsiness sets in **alpha brain waves** are generated. **Hypnagogic hallucinations** can occur during this drowsy, presleep phase.

■ Each sleep stage is characterized by a specific pattern of brain activity. In the first 90 minutes of sleep, four different stages of NREM sleep are followed by a brief episode of REM sleep. Stage 2 of sleep is defined by the appearance of **sleep spindles** and **K complexes.** Throughout the night, episodes of REM sleep become progressively longer and NREM episodes become shorter.

■ As people age, periods of REM sleep and deep sleep become shorter, and more time is spent in stage 2 NREM.

■ Sleep deprivation studies and the phenomenon of **REM rebound** demonstrate the biological need to sleep. The **restorative theory** and the **adaptive theory** offer different explanations for the function of sleep.

■ **Sleep disorders** are serious disturbances in the normal sleep pattern that interfere with daytime functioning and cause subjective distress.

■ The most common sleep disorder is **insomnia;** the next most common is **sleep apnea.** For many, insomnia is related to a condition called **restless legs syndrome (RLS).** The **parasomnias** include **sleepwalking, night terrors,** bruxism, and **REM sleep behavior disorder.** The symptoms of **narcolepsy** are experienced during the day.

Dreams and Mental Activity During Sleep

■ **Sleep thinking** occurs during NREM sleep. A **dream** is a storylike, unfolding episode of mental images that occurs during NREM or REM sleep.

■ During REM sleep, the brain is cut off from external stimuli. The frontal lobes and primary visual cortex are inactivated, but the hippocampus, amygdala, and other visual centers are highly active. REM sleep is needed for the consolidation of certain types of memories.

■ Most dreams reflect everyday concerns and include familiar people and settings. Changes in brain chemistry and functioning that occur during sleep probably contribute to the inability to remember dreams. There are individual differences in dream recall. **Nightmares** are unpleasant anxiety dreams.

■ Sigmund Freud believed that dream images are symbols of unconscious wishes. According to Freud, dreams are composed of **manifest content** and **latent content.** The **activation–synthesis model of dreaming** proposes that dreams reflect our subjective awareness of brain activation during sleep. Some researchers believe that dreaming consciousness is similar in its functions to waking consciousness.

Hypnosis

■ **Hypnosis** is an unusual state of awareness, defined as a cooperative social interaction in which the hypnotic participant responds to suggestions made by the hypnotist. Changes in perception, memory, and behavior may be produced. People vary in hypnotic susceptibility.

■ Under hypnosis, profound sensory and perceptual changes may be experienced, including pain reduction and hallucinations. **Posthypnotic suggestions** influence behavior outside the hypnotic state. Hypnosis is used in habit control, but its effectiveness varies. Hypnosis can produce **posthypnotic amnesia,** but not **hypermnesia.** Although hypnosis does not increase the accuracy of memories, it does increase confidence in memories and can produce false memories. Hypnosis cannot be used to make people perform behaviors that are contrary to their morals or values.

■ The **neodissociation theory** of Ernest Hilgard explains hypnosis as involving **dissociation** and a **hidden observer.** Some psychologists believe that hypnosis is not a special state of consciousness but can be explained by social and cognitive processes.

Meditation

■ **Meditation** refers to techniques used to control attention so as to induce an altered state of focused attention and awareness.

■ Research suggests that regular meditation enhances physical and psychological functioning.

Psychoactive Drugs

■ **Psychoactive drugs** can alter arousal, mood, thinking, sensation, and perception. Many psychoactive drugs are addictive, producing **physical dependence** and **drug tolerance.** The physically dependent person who stops taking a drug experiences **withdrawal symptoms,** which often include the **drug rebound effect.**

■ Psychoactive drugs affect brain activity by influencing synaptic transmission. Drug effects can be influenced by the person's weight, gender, race, metabolism, and the presence of other drugs. Personality characteristics, mood, expectations, experience with the drug, and the setting in which the drug is taken also affect the drug response.

■ **Drug abuse** refers to recurrent drug use that leads to disruptions in academic, social, or occupational functioning and to legal or psychological problems. Many factors contribute to drug abuse, including social and cultural influences.

■ **Depressants** are physically addictive drugs that inhibit central nervous system activity. Depressants include alcohol, **barbiturates, tranquilizers,** and **inhalants.** Psychologically, alcohol lessens inhibitions, but its effects vary, depending on the person's environment and expectations. Barbiturates and inhalants produce relaxation and reduce inhibitions.

■ **Opiates** are addictive drugs that relieve pain and produce feelings of euphoria. The opiates include opium, morphine, codeine, heroin, methadone, and prescription painkillers. Opiates relieve pain by mimicking the effect of endorphins in the brain.

■ **Stimulants** include **caffeine, nicotine, amphetamines,** and **cocaine.** The stimulants increase brain activity, and all stimulants are addictive. Prolonged use of amphetamines or cocaine can lead to **stimulant-induced psychosis.**

■ **Psychedelic drugs** include **mescaline, LSD,** and **marijuana.** The psychedelics create perceptual distortions, alter mood, and affect thinking. Although psychedelic drugs are not physically addictive, they can cause a variety of harmful effects.

■ The "club drugs" are synthetic drugs used at dance clubs, parties, and "raves." These drugs include **MDMA (ecstasy)** and the **dissociative anesthetics** PCP and ketamine.

Key Terms

consciousness, p. 136

circadian rhythm, p. 138

suprachiasmatic nucleus (SCN), p. 139

melatonin, p. 139

electroencephalograph, p. 142

EEG (electroencephalogram), p. 142

REM sleep, p. 142

NREM sleep, p. 142

beta brain waves, p. 143

alpha brain waves, p. 143

hypnagogic hallucinations, p. 143

sleep spindles, p. 144

K complexes, p. 144

REM rebound, p. 147

restorative theory of sleep, p. 148

adaptive theory of sleep, p. 149

sleep disorders, p. 150

insomnia, p. 150

restless legs syndrome (RLS), p. 150

sleep apnea, p. 151

sleepwalking, p. 151

night terrors, p. 152

parasomnias, p. 152

REM sleep behavior disorder, p. 152

narcolepsy, p. 153

sleep thinking, p. 153

dream, p. 155

nightmare, p. 157

manifest content, p. 158

latent content, p. 158

activation–synthesis model of dreaming, p. 158

hypnosis, p. 160

posthypnotic suggestion, p. 162

posthypnotic amnesia, p. 162

hypermnesia, p. 162

dissociation, p. 163

neodissociation theory of hypnosis, p. 163

hidden observer, p. 163

meditation, p. 166

psychoactive drug, p. 169

physical dependence, p. 169

drug tolerance, p. 169

withdrawal symptoms, p. 169

manifest content, p. 158

drug rebound effect, p. 169

drug abuse, p. 170

depressants, p. 171

barbiturates, p. 173

tranquilizers, p. 173

inhalants, p. 174

opiates, p. 174

stimulants, p. 174

caffeine, p. 175

nicotine, p. 175

amphetamines, p. 175

cocaine, p. 176

stimulant-induced psychosis, p. 176

psychedelic drugs, p. 176

mescaline, p. 176

LSD, p. 177

marijuana, p. 177

MDMA (ecstasy), p. 178

dissociative anesthetics, p. 178

sleep inertia, p. 180

Key People

Sigmund Freud (1856–1939) Founder of psychoanalysis; proposed that dream images are disguised and symbolic expressions of unconscious wishes and urges. (p. 158)

Ernest R. Hilgard (1904–2001) American psychologist who extensively studied hypnosis and advanced the *neodissociation theory of hypnosis.* (p. 163)

J. Allan Hobson (b. 1933) Contemporary American psychiatrist and neurobiologist who has extensively researched sleep and dreaming; proposed the *activation–synthesis model* of dreaming. (p. 158)

William James (1842–1910) American psychologist and philosopher who proposed that the subjective experience of consciousness is an ongoing stream of mental activity. (p. 137)

Concept Review Answers

4.1 page 149

1. melatonin
2. suprachiasmatic nucleus; 25
3. sunlight; 24
4. stage 2 NREM
5. REM; dreaming
6. stage 4 NREM

4.2 page 160

1. c   *2.* d   *3.* d   *4.* b   *5.* c

4.3 page 168

1. a   *2.* a   *3.* c   *4.* a

4.4 page 179

1. psychedelic drugs: LSD, mescaline, marijuana
2. depressants: alcohol, barbiturates, tranquilizers, inhalants
3. opiates: opium, morphine, heroin, methadone, Demerol, Percodan
4. stimulants: caffeine, nicotine, amphetamines, methamphetamines, cocaine

Web Companion | Review Activities

You can find additional review activities at **www.worthpublishers.com/hockenbury**
The Psychology 3e Web Companion has a self-scoring practice quiz, flashcards, two interactive crossword puzzles, and other activities to help you master the material in this chapter.

We're More Alike

chapter 5

Learning

Prologue

The Killer Attic

Sandy's parents, Erv and Fern, recently celebrated their fiftieth wedding anniversary. Sometimes it seems truly amazing that they've managed to survive so long together, as you'll see from this true story.

It was a warm summer morning in Chicago. Erv and Fern drank their coffee and made plans for the day. The lawn needed mowing, the garage needed cleaning, and someone had to go to the post office to buy stamps. Fern, who doesn't like driving, said that she would mow the lawn if Erv would go to the post office. Erv, who doesn't like yard work, readily agreed to the deal.

As Erv left for the post office, Fern started cutting the grass in the backyard. When Erv returned, he parked the car around the corner under some large shade trees so that it would stay cool while he puttered around in the garage. Walking through the front door to drop off the stamps, he noticed that the attic fan was squeaking loudly. Switching it off, Erv decided to oil the fan before he tackled the garage. He retrieved the stepladder and oil from the basement, propped the ladder under the attic's trapdoor, and gingerly crawled up into the attic, leaving the trapdoor open.

Meanwhile, Fern was getting thirsty. As she walked past the garage on the way into the house, she noticed the car was still gone. "Why isn't Erv back yet? He must have stopped somewhere on the way back from the post office," she thought. As she got a glass of water, she noticed the stepladder and the open attic door. Muttering that Erv never put anything away, Fern latched the trapdoor shut and dragged the ladder back down to the basement.

Erv, who had crawled to the other side of the attic to oil the fan, never heard the attic trapdoor shut. It was very hot in the well-insulated, airless attic, so he tried to work fast. After oiling the fan, he crawled back to the trapdoor—only to discover that it was latched shut from the outside! "Fern," he hollered, "open the door!" But Fern was already back outside, mowing away, and couldn't hear Erv over the noise of the lawn mower. Erv, dripping with sweat, kept yelling and pounding on the trapdoor.

Outside, Fern was getting hot, too. She stopped to talk to a neighbor, leaving the lawn mower idling. He offered Fern a cold beer, and the two of them leaned over the fence, laughing and talking. From a small, sealed attic window, Erv watched the whole scene. Jealousy was now added to his list of discomforts. He was also seriously beginning to think that he might sweat to death in the attic heat. He could already see the tabloid headlines in the supermarket checkout line: LAUGHING WIFE DRINKS BEER WHILE HUSBAND COOKS IN ATTIC!

Finally, Fern went back to mowing, wondering what in the world had happened to Erv. Meanwhile, up in the attic, Erv was drenched with sweat and his heart was racing. He promised God he'd never complain about Chicago winters again. At last, Fern finished the lawn and walked back to the house. Hearing the back door open, Erv began to yell and pound on the trapdoor again.

"Hey, Fern! Fern!"

Fern froze in her tracks.

"Fern, let me out! I'm going to suffocate up here!"

"Erv! Is that you? Where are you?" she called, looking around.

"I'm in the attic! Let me out!"

"What are you doing in the attic? I thought you were at the store!"

"What do you *think* I'm doing? Let me out of here! Hurry!"

Once Fern was reassured that Erv had suffered no ill effects from being trapped in the attic, she burst out laughing. Later that day, still grumbling about Fern's harebrained sense of humor, Erv removed the latch from the attic door. Ever since, whenever Erv goes up into the attic, he posts a sign on the ladder that reads MAN IN THE ATTIC! And, even today, Erv gets a little anxious whenever he has to go up in the attic.

For her part, Fern is careful to check on Erv's whereabouts before she closes the attic door. But she still laughs when she tells the story of the "killer attic"—which she does frequently, as it never fails to crack up her listeners. Luckily, Erv is a good sport and is used to Fern's sense of humor.

Erv and Fern have both learned from their experience, as is reflected in the changes in their behavior. Learning new behaviors can occur in many ways, but it almost always helps us adapt to changing circumstances, as you'll see in this chapter.

Introduction
What Is Learning?

Key Theme

- Learning refers to a relatively enduring change in behavior or knowledge as a result of experience.

Key Questions

- What is conditioning?
- What are three basic types of learning?

What do we mean when we say that Fern and Erv have "learned" from their experience with the killer attic? In the everyday sense, *learning* often refers to formal methods of acquiring new knowledge or skills, such as learning in the classroom or learning to play the flute.

In psychology, however, the topic of learning is much broader. Psychologists formally define **learning** as a process that produces a relatively enduring change in behavior or knowledge as a result of an individual's experience. For example, Erv has learned to feel anxious and uncomfortable whenever he needs to enter the attic. He's also learned to take simple precautions, such as posting his MAN IN THE ATTIC! sign, to avoid getting locked in the attic again. As Erv's behavior demonstrates, the learning of new behaviors often reflects adapting to your environment. As the result of experience, you acquire new behaviors or modify old behaviors so as to better cope with your surroundings.

In this broad sense of the word, learning occurs in every setting, not just in classrooms. And, learning takes place at every age. Further, the psychological study of learning is not limited to humans. From alligators to zebras, learning is an important aspect of the behavior of virtually all animals.

learning
A process that produces a relatively enduring change in behavior or knowledge as a result of past experience.

Psychologists have often studied learning by observing and recording the learning experiences of animals in carefully controlled laboratory situations. Using animal subjects, researchers can precisely control the conditions under which a particular behavior is learned. The goal of much of this research has been to identify the general principles of learning that apply across a wide range of species, including humans.

Much of this chapter will focus on a very basic form of learning, called *conditioning*. **Conditioning** is the process of learning associations between environmental events and behavioral responses. This description may make you think conditioning has only a limited application to your life. Suppose, however, that at the beginning of your next psychology class, your instructor announced, "There's a surprise test today. Put all your books on the floor and take out a pencil and a clean sheet of paper." Would you feel a twinge of anxiety? If you did, it would be an example of the power of conditioned learning: You've learned to feel anxious when you hear the word *test*.

From simple actions, like answering the telephone, to more complex skills, like programming a cell phone, much of your everyday behavior reflects learning through conditioning. In this chapter, we'll look at basic types of conditioning—classical conditioning and operant conditioning. *Classical conditioning* explains how certain stimuli can trigger an automatic response, as the attic now triggers mild anxiety in Erv. And, as you'll see in a later section, *operant conditioning* is useful in understanding how we acquire new, voluntary actions, such as Erv's posting his sign whenever he climbs into the attic. Finally, toward the end of the chapter, we'll also consider the process of *observational learning,* or how we acquire new behaviors by observing the actions of others.

The study of learning has been a consistent theme throughout the history of psychology. Theories and ideas about the nature of learning have influenced psychology's development as a science since its earliest beginnings at the turn of the last century. In this chapter, you'll meet some of psychology's most influential thinkers and scientists including Ivan Pavlov, John B. Watson, B. F. Skinner, and Albert Bandura. Although the earliest scientific research on the psychology of learning took place more than a hundred years ago, learning continues to be an active and important part of psychological research today. But to fully understand contemporary views on learning, you need to understand how the study of learning evolved. With that thought in mind, we begin our study in the Russian laboratory of a distinguished physiologist in the late 1800s.

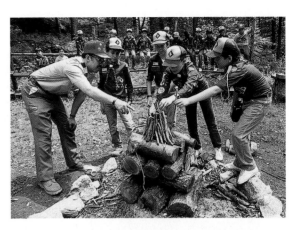

Conditioning, Learning, and Behavior
Through different kinds of experiences, people and animals acquire enduring changes in their behaviors. Psychologists have identified general principles of learning that explain how we acquire new behaviors—from simple responses to complex skills. As other members of their troop look on, these scouts are learning how to build a campfire.

Classical Conditioning
Associating Stimuli

Key Theme

- Classical conditioning is a process of learning associations between stimuli.

Key Questions

- How did Pavlov discover and investigate classical conditioning?
- How does classical conditioning occur?
- What factors can affect the strength of a classically conditioned response?

One of the major contributors to the study of learning was not a psychologist but a Russian physiologist who was awarded a Nobel Prize for his work on digestion. **Ivan Pavlov** was a brilliant scientist who directed several research laboratories in St. Petersburg, Russia, at the turn of the twentieth century.

conditioning
The process of learning associations between environmental events and behavioral responses.

Ivan Pavlov (1849–1936) In his laboratory, Pavlov was known for his meticulous organization, keen memory, and attention to details (Windholz, 1990). But outside his lab, Pavlov was absentminded, forgetful, and impractical, especially regarding money. He often forgot to pick up his paycheck, and he sometimes lent money to people with hard-luck stories who couldn't possibly pay him back (Fancher, 1996). On a trip to New York City, Pavlov carried his money so carelessly that he had his pocket picked in the subway, and his American hosts had to take up a collection to pay his expenses (Skinner, 1966).

classical conditioning
The basic learning process that involves repeatedly pairing a neutral stimulus with a response-producing stimulus until the neutral stimulus elicits the same response; also called *respondent conditioning* or *Pavlovian conditioning.*

unconditioned stimulus (UCS)
The natural stimulus that reflexively elicits a response without the need for prior learning.

unconditioned response (UCR)
The unlearned, reflexive response that is elicited by an unconditioned stimulus.

Pavlov's involvement with psychology began as a result of an observation he made while investigating the role of saliva in digestion, using dogs as his experimental subjects.

In order to get a dog to produce saliva, Pavlov (1904) put food on the dog's tongue. After he had worked with the same dog for several days in a row, Pavlov noticed something curious. The dog began salivating *before* Pavlov put the food on its tongue. In fact, the dog began salivating when Pavlov entered the room or even at the sound of his approaching footsteps. But salivating is a *reflex*—a largely involuntary, automatic response to an external stimulus. The dog should salivate only *after* the food was presented, not before. Why would the reflex occur before the stimulus was presented? What was causing this unexpected behavior?

If you own a dog, you've probably observed the same basic phenomenon. Your dog gets excited and begins to slobber when you shake a box of dog biscuits, even before you've given him a doggie treat. In everyday language, your pet has learned to anticipate food in association with some signal—namely, the sound of dog biscuits rattling in a box.

Pavlov's extraordinary gifts as a researcher enabled him to recognize the important implications of what had at first seemed a problem—a reflex (salivation) that occurred *before* the appropriate stimulus (food) was presented. He also had the discipline to systematically study how such associations are formed. In fact, Pavlov abandoned his research on digestion and devoted the remaining 30 years of his life to investigating different aspects of this phenomenon. Let's look at what he discovered in more detail.

Principles of Classical Conditioning

The process of conditioning that Pavlov discovered was the first to be extensively studied in psychology. Thus, it's called *classical conditioning* (Hilgard & Marquis, 1940). Also called *respondent conditioning* or *Pavlovian conditioning*, **classical conditioning** deals with behaviors that are elicited automatically by some stimulus. *Elicit* means "draw out" or "bring forth." That is, the stimulus doesn't produce a new behavior, but rather *causes an existing behavior to occur.*

Classical conditioning always involves some kind of reflexive behavior. Remember, a reflex is a relatively simple, unlearned behavior, governed by the nervous system, that occurs *automatically* when the appropriate stimulus is presented. In Pavlov's (1904) original studies of digestion, the dogs salivated reflexively when food was placed on their tongues. But when the dogs began salivating in response to the sight of Pavlov or to the sound of his footsteps, a new, *learned* stimulus elicited the salivary response. Thus, in classical conditioning, a *new* stimulus–response sequence is learned.

How does this kind of learning take place? Essentially, classical conditioning is a process of learning an *association between two stimuli.* Classical conditioning involves pairing a *neutral* stimulus (e.g., the sight of Pavlov) with an *unlearned, natural* stimulus (food in the mouth) that automatically elicits a reflexive response (the dog salivates). If the two stimuli (Pavlov + food) are repeatedly paired, eventually the neutral stimulus (Pavlov) elicits the same basic reflexive response as the natural stimulus (food)—even in the absence of the natural stimulus. So, when the dog in the laboratory started salivating at the sight of Pavlov *before* the food was placed on its tongue, it was because the dog had formed a new, *learned association* between the sight of Pavlov and the food.

Pavlov used special terms to describe each element of the classical conditioning process. The natural stimulus that reflexively produces a response without prior learning is called the **unconditioned stimulus** (abbreviated **UCS**). In this example, the unconditioned stimulus is the food in the dog's mouth. The unlearned, reflexive response is called the **unconditioned response** (or **UCR**). The unconditioned response is the dog's salivation.

To learn more about his discovery, Pavlov (1927) controlled the stimuli that preceded the presentation of food. For example, in one set of experiments, he used a bell as a neutral stimulus—neutral because dogs don't normally salivate to the sound of a ringing bell. Pavlov first rang the bell and then gave the dog food. After this procedure was repeated several times, the dog began to salivate when the bell was rung, before the food was put in its mouth. At that point, the dog was *classically conditioned* to salivate to the sound of a bell alone. That is, the dog had *learned a new association* between the sound of the bell and the presentation of food.

Pavlov called the sound of the bell the *conditioned stimulus*. The **conditioned stimulus** (or **CS**) is the stimulus that is originally neutral but comes to elicit a reflexive response. He called the dog's salivation to the sound of the bell the **conditioned response** (or **CR**), which is the *learned* reflexive response to a previously neutral stimulus. The steps of Pavlov's conditioning process are outlined in Figure 5.1.

Classical conditioning terminology can be confusing. You may find it helpful to think of the word *conditioned* as having the same meaning as "learned." Thus, the "conditioned stimulus" refers to the "learned stimulus," the "unconditioned response" refers to the "unlearned response," and so forth.

It's also important to note that in this case the unconditioned response and the conditioned response describe essentially the same behavior—the dog's sali-

conditioned stimulus (CS)
A formerly neutral stimulus that acquires the capacity to elicit a reflexive response.

conditioned response (CR)
The learned, reflexive response to a conditioned stimulus.

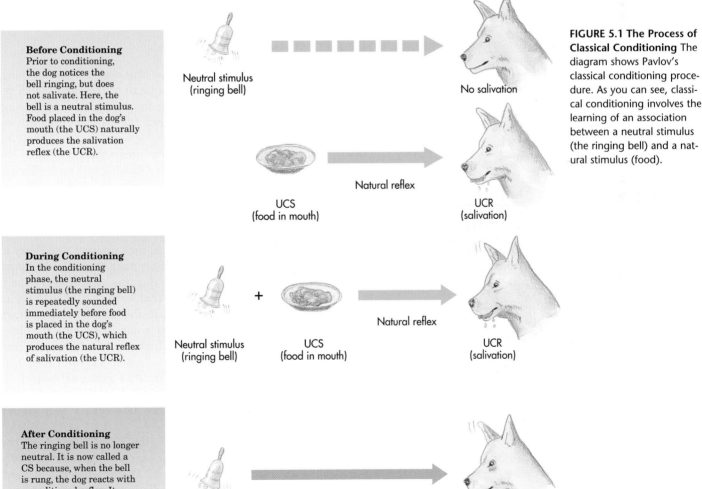

Before Conditioning
Prior to conditioning, the dog notices the bell ringing, but does not salivate. Here, the bell is a neutral stimulus. Food placed in the dog's mouth (the UCS) naturally produces the salivation reflex (the UCR).

Neutral stimulus
(ringing bell)

No salivation

UCS
(food in mouth)

Natural reflex

UCR
(salivation)

During Conditioning
In the conditioning phase, the neutral stimulus (the ringing bell) is repeatedly sounded immediately before food is placed in the dog's mouth (the UCS), which produces the natural reflex of salivation (the UCR).

Neutral stimulus
(ringing bell)

+

UCS
(food in mouth)

Natural reflex

UCR
(salivation)

After Conditioning
The ringing bell is no longer neutral. It is now called a CS because, when the bell is rung, the dog reacts with a conditioned reflex: It salivates even though no food is present. The salivation response is now called a CR.

CS
(ringing bell)

Conditioned reflex

CR
(salivation)

FIGURE 5.1 The Process of Classical Conditioning The diagram shows Pavlov's classical conditioning procedure. As you can see, classical conditioning involves the learning of an association between a neutral stimulus (the ringing bell) and a natural stimulus (food).

Life in Pavlov's Laboratories During Pavlov's four decades of research, more than 140 scientists and students worked in the two laboratories under his direction. Including his daughter, V. I. Pavlova, twenty of his co-researchers were women. Pavlov, who had an extraordinary memory for details, carefully supervised the procedures of dozens of ongoing research projects. Nevertheless, he acknowledged that the scholarly achievements produced by his laboratories represented the collective effort of himself and his co-workers (Windholz, 1990).

Stimulus Generalization: *Any* **White Jacket** Like most babies, our daughter Laura received several rounds of immunizations when she was an infant. And, like the infant in the photo, each painful injection (the UCS) elicited fear and made her cry (the UCR). After only the *second* vaccination, Laura developed a strong classically conditioned response—just the sight of a nurse's white uniform (a CS) triggered an emotional outburst of fear and crying (a CR). Interestingly, Laura's conditioned fear generalized to a wide range of white uniforms. As a toddler, Laura burst into tears in response to a pharmacist's white smock, a cosmetic saleswoman's white jacket, a butcher's white coat, and a veterinarian's white lab coat. These conditioned responses persisted until Laura was almost four years old.

stimulus generalization
The occurrence of a learned response not only to the original stimulus, but to other, similar stimuli as well.

stimulus discrimination
The occurrence of a learned response to a specific stimulus, but not to other, similar stimuli.

vating. Which label is applied depends on which stimulus elicits the response. If the dog is salivating in response to a *natural* stimulus that was not acquired through learning, the salivation is an *unconditioned* response. If, however, the dog has learned to salivate to a *neutral* stimulus that doesn't normally produce the automatic response, the salivation is a *conditioned* response.

Factors That Affect Conditioning

Over the three decades that Pavlov (1928) spent studying classical conditioning, he discovered many factors that could affect the strength of the conditioned response. For example, he discovered that the more frequently the conditioned stimulus and the unconditioned stimulus were paired, the stronger was the association between the two.

Pavlov also discovered that the *timing* of stimulus presentations affected the strength of the conditioned response. He found that conditioning was most effective when the conditioned stimulus was presented immediately *before* the unconditioned stimulus. In his early studies, Pavlov found that a half-second was the optimal time interval between the onset of the conditioned stimulus and the beginning of the unconditioned stimulus. Later, Pavlov and other researchers found that the optimal time interval could vary in different conditioning situations but was rarely more than a few seconds.

Pavlov (1927) also noticed that once a dog was conditioned to salivate to a particular stimulus, new stimuli that were similar to the original conditioned stimulus could also elicit the conditioned salivary response. For example, Pavlov conditioned a dog to salivate to a low-pitched tone. When he sounded a slightly higher-pitched tone, the conditioned salivary response would also be elicited. Pavlov called this phenomenon *stimulus generalization*. **Stimulus generalization** occurs when stimuli that are similar to the original conditioned stimulus also elicit the conditioned response, even though they have never been paired with the unconditioned stimulus.

Just as a dog can learn to respond to similar stimuli, so it can learn the opposite—to *distinguish* between similar stimuli. For example, Pavlov repeatedly gave a dog some food following a high-pitched tone but did not give the dog any food following a low-pitched tone. The dog learned to distinguish between the two tones, salivating to the high-pitched tone but not to the low-pitched tone. This phenomenon, **stimulus discrimination,** occurs when a particular conditioned response is made to one stimulus but not to other, similar stimuli.

Here's an example of stimulus generalization versus discrimination. Recall our example of the dog who drools (the CR) when he hears the rattling sound (the CS) of dog biscuits in a box. If your dog also drools one day when you shake a box of goldfish crackers as you pour them in a serving bowl, *stimulus generalization* has taken place. Eventually, your dog learns that to distinguish between one sound that predicts the delivery of a doggie treat (the rattling dog biscuits) and another sound (the rattle of goldfish crackers) that doesn't. He still drools when you shake the box of dog biscuits, but he doesn't when you shake the box of crackers. At this point, *stimulus discrimination* has taken place.

Once learned, can conditioned responses be eliminated? Pavlov (1927) found that conditioned responses could be gradually weakened. If the conditioned stimulus (the ringing bell) was repeatedly presented *without* being paired with the unconditioned stimulus (the food), the conditioned response seemed to gradually disappear. Pavlov called this process of decline and eventual disappearance of the conditioned response **extinction.**

Pavlov also found that the dog did not simply return to its unconditioned state following extinction (see Figure 5.2). If the animal was allowed a period of rest (such as a few hours) after the response was extinguished, the conditioned response would reappear when the conditioned stimulus was again presented. This reappearance of a previously extinguished conditioned response after a period of time without exposure to the conditioned stimulus is called **spontaneous recovery.** The phenomenon of spontaneous recovery demonstrates that extinction is not unlearning. That is, the learned response may seem to disappear, but it is not eliminated or erased (Bouton, 2000; Rescorla, 2001).

extinction (in classical conditioning)
The gradual weakening and apparent disappearance of conditioned behavior. In classical conditioning, extinction occurs when the conditioned stimulus is repeatedly presented without the unconditioned stimulus.

spontaneous recovery
The reappearance of a previously extinguished conditioned response after a period of time without exposure to the conditioned stimulus.

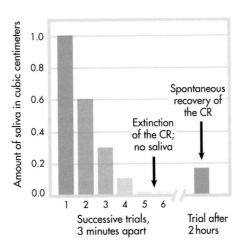

FIGURE 5.2 Extinction and Spontaneous Recovery in Pavlov's Laboratory This demonstration involved a dog that had already been conditioned to salivate (the CR) to just the sight of the meat powder (the CS). During the extinction phase, the CS was repeatedly presented at three-minute intervals and held just out of the dog's reach. As you can see in the graph, over the course of six trials the amount of saliva secreted by the dog quickly decreased to zero. This indicates that *extinction* had occurred. After a two-hour rest period, the CS was presented again. At the sight of the meat powder, the dog secreted saliva once more, evidence for the *spontaneous recovery* of the conditioned response.
SOURCE: Data adapted from Pavlov (1927).

5.1 R·E·V·I·E·W

C·O·N·C·E·P·T

Elements of Classical Conditioning

For each of the following examples, use the diagram below to help identify the neutral stimulus, UCS, UCR, CS, and CR.

1. During a father–daughter tae kwon do class in the school gymnasium, Rick fell and tore his Achilles tendon. The injury was so painful that he almost passed out. A year later, when Rick entered the gym at his daughter's school, he got chills and felt lightheaded.

2. When Cindy's four-month-old infant cried, she would begin breast-feeding him. One evening, Cindy went to a movie with her husband, leaving her baby at home with a sitter. When an infant in the theater began to cry, Cindy experienced the "let-down" reflex, and a few drops of milk stained her new silk blouse.

3. After swimming in the lake near his home one day, Frank emerged from the water covered with slimy, bloodsucking leeches all over his legs and back. He was revolted as he removed the leeches. Now, every time he passes the lake, Frank shudders in disgust.

4. Every time two-year-old Jodie heard the doorbell ring, she raced to open the front door. On Halloween night, Jodie answered the doorbell and encountered a scary monster with nine flashing eyes. Jodie screamed in fear and ran away. Now Jodie screams and hides whenever the doorbell rings.

5. Nine months after two planes hit the World Trade Center, exploded, and demolished Ken's New York City neighborhood, Ken still flinches every time he hears a low-flying jet overhead.

From Pavlov to Watson
The Founding of Behaviorism

Key Theme

- Behaviorism was founded by John Watson, who redefined psychology as the scientific study of behavior.

Key Questions

- What were the fundamental assumptions of behaviorism?
- How did Watson use classical conditioning to explain and produce conditioned emotional responses?
- How did Watson apply classical conditioning techniques to advertising?

John Broadus Watson (1878–1958) Watson founded behaviorism in the early 1900s, emphasizing the scientific study of observable behaviors rather than the study of subjective mental processes. His influence spread far beyond the academic world. He wrote many books and articles for the general public on child rearing and other topics, popularizing the findings of the "new" science of psychology (Rilling, 2000).

behaviorism
School of psychology and theoretical viewpoint that emphasizes the scientific study of observable behaviors, especially as they pertain to the process of learning.

Over the course of three decades, Pavlov systematically investigated different aspects of classical conditioning. Throughout this process, he used dogs almost exclusively as his experimental subjects. Since Pavlov believed he had discovered the mechanism by which all learning occurs, it seems ironic that he had very little to say about applications of classical conditioning to human behavior. This irony is less puzzling when you understand that Pavlov wanted nothing to do with the newly established science of psychology. Why?

At the beginning of the twentieth century, psychology's early founders had defined the field as *the scientific study of the mind* (see Chapter 1). They advocated the use of introspective self-reports to achieve two fundamental goals: describing and explaining conscious thought and perceptions. Because the early psychologists wanted to study subjective states of consciousness, Pavlov did not see psychology as an exact or precise science, like physiology or chemistry. As Pavlov (1927) wrote, "It is still open to discussion whether psychology is a natural science, or whether it can be regarded as a science at all."

At about the same time Pavlov was conducting his systematic studies of classical conditioning in the early 1900s, a young psychologist named **John B. Watson** was attracting attention in the United States. Watson, like Pavlov, believed that psychology was following the wrong path by focusing on the study of subjective mental processes. In 1913, Watson directly challenged the early founders of psychology when he published a landmark article entitled "Psychology as the Behaviorist Views It." Watson's famous article opened with these sentences:

> Psychology as the behaviorist views it is a purely objective experimental branch of natural science. Its theoretical goal is the prediction and control of behavior. Introspection forms no essential part of its methods, nor is the scientific value of its data dependent upon the readiness with which they lend themselves to interpretation in terms of consciousness.

With the publication of this article, Watson founded a new school, or approach, in psychology, called **behaviorism.** Watson strongly advocated that psychology should be redefined as *the scientific study of behavior.* As he later (1924) wrote, "Let us limit ourselves to things that can be observed, and formulate laws concerning only those things. Now what can we observe? We can observe *behavior—what the organism does or says.*"

But having soundly rejected the methods of introspection and the study of consciousness, the young Watson was somewhat at a loss for a new method to replace them (Fancher, 1996). By 1915, when Watson was elected president of the American Psychological Association, he had learned of Pavlov's research. Watson (1916) embraced the idea of the conditioned reflex as the model he had been seeking to investigate and explain human behavior (Evans & Rilling, 2000).

Watson believed that virtually *all* human behavior is a result of conditioning and learning—that is, due to past experience and environmental influences. In championing behaviorism, Watson took his views to an extreme, claiming that neither talent, personality, nor intelligence was inherited. In a characteristically bold statement, Watson (1924) proclaimed:

> I should like to go one step further now and say, "Give me a dozen healthy infants, well-formed, and my own specified world to bring them up in and I'll guarantee to take any one at random and train him to become any type of specialist I might select—doctor, lawyer, artist, merchant-chief and yes, even beggar-man and thief, regardless of his talents, penchants, tendencies, abilities, vocations, and race of his ancestors." I am going beyond my facts and I admit it, but so have the advocates of the contrary and they have been doing it for many thousands of years.

Needless to say, Watson never actually carried out such an experiment, and his boast clearly exaggerated the role of the environment to make his point. Nevertheless, Watson's influence on psychology cannot be overemphasized. Behaviorism was to dominate psychology in the United States for more than 50 years. And, as you'll see in the next section, Watson did carry out a famous and controversial experiment to demonstrate how human behavior could be classically conditioned.

Conditioned Emotional Reactions
The Famous Case of Little Albert

Watson believed that, much as Pavlov's dogs reflexively salivated to food, human emotions could be thought of as reflexive responses involving the muscles and glands. In studies with infants, Watson (1919) identified three emotions that he believed represented inborn and natural unconditioned reflexes—fear, rage, and love. According to Watson, each of these innate emotions could be reflexively triggered by a small number of specific stimuli. For example, he found two stimuli that could trigger the reflexive fear response in infants: a sudden loud noise and a sudden dropping motion.

Watson's interest in the role of classical conditioning in emotions set the stage for one of the most famous and controversial experiments in the history of psychology. In 1920, Watson and a graduate student named Rosalie Rayner set out to demonstrate that classical conditioning could be used to deliberately establish a conditioned emotional response in a human subject. Their subject was a baby, whom they called "Albert B.," but who is now more popularly known as "Little Albert." Little Albert lived with his mother in the Harriet Lane Hospital in Baltimore, where his mother was employed.

Watson and Rayner (1920) first assessed Little Albert when he was only nine months old. Little Albert was a healthy, unusually calm baby who showed no fear when presented with a tame white rat, a rabbit, a dog, and a monkey. He was also unafraid of cotton, masks, and even burning newspapers! But, as with other infants whom Watson had studied, fear could be triggered in Little Albert by a sudden loud sound—clanging a steel bar behind his head. In this case, the sudden clanging noise is the unconditioned stimulus, and the unconditioned response is fear.

Two months after their initial assessment, Watson and Rayner attempted to condition Little Albert to fear the tame white rat (the conditioned stimulus). Watson stood behind Little Albert. Whenever Little Albert reached toward the rat, Watson clanged the steel bar with a hammer. Just as before, of course, the unexpected loud CLANG! (the unconditioned stimulus) startled and scared the daylights out of Little Albert (the unconditioned response).

During the first conditioning session, Little Albert experienced two pairings of the white rat with the loud clanging sound. A week later, he experienced five more pairings of the two stimuli. After only these seven pairings of the loud noise and the white rate, the white rat alone triggered the conditioned response—extreme fear—in Little Albert (see Figure 5.3). As Watson and Rayner (1920) described:

> The instant the rat was shown, the baby began to cry. Almost instantly he turned sharply to the left, fell over on [his] left side, raised himself on all fours and began to crawl away so rapidly that he was caught with difficulty before reaching the edge of the table.

Watson and Rayner also found that stimulus generalization had taken place. Along with fearing the rat, Little Albert was now afraid of other furry animals, including a dog and a rabbit. He had even developed a classically conditioned fear response to a variety of fuzzy objects—a sealskin coat, cotton, Watson's hair, and a white-bearded Santa Claus mask!

Although the Little Albert study has achieved legendary status in psychology, it had several problems (Harris, 1979; Paul & Blumenthal, 1989). One criticism is that the experiment was not carefully designed or conducted. For example, Albert's fear and distress were not objectively measured but were subjectively evaluated by Watson and Rayner.

The experiment is also open to criticism on ethical grounds. Watson and Rayner (1920) did not extinguish Little Albert's fear of furry animals and objects, even though they believed that such conditioned emotional responses would "persist and modify personality throughout life." Whether they had originally intended to extinguish the fear is not completely clear (see Paul & Blumenthal, 1989). Little Albert left the hospital shortly after the completion of the experiment. Watson (1930) later wrote that he and Rayner could not try to eliminate Albert's fear response because the infant had been adopted by a family in another city shortly after the experiment had concluded. Today, conducting such an experiment would be considered unethical.

FIGURE 5.3 A Classically Conditioned Fear Response (a) In the photograph, Rosalie Rayner holds Little Albert as John Watson looks on. Little Albert is petting the white rat, clearly not afraid of it. (b) By repeatedly pairing the white rat with the UCS (a loud noise), the white rat becomes a CS. After conditioning, Little Albert is terrified of the rat and other furry white objects, including rabbits, cotton, Rayner's white fur coat, and Watson in a Santa Claus beard.

(a)

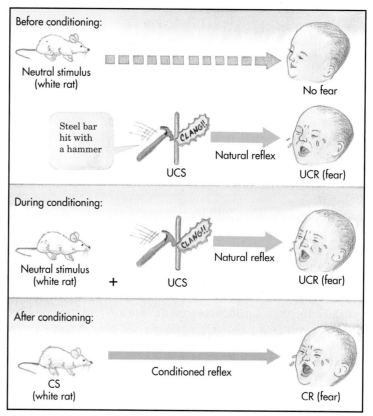

(b)

Watson, Classical Conditioning, and Advertising

From shampoos to soft drinks, advertising campaigns often use sexy models to promote their products. Today, we take this advertising tactic for granted. But it's actually yet another example of Watson's influence.

Shortly after the Little Albert experiment, Watson's wife discovered that he was having an affair with his graduate student Rosalie Rayner. Following a scandalous and highly publicized divorce, Watson was fired from his academic position. Despite his international fame as a scientist, no other university would hire

"Oh dear, I wish my Baby wouldn't cry so much!"

him. Banned from academia, Watson married Rayner and joined the J. Walter Thompson advertising agency (Buckley, 1989).

Watson was a pioneer in the application of classical conditioning principles to advertising. "To make your consumer react," Watson told his colleagues at the ad agency, "tell him something that will tie up with fear, something that will stir up a mild rage, that will call out an affectionate or love response, or strike at a deep psychological or habit need" (quoted in Buckley, 1982).

Watson applied this technique to ad campaigns for Johnson & Johnson Baby Powder and Pebeco toothpaste in the 1920s. For the baby powder ad, Watson intentionally tried to stimulate an anxiety response in young mothers by creating doubts about their ability to care for their infants.

The Pebeco toothpaste campaign targeted the newly independent young woman who smoked. The ad raised the fear that attractiveness might be diminished by the effects of smoking—and Pebeco toothpaste was promoted as a way of increasing sexual attractiveness. One ad read, "Girls! Don't worry any more about smoke-stained teeth or tobacco-tainted breath. You can smoke and still be lovely if you'll just use Pebeco twice a day." Watson also developed ad campaigns for Pond's cold cream, Maxwell House coffee, and Camel cigarettes.

While Watson may have pioneered the strategy of associating products with "sex appeal," modern advertising

Who could Love a girl *with smoke-stained teeth?*

has taken this technique to an extreme. Similarly, some ad campaigns pair products with images of adorable babies, cuddly kittens, happy families, or other "natural" stimuli that elicit warm, emotional responses. If classical conditioning occurs, the product by itself will also elicit a warm emotional response. Are such procedures effective? In a word, yes. Attitudes toward a product or a particular brand can be influenced by advertising and marketing campaigns that use classical conditioning methods (see Grossman & Till, 1998; Olson & Fazio, 2001).

You can probably think of situations, objects, or people that evoke a strong classically conditioned emotional reaction in you, such as fear or anger. One example that many of our students can relate to is that of becoming classically conditioned to cues associated with a person whom you strongly dislike, such as a demeaning boss or a hateful ex-lover. After repeated negative experiences (the UCS) with the person eliciting anger or fear (the UCR), a wide range of cues can become conditioned stimuli (CSs)—the person's name, the sight of the person, locations associated with the person, and so forth—and elicit a strong negative emotional reaction (the CR) in you. Just mentioning the person's name can make your heart pound and send your blood pressure soaring.

In this chapter's Prologue, we saw that Erv became classically conditioned to feel anxious whenever he entered the attic. The attic (the original neutral stimulus) was coupled with being trapped in extreme heat (the UCS), which produced fear (the UCR). Following the episode, Erv found that going into the attic (now a

cathy®   **by Cathy Guisewite**

CS) triggered mild fear and anxiety (the CR). One of our students told us about a similar example. Whenever he drove past a certain intersection where he had been involved in a serious auto accident, his heart would begin to race and his hands would tremble.

Other emotional responses, such as feelings of happiness or sadness, can also be classically conditioned. The sight of a sweater left behind by a loved one (the CS) can trigger a positive emotional reaction because it is associated with pleasant experiences. Someone else looking at the same sweater would probably not experience a conditioned positive emotion.

Aspects of sexual responses involve reflexive elements that also can be subject to classical conditioning, sometimes inadvertently. To illustrate, suppose that a neutral stimulus, such as the scent of a particular cologne, is regularly paired with the person with whom you are romantically involved. In other words, your romantic partner almost always wears his or her "signature" cologne. You, of course, are most aware of the scent when you are physically close to your partner in sexually arousing situations. After repeated pairings, the initially neutral stimulus—the particular cologne scent—can become a conditioned stimulus. Now, the scent of the cologne evokes feelings of romantic excitement or mild sexual arousal even in the absence of your lover or, in some cases, long after the relationship has ended. And, in fact, a wide variety of stimuli can become "sexual turn-ons" through classical conditioning.

Classical Conditioning and Drug Use

Key Theme

- Classical conditioning is involved in several aspects of drug effects, especially responses involving psychoactive drugs.

Key Questions

- How is classical conditioning involved in some placebo responses?
- What are conditioned compensatory responses, and what role do they play in drug tolerance, withdrawal symptoms, and addiction?

Classical conditioning can provide some intriguing insights about drug effects and the use of *psychoactive drugs* like stimulants and opiates. In chapter 4, we described different categories of psychoactive drugs and some of the processes that are involved in drug use and abuse (see pp. 169 to 179). As you'll see in the next few sections, classical conditioning can help explain such important aspects of drug abuse as *addiction, tolerance, withdrawal symptoms,* and drug relapses.

Classically Conditioned Drug Effects: Responses *Similar* to the Drug's Effect

If you're a regular coffee drinker like both of your authors, you may have noticed that you begin to feel more awake and alert after just a few groggy sips of your first cup of coffee in the morning. However, that increased sense of alertness and arousal is *not* due to the caffeine, at least not after the first couple of sips. Why? Because it takes about 20 minutes before the caffeine from the coffee reaches significant levels in your bloodstream. Instead, your sense of increased alertness *before* blood levels of caffeine rise is because you've developed a classically conditioned response to the sight, smell, and taste of coffee. Confirming that everyday experience, such conditioned responses to caffeine-associated stimuli have also been demonstrated experimentally (e.g., Flaten & Blumenthal, 1999; Mikalsen & others, 2001).

Figure 5.4 shows how regular coffee drinkers might acquire such a classically conditioned response. Think of each episode of coffee drinking as a classical conditioning trial. The UCS is the drug caffeine, which automatically triggers increased arousal and alertness, the UCR. The sight, smell, and taste of coffee are the originally neutral stimuli that eventually become conditioned stimuli by being repeatedly paired with caffeine's arousing effect.

Once this classically conditioned drug effect becomes well established, the smell or taste of coffee—even decaffeinated coffee—can trigger the conditioned response of increased arousal and alertness (Knowles, 1963; A. W. Smith & others, 1997). For some habitual coffee drinkers, like your authors, the conditioned response to caffeine-associated cues is so strong that a cup or two of decaffeinated coffee after a late evening meal can cause trouble sleeping.

Interestingly, conditioned drug effects seem to be involved in at least some instances of placebo response. Also called *placebo effect, a* **placebo response** occurs when an individual has a psychological and physiological reaction to what is actually a fake treatment or drug.

For example, in one study patients with hypertension (high blood pressure) were repeatedly given an antihypertensive medication in a particular environment. The effect of the antihypertensive medication was to reduce blood pressure. When given a placebo in the same environment, the fake pill also reduced their blood pressure. Why? Because a classically conditioned drug effect had occurred: The particular situational cues, including the act of taking what was believed to be the medication, elicited a drop in blood pressure. In contrast, other hypertension patients who had *no* prior experience with the medication did *not* experience reduced blood pressure when given the same placebo in the same environment (Suchman & Ader, 1992).

Notice two features that characterize the caffeine and the antihypertensive medication examples. First, the drug is one that is regularly used. Second, the drug is one that essentially restores normal functioning. In regular coffee users, caffeine helps restore and maintain normal levels of arousal and alertness. In the person with high blood pressure, antihypertensive medication helps restore more normal levels of blood pressure.

Here's the important point: In drugs that are regularly used to restore normal levels of functioning, classical conditioning tends to produce a conditioned response that is *similar* to the drug's effect (Flaten, 2001). Clearly, such conditioned drug effects can contribute to the experience of placebo effects (Ader, 2000; Flaten & Blumenthal, 1999). However, classical conditioning can produce very different effects with other kinds of drugs, especially drugs that disrupt the body's normal functioning.

FIGURE 5.4 A Classically Conditioned Drug Effect

placebo response
An individual's psychological and physiological response to what is actually a fake treatment or drug; also called *placebo effect.*

conditioned compensatory response (CCR)

A classically conditioned response in which stimuli that reliably precede the administration of a drug elicit a physiological reaction that counteracts, or is opposite to, the drug's effects.

Classically Conditioned Compensatory Responses: Responses *Opposite* to the Drug's Effect

What kind of a response gets classically conditioned in situations involving drugs that *disrupt* the normal level of functioning? To answer that question, consider a conditioning study done more than 60 years ago that involved placing dogs in a stand and then injecting them with *epinephrine* (*adrenaline*) on repeated occasions (Subkov & Zilov, 1937). Epinephrine disrupts normal body functioning by causing *tachycardia*—an excessively rapid heartbeat. In response to such physiological disruptions, the body automatically tries to compensate and restore normal functioning by triggering the *opposite effect*. The body's opposite, compensatory response to tachycardia is to slow the heart rate down, which is termed *bradycardia*.

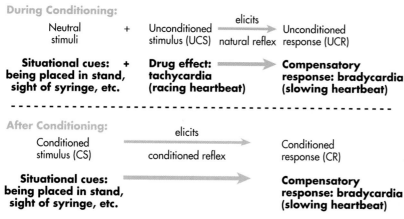

During Conditioning:

Neutral stimuli + Unconditioned stimulus (UCS) — *elicits* *natural reflex* → Unconditioned response (UCR)

Situational cues: + Drug effect: tachycardia (racing heartbeat) → **Compensatory response: bradycardia (slowing heartbeat)**

After Conditioning:

Conditioned stimulus (CS) — *elicits* *conditioned reflex* → Conditioned response (CR)

Situational cues: being placed in stand, sight of syringe, etc. → **Compensatory response: bradycardia (slowing heartbeat)**

FIGURE 5.5 A Classically Conditioned Compensatory Response

After the dogs had experienced several epinephrine-injection conditioning trials, each dog was placed in the stand and injected with plain water. The result? The dog's heart rate *decreased*.

To understand this example in classical conditioning terms, look at Figure 5.5. The UCS is the *drug effect*—tachycardia. The UCR that is elicited is the *opposite, compensatory effect*—bradycardia. Thus, the automatic, reflexive UCS → UCR connection is the drug effect (tachycardia) → eliciting the opposite compensatory response (bradycardia). The initially neutral stimuli are the various situational cues that immediately precede the drug effect, such as the dog being placed in the stand, the sight of the syringe, the actual injection, and so on.

After several conditioning trials, the situational cues become CSs that now elicit a **conditioned compensatory response (CCR)** of bradycardia. Hence, placing the dog in the stand and injecting it with plain water automatically elicited a conditioned compensatory response: The dog's heartbeat decreased.

Conditioned compensatory responses have been extensively studied by Canadian psychologist **Shepard Siegel** at McMaster University. Siegel's research has focused on the role of conditioned compensatory responses in the development of drug tolerance and withdrawal symptoms in addictive opiate drugs like heroin and morphine (for a review, see Siegel, 1999).

To illustrate, consider what happens when a heroin addict repeatedly injects himself with the drug in a particular environment. The situational cues are repeatedly paired with the drug's behavioral and physiological effects (the UCS), which elicits a compensatory response that is opposite to the drug's effects (the UCR). After repeated pairings, the situational cues become conditioned stimuli. Now, exposure to the situational cues (the CS) elicits a conditioned compensatory response (CCR) that is the *opposite* of and counteracts the drug's effects. The heroin user experiences the CCR as *withdrawal symptoms* combined with a powerful craving for the drug's effects (see Siegel & Allan, 1998).

When the heroin is regularly administered in the same environment, *drug tolerance* develops because the conditioned compensatory response becomes stronger over time. To keep experiencing the original "high" in the presence of the same situational cues, the drug user must take increasingly greater amounts of the drug to overcome the stronger conditioned compensatory response. However, if the heroin user takes his usual dose of the drug in an *unfamiliar* situation, the conditioned compensatory response will *not* be elicited. Thus, he runs the risk of a potentially lethal overdose (see Figure 5.6).

As illustrated by the heroin example, Shepard Siegel's model predicts that drug tolerance will be *situationally specific*. That is, drug tolerance should be much more pronounced in the presence of the situational cues (the CSs) in which the addictive drug is regularly taken. However, tolerance will be minimal

*P*avlovian conditioning plays an important role in the acquisition and expression of drug tolerance and withdrawal symptoms. The Pavlovian conditioning analysis of drug tolerance emphasizes that cues present at the time of drug use become associated with drug-induced disturbances.

Shepard Siegel (2001)

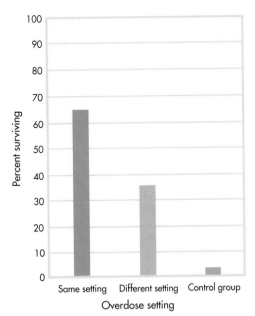

Percent surviving (y-axis: 0, 10, 20, 30, 40, 50, 60, 70, 80, 90, 100)

Overdose setting (x-axis: Same setting, Different setting, Control group)

FIGURE 5.6 Classical Conditioning and Heroin Overdose Deaths Some heroin addicts have died after injecting their usual amount of heroin in an unfamiliar environment (Siegel, 1984). Why? A now-classic study by Siegel and his colleagues (1982) helps explain this phenomenon. Over the course of a month, rats gradually developed tolerance to increasing amounts of heroin. Then, they were injected with an overdose of almost twice as much heroin as they had become accustomed to receiving. Rats who were injected with the heroin overdose in the *same* setting in which they had previously received heroin were twice as likely to survive as were rats who were injected in a *different* setting. The lethal potential of the heroin overdose was underscored by the fate of the rats in the control group who had not previously been exposed to heroin: almost all of them died.

or *not* observed if the drug is taken in the absence of the conditioned stimuli. If the typical CSs are not present, the conditioned compensatory response will *not* be elicited and the full effect of the drug will be felt. This prediction has been confirmed experimentally for many drugs, including heroin, morphine, alcohol, and barbiturates (see Siegel & others, 2000).

Classical conditioning also offers some insight into why it can be so difficult to overcome drug addiction and why so many substance abusers relapse after treatment. Recall that Pavlov discovered that extinguished responses may seem to disappear but are not totally erased. Extinction is *not* unlearning (Bouton, 2000; Rescorla, 2001). Presenting the conditioned stimulus again, even after a lengthy period of time, can produce *spontaneous recovery* of the conditioned response.

Spontaneous recovery of a previously extinguished conditioned response can help explain why people often relapse after they have successfully overcome their physical addiction to cigarettes, alcohol, cocaine, heroin, or other addictive drugs (Bouton, 2000). When the ex-addict encounters a drug-related conditioned stimulus, the CS can trigger *spontaneous recovery* of the previous conditioned compensatory response. In effect, the person experiences the spontaneous recovery of withdrawal symptoms and intense craving for the drug.

The spontaneous recovery of withdrawal symptoms helps explain the experience of people like our friend Randy. Randy has gone "cold turkey" and quit cigarette smoking several times. (For more on Randy, see the Chapter 8 Prologue on pp. 319–320). Each time, Randy manages to get through the three- to four-day process of physically withdrawing from the addictive nicotine in tobacco. Weeks or months go by and Randy rarely thinks about having a cigarette *except* when he encounters stimuli that were previously paired with smoking cigarettes. So, when Randy is at party or in a bar where liquor is being served and other people are smoking—both situations in which he previously would have smoked—he tends to experience sudden and intense cravings for a cigarette. On more than one occasion, Randy has caved in to that sudden and intense craving and started smoking again.

Similarly, people who are addicted to alcohol, cocaine, or heroin might "kick the habit" in a drug rehabilitation center, where they are protected from drug-related cues. Yet when they return to the environment in which the original conditioning took place, associate with drug-taking friends, or encounter other conditioned stimuli associated with drug use, relapses are common (Ciccocioppo & others, 2001; Nestler, 2001a, 2001b). The conditioned stimuli elicit the conditioned compensatory response, and they experience withdrawal symptoms and intense craving for the drug (Bouton, 2000; Siegel & Allan, 1998).

Stuggling with Addiction Gifted actor Robert Downey, Jr., was nominated for an Oscar for his work in film and won a Golden Globe award and an Emmy nomination for his appearances on the *Ally McBeal* show. Yet to many people, Downey is best known for his very public struggles with drug addiction. Downey has been arrested numerous times for drug possession, spending a year in state prison for one conviction. Despite participating in several drug rehabilitation programs, and publicly announcing his determination to give up drugs for good, Downey has experienced repeated relapses, often triggered by his return to environments associated with drug use in the past.

Contemporary Views of Classical Conditioning

Key Theme

■ Contemporary learning researchers acknowledge the importance of both mental factors and evolutionary influences in classical conditioning.

Key Questions

■ How has the involvement of cognitive processes in classical conditioning been demonstrated experimentally?

■ What is meant by the phrase "the animal behaves like a scientist" in classical conditioning?

■ How do taste aversions challenge the basic conditioning principles, and what is biological preparedness?

The traditional behavioral perspective holds that classical conditioning results from a simple association of the conditioned stimulus and the unconditioned stimulus. According to the behaviorists, mental processes such as thinking, anticipating, or deciding were not needed to explain the conditioning process.

However, not all psychologists were convinced that mental processes were so uninvolved in learning. Some wondered whether conditioning procedures did more than simply change how an organism responded. Could conditioning procedures change what the organism *knows* as well as what it *does*? According to the *cognitive perspective* (see Chapter 1), mental processes as well as external events are an important component in the learning of new behaviors. In the next section, we'll look at the role cognitive processes seem to play in classical conditioning. As you'll see, today's psychologists view the classical conditioning process very differently from Pavlov or Watson (see Pearce & Bouton, 2001).

Cognitive Aspects of Classical Conditioning
Reliable Signals

According to Pavlov, classical conditioning occurs simply because two stimuli are associated closely in time. The conditioned stimulus (the bell) precedes the unconditioned stimulus (the food) usually by no more than a few seconds. But is it possible that Pavlov's dogs were learning more than the mere association of two stimuli that occurred very close together in time?

To answer that question, let's begin with an analogy. Suppose that on your way to class you have to go through a railroad crossing. Every time a train approaches the crossing, warning lights flash. Being rather intelligent for your species, after a few weeks you conclude that the flashing lights will be quickly followed by a freight train barreling down the railroad tracks. You've learned an association between the flashing lights and an oncoming train, because the lights are a *reliable signal* that predict the presence of the train.

Now imagine that a friend of yours also has to cross train tracks but at a different location. The railroad has had nothing but problems with the warning lights at that crossing. Sometimes the warning lights flash before a train roars through, but sometimes they don't. And sometimes they flash when no train is coming. Does your friend learn an association between the flashing lights and oncoming trains? No, because here the flashing lights are an *unreliable signal*— they seem to have no relationship to a train's arrival.

Psychologist **Robert A. Rescorla** demonstrated that classically conditioned rats also assess the reliability of signals, much like you and your friend did at the different railroad crossings. In Rescorla's 1968 experiment, one group of rats heard a tone (the conditioned stimulus) that was paired 20 times with a brief

*P*avlovian conditioning is a sophisticated and sensible mechanism by which organisms represent the world. Our current understanding of Pavlovian conditioning leads to its characterization as a mechanism by which the organism encodes relationships between events in the world. The conditioned stimulus and the unconditioned stimulus are simply two events and the organism can be seen as trying to determine the relationship between them. In doing so, the organism is very sophisticated and very demanding in what it takes as evidence that there is a relationship.

Robert A. Rescorla (1997)

Group 1

Conditioned stimulus (tone) ····▸

Unconditioned stimulus (shock) ····▸

Conditioning occurs: tone elicits conditioned response of fear

Time ⟶

Group 2

Conditioned stimulus (tone) ····▸

Unconditioned stimulus (shock) ····▸

Conditioning does *not* occur: tone does not elicit conditioned response of fear

Time ⟶

FIGURE 5.7 Reliable and Unreliable Signals In Rescorla's experiment, both groups of rats experienced the same number of shock–tone pairings. However, the rats in group 1 received a shock only when the tone was sounded, while the rats in group 2 experienced additional shocks that were not paired with the tone. Subsequently, the rats in group 1 displayed a conditioned fear response to the tone and the rats in group 2 did not. Why did only the rats in group 1 become conditioned to display fear when they heard the tone?

shock (the unconditioned stimulus). A second group of rats experienced the *same* number of tone–shock pairings, but this group also experienced an *additional* 20 shocks with *no* tone (see Figure 5.7).

Then Rescorla tested for the conditioned fear response by presenting the tone alone to each group of rats. According to the traditional classical conditioning model, both groups of rats should have displayed the same levels of conditioned fear. After all, each group had received 20 tone–shock pairings. However, this is not what Rescorla found. The rats in the first group displayed a much stronger fear response to the tone than did the rats in the second group. Why?

According to Rescorla (1988), classical conditioning depends on the *information* the conditioned stimulus provides about the unconditioned stimulus. For learning to occur, the conditioned stimulus must be a *reliable signal* that predicts the presentations of the unconditioned stimulus. For the first group of rats, that was certainly the situation. Every time the tone sounded, a shock followed. But for the second group, the tone was an unreliable signal. Sometimes the tone preceded the shock, and sometimes the shock occurred without warning.

Rescorla concluded that the rats in both groups were *actively processing information* about the reliability of the signals they encountered. Rather than merely associating two closely paired stimuli, as Pavlov suggested, the animals assess the *predictive value* of stimuli. Applying this interpretation to classical conditioning, we can conclude that Pavlov's dogs learned that the bell was a signal that *reliably predicted* that food would follow.

According to this view, animals use cognitive processes to draw inferences about the signals they encounter in their environments. To Rescorla (1988), classical conditioning "is not a stupid process by which the organism willy-nilly forms associations between any two stimuli that happen to co-occur." Rather, his research suggests that "the animal behaves like a scientist, detecting causal relations among events and using a range of information about those events to make the relevant inferences" (Rescorla, 1980).

Because of studies by Rescorla and other researchers, today's understanding of how learning occurs in classical conditioning is very different from the explanations offered by Pavlov and Watson. Simply pairing events in time may not be enough for classical conditioning to occur. Instead, a conditioned stimulus must *reliably signal* that the unconditioned stimulus will follow. Put simply, classical conditioning seems to involve *learning the relationships between events* (Klein & Mowrer, 1989; Rescorla, 1988).

Classical Conditioning and Survival Animals quickly learn the signals that predict the approach of a predator. In classical conditioning terms, they learn to associate the approach of a predator (the unconditioned stimuli) with particular sounds, smells, or sights (the originally neutral stimuli that become conditioned stimuli). To survive, animals that are vulnerable to predators, such as this frightened deer, must be able to use environmental signals to predict events in their environment. Thus, a rustle in the underbrush, the faint whiff of a mountain lion, or a glimpse of a human tells this animal that it's time to flee.

taste aversion
A classically conditioned dislike for and avoidance of a particular food that develops when an organism becomes ill after eating the food.

Evolutionary Aspects of Classical Conditioning
Biological Predispositions to Learn

According to Darwin's *theory of evolution by natural selection,* both the physical characteristics and the natural behavior patterns of any species have been shaped by evolution to maximize adaptation to the environment. Thus, just as physical characteristics vary from one species to another, so do natural behavior patterns. Some psychologists wondered whether an animal's natural behavior patterns, as shaped by evolution, would also affect how it learned new behaviors, especially behaviors important to its survival.

According to traditional behaviorists, the general principles of learning applied to virtually all animal species and all learning situations. Thus, they argued that the general learning principles of classical conditioning would be the same regardless of the species or the response being conditioned. However, in the 1960s, some researchers began to report "exceptions" to the well-established principles of classical conditioning (Lockard, 1971; Seligman, 1970). As you'll see in this section, one important exception involved a phenomenon known as a *taste aversion.* The study of taste aversions contributed to a new awareness of the importance of the organism's natural behavior patterns in classical conditioning.

Taste Aversions and Classical Conditioning: Spaghetti? No, Thank You!

A few years ago, Sandy made a pot of super spaghetti, with lots of mushrooms, herbs, spices, and some extra-spicy sausage. Being very fond of Sandy's spaghetti, Don ate two platefuls. Several hours later, in the middle of the night, Don came down with a nasty case of stomach flu. Predictably, Sandy's super spaghetti came up—a colorful spectacle, to say the least. As a result, Don developed a **taste aversion**—he avoided eating spaghetti and felt queasy whenever he smelled spaghetti sauce. Don's taste aversion to spaghetti persisted for more than a year.

Such learned taste aversions are relatively common. Our students have told us about episodes of motion sickness, morning sickness, or illness that resulted in taste aversions to foods as varied as cotton candy, strawberries, and chicken soup. In some cases, a taste aversion can persist for years.

At first glance, it seems as if taste aversions can be explained by classical conditioning. In Don's case, a neutral stimulus (spaghetti) was paired with an unconditioned stimulus (a stomach virus), which produced an unconditioned response (nausea). Now a conditioned stimulus, the spaghetti sauce by itself elicited the conditioned response of nausea.

But notice that this explanation seems to violate two basic principles of classical conditioning. First, the conditioning did not require repeated pairings. Conditioning occurred in a *single pairing* of the conditioned stimulus and the unconditioned stimulus. Second, the time span between these two stimuli was *several hours,* not a matter of seconds. Is this possible? The anecdotal reports of people who develop specific taste aversions seem to suggest it is. But such reports lack the objectivity and systematic control that a scientific explanation of behavior requires.

Enter psychologist **John Garcia,** who demonstrated that taste aversions could be produced in laboratory rats under controlled conditions (Garcia & others, 1966). Garcia's procedure was straightforward. Rats first drank saccharin-flavored water (the neutral stimulus). Hours later, the rats were injected with a drug (the unconditioned stimulus) that produced gastrointestinal distress (the unconditioned response). After the rats recovered from their illness, they refused to drink the flavored water again. The rats had developed a taste aversion to the saccharin-flavored water, which had become a conditioned stimulus.

At first, many psychologists were skeptical of Garcia's findings because they seemed to violate the basic principles of classical conditioning. Several leading

John Garcia (b. 1917) John Garcia grew up working on farms in northern California. In his late twenties, Garcia enrolled at a community college. At the age of 48, Garcia earned his Ph.D. in psychology from the University of California, Berkeley (Garcia, 1997). Garcia was one of the first researchers to experimentally demonstrate the existence of taste aversions and other "exceptions" to the general laws of classical conditioning. His research emphasized the importance of the evolutionary forces that shape the learning process.

Biological Preparedness and Conditioned Fears: What Gives You the Creeps?

Do these photographs make you somewhat uncomfortable?

A *phobia* is an extreme, irrational fear of a specific object, animal, or situation. It was once believed that all phobias were acquired through classical conditioning, as was Little Albert's fear of white rats. But many people develop phobias without having experienced a traumatic event in association with the object of their fear (Merckelbach & others, 1992). Obviously, other forms of learning, such as observational learning, are involved in the development of some fears.

When people do develop conditioned fears as a result of traumatic events, they are more likely to associate fear with certain stimuli rather than others. Erv, not surprisingly, has acquired a conditioned fear response to the "killer attic." But why doesn't Erv shudder every time he hears a lawn mower or sees a ladder, the clothes he was wearing when he got trapped, or his can of oil?

Psychologist Martin Seligman (1971) noticed that phobias seem to be quite selective. Extreme, irrational fears of snakes, spiders, heights, and small enclosed places (like Erv and Fern's attic) are relatively common. But very few people have phobias of stairs, ladders, electrical outlets or appliances, or sharp objects, even though these things are far more likely to be associated with traumatic experiences or accidents.

Seligman proposed that humans are biologically prepared to develop fears of objects or situations—such as snakes, spiders, and heights—that may once have posed a threat to humans' evolutionary ancestors. As Seligman (1971) put it, "The great majority of phobias are about objects of natural importance to the survival of the species." According to this view, people don't commonly develop phobias of knives, stoves, or cars because they're not biologically prepared to do so.

Support for this view is provided by early studies that tried to replicate Watson's Little Albert research. Elsie Bregman (1934) was unable to produce a conditioned fear response to wooden blocks and curtains, although she followed Watson's procedure carefully. And Horace English (1929) was unable to produce a conditioned fear of a wooden duck. Perhaps we're more biologically prepared to learn a fear of furry animals than of wooden ducks, blocks, or curtains!

More recently, Swedish psychologists Arne Öhman and Joaquim Soares (1994) accumulated experimental evidence that seems to support the biological preparedness hypothesis of phobias. For example, people more readily acquire conditioned fear responses to pictures of snakes and spiders paired with an electric shock than they do to pictures of mushrooms and flowers. Furthermore, the conditioned fears of spiders and snakes are much more resistant to extinction (Soares & Öhman, 1993). In accounting for these results, Öhman and Soares suggest that nonconscious perceptual mechanisms in the brain may be "prewired" to react quickly and intensely to threatening environmental stimuli, such as poisonous reptiles and insects.

New experimental research supports the view that human perception evolved in such a way that humans quickly and accurately spot natural threats in their environment. Öhman and his colleagues (2001) discovered that images of snakes and spiders tend to "pop out" when they are displayed among pictures of harmless objects like mushrooms or flowers. Participants in the study were faster at finding snakes and spiders against a background of flowers and mushrooms than they were at finding flowers and mushrooms against a background of snakes and spiders. This implies that humans may have evolved perceptual mechanisms that automatically identify stimuli that are related to threatening encounters in the evolutionary past (Öhman & Mineka, 2001).

Additional support for the evolutionary approach to understanding phobias comes from research on nonhuman animals. Animals also seem to be biologically prepared to fear certain types of stimuli that represent natural threats to survival. For example, monkeys readily learn a conditioned fear response to images of snakes and crocodiles. But under the same conditions, monkeys do *not* acquire a conditioned fear response to images of flowers or toy rabbits (Cook & Mineka, 1990; Mineka & Cook, 1993).

psychological journals refused to publish Garcia's research, saying the results were unconvincing or downright impossible (Garcia, 1981). But Garcia's results have been replicated many times. In fact, later research showed that taste aversions could develop even when a full 24 hours separated the presentation of the flavored water and the drug that produced illness (Etscorn & Stephens, 1973).

biological preparedness
In learning theory, the idea that an organism is innately predisposed to form associations between certain stimuli and responses.

Conditioning Taste Aversions in Coyotes
The fact that coyotes readily form taste aversions has been used to prevent them from preying on livestock (Bower, 1997; Garcia & Gustavson, 1997). To stop coyotes from killing lambs on sheep ranches, sheep carcasses are injected with a drug (lithium chloride) that produces extreme nausea. In the top photo, the coyote has discovered the carcass and is eating it. In the bottom photo, the nauseous coyote is writhing on the ground. In one study, captive coyotes were fed lithium-tainted rabbit and sheep carcasses. When later placed in a pen with live rabbits and sheep, the coyotes avoided them rather than attack them. In fact, some of the coyotes threw up at the sight of a live rabbit (Gustavson & others, 1976).

Conditioned taste aversions also challenged the notion that virtually any stimulus can become a conditioned stimulus. As Pavlov (1928) wrote, "Any natural phenomenon chosen at will may be converted into a conditioned stimulus . . . any visual stimulus, any desired sound, any odor, and the stimulation of any part of the skin." After all, Pavlov had demonstrated that dogs could be classically conditioned to salivate to a ringing bell, a ticking metronome, and even the sight of geometric figures.

But if this were the case, then why didn't Don develop an aversion to other stimuli he encountered between the time he ate the spaghetti and when he got sick? Why was it that only the spaghetti sauce became a conditioned stimulus that triggered nausea, and not the dinner table, the silverware—or even Sandy, for that matter?

Contrary to what Pavlov suggested, Garcia and his colleagues demonstrated that the particular conditioned stimulus that is used *does* make a difference in classical conditioning (Garcia & Koelling, 1966). In another series of experiments, Garcia found that rats did *not* learn to associate a taste with a painful event, such as a shock. Nor did they learn to associate a flashing light and noise with illness. Instead, rats were much more likely to associate a *painful stimulus,* such as a shock, with *external stimuli,* such as flashing lights and noise. And rats were much more likely to associate a *taste stimulus* with *internal stimuli*—the physical discomfort of illness. Garcia and Koelling (1966) humorously suggested that a sick rat, like a sick person, speculates, "It must have been something I ate."

Why is it that certain stimuli are more easy to associate than others? One factor that helps explain Garcia's results is **biological preparedness**—the idea that an organism is innately predisposed to form associations between certain stimuli and responses. If the particular stimulus and response combination is *not* one that an animal is biologically prepared to associate, then the association may not occur or may occur only with great difficulty.

When this concept is applied to taste aversions, rats (and people) seem to be biologically prepared to associate an illness with a taste rather than with a location, a person, or an object. Hence, Don developed an aversion to the spaghetti sauce and not to the fork he used to eat it. Apparently, both humans and rats are biologically prepared to learn taste aversions relatively easily. Thus, taste aversions can be classically conditioned more readily than can more arbitrary associations, such as that between a ringing bell and a plate of food.

Associations that are easily learned may reflect the evolutionary history, and survival mechanisms of the particular animal species. For example, rats in the wild eat a wide variety of foods. If a rat eats a new food and gets sick several hours later, it's likely to survive longer if it learns from this experience to avoid that food in the future (Kalat, 1985; Seligman, 1970).

That different species form some associations more easily than others also probably reflects the unique sensory capabilities and feeding habits that have evolved as a matter of environmental adaptation. Bobwhite quail, for instance, rely primarily on vision for identifying potential meals. In contrast, rats have relatively poor eyesight and rely primarily on taste and odor cues to identify food. Given these species differences, it shouldn't surprise you that quail, but not rats, can easily be conditioned to develop an aversion to blue-colored water—a *visual* stimulus. On the other hand, rats learn more readily than quail to associate illness with sour water—a *taste* stimulus (Wilcoxon & others, 1971). In effect, quail are biologically prepared to associate visual cues with illness, whereas rats are biologically prepared to associate taste cues with illness.

Taste aversion research emphasizes that the study of learning must consider the unique behavior patterns and capabilities of different species. As the result of evolution, animals have developed unique forms of behavior to adapt to their natural environments (Bolles, 1985). These natural behavior patterns and unique characteristics ultimately influence what an animal is capable of learning—and how easily it can be conditioned to learn a new behavior.

Operant Conditioning:
Associating Behaviors and Consequences

Key Theme
- Operant conditioning deals with the learning of active, voluntary behaviors that are shaped and maintained by their consequences.

Key Questions
- How did Edward Thorndike study the acquisition of new behaviors, and what conclusions did he reach?
- What were B. F. Skinner's key assumptions?
- How are positive and negative reinforcement similar, and how are they different?

Classical conditioning can help explain the acquisition of many learned behaviors, including emotional and physiological responses. However, recall that classical conditioning involves reflexive behaviors that are automatically elicited by a specific stimulus. Most everyday behaviors don't fall into this category. Instead, they involve nonreflexive, or *voluntary,* actions that can't be explained with classical conditioning. Raising your hand in class, formatting a computer diskette, operating a vending machine, spiking a volleyball over the net, combing out a child's wet hair, hailing a cab—these are just a few quick examples of the enormous range of nonreflexive, or voluntary, behaviors that people perform every day.

The investigation of how voluntary behaviors are acquired began with a young American psychology student named Edward L. Thorndike. A few years before Pavlov began his extensive studies of classical conditioning, Thorndike was using cats, chicks, and dogs to investigate how voluntary behaviors are acquired. Thorndike's pioneering studies helped set the stage for the later work of another American psychologist named B. F. Skinner. It was Skinner who developed *operant conditioning,* another form of conditioning that explains how we acquire and maintain voluntary behaviors.

Thorndike and the Law of Effect

Edward L. Thorndike was the first psychologist to systematically investigate animal learning and how voluntary behaviors are influenced by their consequences. At the time, Thorndike was only in his early twenties and a psychology graduate student. He conducted his pioneering studies to complete his dissertation and earn his doctorate in psychology. Published in 1898, Thorndike's dissertation, titled *Animal Intelligence: An Experimental Study of the Associative Processes in Animal,* is the most famous dissertation ever published in psychology (Chance, 1999). When Pavlov later learned of Thorndike's studies, he expressed admiration and credited Thorndike with having started objective animal research well before his own studies of classical conditioning (Hearst, 1999).

Thorndike's dissertation focused on the issue of whether animals, like humans, use reasoning to solve problems (Dewsbury, 1998). In an important series of experiments, Thorndike (1898) put hungry cats in specially constructed cages that he called "puzzle boxes." A cat could escape the cage by some simple act, such as pulling a loop or pressing a lever that would unlatch the cage door (see Figure 5.8 on the next page). A plate of food was placed just outside the cage, where the hungry cat could see and smell it.

Thorndike found that when the cat was first put into the puzzle box, it would engage in many different, seemingly random behaviors to escape. For example, the cat would scratch at the cage door, claw at the ceiling, and try to squeeze through the wooden slats (not to mention complain at the top of its lungs). Even-

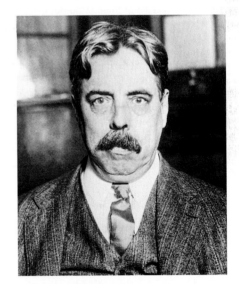

Edward Lee Thorndike (1874–1949) As a graduate student, Thorndike became fascinated by psychology after taking a class taught by William James at Harvard University. Interested in the study of animal behavior, Thorndike's first experiments were conducted with baby chicks. When his landlady protested about the chickens in his room, Thorndike moved his experiments, chicks and all, to the cellar of William James's home—much to the delight of the James children. Following these initial experiments, Thorndike constructed his famous "puzzle boxes" to study learning in cats. Later in life, Thorndike focused his attention on improving educational materials. Among his contributions was the Thorndike Barnhart Student Dictionary for children, which is still published today (R. L. Thorndike, 1991).

FIGURE 5.8 Thorndike's Puzzle Boxes and the Law of Effect Shown above is one of Thorndike's actual puzzle boxes, which were made mostly out of wood slats and wire mesh. Thorndike constructed a total of fifteen different puzzle boxes, which varied in how difficult they were for a cat to escape from. In a simple box, like puzzle box "B₁," shown above, a cat merely had to pull on a loop of string at the back of the cage to escape. More complex boxes required the cat to perform a chain of three responses—step on a treadle, pull on a string, and push a bar up or down (Chance, 1999). The graph shows Thorndike's "law of effect" for cat #12 in puzzle box A, one of the simple puzzle boxes. By the 10th trial, the successful behaviors had become "stamped in," and the cat could escape the puzzle box in 20 seconds or less.

SOURCE: Data from Thorndike, 1898, p. 14

tually, however, the cat would accidentally pull on the loop or step on the lever, opening the door latch and escaping the box. After several trials in the same puzzle box, a cat gradually took less and less time to get the cage door open. Thorndike carefully recorded the time of each trial and plotted the data to create a "time-curve" that depicted the rate of the cat's learning.

Assessing his results, Thorndike (1898) concluded that the cats did *not* display any humanlike insight or reasoning in unlatching the puzzle box door. Instead, he explained the cats' learning as a process of *trial and error*. Thorndike actually preferred the phrase "trial and success" to emphasize the relationship between actions and their consequences (Chance, 1999). Over the course of many trials, the cats gradually learned to associate certain responses with successfully escaping the box and gaining the food reward. According to Thorndike, these successful behaviors became "stamped in," so that a cat was more likely to repeat these behaviors when placed in the puzzle box again. Unsuccessful behaviors were gradually eliminated.

On the basis of his observations, Thorndike (1911) eventually formulated the **law of effect:** Responses followed by a "satisfying state of affairs" are "strengthened" and more likely to occur again in the same situation. Conversely, responses followed by an unpleasant or "annoying state of affairs" are "weakened" and less likely to occur again.

Thorndike's studies and his description of the law of effect were important first steps in the scientific understanding of how active, voluntary behaviors can be modified by their consequences. However, Thorndike never developed his ideas on learning into a formal model or system (Hearst, 1999). And his animal studies ended a few years later.

Thorndike later applied the findings to education, publishing many books on educational psychology (Beatty, 1998). In 1912, Thorndike was elected president of the American Psychological Association. By the end of his long career, Thorndike had more than 500 publications to his credit. But for all his diverse interests, Thorndike remains best known for his puzzle box studies with cats. Some 30 years later, the task of further investigating how voluntary behaviors are acquired and maintained would taken up by another American psychologist, B. F. Skinner.

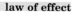

law of effect
Learning principle proposed by Thorndike that responses followed by a satisfying effect become strengthened and are more likely to recur in a particular situation, while responses followed by a dissatisfying effect Leare weakened and less likely to recur in a particular situation.

B. F. Skinner and the Search for "Order in Behavior"

From the time he was a graduate student in psychology until his death, the famous American psychologist **B. F. Skinner** searched for the "lawful processes" that would explain "order in behavior" (Skinner, 1956, 1967). Skinner was a staunch behaviorist. Like Watson, Skinner strongly believed that psychology should restrict itself to studying only phenomena that could be objectively measured and verified—outwardly observable behavior and environmental events.

Skinner (1974) acknowledged the existence of what he called "internal factors," such as thoughts, expectations, and perceptions (Delprato & Midgley, 1992). However, Skinner believed that internal thoughts, beliefs, emotions, or motives could *not* be used to explain behavior. These fell into the category of "private events" that defy direct scientific observation and should not be included in an objective, scientific explanation of behavior (Baum & Heath, 1992).

Along with being influenced by John Watson's writings, Skinner greatly admired Pavlov's work. Prominently displayed in Skinner's university office was one of his most prized possessions—an autographed photo of Pavlov (Catania & Laties, 1999). Skinner acknowledged that Pavlov's classical conditioning could explain the learned association of stimuli in certain reflexive responses (Iversen, 1992). But classical conditioning was limited to existing behaviors that were reflexively elicited. Skinner (1979) was convinced that he had "found a process of conditioning that was different from Pavlov's and much more like most learning in daily life." To Skinner, the most important form of learning was demonstrated by *new* behaviors that were *actively emitted* by the organism, such as the active behaviors produced by Thorndike's cats in trying to escape the puzzle boxes.

Skinner (1953) coined the term **operant** to describe any "active behavior that operates upon the environment to generate consequences." In everyday language, Skinner's principles of operant conditioning explain how we acquire the wide range of *voluntary* behaviors that we perform in daily life. But as a behaviorist who rejected mentalistic explanations, Skinner avoided the term *voluntary* because it would imply that behavior was due to a conscious choice or intention.

Skinner defined operant conditioning concepts in very objective terms and he avoided explanations based on subjective mental states. We'll closely follow Skinner's original terminology and definitions.

Burrhus Frederick Skinner (1904–1990) As a young adult, Skinner had hoped to become a writer. When he graduated from college, he set up a study in the attic of his parents' home and waited for inspiration to strike. After a year of "frittering" away his time, he decided that there were other ways to learn about human nature. As Skinner (1967) later wrote, "A writer might portray human behavior accurately, but he did not understand it. I was to remain interested in human behavior, but the literary method had failed me; I would turn to the scientific. . . . The relevant science appeared to be psychology, though I had only the vaguest idea of what that meant."

Reinforcement

Increasing Future Behavior

In a nutshell, Skinner's **operant conditioning** explains learning as a process in which behavior is shaped and maintained by its consequences. One possible consequence of a behavior is reinforcement. **Reinforcement** is said to occur when a stimulus or an event follows an operant and increases the likelihood of the operant being repeated. Notice that reinforcement is defined by the effect it produces—increasing or strengthening the occurrence of a behavior in the future.

Let's look at reinforcement in action. Suppose you put your money into a soft-drink vending machine and push the button. Nothing happens. You push the button again. Nothing. You try the coin-return lever. Still nothing. Frustrated, you slam the machine with your hand. Bingo! Your can of soda rolls down the chute. In the future, if another vending machine swallows your money without giving you what you want, what are you likely to do? Hit the machine, right?

In this example, slamming the vending machine with your hand is the *operant*—the active response you emitted. The soft drink is the *reinforcing stimulus,* or *reinforcer*—the stimulus or event that is sought in a particular situation. In everyday language, a reinforcing stimulus is typically something desirable, satisfying, or pleasant. Skinner, of course, avoided such terms because they reflected subjective emotional states.

operant
Skinner's term for an actively emitted (or voluntary) behavior that operates on the environment to produce consequences.

operant conditioning
The basic learning process that involves changing the probability of a response being repeated by manipulating the consequences of that response; also called *Skinnerian conditioning.*

reinforcement
The occurrence of a stimulus or event following a response that increases the likelihood of that response being repeated.

Positive and Negative Reinforcement

There are two forms of reinforcement: *positive reinforcement* and *negative reinforcement*. Both increase future behavior, but they do so in different ways (see Table 5.1). It's easier to understand these differences if you note at the outset that Skinner did not use the terms *positive* and *negative* in their everyday sense of meaning "good" and "bad" or "desirable" and "undesirable." Instead, think of the words *positive* and *negative* in terms of their mathematical meanings. *Positive* is the equivalent of a plus sign (+), meaning that something is added. *Negative* is the equivalent of a minus sign (−), meaning that something is subtracted or removed. If you keep that distinction in mind, the principles of positive and negative reinforcement should be easier to understand.

Table 5.1

Comparing Positive and Negative Reinforcement

Process	Operant	Consequence	Effect on Behavior
Positive reinforcement	Studying to make dean's list	Make dean's list	Increase studying in the future
Negative reinforcement	Studying to avoid losing academic scholarship	Avoid loss of academic scholarship	Increase studying in the future

Both positive and negative reinforcement increase the likelihood of a behavior being repeated. Positive reinforcement involves a behavior that leads to a reinforcing or rewarding event. In contrast, negative reinforcement involves behavior that leads to the avoidance of or escape from an aversive or punishing event. Ultimately, both positive and negative reinforcement involve outcomes that strengthen future behavior.

Positive reinforcement involves following an operant with the addition of a reinforcing stimulus. In positive reinforcement situations, a response is strengthened because something is *added* or presented. Everyday examples of positive reinforcement in action are easy to identify. Here are some quick examples:

- Your backhand return of the tennis ball (the operant) is low and fast, and your tennis coach yells "Excellent!" (the reinforcing stimulus).

- A rat presses a lever (the operant) and receives a food pellet (the reinforcing stimulus).

- In the vending machine example, hitting the machine (the operant) was followed by getting your soft drink (the reinforcing stimulus).

- You watch a student production of *Hamlet* and write a short paper about it (the operant) for 10 bonus points (the reinforcing stimulus) in your literature class.

- You reach your sales quota at work (the operant) and you get a bonus check (the reinforcing stimulus).

In each example, if the addition of the reinforcing stimulus has the effect of making you more likely to repeat the operant in similar situations in the future, then positive reinforcement has occurred.

It's important to point out that what constitutes a *reinforcing stimulus* can vary from person to person, species to species, and situation to situation. While gold stars and stickers may be reinforcing to a third-grader, they would probably have little reinforcing value to your average high school student. As Skinner (1953) explained, "The only way to tell whether or not a given event or stimulus is reinforcing to a given organism under given conditions is to make a direct test."

It's also important to note that the reinforcing stimulus is not necessarily something we usually consider positive or desirable. For example, most teachers would not think of a scolding as being a reinforcing stimulus to children. But to children, adult attention can be a powerful reinforcing stimulus. If a child receives attention from the teacher only when he misbehaves, then the teacher may unwittingly be reinforcing misbehavior. The child may actually increase disruptive behavior in order to get the sought-after reinforcing stimulus—adult attention—even if it's in the form of being scolded. To reduce the child's disruptive behavior, the teacher would do better to reinforce the child's appropriate behavior by paying attention to him when he's *not* being disruptive, such as when he is working quietly.

positive reinforcement
A situation in which a response is followed by the addition of a reinforcing stimulus, increasing the likelihood that the response will be repeated in similar situations.

Negative reinforcement involves an operant that is followed by the removal of an aversive stimulus. In negative reinforcement situations, a response is strengthened because something is being *subtracted* or removed. Remember that the word *negative* in negative reinforcement is used like a mathematical minus sign (−). For example, you take two aspirin (the operant) to remove a headache (the aversive stimulus). Thirty minutes later, the headache is gone. Are you now more likely to take aspirin to deal with bodily aches and pain in the future? If you are, then negative reinforcement has occurred.

Aversive stimuli typically involve physical or psychological discomfort that an organism seeks to escape or avoid. Consequently, behaviors are said to be negatively reinforced when they let you either (1) *escape* aversive stimuli that are already present or (2) *avoid* aversive stimuli before they occur. That is, we're more likely to repeat the same escape or avoidance behaviors in similar situations in the future. The headache example illustrates the negative reinforcement of *escape behavior*. By taking two aspirin, you "escaped" the headache. Paying your electric bill on time to avoid a late charge illustrates the negative reinforcement of *avoidance behavior*.

Many students find the concept of negative reinforcement confusing until they realize just how common it is in everyday life. Here are some examples of negative reinforcement involving escape or avoidance behavior:

- You switch on the air conditioning (the operant) to escape the summer heat (the aversive stimulus).

- The addicted cigarette smoker lights a cigarette (the operant) to escape the discomfort of nicotine withdrawal (the aversive stimulus).

- You make backup copies of important computer files (the operant) to avoid losing the data if the computer's hard drive should fail (the aversive stimulus).

- You dab some hydrocortisone cream on an insect bite (the operant) to escape the itching (the aversive stimulus).

- You spray yourself with insect repellent (the operant) to avoid being bitten by mosquitoes (the aversive stimulus).

- You brush your teeth (the operant) to avoid social embarrassment (the aversive stimulus).

- You set a timer (the operant) to avoid burning the cookies in the oven (the aversive stimulus).

- You get to class on time (the operant) to avoid being scolded (the aversive stimulus) by your instructor.

- You get a flu shot in November (the operant) to avoid catching the flu (the aversive stimulus).

In each example, if escaping or avoiding the aversive event has the effect of making you more likely to repeat the operant in similar situations in the future, then negative reinforcement has taken place.

Primary and Conditioned Reinforcers

Skinner also distinguished two kinds of reinforcing stimuli: primary and conditioned. A **primary reinforcer** is one that is *naturally* reinforcing for a given species. That is, even if an individual has not had prior experience with the particular stimulus, the stimulus or event still has reinforcing properties. For example, food, water, adequate warmth, and sexual contact are primary reinforcers for most animals, including humans.

negative reinforcement
A situation in which a response results in the removal, avoidance, or escape from an aversive stimulus, increasing the likelihood that the response will be repeated in similar situations.

primary reinforcer
A stimulus or event that is naturally or inherently reinforcing for a given species, such as food, water, or other biological necessities.

Types of Reinforcers Primary reinforcers, like hugs, are naturally reinforcing—you don't have to learn their value. In contrast, the value of conditioned reinforcers, like grades, and awards, have to be learned through their association with primary reinforcers. But conditioned reinforcers can be just as reinforcing as primary reinforcers. As proof, a beaming Venus Williams holds the 2001 U.S. Open Championship Cup for her first place tennis win. We should also note that Venus's efforts were followed by another potent conditioned reinforcer—a check for $850,000.

conditioned reinforcer

A stimulus or event that has acquired reinforcing value by being associated with a primary reinforcer; also called a *secondary reinforcer.*

punishment

The presentation of a stimulus or event following a behavior that acts to decrease the likelihood of the behavior's being repeated.

punishment by application

A situation in which an operant is followed by the presentation or addition of an aversive stimulus; also called *positive punishment.*

A **conditioned reinforcer,** also called a *secondary reinforcer,* is one that has acquired reinforcing value by being associated with a primary reinforcer. The classic example of a conditioned reinforcer is money. Money is reinforcing not because those flimsy bits of paper and little pieces of metal have value in and of themselves, but because we've learned that we can use them to acquire primary reinforcers and other conditioned reinforcers. Awards, frequent-flyer points, and college degrees are just a few other examples of conditioned reinforcers.

Sometimes there are many links in the association between a conditioned reinforcer and a primary reinforcer. You can't plunk your college diploma down on the counter to purchase a loaf of bread at the grocery store, but your college degree can lead to a job that provides you with money to exchange for the primary reinforcer of food.

Conditioned reinforcers need not be as tangible as money or college degrees. The respect of your peers and the approval of your instructors or managers can be powerful conditioned reinforcers. Conditioned reinforcers can be as subtle as a smile, a touch, or a nod of recognition. Looking back at the Prologue, for example, Fern was reinforced by the laughter of her friends and relatives each time she told the "killer attic" tale—so she keeps telling the story!

Punishment
Using Aversive Consequences to Decrease Behavior

Key Theme

- Punishment is a process that decreases the future occurrence of a behavior.

Key Questions

- What factors influence the effectiveness of punishment?
- What effects are associated with the use of punishment to control behavior, and what are some alternative ways to change behavior?
- What are discriminative stimuli?

Positive and negative reinforcement are processes that *increase* the frequency of a particular behavior. The opposite effect is produced by punishment. **Punishment** is a process in which a behavior is followed by an aversive consequence that *decreases* the likelihood of the behavior being repeated. Many people tend to confuse punishment and negative reinforcement, but these two processes produce entirely different effects on behavior (see Table 5.2). Negative reinforcement *always increases* the likelihood that an operant will be repeated in the future. Punishment *always decreases* the future performance of an operant.

Skinner (1953) identified two types of aversive events that can act as punishment. **Punishment by application,** also called *positive punishment,* in-

Punishment and negative reinforcement are two different processes that produce *opposite* effects on a given behavior. Punishment *decreases* the future performance of the behavior, whereas negative reinforcement *increases* it.

Table | **5.2**

Comparing Punishment and Negative Reinforcement			
Process	**Operant**	**Consequence**	**Effect on Behavior**
Punishment	Using radar detector	Receive ticket and fine for illegal use of radar detector	Decrease use of radar detector in the future
Negative reinforcement	Using radar detector	Avoid speeding ticket and fine	Increase use of radar detector in the future

focus on **Neuroscience**

(a) Reinforcement

(b) Punishment

(c) Reinforcement and Punishment Compared

Reinforcement and Punishment in the Brain How are reinforcement and punishment represented in the brain? In a recent study conducted by British psychologist John O'Doherty and his colleagues (2001a), participants played a computerized gambling game while they were in a functional MRI (fMRI) scanner. The participants viewed geometric figures on a computer screen, "gambled" on which one was correct, and were then told how much "money" they had won (reinforcement) or lost (punishment).

Images (**a**) and (**b**) are fMRI scans of the orbitofrontal cortex. The *orbitofrontal cortex* (OFC) is a region of the prefrontal lobes located just above the skull sockets (or orbits) for the eyes. The fMRI scans show that reinforcement and punishment were associated with increased activity in different OFC areas. Reinforcement, shown in image (**a**), activated the middle region of the orbitofrontal cortex. In contrast, punishment, shown in image (**b**), activated areas on both sides of the orbitofrontal cortex.

Image (**c**) shows the same information projected onto a three-dimensional model of the brain. The blue area shows OFC activation following reward, and the red area depicts OFC activation following punishment. The researchers also discovered that the degree of activation in these OFC areas was directly correlated to the size of the reward or loss—the greater the reward or punishment, the higher the level of activity in these areas.

These findings support other research showing that damage in the prefrontal region is associated with poor decision making in everyday life (Bechara & others, 1997; Damasio, 1999b). Apparently, people with damaged prefrontal lobes are unable to use information from rewarding and punishing outcomes to guide their behavior.

SOURCE: O'Doherty & others (2001a).

---

volves a response being followed by the presentation of an aversive stimulus. The word *positive* in the phrase *positive punishment* signifies that something is added or presented in the situation. In this case, it's an aversive stimulus. Here are some everyday examples of punishment by application:

- An employee wears jeans to work (the operant) and is reprimanded by his supervisor for dressing inappropriately (the punishing stimulus).

- You try to comfort a distraught friend (the operant) only to be angrily told, "Mind your own business!" (the punishing stimulus).

- A child giggles and acts up in the middle of a wedding (the operant), and his parent glares at him and whispers, "Be quiet or else!" (the punishing stimulus).

- You make a comment (the operant) in your workgroup meetings, and a co-worker responds with a sarcastic remark (the punishing stimulus).

In each of these examples, if the presentation of the punishing stimulus has the effect of decreasing the behavior it follows, then punishment has occurred. Although the punishing stimuli in these examples were administered by other people, punishing stimuli also occur as natural consequences for some behaviors. Inadvertently touching a hot iron, a live electrical wire, or a sharp object (the operant) can result in a painful injury (the punishing stimulus).

punishment by removal
A situation in which an operant is followed by the removal or subtraction of a reinforcing stimulus; also called *negative punishment.*

The second type of punishment is **punishment by removal,** also called *negative punishment.* The word negative indicates that some stimulus is subtracted or removed from the situation (see Table 5.3). In this case, it is the loss or withdrawal of a reinforcing stimulus following a behavior. That is, the behavior's consequence is the loss of some privilege, possession, or other desirable object or activity. Here are some everyday examples of punishment by removal:

- After buying stock (the operant) in a "hot" Internet dot-com company, the company fails and the person loses all of her money (loss of reinforcing stimulus).

- After he speeds through a stop sign and broadsides a school bus (the operant), a person's driver's license is suspended (loss of reinforcing stimulus).

- Because he was flirting with another woman (the operant), a guy gets dumped by his girlfriend (loss of reinforcing stimulus).

- After discovering that her child has scribbled all over the new wallpaper (the operant), the parent takes the child's art supplies away (loss of reinforcing stimulus).

- A student fails two classes (the operant) and loses his financial aid (loss of reinforcing stimulus).

Table **5.3**

Types of Reinforcement and Punishment

	Reinforcing stimulus	Aversive stimulus
Stimulus presented	Positive reinforcement	Positive punishment
Stimulus removed	Negative punishment	Negative reinforcement

This table provides a simple way of identifying the type of reinforcement or punishment based on whether a reinforcing or an aversive stimulus is presented or removed following an operant.

In each example, if the behavior decreases in response to the removal of the reinforcing stimulus, then punishment has occurred. It's important to stress that, like reinforcement, punishment is defined by the effect it produces. In everyday usage, people often refer to a particular consequence as a punishment when, strictly speaking, it's not. Why? Because the consequence has *not* reduced future occurrences of the behavior. Hence, many consequences commonly thought of as punishments—being sent to prison, fined, reprimanded, ridiculed, or fired from a job—fail to reduce a particular behavior.

Why is it that aversive consequences don't always function as effective punishments? Skinner (1953) as well as other researchers have noted that several factors influence the effectiveness of punishment (see Axelrod & Apsche, 1983; Kazdin, 2001). For example, punishment is more effective if it immediately follows a response than if it is delayed. Punishment is also more effective if it consistently, rather than occasionally, follows a response. Though speeding tickets and prison sentences are commonly referred to as punishments, these aversive consequences are inconsistently applied and often administered only after a long delay. Thus, they don't always effectively decrease specific behaviors.

Even when punishment works, its use has several drawbacks. First, punishment may decrease a specific response, but it doesn't necessarily teach or promote a more appropriate response to take its place. Second, punishment that is intense may produce undesirable results, such as complete passivity, fear, anxiety, or hostility (Skinner, 1974). Finally, the effects of punishment are likely to be temporary (Estes & Skinner, 1941; Skinner, 1938). A child who is sent to her room for teasing her little brother may well repeat the behavior when her mother's back is turned. As Skinner (1971) noted, "Punished behavior is likely to reappear after the punitive consequences are withdrawn." For some suggestions on how to change behavior without using a punishing stimulus, see In Focus Box 5.3.

Changing the Behavior of Others: Alternatives to Punishment

Although punishment may temporarily decrease the occurrence of a problem behavior, it doesn't promote more desirable or appropriate behaviors in its place. Throughout his life, Skinner remained strongly opposed to the use of punishment. Instead, he advocated the greater use of positive reinforcement to strengthen desirable behaviors (Dinsmoor, 1992; Skinner, 1971). Here are four strategies that can be used to reduce undesirable behaviors without resorting to punishment.

Strategy 1: Reinforce an Incompatible Behavior

The best method to reduce a problem behavior is to reinforce an *alternative* behavior that is both constructive and incompatible with the problem behavior. For example, if you're trying to decrease a child's whining, respond to her requests (the reinforcer) only when she talks in a normal tone of voice.

Strategy 2: Stop Reinforcing the Problem Behavior

Technically, this strategy is called *extinction*. The first step in effectively applying extinction is to observe the behavior carefully and identify the reinforcer that is maintaining the problem behavior. Then eliminate the reinforcer.

Suppose a co-worker is wasting your time with gossip. You want to extinguish his behavior of interrupting your work with needless chitchat. In the past, trying to be polite, you've responded to his behavior by acting interested (a reinforcer). You could eliminate the reinforcer by acting uninterested and continuing to work while he talks.

It's important to note that when the extinction process is initiated, the problem behavior often *temporarily* increases. This situation is more likely to occur if the problem behavior has only occasionally been reinforced in the past. Thus, once you begin, be consistent in nonreinforcement of the problem behavior.

Strategy 3: Reinforce the Nonoccurrence of the Problem Behavior

This strategy involves setting a specific time period after which the individual is reinforced if the unwanted behavior has *not* occurred. For example, if you're trying to reduce bickering between your children, set an appropriate time limit, and then provide positive reinforcement if they have *not* squabbled during that interval.

Strategy 4: Remove the Opportunity to Obtain Positive Reinforcement

It's not always possible to identify and eliminate all the reinforcers that maintain a behavior. For example, a child's obnoxious behavior might be reinforced by the social attention of siblings or classmates.

In a procedure called *time-out from positive reinforcement,* the child is removed from the reinforcing situation for a short time, so that the access to reinforcers is eliminated. When the undesirable behavior occurs, the child is immediately sent to a time-out area that is free of distractions and social contact. The time-out period begins when the child's behavior is under control. For children, a good rule of thumb is one minute of time-out per year of age.

Enhancing the Effectiveness of Positive Reinforcement

Often, these four strategies are used in combination. However, remember the most important behavioral principle: *Positively reinforce the behaviors that you want to increase.* There are several ways in which you can enhance the effectiveness of positive reinforcement:

- Make sure that the reinforcer is *strongly* reinforcing to the individual whose behavior you're trying to modify.

- The positive reinforcer should be delivered *immediately* after the preferred behavior occurs.

- The positive reinforcer should initially be given *every* time the preferred behavior occurs. When the desired behavior is well established, *gradually reduce the frequency of reinforcement.*

- Use a *variety* of positive reinforcers, such as tangible items, praise, special privileges, recognition, and so on. Minimize the use of food as a positive reinforcer.

- Capitalize on what is known as the *Premack principle*—a more preferred activity (e.g., painting) can be used to reinforce a less preferred activity (e.g., picking up toys).

- Encourage the individual to engage in *self-reinforcement* in the form of pride, a sense of accomplishment, and feelings of self-control.

Discriminative Stimuli
Setting the Occasion for Responding

The third component of operant conditioning is the **discriminative stimulus**—the specific stimulus in the presence of which a particular operant is more likely to be reinforced. For example, when do you pick up the telephone and say hello? When it rings, of course. The ringing phone is a discriminative stimulus that sets the occasion for a particular response—picking up the telephone and speaking.

This example illustrates how we've learned from experience to associate certain environmental cues or signals with particular operant responses. We've learned that we're more likely to be reinforced for performing a particular oper-

discriminative stimulus
A specific stimulus in the presence of which a particular response is more likely to be reinforced, and in the absence of which a particular response is not reinforced.

CRITICAL THINKING 5.4

Is Human Freedom Just an Illusion?

Skinner's most famous invention was the *operant chamber,* more popularly known as a *Skinner box,* in which rats or pigeons were conditioned to perform simple behaviors, such as pressing a lever or pecking at a disc, to receive a food reward (see page 216). Had Skinner been content to confine his observations to the behavior of rats or pigeons in a Skinner box, his career might have been relatively uncontroversial. But Skinner was intensely interested in human behavior and social problems (Bjork, 1997a). He believed that operant conditioning principles could, and *should,* be applied on a broad scale to help solve society's problems.

Skinner's most radical—and controversial—belief was that such ideas as free will, self-determination, and individual choice are just an illusion. Skinner (1971) argued that behavior is not simply influenced by the environment but is *determined* by it. Control the environment, he said, and you will control human behavior. As he bluntly asserted in his controversial best-seller, *Beyond Freedom and Dignity* (1971), "A person does not act upon the world, the world acts upon him."

Such views did not sit well with the American public. Following the publication of *Beyond Freedom and Dignity,* one member of Congress denounced Skinner for "advancing ideas which threaten the future of our system of government by denigrating the American tradition of individualism, human dignity, and self-reliance" (quoted in Rutherford, 2000). Why the uproar?

Skinner's ideas clashed with the traditional American ideals of personal responsibility, individual freedom, and self-determination. Such ideals are based on the assumption that behavior arises from causes that are *within* the individual. All individuals are held responsible for their conduct and given credit for their achievements. Skinner labeled such notions the "traditional prescientific view" of human behavior.

According to Skinner, "A scientific analysis [of behavior] shifts both the responsibility and the achievement to the environment." Applying his ideas to social problems, such as alcoholism and crime, Skinner (1971) wrote, "It is the environment which is 'responsible' for objectionable behavior, and it is the environment, not some attribute of the individual, which must be changed."

To understand Skinner's point of view, it helps to think of society as a massive, sophisticated Skinner box. From the moment of birth, the environment shapes and determines your behavior through reinforcing or punishing consequences. Taking this view, you are no more personally responsible for your behavior than is a rat in a Skinner box pressing a lever to obtain a food pellet. Just like the rat's behavior,

©1996, Washington Post Writers Group. Reprinted with permission.

ant response when we do so in the presence of the appropriate discriminative stimulus. Thus, you've learned that you're more likely to be reinforced for screaming at the top of your lungs at a football game (one discriminative stimulus) than in the middle of class (a different discriminative stimulus).

In this way, according to Skinner (1974), behavior is determined and controlled by the stimuli that are present in a given situation. In Skinner's view, an individual's behavior is *not* determined by a personal choice or a conscious decision. Instead, individual behavior is determined by environmental stimuli and the person's reinforcement history in that environment. Skinner's views on this point have some very controversial implications, which are discussed above in Critical Thinking Box 5.4: Is Human Freeddom Just an Illusion?

We now have discussed all the fundamental components of operant conditioning (see Table 5.4). In the presence of a specific environmental stimulus (the discriminative stimulus), we emit a particular behavior (the operant), which is followed by a consequence (reinforcement or punishment). If the consequence is either positive or negative reinforcement, we are *more* likely to repeat the operant when we encounter the same or similar discriminative stimuli in the future. If the consequence is some form of punishment, we are *less* likely to repeat the operant when we encounter the same or similar discriminative stimuli in the future.

Next, we'll build on the basics of operant conditioning by considering how Skinner explained the acquisition of complex behaviors.

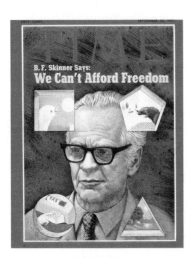

Time for Skinner's Ideas? The impact of the publication of *Beyond Freedom and Dignity* can be measured by Skinner's appearance on the cover of *Time* on September 20, 1971, shortly after the book was published. Skinner is shown in the middle of some of his most famous creations. Clockwise from upper left: pigeons trained to peck at a Ping-Pong ball; a rat pressing a lever in an operant chamber; an idealized rural scene representing the fictional utopia described in Skinner's novel, *Walden Two* (1948b); and a teaching machine, an early mechanical device for programmed instruction based on operant conditioning principles.

your behavior is simply a response to the unique patterns of environmental consequences to which you have been exposed.

Skinner (1971) proposed that "a technology of behavior" be developed, one based on a scientific analysis of behavior. He believed that society could be redesigned using operant conditioning principles to produce more socially desirable behaviors—and happier citizens. He described such an ideal, utopian society in *Walden Two*, a novel he published in 1948. Critics charged Skinner with advocating a totalitarian state. They asked who would determine which behaviors were shaped and maintained (Rutherford, 2000; Todd & Morris, 1992).

As Skinner pointed out, however, human behavior is *already* controlled by various authorities: parents, teachers, politicians, religious leaders, employers, and so forth. Such authorities regularly use reinforcing and punishing consequences to shape and control the behavior of others. Skinner insisted that it is better to control behavior in a rational, humane fashion than to leave the control of behavior to the whims and often selfish aims of those in power. Skinner himself was adamantly opposed to the use of

punishment and other aversive stimuli to control behavior. Instead, he repeatedly advocated the greater use of positive reinforcement (Dinsmoor, 1992).

On the one hand, it may seem convenient to blame your history of environmental consequences for your failures and misdeeds. On the other hand, that means you can't take any credit for your accomplishments and good deeds either!

Critical Thinking Questions:

- If Skinner's vision of a socially engineered society using operant conditioning principles were implemented, would such changes be good or bad for society?

- Are human freedom and personal responsibility illusions? Or is human behavior fundamentally different from a rat's behavior in a Skinner box? If so, how?

- Is your behavior almost entirely the product of environmental conditioning? Think about your answer carefully. After all, exactly *why* are you reading this box?

Table | 5.4

Components of Operant Conditioning

The examples given here illustrate the three key components involved in operant conditioning. The basic operant conditioning process works like this: In the presence of a specific discriminative stimulus, an operant response is emitted, which is followed by a consequence. Depending on the consequence, we are either more or less likely to repeat the operant when we encounter the same or similar discriminative stimuli in the future.

	Discriminative Stimulus	Operant Response	Consequence	Effect on Future Behavior
Definition	The environmental stimulus that precedes an operant response	The actively emitted or voluntary behavior	The environmental stimulus or event that follows the operant response	Reinforcement increases the likelihood of operant being repeated; punishment or lack of reinforcement decreases the likelihood of operant being repeated.
Examples	Wallet on college sidewalk	Give wallet to security	$50 reward from wallet's owner	Positive reinforcement: More likely to turn in lost items to authorities
	Gas gauge almost on "empty"	Fill car with gas	Avoid running out of gas	Negative reinforcement: More likely to fill car when gas gauge shows empty.
	Informal social situation at work	Tell an off-color, sexist joke	Formally reprimanded for sexism and inappropriate workplace behavior	Positive punishment: Less likely to tell jokes at workplace
	Soft-drink vending machine	Put in quarters	No soft drink and lose money	Negative punishment: Less likely to use that vending machine

5.2 R·E·V·I·E·W

Reinforcement and Punishment

Identify the operant conditioning process that is being illustrated in each of the following examples. Choose from: positive reinforcement, negative reinforcement, punishment by application, and punishment by removal.

1. When Joan turns the grocery cart down the candy aisle, her three-year-old son, Connor, starts screaming, "Want candy! Candy!" Joan moves to another aisle, but Connor continues to scream. As other customers begin staring and Joan starts to feel embarrassed, she finally gives Connor a bag of M&Ms. Connor is now more likely to scream in a store when he wants candy because he has experienced _____.

2. If Joan is more likely to give into Connor's temper tantrums in public situations in the future, it is because she has experienced _____.

3. Feeling sorry for a hitchhiker on the side of the road, Howard offered him a ride. The hitchhiker robbed Howard and stole his car. Howard no longer picks up hitchhikers because of _____.

4. Jacob is caught surfing X-rated Web sites on the computer in his office and gets reprimanded by his boss. Jacob no longer accesses X-rated Web sites on his office computer because of _____.

5. As you walk out of the shoe store at the Super Mall and turn toward another store, you spot a person whom you greatly dislike. You immediately duck back into the shoe store to avoid an unpleasant interaction with him. Because _____ has occurred, you are more likely to take evasive action when you encounter people you dislike in the future.

6. Having watched her favorite cartoon characters, the Powderpuff Girls, fly into the air on many episodes, six-year-old Tracey confidently climbs the stepladder with a cape, then launches herself into the air, only to tumble into the yard. Because Tracey experienced _____, she only tried this stunt once.

7. Thinking she was making a good impression in her new job by showing how knowledgeable she was, Tanya corrected her supervisor's erroneous comments in two different meetings. Not long after the second meeting, Tanya was "let go" because the company said it was eliminating her position. Because she experienced _____, Tanya no longer publicly corrects her superiors.

Shaping and Maintaining Behavior

Key Theme

- New behaviors are acquired through shaping and can be maintained through different patterns of reinforcement.

Key Questions

- How does shaping work?
- What is the partial reinforcement effect, and how do the four schedules of reinforcement differ in their effects?
- What is behavior modification?

To scientifically study the relationship between behavior and its consequences in the laboratory, Skinner invented the **operant chamber,** more popularly known as the **Skinner box.** An operant chamber is a small cage with a food dispenser. Attached to the cage is a device that automatically records the number of operants made by an experimental animal, usually a rat or pigeon. For a rat, the typical operant is pressing a bar; for a pigeon, it is pecking at a small disk. Food pellets are usually used for positive reinforcement. Often, a light in the cage functions as a discriminative stimulus. When the light is on, pressing the bar or pecking the disk is reinforced with a food pellet. When the light is off, these responses do not result in reinforcement.

When a rat is first placed in a Skinner box, it typically explores its new environment, occasionally nudging or pressing the bar in the process. The researcher can accelerate the rat's bar-pressing behavior through a process called shaping. **Shaping** involves reinforcing successively closer approximations of a

operant chamber or **Skinner box**
The experimental apparatus invented by B. F. Skinner to study the relationship between environmental events and active behaviors.

shaping
The operant conditioning procedure of selectively reinforcing successively closer approximations of a goal behavior until the goal behavior is displayed.

behavior until the correct behavior is displayed. For example, the researcher might first reinforce the rat with a food pellet whenever it moves to the half of the Skinner box in which the bar is located. Other responses would be ignored. Once that response has been learned, reinforcement is withheld until the rat moves even closer to the bar. Then the rat might be reinforced only when it touches the bar. Step by step, the rat is reinforced for behaviors that correspond ever more closely to the final goal behavior—pressing the bar.

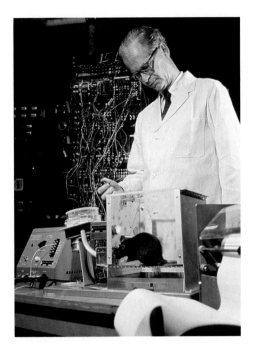

The Skinner Box Popularly called a Skinner box, after its inventor, an operant chamber is used to experimentally study operant conditioning in laboratory animals.

Skinner believed that shaping could explain how people acquire a wide variety of abilities and skills—everything from tying shoes to operating sophisticated computer programs. To illustrate, consider how parents can use shaping to teach a toddler to dress herself. At first they might praise her for simply picking up a shirt, and then for managing to pull it over her head. Once that step is mastered, she would be reinforced only when she poked her head and arms through the appropriate shirt holes. Eventually, praise is forthcoming only when, as a preschooler, she picks out clothes that match, or when, as an adolescent, she chooses an outfit that doesn't mortify her parents.

Athletic coaches, teachers, parents, and child-care workers all use shaping techniques. Psychologist Judith Mathews and her colleagues (1992) used shaping to teach visually impaired children as young as two years of age to wear contact lenses. Toys, bubbles, and stickers were used as reinforcers. First, the children were positively reinforced for allowing their faces to be touched. Then, the children were reinforced for pulling open an eyelid, allowing an adult's finger to approach their eyes, touching the contact lens, and so forth. By the end of the study, the children were wearing their contact lenses every day, and it took an average of only two minutes for an adult to insert or remove the lenses.

Operant Conditioning at SeaWorld This sequence shows a SeaWorld trainer using operant conditioning principles with a dolphin that has already been shaped to perform somersaults. **(a)** The trainer gives the dolphin two discriminative stimuli—a distinct vocal sound and a specific hand gesture. **(b)** The dolphin quickly responds with the correct operant—a perfect somersault in the air. **(c)** The operant is positively reinforced with a piece of fish. The same basic techniques are also used to teach seals, sea lions, walruses, and killer whales to perform different tricks on cue.

(a)   (b)   (c)

continuous reinforcement
A schedule of reinforcement in which every occurrence of a particular response is reinforced.

partial reinforcement
A situation in which the occurrence of a particular response is only sometimes followed by a reinforcer.

extinction (in operant conditioning)
The gradual weakening and disappearance of conditioned behavior. In operant conditioning, extinction occurs when an emitted behavior is no longer followed by a reinforcer.

partial reinforcement effect
The phenomenon in which behaviors that are conditioned using partial reinforcement are more resistant to extinction than behaviors that are conditioned using continuous reinforcement.

schedule of reinforcement
The delivery of a reinforcer according to a preset pattern based on the number of responses or the time interval between responses.

fixed-ratio (FR) schedule
A reinforcement schedule in which a reinforcer is delivered after a fixed number of responses has occurred.

The Partial Reinforcement Effect: Building Resistance to Extinction

Once a rat had acquired a bar-pressing behavior, Skinner found that the most efficient way to strengthen the response was to immediately reinforce *every* occurrence of bar pressing. This pattern of reinforcement is called **continuous reinforcement.** In everyday life, of course, it's common for responses to be reinforced only sometimes—a pattern called **partial reinforcement.** For example, practicing your basketball skills isn't followed by putting the ball through the hoop on every shot. Sometimes you're reinforced by making a basket, and sometimes you're not.

Now suppose that despite all your hard work, your basketball skills are dismal. If practicing free throws was *never* reinforced by making a basket, what would you do? You'd probably eventually quit playing basketball. This is an example of **extinction.** In operant conditioning, when a learned response no longer results in reinforcement, the likelihood of the behavior being repeated gradually declines.

Skinner (1956) first noticed the effects of partial reinforcement when he began running low on food pellets one day. Rather than reinforcing every bar press, Skinner tried to stretch out his supply of pellets by rewarding responses only periodically. He found that the rats not only continued to respond, but actually increased their rate of bar pressing.

One important consequence of partially reinforcing behavior is that partially reinforced behaviors tend to be more resistant to extinction than are behaviors conditioned using continuous reinforcement. This phenomenon is called the **partial reinforcement effect.** For example, when Skinner shut off the food-dispensing mechanism, a pigeon conditioned using continuous reinforcement would continue pecking at the disk 100 times or so before the behavior decreased significantly, indicating extinction. In contrast, a pigeon conditioned with partial reinforcement continued to peck at the disk thousands of times! If you think about it, this is not surprising. When pigeons, rats, or humans have experienced partial reinforcement, they've learned that reinforcement may yet occur, despite delays and nonreinforced responses, if persistent responses are made.

In everyday life, the partial reinforcement effect is reflected in behaviors that persist despite the lack of reinforcement. Gamblers may persist despite a string of losses, writers will persevere in the face of repeated rejection slips, and the family dog will continue begging for the scraps of food that it has only occasionally received at the dinner table in the past.

The Schedules of Reinforcement

Skinner (1956) found that specific preset arrangements of partial reinforcement produced different patterns and rates of responding. Collectively, these different reinforcement arrangements are called **schedules of reinforcement.** As we describe the four basic schedules of reinforcement, you'll find it helpful to refer to Figures 5.9 and 5.10, which show the typical pattern of responses produced by each schedule.

Superstitious Behavior and Accidental Reinforcement Like these New York Mets baseball players, professional athletes sometimes develop quirky superstitious rituals. Skinner (1948b) pointed out that superstitions may result when a behavior is *accidentally* reinforced—that is, when reinforcement is just a coincidence. If you win a lottery when you play your "lucky" number, will you be more likely to play that number again?

Fixed-Ratio Schedule With a **fixed-ratio (FR) schedule,** reinforcement occurs after a fixed number of responses. For example, a rat might be on a 25-to-1 fixed-ratio (abbreviated FR-25), meaning it has to press the bar 25 times in order to receive one food pellet. Not surprisingly, shaping is usually needed to get a rat to the point at which it will press the bar 25 times in order to get one food pellet. The rat may start on continuous reinforcement, followed by an FR-2 schedule, then an FR-4 schedule, and so on. In this way, the rat's behavior is eventually shaped to produce responding on an FR-25 schedule of reinforcement. Once the behavior is shaped, the ratio of reinforcements to responses is fixed and predictable.

Fixed-ratio schedules typically produce a high rate of responding that follows a burst–pause–burst pattern. The rat displays a burst of bar pressing, receives a pellet of food, pauses briefly, then displays another burst of responding (see Figure 5.9). In everyday life, the fixed-ratio schedule is reflected in any activity that requires a precise number of responses in order to obtain reinforcement. Piecework—work for which you are paid for producing a specific number of items, such as being paid $1 for every 100 envelopes you stuff—is an example of an FR-100 schedule. On this sort of schedule, you might work steadily until you've stuffed 100 envelopes and then take a short break before you began working again (Skinner, 1953).

Variable-Ratio Schedule   With a **variable-ratio (VR) schedule,** reinforcement occurs after an *average* number of responses, which *varies* from trial to trial. For example, a rat on a variable-ratio-20 schedule (abbreviated VR-20) would be reinforced after an average of 20 responses. But the rat might have to press the bar 25 times on the first trial before being reinforced and only 15 times on the second trial before reinforcement. Although the number of responses required on any specific trial is *unpredictable,* over repeated trials the ratio of responses to reinforcers works out to the predetermined average.

As you can see in Figure 5.9, variable-ratio schedules of reinforcement produce high, steady rates of responding with hardly any pausing between trials or after reinforcement. Why do variable-ratio schedules produce such persistent responses? One explanation is that although it's impossible to predict *which* response will result in reinforcement, the more responses that are made, the greater the likelihood of reinforcement. The combination of these two factors can make some behaviors, such as gambling, "addictive" for some people (Skinner, 1953). Gambling is the classic example of a variable-ratio schedule in real life. Each spin of the roulette wheel, toss of the dice, or purchase of a lottery ticket could be the big one, and the more often you gamble, the more opportunities you have to win. (And lose, as casino owners are well aware.)

Fixed-Interval Schedule   With a **fixed-interval (FI) schedule,** a reinforcer is delivered for the first response emitted *after* the preset time interval has elapsed. A rat on a two-minute fixed-interval schedule (abbreviated FI-2 minutes) would receive no food pellets for any bar presses made during the first two minutes, whether it pressed the bar twice or 100 times. But the first bar press *after* the two-minute interval had elapsed would be reinforced.

Fixed-interval schedules typically produce a pattern of responding in which the number of responses tends to increase as the time for the next reinforcer draws near. As you can see in Figure 5.10, this produces a scallop-shaped pattern of responses. Long pauses in responding after reinforcement are especially common when the fixed interval is large. For example, a rat conditioned to an FI-10 minutes schedule may go for several minutes without pressing the bar. But as the end of the 10-minute interval draws near, bar pressing steadily increases until reinforcement occurs.

Daily life contains examples of reinforcement that follow a very similar pattern to the laboratory example of fixed-interval reinforcement. For instance, if your instructor gives you a test every four weeks, your studying behavior would probably follow the same scallop-shaped pattern of responding as the rat's bar-pressing behavior. As the end of the four-week interval draws near, studying behavior increases. After the test, studying behavior drops off until the end of the next four-week interval draws near. The same effect can occur with an employee's annual performance review. As the time for the performance review gets closer, the employee's productive behaviors (the operant) tend to increase.

FIGURE 5.9 Fixed-Ratio and Variable-Ratio Schedules of Reinforcement The predictable nature of fixed-ratio schedules produces a high rate of responding, with a pause after the reinforcer is delivered. In contrast, the unpredictable nature of variable-ratio schedules produces high, steady rates of responding with hardly any pausing between reinforcers.

SOURCE: Based on Skinner (1961).

FIGURE 5.10 Fixed-Interval and Variable-Interval Schedules of Reinforcement The predictable nature of fixed-interval schedules produces a scallop-shaped pattern of responding. As the end of the interval draws near, the rate of responding increases steadily until a reinforcer is delivered; then comes a sharp decrease in responding until the end of the interval draws near again. In contrast, the unpredictable nature of variable-interval schedules produces a moderate, but steady, rate of responding.

SOURCE: Based on Skinner (1961).

variable-ratio (VR) schedule
A reinforcement schedule in which a reinforcer is delivered after an average number of responses, which varies unpredictably from trial to trial.

fixed-interval (FI) schedule
A reinforcement schedule in which a reinforcer is delivered for the first response that occurs after a fixed-time interval has elapsed.

variable-interval (VI) schedule
A reinforcement schedule in which a reinforcer is delivered for the first response that occurs after an average time interval, which varies unpredictably from trial to trial.

behavior modification
The application of learning principles to help people develop more effective or adaptive behaviors.

Variable-Interval Schedule On a **variable-interval (VI) schedule,** reinforcement occurs for the first response emitted after an *average* amount of time has elapsed, but the interval varies from trial to trial. In other words, the length of time that must pass before a particular reinforcement is delivered is unpredictable, but over a *series* of trials, it works out to a predetermined average. A rat on a VI-30 seconds schedule might be reinforced on trial 1 for the first bar press after only 10 seconds have elapsed, for the first bar press after 50 seconds have elapsed on trial 2, and for the first bar press after 30 seconds have elapsed on trial 3. This works out to an average of one reinforcer every 30 seconds.

Generally, the unpredictable nature of variable-interval schedules tends to produce moderate but steady rates of responding, especially when the average interval is relatively short (see Figure 5.10). In daily life, we experience variable-interval schedules when we have to wait for events that follow an approximate, rather than a precise, schedule. Trying to connect to the Internet via a dial-up modem during peak usage hours is one example. When you encounter a busy signal, you periodically try connecting because you know that at some point you'll be able to access the network. However, it's impossible to predict exactly when your attempt to connect to the network (the operant response) will be reinforced (the modem squeals, and you hear the familiar, "Welcome! You've got mail!").

On a variable-interval schedule, reinforcement depends on the passage of time rather than on the number of responses. Dramatically increasing the number of responses probably won't result in increased reinforcement. But reinforcement is unpredictable and *might* occur at any time. Thus, a moderately steady rate of responses will pay off in the long run.

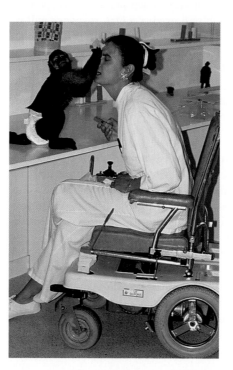

Using Operant Conditioning An organization called Helping Hands, founded by behavioral psychologist Mary Joan Willard, trains capuchin monkeys to help people who are paralyzed or otherwise disabled. During the training phase, operant conditioning is used to teach the monkeys a wide range of helping skills, such as feeding a person, turning lights on and off, and so forth. A monkey may undergo training for up to four years before being placed with a disabled person.

Applications of Operant Conditioning

In a previous section we described how operant conditioning principles have been applied to help visually impaired children wear contact lenses. This example illustrates **behavior modification,** the application of learning principles to help people develop more effective or adaptive behaviors. Most often, behavior modification involves applying the principles of operant conditioning to bring about changes in behavior.

Behavior modification has been used in such diverse situations as improving worker performance, increasing social skills in schoolchildren, promoting sleep at night, and increasing the use of automobile seatbelts (e.g., Kamps & others, 1992; Lilie & Rosenberg, 1990; Martens & others, 1992; Stajkovic & Luthans, 1997). Behavior modification has even been used to reduce "goofing off" by competitive athletes during practice sessions (Hume & Crossman, 1992). When swimmers were reinforced with music for focusing on practicing their skills, productive behavior increased dramatically. In each of these situations, the systematic use of reinforcement and shaping resulted in the increased occurrence of desirable behaviors. In Chapter 15, on therapies, we'll look at behavior modification techniques in more detail.

The principles of operant conditioning have also been used in the specialized training of animals to help people who are physically challenged. Seeing Eye dogs and dogs who assist people who are hearing-impaired are just two examples.

5.3 R·E·V·I·E·W

C·O·N·C·E·P·T

Schedules of Reinforcement

Indicate which of the following schedules of reinforcement is being used for each example: variable interval (VI); fixed interval (FI); variable ratio (VR); fixed ratio (FR).

1. _____ A keypunch clerk is paid $1 for every 100 correct accounting entries made on the computer.

2. _____ At the beginning of the new term, your instructor announces that there will be five surprise quizzes over the course of the semester.

3. _____ At the beginning of the semester, your instructor announces that there will be a test every two weeks.

4. _____ On the average, the campus shuttle bus passes the library about once every hour.

5. _____ Michael loves to play the slot machines, and, occasionally, he wins.

6. _____ Miguel works 40 hours a week in an office and gets paid every Friday afternoon.

Contemporary Views of Operant Conditioning

Key Theme

■ In contrast to Skinner's views, today's learning researchers acknowledge the importance of both cognitive and evolutionary factors in operant conditioning.

Key Questions

■ How did Tolman's research demonstrate the involvement of cognitive processes in learning?

■ What are cognitive maps, latent learning, and learned helplessness?

■ How do an animal's natural behavior patterns affect the conditioning of operant behaviors?

In our discussion of classical conditioning, we noted that contemporary psychologists acknowledge the important roles played by cognitive factors and biological predispositions in classical conditioning. The situation is much the same with operant conditioning. The basic principles of operant conditioning have been confirmed in thousands of studies. However, our understanding of operant conditioning has been broadened by the consideration of cognitive factors and the recognition of the importance of natural behavior patterns.

Cognitive Aspects of Operant Conditioning

Rats! I Thought *You* Had the Map!

In Skinner's view, operant conditioning did not need to invoke cognitive factors to explain the acquisition of operant behaviors. Words such as *expect, prefer, choose,* and *decide* could not be used to explain how behaviors were acquired, maintained, or extinguished. Similarly, Thorndike and other early behaviorists believed that complex, active behaviors were no more than a chain of stimulus–response connections that had been "stamped in" by their effects.

Edward Chase Tolman (1898–1956)
Although he looks rather solemn in this photo, Tolman was known for his openness to new ideas, energetic teaching style, and playful sense of humor. During an important speech, he showed a film of a rat in a maze with a short clip from a Mickey Mouse cartoon spliced in at the end (Gleitman, 1991). Tolman's research demonstrated that cognitive processes are an important part of learning, even in the rat.

However, not all learning researchers agreed with Skinner and Thorndike. **Edward C. Tolman** firmly believed that cognitive processes played an important role in the learning of complex behaviors—even in the lowly laboratory rat. According to Tolman, although such cognitive processes could not be observed directly, they could still be experimentally verified and inferred by careful observation of outward behavior (Tolman, 1932).

Much of Tolman's research involved rats in mazes. When Tolman began his research in the 1920s, many studies of rats in mazes had been done. In a typical experiment, a rat would be placed in the "start" box. A food reward would be put in the "goal" box at the end of the maze. The rat would initially make many mistakes in running the maze. After several trials, it would eventually learn to run the maze quickly and with very few errors.

But what had the rats learned? According to traditional behaviorists, the rats had learned a *sequence of responses,* such as "first-corner—turn left; second corner—turn left; third corner—turn right," and so on. Each response was associated with the "stimulus" of the rat's position in the maze. And the entire sequence of responses was "stamped in" by the food reward at the end of the maze.

Tolman (1948) disagreed with that view. He noted that several investigators had reported as incidental findings that their maze-running rats had occasionally taken their own shortcuts to the food box. In one case, an enterprising rat had knocked the cover off the maze, climbed over the maze wall and out of the maze, and scampered directly to the food box (Lashley, 1929; Tolman & others, 1946). To Tolman, such reports indicated that the rats had learned more than simply the sequence of responses required to get to the food. Tolman believed instead that the rats eventually built up, through experience, a **cognitive map** of the maze—a mental representation of its layout.

As an analogy, think of the route you typically take to get to your psychology classroom. If a hallway along the way were blocked off for repairs, you would use your cognitive map of the building to come up with an alternative route to class. Tolman showed experimentally that rats, like people, seem to form cognitive maps (Tolman, 1948). And, like us, rats can use their cognitive maps to come up with an alternative route to a goal when the customary route is blocked (Tolman & Honzik, 1930a).

Tolman challenged the prevailing behaviorist model on another important point. According to Thorndike, for example, learning would not occur unless the behavior was "strengthened," or "stamped in," by a rewarding consequence. But Tolman showed that this was not necessarily the case. In a classic experiment, three groups of rats were put in the same maze once a day for several days (Tolman & Honzik, 1930b). For group 1, a food reward awaited the rats at the end of the maze. Their performance in the maze steadily improved; the number of errors and the time it took the rats to reach the goal box showed a steady decline with each trial. The rats in group 2 were placed in the maze each day with *no* food reward. They consistently made many errors, and their performance showed only slight improvement. The performance of the rats in groups 1 and 2 was exactly what the traditional behaviorist model would have predicted.

Now consider the behavior of the rats in group 3. These rats were placed in the maze with no food reward for the first 10 days of the experiment. Like the rats in group 2, they made many errors as they wandered about the maze. But, beginning on day 11, they received a food reward at the end of the maze. As you can see in Figure 5.11, there was a dramatic improvement in group 3's performance from day 11 to day 12. Once the rats had discovered that food awaited them at the end of the maze, they made a beeline for the goal. On day 12, the rats in group 3 ran the maze with very few errors, improving their performance to the level of the rats in group 1 that had been rewarded on every trial!

Tolman concluded that *reward*—or reinforcement—is *not necessary* for learning to take place (Tolman & Honzik, 1930b). The rats in group 3 had learned the layout of the maze and formed a cognitive map of the maze simply by exploring

cognitive map
Tolman's term that describes the mental representation of the layout of a familiar environment.

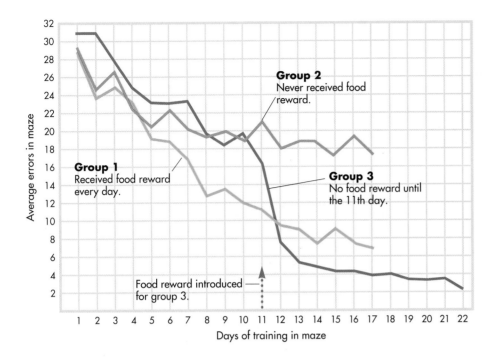

FIGURE 5.11 Latent Learning Beginning with day 1, the rats in group 1 received a food reward at the end of the maze, and the number of errors they made steadily decreased each day. The rats in group 2 never received a food reward; they made many errors as they wandered about in the maze. Beginning on day 11, the rats in group 3 received a food reward at the end of the maze. Notice the sharp decrease in errors on day 12 and thereafter. According to Tolman, the rats in group 3 had formed a cognitive map of the maze during the first 11 days of the experiment. Learning had taken place, but this learning was not demonstrated until reinforcement was present—a phenomenon that Tolman called latent learning.

SOURCE: Tolman & Honzik (1930b).

it for 10 days. However, they had not been motivated to *demonstrate* that learning until a reward was introduced. Rewards, then, seem to affect the *performance* of what has been learned rather than learning itself. To describe learning that is not immediately demonstrated in overt behavior, Tolman used the term **latent learning.**

From these and other experiments, Tolman concluded that learning involves the acquisition of knowledge rather than simply changes in outward behavior. According to Tolman (1932), an organism essentially learns "what leads to what." It learns to "expect" that a certain behavior will lead to a particular outcome in a specific situation.

Tolman is now recognized as an important forerunner of modern cognitive learning theorists (Gleitman, 1991; Olton, 1992). Many contemporary cognitive learning theorists follow Tolman in their belief that operant conditioning involves the *cognitive representation* of the relationship between a behavior and its consequence. Today, operant conditioning is seen as involving the cognitive *expectancy* that a given consequence will follow a given behavior (Bolles, 1972; Dickinson, 1997; Dickinson & Balleine, 2000).

Learned Helplessness

Expectations of Failure and Learning to Quit

Cognitive factors, particularly the role of expectation, are involved in another learning phenomenon, called *learned helplessness.* Learned helplessness was first discovered by accident. Psychologists were trying to find out if classically conditioned responses would affect the process of operant conditioning in dogs. The dogs were strapped into harnesses and then exposed to a tone (the neutral stimulus) paired with a mild electric shock (the UCS), which elicited fear (the UCR). After conditioning, the tone alone—now a CS—elicited the conditioned response of fear.

In the classical conditioning setup, the dogs were unable to escape or avoid the shock. But the next part of the experiment involved an operant conditioning procedure in which the dogs *could* escape the shock. The dogs were transferred to a special kind of operant chamber called a *shuttlebox,* which has a low barrier in the middle that separates the two ends of the chamber. In the

latent learning
Term coined by Tolman to describe learning that occurs in the absence of reinforcement but is not behaviorally demonstrated until a reinforcer becomes available.

Learned Helplessness on the Court When aversive events appear to be beyond your control, you may experience learned helplessness. These basketball players have given up all hope of winning the game. If learned helplessness develops in these teammates—the sense that there is nothing they can do to avoid failure—there is a good chance they will play badly in the *next* game as well (Reisel & Kopelman, 1995).

learned helplessness
A phenomenon in which exposure to inescapable and uncontrollable aversive events produces passive behavior.

operant conditioning setup, the floor on one side of the cage became electrified. To escape the shock, all the dogs had to do was learn a simple escape behavior: Jump over the barrier when the floor was electrified. Normally, dogs learn this simple operant very quickly.

However, when the classically conditioned dogs were placed in the shuttlebox and one side became electrified, the dogs did *not* try to jump over the barrier. Rather than perform the operant to escape the punishing shock, they just lay down and whined. Why?

To Steven F. Maier and Martin Seligman, two young psychology graduate students at the time, the explanation of the dogs' passive behavior seemed obvious. During the tone–shock pairings in the classical conditioning setup, the dogs *had learned that shocks were inescapable.* No active behavior that they engaged in—whether whining, barking, or struggling in the harness—would allow them to avoid or escape the shock. In other words, the dogs had "learned" to be helpless: They had developed the *cognitive expectation* that their behavior had no effect on the environment.

To test this idea, Seligman and Maier (1967) designed a simple experiment. Dogs were arranged in groups of three. The first dog received shocks that it could escape by pushing a panel with its nose. The second dog was "yoked" to the first and received the same number of shocks. However, nothing the second dog did could stop the shock—they stopped only if the first dog pushed the panel. The third dog was the control and got no shocks at all.

After this initial training, the dogs were transferred to the shuttlebox. As Seligman and Maier had predicted, the first and third dogs quickly learned to jump over the barrier when the floor became electrified. But the second dog, the one that had learned that nothing it did would stop the shock, made no effort to jump over the barrier. Because the dog had developed the cognitive expectation that its behavior had no effect on the environment, it had become passive (Seligman & Maier, 1967). The name of this phenomenon is **learned helplessness**—a phenomenon in which exposure to inescapable and uncontrollable aversive events produces passive behavior (Maier & others, 1969).

Since these early experiments, learned helplessness has been demonstrated in many different species, including primates, cats, rats, and fish (LoLordo, 2001). Even cockroaches demonstrate learned helplessness in a cockroach-sized shuttlebox after being exposed to inescapable shock (G. E. Brown & others, 1999).

In humans, numerous studies have found that exposure to uncontrollable, aversive events can produce passivity and learned helplessness. For example, college students who have experienced failure in previous academic settings may feel that academic tasks and setbacks are beyond their control. Thus, when faced with the demands of exams, papers, and studying, rather than rising to the challenge, they may experience feelings of learned helplessness (McKean, 1994). If a student believes that academic tasks are unpleasant, unavoidable, and beyond her control, even the slightest setback can trigger a sense of helpless passivity. Such students may be prone to engage in self-defeating responses, such as procrastinating or giving up prematurely.

Groups of people—even highly motivated people—can also succumb to learned helplessness, as a study of National Football League teams showed (Reisel & Kopelman, 1995). A survey of three years of NFL league records showed that teams that were badly beaten in one game tended to perform even worse than expected in the next game. Because the experience of being creamed by an opponent was so demoralizing, the team members stopped trying to succeed and simply "gave up" the next time they took the field. The team's performance plummeted to even lower levels if its next game was against a highly ranked opponent. As the learned helplessness model predicts, failure has the potential to breed further failure.

How can learned helplessness be overcome? In their early experiments, Seligman and Maier discovered that if they forcibly dragged the dogs over the shuttlebox barrier when the floor on one side became electrified, the dogs would eventually overcome their passivity and begin to jump over the barrier on their own (LoLordo, 2001; Seligman, 1992). For students who experience academic learned helplessness, establishing a sense of control over their schoolwork is the first step. Seeking knowledge about course requirements and assignments and setting goals, however modest, that can be successfully met can help students begin to acquire a sense of mastery over environmental challenges (McKean, 1994).

Since the early demonstrations of learned helplessness in dogs, the notion of learned helplessness has undergone several revisions and refinements (Abramson & others, 1978; Gillham & others, 2001). Learned helplessness has been shown to play a role in psychological disorders, particularly depression, and in the ways that people respond to stressful events. Learned helplessness has also been applied in such diverse fields as management, sales, and health psychology (Peterson & others, 1993). In Chapter 13, on stress, health, and coping, we will take up the topic of learned helplessness again.

Operant Conditioning and Biological Predispositions
Misbehaving Chickens

B. F. Skinner and other behaviorists firmly believed that the general laws of operant conditioning applied to all animal species—whether they were pecking pigeons or bar-pressing rats. As Skinner (1956) wrote:

> Pigeon, rat, monkey, which is which? It doesn't matter. Of course, these species have behavioral repertoires which are as different as their anatomies. But once you have allowed for differences in the ways in which they make contact with the environment, and in the ways in which they act upon the environment, what remains of their behavior shows astonishingly similar properties.

However, psychologists studying operant conditioning, like those studying classical conditioning, found that an animal's natural behavior patterns *could* influence the learning of new behaviors. Consider the experiences of Keller and Marian Breland, two of B. F. Skinner's students. The Brelands established a successful business training animals for television commercials, trade shows, fairs, and even displays in department stores (Bailey & Bailey, 1993; Breland & Breland, 1961). Using operant conditioning, the Brelands trained thousands of animals of many different species to perform all sorts of complex tricks.

But the Brelands weren't always successful in training the animals. For example, they tried to train a chicken to play baseball. The chicken learned to pull a loop that activated a swinging bat. After hitting the ball, the chicken was supposed to run to first base. The chicken had little trouble learning to pull the loop, but instead of running to first base, the chicken would chase the ball.

The Brelands also tried to train a raccoon to pick up two coins and deposit them into a metal box. The raccoon easily learned to pick up the coins, but seemed to resist putting them into the box. Like a furry little miser, it would rub the coins together. And rather than dropping the coins in the box, it would dip the coins in the box and take them out again. As time went on, this behavior became more persistent, even though the raccoon was not being reinforced for it. In fact, the raccoon's "misbehavior" was actually *preventing* it from getting reinforced for correct behavior.

The Brelands noted that such nonreinforced behaviors seemed to reflect innate, instinctive responses. The chicken chasing the ball was behaving like a chicken chasing a bug. Raccoons in the wild instinctively clean and moisten their

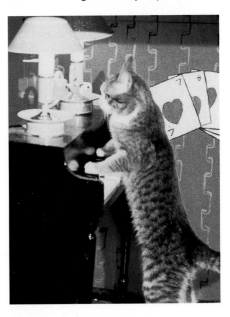

Animal Behavior and Misbehavior Marian and Keller Breland used the operant conditioning principles of shaping and reinforcement to train animals to perform all sorts of behaviors. For example, this cat has been trained to "play" the piano—a difficult feat, since pressing keys to obtain food is not a natural food-seeking behavior pattern for cats. The Brelands discovered that an animal's natural behavior patterns, even though they were not reinforced, can sometimes interfere with the learning of arbitrary responses.

Table | **5.5**

Comparing Classical and Operant Conditioning

	Classical Conditioning	**Operant Conditioning**
Type of behavior	Reflexive, involuntary behaviors	Nonreflexive, voluntary behaviors
Source of behavior	Elicited by stimulus	Emitted by organism
Basis of learning	Associating two stimuli: CS + UCS	Associating a response and the consequence that follows it
Responses conditioned	Physiological and emotional responses	Active behaviors that operate on the environment
Extinction process	Conditioned response decreases when conditioned stimulus is repeatedly presented alone	Responding decreases with elimination of reinforcing consequences
Cognitive aspects	Expectation that CS reliably predicts the UCS	Performance of behavior influenced by the expectation of reinforcement or punishment
Biological predispositions	Innate predispositions influence how easily an association is formed between a particular stimulus and response	Behaviors similar to natural or instinctive behaviors are more readily conditioned

food by dipping it in streams or rubbing it between their forepaws. These natural behaviors interfered with the operant behaviors the Brelands were attempting to condition—a phenomenon called **instinctive drift.**

The biological predisposition to perform such natural behaviors was strong enough to overcome the lack of reinforcement. These instinctual behaviors also prevented the animals from engaging in the learned behaviors that would result in reinforcement. Clearly, reinforcement is not the sole determinant of behavior. And, inborn or instinctive behavior patterns can interfere with the operant conditioning of arbitrary responses.

Before you go on to the next section, take a few minutes to review Table 5.5 and make sure you understand the differences between classical and operant conditioning.

Observational Learning
Imitating the Actions of Others

Key Theme
▓ In observational learning, we learn through watching and imitating the behaviors of others.

Key Questions
▓ How did Albert Bandura demonstrate the principles of observational learning?
▓ What four mental processes are involved in observational learning?
▓ How has observational learning been shown in nonhuman animals?

instinctive drift
The tendency of an animal to revert to instinctive behaviors that can interfere with the performance of an operantly conditioned response.

observational learning
Learning that occurs through observing the actions of others.

Classical conditioning and operant conditioning emphasize the role of direct experiences in learning, such as directly experiencing a reinforcing or punishing stimulus following a particular behavior. But much human learning occurs *indirectly,* by watching what others do, then imitating it. In **observational learning,** learning takes place through observing the actions of others.

Humans develop the capacity to learn through observation at a very early age. Studies of 21-day-old infants have shown that they will imitate a variety of actions, including opening their mouths, sticking out their tongues, and making other facial expressions (Field & others, 1982; Meltzoff & Moore, 1977, 1983).

Albert Bandura is the psychologist most strongly identified with observational learning. Bandura (1974) believes that observational learning is the result of cognitive processes that are "actively judgmental and constructive," not merely "mechanical copying." To illustrate his theory, let's consider his famous experiment involving the imitation of aggressive behaviors (Bandura, 1965). In the experiment, four-year-old children separately watched a short film showing an adult playing aggressively with a Bobo doll—a large, inflated balloon doll that stands upright because the bottom is weighted with sand. All the children saw the adult hit, kick, and punch the Bobo doll in the film.

However, there were three different versions of the film, each with a different ending. Some children saw the adult *reinforced* with soft drinks, candy, and snacks after performing the aggressive actions. Other children saw a version in which the aggressive adult was *punished* for the actions with a scolding and a spanking by another adult. Finally, some children watched a version of the film in which the aggressive adult experienced *no consequences*.

After seeing the film, each child was allowed to play alone in a room with several toys, including a Bobo doll. The playroom was equipped with a one-way window so that the child's behavior could be observed. Bandura found that the consequences the children observed in the film made a difference. Children who watched the film in which the adult was punished were much less likely to imitate the aggressive behaviors than were children who watched either of the other two film endings.

Then Bandura added an interesting twist to the experiment. Each child was asked to show the experimenter what the adult did in the film. For every behavior they could imitate, the child was rewarded with snacks and stickers. Virtually all the children imitated the adult's behaviors they had observed in the film, including the aggressive behaviors. The particular version of the film the children had seen made no difference.

Bandura (1965) explained these results much as Tolman explained latent learning. Reinforcement is *not* essential for learning to occur. Rather, the *expectation of reinforcement* affects the *performance* of what has been learned.

Bandura (1986) suggests that four cognitive processes interact to determine whether imitation will occur. First, you must pay *attention* to the other person's behavior. Second, you must *remember* the other person's behavior so that you can

Albert Bandura Bandura contends that most human behavior is acquired through observational learning rather than through trial and error or direct experience of the consequences of our actions. Watching and processing information about the actions of others, including the consequences that occur, influence the likelihood that behavior will be imitated.

The Classic Bobo Doll Experiment Bandura demonstrated the powerful influence of observational learning in a series of experiments conducted in the early 1960s. Children watched a film showing an adult playing aggressively with an inflated Bobo doll. If they saw the adult rewarded with candy for the aggressive behavior or experience no consequences, the children were much more likely to imitate the behavior than if they saw the adult punished for the aggressive behavior (Bandura, 1965; Bandura & others, 1963).

CRITICAL THINKING 5.5

Does "Reel" Violence Cause Real Aggressive Behavior?

Bandura's early observational learning studies showing preschoolers mimicking the movie actions of an adult and pummeling a Bobo doll provided a powerful paradigm to study the effects of "entertainment" violence. Since Bandura's pioneering research, more than 1,000 studies have investigated the relationship between television and movie depictions of violence and increases in aggressive behavior in the real world (Cantor, 2000). Here we'll highlight some of the key issues and findings from more than three decades of research.

How Prevalent Is Violence on American Television?

The amount of violence depicted on American television is truly staggering. A major research project, the National Television Violence Study (NTVS, 1996, 1997, 1998), was designed to measure the amount of violence and how violence is depicted. Conducted by four major American universities, the NTVS compiled data on more than 8,000 hours of randomly sampled cable and network television programming over a three-year period. Here are some of the NTVS findings:

- Television programs that contain violence: 60 percent

- Violent interactions that did *not* include any expression of pain: 55 percent

- Violent programs that did *not* show any long-term negative consequences of the violence: 80 percent

- Violent scenes in which aggression is *not* punished: 58 percent

- Violent scenes in which humor was used to downplay the violence: 40 percent

- Violent scenes perpetrated by the "good guys" in their roles as heroes: 40 percent

- Number of violent incidents a pre-schooler would observe if he watched two hours of cartoons a day for a year: 10,000

Do These Violent Scenes Fulfill the Criteria for Actions That Are Likely to Be Imitated?

The observational learning research has shown that the following qualities make observed actions more likely to be imitated:

- The model is attractive, of high status, and/or a dominant member of the viewer's social group.

- The model is rewarded for his or her behavior.

- The model is not punished for his or her actions.

Clearly, depictions of violence on television fulfill the criteria that are most likely to lead to imitation, especially by children. As psychologist Joanne Cantor (1999) observes, "The context in which television violence is typically presented—attractive characters performing unpunished violence that produces no pain—is destined to promote children's imitation of aggression and the acquisition of violent attitudes and behaviors."

Can Media Portrayals *Cause* Behavior Changes?

Absolutely. When you combine the power of observational learning with the ability of the television to capture attention, both positive and negative behavior changes can be produced in whole societies. Consider this positive example: In Mexico, a soap opera was developed using observational learning principles to improve literacy. The main storyline centered on the experiences of a group of people in a liter-acy self-instruction group. Millions of viewers faithfully watched the series. In the year before the televised series, about 90,000 people were enrolled in such literacy groups. In the year *during* the series, enrollment jumped to 840,000 people (see Bandura, 1997).

Now consider this negative example: When regular televised showings of the wrestling mayhem of the World Wrestling Federation were introduced on Israeli television, the "fantasy" violence quickly became real violence on middle school playgrounds. The widespread imitation of the wrestlers' behavior produced an epidemic of serious playground injuries, including concussions and broken bones (Lemish, 1998). Although all the children were old enough to recognize that the televised violence was fake, that didn't stop them from imitating it.

Isn't There Only a "Modest" Correlation Between Media Violence and Aggressive Behavior?

A large-scale meta-analysis pooled the results of more than 200 studies on the effects of violent media (Paik & Comstock, 1994). The meta-analysis found a positive and statistically significant overall correlation of +.31 between media violence and aggressive behavior. In other words, the greater the exposure to media violence, the greater the likelihood that someone will behave aggressively. This finding held true regardless of the age of the participants—preschool, elementary school, high school, college, or adults.

Dissenters, many of whom are in the entertainment or media industry, argue that the +.31 correlation is only a "modest" correlation (e.g., Rhodes, 2000). But is it? Compare the magnitude of the relationship between media violence and aggressive behavior with other known correlations, shown in the accompanying table. For example, the +.09 correlation between asbestos and cancer is much lower than the +.31 correlation between media violence and aggressive behavior. Nevertheless, it led to a massive national effort to remove asbestos from schools and other buildings.

Psychologists Brad Bushman and Craig Anderson (2001) at Iowa State University note several parallels between the +.39 smoking–cancer correlation and the +.31 media violence–aggressive behavior corre-

CALVIN AND HOBBES   **BILL WATTERSON**

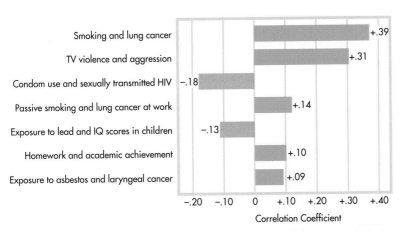

Comparing the Effect of Violent Media on Aggression with Other Known Effects

SOURCE: Adapted from data presented in Bushman & Anderson (2001)

lation. As they point out, not everyone who smokes gets lung cancer, and not everyone who gets lung cancer is a smoker. Similarly, not everyone who watches violent television becomes aggressive, and not everyone who is aggressive watches violent media.

Second, smoking is not the only factor that contributes to lung cancer, but it is a very important factor. Similarly, watching violent media is not the *only* factor that causes aggressive behavior, but it is a very important factor.

Third, the effect of smoking one cigarette fades quickly and has little impact on developing lung cancer. However, smoking cigarettes every day over the course of years dramatically increases the likelihood of developing lung cancer. Similarly, watching one violent TV show produces a temporary increase—of about an hour or so—in aggressive thoughts, feelings, and behavior. But repeated daily exposure to violent media significantly increases the likelihood of a person becoming a habitually aggressive person (Bushman & Huesmann, 2001).

How Is Exposure to Media Violence Linked to Aggressive Behavior, Especially in Children?

The American Psychological Association, American Academy of Pediatrics, and four other public health organizations recently issued a joint statement on the impact of entertainment violence on children (*Congressional Public Health Summit,* 2000). The joint statement noted that well over 1,000 studies "point overwhelmingly to a causal connection between media violence

and aggressive behavior in some children." The essence of that causal connection includes the following:

■ Children who see a lot of violence are more likely to view violence as an effective way of settling conflicts and are more likely to assume that violence is acceptable behavior.

■ Viewing violence can lead to emotional desensitization in real life and can decrease the likelihood that people will help a victim of violence in real life.

■ Children who are exposed to violent programming at a young age have a greater tendency for violent and aggressive behavior later in life than children who are not exposed.

Can Reduced Television Exposure Reduce Aggressive Behavior in the Real World?

Yes. Consider what happened in two California schools when third- and fourth-graders were encouraged to turn off the TV, VCR, and video games completely for ten days and then follow a media diet of no more than seven hours per week for six months. The actual violent content of the abandoned television, video, or video games was not measured, although it's safe to assume that some were violent. At the end of the study, aggressive behavior in the children in the intervention school dropped by 25 percent as compared to aggressive behavior in the control group of students who did not reduce their video exposure (Robinson & others, 2001).

But What About the Fact That Most People Who Watch Violent Scenes on Television Don't Commit Crimes?

As Brad Bushman and Colleen Phillips (2001) point out, "The fact that TV violence does not noticeably increase violence in everybody does not mean that TV does not increase violence in anybody." Most people don't commit murders, rapes, or assaults, either, but that doesn't mean that we don't need crime-prevention programs and a police force. *Some* people *are* affected by media violence. Laboratory experiments have shown that viewing just 15 minutes of a program featuring relatively mild violence increases the aggressiveness of more than one-quarter of the viewers (Bushman, 1995). Further, highly aggressive people are more likely to be drawn to violent media. After watching a violent movie, their levels of aggression increased to even higher levels (Black & Bevan, 1992).

In other words, even if *you* are not likely to be affected by the violent images that permeate our media culture, there is a substantial minority of other people who probably *are* susceptible to such influences. Because so many people are exposed to violent media, the effect on society can be immense even if only a small percentage of people are affected by them (Bushman & Anderson, 2001). Remember, the average prime-time television show has millions of viewers. If just 5 percent of people become more aggressive after absorbing the show's violent message, we're talking about hundreds of thousands of individuals.

Critical Thinking Questions

■ Given the evidence summarized here, what conclusions can you draw about the effect of violent media images on aggressive behavior?

■ What, if anything, should be done to curb media depictions of violence? What about depictions of violence in cartoons?

■ How would you respond to the claim that "no direct, causal link between exposure to mock violence in the media and subsequent violent behavior has ever been demonstrated" (Rhodes, 2000)?

Table | **5.6**

Factors That Increase Imitation

You're more likely to imitate:

- People who are rewarded for their behavior
- Warm, nurturant people
- People who have control over you or have the power to influence your life
- People who are similar to you in terms of age, sex, and interests
- People you perceive as having higher social status
- When the task to be imitated is not extremely easy or difficult
- If you lack confidence in your own abilities in a particular situation
- If the situation is unfamiliar or ambiguous
- If you've been rewarded for imitating the same behavior in the past

SOURCE: Based on research summarized in Bandura (1977, 1986, 1997).

perform it at a later time. That is, you must form and store a mental representation of the behavior to be imitated. Third, you must be able to transform this mental representation into *actions that you are capable of reproducing*. These three factors—attention, memory, and motor skills—are necessary for learning to take place through observation.

Fourth, there must be some *motivation* for you to imitate the behavior. This factor is crucial to the actual performance of the learned behavior. You are more likely to imitate a behavior if there is some expectation that doing so will produce reinforcement or reward. Thus, all the children were capable of imitating the adult's aggressive behavior. But the children who saw the aggressive adult being rewarded were much more likely to imitate the aggressive behavior than were the children who saw the adult punished. Table 5.6 summarizes other factors that increase the likelihood of imitation.

Observational Learning in Animals

Like humans, nonhuman animals are also capable of learning new behaviors through observation and imitation. One study involved German shepherd puppies whose mothers were specially trained to locate and retrieve hidden drugs (Slabbert & Rasa, 1997). Puppies who had observed their mothers locate and retrieve the packets of narcotics were significantly better at performing the same task three months later than were puppies who had *not* seen adult dogs perform this behavior.

The ability to learn a novel behavior through observation of other animals has been demonstrated in animals as diverse as golden hamsters (Previde & Poli, 1996), pigeons (Kaiser & others, 1997), starlings (Templeton, 1998), grackles (Lefebvre & others, 1997), and Japanese quail (Akins & Zentall, 1996). Along with learning new behaviors, animals learn to modify existing behaviors by observing others of their species. For example, young rats that observed the eating preferences of older rats mimicked the food choices of the older rats (Galef & Whiskin, 1995).

Not surprisingly, chimpanzees, apes, and other primates are quite adept at learning through observation (e.g., Whiten & others, 1996). After observing another monkey's fearful reaction to snakes, captive monkeys with no prior exposure to snakes quickly developed an intense and persistent fear of snakes (Mineka & Cook, 1988, 1993).

Just as with humans, motivational factors seem to play a role in observational learning by primates. For example, researchers studied the imitative behavior of free-ranging orangutans in a preserve located in central Indonesia (Russon & Galdikas, 1995). The orangutans imitated the behavior of both humans and other orangutans, but they were more likely to imitate high-status or dominant models than low-status models. The orangutans were also more likely to imitate models with whom they had close relationships, such as biological parents, siblings, or their human caregivers. Human strangers were virtually never imitated.

Applications of Observational Learning

Like classical and operant conditioning, observational learning has been applied in a variety of settings, including in education, vocational and job training, psychotherapy, and counseling. For example, observational learning has been used to help people develop more effective interpersonal skills (see Gambrill, 1995b). Training for nurses, electricians, pilots, and police officers routinely involves watching an experienced professional correctly perform a particular task, then imitating it. Clearly, this is advantageous. After all, would you want to be operated on by a surgeon who was learning strictly by trial and error?

5.4 R·E·V·I·E·W

C·O·N·C·E·P·T

Learning Researchers and Processes

For each of the situations described, name the process involved (classical conditioning, operant conditioning, latent learning, instinctive drift, observational learning) and the psychologist(s) associated with it.

1. Lisa transfers to a new college and spends her first few days on campus getting oriented. A week later she decides to have lunch at the college cafeteria. Although she has never eaten there before, she has no problem finding it.

   Process _____ Psychologist(s) _____

2. Little Ben rarely brushed his teeth. Ben's parents began giving him a sticker every time he brushed his teeth. Now, Ben brushes his teeth frequently.

   Process _____ Psychologist(s) _____

3. When Brittany's grandmother gave her a toy broom, the two-year-old immediately tried to sweep the floor with it.

   Process _____ Psychologist(s) _____

4. One of Jordan's first jobs as an animal trainer was to train a pig to pick up a coin and deposit it into a piggy bank. Through shaping and reinforcement with food, Jordan had some initial success, but soon the pig was more interested in pushing the coin along the ground with its snout than in putting it in the bank.

   Process _____ Psychologist(s) _____

5. Jan's ex-husband always wore Old Spice aftershave. Five years after her divorce, Jan still cringes whenever she encounters someone who smells like Old Spice.

   Process _____ Psychologist(s) _____

Summing Up

Learning

One theme throughout this chapter has been the quest to discover general laws of learning that would apply across virtually all species and situations. Watson was convinced that these laws were contained in the principles of classical conditioning. Skinner contended that they were to be found in the principles of operant conditioning. In a sense, they were both right. Thousands of experiments have shown that behavior can be reliably and predictably influenced by classical and operant conditioning procedures. By and large, the general principles of classical and operant conditioning hold up quite well across a wide range of species and situations.

But you've also seen that the general principles of classical and operant conditioning are just that—general, not absolute. Such researchers as John Garcia and Marian and Keller Breland recognized the importance of a species' evolutionary and biological heritage in acquiring new behaviors. Other researchers, such as Edward Tolman and Robert Rescorla, drew attention to the important role played by cognitive processes in learning. And Albert Bandura's investigations of observational learning underscored that classical and operant conditioning principles could not account for all learning.

Another prominent theme has been the adaptive nature of learning. Faced with an ever-changing environment, an organism's capacity to learn is critical to adaptation and survival. Clearly, there are survival advantages in being able to learn that a neutral stimulus can signal an important upcoming event, as in classical conditioning. An organism also enhances its odds of survival by being responsive to the consequences of its actions, as in operant conditioning. And, by observing the actions and consequences experienced by others, behaviors can be acquired through imitation. Thus, it is probably because these abilities are so useful in so many environments that the basic principles of learning are demonstrated with such consistency across so many species (Beecher, 1988; Staddon, 1988).

In the final analysis, it's probably safe to say that the most important consequence of learning is that it promotes the adaptation of many species, including humans, to their unique environments. Were it not for the adaptive nature of learning, Erv would probably get trapped in the attic again!

Self-control often involves choosing between two reinforcers: (1) a *long-term reinforcer* that will provide a gratification at some point in the future or (2) a *short-term reinforcer* that provides immediate gratification but gets in the way of obtaining a long-term reinforcer. Objectively, the benefits of the long-term reinforcer far outweigh the benefits associated with the short-term, immediate reinforcer. Yet despite our commitment to the long-term goal, sometimes we choose a short-term reinforcer that conflicts with it. Why?

The Shifting Value of Reinforcers

The key is that *the relative value of reinforcers can shift over time* (Ainslie, 1975, 1992; Rachlin, 1974, 2000). Let's use an example to illustrate this principle. Suppose you sign up for an 8:00 A.M. class that meets every Tuesday morning. On Monday night, the short-term reinforcer (getting extra sleep on Tuesday morning) and the long-term reinforcer (getting a good course grade at the end of the semester) are both potential future reinforcers. Neither reinforcer is immediately available. So, when you compare these two future reinforcers, the value of making a good grade easily outweighs the value of getting extra sleep on Tuesday morning. That's why you duly set the alarm clock for 6:00 A.M. so you will get to class on time.

However, as the availability of a reinforcer gets closer, the subjective value of the reinforcer increases. Consequently, when your alarm goes off on Tuesday morning, the situation is fundamentally different. The short-term reinforcer is now immediately available: staying in that warm, comfy bed. Compared with Monday night when you set the alarm, the subjective value of extra sleep has increased significantly. Although making a good grade in the course is still important to you, its subjective value has not increased on Tuesday morning. After all, that long-term reinforcer is still in the distant future.

At the moment you make your decision, you choose whichever reinforcer has the greatest apparent value to you. At that moment, if the subjective value of the short-term reinforcer outweighs that of the long-term reinforcer, you're very likely to choose the short-term reinforcer (Rachlin, 1995, 2000). In other words, you'll probably stay in bed.

When you understand how the subjective values of reinforcers shift over time, the tendency to impulsively cave in to available short-term reinforcers starts to make more sense. The availability of an immediate, short-term reinforcer can temporarily outweigh the subjective value of a long-term reinforcer in the distant future. How can you counteract these momentary surges in the subjective value of short-term reinforcers? Fortunately, there are several strategies that can help you overcome the temptation of short-term reinforcers and improve self-control (Trope & Fishback, 2000).

Strategy 1: Precommitment

Precommitment involves making an advance commitment to your long-term goal, one that will be difficult to change when a conflicting reinforcer becomes available (Green & Rachlin, 1996). In the case of getting to class on time, a precommitment could involve setting multiple alarms and putting them far enough away that you will be forced to get out of bed to shut each of them off. Or you could ask an early-rising friend to call you on the phone and make sure you're awake.

Strategy 2: Self-Reinforcement

Sometimes long-term goals seem so far away that your sense of potential future reinforcement seems weak compared with immediate reinforcers. One strategy to increase the subjective value of the long-term reinforcer is to use self-reinforcement for current behaviors related to your long-term goal. For example, promise yourself that if you spend two hours studying in the library, you'll reward yourself by watching a favorite television show.

It's important, however, to reward yourself only *after* you perform the desired behavior. If you say to yourself, "Rather than study tonight, I'll go to this party and make up for it by studying tomorrow," you've blown it. You've just reinforced yourself for *not* studying! This would be akin to trying to increase bar-pressing behavior in a rat by giving the rat a pellet of food *before* it pressed the bar. Obviously, this contradicts the basic principle of positive reinforcement in which behavior is *followed* by the reinforcing stimulus.

Strategy 3: Stimulus Control

Remember, environmental stimuli can act as discriminative stimuli that "set the occasion" for a particular response. In effect, the environmental cues that precede a behavior can acquire some control over future occurrences of that behavior. So be aware of the environmental cues that are likely to trigger unwanted behaviors, such as studying in the kitchen (a cue for eating) or in an easy chair in the living room (a cue for watching television). Then replace those cues with others that will help you achieve your long-term goals.

For example, always study in a specific location, whether it's the library, an empty classroom, or at a table or desk in a certain corner of your apartment. Over time, these environmental cues will become associated with the behavior of studying.

Strategy 4: Focus on the Delayed Reinforcer

The cognitive aspects of learning also play a role in choosing behaviors associated with long-term reinforcers (Metcalfe & Mischel, 1999; Mischel, 1996). When faced with a choice between an immediate and a delayed reinforcer, focus your attention on the delayed reinforcer. You'll be less likely to impulsively choose the short-term reinforcer (Ainslie, 1975).

Practically speaking, this means that if your goal is to save money for school, don't fantasize about a new stereo system or expensive running shoes. Focus instead on the delayed reinforcement of achieving your long-term goal (see Mischel & others, 1989). Imagine yourself proudly walking across the stage and receiving your college degree. Visualize yourself fulfilling your long-term career goals. The idea in selectively focusing on the delayed reinforcer is to mentally bridge the gap between the present and the ultimate attainment of your future goal. One of our students, a biology major, put a picture of a famous woman biologist next to her desk to help inspire her to study.

Strategy 5: Observe Good Role Models

Observational learning is another strategy you can use to improve self-control. Psychologist Walter Mischel (1966) found that children who observed others choose a delayed reinforcer over an immediate reinforcer were more likely to choose the delayed reinforcer themselves. So look for good role models. Observing others who are currently behaving in ways that will ultimately help them realize their long-term goals can make it easier for you to do the same.

Chapter Review

Key Points

Introduction: What Is Learning?

■ **Learning** is defined as a relatively enduring change in behavior or knowledge that is due to past experience. Learning often reflects adaptation to the environment. **Conditioning** is the process of learning associations between environmental events and behavioral responses. Classical conditioning, operant conditioning, and observational learning are three types of learning.

Classical Conditioning: *Associating Stimuli*

■ Ivan Pavlov, a Russian physiologist, discovered the principles of classical conditioning while studying the digestive system of dogs.

■ **Classical conditioning** deals with reflexive behaviors that are elicited by a stimulus and results from learning an association between two stimuli. A neutral stimulus is repeatedly paired with an unlearned, natural stimulus (the **unconditioned stimulus, or UCS**), producing a reflexive response (the **unconditioned response, or UCR**). Eventually, the neutral stimulus (now called a **conditioned stimulus, or CS**) elicits the same reflexive response (the **conditioned response, or CR**) that was initially elicited by the natural stimulus.

■ Factors that affect the strength of the conditioned response include the frequency with which the conditioned and unconditioned stimuli are paired and the timing of the stimulus presentations.

■ In **stimulus generalization,** a new stimulus that is similar to the conditioned stimulus produces the conditioned response. In **stimulus discrimination,** one stimulus elicits the conditioned response but another, similar stimulus does not.

■ In classical conditioning, **extinction** occurs when the conditioned stimulus no longer elicits the conditioned response. However, extinction is not unlearning. **Spontaneous recovery** of the conditioned response may occur.

■ John B. Watson defined psychology as the scientific study of behavior and founded **behaviorism.** According to Watson, all human behavior is a result of conditioning and learning.

■ As Watson demonstrated in his famous Little Albert study, emotional responses can be classically conditioned.

■ Classical conditioning can also contribute to the **placebo response** and other drug effects. **Conditioned compensatory responses** are implicated in the development of drug tolerance, withdrawal symptoms, and accidental overdoses.

Contemporary Views of Classical Conditioning

■ Modern learning researchers acknowledge that mental processes and natural behavior patterns influence the learning process. Robert Rescorla demonstrated that classical conditioning involves learning the relations between events and assessing the reliability of signals.

■ John Garcia's research showed that **taste aversions** violate key principles of classical conditioning. Classical conditioning is affected by **biological preparedness.** For a given species, some stimuli are more readily associated than others.

Operant Conditioning: *Associating Behaviors and Consequences*

■ Edward Thorndike investigated the learning of active behaviors and formulated the **law of effect.** B. F. Skinner's operant conditioning principles explain how **operants,** or new, voluntary behaviors, are acquired.

■ **Operant conditioning** explains learning as a process in which behavior is shaped and modified by its consequences. **Reinforcement** increases the likelihood of an operant being repeated. In **positive reinforcement,** a response is strengthened because a reinforcing stimulus is added or presented. In **negative reinforcement,** a response is strengthened because an aversive stimulus is subtracted or removed. Reinforcers may be **primary reinforcers** or **conditioned reinforcers.**

■ **Punishment** decreases the likelihood of an operant being repeated. Two forms of punishment are **punishment by application** and **punishment by removal.** Aversive consequences do not always function as effective punishments. As a method of controlling behavior, punishment has many drawbacks.

■ The **discriminative stimulus** is the stimulus in the presence of which a particular operant is likely to be reinforced; it sets the occasion for a particular response.

■ New behaviors can be acquired through the process of **shaping.** An **operant chamber,** or **Skinner box,** is often used to study the acquisition of new behaviors by laboratory animals. Shaping is frequently used in everyday life to teach new behaviors.

■ Once acquired, behaviors are maintained through **continuous reinforcement** or **partial reinforcement.** Behaviors on a partial reinforcement schedule are more resistant to **extinction** than are behaviors on a continuous reinforcement schedule. This phenomenon is known as the **partial reinforcement effect. Schedules of reinforcement** include the **fixed-ratio (FR), variable-ratio (VR), fixed-interval (FI),** and **variable-interval (VI) schedules.**

■ In **behavior modification,** the principles of operant conditioning are applied to help people develop more adaptive behaviors.

Contemporary Views of Operant Conditioning

■ Modern learning researchers acknowledge that operant conditioning involves cognitive processes and is influenced by natural behavior patterns. Edward Tolman's research on **cognitive maps** and **latent learning** demonstrated the involvement of cognitive processes in learning active behaviors. **Learned helplessness** may result when a person or an animal develops the cognitive expectation that aversive stimuli are unavoidable or uncontrollable.

- The phenomenon of **instinctive drift** refers to the fact that an animal's natural behavior patterns can affect operant conditioning by influencing what it is capable of learning.

Observational Learning: *Imitating the Actions of Others*

- Albert Bandura systematically investigated how new behaviors could be acquired through **observational learning.** Observational learning involves the cognitive processes of attention, memory, motor skills, and motivation.

- Like humans, nonhuman animals learn new behaviors through observation and imitation. Observational learning has been applied in educational settings, job training, psychotherapy, and counseling.

Key Terms

learning, p. 186

conditioning, p. 187

classical conditioning, p. 188

unconditioned stimulus (UCS), p. 188

unconditioned response (UCR), p. 188

conditioned stimulus (CS), p. 189

conditioned response (CR), p. 189

stimulus generalization, p. 190

stimulus discrimination, p. 190

extinction (in classical conditioning), p. 191

spontaneous recovery, p. 191

behaviorism, p. 192

placebo response, p. 197

conditioned compensatory response (CCR), p. 198

taste aversion, p. 202

biological preparedness, p. 204

law of effect, p. 206

operant, p. 207

operant conditioning, p. 207

reinforcement, p. 207

positive reinforcement, p. 208

negative reinforcement, p. 209

primary reinforcer, p. 209

conditioned reinforcer, p. 210

punishment, p. 210

punishment by application, p. 210

punishment by removal, p. 212

discriminative stimulus, p. 213

operant chamber (Skinner box), p. 216

shaping, p. 216

continuous reinforcement, p. 218

partial reinforcement, p. 218

extinction (in operant conditioning), p. 218

partial reinforcement effect, p. 218

schedule of reinforcement, p. 218

fixed-ratio (FR) schedule, p. 218

variable-ratio (VR) schedule, p. 219

fixed-interval (FI) schedule, p. 219

variable-interval (VI) schedule, p. 220

behavior modification, p. 220

cognitive map, p. 222

latent learning, p. 223

learned helplessness, p. 224

instinctive drift, p. 226

observational learning, p. 226

Key People

Albert Bandura (b. 1925) American psychologist who experimentally investigated observational learning, emphasizing the role of cognitive factors. (p. 227)

John Garcia (b. 1917) American psychologist who experimentally demonstrated the learning of taste aversions in animals, a finding that challenged several basic assumptions of classical conditioning. (p. 202)

Ivan Pavlov (1849–1936) Russian physiologist who first described the basic learning process of associating stimuli that is now called classical conditioning. (p. 187)

Robert A. Rescorla (b. 1940) American psychologist who experimentally demonstrated the involvement of cognitive processes in classical conditioning. (p. 200)

Shepard Siegel (b. 1940) Canadian psychologist who has extensively studied the role of classical conditioning and conditioned compensatory responses in the development of drug tolerance, drug withdrawal symptoms, and drug relapse. (p. 198)

B. F. Skinner (1904–1990) American psychologist who developed the operant conditioning model of learning; emphasized studying the relationship between environmental factors and observable actions, not mental processes, in trying to achieve a scientific explanation of behavior. (p. 207)

Edward L. Thorndike (1874–1949) American psychologist who was the first to experimentally study animal behavior and document how active behaviors are influenced by their consequences; postulated the law of effect. (p. 205)

Edward C. Tolman (1898–1956) American psychologist who used the terms cognitive map and latent learning to describe experimental findings that strongly suggested that cognitive factors play a role in animal learning. (p. 222)

John B. Watson (1878–1958) American psychologist who, in the early 1900s, founded behaviorism, an approach that emphasized the scientific study of outwardly observable behavior rather than subjective mental states. (p. 192)

Concept Review Answers

5.1 page 191

1. (a) school gym; (b) painful injury; (c) faintness, chills; (d) school gym; (e) faintness, chills

2. (a) baby crying; (b) nursing baby; (c) let-down reflex, breast milk flows; (d) baby's cry; (e) let-down reflex, breast milk flows

3. (a) lake; (b) leeches; (c) disgust; (d) lake; (e) disgust

4. (a) doorbell; (b) scary monster; (c) fear; (d) doorbell; (e) fear

5. (a) sound of plane; (b) explosion; (c) flinching, fear; (d) sound of plane; (e) flinching, fear

5.2 page 216

1. positive reinforcement
2. negative reinforcement
3. punishment by removal
4. punishment by application
5. negative reinforcement

6. punishment by application
7. punishment by removal

5.3 page 221

1. fixed ratio
2. variable interval
3. fixed interval
4. variable interval
5. variable ratio
6. fixed interval

5.4 page 231

1. latent learning; Edward L. Tolman
2. operant conditioning; B. F. Skinner
3. observational learning; Albert Bandura
4. instinctive drift; Marian and Keller Breland
5. classical conditioning; John B. Watson

| Web Companion | Review Activities |

You can find additional review activities at **www.worthpublishers.com/hockenbury** The Psychology 3e Web Companion has a self-scoring practice quiz, flashcards, two interactive crossword puzzles, and other activities to help you master the material in this chapter.

Freeze Frame Memories

chapter 6

Memory

Prologue

The Drowning

Elizabeth was only 14 years old when her mother drowned. Although Elizabeth remembered many things about visiting her Uncle Joe's home in Pennsylvania that summer, her memory of the details surrounding her mother's death had always been hazy. As she explained:

> In my mind I've returned to that scene many times, and each time the memory gains weight and substance. I can see the cool pine trees, smell their fresh tarry breath, feel the lake's algae-green water on my skin, taste Uncle Joe's iced tea with fresh-squeezed lemon. But the death itself was always vague and unfocused. I never saw my mother's body, and I could not imagine her dead. The last memory I have of my mother was her tiptoed visit the evening before her death, the quick hug, the whispered, "I love you."

Some 30 years later, Elizabeth began to remember the details of her mother's death. While at her Uncle Joe's 90th birthday party, Elizabeth learned from a relative that she had been the one to discover her mother's body in Uncle Joe's swimming pool. With this realization, memories that had eluded Elizabeth for decades began to come back.

> The memories began to drift back, slow and unpredictable, like the crisp piney smoke from the evening campfires. I could see myself, a thin, dark-haired girl, looking into the flickering blue-and-white pool. My mother, dressed in her nightgown, is floating face down. "Mom? Mom?" I ask the question several times, my voice rising in terror. I start screaming. I remember the police cars, their lights flashing, and the stretcher with the clean, white blanket tucked in around the edges of the body. The memory had been there all along, but I just couldn't reach it.

As the memory crystallized, it suddenly made sense to Elizabeth why she had always felt haunted by her vague memories of the circumstances surrounding her mother's death. And it also seemed to explain, in part, why she had always been so fascinated by the topic of memory.

However, several days later, Elizabeth learned that the relative had been wrong—it was *not* Elizabeth who discovered her mother's body, but her Aunt Pearl. Other relatives confirmed that Aunt Pearl had been the one who found Elizabeth's mother in the swimming pool. Yet Elizabeth's memory had seemed so real.

The Elizabeth in this true story is Elizabeth Loftus, a psychologist who is nationally recognized as the leading expert on the distortions that can occur in the memories of eyewitnesses. Loftus shares this personal story in her book *The Myth of Repressed Memory: False Memories and Allegations of Sexual Abuse,* which she co-wrote with science writer Katherine Ketcham in 1994.

Even though she is an expert on memory distortions and false memories, Loftus herself wasn't immune to the phenomenon. She experienced firsthand just how convincing a false memory can be. In retrospect, Loftus could see how she actively created information in her own mind that corresponded to the inaccurate information that she had been the one to discover her mother's body. She wrote, "That elaborate but completely fabricated memory confronted me with its detail and precision, its utter lack of ambiguity" (Loftus & Ketcham, 1994).

In this chapter, we'll consider the psychological and biological processes that underlie how memories are formed and forgotten. As you'll see, memory distortions such as the one Elizabeth Loftus experienced are relatively common. By the end of this chapter, you'll have a much better understanding of the memory process, including the reason that Elizabeth's "memory" of finding her mother's body seemed so real.

Introduction

What Is Memory?

Key Theme

- Memory is not a single process, but rather a group of related mental processes that are involved in acquiring, storing, and retrieving information.

Key Question

- What are encoding, storage, and retrieval?

Like Elizabeth's memories of her uncle's home, memories can be vivid and evoke intense emotions. We can conjure up distinct memories that involve all our senses, including smells, sounds, and even tactile sensations. The feeling of rain-soaked clothes against your skin, the smell of popcorn, and how cold your feet felt after playing in the snow as a child are a few examples of such memories.

On the one hand, it's incredible how much information is stored in memory and how much we rely on those memories. With next to no conscious effort, you can remember what you did last Saturday, how to set your alarm clock, and the names of hundreds of relatives, friends, and acquaintances. Your very sense of identity relies on the memory of your personal history. Without memory, who would you be?

On the other hand, memories can be fleeting and frustratingly unreliable. Everyday life is filled with examples of embarrassing memory lapses. Have you ever put a soft-drink cup on top of a car, then watched it roll down your back windshield as you drove off? Or shown up on the wrong day for a test?

As we explore how human memory works, we encourage you to take a few minutes to try each of the memory demonstrations included in this chapter. These demonstrations will help you gain firsthand insights into fundamental memory processes as well as memory quirks, such as the familiar feeling of having a memory on the tip of your tongue. We'll also consider some unusual and controversial memory experiences, such as "memories" of previous lives. And in the chapter's Application, we'll tell you how to improve your ability to remember information.

Memories Can Involve All Your Senses Think back to a particularly memorable experience from your high school years. Can you conjure up vivid memories of smells, tastes, sounds, or emotions associated with that experience? In the years to come, these teenagers may remember many sensory details associated with this impromptu football game on a crisp autumn afternoon.

Memory Processes

An Overview

Let's begin with an overview of some of the basic concepts that we'll be discussing throughout this chapter. First, **memory** refers to the mental processes that enable us to acquire, retain, and retrieve information. Rather than being a single process, memory involves three fundamental processes: *encoding, storage,* and *retrieval.*

Encoding refers to the process of transforming information into a form that can be entered and retained by the memory system. For example, to memorize the definition of a key term that appears on a text page, you would visually *encode* the patterns of lines and dots on the page as meaningful words that could be retained by your memory. **Storage** is the process of retaining information in memory so that it can be used at a later time. **Retrieval** involves recovering the stored information so that we are consciously aware of it (Butters & Delis, 1995).

memory
The mental processes that enable us to retain and use information over time.

encoding
The process of transforming information into a form that can be entered into and retained by the memory system.

storage
The process of retaining information in memory so that it can be used at a later time.

retrieval
The process of recovering information stored in memory so that we are consciously aware of it.

stage model of memory
A model describing memory as consisting of three distinct stages: sensory memory, short-term memory, and long-term memory.

The Stage Model of Memory

Key Theme

- The stage model of memory is based on the idea that memory is transferred from one memory stage to another.

Key Questions

- What are the three stages of memory, and how are their functions related?
- What are the nature and function of sensory memory?
- How did Sperling's research establish the duration of visual memory?

No single model has been shown to capture all aspects of human memory (Tulving, 1997). However, one very influential model, the **stage model of memory,** is useful in explaining the basic workings of memory. In this model, shown in Figure 6.1, memory involves three distinct stages: *sensory memory, short-term memory,* and *long-term memory* (Atkinson & Shiffrin, 1968). The stage model is based on the idea that information is *transferred* from one memory stage to another. Each memory stage is thought to differ in terms of the following:

- *Capacity*—how much information can be stored
- *Duration*—how long the information can be stored
- *Function*—what is done with the stored information

FIGURE 6.1 Overview of the Stage Model of Memory

Sensory Memory

- Environmental information is registered
- Large capacity for information
- Duration: 1/4 second to 3 seconds

Attention →

Short-Term (Working) Memory

- New information is transferred from sensory memory
- Old information is retrieved from long-term memory
- Limited capacity for information
- Duration: approx. 30 seconds

Encoding and Storage →

← Retrieval

Long-Term Memory

- Information that has been encoded in short-term memory is stored
- Unlimited capacity for information
- Duration: potentially permanent

sensory memory
The stage of memory that registers information from the environment and holds it for a very brief period of time.

short-term memory or **working memory**
The active stage of memory in which information is stored for about 30 seconds.

long-term memory
The stage of memory that represents the long-term storage of information.

The Interaction of Memory Stages in Everyday Life Imagine driving on a busy street in pouring rain. How might each of your memory stages be involved in successfully navigating the wet streets? What kinds of information would be transferred from sensory memory and retrieved from long-term memory?

The first stage of memory is called *sensory memory*. **Sensory memory** registers a great deal of information from the environment and holds it for a very brief period of time. After a few seconds or less, the information fades. Think of your sensory memory as an internal camera that continuously takes "snapshots" of your surroundings. With each snapshot, you momentarily focus your attention on specific details. Almost instantly, the snapshot fades, only to be replaced by another.

During the very brief time the information is held in sensory memory, you "select," or pay *attention* to, just a few aspects of all the environmental information that's being registered. While studying, for example, you focus your attention on one page of your textbook, ignoring other environmental stimuli. The information you select from sensory memory is important, because this information is transferred to the second stage of memory, *short-term memory*.

Short-term memory refers to the active, working memory system (Cowan & others, 1994). Your short-term memory temporarily holds all the information you are currently thinking about or consciously aware of. That information is stored briefly in short-term memory—for up to about 30 seconds (Cowan, 1994). Because you use your short-term memory to actively process conscious information in a variety of ways, short-term memory is often referred to as **working memory** (Baddeley, 1995, 1998). Imagining, remembering, and problem solving all take place in short-term memory.

Over the course of any given day, vast amounts of information flow through your short-term memory. Most of this information quickly fades and is forgotten in a matter of seconds. However, some of the information that is actively processed in short-term memory may be encoded for storage in long-term memory.

Long-term memory, the third memory stage, represents what most people typically think of as memory—the long-term storage of information, potentially for a lifetime. It's important to note that the transfer of information between short-term and long-term memory goes two ways. Not only does information flow from short-term memory to long-term memory, but much information also flows in the other direction, from long-term memory to short-term memory (Shiffrin & Nosofsky, 1994).

If you think about it, this makes a great deal of sense. Consider a routine cognitive task, such as carrying on a conversation. Such tasks involve processing current sensory data and retrieving relevant stored information, such as the meaning of individual words (Goldman-Rakic, 1992). In the next few sections, we'll describe each of the stages of memory in more detail.

Sensory Memory
Fleeting Impressions of the World

Has something like this ever happened to you? You're engrossed in a suspenseful movie video. From another room, a family member calls out, "Where'd you put the phone book?" You respond with, "What?" Then, a split second later, the question registers in your mind. Before the other person can repeat the question, you reply, "Oh. It's on the kitchen counter."

You were able to answer the question because your *sensory memory* registered and preserved the other person's words for a few fleeting seconds—just long enough for you to recall what had been said to you while your attention was focused on the movie. Sensory memory stores a detailed record of a sensory experience, but only for a few seconds at the most.

The Duration of Sensory Memory: It Was There Just a Split Second Ago!

The characteristics of visual sensory memory were first identified largely through the research of psychologist **George Sperling** in 1960. In his experiment, Sperling flashed the images of 12 letters on a screen for one-twentieth of a second. The letters were arranged in four rows of three letters each. Subjects focused their attention on the screen and, immediately after the screen went blank, reported as many letters as they could remember.

On average, subjects could report only 4 or 5 of the 12 letters. However, several subjects claimed that they had actually seen *all* the letters but that the complete image had faded from their memory as they spoke, disappearing before they could verbally report more than 4 or 5 letters.

Based on this information, Sperling tried a simple variation on the original experiment (see Figure 6.2). He arranged the 12 letters in three rows of 4 letters each. Then, immediately *after* the screen went blank, he sounded a high-pitched, medium-pitched, or low-pitched tone. If the subjects heard the high-pitched tone, they were to report the letters in the top row; the medium-pitched tone signaled the middle row; and the low-pitched tone signaled the bottom row. If the subjects actually did see all the letters, Sperling reasoned, then they should be able to report the letters in a given row by focusing their attention on the indicated row *before* their visual sensory memory faded.

This is exactly what happened. If the tone followed the letter display in under one-third of a second, subjects could accurately report about three of the four letters in whichever row was indicated by the tone. However, if the interval between the screen going blank and the sound of the tone was more than one-third of a second, the accuracy of the reports decreased dramatically. By the time one second had elapsed, the image in the subject's visual sensory memory had already faded beyond recall.

FIGURE 6.2 Sperling's Experiment Demonstrating the Duration of Sensory Memory In George Sperling's (1960) classic experiment, subjects stared at a screen on which rows of letters were projected for just one-twentieth of a second (1). The screen then went blank (2). After intervals varying up to one second, a tone was sounded that indicated the row of letters the subject should report (3). If the tone was sounded within about one-third of a second, subjects were able to report the letters in the indicated row (4), because the image of *all* the letters was still in sensory memory.

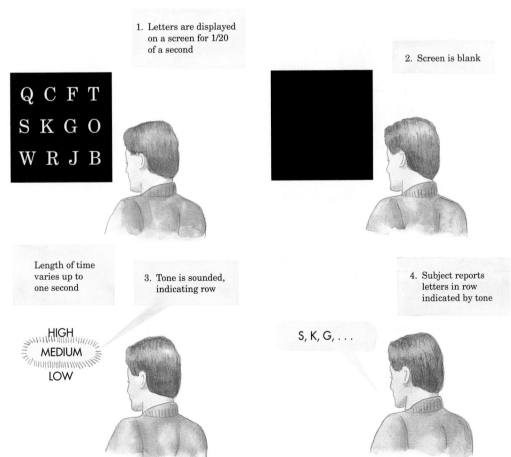

1. Letters are displayed on a screen for 1/20 of a second

2. Screen is blank

Length of time varies up to one second

3. Tone is sounded, indicating row

4. Subject reports letters in row indicated by tone

HIGH
MEDIUM
LOW

S, K, G, . . .

Sperling's classic experiment demonstrated that our visual sensory memory holds a great deal of information very briefly, for about half a second. This information is available just long enough for us to pay attention to specific elements that are significant to us at that moment. This meaningful information is then transferred from the very brief storage of sensory memory to the somewhat longer storage of short-term memory.

Types of Sensory Memory: Pick a Sense, Any Sense!

Memory researchers believe there is a separate sensory memory for each sense—vision, hearing, touch, smell, and so on. Of the different senses, however, visual and auditory sensory memories have been the most thoroughly studied. *Visual sensory memory* is sometimes referred to as *iconic memory*, because it is the brief memory of an image, or *icon*. *Auditory sensory memory* is sometimes referred to as *echoic memory*, meaning a brief memory that is like an *echo*.

Researchers have found slight differences in the duration of sensory memory for visual and auditory information. Your visual sensory memory typically holds an image of your environment for about one-quarter to one-half second before it is replaced by yet another overlapping "snapshot." This is easy to demonstrate. Quickly wave a pencil back and forth in front of your face. Do you see the fading image of the pencil trailing behind it? That's your visual sensory memory at work. It momentarily holds the snapshot of the environmental image you see before it is almost instantly replaced by another overlapping image.

Your auditory sensory memory holds sound information a little longer, up to a few seconds. This brief auditory sensory trace for sound allows you to hear speech as continuous words, or a series of musical notes as a melody, rather than as disjointed sounds. It also explains why you are able to "remember" something that you momentarily don't "hear," as in the example of the family member asking you where the phone book is.

An important function of sensory memory is to very briefly store sensory impressions so that they overlap slightly with one another. Thus, we perceive the world around us as continuous, rather than as a series of disconnected visual images or disjointed sounds.

Perception and Sensory Memory Traces
Because our visual sensory memory holds information for a fraction of a second before it fades, rapidly presented stimuli overlap and appear continuous. Thus, we perceive the separate blades of a rapidly spinning windmill as a smooth blur of motion. Similarly, we perceive a lightning bolt streaking across the sky as continuous even though it is actually three or more separate bolts of electricity.

Short-Term, Working Memory
The Workshop of Consciousness

Key Theme

- Short-term or working memory provides temporary storage for information transferred from sensory and long-term memory.

Key Questions

- What are the duration and capacity of short-term memory?
- How can you overcome the limitations of short-term memory?

You can think of *short-term memory,* or *working memory,* as the "workshop" of consciousness. It is the stage of memory in which information transferred from sensory memory *and* information retrieved from long-term memory become conscious (Ericsson & Kintsch, 1995). When you recall a past event or mentally add two numbers, the information is temporarily held and processed in your short-term memory. Your short-term memory also allows you to make sense out of this sentence by holding the beginning of the sentence in active memory while you read the rest of the sentence. Thus, working memory provides temporary storage for information that is currently being used in some conscious cognitive activity (Baddeley, 1995, 1998).

The Duration of Short-Term Memory: Going, Going, Gone!

Information in short-term memory lasts longer that information in sensory memory, but its duration is still very short. At best, you can hold most types of information in short-term memory up to about 30 seconds before it's forgotten (Cowan, 1994). However, information can be maintained in short-term memory longer than 30 seconds if it is *rehearsed,* or repeated, over and over. Because consciously rehearing information will maintain it in short-term memory, this process is called **maintenance rehearsal.** For example, when you look up an office number on a building directory, you use maintenance rehearsal to maintain it in short-term memory until you reach the office. Another example is repeating an unfamiliar phone number until you dial it.

Information that is not actively rehearsed quickly fades, or *decays,* from short-term memory. That's why you sometimes forget an important point that comes to mind while you wait for a talkative friend to pause. Your idea quickly faded from short-term memory because listening to your friend's comments prevented you from rehearsing—and remembering—the point you wanted to make.

The Capacity of Short-Term Memory: So That's Why There Were Seven Dwarfs!

Along with having a relatively short duration, short-term memory also has a relatively limited capacity. This is easy to demonstrate. Take a look at the numbers in Figure 6.3. If you've got a friend handy who's willing to serve as your research subject, simply read the numbers out loud, one row at a time, and ask your friend to repeat them back to you in the same order. Try to read the numbers at a steady rate, about one per second. Note each row that she correctly remembers.

How many numbers could your friend repeat accurately? Most likely, she could correctly repeat between five and nine numbers. That's what psychologist George Miller (1956) described as the limits of short-term memory in a classic paper entitled "The Magical Number Seven, Plus or Minus Two." Miller found that the capacity of short-term memory is limited to about seven items, or bits of information, at one time. So it's no accident that local telephone numbers are seven digits long. And had Snow White met more than seven dwarfs, it would be even more difficult to remember all their names.

This seven-item limit to short-term memory seems to be universal. For example, it's been demonstrated in non-Western cultures in studies using Chinese characters instead of English-language materials (Yu & others, 1985).

So what happens when your short-term memory store is filled to capacity? New information *displaces,* or bumps out, currently held information. Maintenance rehearsal is one way to avoid the loss of information from short-term memory. By consciously repeating the information you want to remember, you keep it active in short-term memory and prevent it from being displaced by new information (Cowan & others, 1994).

Although the capacity of your short-term memory is limited, there are ways to increase the amount of information you can hold in short-term memory at any given moment. To illustrate this point, let's try another short-term memory demonstration. Read the sequence of letters in the margin, then close your eyes and try to repeat the letters out loud in the same order.

How many letters were you able to remember? Unless you have an exceptional short-term memory, you probably could not repeat the whole sequence correctly. Now try this sequence of letters: V C R F B I U S A C I A.

maintenance rehearsal
The mental or verbal repetition of information in order to maintain it beyond the usual 30-second duration of short-term memory.

Row 1 — 8 7 4 6
Row 2 — 3 4 9 6 2
Row 3 — 4 2 7 7 1 6
Row 4 — 5 1 4 0 8 1 3
Row 5 — 1 8 3 9 5 5 2 1
Row 6 — 2 1 4 9 7 5 2 4 8
Row 7 — 9 3 7 1 0 4 2 8 9 7
Row 8 — 7 1 9 0 4 2 6 0 4 1 8

FIGURE 6.3 Demonstration of Short-Term Memory Capacity

U V A F C I C R B S A I

chunking
Increasing the amount of information that can be held in short-term memory by grouping related items together into a single unit, or *chunk*.

You probably managed the second sequence with no trouble at all, even though it is made up of exactly the same letters as the first sequence. The ease with which you handled the second sequence demonstrates **chunking**—the grouping of related items together into a single unit. The first letter sequence was perceived as 12 separate items and probably exceeded your short-term memory's capacity. But the second letter sequence was perceived as only four "chunks" of information, which you easily remembered: VCR, FBI, USA, and CIA. Thus, chunking can increase the amount of information held in short-term memory. But to do so, chunking also often involves the retrieval of meaningful information from *long-term memory,* such as the meaning of the initials FBI (Ericsson & Kintsch, 1995).

The basic principle of chunking is incorporated into many numbers that we need to remember. Long strings of identification numbers, such as Social Security numbers or bank account numbers, are usually broken up by hyphens so that you can chunk them easily. Notice, however, that short-term memory is still limited to seven chunks. It's as if short-term memory has about seven mental slots for information. Each slot can hold a simple message or a complex message, but only about seven slots are available.

Long-Term Memory

Key Theme

- Once encoded, an unlimited amount of information can be stored in long-term memory, which has different memory systems.

Key Questions

- What are two ways to improve the effectiveness of encoding?
- How do procedural, episodic, and semantic memories differ, and what are implicit and explicit memory?
- How does the semantic network model explain the organization of long-term memory?

Long-term memory refers to the storage of information over extended periods of time. Technically, any information stored longer than the roughly 30-second duration of short-term memory is considered to be stored in long-term memory. So, a long-term memory can be recalling what you were doing 5 minutes ago or 10 years ago. In terms of maximum duration, some long-term memories can last a lifetime.

Compared with the limited bits of information that can be stored in sensory memory and short-term memory, the amount of information that can be held in long-term memory is limitless. Granted, it doesn't always feel limitless, but consider this: Every day, you remember the directions to your college, your home phone number, and how to start your car. And, simply to read this chapter, you will have retrieved the meaning of thousands of words from your long-term memory. These examples illustrate not only the range and quantity of information stored in long-term memory, but also the fact that retrieving information from long-term memory happens quickly and with little effort—most of the time.

Encoding Long-Term Memories

How does information get "into" long-term memory? One very important function that takes place in short-term memory is *encoding,* or transforming the new information into a

"The matters about which I'm being questioned, Your Honor, are all things I should have included in my long-term memory but which I mistakenly inserted in my short-term memory."

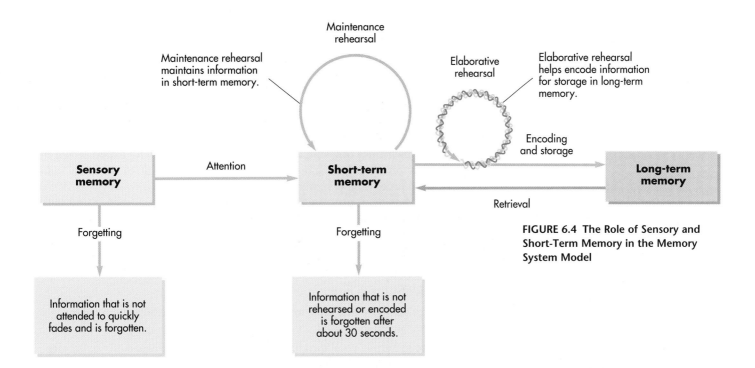

FIGURE 6.4 The Role of Sensory and Short-Term Memory in the Memory System Model

form that can be retrieved later (see Figure 6.4). As a student, you may have tried to memorize dates, facts, or definitions by simply repeating them to yourself over and over. This strategy reflects an attempt to use maintenance rehearsal to encode material into long-term memory. However, maintenance rehearsal is *not* a very effective strategy for encoding information into long-term memory.

A much more effective encoding strategy is **elaborative rehearsal,** which involves focusing on the *meaning* of information to help encode and transfer it to long-term memory. With elaborative rehearsal, you relate the information to other information you already know. That is, rather than simply repeating the information over and over to yourself, you *elaborate* on the new information in some meaningful way.

Elaborative rehearsal significantly improves memory for new material. This point is especially important for students, because elaborative rehearsal is a helpful study strategy. Here's an example of how you might use elaborative rehearsal to improve your memory for new information. In Chapter 2 we discussed three brain structures that are part of the limbic system: the *hypothalamus,* the *hippocampus,* and the *amygdala.* If you tried to memorize the definitions of these structures by reciting them over and over to yourself, you engaged in the not-so-effective memory strategy of maintenance rehearsal.

But if you elaborated on the information in some meaningful way, you would be more likely to recall it. For example, you could think about the limbic system's involvement in emotions, memory, and motivation by constructing a simple story. "I knew it was lunchtime because my hypothalamus told me I was *h*ungry, *th*irsty, and cold. My hippocampus helped me remember a new restaurant that opened on *campus,* but when I got there I had to wait in line and my amygdala reacted with *anger.*" The story may be a bit silly, but many studies have shown that elaborative rehearsal leads to better retention (Lockhart & Craik, 1990).

Creating this simple story to help you remember the limbic system illustrates two additional factors that enhance encoding. First, applying information to yourself, called the *self-reference effect,* improves your memory for information (Rogers & others, 1977). Second, the use of *visual imagery,* especially vivid images, also enhances encoding (Paivio, 1986; Tindall-Ford & others, 1997).

Why should elaborative rehearsal be a more effective way of encoding new information than maintenance rehearsal? Psychologists Fergus Craik and Robert

elaborative rehearsal
Rehearsal that involves focusing on the meaning of information to help encode and transfer it to long-term memory.

levels-of-processing framework
The view that information that is processed at a deeper (more meaningful) level is more likely to be remembered than information that is processed at a shallow (less meaningful) level.

procedural memory
Category of long-term memory that includes memories of different skills, operations, and actions.

episodic memory
Category of long-term memory that includes memories of particular events.

semantic memory
Category of long-term memory that includes memories of general knowledge of facts, names, and concepts.

Types of Information Stored in Long-Term Memory Playing Ping-Pong can involve all three types of information stored in long-term memory. Examples of *procedural memory* might be how to hold the paddle and how to hit the ball. Remembering the rules of the game would be an example of *semantic memory*. Your vivid recollection of the time you beat your brother-in-law in a close game right before Thanksgiving dinner would be an example of an *episodic memory*.

Lockhart (1972) proposed that the *level* at which new information is processed determines how well the new information will be encoded and remembered. Craik and Lockhart's approach to understanding the relationship between coding processes and memory is called the **levels-of-processing framework** (Lockhart & Craik, 1990).

According to the levels-of-processing framework, information processed at a "deeper" level is more likely to be remembered than information processed at a "shallow" level (Craik & Tulving, 1975). Deep processing involves processing the *meaning* of the new information, rather than its more superficial characteristics. According to this framework, simple repetition, or maintenance rehearsal, would represent shallow processing of information. In contrast, elaborative rehearsal would represent deep processing of material.

The fact that deep processing results in more effective encoding and better memory of new information has many practical applications for students. How can you process new information at a deep, rather than a shallow, level? You can do the following:

- Actively question new information.
- Think about the implications of information.
- Figure out how new information relates to information you already know.
- Try to generate your own examples of the concept, especially examples from your own experiences.
- Make sure you understand and question the evidence.

Such mental activities promote "deeper" processing and enhance your memory for new information. In the Application, we'll give you more suggestions for strategies you can use to improve your memory.

Types of Information in Long-Term Memory

There are three major categories of information stored in long-term memory (Tulving, 1985, 1995). **Procedural memory** refers to the long-term memory of how to perform different skills, operations, and actions. Typing, riding a bike, running, and making scrambled eggs are all examples of procedural information stored in long-term memory. We begin forming procedural memories early in life when we learn to walk, talk, feed ourselves, and so on.

Often, we can't recall exactly when or how we learned procedural information. And usually it's difficult to describe procedural memories in words. For example, try to describe *precisely* and *exactly* what you do when you blow-dry your hair, play the guitar, or ride a bicycle. A particular skill may be easy to demonstrate but very difficult to describe.

In contrast to procedural memory, **episodic memory** refers to your long-term memory of specific events or episodes, including the time and place that they occurred (Squire & Kandel, 1999). Your memory of attending a friend's wedding or your first day at college would both be examples of episodic memories. Closely related to episodic memory is *autobiographical memory,* which refers to the events of your life—your personal life history (Nelson, 1993). Autobiographical memory plays a key role in your sense of self. Does culture affect autobiographical memory? In Culture and Human Behavior Box 6.1, we examine the impact of culture on earliest memories.

The third category of long-term memory is **semantic memory**—general knowledge that includes facts, names, definitions, concepts, and ideas. Semantic memory represents your personal encyclopedia of accumulated data and trivia stored in your long-term memory. Typically, you store semantic memories in long-term memory *without* remembering when or where you originally acquired the information. For example, can you remember when or where you learned that there are different time zones across the United States? Or when you learned that there are nine innings in a baseball game?

Cultural Differences in Earliest Memories

Here's the assignment: Rummage through your mental storage closet and retrieve your very earliest memory. How old are you? Where are you? Are you alone or with others? What are you doing? Feeling? Thinking about?

For most adults, earliest memories are for events that occurred between the ages of two and four. Such early memories form the beginnings of *autobiographical memory*— episodic memories for information related to the self. Autobiographical memory reflects your unique life experiences, providing a basis for your sense of self.

In various places in this text, we've talked about the ways that the sense of self varies among cultures. In individualistic cultures, such as the United States, Australia, and many Western European countries, the self is construed as *independent,* autonomous, and separate from other people or social contexts. In contrast, in collectivistic cultures, such as Japan, China, and other Asian countries, the self is construed as *interdependent* and defined in terms of social relationships, roles, and responsibilities. Can these cultural differences influence the content of our earliest memories?

Developmental psychologist Qi (pronounced "chee") Wang set out to determine whether—and how—cultural beliefs about the self might affect autobiographical memory. Wang (2001) asked American college students and Chinese college students in Beijing to report their earliest childhood recollections. All of the college students were young adults, ranging in age from the late teens to the late twenties. Analyzing the reports, Wang found a number of significant differences between the earliest memories of the Chinese and American students.

First, the average age for earliest memory was about three and a half for the U.S.-born students and four for the China-born students. This finding confirmed earlier research that the age of earliest memory for Asian adults tends

Culture and Earliest Memories The earliest memories of American adults tend to focus on a specific event and include many details about the person's feelings and thoughts at the time. In contrast, the earliest memories of Chinese adults tend to focus on routine activities that they shared with other members of their family or social group. Perhaps years from now, these children will remember eating meals or playing with their friends in this child care center in Beijing.

to be about six months later than for Americans (Mullen, 1994). Wang also found striking differences in the content of the students' early memories. The Americans' memories were more likely to be discrete, one-point-in-time events focused on individual experiences or feelings, such as "I remember getting stung by a bee when I was three years old." The Chinese students' memories were more likely to be of general, routine activities that were centered on group activities with family or community members, such as "I remember walking to school every day with my friends."

The memories as narrated by the American students were lengthier, more elaborate, and more self-focused than those of the Chinese students. Themes of self-awareness and individual autonomy were more common in the American students' memories, which tended to focus on

their own experiences, emotions, and thoughts. These qualities are evident in the earliest memory of one American female student, who was three and a half years old when this event occurred:

> I was at a party at my great-aunt's house. I was wearing my purple-flowered party dress. I crawled into a crib on the floor and lay on my back. My feet stuck out, but I fit pretty well. I remember I was trying to get the attention of people passing by. I was having fun and feeling slightly mischievous. When I picture the memory, I am lying down in the crib, looking at my party-shoed feet sticking out of the end of the crib.

In contrast, Chinese students were more likely to include other people in their memories. Rather than focusing exclusively on their own behavior and thoughts, their earliest memories were typically brief accounts that centered on collective activities. These characteristics are reflected in the early memory of a Chinese male student, who was four and a half years old at the time of this memory:

> I used to play with friends when I was little. We went to the bush to pick up wild fruits to eat. And I watched them catch birds.

For Americans, Wang notes, the past is like a drama—in which the self plays the lead role. But for the Chinese students, the self is not easily separated from its social context. As Wang (2001) summarizes, "The individual-focused, self-assured self-descriptions of Americans reflect a cultural emphasis on individuality and self-enhancement, whereas the group-oriented, modest self-descriptions of Chinese reflect a cultural emphasis on interconnectedness and personal humility." Wang's findings indicate that cultural differences in autobiographical memory may well be formed in very early childhood. Like your sense of self, your autobiographical memory is shaped by your cultural and social context.

Memory is composed of several different abilities that depend on different brain systems. A fundamental distinction is between the capacity for conscious recollection and facts (declarative or explicit memory) and various nondeclarative (implicit) forms of memory that are expressed in skills, habits, and simple forms of conditioning.

Robert E. Clark and Larry R. Squire (1998)

Implicit and Explicit Memory: Two Dimensions of Long-Term Memory

Studies with patients who have suffered different types of amnesia as a result of damage to particular brain areas have led memory researchers to recognize that long-term memory is *not* a simple, unitary system. Instead, long-term memory appears to be composed of separate but interacting subsystems and abilities (Clark & Squire, 1998; Schacter & others, 1993).

What are these subsystems? One basic distinction that has been made is between *explicit memory* and *implicit memory*. **Explicit memory** is *memory with awareness*—information or knowledge that can be consciously recollected, including episodic and semantic information. Thus, remembering what you did last New Year's Day or the topics discussed in your last psychology class are both examples of explicit memory. Explicit memories are also called *declarative memories,* because, if asked, you can "declare" the information.

In contrast, **implicit memory** is *memory without awareness*. Implicit memories cannot be consciously recollected, but they still affect your behavior, knowledge, or performance of some task. For example, let's assume that you are a pretty good typist. Imagine that we asked you to type the following phrase with your eyes closed: "most zebras cannot be extravagant." Easy, right? Now, without looking at a typewriter or computer keyboard, try reciting, from left to right, the seven letters of the alphabet that appear on the bottom row of a keyboard. Can you do it? Your authors are both expert typists, and neither one of us could do this. Chances are, you can't either. (In case you're wondering, the letters are *ZXCVBNM.*)

Here's the point of this simple demonstration. Your ability to type the phrase "most zebras cannot be extravagant" without looking demonstrates that you *do* know the location of the letters *Z, X, C, V, B, N,* and *M.* But your inability to recite that knowledge demonstrates that your memory of each key's location cannot be consciously recollected. Even though you're not consciously aware of the memory, it still affects your behavior. Implicit memories are also called *nondeclarative memories,* because you're unable to "declare" the information. Procedural memories, including skills and habits, typically reflect implicit memory processes. Figure 6.5 summarizes the different types of long-term memory.

Although much of the memory research covered in this chapter centers on explicit memory, psychologists and neuroscientists have become increasingly interested in implicit memory (Schacter, 1995c, 1998). As we'll see in a later section, there is growing evidence that implicit memory and explicit memory involve different brain regions. Some memory theorists believe that implicit memory and explicit memory are two distinct memory systems (Schacter & others, 1993; Squire & Kandel, 1999). Other researchers are more inclined to think that implicit and explicit memory simply involve the use of different types of encoding and retrieval processes (Roediger, 1990).

The Organization of Information in Long-Term Memory

You can probably recite the days of the week in about three or four seconds. Now try timing how long it takes you to recite the weekdays in alphabetical order. Probably a minute or more, right? This simple demonstration illustrates that information in long-term memory is organized in some way. Exactly *how* information is organized is not completely understood by memory researchers.

FIGURE 6.5 Types of Long-Term Memory

explicit memory
Information or knowledge that can be consciously recollected; also called *declarative memory.*

implicit memory
Information or knowledge that affects behavior or task performance but cannot be consciously recollected; also called *nondeclarative memory.*

clustering
Organizing items into related groups during recall from long-term memory.

semantic network model
A model that describes units of information in long-term memory as being organized in a complex network of associations.

Nonetheless, memory researchers know that information in long-term memory is *clustered* and *associated*.

Clustering means organizing items into related groups, or *clusters,* during recall. You can experience clustering firsthand by trying the demonstration in Figure 6.6. Even though the words are presented in random order, you probably recalled groups of vehicles, fruits, and furniture. In other words, you organized the bits of information by clustering them into related categories.

Different bits and pieces of information in long-term memory are also logically linked, or associated. For example, what's the first word that comes to your mind in response to the word *red?* When we asked our students that same question, their top five responses were "blue," "apple," "color," "green," and "rose." Even if you didn't answer with one of the same associations, your response was based on some kind of logical association that you could explain if asked. Some of the less common but still logical associations that our students made with the word *red* were "hair," "coat," "hot," "flag," "tag," "wine," "alert," "embarrassment," and "ink."

Based on the finding that items stored in long-term memory are both organized and associated, memory researchers have developed several models to show *how* information is organized in long-term memory (Ratcliff & McKoon, 1994). One of the best-known models is called the **semantic network model** (Collins & Loftus, 1975).

A semantic network works like this: You can make many kinds of associations between concepts. For example, you can associate an object with its characteristics (ball → round), a location with an activity (library → study), or an activity with an emotion (dancing → excitement). All these associations can in turn be linked with additional associations in a massive network in long-term memory. However, some concepts in the network are more strongly linked than others.

When one concept is activated in the semantic network, it can *spread* in any number of directions, *activating* other associations in the semantic network. For example, the word *red* might activate "blue" (another color), "apple" or "fire truck" (objects that are red), or "alert" (as in the phrase, "red alert").

Figure 6.7 illustrates the potential associations in a greatly simplified semantic network. Each oval represents a piece of information stored in long-term memory. The lines connecting the ovals represent a network of possible associations. The length of the lines between the ovals indicates the strength of the association between two concepts. The shorter the line, the stronger the association and the less time it takes to make that association. Thus, in the semantic network shown in Figure 6.7, if the concept "red" is activated in long-term memory, it's more likely to activate an association with the concepts "apple" or "blue" than with the concepts "fire truck" or "flag."

While the semantic network model is a useful way of conceptualizing how information is organized in long-term memory, keep in mind that it is just a metaphor, not a physical structure in the brain. However, information *is* organized in long-term memory. This fact has some very important implications for the retrieval process, as you'll see in the next section.

chair	apple
boat	car
footstool	airplane
orange	lamp
pear	banana
peach	dresser
bed	sofa
bus	bookcase
train	truck
plum	table
grapes	strawberry
motorcycle	bicycle

FIGURE 6.6 Clustering Demonstration
Study the words on this list for one minute. Then count backward by threes from 108 to 0. When you've completed that task, write down as many of the words from the list as you can remember.

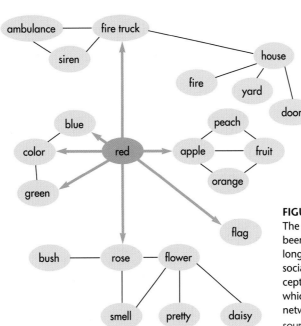

FIGURE 6.7 A Semantic Network Model
The semantic network is one model that has been proposed to show how information in long-term memory is organized through associations and clustering. Activating one concept can trigger a variety of other concepts, which, in turn, can spread throughout the network.

SOURCE: Based on Collins & Loftus (1975).

C·O·N·C·E·P·T

6.1 R·E·V·I·E·W

Comparing the Three Stages of Memory

Identify each of the following descriptions as characteristic of sensory memory (SM), short-term memory (STM), or long-term memory (LTM).

Function

1. Storage of information for later retrieval _____

2. Brief storage of sensory impressions _____

3. Temporary storage of new information; interaction with stored information _____

Duration

4. Potentially permanent _____

5. Approximately 20 to 30 seconds _____

6. Approximately ½ to 3 seconds _____

Capacity

7. Limited capacity of about seven items _____

8. Large but fleeting capacity _____

9. Unlimited capacity _____

Retrieval

Getting Information from Long-Term Memory

Key Theme

▨ Retrieval refers to the process of accessing and retrieving stored information in long-term memory.

Key Questions

▨ What are retrieval cues and how do they work?

▨ What do tip-of-the-tongue experiences tell us about the nature of memory?

▨ How is retrieval tested, and what is the serial position effect?

So far, we've discussed some of the important factors that affect encoding and storing information in memory. In this section, we will consider factors that influence the retrieval process. Before you read any further, try the demonstration in Figure 6.8. After completing part (a) on this page, go to page 254 and try part (b). We'll refer to this demonstration throughout this section, so please take a shot at it. After you've completed both parts of the demonstration, continue reading.

Instructions: Spend 3 to 5 seconds reading each of the following sentences, and read through the list only once. As soon as you are finished, cover the list and write down as many of the sentences as you can remember (you need not write "can be used" each time). Please begin now.

A brick can be used as a doorstop.
A ladder can be used as a bookshelf.
A wine bottle can be used as a candleholder.
A pan can be used as a drum.
A record can be used to serve potato chips.
A guitar can be used as a canoe paddle.
A leaf can be used as a bookmark.
An orange can be used to play catch.
A newspaper can be used to swat flies.
A TV antenna can be used as a clothes rack.
A sheet can be used as a sail.
A boat can be used as a shelter.
A bathtub can be used as a punch bowl.

A flashlight can be used to hold water.
A rock can be used as a paperweight.
A knife can be used to stir paint.
A pen can be used as an arrow.
A barrel can be used as a chair.
A rug can be used as a bedspread.
A telephone can be used as an alarm clock.
A scissors can be used to cut grass.
A board can be used as a ruler.
A balloon can be used as a pillow.
A shoe can be used to pound nails.
A dime can be used as a screwdriver.
A lampshade can be used as a hat.

FIGURE 6.8(a) Demonstration of Retrieval Cues

SOURCE: Bransford & Stein (1993).

Now that you've recalled as many sentences as you can, turn to Figure 6.8 (b) on page 254.

The Importance of Retrieval Cues

Retrieval refers to the process of accessing, or *retrieving,* stored information. There's a vast difference between what is stored in our long-term memory and what we can actually access. In many instances, our ability to retrieve stored memories hinges on having an appropriate retrieval cue. A **retrieval cue** is a clue, prompt, or hint that can help trigger recall of a stored memory. If your performance on the demonstration experiment in Figure 6.8 was like ours, the importance of retrieval cues should have been vividly illustrated.

Let's compare results. How did you do on the first part of the demonstration, in Figure 6.8a? Don remembered 12 pairs of items. Sandy blew Don out of the water on the first part—she remembered 19 pairs of items. Like us, you undoubtedly reached a point at which you were unable to remember any more pairs. At that point, you experienced **retrieval cue failure,** which refers to the inability to recall long-term memories because of inadequate or missing retrieval cues.

Your authors both did much better on the demonstration in Figure 6.8b, and you probably did, too. (Sandy got 24 of 26, and Don got 26 of 26 words, except that he remembered "clothes rack" as "clothesline.") Why the improvement? In part (b) you were presented with retrieval cues that helped you access your stored memories.

The point of this exercise is to demonstrate the difference between information that is *stored* in long-term memory and information that you can *access.* Many of the items on the list that you could not recall in part (a) were not forgotten. They were simply inaccessible—until you had a retrieval cue to work with. This exercise illustrates that many memories only *appear* to be forgotten. With the right retrieval cue, you can often access stored information that seemed to be completely unavailable.

Retrieval Glitches in Daily Life: The Tip-of-the-Tongue Experience

One of the most common, and most frustrating, experiences of retrieval failure is called the **tip-of-the-tongue (TOT) experience.** The TOT experience refers to the inability to get at a bit of information that you're absolutely certain is stored in your memory. Subjectively, it feels as though the information is very close, but just out of reach—or on the tip of your tongue (Koriat, 1993).

When experiencing this sort of retrieval failure, people can almost always dredge up partial responses or related bits of information from their memory. About half the time, people can accurately identify the first letter of the target word and the number of syllables in it. They can also often produce words with similar meanings or sounds (A. S. Brown, 1991). While momentarily frustrating, most TOT experiences are quickly resolved, sometimes within a few minutes. In one study, more than half the blocked words spontaneously came to the participants' minds within two days (D. M. Burke & others, 1991).

Tip-of-the-tongue experiences illustrate that retrieving information is not an all-or-nothing process. Often, we remember bits and pieces of what we want to remember. In many instances, information is stored in memory, but not accessible without the right retrieval cues. TOT experiences also emphasize a point that we made earlier. Information stored in memory is *organized* and connected in relatively logical ways. As you mentally struggle to retrieve the blocked information, logically connected bits of information are frequently triggered (Riefer & others, 1995). In many instances, these related tidbits of information act as additional retrieval cues, helping you access the desired memory.

retrieval
The process of accessing stored information.

retrieval cue
A clue, prompt, or hint that helps trigger recall of a given piece of information stored in long-term memory.

retrieval cue failure
The inability to recall long-term memories because of inadequate or missing retrieval cues.

tip-of-the-tongue (TOT) experience
A memory phenomenon that involves the sensation of knowing that specific information is stored in long-term memory, but being temporarily unable to retrieve it.

"And here I am at two years of age. Remember? Mom? Pop? No? Or how about this one. My first day of school. Anyone?"

recall
A test of long-term memory that involves retrieving information without the aid of retrieval cues; also called *free recall*.

cued recall
A test of long-term memory that involves remembering an item of information in response to a retrieval cue.

recognition
A test of long-term memory that involves identifying correct information out of several possible choices.

serial position effect
The tendency to remember items at the beginning and end of a list better than items in the middle.

encoding specificity principle
The principle that when the conditions of information retrieval are similar to the conditions of information encoding, retrieval is more likely to be successful.

Testing Retrieval: Recall, Cued Recall, and Recognition

The first part of the demonstration in Figure 6.8 illustrated the use of recall as a strategy to measure memory. **Recall,** also called *free recall,* involves producing information using no retrieval cues. This is the memory measure that's used on essay tests. Other than the questions themselves, an essay test provides no retrieval cues to help jog your memory.

The second part of the demonstration used a different memory measurement, called **cued recall.** Cued recall involves remembering an item of information in response to a retrieval cue. Fill-in-the-blank and matching questions are examples of cued-recall tests.

A third memory measurement is **recognition,** which involves identifying the correct information from several possible choices. Multiple-choice tests involve recognition as a measure of long-term memory. The multiple-choice question provides you with one correct answer and several wrong answers. If you have stored the information in your long-term memory, you should be able to recognize the correct answer.

Cued-recall and recognition tests are clearly to the student's advantage. Because these kinds of tests provide retrieval cues, the likelihood that you will be able to access stored information is increased.

The Serial Position Effect

Notice that the first part of the demonstration in Figure 6.8 did not ask you to recall the sentences in any particular order. Instead, the demonstration tested *free recall*—you could recall the items in any order. Take another look at your answers to Figure 6.8a. Do you notice any sort of pattern to the items that you did recall?

Both your authors were least likely to recall items from the middle of the list. This pattern of responses is called the **serial position effect,** which refers to the tendency to retrieve information more easily from the beginning and the end of a list rather than from the middle. There are two parts to the serial position effect. The tendency to recall the first items in a list is called the *primacy effect,* and the tendency to recall the final items in a list is called the *recency effect.*

The primacy effect is especially prominent when you have to engage in *serial recall,* that is, when you need to remember a list of items in their original order. Remembering speeches, ordered lists, and directions are a few examples of serial recall.

A Demonstration of the Serial Position Effect Without singing them, try to recite the words of "The Star-Spangled Banner." If you're like most people, you'll correctly remember the words at the beginning and the end of "The Star-Spangled Banner" but have difficulty recalling the words and phrases in the middle—the essence of the serial position effect.

The Encoding Specificity Principle

Key Theme
■ According to the encoding specificity principle, re-creating the original learning conditions makes retrieval easier.

Key Questions
■ What are the context effect, state-dependent retrieval, and mood congruence?
■ What role does distinctiveness play in retrieval, and how accurate are flashbulb memories?

One of the best ways to increase access to information in memory is to re-create the original learning conditions. This simple idea is formally called the **encoding specificity principle** (Tulving, 1983). As a general rule, the more closely retrieval cues match the original learning conditions, the more likely it is that retrieval will occur. The encoding specificity principle can take several forms. Examples include the context effect, state-dependent retrieval, and mood congruence.

The Context Effect

The encoding specificity principle can explain some common experiences. Have you ever had trouble remembering some bit of information during a test but immediately recalled it as you entered the library where you normally study?

When you intentionally try to remember some bit of information, such as the definition of a term, you often encode into memory much more than just that isolated bit of information. As you study in the library, for example, at some level you're aware of all kinds of environmental cues. These cues might include the sights, sounds, and aromas within that particular situation. *The environmental cues in a particular context can become encoded as part of the unique memories you form while in that context.* These same environmental cues can act as retrieval cues to help you access the memories formed in that context. This particular form of encoding specificity is called the context effect. The **context effect** is the tendency to remember information more easily when the retrieval occurs in the same setting in which you originally learned the information (see Figure 6.9).

Thus, the environmental cues in the library where you normally study act as additional retrieval cues that help jog your memory. Of course, it's too late to help your test score, but the memory *was* there. Just for the record, studies have confirmed that when students are tested in the same room in which they learned the material, they perform better (e.g., Saufley & others, 1985).

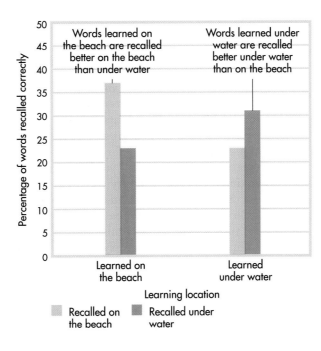

FIGURE 6.9 The Context Effect The influence of the context effect was seen in a clever study in which subjects learned lists of words either while on the beach or while submerged under 15 feet of water. In this graph, you see that when the conditions of learning and retrieval matched, subjects were able to remember more words.

SOURCE: From Godden & Baddeley (1975).

State-Dependent Retrieval

Whereas context effects are due to *external* environmental cues, state-dependent retrieval is a form of encoding specificity in which the critical factor is the influence of drugs on a person's *internal* state. Taking a drug can produce an internal state with unique psychological and physiological characteristics, aspects of which can become encoded with new memories. At a later point, the same intoxicated state can provide additional retrieval cues. Thus, **state-dependent retrieval** involves better recall of information when the pharmacological states of learning and retrieval match.

Studies have shown that when subjects learn information while under the influence of alcohol or marijuana, they recall the information better when they are under the influence of the drugs than when they are not. Similar effects have been shown with caffeine, nicotine, and other drugs (Eich, 1980; Horton & Mills, 1984; Peters & McGee, 1982).

Does this mean that drugs such as alcohol or marijuana improve memory? Absolutely not. As we noted in Chapter 4 on consciousness, these drugs tend to *impair* memory. It's also important to note that state-dependent effects are very weak and limited to free-recall tasks. On cued-recall or recognition memory

context effect
The tendency to recover information more easily when the retrieval occurs in the same setting as the original learning of the information.

state-dependent retrieval
An encoding specificity phenomenon in which information that is learned in a particular drug state is more likely to be recalled while the person is in the same drug state.

Mood and Memory Your emotional state tends to evoke memories that are consistent with the mood you are experiencing. When you're in a good mood, happy memories more easily come to mind. When you're feeling despondent, you're more likely to recall sad memories.

FIGURE 6.8(b) Demonstration of Retrieval Cues

SOURCE: Bransford & Stein (1993).

Instructions: *Do not* look back at the list of sentences in Figure 6.8(a). Use the following list as retrieval cues, and now write as many sentences as you can. Be sure to keep track of how many you can write down.

flashlight	lampshade
sheet	shoe
rock	guitar
telephone	scissors
boat	leaf
dime	brick
wine bottle	knife
board	newspaper
pen	pan
balloon	barrel
ladder	rug
record	orange
TV antenna	bathtub

mood congruence
An encoding specificity phenomenon in which a given mood tends to evoke memories that are consistent with that mood.

flashbulb memory
The recall of very specific images or details surrounding a vivid, rare, or significant personal event.

schema
(SKEE-muh) An organized cluster of information about a particular topic.

tasks, performance is superior when a person is in a *sober* state, even if the information was encoded in an *intoxicated* state. The strong retrieval cues of recognition or cued-recall tasks easily outweigh the very weak state-dependent retrieval effect (Eich, 1989).

Mood Congruence

Mood congruence refers to the idea that a given mood tends to evoke memories that are consistent with that mood. Research has consistently shown that your current mood influences the kinds of memories you recall (Eich, 1995; Eich & Macaulay, 2000). A specific emotional state can act as a retrieval cue that evokes memories of events involving the same emotion. So, when you're in a positive mood, you're more likely to recall positive memories. When you're feeling blue, you're more likely to recall negative or unpleasant memories.

In seriously depressed individuals, the mood-congruence effect can actually prolong depression (Eich & others, 1997; Mineka & Nugent, 1995). The depressed mood enhances memory retrieval of sad experiences, such as personal failures or losses. In turn, dwelling on negative memories can intensify or prolong the depression.

Flashbulb Memories
Vivid Events, Accurate Memories?

If you rummage around your own memories, you'll quickly discover that highly unusual, surprising, or even bizarre experiences are easier to retrieve from memory than are routine events (Pillemer, 1998). Such memories are said to be characterized by a high degree of *distinctiveness*. That is, the encoded information represents a unique, different, or unusual memory. In the retrieval cue demonstration in Figure 6.8, if you were more likely to remember the unusual combinations than the ordinary combinations, distinctiveness probably played a role.

Significant events can create vivid, distinctive memories that are sometimes referred to as *flashbulb memories* (Brown & Kulik, 1982). Just as a camera flash captures the specific details of a scene on film, a **flashbulb memory** is thought to involve the recall of very specific images or details surrounding a significant, rare, or vivid event. Do flashbulb memories literally capture specific details, like the details of a photograph, that are unaffected by the passage of time? Clearly, confidence in a memory is no guarantee of accuracy.

A recent study helps shed some light—so to speak—on flashbulb memories and how they compare to more normal episodic memories (Schmolck & others, 2000). Three days after the verdict in the 1995 O. J. Simpson murder trial was announced, California college students completed a questionnaire describing their reaction to the verdict and how they had learned about it. Half of the students were contacted 15 months later and asked to recall the event, while the other half of the students were contacted 32 months later.

When the researchers compared the later recollections against the students' original reports, they found that there were far more inaccuracies and distortions in the memories recalled 32 months after the event than in the memories recalled only 15 months after the events. Almost 40 percent of the highly detailed, flashbulb memories of the O. J. Simpson verdict were completely *inaccurate* 32 months later. Nevertheless, these participants were very confident of the accuracy of their memories. It seems, then, that the accuracy of flashbulb memories—like that of normal memories—declines over time. Clearly, confidence in a memory is no guarantee of accuracy.

Although flashbulb memories can seem incredibly vivid, they appear to function just as normal, everyday memories do. We remember some details, forget some details, and *think* we remember some details. What does seem to distinguish flashbulb memories from ordinary memories is the high degree of confidence the person has in the accuracy of these memories (Weaver, 1993).

Reconstructing Memories
Sources of Potential Errors

Key Theme
- Because retrieval involves the active reconstruction of memories, details of memories can change.

Key Questions
- What are schemas, and how can they contribute to memory distortions?
- What is source confusion, and how can it produce false memories?
- What factors reduce the accuracy of eyewitness testimony?

Flashbulb Memories Can you remember where you were when you heard about the attacks on the World Trade Center and the Pentagon? The verdict in the O. J. Simpson trial? Significant events can trigger flashbulb memories. Along with public events and national tragedies, meaningful personal events, such as your wedding day, can also produce flashbulb memories. But are flashbulb memories more accurate than ordinary memories?

For the most part, you remember the general gist of what you see or hear. But the specific details that you remember can change over time. Unintentionally and without your awareness, details can be added, subtracted, exaggerated, or down-played in your memories (Koriat & others, 2000).

How do errors and distortions creep into your memories? First, you need to understand that every new memory you form is not simply recorded, but *actively constructed*. To form a new memory, you actively organize and encode information. When you later attempt to retrieve those details from memory, you actively *reconstruct*, or rebuild, the memory (Bartlett, 1932; Schacter & others, 1998). In the process of constructing and reconstructing a memory, two general factors can contribute to errors and distortions: (1) the information you stored *before* the memory occurred and (2) the information you acquired *after* the memory occurred. Let's look at how each of these factors can contribute to memory errors and distortions.

Schemas and Memory Distortions

Since very early in life, you have been actively forming **schemas**—organized clusters of knowledge and information about particular topics. The topic can be almost anything—an event, an object, a situation, or a concept. For example, consider the schema you have for a typical kitchen. It probably includes food, a refrigerator, a toaster, a sink, cabinets, silverware, and so forth. You started forming your kitchen schema early in life by gradually identifying the common elements first in your own kitchen, then in other people's kitchens. Over time, these common elements became associated and organized into a cluster of knowledge, producing the working schema you have for a kitchen.

On the one hand, schemas are useful in forming new memories. Using the schemas you already have stored in long-term memory allows you to quickly integrate new experiences into your knowledge base. For example, if you hear about some handy new cooking gadget like a pasta machine, you can easily incorporate that new information into your kitchen schema. On the other hand, schemas can also contribute to memory distortions.

To illustrate this point, let's try to re-create some of the conditions in an ingenious study by William Brewer and James Treyens (1981). Imagine that you've signed up to participate in a psychology experiment. When you show up at the psychology professor's office for the study, the professor asks you to wait briefly in his office. Take a few moments now to "glance around" the office, which is depicted in the accompanying photograph.

The Psychology Professor's Office in the Brewer and Treyens (1981) Study Take a few moments to "look around" the office, then continue reading.

The professor comes back and escorts you to a different room. After you sit down, you are told the real purpose of the study: to test your memory of the details of the professor's office. Without looking at the photograph again, take out a piece of paper and write down as many details as you can remember about the office, then continue reading.

Did you remember that the office contained books, a filing cabinet, a telephone, a lamp, pens, pencils, and a coffee cup? That's what many of the participants in this study remembered. But *none* of these items were in the professor's office. Compare what you remembered with what is actually shown in the photograph. How accurate was *your* memory?

Why did the participants in this study erroneously "remember" items that weren't there? When the participants reconstructed their memories of the office, they remembered objects that were not in the room but that *did* fit the schema of a professor's office. Thus, the incorrect details that they thought they remembered were all items that would be consistent with a typical professor's office.

Schemas can also contribute to memory distortions when we learn new information that is inconsistent with previously learned information. When we try to account for or incorporate the new information, memories can become distorted to resolve the inconsistencies.

In one clever study, subjects read a brief story about "Bob" and "Margie," a happy, compatible couple engaged to be married (Spiro, 1980). Just before the subjects left the experiment, the experimenter casually mentioned that Bob and Margie broke up and never did get married. When the subjects were later tested for their recall of the written story, they introduced new, inaccurate details to make the story more consistent with the experimenter's remark. For example, one subject recalled that there were problems with Bob's or Margie's parents and that these troubles led to the breakup. Unknowingly, the subjects had fabricated or distorted details of the story to make it consistent with the experimenter's remark and with their own schemas about relationships and marriage.

In combination, the office study and the Bob and Margie study underscore several important points. First, they show how the schemas we already hold can influence what we remember. Second, they demonstrate that once a memory is formed, it has the potential to be changed by new information. And third, they demonstrate how easily memories can become distorted. Notice that neither of these studies involved elaborate efforts to get subjects to distort the memories being formed or remembered.

Source Confusion and False Memories

Memory distortions can also occur because of **source confusion,** which arises when the true source of the memory is forgotten (Johnson & others, 1993; Leichtman & Ceci, 1995). One of the most easily forgotten parts of a memory is its source—how, when, or where it was acquired. Elizabeth's story in the Prologue demonstrated how confusion about the source of a memory can give rise to an extremely vivid, but inaccurate, recollection. Vivid and accurate memories of her uncle's home, such as the smell of the pine trees and the feel of the lake water, became blended with her fantasy of finding her mother's body. The result was a *false memory*, which is a distorted or inaccurate memory that feels completely real and is often accompanied by all the emotional impact of a real memory.

Confusion about the source of a memory is a common cause of false memories. Such false memories can arise when you confuse something that you've only imagined, heard about, read about, or seen in a film with something that really happened to you (Henkel & others, 2000; Johnson & others, 1993). In Science Versus Pseudoscience Box 6.2, we discuss some unusual examples of false memories that seem to involve source confusion.

source confusion
A memory distortion that occurs when the true source of the memory is forgotten.

cryptomnesia
A memory distortion in which a seemingly "new," or "original," memory is actually based on an unrecalled previous memory.

SCIENCE VERSUS PSEUDOSCIENCE 6.2

Remembering Past Lives

While under hypnosis, people sometimes recover memories of past lives (Baker, 1992; Spanos, 1987–1988). When such memories surface, individuals may report very specific details about the time period of their previously remembered life. Current events, buildings, local customs, people's names, and even previously spoken languages are sometimes recalled. Consider the following cases.

Case 1.

Under hypnosis, a Colorado woman named Virginia Tighe recalled her previous life in Ireland in the 1800s (Rogo, 1985). Speaking with an Irish accent, Tighe remembered many details of her past life as Bridey Murphy, including her marriage to a Brian Joseph McCarthy.

Case 2.

Jane Evans, a Welsh woman, recalled several previous lives (Hines, 1988). In one past life, in the fifteenth century, Evans was maid to the wealthy Frenchman Jacques Coeur. Evans recalled very specific details of Coeur's magnificent home, such as carvings over the fireplace. She also remembered that Coeur was unmarried and had no children.

Past-life memories such as these are frequently offered as evidence of reincarnation. Whether or not you believe in reincarnation, consider the most basic evidence that any reasonably objective person would need to regard such memories as credible.

First, the reincarnation memory must contain information that could not be obtained through relatively ordinary means, such as books, conversations, movies, and newspaper articles. Second, it should not be possible to attribute the demonstration of a complex skill, such as recalling a foreign language, to learning acquired in the person's current life.

Third, the individual reporting the reincarnation memory should be able to provide ordinary information that virtually anyone living at that time would know. So if a person reports that he was a Japanese fighter pilot during World War II, he could reasonably be expected to know who the emperor of Japan was at the time.

Fourth, most of the information in a previous-life memory should mesh with valid historical records. If an individual reports a previous life as the composer Wolfgang Amadeus Mozart living in England in the 1400s, there are some credibility problems, because Mozart was born in 1756 and lived most of his life in Vienna, Austria. Given these basic criteria, let's look at each reincarnation case again.

Case 1 Reconsidered.

In the Virginia Tighe case, historical searches failed to uncover evidence for many details of her past-life memories, including any records of either Bridey Murphy or her husband (Rogo, 1985). But investigators learned that while Virginia Tighe was growing up, she lived across the street from an Irish woman who told her stories about Ireland. The neighbor's name? Bridie Murphy Corkell. It also turns out that in high school, Virginia Tighe had been involved in theater and had performed several Irish monologues, complete with Irish accent (Alcock, 1978–1979; R. A. Baker, 1996).

Case 2 Reconsidered.

Jane Evans's reincarnation memories seem pretty convincing, especially to those of us who have never heard of the fifteenth-century Frenchman Jacques Coeur. But as it turns out, Coeur's home exists today and is one of France's most photographed homes. Further, Evans's recollections of her life as Coeur's maid contained incorrect details. For instance, Coeur was married and had five children. Jane Evans's memories do, however, mesh very nicely with a detailed novel about Coeur's life, entitled *The Moneyman,* by Thomas B. Costain—which makes no mention of Coeur's wife or five children (Hines, 1988).

So how are we to explain these memories of past lives? There is good reason to believe that many reincarnation memories are examples of cryptomnesia, which literally means "hidden memories" (R. A. Baker, 1992). **Cryptomnesia** is a memory distortion in which a seemingly "new," or "original," memory is actually based on an unrecalled previous memory. In the two cases we've described, existing information seems to form the basis for what the person believes is a genuine reincarnation memory.

Notice that this explanation doesn't necessarily rule out the possibility of reincarnation, which is a religious belief held by many people. It just means that pseudoscientific claims of proof for reincarnation are often made with little or no objective consideration of the evidence. In many cases, common psychological processes, such as cryptomnesia, seem to provide simpler and more likely explanations of the phenomenon. So beware. The past life that you remember just might be your own.

Doonesbury   BY GARRY TRUDEAU

© 1988 G. B. Trudeau. Reprinted with permission of Universal Press Syndicate. All Rights Reserved.

Do These Men Look Alike? Seven eyewitnesses identified Father Pagano (*top photo*) as the armed robber that the press dubbed the "Gentleman Bandit." But Ronald Clouser (*bottom photo*) confessed to the crimes during Pagano's trial. How could seven eyewitnesses confuse these two men?

Word Used in Question	Average Speed Estimate
smashed	41 m.p.h.
collided	39 m.p.h.
bumped	38 m.p.h.
hit	34 m.p.h.
contacted	32 m.p.h.

FIGURE 6.10 Estimated Speeds

SOURCE: After Loftus & Palmer (1974).

misinformation effect

A memory-distortion phenomenon in which a person's existing memories can be altered if the person is exposed to misleading information.

Distortions in Eyewitness Testimony

Given the fallibility of human memory, it's understandable that precautions are often taken when specific details may be critically important. For example, if you dial 911, your emergency report and the dispatcher's response are recorded. In such situations, steps have been taken to guard against memory distortions *before* a crucial event or dialogue occurs.

One important area in which it's often impossible to take such precautions is eyewitness testimony. The guilt or innocence of people in criminal and civil cases often hinges on the accuracy of witnesses' memories (Wells & others, 2000). Psychologists are well aware of how easily memories can be distorted in the laboratory. If such distortions also occur in real life, they could have serious implications.

As a case in point, consider the differences in appearance between the two men in the accompanying photographs. The older, bald man in the top picture is Father Bernard Pagano, a Roman Catholic priest who was arrested and charged with six armed robberies (Beck & Borger, 1979). The trial was dubbed the trial of the "Gentleman Bandit" because the robber had been very polite and courteous to his victims. At Father Pagano's trial, *seven* eyewitnesses positively identified the priest as the robber.

Now look at the lower picture. That man is Ronald Clouser, who actually committed the robberies. Had Clouser not confessed to the robberies during Father Pagano's trial, Pagano would probably have been convicted of the crimes. But Clouser reported specific details of the robberies that were known only by the police, so there was no doubt that he was the real crook.

How could seven eyewitnesses positively identify Father Pagano as the robber? Before we answer that question, we need to consider some of the research into how the memory of eyewitnesses can become distorted. Psychologist **Elizabeth Loftus,** whose story we told in the Prologue, is one of the most widely recognized authorities on eyewitness testimony. Loftus has not only conducted extensive research in this area but has also testified as an expert witness in many high-profile cases (Loftus & Ketcham, 1991).

To illustrate how eyewitness testimony can become distorted, let's consider a study that has become a classic piece of research (Loftus & Palmer, 1974). Loftus had subjects watch a film of an automobile accident, write a description of what they saw, and then answer a series of questions. There was one critical question in the series: "About how fast were the cars going when they contacted each other?" Different subjects were given different versions of that question. For some subjects, the word *contacted* was replaced with *hit.* Other subjects were given *bumped, collided,* or *smashed.*

Depending on the specific word used in the question, subjects provided very different estimates of the speed at which the cars in the film were traveling. As shown in Figure 6.10, the subjects who gave the highest speed estimates got *smashed* (so to speak). Clearly, how a question is asked can influence what is remembered.

A week after seeing the film, the subjects were asked another series of questions. This time, the critical question was "Did you see any broken glass?" Although no broken glass was shown in the film, the majority of the subjects whose question had used the word *smashed* a week earlier said "yes." Once again, following the initial memory (the film of the automobile accident), new information (the word *smashed*) distorted the reconstruction of the memory (remembering broken glass that wasn't really there).

More recently, Loftus and her colleagues demonstrated that subjects can intentionally be led to make inaccurate reports after being exposed to misleading information (Loftus, 1992; Loftus & others, 1989). This **misinformation effect** is relatively easy to produce. In one study, subjects watched a series of slides about a burglary in which a screwdriver was a key element. The subjects then read a written account of the event. However, the written account contained misleading information: It referred to a hammer instead of a screwdriver. The subjects were then tested for their memory of the event.

The results? After exposure to the misleading information, about 60 percent of the subjects quickly and confidently said that a hammer, rather than a screwdriver, had been used in the burglary. Subjects were as confident about their fabricated memories as they were about their genuine memories of other details of the original event. Many other studies have confirmed that misleading questions, misinformation, and other factors can distort eyewitness memories (Loftus & others, 1998; Wells & others, 2000).

Now we can begin to make sense of Father Pagano's experience. Remember, seven eyewitnesses *confidently,* but *mistakenly,* identified him as the armed robber. As you consider the following additional bits of information that led to his arrest, notice the roles played by schemas and misinformation:

- After the victims experienced the robberies (the original memories), the local media showed a composite sketch of the robber (potentially inaccurate information) based on details remembered by the victims.
- A former member of Father Pagano's parish "recognized" the priest from the sketch and notified the police (Beck & Borger, 1979).
- The behavior of the "Gentleman Bandit" fit the schema of a priest: The robber was very courteous and even apologized when he robbed people, saying he needed the money (schema distortion).
- When police investigators interviewed the witnesses, the officers mentioned that the robber *might* be a priest (misleading information; source confusion).
- *After* witnesses saw news photos of the priest being arrested (more misleading information), they were shown photographs of possible suspects. Only *one* photograph showed a suspect wearing a clerical collar—the picture of Father Pagano.

In combination, these factors contributed to the memory distortions of the seven eyewitnesses. Is the case of Father Pagano an isolated example of eyewitnesses' mistaken identification of the wrong person? Not at all. As psychologists Gary Wells and Amy Bradfield (1999) note, "Analyses of cases in which people were mistakenly convicted by juries have shown eyewitness misidentification to account for more cases than all other causes of wrongful conviction combined." Because of the potential for errors in eyewitness identification in criminal cases, the United States Department of Justice (1999) has recently developed new guidelines to minimize such mistakes. These guidelines are based on years of psychological research into eyewitness testimony (Foxhall, 2000; Wells & others, 2000).

Finally, we don't want to leave you with the impression that it's astonishing that anybody remembers *anything* accurately. In reality, people's memories tend to be quite accurate for overall details. When memory distortions occur, they usually involve limited bits of information. In all the examples we've discussed in this section, the general memories were accurate, even though some specific details were wrong.

Still, the surprising ease with which bits of memory can become distorted is unnerving. The distorted memories can ring true in our minds and feel just as real as accurate memories (Loftus, 1997; Payne & others, 1997). In the chapter Prologue, you saw how easily Elizabeth Loftus created a false memory. You also saw how quickly she became convinced of the false memory's authenticity and the strong emotional impact it had on her. Rather than being set in stone, human memories are more like clay: They can change shape with just a little bit of pressure.

*M*isleading information can turn a lie into memory's truth. It can cause people to believe that they saw things that never really existed, or that they saw things differently from the way things actually were. It can make people confident about these false memories and also, apparently, impair earlier recollections. Once adopted, the newly created memories can be believed as strongly as genuine memories.

Elizabeth Loftus (1992)

The Accuracy of Memory Will these people accurately remember the details of this day? Despite the potential for errors in the recall of specific details, our memories are usually accurate for overall themes and general information.

forgetting
The inability to recall information that
was previously available.

Forgetting
You *Forgot* the Plane Tickets?!

Key Theme
- Since Ebbinghaus first studied memory over a century ago, researchers have identified several factors that contribute to forgetting stored information.

Key Questions
- What is the Ebbinghaus Forgetting Curve?
- What roles do encoding failure, interference, motivation, and decay play in forgetting?

Forgetting is the inability to recall information that was previously available. Forgetting is so common that our lives are filled with automatic reminders to safeguard against forgetting important information. Cars are equipped with buzzers so you don't forget to put on your seatbelt or turn off your lights. News announcements remind you to reset your clocks as daylight saving time begins or ends. Dentists thoughtfully send brightly colored postcards so that your appointment doesn't slip your mind.

Sometimes, of course, we *want* to forget. From the standpoint of a person's psychological well-being, it's probably just as well that we tend to forget the details of unpleasant memories, such as past failures, social embarrassments, and unhappy relationships. Even more generally, our minds would be cluttered with mountains of useless information if we remembered every television program, magazine article, billboard, or conversation we'd ever experienced. So forgetting *does* have some adaptive value (Squire & Kandel, 1999).

Hermann Ebbinghaus
The Forgetting Curve

German psychologist **Hermann Ebbinghaus** began the scientific study of forgetting over a century ago. Because there was a seven-year gap between his completion of college and his first university teaching position, Ebbinghaus couldn't use university students for experimental subjects (Fancher, 1996). So to study *forgetting*, Ebbinghaus had to rely on the only available research subject: himself.

Ebbinghaus's goal was to determine how much information was forgotten after different lengths of time. But he wanted to make sure that he was studying the memory and forgetting of completely new material, rather than information that had preexisting associations in his memory. To solve this problem, Ebbinghaus (1885) created new material to memorize: thousands of nonsense syllables. A *nonsense syllable* is a three-letter combination, made up of two consonants and a vowel, such as WIB or MEP. It almost sounds like a word, but it is meaningless.

Ebbinghaus carefully noted how many times he had to repeat a list of 13 nonsense syllables before he could recall the list perfectly. To give you a feeling for this task, here's a typical list:

ROH, LEZ, SUW, QOV, XAR, KUF, WEP, BIW, CUL, TIX, QAP, WEJ, ZOD

Once he had learned the nonsense syllables, Ebbinghaus tested his recall of them after varying amounts of time, ranging from 20 minutes to 31 days. He plotted his results in the now-famous Ebbinghaus *forgetting curve,* shown in Figure 6.11a.

Hermann Ebbinghaus (1850–1909) After earning his Ph.D. in philosophy in 1873, Ebbinghaus worked as a private tutor for several years. It was during this time that he conducted his famous research on the memory of nonsense syllables. In 1885, he published his results in *Memory: A Contribution to Experimental Psychology.* In that text, Ebbinghaus observed, "Left to itself, every mental content gradually loses its capacity for being revived. Facts crammed at examination time soon vanish, if they were not sufficiently grounded by other study and later subjected to a sufficient review." Among his other notable contributions, he developed an early intelligence test, called the *Ebbinghaus Completion Test* (Lander, 1997).

(a)

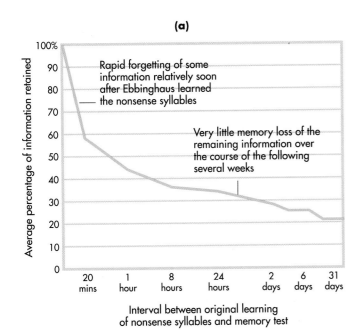

Rapid forgetting of some information relatively soon after Ebbinghaus learned the nonsense syllables

Very little memory loss of the remaining information over the course of the following several weeks

Average percentage of information retained

Interval between original learning of nonsense syllables and memory test

(b)

Rapid forgetting of some information during the first several months after the psychology class

Very little memory loss over a period of 10 years for the remaining concepts and names learned in the psychology class

Names

Concepts

Average percentage of information recalled

Interval in months between completion of psychology class and memory test for concepts and names

FIGURE 6.11 (a) The Ebbinghaus Forgetting Curve Ebbinghaus's research demonstrated the basic pattern of forgetting: relatively rapid loss of some information, followed by stable memories of the remaining information.
SOURCE: Adapted from Ebbinghaus (1885).

(b) Forgetting Information Learned in a Psychology Class Most of the information that the students forgot was lost during the first several months immediately following the class. During the following 10-year period, memory for the remaining information was relatively stable. Notice that the curve closely parallels the shape of the Ebbinghaus forgetting curve.
SOURCE: Adapted from Conway & others (1991).

The Ebbinghaus forgetting curve reveals two distinct patterns in the relationship between forgetting and the passage of time. First, much of what we forget is lost relatively soon after we originally learned it. How quickly we forget material depends on several factors, such as how well the material was encoded in the first place, how deeply it was processed, and how often it was rehearsed.

In general, if you learn something in a matter of minutes on just one occasion, most forgetting will occur very soon after the original learning—also in a matter of minutes. However, if you spend many sessions over weeks or months encoding new information into memory, the period of most rapid forgetting will be the first several months after such learning.

The basic pattern of Ebbinghaus's forgetting curve has been demonstrated using a wide variety of learning materials. For example, a similar pattern emerged when researchers measured the retention of psychology concepts from 3 months to over 10 years after students took a psychology course (Conway & others, 1991). Memory for names and concepts learned in the course declined very rapidly over the first several months, as shown in Figure 6.11b.

Second, the Ebbinghaus forgetting curve shows that the amount of forgetting eventually levels off. As you can see in Figure 6.11, there's very little difference between how much Ebbinghaus forgot eight hours later and a month later. The information that is *not* quickly forgotten seems to be remarkably stable in memory over long periods of time. This same pattern is also evident in the study of former psychology students. The amount of forgotten psychology information leveled off after about three years, then remained essentially the same for the next seven years (Conway & others, 1991).

Ebbinghaus was a pioneer in the study of memory. His major contribution was to identify the basic pattern of forgetting: rapid forgetting of some information relatively soon after the original learning, followed by stability of the memories that remain.

Factors That Influence Forgetting

Why do we forget? Research on forgetting, both in the laboratory and in everyday life, has identified four potential causes of forgetting: encoding failure, interference, motivated forgetting, and decay. Let's consider how each of these causes can help explain instances of forgetting.

Encoding Failure: It Never Got to Long-Term Memory

Without rummaging through your loose change, look at each drawing in Figure 6.12, then circle the one that accurately depicts the details of a penny. Now, check your answer against a real penny. Was your answer correct?

FIGURE 6.12 Test for Memory of Details of a Common Object Which of these drawings is an accurate picture of a real penny?

When this task was presented to subjects in one study, less than half of them picked the correct drawing (Nickerson & Adams, 1982). The explanation? Unless you're a coin collector, you've probably never really looked carefully at a penny. Even though you've handled thousands of pennies, you've only encoded a penny's essential characteristics—its color, size, and texture—into your long-term memory.

As this simple demonstration illustrates, one of the most common reasons for forgetting is that we never *encoded* the information into long-term memory in the first place. This phenomenon is called **encoding failure.** Encoding failure explains why you forget where you put your car keys or a person's name five minutes after meeting her. The information momentarily entered your short-term memory, but it was never encoded into long-term memory. As we discussed earlier, information that is not transferred from short-term memory to long-term memory lasts up to about 30 seconds, then evaporates. (You *do* remember that, don't you?) Although we may notice important details, the memory of those details will be fleeting if we don't quickly make a conscious effort to store it.

Interference Theory: Memories Interfering with Memories

A second reason for forgetting is that memories can interfere with one another. According to the **interference theory** of forgetting, forgetting is caused by one memory competing with or replacing another memory. The most critical factor is the similarity of the information. The more similar the information is in two memories, the more likely it is that interference will be produced.

There are two basic types of interference. **Retroactive interference** occurs when a *new* memory (your new phone number) interferes with remembering an *old* memory (your old phone number). Retroactive interference can also help explain how misinformation can contribute to the distortions that sometimes occur in eyewitness memories. After the original memory (being robbed), the witness is given inaccurate information that forms a new memory (the robber might be a priest). The new memory then interferes with the old memory, causing the forgetting of details or distortions of the old memory (Riccio & others, 1994). Thus, the misinformation effect that we discussed earlier can be a form of retroactive interference.

Proactive interference is the opposite of retroactive interference. It occurs when an *old* memory interferes with a *new* memory. This is a relatively common experience. For example, proactive interference can occur when you get a new car or borrow someone else's car. You want to switch on the headlights, but you keep turning on the windshield wipers. The old memory (the switch's location in your car) interferes with the more recent memory (the switch's location in the new car). A rather embarrassing example of

MEMORY CHIPS

JOYOUS   BITTERSWEET   BEST FORGOTTEN

MCCALLISTER

proactive interference occurs when you refer to your current partner by a previous partner's name. Such momentary memory glitches seem to occur spontaneously, often in the thralls of passion or anger.

Motivated Forgetting

Motivated forgetting refers to the idea that we forget because we are motivated to forget, usually because a memory is unpleasant or disturbing. In one form of motivated forgetting, called **suppression,** a person makes a deliberate, conscious effort to forget information. Although the person remains aware that a particular event did occur, he or she consciously chooses not to think about it. In effect, the goal is to put it out of your mind. However, research is mixed on whether it's really possible to deliberately forget information (H. Johnson, 1994; Wegner, 1989).

There is another form of motivated forgetting that is much more controversial. **Repression** is motivated forgetting that occurs *unconsciously.* With repression, all memory of an event or experience is blocked

Doonesbury   BY GARRY TRUDEAU

Doonesbury © 1994 G. B. Trudeau. Reprinted with permission of UNIVERSAL PRESS SYNDICATE. All Rights Reserved.

from conscious awareness. Thus, repression is fundamentally different from suppression, in which people know that a particular event happened but intentionally avoid thinking about it (Ceci & Loftus, 1994). As we'll discuss in greater detail in Chapters 11 and 15, the idea of repression is the cornerstone of Sigmund Freud's famous theory of personality and psychotherapy, *psychoanalysis.*

Freud (1904) believed that psychologically threatening feelings and traumatic events, especially ones that occurred during childhood, become repressed. Even though such memories are blocked and unavailable to consciousness, the repressed memories continue to unconsciously influence the person's behavior and personality, often in maladaptive or unhealthy ways.

Among clinical psychologists who work with psychologically troubled people, the notion that a person's behavior can be influenced by repressed memories is widely, but certainly not universally, accepted (Yapko, 1994a, 1994b). Among the general public, many people believe that we are capable of repressing memories of unpleasant events (Loftus & others, 1994). However, trying to scientifically study the influence of memories that a person does *not* remember is tricky, if not impossible (Loftus, 1993).

Today, much remains unknown about repression, and the topic is controversial (Erdelyi, 1993; Yapko, 1994b). At one extreme are some psychologists who do not believe that true repression ever occurs (Holmes, 1990). At the other extreme are psychologists who are convinced that repressed memories are at the root of many psychological problems, particularly repressed memories of childhood sexual abuse (Briere & Conte, 1993). In the middle are memory researchers who agree that extreme emotion can disrupt memory yet believe that the evidence for repression is far from conclusive (Bowers & Favolden, 1996).

In the past several years, a type of psychotherapy that focuses on the recovery of repressed memories of sexual abuse has become widespread (Pendergrast, 1996). This therapy has led to a heated controversy. Are the "recovered" memories true memories, or have they been inadvertently created by the therapist's suggestions? In Critical Thinking Box 6.3, we explore this controversy.

encoding failure
The inability to recall specific information because of insufficient encoding for storage in long-term memory.

interference theory
The theory that forgetting is caused by one memory competing with or replacing another.

retroactive interference
Forgetting in which a new memory interferes with remembering an old memory; backward-acting memory interference.

proactive interference
Forgetting in which an old memory interferes with remembering a new memory; forward-acting memory interference.

motivated forgetting
The theory that forgetting occurs because an undesired memory is held back from awareness.

suppression
Motivated forgetting that occurs consciously.

repression
Motivated forgetting that occurs unconsciously.

CRITICAL THINKING 6.3

Recovering "Repressed" Memories of Childhood Sexual Abuse

Sexual abuse of children is a serious problem in our society. It is estimated that approximately 25 percent of all girls and 10 percent of all boys are sexually abused (Zgourides, 1996). Every year, approximately 45,000 cases of child sexual abuse are reported to the authorities (Nevid & others, 1995). Without question, the physical and sexual abuse of children can contribute to psychological problems in adulthood (Brewin & others, 1993; Wenar, 1994).

In recent years, some psychotherapists, counselors, social workers, and other mental health workers have embraced a new form of treatment, called *recovery therapy, trauma therapy,* or *repressed memory therapy.* Recovery therapy asserts that many adult "survivors" of childhood sexual abuse have completely repressed all memories of the sexual abuse, although it may have gone on for years and involved multiple family members. Because they are "in denial," these adults consciously remember their childhood as being relatively uneventful—until they enter therapy.

Recovery therapists claim that even though all memories of the abuse are blocked, the repressed memories cause a wide range of psychological problems. Symptoms range from eating disorders, substance abuse, and sexual problems to headaches, anxiety, lack of motivation, relationship problems, and career problems (see Pendergrast, 1996).

The goal of repressed memory therapy is to help adults "recover" their memories of sexual abuse in childhood that have presumably been repressed from conscious awareness. As they do so, they can begin "the healing process" of working through their anger and other intense emotions (Bass & Davis, 1994).

The Controversy: Methods Used to "Recover" Repressed Memories

Repressed memory therapy is at the center of what has become a highly publicized and emotionally charged controversy (Baker, 1998). This controversy is focused on the methods used to help people unblock, or recover, repressed memories.

Through the use of hypnosis and other highly suggestive techniques, vivid memories of childhood sexual abuse can supposedly be recovered and brought to conscious awareness (Lindsay & Read,

1994). In extreme cases, patients have recovered repressed memories of years of ritual satanic abuse involving secret cults practicing infanticide (the murder of babies), torture, and ritual murder (Sakheim & Devine, 1992).

The Critical Issue: Recovered Memories or False Memories?

Critics of recovery therapy contend that many of the supposedly "recovered" memories are actually *false memories* produced by the suggestions of well-intentioned but misguided therapists (de Rivera, 2000). These critics note that in documented cases of trauma, most survivors are troubled by the *opposite* problem—they cannot forget their traumatic memories (Yapko, 1994b). Rather than being unable to remember the experience, the person suffers from recurring flashbacks, intrusive thoughts and memories of the trauma, and nightmares (Loftus, 1993; Loftus & Ketcham, 1994).

The issue of repression in general is also controversial. Most psychologists accept the notion that repression can occur, but with important qualifications (Schacter, 1995c). For example, it is relatively common for a person to be unable to remember *some* of the specific details of a traumatic event. Thus, people might experience amnesia for a single traumatic incident or the events surrounding the incident. However, most memory researchers are skeptical that anyone could repress *all* memories of *repeated* incidents of abuse, especially when those incidents occurred over a period of several years (Loftus & Ketcham, 1994; Schacter, 1995b).

Memory experts also have many objections to the use of hypnosis and other highly suggestive techniques to recover repressed memories (Ceci & Loftus, 1994; Lindsay & Read, 1994; Lynn & others, 1997). As discussed in Chapter 4, hypnosis does *not* increase the accuracy of memories (Kihlstrom & Barnhardt, 1993; Nash, 1987). However, hypnosis does increase a person's *confidence* in the memories that are recalled.

As you've seen in this chapter, compelling evidence shows the power of suggestion and misinformation in the creation of vivid, but false, memories (e.g., Garry & Loftus, 1994; Hyman & others, 1998; Loftus & others, 1998).

What Conclusions Can Be Drawn?

There is no question that physical and sexual abuse in childhood can contribute to psychological problems in adulthood (Wenar, 1994). Many psychologists believe it is *possible* for memories of abuse to be repressed in childhood, only to surface many years later in adulthood (Brenneis, 2000). Nevertheless, it's clear that repressed memories that have been recovered in psychotherapy need to be regarded with caution (Bowers & Favolden, 1996). There are some key points to remember in weighing such claims.

First, having confidence in a memory is no guarantee that the memory is accurate. False or fabricated memories can seem just as detailed, vivid, and real as accurate memories (Payne & others, 1997). As we've seen in this chapter, the ease with which the details of memories can be distorted is disturbing. Consequently, the use of highly suggestive techniques to recover memories of abuse raises serious concerns about the accuracy of such memories.

Second, keep in mind that every act of remembering involves reconstructing a memory. The human memory system does not function like a video camera, perfectly preserving the details of an experience. Remembering an experience is not like popping a videotape into your VCR. Memories can change over time. Without our awareness, memories grow and evolve, sometimes in unexpected ways.

Third, psychologists have become more aware of the possibility of inadvertently creating false memories in therapy (Palm & Gibson, 1998). Guidelines have been developed to help mental health professionals avoid unintentionally creating false memories in clients (Pope & Brown, 1996).

Critical Thinking Questions

- Why is it difficult to determine the accuracy of a "memory" that is recovered in therapy?

- What problems do you see in the use of suggestive techniques, such as hypnosis, to retrieve repressed memories?

- How could the phenomenon of source confusion be used to explain the production of false memories?

Decay Theory

Earlier in the chapter we noted that information in sensory memory and short-term memory quickly fades, or *decays*, if it is not transferred to long-term memory. Can the same thing happen with information that *is* stored in long-term memory?

According to **decay theory,** we forget memories because we don't use them and they fade away over time as a matter of normal brain processes. The idea is that when a new memory is formed, it creates a *memory trace*—a distinct change in brain structure or chemistry. Through disuse over time, the normal metabolic processes of the brain are thought to erode the memory trace. The gradual fading of memories, then, would be similar to the fading of letters on billboards or newsprint exposed to environmental elements, such as sunlight.

Like motivated forgetting, decay theory makes a good deal of sense intuitively. However, most memory researchers today do not think that long-term memories simply fade or decay from disuse. Why? Because too much evidence contradicts the basic assumptions of decay theory.

For example, many studies have shown that information can be remembered for decades after it was originally learned, even though it has not been rehearsed or recalled since the original memory was formed (Bahrick & Hall, 1991; Bahrick & Phelps, 1987). As we discussed earlier, the ability to access memories is strongly influenced by the kinds of retrieval cues provided when memory is tested (Slamecka, 1992). If the memory trace simply decayed over time, the presentation of potent retrieval cues should have no effect on the retrieval of information or events experienced long ago—but they do.

Although researchers have not been able to muster compelling evidence for decay theory, there has been enormous interest in trying to explain the physiological basis of memory and forgetting. In the next section of this chapter, we'll look at how memories seem to be created and stored in the brain.

decay theory
The view that forgetting is due to normal metabolic processes that occur in the brain over time.

6.2 R·E·V·I·E·W

C·O·N·C·E·P·T

Factors That Affect Retrieval and Forgetting

Circle the letter of the correct answer.

1. Lila discovered an old box of childhood toys stored in her attic. As she sorted through the box, she was flooded with memories of long-forgotten friends and experiences, including her first day of school and the games she played with neighborhood children. The toys were acting as:

   a. cues that activated repressed memories

   b. chunking cues

   c. serial position cues

   d. retrieval cues

2. Juan always studied alone in the college library. He was surprised when he had difficulty remembering some information during his final exam, which he took in a large gymnasium with several hundred other students. One explanation for his forgetting information that he had studied could be:

   a. the context effect

   b. mood-dependent retrieval

   c. the primacy effect

   d. source confusion

3. Renee asked her husband what his secretary had worn to the office party, and he could not remember. The most likely explanation is:

   a. suppression   c. the interference effect

   b. encoding failure   d. He was lying.

4. Professor Ivanovich has many vivid memories of her students from last semester and can recall most of their names. Because of _____, she is having problems remembering her new students' names this semester.

   a. retroactive interference   c. decay

   b. proactive interference   d. suppression

5. Rob has a very vivid memory of a bad traffic accident that occurred near his home when he was a child. His mother, however, claims that Rob couldn't have witnessed the incident because he was in bed, asleep, when it occurred, and that he had learned about the accident from television news reports. Rob's false memory is probably the result of:

   a. retrieval cue failure   c. flashbulb interference

   b. repression   d. source confusion

memory trace
The brain changes associated with a
particular stored memory.

The Search for the Biological Basis of Memory

Key Theme

▪ Early researchers believed that memory was associated with physical changes in the brain, but these changes were only discovered in the last few decades.

Key Questions

▪ How are memories both localized and distributed in the brain?
▪ How do neurons change when a memory is formed?

Does the name *Ivan Pavlov* ring a bell? We hope so. As you should recall from Chapter 5, Pavlov was the Russian physiologist who classically conditioned dogs to salivate to the sound of a bell and other neutral stimuli. Without question, learning and memory are intimately connected. Learning an adaptive response depends on our ability to form new memories in which we associate environmental stimuli, behaviors, and consequences.

Pavlov (1927) believed that the memory involved in learning a classically conditioned response would ultimately be explained as a matter of changes in the brain. However, he only speculated about the kinds of brain changes that would produce the memories needed for classical conditioning to occur. Other researchers would take up the search for the physical changes associated with learning and memory. In this section, we look at some of the key discoveries that have been made in trying to understand the biological basis of memory.

The Search for the Elusive Memory Trace

An American physiological psychologist named **Karl Lashley** set out to find evidence for Pavlov's speculations. In the 1920s, Lashley began the search for the **memory trace,** or *engram*—the brain changes associated with the formation of a long-term memory. Guiding Lashley's research was his belief that memory was *localized,* meaning that a particular memory was stored in a specific brain area.

Lashley searched for the specific location of the memory that a rat forms for

Karl S. Lashley (1890–1958) Lashley was trained as a zoologist but turned to psychology after he became friends with John B. Watson, the founder of behaviorism. Interested in discovering the physical basis of the conditioned reflex, Lashley focused his research on how learning and memory were represented in the brain. After years of frustrating research, Lashley (1950) humorously concluded, "This series of experiments has yielded a good bit of information about what and where memory is not. It has discovered nothing directly of the real nature of the engram. I sometimes feel in reviewing the evidence on the localization of the memory trace, that the necessary conclusion is that learning just is not possible."

running a maze. Lashley (1929) suspected that the specific memory was localized at a specific site in the *cerebral cortex,* the outermost covering of the brain that contains the most sophisticated brain areas. Once a rat had learned to run the maze, Lashley surgically removed tiny portions of the rat's cortex. After the rat recovered, Lashley tested the rat in the maze again. Obviously, if the rat could still run the maze, then the portion of the brain removed did not contain the memory.

Over the course of 30 years, Lashley systematically removed different sections of the cortex in trained rats. The result of Lashley's painstaking research? No matter which part of the cortex he removed, the rats were still able to run the maze (Lashley, 1929, 1950). At the end of his professional career, Karl Lashley concluded that memories are not localized in specific locations but instead are *distributed,* or stored, throughout the brain.

Lashley was wrong, but not completely wrong. Some memories *do* seem to be localized at specific spots in the brain. Some 20 years after Lashley's death, psy-

chologist **Richard F. Thompson** and his colleagues resumed the search for the location of
the memory trace that would confirm
Pavlov's speculations. Thompson classically
conditioned rabbits to perform a very simple
behavior—an eye blink. By pairing a tone
with a puff of air administered to the rabbit's
eye, he classically conditioned rabbits to blink
reflexively in response to the tone alone
(Thompson, 1994, 2000).

Thompson discovered that after a rabbit
had learned this simple behavior, there was a
change in the brain activity in a small area of
the rabbit's *cerebellum,* a lower-brain struc-
ture involved in physical movements. When this tiny area of the cerebellum was
removed, the rabbit's memory of the learned response disappeared. It no longer
blinked at the sound of the tone. However, the puff of air still caused the rabbit
to blink reflexively, so the reflex itself had not been destroyed.

Thompson and his colleagues had confirmed Pavlov's speculations. The long-
term memory trace of the classically conditioned eye blink was formed and stored
in a very localized region of the cerebellum. So why had Karl Lashley failed? Unlike Thompson, Lashley was working with a relatively complex behavior. Running a maze involves the use of several senses, including vision, smell, and touch.
In comparison, Thompson's rabbits had learned a very simple reflexive behavior—a classically conditioned eye blink.

Thus, part of the reason Lashley failed to find a specific location for a rat's
memory of a maze was that the memory was not a single memory. Instead, the
rat had developed a complex set of *interrelated memories* involving information
from multiple senses. These interrelated memories were processed and stored in
different brain areas. As a result, the rat's memories were *distributed* and stored
across multiple brain locations. Hence, no matter which small brain area Lashley removed, the rat could still run the maze. So Lashley seems to have been right
in suggesting that some memories are distributed throughout the brain.

When you combine the findings of Lashley and Thompson, they suggest that
memories have the potential to be *both localized and distributed* (Squire & Kandel, 1999). Very simple memories may be localized in a specific area, whereas
more complex memories seem to be distributed throughout the brain. A complex
memory involves clusters of information, and each part of the memory may be
stored in the brain area that originally processed the information (Squire & Butters, 1992).

More recently, researchers have used PET scans to confirm that many kinds
of memories are distributed in the human brain. When we are performing a relatively complex memory task, multiple brain regions are activated—evidence of
the distribution of memories involved in complex tasks (Squire & others, 1992).

If multiple brain areas are involved when we form a new memory, are they
also involved when we retrieve an existing memory? In this chapter's Focus on
Neuroscience, we take a look at a clever study that investigated this question.

Richard F. Thompson (b. 1930) Like Karl
Lashley, Richard Thompson, an American
psychologist and neuroscientist, wished
to discover the neurobiological basis for
learning and memory. But, unlike Lashley,
Thompson decided to use a very simple behavior—a classically conditioned eye blink—
as a model system to locate a memory trace
in the brain. He succeeded, identifying the
critical region in the cerebellum where the
memory of the learned behavior was stored.

The Role of Neurons in Long-Term Memory

What exactly is it that is localized or distributed? Memories don't just float
around in your brain. The notion of a memory trace suggests that some change
must occur in the workings of the brain when a new long-term memory is stored.
Logically, two possible changes could occur. First, the *functioning* of the neurons
in the brain could somehow change. Second, the *structure* of the neurons could
somehow change.

Perception   **Recall**

Picture

(a)   (b)

Sound

(c)   (d)

Retrieving the Memory of a Sensory Experience

Top row: (a) Perceiving a picture activates areas of the visual cortex. (b) When the memory of the picture is recalled, it reactivates some of the same areas of the visual cortex (*arrow*) that were involved in the initial perception of the picture. Bottom row: (c) Perceiving a sound activates areas of the auditory cortex. (d) When the memory of the sound is recalled, it reactivates some of the same areas of the auditory cortex (*arrow*) that were involved in the initial perception of the sound.

SOURCE: Wheeler & others (2000).

Assembling Memories: Echoes and Reflections of Perception If we asked you to remember Paul McCartney's rendition of "Yesterday" or the theme from *Star Wars,* you would "hear" the song in your head. Conjure up a memory of your elementary school, and you "see" it in your mind. Vivid memories can include a great deal of sensory information—sounds, sights, and even odors and tastes. How are such rich sensory aspects of an experience incorporated into the memory that is retrieved?

Psychologists Mark Wheeler, Steven Peterson, and Randy Buckner (2000) set out to investigate this question using a simple memory task and fMRI. First, the participants spent two days studying labels for common objects that were paired with either a picture or a sound. For example, half of the participants memorized the word *dog* paired with a picture of a dog, and half memorized the word *dog* paired with the sound of a dog barking. The researchers then used fMRI to measure brain activity in the volunteers under two conditions: (1) a *perception* condition, in which the participants simply reviewed the pairings that they had learned, and (2) a *recall* condition, in which the volunteers were given the label and told to retrieve the memory and indicate whether the word was associated with a picture or a sound.

The results? Retrieving the memory activated a subset of the same brain areas that were involved in perceiving the sensory stimulus. In other words, participants who had memorized the label "dog" with a *picture* of a dog showed a high level of activation in the *visual cortex* when they retrieved the memory. And, participants who had memorized the label "dog" with the *sound* of a barking dog showed a high level of activation in the *auditory cortex* when they retrieved the memory.

Other studies have confirmed that retrieving a sensory memory reactivates the sensory area of the cortex that was involved in the initial perception of the event (see Buckner & Wheeler, 2001). What about memories that involve more than a single sense? These memories tend to reactivate *multiple* sensory areas of the brain—the same areas that were activated during the initial encoding of the information (Nyberg & others, 2000). Of course, many of our memories are highly complex, involving not just sensations but also thoughts and emotions. Neuroscientists assume that such complex memories involve traces that are widely distributed throughout the brain. However, they still don't understand how all these neural records are bound together and interrelated to form a single, highly elaborate memory (Buckner & Wheeler, 2001).

Given those two possibilities, the challenge for memory researchers has been to identify the specific neurons involved in a given memory, a task that is virtually impossible with the human brain because of its enormous complexity. What this task requires is a creature with a limited number of neurons that is also capable of learning new memories.

Enter *Aplysia,* a gentle, seaweed-munching sea snail that resides off the California coast. The study of *Aplysia* in the last 30 years has given memory researchers important clues to the brain changes involved in memory. *Aplysia* has only about 20,000 good-sized neurons. Thus, memory researchers, such as **Eric Kandel** (2001) at Columbia University, have been able to study the neuronal changes that occur when *Aplysia* forms a new memory for a simple classically conditioned response.

If you give *Aplysia* a gentle squirt with a WaterPik, followed by a mild electric shock to its tail, the snail reflexively withdraws its gill flap. When the process is repeated several times, *Aplysia* wises up and acquires a new memory of a classically conditioned response—it withdraws its gill when squirted with the

long-term potentiation
A long-lasting increase in synaptic strength between two neurons.

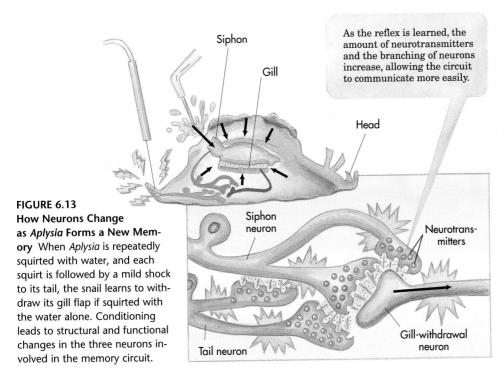

As the reflex is learned, the amount of neurotransmitters and the branching of neurons increase, allowing the circuit to communicate more easily.

Siphon

Gill

Head

Siphon neuron

Neurotrans-mitters

Tail neuron

Gill-withdrawal neuron

FIGURE 6.13
How Neurons Change as *Aplysia* Forms a New Memory When *Aplysia* is repeatedly squirted with water, and each squirt is followed by a mild shock to its tail, the snail learns to withdraw its gill flap if squirted with the water alone. Conditioning leads to structural and functional changes in the three neurons involved in the memory circuit.

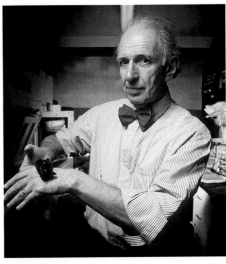

Aplysia, **the Supersnail of Memory Research** Eric Kandel holds *Aplysia,* the sea snail that is used to study how neurons change when simple behaviors are learned and remembered. Kandel won the Nobel Prize in 2000 for his discoveries on the neural basis of memory.

WaterPik alone. This learned gill-withdrawal reflex seems to involve a circuit of just three neurons: one that detects the water squirt, one that detects the tail shock, and one that signals the gill-withdrawal reflex (see Figure 6.13).

When *Aplysia* acquires this new memory through repeated training trials, significant changes occur in the three-neuron circuit (2001). First, the *function* of the neurons is altered: There is an increase in the amount of the neurotransmitters produced by the neurons. Second, the *structure* of the snail's neurons changes: The number of interconnecting branches between the neurons increases, as do the number of synapses or communication points on each branch. These changes allow the neurons involved in the particular memory circuit to communicate more easily. Collectively, these changes are called **long-term potentiation,** which refers to a long-lasting increase in synaptic strength (Malenka & Nicoll, 1999; Tsien, 2000).

The same kinds of brain changes have been observed in more sophisticated mammals (McKernan & Shinnick-Gallagher, 1997). Chicks, rats, and rabbits also show structural and functional neuron changes associated with new learning experiences and memories (Martin & others, 2000; Rioult-Pedotti & others, 2000). And, as you may recall from the Chapter 2 Application, there is indirect evidence that the same kinds of changes occur in humans (Jacobs & others, 1993; Stern & others, 1992, 1994).

In terms of our understanding of the memory trace, what do these findings suggest? Although there are vast differences between the nervous system of a simple creature such as *Aplysia* and the enormously complex human brain, some tentative generalizations are possible. Forming a memory seems to produce distinct functional and structural changes in specific neurons (Tsien, 2000). These changes create a memory circuit. Each time the memory is recalled, the neurons in this circuit are activated. As the structural and functional changes in the neurons strengthen the communication links in this circuit, the memory becomes established as a long-term memory (Kandel, 2001).

Creating New Synaptic Connections Forming new memories involves strengthening existing synaptic connections and creating new synaptic connections between neurons in the brain. Neuroscientist Michael Colicos and his colleagues at the University of California-San Diego (2001) photographed structural changes in a single hippocampus neuron that occurred in response to repeated electrical stimulation. The spidery blue lines in the photo are physical changes in the neuron's structure that represent the first steps toward the formation of new synaptic connections with other neurons.

C·O·N·C·E·P·T

6.3 R·E·V·I·E·W

Remembering Famous Names

Match each of the following names with one of the descriptions below: Eric Kandel, George Sperling, Hermann Ebbinghaus, Richard F. Thompson, Elizabeth Loftus, Karl Lashley.

1. The psychologist who identified the duration of visual sensory memory _____

2. One of the most widely recognized experts on memory distortions, eyewitness testimony, and false memories _____

3. The psychologist who was one of the first people to scientifically study memory and forgetting _____

4. The physiological psychologist who tried but failed to find the specific location of individual memories in the brain _____

5. The physiological psychologist who succeeded in identifying the specific brain location of a simple classically conditioned response

_____

6. The neuroscientist who won a Nobel Prize for his success in determining the neural basis of memory in *Aplysia*._____

Processing Memories in the Brain
Clues from Amnesia

Key Theme

▨ Important insights into the brain structures involved in normal memory have been provided by case studies of people with amnesia caused by damaged brain tissue.

Key Questions

▨ What are anterograde and retrograde amnesia, and what do they reveal about normal memory processes?
▨ What brain structures are involved in normal memory?
▨ What are senile dementia and Alzheimer's disease?

The complexity and inaccessibility of the human brain have made it virtually impossible to study the role of individual neurons in human memory. However, memory researchers have been able to study the role of specific brain structures in processing memories. Much of this research has involved studying individuals who have sustained a brain injury or had part of their brain surgically removed for medical reasons. Often, such individuals experience **amnesia,** or severe memory loss (Butters & Delis, 1995). By relating the type and extent of amnesia to the specific brain areas that have been damaged, researchers have uncovered clues as to how the human brain processes memories.

Retrograde Amnesia: Disrupting Memory Consolidation

One type of amnesia is **retrograde amnesia.** *Retrograde* means "backward moving." People who have retrograde amnesia are unable to remember some or all of their past, especially episodic memories for recent events. Retrograde amnesia often results from a blow to the head. Boxers sometimes suffer such memory losses after years of fighting. Head injuries from automobile and motorcycle acci-

amnesia
(am-NEE-zha) Severe memory loss.

retrograde amnesia
Loss of memory, especially for episodic information; backward-acting amnesia.

dents are another common cause of retrograde amnesia. Typically, memories of the events that immediately preceded the injury are completely lost, as in the case of accident victims who cannot remember details about what led up to the accident.

Apparently, establishing a long-term memory is like creating a cement wall—it needs time to "set" before it becomes permanent. This process of "setting" a new memory permanently in the brain is called memory consolidation. More specifically, **memory consolidation** is the gradual, physical process of converting new long-term memories to stable, enduring memory codes. If memory consolidation is disrupted before the process is complete, a long-term memory is vulnerable and may be lost. In humans, memory consolidation can be disrupted by brain trauma, such as a sudden blow, concussion, electric shock, or encephalitis (Squire & Kandel, 1999).

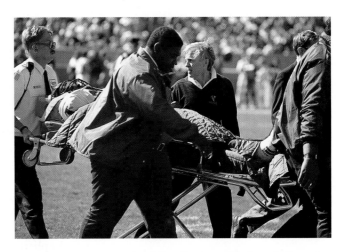

Disrupting the Consolidation of Memories
Head injuries are common in football and many other sports. In one study, football players who were questioned immediately after a concussion or other head injury could remember how they were injured and the name of the play just performed. But if questioned 30 minutes later for the same information, they could not. Because the head injury had disrupted the memory consolidation process, the memories were permanently lost (Yarnell & Lynch, 1970).

Anterograde Amnesia: Disrupting Explicit Memory Formation

Another form of amnesia is **anterograde amnesia**—the inability to form new memories. *Anterograde* means "forward moving." The most famous case of anterograde amnesia is that of a man identified only by the initials H. M. to protect his identity.

In 1953, H. M. was 27 years old and had a history of severe, untreatable epileptic seizures. H. M.'s doctors located the brain area where the seizures seemed to originate. In desperation, they surgically removed portions of the medial (inner) temporal lobe on each side of H. M.'s brain, including the brain structure called the *hippocampus* (Corkin & others, 1997; Ogden & Corkin, 1991).

After the surgery, the frequency and severity of H. M.'s seizures were greatly reduced. However, another effect was quickly discovered. H. M.'s ability to form new memories of events and information had been destroyed. Although intended to treat H. M.'s seizures, the surgery had dramatically revealed the role of the hippocampus in forming new explicit memories for episodic and semantic information.

Canadian psychologist Brenda Milner (1965, 1970) has studied H. M. extensively over the last 40 years. If you were to meet H. M. today, you could carry on a conversation with him, and he would appear normal enough. He has a good vocabulary, normal language skills, and above-average intelligence. But he lives in the eternal present. If you left his room and returned five minutes later, he wouldn't remember your name or having seen you before. He must be reintroduced to his doctors each time he sees them, even though some of them have been treating him for years (Ogden & Corkin, 1991).

For the most part, H. M.'s short-term memory seems to work just fine. If he actively repeats or rehearses information, he can hold it in short-term memory for an hour or more. However, he forgets the information if he switches his attention to something else and stops rehearsing it (Ogden & Corkin, 1991). H. M.'s long-term memory is also partially intact. He can retrieve long-term memories from before the time he was 16 years old, when the severe epileptic seizures began.

But H. M. is unable to form new long-term memories of events (episodic information) or general knowledge (semantic information). Thus, H. M.'s case suggests that the hippocampus is not involved in most short-term memory tasks, nor is it the storage site for already established long-term memories. Instead, the critical role played by the hippocampus seems to be the *encoding* of new memories for events and information and the *transfer* of them from short-term to long-term memory (Squire & Knowlton, 1995). When the same brain sections are surgically removed from monkeys, the monkeys show the same kind of massive anterograde amnesia displayed by H. M. (Zola-Morgan & Squire, 1993).

memory consolidation
The gradual, physical process of converting new long-term memories to stable, enduring long-term memory codes.

anterograde amnesia
Loss of memory caused by the inability to store new memories; forward-acting amnesia.

Implicit and Explicit Memory in Anterograde Amnesia   The case of H. M. and those of other patients with anterograde amnesia have also contributed to our understanding of the distinction between implicit and explicit memory. As discussed earlier in the chapter, *implicit memories* are memories without conscious awareness. In contrast, *explicit memories* are memories with conscious awareness.

H. M. cannot form new episodic or semantic memories, which reflect the explicit memory system. But it turns out that H. M. *can* form new procedural memories, which reflect the implicit memory system. For example, when H. M. was given the same logical puzzle to solve several days in a row, he was able to solve it more quickly each day. This improvement showed that at some level he implicitly "remembered" the procedure involved in solving the puzzle. But if you asked H. M. if he had ever seen the puzzle before, he would answer "no," because he could not consciously (or explicitly) remember having learned how to solve the puzzle. It seems, then, that the hippocampus is less crucial to the formation of new implicit memories, such as procedural memories, than it is to the formation of new explicit memories (Zola-Morgan & Squire, 1993).

Is H. M. an exception? No. Many studies have been conducted with other amnesia patients who have experienced damage to the hippocampus and related brain structures. Like H. M., these patients are unable to form new explicit memories, but their performances on implicit memory tasks, which do not require conscious recollection of the new information, are normal (Schacter, 1998). Such findings suggest that implicit and explicit memory processes involve different brain regions. The research has also led to a new understanding of the roles played by different brain regions in different types of memory abilities (Clark & Squire, 1998; Rugg & others, 1998).

Infantile Amnesia: Parallels with H. M.?   Most people are unable to remember any events from their first few years of life. This inability to remember infant experiences during adulthood is called *infantile amnesia* (Bauer, 1996; Howe & Courage, 1993). One explanation for infantile amnesia relies on the *encoding specificity principle* discussed earlier in the chapter. That is, retrieval of early memories is not possible because there are simply too many differences between the world of the infant and that of the adult. According to this idea, as adults we no longer possess the appropriate retrieval cues to access memories from infancy (Hartshorn & others, 1998; Rovee-Collier, 1997, 1999).

Another explanation for infantile amnesia involves brain development and rests partly on the similarities between infant memory and anterograde amnesia. Infants, like adults with hippocampus damage, lack the ability to encode and store new *episodic* memories (Moscovitch, 1985; Schacter & Moscovitch, 1984). However, like H. M., infants do have the ability to form *procedural* memories.

Some researchers believe that the hippocampus does not mature until about two years of age. If this is the case, the infant's hippocampus may not be able to encode and store events and experiences in long-term memory. Other late-maturing brain structures, such as the cortex, may also play a role in memory development (Goldman-Rakic, 1992; C. A. Nelson, 1995, 1998). As the critical brain structures necessary for episodic memory become more fully functional, around the ages of two to three, the beginnings of episodic memory traces become solidified as long-term memories (Newcombe & others, 2000).

Brain Structures Involved in Memory

Along with the hippocampus, several other brain regions are involved in memory tasks, including the amygdala, the cerebellum, and the frontal cortex (see Figure 6.14). As we've already seen, the *cerebellum* is involved in classically conditioning simple reflexes, such as the eye-blink reflex. The cerebellum is also involved in procedural memories and other motor skill memories.

The *amygdala,* which is situated very close to the hippocampus, seems to encode the emotional qualities associated with particular memories, such as fear or

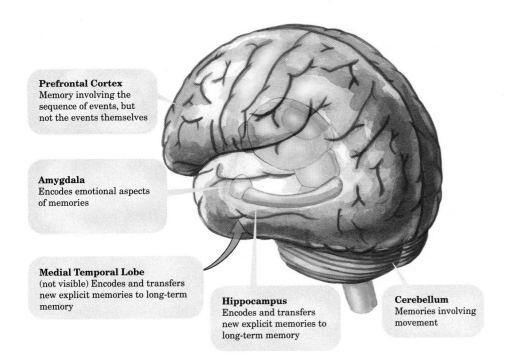

Prefrontal Cortex
Memory involving the sequence of events, but not the events themselves

Amygdala
Encodes emotional aspects of memories

Medial Temporal Lobe
(not visible) Encodes and transfers new explicit memories to long-term memory

Hippocampus
Encodes and transfers new explicit memories to long-term memory

Cerebellum
Memories involving movement

FIGURE 6.14 Brain Structures Involved in Human Memory Shown here are some of the key brain structures involved in encoding and storing memories.

anger (Davis, 1992). For example, normal monkeys are afraid of snakes. But if the amygdala is damaged, a monkey loses its fear of snakes and other natural predators. The amygdala is also associated with memories of sensory stimuli that are associated with rewards and punishments (Rolls, 2000).

The *prefrontal cortex* seems to play an important role in memory as well, especially in the ability to remember the order of information (Chiba & others, 1997; Parkin & others, 1995). In one study, patients with damage to the frontal lobes showed no deficit in remembering key words from a story. However, they were impaired in their ability to remember the order in which the words were presented in the story (Swain & others, 1998).

Neuroscientists are far from a comprehensive understanding of the brain mechanisms involved in memory. Nevertheless, enormous strides have been made in the last 30 years. Clearly, certain brain structures, most notably the hippocampus, are involved in the initial processing of episodic memories (Squire & Knowlton, 1995). Distinct structural and functional changes in circuits of neurons seem to be associated with enduring memories (Kandel, 2001). Researchers are also making gains in understanding which neurotransmitters seem to be most involved in the memory process (Baudry & Davis, 1992).

The goals of such research are not purely academic. *Senile dementia* is a condition characterized by impairment of memory and intellectual functions. The most common cause of senile dementia is *Alzheimer's disease,* which occurs in about 10 percent of the population over the age of 65. The symptoms of Alzheimer's disease are caused by the progressive degeneration of neurons in the brain (Patrick & others, 1999). In the early stages of Alzheimer's disease, the symptoms of memory impairment are often mild, such as forgetting to lock the front door. But as the disease progresses, the loss of memory becomes pervasive. The person becomes unable to remember what month it is or the names of family members. Eventually, the person becomes completely incapacitated and dies (Soukup, 1996).

The prevalence of the different forms of dementia increases with advancing age (Butters & Delis, 1995). Through the efforts of memory researchers, combined with advances in technology, it may one day be possible to treat these conditions or at least to minimize the devastating loss of human memory that accompanies them. However, it's important to keep in mind that factors other than disease and the aging process can potentially influence memory in old age. In Culture and Human Behavior Box 6.4, we consider an intriguing notion—that the memory abilities of elderly people may partly reflect cultural expectations.

CULTURE AND HUMAN BEHAVIOR 6.4

Do Cultural Beliefs Affect Memory in Old Age?

Many researchers believe that declines in memory ability are part of the natural biological aging process (Salthouse, 1993). However, psychologists Becca Levy and Ellen Langer (1994) have offered a very different explanation. They believe that cultural expectations about aging can affect memory abilities in the elderly.

While most Americans believe that memory loss inevitably accompanies old age (Ryan, 1992), Levy and Langer point out that this belief is far from universal. In many cultures, the elderly are accorded high status and revered for their wisdom and accumulated knowledge.

To test the notion that cultural stereotypes of the elderly can influence memory ability, Levy and Langer (1994) first identified two cultural groups that hold a very positive view of aging. One group was people living in mainland China. The other group consisted of hearing-impaired Americans who used American Sign Language and strongly identified with the Deaf culture.

Next, Levy and Langer recruited three groups of subjects: (1) residents of Beijing, China; (2) American members of the Deaf culture who communicated with American Sign Language; and (3) Americans who were part of the mainstream hearing culture. Half of each group consisted of people aged 15 to 30; the other half consisted of adults aged 59 to 91. Participants in all groups were tested on four different memory tasks. In addition, their attitudes toward old age were measured.

On the memory tasks, Levy and Langer found no significant difference among all three groups of younger adults. But, although the younger adults in the three cultural groups performed very similarly, the older adults did not. The older American hearing participants had the *lowest* memory-test scores. The elderly Deaf participants had the next highest memory-test scores. And the elderly Chinese subjects had the *highest* scores of all the older adults. In fact, their scores did not differ from the scores of the young Chinese subjects.

Levy and Langer note that the pattern of memory test scores was directly correlated with each group's view of aging. The more positive the view of aging, the better the performance on actual memory tasks. The Chinese reported the most positive view of aging, and the older Chinese participants scored the highest on the memory tasks. The hearing Americans reported the *least* positive view of aging, and the elderly members of this group scored the lowest on the memory tasks. The Deaf participants' views about aging fell between those of the Chinese and those of the American hearing group, and their scores on the memory tests also fell between those of the other two groups.

How can we interpret these findings? Levy and Langer point out that the Chinese and Deaf cultures have little in common other than their esteem for old age. If biological processes were responsible for memory in old age, the Chinese and Deaf participants should not have outperformed the older American hearing participants on all four memory tasks.

Levy and Langer (1994) concluded that cultural beliefs about aging may well play an important role in determining the degree of memory loss that people experience in old age. They suggest that the negative stereotypes about aging that are common in mainstream American culture may function as a self-fulfilling prophecy for many older Americans (Levy, 1996).

Summing Up

Memory

Human memory is at once both perfectly ordinary and quite extraordinary. With next to no mental effort, you form and recall countless memories as you go through daily life. As you've seen in this chapter, psychologists have made enormous progress in explaining how those memories are encoded, stored, retrieved, and forgotten.

Yet perhaps the most fascinating aspect of human memory is its fallibility. Memory is surprisingly susceptible to errors and distortions. Under some conditions, completely false memories can be experienced, such as Elizabeth Loftus's memory of discovering her mother's body in the swimming pool. Such false memories can be so subjectively compelling that they feel like authentic memories.

Many mysteries of human memory remain, including exactly how memories are stored in and retrieved from the brain. Nevertheless, reliable ways of improving memory in everyday life have been discovered. In the Application we provide several suggestions to enhance your memory for new information.

None of us is immune to the pitfalls of forgetting. Fortunately, there are several very effective strategies to boost your memory for important information, whether it's textbook material or the location of that extra set of house keys. Based on memory research, we've compiled 10 effective techniques to enhance your memory.

1. Focus your attention.
Problems in absorbing new information arise when distracting thoughts, background noise, and other interruptions sidetrack your attention. Television is one common culprit (Armstrong & Sopory, 1997). Rather than studying in front of the tube, locate a quiet study space that's free from distractions so you can focus your attention. If distracting thoughts are competing for your attention, start your study session by reading aloud part of what you need to study (Hertel & Rude, 1991).

2. Commit the necessary time.
The more time you spend learning material, the better you will understand it and the longer you will remember it. So don't rely on skimming material the night before a test. Budget enough time to read the assigned material carefully. If you read material faster than you can comprehend it, you not only won't understand the material, you also won't remember it.

3. Space your study sessions.
Distributed practice means that you learn information over several sessions, which gives you time to mentally process and incorporate the information (Bjork, 2001). Students who take the distributed-practice approach to learning retain significantly more information than students who use cramming, or *massed practice*. It's also been shown that sleep, particularly REM or dreaming sleep, helps consolidate new memories (Karni & others, 1994; Smith & Lapp, 1991). All-night cram sessions just before an exam are one of the *least* effective ways to learn new material.

4. Organize the information.
We have a strong natural tendency to organize information in long-term memory into categories. You can capitalize on this tendency by actively organizing information you want to remember. One way to accomplish this is by outlining chapters or your lecture notes. Use the chapter headings and subheadings as categories, or, better yet, create your own categories. Under each category, list and describe the relevant terms, concepts, and ideas. This strategy can double the amount of information you can recall.

5. Elaborate on the material.
You've probably noticed that virtually every term or concept in this text is formally defined in just a sentence or two. But we also spend a paragraph or more explaining what the concept means. In order to remember the information you read, you have to do the same thing—engage in elaborative rehearsal and actively process the information for meaning.

How can you actively process information for meaning? Actively question new information and think about its implications. Form memory associations by relating the material to what you already know. Try to come up with examples that relate to your own life. React to what you read by writing your comments or questions in the margin of the textbook. Create sentences that accurately use the concept or term.

6. Use visual imagery.
Two memory codes are better than one (Paivio, 1986). Rather than merely encoding the information verbally, use mental imagery (Tindall-Ford & others, 1997). Much of the information in this text easily lends itself to visual imagery. Use the photographs and other illustrations to help form visual memories of the information. A simple way to make text information visually distinct is to highlight different concepts in different colors.

7. Explain it to a friend.
Memory research clearly supports the benefits of explaining new material out loud (Muth & others, 1988). After you read a section of material, stop. Summarize what you have read in your mind. When you think you understand it, try to explain the information to a friend or a family member.

8. Reduce interference within a topic.
If you occasionally confuse related terms and concepts, it may be because you're experiencing *interference* in your memories for similar information. To minimize memory interference for related information, first break the chapter into manageable sections, then learn the key information one section at a time. As you encounter new concepts, compare them with previously learned concepts, looking for differences and similarities. By building distinct memories for important information as you progress through a topic, you're more likely to distinguish between concepts so they don't get confused in your memory.

9. Counteract the serial position effect.
The serial position effect is our tendency to remember information at the beginning and end of a sequence. To counteract it, spend extra time with the information that falls in the middle. Once you've mastered a sequence of material, start at a different point each time you review the information.

10. Use contextual cues to jog memories.
Ideally, study in the setting in which you're going to be tested. If that's not possible, when you're taking a test and a specific memory gets blocked, imagine that your books and notes are in front of you and that you're sitting where you normally study. Simply imagining the surroundings where you learned the material can help jog those memories (Smith & others, 1978).

Garfield BY JIM DAVIS

Chapter Review

Key Points

Introduction: What Is Memory?

■ **Memory** refers to the mental processes that enable us to acquire, retain, and retrieve information. Key memory processes are **encoding, storage,** and **retrieval.**

The Stage Model of Memory

■ The **stage model of memory** describes human memory as the process of transferring information from one memory stage to another. The three stages of memory are sensory memory, short-term memory, and long-term memory. Short-term memory is also called working memory.

■ **Sensory memory** briefly stores information about the environment. Information that we attend to is transferred from sensory memory to short-term memory; other information fades quickly.

■ George Sperling discovered that visual sensory memory holds information for about half a second before the information fades.

■ There is a separate sensory memory for each sense. Visual and auditory sensory memory are the most thoroughly studied. Auditory sensory memory lasts up to a few seconds.

■ **Short-term memory,** also called **working memory,** provides temporary storage for information transferred from sensory memory and information recalled from **long-term memory.** Most information fades from short-term memory within about 30 seconds. **Maintenance rehearsal** keeps information active in short-term memory.

■ The capacity of short-term memory is limited to about seven items, plus or minus two. When the capacity of short-term memory is reached, new information will displace existing information. **Chunking** can be used to increase the amount of information held in short-term memory.

■ Long-term memory stores a limitless amount of information for extended periods of time.

■ Encoding transforms information into a form that can be stored and retrieved later. The most effective encoding strategies involve **elaborative rehearsal.** The **levels-of-processing framework** suggests that information that is processed deeply will be encoded more effectively.

■ Long-term memory includes **procedural, episodic,** and **semantic memory. Explicit memories** can be consciously recalled. **Implicit memories** cannot be consciously recalled, but affect behavior or performance. Information in long-term memory is **clustered** into related groups during recall. The **semantic network model** describes the organization of long-term memory.

Retrieval: *Getting Information from Long-Term Memory*

■ **Retrieval** refers to the process of accessing information stored in long-term memory.

■ **Retrieval cues** are hints that help us retrieve stored memories. Sometimes stored memories cannot be retrieved because of **retrieval cue failure,** such as in **tip-of-the-tongue experiences (TOT).**

■ Retrieval can be tested using **recall, cued recall,** and **recognition** measures. The **serial position effect** is our tendency to remember best the first and last items in a series.

■ According to the **encoding specificity principle,** recreating aspects of the original learning conditions is one way to increase retrieval effectiveness. Examples of the encoding specificity principle include the **context effect, state-dependent retrieval,** and **mood congruence.**

■ Memories that are highly unusual tend to be easier to retrieve from long-term memory. **Flashbulb memories** can be extremely vivid, but, like normal memories, they are not always accurate.

Reconstructing Memories: *Sources of Potential Errors*

■ Because retrieval involves the reconstruction of memories, memory details can change. Memories can be distorted by **schemas** and other preexisting information that we have stored before acquiring a new memory. Schemas can also contribute to memory distortions when we learn new information that is inconsistent with previously learned information. **Source confusion** occurs when we either don't remember or misidentify the source of a memory.

■ The **misinformation effect,** schema distortion, and source confusion can contribute to inaccuracies in eyewitness testimony.

■ Memory tends to be fairly accurate for the general gist of experiences. Meaningful or important details are least likely to be forgotten. Distorted or false memories can be just as vivid as accurate memories.

Forgetting: *You Forgot the Plane Tickets?!*

■ **Forgetting** refers to the inability to recall information that was previously available. The general pattern of forgetting is reflected in the forgetting curve, which is based on the classic research of Hermann Ebbinghaus.

■ **Encoding failure** is one cause of forgetting. According to **interference theory,** forgetting results from **retroactive** and **proactive interference** with other information. **Motivated forgetting** can result from **suppression** or **repression.** Research support for repression is mixed. **Decay theory** is another explanation for forgetting.

The Search for the Biological Basis of Memory

■ After extensive research, Karl Lashley concluded that memories are distributed rather than localized as a **memory trace.** Richard Thompson showed the physical changes that are associated with a simple conditioned reflex in rabbits. Today, it is believed that memories are both localized and distributed. Complex memories involve interrelated changes among many different brain areas.

■ Eric Kandel showed that functional and structural changes in neurons are associated with acquiring a conditioned reflex in the sea snail *Aplysia*. Enduring memories are believed to be stored through **long-term potentiation,** a long-lasting increase in synaptic strength.

■ **Retrograde amnesia** results when **memory consolidation** is disrupted. **Anterograde amnesia** results when the hippocampus is damaged, as in the case of H. M. **Amnesia** affects episodic memories rather than procedural memories, and explicit memory rather than implicit memory. Brain structures involved in memory include the hippocampus, the amygdala, the cerebellum, and the prefrontal cortex. Impaired memory is a symptom of senile dementia and Alzheimer's disease.

Key Terms

memory, p. 239

encoding, p. 239

storage, p. 239

retrieval, p. 239

stage model of memory, p. 239

sensory memory, p. 240

short-term memory (working memory), p. 240

long-term memory, p. 240

maintenance rehearsal, p. 243

chunking, p. 244

elaborative rehearsal, p. 245

levels-of-processing framework, p. 246

procedural memory, p. 246

episodic memory, p. 246

semantic memory, p. 246

explicit memory, p. 248

implicit memory, p. 248

clustering, p. 249

semantic network model, p. 249

retrieval, p. 251

retrieval cue, p. 251

retrieval cue failure, p. 251

tip-of-the-tongue (TOT) experience, p. 251

recall, p. 252

cued recall, p. 252

recognition, p. 252

serial position effect, p. 252

encoding specificity principle, p. 252

context effect, p. 253

state-dependent retrieval, p. 253

mood congruence, p. 254

flashbulb memory, p. 254

schema, p. 255

source confusion, p. 256

cryptomnesia, p. 257

misinformation effect, p. 258

forgetting, p. 260

encoding failure, p. 262

interference theory, p. 262

retroactive interference, p. 262

proactive interference, p. 262

motivated forgetting, p. 263

suppression, p. 263

repression, p. 263

decay theory, p. 265

memory trace, p. 266

long-term potentiation, p. 269

amnesia, p. 270

retrograde amnesia, p. 270

memory consolidation, p. 271

anterograde amnesia, p. 271

Key People

Hermann Ebbinghaus (1850–1909)   German psychologist who originated the scientific study of forgetting; plotted the first forgetting curve, which describes the basic pattern of forgetting learned information over time. (p. 260)

Eric Kandel (b. 1929)   American neurobiologist, born in Austria, who won the Nobel Prize in 2000 for his work on the neural basis of learning and memory in the sea snail *Aplysia*. (p. 268)

Karl Lashley (1890–1958)   American physiological psychologist who attempted to find the specific brain location of particular memories. (p. 266)

Elizabeth F. Loftus (b. 1944)   American psychologist who has conducted extensive research on the memory distortions that can occur in eyewitness testimony. (p. 258)

George Sperling (b. 1934)   American psychologist who identified the duration of visual sensory memory in a series of classic experiments in 1960. (p. 241)

Richard F. Thompson (b. 1930)   American psychologist and neuroscientist who has conducted extensive research on the neurobiological foundations of learning and memory. (p. 267).

Concept Review Answers

6.1   page 250

1. LTM   *2.* SM   *3.* STM   *4.* LTM

5. STM   *6.* SM   *7.* STM   *8.* SM   *9.* LTM

6.2   page 265

1. d   *2.* a   *3.* b   *4.* b   *5.* d

6.3   page 270

1. George Sperling

2. Elizabeth Loftus

3. Hermann Ebbinghaus

4. Karl Lashley

5. Richard F. Thompson

6. Eric Kandel

Judgment Day

Thinking, Language, and Intelligence

Prologue

Mr. and Ms. Fix-It

"I found it! The rubber gasket between the sink and faucet is leaking!" Don yelled from under the kitchen sink.

"The *basket* is leaking!" our then three-year-old daughter, Laura, who was holding the flashlight, enthusiastically relayed to Sandy.

"The *basket* is leaking?" Sandy asked. "What basket?"

"No, it's called a *gasket,* not a *basket,* honey," Don explained to Laura.

"Can you fix it?" Sandy asked.

"Piece of cake," Don replied as he crawled out from under the sink. "Laura and I will run down to the hardware store and just buy a new gasket."

Of course, the solution would not be that simple. "They don't sell *just* the gasket," the clerk at the hardware store explained. "You have to buy a whole new faucet."

"What's that going to run me?"

"Kitchen faucets start at $39.95 plus tax," the hardware guy smiled. "Then you'll need some replacement tubing for when you weld the new faucet in place. You have a welding torch, don't you? If you don't, a plumber probably wouldn't charge more than $150 or so to install it, not including the cost of the parts."

"Let me think about it," Don replied, frowning.

"Why didn't we buy a new basket?" Laura asked as she and Don walked out of the hardware store.

"It's called a *gasket,* Laura," Don explained. "It's just a piece of rubber that fits between two pieces of metal. It keeps the water that splashes around the faucet from dripping under the sink. Does that make sense?"

"I think so," Laura said thoughtfully. "Why didn't we buy one?"

"Because they want too much money for it," Don answered as he buckled Laura into her car seat.

As Laura chattered away on the drive home, Don mulled over calling a plumber. *A couple hundred bucks to replace a lousy piece of rubber. That's ridiculous.*

"We'll make one!" Don suddenly exclaimed.

"Make what, Daddy?" Laura responded, slightly startled.

"A new gasket! And best of all, Laura, it won't cost a cent!"

Less than five minutes later, Don and Laura were at a General Tire store. "Help yourself," the manager replied when Don asked if he could have a discarded inner tube. An hour later, the new "gasket" was in place—a piece of black rubber inner tube that Don had cut to the same shape as the original gasket. It worked like a charm. No drips.

"You missed your calling in life," Sandy quipped as Don stood basking in the glory of the moment.

cognition
The mental activities involved in acquiring, retaining, and using knowledge.

thinking
The manipulation of mental representations of information in order to draw inferences and conclusions.

mental image
A mental representation of objects or events that are not physically present.

"Hey, you just have to think creatively," Don smiled back.

Unfortunately, creative thinking is not always the answer. A few weeks later, when the upstairs toilet wouldn't flush properly, Mr. Fix-It spent almost two hours dismantling and lifting the entire toilet off the floor drain in search of the cause.

"You're sure you didn't flush one of your toys down the toilet?" Don asked Laura again.

"No, Daddy," Laura said solemnly, shaking her head, as she peered down the ominous-looking drain in the floor with her Barney flashlight.

"Well, I don't know what the hell is wrong with it," Don announced in frustration, wiping the sweat from his brow.

Sitting on the floor in the corner of the bathroom, Sandy flipped through the pages of a book called *The Complete Home Fix-It-Yourself Manual.* "Did you look at this book? There's a troubleshooting guide for toilets on this page."

"No, I did *not* look at it," Don huffed cynically. "I *know* how to unblock a toilet. First, you try a plunger. If that doesn't work, then you take the toilet off to find whatever is blocking the drain."

"That's what it lists to try *third* in this book," Sandy pointed out calmly. "What was the water level inside the tank?"

"It was a couple inches down from the fill line," Don answered.

"Well, it says here that if the water level is too low, the toilet bowl will drain sluggishly," Sandy explained matter-of-factly, then glanced up. "Did you try raising the water level to the fill line *before* you took the toilet apart?"

Silence loomed in the bathroom.

Well over an hour later Laura excitedly called downstairs to Sandy, "Mama! Mama! Come see! Daddy fixed the toilet."

"What was wrong with it?" Sandy innocently asked as she watched the toilet flush perfectly.

"The water level was just too low," Don replied, then cleared his throat.

"You're kidding!" Sandy feigned disbelief. "That must have been why it was listed as the *first* thing to check in that troubleshooting guide."

"I think you missed your calling in life," Don muttered.

"Well, you know what I always say, 'When in doubt, look it up!'" Sandy smiled.

All of us rely on a variety of cognitive processes to imagine, think, make decisions, and solve problems in daily life. In this chapter, we'll look at the broad issue of how we think, including how we solve problems, make decisions, and occasionally arrive at creative solutions. In the process, we'll come back to this story of Mr. and Ms. Fix-It to help illustrate several important concepts and ideas.

Introduction
Thinking, Language, and Intelligence

Key Theme
▪ *Thinking* is a broad term that refers to how we use knowledge to analyze situations, solve problems, and make decisions.

Key Questions
▪ What are some of the basic characteristics of mental images?
▪ How do we manipulate mental images?
▪ What are concepts, and how are they formed?

Cognition is a general term that refers to the mental activities involved in acquiring, retaining, and using knowledge. In previous chapters, we've looked at fundamental cognitive processes such as perception, learning, and memory. These processes are critical in order for us to acquire and retain new knowledge.

In this chapter, we will focus on how we *use* that knowledge to analyze situations, solve problems, make decisions, and use language. As you'll see, such cognitive abilities are widely regarded as key dimensions of *intelligence*—a concept that we will also explore.

The Building Blocks of Thought
Mental Imagery and Concepts

In the most general sense, *thinking* is involved in all conscious mental activity, whether it is acquiring new knowledge, remembering, planning ahead, or daydreaming (Holyoak & Spellman, 1993). More narrowly, we can say that **thinking** involves manipulating mental representations of information in order to draw inferences and conclusions. Thinking, then, involves active mental processes and is often directed toward some goal, purpose, or conclusion.

What exactly is it that we think *with*? Thinking often involves the manipulation of two forms of mental representations: *mental images* and *concepts*. We'll look first at mental images.

Mental Images

When you read the Prologue, did you form a mental picture of a little girl peering down a cavernous floor drain with her Barney flashlight? Or Sandy sitting in the corner of the bathroom, looking at the home repair manual? The stories we tell in our prologues typically lend themselves to the creation of mental images. Formally, a **mental image** is a mental representation of objects or events that are not physically present.

We often rely on mental images to accomplish some cognitive task (Farah, 1995). For example, try reciting the letters of the alphabet that consist of only curved lines. To accomplish this task, you have to mentally visualize and then inspect an image of each letter of the alphabet.

Note that mental imagery is not strictly limited to visual "pictures." Most people are able to form images that involve senses other than vision (McKellar, 1972). For example, you can probably easily create a mental representation for the taste and texture of a chocolate milk shake, or the feel of wet clothing sticking to your skin. Nonetheless, most research on mental images has looked at how we manipulate visual images, and we'll focus on visual images in our discussion here.

Do people manipulate mental images in the same way that they manipulate their visual images of actual objects? Suppose we gave you a map of the United States and asked you to visually locate San Francisco. Then suppose we asked you to fix your gaze on another city. If the other city was far away from San Francisco (like New York), it would take you longer to visually locate it than if it was close by (like Los Angeles). If you were scanning a *mental* image rather than an actual map, would it also take you longer to scan across a greater distance?

In a classic study by Stephen Kosslyn and his colleagues (1978), participants first viewed and memorized a map of a fictitious island with distinct locations, such as a lake, a hut, and grass (see Figure 7.1). After the map was removed, participants were asked to imagine a specific location on the island, such as the sandy beach. Then a second location, such as the rock, was named. The participants mentally scanned across their mental image of the map and pushed a button when they reached the rock.

The researchers found that the amount of time it took to mentally scan to the new location was directly related to the distance between the two points. The greater the distance between the two points, the longer it took to scan the mental image of the map (Kosslyn & others, 1978).

It seems, then, that we tend to scan a mental image in much the same way that we visually scan an actual image (Kosslyn & Thompson, 2000).

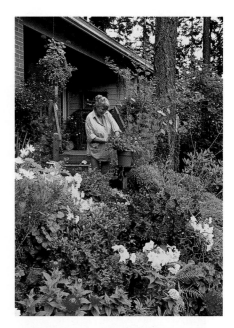

A Flower for Your Thoughts? What types of cognitive activities might be involved in growing an elaborate flower garden? Planning, forming mental images, making decisions, and problem solving are some of the mental activities that successful gardening requires.

FIGURE 7.1 Mentally Scanning Images This is a reduced version of the map used by Stephen Kosslyn and his colleagues (1978) to study the scanning of mental images. After subjects memorized the map, the map was removed. Subjects then mentally scanned from one location to another. As you can see by the average scanning times, it took subjects longer to scan greater distances on their mental images of the map, just as it takes longer to scan greater distances on an actual map.

*focus on*Neuroscience

FACE

Subject 1 — perception
Subject 2 — perception

imagery — imagery

PLACE

Subject 1 — perception
Subject 2 — perception

imagery — imagery

Brain Activation During Perception and Mental Imagery
Shown here are the fMRIs of two participants in O'Craven and Kanwisher's (2000) study. Notice that the same brain areas are activated while perceiving or imagining a familiar face. Likewise, the same brain areas are activated while perceiving or imagining a familiar place. Also notice that the brain activation is slightly stronger in the perception condition than in the mental imagery condition.

Seeing Faces and Places in the Mind's Eye Until the advent of sophisticated brain-scanning techniques, studying mental imagery relied on cognitive tasks, such as measuring how long participants reported it took to scan a mental image (see Kosslyn & others, 2001). Today, however, psychologists are using brain-imaging techniques to study mental imagery. One important issue is whether mental images activate the same brain areas that are involved in perception. Remember, perception takes place when the brain registers information that is received directly from sensory organs.

Previously, researchers have found that perceiving certain types of scenes or objects activates specific brain areas. For example, when we look at *faces,* a brain area dubbed the *fusiform facial area (FFA)* is activated. When we look at pictures of *places,* a different brain area, called the *parahippocampal place area,* or *PPA,* is activated (Epstein & Kanwisher, 1998; Kanwisher, 2001). Given those findings, the critical question is this: If we simply *imagine* faces or places, would the same brain areas be activated?

To answer that question, psychologists Kathleen O'Craven and Nancy Kanwisher (2000) used functional magnetic resonance imaging (fMRI) to compare brain activity during perception and imagery. Study participants underwent fMRI scans while they looked at pho-

tographs of familiar faces and places (scenes from their college campus). Next, the participants were asked to close their eyes and form a vivid mental image of each of the photographs that they had just viewed.

Three key findings emerged from the study. First, as you can see from the fMRI scans of two participants shown here, *imagining* a face or place activated the same brain region that is activated when *perceiving* a face or a place. More specifically, forming a mental image of a place activated the parahippocampal place area. And forming a mental image of a face activated the fusiform facial area.

Second, compared to imaging a face or place, the perception of an actual face or place evoked a stronger brain response, as indicated by the slightly larger red and yellow areas in the perception fMRIs (upper row). Third, because the brain responses between the two conditions were so distinctive, O'Craven and Kanwisher could determine what the participants were imagining—faces or places—simply from looking at the fMRI scans.

Clearly, perception and mental images share common brain mechanisms. So at least as far as the brain is concerned, "the next best thing to being there" might just be closing your eyes and going there in your mind's eye.

concept
A mental category of objects or ideas based on properties they share.

formal concept
A mental category that is formed by learning the rules or features that define it.

natural concept
A mental category that is formed as a result of everyday experience.

However, we don't simply look at mental images in our minds. Sometimes thinking involves the *manipulation* of mental images before we can arrive at an answer. For example, try the problem in Figure 7.2.

It probably took you longer to determine that the 3 in the middle was backward than to determine that the 3 on the far left was backward. Determining which 3s were backward required you to mentally *rotate* each one to an upright position. Just as it takes time to rotate a physical object, it takes time to mentally rotate an image. Furthermore, the greater the degree of rotation required, the longer it takes you to rotate the image mentally (Wohlschläger & Wohlschläger, 1998). Thus, it probably took you longer to mentally rotate the 3 in the middle, which you had to rotate 180 degrees, than it did to mentally rotate the 3 on the far left, which you only had to rotate 60 degrees.

Collectively, research seems to indicate that we manipulate mental images much as we manipulate the actual objects they represent (Rosenbaum & others, 2001). However, mental images are not perfect duplicates of our actual sensory experience. The mental images we use in thinking have some features in common with actual visual images, but they are not like photographs. Instead, they are *memories* of visual images. And, like memories, visual images are actively constructed and potentially subject to error (Reisberg & Chambers, 1991).

FIGURE 7.2 Manipulating Mental Images Two of these threes are backward. Which ones?

Concepts

Along with mental images, thinking also involves the use of concepts. A **concept** is a mental category we have formed to group objects, events, or situations that share similar features or characteristics. Concepts provide a kind of mental shorthand, economizing the cognitive effort required for thinking and communication.

Using concepts makes it easier to communicate with others, remember information, and learn new information. For example, the concept "food" might include anything from a sardine to a rutabaga. Although very different, we can still group rutabagas and sardines together because they share the central feature of being edible. If someone introduces us to a new delicacy and tells us it is *food*, we immediately know that it is something to eat—even if it is something we've never seen before.

Adding to the efficiency of our thinking is our tendency to organize the concepts we hold into orderly hierarchies composed of main categories and subcategories (Markman & Gentner, 2001). Thus a very general concept, such as "furniture," can be mentally divided into a variety of subcategories: tables, chairs, lamps, and so forth. As we learn the key properties that define general concepts, we also learn how members of the concept are related to one another.

How are concepts formed? When we form a concept by learning the *rules* or *features* that define the particular concept, it is called a **formal concept.** Children are taught the specific rules or features that define many simple formal concepts, such as geometric shapes. These defining rules or features can be simple or complex. In either case, the rules are logical but rigid. If the defining features, or *attributes,* are present, then the object is included as a member or example of that concept. For some formal concepts, this rigid all-or-nothing categorization procedure works well. For example, a substance can be categorized as a solid, liquid, or gas. The rules defining these formal concepts are very clear-cut.

However, as psychologist Eleanor Rosch (1973) pointed out, the features that define categories of natural objects and events in everyday life are seldom as clear-cut as the features that define formal concepts. A **natural concept** is a concept formed as a result of everyday experience rather than by logically determining whether an object or event fits a specific set of rules. Rosch suggested that, unlike formal concepts, natural concepts have "fuzzy boundaries." That is, the rules or attributes that define natural concepts are not always sharply defined.

Because natural concepts have fuzzy boundaries, it's often easier to classify some members of natural concepts than others (Rosch & Mervis, 1975). To illustrate this point, think about the defining features or rules that you usually associate with the natural concept "vehicle." With virtually no hesitation, you can say that a car, truck, and bus are all examples of this natural concept. How about a sled? Wheelbarrow? Raft? Elevator? It probably took you a few seconds to determine whether these objects are also vehicles. Why are some members of natural concepts easier to classify than others?

Are These Mammals? The more closely an item matches the prototype of a concept, the more quickly we can identify the item as being an example of that concept. Because bats and dolphins don't fit our prototype for a mammal, it takes us longer to decide whether they belong to the category "mammal" than it does to classify animals that are closer to the prototype.

Table | **7.1**

From Prototypes to Atypical Examples

Vehicles	Fruit
car	orange
truck	apple
bus	banana
motorcycle	peach
train	pear
trolley car	apricot
bicycle	plum
airplane	grape
boat	strawberry
tractor	grapefruit
cart	pineapple
wheelchair	blueberry
tank	lemon
raft	watermelon
sled	honeydew
horse	pomegranate
blimp	date
skates	coconut
wheelbarrow	tomato
elevator	olive

SOURCE: Rosch & Mervis (1975).

The first items listed under each general concept are the ones most people tend to think of as the prototype examples of that concept. Farther down the list, the items become progressively less similar to the prototype examples.

prototype
The most typical instance of a particular concept.

problem solving
Thinking and behavior directed toward attaining a goal that is not readily available.

trial and error
A problem-solving strategy that involves attempting different solutions and eliminating those that do not work.

According to Rosch (1978), some members are better representatives of a natural concept than are others. The "best," or most typical, instance of a particular concept is called a **prototype** (Mervis & Rosch, 1981; Rosch, 1978). We tend to determine whether an object is an instance of a natural concept by comparing it to the prototype we have developed rather than by logically evaluating whether the defining features are present or absent.

The more closely an item matches the prototype, the more quickly we can identify it as being an example of that concept. For example, it usually takes us longer to identify an olive or a coconut as being a fruit because they are so dissimilar from the prototypes we typically think of as fruit, such as apples and oranges (Rosch & Mervis, 1975) (see Table 7.1).

As the two building blocks of thinking, mental images and concepts help us impose order on the phenomena we encounter and think about. We often rely on this knowledge when we engage in complex cognitive tasks, such as solving problems and making decisions, which we'll consider next.

Solving Problems and Making Decisions

Key Theme

▥ *Problem solving* refers to thinking and behavior directed toward attaining a goal that is not readily available.

Key Questions

▥ **What are some advantages and disadvantages of each problem-solving strategy?**

▥ **What is insight and how does intuition work?**

▥ **How can functional fixedness and mental set interfere with problem solving?**

From fixing flat tires to figuring out how to pay for college classes, we engage in the cognitive task of problem solving so routinely that we often don't even notice the processes we follow. Formally, **problem solving** refers to thinking and behavior directed toward attaining a goal that is not readily available.

Before you can solve a problem, you must develop an accurate understanding of the problem. Correctly identifying the problem is a key step in successful problem solving (Bransford & Stein, 1993). If your representation of the problem is flawed, your attempts to solve it will also be flawed. This is exactly what happened when Mr. Fix-It attempted to fix the upstairs toilet. Because the water drained sluggishly, Don assumed that something was blocking the drain. Armed with an erroneous representation of the problem, Don launched a strategy to solve a problem that didn't even exist.

Problem-Solving Strategies

As a general rule, people tend to attack a problem in an organized or systematic way. Usually, the strategy you select is influenced by the nature of the problem and the amount of time you're willing to invest in solving it. In this section, we'll look at some of the common strategies used in problem solving.

Trial and Error: A Process of Elimination

The strategy of **trial and error** involves actually trying a variety of solutions and eliminating those that don't work. When there is a limited range of possible solutions, trial and error can be a useful problem-solving strategy. If you were try-

DRABBLE

ing to develop a new spaghetti sauce recipe, for example, you might use trial and error to fine-tune the seasonings.

When the range of possible answers or solutions is large, however, trial and error can be very time-consuming. For example, our friend Thomas typically learns new computer programs by trial and error. Rather than taking 20 minutes to look through the manual, he'll spend hours trying different menu commands to see if he can make the software do what it's supposed to do.

Algorithms: Guaranteed to Work

Unlike trial and error, an **algorithm** is a procedure or method that, when followed step by step, always produces the correct solution. Mathematical formulas are examples of algorithms. For instance, the formula used to convert temperatures from Celsius to Fahrenheit—multiply C by 9/5, then add 32—is an algorithm.

Even though an algorithm may be guaranteed to eventually produce a solution, using an algorithm is not always practical. For example, imagine that while rummaging in a closet you find a combination lock with no combination attached. Using an algorithm will eventually produce the correct combination. You can start with 0–0–0, then try 0–0–1, followed by 0–0–2, and so forth, and systematically work your way through combinations to 36–36–36. But this solution would take a while, because there are 46,656 potential combinations to try. So, although using an algorithm to generate the correct combination for the combination lock is guaranteed to work eventually, it's not a very practical approach to solving this particular problem.

Heuristics: Rules of Thumb

In contrast to an algorithm, a **heuristic** is a general rule-of-thumb strategy that may or may not work. Although heuristic strategies are not guaranteed to solve a given problem, they tend to simplify problem solving because they let you reduce the number of possible solutions. With a more limited range of solutions, you can use trial and error to eventually arrive at the correct one.

Here's an example. Creating footnotes is described somewhere in the manual for a word-processing computer program. If you use the algorithm of reading every page of the manual, you're guaranteed to solve the problem eventually. But you can greatly simplify your task by using the heuristic of looking up "footnotes" in the manual's index. This strategy does not guarantee success, because the procedure may not be listed in the index.

The Prologue to this chapter contained a couple of examples of heuristics. In the case of the leaking faucet, Don resorted to the familiar homeowner's heuristic of going to the hardware store to buy a replacement. Notice, however, that this heuristic did not result in an acceptable solution. And in trying to solve the problem of the malfunctioning toilet, Sandy relied on her favorite heuristic: She looked for potential solutions in a book on the subject. Of course, this particular heuristic will work only when there's a book available that describes how to solve a specific problem.

algorithm
A problem-solving strategy that involves following a specific rule, procedure, or method that inevitably produces the correct solution.

heuristic
A problem-solving strategy that involves following a general rule of thumb to reduce the number of possible solutions.

One common heuristic is to break a problem into a series of *subgoals.* This strategy is often used in writing a term paper. Choosing a topic, locating information about the topic, organizing the information, and so on become a series of subproblems. As you solve each subproblem, you move closer to solving the larger problem.

Another useful heuristic involves *working backward* from the goal. Starting with the end point, you determine the steps necessary to reach your final goal. For example, when making a budget, people often start off with the goal of spending no more than a certain total each month, then work backward to determine how much of the target amount they will allot for each category of expenses.

Insight and Intuition

Finally, the solution to some problems seems to arrive in a sudden realization, or flash of **insight,** that happens after you mull a problem over (Kaplan & Simon, 1990). Sometimes an insight will occur when you recognize how the problem is similar to a previously solved problem. Or an insight can involve the sudden realization that an object can be used in a novel way, such as Don's realization that he could make an inexpensive replacement gasket for the kitchen sink from a discarded inner tube. Try your hand at the two problems in Figure 7.3. The solution to each of those problems is often achieved by insight.

Problem 1	Six drinking glasses are lined up in a row. The first three are full of water, the last three are empty. By handling and moving only one glass, change the arrangement so that no full glass is next to another full one, and no empty glass is next to another empty one.
Problem 2	A man who lived in a small town married 20 different women in that same town. All of them are still living, and he never divorced any of them. Yet he broke no laws. How could he do this?

FIGURE 7.3 A Demonstration of Insightful Solutions The solutions to these problems are often characterized by sudden flashes of insight. See if you have the "That's it!" experience in solving these problems without looking at the solutions on page 288.

SOURCE: Adapted from Ashcraft (1994); problem 2 adapted from Sternberg (1986).

Insights rarely occur through the conscious manipulation of concepts or information (Schooler & others, 1993). In fact, you're usually not aware of the thought processes that led to an insight. Increasingly, cognitive psychologists and neuroscientists are investigating nonconscious processes, including unconscious problem solving, insight, and intuition (M. Lieberman, 2000; Underwood, 1996). **Intuition** means coming to a conclusion or making a judgment without conscious awareness of the thought processes involved.

Canadian psychologist Kenneth Bowers and his colleagues (1990) have proposed a two-stage model of intuition. In the first stage, called the *guiding stage,* you perceive a pattern in the information you're considering, but not consciously. The perception of such patterns is based on your expertise in a given area and your memories of related information.

In the second stage, the *integrative stage,* a representation of the pattern becomes conscious, usually in the form of a hunch or hypothesis. At this point, conscious analytic thought processes take over. You systematically attempt to prove or disprove the hypothesis. For example, an experienced doctor might integrate both obvious and subtle cues to recognize a pattern in a patient's symptoms, a pattern that takes the form of a hunch or an educated guess. Once the hunch is consciously formulated, she might order lab tests to confirm or disprove her tentative diagnosis.

An intuitive hunch, then, is a new idea that integrates new information with existing knowledge stored in long-term memory. Such hunches are likely to be accurate only in contexts in which you already have a broad base of knowledge and experience (M. Lieberman, 2000).

Obstacles to Solving Problems
Functional Fixedness and Mental Sets

When we view objects as functioning only in the usual or customary way, we're engaging in a tendency called **functional fixedness.** Functional fixedness often prevents us from seeing the full range of ways in which an object can be used. To get a feel for how functional fixedness can interfere with your ability to find a solution, try the problem in Figure 7.4.

Here's an example of functional fixedness. When pilots fly through clouds, they watch an instrument called an artificial horizon, which shows an outline of an airplane against a horizontal line that represents the horizon. By watching the movement of the outline, they can tell if the aircraft is tilting up or down, or banking to the left or right.

When Don was first learning to fly, he was publicly chastised by a salty old flight instructor for failing to wear a St. Christopher's medal around his neck when flying. Since St. Christopher is the patron saint of travelers, Don assumed that the flight instructor was a bit superstitious. Don's functional fixedness kept him from thinking of any other reason for a pilot to wear a St. Christopher's medal. Finally, Don asked the instructor.

It turned out that a St. Christopher's medal or any other object on a chain can be used to create a makeshift artificial horizon if the flight instrument should fail. You simply drape the chain over the throttle stick. If the aircraft starts pointing down, the medal swings forward; if the aircraft starts pointing upward, the medal swings back. When the aircraft banks, the medal swings to one side or the other. This novel use of an object could literally save the lives of the people in the plane.

Another common obstacle to problem solving is **mental set**—the tendency to persist in solving problems with solutions that have worked in the past. Obviously, if a solution has worked in the past, there's good reason to consider using it again. However, if we approach a problem with a rigid mental set, we may not see other possible solutions. For example, Don's initial attempt to fix the toilet reflected his mental set that when the water in a toilet doesn't drain properly, the drain is probably clogged. Since using a plunger had solved such problems in the past, it made sense to try that solution again.

Mental sets can sometimes suggest a useful heuristic. But they can also prevent us from coming up with new, and possibly more effective, solutions. If we try to be flexible in our thinking and overcome the tendency toward mental sets, we can often identify simpler solutions to many common problems. Because Sandy did not have any particular mental sets about malfunctioning toilets, she was able to search for and identify an alternative solution that not only worked, but was also much simpler than Don's attempted solution to the problem.

FIGURE 7.4 Overcoming Functional Fixedness Here's a classic problem for you to solve. You have two candles, some thumbtacks, and a box of matches. Using just these objects, try to figure out how to mount the candles on a wall. (The solution is on p. 288.)

SOURCE: Adapted from Duncker (1945).

Decision-Making Strategies

Key Theme

- Different cognitive strategies are used when making decisions, depending on the type and number of options available to us.

Key Questions

- What are the single-feature model, the additive model, and the elimination by aspects model of decision making?
- Under what conditions is each strategy most appropriate?
- How do we use the availability and representativeness heuristics to help us estimate the likelihood of an event?

Who hasn't felt like flipping a coin when faced with an important or complicated decision? Fortunately, most of the decisions we make in everyday life are relatively minor. But every now and then we have to make a decision where much more is at stake. When a decision is important or complex, we're more likely to invest time, effort, and other resources in considering different options.

The decision-making process becomes complicated when each option involves the consideration of several features. It's rare that one alternative is superior in every category. So, what do you do when each alternative has pros and cons? In this section, we'll describe three common decision-making strategies.

insight
The sudden realization of how a problem can be solved.

intuition
Coming to a conclusion or making a judgment without conscious awareness of the thought processes involved.

functional fixedness
The tendency to view objects as functioning only in their usual or customary way.

mental set
The tendency to persist in solving problems with solutions that have worked in the past.

| **Problem 1** | Pour the water in glass number 2 into glass number 5. |
| **Problem 2** | The man is a minister. |

Solutions to the Problems in Figure 7.3

The Single-Feature Model

One decision-making strategy is called the *single-feature model*. In order to simplify the choice among many alternatives, you base your decision on a single feature. When the decision is a minor one, the single-feature model can be a good decision-making strategy. For example, faced with an entire aisle of laundry detergents, you could simplify your decision by deciding to buy the cheapest brand. When a decision is important or complex, however, making decisions on the basis of a single feature can increase the riskiness of the decision.

The Additive Model

A better strategy for complex decisions is to systematically evaluate the important features of each alternative. One such decision-making model is called the *additive model.*

In this model, you first generate a list of the factors that are most important to you. Then, you rate each alternative on each factor using an arbitrary scale, such as −5 to +5. If a particular factor has strong advantages or appeal, you give it the maximum rating (+5). If a particular factor has strong drawbacks or disadvantages, you give it the minimum rating (−5). Finally, you add up the ratings for each alternative. This strategy can often reveal the best overall choice. If the decision involves a situation in which some factors are more important than others, you can emphasize the more important factors by multiplying the rating.

Taking the time to apply the additive model to important decisions can greatly improve your decision making. By allowing you to evaluate the features of one alternative at a time, then comparing the alternatives, the additive model provides a logical strategy for identifying the most acceptable choice from a range of possible decisions. Although we seldom formally calculate the subjective value of individual features for different options, we often informally use the additive model by comparing two choices feature by feature. The alternative with the "best" collection of features is then selected.

The Elimination by Aspects Model

Psychologist Amos Tversky (1972) proposed another decision-making model called the *elimination by aspects model.* Using this model, you evaluate all the alternatives one characteristic at a time, typically starting with the feature you consider most important. If a particular alternative fails to meet that criterion, you scratch it off your list of possible choices, even if it possesses other desirable attributes. As the range of possible choices is narrowed down, you continue to compare the remaining alternatives, one feature at a time, until just one alternative is left.

For example, suppose you want to buy a new computer. You might initially eliminate all the models that aren't powerful enough to run the software you need to use, then the models outside your budget, and so forth. Continuing in this fashion, you would progressively narrow down the range of possible choices to the one choice that satisfies all your criteria.

Good decision makers adapt their strategy to the demands of the specific situation (Payne & others, 1993). If there are just a few choices and features to compare, people tend to use the additive method, at least informally. However, when the decision is complex, involving the comparison of many choices that have multiple features, people often use *both* strategies. That is, we usually begin by focusing on the critical features, using the elimination by aspects strategy to quickly narrow down the range of acceptable choices. Once we have narrowed the list of choices down to a more manageable shortlist, we tend to use the additive model to make a final decision.

Solution to Figure 7.4

Decisions Involving Uncertainty
Estimating the Probability of Events

Some decisions involve a high degree of uncertainty. In these cases, you need to make a decision, but you are unable to predict with certainty that a given event will occur. Instead, you have to estimate the probability of an event occurring. But how do you actually make that estimation?

For example, imagine that you're running late for a very important appointment. You may be faced with this decision: "Should I risk a speeding ticket to get to the appointment on time?" In this case, you would have to estimate the probability of a particular event occurring—getting pulled over for speeding.

In such instances, we often estimate the likelihood that certain events will occur, then gamble. In deciding what the odds are that a particular gamble will go our way, we tend to rely on two rule-of-thumb strategies to help us estimate the likelihood of events: the *availability heuristic* and the *representativeness heuristic* (Tversky & Kahneman, 1982).

The Availability Heuristic

When we use the **availability heuristic,** we estimate the likelihood of an event on the basis of how readily available other instances of the event are in our memory. When instances of an event are easily recalled, we tend to consider the event as being more likely to occur. So, we're less likely to exceed the speed limit if we can readily recall that a friend recently got a speeding ticket.

However, when a rare event makes a vivid impression on us, we may overestimate its likelihood (Tversky & Kahneman, 1982). Companies like Publishers Clearing House and American Family Publishers capitalize on this cognitive tendency by running many TV commercials showing that lucky person who won the $10 million sweepstakes prize. A vivid memory is created, which leads viewers to an inaccurate estimate of the likelihood that the event will happen to them.

The key point here is that the less accurately our memory of an event reflects the actual frequency of the event, the less accurate our estimate of the event's likelihood will be. That's why the sweepstakes commercials don't show the other 50 million people staring dejectedly at their mailboxes because they did *not* win the $10 million.

The Representativeness Heuristic

The other heuristic we often use to make estimates is called the **representativeness heuristic** (Kahneman & Tversky, 1982). Here, we estimate an event's likelihood by comparing how similar its essential features are to our prototype of the event. Remember, a *prototype* is the most typical example of an object or an event.

To go back to our example of deciding whether to speed, we are more likely to risk speeding if we think that we're somehow significantly different from the prototype of the driver who gets a speeding ticket. If our prototype of a speeder is a teenager driving a flashy, high-performance car, and we're an adult driving a minivan with a baby seat, then we will probably estimate the likelihood of our getting a speeding ticket as low.

Like the availability heuristic, the representativeness heuristic can lead to inaccurate judgments. Consider the following description:

> Maria is a perceptive, sensitive, introspective woman. She is very articulate, but measures her words carefully. Once she's certain she knows what she wants to say, she expresses herself easily and confidently. She has a strong preference to work alone.

availability heuristic
A strategy in which the likelihood of an event is estimated on the basis of how readily available other instances of the event are in memory.

representativeness heuristic
A strategy in which the likelihood of an event is estimated by comparing how similar it is to the prototype of the event.

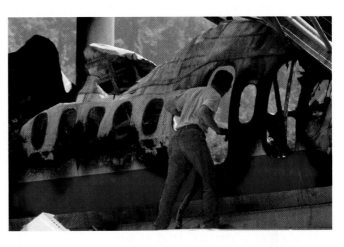

Vivid Images and the Availability Heuristic This American Airlines jet crashed while attempting to land during a thunderstorm in Little Rock, Arkansas. The jet broke into pieces and then burst into flames, killing the pilot and several passengers. After seeing such vivid images in the media coverage of a plane crash, many people become more fearful about air travel, because they overestimate the likelihood that the plane they're traveling in might crash. How does the availability heuristic explain this phenomenon?

The Persistence of Unwarranted Beliefs

Throughout this text, we show how many pseudoscientific claims have been scientifically investigated and disproven. However, once a belief in a pseudoscience or paranormal phenomenon is established, the presentation of contradictory evidence often has little impact (Lester, 2000). Ironically, contradictory evidence can actually *strengthen* a person's established beliefs (Lord & others, 1979). How do psychologists account for this?

Several psychological studies have explored how people deal with evidence, especially evidence that contradicts their beliefs (see Ross & Anderson, 1982; Zusne & Jones, 1989). The four obstacles to logical thinking described here can account for much of the persistence of unwarranted beliefs in pseudosciences or other areas.

Obstacle 1: The Belief-Bias Effect

The *belief-bias effect* occurs when people accept only the evidence that conforms to their belief, rejecting or ignoring any evidence that does not. For example, in a classic study conducted by Warren Jones and Dan Russell (1980), ESP believers and ESP disbelievers watched two attempts at telepathic communication. In each attempt, a "receiver" tried to indicate what card the "sender" was holding.

In reality, both attempts were rigged. One attempt was designed to appear to be a successful demonstration of telepathy, with a significant number of accurate responses. The other attempt was designed to convincingly demonstrate failure. In this case, the number of accurate guesses was no more than chance and could be produced by simple random guessing.

Following the demonstration, the participants were asked what they believed had taken place. Both believers and disbelievers indicated that ESP had occurred in the successful attempt. But only the believers said that ESP had also taken place in the clearly *unsuccessful* attempt. In other words, the ESP believers ignored or discounted the evidence in the failed attempt. This is the essence of the belief-bias effect.

Obstacle 2: Confirmation Bias

Confirmation bias is the strong tendency to search for information or evidence that confirms a belief, while making lit-

By Sidney Harris

"WHAT'S NICE ABOUT WORKING IN THIS PLACE IS WE DON'T HAVE TO FINISH ANY OF OUR EXPERIMENTS."

tle or no effort to search for information that might disprove the belief (Gilovich, 1997). For example, we tend to read the newspaper and magazine columns of editorial writers who interpret events from our perspective and to avoid the columns of writers who don't see things our way (Ruscio, 1998).

Obstacle 3: The Fallacy of Positive Instances

The *fallacy of positive instances* is the tendency to remember uncommon events that seem to confirm our beliefs and to forget events that disconfirm our beliefs. Often, the occurrence is really nothing more than coincidence. For example, you find yourself thinking of an old friend. A few moments later, the phone rings and it's him. You remember this seemingly telepathic event, but forget all the times that you've thought of your old friend and he did *not* call. In other words, you remember the positive instance but fail to notice the negative instances when the anticipated event did not occur (Gilovich, 1997).

Obstacle 4: The Overestimation Effect

The tendency to overestimate the rarity of events is referred to as the *overestimation effect*. Suppose a "psychic" comes to your class of 23 students. Using his psychic abilities, the visitor "senses" that two people in the class were born on the same

day. A quick survey finds that, indeed, two people share the same month and day of birth. This is pretty impressive evidence of clairvoyance, right? After all, what are the odds that two people in a class of 23 would have the same birthday?

When we perform this "psychic" demonstration in class, our students usually estimate that it is very unlikely that 2 people in a class of 23 will share a birthday. In reality, the odds are *1 in 2*, or 50–50 (Martin, 1998). Our students' overestimation of the rarity of this event is an example of the *overestimation effect*.

Thinking Critically About the Evidence

On the one hand, it is important to keep an open mind. Simply dismissing an idea as impossible shuts out the consideration of evidence for new and potentially promising ideas or phenomena. At one time, for example, scientists thought it impossible that rocks could fall from the sky (Hines, 1988).

On the other hand, the obstacles described here underscore the importance of choosing ways to gather and think about evidence that will help us avoid unwarranted beliefs and self-deception.

The critical thinking skills we described in Chapter 1 are especially useful in this respect. Both Box 1.2, "What Is Critical Thinking?" (page 17) and Box 1.3, "What Is a Pseudoscience?" (page 34) provided guidelines that can be used to evaluate all claims, including pseudoscientific or paranormal claims. In particular, it's important to stress again that good critical thinkers strive to evaluate *all* the available evidence before reaching a conclusion, not just the evidence that supports what they want to believe.

Critical Thinking Questions

- How can using critical thinking skills help you avoid these obstacles to logical thinking?

- Beyond the logical fallacies described here, what might motivate people to maintain beliefs in the face of contradictory evidence?

On the basis of this description, is it more likely that Maria is a successful fiction writer or that Maria is a nurse? Most people guess that she is a successful fiction writer. Why? Because the description seems to mesh with what many people think of as the typical characteristics of a writer.

However, when you compare the number of nurses (which is very large) to the number of successful female fiction writers (which is very small), it's actually much more likely that Maria is a nurse. Thus, the representativeness heuristic can produce faulty estimates if (1) we fail to consider possible variations from the prototype or (2) we fail to consider the approximate number of prototypes that actually exist.

Critical Thinking Box 7.1 discusses some of the other psychological factors that can influence the way in which we evaluate evidence, make decisions, and draw conclusions.

7.1 R·E·V·I·E·W

CONCEPT

Problem Solving and Decision-Making Strategies

Identify the strategy used in each of the following examples. Choose from: trial and error, algorithm, heuristic, insight, representativeness heuristic, availability heuristic, single-feature model.

_____ 1. As you try to spell the word *deceive*, you recite "*i* before *e* except after *c*."

_____ 2. You are asked to complete the following sequence: O, T, T, F, F, _____, _____, _____. You suddenly realize that the answer is obvious: S, S, E, N, T.

_____ 3. One by one, Professor Goldstein tries each key on the key chain until she finds the one that opens the locked filing cabinet.

_____ 4. Laura is trying to construct a house out of Lego building blocks. She tries blocks of different shapes until she finds one that fits.

_____ 5. After seeing news reports about a teenager being killed in a freak accident on a roller coaster, Angela refuses to allow her son to go to an amusement park with his friends.

_____ 6. Jacob decided to rent an apartment at the apartment complex that was closest to his college campus.

_____ 7. Jack, who works as a bank teller, is stunned when a well-dressed, elderly woman pulls out a gun and tells him to hand over all the money in his cash drawer.

Language and Thought

Key Theme

- Language is a system for combining arbitrary symbols to produce an infinite number of meaningful statements.

Key Questions

- What are the characteristics of language?
- How does language affect thinking?
- How have nonhuman animals been shown to use language?

The human capacity for language is surely one of the most remarkable of all our cognitive abilities. With little effort, you produce hundreds of new sentences every day. And you're able to understand the vast majority of the thousands of words contained in this chapter without consulting a dictionary.

The primary function of language is, of course, to communicate. Human language has many special qualities—qualities that make it flexible, versatile, and complex. **Language** can be formally defined as a system for combining arbitrary symbols to produce an infinite number of meaningful statements. We'll begin our discussion of the relationship between language and thought by describing these special characteristics of language. In Chapter 9, we'll discuss language development in children.

The Characteristics of Language

*T*he word **duck** *does not look like a duck, walk like a duck, or quack like a duck, but refers to a duck all the same, because the members of a language community, as children, all memorized the pairing [between a sound and a meaning].*

Steven Pinker (1995)

The purpose of language is to communicate—to express meaningful information in a way that can be understood by others. To do so, language requires the use of *symbols*. These symbols may be sounds, written words, or, as in American Sign Language, formalized gestures.

A few symbols may be similar in form to the meaning they signify, such as the English words *boom* and *pop*. However, for most words, the connection between the symbol and the meaning is completely *arbitrary* (Pinker, 1995). For example, *ton* is a small word that stands for a vast quantity, whereas *nanogram* is a large word that stands for a very small quantity. Because the relationship between the symbol and its meaning is arbitrary, language is tremendously flexible (Pinker, 1994). New words can be invented, such as *cyberspace, Internet,* and *e-mail*. And the meanings of words can change and evolve, such as *gay, stock market,* and *union*.

The meaning of these symbols is *shared* by others who speak the same language. That is, speakers of the same language agree on the connection between the sound and what it symbolizes. Consequently, a foreign language sounds like a stream of meaningless sounds because we do not share the memory of the connection between the arbitrary sounds and the concrete meanings they symbolize.

Further, language is a highly structured system that follows specific rules. Every language has its own unique *syntax,* or set of rules for combining words. Although you're usually unaware of these rules as you're speaking or writing, you immediately notice when a rule has been violated.

The rules of language help determine the meaning that is being communicated. For example, word-order rules are very important in determining the meaning of an English phrase. "The boy ate the giant pumpkin" has an entirely different meaning from "The giant pumpkin ate the boy." In other languages, meaning may be conveyed by different rule-based distinctions, such as specific pronouns, the class or category of word, or word endings (Hunt & Agnoli, 1991).

Another important characteristic of language is that it is creative, or *generative*. That is, you can generate an infinite number of new and different phrases and sentences.

A final important characteristic of human language is called *displacement*. You can communicate meaningfully about ideas, objects, and activities that are not physically present. You can refer to activities that will take place in the future, that took place in the past, or that will take place only if certain conditions are met ("If you get that promotion, maybe we can afford a new car."). You can also carry on a vivid conversation about abstract ideas ("What is justice?") or strictly imaginary topics ("If you were going to spend a year in a space station orbiting Neptune, what would you bring along?").

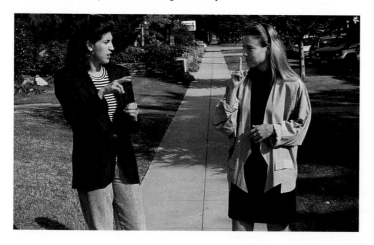

American Sign Language American Sign Language, used by the hearing impaired, meets all the formal requirements for language, including syntax, displacement, and generativity.

How Language Influences Thinking

All your cognitive abilities are involved in understanding and producing language. Using learning and memory, you acquire and remember the meaning of words. You interpret the words you hear or read (or see, in the case of American Sign Language) through the use of perception. You use language to help you reason, represent and solve problems, and make decisions (Polk & Newell, 1995).

Language can influence thinking in several ways (Matlin, 1985). In this section, we'll consider just a few of the ways in which language affects cognitive processes.

Language and Social Perception

An important way in which language can influence thought has to do with our social perceptions of others. Consider the different images produced in your mind by these pairs of terms:

jock	versus	athlete
ambulance chaser	versus	personal-injury lawyer
statuesque brunette	versus	tall, dark-haired woman

The nuances of words influence our social perceptions of others, reinforcing or minimizing negative stereotypes. Language that promotes stereotypical thinking can encourage discrimination against women, elderly adults, and members of racial or ethnic minorities. In Chapter 12, on social psychology, we'll discuss the effects of stereotypes in more detail.

Language and Gender Bias

When you hear about a course titled "Man and His Environment," what image comes to mind? Do you visualize a group of men tromping through the forest, or do you imagine a mixed group of men and women?

The word *man* or the pronouns *he* and *his* can refer to either a male or a female in English, because English has no gender-neutral pronoun. So, according to the rules of the English language, the course title "Man and His Environment" refers to both men and women. Similarly, the cover story "How Man Evolved" featured in a *Time* magazine was not intended to apply to men alone, but rather the entire human race.

However, what do people actually understand by this style of language? Several studies have shown that using the masculine pronoun tends to produce images of males and exclude females (Foertsch & Gernsbacher, 1997; Gastil, 1990). In a study by Nancy Henley (1989), participants were given identical sentence fragments to complete. Examples included "If a writer expects to get a book published . . ." and "If an employee wants a raise . . ." Participants in the first group were given the masculine generic *he* to use in finishing the sentences. Participants in the second group were given either *they* or *he or she* to use in completing the sentences.

After completing the sentences, the subjects were asked to describe their mental imagery for each sentence and to provide a first name for the person they visualized. When the word *he* was used, subjects were much more likely to produce a male image and name than a female image and name. When the phrase *he or she* was used, subjects were only slightly more likely to use a male rather than a female image and name.

Using the masculine generic pronoun influences people to visualize a male, even when they "know" that *he* supposedly includes both men and women (Hamilton, 1988, 1991). Thus, using *he* to refer to both men and women in speech and writing tends to increase male bias.

language
A system for combining arbitrary symbols to produce an infinite number of meaningful statements.

CULTURE AND HUMAN BEHAVIOR 7.2

The Effect of Language on Perception

Professionally, Benjamin Whorf was an insurance company inspector. But his passion was the study of languages, particularly Native American languages. In the 1950s, Whorf proposed an intriguing theory that became known as the *Whorfian hypothesis.*

Whorf (1956) believed that a person's language determines the very structure of his or her thought and perception. Your language, he claimed, determines how you perceive and "carve up" the phenomena of your world. He argued that people who speak very different languages have completely different worldviews. More formally, the Whorfian hypothesis is called the **linguistic relativity hypothesis**—the notion that differences among languages cause differences in the thoughts of their speakers (Pinker, 1994).

To illustrate his hypothesis, Whorf contended that the Eskimos had many different words for "snow." But English, he pointed out, has only the word *snow.* According to Whorf (1956):

> We have the same word for falling snow, snow on the ground, snow packed hard like ice, slushy snow, wind-driven flying snow—whatever the situation may be. To an Eskimo, this all-inclusive word would be almost unthinkable; he would say that falling snow, slushy snow, and so on, are sensuously and operationally different, different things to contend with; he uses different words for them and for other kinds of snow.

Whorf's example would be compelling except for one problem: The Eskimos do *not* have dozens of different words for "snow." Rather, they have just a few words for "snow" (Martin, 1986; Pullum, 1991). Beyond that minor sticking point, think carefully about Whorf's example. Is it really true that English-speaking people have a limited capacity to describe snow? Or do not discriminate between different types of snow? The English language includes *snowflake, snowfall, slush, sleet, flurry, blizzard,* and *avalanche.* Avid skiers have many additional words to describe snow, from *powder* to *mogul* to *hardpack.*

More generally, people with expertise in a particular area tend to perceive and make finer distinctions than nonexperts do. Experts are also more likely to know the specialized terms that reflect those distinctions (Pinker, 1994). To the knowledgeable bird-watcher, for example, there are distinct differences between a cedar waxwing and a bohemian waxwing. To the nonexpert, they're just two brownish birds with yellow tail feathers.

Despite expert/nonexpert differences in noticing and naming details, we don't claim that the expert "sees" a different reality than a nonexpert. In other words, our perceptions and thought processes influence the language we use to describe those perceptions (Rosch, 1987). Notice that this conclusion is the exact *opposite* of the linguistic relativity hypothesis.

Whorf also pointed out that many languages have different color-naming systems. English has names for 11 basic colors: *black, white, red, green, yellow, blue, brown, purple, pink, orange,* and *gray.* However, some languages have only a few color terms. Navajo, for example, has only one word to describe both blue and green, but two different words for black (Fishman, 1960/1974). Would people who had just a few words for colors "carve up" and perceive the electromagnetic spectrum differently?

Eleanor Rosch set out to answer this question (Heider & Olivier, 1972). The people of New Guinea who speak a language called Dani have words for only two colors. *Mili* is used for the dark, cool colors of black, green, and blue. *Mola* is used for light, warm colors, such as white, red, and yellow. According to the Whorfian hypothesis, the people of New Guinea, with names for only two classes of colors, should perceive color differently than English-speaking people, with names for 11 basic colors.

Rosch showed Dani speakers a brightly colored chip and then, 30 seconds later, asked them to pick out the color they had seen from an array of other colors. Her results? The Dani-speaking people perceived colors in much the same way as English-speaking people. For example, even though both red and yellow are called *mola,* the Dani could distinguish between them. Despite their lack of a specific word for the color they were shown, the Dani could remember and identify the color from a range of other colors as readily as English-speaking Americans given the same test.

Whorf's strong contention that language *determines* perception and the structure of thought has not been supported. However, cultural and cognitive psychologists today are actively investigating the ways in which language can *influence* perception and thought (Krauss & Chiu, 1998; Lillard, 1998).

For example, consider the difference between number names in Chinese and English. English has unique names for the numbers 11 and 12, and irregular names for numbers 13 through 19. In contrast, Chinese does not have special words for 11 through 19. Eleven is literally "ten and one," twelve is "ten and two," and so forth.

This language difference in number names *does* seem to have an effect on mathematics comprehension in children (Miller & others, 1995). English-speaking and Chinese-speaking preschoolers learn to count from 1 to 10 at the same age. But Chinese children learn to count from 10 to 20 at a much younger age than English-speaking children, who typically have trouble learning the irregular names for the numbers 11 through 19. As this example shows, the same concepts can be expressed in both languages, but some concepts are *easier* to express in one language than another (Hunt & Agnoli, 1991).

Animal Communication

Can Animals Learn Language?

Without question, animals communicate. Chimpanzees "chutter" to warn of snakes, "rraup" to warn of an eagle, and "chirp" to let the others know that a leopard is nearby (Marler, 1967). Each of the warning calls of the vervet monkey of East Africa triggers specific behaviors for a particular danger, such as scurrying for cover in the bushes when the warning for an airborne predator is sounded (Cheney & Seyfarth, 1990). Even insects have complex communication systems. For example, honeybees perform a dance to report information about the distance, location, and quality of a pollen source to their hive mates (Esch & others, 2001; Gould & Gould, 1994).

Clearly, animals communicate with one another, but are they capable of mastering language? Some of the most promising results have come from the research of psychologists Sue Savage-Rumbaugh, Duane Rumbaugh, and their co-workers. These researchers are working with a rare chimpanzee species called the *bonobo*. In the mid-1980s, they taught a female bonobo, named Matata, to press symbols on a computer keyboard. Although Matata did not learn many symbols, her infant son, Kanzi, appeared to learn how to use the keyboard simply from watching his mother and her caretakers (Savage-Rumbaugh & Lewin, 1994).

Kanzi never received formal training, yet he quickly learned many symbols. Altogether, Kanzi understands more than 150 spoken English words. Kanzi can respond to new, complex spoken commands, such as "Go to the refrigerator and get out a tomato" (Savage-Rumbaugh, 1993). Because these spoken commands are made by an assistant out of Kanzi's view, he cannot be responding to nonverbal cues.

Kanzi also seems to demonstrate an elementary understanding of syntax. He is able to respond correctly to commands whose meaning is determined by word order. For example, using a toy dog and toy snake, he responds appropriately to such commands as "Make the dog bite the snake" and "Make the snake bite the dog" (Savage-Rumbaugh & others, 1998). Kanzi seems to demonstrate a level of language comprehension that is roughly equivalent to that of a two-and-a-half-year-old human child.

Research with other species has produced evidence that nonprimates also can acquire limited aspects of language. Louis Herman and his co-workers (1993) have trained bottle-nosed dolphins to respond to sounds and gestures, each of which stands for a word. The artificial languages taught to the dolphins incorporate syntax rules governing word order.

Finally, consider Alex, an African gray parrot. Trained by Irene Pepperberg (1993, 2000), Alex can answer spoken questions with spoken words. After two decades of training, Alex has about a 100-word vocabulary, which includes words for objects, names, shapes, numbers, and simple phrases, such as "Come here," "How many," and "Want to go." Alex can accurately answer questions about the color and number of objects. He can also categorize objects by color, shape, and material, which suggests that he comprehends simple concepts (Pepperberg, 2000, 2001).

When animal language research began in the 1960s and 1970s, some critics contended that primates were simply producing learned responses to their trainers' nonverbal cues rather than demonstrating true language skills (Terrace, 1985). In the last decade, however, studies conducted under more carefully controlled conditions have produced

Vervet Monkeys Vervet monkeys sound different alarm calls for different kinds of predators. The "leopard" call sends the troop into the trees to avoid leopards and other ground predators. In response to the "eagle" call, the monkeys look up and take cover in bushes to hide from aerial predators.

linguistic relativity hypothesis The notion that differences among languages cause differences in the thoughts of their speakers.

Sue Savage-Rumbaugh with Kanzi Kanzi, a bonobo, communicates by pressing symbols on a computer keyboard.

Irene Pepperberg with Alex Along with his language abilities, Alex seems to understand some simple concepts. For example, when shown a blue key and a blue cork and asked, "What's the same?" Alex responds, "Color." Here, in response to Pepperberg's request, Alex correctly selects the object that is "blue." Alex does just as well with new objects as with familiar objects. This implies that he understands the concept of color and size and is not just responding to conditioning cues.

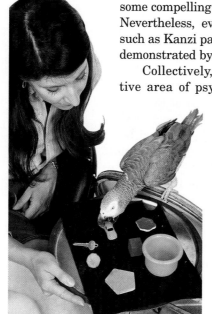

some compelling demonstrations of animal language learning. Nevertheless, even the performance of primate superstars such as Kanzi pales in comparison with the language learning demonstrated by a three-year-old child (Pinker, 1994).

Collectively, animal language research reflects an active area of psychological research that is referred to as **animal cognition** or *comparative cognition* (Boysen & Hines, 1999; Papini, 2002). Although the results of these studies are fascinating, a great deal remains to be discovered about the potential of different species of animals to communicate, produce language, and solve problems—and their limitations in doing so. Many psychologists caution against jumping to the conclusion that animals can "think" or that they possess self-awareness, because such conclusions are far from proven (Blumberg & Wasserman, 1995).

Measuring Intelligence

Key Theme

- *Intelligence* is defined as the global capacity to think rationally, act purposefully, and deal effectively with the environment.

Key Questions

- What roles did Binet, Terman, and Wechsler play in the development of intelligence tests?
- How did Binet, Terman, and Wechsler differ in their beliefs about intelligence and its measurement?
- Why are standardization, validity, and reliability important components of psychological tests?

Up to this point, we have talked about a broad range of cognitive abilities—the use of mental images and concepts, problem solving and decision making, and the use of language. All these mental abilities are aspects of what we commonly call *intelligence*.

What exactly is intelligence? We will rely on a formal definition developed by psychologist David Wechsler. Wechsler (1944, 1977) defined **intelligence** as the global capacity to think rationally, act purposefully, and deal effectively with the environment. Although many people commonly equate intelligence with "book smarts," notice that Wechsler's definition is much broader. To Wechsler, intelligence is reflected in effective, rational, and goal-directed behavior.

The Development of Intelligence Tests

To judge well, to comprehend well, to reason well, these are the essential activities of intelligence.

Alfred Binet and Théodore Simon (1905)

Can intelligence be measured? If so, how? Intelligence tests attempt to measure general mental abilities, rather than accumulated knowledge or aptitude for a specific subject or area. In the next several sections, we will describe the evolution of intelligence tests, including the qualities that make any psychological test scientifically acceptable.

Alfred Binet: Identifying Students Who Needed Special Help

In the early 1900s, the French government passed a law requiring all children to attend school. Faced with the need to educate children from a wide variety of backgrounds, the French government commissioned psychologist **Alfred Binet** to develop procedures to identify students who might require special help.

With the help of French psychiatrist Théodore Simon, Binet devised a series of tests to measure different mental abilities. Binet deliberately did not test abilities, such as reading or mathematics, that the students might have been taught. Instead, he focused on elementary mental abilities, such as memory, attention, and the ability to understand similarities and differences.

Binet arranged the questions on his test in order of difficulty, with the simplest tasks first. He found that brighter children performed like older children. That is, a bright seven-year-old might be able to answer the same number of questions as an average nine-year-old, while a less capable seven-year-old might only do as well as an average five-year-old.

This observation led Binet to the idea of a mental level or **mental age** that was different from a child's chronological age. An "advanced" seven-year-old might have a mental age of nine, while a "slow" seven-year-old might demonstrate a mental age of five.

It is somewhat ironic that Binet's early tests became the basis for modern intelligence tests. First, Binet did *not* believe that he was measuring an inborn or permanent level of intelligence (Kamin, 1995). Rather, he believed that his tests could help identify "slow" children who could benefit from special help.

Second, Binet believed that intelligence was too complex a quality to describe with a single number (Siegler, 1992). He steadfastly refused to rank "normal" children on the basis of their scores, believing that such rankings would be unfair. He recognized that many individual factors, such as a child's level of motivation, might affect the child's score. Finally, Binet noted that an individual's score could vary from time to time (Fancher, 1996; Gould, 1993).

Alfred Binet French psychologist Alfred Binet (1857–1911) is shown here with an unidentified child and an instrument from his laboratory that was used to measure his young subjects' breathing rates while they performed different tasks (Cunningham, 1997). Although Binet developed the first systematic intelligence tests, he did not believe that he was measuring innate ability. Instead, he believed that his tests could identify schoolchildren who could benefit from special help.

Lewis Terman and the Stanford-Binet Intelligence Test

There was enormous interest in Binet's test in the United States. The test was translated and adapted by Stanford University psychologist **Lewis Terman.** Terman's revision was called the *Stanford-Binet Intelligence Scale.* First published in 1916, the Stanford-Binet was for many years the standard for intelligence tests in the United States.

Terman adopted the suggestion of a German psychologist that scores on the Stanford-Binet test be expressed in terms of a single number, called the **intelligence quotient,** or **IQ.** This number was derived by dividing the individual's mental age by the chronological age and multiplying the result by 100. Thus, a child of average intelligence, whose mental age and chronological age were the same, would have an IQ score of 100. A "bright" 10-year-old child with a mental age of 13 would have an IQ of 130 ($^{13}/_{10} \times 100$). A "slow" child with a chronological age of 10 and a mental age of 7 would have an IQ of 70 ($^{7}/_{10} \times 100$). It was Terman's use of the intelligence quotient that resulted in the popularization of the phrase "IQ test."

World War I and Group Intelligence Testing

When the United States entered World War I in 1917, the U.S. military was faced with the need to rapidly screen 2 million army recruits. Using a group intelligence test designed by one of Terman's students, army psychologists developed the Army Alpha and Beta tests. The *Army Alpha* test was administered in writing, and the *Army Beta* test was administered orally to recruits and draftees who could not read.

animal cognition
The study of animal learning, memory, thinking, and language.

intelligence
The global capacity to think rationally, act purposefully, and deal effectively with the environment.

mental age
A measurement of intelligence in which an individual's mental level is expressed in terms of the average abilities of a given age group.

intelligence quotient (IQ)
A global measure of intelligence derived by comparing an individual's score with the scores of others in the same age group.

Testing Immigrants at Ellis Island This photograph, taken in 1917, shows an examiner administering a mental test to a newly arrived immigrant at Ellis Island. According to one intelligence "expert" of the time, 80 percent of the Hungarians, 79 percent of the Italians, and 87 percent of the Russians were "feeble-minded" (see Kamin, 1995). The new science of "mental testing" was used to argue for restrictions on immigration.

After World War I ended, the Army Alpha and Army Beta group intelligence tests were adapted for civilian use. The result was a tremendous surge in the intelligence-testing movement. Group intelligence tests were designed to test virtually all ages and types of people, including preschool children, prisoners, and newly arriving immigrants (Anastasi, 1988; Kamin, 1995). However, the indiscriminate use of the tests also resulted in skepticism and hostility.

For example, newly arriving immigrants were screened as they arrived at Ellis Island. The result was sweeping generalizations about the intelligence of different nationalities and races. During the 1920s, a few intelligence testing experts even urged the U.S. Congress to severely limit the immigration of certain nationalities to keep the country from being "overrun with a horde of the unfit" (see Kamin, 1995).

Despite concerns about the misuse of the so-called IQ tests, the tests quickly became very popular. Lost was Binet's belief that intelligence tests were useful only to identify those who might benefit from special educational help. Contrary to Binet's contention, it soon came to be believed that the IQ score was a fixed, inborn characteristic that was resistant to change (Gould, 1993).

Terman and other American psychologists also believed that a high IQ predicted more than success in school. To investigate the relationship between IQ and success in life, Terman (1926) identified 1,500 Californian schoolchildren with "genius" IQ scores. He set up a longitudinal research study to follow their careers throughout their lives. Some of the findings of this landmark study are described in In Focus Box 7.3.

David Wechsler and the Wechsler Intelligence Scales

The next major advance in intelligence testing came as a result of a young psychologist's dissatisfaction with the Stanford-Binet and other intelligence tests in widespread use. **David Wechsler** was in charge of testing adults of widely varying cultural and socioeconomic backgrounds and ages at a large hospital in New York City. He designed a new intelligence test, called the *Wechsler Adult Intelligence Scale (WAIS),* which was first published in 1955.

The WAIS had two advantages over the Stanford-Binet. First, the WAIS was specifically designed for adults, rather than for children. Second, Wechsler's test provided scores on 11 subtests measuring different abilities. The subtest scores were grouped to provide an overall verbal score and performance score. The *verbal score* represented scores on subtests of vocabulary, comprehension, knowledge of general information, and other verbal tasks. The *performance score* reflected scores on largely nonverbal subtests, such as identifying the missing part in incomplete pictures, arranging pictures to tell a story, or arranging blocks to match a given pattern.

The design of the WAIS reflected Wechsler's belief that intelligence involves a variety of mental abilities. Because the WAIS provided an individualized profile of the subject's strengths and weaknesses on specific tasks, it marked a return to the attitudes and goals of Alfred Binet (Fancher, 1996; Sternberg, 1990).

The subtest scores on the WAIS also proved to have practical and clinical value. For example, a pattern of low scores on some subtests combined with high scores on other subtests might indicate a specific learning disability (Kaufman, 1990). Or, someone who did well on the performance subtests but poorly on the verbal subtests might be unfamiliar with the culture rather than deficient in these skills (Aiken, 1997). That's because many items included on the verbal subtests draw on cultural knowledge.

David Wechsler Born in Romania, David Wechsler (1896–1981) emigrated with his family to New York when he was six years old. Like Binet, Wechsler believed that intelligence involved a variety of mental abilities. He also strongly believed that IQ scores could be influenced by personality, motivation, and cultural factors (Matarazzo, 1981).

IN FOCUS 7.3

Does a High IQ Score Predict Success in Life?

Starting in 1921, Lewis M. Terman set out to investigate the common notion that genius-level intelligence is related to social and personal maladjustment, physical weakness, and mental instability. Terman identified 1,500 California children between the ages of 8 and 12 who had IQs above 140, the minimum IQ score for genius-level intelligence. The average IQ of the children was 150, and 80 children had scores above 170. Terman's goal was to track these children by conducting periodic surveys and interviews to see how genius-level intelligence would affect the course of their lives.

Within a few years, Terman (1926) showed that the highly intelligent children were far from being socially and physically inept. In fact, his findings indicated just the opposite. Those children tended to be socially well-adjusted. They were also taller, stronger, and healthier than average children, with fewer illnesses and accidents. Not surprisingly, those children performed exceptionally well in school.

Since Terman's death in 1956, the study has been continued by other psychologists, most notably Melita Oden, Robert Sears, and Pauline Sears. These collaborators in Terman's study kept track of the subjects, by then well into adulthood. Today, more than 70 years after the

With the exception of moral character, there is nothing as significant for a child's future as his grade of intelligence.

Lewis M. Terman (1916)

study began, psychologists continue to assess the professional and personal accomplishments of the surviving original subjects (Holahan & Sears, 1995).

How did Terman's "gifted" children fare in the real world as adults? As a group, they showed an astonishing range of accomplishments (Terman & Oden, 1947, 1959). In 1955, when average income was $5,000 a year, the average income for the group was $33,000. Two-thirds had graduated from college, and a sizable proportion had earned advanced academic or professional degrees. There were no "creative geniuses"—no Picassos, Einsteins, or Mozarts—but there were many doctors, lawyers, scientists, university professors, business executives, and other professionals in the group. Collectively, the gifted group had produced 2,200 scientific articles, 92 books, 235 patents, and 38 novels (Goleman, 1980). One individual had become a famous science fiction writer, and another was an Oscar-winning movie director.

However, not all of Terman's subjects were so successful. To find out why, Terman's colleague Melita Oden compared the 100 most successful men (the "A" group) and the 100 least successful men (the "C" group) in Terman's sample. Despite their high IQ scores, only a handful of the C group were professionals, and none was doing exceptionally well. Whereas the Cs were earning slightly above the national average income, the As were earning almost five times the national income and better than three times the average C-group income. In terms of their personal lives, the Cs were less healthy, had higher rates of alcoholism, and were three times more likely to be divorced than the As (Terman & Oden, 1959).

Given that the IQ scores of the A and C groups were essentially the same, what accounted for the difference in their levels of accomplishment? Terman noted that, as children, the As were much more likely to display "prudence and forethought, will power, perseverance, and the desire to excel." As adults, the As were rated differently from the Cs on

only three traits: They were more goal-oriented, had greater perseverance, and had greater self-confidence. Overall, the As seemed to have greater ambition and a greater drive to achieve. In other words, *personality factors* seemed to account for the differences in level of accomplishment between the A group and the C group (Terman & Oden, 1959).

As the general success of Terman's gifted children demonstrates, high intelligence can certainly contribute to success in life. But intelligence alone is not enough. Although IQ scores do reliably predict academic success, success in school is no guarantee of success beyond school. Many different personality factors are involved in achieving success, such as motivation, emotional maturity, commitment to goals, creativity, and—perhaps most important—a willingness to work hard (Goleman, 1995; Renzulli, 1986; Sternberg, 1982, 1985). None of these attributes are measured by traditional IQ tests.

Terman's findings may have been overly optimistic about the relationship between high IQ scores and social and personal adjustment. Why? The children in Terman's study were first nominated by their teachers before having their IQ tested. Thus, it's possible that the teachers were more likely to select well-adjusted bright children over children who were just as intelligent but less socially adept. And, subsequent research has found that children with exceptionally high academic abilities are somewhat more likely to suffer personal problems, such as social isolation, than their less gifted peers (Winner, 1998).

Intelligence researchers continue to debate the degree to which IQ relates to success in life (Brody, 1997; Sternberg, 1997). However, contemporary research on IQ and professional eminence seems to confirm the essential findings of the original Terman study (Winner, 1997). Although intelligence is necessary for success in any field, the kind of intelligence that is reflected by high scores on traditional IQ tests is no guarantee of vocational success or professional eminence.

The Wechsler Intelligence Scale for Children (WISC) Revised and updated in 1991, the WISC-III is designed to assess the intelligence of children ages 6 to 16. This psychologist is administering the WISC-III picture completion subtest to a 6-year-old girl. Other WISC-III subtests include vocabulary, arithmetic, arranging blocks to match a design, and arranging pictures so that they correctly tell a story.

Wechsler's test also provided a global IQ score, but he changed the way that the IQ score was calculated. On the Stanford-Binet and other early tests, the IQ represented the mental age divided by chronological age. But this approach makes little sense when applied to adult subjects. Although a 12-year-old is typically able to answer more questions than an 8-year-old because of developmental differences, such year-by-year age differences lose their meaning in adulthood.

Instead, Wechsler calculated the IQ by comparing an individual's score with the scores of others in the same general age group, such as young adults. The average score for a particular age group was statistically fixed at 100. The range of scores is statistically defined so that two-thirds of all scores fall between 85 and 115—the range considered to indicate "normal" or "average" intelligence. This procedure proved so successful that it was adopted by the administrators of other tests, including the current version of the Stanford-Binet. Today, IQ scores continue to be calculated by this method.

The WAIS was revised in 1981 and again in 1997. Today the third edition of the WAIS is known as the WAIS-III. Since the 1960s, the WAIS has remained the most commonly administered intelligence test. Wechsler also developed two tests for children: the *Wechsler Intelligence Scale for Children (WISC)* and the *Wechsler Preschool and Primary Scale of Intelligence (WPPSI)*.

Principles of Test Construction
What Makes a Good Test?

Many kinds of psychological tests measure various aspects of intelligence or mental ability. **Achievement tests** are designed to measure a person's level of knowledge, skill, or accomplishment in a particular area, such as mathematics or a foreign language. In contrast, **aptitude tests** are designed to assess a person's capacity to benefit from education or training. The overall goal of an aptitude test is to predict your ability to learn certain types of information or perform certain skills.

Any psychological test must fulfill certain requirements to be considered scientifically acceptable. The three basic requirements of good test design are standardization, reliability, and validity. Let's briefly look at what each of those requirements entails.

Standardization

If you answer 75 of 100 questions correctly, what does that score mean? Is it high, low, or average? For an individual's test score to be interpreted, it has to be compared against some sort of standard of performance.

Standardization means that the test is given to a large number of subjects who are representative of the group of people for whom the test is designed. All the subjects take the same version of the test under uniform conditions. The scores of this group establish the *norms,* or the standards against which an individual score is compared and interpreted.

achievement test
A test designed to measure a person's level of knowledge, skill, or accomplishment in a particular area.

aptitude test
A test designed to assess a person's capacity to benefit from education or training.

standardization
The administration of a test to a large, representative sample of people under uniform conditions for the purpose of establishing norms.

normal curve or **normal distribution**
A bell-shaped distribution of individual differences in a normal population in which most scores cluster around the average score.

reliability
The ability of a test to produce consistent results when administered on repeated occasions under similar conditions.

validity
The ability of a test to measure what it is intended to measure.

For IQ tests, such norms closely follow a pattern of individual differences called the **normal curve,** or **normal distribution.** In this bell-shaped pattern, most scores cluster around the average score. As scores become more extreme, fewer instances of the scores occur. In Figure 7.5, you can see the normal distribution of IQ scores on the WAIS-III. About 68 percent of subjects taking the WAIS-III will score between 85 and 115, the IQ range for "normal" intelligence. Less than 1 percent of the population have extreme scores that are above 145 or below 55.

FIGURE 7.5 The Normal Curve of Distribution of IQ Scores The distribution of IQ scores on the WAIS-III in the general population tends to follow a bell-shaped normal curve, with the average score defined as 100. Notice that 68 percent of the scores fall within the "normal" IQ range of 85 to 115. Ninety-five percent of the general population score between 70 and 130, while only one-tenth of 1 percent score lower than 55 or higher than 145.

Reliability

A good test must also have **reliability.** That is, it must consistently produce similar scores on different occasions. How do psychologists determine whether a psychological test is reliable? One method is to administer two similar, but not identical, versions of the test at different times. Another procedure is to compare the scores on one half of the test with the scores on the other half of the test. A test is considered reliable if the test and retest scores are highly similar when such strategies are used.

Validity

Finally, a good test must demonstrate **validity,** which means that the test measures what it is supposed to measure. One way to establish the validity of a test is by demonstrating its predictive value. For example, if a test is designed to measure mechanical aptitude, people who received high scores should ultimately prove more successful in mechanical jobs than people who received low scores. Figure 7.6 shows sample items from a valid test of mechanical aptitude.

FIGURE 7.6 Demonstrating Validity A good test measures what it claims to measure. Shown here are two sample items from an aptitude test, the Bennett Mechanical Comprehension Test. Because scores on this test are correlated with job performance in occupations requiring mechanical ability, the test is considered valid.

g factor or **general intelligence**
The notion of a general intelligence factor that is responsible for a person's overall performance on tests of mental ability.

The Nature of Intelligence

Key Theme

■ Psychologists do not agree about the basic nature of intelligence, including whether it is a single, general ability and whether it includes skills and talents as well as mental aptitude.

Key Questions

■ What is *g,* and how did Spearman and Thurstone view intelligence?
■ What is Gardner's theory of multiple intelligences?
■ What is Sternberg's triarchic theory of intelligence?

The Wechsler Adult Intelligence Scale and the Stanford-Binet Intelligence Scale are standardized, reliable, and valid. But do they adequately measure intelligence? Psychologists do not agree on the answer to this question. Put simply, there is considerable disagreement about the nature of intelligence, including how intelligence should best be defined (Neisser & others, 1996).

For example, take another look at the Prologue to this chapter, which described solving two real problems: a leaking faucet and a malfunctioning toilet. Obviously, solving these problems required a certain level of intelligence. But could that intelligence be adequately measured by an IQ test? Does an IQ test measure the ingenuity that Don demonstrated? Or Sandy's enterprising ability to find a resource to supply the knowledge that she knew she didn't have?

Theories of Intelligence

Much of the controversy over the definition of *intelligence* centers on two key issues. First, is intelligence a single, general ability, or is it better described as a cluster of different mental abilities? And second, should the definition of intelligence be restricted to the mental abilities measured by IQ and other intelligence tests? Or should intelligence be defined more broadly?

Although these issues have been debated for decades, they are far from being resolved. In this section, we'll describe the views of four influential psychologists on both issues.

Charles Spearman: Intelligence Is a General Ability

Some psychologists believe that a common factor, or general mental capacity, is at the core of different mental abilities. This approach originated with British psychologist **Charles Spearman.** Although Spearman agreed that an individual's scores could vary on tests of different mental abilities, he found that the scores on different tests tended to be similar. That is, people who did well or poorly on a test of one mental ability, such as verbal ability, tended also to do well or poorly on the other tests.

Spearman recognized that particular individuals might excel in specific areas. However, Spearman (1904) believed that a factor he called **general intelligence,** or the **g factor,** was responsible for their overall performance on tests of mental ability. Psychologists who follow this approach today think that intelligence can be described as a single measure of general cognitive ability, or *g* factor (Gottfredson, 1998). Thus, general mental ability could accurately be expressed by a single number, such as the IQ score. Lewis Terman's approach to measuring and defining intelligence as a single, overall IQ score was in the tradition of Charles Spearman.

Charles Spearman (1863–1945) British psychologist Charles Spearman (1904) believed that a single factor, which he called the *g factor,* underlies many different kinds of mental abilities. To Spearman, a person's level of general intelligence was equivalent to their level of "mental energy."

Louis L. Thurstone: Intelligence Is a Cluster of Abilities

Psychologist **Louis L. Thurstone** disagreed with Spearman's notion that intelligence is a single, general mental capacity. Instead, Thurstone believed that there were seven different "primary mental abilities," each a relatively independent element of intelligence. Abilities such as verbal comprehension, numerical ability, reasoning, and perceptual speed are examples Thurstone gave of independent "primary mental abilities."

To Thurstone, the so-called *g* factor was simply an overall average score of such independent abilities and consequently was less important than an individual's specific *pattern* of mental abilities (Thurstone, 1937). David Wechsler's approach to measuring and defining intelligence as a pattern of different abilities was very similar to Thurstone's approach.

Howard Gardner: "Multiple Intelligences"

More recently, **Howard Gardner** has expanded Thurstone's basic notion of intelligence as different mental abilities that operate independently. However, Gardner has stretched the definition of intelligence (Gardner & Taub, 1999). Rather than analyzing intelligence test results, Gardner (1985, 1993) looked at the kinds of skills and products that are valued in different cultures. He also studied brain-damaged individuals, noting that some mental abilities are spared when others are lost. To Gardner, this phenomenon implies that different mental abilities are biologically distinct and controlled by different parts of the brain.

Like Thurstone, Gardner has suggested that such mental abilities are independent of each other and cannot be accurately reflected in a single measure of intelligence. Rather than one intelligence, Gardner (1993, 1998a) believes, there are "multiple intelligences." To Gardner, "an intelligence" is the ability to solve problems, or to create products, that are valued within one or more cultural settings. Thus, he believes that intelligence must be defined within the context of a particular culture. Gardner (1998b) has proposed eight distinct, independent intelligences, which are summarized in Figure 7.7.

Some of the abilities emphasized by Gardner, such as logical-mathematical intelligence, might be tapped by a standard intelligence test. However, other abilities, such as bodily-kinesthetic intelligence or musical intelligence, do not seem to be reflected on standard intelligence tests. Yet, as Gardner points out, such abilities are recognized and highly valued in many different cultures, including our own.

Louis L. Thurstone (1887–1955) American psychologist Lewis Thurstone studied electrical engineering and was an assistant to Thomas Edison before he became interested in the psychology of learning. Thurstone was especially interested in the measurements of people's attitudes and intelligence, and was an early critic of the idea of "mental age," believing that intelligence was too diverse to be quantified in a single number or IQ score.

Linguistic intelligence	Adept use of language: poet, writer, public speaker, native storyteller
Logical-mathematical intelligence	Logical, mathematical, and scientific ability: scientist, mathematician, navigator, surveyor
Musical intelligence	Ability to create, synthesize, or perform music: Musician, composer, singer
Spatial intelligence	Ability to mentally visualize the relationships of objects or movements: sculptor, painter, expert chess player, architect
Bodily-kinesthetic intelligence	Control of bodily motions and capacity to handle objects skillfully: athlete, dancer, craftsperson
Interpersonal intelligence	Understanding of other people's emotions, motives, intentions: politician, salesperson, clinical psychologist
Intrapersonal intelligence	Understanding of one's own emotions, motives, and intentions: essayist, philosopher
Naturalist intelligence	Ability to discern patterns in nature: ecologist, zoologist, botanist.

FIGURE 7.7 Gardner's Multiple Intelligences

Examples of Gardner's Theory of Multiple Intelligences Gardner points out that many forms of mental ability are not adequately measured by traditional intelligence tests. Examples are the complex, perfectly balanced designs of this Navajo weaver (spatial intelligence), the electrifying performances of country music singer Garth Brooks (musical intelligence), and the extraordinary athletic talents of Michael Jordan (bodily-kinesthetic intelligence).

Robert Sternberg: Three Forms of Intelligence

Robert Sternberg agrees with Gardner that intelligence is a much broader quality than is reflected in the narrow range of mental abilities measured by a conventional IQ test. However, Sternberg (1988, 1995) disagrees with Gardner's notion of multiple, independent intelligences. He believes that some of Gardner's intelligences are more accurately described as specialized talents, whereas intelligence is a more general quality. Sternberg (1988) points out that you would be able to manage just fine if you were tone-deaf and lacked "musical intelligence" in most societies. However, if you didn't have the ability to reason and plan ahead, you would be unable to function in any culture.

Sternberg's **triarchic theory of intelligence** emphasizes both the universal aspects of intelligent behavior and the importance of adapting to a particular social and cultural environment. More specifically, Sternberg (1997) has proposed a different conception of intelligence, which he calls *successful intelligence*. Successful intelligence involves three distinct types of mental abilities: analytic, creative, and practical.

Analytic intelligence refers to the mental processes used in learning how to solve problems, such as picking a problem-solving strategy and applying it. Although conventional intelligence tests measure mental abilities, they do not evaluate the strategies used to solve problems, which Sternberg considers important in determining analytic intelligence. In the Prologue, Sandy's ability to review and select a problem-solving strategy from the "Fix-It" book reflected analytic intelligence.

Creative intelligence is the ability to deal with novel situations by drawing on existing skills and knowledge. The intelligent person effectively draws on past experiences to cope with new situations, which often involves finding an unusual way to relate old information to new. Don displayed creative intelligence when he came up with a novel way to fix the leaky kitchen faucet.

Practical intelligence involves the ability to adapt to the environment and often reflects what is commonly called "street smarts." Sternberg notes that what is required to adapt successfully in one particular situation or culture may be very different from what is needed in another situation or culture. He stresses that the behaviors that reflect practical intelligence can vary depending on the particular situation, environment, or culture.

Despite disagreements on the specific nature and definition of intelligence, there is evidence that psychologists *do* generally agree on the characteristics of intelligent behavior. A survey of several hundred psychologists who were experts in intelligence testing revealed several points of agreement (Snyderman & Rothman, 1987, 1988). The psychologists were virtually unanimous in considering factors such as abstract thinking, problem solving, and the capacity to acquire knowledge important elements of intelligence. These aspects of intelligence are typically assessed in intelligence tests such as the WAIS and Stanford-Binet.

However, many experts also agreed that other important aspects of intelligence exist but are not measured in conventional intelligence tests. These aspects include creativity, achievement motivation, and goal-directed behavior. Although there was overall agreement that adaptation to one's environment is a significant factor in intelligence, three-fourths of those who agreed with this statement thought that existing tests did not adequately measure this quality. Thus, the respondents generally agreed that conventional intelligence tests have some important limitations.

The exact nature of intelligence will no doubt be debated for some time. However, the intensity of this debate pales in comparison with the next issue we consider: the origins of intelligence.

triarchic theory of intelligence
Sternberg's theory that there are three distinct forms of intelligence: analytic, creative, and practical.

7.2 R·E·V·I·E·W

C·O·N·C·E·P·T

Major Contributors to the Intelligence Debate

Identify the psychologist who is described by each statement. Choose from: Binet, Terman, Wechsler, Spearman, Thurstone, Gardner, Sternberg.

_____ 1. Contemporary American psychologist who proposed that there are three aspects of intelligence: analytic, creative, and practical.

_____ 2. French psychologist who is credited with developing the first practical intelligence test.

_____ 3. American psychologist whose widely used intelligence test provides both a global IQ score and scores on verbal and performance tests.

_____ 4. British psychologist who advanced the theory that overall intellectual ability

is a function of a general intelligence factor, called the *g* factor.

_____ 5. Contemporary American psychologist who proposed that there are multiple independent intelligences and that an intelligence is an ability that is valued within a particular cultural setting.

_____ 6. American psychologist who believed that there are seven different primary mental abilities rather than a single *g* factor.

_____ 7. American psychologist who translated and adapted Binet's intelligence test for use in the United States.

The Roles of Genetics and Environment in Determining Intelligence

Key Theme

▪ Both genes and environment contribute to intelligence, but the relationship is complex.

Key Questions

▪ How are twin studies used to measure genetic and environmental influences on intelligence?

▪ What is a heritability estimate, and why can't it be used to explain differences between groups?

▪ What social and cultural factors affect performance on intelligence tests?

Given that psychologists do not agree on the definition or nature of intelligence, it probably won't surprise you to learn that psychologists also do not agree on the *origin of intelligence*. On the surface, the debate comes down to this: Do we

*T*he nature-versus-nurture debate is now informed by current research on molecular biology that moves the question from which factor is more important to how and when expression of the human genome is triggered and maintained. The basic behavior genetics issue has become how environment influences gene expression.

Bernard Brown (1999)

essentially *inherit* our intellectual potential from our parents, grandparents, and great-grandparents? Or is our intellectual potential primarily determined by our *environment* and upbringing?

The simple answer to both these questions is "yes." In a nutshell, virtually all psychologists agree that *both* heredity and environment are important in determining intelligence level. Where psychologists disagree is in identifying how much of intelligence is determined by heredity, how much by environment. The implications of this debate have provoked some of the most heated arguments in the history of psychology. In this section, we'll try to clarify some of the critical issues involved in this ongoing controversy.

To make sense of the IQ controversy, let's start with some basic points about the relationship between genes and the environment. At one time, it was commonly believed that genes provided the blueprint for human potential and development. Today, the "genes as blueprint" metaphor has been replaced by a "genes as data bank" metaphor (Brown, 1999). It's now known that environmental factors influence *which* of the many genes we inherit are actually switched on, or activated. As psychologist Bernard Brown (1999) writes, "Genes are not destiny. There are many places along the gene–behavior pathway where genetic expression can be regulated."

Take the example of height. You inherit a potential *range* for height, rather than an absolute number of inches. Environmental factors influence how close you come to realizing that genetic potential. If you are healthy and well-nourished, you may reach the maximum of your genetic height potential. But if you are poorly nourished and not healthy, you probably won't.

To underscore the interplay between heredity and environment, consider the fact that in the last 50 years, the average height of Americans has increased by several inches. The explanation for this increase is that nutritional and health standards have steadily improved, not that the genetic heritage of Americans has fundamentally changed. However, heredity does play a role in establishing *limits* on height. If you're born with "short" genes (like your authors), you're unlikely to reach six foot four, no matter how good your nutrition.

The roles of heredity and environment in determining intelligence and personality factors are much more complex than the simple examples of height or eye color (Plomin & others, 1994). However narrowly intelligence is defined, the genetic range of intellectual potential is influenced by *many* genes, not by one single gene (Gottesman, 1997; Rose, 1995). No one knows how many genes might be involved. Given the complexity of genetic and environmental influences, how do scientists estimate how much of intelligence is due to genetics, how much to environment?

Genetics or Environment? These identical twins have a lot in common—including a beautiful smile. Twins are often used in studies of the relative contributions that heredity and environment make to personality and other characteristics.

Twin Studies: Sorting Out the Influence of Genetics Versus Environment

One way this issue has been explored is by comparing the IQ scores of individuals who are genetically related to different degrees. *Identical twins* share exactly the same genes, because they developed from a single fertilized egg that split into two. Hence, any dissimilarities between them must be due to environmental factors rather than hereditary differences. *Fraternal twins* are like any other pair of siblings, because they develop from two different fertilized eggs.

As you can see in Figure 7.8, comparing IQ scores in this way shows the effects of both heredity and environment. Identical twins raised together have very similar IQ scores, whereas fraternal twins raised together have IQs that are less similar (McClearn & others, 1997; Plomin & DeFries, 1998).

However, notice that identical twins raised in separate homes have IQs that are slightly less similar, indicating the effect of different environments. And, although fraternal twins raised together have less similar IQ scores than do identical twins, they show more similarity in IQs than do nontwin siblings. Recall

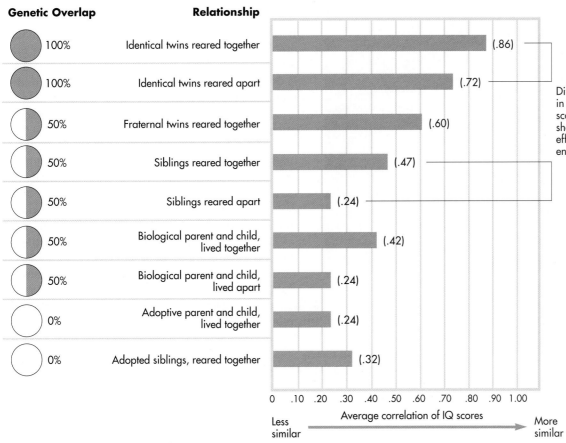

Genetic Overlap   **Relationship**

Genetic Overlap	Relationship
100%	Identical twins reared together
100%	Identical twins reared apart
50%	Fraternal twins reared together
50%	Siblings reared together
50%	Siblings reared apart
50%	Biological parent and child, lived together
50%	Biological parent and child, lived apart
0%	Adoptive parent and child, lived together
0%	Adopted siblings, reared together

(.86)
(.72)
(.60)
(.47)
(.24)
(.42)
(.24)
(.24)
(.32)

Difference in IQ scores shows effect of environment

0   .10   .20   .30   .40   .50   .60   .70   .80   .90   1.00
Average correlation of IQ scores
Less similar → More similar

FIGURE 7.8 Genetics, Environment, and IQ Scores This graph shows the average correlations of IQ scores for individuals who are genetically related to different degrees. The graph is based on research by psychologists Thomas Bouchard and Matt McGue, who summarized the results from more than 100 separate studies on over 100,000 pairs of relatives (McGue & others, 1993). The data show that both genetics and environment have an effect on IQ scores. The more closely two individuals are related genetically, the more similar their IQ scores: Identical twins reared together are more alike than are fraternal twins reared together. However, the same data also show the importance of environmental influences: Identical twins reared together are more alike than are identical twins reared apart, and siblings who are reared together are more alike than are siblings reared in different homes.

that the degree of genetic relatedness between fraternal twins and nontwin siblings is essentially the same. But because fraternal twins are the same age, their environmental experiences are likely to be more similar than are those of siblings who are of different ages.

Thus, *both* genetic *and* environmental influences are important. Genetic influence is shown by the fact that the closer the genetic relationship, the more similar the IQ scores. Environmental influences are demonstrated by two findings: First, two people who are genetically identical but are raised in different homes have different IQ scores. And second, two people who are genetically unrelated but are raised in the same home have IQs that are much more similar than are those of two unrelated people from randomly selected homes.

Using studies based on degree of genetic relatedness and using sophisticated statistical techniques to analyze the data, researchers have scientifically estimated **heritability**—the percentage of variation within a given population that is due to heredity. The currently accepted *heritability estimate* is about 50 percent for the general population (Plomin & DeFries, 1998; Plomin & others, 1994).

In other words, approximately 50 percent of the difference in IQ scores *within* a given population is due to genetic factors. But there is disagreement even over this figure, depending on the statistical techniques and data sources used. Some researchers estimate the heritability of IQ to be as high as 65 percent (T. Bouchard & others, 1990).

It is important to stress that the 50 percent figure does *not* apply to a single individual's IQ score. If Mike's IQ is 120, it does not mean that 60 IQ points are due to Mike's environment and 60 points are genetically inherited. Instead, the 50 percent heritability estimate means that approximately 50 percent of the difference in IQ scores *within a specific group of people* is due to differences in their genetic makeup. More on this key point shortly.

heritability
The percentage of variation within a given population that is due to heredity.

Culture and Educational Achievement
These children attend kindergarten in Kawasaki, Japan. Children in Japan attend school six days a week. Along with spending more time in school each year than American children, Japanese children grow up in a culture that places a strong emphasis on academic success as the key to occupational success.

Group Differences in IQ Scores

If the contributions of heredity and environment are roughly equal, why all the fuss? Much of the controversy over the role of heredity in intelligence is due to attempts to explain the differences in average IQ scores for different racial groups.

In comparing the *average IQ* for various racial groups, several studies have shown differences. For example, Japanese and Chinese schoolchildren tend to score above European-American children on intelligence and achievement tests, especially in math (Lynn, 1987; Stevenson & Lee, 1990). Are Japanese and Chinese children genetically more intelligent than European-American children?

Consider this finding: In early childhood, there are *no* significant differences in IQ among European-American, Japanese, and Chinese schoolchildren. The scores of the three groups are essentially the same (Stevenson & Stigler, 1992). The gap begins to appear only after the children start school, and it increases with every year of school attended. By middle school, Asian students tend to score much higher than American students on both math and reading tests.

Why the increasing gap once children enter school? Japanese and Chinese students spend more time in school, spend more time doing homework, and experience more pressure and support from their parents to achieve academically. In addition, the Japanese and Chinese cultures place a high value on academic achievement (Gardner, 1995). Clearly, the difference between American and Asian students is due not to genetics but to the educational system.

In the United States, the most controversy has been caused by the differences in average IQ scores between black and white Americans. *As a group,* black Americans once scored about 15 points lower than white Americans *as a group* (MacKenzie, 1984). However, this gap has narrowed over the past few decades to 10 points or less (Flynn, 1999; Neisser & others, 1996).

Once again, it is important to note that such group differences do not predict *individual* differences in IQ scores. Many individual black Americans receive higher IQ scores than many individual white Americans. Also, the range and degree of IQ variation *within* each group—the variation of IQs among individual blacks or among individual whites—is much greater than the 10-point average difference *between* the two groups.

Differences *Within* Groups Versus Differences *Between* Groups

Some group differences in average IQ scores do exist. But heritability cannot be used to explain group differences. Although it is possible to estimate the degree of difference *within* a specific group that is due to genetics, it makes no sense to apply this estimate to the differences *between* groups (Rutter, 1997). Why? An analogy provided by geneticist Richard Lewontin (1970) may help you understand this important point.

Suppose you have a 50-pound bag of corn seeds and two pots. A handful of seeds is scooped out and planted in pot A, which has rich, well-fertilized soil. A second handful is scooped out and planted in pot B, which has poor soil with few nutrients (see Figure 7.9).

Because the seeds are not genetically identical, the plants *within group A* will vary in height. So will the plants *within group B.* Given that the environment (the soil) is the same for all the plants in one particular pot, this variation within each group of seeds is *completely* due to heredity—nothing differs but the plants' genes.

However, when we compare the average height of the corn plants in the two pots, pot A's plants have a higher average height than pot B's. Can the difference in these average heights be explained in terms of overall genetic differences between the seeds in each pot? No. The overall differences can be attributed to the two different environments, the good soil and the poor soil. In fact, because the environments are so different, it is impossible to estimate what the overall genetic differences are between the two groups of seeds.

Note also that even though, on the average, the plants in pot A are taller than the plants in pot B, some of the plants in pot B are taller than some of the plants in pot A. In other words, the average differences *within a group* of plants tell us nothing about whether an *individual* member of that group is likely to be tall or short.

The same point can be extended to the issue of average IQ differences between racial groups. Unless the environmental conditions of two racial groups are virtually identical, it is impossible to estimate the overall genetic differences between the two groups. Even if intelligence were *primarily* determined by heredity, which is not the case, IQ differences between groups could still be due entirely to the environment.

In the United States, black children, like members of many other minority groups, are more likely than white children to be raised in poverty and to have fewer educational opportunities. Environmental factors associated with poverty, such as poor nutrition and lack of prenatal care, can have a negative impact on intelligence. And, even when their socioeconomic status is roughly equal to that of white Americans, black Americans experience many forms of overt and subtle social discrimination (Steele & Aronson, 1995).

An important study by psychologists Sandra Scarr and Richard Weinberg (1976) explored the relationship between racial IQ differences and the environment in which children are raised. Scarr and Weinberg looked at the IQ scores of black children who had been adopted by white families that were highly educated and above average in occupational status and income. When tested, the black children's IQ scores were several points higher than the average scores of *both* black and white children.

Scarr and Weinberg concluded that IQ differences are due not to race but rather to the socioeconomic conditions and cultural values to which children are exposed. According to Weinberg (1989), the adopted black children performed well above average because they were provided with home environments in which they were taught the vocabulary and cognitive skills that IQ and achievement tests reward. A follow-up study of the children a decade later demonstrated the "persisting beneficial effects [on IQ scores] of being reared in the culture of the school and tests" (Weinberg & others, 1992; see also Waldman & others, 1994).

Other evidence for the importance of the environment in determining IQ scores derives from the improvement in average IQ scores that has occurred in several cultures and countries during the last few generations (Flynn, 1999; Neisser & others, 1996). For example, average IQ scores in Japan have risen dramatically since World War II.

In a survey of intelligence test scores around the world, 14 nations were found to have shown significant gains in average IQ scores in just one generation (Flynn, 1994, 1999). The average IQ score in the United States has also steadily increased over the past century (Kaufman, 1990). Such changes in a population can be accounted for only by environmental changes, because the amount of time involved is far too short for genetically influenced changes to have occurred.

FIGURE 7.9 The Two Pots Analogy Because the two environments are very different, no conclusions can be drawn about possible overall genetic differences between the plants in pot A and the plants in pot B.

Individual differences in height *within* the group are due to genetics because environment is the same

Corn plants

Pot A
Rich soil, many nutrients

Pot B
Poor soil, few nutrients

Difference in average height *between* groups is due to environment

*W*e need to appreciate that all human behavior is based on biology and, hence, will involve some degree of genetic influence. But, equally, all social behavior is bound to be affected by social context and, hence, will involve an important environmental influence.

Michael R. Rutter (1997)

stereotype threat
A psychological predicament in which fear that you will be evaluated in terms of a negative stereotype about a group to which you belong creates anxiety and self-doubt, lowering performance in a particular domain that is important to you.

Table 7.2

The Effects of Discrimination on Scores in Japan

Percentage of Children Scoring in a Given Range

Range of IQ Scores	Non-Burakumin	Burakumin
Above 125	23.3	2.6
124–109	31.8	19.5
108–93	23.3	22.1
92–77	11.7	18.2
Below 76	9.9	37.6

SOURCE: Adapted from De Vos & Wagatsuma (1967), Table 2, p. 261.

The Burakumin of Japan are not racially different from other Japanese, but they have suffered from generations of discrimination. Their average IQ scores are about 10 to 15 points below those of mainstream Japanese (Ogbu, 1986). In many other cultures, a similar gap in IQ scores exists between the discriminated-against minority and the dominant group.

Cross-Cultural Studies of Group Discrimination and IQ Differences

The effect of social discrimination on intelligence test scores has been shown in numerous cross-cultural studies (see Ogbu, 1986). In many different societies, average IQ is lower for members of a discriminated-against minority group, even when that group is not racially different from the dominant group.

Take the case of the Burakumin people of Japan. Americans typically think of Japan as relatively homogeneous, and indeed the Burakumin are not racially different from other Japanese. They look the same and speak the same language. However, the Burakumin are the descendants of an outcast group that for generations worked as tanners and butchers. Because they handled dead bodies and killed animals, the Burakumin were long considered unclean and unfit for social contact. For centuries, they were forced to live in isolated enclaves, apart from the rest of Japanese society (De Vos, 1992; De Vos & Wagatsuma, 1967).

Today, there are about 3 million Burakumin in Japan. Although the Burakumin were legally emancipated from their outcast status many years ago, substantial social discrimination against them persists (Payton, 1992). Because there is no way to tell if a Japanese citizen is of Burakumin descent, there are dozens of private detective agencies in Tokyo and other Japanese cities that openly specialize in tracking Burakumin who are trying to "pass" and hide their background. Corporations in Japan routinely consult computer databanks to identify Burakumin who apply for jobs, as do individuals who wish to investigate the ancestral background of prospective marriage partners.

The Burakumin are the poorest people in Japan. They are only half as likely as other Japanese to graduate from high school or attend college. Although there are no racial differences between the Burakumin and other Japanese, the average IQ scores of the Burakumin in Japan are well below those of other Japanese. As shown in Table 7.2, their average IQ scores are about 10 to 15 points below those of mainstream Japanese. However, when Burakumin families immigrate to the United States, they are treated like any other Japanese. The children do just as well in school—and on IQ tests—as any other Japanese-Americans (Ogbu, 1986).

Of course, Japan is not the only society that discriminates against a particular social group. Many societies discriminate against specific minority groups, such as the Harijans in India (formerly called the untouchables), West Indians in Great Britain, Maoris in New Zealand, and Jews of non-European descent in Israel.

Children belonging to these minority groups score 10 to 15 points lower on intelligence tests than do children belonging to the dominant group in their societies. Children of the minority groups are often one or two years behind dominant-group children in basic reading skills and mathematical skills. Minority-group children are overrepresented in remedial programs and in school dropout rates. They are also underrepresented in higher education. The impact of discrimination on group differences in IQ remains even when the minority-group and dominant-group members are of similar socioeconomic backgrounds (Ogbu, 1986). In many ways, the educational experiences of these minority groups seem to parallel those of black Americans, providing a cross-cultural perspective on the consistent effects of discrimination in many different societies.

In Culture and Human Behavior Box 7.4, we discuss another way that belonging to a stigmatized group can affect test performance.

The Burakumin Protest Centuries of Discrimination Members of the Burakumin Emancipation Alliance protest discrimination in a peaceful demonstration in Tokyo. Their vests proclaim their demand for basic human rights for the Burakumin people. Today, the Burakumin are the poorest group in Japan. Compared to the general population of Japan, only about half as many Burakumin graduate from high school or attend college.

CULTURE AND HUMAN BEHAVIOR 7.4

Stereotype Threat: Performing When There's a "Threat in the Air"

Tests such as the Wechsler Adult Intelligence Scale (WAIS), SAT, and the American College Test (ACT) are *standardized*. That means that every individual experiences the same testing conditions, instructions, materials, and test questions. Obviously, one goal of standardization is to help ensure that such tests are as fair and unbiased as possible. However, it is impossible to standardize all conditions, including the expectations that we think other people might have about our performance in a particular situation.

As psychologist Claude Steele has discovered, if those expectations are negative, they can cause us to perform below our actual ability level. Steele coined the term **stereotype threat** to describe this phenomenon, which occurs when members of a particular group fear that they will be evaluated in terms of a negative stereotype about their group. As Steele (1997) explains, "It's a situational threat—a threat in the air—that, in general form, can affect the members of any group about whom a negative stereotype exists, whether it's skateboarders, older adults, white men, or gang members. Where bad stereotypes about these groups apply, members of these groups can fear being reduced to that stereotype."

Stanford Psychologist Claude Steele As Claude Steele has discovered, the awareness of threatening stereotypes can affect performance. The anxiety and self-doubt caused by stereotype threat may help explain group differences in intelligence, math, and other test scores.

To illustrate, consider the gender stereotype that females are poor at math, especially advanced mathematics. (We dispel this myth in chapter 10, on gender and sexuality.) In one study, when female students took a difficult math test that was described in advance as producing gender differences, their scores were much lower than that of male students taking the same test. But when a matched group of female students took the same test but were told that it did *not* produce gender differences, their scores were equal to those of the male students (Spencer & others, 1999). Simply reminding the female students of the stereotype that women are less skilled in mathematics than men was enough to lower their scores.

Now consider a study by Margaret Shih and her colleagues (1999) showing just how easily stereotype awareness can be manipulated to affect test performance. Mathematically gifted Asian-American female college students were randomly assigned to two groups. One group filled out a questionnaire asking them several questions that were likely to remind them of their Asian background and activate the cultural stereotype that Asian-Americans have superior math abilities. The other group filled out a questionnaire asking them questions that were likely to remind them of their gender identity as females and activate the gender stereotype that women are not good at math. Then each group took a challenging math test.

The results? Those students who were reminded of their racial identity as Asians scored significantly higher on the exam than the students who were reminded of their gender identity as women. A control group of students, who filled out a neutral questionnaire, had scores in the middle of the two groups.

Why would being reminded of a negative stereotype undermine your performance on a test? Fear that you might confirm the negative stereotype creates self-doubt and anxiety (Blascovich & others, 2001; Stone & others, 1999). In turn, anxiety, apprehension, and nervousness interfere with your thinking and problem-solving abilities (Osborne, 2001;

Quinn & Spencer, 2001). Perhaps not surprisingly, those students who are most highly motivated to perform well are the ones most likely to be affected by stereotype threat (Wheeler & Petty, 2001).

The influence of stereotype threats is not confined to Asian-American or female students taking math tests or, for that matter, limited to tests of academic ability. Consider these additional examples:

- When told that a test was simply a laboratory task investigating problem-solving strategies and did not measure intellectual ability, black and white students scored equally well. But when a matched group of students were given the same test and told that it was a test of intellectual ability, black students did much more poorly than white students (Steele & Aronson, 1995).

- When reminded of the stereotype of the elderly being more forgetful, senior adults scored more poorly on memory tests than when they were not reminded of the stereotype. But when reminded of the *positive* stereotype that elderly people are wise, older individuals scored higher on the same memory tests (Levy, 1996).

- After completing questionnaires about their social and economic background, French students from a low socioeconomic background who took a test described as a measure of intellectual ability performed worse than students from a wealthy background. But when the test was presented as *not* reflecting intellectual ability, the students performed just as well as the students from a wealthy background (Croizet & Claire, 1998).

The key point here is that performance on tests, even tests that are carefully designed to be fair and objective, is surprisingly susceptible to social and cultural influences. How can the influence of stereotype threats be overcome? One way is for the test-giver to tackle the issue head-on: Simply saying that a particular test is racially fair or gender-neutral has been shown to reduce the effects of stereotype threat (Spencer & others, 1999).

Testing, Testing, Testing . . . Virtually all college students will be evaluated with standardized tests at some point in their college career. Although great lengths are taken to make tests as unbiased and objective as possible, many factors, both personal and situational, can affect performance on tests. Cultural factors, familiarity with the testing process, and the presence or absence of stereotype threat are just a few of the factors that can skew test results. So perhaps the best way to view standardized tests is as just one of many possible indicators of a student's level of knowledge—and of his or her potential to learn.

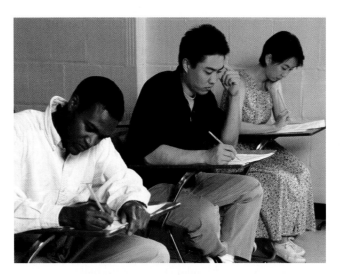

Are IQ Tests Culturally Biased?

Another approach to explaining group differences in IQ scores has been to look at cultural bias in the tests themselves. If standardized intelligence tests reflect white, middle-class cultural knowledge and values, minority-group members might do poorly on the tests not because of lower intelligence but because of unfamiliarity with the white, middle-class culture.

Researchers have attempted to create tests that are "culture-fair" or "culture-free." However, it is now generally recognized that it is virtually impossible to design a test that is completely culture-free. As cross-cultural psychologist Patricia Greenfield (1997) argues, ability tests "reflect the values, knowledge, and communication strategies of their culture of origin." Within that culture, the intelligence test may be a valid measure. Thus, a test will tend to favor the people from the culture in which it was developed.

Cultural differences may also be involved in *test-taking behavior* (Sternberg, 1995). People from different cultural backgrounds may use strategies in solving problems or organizing information that are different from those required on standard intelligence tests (Miller-Jones, 1989). In addition, such cultural factors as motivation, attitudes toward test taking, and previous experiences with tests can affect performance and scores on tests.

7.3 R·E·V·I·E·W

C·O·N·C·E·P·T

Determinants of Intelligence

1. Most intelligence experts agree that observed differences in average IQ scores between racial groups are due to _____.
   a. genetic factors
   b. environmental factors
   c. the deliberate construction of biased tests
   d. the use of culture-free tests

2. A researcher tests a group of identical twins raised together and a different group of identical twins who were separated at birth and raised in different environments. She finds that the IQ scores of each pair of twins in the first group are more similar than are the IQ scores of each pair of twins in the second group. This difference between groups is the result of _____.
   a. genetic influences
   b. environmental influences
   c. neither environmental nor genetic influences
   d. an equal degree of environmental and genetic influences

3. One scoop of seeds is planted in a plot of farmland with rich soil and adequate rainfall. Another scoop of seeds from the same batch is planted in a backyard with poor soil that is never watered or fertilized. On the average, the seeds in the rich soil grow taller than the seeds in the poor soil. The difference between the average height of the plants in the rich soil and that of the plants in the poor soil is best accounted for by _____.
   a. genetic factors
   b. environmental factors
   c. 30 percent genetics and 70 percent environment
   d. 70 percent genetics and 30 percent environment

4. In question 3, the plants in the rich farmland vary in height. Some of the plants are taller than others. The same is true of the plants in the backyard. The differences in heights of the plants in the same plot of soil is best accounted for by _____.
   a. genetics
   b. environment
   c. 30 percent genetics and 70 percent environment
   d. 70 percent genetics and 30 percent environment

Summing Up
Thinking, Language, and Intelligence

On the basis of our discussion about the influences of heredity and environment on intelligence, we can draw three broad conclusions about the debate surrounding intelligence and race.

First, it's clear that the IQ of any given individual, regardless of what racial group that person belongs to, is the result of the complex interaction of hereditary and environmental factors. Second, as far as the IQ differences between racial groups are concerned, environmental factors are much more likely to account for such differences than are genetic factors (Neisser & others, 1996). Third, within any given racial group, the differences among people are due at least as much to environmental influences as they are to genetic influences (Plomin & others, 1994).

IQ scores measure only the selected aspects of intelligence they are designed to measure. We draw on many different types of mental abilities to solve problems, adapt to our environment, and communicate with others. As the story of Mr. and Ms. Fix-It in the Prologue illustrated, solving even the most mundane problems of life often involves creative and flexible thinking. In the Application section, we provide a variety of suggestions for enhancing your creativity.

APPLICATION   A Workshop on Creativity

Creativity can be defined as a group of cognitive processes used to generate useful, original, and novel ideas or solutions to problems (Amabile & Tighe, 1993; Ochse, 1990). Notice that usefulness, along with originality, is involved in judging creativity. An idea can be highly original, but if it lacks usefulness it is not regarded as creative.

Although we typically think of creativity in terms of artistic expression, the act of creativity is almost always linked to the process of solving some problem. In that sense, creativity can occur in virtually any area of life.

Can you learn to be more creative? In general, creativity experts agree that you can. Although there is no simple formula that guarantees creative success, a few basic ingredients are central to the process of creative thinking. Here are several suggestions that can enhance your ability to think creatively.

1. Choose the goal of creativity.

Psychologists have found that virtually everyone possesses the intelligence and cognitive processes needed to be creative (Weisberg, 1988, 1993). But the creative individual values creativity as a personal goal. Without the personal goal of creativity, the likelihood of doing something creative is slim.

CALVIN AND HOBBS

2. Reinforce creative behavior.

People are most creative when motivated by their own interest, the enjoyment of a challenge, and a personal sense of satisfaction and fulfillment (Amabile, 1996, 2001). This is called *intrinsic motivation.* In contrast, when people are motivated by external rewards, such as money or grades, they are displaying *extrinsic motivation.*

Researchers used to believe that extrinsic rewards made creative behavior much less likely. New research, however, seems to demonstrate that rewards can increase creative behavior in a person who has some training in generating creative solutions to problems (Eisenberger & others, 1998). When people know that creative behavior will be rewarded, they are more likely to behave in a creative way (Eisenberger & Cameron, 1996).

3. Engage in problem finding.

In many cases, the real creative leap involves recognizing that a problem exists. This is referred to as *problem finding.* We often overlook creative opportunities by dismissing trivial annoyances rather than recognizing them as potential problems to be solved.

For example, consider the minor annoyance experienced by a man named Art Fry. Fry, a researcher for 3M Corporation, regularly sang in his church choir. In order to locate the hymns quickly during the Sunday service, Fry used little scraps of paper to mark their places. But the scraps of paper would sometimes fall out when Fry stood up to sing, and he'd have to fumble to find the right page (Kaplan, 1990).

While sitting in church, Fry recognized the "problem" and came up with a relatively simple solution. If you put a substance that is sticky, but not *too* sticky, on the scraps of paper, they'll stay on the page and you can take them off when they are not needed anymore.

If you haven't already guessed, Art Fry invented Post-it notes. The formula for the adhesive had been discovered years earlier at 3M, but nobody could imagine a use for a glue that did not bond permanently. The mental set of the 3M researchers was to find *stronger* glues, not weaker ones. Fry's story demonstrates the creative value of recognizing problems instead of simply dismissing them.

A technique called *bug listing* is one useful strategy to identify potential problems (Adams, 1979). Bug listing involves creating a list of things that annoy, irritate, or bug you. Such everyday annoyances are problems in need of creative solutions.

4. Acquire relevant knowledge.

Creativity requires a good deal of preparation (Weisberg, 1993). Acquiring a solid knowledge base increases your potential for recognizing how to creatively extend your knowledge or apply it in a new way. For example, if Don did not understand how the faucet in the kitchen functioned, he would never have been able to come up with a creative way to repair it. As the famous French chemist Louis Pasteur said, "Chance favors the prepared mind."

5. Try different approaches.

Creative people are flexible in their thinking. They step back from problems, turn them over, and mentally play with possibilities. By being flexible and imagi-

The Prairie Dog Vacuum Gay Balfour's invention harmlessly sucks prairie dogs out of their burrows and deposits them into a holding tank in his truck so that they can be relocated. According to Balfour, "It's quite a ride but the prairie dogs are not too disturbed about it."

native, people seeking creative solutions generate many different responses. This is called *divergent thinking*, because it involves moving away (or diverging) from the problem and considering it from a variety of perspectives (Baer, 1993).

Looking for analogies is one technique to encourage divergent thinking. In problem solving, an *analogy* is the recognition of some similarity or parallel between two objects or events that are not usually compared. Similarities can be drawn in terms of the objects' operation, function, purpose, materials, or other characteristics.

For example, Gay Balfour of Colorado recognized a problem—the need to re-

move prairie dogs from an area without killing them. ("New Prairie Dog Vacuum," 1992). When trying to come up with a way to get the prairie dogs out of their burrows, Balfour was struck by the analogy between a vacuum cleaner and the suction devices used to clean out septic tanks. Balfour devised a machine that sucked the critters out of the ground without harming them so they could be relocated. On one occasion, he vacuumed up 53 prairie dogs in a little over an hour.

6. Exert effort and expect setbacks.

Flashes of insight or inspiration can play a role in creativity, but they usually occur only after a great deal of work. Whether you're trying to write a brilliant term paper or design the next Beanie Baby, creativity requires effort and persistence.

Finally, the creative process is typically filled with obstacles and setbacks. The best-selling novelist Stephen King endured years of rejection of his manuscripts before his first book was published. Thomas Edison tried thousands of filaments before he created the first working light bulb. But in the face of obstacles and setbacks, the creative person perseveres.

To summarize our workshop on creativity, we'll use the letters of the word *create* as an acronym. Thus, the basic ingredients of creativity are

- **C**hoose the goal of creativity.
- **R**einforce creative behavior.
- **E**ngage in problem finding.
- **A**cquire relevant knowledge.
- **T**ry different approaches.
- **E**xert effort and expect setbacks.

Chapter Review
Thinking, Language, and Intelligence

Key Points

Introduction: Thinking, Language, and Intelligence

- **Cognition** refers to the mental activities involved in acquiring, retaining, and using knowledge.

- **Thinking** involves manipulating internal, mental representations of information in order to draw inferences and conclusions. Thinking often involves the manipulation of two kinds of mental representations: **mental images** and **concepts.**

- Most research has been done on visual mental images. We seem to treat mental images much as we do actual visual images or physical objects.

- Thinking also involves the use of concepts. **Formal concepts** are defined by logical rules. **Natural concepts** are likely to have fuzzy rather than rigid boundaries. We determine membership in natural concepts by comparing an object with our **prototype** for the natural concept. The more similar an item is to the prototype, the more quickly and easily we can determine whether it is an instance of the concept.

Solving Problems and Making Decisions

- **Problem solving** refers to thinking and behavior directed toward attaining a goal that is not readily available.

- Strategies commonly used in problem solving include **trial and error, algorithms,** and **heuristics.** Heuristics include breaking a problem into a series of subgoals and working backward from the goal. Sometimes problems are resolved through **insight** or **intuition.**

- **Functional fixedness** and **mental set** are two common obstacles to problem solving.

- Decision-making models include the single-feature model, the additive model, and the elimination by aspects model. Different strategies may be most helpful in different situations.

- When making risky decisions, we often use the **availability heuristic** and the **representativeness heuristic** to help us estimate the likelihood of events.

Language and Thought

- **Language** is a system for combining arbitrary symbols to produce an infinite number of meaningful statements.

- Language has the following characteristics: Meaning is conveyed by arbitrary symbols whose meaning is shared by speakers of the same language; language is a rule-based system; language is generative; and language involves displacement. Language influences thinking by affecting our perceptions of others.

- Animals communicate with members of their own species, sometimes in a complex fashion. They can also be taught to communicate with humans. Bonobos and dolphins seem to have demonstrated an elementary grasp of the rules of syntax. **Animal cognition** is an active field of research in comparative psychology.

Measuring Intelligence

- **Intelligence** can be defined as the global capacity to think rationally, act purposefully, and deal effectively with the environment. Intelligence tests are designed to measure general mental abilities.

- Alfred Binet developed the first widely accepted intelligence test, which incorporated the idea of a **mental age** that was different from chronological age. Binet did not believe that intelligence was inborn or fixed or that it could be described by a single number.

- Lewis Terman adapted Binet's test for use in the United States and developed the concept of the **intelligence quotient,** or **IQ** score. Terman believed that success in life was primarily determined by IQ.

- Group intelligence tests were developed for screening military recruits during World War I.

- David Wechsler developed the Wechsler Adult Intelligence Scale (WAIS), which included scores on subtests that measured different mental abilities. Wechsler also changed the method of calculating overall IQ scores.

- **Achievement tests** and **aptitude tests** are two types of psychological tests. Psychological tests must meet the requirements of **standardization, reliability,** and **validity.** The norms, or standards, for intelligence tests follow the **normal curve,** or **normal distribution,** of scores.

The Nature of Intelligence

- Debate over the nature of intelligence centers on two key issues: (1) whether intelligence is a single factor or a cluster of different abilities and (2) how narrowly intelligence should be defined.

- Charles Spearman believed that intelligence could be described as a single factor, called **general intelligence,** or the **g factor.**

- Louis L. Thurstone believed that there were seven primary mental abilities.

- Howard Gardner believes that there are multiple intelligences. He defines *intelligence* as the ability to solve problems or create products that are valued within a cultural setting.

- Robert Sternberg's **triarchic theory of intelligence** emphasizes both the universal aspects of intelligence and the importance of adapting to a particular cultural environment. He identifies three forms of intelligence: analytic, creative, and practical intelligence.

■ The IQ of any individual is the result of a complex interaction between heredity and environment. Intelligence is not determined by a single gene, but by the interaction of multiple genes.

■ Twin studies are used to determine the degree to which genetics contributes to complex characteristics such as intelligence. **Heritability** refers to the percentage of variation within a given population that is due to heredity. Within a given racial group, the effects of environment and genetics are roughly equal.

■ There are differences in the average IQ scores for different racial groups. However, there is more variation within a particular group than there is between groups.

■ Although it is possible to calculate the differences within a given group that are due to heredity, it is not possible to calculate the differences between groups that are due to heredity. Unless the environments are identical, no comparisons can be drawn. Rather than genetic factors, environmental factors are more likely to be the cause of average IQ differences among groups.

■ Cross-cultural studies have demonstrated that the average IQ scores of groups subject to social discrimination are frequently lower than the average IQ scores of the dominant social group, even when the groups are not racially different.

■ Intelligence tests can be culturally biased. All intelligence tests reflect the culture in which they are developed. Cultural factors may also influence test-taking behavior and individual performance. IQ scores reflect only selected aspects of intelligence.

Key Terms

cognition, p. 280

thinking, p. 281

mental image, p. 281

concept, p. 283

formal concept, p. 283

natural concept, p. 283

prototype, p. 284

problem solving, p. 284

trial and error, p. 284

algorithm, p. 285

heuristic, p. 285

insight, p. 286

intuition, p. 286

functional fixedness, p. 286

mental set, p. 287

availability heuristic, p. 289

representativeness heuristic, p. 289

language, p. 292

linguistic relativity hypothesis, p. 294

animal cognition, p. 296

intelligence, p. 296

mental age, p. 297

intelligence quotient (IQ), p. 297

achievement test, p. 300

aptitude test, p. 300

standardization, p. 300

normal curve (normal distribution), p. 301

reliability, p. 301

validity, p. 301

g factor (general intelligence), p. 302

triarchic theory of intelligence, p. 305

heritability, p. 307

stereotype threat, p. 311

creativity, p. 313

Key People

Alfred Binet (1857–1911) French psychologist who, along with French psychiatrist Théodore Simon, developed the first widely used intelligence test. (p. 297)

Howard Gardner (b. 1943) Contemporary American psychologist whose theory of intelligence states that there is not one intelligence, but multiple independent intelligences. (p. 303)

Charles Spearman (1863–1945) British psychologist who advanced the theory that a general intelligence factor, called the *g* factor, is responsible for overall intellectual functioning. (p. 302)

Robert Sternberg (b. 1949) Contemporary American psychologist whose *triarchic theory of intelligence* includes three forms of intelligence (analytic, creative, and practical). (p. 304)

Lewis Terman (1877–1956) American psychologist who translated and adapted the Binet-Simon intelligence test for use in the United States; he also began a major longitudinal study of the lives of gifted children in 1921. (p. 297)

Louis L. Thurstone (1887–1955) American psychologist who advanced the theory that intelligence is composed of several primary mental abilities and cannot be accurately described by an overall general or *g* factor measure. (p. 303)

David Wechsler (1896–1981) American psychologist who developed the Wechsler Adult Intelligence Scale, the most widely used intelligence test. (p. 298)

Concept Review Answers

7.1   page 291

1. heuristic
2. insight (O = one, T = two, etc.)
3. algorithm
4. trial and error

5. availability heuristic
6. single-feature model
7. representativeness heuristic

7.2   page 305

1. Sternberg
2. Binet
3. Wechsler

4. Spearman
5. Gardner

6. Thurstone
7. Terman

7.3   page 313

1. b   2. b   3. b   4. a

Web Companion   Review Activities

You can find additional review activities at **www.worthpublishers.com/hockenbury**
The Psychology 3e Web Companion has a self-scoring practice quiz, flashcards, two interactive crossword puzzles, and other activities to help you master the material in this chapter.

LA Marathon 2000

chapter 8

Motivation and Emotion

Prologue

One Step at a Time

"Nonsmoking section, please," Randy said to the hostess.

The request caught Don off guard. "Quit smoking again?" Don asked, trying not to sound too unconvinced.

"Yep, and this time it's for good," Randy said flatly as they walked toward the table. "I'm going to clean up my act. I quit coffee about three weeks ago, cigarettes about two weeks ago, and I joined a health club one week ago."

"And what motivated you to make all these changes?"

"I'm going to run this year's Tulsa Run," Randy explained matter-of-factly.

Don looked at Randy with a deadpan expression. "The Tulsa Run? Let me get this straight, Randy. You quit smoking and joined a health club so you can run nine miles in a race with 10,000 other runners. Why?!"

Randy smiled his trademark, funny little smile, the one that usually means he's thinking about four steps ahead of you. "To see if I can do it," he explained.

"Got'cha," Don said, nodding. "So, tell me, does Sara feel like she's dating a whole new guy?"

"I hope Sara *is* dating a whole new guy," Randy replied, his facial expression tensing as he glanced down at the menu. "Sara and I broke up last month."

Now it was Don's turn to glance away as he considered the unexpected comment. After a moment, Don quietly said, "I'm sorry to hear that, Randy. I know that you and Sara were having . . ."

"Nothing to be sorry about," Randy interrupted. "I just got to the point that I couldn't handle her emotional swings any more. She was just so unpredictable. Actually, Don, I'm relieved that it's over."

"You want to talk about it?"

"We just did," Randy said, and smiled again, ready to change topics. "Have you still got that book on running?"

"*Galloway's Book on Running*? Sure, you want to borrow it?"

It was early May when that conversation took place. The Tulsa Run happens every year on the last Saturday in October. That meant that Randy had about five months to train for the race. His training began very slowly at first, largely because he had no choice but to start slowly. He could jog about half a block before he was gasping for breath. After regaining his breath, he'd jog another half a block. Nonetheless, Randy would jog/walk about three miles a day.

By late June, Randy had made significant progress and crossed an important threshold. He could jog a mile before he had to stop and catch his breath. Don assumed that

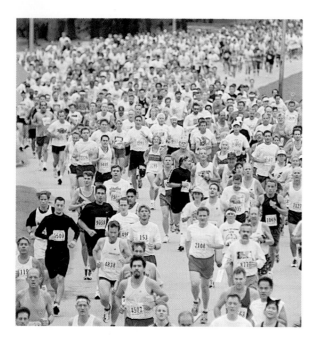

Motivation: What Makes Them Run? Every October, some 10,000 runners compete in the annual Tulsa Run. What motivates people to run this grueling 9.3-mile race? Why do they do it? Motivation researchers study the "why" of human behavior—the forces that motivate an individual to act.

Randy would abandon his Tulsa Run goal by midsummer, when the sweltering Tulsa heat makes running at any time of day uncomfortable. But Randy persevered. He switched to a morning routine, arriving at the Riverparks jogging trail around 6:00 A.M. His new girlfriend, Linda, bicycled alongside Randy as he plodded along the scenic trails. By mid-July, Randy's confidence soared as he passed another threshold. He could jog two miles nonstop.

In early September, Randy ran in his first official race—a three-mile run. Although he had to walk briefly during the middle of the race, he finished with an average time of about nine minutes per mile. And in all fairness, it was pretty impressive for a guy who couldn't even jog a block three months earlier.

In early October, Randy twisted his ankle while running, and Don was certain Randy's Tulsa Run goal would finally evaporate. It didn't. Instead, Randy worked out at the health club, "running" in the swimming pool as his ankle healed. Less than two weeks later, he was back on the jogging path, Linda riding along beside him.

The last Saturday in October finally arrived. As the starting gun sounded on that glorious fall morning, some 10,000 runners surged forward to cover 9.3 miles. Randy was somewhere in the throng of runners. The professional runners, of course, always win the race with extraordinary times. So what are all the other runners trying to accomplish? Many of them are trying to achieve a personal "best" time. Regular local runners are often trying to improve their standing in their age and gender categories. And many people, like Randy, are simply trying to prove that they can do it.

Randy's personal goal was to finish the Tulsa Run in eight-minute miles or better—the ambitious goal he had set for himself back in May. Although Randy had never run more than six miles at a time in all of his training, he was certain he could finish the Tulsa Run. And finish he did. In the final stretch of the Tulsa Run, Randy flat out sprinted the last four blocks, blazing across the finish line at 1 hour, 14 minutes, and 10 seconds. His average time? *Exactly* eight minutes per mile.

It is impossible to capture in words the exhilaration that Randy felt on that Saturday. He was on an emotional high for the rest of the weekend. His sense of achievement was complete: He had set a very challenging goal for himself, worked toward it literally one step at a time, and attained it.

Introduction

Motivation and Emotion

Key Theme

■ **Motivation refers to the forces acting on or within an organism to initiate and direct behavior.**

Key Questions

■ **What three characteristics are associated with motivation?**
■ **How is emotion related to the topic of motivation?**

There's no question that "something" energized Randy's behavior, not just to start jogging but also to make sweeping changes in his life. For that matter, "something" inspired you to pick up this text, so that you are reading these words right now. And, going a step further, "something" moved us to write these words.

That "something" is what the topic of **motivation** is about—the biological, emotional, cognitive, or social forces that act on or within you, initiating and directing your behavior. Typically, psychologists don't measure motivation directly. Instead, some type of motivation is *inferred* when an organism performs a particular behavior, such as curiosity motivating exploratory behavior or hunger

motivation
The biological, emotional, cognitive, or social forces that activate and direct behavior.

motivating eating behavior. Indeed, the forces that activate your behavior can take many different forms, including biological, psychological, or social forces.

As an explanatory concept, motivation is very useful in both the scientific sense and the everyday sense. In conversations, people routinely use the word *motivation* to understand or explain the "why" behind the behavior of others. "And what motivated you to join a health club?" "She is so motivated to get her pilot's license that she started going to the library every night to study for the written exam." Everyday statements like these reflect three basic characteristics commonly associated with motivation: activation, persistence, and intensity.

Activation is demonstrated by the initiation or production of behavior, such as Randy's initiating his daily training to prepare for the Tulsa Run. *Persistence* is demonstrated by continued efforts or the determination to achieve a particular goal, often in the face of obstacles. Despite scorching summer heat and an injury, Randy never wavered in his dogged determination to accomplish the goal he had set for himself. Finally, *intensity* is seen in the greater vigor of responding that usually accompanies motivated behavior. In Randy's case, he pursued his goal with considerable intensity, practicing harder and longer as the date of the Tulsa Run approached.

Motivation is closely tied to emotional processes, and vice versa. Often we are motivated to experience a particular emotion, such as feeling victorious. And the experience of different emotions—such as love, fear, or dissatisfaction—can motivate us to take action. Many forms of motivation have an emotional component, which is involved in the initiation and persistence of behavior. One reflection of the emotional intensity of Randy's motivation was the exhilaration he experienced when he finally achieved the goal he had set for himself. In the second half of the chapter, we'll take a detailed look at emotion. As you'll see, *emotion* is a psychological state involving three distinct components: subjective experience, a physiological response, and a behavioral or expressive component.

© 2002 The New Yorker Collection from cartoonbank.com. Barbara Smaller.

"Could you give me a little push?"

Motivational Concepts and Theories

Key Theme
- Over the past century, instinct, drive, incentive, arousal, and humanistic theories were proposed to explain the general principles of motivation.

Key Questions
- How does each theory explain motivation?
- What were the limitations of each theory?
- What lasting ideas did each theory contribute to the study of motivation?

During the twentieth century, several broad theories of motivation were proposed. Each model eventually proved to be limited, explaining only certain aspects of motivation. However, key ideas and concepts from each model became essential to a complete understanding of motivation and were incorporated into newer theories. As you'll see in this section, the concepts used to explain motivation have become progressively more diverse.

Instinct Theories
Inborn Behaviors as Motivators

In the late 1800s, the fledgling science of psychology initially embraced instinct theories to explain motivation. According to **instinct theories,** people are motivated to engage in certain behaviors because of evolutionary

instinct theories
The view that certain human behaviors are innate and due to evolutionary programming.

drive theories
The view that behavior is motivated by the desire to reduce internal tension caused by unmet biological needs.

homeostasis
(home-ee-oh-STAY-sis) The idea that the body monitors and maintains internal states, such as body temperature and energy supplies, at relatively constant levels; in general, the tendency to reach or maintain equilibrium.

Table 8.1

James's List of Instincts

Attachment	Resentment
Fear	Curiosity
Disgust	Shyness
Rivalry	Sociability
Greediness	Bashfulness
Suspicion	Secretiveness
Hunting	Cleanliness
Play	Modesty
Shame	Love
Anger	Parental Love

In his famous text *The Principles of Psychology,* William James (1890) devoted a lengthy chapter to the topic of instinct. Listed above are some of the human instincts that James noted.

programming. Just as animals display automatic and innate instinctual behavior patterns called *fixed action patterns,* such as migration or mating rituals, human behavior was also thought to be motivated by inborn instinctual behavior patterns.

Inspired by Charles Darwin's (1859, 1871) landmark theory of evolution, early psychologists like William James and William McDougall (1908) devised lists of human instincts. Table 8.1 is a collection of the human instincts that William James included in his famous text, *Principles of Psychology.* In discussing instincts, James (1890) noted with an air of superiority, "It will be observed that no other mammal, not even the monkey, shows so large an array of instincts."

By the early 1900s, thousands of instincts had been proposed in one expert's list or another to account for just about every conceivable human behavior (Bernard, 1924). (The early instinct theorists were, no doubt, motivated by a "listing instinct.") But what does it mean to say that an assertive person has a "self-assertion instinct"? Or to say that our friend Randy had a "jogging instinct"? The obvious problem with the early instinct theories was that merely describing and labeling behaviors did not explain them.

By the 1920s, instinct theories had fallen out of favor as an explanation of human motivation, primarily because of their lack of explanatory power. But the more general idea that some human behaviors are innate and genetically influenced remained an important element in the overall understanding of motivation. Today, psychologists taking the *evolutionary perspective* consider how our evolutionary heritage may influence patterns of human behaviors, such as eating behaviors or the expression of emotions. We'll consider what the evolutionary perspective has to say about both of those examples later in the chapter.

Drive Theories
Biological Needs as Motivators

Beginning in the 1920s, instinct theories were replaced by drive theories. In general, **drive theories** asserted that behavior is motivated by the desire to reduce internal tension caused by unmet biological needs, such as hunger or thirst. The basic idea was that these unmet biological needs "drive" or "push" us to behave in certain ways that will lead to a reduction in the drive. When a particular behavior successfully reduces a drive, the behavior becomes more likely to be repeated when the same need state arises again.

Leading drive theorists, including psychologists Robert S. Woodworth (1918, 1921) and Clark L. Hull (1943, 1952), believed that drives are triggered by the internal mechanisms of homeostasis. The principle of **homeostasis** states that the body monitors and maintains relatively constant levels of internal states, such as body temperature, fluid levels, and energy supplies. If any of these internal conditions deviates very far from the

Motivation and Drive Theories According to drive theories of motivation, behavior is motivated by biological drives to maintain homeostasis, or an optimal internal balance. After a long soccer practice on a hot day, these high school students are motivated to sit down, cool off, and drink water. Drive theories of motivation are useful in explaining biological motives like hunger, thirst, and fatigue, but are less useful in explaining psychological motives. For example, how could we explain their motivation to play competitive soccer? To practice long and hard on a hot summer day?

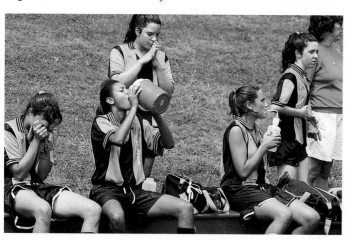

optimal level, the body initiates processes to bring the condition back to the normal or optimal range. Thus, the body automatically tries to maintain a "steady state," which is what *homeostasis* means.

According to drive theorists, when an internal imbalance is detected by homeostatic mechanisms, a **drive** to restore balance is produced. The drive activates behavior to reduce the need and to reestablish the balance of internal conditions. For example, after you have not eaten anything for several hours, the internal pangs of hunger signal an imbalance in your body's energy level. According to drive theorists, this unmet biological need creates a *drive state*—hunger—that motivates or energizes your behavior. And how might the drive of hunger energize you to behave? You might make your way to the kitchen and forage in the refrigerator for some leftover guacamole dip or chocolate cake.

Today, the drive concept remains useful in explaining motivated behaviors that clearly have biological components, such as hunger, thirst, and sexuality. However, drive theories also have limitations. Let's consider hunger again. Is the motivation of eating behavior strictly a matter of physiological need? Obviously not. People often eat when they're not hungry and don't eat when they are hungry. And how could drive theories account for the motivation to buy a lottery ticket or run a marathon?

Incentive Motivation
Goal Objects as Motivators

Building on the base established by drive theories, incentive theories emerged in the 1940s and 1950s. **Incentive theories** proposed that behavior is motivated by the "pull" of external goals, such as rewards, money, or recognition. It's easy to think of many situations in which a particular goal, such as a promotion at work, can serve as an external incentive that helps activate particular behaviors.

Incentive theories drew heavily from well-established learning principles, such as *reinforcement,* and the work of influential learning theorists, such as Pavlov, Watson, Skinner, and Tolman (see Chapter 5). Edward Tolman (1932) also stressed the importance of cognitive factors in learning and motivation, especially the *expectation* that a particular behavior will lead to a particular goal.

When combined, drive and incentive theories account for a broad range of the "pushes" and "pulls" motivating many of our behaviors. But even in combination, drive and incentive explanations of motivation still had limitations. In some situations, such as playing a rapid-response video game, our behavior seems to be directed toward *increasing* tension and physiological arousal. If you think about it, our friend Randy's decision to take up running was not motivated by either an internal, biological drive or an external incentive.

Arousal Theory
Optimal Stimulation as a Motivator

Racing your car down a barren stretch of highway, going to a suspenseful movie, shooting down the Super Slide at a water park—none of these activities seem to involve tension reduction, the satisfaction of some biological need, or the lure of some reward. Rather, performing the activity itself seems to motivate us. Why?

Arousal theory is based on the observation that people find both very high levels of arousal and very low levels of arousal quite unpleasant. When arousal is too low, we experience boredom and become motivated to *increase* arousal by seeking

drive
A need or internal motivational state that activates behavior to reduce the need and restore homeostasis.

incentive theories
The view that behavior is motivated by the pull of external goals, such as rewards.

arousal theory
The view that people are motivated to maintain an optimal level of arousal that is neither too high nor too low.

Motivated to an Extreme They are aptly called "extreme sports," and they include such diverse activities as hang gliding, ice climbing, white-water kayaking, bungee jumping, and parachuting from mountain cliffs and radio towers. People who enjoy such high-risk activities are usually sensation seekers. For them, the rush of adrenaline that they experience when they push the outer limit is an exhilarating and rewarding experience.

out stimulating experiences (Berlyne, 1960, 1971). But when arousal is too high, we seek to *reduce* arousal in a less stimulating environment. Thus, people are motivated to maintain an *optimal* level of arousal, one that is neither too high nor too low (Hebb, 1955). This optimal level of arousal varies from person to person, from time to time, and from one situation to another.

That the optimal level of arousal varies from person to person is especially evident in people dubbed *sensation seekers*. Sensation seekers find the heightened arousal of novel experiences very pleasurable. According to psychologist Marvin Zuckerman (1979, 1994), people who rank high on the dimension of **sensation seeking** have a need for varied, complex, and unique sensory experiences. No doubt Don ranks high on this dimension, since he has tried skydiving, aerobatic flying, and white-water rafting. (He also once ate a handful of biodegradable packing peanuts, much to the horror of a college secretary.) Although such experiences can sometimes involve physical or social risks, sensation seekers aren't necessarily drawn to danger—but rather to the novel experience itself. For example, college students who study abroad score significantly higher on sensation seeking than college students who stay in their country of origin (Schroth & McCormack, 2000).

Seeking Stimulation Like humans, animals are also motivated to seek out stimulation and explore novel environments. In his research with monkeys, Harry Harlow (1953c) found that arousal was a powerful motive. These young monkeys are trying to open a complicated lock, despite the lack of an incentive or reward for their behavior.

Like people, animals also seem to seek out novel environmental stimulation. Rats, cats, dogs, and other animals actively explore a new environment. In a series of classic studies, psychologist Harry Harlow (1953a, 1953b) showed that a monkey will spend hours trying to open a complicated lock, even when there is no incentive or reward for doing so. And, when kept in a boring cage, a monkey will "work" for the opportunity to open a window to peek into another monkey's cage or to watch an electric train run (Butler & Harlow, 1954).

Humanistic Theory
Human Potential as a Motivator

In the late 1950s, **humanistic theories of motivation** were championed by psychologists Carl Rogers and Abraham Maslow. Although not discounting the role of biological and external motivators, humanistic theories emphasized psychological and cognitive components in human motivation. Motivation was thought to be affected by how we perceive the world, how we think about ourselves and others, and our beliefs about our abilities and skills (Rogers, 1961, 1977).

According to the humanistic perspective, people are motivated to realize their highest personal potential. Although the motivation to strive for a positive self-concept and personal potential was thought to be inborn, humanistic theories also recognized the importance of the environment (Maslow, 1970). Without a supportive and encouraging environment—personal, social, and cultural—the motivation to strive toward one's highest potential could be jeopardized. Later in the chapter, we'll consider the most famous humanistic model of motivation, Maslow's *hierarchy of needs*.

In the next several sections, we'll look at several basic motives, starting with the fundamentally biological motive of hunger and eating. Later, we'll consider psychological motives, including competence and achievement motivation. As you'll see, the motivation concepts of drive, homeostasis, incentive, and arousal all come into play in understanding diverse human behaviors.

sensation seeking
The degree to which an individual is motivated to experience high levels of sensory and physical arousal associated with varied and novel activities.

humanistic theories of motivation
The view that emphasizes the importance of psychological and cognitive factors in motivation, especially the notion that people are motivated to realize their personal potential.

Biological Motivation
Hunger and Eating

Key Theme
- Hunger is a biological motive, but eating behavior is motivated by a complex interaction of biological, social, and psychological factors.

Key Questions
- What is energy homeostasis, and how does it relate to energy balance?
- What are the short-term signals that regulate eating behavior?
- What four chemical signals are involved in the long-term regulation of a stable body weight?
- How do set-point and settling-point theories differ?

Delicious or Disgusting? The need to eat is a universal human motive. However, culture influences *what* we eat, *when* we eat, and *how* we eat. At a market in Beijing, this eight-year-old is clearly enjoying her tasty treat—deep-fried grasshopper kabob. While not a feature at your typical U.S. restaurant, insects are standard fare in many countries. For example, grasshoppers, ant and fly larvae, and worms can be purchased as snacks in traditional markets in Mexico, where they have been a staple of the diet for thousands of years.

It seems simple: You're hungry, so you eat. But even a moment's reflection will tell you that eating behavior is not that straightforward. When, what, how much, and how often you eat is influenced by an array of psychological, biological, social, and cultural factors.

For example, think about what you ate yesterday. Now contrast your choices with food preferences in other cultures. A typical diet for the Dusan of northern Borneo in Southeast Asia includes anteater, gibbon (a small ape), snake, mouse, and rat meat. After these meats have spoiled to the point of being liquefied, the Dusan consume them with rice. South American Indians eat head lice, bees, iguanas, and monkeys. The Guianese of South America eat pebbles as a regular part of their diet, while the Vedda of Sri Lanka like rotted wood (see Fieldhouse, 1986). Clearly, cultural experience shapes our food choices (Rozin, 1996).

Themes of food and eating permeate many different dimensions of our lives. Psychologically, eating can be related to emotional states, such as depression, anxiety, or stress (Greeno & Wing, 1994; Tuomisto & others, 1998). Interpersonally, eating is often used to foster relationships, as when you have friends over for dinner or take a potential customer to lunch. We often rely on food-related adjectives to describe other people, as when we say that someone has a *sweet disposition* or a *sour outlook* on life. And, interestingly, our judgments about others may be influenced by what they eat (Stein & Nemeroff, 1995).

In the next several sections, we look at what researchers have learned about the motivational factors that trigger hunger and eating behavior. As you'll see, these research efforts have focused on answering several key questions:

- What signals regulate the motivation to start and stop eating?
- How do people maintain a stable body weight over time?
- Why do people become overweight or obese?
- What causes eating disorders?

*N*ot one man in a billion, when taking his dinner, ever thinks of utility. He eats because the food tastes good and makes him want more.

William James *Principles of Psychology* (1890)

Energy Homeostasis
Calories Consumed = Calories Expended

In order to understand the regulation of hunger and eating behavior, we need to begin with some basics on how food is converted to energy in the body. Once you understand how these mechanisms normally regulate body weight, we'll look at how these mechanisms become disrupted in obesity and eating disorders.

The food that you eat is broken down by enzymes and gradually absorbed in your intestines. As part of this process, food is converted into amino acids, fatty acids, and simple sugars, providing "fuel" for your body. The simple sugar **glucose,** commonly called *blood sugar,* provides the main source of energy for all mammals, including humans. In the liver, glucose is converted to and stored as

glucose
Simple sugar that provides energy and is primarily produced by the conversion of carbohydrates and fats; commonly called *blood sugar.*

insulin
Hormone produced by the pancreas that regulates blood levels of glucose and signals the hypothalamus, regulating hunger and eating behavior.

basal metabolic rate (BMR)
When the body is at rest, the rate at which it uses energy for vital functions, such as heartbeat and respiration.

adipose tissue
Body fat that is the main source of stored, or reserve, energy.

energy homeostasis
The long-term matching of food intake to energy expenditure.

glycogen, which can be easily converted back to glucose for energy. The hormone **insulin,** secreted by the pancreas, helps control blood levels of glucose and promotes the uptake of glucose by the muscles and other body tissues. Insulin also helps in regulating eating behavior and maintaining a stable body weight.

About one-third of your body's energy is expended for the routine physical activities of daily life, such as walking, lifting objects, brushing your teeth, and digesting the food you eat. The remaining two-thirds of your body's energy is used for continuous bodily functions that are essential to life, such as generating body heat, heartbeat, respiration, and brain activity. When you are lying down and resting, the rate at which your body uses energy for vital body functions is referred to as your **basal metabolic rate (BMR)** (Ravussin, 1995).

Obviously, you have to eat in order to have sufficient immediate energy for vital body functions and to survive. But another reason you eat is to maintain a reserve of stored energy. **Adipose tissue,** or body fat, is the main source of stored calories. Your liver, which monitors glucose levels in your bloodstream, can utilize this stored energy if necessary.

How much reserve energy is stored in your adipose tissue? People who are lean have about a month's worth of stored energy in their body fat, while people who are of normal weight have at least two months worth of stored energy. Someone who is seriously overweight has enough reserve energy stored in fat tissues to fuel basic energy requirements for more than a year (Levine & others, 1999).

Positive Versus Negative Energy Balance

For most of us there is considerable daily variation in what, when, how often, and how much we eat (de Castro & others, 2000; Marcelino & others, 2001). Yet despite this day-to-day variability in eating behavior, our body weight, including our stores of body fat, tends to stay relatively constant over the course of weeks, months, and even years (Keesey & Hirvonen, 1997). Your typical or average body weight is called your *baseline body weight.*

The tendency of our bodies to "defend" or maintain our baseline body weight and keep it stable over time is well documented (Schwartz & others, 2000). In numerous experiments, researchers have overfed or underfed animals, resulting in weight gain or loss. When the experimental feeding manipulation ends and the animals are allowed to eat as they wish, their body weight returns to baseline, usually within a few weeks (see Keesey & Hirvonen, 1997; Woods & others, 2000). In studies with humans, the same return to baseline body weight occurs after participants have gained or lost weight due to deliberate overeating or undereating (Leibel & others, 1995).

A regulatory process called **energy homeostasis** helps you maintain your baseline body weight. Over time, most people experience *energy balance* (see Figure 8.1). This means that the number of calories you consume almost exactly matches the number of calories you expend for energy. The result is that your body weight, including body fat stores, tends to stay stable.

However, energy balance can become disrupted if you eat more or less food than you need. If your caloric intake exceeds the amount of calories expended for energy, you experience a *positive energy balance.* When there is more glucose than your body needs for its energy requirements, the excess glucose is converted into reserve energy—fat. If positive energy balance persists over time, the size and number of the body fat cells that make up the adipose tissue increase. Conversely, if you diet or fast, *negative energy balance* occurs: Caloric intake falls short of the calories expended for energy. If this imbalance continues, body fat stores shrink as the reserve energy in fat cells is used for physical activity and metabolic functions.

These findings imply that energy homeostasis and a stable body weight are actively regulated by internal signals and mechanisms that influence eating behavior. But what exactly are these signals or mechanisms? To begin to answer that question, let's first consider some of the short-term influences motivating us to eat any given meal.

FIGURE 8.1

SOURCE: Adapted from Ravussin & Danforth (1999).

Short-Term Signals That Regulate Eating

Stopping to eat sometimes is so routine in our lives that most of us don't give it much thought. But in eating any given meal, both physiological and psychological factors are involved in motivating our behavior.

Physiological Changes That Predict Eating

Many people believe that eating is triggered by a drastic drop in blood glucose levels, which are rapidly restored by food consumption. This popular belief is *not* accurate. Actually, your blood levels of glucose and fats fluctuate very little over the course of a typical day. However, about 30 minutes before you eat, you experience a *slight* increase in blood levels of insulin and a *slight* decrease in blood levels of glucose. In experimental studies with both humans and rats, these small changes reliably predict the initiation of eating (Campfield & others, 1996; Melanson & others, 1999).

Once the meal is begun, blood glucose levels return to their baseline level. Interestingly, glucose returns to its baseline level well *before* the food is actually digested and absorbed. And, in fact, glucose will return to its baseline level even if you do *not* eat (see Figure 8.2).

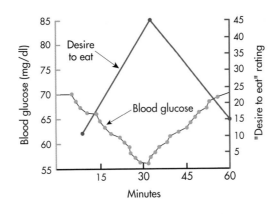

Two other internal factors are correlated with meal onset—body temperature and metabolism rate. Prior to eating, body temperature increases and metabolism decreases. As the meal is consumed, this internal physiological pattern reverses: Body temperature decreases and metabolism increases (De Vries & others, 1993; LeBlanc, 2000). This slight post-eating decrease in body temperature might explain why some people, including about a third of our students, occasionally feel cold after eating a meal.

FIGURE 8.2 **Blood Glucose and the Motivation to Eat** In this graph, the red dots depict the effects of insulin triggering a small decline in blood glucose over the course of about 30 minutes. As blood glucose decreases, the person's subjective desire to eat increases sharply, depicted by the blue line. Also notice that although this person did not eat, his blood glucose level returned to normal within the hour and his desire to eat diminished. In daily life, a small decline in blood glucose level is one of the factors that reliably predicts our motivation to eat (Campfield & others, 1996).

Psychological Factors That Trigger Eating

In Chapter 5, we described classical and operant conditioning. Both forms of conditioning can affect your eating behavior. Recall that *classical conditioning* involves acquiring a reflexive response to a stimulus that does not normally elicit that reflex. Using dogs as his experimental subjects, Pavlov repeatedly paired a sound (the initially neutral stimulus) with food (the unconditioned stimulus, or UCS), which reflexively triggered salivation (the unconditioned response, or UCR). After experiencing this pairing several times, the dogs became classically conditioned. The sound alone became a conditioned stimulus (CS) that elicited the conditioned response (CR) of salivation. Look back at Figure 5.1 on page 189 if you need to review the basic principles of classical conditioning.

Pavlov (1927) also showed that a *time interval* could become a conditioned stimulus. Exactly every 30 minutes, a dog was presented with food, which reflexively triggered salivation. Eventually, the dog became classically conditioned: As the end of the 30-minute interval neared, the dog began salivating even though no food had been presented.

Your eating behavior has probably also been influenced by years of classical conditioning. Much like Pavlov's dogs, you may be classically conditioned. The time of day at which you normally eat (the CS) elicits reflexive internal physiological changes (the CR), such as the slight changes in blood levels of insulin and glucose, increased body temperature, and decreased metabolism. In turn, these

Is Your Mouth Watering?
Does the sight of this freshly baked chocolate chip cookie make you feel hungry? Some foods—like chocolate chip cookies—have a strong positive incentive value. Even if you've just eaten a large meal, the reinforcing value of a chocolate chip cookie might tempt you to keep eating. Even if you weren't particularly hungry before you read this page, looking at this photograph might send you to the kitchen in search of a sweet snack—which is exactly what happened to your authors!

internal physiological changes increase your sense of hunger. Other stimuli, such as the setting in which you normally eat or just the sight of food utensils, can become associated with the anticipation of eating (T. L. Davidson, 2000; Nederkoorn & others, 2000; Tuomisto & others, 1998).

Operant conditioning also affects the motivation to eat. The premise of Skinner's operant conditioning is that behavior is shaped and maintained by its consequences. *Positive reinforcement* clearly plays a role in eating. Voluntary eating behaviors are followed by the addition of a *reinforcing stimulus*—food.

Granted, not all foods are equally reinforcing. Because of prior reinforcement experiences, people develop preferences for certain tastes, especially sweet, salty, and fatty tastes (Capaldi, 1996; Mennella & Beauchamp, 1996). Assuming you're not starving, a steaming plate of fried liver and onions probably holds less reinforcing appeal to you than tacos, Doritos, or Hostess Ho-Hos. In other word, these foods hold greater **positive incentive value** to you. Hence, your motivation to eat is influenced by prior learning experiences that have shaped your expectations, especially the anticipated pleasure of eating certain foods.

Satiation Signals: Sensing When to Stop Eating

The feeling of fullness and diminished desire to eat that accompanies eating a meal is termed **satiation.** Several signals combine to help trigger satiation. As you taste, chew, and swallow food, the specialized receptor cells called *taste buds* on your tongue, the roof of your mouth, and your throat are activated. Your taste buds register differences in the temperature, shape, size, texture, and taste qualities of the different food molecules (Schiffman & others, 1998). These taste receptor cells also activate chemical signals in your stomach and intestines to prepare for digesting the food. All of these signals are involved in eventually producing satiation (Cecil & others, 1998; Katz & others, 2000).

Another satiation signal involves *stretch receptors* in the stomach that communicate sensory information to the brainstem (Furness & others, 1999). The sensitivity of the stomach stretch receptors is increased by a hormone called **cholecystokinin,** thankfully abbreviated **CCK.** During meals, cholecystokinin is secreted by the small intestines and enters the bloodstream. In the brain, CCK acts as a neurotransmitter. Many studies have shown that CCK promotes satiation and reduces or stops eating (G. P. Smith & Gibbs, 1998). CCK also magnifies the satiety-producing effects of food in the stomach by slowing the rate at which the stomach empties (Liddle, 1997).

Psychological factors play a role in satiation, too. As you eat a meal, there is a decline in the positive incentive value of any available food, but especially the specific foods you are eating. So, after you have wolfed down four slices of pizza, the pizza's appeal begins to diminish. This phenomenon is termed **sensory-specific satiety** (Guinard & Brun, 1998; Hetherington & Rolls, 1996). Of course, if a *different* appealing food becomes available, your willingness to eat might return. Restaurants are well aware of this, which is why servers will bring a tempting platter of scrumptious desserts to your table after you've finished a large and otherwise satisfying dinner.

Long-Term Signals That Regulate Body Weight

In the last decade, researchers have discovered more than 20 different chemical messengers that monitor and help us maintain a stable body weight over time (see Schwartz & others, 2000; Woods & others, 2000). In this section we'll look at

positive incentive value
In eating behavior, the anticipated pleasure of consuming a particular food; in general, the expectation of pleasure or satisfaction in performing a particular behavior.

satiation
(say-she-A-shun) In eating behavior, the feeling of fullness and diminished desire to eat that accompanies eating a meal; in general, the sensation of having an appetite or desire fully or excessively satisfied.

cholecystokinin (CCK)
(kola-sis-tow-KINE-in) Hormone secreted primarily by the small intestines that promotes satiation; also found in the brain.

sensory-specific satiety
(sah-TIE-it-tee) The reduced desire to continue consuming a particular food.

four of the best-documented internal signals, including *leptin, insulin, neuropeptide Y,* and *corticotropin-releasing hormone.* Some of these signals act as very precise barometers of the amount of body fat we have at any given moment. We'll also look at how the hypothalamus in the brain responds to these internal signals, influencing eating behavior and the body's energy expenditure.

Leptin and Insulin

In 1995, researcher Jeffrey Friedman and his colleagues discovered a new hormone that they named **leptin,** from the Greek root *leptos,* meaning "thin" (Halaas & others, 1995). Leptin is secreted by the body's adipose tissue into the bloodstream. The amount of leptin that is secreted is directly correlated with the amount of body fat.

The brain receptor sites for leptin are located in several areas of the hypothalamus, including the *ventromedial hypothalamus* and the *lateral hypothalamus* (Friedman & Halaas, 1998). It's been known since the 1950s that the ventromedial and lateral areas of the hypothalamus are involved in regulating eating behavior. Neurons in the stomach and the gut also have leptin receptor sites (Kirchgessner & Liu, 1999).

Leptin is a key element in the feedback loop that regulates energy homeostasis. If positive energy balance occurs, the body's fat stores increase, and so do blood levels of leptin. When the leptin level in the brain increases, food intake is reduced and the size of fat stores shrink over time (Elmquist & others, 1998). Increased leptin levels also intensify the satiety-producing effects of CCK, further decreasing the amount of food consumed (Matson & others, 2000). Should negative energy balance occur, body fat stores shrink and there is a corresponding decrease in leptin blood levels, which triggers eating behavior.

The hormone *insulin* is also involved in brain mechanisms that control food intake and body weight. Like leptin, the amount of insulin secreted by the pancreas is directly proportional to the amount of body fat. In the brain, insulin receptors are located in the same hypothalamus areas as leptin receptors (Brüning & others, 2000). Increased brain levels of insulin are also associated with a reduction in food intake and body weight (Baskin & others, 1999). So in much the same way as leptin, insulin levels vary in response to positive or negative energy balance, triggering an increase or decrease in eating.

In combination, the coordinated fluctuations in leptin and insulin levels systematically influence the activity of other chemical signals in the brain, including *neuropeptide Y* and *corticotropin-releasing hormone.*

Neuropeptide Y and Corticotropin-Releasing Hormone

Abbreviated **NPY, neuropeptide Y** is a neurotransmitter manufactured throughout the brain, including the hypothalamus. During periods of negative energy balance and weight loss, decreased leptin and insulin levels promote the secretion of NPY by the hypothalamus. In turn, increased brain levels of neuropeptide Y trigger eating behavior, reduce body metabolism, and promote fat storage. Conversely, if positive energy balance and weight gain occur, neuropeptide Y activity decreases (A. Levine & Billington, 1997; Naveilhan & others, 1999).

Abbreviated **CRH, corticotropin-releasing hormone** is primarily manufactured in the hypothalamus and adjacent brain regions (Rowland & others, 1995). In the brain, the receptor sites for CRH are located in the same hypothalamus areas as those for leptin, insulin, and neuropeptide Y. When leptin and insulin signaling increases in the brain, CRH activity increases in the hypothalamus and surrounding areas (Van Dijk & others, 1999). This increased CRH activity reduces food intake and increases body metabolism, actions that promote weight loss. The opposite effects occur in response to negative energy balance and weight loss. CRH activity decreases, which helps promote eating and weight gain (see Schwartz & others, 1999; Seeley & others, 1996).

Ob/ob Mice, Before and After Leptin Leptin is a hormone produced by body fat. Because of a genetic mutation, these mice, dubbed *ob/ob* mice, lack the ability to produce leptin. Consequently, *ob/ob* mice behave as though their brain were telling them that their body fat reserves are completely depleted and that they are starving. *Ob/ob* mice have voracious appetites and five times as much body fat as normal weight mice. Yet they display the characteristics of a starving animal, including decreased immune system functioning, low body temperature, and lack of energy. When the *ob/ob* mouse on the right was given supplemental leptin, it lost the excess fat and began eating normally. Its body temperature, immune system, and metabolism also became normal (Friedman & Halaas, 1998). Unfortunately, what worked for obese mice has not worked as easily for obese people, although researchers remain hopeful.

leptin
Hormone produced by fat cells that signals the hypothalamus, regulating hunger and eating behavior.

neuropeptide Y (NPY)
Neurotransmitter found in several brain areas, most notably the hypothalamus, that stimulates eating behavior and reduces metabolism, promoting positive energy balance and weight gain.

corticotropin-releasing hormone (CRH)
Hormone manufactured primarily in the hypothalamus that reduces eating behavior and increases metabolism, promoting negative energy balance and weight loss; also spelled *corticotrophin.*

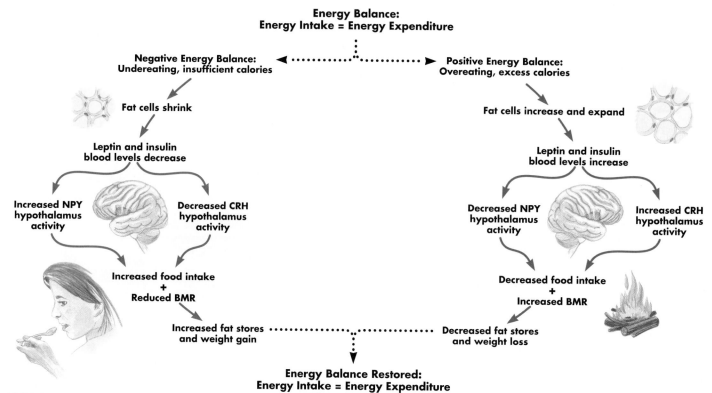

FIGURE 8.3 Maintaining a Stable Body Weight Over Time Multiple internal signals and mechanisms are involved in regulating our eating patterns and energy expenditure so that we maintain a stable body weight over time. In the above figure you can track the sequence of internal events that occur when energy balance is disrupted.

Figure 8.3 shows how these four internal signals interact to maintain a stable body weight over time. As the hypothalamus detects changes in leptin and insulin, the activity of NPY and CRH neural pathways increases or decreases. In turn, food intake and BMR are adjusted to promote or reduce weight gain. The end result? Over the course of time, energy balance is achieved. Your average baseline body weight stays stable because the number of calories you consume closely matches the calories you expend for energy. Or, at least, that's how it's supposed to work.

Eating and Body Weight over the Lifespan: Set Point or Settling Point?

So far we've discussed the regulation of eating in terms of the energy balance model, which is the essence of a popular theory called *set-point theory.* According to **set-point theory,** the body has a natural or optimal weight, called the *set-point weight,* that it is set to maintain. Much like a thermostat set to a particular temperature, your body vigorously defends this set-point weight from becoming lower or higher by regulating feelings of hunger and body metabolism (Keesey & Hirvonen, 1997; Keesey & Powley, 1986)

Although body weight tends to stay stable over extended periods of time, that does not necessarily mean that your baseline body weight is fixed at an optimal level throughout the lifespan. Instead, many people experience a strong tendency to drift to a heavier average body weight throughout adulthood. Why?

Settling-point models of weight regulation provide an alternate view that seems to better explain this tendency (see Pinel & others, 2000). According to settling-point models of weight regulation, your body weight tends to "settle" around the point at which equilibrium is achieved between energy expenditure and food consumption. Your *settling-point weight* will stay relatively stable as long as the factors influencing food consumption and energy expenditure don't change. However, if these factors do change, creating positive or negative energy balance, you will drift to a higher or lower settling-point body weight. In the next few sections, we'll consider some of the factors that contribute to the upward drift of body weight.

set-point theory
Theory that proposes that humans and other animals have a natural or optimal body weight, called the *set-point weight,* that the body defends from becoming higher or lower by regulating feelings of hunger and body metabolism.

settling-point models of weight regulation
General model of weight regulation suggesting that body weight settles, or stabilizes, around the point at which there is balance between the factors influencing energy intake and energy expenditure.

Excess Weight and Obesity
The Epidemic

Key Theme
- Overweight, obesity, and eating disorders are characterized by unhealthy body weight and maladaptive patterns of eating behavior.

Key Questions
- What is BMI, and why do people become overweight?
- What factors are involved in the development of obesity?
- What are the symptoms, characteristics, and causes of anorexia and bulimia nervosa?

In the United States today, six out of ten adults—approximately 100 million Americans—are either overweight or obese (National Center for Health Statistics, 2000b). As you can see in Figure 8.4a, the trend toward obesity has accelerated in recent years. This problem is not limited to the United States. Other countries also face the problem of an overweight population (see Table 8.2).

Figure 8.4b shows how the percentage of overweight Americans escalates throughout adulthood, peaking in the fifth and sixth decades of life. But even early in life, approximately one out of nine children and adolescents are overweight (National Center for Health Statistics, 2000a).

The national trend toward excessive weight gain contrasts sharply with our cultural ideal of beauty and physical attractiveness—a very slender body. A normal, healthy woman with a body weight that is appropriate for her height has approximately 22 to 25 percent body fat. But the standard for female beauty in our society is set by media depictions of supermodels, *Playboy* centerfolds, and Miss America contestants who are often 15 percent or more below their appropriate weight (Wilfley & Rodin, 1995). Thus, there is enormous cultural pressure, especially for women, to strive for unhealthy levels of thinness.

Not surprisingly, at any given time one out of three women *and* one out of four men are trying to lose weight. Annually, Americans spend $33 *billion* on weight-reduction programs and diet foods (National Institutes of Health, 2000). Along with cosmetic considerations, the motivation to lose weight also often involves health considerations.

Table **8.2**

Overweight People in Other Countries	
Australia	56%
Russian Federation	54%
Great Britain	51%
Germany	50%
Canada	48%
Colombia	41%
Italy	39%
France	38%
Spain	37%
Brazil	36%
Japan	18%
China	15%

SOURCES: Australian Institute of Health and Welfare (1999); Gardner & Halwell (2000); Heart and Stroke Foundation of Canada (1999).

FIGURE 8.4 The Growing Epidemic of Overweight and Obesity In graph **(a)**, you can see how the percentage of U.S. adults who are overweight or obese has rapidly increased in a very short period of time. Today, almost two-thirds of all American adults are overweight or obese. In graph **(b)**, you can see that the problem of being overweight escalates during young and middle adulthood. Males outpace females in being overweight in each age group. But although the data are not shown, more women than men are obese in each age group.

SOURCES: Adapted from National Center for Health Statistics (2000a, 2000b, 2001).

(a)

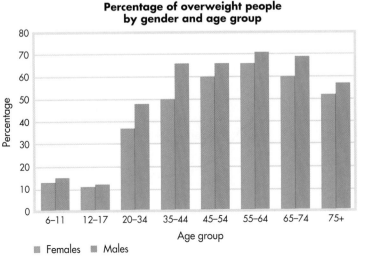

(b)

FIGURE 8.5 Calculating Your BMI: Where Do You Weigh In?

The **body mass index**, or **BMI**, is one measure of weight status. The BMI provides a single numerical value that represents your height in relation to your weight. To determine your BMI, grab a calculator and follow these steps:

Step 1. Multiply your weight in pounds by 704.5 _____

Step 2. Square your height in inches _____

Step 3. Divide step 1 by step 2 _____
This is your BMI.

If your BMI is:	You are:
18.4 or below	Underweight
18.5 to 24.9	Healthy weight
25.0 to 29.9	Overweight
30.0 and above	Obese

SOURCES: Centers for Disease Control and Prevention (2001); National Institutes of Health (2000).

FIGURE 8.6 Age and Gender Differences in Metabolism From infancy through adolescence, there is a steep decline in the rate at which your body uses energy for vital functions, such as heartbeat, breathing, and body heat. Your BMR continues to decrease by about 2 to 3 percent during each decade of adulthood. At all points in the lifespan, women's metabolic rate is 3 to 5 percent lower than men's (Arciero & others, 1993).

SOURCE: Stuart & Davis (1972).

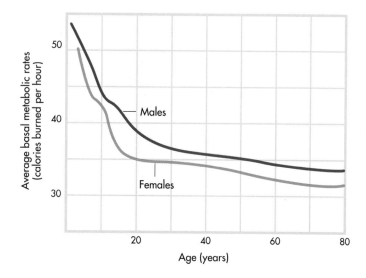

How do you know if you are at a healthy weight? The most widely used method to determine weight status is the **body mass index,** abbreviated **BMI.** For adults, the body mass index provides a single numerical value that reflects your weight in relation to your height (Figure 8.5).

Keep in mind that someone who is overweight has excess weight that may be attributable to muscle, bone, body water, or fat. It is possible to be overweight and very healthy, such as a bodybuilder or an athlete who has developed his or her muscle mass. In contrast, someone who is **obese** has an abnormally high proportion of body fat. Because the factors that contribute to becoming overweight are different from the critical factors involved in obesity, we'll consider each separately.

Factors Involved in Becoming Overweight

At the simplest level, the only way you can become overweight is if your caloric intake consistently exceeds your energy expenditure—the essence of *positive energy balance.* So the critical question is this: What kinds of factors are creating positive energy balance for so many people?

Positive Incentive Value: Highly Palatable Foods Rather than hunger, we are often enticed to eat by the *positive incentive value* of the available foods and the anticipated pleasures of consuming those highly palatable foods. Did someone say *Godiva chocolate?*

The "SuperSize It" Syndrome: Overeating In the last two decades, average daily caloric intake has increased nearly 10 percent for men and 7 percent for women (Koplan & Dietz, 1999). Every day, we are faced with the opportunity to overeat at all-you-can-eat brunches, pizza buffets, and fast-food restaurants that offer to "SuperSize" your portions for only a few cents more.

The Cafeteria Diet Effect: Variety = More Consumed If variety is the spice of life, it's also a sure-fire formula to pack on the pounds. Offered just one choice or the same old choice for a meal, we consume less. But when offered a variety of highly palatable foods, such as at a cafeteria or an all-you-can-eat buffet, we consume more (Zandstra & others, 2000). This is sometimes called the **cafeteria diet effect** (Raynor & Epstein, 2001).

Snacks and Appetizers: Preloading Calories Bad news: Research contradicts the commonsense notion that a snack an hour or two before dinner will curb your appetite and reduce consumption during the meal. In one study, presenting a snack soon after lunch, in the middle of the afternoon, or two hours before dinner had *no* impact on how much food was consumed at dinner. The snack simply added more calories on top of those later consumed at the meal (Marmonier & others, 1999). And there's more bad news: Having a small but scrumptious appetizer shortly before eating acts to stimulate your appetite, increasing the rate of consumption at the subsequent meal (Yeomans & others, 1997).

BMR: Individual Differences and Lifespan Changes Not everyone who overeats gains excess weight. One reason is that people vary greatly in their basal metabolic rate, which accounts for about two-thirds of your energy expenditure. On average, women have a metabolic rate that is 3 to 5 percent lower than men's (Arciero & others, 1993). Metabolism also decreases with age (Pannemans & Westerterp, 1995). Body metabolism is highest during growth periods early in the lifespan (see Figure 8.6). After declining sharply between infancy

CRITICAL THINKING 8.1

Has Evolution Programmed Us to Overeat?

Consider this fact: Numerous correlational studies of humans and experiments with rodents and Rhesus monkeys have consistently come to the same conclusion: Eating a restricted but balanced diet produces a variety of health benefits and promotes longevity (e.g., Barzilia & Gupta, 1999; Cefalu & others, 1997; Weindruch, 1996). So if eating a calorically restricted but balanced diet confers numerous health benefits and promotes longevity, *why* do so many people overeat?

University of British Columbia psychologists John P. J. Pinel, Sunaina Assanand, and Darrin R. Lehman (2000) believe that the evolutionary perspective provides several insights. For animals in the wild, food sources are often sporadic and unpredictable. When animals do find food, competition for it can be fierce, even deadly. If an animal waited to eat until it was hungry and its energy reserves were significantly diminished, it would run the risk of starving or falling prey to another animal.

Thus, the eating patterns of many animals have evolved so that they readily eat even if not hungry. Overeating when food is available ensures ample energy reserves to survive times when food is *not* available. As Pinel and his colleagues (2000) explain, "Warm-blooded animals survive in natural environments because they spend a large proportion of their waking hours foraging for food and consuming it when they find it, whether or not they have an immediate need for the energy it contains. As a result, excess energy is stored in the body as a buffer against future food shortages."

For most people living in food-abundant Western societies, foraging for

your next meal is usually about as life-threatening as waiting your turn in the Taco Bell drive-through lane. According to Pinel and his colleagues, people in food-rich societies do *not* eat because they are hungry or because their bodies are suffering from depleted energy resources. Rather, the key reason that humans in developed societies eat is because we are enticed by the anticipated pleasure of devouring that SuperSize burrito or calzone ring. In other words, we are motivated to eat by the *positive incentive value* of highly palatable foods.

Pinel and his colleagues (2000) note several well-established and evolutionarily adaptive behavioral patterns related to the positive incentive value of foods. When a food with a high positive incentive value is readily available, we eat, and often overeat, until we are satiated by that specific taste, which is termed *sensory-specific satiety*. Should another food with high positive incentive value become available, we continue eating and overconsume (Raynor & Epstein, 2001). As noted in the text, this is referred to

as the *cafeteria diet effect*. From the evolutionary perspective, there is adaptive pressure to consume a variety of foods. Why? Because consuming a varied diet helps promote survival by ensuring that essential nutrients, vitamins, and minerals are obtained.

The evolution of a hunger and eating system with such characteristics no doubt increased the odds of survival among our ancient ancestors living eons ago. But rather than scrounging through the woods for seeds, fruits, and vegetables, today's humans are confronted with foraging for burgers, cheese fries, and Oreo McFlurries. Therein lies the crux of the problem. As Pinel and his colleagues (2000) explain, "The increases in the availability of high positive-incentive value foods that have occurred over the past few decades in industrialized nations—increases that have been much too rapid to produce adaptive evolutionary change—have promoted levels of ad libitum consumption that are far higher than those that are compatible with optimal health and long life."

Critical Thinking Questions

- Look back at the section on motivation theories. How might each theory (instinct, drive, incentive, arousal, and humanistic) explain the behavior of overeating?

- How might the insights provided by the evolutionary explanation be used to resist the temptation to overeat?

and early adulthood, BMR decreases more slowly, by about 2 to 3 percent per decade of life (Poehlman & Horton, 1995). As your BMR decreases with age, less food is required to meet your basic energy needs. Consequently, it's not surprising that many people, upon reaching early adulthood, must begin to watch how much they eat.

Sedentary Lifestyles   Sloth may be one of the seven deadly sins, but that doesn't seem to deter the couch potato behavior that plays a significant role in the expanding waistlines of many adults. Four out of ten American adults report that they *never* exercise, play sports, or engage in physically active hobbies like

body mass index (BMI)
A numerical scale indicating adult height in relation to weight; calculated as ($704.5 \times$ weight in pounds)/(height in inches)^2.

obese
Condition characterized by excessive body fat and a body mass index equal to or greater than 30.0.

cafeteria diet effect
The tendency to eat more when a wide variety of palatable foods is available.

Prevalence of sedentary leisure-time behavior by age group and gender

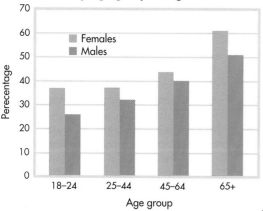

FIGURE 8.7 Sedentary Lifestyles Among U.S. Adults This graph depicts a positive correlation, showing the increasing prevalence of sedentary leisure time as adults get older. Notice that in each of the age groups, more women than men lead sedentary lifestyles.

SOURCE: Data adapted from CDC/NCHS, National Health Interview Survey, 1997 and National Center for Health Statistics (2000c).

FIGURE 8.8 Genetic Susceptibility and Environmental Conditions If different populations have similar percentages of people who are genetically susceptive to obesity, then the critical factor becomes environmental conditions. In a low-risk environment, the availability of food, especially high-calorie foods, is limited. In countries with poorly developed economies and food supplies, the prevalence of underfed people (BMI<17) is higher than the prevalence of obesity (BMI>30). But in countries with established or well-developed economies, such as most Western countries, food is plentiful and easily attainable, creating high-risk conditions for obesity. In highly developed market economies, obesity rates have soared.

SOURCES: Barsh & others, 2000; World Health Organization, 2001.

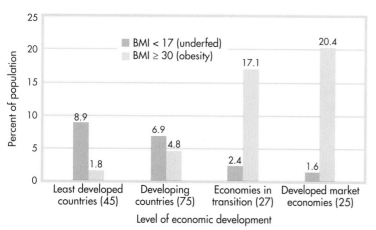

gardening or walking the dog. When the averages are broken down by gender, more women (43 percent) than men (37 percent) lead sedentary lifestyles (National Center for Health Statistics, 2000b). As you can see in Figure 8.7, both men and women tend to become more sedentary with age.

Of the six factors we've covered here, you can exert control over five of them to counteract becoming or remaining overweight. The bad news is that if we don't exercise control, all six factors can contribute to becoming obese.

Factors Involved in Obesity

Especially in the last decade, there has been intensive research investigating the causes of obesity—and for good reason. Health care costs directly attributable to obesity exceed $50 *billion* a year (National Institutes of Health, 2000). Regardless of how it develops, a BMI of 30 or above has life-threatening consequences (Kopelman, 2000). Annually, about 300,000 adult deaths in the United States are *directly* attributable to obesity (Allison & others, 1999). Several variables derail the normal mechanisms of energy homeostasis in obesity (see Friedman, 2000). In this section, we'll summarize some of those factors.

GEECH, reprinted by permission of United Feature Syndicate, Inc. / ©2001 Jerry Bittle / dist. by United Feature Syndicate, Inc.

The Interaction of Genetics and Environment Current research suggests that multiple genes on multiple chromosomes are involved in creating susceptibility to obesity (Barsh & others, 2000; Comuzzie & Allison, 1998). People with a family history of obesity are two to three times more likely than people with no such family history to become obese (Bouchard, 1997). And the more closely related two people are genetically, the more likely they are to have similar body mass indexes (Maes & others, 1997).

But, once again, we need to stress that genetics is not necessarily destiny. About 30 percent of the time, obese children have obese parents. However, obesity also occurs about 30 percent of the time among children with parents who are of normal weight (Bouchard, 1997).

The key phrase here is *susceptibility to obesity.* Even though someone may be genetically predisposed to obesity, environmental factors still play a role. If an individual is genetically susceptible and lives in a high-risk environment, obesity is more likely to occur. And what constitutes a high-risk environment for obesity? An environment characterized by ample and easily obtainable high-fat, high-calorie, palatable foods. A real-world example of this interaction is shown in Figure 8.8. As countries develop stable economies and food supplies, the prevalence of obesity rapidly escalates.

Leptin Resistance Having greater fat stores, most obese people have high blood levels of leptin. So why don't these high blood levels of the leptin hormone reduce eating behavior and induce weight loss? Many obese people experience **leptin resistance,** in which the normal mechanisms through which leptin regulates body weight and energy balance are disrupted. Although leptin levels are high in the blood, they are often low in the obese person's cerebrospinal fluid (Caro & others, 1996). This suggests that leptin is not sufficiently transported from the blood to the brain. One possibility is that the obese person's high blood levels of leptin are overwhelming the transport system to the brain (Schwartz & others, 2000).

Dieting: BMR Resistance to Maintaining Weight Loss Any diet that reduces caloric intake will result in weight loss. The difficult challenge is to maintain the weight loss. Many overweight or obese dieters experience **weight cycling,** or *yo-yo dieting*—the weight lost through dieting is regained in weeks or months and maintained until the next attempt at dieting (Venditti & others, 1996).

focus on **Neuroscience**

Normal   **Obese**

Dopamine Receptors and Obesity: Eating to Stimulate Brain Reward? In Chapter 2, we noted that dopamine brain pathways are involved in the reinforcing feelings of pleasure and satisfaction. In chapter 4, we also noted that many addictive drugs produce their pleasurable effects by increasing brain dopamine levels. These pleasurable effects are most reinforcing in people who have a low level of dopamine brain receptors (Volkow & others, 1999a, 1999b).

Given that eating can be highly reinforcing and produces pleasurable sensations, could the same mechanisms also play a role in obesity?

In a recent study, researchers injected obese and normal weight individuals with a slightly radioactive chemical "tag" that binds to brain dopamine receptors. Positron emission tomography (PET) scans detected where the chemical tag bound with dopamine receptors, shown in red. The two PET scans reveal significantly fewer dopamine receptors for obese individuals (left) as compared to the normal weight control subjects (right). And, among the obese people in the study, the number of dopamine receptors decreased as BMI increased (Wang & others, 2001).

Researchers don't know yet whether the reduced number of dopamine receptors is a cause or a consequence of obesity. Nevertheless, the finding tentatively suggests that compulsive or binge eating might stimulate the brain's reward system and compensate for reduced dopamine signaling.

One reason this occurs is because the human body is much more effective at vigorously defending against weight *loss* than it is at protecting against weight *gain*. As caloric intake is reduced and fat cells begin to shrink, the person's body actively defends against weight loss by decreasing metabolism rate and energy level. With energy expenditure reduced, far fewer calories are needed to maintain the excess weight. In effect, the body is using energy much more efficiently. If the person continues to restrict caloric intake, weight loss will plateau in a matter of weeks. When they go off the diet, their now more energy-efficient bodies quickly utilize the additional calories, and they regain the weight they lost. Even among obese individuals who successfully maintain their weight loss, BMR often continues to be reduced (Astrup & others, 1999; Wyatt & others, 1999).

For people who are obese, the implications of the factors we've discussed in this section are discouraging. Obesity is maintained by a complex system of biological, psychological, and environmental factors (Kopelman, 2000). On a more encouraging note, new and promising treatments for obesity are being developed (Bray & Tartaglia, 2000). But researchers have yet to discover a "magic bullet" treatment that will help the millions of obese people shed their dangerous levels of body fat.

Eating Disorders
Anorexia and Bulimia

Eating disorders involve serious and maladaptive disturbances in eating behavior. These disturbances can include extreme reduction of food intake, severe bouts of overeating, and obsessive concerns about body shape or weight (DSM-IV-TR, 2000). The two main types of eating disorders are *anorexia nervosa* and *bulimia nervosa,* which usually begin during adolescence or early adulthood. Ninety to 95 percent of the people who experience an eating disorder are female (Kaye & others, 2000). Despite the 10-to-1 gender-difference ratio, the central features of eating disorders are similar for males and females (Andersen, 1995; Crosscope-Happel & others, 2000).

leptin resistance
A condition in which higher-than-normal blood levels of the hormone leptin do not produce the expected physiological response.

weight cycling
Repeated cycles of dieting, weight loss, and weight regain; also called *yo-yo dieting.*

eating disorder
A category of mental disorders characterized by severe disturbances in eating behavior.

Barbie, the American Ideal? If a normal-sized woman *(left)* was proportioned like a Barbie doll, she would look like the photograph on the right. Yale psychologist Kelly Brownell calculated that if a woman's hips stayed the same size, she would have to gain nearly a foot in height, add four inches to her chest, and lose five inches from her waist to meet the impossible standard set by Barbie. Many psychologists believe that such unrealistic standards contribute to the incidence of eating disorders in Western cultures.

anorexia nervosa
An eating disorder characterized by excessive weight loss, an irrational fear of gaining weight, and distorted body self-perception.

bulimia nervosa
An eating disorder characterized by binges of extreme overeating followed by self-induced vomiting, misuse of laxatives, or other inappropriate methods to purge the excessive food and prevent weight gain.

binge-eating disorder
A proposed category of eating disorder characterized by recurring episodes of binge eating that are not followed by purging.

Anorexia Nervosa: Life-Threatening Weight Loss

Four key features define **anorexia nervosa.** First, the person refuses to maintain a minimally normal body weight. With a body weight that is 15 percent or more below normal, body mass index can drop to 12 or lower. Second, despite being dangerously underweight, the person with anorexia is intensely afraid of gaining weight or becoming fat. Third, she has a distorted perception about the size of her body. Although emaciated, she looks in the mirror and sees herself as fat or obese. And fourth, she denies the seriousness of her weight loss (American Psychiatric Association, 2000b).

There are two basic subtypes of anorexia nervosa. The *restricting subtype* involves severe food restriction and maladaptive dieting. Although often obsessed with food, the individual severely undereats, rejecting many foods and limiting herself to just a few. The person develops numerous maladaptive strategies to prevent weight gain, such as excessive fluid intake, fasting, or secretly throwing away food. Overactivity and compulsive exercising to burn off calories are also common. The *binge–purge subtype* involves episodes of binge eating, followed by purging the food through self-induced vomiting or misusing laxatives to induce diarrhea and flush the food from her system. During the course of anorexia, the individual can alternate between the restricting and binge–purge subtypes.

The severe malnutrition caused by anorexia disrupts body chemistry in ways that are very similar to those caused by starvation (Fairburn, 1995). BMR decreases, as do blood levels of glucose, insulin, and leptin. Other hormonal levels drop, including the level of reproductive hormones. In women, reduced estrogen results in the menstrual cycle stopping. In males, decreased testosterone disrupts sex drive and sexual function (Crosscope-Happel & others, 2000). Because the ability to retain body heat is greatly diminished, people with severe anorexia often develop a soft, fine body hair called *lanugo* (Beumont, 1995).

Perfectionism and rigid thinking, poor peer relations, social isolation, and low self-esteem are common (Halmi & others, 2000). Although estimates vary, approximately 10 percent of people with anorexia nervosa die from starvation, suicide, or physical complications accompanying extreme weight loss (American Psychiatric Association, 2000b; Kaye & others, 2000).

Bulimia Nervosa: Binging and Purging

People with **bulimia nervosa** share many of the characteristics associated with the binge–purge subtype of anorexia. Like people with anorexia, people with bulimia fear gaining weight. Intense preoccupation and dissatisfaction with their bodies are also apparent. However, people with bulimia stay within a normal weight range or may even be slightly overweight. Another difference is that people with bulimia usually recognize that they have an eating disorder.

People with bulimia nervosa experience extreme episodes of binge eating, consuming as many as 50,000 calories in a single binge. Binges typically occur as often as twice a week and are often triggered by negative feelings or hunger (Agras & Apple, 1997). During the binge, the person usually consumes sweet, high-calorie foods that can be swallowed quickly, such as ice cream, cake, and candy. Binges typically occur in secrecy, leaving the person feeling ashamed, guilty, and disgusted by their own behavior. After binging, they compensate by purging themselves of the excessive food by self-induced vomiting or by misuse of laxatives or enemas. Once they purge, they often feel psychologically relieved. Some people with bulimia don't purge themselves of the excess food. Rather, they use fasting and excessive exercise to keep their body weight within the normal, healthy range (American Psychiatric Association, 2000b).

A related but different syndrome is **binge-eating disorder** (Bulik & others, 2000). In binge-eating disorder, food binges occur at least two days a week over the course of six months or longer. However, the person does not compensate for the excessive food intake with self-induced vomiting, laxatives, or fasting. Not surprisingly, people with binge-eating disorder are more prone to obesity (Striegel-Moore & others, 1998). And as with anorexia and bulimia, females are more likely than males to display binge-eating disorder (DSM-IV-TR, 2000).

Causes of Eating Disorders: A Complex Picture

In trying to understand the causes of eating disorders, familiar themes emerge. Family and twin studies point to the role of genetic factors in both anorexia and bulimia, suggesting that some people are at greater risk to develop an eating disorder (e.g., Strober & others, 2001; Walters & Kendler, 1995). Researchers have also identified specific genes that are involved in eating disorders (Fumeron & others, 2001; Vink & others, 2001).

Both anorexia and bulimia involve decreases in brain activity of the neurotransmitter *serotonin* (Fumeron & others, 2001). Disrupted brain chemistry probably also contributes to the fact that eating disorders frequently co-occur with other psychiatric disorders, such as depression, substance abuse, personality disorders, and anxiety disorders, including obsessive–compulsive disorder (Bulik & others, 2000; Herzog & others, 1996).

The chemical signals that normally regulate eating behavior are also disrupted in the eating disorders. For example, in Figure 8.3 on page 330, we noted that the activity of corticotropin-releasing hormone (CRH) usually decreases when weight loss occurs. But in people with anorexia, CRH activity is increased (Strober & others, 2000). And earlier we noted that the hormone CCK helps trigger satiation. When compared with healthy volunteers, people with bulimia have reduced levels of CCK after a meal. This may partly explain why people with bulimia don't feel satiated until they have eaten extreme amounts (Pirke, 1995).

Although anorexia and bulimia have been documented for at least 150 years, contemporary Western cultural attitudes toward thinness and dieting probably contribute to the increased incidence of eating disorders today. This seems to be especially true with anorexia, which occurs predominantly in developed countries (Wilfley & Rodin, 1995). Still, it's important to remember that the vast majority of people who diet do *not* develop an eating disorder.

8.1 R·E·V·I·E·W

C·O·N·C·E·P·T

Motivational Concepts and Eating Behavior

True or false?

____ 1. Because they had so much difficulty trying to identify human behaviors that might be instinctual, early psychologists abandoned instinct theories as an explanation of human motivation.

____ 2. Whereas drive theories "pull" us to behave in certain ways, incentive theories describe the motivational "push" of external goals.

____ 3. Studies with both humans and nonhuman animals have shown that lower-than-normal brain levels of neuropeptide Y are correlated with sensation-seeking behavior.

____ 4. The basal metabolic rate tends to gradually decrease throughout adulthood.

____ 5. There has been virtually no change in the average daily caloric intake of U.S. males and females over the last two decades.

____ 6. Research by comparative psychologists has shown that most wild animals eat only when their immediate energy reserves are depleted.

____ 7. A small late-afternoon snack is an excellent strategy to reduce the amount of calories consumed at dinner.

____ 8. Despite binging on high calorie foods, people with bulimia nervosa maintain a dangerously low body weight because they vomit or use laxatives after bingeing.

Psychological Needs as Motivators

Key Theme

- According to the motivation theories of Maslow and of Deci and Ryan, psychological needs must be fulfilled for optimal human functioning.

Key Questions

- How does Maslow's hierarchy of needs explain human motivation?
- What are some important criticisms of Maslow's theory?
- What are the basic premises of self-determination theory?

The idea that we are motivated to satisfy fundamental psychological needs has a long, rich history in psychology. Theorists as diverse as Sigmund Freud, Erik Erikson, Henry Murry, Carl Rogers, and Seymour Epstein have advocated the importance of various psychological needs. In studying this idea, psychologists have grappled with several key questions:

- Are there universal psychological needs?
- Are we internally or externally motivated to satisfy psychological needs?
- What psychological needs must be satisfied for optimal human functioning?

In this section, we'll first consider two theories that have tried to answer those questions: Abraham Maslow's famous *hierarchy of needs* and the more recent *self-determination theory* of Edward L. Deci and Richard M. Ryan. Then, we'll look at the research on two specific psychological motives: *achievement motivation* and *curiosity*.

Maslow's Hierarchy of Needs

A major turning point in the discussion of human needs occurred when humanistic psychologist **Abraham Maslow** developed his model of human motivation in the 1940s and 1950s. Maslow acknowledged the importance of biological needs as motivators. But once basic biological needs are satisfied, he believed that "higher" psychological needs emerge to motivate human behavior.

The centerpiece of Maslow's (1954, 1968) model of motivation was his famous **hierarchy of needs,** summarized in Figure 8.9. Maslow believed that people are motivated to satisfy the needs at each level of the hierarchy before moving up to the next level. As people progressively move up the hierarchy, they are ultimately motivated by the desire to achieve self-actualization. The lowest levels of Maslow's hierarchy emphasize fundamental biological and safety needs. At the higher levels, the needs become more social and psychologically growth-oriented, culminating in the need to achieve *self-actualization*.

What exactly is self-actualization? Maslow (1970) himself had trouble defining the term, saying that self-actualization is "a difficult syndrome to describe accurately." Nonetheless, Maslow defined **self-actualization** in the following way:

FIGURE 8.9 Maslow's Hierarchy of Needs Abraham Maslow believed that people are innately motivated to satisfy a progression of needs, beginning with the most basic psychological needs. Once the needs at a particular level are satisfied, the individual is motivated to satisfy the needs at the next level, steadily progressing upward. The ultimate goal is self-actualization, the realization of personal potential.

SOURCE: Based on Maslow (1970).

It may be loosely described as the full use and exploitation of talents, capacities, potentialities, etc. Such people seem to be fulfilling themselves and to be doing the best that they are capable of doing. . . . They are people who have developed or are developing to the full stature of which they are capable.

Beyond that general description, Maslow's research identified several characteristics of self-actualized people which are summarized in Table 8.3.

Maslow's model of motivation generated considerable research, especially during the 1970s and 1980s. Some studies found support for Maslow's ideas (e.g., Graham & Balloun, 1973). Others, however, criticized his hierarchy of needs on several points (e.g., Fox, 1982; Neher, 1991; Wahba & Bridwell, 1976). Maslow's concept of self-actualization is very vague and almost impossible to define in a way that would allow it to be tested scientifically. And Maslow's initial studies on self-actualization were based on limited samples with questionable reliability. For example, Maslow (1970) often relied on the life stories of acquaintances whose identities were never revealed. He also studied the biographies and autobiographies of famous historical figures he believed had achieved self-actualization, such as Eleanor Roosevelt, Abraham Lincoln, and Albert Einstein.

There is a more important criticism. Despite the claim that self-actualization is an inborn motivational goal toward which all people supposedly strive, most people do *not* experience or achieve self-actualization. Maslow (1970) himself wrote that self-actualization "can seem like a miracle, so improbable an event as to be awe-inspiring." Maslow explained this basic contradiction in a number of different ways. For instance, he suggested that few people experience the supportive environment that is required to achieve self-actualization.

Although interest in Maslow's theory has waned, it continues to generate occasional research (e.g., Hagerty, 1999; Sumerlin & Bundrick, 1996). But in general, Maslow's notion that we must satisfy needs at one level before moving to the next level has not stood up (Sheldon & others, 2001). Perhaps Maslow's most important contribution was to encourage psychology to focus on the motivation and development of psychologically healthy people. In advocating that idea, he helped focus attention on psychological needs as motivators.

hierarchy of needs
Maslow's hierarchical division of motivation into levels that progress from basic physical needs to psychological needs to self-fulfillment needs.

self-actualization
Defined by Maslow as "the full use and exploitation of talents, capacities, and potentialities."

It is quite true that man lives by bread alone—where there is no bread. But what happens to man's desires when there is plenty of bread and when his belly is chronically filled? At once other (and "higher") needs emerge and these, rather than physiological hungers, dominant the organism. And when these in turn are satisfied, again new (and still "higher") needs emerge, and so on. That is what we mean by saying that the basic human needs are organized into a hierarchy of relative prepotency.

Abraham Maslow (1943)

Table | 8.3

Maslow's Characteristics of Self-Actualized People

Realism and acceptance	Self-actualized people have accurate perceptions of themselves, others, and external reality. They easily accept themselves and others as they are.
Spontaneity	Self-actualized people are spontaneous, natural, and open in their behavior and thoughts. However, they can easily conform to conventional rules and expectations when situations demand such behavior.
Problem centering	Self-actualized people focus on problems outside themselves. They often dedicate themselves to a larger purpose in life, which is based on ethics or a sense of personal responsibility.
Autonomy	Although they accept and enjoy other people, self-actualized individuals have a strong need for privacy and independence. They focus on their own potential and development rather than on the opinions of others.
Continued freshness of appreciation	Self-actualized people continue to appreciate the simple pleasures of life with awe and wonder.
Peak experiences	Self-actualized people commonly have *peak experiences*, or moments of intense ecstasy, wonder, and awe during which their sense of self is lost or transcended. The self-actualized person may feel transformed and strengthened by these peak experiences.

SOURCE: Based on Maslow (1970).

Deci and Ryan's Self-Determination Theory

University of Rochester psychologists **Edward L. Deci** and **Richard M. Ryan** (1985, 2000) have developed **self-determination theory,** abbreviated **SDT.** Much like Maslow's theory, SDT moves on the premise that people are actively growth-oriented and that they move toward a unified sense of self and integration with others. To realize optimal psychological functioning and growth throughout the lifespan, Ryan and Deci contend that three innate and universal psychological needs must be satisfied:

- *Autonomy*—the need to determine, control, and organize one's own behavior and goals so that they are in harmony with one's own interests and values.

- *Competence*—the need to effectively learn and master appropriately challenging tasks.

- *Relatedness*—the need to feel attached to others and experience a sense of belongingness, security, and intimacy.

Like Maslow, Deci and Ryan view the need for social relationships as a fundamental psychological motive. The benefits of having strong, positive social relationships are well documented and uncontroversial (Baumeister & Leary, 1995). Another well-established psychological need is having a sense of competence or mastery (Bandura, 1997; R. White, 1959).

One subtle difference in Maslow's views compared to those of Deci and Ryan has to do with the definition of *autonomy*. Deci and Ryan's definition of *autonomy* emphasizes the need to feel that your activities are self-chosen and self-endorsed. This reflects the importance of self-determination in Deci and Ryan's theory. In contrast, Maslow's view of *autonomy* stressed the need to feel independent and focused on your own potential (see Table 8.3).

How does a person satisfy the needs for autonomy, competence, and relatedness? In a supportive social, psychological, and physical environment, an individual will pursue interests, goals, and relationships that tend to satisfy these psychological needs. In turn, this enhances the person's psychological growth and intrinsic motivation. **Intrinsic motivation** is behavior motivated by the desire to engage in tasks that the person finds inherently satisfying and enjoyable, novel, or optimally challenging.

Of course, much of our behavior in daily life is driven by extrinsic motivation (Ryan & La Guardia, 2000). **Extrinsic motivation** is behavior that is motivated by external influences, such as rewards, social evaluations, rules, and responsibilities. According to Ryan and Deci, the person who has satisfied the needs for competence, autonomy, and relatedness actively *internalizes* and *integrates* different external motivators as part of their identity and values. In effect, the person incorporates societal expectations, rules, and regulations as values or rules that he or she personally endorses.

What if one or more of the psychological needs are thwarted by an unfavorable environment, one that is overly challenging, controlling, rejecting, punishing, or even abusive? According to SDT, the person may compensate with substitute needs, defensive behaviors, or maladaptive behaviors. For example, if someone is frustrated in satisfying the need for relatedness, he or she may compensate by chronically seeking the approval of others or by pursuing substitute goals, such as accumulating money or material possessions.

In support of self-determination theory, Deci and Ryan have compiled an impressive array of studies, including cross-cultural studies (see Deci & Ryan, 2000; Ryan & Deci, 2000, 2001). Taking the evolutionary perspective, they also contend that the needs for autonomy, competence, and relatedness have adaptive advantages. For example, the need for relatedness promoted resource sharing, mutual protection, and the division of work, increasing the likelihood that both the individual and the group would survive.

As with any theory as broad in scope as self-determination theory, research will point to ways that the theory can be refined to make it more accurate. But even as it currently exists, self-determination theory is widely regarded as a well-integrated theory that explains many diverse findings in motivational research.

Competence and Achievement Motivation

Key Theme

- Competence and achievement motivation are important psychological motives.

Key Questions

- How does competence motivation differ from achievement motivation, and how is achievement motivation measured?
- What characteristics are associated with a high level of achievement motivation, and how does culture affect achievement motivation?

In self-determination theory, Deci and Ryan identified *competence* as a universal motive. You are displaying **competence motivation** when you strive to use your cognitive, social, and behavioral skills to be capable and exercise control in a situation (R. White, 1959). Competence motivation provides much of the motivational "push" to prove to yourself that you can successfully tackle new challenges, such as striving to do well in this class.

A step beyond competence motivation is **achievement motivation**—the drive to excel, succeed, or outperform others at some task. Creaming your rival in a competitive game and trying to outdo your own previous level of performance, as did our running friend Randy in the chapter Prologue, are examples of achievement motivation.

In the 1930s, Henry Murray identified 20 fundamental human needs or motives, including achievement motivation. Murray (1938) defined the "need to achieve" as the tendency "to overcome obstacles, to exercise power, [and] to strive to do something difficult as well and as quickly as possible." Also in the 1930s, Christiana Morgan and Henry Murray (1935) developed a test to measure human motives called the **Thematic Apperception Test (TAT).** The TAT consists of a series of ambiguous pictures. The person being tested is asked to make up a story about each picture, and the story is then coded for different motivational themes, including achievement. In Chapter 11, on personality, we'll look at the TAT in more detail.

In the 1950s, David McClelland, John Atkinson, and their colleagues (1953) developed a specific TAT scoring system to measure the *need for achievement,* often abbreviated *nAch.* Other researchers also developed questionnaire measures of achievement motivation (Spangler, 1992). Over the next four decades, McClelland and his associates investigated many different aspects of achievement motivation, especially its application in work settings. In cross-cultural studies, McClelland explored how differences in achievement motivation at the national level have influenced economic development (McClelland, 1961; McClelland & Winter, 1971). He also studied organizational leadership and *power motivation*—striving to attain power to control or influence the behavior of other people or groups (McClelland, 1975, 1989).

Hundreds of studies have shown that measures of achievement motivation generally correlate well with various areas of success, such as school grades, job performance, and worker output (Spangler, 1992). This is understandable, since people who score in high in achievement motivation expend their greatest efforts when faced with moderately challenging tasks. In striving to achieve the task,

competence motivation
Motivated behavior directed toward demonstrating competence and exercising control in a situation.

achievement motivation
Motivated behavior directed toward excelling, succeeding, or outperforming others at some task.

Thematic Apperception Test (TAT)
A projective test developed by Henry Murray and his colleagues that involves creating stories about ambiguous scenes that can be interpreted in a variety of ways.

Extraordinary Achievement Motivation
The U.S. women's soccer team thrilled onlookers at the Rose Bowl stadium with their overtime win against China in the Women's World Cup Final. Some of the team members had been playing competitive soccer for more than a decade. Here, team captain Carla Overbeck holds the trophy after Brandi Chastain's winning penalty kick.

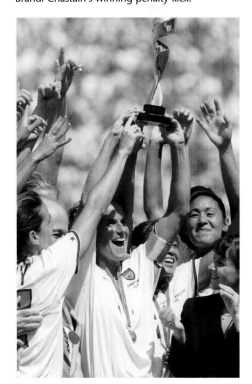

SCIENCE VERSUS PSEUDOSCIENCE 8.2

Subliminal Self-Help Tapes: Effortless Motivation?

A typical subliminal self-help tape contains the sounds of ocean waves or relaxing music. "Subliminal messages," or messages that are below one's level of subjective awareness, are supposedly embedded in the sounds.

The notion that simply listening to a subliminal self-help tape will quickly and easily produce changes in our motivation, behavior, and attitudes is very appealing. Who doesn't want to have "effortless weight control," "peak performance in work, studies, the arts, or sports," and the ability to "conquer habits like smoking, alcohol, and drugs without struggle," to quote a few claims we read in a recent advertisement.

As is the case with many pseudoscientific claims, the illusion of scientific credibility in selling subliminal self-help tapes is often promoted by the use of phrases that certainly *sound* scientific, like "technological breakthrough," "scientific research," and the testimony of "leading authorities." And, in fact, people spend millions of dollars each year on subliminal self-help tapes on the basis of the unsubstantiated claims contained in such ads (Pratkanis, 1992).

How do subliminal self-help tapes stand up to scientific scrutiny? Consider a carefully controlled study involving 79 college students who were enrolled in a career development class (Russell & others, 1991). The students were randomly assigned to one of three groups. The experimental group listened to two sub-

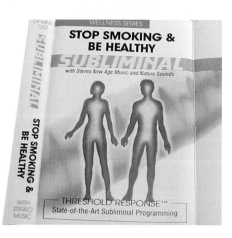

Effortless Motivation? Can you really achieve your toughest goals just by listening to a tape playing soothing music or nature sounds? If only it were true!

liminal self-help tapes, one on improving study habits and the other on passing exams. The placebo control group listened to what they *thought* were subliminal self-help tapes. In reality, the placebo tapes contained no subliminal messages, just the sound of ocean waves. The real and fake subliminal tapes were provided by the largest manufacturer of subliminal tapes in the United States. The third group was a no-treatment control group that didn't listen to any tapes.

According to the subliminal-tape manufacturer, an individual should listen to the tapes for 20 to 25 hours before expecting significant results. Over 10 weeks of

the semester, the students listened to the tapes for an average of *120* hours. Some students listened to the tapes for more than 250 hours. At the end of the semester, the final examination scores of the students in the three experimental groups were compared. The researchers also compared the three groups in terms of their semester grade-point average.

The result? There were *no* significant differences among the three groups in terms of their final examination scores or their semester grade-point average. In other words, the tapes produced *none* of the effects claimed by the manufacturer. This finding is consistent with numerous other studies that also found no evidence to support the claim that subliminal self-help tapes can influence motivation or complex behaviors (Greenwald & others, 1991; Merikle & Skanes, 1992; Pratkanis & others, 1994).

The moral? Don't be fooled by the advertising claims for subliminal self-help tapes. Their not-so-subliminal claims are designed to get you to spend your money by promising easy answers to life's difficulties. If you want to enhance your motivation and achieve your goals, try the research-based suggestions we present in the chapter Application. If you absolutely feel compelled to spend your money on something that will help you do better in your classes, buy a fluorescent highlighting pen to use when reading your textbooks. Plus, if you hold the pen's cap up to your ear, you can hear ocean waves. Honest!

they often choose to work long hours and have the capacity to delay gratification and focus on the goal. They also tend to display original thinking, seek expert advice, and value feedback about their performance (McClelland, 1985b).

Although people high in achievement motivation prefer to work independently, the most successful people also have the ability to work well with others (McClelland, 1985a, 1987). And in assessing their own performance, high achievers tend to attribute their successes to their own abilities and efforts, and to explain their failures as being due to external factors or bad luck (Weiner, 1985).

Achievement Motivation and Culture

When it is broadly defined as the "desire for excellence," achievement motivation is found in many, if not all, cultures. In individualistic cultures, like those that characterize North American and European countries, the need to achieve emphasizes personal, individual success rather than the success of the group. In these cultures, achievement motivation is also closely linked with succeeding in competitive tasks (Markus & Kitayama, 1991).

In collectivistic cultures, like those of many Asian countries, achievement motivation tends to have a different focus. Instead of being oriented toward the individual, achievement orientation is more *socially* oriented (Bond, 1986). For example, students in China felt that it was unacceptable to express pride for personal achievements but that it was acceptable to feel proud of achievements that benefited others (Stipek, 1998). The person strives to achieve not to promote himself or herself but to promote the status or well-being of other members of the relevant social group, such as family members (Matsumoto & others, 1994).

Achievement in a Collectivistic Culture In many collectivistic cultures, achievements are viewed as a way of bringing glory to one's family, group, or country rather than to one's self. Here, Tang Lin of China celebrates her 2000 Olympic gold medal in judo by proudly displaying her country's flag on the winner's platform.

Individuals in collectivistic cultures may persevere or aspire to do well in order to fulfill the expectations of family members and to fit into the larger group. For example, the Japanese student who strives to do well academically is typically not motivated by the desire for personal recognition. Rather, the student's behavior is more likely to be motivated by the desire to enhance the social standing of his or her family by gaining admission to a top university (Hawkins, 1994).

8.2 R·E·V·I·E·W

C·O·N·C·E·P·T

Psychological Needs as Motivators

1. Compared to those in individualistic cultures, people in collectivistic cultures:
   a. are much less likely to achieve self-actualization.
   b. are more likely to value extrinsic motivation over intrinsic motivation.
   c. are more likely to be motivated to pursue achievements to promote the social status of their family group.
   d. place much less value on the importance of self-esteem in psychological well-being.

2. Deci and Ryan's self-determination theory:
   a. accurately describes psychological motives in individualistic but not collectivistic cultures.
   b. has shown that self-actualization can be achieved even if only one of the innate psychological needs has been satisfied.
   c. challenged the evolutionary perspective's notion that the need for relatedness has adaptive advantages.
   d. contends that psychologically healthy people internalize external motivators as part of their identity and values.

3. Who said, "[It] can seem like a miracle, so improbable an event as to be awe-inspiring," and what is he or she describing?
   a. Edward Deci, describing *intrinsic motivation*.
   b. Abraham Maslow, describing *self-actualization*.
   c. Henry Murray, describing the development of the *Thematic Apperception Test*.
   d. Julia Roberts, describing how difficult it is to achieve stardom in Hollywood.

4. People who rate high on achievement motivation:
   a. have the capacity to delay gratification in working hard to achieve goals.
   b. explain their failures as being due to a lack of effort or abilities.
   c. are no more likely to achieve challenging goals than someone who rates low on achievement motivation.
   d. avoid competing with others.

emotion
A complex psychological state that involves subjective experience, a physiological response, and a behavioral or expressive response.

emotional intelligence
The capacity to understand and manage your own emotional experiences and to perceive, comprehend, and respond appropriately to the emotional responses of others.

Emotion

Key Theme
- Emotions are complex psychological states that serve many functions in human behavior and relationships.

Key Questions
- What are the three components of emotion, and what functions do emotions serve?
- How do evolutionary psychologists view emotion?
- What are the basic emotions, and how are emotions classified?

With a final score of 8 to 6, our daughter Laura's soccer team had just won its first game of the season. After lining up for the ceremonial "high-fives" with the defeated team, Laura's team erupted in shouts of joy, leaping into the air, hugging, and slapping more high-fives. In contrast, the girls on the defeated team maintained polite but resigned smiles. One seemed to fight back tears. The girls, their coaches, and many of the spectators were clearly having an emotional experience—one that is familiar to everyone. But what, exactly, is emotion?

Emotion is a complex psychological state that involves three distinct components: a *subjective experience,* a *physiological response,* and a *behavioral* or *expressive response.* How are emotions different from moods? Generally, emotions are intense but rather short-lived. Emotions are also more likely to have a specific cause, to be directed toward some particular object, and to motivate a person to take some sort of action (Frijda, 1994). In contrast, a *mood* involves a milder emotional state that is more general and pervasive, such as gloominess or contentment. Moods may last for a few hours or even days (Gendolla, 2000).

The Many Functions of Emotion Emotions play an important role in relationships and social communication. If a friend tells you that she is thrilled, happy, or excited, you immediately understand her internal emotional state.

The Functions of Emotion

Emotional processes are closely tied to motivational processes. Like the word *motivation,* the root of the word *emotion* is the Latin word *movere,* which means "to move." And indeed, emotions can move us to act, triggering motivated behavior. In the Prologue, Randy's dissatisfaction and frustration in his relationship with Sara motivated him to end the relationship. Similarly, anger might motivate you to seek another job when you feel you've been treated unfairly.

Emotions help us to set goals, but emotional states can also be goals in themselves. We ride a roller-coaster to achieve emotional excitement or practice every day to relish the satisfaction of eventually winning a piano competition. And most of us direct our lives so as to maximize the experience of positive emotions and minimize the experience of negative emotions (Gendolla, 2000).

At one time, psychologists considered emotions to be disruptive forces that interfered with rational behavior (Cacioppo & Gardner, 1999). Emotions were thought of as primitive impulses that needed to be suppressed or controlled.

Today, psychologists are much more attuned to the importance of emotions in many different areas of behavior, *including* rational decision making and purposeful behavior (Loewenstein & others, 2001; Mellers, 2000). Consider goal-directed behavior. At any given moment, we are faced with choosing among many different goals—goals that involve the activation of different motives. Should I study for my psychology test (achievement), call a friend (relatedness), or go to a movie (arousal)? Emotions shape our decisions by helping us choose which goal to pursue and how strongly to pursue it.

*T*he emotions are mechanisms that set the brain's highest-level goals. Once triggered by a propitious moment, an emotion triggers the cascade of subgoals and sub-sub-goals that we call thinking and acting.

Steven Pinker (1997)

Far from interfering with rational behavior and appropriate goal setting, emotions are now known to be essential to successful living. Most of our choices are guided by our feelings, sometimes without our awareness (Bechara & others, 1997; Kihlstrom & others, 2000). But consider the fate of people who have lost the capacity to feel emotion because of damage to specific brain areas. Despite having an intact ability to reason, such people tend to make disastrous decisions (Damasio, 1994).

Similarly, people who are low in what is termed **emotional intelligence** may have superior reasoning powers, but they sometimes experience one failure in life after another (Goleman, 1995; Mayer & Salovey, 1993). Why? Because they lack the ability to manage their own emotions, comprehend the emotional responses of others, and respond appropriately to the emotions of other people. In contrast, people who are high in emotional intelligence possess these abilities, and they are able to understand and use their emotions to help motivate themselves (Mayer & Salovey, 1997).

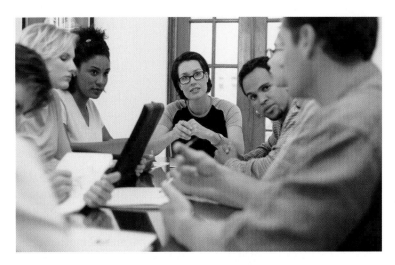

Emotional Intelligence on the Job Have you ever known people who were very intelligent but couldn't hold down a job because they constantly alienated supervisors and coworkers? Success in any field is at least partly dependent on your ability to manage your own emotions and understand the emotions of others–key aspects of *emotional intelligence*. Resolving conflicts in a constructive way, getting along with other workers, and functioning well as part of a team are the kinds of abilities that require a high degree of emotional intelligence.

Evolutionary Explanations of Emotion

One of the earliest scientists to systematically study emotions was **Charles Darwin.** Darwin published *The Expression of the Emotions in Man and Animals* in 1872, 13 years after he had laid out his general theory of evolution in *On the Origin of Species by Means of Natural Selection* and only a year after his book on the evolution of humans, *The Descent of Man* (1871). Darwin (1872) described the facial expressions, body movements, and postures used to express specific emotions in animals and humans. He argued that emotions reflect evolutionary adaptations to the problems of survival and reproduction.

Like Darwin, today's evolutionary psychologists believe that emotions are the product of evolution (Tooby & Cosmides, 2000). Emotions help us solve adaptive problems posed by our environment. They "move" us toward potential resources, and they move us away from potential dangers. Fear prompts us to flee an attacker or evade a threat. Anger moves us to turn and fight a rival. Love propels us to seek out a mate and care for our offspring. Disgust prompts us to avoid a sickening stimulus. Obviously, the capacity to feel and be moved by emotion has adaptive value: An organism that is able to quickly respond to rewards or threats is more likely to survive and successfully reproduce.

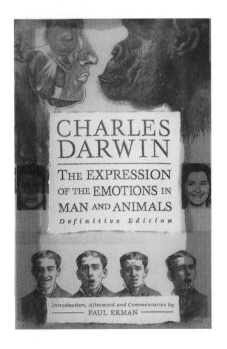

Darwin and Emotion *The Expression of the Emotions in Man and Animals* was a best-seller when it was first published in 1872. It was also the first scientific book to take advantage of the new technology of photography. Charles Darwin was one of the first scientists to systematically study emotional expressions. His purpose was to show the continuity of emotional expressions among nonhuman animals and humans—additional evidence for his evolutionary theory.

Darwin (1872) also pointed out that emotional displays serve the important function of informing other organisms about an individual's internal state. When facing an aggressive rival, the snarl of a baboon signals its readiness to fight. A wolf rolling submissively on its back telegraphs its willingness to back down and avoid a fight.

Emotions are also important in situations that go well beyond physical survival. Virtually all human relationships are heavily influenced by emotions. Our emotional experience and expression, as well as our ability to understand the emotions of others, are crucial to the maintenance of social relationships (Reis & others, 2000).

In the next several sections, we'll consider each of the components of emotion in turn, beginning with the component that is most familiar: the subjective experience of emotion.

The Subjective Experience of Emotion

Do you know people who are very low key and rarely get very excited about anything? Or, at the other extreme, people who seem to be either on top of the world or in the depths of despair? Even casual people-watching confirms the observation that people vary greatly in the *intensity* of their emotions. Some people really are "more emotional" than others (Gross & others, 2000).

People who experience very intense positive emotions also tend to experience very intense negative emotions (Diener & others, 1985). When things go well, they experience great joy. But when things go poorly, they are equally miserable. In general, emotionally expressive people tend to be better liked than people who are more inhibited in their expressions of emotions (DePaulo, 1992).

Along this line, a common belief is that women are "naturally" more emotional than men. In fact, *both* men and women tend to view women as the more emotional sex (Hess & others, 2000). But are women really more emotional? Several studies have shown that men and women do *not* differ in their self-ratings of experiencing different emotions (Kring & Gordon, 1998; Thunberg & Dimberg, 2000). In other words, men and women differ little in the *experience* of emotions. However, the sexes do differ in the *expression* of emotions. In a nutshell, women are more emotionally expressive. Women tend to be much more at ease expressing their emotions, thinking about emotions, and recalling emotional experiences (Feldman Barrett & others, 2000). Although guys tend to feel equally confident in their ability to express their emotions, they are more likely to mask them (Gross & John, 1998). We discuss gender differences in emotion in more detail in Chapter 10.

The Basic Emotions

Given the range and variety of emotions that people experience, it's not surprising that psychologists have tried to classify emotions into distinct categories. It is perhaps even less surprising that many psychologists disagree about the best way to classify emotions. Nevertheless, most emotion researchers today agree that there are a limited number of **basic emotions** that all humans, in every culture, experience. These basic emotions are thought to be biologically determined, the products of evolution. And what are these basic emotions? As shown in Table 8.4, happiness, sadness, anger, fear, surprise, and disgust are most commonly cited as the basic emotions (Ekman, 1992a; Matsumoto, 2000).

Many psychologists contend that each basic emotion represents a sequence of responses that is innate and hard-wired in the brain (Tooby & Cosmides, 2000). But your emotional experience is not limited to pure forms of each basic emotion. Rather, each basic emotion represents a family of related emotional states (Ekman, 1994a, b). For example, consider the many types of angry feelings, which can range from mild annoyance to bitter resentment or fierce rage.

Further, psychologists recognize that emotional experience can be complex and multifaceted (Cacioppo & Gardner, 1999). People often experience a *blend* of emotions. As he was milling around with the other 10,000 runners waiting for the starting gun of the Tulsa Run, Randy simultaneously felt excited and anxious. In more complex situations people may experience *mixed emotions,* in which very different emotions are experienced simultaneously or in rapid succession. As he talked about the ending of his relationship with Sara, for example, Randy expressed anger, sadness, regret, and relief.

Despite their variety, emotions can be classified along two dimensions: (1) the degree to which the emotion is *pleasant* or *unpleasant* and (2) the level of *activation,* or arousal, associated with the emotion (Feldman Barrett & Russell, 1999; Russell, 1980). For example, joy and contentment are both classified as positive emotions, but joy is higher in activation. Similarly, you can distinguish between the highly activated emotion of rage and the slow burn of resentment.

Table | **8.4**

The Basic Emotions

Fear	Disgust
Surprise	Happiness
Anger	Sadness

Although there is some disagreement as to exactly which emotions best represent the universal set of basic emotions, most emotion researchers today agree on the six emotions shown above. Other possible candidates are contempt or disdain, pride, and excitement.

The basic emotions blend with our experiences, personality, and sociocultural milieu to create an infinite degree of shading, blends, and coloring in our emotional world. Much like colors on a color wheel, the existence of basic emotions suggests that cultures shape, mold, and color our emotional lives by using the set of basic emotions as a starting point to create other emotions.

David Matsumoto (2000)

Culture and Emotional Experience

Are the dimensions of emotion universal? In diverse cultures, psychologists have found general agreement regarding the subjective experience and meaning of different basic emotions (Scherer & Wallbott, 1994). Canadian psychologist James Russell (1991) compared the emotion rankings of people from several different cultures. He found that the "pleasant/unpleasant" and "activated/not activated" emotional dimensions were most commonly identified across a wide range of cultures. While these may be the most fundamental dimensions of emotion, cultural variations in classifying emotions do exist (White, 1994).

For example, Hazel Rose Markus and Shinobu Kitayama (1991, 1994) found that Japanese subjects classified emotions in terms of not two but three important dimensions. Along with the pleasantness and activation dimensions, they also categorized emotions along a dimension of **interpersonal engagement.** This dimension reflects the idea that some emotions result from your connections and interactions with other people (Kitayama & others, 2000). Japanese participants rated anger and shame as being about the same in terms of unpleasantness and activation, but they rated shame as being much higher than anger on the dimension of interpersonal engagement.

Why would the Japanese emphasize interpersonal engagement as a dimension of emotion? Because Japan is a collectivistic culture, a person's identity is seen as interdependent with those of other people, rather than independent, as is characteristic of the more individualistic cultures. Thus, social context is an important part of private emotional experience (Markus & Kitayama, 1991).

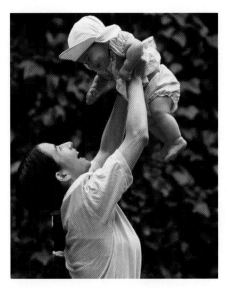

Socially engaged emotions in Japan
Closeness and interdependence are fostered by Japanese child-rearing practices, and some psychologists believe they also form the basis for such other-focused emotions as *amae,* a central emotion in Japanese culture (Markus & Kitayama, 1991). *Amae* can be defined as the sense of being lovingly cared for and unconditionally accepted by another person. *Amae* can only be achieved within a reciprocal, interdependent relationship with someone else. Thus, *amae* is a prototypical example of a socially engaged emotion–an other-focused emotion that creates and fosters interdependence with significant others.

The Neuroscience of Emotion

Key Theme

- Emotions are associated with distinct patterns of responses by the sympathetic nervous system and in the brain.

Key Questions

- How is the sympathetic nervous system involved in intense emotional responses?
- What brain structures are involved in emotional experience, and what neural pathways make up the brain's fear circuit?
- How does the evolutionary perspective explain the dual brain pathways for transmitting fear-related information?

Psychologists have long studied the physiological aspects of emotion. Early research focused on the autonomic nervous system's role in triggering physiological arousal. More recently, brain-imaging techniques have identified specific brain regions involved in emotions. In this section, we'll look at both areas of research.

Emotion and the Sympathetic Nervous System: Hot Heads and Cold Feet

The pounding heart, rapid breathing, trembling hands and feet, and churning stomach that occur when you experience an intense emotion like fear reflect the activation of the sympathetic branch of the *autonomic nervous system.* When you are threatened, the *sympathetic nervous system* triggers the *fight-or-flight response,* a rapidly occurring series of automatic physical reactions. Breathing and heart rate accelerate, and blood pressure surges. You perspire, your mouth goes dry, and the hairs on your skin may stand up, giving you the familiar sensation of goose bumps. Your pupils dilate, allowing you to take in a wider visual field. Blood sugar levels increase, giving you immediate energy to expend. Digestion stops as

basic emotions
The most fundamental set of emotion categories, which are biologically innate, evolutionarily determined, and culturally universal.

interpersonal engagement
Emotion dimension reflecting the degree to which emotions involve a relationship with another person or other people.

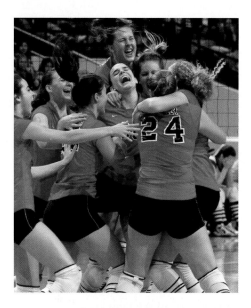

Arousal and Extremes of Emotion The ecstatic members of this volleyball team have just won the state championship trophy after a three-game set. Many intense emotions involve the activation of the sympathetic nervous system. Although emotions like extreme joy, fear, and grief subjectively *feel* very different, they are all associated with increases in heart rate, breathing, and blood pressure. From a functional perspective, the physical arousal associated with extreme emotion helps gear people up for action.

amygdala
(uh-MIG-dull-uh) Almond-shaped cluster of neurons in the brain's temporal lobe, involved in memory and emotional responses, especially fear.

brain fingerprinting
Technique to detect lies or deception, which uses an electroencephalograph to analyze brain waves; determines whether a stimulus is familiar (i.e., recognized because it is stored in the suspect's memory) or unfamiliar.

blood is diverted from the stomach and intestines to the brain and skeletal muscles, sometimes causing the sensations of light-headedness or "butterflies" fluttering in your stomach. The polygraph or "lie detector" measures these physiological reactions associated with emotional arousal (see In Focus Box 8.3).

The sympathetic nervous system is also activated by other intense emotions, such as excitement, passionate love, or extreme joy. If you've ever ridden an exciting roller-coaster, self-consciously given a speech in front of your peers, or been reunited with a loved one after a long absence, you've experienced the high levels of physiological arousal that can be induced by other types of emotions. Obviously, not all emotions involve intense physical reactions. And some emotions, such as contentment, are characterized by decreased physical arousal and the slowing of some body processes (Levenson & others, 1990, 1992).

Studies have found that there are differing patterns of physiological arousal for different emotions. In a series of studies, psychologist Robert W. Levenson (1992) found that fear, anger, and sadness are all associated with accelerated heart rate. But comparing anger and fear showed differences that confirm everyday experience. Anger produces greater increases in blood pressure than fear. And while anger produces an increase in skin temperature, fear produces a *decrease* in skin temperature. Perhaps that's why when we are angry, we speak of "getting hot under the collar," and when fearful, we feel clammy and complain of having "cold feet."

Levenson (1992) believes that these differing patterns of sympathetic nervous system activation are universal, reflecting biological responses to the basic emotions that are hard-wired by evolution into all humans. Supporting this contention, Levenson found that male and female subjects, as well as young and elderly subjects, experience the *same* patterns of autonomic nervous system activity for different basic emotions. These distinctive patterns of emotional physiological arousal were also found in members of a remote culture in western Sumatra, an island in Indonesia (Levenson & others, 1992). Broader surveys of different cultures have also demonstrated that the basic emotions are associated with distinct patterns of autonomic nervous system activity (Scherer & Wallbott, 1994).

The Emotional Brain: Fear and the Amygdala

Sophisticated brain-imaging techniques have led to an explosion of new knowledge about the brain's role in emotion. Of all the emotions, the brain processes involved in *fear* have been most thoroughly studied. Many brain areas are implicated in emotional responses, but the brain structure called the **amygdala** has long been known to be important. The amygdala is part of the *limbic system,* a group of brain structures involved in emotion, memory, and basic motivational drives, such as hunger, thirst, and sex. As described in Chapter 2, the amygdala is an almond-shaped cluster of neurons located deep in the temporal lobe on each side of the brain. Neural pathways connect the amygdala with other brain structures.

Several studies have shown that the amygdala is a key brain structure in the emotional response of fear in humans (Davis & Whalen, 2001). For example, brain-imaging techniques have demonstrated that the amygdala activates when you view threatening or fearful faces, or hear people make nonverbal sounds expressing fear (Morris & others, 1999). Even when people simply anticipate a threatening stimulus, the amygdala activates as part of the fear circuit in the brain (Phelps & others, 2001).

In rats, amygdala damage disrupts the neural circuits involved in the fear response. For example, rats with a damaged amygdala can't be classically conditioned to acquire a fear response (Davidson & others, 2000). In humans, damage to the amygdala also disrupts elements of the fear response. For example, people with amygdala damage lose the ability to distinguish between friendly and threatening faces (Adolphs & others, 1998).

Detecting Lies: From Polygraphs to the P300

The *polygraph,* commonly called a lie detector, doesn't really detect lies or deception. Rather, a polygraph measures physiological changes associated with emotions like fear, tension, and anxiety. Heart rate, blood pressure, respiration, and other indicators are monitored during a polygraph interview. When people show arousal patterns typically associated with anxiety or fear, lying is inferred (Rosenfeld, 1995).

There are many potential problems with using a polygraph to detect lying. First, there is *no* unique pattern of physiological arousal associated specifically with lying (Lykken, 1983, 1998). Second, some people can lie *without* experiencing anxiety or arousal. This produces a *false negative* result—the liar is judged to be telling the truth. Third, when innocent people are asked incriminating questions, they may respond with anxiety or fear. This can lead to *false positive* results— innocent people are judged as being guilty. In fact, polygraph tests are more likely to wrongly identify innocent people as guilty than guilty people as innocent (Bashore & Rapp, 1993).

Finally, interpreting polygraph results can be highly subjective. In one study, polygraph results were compared to later confessions of guilt in criminal cases. Lying was accurately detected by the polygraph examiners at a rate just slightly better than flipping a coin (Phillips, 1999).

In the scientific community, it is generally agreed that polygraphs are *not* a valid method to detect lies and that their results should not be used as evidence (Iacono & Lykken, 1997). Because of the polygraph's high error rate, many states do not allow polygraph tests as evidence in court. However, the U.S. government uses polygraph testing in several agencies, including the CIA and the Department of Energy (Holden, 2001).

Microexpressions: Fleeting Indicators of Deceit

Emotion researcher Paul Ekman and his colleagues (1999) have found that deception is associated with a variety of *nonverbal cues,* such as fleeting facial expressions, vocal cues, and nervous body

Harrington's response to information that was:
- Familiar
- Unfamiliar
- Related to crime scene

Voltage (mV) — Time (msec) — P300 wave

Brain Fingerprinting Lawrence Farwell, inventor of the brain-fingerprinting technique, is shown measuring Terry Harrington's brain response to information flashed on a computer screen. Harrington was convicted in 1997 for a murder that he steadfastly contends he did not commit. Brain fingerprinting results showed that he did *not* respond to information about the crime scene with a P300 wave—results that suggest that the crime scene information was unfamiliar to him. Harrington remains in prison for the crime, but his case is under appeal.

movements. Especially revealing are the fleeting facial expressions, called *microexpressions,* that last about 1/25 of a second. When people lie and try to control their facial expressions, microexpressions of fear, guilt, or anxiety often "leak" through. Even so, no single nonverbal cue indicates that someone is lying (Frank & Ekman, 1997). However, people who are skilled at decoding nonverbal cues—like clinical psychologists—are better than other people at detecting deception (Ekman & others, 1999).

Brain Fingerprinting: The P300 Brain Wave and "Guilty Knowledge"

A new strategy to detect deception, called **brain fingerprinting,** uses the *electroencephalograph,* or *EEG,* to detect brainwave responses. Brain fingerprinting is based on the well-established finding that the brain emits a distinctive brainwave response, called a *P300 wave,* when presented with a stimulus that is distinctive in some way (Farwell & Donchin, 1991; Farwell & Smith, 2001). For example, if you're looking at random numbers scrolling across a computer screen and your Social Security number suddenly appears in the sequence, your brain would respond to the familiar stimulus with a P300 wave. From this response, the examiner would conclude that you

recognized the stimulus—that the information was familiar and relevant to you. So, brain fingerprinting detects information already stored in your brain.

In a criminal investigation, brain fingerprinting works like this: Details that only the actual criminal would know are mingled with neutral details, and all are presented to the suspect. In one case, the fleeing murderer ran through waist-high weeds behind a house (Boyce, 2001). In the brain-fingerprinting interview, the suspect was asked, "What is located behind the house where the murder occurred?" Different choices were then provided: "Cement and blacktop?" "Sand and gravel?" "Weeds and grass?" If a P300 wave is emitted in response to details that only the criminal would know (weeds and grass), the examiner would conclude that the suspect possessed "guilty knowledge" of the crime.

Brain fingerprinting is still controversial and has only recently become admissible as evidence in court. One problem is that criminals might not encode memories of incidental details that would indicate guilty knowledge, especially if they are intoxicated or using drugs at the time of the crime. Caution also needs to be exercised because brain fingerprinting has not been thoroughly field tested ("Forensic Neuroscience," 2001).

Activating the Amygdala: Direct and Indirect Neural Pathways Let's use an example to show how the amygdala participates in the brain's fear circuit. Imagine that your sister's eight-year-old son sneaks up behind you at a family picnic and pokes you in the back with a long stick. As you quickly wheel around, he shouts, "Look what I found in the woods!" Dangling from the stick is a wriggling, slimy-looking, three-foot-long snake. He tosses the snake into your face, and you let out a yell and jump two feet into the air. As he bursts into hysterical laughter, you quickly realize that the realistic-looking snake is made of rubber, your nephew is a twit, and your sister is laughing as hard as her son.

Even if you don't know any obnoxious eight-year-old boys, you've probably experienced a sudden fright where you instantly reacted to a threatening stimulus, like a snake, a spider, or an oncoming car. Typically, you respond instinctively, without taking time to consciously or deliberately evaluate the situation.

So, how can we respond to potentially dangerous stimuli before we've had time to think about them? Let's stay with our example. When you saw the dangling snake, the visual stimulus was first routed to the *thalamus* (see Figure 8.10). As we explained in Chapter 2, all incoming sensory information, with the exception of olfactory sensations, is processed in the thalamus before being relayed to sensory centers in the cerebral cortex.

However, neuroscientist Joseph LeDoux (1996, 2000) discovered that there are *two* neural pathways for sensory information that project from the thalamus. One leads to the cortex, as previously described, but the other leads directly to the amygdala, bypassing the cortex. When we are faced with a potential threat, sensory information about the threatening stimulus is routed simultaneously along both pathways.

LeDoux (1996) describes the direct thalamus→amygdala pathway as a "shortcut" from the thalamus to the amygdala. This is a "quick-and-dirty" route that transmits crude, almost archetypal, information about the stimulus directly to the amygdala. This rapid transmission allows the brain to start to respond to the possible danger represented by a writhing, curved snake dangling from a stick *before* you have time to consciously think about the stimulus. The amygdala activates and triggers the brain's alarm system.

What happens next? The amygdala sends information along neural pathways that project to other brain regions that make up the rest of the brain's fear circuit. One pathway leads to an area of the *hypothalamus*, then on to the *medulla* at the base of the brain. In combination, the hypothalamus and medulla trigger arousal of the sympathetic nervous system. Another pathway projects from the amygdala to a different hypothalamus area that, in concert with the *pituitary gland*, triggers the release of stress hormones (LeDoux, 1995, 2000).

The result? You respond instantly to the threat—"SNAKE!"—by leaping backwards, heartbeat and breathing accelerating. But even as you respond to the threat, information is speeding along the other neural pathway that reaches the amygdala by traveling through the cortex. The thalamus sends information to the visual cortex, which creates a detailed and more accurate representation of the visual stimulus. You can also reevaluate the signal that prompted the initial instinctive response.

Now you realize that the "snake" is actually just a rubber toy. The cortex sends the "false alarm" message to the amygdala. But note that information traveling the thalamus→cortex→amygdala route takes about twice as long to reach the amygdala as the information traveling along the direct thalamus→amygdala route. Thus, the alarm reaction is already in full swing before signals from the cortex reach the amygdala.

FIGURE 8.10 Fear Circuits in the Brain
When you're faced with a potentially threatening stimulus—like a snake dangling from a stick—information arrives in the thalamus (blue) and is relayed simultaneously along two pathways. Crude, archetypal information rapidly travels the direct route to the amygdala (red), triggering an almost instantaneous fear response. More detailed information is sent along the pathway to the visual cortex (blue), where the stimulus is interpreted. If the cortex determines that a threat exists, the information is relayed to the amygdala along the longer, slower pathway. The amygdala triggers other brain structures, such as the hypothalamus, which activate the sympathetic nervous system and the endocrine system's release of stress hormones.

SOURCE: Adapted from LeDoux (1994a, b).

Thalamus

Visual cortex

Amygdala

Sympathetic nervous system

Endocrine system

focus on Neuroscience

Sadness   **Happiness**

Anger   **Fear**

Do Different Emotions Activate Different Brain Areas? How does the brain process basic emotions other than fear? Is there a single "emotion center" in the brain? Or, are multiple brain areas involved in emotional responses? The idea that different combinations of brain regions are activated by different emotions received considerable support in a brain-imaging study by neuroscientist Antonio Damasio and his colleagues

(2000). In the study, participants were scanned using positron emission tomography (PET) while they recalled emotionally charged memories to generate different emotions—sadness, happiness, anger, and fear.

Each of the four PET scans shown here is an averaged composite of all thirty-nine participants in the study. Significant areas of brain activation are indicated in red, while significant areas of deactivation are indicated in purple. As you take a few moments to compare the scans, notice that sadness, happiness, anger, and fear each produced a distinct pattern of brain activation and deactivation. These findings confirmed the idea that each emotion involves distinct neural circuits in the brain (Lane & others, 1997; Reiman & others, 1997).

Interestingly, the emotional memory triggered increases in autonomic nervous system activity and physiological arousal before the volunteers signaled that they were subjectively "feeling" the target emotion. Areas of the somatosensory cortex, which processes sensory information from the skin, muscles, and internal organs, were also activated. These sensory signals from the body's peripheral nervous system contributed to the overall subjective "feeling" of a particular emotion. Remember the findings of this study, because we'll refer to Damasio's study again in the next section when we discuss theories of emotion.

LeDoux believes these dual alarm pathways serve several adaptive functions. The direct thalamus→amygdala pathway rapidly triggers an emotional response to threats that, through evolution, we are biologically prepared to fear, such as snakes, snarling animals, or rapidly moving, looming objects. In contrast, the indirect pathway allows more complex stimuli to be evaluated in the cortex before triggering the amygdala's alarm system. So, for example, the gradually dawning awareness that your job is in jeopardy as your boss starts talking about the need to reduce staff in your department probably has to travel the thalamus→cortex→amygdala pathway before you begin to feel the cold sweat break out on your palms.

In situations of potential danger, it is clearly advantageous to be able to respond quickly. According to LeDoux (1995, 2000), the direct thalamus→amygdala connection represents an adaptive response that has been hard-wired by evolution in the human brain. From the point of view of survival, as LeDoux (1996) remarks, "The time saved by the amygdala in acting on the thalamic interpretation, rather than waiting for the cortical input, may be the difference between life and death."

In support of this evolutionary explanation, Swedish psychologist Arne Öhman and his colleagues (2001b) have found that people pick out angry or threatening faces from a crowd of other faces much more quickly than they detect friendly or neutral faces. Presumably, this reflects the faster processing of threatening stimuli via the direct thalamus→amygdala route.

The Expression of Emotion
Making Faces

Key Theme

▪ The behavioral components of emotion include facial expressions and nonverbal behavior.

Key Questions

▪ What evidence supports the idea that facial expressions for basic emotions are universal?

▪ How does culture affect the behavioral expression of emotion?

▪ How can emotional expression be explained in terms of evolutionary theory?

Every day, we witness the behavioral components of emotions in ourselves and others. We laugh with pleasure, slam a door in frustration, or frown at a clueless remark. But of all the ways that we express and communicate our emotional responses, facial expressions are the most important.

Which Is the "True" Smile? Psychologist and emotion researcher Paul Ekman demonstrates the difference between a fake smile *(left)* and the true smile *(right).* If you were able to pick out the true smile, it was because you, like most people, are able to decipher the subtle differences in the facial muscles, especially around the eyes and lips.

In *The Expression of the Emotions in Man and Animals,* Darwin (1872) argued that human emotional expressions are innate and culturally universal. He also noted the continuity of emotional expression between humans and many other species, citing it as evidence of the common evolutionary ancestry of humans and other animals. But do nonhuman animals actually experience emotions? We explore this question on pages 354–355 in Critical Thinking Box 8.4, "Emotion in Nonhuman Animals: Laughing Rats, Silly Elephants, and Smiling Dolphins?"

Of course, humans are the animals that exhibit the greatest range of facial expressions. Psychologist **Paul Ekman** has studied the facial expression of emotions for more than four decades. Ekman (1980) estimates that the human face is capable of creating more than *7,000* different expressions. This enormous flexibility allows us considerable versatility in expressing emotion in all its subtle variations.

To study facial expressions, Ekman and his colleague Walter Friesen (1978) coded different facial expressions by painstakingly analyzing the facial muscles involved in producing each expression. In doing so, they precisely classified the facial expressions that characterize the basic emotions of happiness, sadness, surprise, fear, and disgust. When shown photographs of these facial expressions, research participants were able to correctly identify the emotion being displayed (Ekman, 1982, 1992b, 1993).

Ekman concluded that facial expressions for the basic emotions are innate and probably hard-wired into the brain. Other studies support this view. In infants, the social smile emerges three to four weeks after birth. Facial expressions of pain, interest, disgust, sadness, and anger are evident by two to three months of age, and fear by the age of six or seven months (Izard, 1989, 1994).

Facial Expressions Are Innate Born deaf and blind, this seven-year-old girl has never observed the facial expressions of those around her. Yet her smile and laughter are unmistakable and identical to those of other children. Facial expressions, especially for basic emotions, seem to be innate rather than learned.

These inborn expressions are also evident in children who are born blind and deaf. Despite their inability to observe or hear others, these children express joy, anger, and pleasure using the same expressions as sighted children (Eibl-Eibesfeldt, 1973; Goodenough, 1932). Similarly, when the spontaneous facial expressions of young adults who were born blind are compared with those of sighted adults, no significant differences emerge (Galati & others, 1997).

Culture and Emotional Expression

Recognizing facial expressions for the basic emotions seems to be universal across different cultures. Ekman (1982) and other researchers showed photographs of facial expressions to people in 21 different countries. Despite their different cultural experiences, all the participants identified the emotions being expressed with a high degree of accuracy (see Ekman, 1998). Even the inhabitants of remote, isolated villages in New Guinea, who had never been exposed to movies or other aspects of Western culture, were able to identify the emotions being expressed. Other research has confirmed and extended Ekman's original findings (see Frank & Stennett, 2001).

As anyone who has ever been the victim of a sarcastic comment is well aware, the human voice also conveys emotion. Several studies have found that people can correctly infer the emotion being expressed by voices, suggesting that there may be distinct acoustic profiles for different emotions (see Banse & Scherer, 1996). And, once again, this ability crosses cultural boundaries. In a clever study by Walter Scherer and his colleagues (2001), professional actors used tone of voice to communicate different emotions while speaking nonsense syllables made up of several foreign languages. On the basis of just the vocal qualities, judges from nine countries—speaking seven different languages—accurately determined the emotion being expressed.

Some specific nonverbal gestures, which are termed *emblems,* vary across cultures. For example, shaking your head means "no" in the United States but "yes" in southern India and Bulgaria. Nodding your head means "yes" in the United States, but in Japan it could mean "maybe" or even "no way!"

Nevertheless, some body language is probably universal. For example, a typical display of embarrassment involves a sequence of gaze aversion, sheepish smiles, and movements of the shoulder and head. People from different countries, including India, Japan, and the United States, display and easily recognize these nonverbal behaviors as indicating embarrassment (Keltner & Anderson, 2000; Keltner & Buswell, 1997).

Cultural Display Rules In many situations, you adjust your emotional expressions to make them appropriate in that particular social context. For example, even if you are deeply angered by your supervisor's comments at work, you might consciously restrain yourself and maintain a neutral facial expression. How, when, and where we display our emotional expressions are strongly influenced by cultural norms. Cultural differences in the management of facial expressions are called **display rules** (Ekman & others, 1987).

Happiness

Surprise

Sadness

Anger

Disgust

Fear

Basic Emotions and Universal Facial Expressions Paul Ekman and his colleagues have precisely calibrated the muscles used in facial expressions for basic emotions. When photographs like these are shown to people in a wide variety of cultures, they recognize the basic emotions that are being expressed.

display rules
Social and cultural rules that regulate emotional expression, especially facial expressions.

Expressing Emotion in Universal Body Language Embarrassment is expressed by a characteristic sequence of physical responses: the person averts his gaze; gives a controlled, sheepish smile; moves his head down and to the left; shifts his gaze again; displays another sheepish smile; and again looks off to the side. People from many different cultures, including India, Japan, and the United States, both display and recognize these nonverbal behaviors as indicating embarrassment (Keltner & Anderson, 2000; Keltner & Buswell, 1997).

CRITICAL THINKING 8.4

Emotion in Nonhuman Animals: Laughing Rats, Silly Elephants, and Smiling Dolphins?

Do rats laugh? Neurobiologist and psychologist Jaak Panksepp (1998, 2000) thinks that they do. When young rats play, they emit high-frequency ultrasonic "chirps" that Panksepp believes are analogous to human laughter. Rats also chirp when they are tickled, when they're anticipating tasty rat treats, and during positive social interactions. Conversely, when infant rats are separated from their mothers, or when they're cold, they emit a distress cry that is much lower in frequency than the ultrasonic chirps that are associated with pleasant experiences.

At the other end of the size spectrum, elephants seem to experience joy, compassion, empathy, grief, and depression. For example, when elephants belonging to a family group are reunited after a long separation, they perform an elaborate greeting ceremony—rumbling, trumpeting, flapping their ears, and spinning

Laughing Rats? Rats are sociable, playful creatures. They emit distinct, high-pitched chirps when they play, anticipate treats, and during positive social interactions. They also chirp when they're tickled by researchers like neuroscientist Jaak Panksepp (2000).

around as they rush together, exuberantly intertwining their trunks. Even adult elephants play, sometimes with great enthusiasm, which veteran elephant researcher Cynthia Moss (2000) describes as "elephants acting silly." But when an elephant is injured or sick, other members of its family group band together to try to raise it to its feet. They will feed a sick elephant and cover a dead one with vegetation. One female elephant stood guard over her stillborn baby for several days. With tail, ears, and trunk drooping, she moved slowly, the corners of her mouth turned down—behavioral signs that suggest extreme grief (Moss, 2000; Poole, 2000).

Do animals experience emotions? If you've ever frolicked with a playful puppy or shared the contagious contentment of a cat purring on your lap, the answer seems obvious. But before you accept that answer, remember that emotion involves three components: physiological arousal, behavioral expression, *and* subjective experience. In many animals, fear and other "emotional" responses appear to involve physiological and brain processes that are similar to those involved in human emotional experience. In mammals, it's also easy to observe behavioral responses for many basic emotions, such as fear responses when an animal is menaced by a predator or the anger shown in aggressive displays. But what about subjective experience?

Darwin on Animal Emotions

Charles Darwin never doubted that animals experience emotions. In his landmark work *The Expression of the Emotions in Man and Animals,* Darwin

Foxes in love? Rather than living in a pack like coyotes or wolves, their evolutionary relatives, red foxes form a monogamous pair bond and often mate for life. They live, play, and hunt together, and share in the care of their offspring. It's tempting, but unscientific, to label their bond as "love."

(1872) contended that differences in emotional experience between nonhuman animals and humans are a matter of degree, not kind. "The lower animals, like man, manifestly feel pleasure and pain, happiness and misery," he wrote in *The Descent of Man* in 1871. From Darwin's perspective, the capacity to experience emotion is yet another evolved trait that humans share with lower animals.

Not all psychologists agree with that stance. Staunch behaviorists like Mark Blumberg and his colleagues (2000) argue that there is no need to assume that the behaviors of animals have an emotional or mental component. For example, they contend that the distress cry of infant rats is *not* the expression of an emotional state. Rather, the cries are an "acoustic by-product" of a physiological process, more like a cough or a sneeze than a human cry (Blumberg & Sokoloff, 2001).

Consider an experiment in which a hidden camera recorded the facial expressions of Japanese and Americans as they watched films that showed grisly images of surgery, amputations, and so forth (Ekman & others, 1987; Friesen, 1972). When they watched the films alone, the Japanese and American participants displayed virtually identical facial expressions, grimacing with disgust and distaste at the gruesome scenes. But when a scientist was present while the participants watched the films, the Japanese masked their negative facial expressions of disgust or fear with smiles. Why? In Japan an important display rule is that you should not reveal negative emotions in the presence of an authority figure, so as not to offend the higher-status individual.

Display rules can also vary for different groups within a given culture. For example, recall our earlier discussion about gender differences in emotional expression. In many cultures, including the United States, women are allowed a wider range of emotional expressiveness and responsiveness than men. For men, it's considered

One problem in establishing whether animals experience emotion is the difficulty of determining the nature of an animal's subjective experience. Even Darwin (1871) readily acknowledged this problem, writing, "Who can say what cows feel, when they surround and stare intently on a dying or dead companion?"

Anthropomorphism: Happy Dolphins?

Despite the problem of knowing just what an animal is feeling, we often *think* that we do. For example, one reason that dolphins are so appealing is the wide, happy grin they seem to wear. But the dolphin's "smile" is *not* a true facial expression—it's simply the bony curvature of its mouth. If you comment on the friendly, happy appearance of the dolphins frolicking at Sea World or another aquarium, you're *projecting* those human emotions onto the dolphins.

You also just committed **anthropomorphism**—you attributed human traits, qualities, or behaviors to a nonhuman animal. The tendency of people to be anthropomorphic is understandable when you consider how extensively most of us were conditioned as children via books, cartoons, and Disney characters to believe that animals are just like people, only with fur or feathers.

From a scientific perspective, anthropomorphism can hinder progress in understanding animal emotions. By assuming that an animal thinks and feels as we do, we run the risk of distorting or obscuring the reality of the animal's own unique experience (Hauser, 2000). Rather than understanding the

Maternal love, elephant style An elephant herd is a tight-knit group, and female elephants are intensely devoted to their offspring (Moss, 2000). Elephants in a family group often touch one another with seeming affection.

animal's experience, we see only our own reflection. On the other hand, biologist Mark Bekoff (2000) notes that using human terms to explain animals' emotions and feelings helps make their worlds more accessible to us.

Still, we must acknowledge that other animals are not happy or sad in the same way that humans subjectively experience happiness or sadness. As psychologist Mark Hauser (2000) puts it, "Animal minds are wild minds, shaped by a history of environmental pressures. The problem we face is to figure out what kinds of feelings and thoughts animals have, and why they evolved such capacities."

Animals clearly demonstrate diverse emotions—fear, anger, surprise. But to understand how they subjectively *experience* such feelings—and, indeed, whether they do at all—raises questions that cannot be fully answered at this time. Nonetheless, it seems safe to assume that more primitive animals, like fish, turtles, and snakes, probably do not possess a level of self-awareness that would allow them to experience complex emotions like grief, empathy, or altruism (Hauser, 2000). For more sophisticated animals, like dolphins, primates, and elephants, the evidence is more compelling (Griffin, 2001; Reiss & Marino, 2001).

One subjective aspect of the scientific method is how to interpret evidence and data. In the case of the evidence for animal emotions, the scientific debate is far from over. Although the lack of a definitive answer can be frustrating, keep in mind that such scientific debates play an important role in avoiding erroneous conclusions and shaping future research.

Critical Thinking Questions

■ What evidence would lead you to conclude that primates, dolphins, or elephants experience emotions?

■ Would you accept different evidence to conclude that a six-month-old human infant can experience emotions? If so, why?

■ Is it possible to be completely free of anthropomorphic tendencies in studying animal emotions?

"unmasculine" to be too open in expressing emotions (Grossman & Wood, 1993). Crying is especially taboo (Vingerhoets & others, 2000).

So what overall conclusions emerge from the research findings on emotional expressions? First, Paul Ekman and other researchers have amassed considerable evidence that facial expressions for the basic emotions—happiness, sadness, anger, fear, surprise, and disgust—are hard-wired into the brain. They also contend that the basic emotions are biologically determined, the result of evolutionary processes.

Second, these emotional expressions serve the adaptive problem of communicating internal states to friends and enemies. Like the survival of other social animals, human survival depends on being able to recognize and respond quickly to the emotional state of others. Third, although facial expressions for the basic emotions may be biologically programmed, cultural conditioning, gender-role expectations, and other learning experiences shape how, when, and whether emotional responses are displayed.

anthropomorphism
The attribution of human traits, motives, emotions, or behaviors to nonhuman animals or inanimate objects.

James–Lange theory of emotion
The theory that emotions arise from the perception of body changes.

Cannon–Bard theory of emotion
The theory that emotions arise from the simultaneous activation of the sympathetic nervous system, which causes physical arousal, and the cortex, which causes the subjective experience of emotion.

*C*ommon sense says we lose our fortune, are sorry and weep; we meet a bear, are frightened and run; we are insulted by a rival, are angry and strike. The hypothesis here to be defended says that this order of sequence is incorrect, that the one mental state is not immediately induced by the other, that the bodily manifestations must first be interposed between, and that the more rational statement is that we feel sorry because we cry, angry because we strike, afraid because we tremble.

William James (1894)

Theories of Emotion
Explaining Emotion

Key Theme
- Emotion theories emphasize different aspects of emotion, but all have influenced the direction of emotion research.

Key Questions
- What are the basic principles and key criticisms of the James–Lange theory of emotion?
- How do the facial feedback hypothesis and other contemporary research support aspects of the James–Lange theory?
- What is the two-factor theory and the cognitive-mediational theory of emotion, and how do they emphasize cognitive factors in emotion?

For more than a century, American psychologists have actively debated theories to explain emotion. Like many controversies in psychology, the debate helped shape the direction of psychological research. And, in fact, the earliest psychological theory of emotion, proposed by William James more than a century ago, continues to influence psychological research (Davidson & others, 2000).

In this section, we'll look at the most influential theories of emotion. As you'll see, theories of emotion differ in terms of *which* component of emotion receives the most emphasis—subjective experience, physiological arousal, or expressive behavior.

The James–Lange Theory of Emotion
Do You Run Because You're Afraid? Or Are You Afraid Because You Run?

Imagine that you're walking to your car through the deserted college parking lot late at night. Suddenly, a shadowy figure emerges from behind a parked car. As he starts to move toward you, you walk more quickly. "Hey, what's your hurry?" he calls out, and he picks up his pace.

Your heart starts pounding as you break into a run. Reaching your car, you fumble with the keys, then jump in and lock the doors. Your hands are trembling so badly you can barely get the key into the ignition, but somehow you manage, and you hit the accelerator, zooming out of the parking lot and onto a main street. Still feeling shaky, you ease off the accelerator pedal a bit, wipe your sweaty palms on your jeans, and will yourself to calm down. After several minutes, you breathe a sigh of relief.

In this example, all three emotion components are clearly present. You experienced a subjective feeling that you labeled as "fear." You experienced physical arousal—trembling, sweating, pounding heart, and rapid breathing. And you expressed the fear, both in your facial expression and by bolting into a run. What caused this constellation of effects that you experienced as fear?

The commonsense view of emotion would suggest that you (1) recognized a threatening situation and (2) reacted by feeling fearful. This subjective experience of fear (3) activated your sympathetic nervous system and (4) triggered fearful behavior. In one of the first psychological theories of emotion, **William James** (1884) disagreed with this commonsense view, proposing a very different explanation of emotion. Danish psychologist Carl Lange proposed a very similar theory at about the same time (see James, 1894; Lange & James, 1922). Thus, this theory, illustrated in Figure 8.11, is known as the **James–Lange theory of emotion.**

Consider our example again. According to the James–Lange theory, your heart didn't pound and you didn't run because you were afraid. Rather, the James–Lange theory holds that you felt afraid *because* your heart pounded and you ran. Feedback from your physiological arousal and from the muscles involved in your behavior caused your subjective feeling of fearfulness. Thus, James believed that emotion follows this sequence: (1) We perceive a stimulus; (2) physiological and behavioral changes occur, which (3) we experience as a particular emotion.

The James–Lange theory stimulated a great deal of research, much of it consisting of attempts to disprove the theory. In 1927, the famous American physiologist **Walter Cannon** challenged the James–Lange theory. Cannon pointed out that body reactions are similar for many emotions, yet our subjective experience of various emotions is very different. For example, both fear and rage are accompanied by increased heart rate, but we have no difficulty distinguishing between the two emotions.

Second, Cannon (1927) argued that our emotional reaction to a stimulus is often faster than our physiological reaction. Here's an example to illustrate this point: Sandy's car started to slide out of control on a wet road. She felt fear as the car began to skid, but it was only *after* the car was under control, a few moments later, that her heart began to pound and her hands started to tremble. Cannon correctly noted that it can take several seconds for the physiological changes caused by activation of the sympathetic nervous system to take effect, but the subjective experience of emotion is often virtually instantaneous.

Third, artificially inducing physiological changes does not necessarily produce a related emotional experience. In one early test of the James–Lange theory, Spanish psychologist Gregorio Marañón (1924) injected several subjects with the hormone *epinephrine,* more commonly known as *adrenaline.* Epinephrine activates the sympathetic nervous system. When asked how they felt, the subjects simply reported the physical changes produced by the drug, saying, "My heart is beating very fast." Some reported feeling "as if" they should be feeling an emotion, but they said they did not feel the emotion itself: "I feel *as if* I were afraid."

James (1894) also proposed that if a person were cut off from feeling body changes, he would not experience true emotions. If he felt anything, he would experience only intellectualized, or "cold," emotions. To test this hypothesis, Cannon and his colleagues (1927) disabled the sympathetic nervous system of cats. But the cats still reacted with catlike rage when barking dogs were present: They hissed, growled, and lifted one paw to defend themselves.

What about humans? The sympathetic nervous system operates via the spinal cord. Thus, it made sense to James (1894) that people with spinal cord injuries would experience a decrease in emotional intensity, because they would not be aware of physical arousal or other bodily changes.

Once again, however, research has not supported the James–Lange theory. For example, Dutch psychologist Bob Bermond and his colleagues (1991) found that individuals with spinal cord injuries reported that their experience of fear, anger, grief, sentimentality, and joyfulness had either increased in intensity or was unchanged since their injury. Other researchers have reported similar results (e.g., Chwalisz & others, 1988).

Along with challenging the James–Lange theory of emotion, Walter Cannon (1927) proposed his own theory. Because American physiologist Philip Bard later joined with him in endorsing the theory, it became known as the **Cannon–Bard theory of emotion.** According to the Cannon–Bard theory of emotion, illustrated in Figure 8.12, when an emotion-arousing stimulus is perceived, information is relayed *simultaneously* to the brain's cerebral cortex and to the sympathetic nervous system. Cortical activation causes the subjective

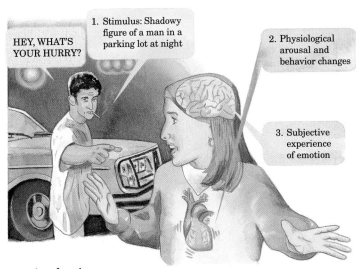

1. I see a man by that parked car.
2. I am trembling and running away.
3. I am afraid!

FIGURE 8.11 The James–Lange Theory of Emotion According to William James, we don't tremble and run because we are afraid, we are afraid because we tremble and run. James believed that body signals trigger emotional experience. These signals include physiological arousal and feedback from the muscles involved in behavior. The James–Lange theory inspired a great deal of research, but only limited aspects of the theory have been supported by research evidence.

FIGURE 8.12 The Cannon–Bard Theory of Emotion According to Walter Cannon, emotion is a two-pronged response, including both conscious experience and psychological arousal. Cannon believed that the sympathetic nervous system and the cortex in the brain were simultaneously activated. The subjective, conscious experience of emotion and physiological arousal are triggered at the same time: Neither causes the other.

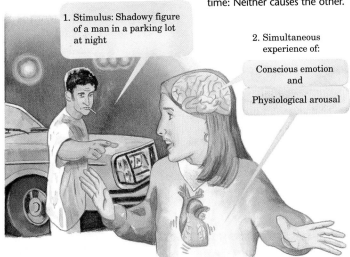

1. I see a man by that parked car.
2. I am afraid *and* trembling!

emotional experience, and sympathetic nervous system activation causes the physical response, which lags by a few seconds. Thus, according to Cannon and Bard, subjective experience and physiological arousal are triggered *at the same time:* neither causes the other.

Evidence Supporting the James–Lange Theory

On the one hand, you'd think that the James–Lange theory of emotion should be nothing more than a historical artifact at this point. Cannon's critique certainly seemed to demolish it. On the other hand, the brilliance of William James is reflected in the fact that researchers keep finding research support for key points in his theory of emotion.

For example, earlier we discussed the PET scan study by Antonio Damasio and his colleagues (2000). Damasio's study showed that each of the basic emotions produced a distinct pattern of neural responses, a finding that lends support to the James–Lange theory. It also demonstrated the importance of internal physiological feedback from the skin, muscles, internal organs, and sympathetic nervous system in generating the subjective sense of "feeling" an emotion.

Most important, Damasio found that these internal changes were registered in the brain's somatosensory cortex of the brain *before* the research volunteers reported "feeling" the emotion. This supports the most basic premise of the James–Lange theory—that physiological changes occur *before* we interpret them as an emotion.

Say "Cheese!" Here's a simple test of the facial feedback hypothesis. In a clever study by Fritz Strack and his colleagues (1988), participants who held a pen between their teeth *(left)* thought that cartoons were funnier than participants who held a pen between their lips *(right)*. How does this finding support the facial feedback hypothesis?

Research on the **facial feedback hypothesis** also supports the notion that our bodily responses affect our subjective experience. The facial feedback hypothesis states that expressing a specific emotion, especially facially, causes us to subjectively experience that emotion. Supporting this are studies showing that when people mimic the facial expressions characteristic of a given emotion, such as anger or fear, they tend to report *feeling* the emotion (Duclos & others, 1989; Flack & others, 1999).

The basic explanation for this phenomenon is that the facial muscles send feedback signals to the brain. In turn, the brain uses this information to activate and regulate emotional experience, intensifying or lessening emotion (Izard, 1990a, 1990b). In line with this explanation, Paul Ekman and Richard Davidson (1993) demonstrated that deliberately creating a "happy" smile produces brain-activity changes similar to those caused by spontaneously producing a happy smile in response to a real event. Collectively, the evidence for the facial feedback hypothesis adds support for aspects of the James–Lange theory.

Cognitive Theories of Emotion

facial feedback hypothesis
The view that expressing a specific emotion, especially facially, causes the subjective experience of that emotion.

two-factor theory of emotion
Schachter and Singer's theory that emotion is the interaction of physiological arousal and the cognitive label that we apply to explain the arousal.

cognitive-mediational theory of emotion
Lazarus's theory that emotions result from the cognitive appraisal of a situation's effect on personal well-being.

A third theory of emotion, proposed by Stanley Schachter and Jerome Singer, was influential for a short time. Schachter and Singer (1962) agreed with James that physiological arousal is a central element in emotion. But they also agreed with Cannon that physiological arousal is very similar for different emotions. Thus, arousal alone would not produce an emotional response.

Instead, Schachter and Singer proposed that we cognitively label physiological arousal as a given emotion based on our appraisal of a situation. Thus, according to the **two-factor theory of emotion,** illustrated in Figure 8.13, emotion is the result of the *interaction* of physiological arousal and the cognitive label we use to explain our stirred-up state.

Schachter and Singer (1962) tested their theory in a clever, but flawed, experiment. Male volunteers were injected with epinephrine, which produces sympathetic nervous system arousal: accelerated heartbeat, rapid breathing, trembling, and so forth. One group was informed that their symptoms were caused by the injection, but the other group was not given this explanation.

One at a time, the volunteers experienced a situation that was designed to be either irritating or humorous. Schachter and Singer predicted that the subjects who were *informed* that their physical symptoms were caused by the drug injection would be less likely to attribute their symptoms to an emotion caused by the situation. Conversely, the subjects who were *not informed* that their physical symptoms were caused by the drug injection would label their symptoms as an emotion produced by the situation.

The results partially supported their predictions. The subjects who were not informed tended to report feeling either happier or angrier than the informed subjects. Despite several problems with the experiment, Schachter and Singer's theory inspired a flurry of research. The bottom line of those research efforts? The two-factor theory of emotion received little support (Reisenzein, 1983). Nevertheless, Schachter and Singer's theory stimulated a new line of research on the importance of cognition in emotion.

To help illustrate the final theory of emotion that we'll consider, let's go back to the shadowy figure lurking in your college parking lot. Suppose that as the guy called out to you, "Hey, what's your hurry?" you recognized his voice as that of a good friend. Your emotional reaction, of course, would be very different. This simple observation is the basic premise of the **cognitive-mediational theory of emotion.**

Developed by psychologist **Richard Lazarus,** the cognitive-mediational theory of emotion asserts that the most important aspect of an emotional experience is your cognitive interpretation, or *appraisal,* of a stimulus that is potentially emotion-causing. As the name of the theory suggests, your cognitive appraisal of a stimulus "mediates," or determines, your emotional response to it.

Lazarus (1991) contends that *all* emotions are the result of cognitive appraisals of the *personal meaning* of events and experiences. If we think that we have something to gain or lose, we experience emotion. In this way, our cognitive appraisals of situations are closely tied to motivation. The more personally important the outcome, the more intense the emotion.

In the case of the shadowy figure in the parking lot, your relief that you were not on the verge of being attacked by a mugger could quickly turn to another emotion. If it's a good friend you hadn't seen for a while, your relief might turn to pleasure, even happiness. If it's an obnoxious acquaintance you'd prefer to avoid, your relief might turn to annoyance or dread.

At first glance, Lazarus's cognitive-mediational theory and the Schachter–Singer two-factor theory seem very similar. Both theories emphasize the importance of cognitive appraisal. However, the two-factor theory says that emotion results from physiological arousal *plus* a cognitive label. In contrast, Lazarus stresses that cognitive appraisal *is* the essential trigger for an emotional response. According to Lazarus (1995), all other components of emotion, including physiological arousal, *follow* the initial cognitive appraisal.

Some critics of the cognitive-mediational approach object that emotional reactions to events are virtually instantaneous—too rapid to allow for the process of cognitive appraisal. Instead, as Robert Zajonc suggested (1984, 1998), *we feel first and think later.* However, today's emotion researchers recognize that emotions can be triggered in multiple ways.

1. I see a man by that parked car.
2. I am trembling.
3. My trembling is caused by fear.
4. I am afraid!

FIGURE 8.13 The Two-Factor Theory of Emotion According to Stanley Schachter and Jerome Singer, emotional experience requires the interaction of two separate factors: (1) physiological arousal and (2) a cognitive *label* for that arousal. Both factors are necessary for the subjective experience of emotion.

Appraisal and Emotion Lazarus believes that how you cognitively appraise the personal significance of any event will determine the emotion that you experience.

Complex stimuli—like social situations or personal interactions—must be cognitively appraised before an emotion is generated. And complex emotional responses—like mixed emotions, pride, shame, or guilt—are likely to require conscious, cognitive processes.

On the other hand, cognitive appraisals are more important for some types of emotion-triggers than others (Cacioppo & Gardner, 1999). For a very simple stimulus—like a long, wriggling object dangling from a stick—emotional responses can be virtually instantaneous, bypassing conscious consideration. As Joseph LeDoux and other neuroscientists have demonstrated, the human brain can respond to biologically significant threats *without* involving conscious cognitive processes (Kihlstrom & others, 2000). So at least in some instances, we do seem to feel first and think later.

8.3 R·E·V·I·E·W

C·O·N·C·E·P·T

Emotion

Fill in the blank with the missing name or term.

1. Damage to the brain structure called the _____ disrupts the fear response in human and nonhuman animals.

2. The _____ theory of emotion claims that emotion results from our perceptions of bodily changes; it was challenged by _____.

3. According to the _____ perspective, emotions promote survival by helping us solve adaptive problems posed by our environment.

4. _____ control how people express their emotions in a particular culture.

5. According to the _____ theory of emotion, emotion results from the label we apply to physiological arousal.

6. We are able to most rapidly pick out _____ or _____ facial expressions in a crowd.

7. Intense emotions like fear, anger, and joy, activate the _____ _____ system.

8. According to the _____ theory of emotion, the emotion we feel results from how we evaluate the personal meaning of an event.

9. As you are cleaning out the debris under your grandmother's back porch, you disturb a hissing possum and instinctively jump back in alarm. Your response probably involved a neural pathway connecting the _____ and the _____ in your brain.

Summing Up
Motivation and Emotion

As you've seen in the second half of this chapter, psychologists have been interested in the nature of emotion since the beginning of the last century. And the topic of emotion involves some familiar themes in psychology. Emotions display the complex interaction of biological responses that are the result of evolutionary forces, cultural factors that shape the expression and antecedents of emotion, and individual differences in experiencing, expressing, and coping with emotion.

Like emotions, motives reflect the complex interaction of a variety of factors, including cognitive, biological, behavioral, and cultural factors. And motivation and emotion are closely intertwined in every person's life. Think back to the story of Randy, whom we introduced in the Prologue to this chapter. Randy's completion of the Tulsa Run is just one example of how motivational and emotional factors interact to cause behavior. As you've read this chapter, we hope you've also thought about the multiple factors that influence your own motivation and emotional experiences. In the chapter Application, we'll show you how you can use psychological research to help you achieve *your* goals and aspirations.

self-efficacy
The degree to which a person is convinced of his or her ability to effectively meet the demands of a particular situation.

APPLICATION Turning Your Goals into Reality

In the chapter Prologue, we described Randy's efforts to set and achieve several goals. His lifestyle changes were partly triggered by some serious self-evaluation after his long-term relationship with Sara ended.

Of course, most people can identify different aspects of their lives they'd like to change. Identifying goals we'd like to achieve is usually easy. Successfully accomplishing these goals is the tricky part. Fortunately, psychological research has identified several strategies and suggestions that can help you get motivated, act, and achieve your goals.

Self-Efficacy: Optimistic Beliefs About Your Capabilities

Your motivation to strive for achievement is closely linked to what you believe about your abilities to produce the necessary or desired results in a situation. This is what psychologist Albert Bandura calls **self-efficacy**—the degree to which you are convinced of your ability to effectively meet the demands of a particular situation.

Bandura (1997) has found that if you have an optimistic sense of self-efficacy, you will approach a difficult task as a challenge to be mastered. You will also exert strong motivational effort, persist in the face of obstacles, and look for creative ways to overcome obstacles. If you see yourself as competent and capable, you are more likely to strive for higher personal goals (Wood & Bandura, 1991).

People tend to avoid challenging situations or tasks that they *believe* exceed their capabilities (Bandura, 1989a). If self-doubts occur, motivation quickly dwindles because the task is perceived as too difficult and threatening. So how do you build your sense of self-efficacy, especially in situations in which your confidence is shaky?

According to Bandura (1991), the most effective way to strengthen your sense of self-efficacy is through *mastery experiences*—experiencing success at moderately challenging tasks in which you have to overcome obstacles and persevere. As you tackle a challenging task, you should strive for progressive improvement rather than perfection on your first attempt. Understand that setbacks serve a useful purpose in teaching that success usually requires sustained effort. If you experienced only easy successes, you'd be more likely to become disappointed and discouraged, and to abandon your efforts when you did experience failure (Miceli & Castelfranchi, 2000).

A second strategy is *social modeling* or *observational learning*. In some situations, the motivation to succeed is present, but you lack the knowledge of exactly how to achieve your goals. In such circumstances, it can be helpful to observe and imitate the behavior of someone who is already competent at the task you want to master (Bandura, 1986, 1990). For example, if you're not certain how to prepare effectively for a test or a class presentation, talk with fellow students who *are* successful in doing this. Ask how they study and what they do when they have difficulty understanding material. Knowing what works is often the critical element in ensuring success.

Implementation Intentions: Turning Goals into Actions

Suppose your sense of self-efficacy is strong, but you still have trouble putting your intentions into action. For example, have you ever made a list of New Year's resolutions and looked back at it six months later? If you're like most people, you'll wonder what went wrong.

How can you bridge the gap between good intentions and effective, goal-directed behavior? German psychologist Peter Gollwitzer (1999) points out that many people have trouble *initiating* the actions required to fulfill their goals and then *persisting* in these behaviors until the goals are achieved. Gollwitzer has identified some simple yet effective techniques that help people translate their good intentions into actual behavior.

Step 1: Form a goal intention.
This step involves translating vague, general intentions ("I'm going to do my best") into a specific, concrete, and binding goal. Express the specific goal in terms of "I intend to achieve _____," filling in the blank with the particular behavior or outcome that you wish to achieve. For example, suppose you made a New Year's resolution to exercise more regularly. Transform that general goal into a much more specific goal intention, such as "I intend to go to aerobics class three times a week." Forming the specific goal intention enhances your sense of personal commitment to the goal, and it also heightens your sense of obligation to realize the goal.

Step 2: Create implementation intentions.
This step involves making a specific plan for turning your good intention into reality. The trick is to specify exactly where, when, and how you will carry out your intended behavior. Mentally link the intended behaviors to specific situational cues, such as saying, "After my psychology class, I will go to the campus athletic center and attend the noon aerobics class in Room 201." By linking the behavior to specific situational cues, you're more likely to initiate the goal behavior when the critical situation is encountered (Oettingen & Gollwitzer, 2001). The ultimate goal of implementation intentions is to create new habits or routines in your life (Aarts & Dijksterhuis, 2000).

As simple as this seems, research has demonstrated that forming specific implementation intentions is very effective (Milne & others, 2000; Verplanken & Faes, 1999). For example, one study involved student volunteers with no enticement for participating in the research, such as money or course credit.

GARFIELD   Jim Davis

IT'S FIVE A.M., GARFIELD. A GREAT TIME TO JOG

YAWN

I KNEW THAT NONSENSE WOULDN'T LAST LONG

Just before the students left for the holidays, they were instructed to write an essay describing how they spent Christmas Eve. The essay had to be written and mailed within two days after Christmas Eve.

Half of the participants were instructed to write out specific implementation intentions describing exactly when and where they would write the report during the critical 48-hour period. They were also instructed to visualize the chosen opportunity and mentally commit themselves to it.

The other half of the participants were not asked to identify a specific time or place, but just instructed to write and mail the report within the 48 hours. The results? Of those in the implementation intention group, 71 percent wrote and mailed the report by the deadline. Only 32 percent of the other group did so (Gollwitzer & Brandstatter, 1997).

Mental Rehearsal: Visualize the Process

The mental images you create in anticipation of a situation can strongly influence your sense of self-efficacy and self-control as well as the effectiveness of your implementation intentions (Gollwizer, 1999; Ozer & Bandura, 1990). For example, students sometimes undermine their own performance by vividly imagining their worst fears, such as becoming overwhelmed by anxiety during a class presentation or going completely blank during a test.

However, the opposite is also possible. Mentally visualizing yourself dealing *effectively* with a situation can enhance your performance (Rivkin & Taylor, 1999; Sanna, 1999, 2000). Athletes, in particular, are aware of this and mentally rehearse their performance prior to competition.

So strive to control your thoughts in an optimistic way by mentally focusing on your capabilities and a positive outcome, not your limitations and worst fears. The key here is not just imagining a positive outcome. Instead, imagine and mentally rehearse the *process*—the skills you will effectively use and the steps you will take—to achieve the outcome *you* want (Pham & Taylor, 1999). Go for it!

Chapter Review
Motivation and Emotion

Key Points

Introduction: Motivation and Emotion

- **Motivation** refers to the forces that act on or within an organism to initiate and direct behavior. Three characteristics associated with motivation are activation, persistence, and intensity. Motivation is closely tied to emotion—we may be motivated to achieve certain emotions, and emotions may motivate us to take action.

Motivational Concepts and Theories

- During the twentieth century, many psychologists tried to develop general theories of motivation, but each model was too limited to explain all motivated behavior.

- **Instinct theories** of motivation, inspired by evolutionary theory, were limited in that they described and labeled behaviors but did not explain them.

- According to **drive theories,** behavior is motivated by the need to maintain **homeostasis.** Drive theories could not account for psychological motives or motives that are not related to a **drive,** or unmet need.

- According to **incentive theories,** behavior is motivated by external rewards.

- **Arousal theory** is based on the notion that people are motivated to maintain an optimal level of arousal, which can vary from one person to another. People who are high in **sensation seeking** seek high levels of arousal.

- **Humanistic theories of motivation** were based on the idea that people are motivated to achieve their highest potential.

Biological Motivation: *Hunger and Eating*

- Hunger is a biological motive, but eating behavior is also influenced by psychological, social, and cultural factors.

- Food provides **glucose,** the main source of the body's energy, which is regulated by **insulin.** Excess glucose is stored in **adipose tissue.** The **basal metabolic rate (BMR)** is the rate at which your body uses energy for vital body functions. **Energy homeostasis** helps people maintain their baseline body weight, which tends to remain stable over time unless conditions of positive or negative energy balance occur.

- Physiological factors that are correlated with eating are small changes in glucose, insulin, body temperature, and metabolism. Psychological factors that trigger eating behavior include classically conditioned stimuli; and foods that, through operant conditioning and reinforcement, have acquired a **positive incentive value**. **Satiation** signals include **cholecystokinin (CCK)** and other physiological signals, as well as **sensory-specific satiety.**

- Chemical signals that regulate body weight and help maintain a stable body weight over time include **leptin**, insulin, **neuropeptide Y (NPY)**, and **corticotropin-releasing hormone (CRH).** These factors are part of a complex feedback loop that also involves the hypothalamus in the brain. Leptin and insulin levels vary in response to positive or negative energy balance. As the hypothalamus detects changes in leptin and insulin, NPY and CRH activity increases or decreases, adjusting food intake and BMR. The energy balance model is based on **set-point theory.** An alternative view, **settling-point models of weight regulation,** helps explain why baseline body weight can change in response to positive or negative energy balance.

- The number of overweight people in the United States and other developed countries has steadily increased in the past decades. **Body mass index (BMI)** is one way to calculate weight status. Someone who is **obese** has a high BMI and an abnormally high proportion of body fat. Factors involved in becoming overweight include the ready availability of foods with a positive incentive value, overeating, the **cafeteria diet effect,** preloading calories, individual differences in BMR, and sedentary lifestyles.

- Obesity leads to many health problems, some of which are life-threatening. Several factors contribute to obesity, including genetic susceptibility, **leptin resistance,** and frequent dieting, which may lead to **weight cycling.** Obese people tend to have fewer dopamine receptors in their brains than normal-weight individuals, which may lead to compulsive eating to stimulate brain reward centers.

- **Eating disorders** include **anorexia nervosa, bulimia nervosa,** and **binge-eating disorder.** Eating disorders are more common in females. Subtypes of anorexia include restricting and binge–purge. Factors that contribute to the development of eating disorders include genetics, disruptions in serotonin, and disruptions in the chemical signals that normally regulate eating behavior. Cultural attitudes also contribute to eating disorders.

Psychological Needs as Motivators

- According to Abraham Maslow's **hierarchy of needs,** people must fulfill basic needs before they can be motivated by higher psychological needs, such as **self-actualization.** Maslow's model has been very influential, but lacks empirical support.

- **Self-determination theory (SDT),** developed by Edward Deci and Richard Ryan, is based on the premise that people are motivated to achieve a unified sense of self and integration with others. SDT includes three innate, universal psychological needs: autonomy, competence, and relatedness. **Intrinsic motivation** and **extrinsic motivation** are important principles in SDT.

- **Competence motivation** refers to striving to be capable and exercise control, while **achievement motivation** refers to striving to excel or outperform others. The **Thematic Apperception Test (TAT)** is one way to measure achievement motivation. Achievement motivation is expressed differently in individualistic and collectivistic cultures.

Emotion

- An **emotion** has three basic components: subjective experience, a physiological response, and a behavioral or expressive response.

- Emotions have many functions, including triggering motivated behavior, and contribute to rational decision making and purposeful behavior. **Emotional intelligence** is needed to succeed in life. According to evolutionary psychologists, emotions are the product of evolution and help us solve important adaptive problems.

- People differ in the intensity of their emotional experiences and in how readily they express their emotions. Women tend to be more emotionally expressive than men. The **basic emotions** are innate and the product of evolution. Emotions can be classified in terms of their degree of activation and pleasantness, and, in collectivistic societies, their level of **interpersonal engagement.**

- Some emotions, such as fear, anger, and happiness, involve arousal of the sympathetic nervous system. The **amygdala** is a key structure in the brain's fear circuit, which also involves the thalamus, the cortex, and the hypothalamus. The amygdala can be activated by threatening stimuli before we are consciously aware of the stimulus, an ability that has adaptive survival value. PET scans show that different emotions involve distinct patterns of brain region activation.

- Facial expressions of the basic emotions are biologically innate, culturally universal, and the result of evolution. People from diverse cultures can also accurately recognize emotions expressed vocally. However, emotional expression is controlled by cultural **display rules.** Display rules also vary by gender, with men more like to mask their emotions than women.

Theories of Emotion: *Explaining Emotion*

- Emotion theories differ in terms of which emotion component is emphasized. The **James–Lange theory** holds that emotion results from our perception of biological and behavioral responses. The **Cannon–Bard theory** holds that subjective experience and physiological arousal are experienced simultaneously. Contemporary evidence supporting the James–Lange theory includes neuroscience research demonstrating that we "feel" emotions in our body and the **facial feedback hypothesis.**

- There are two main cognitive theories of emotion. The **two-factor theory,** proposed by Schachter and Singer, holds that emotion results from applying a cognitive label to feelings of arousal. The **cognitive-mediational theory,** developed by Richard Lazarus, states that emotions result from the cognitive appraisal of the personal meaning of an event or stimulus. Emotion researchers today tend to agree that emotions can be triggered in multiple ways and that instinctive emotional responses may not require a conscious cognitive appraisal.

Key Terms

motivation, p. 320

instinct theories, p. 321

drive theories, p. 322

homeostasis, p. 322

drive, p. 323

incentive theories, p. 323

arousal theory, p. 323

sensation seeking, p. 324

humanistic theories of motivation, p. 324

glucose, p. 325

insulin, p. 326

basal metabolic rate (BMR), p. 326

adipose tissue, p. 326

energy homeostasis, p. 326

positive incentive value, p. 328

satiation, p. 328

cholecystokinin (CCK), p. 328

sensory-specific satiety, p. 328

leptin, p. 329

neuropeptide Y (NPY), p. 329

corticotropin-releasing hormone (CRH), p. 329

set-point theory, p. 330

settling-point models of weight regulation, p. 330

body mass index (BMI), p. 332

obese, p. 332

cafeteria diet effect, p. 332

leptin resistance, p. 334

weight cycling, p. 335

eating disorder, p. 335

anorexia nervosa, p. 336

bulimia nervosa, p. 336

binge-eating disorder, p. 336

hierarchy of needs, p. 338

self-actualization, p. 338

self-determination theory (SDT), p. 340

intrinsic motivation, p. 340

extrinsic motivation, p. 340

competence motivation, p. 341

achievement motivation, p. 341

Thematic Apperception Test (TAT), p. 341

emotion, p. 344

emotional intelligence, p. 345

basic emotions, p. 346

interpersonal engagement, p. 347

amygdala, p. 348

brain fingerprinting, p. 349

display rules, p. 353

anthropomorphism, p. 355

James–Lange theory of emotion, p. 356

Cannon–Bard theory of emotion, p. 357

facial feedback hypothesis, p. 358

two-factor theory of emotion, p. 358

cognitive-mediational theory of emotion, p. 359

self-efficacy, p. 361

Key People

Walter Cannon (1871–1945) American physiologist who developed an influential theory of emotion called the Cannon–Bard theory of emotion. (p. 357)

Charles Darwin (1809–1882) English naturalist and scientist (also see Chapter 1) whose theory of evolution through natural selection was first published in *On the Origin of the Species by Means of Natural Selection* in 1859. (p. 345)

Edward L. Deci (b. 1942) American psychologist who, along with Richard M. Ryan, developed self-determination theory, which contends that optimal psychological functioning and growth can occur only if the psychological needs of autonomy, competence, and relatedness are satisfied. (p. 340)

Paul Ekman (b. 1934) American psychologist and emotion researcher who is best known for his work in classifying basic emotions, analyzing facial expressions, and demonstrating that basic emotions and facial expressions are culturally universal. (p. 352)

William James (1842–1910) American psychologist (also see Chapters 1 and 4) who developed an influential theory of emotion called the James–Lange theory. (p. 356)

Richard Lazarus (b. 1922) American psychologist who promoted the cognitive perspective in the study of emotion; proposed the cognitive-mediational theory of emotion. (p. 359)

Abraham Maslow (1908–1970) American psychologist and a founder of humanistic psychology who developed a hierarchical model of human motivation in which basic needs must first be satisfied before people can strive for self-actualization. (p. 338)

Richard M. Ryan (b. 1953) American psychologist who, along with Edward L. Deci, developed self-determination theory, which contends that optimal psychological functioning and growth can occur only if the psychological needs of autonomy, competence, and relatedness are satisfied. (p. 340)

Concept Review Answers

8.1   page 337

1. False   5. True   9. True
2. False   6. False   10. False
3. False   7. False   11. False
4. True   8. False   12. True

8.2   page 343

1. c   2. d   3. b   4. a

8.3   page 360

1. amygdala
2. James–Lange;
   Walter Cannon
3. evolutionary
4. Display rules

5. two-factor
6. angry or threatening
7. sympathetic nervous
8. cognitive-mediational
9. thalamus; amygdala

| Web Companion | Review Activities |

You can find additional review activities at **www.worthpublishers.com/hockenbury**
The Psychology 3e Web Companion has a self-scoring practice quiz, flashcards, two interactive
crossword puzzles, and other activities to help you master the material in this chapter.

Fine China

Lifespan Development

Prologue

Themes and Variations

"I don't get it," nine-year-old Laura sighed. "Three is more than 2, right? So how can one-third of 12 be less than one-half of 12?"

"Look," Sandy said, drawing a square on a piece of paper. "Imagine that this is a brownie. Now, I cut it into two parts. Each part is one-half, right?"

"Right," Laura said, concentrating.

"OK. Now cut it again. Now each part is one-fourth. See? So, which would you rather have, half of a brownie or one-fourth of a brownie?"

"Mom? Couldn't I have the whole thing?"

"Very funny," Sandy smiled. "Maybe we should be trying this with paper clips. See, fractions are like dividing something. This line between the top and bottom numbers is telling you that you're dividing the top number by the bottom number. Try it with a circle. See what happens if you split it up into halves and fourths and eighths."

Frowning, Laura went to work. Suddenly her face relaxed. "Oh, I get it!" she exclaimed. "It's not really 2s and 4s and 8s. It's how many pieces you cut it up into!"

"Right! Now let's get out those paper clips and see if we can figure out the problem. Which is more, one-half or one-third of 12?"

This time, Laura could solve the problem—and the rest of her math homework. Fourth grade had presented our daughter with many new challenges, not the least of which was the move from simple addition and subtraction to more abstract math concepts, like fractions and geometry. But, as with earlier challenges in her life, Laura took it in stride.

From the very beginning of her life, Laura's growth and development have been inextricably intertwined with the development of the book that you are holding in your hands. She was born in 1990 on the day after we received our contract to write our first psychology textbook. When Laura was a newborn, Sandy became adept at typing with one hand so she could hold Laura in her lap with the other. As an infant, Laura would nap in her baby swing next to Don's desk as he wrote and rewrote chapters. And by the time she entered first grade, Laura had become proficient at putting journals and books back on the bookshelves.

Many children, of course, grow up being familiar with their parents' work. In Laura's life, that's meant living in a house filled with mountains of psychology journals, books, manuscript drafts, and a photocopier just outside her bedroom door. It's also meant putting off many of the simple pleasures of childhood because we were trying to meet a deadline. And at different times, Laura has directly participated in our work.

When she was almost six years old, for example, Laura patiently endured two three-hour photo shoots to produce the pictures you'll see of her later in this chapter.

As we've experienced Laura's development from infancy to middle childhood, we've also experienced some transitions ourselves. Your authors met and married when we were in our mid-thirties. Laura was born a month after our first wedding anniversary. Thus, we were beginning our family at a relatively late age. In fact, we were the second-oldest couple in our childbirth class.

In one sense, the first 12 years of our marriage have been exciting and eventful. We've learned that you never really know what life has in store for you. In our case, we never anticipated working side by side on a daily basis writing psychology textbooks. Nor did we anticipate how that goal would come to dominate our lives and our daughter's life.

In another sense, the last 12 years of our lives have underscored some of the typical patterns of development that we will discuss in this chapter. Just as Laura learned to walk, talk, and ride her bicycle in a predictable fashion, we've grown and developed as parents and marital partners in a relatively predictable fashion.

Without question, virtually every life follows well-established, sometimes universal, patterns of physical, social, and mental changes. Yet at the same time, every life is distinct and different—a unique combination of the predictable and the unexpected. So although certain themes are common in the life stories of almost every person, how those themes are played out remains highly individual. As you read this chapter, we hope you'll come to better understand some of the universal themes—and individual variations—in your life as well.

Introduction
Your Life Story

Key Theme
- **Developmental psychology is the study of how people change over the lifespan.**

Key Questions
- **What are the eight basic stages of the lifespan?**
- **What are some of the key themes in developmental psychology?**

One way to look at the "big picture" of your life is to think of your life as a story. You, of course, are the main character. Your life story so far has had a distinct plot, occasional subplots, and a cast of supporting characters, including family, friends, and lovers.

Like every other person, your life story has been influenced by factors beyond your control. One such factor is the unique combination of genes you inherited from your biological mother and father. Another is the historical era during which you grew up. Your individual development has also been shaped by the cultural, social, and family contexts within which you were raised.

The patterns of your life story, and the life stories of countless other people, are the focus of **developmental psychology**—the study of how people change physically, mentally, and socially throughout the lifespan. At every age and stage of life, developmental psychologists investigate the influence of multiple factors on development, including biological, environmental, social, cultural, and behavioral factors.

However, the impact of these factors on individual development is greatly influenced by attitudes, perceptions, and personality characteristics. For example, the adjustment to middle school may be a breeze for one child, but a nightmare for another. So although we are influenced by the events we experience, we also shape the meaning and consequences of those events.

developmental psychology
The branch of psychology that studies how people change over the lifespan.

Along with studying common patterns of growth and change, developmental psychologists look at the ways in which people *differ* in their development and life stories. As the prologue illustrates, there is considerable individual variation among adults in the timing of social, occupational, and interpersonal accomplishments. As we'll note several times in this chapter, the typical, or "normal," pattern of development can also vary among cultures.

Developmental psychologists often conceptualize the lifespan in terms of basic *stages* of development (see Table 9.1). Traditionally, the stages of the lifespan are defined by age, which implies that we experience relatively sudden, age-related changes as we move from one stage to the next. Indeed, some of life's transitions *are* rather abrupt, such as entering the workforce, becoming a parent, or retiring. And some aspects of development, such as prenatal development and language development, are closely tied to *critical periods,* which are periods during which a child is maximally sensitive to environmental influences.

Still, most of our physical, mental, and social changes occur gradually. As we trace the typical course of human development in this chapter, the theme of *gradually unfolding changes* throughout the ages and stages of life will become more evident.

Another important theme in developmental psychology is the *interaction between heredity and environment.* Traditionally, this is called the *nature–nurture* issue (see Chapter 1). Although we are born with a specific genetic potential that we inherit from our biological parents, our environment influences and shapes how that potential is expressed. In turn, our genetic inheritance influences the ways in which we experience and interact with the environment.

Developmental psychology is a broad field, covering a wide range of topics from many different perspectives. Our goal in this chapter is not to try to survey the entire field of lifespan development. Rather, we'll focus on presenting some of the most influential theories in developmental psychology and the key themes that have guided research on each stage of the lifespan. As we do so, we'll describe the typical patterns of development while noting the importance of individual variation.

Table **9.1**

The Eight Stages of the Lifespan

Stage	Age Range
Prenatal	Conception to birth
Infancy	0–2 years
Early childhood	2–6 years
Middle childhood	6–12 years
Adolescence	12–18 years
Young adulthood	18–40 years
Middle adulthood	40–65 years
Late adulthood	65+ years

One useful way to conceptualize the human lifespan is in terms of eight major developmental stages. Each stage is characterized by different kinds of physical, cognitive, and social changes.

Continuity and Change over the Lifespan The twin themes of continuity and change throughout the lifespan are evident in the changing nature of relationships. Childhood friendships center on sharing activities, whereas peer relationships in adolescence emphasize sharing thoughts and feelings. Early adulthood brings the challenge of forming intimate relationships and beginning a family. Close relationships with friends and family continue to contribute to psychological well-being in late adulthood.

Human Chromosomes A person's unique genetic blueprint is contained in the 23 pairs of chromosomes found in every body cell. By convention, chromosomes are numbered from 1 to 22 according to descending size. Hence, the first pair of chromosomes is the largest. The 23rd pair, which is labeled X in this micrograph, determines a person's sex. An XX combination, which is shown, indicates a female. An XY combination indicates a male.

Genetic Contributions to Your Life Story

Key Theme

▨ Your unique genetic makeup results from the pairing of one set of chromosomes from each biological parent.

Key Questions

▨ What is the relationship among genotype, phenotype, and environment?

▨ How do dominant and recessive genes differ?

At the moment of your conception, you were a single cell no larger than the period at the end of this sentence. Packed in that tiny cell was the unique genetic blueprint that you inherited from your biological parents. Today, that same genetic blueprint is found in the **chromosomes** in every cell of your body. Each chromosome is a long, threadlike structure composed of twisted parallel strands of **deoxyribonucleic acid,** abbreviated **DNA.** Put simply, DNA is the chemical basis of all heredity. It contains the chemical genetic code that has directed the growth and development of many of your unique characteristics.

The DNA code carried on each chromosome is arranged in thousands of segments called genes (see Figure 9.1). Each **gene** is a unit of DNA instructions pertaining to some characteristic, such as eye or hair color, height, or handedness.

At conception, the genes carried on the 23 chromosomes contributed by your biological mother's ovum were paired with the genes carried on the 23

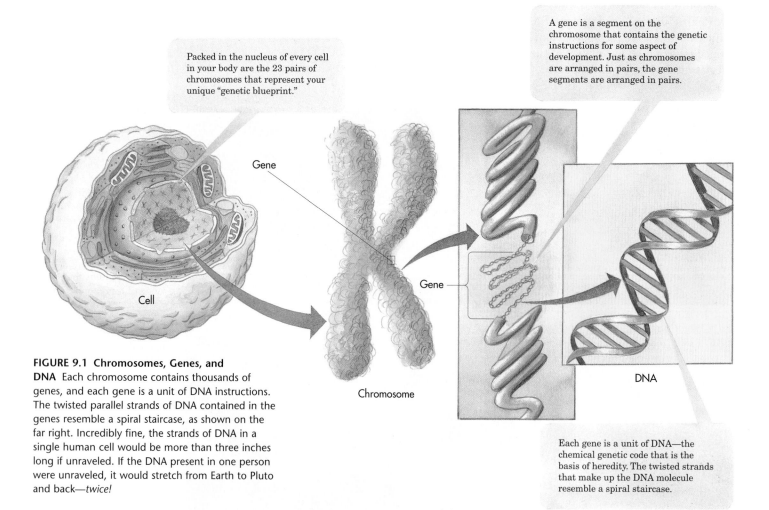

Packed in the nucleus of every cell in your body are the 23 pairs of chromosomes that represent your unique "genetic blueprint."

A gene is a segment on the chromosome that contains the genetic instructions for some aspect of development. Just as chromosomes are arranged in pairs, the gene segments are arranged in pairs.

Gene

Cell

Gene

Chromosome

DNA

Each gene is a unit of DNA—the chemical genetic code that is the basis of heredity. The twisted strands that make up the DNA molecule resemble a spiral staircase.

FIGURE 9.1 Chromosomes, Genes, and DNA Each chromosome contains thousands of genes, and each gene is a unit of DNA instructions. The twisted parallel strands of DNA contained in the genes resemble a spiral staircase, as shown on the far right. Incredibly fine, the strands of DNA in a single human cell would be more than three inches long if unraveled. If the DNA present in one person were unraveled, it would stretch from Earth to Pluto and back—*twice!*

chromosomes contributed by your biological father's sperm. The resulting 23 pairs of chromosomes contained an estimated 100,000 pairs of genes—your unique genetic blueprint.

Multiple gene pairs are involved in directing many complex features of development, such as brain organization, body build, and even some personality characteristics. Height, for example, seems to be determined by four different pairs of genes. But some relatively simple traits are determined by the interaction of a single gene pair, such as light or dark eye color, freckles, and dimples. In the next section, we'll illustrate some basic genetic mechanisms by looking at a trait that is determined by a single gene pair—freckles.

Dominant and Recessive Characteristics

The term **genotype** refers to the underlying genetic makeup of a particular individual, and the term **phenotype** refers to the traits that are actually displayed. For the sake of our discussion, let's suppose that your genotype includes one gene from your mother with the genetic code for freckles. This gene is paired with the gene you inherited from your father, which contains the genetic code for no freckles.

When a genotype combines such conflicting genetic information, the **dominant gene** will influence the trait actually displayed. In this case, the dominant gene is the one for freckles, and you'll inherit the tendency to develop freckles. Traits like freckles, dark eyes, dark hair, and dimples are referred to as *dominant characteristics* because they require *only one member of a gene pair to be dominant for the trait to be displayed*. If both members of the gene pair happen to be dominant, the genes will simply act in harmony. In either case, your phenotype will express the dominant characteristic.

How do you get a phenotype displaying nondominant characteristics, such as skin without freckles or dimples? *Each* gene in the gene pair must be a **recessive gene**—a gene whose instructions are not expressed if combined with a dominant gene. In other words, recessive genes are expressed only if paired with an identical recessive gene. In order to be freckle-free, you'd have to inherit a NO FRECKLES/NO FRECKLES gene combination as your genotype. Traits whose expression requires two identical recessive genes, such as light hair and being dimple-free, are called *recessive characteristics*. Examples of other dominant and recessive characteristics are listed in Table 9.2.

But let's not forget the interplay between heredity and environment. What we really inherit from our biological parents is a *genetic potential, the expression of which can be influenced by environmental conditions*. For example, suppose you inherited a FRECKLES/FRECKLES genotype. Because both genes are dominant, you would be genetically predisposed to develop freckles. But would you be destined to have freckles? No. The phenotype *expression* of that genetic potential will occur only if triggered by some environmental factor. In the case of freckles, exposure to sunlight activates the phenotype expression of freckles. So, if you minimized your exposure to the sun, you might never develop freckles, despite having the genetic potential to do so.

The Sex Chromosomes and Sex-Linked Recessive Characteristics

Some recessive characteristics, such as color blindness and hemophilia (inability of the blood to clot properly), are much more common in males than in females. Why? The answer has to do with the **sex chromosomes**, the 23rd pair of chromosomes—the ones that determine biological sex.

chromosome
A long, threadlike structure composed of twisted parallel strands of DNA; found in the nucleus of the cell.

deoxyribonucleic acid (DNA)
The chemical basis of heredity; carries the genetic instructions in the cell.

gene
The basic unit of heredity that directs the development of a particular characteristic; the individual unit of DNA instructions on a chromosome.

genotype
(JEEN-oh-type) The underlying genetic makeup of a particular organism, including the genetic instructions for traits that are not actually displayed.

phenotype
(FEEN-oh-type) The observable traits or characteristics of an organism as determined by the interaction of genetics and environmental factors.

dominant gene
In a pair of genes, the gene containing genetic instructions that will be expressed whether paired with another dominant gene or with a recessive gene.

recessive gene
In a pair of genes, the gene containing genetic instructions that will not be expressed unless paired with another recessive gene.

sex chromosomes
Chromosomes designated as X or Y that determine biological sex; the 23rd pair of chromosomes in humans.

Table **9.2**

Dominant and Recessive Characteristics

Dominant Characteristics	Recessive Characteristics
Full lips	Thin lips
Curly hair	Straight hair
Dark hair	Light hair
Free earlobes	Attached earlobes
Normal hearing	Congenital deafness
Freckles	No freckles
Ability to make U-shape with tongue	Inability to make U-shape with tongue
Dimples	No dimples
Feet with normal arches	Flat feet

Human Sex Chromosomes The human sex chromosomes are contained in the 23rd pair of chromosomes. On the left is the large X chromosome, which carries many more genes than the smaller Y chromosome, shown on the right.

There are two types of sex chromosomes, the large *X chromosome* and the smaller *Y chromosome.* The large X chromosome carries more genes than does the smaller Y chromosome, including genes for traits unrelated to sex. In females, the 23rd pair of chromosomes is made up of two large X chromosomes. In males, a large X chromosome and a smaller Y chromosome make up the 23rd pair.

As we've already seen, recessive characteristics normally require the presence of *two* identical recessive genes for the trait to be displayed, one on each chromosome in a particular pair. This continues to be true for females for recessive characteristics communicated on the 23rd chromosome pair. Females require the presence of *two* recessive genes, one on each X chromosome.

For males, however, the smaller Y chromosome often does *not* contain a corresponding gene segment to match the one on the X chromosome. This means that a male can display certain recessive characteristics as the result of having only *one recessive gene carried on the X chromosome of his XY pair.*

Traits determined by recessive genes on the X chromosomes are referred to as **sex-linked recessive characteristics.** Red–green color blindness, congenital night blindness, hemophilia, and brown tooth enamel are examples of sex-linked recessive characteristics. Because males require only one recessive gene on their X chromosome to display the recessive trait, they are more likely than are females to display these sex-linked recessive characteristics. Thus, males and females show different patterns of inheritance for recessive characteristics that are communicated on the sex chromosomes.

Beyond the special case of sex-linked recessive characteristics, other patterns of genetic influence exist. Some traits, for example, are expressed as the *average* of the genetic instructions inherited from the mother and the father. For example, skin color is usually an intermediate value between the skin color of each parent. In addition, the genetic code can *mutate,* or spontaneously change, from one generation to the next.

Prenatal Development

Key Theme

- During the prenatal stage, the single-cell zygote develops into a full-term fetus.

Key Questions

- What are the three stages of prenatal development?
- What are teratogens, and what general principles seem to govern their impact on the fetus?

sex-linked recessive characteristics
Traits determined by recessive genes located on the X chromosome; in males, these characteristics require only one recessive gene to be expressed.

prenatal stage
The stage of development before birth; divided into the germinal, embryonic, and fetal periods.

germinal period
The first two weeks of prenatal development.

At conception, chromosomes from the biological mother and father combine to form a single cell—the fertilized egg, or *zygote.* Over the relatively brief span of nine months, that single cell develops into the estimated trillion cells that make up a newborn baby. This **prenatal stage** has three distinct phases: the germinal period, the embryonic period, and the fetal period.

The **germinal period,** also called the *zygotic period,* represents the first two weeks of prenatal development. During this time, the zygote undergoes rapid cell division before becoming implanted on the mother's uterine wall. Some of the zygote's cells will eventually form the structures that house and protect the developing fetus and will provide nourishment from the mother. By the end of the two-week germinal period, the single-celled zygote has developed into a cluster of cells called the *embryo.*

The **embryonic period** begins with week 3 and extends through week 8. During this time of rapid growth and intensive cell differentiation, the organs and major systems of the body form. Genes on the sex chromosomes and hormonal influences also trigger the initial development of the sex organs.

Protectively housed in the fluid-filled *amniotic sac,* the embryo's lifeline is the umbilical cord. Via the *umbilical cord,* the embryo receives nutrients, oxygen, and water and gets rid of carbon monoxide and other wastes. The umbilical cord attaches the embryo to the *placenta,* a disk-shaped tissue on the mother's uterine wall. The placenta prevents the mother's blood from mingling with that of the developing embryo, acting as a filter to prevent harmful substances that might be present in the mother's blood from reaching the embryo.

The placenta cannot, however, filter out all harmful agents from the mother's blood. Harmful agents or substances that can cause abnormal development or birth defects are called **teratogens.** Generally, the greatest vulnerability to teratogens occurs during the embryonic stage, when major body systems are forming. Known teratogens include:

- Exposure to radiation
- Toxic industrial chemicals, such as mercury and PCBs
- Diseases, such as rubella, syphilis, genital herpes, and AIDS
- Drugs taken by the mother, such as alcohol, cocaine, and heroin

By the end of the embryonic period, the embryo has grown from a cluster of a few hundred cells no bigger than the head of a pin to over an inch in length. Now weighing about an ounce, the embryo looks distinctly human, even though its head accounts for about half its body size.

The third month heralds the beginning of the **fetal period**—the final and longest stage of prenatal development. The main task during the next seven months is for body systems to grow and reach maturity in preparation for life outside the mother's body. By the end of the third month, the *fetus* can move its arms, legs, mouth, and head. The fetus becomes capable of reflexive responses, such as fanning its toes if the sole of the foot is stroked and squinting if its eyelids are touched. During the fourth month, the mother experiences *quickening*—she can feel the fetus moving.

By the fifth month, all the brain cells the person will have at birth are present. After birth, the communication links between these brain cells continue to develop in complexity. The fetus has distinct sleep–wake cycles and periods of activity. During the sixth month, the fetus's brain activity becomes similar to that of a newborn baby.

During the final two months of this period, the fetus will double in weight, gaining an additional three to four pounds of body fat. This additional body fat will help the newborn adjust to changing temperatures outside the womb. It also contributes to the newborn's chubby appearance. As birth approaches, growth slows and the fetus's body systems become more active.

embryonic period
The second period of prenatal development, extending from the third week through the eighth week.

teratogens
Harmful agents or substances that can cause malformations or defects in an embryo or fetus.

fetal period
The third and longest period of prenatal development, extending from the ninth week until birth.

Prenatal Development Although it is less than an inch long, the beginnings of arms, legs, and fingers can already be distinguished in the 7-week-old embryo (*left*). The amniotic sac and the placenta can be clearly seen in this photograph. The fetus at 4 months (*center*) measures 6 to 10 inches long, and the mother may be able to feel the fetus's movements. Notice the well-formed umbilical cord. Near full term (*right*), the 8-month-old fetus gains body fat to help the newborn survive outside the mother's uterus.

Development During Infancy and Childhood

Key Theme

- Although physically helpless, newborn infants are equipped with reflexes and sensory capabilities that enhance their chances for survival.

Key Questions

- How do the senses and the brain develop after birth?
- What roles do temperament and attachment play in social and personality development?
- What are the stages of language development?

The newly born infant enters the world with an impressive array of physical and sensory capabilities. Initially, his behavior is mostly limited to reflexes that enhance his chances for survival. Touching the newborn's cheek triggers the *rooting reflex*—the infant turns toward the source of the touch and opens his mouth. Touching the newborn's lips evokes the *sucking reflex*. If you put a finger on each of the newborn's palms, he will respond with the *grasping reflex*—the baby will grip your fingers so tightly that he can be lifted upright. As motor areas of the infant's brain develop over the first year of life, the rooting, sucking, and grasping reflexes are replaced by voluntary behaviors.

The newborn's senses—vision, hearing, smell, and touch—are keenly attuned to people, helping her quickly learn to differentiate between her mother and other humans. In a classic study, Robert Fantz (1961) demonstrated that the image of a human face holds the newborn's gaze longer than do other images. Other researchers have also confirmed the newborn's visual preference for the human face. Newborns only 10 *minutes* old will turn their heads to continue gazing at the image of a human face as it passes in front of them, but they will not visually follow other images (Johnson & others, 1991).

Vision is the least developed sense at birth. A newborn infant is extremely nearsighted, meaning she can see close objects more clearly than distant objects. The optimal viewing distance for the newborn is about 6 to 12 inches, the perfect distance for a nursing baby to focus easily on her mother's face and make eye contact. Nevertheless, the infant's view of the world is pretty fuzzy for the first several months, even for objects that are within close range.

The interaction between adults and infants seems to compensate naturally for the newborn's poor vision. When adults interact with very young infants, they almost always position themselves so that their face is about 8 to 12 inches away from the baby's face. Adults also have a strong natural tendency to exaggerate head movements and facial expressions, such as smiles and frowns, again making it easier for the baby to see them.

The newborn also responds with increased alertness to the sound of human voices. Even at birth, he can distinguish between his mother's voice and that of another woman (DeCasper & Fifer, 1980). Especially if breast-fed, the newborn quickly becomes sensitized to the scent of his mother's body (Makin, 1989). For her part, the mother becomes keenly attuned to her infant's characteristic appearance, smell, and skin texture (Kaitz & others, 1992).

Newborn Reflexes When this 2-week-old baby (*left*) is held upright with her feet touching a flat surface, she displays the *stepping reflex,* moving her legs as if trying to walk. Another reflex that is present at birth is the *grasping reflex* (*right*). The infant's grip is so strong that he can support his own weight. Thought to enhance the newborn's chances for survival, these involuntary reflexes disappear after the first few months of life.

Physical Development

By the time infants begin crawling, at around 7 to 8 months of age, their view of the world, including distant objects, will be as clear as that of their parents. The increasing maturation of the infant's visual system reflects the development of her brain. At birth, her brain is an impressive 25 percent of its adult weight. In contrast, her birth weight is only about 5 percent of her eventual adult weight. During infancy, her brain will grow to about 75 percent of its adult weight, while her body weight will reach only about 20 percent of her adult weight.

That's Using Your Head! Although the sequence of motor development is universal, there is a great deal of individual variation in when and how these developmental milestones are reached. At 8 months of age, Laura crawled like an inchworm, relying on her head and toes to get around instead of her hands and knees. Some children scoot or roll to get where they want to go.

Newborns enter the world with an estimated 100 billion neurons. After birth, the brain continues to develop rapidly. The number of *dendrites* increases dramatically during the first two years of life. The axons of many neurons acquire *myelin*—the white, fatty covering that increases a neuron's communication speed (see Chapter 2).

One outward reflection of the infant's developing brain is the attainment of more sophisticated motor skills. Figure 9.2 illustrates the sequence and average ages of motor skill development during infancy. The basic *sequence* of motor skill development is universal, but the *average ages* can be a little deceptive. Infants vary a great deal in the ages at which they master each skill. Although virtually all infants are walking well by 15 months of age, some infants will walk as early as 10 months. Each infant has her own genetically programmed timetable of physical maturation and developmental readiness to master different motor skills.

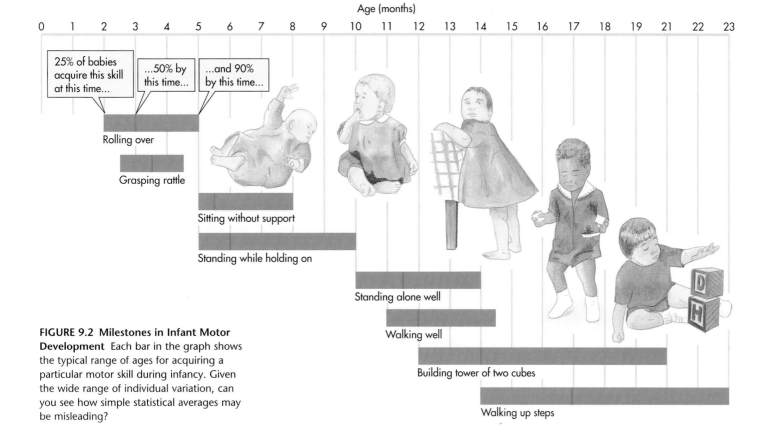

FIGURE 9.2 Milestones in Infant Motor Development Each bar in the graph shows the typical range of ages for acquiring a particular motor skill during infancy. Given the wide range of individual variation, can you see how simple statistical averages may be misleading?

temperament
Inborn predispositions to consistently behave and react in a certain way.

attachment
The emotional bond that forms between an infant and caregiver(s), especially his or her parents.

Social and Personality Development

From birth, forming close social and emotional relationships with caregivers is essential to the infant's physical and psychological well-being. Although physically helpless, the young infant does not play a passive role in forming these relationships. As you'll see in this section, the infant's individual traits play an important role in the development of the relationship between infant and caregiver.

Temperamental Qualities: Babies Are Different!

Infants come into the world with very distinct and consistent behavioral styles. Some babies are consistently calm and easy to soothe. Other babies are fussy, irritable, and hard to comfort. Some babies are active and outgoing; others seem shy and wary of new experiences. Psychologists refer to these inborn predispositions to consistently behave and react in a certain way as an infant's **temperament.**

Interest in infant temperament was triggered by a classic longitudinal study launched in the 1950s by psychiatrists Alexander Thomas and Stella Chess. The focus of the study was on how temperamental qualities influence adjustment throughout life. Chess and Thomas rated young infants on a variety of characteristics, such as activity level, mood, regularity, and attention span. They found that about two-thirds of the babies could be classified into one of three broad temperamental patterns: *easy, difficult,* and *slow-to-warm-up.* About a third of the infants were characterized as *average* babies because they did not fit neatly into one of these three categories (Thomas & Chess, 1977).

Easy babies readily adapt to new experiences, generally display positive moods and emotions, and have regular sleeping and eating patterns. *Difficult* babies tend to be intensely emotional, are irritable and fussy, and cry a lot. They also tend to have irregular sleeping and eating patterns. *Slow-to-warm-up* babies have a low activity level, withdraw from new situations and people, and adapt to new experiences very gradually. After studying the same children from infancy through childhood, Thomas and Chess (1986) found that these broad patterns of temperamental qualities are remarkably stable.

Virtually all temperament researchers agree that individual differences in temperament have a genetic and biological basis (Calkins & Fox, 1994; Rothbart & others, 1994). However, researchers also agree that environmental experiences can modify a child's basic temperament (Goldsmith & others, 1987; Gunnar, 1994). For example, a slow-to-warm-up child with a temperamental predisposition to be shy can be encouraged by his parents to be more sociable. In a supportive environment, he may well overcome much of his tendency toward shyness. Thus, the display of temperamental qualities is yet another example of the complex interaction between genetic and environmental factors.

Attachment: Forming Emotional Bonds

During the first year of life, the emotional bond that forms between the infant and his caregivers, especially his parents, is called **attachment.** According to *attachment theory,* an infant's ability to thrive physically and psychologically depends in part on the quality of attachment (Ainsworth & others, 1978).

In all cultures, the emotional bond between infants and their caregivers is an important relationship (Grossmann & Grossmann, 1990). But not surprisingly, there are cultural differences in how the attachment relationship is conceptualized and encouraged. In Culture and Human Behavior Box 9.1, we describe one example of how cultural differences in child-rearing practices reflect different ideas about the appropriate relationship between infants and parents.

In studying attachment, psychologists have typically focused on the infant's bond with the mother, since the mother is often the infant's primary caregiver. Still, it's important to note that most fathers are also directly involved with the

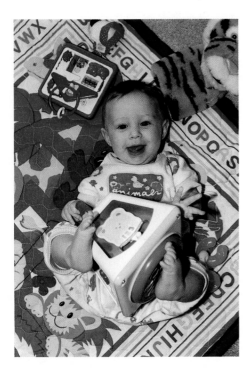

Hello, World! Some babies seem to be born wearing a smile. An "easy" baby is calm, easy to soothe, and usually cheerful. At the opposite extreme, "difficult" babies are more likely to be irritable and fussy. "Slow-to-warm-up" babies adapt to new experiences very slowly.

Where Does the Baby Sleep?

In most U.S. families, infants sleep in their own bed, usually in a separate room from their parents. It may surprise you to discover that the United States is very unusual in this respect. In one survey of 100 societies, the United States was the *only* one in which babies slept in separate rooms. Another survey of 136 societies found that in two-thirds of the societies, infants slept in the same beds as their mothers. In the remainder, infants generally slept in the same room as their mothers (Morelli & others, 1992).

Gilda Morelli and her colleagues (1992) compared the sleeping arrangements of several middle-class U.S. families with those of Mayan families in a small town in Guatemala. They found that infants in the Mayan families slept with their mothers until they were two or three, usually until another baby was about to be born. At that point, toddlers moved to the bed of another family member, usually the father or an older sibling. Children continued to sleep with other family members throughout childhood.

Mayan mothers were shocked when the American researchers told them that infants in the United States slept alone and often in a different room from their parents. The Mayan mothers reacted with disapproval and pity for the infant. They believed that the practice was cruel and unnatural and would have negative effects on the infant's development.

In the United States, bedtime marks the separation of the infant or small child from the family. To ease the child's transition to sleeping—and to spending long hours alone—"putting the baby to bed" often involves lengthy bedtime rituals, including stories and lullabies. Small children often take comforting items, such as a favorite blanket or teddy bear, to bed with them to ease the stressful transition to falling asleep alone. The child may also use his "security blanket" or "cuddly" to comfort himself when he wakes up in the night, as most small children do.

In contrast, the Mayan babies did not take cuddly items to bed, and no special routines marked the transition between wakefulness and sleep. Mayan parents were puzzled by the very idea. Instead, the Mayan babies simply went to bed when their parents did or fell asleep in the middle of the family's social activities.

Morelli and her colleagues (1992) found that the different sleeping customs of the American and Mayan families reflect different cultural values. Some of the American babies slept in the same room as their parents when they were first born, which the parents felt helped foster feelings of closeness and emotional security in the newborns. Nonetheless, most of the American parents moved their babies to a separate room when they felt that the babies were ready to sleep alone, usually by the time they were three to six months of age. These parents explained their decision by saying that it was time for the baby to learn to be "independent" and "self-reliant."

In contrast, the Mayan parents felt that it was important to develop and encourage the infant's feelings of *interdependence* with other members of the family. Thus, in both Mayan and U.S. families, sleeping arrangements reflect cultural goals for child rearing and cultural values for relations among family members.

---

basic care of their infants and children (Blair & Lichter, 1991). In homes where both parents are present, infants who are attached to one parent are also attached to the other (Fox & others, 1991). Infants tend to form attachments to both parents at about the same time. Infants are also capable of forming attachments to other consistent caregivers in their lives, such as relatives or workers at a day-care center. Thus, an infant can form *multiple* attachments (Field, 1996).

Generally, when parents are consistently warm, responsive, and sensitive to their infant's needs, the infant develops a *secure attachment* to her parents (Goldsmith & Harman, 1994). The infant's expectations that her needs will be met are essential to forming a secure attachment to her parents.

In contrast, *insecure attachment* may develop when an infant's parents are neglectful, inconsistent, or insensitive to his moods or behaviors. Insecure attachment seems to reflect an ambivalent or detached emotional relationship between an infant and his parents (Ainsworth, 1979; Isabella & others, 1989).

How do researchers measure attachment? The most commonly used procedure, called the *Strange Situation*, was devised by **Mary D. Salter Ainsworth.** The Strange Situation is typically used with infants who are between 1 and 2 years old (Ainsworth & others, 1978). In this technique, the baby and his mother are brought into an unfamiliar room with a variety of toys. A few minutes later, a stranger enters the room. The mother stays with the child for a few moments, then departs, leaving the child alone with the stranger. After a few minutes, the mother returns, spends a few minutes in the room, leaves, and returns again. Through a one-way window, observers record the infant's behavior throughout this sequence of separations and reunions with his mother.

The Importance of Attachment Secure attachment in infancy forms the basis for emotional bonds in later childhood. At one time, attachment researchers focused only on the relationship between mothers and infants. Today, the importance of the attachment relationship between fathers and children is also recognized.

Psychologists assess attachment by observing the infant's behavior toward his mother during the Strange Situation procedure. When his mother is present, the *securely attached* infant will use her as a "secure base" from which to explore the new environment, periodically returning to her side. He will show distress when his mother leaves the room and will greet her warmly when she returns. A securely attached baby is easily soothed by his mother (Ainsworth & others, 1978; Lamb & others, 1985).

In contrast, an *insecurely attached* infant is less likely to explore the environment, even when her mother is present. In the Strange Situation, insecurely attached infants may appear either very anxious or completely indifferent. Such infants tend to ignore or avoid their mothers when they are present. Some insecurely attached infants become extremely distressed when their mothers leave the room. When insecurely attached infants are reunited with their mothers, they are hard to soothe and may resist their mothers' attempts to comfort them.

The quality of attachment during infancy is associated with a variety of long-term effects (Goldsmith & Harman, 1994). Preschoolers with a history of being securely attached tend to be more prosocial, empathic, and socially competent than are preschoolers with a history of insecure attachment (Collins & Gunnar, 1990; Suess & others, 1992). Adolescents who were securely attached in infancy have fewer problems, do better in school, and have more successful relationships with their peers than do adolescents who were insecurely attached in infancy (Sroufe, 1995).

Because attachment in infancy seems to be so important, psychologists have extensively investigated the impact of day care on attachment. In Critical Thinking Box 9.2, we take a close look at this issue.

Language Development

Probably no other accomplishment in early life is as astounding as language development. By the time a child reaches 3 years of age, he will have learned approximately 3,000 words and the complex rules of his language.

According to linguist **Noam Chomsky,** every child is born with a biological predisposition to learn language—*any* language. In effect, children possess a "universal grammar"—a basic understanding of the common principles of language organization. Infants are innately equipped not only to understand language but also to extract grammatical rules from what they hear (Chomsky, 1965).

At birth, infants can distinguish among the speech sounds of all the world's languages, no matter what language is spoken in their homes (Werker & Desjardins, 1995). For example, adult native speakers of English cannot distinguish between two different /t/ sounds in Hindi. And adult native speakers of Japanese cannot distinguish between /l/ and /r/ sounds—"rake" and "lake" sound the same. But infants just a few months old can distinguish among all these different sounds.

Infants lose this ability by 10 months of age (Kuhl & others, 1992). Instead, they can distinguish only among the speech sounds that are present in the language to which they have been exposed. Thus, during the first year of life, infants begin to master the sound structure of their own native language.

Encouraging Language Development: Motherese

Just as infants seem to be biologically programmed to learn language, parents seem to be biologically programmed to encourage language development by the way they speak to infants and toddlers. People in every culture, especially parents, use a style of speech called *motherese,* or *infant-directed speech,* with babies (Kuhl & others, 1997).

CRITICAL THINKING 9.2

The Effects of Child Care on Attachment and Development

The majority of infants and toddlers in the United States routinely experience care by someone other than their mother or father (Phillips, 1991). Given the importance of the emotional bond between infant and parent, should we be concerned that many young children experience daily separation from their parents?

Developmental psychologist Jay Belsky created considerable controversy when he published studies showing that infants under a year old were more likely to demonstrate insecure attachment if they experienced over 30 hours of day care per week (Belsky, 1986, 2001; Belsky & Rovine, 1988). Belsky also reviewed evidence showing that grade school children with extensive infant day-care experience were more aggressive and less compliant than children who had not been in day care. Belsky (1992) concluded that children who entered full-time day care before their first birthday were "at risk" to be insecurely attached and to suffer later behavioral and emotional problems.

Belsky's conclusions sparked a heated debate over the effects of day care on infants. Does extensive experience with day care during the first year of life create insecurely attached infants and toddlers? Does it produce negative effects in later childhood? Let's look at the evidence.

Belsky did not claim that *all* infants in day care were likely to experience insecure attachment. Reviewing the data in Belsky's studies and others, psychologist Alison Clarke-Stewart (1989, 1992) pointed out that the actual difference in attachment was quite small when infants experiencing day care were compared with infants cared for by a parent. The proportion of insecurely attached infants in day care is only slightly higher than the proportion typically found in the general population (Lamb & others, 1992). In other words, *most* of the children who had started day care in infancy were securely attached, just like most of the children who had not experienced extensive day care during infancy.

So what about the long-term effects of day care? One study found that third-graders with extensive infant day-care experience were more likely to demonstrate a variety of social and academic problems (Vandell & Corasaniti, 1990). However, these children were not enrolled in high-quality day care, as defined in the accompanying table. Rather, they experienced average day-care conditions in a state with relatively low standards for day-care centers. But even in this case, it's difficult to assign the cause of these problems to day care itself. Why? Because developmental problems in the third-graders studied were also associated with being raised exclusively by their mothers at home.

Most psychologists today agree that the *quality* of child care is a key factor in promoting secure attachment in early childhood and preventing problems in later childhood (Scarr & Eisenberg, 1993). Many studies have found that children who experience high-quality care tend to be more sociable, better adjusted, and more academically competent than children who experience poor-quality care (Howes, 1991; Phillips & Howes, 1987). In fact, when psychologist Tiffany Field studied grade school children who had been enrolled in high-quality day care from infancy, she found *no* negative effects of the day-care experience (Field, 1991; Field & others, 1988).

Swedish psychologist Bengt-Erik Andersson (1989, 1992) arrived at the same conclusion. Andersson studied children who had experienced day care before one year of age in Sweden, where high-quality day care is widely available. These children were assessed at the ages of 8 and 13 and compared to children who had been cared for by a parent at home or who had started day care later in childhood. The

The Characteristics of High-Quality Day Care

- Whether care is in someone's home or in a day-care center, caregivers should be warm and responsive.
- Developmentally appropriate activities and a variety of play materials should be available.
- Caregivers should have some training and education in child development.
- Low staff turnover is essential, as consistency is especially important for infants and toddlers.
- The ratio of caregivers to children should be low. Two adults should care for no more than 8 infants, no more than 14 toddlers, or no more than 20 four- and five-year-olds.

The National Association for the Education of Young Children (1998) has identified several key characteristics of high-quality day care, which are supported by child development research.

children who had started day care in infancy performed better in school and were rated more highly on their social and emotional competence by their teachers.

Clearly, then, day care in itself does not necessarily lead to undesirable outcomes. The critical factor is the *quality* of care. High-quality day care can potentially benefit children, even when it begins in early infancy. In contrast, low-quality care can potentially contribute to social and academic problems in later childhood. Unfortunately, high-quality day care is not readily available in many areas of the United States (Pope, 1997). High-quality day-care centers, where they do exist, tend to be expensive and may have long waiting lists.

Critical Thinking Questions

- Why do you think there is so much controversy surrounding the issue of day care and mothers working outside the home?

- How can we best ensure that high quality day care is much more available to those who need it?

High-Quality Day Care A high-quality day-care center offers a variety of age-appropriate activities and toys, and sometimes even a furry friend or two, as in this classroom. For toddlers and infants, consistency in caregivers is also extremely important.

Motherese is characterized by very distinct pronunciation, a simplified vocabulary, short sentences, high pitch, and exaggerated intonation and expression. Content is restricted to topics that are familiar to the child, and "baby talk" is often used—simplified words such as "go bye-bye" and "night-night." Questions are often asked, encouraging a response from the infant. Research by psychologist Ann Fernald (1985) has shown that infants prefer infant-directed speech to language spoken in an adult conversational style.

The adult use of infant-directed speech seems to be instinctive. Deaf mothers who use sign language modify their hand gestures when they communicate with infants and toddlers in a way that is very similar to the infant-directed speech of hearing mothers. Furthermore, as infants mature, the speech patterns of parents change to fit the child's developing language abilities (Papoušek & others, 1985).

The Cooing and Babbling Stage of Language Development

As with many other aspects of development, the stages of language development appear to be universal. In virtually every culture, infants follow the same sequence of language development and at roughly similar ages (see Figure 9.3).

At about 3 months of age, infants begin to "coo," repeating vowel sounds such as *ahhhh* or *ooooo*, varying the pitch up or down. At about 5 months of age, infants begin to *babble*. They add consonants to the vowels and string the sounds together in sometimes long-winded productions of babbling, such as *ba-ba-ba-ba, de-de-de-de,* or *ma-ma-ma-ma.*

When infants babble, they are not simply imitating adult speech. Infants all over the world use the *same* sounds when they babble, including sounds that do not occur in the language of their parents and other caregivers. At around 9 months of age, babies begin to babble more in the sounds specific to their language. Babbling, then, seems to be a biologically programmed stage of language development.

Deaf Babies Babble with Their Hands
Deaf babies whose parents use American Sign Language (ASL) babble with their hands, rather than their voices. Just as hearing babies repeat the same syllables over and over, deaf babies repeat the same simple hand gestures. The hand shapes represent basic components of ASL gestures, much like the syllables that make up the words of spoken language. Here, a baby repeats the sign for "A."

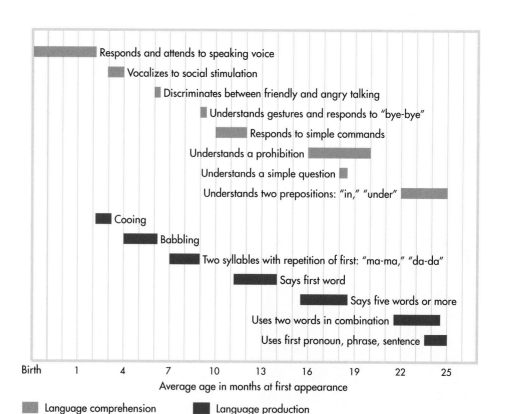

FIGURE 9.3 Milestones in Language Comprehension and Production Approximate average ages for the first appearance of different stages of language development are shown here. Notice that language comprehension occurs much earlier than language production.

SOURCE: Based on Bornstein & Lamb (1992).

Responds and attends to speaking voice
Vocalizes to social stimulation
Discriminates between friendly and angry talking
Understands gestures and responds to "bye-bye"
Responds to simple commands
Understands a prohibition
Understands a simple question
Understands two prepositions: "in," "under"
Cooing
Babbling
Two syllables with repetition of first: "ma-ma," "da-da"
Says first word
Says five words or more
Uses two words in combination
Uses first pronoun, phrase, sentence

Birth   1   4   7   10   13   16   19   22   25
Average age in months at first appearance

■ Language comprehension   ■ Language production

The One-Word Stage of Language Development

Long before babies become accomplished talkers, they understand much of what is said to them (Woodward & others, 1994). Before they are a year old, most infants can understand simple commands, such as "Bring Daddy the block," even though they cannot *say* the words *bring, Daddy,* or *block.* This reflects the fact that an infant's **comprehension vocabulary** (the words she understands) is much larger than her **production vocabulary** (the words she can say). Generally, infants acquire comprehension of words more than twice as fast as they learn to speak new words.

Somewhere around their first birthday, infants produce their first real words. First words usually refer to concrete objects or people that are important to the child, such as *mama, daddy,* or *ba-ba* (bottle). First words are also often made up of the syllables that were used in babbling.

During the *one-word stage,* babies use a single word and vocal intonation to stand for an entire sentence. With the proper intonation and context, *baba* can mean "I want my bottle!" "There's my bottle!" or "Where's my bottle?"

The Two-Word Stage of Language Development

Around their second birthday, infants begin putting words together. During the *two-word stage,* infants combine two words to construct a simple "sentence," such as "Mama go," "Where kitty?" and "No potty!" During this stage, the words used are primarily content words—nouns, verbs, and sometimes adjectives or adverbs. Articles (*a, an, the*) and prepositions (*in, under, on*) are omitted. Two-word sentences reflect the first understandings of grammar. Although these utterances include only the most essential words, they basically follow a grammatically correct sequence.

At around two and a half years of age, children move beyond the two-word stage. They rapidly increase the length and grammatical complexity of their sentences. There is a dramatic increase in the number of words they can comprehend and produce. By the age of 3, the typical child has a production vocabulary of over 3,000 words. Acquiring about a dozen new words per day, a child may have a production vocabulary of over 10,000 words by school age (Bjorklund, 1995).

> **comprehension vocabulary**
> The words that are understood by an infant or child.
>
> **production vocabulary**
> The words that an infant or child understands and can speak.

9.1 R·E·V·I·E·W

C·O·N·C·E·P·T

Early Development

Indicate whether each of the following statements is true or false. If a statement is false, write in the correct statement.

_____ *1.* Mary's genotype (Dd) includes one dominant gene (D) for DIMPLES and a recessive gene (d) for NO DIMPLES. Mary's phenotype will be to have dimples.

_____ *2.* Each chromosome has exactly 23 genes.

_____ *3.* The greatest vulnerability to teratogens usually occurs during the embryonic stage.

_____ *4.* Vision is the least well-developed sense in the human newborn.

_____ *5.* Sam, who is 4 years old, adapts easily to new situations. Sam would probably be classified as "slow-to-warm-up" in temperament.

_____ *6.* Instead of happily exploring the toys in the doctor's waiting room, Amy clings to her mother's hand, a behavior that characterizes an insecurely attached toddler.

_____ *7.* Research has confirmed that most children who enter full-time day care before the age of 18 months are insecurely attached to their parents.

Cognitive Development

Key Theme

- According to Piaget's theory, children progress through four distinct cognitive stages, and each stage marks a shift in how they think and understand the world.

Key Questions

- What are Piaget's four stages of cognitive development?
- What are three criticisms of Piaget's theory?
- How do Vygotsky's ideas about cognitive development differ from Piaget's theory?

When Laura was almost 3, Sandy and Laura were investigating the tadpoles in the creek behind our home. "Do you know what tadpoles become when they grow up? They become frogs," Sandy explained. Laura looked very serious. After considering this new bit of information for a few moments, she asked, "Laura grow up to be a frog, too?"

Just as children advance in motor skill and language development, they also develop increasing sophistication in cognitive processes—thinking, remembering, and processing information. The most influential theory of cognitive development is that of Swiss psychologist **Jean Piaget.** Originally trained as a biologist, Piaget combined a boundless curiosity about the nature of the human mind with a gift for scientific observation (Brainerd, 1996).

Piaget (1952, 1972) believed that children *actively* try to make sense out of their environment rather than passively soaking up information about the world. To Piaget, many of the "cute" things children say actually reflect their sincere attempts to make sense of their world. In fact, Piaget carefully observed his own three children in developing his theory (Fischer & Hencke, 1996).

According to Piaget, children progress through four distinct cognitive stages: the sensorimotor stage, from birth to age 2; the preoperational stage, from age 2 to age 7; the concrete operational stage, from age 7 to age 11; and the formal operational stage, which begins during adolescence and continues into adulthood. As a child advances to a new stage, his thinking is *qualitatively different* from that of the previous stage. In other words, each new stage represents a fundamental shift in *how* the child thinks and understands the world.

Piaget saw this progression of cognitive development as a continuous, gradual process. As a child develops and matures, she does not simply acquire more information. Rather, she develops a new understanding of the world in each progressive stage, building on the understandings acquired in the previous stage (Siegler & Ellis, 1996). As the child *assimilates* new information and experiences, he eventually changes his way of thinking to *accommodate* new knowledge (P. H. Miller, 1993).

Piaget believed that these stages were biologically programmed to unfold at their respective ages (Flavell, 1996). He also believed that children in every culture progressed through the same sequence of stages at roughly similar ages. However, Piaget also recognized that hereditary and environmental differences could influence the rate at which a given child progressed through the stages (Fischer & Hencke, 1996; Wadsworth, 1996).

For example, a "bright" child may progress through the stages faster than a child who is less intellectually capable. A child whose environment provides ample and varied opportunities for exploration is likely to progress faster than a child who has limited environmental opportunities. Thus, even though the sequence of stages is universal, there can be individual variation in the rate of cognitive development.

Jean Piaget Swiss psychologist Jean Piaget (1896–1980) viewed the child as a little scientist, actively exploring his or her world. Much of Piaget's theory was based on his careful observation of individual children, especially his own children.

The Sensorimotor Stage

The **sensorimotor stage** extends from birth until about 2 years of age. During this stage, infants acquire knowledge about the world through actions that allow them to directly experience and manipulate objects. Infants discover a wealth of very practical sensory knowledge, such as what objects look like and how they taste, feel, smell, and sound.

Infants in this stage also expand their practical knowledge about motor actions—reaching, grasping, pushing, pulling, and pouring. In the process, they gain a basic understanding of the effects their own actions can produce, such as pushing a button to turn on the television or knocking over a pile of blocks to make them crash and tumble.

At the beginning of the sensorimotor stage, the infant's motto seems to be, "Out of sight, out of mind." An object exists only if she can directly sense it. For example, if a 4-month-old infant knocks a ball underneath the couch and it rolls out of sight, she will not look for it. Piaget interpreted this response to mean that to the infant, the ball no longer exists.

However, by the end of the sensorimotor stage, children acquire a new cognitive understanding, called object permanence. **Object permanence** is the understanding that an object continues to exist even if it can't be seen. Now the infant will actively search for a ball that she has watched roll out of sight. Infants gradually acquire an understanding of object permanence as they gain experience with objects, as their memory abilities improve, and as they develop mental representations of the world, which Piaget called *schemas*.

This Feels Different! During the sensorimotor stage, infants and toddlers rely on sensory and motor skills to explore and make sense of the world around them.

The Preoperational Stage

The **preoperational stage** lasts from roughly age 2 to age 7. In Piaget's theory, the word *operations* refers to logical mental activities. Thus, the "preoperational" stage is a prelogical stage.

The hallmark of preoperational thought is the child's capacity to engage in symbolic thought. **Symbolic thought** refers to the ability to use words, images, and symbols to represent the world (DeLoache, 1995). One indication of the expanding capacity for symbolic thought is the child's impressive gains in language during this stage.

The child's increasing capacity for symbolic thought is also apparent in her use of fantasy and imagination while playing (Golomb & Galasso, 1995). A discarded box becomes a spaceship, a house, or a fort, as children imaginatively take on the roles of different characters. In doing so, children imitate (or try to imitate) actions they have mentally symbolized from situations observed days, or even weeks, earlier.

Still, the preoperational child's understanding of symbols remains immature. A 2-year-old shown a picture of a flower, for example, may try to smell it. A young child may be puzzled by the notion that a map symbolizes an actual location—as in the cartoon below. In short, preoperational children are still actively figuring out the relationship between symbols and the actual objects they represent (DeLoache, 1995).

sensorimotor stage
In Piaget's theory, the first stage of cognitive development, from birth to about age 2; the period during which the infant explores the environment and acquires knowledge through sensing and manipulating objects.

object permanence
The understanding that an object continues to exist even when it can no longer be seen.

preoperational stage
In Piaget's theory, the second stage of cognitive development, which lasts from about age 2 to age 7; characterized by increasing use of symbols and prelogical thought processes.

symbolic thought
The ability to use words, images, and symbols to represent the world.

FOR BETTER OR FOR WORSE

Preoperational Thinking: Manipulating Mental Symbols With a hodge-podge of toys, some fake fruit, a couple of scarves, and a firefighter's helmet, these two are having great fun. The preschool child's increasing capacity for symbolic thought is delightfully reflected in symbolic play and deferred imitation. In *symbolic play,* one object stands for another: a scarf can become a magic cape, a coat, a mask, or a tablecloth. *Deferred imitation* is the capacity to repeat an action observed earlier, such as the action of a checker in a store.

egocentrism
In Piaget's theory, the inability to take another person's perspective or point of view.

irreversibility
In Piaget's theory, the inability to mentally reverse a sequence of events or logical operations.

centration
In Piaget's theory, the tendency to focus, or *center,* on only one aspect of a situation and ignore other important aspects of the situation.

conservation
In Piaget's theory, the understanding that two equal quantities remain equal even though the form or appearance is rearranged, as long as nothing is added or subtracted.

The thinking of preoperational children often displays **egocentrism.** By *egocentrism,* Piaget did not mean selfishness or conceit. Rather, egocentric children lack the ability to consider events from another person's point of view. Thus, the young child genuinely thinks that Grandma would like a new Beanie Baby or a Spiderman video for her upcoming birthday because that's what *he* wants. Egocentric thought is also operating when the child silently nods his head in answer to Grandpa's question on the telephone.

The preoperational child's thought is also characterized by irreversibility and centration. **Irreversibility** means that the child cannot mentally reverse a sequence of events or logical operations back to the starting point. For example, the child doesn't understand that adding "3 plus 1" and adding "1 plus 3" refer to the same logical operation. **Centration** refers to the tendency to focus, or center, on only one aspect of a situation, usually a perceptual aspect. In doing so, the child ignores other relevant aspects of the situation.

The classic demonstration of both irreversibility and centration involves a task devised by Piaget. When Laura was 5, we tried this task with her. First, we showed her two identical glasses, each containing exactly the same amount of liquid. Laura easily recognized the two amounts of liquid as being the same.

Then, while Laura watched intently, we poured the liquid from one of the glasses into a third container that was much taller and narrower than the others. "Which container," we asked, "holds more liquid?" Like any other preoperational child, Laura answered confidently, "The taller one!" Even when we repeated the procedure, reversing the steps over and over again, Laura remained convinced that the taller container held more liquid than did the shorter container.

This classic demonstration illustrates the preoperational child's inability to understand conservation. The principle of **conservation** holds that two equal physical quantities remain equal even if the appearance of one is changed, as long as nothing is added or subtracted (Piaget & Inhelder, 1974). Because of *centration,* the child cannot simultaneously consider the height and the width of the liquid in the container. Instead, the child focuses on only one aspect of the situation, the height of the liquid. And because of *irreversibility,* the child cannot cognitively reverse the series of events, mentally returning the poured liquid to its original container. Thus, she fails to understand that the two amounts of liquid are still the same.

Piaget's Conservation Task Laura compares the liquid in the two short beakers, then watches as Sandy pours the liquid into a tall, narrow beaker. When asked which has more, she insists that there is more liquid in the tall beaker. As Piaget's classic task demonstrates, the average 5-year-old doesn't grasp this principle of conservation. Even though Laura repeated this demonstration several times for the photographer, she persisted in her belief that the tall beaker had more liquid. We tried the demonstration again when Laura was 7. Now in the concrete operational stage, Laura immediately understood that both beakers held the same amount of liquid—just as Piaget's theory predicts.

The Concrete Operational Stage

With the beginning of the **concrete operational stage,** at around age 7, children become capable of true logical thought. They are much less egocentric in their thinking, can reverse mental operations, and can focus simultaneously on two aspects of a problem. In short, they understand the principle of conservation. When presented with two rows of pennies, each row equally spaced, concrete operational children understand that the number of pennies in each row remains the same even when the spacing between the pennies in one row is increased.

As the name of this stage implies, thinking and use of logic tend to be limited to concrete reality—to tangible objects and events. Children in the concrete operational stage often have difficulty thinking logically about hypothetical situations or abstract ideas. For example, an 8-year-old will explain the concept of friendship in very tangible terms, such as, "Friendship is when someone plays with me." In effect, the concrete operational child's ability to deal with abstract ideas and hypothetical situations is limited to his or her personal experiences and actual events.

The Formal Operational Stage

At the beginning of adolescence, children enter the **formal operational stage.** In terms of problem solving, the formal operational adolescent is much more systematic and logical than the concrete operational child.

Formal operational thought reflects the ability to think logically even when dealing with abstract concepts or hypothetical situations (Piaget, 1972; Piaget & Inhelder, 1958). In contrast to the concrete operational child, the formal operational adolescent explains *friendship* by emphasizing more global and abstract characteristics, such as mutual trust, empathy, loyalty, consistency, and shared beliefs (Beal, 1994; Harter, 1990).

But, like the development of cognitive abilities during infancy and childhood, formal operational thought emerges only gradually (Wood, 1988). Formal operational thought continues to increase in sophistication throughout adolescence and adulthood. Although an adolescent may deal effectively with abstract ideas in one domain of knowledge, his thinking may not reflect the same degree of sophistication in other areas (Keating, 1990). Piaget (1973) acknowledged that even among many adults, formal operational thinking is often limited to areas in which they have developed expertise or a special interest.

Table 9.3 summarizes Piaget's stages of cognitive development.

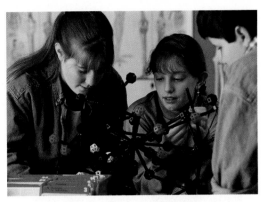

From Concrete Operations to Formal Operations Logical thinking is evident during the concrete operational stage, but develops more fully during the formal operational stage. At about the age of 12, the young person becomes capable of applying logical thinking to hypothetical situations and abstract concepts, such as the principles of molecular bonds in this chemistry class. But as is true of each of Piaget's stages, new cognitive abilities emerge gradually. Having a tangible model to manipulate helps these students grasp abstract chemistry concepts.

concrete operational stage
In Piaget's theory, the third stage of cognitive development, which lasts from about age 7 to adolescence; characterized by the ability to think logically about concrete objects and situations.

formal operational stage
In Piaget's theory, the fourth stage of cognitive development, which lasts from adolescence through adulthood; characterized by the ability to think logically about abstract principles and hypothetical situations.

Table | 9.3

Piaget's Stages of Cognitive Development

Stage	Characteristics of the Stage	Major Change of the Stage
Sensorimotor (0–2 years)	Acquires understanding of object permanence. First understandings of cause-and-effect relationships.	Development proceeds from reflexes to actively using sensory and motor skills to explore environment.
Preoperational (2–7 years)	Symbolic thought emerges. Language development occurs (2–4 years). Thought and language both tend to be egocentric. Cannot solve conservation problems.	Development proceeds from understanding simple cause-and-effect relationships to prelogical thought processes involving the use of imagination and symbols to represent objects, actions, and situations.
Concrete operations (7–11 years)	Reversibility attained. Can solve conservation problems. Logical thought develops and is applied to concrete problems. Cannot solve complex verbal problems and hypothetical problems.	Development proceeds from prelogical thought to logical solutions to concrete problems.
Formal operations (from adolescence through adulthood)	Logically solves all types of problems. Thinks scientifically. Solves complex verbal and hypothetical problems. Is able to think in abstract terms.	Development proceeds from logical solving of concrete problems to logical solving of all classes of problems, including abstract problems.

Renée Baillargeon Canadian-born psychologist Renée Baillargeon's ingenious studies of cognitive development during infancy, using visual rather than manual tasks, challenged Piaget's beliefs about the age at which object permanence first appears.

Criticisms of Piaget's Theory

Piaget's theory has inspired hundreds of research studies (Kessen, 1996). Generally, scientific research has supported Piaget's most fundamental idea: that infants, young children, and older children use distinctly different cognitive abilities to construct their understanding of the world. However, other aspects of Piaget's theory have been criticized.

One criticism is that Piaget underestimated the cognitive abilities of infants and young children. For example, to test for object permanence, Piaget would show the infant an object, cover it with a cloth, and then observe whether the infant tried to reach under the cloth for the object. But this action requires the infant to have a certain level of motor skill development. Using this procedure, Piaget found that it wasn't until an infant was about 9 months old that she behaved as if she understood that an object continued to exist after it was hidden. Even at this age, Piaget maintained, an infant's understanding of object permanence was immature and would not be fully developed for another year or so.

Today, many researchers believe that Piaget confused *motor skill limitations* with *cognitive limitations* in assessing object permanence during infancy (Mandler, 1990). In other words, perhaps the infant "knew" that the object was under the cloth but simply lacked the physical coordination to reach for it.

To test this hypothesis, psychologist **Renée Baillargeon** has used *visual* tasks, rather than *manual* tasks, in several studies to assess an infant's understanding of object permanence (1987, 1994). Baillargeon's research is based on the premise that infants, like adults, will look longer at "surprising" events that appear to contradict their understanding of the world.

Let's briefly examine a simple but ingenious study that Baillargeon conducted with co-researcher Julie De Vos (1991), using 3½-month-old infants. During the pretest phase, the infants watched a short carrot as it moved behind a panel, briefly disappeared, and then reappeared on the other side of the panel. After the babies became accustomed to the short carrot event, the same procedure was repeated with a tall carrot. (See the upper portion of Figure 9.4.)

In the test phase, the event was changed slightly: The solid panel was replaced by a panel with a window. The window was too high for the short carrot to be seen as it passed behind the panel, but not the tall carrot. Now, as the infants

FIGURE 9.4 Testing Object Permanence in Very Young Infants

Pretest Events

Short Carrot Event

Tall Carrot Event

Test Events

Possible Event

Impossible Event

watched, the tall carrot started to pass behind the screen. Although the top of the tall carrot should have been visible in the window, it *failed* to appear in the window before reappearing on the opposite side. (See the lower portion of Figure 9.4.)

Baillargeon and De Vos (1991) reasoned that if 3½-month-old infants displayed object permanence, they would remember the size of the carrots. Because the short carrot was too short to be seen in the window, the infants should not have been surprised when the short carrot passed behind the panel without appearing in the window. However, they should have expected the tall carrot to appear in the window as it moved behind the panel—and should have been surprised when it didn't appear in the window before reappearing on the opposite side.

This is exactly what Baillargeon and De Vos (1991) found. When infants *failed* to see the anticipated event—the tall carrot passing the window—they looked much longer at the scene than when the short carrot passed behind the screen without being seen. This finding suggests that 3½-month-old infants mentally represented the existence, height, and path of each carrot as it moved behind the panel. Piaget believed that such cognitive understandings were not possible until infants were at least nine months of age.

Piaget's notion that the stages unfold universally has also been challenged. Researchers have found that many adults display abstract hypothetical thinking only in limited areas of knowledge. Some adults never display formal operational thought processes. College students, for example, may not display formal operational thinking when given problems outside their major, as when an English major is presented with a physics problem (DeLisi & Staudt, 1980). Late in his life, Piaget (1972, 1973) suggested that the attainment of formal operational thinking may not be a universal phenomenon. Instead, it might be the product of and limited to an individual's expertise in a specific area.

Rather than distinct stages of cognitive development, some developmental psychologists emphasize the **information-processing model of cognitive development** (Klahr, 1992; Siegler, 1991). This model focuses on the development of fundamental mental processes, such as attention, memory, and problem solving (Rose & Feldman, 1995). In this approach, cognitive development is viewed as a process of continuous change over the lifespan. Through life experiences, we continue to acquire new knowledge, including more sophisticated cognitive skills and strategies. In turn, this improves our ability to process, learn, and remember information (Kail, 1991).

Another criticism is that Piaget underestimated the impact of the social and cultural environment on cognitive development (Gopnik, 1996). Other theorists, including the highly regarded Russian psychologist **Lev Vygotsky,** have offered very different viewpoints. Vygotsky was born the same year as Piaget and developed his theory of cognitive development at about the same time as Piaget. Vygotsky's influence in psychology has increased dramatically in the last few decades (van Geert, 1998; Wertsch & Tulviste, 1994).

Vygotsky agreed with Piaget that children may be able to reach a particular cognitive level through their own independent efforts. However, unlike Piaget, Vygotsky (1978, 1987) believed that cognitive development is strongly influenced by social and cultural factors, such as the support and guidance that children receive from parents, other adults, and older children. Such guidance can help "stretch" the child's cognitive abilities to new levels. Indeed, researchers have confirmed that such social interactions play a significant role in a child's cognitive development (Gopnik, 1996; Wertsch & Tulviste, 1992).

How these supportive social interactions are displayed varies from culture to culture (Rogoff & Chavajay, 1995). In middle-class American families, for example, adults often interact with children by posing questions to which the adult already knows the answer, such as asking, "How much is 2 times 2?" It's also considered culturally acceptable for children to show off their knowledge. In other cultures, however, these behaviors are not necessarily considered appropriate or

Lev Vygotsky Russian psychologist Lev Vygotsky was born in 1896, the same year as Piaget. He died in 1934 of tuberculosis. Recent decades have seen a resurgence of interest in Vygotsky's theoretical writings. Vygotsky emphasized the impact of social and cultural factors on cognitive development. According to Vygotsky, cognitive development always takes place within a social and cultural context.

information-processing model of cognitive development
The model that views cognitive development as a process that is continuous over the lifespan and that studies the development of basic mental processes such as attention, memory, and problem solving.

focus on **Neuroscience**

At Birth **6 Years Old** **14 Years Old**

Proliferation and decline in synaptic connections in children

Brain Changes During Childhood: Pruning Synaptic Connections By about 6 years of age, the volume of a child's brain is about 95 percent of its adult size. Although the overall size of the brain changes little during late childhood and the adolescent years, dramatic changes are occurring in the number of interconnections among the brain's neurons. In the left and center images, you can see the explosive proliferation of synaptic connections occurring during infancy and early childhood. But between age 6 and the early adolescent years, unused dendrites, synaptic connections, and neurons in the brain are selectively pruned and discarded. Those neurons that are most used survive, flourish, and strengthen their interconnections with other neurons, communicating more efficiently (Seeman, 1999; Thompson & others, 2000).

acceptable. Cross-cultural studies have also shown that cognitive development is strongly influenced by the skills that are valued and encouraged in a particular environment.

Despite these criticisms, Piaget's documentation of the many cognitive changes that occur during infancy and childhood ranks as one of the most outstanding contributions to developmental psychology (Beilin, 1994). With the exceptions that have been noted, Piaget's observations of the changes in children's cognitive abilities are fundamentally accurate.

9.2 R·E·V·I·E·W

C·O·N·C·E·P·T

Piaget's Stages of Cognitive Development

Indicate which stage of cognitive development is illustrated by each of the following examples. Choose from:

    a. sensorimotor   c. concrete operational

    b. preoperational   d. formal operational

_____ *1.* When confronted with a lawn mower that would not start, Jason approached the problem very systematically, checking and eliminating possible causes one at a time.

_____ *2.* Lynn rolls identical amounts of clay into two balls and is quite sure they are exactly the same. However, when her dad flattens one ball into a pancake shape, Lynn is confident that the pancake has more clay than the ball.

_____ *3.* When Carla's mother hides her favorite toy under a cushion, Carla starts playing with another toy and acts as though her favorite toy no longer exists.

_____ *4.* Andrew is told that Michael is taller than Bridget and Bridget is taller than Patrick. When asked who is the smallest child, Andrew thinks carefully, then answers, "Patrick."

Adolescence

Key Theme
- Adolescence is the stage that marks the transition from childhood to adulthood.

Key Questions
- What characterizes adolescent relationships with parents and peers?
- What is Erikson's psychosocial theory of lifespan development?
- What is Kohlberg's theory of moral development, and how is moral reasoning affected by gender and culture?

adolescence
The transitional stage between late childhood and the beginning of adulthood, during which sexual maturity is reached.

Adolescence is the transitional stage between late childhood and the beginning of adulthood. Adolescence begins at around age 12 and lasts until the individual assumes adult roles and responsibilities. Outwardly, the most noticeable changes that occur during adolescence are the physical changes that accompany the development of sexual maturity, a topic we'll discuss in detail in Chapter 10.

We'll start this section by looking at aspects of social development during adolescence, including the question of how the adolescent begins to build a unique sense of identity. Following that discussion, we'll consider some of the cognitive changes that occur during adolescence, especially the development of moral reasoning.

Social Development

Contrary to what many people think, parent–adolescent relationships are generally positive. In fact, most teenagers report that they admire their parents and turn to them for advice (Steinberg, 1990). As a general rule, when parent–child relationships have been good before adolescence, they continue to be relatively smooth during adolescence (Buchanan & others, 1992). Nevertheless, some friction seems to be inevitable as children make the transition to adolescence. We discuss the issue of conflict between adolescents and parents in Culture and Human Behavior Box 9.3 on page 390.

Although parents remain influential throughout adolescence, relationships with friends and peers become increasingly important. Adolescents usually encounter greater diversity among their peers as they make the transitions to middle school and high school. To a much greater degree than during childhood, the adolescent's social network, social context, and community influence his or her values, norms, and expectations (Steinberg & others, 1995).

Parents often worry that peer influences will lead to undesirable behavior. Researchers have found, however, that peer relationships tend to *reinforce* the traits and goals that parents fostered during childhood (Steinberg & others, 1995). This finding is not as surprising as it might seem. Adolescents tend to form friendships with peers who are similar in age, social class, race, and beliefs about drinking, dating, church attendance, and educational goals (Savin-Williams & Berndt, 1990).

Friends often exert pressure on one another to study, make good grades, attend college, and engage in prosocial behaviors. So, although peer influence can lead to undesirable behaviors in some instances, peers can also influence one another in positive ways (Berndt, 1992; Mounts & Steinberg, 1995).

Peer Relationships in Adolescence Peer relationships become increasingly important in adolescence. Although parents often worry about the negative effects of peer influence, peers can also have a positive influence on one another. These teenage volunteers are helping plant trees in a public park in Austin, Texas.

CULTURE AND HUMAN BEHAVIOR 9.3

Conflict Between Adolescents and Their Parents

Many people believe that relations between parents and their adolescent children are generally poor, marked by frequent and heated conflicts. Are the adolescent years a battleground?

Research on adolescents in the United States has shown that skirmishes between parents and their adolescent children *do* tend to increase, particularly during the early adolescent years (Buchanan & others, 1992; Laursen & Collins, 1994). Usually, conflicts focus on issues of control and authority and often revolve around parents' attempts to regulate everyday aspects of their children's lives.

As they enter adolescence, children are less willing to accept their parents' authority over their activities, choice of friends, and other aspects of their personal lives. In the same vein, they also tend to be more willing to disagree with their parents, argue with them, and challenge their authority. These tendencies naturally lead to an increase in bickering and sometimes even heated disputes.

Many developmental psychologists, however, view the increased conflict in early and middle adolescence as healthy, a necessary stage in the adolescent's development of increased independence and autonomy. After middle adolescence, conflicts with parents begin to decline and continue to do so throughout late adolescence (Laursen & Collins, 1994). As the adolescent matures, both parents and adolescent children become more comfortable with the adolescent's greater independence and autonomy.

Given the individualistic nature of U.S. culture, it's not surprising that developing a separate, autonomous identity

would be seen as a key developmental milestone on the path to adulthood. What about adolescents in collectivistic cultures? Is adolescence also marked by conflict in other cultures, especially collectivistic cultures?

To answer that question, psychologists have conducted research on adolescent development in non-Western collectivistic cultures and among adolescents of non-European descent (B. Schneider, 1998). Collectivistic cultures tend to be marked by a greater respect for authority, especially parental authority; a strong sense of family obligation; and a greater emphasis on harmony among family members. Is achieving identity as a separate individual as highly valued in these cultural contexts?

One study compared American adolescents of European descent with Chinese-American adolescents; Chinese adolescents living in Beijing, China; and Chinese adolescents living in Taipei, Taiwan (Chen & others, 1998). On the average, the European-American teenagers reported the *highest* level of conflict with their parents, while the Chinese adolescents living in Beijing and Taipei

reported the *lowest* levels. The Chinese-American teens fell between the European-Americans and the two Chinese groups. Although there was significantly more conflict in the European-American families, it's important to note that conflict between parents and adolescent children was present in *all* groups. This suggests that parent–adolescent conflict is a common dimension of family life in very different cultures.

Another perspective was provided by a wide-ranging study conducted by Andrew Fuligni (1998). Fuligni compared parent–adolescent conflict among different ethnic groups living in California: adolescents of Mexican, Chinese, Filipino, and European descent. The Filipino-, Chinese-, and Mexican-American adolescents generally demonstrated a greater respect for parental authority and less of an emphasis on individual autonomy.

Nevertheless, adolescents of all four ethnic groups reported very similar levels of conflict with their parents. As Fuligni (1998) observes, "Members of these different ethnic groups showed similar developmental trends in their ideas about authority and autonomy." As they progressed through adolescence, these teens became more willing to openly disagree with their parents. They also became increasingly more willing to challenge their parents' attempts to control various aspects of their personal lives. Thus, even within cultural and ethnic groups that traditionally emphasize parental authority, it seems that adolescents are motivated to assert their independence and developing autonomy.

Identity Formation: Erikson's Theory of Psychosocial Development

When psychologists talk about a person's **identity,** they are referring to the values, beliefs, and ideals that guide an individual's behavior (Erikson, 1964a; Marcia, 1991). Our sense of personal identity gives us an integrated and continuing sense of self over time. Identity formation is a process that continues throughout the lifespan. As we embrace new and different roles over the course of our lives, we define ourselves in new ways (Erikson & others, 1986; Grotevant, 1992).

For the first time in the lifespan, the adolescent possesses the cognitive skills necessary for dealing with identity issues in a meaningful way (Habermas & Bluck, 2000). Beginning in early adolescence, self-definition shifts. Preadolescent

identity
A person's definition or description of himself or herself, including the values, beliefs, and ideals that guide the individual's behavior.

ZITS

Zits cartoon, © Zits Partnership. Reprinted with special permission of King Features Syndicate.

children tend to describe themselves in very concrete social and behavioral terms. An 8-year-old might describe himself by saying, "I play with Mark and I like to ride my bike." In contrast, adolescents use more abstract self-descriptions that reflect personal attributes, values, beliefs, and goals (Harter, 1990). Thus, a 14-year-old might say, "I have strong religious beliefs, love animals, and hope to become a veterinarian."

Some aspects of personal identity involve characteristics over which the adolescent has no control, such as gender, race, ethnic background, and socioeconomic level. In effect, these identity characteristics are fixed and already internalized by the time an individual reaches the adolescent years.

Beyond such fixed characteristics, the adolescent begins to evaluate herself on several different dimensions. Social acceptance by peers, academic and athletic abilities, work abilities, personal appearance, and romantic appeal are some important aspects of self-definition. Another challenge facing the adolescent is to develop an identity that is independent of her parents while retaining a sense of connection to her family. Thus, the adolescent has not one but several self-concepts that she must integrate into a coherent and unified whole to answer the question "Who am I?"

The adolescent's task of achieving an integrated identity is one important aspect of psychoanalyst **Erik Erikson's** influential theory of psychosocial development. Briefly, Erikson (1968) proposed that each of eight stages of life is associated with a particular psychosocial conflict that can be resolved in either a positive or a negative direction (see Table 9.4 on page 392). Relationships with others play an important role in determining the outcome of each conflict. According to Erikson, the key psychosocial conflict facing adolescents is *identity versus identity diffusion.*

To successfully form an identity, adolescents not only must integrate various dimensions of their personality into a coherent whole, but they also must define the roles that they will adopt within the larger society on becoming an adult (Habermas & Bluck, 2000). To accomplish this, adolescents grapple with a wide variety of issues, such as selecting a potential career and formulating religious, moral, and political beliefs. They must also adopt social roles involving interpersonal relationships, sexuality, and long-term commitments such as marriage and parenthood.

In Erikson's (1968) theory, the adolescent's path to successful identity achievement begins with *identity diffusion,* which is characterized by little sense of commitment on any of these issues. This period is followed by a *moratorium period,* during which the adolescent experiments with different roles, values, and beliefs. Gradually, by choosing among the alternatives and making commitments, the adolescent arrives at an *integrated identity.*

Psychological research has generally supported Erikson's description of the process of identity formation (Grotevant, 1987; Marcia, 1991). However, it's important to keep in mind that identity continues to evolve over the entire lifespan, not just during the adolescent years (Grotevant, 1992). Adolescents and young adults seem to achieve a stable sense of identity in some areas earlier than in others. Far fewer adolescents and young adults have attained a stable sense of identity in the realm of religious and political beliefs than in the realm of vocational choice.

Psychoanalyst Erik Erikson Erikson (1902–1994) is shown here with his wife, Joan, in 1988. Erikson's landmark theory of psychosocial development stressed the importance of social and cultural influences on personality throughout the stages of life.

Table **9.4**

Erik Erikson's Psychosocial Stages of Development

Life Stage	Psychosocial Conflict	Positive Resolution	Negative Resolution
Infancy (birth to 18 months)	Trust vs. mistrust	Reliance on consistent and warm caregivers produces a sense of predictability and trust in the environment.	Physical and psychological neglect by caregivers leads to fear, anxiety, and mistrust of the environment.
Toddlerhood (18 months to 3 years)	Autonomy vs. doubt	Caregivers encourage independence and self-sufficiency, promoting positive self-esteem.	Overly restrictive caregiving leads to self-doubt in abilities and low self-esteem.
Early childhood (3 to 6 years)	Initiative vs. guilt	The child learns to initiate activities and develops a sense of social responsibility concerning the rights of others; promotes self-confidence.	Parental overcontrol stifles the child's spontaneity, sense of purpose, and social learning; promotes guilt and fear of punishment.
Middle and late childhood (6 to 12 years)	Industry vs. inferiority	Through experiences with parents and "keeping up" with peers, the child develops a sense of pride and competence in schoolwork and home and social activities.	Negative experiences with parents or failure to "keep up" with peers leads to pervasive feelings of inferiority and inadequacy.
Adolescence	Identity vs. identity diffusion	Through experimentation with different roles, the adolescent develops an integrated and stable self-definition; forms commitments to future adult roles.	An apathetic adolescent or one who experiences pressures and demands from others may feel confusion about his or her identity and role in society.
Young adulthood	Intimacy vs. isolation	By establishing lasting and meaningful relationships, the young adult develops a sense of connectedness and intimacy with others.	Because of fear of rejection or excessive self-preoccupation, the young adult is unable to form close, meaningful relationships and becomes psychologically isolated.
Middle adulthood	Generativity vs. stagnation	Through child rearing, caring for others, productive work, and community involvement, the adult expresses unselfish concern for the welfare of the next generation.	Self-indulgence, self-absorption, and a preoccupation with one's own needs lead to a sense of stagnation, boredom, and a lack of meaningful accomplishments.
Late adulthood	Ego integrity vs. despair	In reviewing his or her life, the older adult experiences a strong sense of self-acceptance and meaningfulness in his or her accomplishments.	In looking back on his or her life, the older adult experiences regret, dissatisfaction, and disappointment about his or her life and accomplishments.

SOURCE: Adapted from Erikson (1964a).

So, although Erikson believed that identity formation was a critical goal for the adolescent, it appears that the process of identity formation only begins to take on serious meaning during adolescence. For most people, a stable and fully integrated identity doesn't occur until well into the adult years.

The Development of Moral Reasoning

An important aspect of cognitive development during adolescence is a change in **moral reasoning**—how an individual thinks about moral decisions. The adolescent's increased capacities to think abstractly, imagine hypothetical situations, and compare ideals to the real world all affect his thinking about moral issues (Darley & Shultz, 1990).

The most influential theory of moral development was proposed by psychologist **Lawrence Kohlberg.** Kohlberg used stories like the one below to investigate moral reasoning. Read the story and, before going on, answer the questions.

A woman was near death from a rare form of cancer. There was one drug that the doctors thought might save her, recently discovered by a druggist in the same town. The drug was expensive to make—about $400 for a small

moral reasoning
The aspect of cognitive development that has to do with how an individual reasons about moral decisions.

dose. But the druggist was charging ten times what the drug cost him to make—$4,000 for a small dose.

The sick woman's husband, Heinz, went to everyone he knew to borrow the money, but he could only get together about $2,000, half of what the druggist was charging. He told the druggist that his wife was dying and asked him to sell it cheaper or let him pay the rest later. But the druggist refused, saying, "No, I discovered the drug and I'm going to make money from it." So Heinz gets desperate and considers breaking into the man's store to steal the drug for his wife.

Should Heinz steal the drug? Why or why not? (Adapted from Colby & others, 1983)

In Kohlberg's (1976, 1984) theory, whether you think Heinz should or should not steal the drug is not the critical issue. Instead, it is the *reasoning* you use to justify your answer that is significant. Kohlberg analyzed the responses of children, adolescents, and adults to hypothetical moral dilemmas like the one in the Heinz story. He concluded that there were distinct *stages* of moral development. These stages unfold in an age-related step-by-step fashion, much like Piaget's stages of cognitive development (Kohlberg, 1981).

Kohlberg proposed three distinct *levels* of moral reasoning: preconventional, conventional, and postconventional. Each level is based on the degree to which a person conforms to conventional standards of society. Furthermore, each level has two *stages* that represent different degrees of sophistication in moral reasoning. Table 9.5 describes the characteristics of the moral reasoning associated with each of Kohlberg's levels and stages.

HAGAR

Reprinted with special permission of King Features Syndicate.

Table 9.5

Kohlberg's Levels and Stages of Moral Development

I. Preconventional Level
Moral reasoning is guided by external consequences. No internalization of values or rules.

Stage 1: Punishment and Obedience
"Right" is obeying the rules simply to avoid punishment because others have power over you and can punish you.

Example: Heinz shouldn't steal the drug because he'd go to jail if he got caught.

Stage 2: Mutual Benefit
"Right" is an even or fair exchange, so that both parties benefit. Moral reasoning guided by a sense of "fair play."

Example: Heinz should steal the drug because the druggist is being greedy by charging so much.

II. Conventional Level
Moral reasoning is guided by conformity to social roles, rules, and expectations that the person has learned and internalized.

Stage 3: Interpersonal Expectations
"Right" is being a "good" person by conforming to social expectations, such as showing concern for others and following rules set by others so as to win their approval. For example, behaving like a "good" child, student, citizen, spouse, friend, or employee.

Example: Heinz should try to steal the drug because that's what a devoted husband would do.

Stage 4: Law and Order
"Right" is helping maintain social order by doing one's duty, obeying laws simply because they are laws, and showing respect for authorities simply because they are authorities.

Example: Heinz should not steal the drug because that would be against the law and he has a duty to uphold the law.

III. Postconventional Level
Moral reasoning is guided by internalized legal and moral principles that protect the rights of all members of society.

Stage 5: Legal Principles
"Right" is helping protect the basic rights of all members of society by upholding legalistic principles that promote the values of fairness, justice, equality, and democracy.

Example: Heinz should steal the drug because his obligation to save his wife's life must take precedence over his obligation to respect the druggist's property rights.

Stage 6: Universal Moral Principles
"Right" is determined by self-chosen ethical principles that underscore the person's profound respect for ideals such as the sanctity of human life, nonviolence, equality, and human dignity. If these moral principles conflict with democratically determined laws, the person's self-chosen moral principles would take precedence, such as the conscientious objector who refuses to be drafted because of moral principles against war.

Example: Even if it were a stranger and not his wife, Heinz should steal the drug because he must follow his own conscience and not let another person's desire for monetary gain outweigh the value of a human life.

SOURCES: Based on Kohlberg (1981) and Colby & others (1983).

Unlike the hypothetical dilemmas posed by Lawrence Kohlberg, political debates often focus on real-life moral decisions that affect many lives. When you apply Kohlberg's theory to just about any controversial political issue, such as abortion rights or gun control, it can help you identify different levels of moral reasoning used to support or oppose a particular decision. Psychology professor Johnna Shapiro (1995) did just that, asking her students to analyze U.S. congressional debates over the resolution to attack Iraq because of its invasion of Kuwait in 1990. Listed here are quotations that Shapiro's students compiled from those congressional debates, along with the stage of Kohlberg's theory that each quote reflects.

Table | 9.6

Applying Kohlberg's Theory to Political Debates

Stage	Arguments Against U.S. Involvement	Arguments for U.S. Involvement
	"We shouldn't consider war because . . .	"We should consider war because . . .
1	"it would hurt our economy."	"our oil is threatened."
2	"we'll have more money for domestic issues."	"we can gain security of the oil supply."
3	"we don't want to appear too militaristic."	"we don't want the world to see us as weak."
4	"war is killing and killing is against the law."	"the U.N. has laid down written resolutions which should be upheld."
5	"even though the situation is bad, war is damaging to people and property and society agrees *that* is bad."	"the situation is extreme enough that society's rights are threatened and need to be defended."
6	"although atrocities have been committed, it would be an even greater atrocity to wage war."	"evil is on the march, and it would be morally wrong to allow it to continue."

SOURCE: Adapted from J. Shapiro (1995).

Kohlberg and his colleagues found that the responses of children under the age of 10 reflected *preconventional* moral reasoning based on self-interest—avoiding punishment and maximizing personal gain. Beginning in late childhood and continuing through adolescence and adulthood, responses typically reflected *conventional* moral reasoning, which emphasizes social roles, rules, and obligations. Thus, the progression from preconventional to conventional moral reasoning is closely associated with age-related cognitive abilities (Kohlberg, 1984; Walker, 1989).

Do people inevitably advance from conventional to postconventional moral reasoning, as Kohlberg once thought? In a 20-year longitudinal study, Kohlberg followed a group of boys from late childhood through early adulthood. Of the 58 subjects in the study, only 8 subjects occasionally displayed stage 5 reasoning, which emphasizes respect for legal principles that protect all members of society. *None* of the subjects showed stage 6 reasoning, which reflects self-chosen ethical principles that are universally applied (Colby & others, 1983). Kohlberg and his colleagues eventually dropped stage 6 from the theory, partly because clear-cut expressions of "universal moral principles" were so rare (Rest, 1983).

Thus, Kohlberg's original belief that the development of abstract thinking in adolescence naturally and invariably leads people to the formation of idealistic moral principles has not been supported. Only a few exceptional people display the philosophical ideals in Kohlberg's highest level of moral reasoning. The normal course of changes in moral reasoning for most people seems to be captured by Kohlberg's first four stages (Colby & Kohlberg, 1984). By adulthood, the predominant form of moral reasoning is conventional moral reasoning, reflecting the importance of social roles and rules. See Table 9.6 for an interesting application of Kohlberg's theory.

Gender and Moral Reasoning

Kohlberg's theory of moral development has many critics (see Modgil & Modgil, 1986). For example, psychologist Carol Gilligan (1982) pointed out that Kohlberg's early research was conducted entirely with male subjects, yet it became the basis for a theory applied to both males *and* females. Gilligan has also noted that in most of Kohlberg's stories, the main actor who faces the moral dilemma to be resolved is a male. When females are present in the stories, they often play a subordinate role, such as the female patient in the Heinz story. Thus, Gilligan believes that Kohlberg's model reflects a male perspective that may not accurately depict the development of moral reasoning in women.

To Gilligan, Kohlberg's model is based on an *ethic of individual rights and justice,* which is a more common perspective for men. In contrast, Gilligan (1982) has developed a model of women's moral development that is based on an *ethic of care and responsibility.* In her studies of women's moral reasoning, Gilligan found that women tend to stress the importance of maintaining interpersonal relationships and responding to the needs of others, rather than focusing primarily on individual rights (Gilligan & Attanucci, 1988).

Gilligan's model has sparked considerable research and debate. Several studies have reviewed gender differences in moral reasoning (Jaffee & Hyde, 2000). In general, researchers have found that men and women may approach moral matters from slightly different perspectives. However, when subjects are carefully matched on critical factors, such as level of education, there do not seem to be systematic gender differences in moral reasoning.

Culture and Moral Reasoning

Culture also seems to have an effect on moral reasoning (Eckensberger, 1994; Haidt & others, 1993). Some cross-cultural psychologists argue that Kohlberg's stories and scoring system reflect a Western emphasis on individual rights, harm, and justice that is not shared in many cultures (Shweder & others, 1990a).

For example, Kohlberg's moral stages do not reflect the sense of interdependence and the concern for the overall welfare of the group that is more common in collectivistic cultures. Cross-cultural psychologist Harry Triandis (1994) reports an example of a response that does not fit into Kohlberg's moral scheme. In response to the scenario, "Heinz steals the drug to save his wife's life," a man in New Guinea said, "If nobody helped him, I would say that *we* had caused the crime." Thus, there are aspects of moral reasoning in other cultures that do not seem to be reflected in Kohlberg's theory (Shweder & Haidt, 1993).

9.3 R·E·V·I·E·W

C·O·N·C·E·P·T

Stages of Moral Reasoning

The examples below represent moral reasoning typically associated with different levels in Kohlberg's stages of moral development. Identify each one as preconventional, conventional, or postconventional.

1. Because he believed that all war is immoral, Adrian burned his draft card and refused to be inducted into the military, even though he was risking imprisonment. _____

2. While his brother was in the washroom, Jerry resisted sneaking a bit of his dessert because he was afraid his brother would punch him if he did. _____

3. When her daughter chided her about driving so slowly, Barbara replied, "I can't drive faster than the posted speed limit because responsible drivers obey the traffic laws." _____

4. Jeremiah organized a demonstration outside the state prison to protest the upcoming execution of a convicted murderer. He held a sign that read, "Every human life is worth preserving."

_____

menopause
The natural cessation of menstruation and the end of reproductive capacity in women.

Adult Development

Key Theme
- Development during adulthood is marked by physical changes and the adoption of new social roles.

Key Question
- What physical changes take place in adulthood?
- What are some general patterns of adult social development?
- What characterizes career paths in adulthood?

You can think of the developmental changes you experienced during infancy, childhood, and adolescence as early chapters in your life story. Those early life chapters helped set the tone and some of the themes for the primary focus of your life story—adulthood. During the half-century or more that constitutes adulthood, predictable changes continue to occur. Self-definition evolves as people achieve independence and take on new roles and responsibilities. As you'll see in this section, the story of adulthood also reflects the increasing importance of individual variation. Although general patterns of aging exist, our life stories become more distinct and individualized with each passing decade of life (Schaie & Willis, 1996).

Physical Changes

Your unique genetic blueprint greatly influences the unfolding of certain physical changes during adulthood, such as when your hair begins to thin, lose its color, and turn gray. Such genetically influenced changes can vary significantly from one person to another. For example, **menopause,** the cessation of menstruation that signals the end of reproductive capacity in women, may occur anywhere from the late thirties to the early fifties.

But your destiny is not completely ruled by genetics. Your lifestyle is one key environmental factor that can influence the aging process. Staying mentally and physically active and eating a proper diet can both slow and minimize the degree of physical decline associated with aging.

Another potent environmental force is simply the passage of time. Decades of use and environmental exposure take a toll on the body. Wrinkles begin to appear as we approach the age of 40, largely because of a loss of skin elasticity combined with years of making the same facial expressions. With each decade after age 20, the efficiency of various body organs declines. For example, lung capacity decreases, as does the amount of blood pumped by the heart.

Physical strength typically peaks in *early adulthood,* the twenties and thirties. By *middle adulthood,* roughly from the forties to the mid-sixties, physical strength and endurance gradually decline. Physical and mental reaction times also begin to slow during middle adulthood. During *late adulthood,* from the mid-sixties on, physical stamina and reaction time tend to decline further and faster.

Psychosocial Development in Young Adulthood Young adulthood brings many psychological challenges and transitions, not the least of which is choosing a life partner. To psychoanalyst Erik Erikson (1968), the key psychosocial task of young adulthood was intimacy versus isolation. Erikson believed that the ability to establish a meaningful, intimate, and lasting relationship helps set the stage for healthy adult development.

Social Development

In his theory of psychosocial development, Erik Erikson (1982) described the two fundamental themes that dominate adulthood: love and work. According to Erikson (1964b, 1968), the primary psychosocial task of early adulthood is to form a committed, mutually enhancing, intimate relationship with another person. During middle adulthood, the primary psychosocial task becomes one of *generativity*—to contribute to future generations through your children, your career, and other meaningful activities. In this section, we'll consider the themes of love and work by examining adult friendships, marriage, family life, and careers.

Friends and Lovers in Adulthood

Largely because of competing demands on their time, adults typically have fewer friends than adolescents do. The focus of adult friendships is somewhat different for men and women. Female friends tend to confide in one another about their feelings, problems, and interpersonal relationships. In contrast, male friends typically minimize discussions about relationships or personal feelings or problems. Instead, male friends tend to do things together that they find mutually interesting, such as activities related to sports or hobbies (Norris & Tindale, 1994; Winstead, 1986).

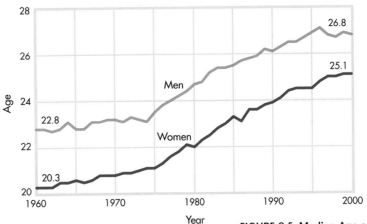

FIGURE 9.5 Median Age at First Marriage, United States

SOURCE: Fields (2001).

Beyond friendship, establishing a committed, intimate relationship takes on a new urgency in adulthood. Looking for Mr. or Ms. Right, getting married, and starting a family are the traditional tasks of early adulthood. However, in contrast to their parents, today's young adults are marrying at a later average age. As Figure 9.5 shows, in 1960 the median age for a first marriage was 23 for men and 20 for women. By 1996 those averages had increased to age 27 for men and age 25 for women. Many young adults postpone marriage until their late twenties or early thirties so they can finish their education and become established in a career.

Whom are we most likely to marry? As a general rule, the old adage "Birds of a feather flock together" seems to hold. We tend to be attracted to and marry people who are similar to us on a variety of dimensions, including physical attractiveness, social and educational status, ethnic background, attitudes, values, and beliefs (Brehm, 1992).

The Transition to Parenthood: Kids 'R' Us?

Although it is commonly believed that children strengthen the marital bond, marital satisfaction tends to decline after the birth of the first child (Hackel & Ruble, 1992; Levy-Shiff, 1994). For all the joy that can be derived from watching a child grow and experience the world, the first child's arrival creates a whole new set of responsibilities, pushes, and pulls on the marital relationship.

Without question, parenthood fundamentally alters your identity as an adult. With the birth or adoption of your first child, you take on a commitment to nurture the physical, emotional, social, and intellectual well-being of the next generation. This change in your identity can be a struggle, especially if the transition to parenthood was more of a surprise than a planned event (Mebert, 1991; Sandelowski & others, 1992).

Parenthood is further complicated by the fact that children are not born speaking fluently so that you can immediately enlighten them about the constraints of adult schedules, deadlines, finances, and physical energy. Instead, you must continually strive to adapt lovingly and patiently to your child's needs while managing all the other priorities in your life.

Not all couples experience a decline in marital satisfaction after the birth of a child. The hassles and headaches of child rearing can be minimized if the marital relationship is warm and positive, and if both husband and wife share household and child-care responsibilities. It also helps if you're blessed with a child who is born with a good disposition and an easy temperament. When infants are irritable, cry a lot, or are otherwise "difficult," parents find it harder to adjust to their new role (van den Boom & Hoeksma, 1994).

That many couples are marrying at a later age and waiting until their thirties to start a family also seems to be advantageous. Becoming a parent at an older age and waiting longer after marriage to start a family help ease the

NON SEQUITUR

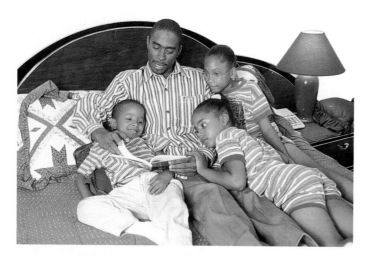

Single-Parent Families Today, more than 30 percent of all children are being raised by a single parent. Many single parents provide their children with a warm, stable, and loving environment. In terms of school achievement and emotional stability, children in stable single-parent households do just as well as children with two parents living in the same home (Dawson, 1991).

FIGURE 9.6 The Changing Structure of American Families and Households Between 1970 and 2000, the number of American households increased from 63 million to 105 million. During that same period, however, the average size of the American household decreased from 3.14 to 2.59 persons. The two pie charts show how the structure of American households has undergone major shifts in a relatively short period of time. Notice how the percentage of single-parent households has more than doubled, while the number of "traditional" families consisting of a married couple with children has decreased dramatically.

SOURCES: J. Fields (2001), U.S. Census Bureau (2001).

adjustment to parenthood. Why? Largely because the couple is more mature and the marital relationship is typically more stable.

Although marital satisfaction often declines when people first become parents, it rises again after children leave home (Norris & Tindale, 1994). Successfully launching your children into the adult world represents the attainment of the ultimate parental goal. It also means there is more time to spend in leisure activities with your spouse. Not surprisingly, then, marital satisfaction tends to increase steadily once children are out of the nest and flying on their own.

Variations in the Paths of Adult Social Development

Up to this point, we've described the "traditional" track of adult social development: finding a mate, getting married, starting and raising a family. However, there is enormous diversity in how the goal of intimacy is realized during adulthood (Edwards, 1995b). The nature of intimate relationships and family structures varies widely in the United States (see Figure 9.6).

For example, the number of unmarried couples living together increased dramatically at the end of the twentieth century—to well over 3 million couples. Currently, more than 30 percent of children are being raised by a single parent (Rawlings & Saluter, 1995). Given that more than half of all first marriages end in divorce, the phenomenon of remarrying and starting a "second family" later in life is not unusual (Karney & Bradbury, 1995). As divorce has become more common, the number of single parents and stepfamilies has also risen. And among married couples, some opt for a "child-free" life together. There are also gay and lesbian couples who, like many married couples, are committed to a long-term, monogamous relationship (Kurdek, 1995).

Such diversity in adult relationships reflects the fact that adult social development does not always follow a predictable pattern. As you travel through adulthood, your life story may include many unanticipated twists in the plot and changes in the cast of characters. Just as the "traditional" family structure has its joys and heartaches, so do other configurations of intimate and family relationships. In the final analysis, *any* relationship that promotes the overall sense of happiness and well-being of the people involved is a successful one.

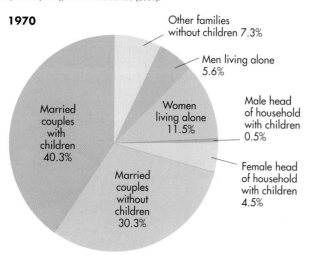

1970

Other families without children 7.3%
Men living alone 5.6%
Women living alone 11.5%
Male head of household with children 0.5%
Married couples with children 40.3%
Married couples without children 30.3%
Female head of household with children 4.5%

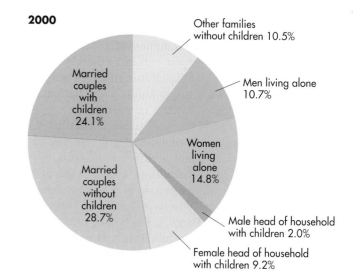

2000

Other families without children 10.5%
Men living alone 10.7%
Married couples with children 24.1%
Women living alone 14.8%
Married couples without children 28.7%
Male head of household with children 2.0%
Female head of household with children 9.2%

Careers in Adulthood

People follow a variety of routes in developing careers. Most people explore different career options, narrow down those options, and tentatively commit to a particular job in a particular field in young adulthood (Super, 1990). However, researchers have found that close to a third of people in their late twenties and early thirties do not just change jobs within a particular field—they completely switch occupational fields (Phillips & Blustein, 1994).

Dual-career families have become increasingly common (Gilbert, 1993). However, the career tracks of men and women often differ if they have children. Although today's fathers are more actively involved in child rearing than were fathers in previous generations, women still tend to have primary responsibility for child care. Thus, married women with children are much more likely than are single women or childless women to interrupt their careers, leave their jobs, or switch to part-time work because of child-rearing responsibilities.

Do adults, particularly women, experience greater stress because of the conflicting demands of career, marriage, and family? Not necessarily. Generally, multiple roles seem to provide both men and women with a greater potential for increased feelings of self-esteem, happiness, and competence (Gilbert, 1994). The critical factor is not so much the number of roles that people take on, but the *quality* of their experiences on the job, in marriage, and as a parent (Barnett & others, 1992). When experiences in these different roles are positive and satisfying, psychological well-being is enhanced. However, when work is dissatisfying, finding high-quality child care is difficult, and making ends meet is a never-ending struggle, stress can escalate and psychological well-being can plummet—for either sex (Clay, 1995).

Blended Families Today, about 17% of all children live in *blended families,* sharing their home with the children from a stepparent's previous marriage (U.S. Census Bureau, 2002a). Sometimes, as is the case with this family, the children of the first marriage are much older than the children of the second marriage.

Late Adulthood and Aging

Key Theme
■ Late adulthood does not necessarily involve a steep decline in physical or cognitive capabilities.

Key Questions
■ What cognitive changes take place in late adulthood?
■ What factors influence social development in late adulthood?

The average life expectancy for men in the U. S. is about 74 years. For women, the average life expectancy is about 79 years. So the stage of late adulthood can easily last for 20 years or more. Although we experience many physical and sensory changes throughout adulthood, that's not to say that we completely fall apart when we reach our sixties, seventies, or even eighties. Some people in their nineties are healthier and more active than other people who are 20 years younger (Baltes & Mayer, 2001).

In American culture, but certainly not in all cultures, the phrase "old age" is often associated with images of poor health, inactivity, social isolation, and mental and physical incompetence. Are those images accurate? Far from it. The majority of older adults live healthy, active, and self-sufficient lives (Schaie & Willis, 1996).

In fact, the stereotypical image that most elderly people live in nursing homes is a major myth. In Table 9.7, you can see that of *all* American adults aged 65 and over, only 4.5 percent live in nursing homes. It's also interesting to note the downward trend that has occurred over the last decade in the percentages of senior adults who live in nursing homes. Even among those aged 85 and over, fewer than 20 percent live in nursing homes. Some older adults live with relatives, but most live in their own homes (U.S. Census Bureau, 2002b).

Table | **9.7**

U.S. Population Aged 65 and Older in Nursing Homes by Age: 1990 and 2000

Age	Percent of Age Group	
	1990	2000
65 years and over	**5.1**	**4.5**
65 to 74 years	1.4	1.1
75 to 84 years	6.1	4.7
85 years and over	24.5	18.2

SOURCE: Hetzel & Smith (2001).

Stereotypes of Aging What are your thoughts about the personalities and abilities of these two gentlemen? When U.S. college students were shown pictures of the same man at ages 25, 52, and 74, they rated the 74-year-old as least active, intelligent, healthy, and competent (Levin, 1988). After reading this section, can you explain why these stereotypes are inaccurate?

Although they have more chronic medical conditions, elderly individuals tend to see themselves as relatively healthy, partly because they have fewer acute illnesses, such as colds and flu, than do younger people (U.S. National Center for Health Statistics, 1990). Even during the final year of life, the majority of older adults enjoy relatively good health, mental alertness, and self-sufficiency (Brock & others, 1994).

The number of older adults in the United States has been gradually increasing over the past several decades. At the beginning of the twentieth century, only about 1 American in 20 was 65 or older; today, 1 of every 8 Americans is. By the year 2030, 1 of 5 Americans will be an older adult (Kinsella & Velkoff, 2001).

Cognitive Changes

During which decade of life do you think people reach their intellectual peak? If you answered the twenties or thirties, you may be surprised by the results of longitudinal studies done by psychologist K. Warner Schaie. Since the 1950s, Schaie and his colleagues have followed some 5,000 people as they have aged to learn what happens to intellectual abilities.

Schaie (1995) found that general intellectual abilities gradually increase until one's early forties, then become relatively stable until about age 60. After age 60, a small but steadily increasing percentage of older adults experienced slight declines on tests of general intellectual abilities, such as logical reasoning, math skills, word recall, and the ability to mentally manipulate images. But even after age 60, most older adults maintain these previous levels of abilities.

When declines in mental abilities occur during old age, Schaie found, the explanation is often simply a lack of practice or experience with the kinds of tasks used in mental ability tests. Even just a few hours of training on mental skills can improve test scores for most older adults (Schaie & Willis, 1986).

Is it possible to minimize declines in mental abilities in old age? In a word, yes. Schaie (1994) found that those who were better educated and engaged in physical and mental activities throughout older adulthood showed the smallest declines in mental abilities. In contrast, the greatest intellectual declines tended to occur in older adults with unstimulating lifestyles, such as people who lived alone, were dissatisfied with their lives, and engaged in few activities.

Social Development

At one time it was believed that older adults gradually "disengage," or withdraw, from vocational, social, and relationship roles as they face the prospect of their lives ending (Cumming & Henry, 1961). But consider Sandy's father, Erv, who is about to turn 83. Erv and about a dozen other retired men in their seventies and eighties belong to what they call the "Golden Agers' Club." They regularly get together to play cards, go out to lunch, and forage used bookstores and flea markets for treasures. About once a year, they take a fishing trip.

What Erv and his buddies epitomize is the activity theory of aging. According to the **activity theory of aging,** life satisfaction in late adulthood is highest when you maintain your previous level of activity, either by continuing old activities or by finding new ones (Havighurst & others, 1968).

Just like younger adults, older adults differ in the level of activity they find personally optimal. Some older adults pursue a busy lifestyle of social activities, travel, college classes, and volunteer work. Other older adults are happier with a quieter lifestyle, pursuing hobbies, reading, or simply puttering around their homes. Such individual preferences reflect lifelong temperamental and personality qualities that continue to be evident as a person ages (Costa & McCrae, 1989).

activity theory of aging
The psychosocial theory that life satisfaction in late adulthood is highest when people maintain the level of activity they displayed earlier in life.

For many older adults, caregiving responsibilities can persist well into late adulthood. Sandy's parents, Fern and Erv, for example, spend a great deal of time helping out with their young grandchildren and caring for some of their older relatives. They're not unusual in that respect. Many older adults who are healthy and active find themselves taking care of other older adults who are sick or have physical limitations (Norris & Tindale, 1994).

Even for an older adult who is not very socially active, it's still important to have at least one confidant. Some-times the confidant is simply a very close friend. For older men, the confidant is often the spouse. The social support provided by the confidant yields important psychological benefits for the older adult, such as higher morale, better mental health, and better psychological well-being (Rawlins, 1992). A confidant can also provide an important buffer for the older adult in coping with stressful events, such as health problems or the deaths of friends or family members.

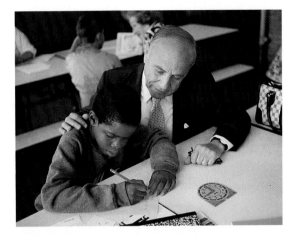

A Lifetime of Experience to Share Like many other senior adults, Ettore Buonomo of New York City derives great personal satisfaction as a volunteer helping grade school students. Contributing to society, taking care of others, and helping people both younger and older than themselves often takes on renewed importance to senior adults.

Along with satisfying social relationships, the prescription for psychological well-being in old age includes achieving what Erik Erikson called *ego integrity*—the feeling that one's life has been meaningful (Erikson & others, 1986). Older adults experience ego integrity when they look back on their lives and feel satisfied with their accomplishments, accepting whatever mistakes or missteps they may have made.

In contrast, those who are filled with regrets or bitterness about past mistakes, missed opportunities, or bad decisions experience *despair*—a sense of disappointment in life. Often the themes of ego integrity or despair emerge as older adults engage in a *life review,* thinking about or retelling their life story to others (Haight, 1992; Taft & Nehrke, 1990).

9.4 R·E·V·I·E·W

C·O·N·C·E·P·T

Adulthood and Late Adulthood

Mark each of the following statements as true or false. If a statement is false, write in the correct statement.

_____ **1.** The adage "Use it or lose it" seems to apply to your brain's abilities as you grow older.

_____ **2.** In general, people tend to marry people who are like themselves.

_____ **3.** Women tend to experience much greater stress than do men when faced with the demands of career, marriage, and family roles.

_____ **4.** Younger parents adjust more easily to parenthood than do older parents.

_____ **5.** The percentage of married couples with children has remained consistent since 1960.

_____ **6.** After the last child leaves home, parents suffer from the "empty-nest syndrome," and marital satisfaction declines significantly.

The Final Chapter

Dying and Death

Key Theme

▪ Attitudes toward dying and death are as diverse in late adulthood as they are throughout the lifespan.

Key Questions

▪ How did Kübler-Ross describe the stages of dying?

▪ What are some individual variations in attitudes toward death and dying?

It is tempting to view death as the special province of the very old. Of course, death can occur at any point during the lifespan. It's also tempting to assume that older adults have come to a special understanding about death—that they view the prospect of dying with wisdom and serenity. In reality, attitudes toward death in old age show the same diversity that is reflected in other aspects of adult development. Not all older adults are resigned to death, even when poor health has severely restricted their activities (Kastenbaum, 1986, 1992).

As psychologist Robert Kastenbaum (1992) wrote, "Everyone lives in relationship to death at every point in the lifespan." In other words, long before encountering old age, each individual has a personal history of thinking about death. Some people are obsessed with issues of life and death from adolescence or early adulthood, while others, even in advanced old age, take more of a one-day-at-a-time approach to living.

In general, anxiety about death tends to peak in middle adulthood, then tends to *decrease* in late adulthood (Lonetto & Templer, 1986). At any age, people respond with a wide variety of emotions when faced with the prospect of imminent death, such as when they are diagnosed with a terminal illness.

Elisabeth Kübler-Ross (1969) interviewed more than 200 terminally ill patients and proposed that the dying go through five stages. First, they *deny* that death is imminent, perhaps insisting that their doctors are wrong or denying the seriousness of their illness. Second, they feel and express *anger* that they are dying. Third, they *bargain*—they try to "make a deal" with doctors, relatives, or God, promising to behave in a certain way if only they may be allowed to live. Fourth, they become *depressed*. Finally, they *accept* their fate.

Although Kübler-Ross's research did much to sensitize the public and the medical community to the emotional experience of dying, it now seems clear that the dying individual does *not* progress through a predictable sequence of stages (Kastenbaum, 1992). Dying is as individual a process as living. People cope with the prospect of dying much as they have coped with other stresses in their lives (Schulz & Schlarb, 1987–1988).

Faced with impending death, some older adults react with passive resignation, others with bitterness and anger. Some people plunge into activity and focus their attention on external matters, such as making funeral arrangements, disposing of their property, or arranging for the care of other family members. And others turn inward, searching for the meaning of their life's story as the close of the final chapter draws near (Kastenbaum, 1992).

But even in dying, our life story doesn't just end. Each of us leaves behind a legacy of memo-

FOR BETTER OR FOR WORSE

ries in the minds of those who survive us. As we live each day, we are building this legacy, through our words, our actions, and the choices we make.

Each of us began life being completely dependent upon others for our survival. Over the course of our lifespan, others come to depend upon us. It is those people whose lives we have touched in some way, whether for good or for ill, who will remember us. In this sense, the final chapter of our lives will be written not by us, but by those whose life stories have intersected with our own.

Summing Up
Lifespan Development

Traditionally, development in childhood has received the most attention from developmental psychologists. Yet, as we have emphasized throughout this chapter, development is a lifelong process. Despite being firmly entrenched in middle adulthood, we, your authors, for example, have grown and changed at the same time that our daughter has developed from being a newborn to an exuberant middle-schooler. And, as Sandy's parents, Erv and Fern, clearly demonstrate, development continues well beyond retirement. For many older adults, the responsibility for others does not end with retirement. Rather, it takes on new dimensions.

Throughout this chapter, you've seen that every life is a unique combination of universal and individualized patterns of development. Although some aspects of development unfold in a predictable fashion, every life story, including yours, is influenced by unexpected events and plot twists. In our case, when we signed the contract to write this book, we never envisioned how dramatically it would affect our lives—and our daughter's life. So despite predictable changes, the wonderful thing about the developmental process is that you never *really* know what the next chapter of your life story may hold.

authoritarian parenting style
Parenting style in which parents are demanding and unresponsive toward their children's needs or wishes.

permissive parenting style
Parenting style in which parents are extremely tolerant and not demanding; permissive-indulgent parents are responsive to their children, whereas permissive-indifferent parents are not.

authoritative parenting style
Parenting style in which parents set clear standards for their children's behavior but are also responsive to their children's needs and wishes.

induction
A discipline technique that combines parental control with explaining why a behavior is prohibited.

APPLICATION   Raising Psychologically Healthy Children

Unfortunately, kids don't come with owners' manuals. Maybe that's why if you walk into any bookstore and head for the "parenting" section, you'll see shelves of books offering advice on topics ranging from "how to toilet-train your toddler" to "how to talk to your teenager." We're not going to attempt to cover that range in this brief chapter Application. However, we will present some basic principles of parenting that have been shown to foster the development of children who are psychologically well-adjusted, competent, and in control of their own behavior.

Basic Parenting Styles and Their Effects on Children
Psychologist Diana Baumrind (1971, 1991) has described three basic parenting styles: authoritarian, permissive, and authoritative. These parenting styles differ in terms of (1) *parental control* and (2) *parental responsiveness* to the child's needs and wishes.

Parents with an **authoritarian parenting style** are demanding but unresponsive to their children's needs or wishes. Authoritarian parents believe that they should shape and control the child's behavior so that it corresponds to an absolute set of standards. Put simply, they expect children to obey the rules, no questions asked. Rules are made without input from the child, and they are enforced by punishment, often physical.

At the opposite extreme are two **permissive parenting styles** (Maccoby & Martin, 1983). *Permissive-indulgent parents* are responsive, warm, and accepting of their children but impose few rules and rarely punish their children.

Permissive-indifferent parents are both unresponsive and uncontrolling. Establishing firm rules and consistently enforcing them is simply too much trouble for permissive-indifferent parents. If taken to an extreme, the lack of involvement of permissive-indifferent parenting can amount to child neglect.

The third style is the **authoritative parenting style.** Authoritative parents are warm, responsive, and involved with their children. They set clear standards for mature, age-appropriate behavior and expect their children to be responsive to parental demands. However, authoritative parents also feel a *reciprocal* responsibility to consider their children's reasonable demands and points of view. Thus, there is considerable give-and-take between parent and child. Rules are firm and consistently enforced, but the parents discuss the reasons for the rules with the child (Maccoby & Martin, 1983).

How do these different parenting styles affect young children? Baumrind (1971) found that the children of authoritarian parents are likely to be moody, unhappy, fearful, withdrawn, unspontaneous, and irritable. The children of permissive parents tend to be more cheerful than the children of authoritarian parents, but they are more immature, impulsive, and aggressive. In contrast, the children of authoritative parents are likely to be cheerful, socially competent, energetic, and friendly. They show high levels of self-esteem, self-reliance, and self-control (Buri & others, 1988).

These different parenting styles also affect children's competence, adjustment, and delinquent behavior (Kaufmann & others, 2000; Palmer & Hollin, 2001). Authoritative parenting is associated with higher grades than authoritarian or permissive parenting (Kawamura & others, 2002). In one study of several hundred adolescents, this finding was consistent for virtually all adolescents, regardless of ethnic or socioeconomic background (Dornbusch & others, 1987).

Adding to the evidence, psychologist Laurence Steinberg and his colleagues (1995) conducted a three-year longitudinal study involving more than 20,000 U.S. high school students. Steinberg found that authoritative parenting is associated with a broad range of beneficial effects for the adolescent, regardless of socioeconomic or ethnic background. As Steinberg summarized, "Adolescents raised in authoritative homes are better adjusted and more competent, they are confident about their abilities, competent in areas of achievement, and less likely than their peers to get into trouble" (Steinberg & others, 1995).

Why does an authoritative parenting style provide such clear advantages over other parenting styles? First, when children perceive their parents' requests as fair and reasonable, they are more likely to comply with the requests. Second, the children are more likely to *internalize* (or accept as their own) the reasons for behaving in a certain way and thus to achieve greater self-control (Hoffman, 1977, 1994).

In contrast, authoritarian parenting promotes resentment and rebellion (Hoffman, 1977, 1988). Because compliance is based on external control and punishment, the child often learns to avoid the

parent rather than independently control his or her own behavior. Finally, the child with permissive parents may never learn self-control. And because permissive parents have low expectations, the child may well live up to those expectations by failing to strive to fulfill his or her potential (Baumrind, 1971).

How to Be an Authoritative Parent: Some Practical Suggestions

Authoritative parents are high in both responsiveness and control. How can you successfully achieve that balance? Here are several suggestions based on psychological research.

1. Let your children know that you love them.

Attention, hugs, and other demonstrations of physical affection, coupled with a positive attitude toward your child, are some of the most important aspects of parenting, aspects that have enduring effects. Children who experience warm, positive relationships with their parents are more likely to become happy adults with stable marriages and good relationships with friends (Franz & others, 1991). So the question is simple: Have you hugged your kids today?

2. Listen to your children.

Let your children express their opinions, and respect their preferences when it's reasonable to do so. In making rules and decisions, ask for their input and give it genuine consideration. Strive to be fair and flexible, especially on issues that are less than earthshaking, such as which clothes they wear to school.

3. Use induction to teach as you discipline.

The most effective form of discipline is called **induction,** because it *induces* understanding in the child. Induction combines controlling a child's behavior with *teaching* (Hoffman, 1977, 1994). Put simply, induction involves consistently explaining (a) the *reason* for prohibiting or performing certain behaviors; (b) the *consequences* of the action for the child; and (c) the *effect* of the child's behavior on others. When parents use induction, the child begins to understand that their actions are not completely arbitrary or unfair. The child is also more likely to internalize the reasoning and apply it in new situations (Schulman & Mekler, 1985).

4. Work with your child's temperamental qualities.

Think back to our earlier discussion of temperamental qualities. Be aware of your child's natural temperament and work with it, not against it. If your child is very active, for example, it is unrealistic to expect him to sit quietly during a four-hour plane or bus trip. Knowing that, you can increase the likelihood of positive experiences by planning ahead. Bring coloring books, picture books, or small toys to occupy the young child in a restaurant or at a family gathering. Take frequent "exercise stops" on a long car trip. If your child is unusually sensitive, shy, or "slow-to-warm-up," give her plenty of time to make the transition to new situations and provide lots of preparation so that she knows what to expect.

Situation: Nine-year-old Jeff wants to stay up late to watch a special program on television.

	Low responsiveness	High responsiveness
Low control	**Permissive-Indifferent** Doesn't notice that Jeff is up late; Jeff has no regular bedtime.	**Permissive-Indulgent** Says, "Fine, if it's that important to you."
High control	**Authoritarian** Says, "You know the rules. Bedtime is nine o'clock. No exceptions!"	**Authoritative** Asks why program is so important. Offers to tape program so Jeff can watch it at a later time, or agrees that Jeff can stay up late tonight if he promises to go to bed early tomorrow.

Four Parenting Styles Researchers have identified four basic parenting styles, based on the dimensions of parental control and parental responsiveness.

5. Understand your child's age-related cognitive abilities and limitations.

Some parents make the mistake of assuming that children think in the same way adults do. They may see a toddler or even an infant as purposely "misbehaving," "being naughty," or "rebelling," when the little one is simply doing what 1-year-olds or 3-year-olds do. Your expectations for appropriate behavior should be geared to the child's age and developmental stage (Barclay & Houts, 1995b). Having a thorough understanding of the information in this chapter is a good start. You might also consider taking a developmental psychology or child development class. Or go to your college library and check out some of the developmental psychology texts. By understanding your child's cognitive abilities and limitations at each stage of development, you're less likely to misinterpret behavior or to place inappropriate demands on him.

ZITS

Zits cartoon, © Zits Partnership. Reprinted with special permission of King Features Syndicate.

6. Don't expect perfection, and learn to go with the flow.

Accidents happen. Mistakes occur. Children get cranky or grumpy, especially when they're tired or hungry. Don't get too bent out of shape when your child's behavior is less than perfect. Be patient. Moments of conflict with children are a natural, inevitable, and healthy part of growing up. Look at them as part of the process by which a child achieves autonomy and a sense of self.

Finally, effective parenting is an ongoing process in which you, as the parent, should be regularly assessing your impact on your child. It's not always easy to combine responsiveness with control, or flexibility with an appropriate level of firmness. When you make a mistake, admit it not just to yourself, but also to your child. In doing so, you'll teach your child how to behave when she makes a mistake. As you'll discover, children are remarkably forgiving—and also resilient.

Chapter Review
Lifespan Development

Key Points

Your Life Story

■ Developmental psychologists study the many ways in which people change over the lifespan. Key themes in **developmental psychology** include understanding the stages of lifespan development, the nature of change, and the interaction between heredity and environment.

Genetic Contributions to Your Life Story

■ The genetic blueprint is determined at conception by the pairing of **chromosomes** from the biological parents. The chromosomes are made of **DNA,** which is arranged in thousands of segments called **genes.**

■ The **genotype** refers to the underlying genetic makeup; the **phenotype** refers to the traits that are displayed. When paired with a **recessive gene,** a **dominant gene** determines the trait that will be displayed. Recessive traits are displayed only if there are two recessive genes. Environmental conditions can influence the phenotype.

■ **Sex chromosomes** are the 23rd pair of chromosomes and determine whether male or female sexual characteristics will develop. Females have two X chromosomes, and males have an X and a Y chromosome. Females require two recessive genes for **sex-linked recessive characteristics** to be displayed. However, males require only one recessive gene for the same sex-linked recessive characteristic to be displayed.

Prenatal Development

■ During the nine months that make up the **prenatal stage,** the zygote develops into a full-term fetus. The prenatal stage includes the **germinal period,** the **embryonic period,** and the **fetal period.** The greatest vulnerability to **teratogens** occurs during the embryonic stage, when major bodily systems are forming.

Development During Infancy and Childhood

■ Although physically helpless, newborns are equipped with reflexes and sensory capabilities that seem to enhance their chances for survival. Vision, hearing, and smell are attuned to interaction with caregivers. The brain develops rapidly after birth. The sequence of motor skill development is generally universal, although there is individual variation in the rate of development.

- Thomas and Chess demonstrated that infants seem to be born with different **temperaments.** They identified three basic temperamental patterns: easy, difficult, and slow-to-warm-up. Temperamental qualities seem to have a biological basis and persist through life, although they can be modified by environmental influences.

- According to attachment theory, the infant's ability to thrive is dependent on the quality of his or her **attachment** to caregivers. Secure attachment develops when parents are sensitive and responsive to the infant's needs. Insecure attachment may develop when parents are insensitive to the infant's needs.

- Infants are biologically predisposed to learn language. At birth, infants can distinguish between the sounds that are present in any language, but they soon become sensitized to the sounds of the language that is spoken in their home. Adults encourage language development in infants by using motherese, also called infant-directed speech.

- The stages of language development include cooing and babbling. Other stages of language development are the one-word stage and the two-word stage. At every stage, the infant's **comprehension vocabulary** is larger than his or her **production vocabulary.**

- According to Jean Piaget's theory of cognitive development, children progress through distinct cognitive stages, each of which represents a shift in how they think and understand the world.

- **Object permanence** is acquired during the **sensorimotor stage. Symbolic thought** is acquired during the **preoperational stage.** Preoperational thought is **egocentric** and characterized by **irreversibility** and **centration.** Thus, the preoperational child is unable to grasp the principles of **conservation.** Children become capable of logical thought during the **concrete operational stage,** but thinking is limited to tangible objects and events. During the **formal operational stage,** the adolescent can engage in logical mental operations involving abstract concepts and hypothetical situations.

- Criticisms of Piaget's theory include: Piaget underestimated the cognitive abilities of infants and children; Piaget's stages are not as universal as he believed; and Piaget underestimated the influence of social and cultural factors on cognitive development.

- The **information-processing model** is an alternative description of cognitive development that emphasizes fundamental mental processes and stresses that cognitive development is a process of continuous change.

Adolescence

- In general, when parent–child relationships are good before **adolescence,** they continue to be positive during adolescence. Relationships with peers become increasingly important. Peer influence is just as likely to be positive as negative.

- Erik Erikson's theory of psychosocial development stresses that every stage of life is marked by a particular psychosocial conflict. **Identity** versus identity diffusion is the conflict associated with adolescence; however, the process of identity formation does not end in adolescence.

- Lawrence Kohlberg described **moral reasoning,** which is used in making moral decisions. His theory of moral development includes the preconventional, conventional, and postconventional levels, with each level having two stages. Some researchers believe that moral reasoning is affected by both gender and culture.

Adult Development

- Although there are general patterns in adult development, individual variation becomes increasingly significant. The three phases of adulthood are early adulthood, middle adulthood, and late adulthood. Genetics, environment, and an individual's lifestyle all influence physical changes during adulthood and aging. **Menopause** is one such physical change in adult women.

- Love and work are two key themes that dominate adult development. Friends continue to be important in adulthood. Forming a committed, intimate relationship is one important task traditionally associated with early adulthood.

- Marital satisfaction tends to decline after the first child is born and to increase after children leave home. Family structures and relationships have become increasingly diverse in the United States. Although the combination of work, marital, and family roles can be demanding, especially for women, multiple roles can lead to increased personal satisfaction when the quality of experience in each role is high.

Late Adulthood and Aging

- Late adulthood does not necessarily involve a steep decline in physical and cognitive functioning. Mental abilities only begin to decline slightly at around age 60, and these declines can be minimized or eliminated with an active and mentally stimulating lifestyle.

- Many older adults do not disengage from life but rather remain socially active. According to the **activity theory of aging,** life satisfaction in late adulthood is highest when people maintain their previous levels of activity. Older adults differ in their optimal level of activity. Erikson identified the task of ego integrity as the key psychosocial task of old age.

The Final Chapter: *Dying and Death*

- Although commonly associated with old age, death can occur at any point in the lifespan. Anxiety about death tends to peak in middle adulthood and decrease in late adulthood. Elisabeth Kübler-Ross proposed a five-stage model of dying: denial, anger, bargaining, depression, and acceptance. However, individuals respond in diverse ways to impending death.

Key Terms

developmental psychology, p. 368

chromosome, p. 370

deoxyribonucleic acid (DNA), p. 370

gene, p. 370

genotype, p. 371

phenotype, p. 371

dominant gene, p. 371

recessive gene, p. 371

sex chromosomes, p. 371

sex-linked recessive characteristics, p. 372

prenatal stage, p. 372

germinal period, p. 372

embryonic period, p. 373

teratogens, p. 373

fetal period, p. 373

temperament, p. 376

attachment, p. 376

comprehension vocabulary, p. 381

production vocabulary, p. 381

sensorimotor stage, p. 383

object permanence, p. 383

preoperational stage, p. 383

symbolic thought, p. 383

egocentrism, p. 384

irreversibility, p. 384

centration, p. 384

conservation, p. 384

concrete operational stage, p. 385

formal operational stage, p. 385

information-processing model of cognitive development, p. 387

adolescence, p. 389

identity, p. 390

moral reasoning, p. 392

menopause, p. 396

activity theory of aging, p. 400

authoritarian parenting style, p. 403

permissive parenting style, p. 403

authoritative parenting style, p. 403

induction, p. 404

Key People

Mary D. Salter Ainsworth (1913–1999) American psychologist who devised the Strange Situation procedure to measure attachment; contributed to attachment theory. (p. 377)

Renée Baillargeon (b. 1954) Canadian-born psychologist whose studies of cognitive development during infancy using visual rather than manual tasks challenged beliefs about the age at which object permanence first appears. (p. 386)

Noam Chomsky (b. 1928) American linguist who proposed that people have an innate understanding of the basic principles of language, which he called a "universal grammar." (p. 378)

Erik Erikson (1902–1994) German-born American psychoanalyst who proposed an influential theory of psychological development throughout the lifespan. (p. 390)

Lawrence Kohlberg (1927–1987) American psychologist who proposed an influential theory of moral development. (p. 392)

Jean Piaget (1896–1980) Swiss child psychologist whose influential theory proposed that children progress through distinct stages of cognitive development. (p. 382)

Lev Vygotsky (1896–1934) Russian psychologist who stressed the importance of social and cultural influences in cognitive development. (p. 387)

Concept Review Answers

9.1 page 381

1. True
2. False. With the exception of the Y chromosome, each human chromosome contains thousands of genes.
3. True
4. True.
5. False. Sam would be classified as an "easy" baby.
6. True
7. False. Most children who enter day care in infancy are securely attached to their parent or other primary caregiver.

9.2 page 388

1. d 2. b 3. a 4. c

9.3 page 395

1. postconventional 3. conventional
2. preconventional 4. postconventional

9.4 page 401

1. True
2. True
3. False. Rather than gender, the critical factor for both men and women is the quality of experiences in different roles.
4. False. Older parents tend to adjust more easily to parenthood than do younger parents.
5. False. The percentage has decreased significantly.
6. False. Marital satisfaction typically increases after the last child leaves home.

Wolf's Clothing #2

Gender and Sexuality

Prologue

Soaring with Angels

Richard and I had been best friends since our paths first crossed at Central High School in Sioux City, Iowa. Even then, Richard was extraordinary. He was good-looking and liked by everyone. He maintained almost a straight-A average in his classes. In our senior year, he was elected student body president. (To be perfectly honest, he beat me in the race for student body president.) And his talent as a diver had attracted the attention of college swimming coaches. Coming from a family of very modest means, Richard hoped for an athletic scholarship to attend college. He got one: The University of Arkansas awarded him a four-year athletic scholarship.

Richard met Becky when they were freshmen at the University of Arkansas. They seemed like a good match. Becky was smart, pretty, athletic, and had a wonderful sense of humor. They were also both Catholic, which greatly pleased Becky's parents. So, it came as no surprise when Richard and Becky announced their plans to marry after graduating. But, in retrospect, I can't help thinking that Richard's timing was deliberate when he asked me, in front of Becky, to be his best man.

"You're *sure* you want to marry this guy?" I half-jokingly asked Becky.

"Only if he takes nationals on the three-meter board," Becky quipped. As it turned out, Richard did place third on the three-meter board the following spring at the national collegiate swimming competition.

Three months before their wedding, Richard and I had the only argument we've ever had. At the time we had the argument, the word *gay* meant lighthearted and cheerful, so the word never came up in our heated exchange.

"What do you mean, you haven't told her!?"

"I don't need to tell her about the past," Richard insisted.

"That's bull, Richard," I shouted. "This woman loves you and if you don't tell her about your homosexual urges, then you are marrying her under false pretenses."

"I do *not* have those feelings anymore!" Richard yelled back.

"If that's true, then tell her!" I demanded.

But it wasn't true, of course. Although Richard would not admit it to himself, he had only become adept at suppressing his sexual attraction to other men. At the time we had that argument, I was still the only person who knew that Richard harbored what he called "homosexual urges." Richard had first told me when we were juniors in high school. I was stunned. But Richard was also adamant that he did not want to feel the way he did. In fact, he felt ashamed and guilty. Back then, being homosexual carried a much greater social stigma than it does today.

So when Richard and I were still in high school, we scraped up enough money to secretly send him to a psychologist for a few sessions. Despite our naive hopes for a quick "cure," Richard's troubling feelings remained. When he got to the University of Arkansas, Richard saw a counselor on a regular basis. After months of counseling, Richard believed he was capable of leading a heterosexual life.

Richard and Becky's wedding was magnificent. And, yes, I was the best man. After the wedding, they decided to stay in Fayetteville so that Richard could start graduate school. The inevitable happened less than a year later. Becky called me.

"I'm driving to Tulsa tonight. Don, you've *got* to tell me what's going on," she said, her voice strained, shaking. And I did, as gently as I could.

Richard and Becky's marriage was annulled. In time, Becky recovered psychologically, remarried, and had two children. Her bitterness toward Richard softened over the years. The last time we talked, she seemed genuinely forgiving of Richard.

For his part, Richard gave up trying to be something he was not. Instead, he came to grips with his sexual orientation, moved to San Francisco, and became a co-owner of two health clubs. True to form, Richard quickly became a respected and well-liked member of San Francisco's large gay community. He eventually met John, an accountant, with whom he formed a long-term relationship. But after Richard's move to San Francisco, our friendship faded.

It was our 20-year high school reunion that triggered Richard's unexpected call. When I told him I simply did not have the time to attend, he suggested stopping in Tulsa on his way to the reunion to meet Sandy and our daughter, Laura.

So on a warm May evening, Richard, Sandy, and I drank some margaritas, ate Chinese carryout, and talked until midnight. Just as I had expected, Sandy was quite taken with Richard. Indeed, Richard *was* a wonderful man—smart, funny, thoughtful, and sensitive. Laura, who was not quite two years old, was also enchanted by Richard. My only regret about that evening is that I did not take a picture of Richard sitting on our back deck as Laura brought him first one toy, then another, then another. As it turned out, it would be the last time I saw Richard.

About a year after he visited us in Tulsa, Richard was killed in a hang-gliding accident. As he was soaring over the rocky California coast, Richard swerved to miss an inexperienced flyer who crossed his path in the air. Richard lost control of his hang glider and was killed on impact when he plummeted into the rocky coastline.

A week later, more than 300 people crowded into St. Mary's Catholic Church in Sioux City, where Richard had been an altar boy in his youth. The outpouring of love and respect for Richard at the memorial service was a testament to the remarkable man he was.

What Richard's story illustrates is that who we are in this life—our identity—is not determined by any single characteristic or quality. Richard was gay, but that's not all Richard was, just as your sexual orientation is not the only characteristic that defines you. Nonetheless, Richard's story illustrates that sexual orientation and gender identity are potent forces that shape and direct each of our lives, including the relationships we form. In this chapter, we'll explore these topics in detail. In the process, we'll come back to Richard's story.

Introduction

Gender and Sexuality

Key Theme

- Although the words are sometimes used interchangeably, *sex* refers to the biological aspects of being male and female, while *gender* refers to the psychological, social, and cultural aspects of masculinity and femininity.

Key Questions

- What are gender roles?
- How do the terms *gender identity* and *sexual orientation* differ in meaning?

As our description of Richard's life demonstrates, gender and sexuality are important components of everyone's personal destiny. As you read this chapter, we encourage you to think about how *your* life has been shaped by your sexual orientation and gender. Some of the information we present in this chapter may challenge your preconceptions about sexual attitudes and behavior. Certain topics related to gender and sexuality are controversial for some people. However, our primary goal in this chapter is to present research findings in an unbiased and evenhanded fashion.

Before we begin, we need to clarify terminology. The English language is less than precise in the arena of gender and sexuality. For example, the word *sex* can be used to describe an activity, as in the phrase "having sex." But the word *sex* is also used to indicate whether someone is biologically male or female. In this sense, the term **sex** refers to biologically determined physical characteristics, such as differences in genetic composition and reproductive anatomy and function (Pryzgoda & Chrisler, 2000).

In contrast, **gender** refers to the cultural, social, and psychological meanings that are associated with maleness and femaleness (Eagly, 1995a). Think of "male" and "female" as designating the biological categories of *sex,* while "masculine" and "feminine" designate the social, cultural, and psychological categories of *gender.* As psychologists Rhoda Unger and Mary Crawford (1993) put it, "Gender is what culture makes out of the 'raw material' of biological sex."

Gender roles consist of the behaviors, attitudes, and personality traits that a given culture designates as either masculine or feminine (Bailey & Zucker, 1995). **Gender identity** refers to a person's psychological sense of being male or female (Egan & Perry, 2001). Finally, **sexual orientation** refers to the *direction* of a person's emotional and erotic attraction, whether toward members of the opposite sex, the same sex, or both sexes.

By the time most people reach adulthood, both gender identity and sexual orientation are well established. Often without our awareness, our behavior, attitudes, and aspirations have been strongly influenced by the gender-role expectations of our particular culture. But it's important to note that gender identity and sexual orientation can be independent of one another. For example, Richard's gender identity was very definitely male. He did not think of himself as anything but masculine. Nevertheless, his sexual orientation was toward other men, not toward women.

In this chapter, we'll take a close look at the development and consequences of male and female gender roles. We'll also examine how sexuality develops. Later in the chapter, we'll consider some of the ways in which the expression of sexuality can become disrupted and psychologically troubling. In the chapter Application, we'll look at how gender differences can short-circuit attempts to resolve conflicts in intimate relationships, and we'll show you how these communication problems can be overcome.

---

sex
(1) The biological category of male or female as defined by physical differences in genetic composition and in reproductive anatomy and function. (2) The behavioral manifestation of the sexual urge; sexual intercourse.

gender
The cultural, social, and psychological meanings that are associated with masculinity or femininity.

gender roles
The behaviors, attitudes, and personality traits that are designated as either masculine or feminine in a given culture.

gender identity
A person's psychological sense of being male or female.

sexual orientation
The direction of a person's emotional and erotic attraction toward members of the opposite sex, the same sex, or both sexes.

Life Themes: Gender and Sexuality From childhood to old age, gender identity and sexuality play an important role in our lives. How has your gender identity influenced the course of your life? The choices you've made? The relationships you've formed?

gender-role stereotypes
The beliefs and expectations people hold about the typical characteristics, preferences, and behavior of men and women.

Gender Stereotypes and Gender Roles

Key Theme

- Gender-role stereotypes are the beliefs and expectations that people hold about the characteristics and behaviors of each sex.

Key Questions

- How do men and women compare in personality characteristics and cognitive abilities?
- How do men and women compare in terms of sexual attitudes and behaviors?

The beliefs people have about the typical characteristics and behaviors of each sex are referred to as **gender-role stereotypes.** In our culture, gender-role stereotypes for men and women are very different. Women are thought (and expected) to be more emotional, nurturing, and patient than are men. Men are thought (and expected) to be more aggressive, decisive, and mechanically minded than are women. People often assume that gender stereotypes are derogatory toward women. In the United States, however, both men and women view the female gender-role stereotype more positively than the male gender-role stereotype (Swim, 1994). However, psychologists Peter Glick and Susan Fiske (2001) argue that accepting positive stereotypes of women can produce a type of prejudice they call *benevolent sexism.* While benevolent sexism is more socially acceptable than hostile sexism, it can contribute to gender inequality. As Glick and Fiske observe, "Characterizing women as pure creatures who ought to be protected, supported, and adored . . . implies that they are weak and best suited for conventional gender roles."

What about gender-role stereotypes in other cultures? In a survey of more than 25 cultures, psychologists John Williams (1999) and Deborah Best (2001) discovered a high degree of agreement on the characteristics associated with each sex (see Table 10.1). In general, the characteristics associated with males tended to be stronger and more active than the characteristics associated with females. In countries such as Japan, South Africa, and Nigeria, characteristics associated with the male stereotype were viewed more favorably than were characteristics associated with the female stereotype. However, the reverse was true in other countries, such as Italy, Peru, and Australia.

Gender Roles, Gender Stereotypes
Lieutenant Susan Hart, a jet fighter pilot, is shown here in her F-16 jet. Many women have challenged traditional gender-role stereotypes in their choice of professions. How does Hart's occupation violate gender-role stereotypes?

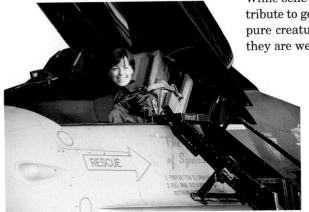

Table | 10.1

Gender Stereotypes Across Cultures

Characteristics Associated with Males			Characteristics Associated with Females		
Active	Dominant	Progressive	Affected	Emotional	Shy
Adventurous	Energetic	Robust	Affectionate	Fearful	Soft-hearted
Aggressive	Enterprising	Rude	Anxious	Feminine	Submissive
Ambitious	Forceful	Self-confident	Attractive	Fussy	Superstitious
Autocratic	Independent	Stern	Charming	Meek	Talkative
Coarse	Inventive	Strong	Complaining	Mild	Timid
Courageous	Logical	Tough	Curious	Sensitive	Weak
Cruel	Masculine	Unemotional	Dependent	Sexy	Whiny
Daring			Dreamy		

SOURCE: Adapted from Williams & others (1999).

Psychologists John Williams (1999) and Deborah Best (2001) surveyed the characteristics commonly associated with men and women in 25 countries. Overall, characteristics associated with the male stereotype tended to be more active and stronger than the characteristics associated with the female stereotype.

Gender-Related Differences

The *Opposite* Sex?

The notion that men and women are radically different is routinely touted in the media. Consider John Gray's (1992) first best-selling self-help book, *Men Are from Mars, Women Are from Venus*. According to Gray:

> Men and women differ in all areas of their lives. Not only do men and women communicate differently but they think, feel, perceive, react, respond, love, need, and appreciate differently. They almost seem to be from different planets, speaking different languages and needing different nourishment.

When psychologists scientifically investigate the issue of gender differences, what do they find? *Are* men and women fundamentally different in *all* areas of their lives, as is often claimed in the popular media? Not really. In many aspects of behavior, including social, personality, and cognitive aspects, men and women are very similar (Hyde & Plant, 1995). And despite the claims of popular self-help books, men and women do not tend to *perceive* themselves as being diametrically opposite (Swim, 1994).

Of course, men and women are not similar in every respect. Some significant differences between the sexes do exist (Eagly, 1995a). However, many psychologists (including many of those who write textbooks) are often reluctant to point out the gender differences that have been substantiated. Why? Basically, because some people are quick to equate a gender *difference* with a gender *deficiency*. For example, women's differences from men have historically been used to suggest that women are inferior to men (Eagly, 1995b; Spence & Buckner, 1995). And, not surprisingly, the gender-difference-equals-inferiority argument has also been used by some to suggest that men are inferior to women.

Regardless of such inappropriate (and sexist) conclusions, we think it's important to present the findings on gender differences that have been supported by research. We've already noted some gender differences in previous chapters, such as male–female differences in friendship patterns (Chapter 9). But before we note other differences two important qualifications need to be stressed.

First, the differences between men and women are *average* differences, not absolute differences. As with other generalizations in psychology, no single finding will apply to *all* men and women. For example, consider the general finding that men tend to think about sex more often than do women (Michael & others, 1994). When you look at the actual data from one national survey in Figure 10.1, you quickly see that *some* women (19%) think about sex more often than almost half the male population. The point here is that for any given gender difference, there is a wide range of individual variation within each group. There is also quite a bit of overlap between the two groups.

Second, finding that a gender difference exists is one matter. Explaining what *caused* that difference is another matter altogether. For instance, consider the observation that women are more likely than men to wear earrings. This finding says nothing about the *cause* of that difference. Acknowledging that a gender difference exists does not automatically mean that such differences are "natural," "inevitable," or "unchangeable." Nor does it necessarily mean that the differences are biologically based.

Bearing these qualifications in mind, let's look at three areas of gender differences: personality, cognitive abilities, and sexual attitudes and behaviors. Although some differences do exist in these areas, men and women are more similar than they are different (Hyde & Plant, 1995).

"Sex brought us together, but gender drove us apart."

© 2001 The New Yorker Collection from cartoonbank.com. Barbara Smaller.

FIGURE 10.1 "How Often Do You Think About Sex?" The percentages shown here were derived from a national survey based on a random sample of American adults between the ages of 18 and 59. As you can see, although *most* men seem to think about sex more often than *most* women do, there is overlap between the sexes in this respect.

SOURCE: Michael & others (1994).

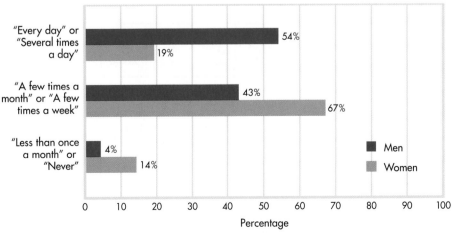

Percentage

Personality Differences

For *most* personality characteristics, there are *no* significant average differences between men and women. For example, women and men are, on average, very similar on such characteristics as impulsiveness and orderliness. However, men and women consistently differ on two personality dimensions. The first is that women tend to be more *nurturant* than men. The second is that men tend to be more *assertive* than women (Feingold, 1994; Helgeson, 1994). As psychologist Alice Eagly (1995a) summarized, "In general, women tend to manifest behaviors that can be described as socially sensitive, friendly, and concerned with others' welfare, whereas men tend to manifest behaviors that can be described as dominant, controlling, and independent." Many people believe that women are much more emotional than men. We explore that issue in Critical Thinking Box 10.1.

Cognitive Differences

Is one sex smarter, more logical, or more creative than the other? No. For *most* cognitive abilities, there are *no* significant differences between males and females (Buss, 1995b; Hyde, 1996; Hyde & Plant, 1995). However, once again, some limited differences do exist in this area (see Figure 10.2). Here are some of the best-substantiated gender-related cognitive differences.

FIGURE 10.2 Sample Test Items Favoring Females or Males Women tend to outscore men on tests of verbal fluency, spelling, perceptual speed, and writing skills. Men, in contrast, tend to outscore women on some tests involving spatial skills, particularly mental rotation tasks.

SOURCE: Kimura (1992).

Women generally do better on tests of:

(a) Perceptual Speed

Which house on the right is exactly the same as the house on the far left?

(b) Verbal Fluency

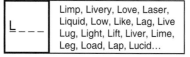

List as many words as you can think of that begin with the letter shown at left.

Men generally do better on tests of:

(c) Mental Rotation

Which item on the right is the rotated image of the item on the far left?

(d) Manipulating Mental Images

A hole has been punched through the folded sheet of paper on the far left. Which item on the right accurately shows where the holes will fall when the paper is unfolded?

■ **Verbal, reading, and writing skills.** Females consistently score much higher than males on tests of verbal fluency, reading comprehension, spelling, and, especially, basic writing skills (Eagly, 1995a; Hedges & Nowell, 1995). Although you rarely read about the "gender gap" in writing skills, researchers Larry Hedges and Amy Nowell (1995) have pointed out, "The data imply that males are, on average, at a rather profound disadvantage in the performance of this basic skill."

■ **Spatial skills.** Males outscore females on some, but not all, tests of spatial skills (Voyer & others, 1995). For example, males consistently outperform females on tests measuring the ability to mentally rotate three-dimensional figures (Kimura, 1999). On the other hand, women are significantly better than men at remembering the location of objects (Silverman & Eals, 1996).

■ **Math skills.** On average, males do slightly better than females on tests of mathematical ability (Hedges & Nowell, 1995; Hyde, 1996).

The difference in math skills deserves more comment. After all, hasn't everyone heard that "boys are much better than girls at math"? That assertion is simply not true. Over the last several decades, the so-called gender gap in mathematics has been steadily narrowing (Hyde & Plant, 1995; Murray, 1995). Today, the average difference between males and females on national math tests is very small. However, it is true that twice as many males as females score in the very highest range—the top 3 percent—in math ability tests (Casey & others, 1995; Hedges & Nowell, 1995).

Some researchers believe that cognitive differences between the sexes, such as the female advantage on verbal skills and the male advantage on spatial skills, are due to sex differences in brain function or organization (e.g., Kimura, 1999). For more on this controversial topic, see Critical Thinking Box 10.2.

CRITICAL THINKING 10.1

Are Women Really *More Emotional Than Men?*

"You never talk about your feelings!!" *she* said in exasperation. "And you *never* stop talking about yours!!" *he* shot back, frowning. Is this scene familiar?

One of our culture's most pervasive gender stereotypes is that women express their emotions more frequently and intensely than men do. In contrast, men supposedly are calmer and possess greater emotional control (Plant & others, 2000). Women, it's thought, cry easily. *Real* men don't cry at all.

Studies have shown that *both* men and women tend to view women as the more emotional sex (Grossman & Wood, 1993; Hess & others, 2000). As compared to men, women also place a higher value on emotional expressiveness (Shields, 1987). But do such widely held stereotypes reflect actual gender differences in behavior?

Consider a study by Ann Kring and Albert Gordon (1998), in which participants separately watched film clips that typically evoke happiness, fear, or sadness. For example, a fear-evoking film clip depicted a man almost falling off the ledge of a tall building. During the film, the participants' facial expressions were secretly videotaped from behind a one-way mirror. Galvanic skin response was also monitored as an index of physiological arousal. *Galvanic skin response* (GSR) measures the skin's electrical conductivity, which changes in response to sweating and increased blood flow. After the film clip, the participants rated the extent to which they experienced different emotions.

Kring and Gordon found that men and women did *not* differ in their self-ratings of the emotions they experienced in response to the film clips. However, the women *were* more emotionally expressive than men. Women displayed more positive facial expressions in response to happy film clips and more negative facial expressions in response to the sad or fearful scenes. Although the sexes did not differ in their physiological reaction to happy or sad films, the men were more physiologically reactive to the fear-inducing film clips.

In a similar study, electrodes monitored facial muscle activity of male and female participants as they looked at fear-evoking pictures (Thunberg & Dimberg, 2000). Even though men and women rated the pictures as equally unpleasant,

ZITS

© Zits Partnership. Reprinted with special permission of King Features Syndicate.

the women's facial muscles reacted much more strongly to the fearful images.

Collectively, such findings suggest that men and women differ little in the *experience* of emotions, but they do differ in the *expression* of emotions. How can we account for these gender differences in emotional expression? Are men just less confident about expressing their emotions? Not according to researchers James Gross and Oliver John (1998). They found that men feel equally confident about their expressive skills but reported masking their emotions more than women. So why are guys more inclined to mask or hide their emotions?

For both men and women, the expression of emotions is strongly influenced by *culturally determined display rules,* or societal norms of appropriate behavior in different situations. In many cultures, including the United States, women are allowed a wider range of emotional expressiveness and responsiveness than men. For men, it's considered "unmasculine" to be too open in expressing emotions (Grossman & Wood, 1993). Crying is especially taboo (Vingerhoets & others, 2000). Thus, there are strong cultural and gender-role expectations concerning emotional expressiveness and sensitivity.

These cultural norms influence what parents teach their children about emotional expression and control, and what children see modeled by adults. For example, mothers talk more to their preschool children about emotions than fathers do. They also emphasize emotion management more with their daughters than their sons (Fivush & others, 2000). By the time they reach third grade, children are already attuned to gender differences in the display rules for emotional expres-

sion (McDowell & Parke, 2000). Thus, it's not surprising that even as children, girls generally are more emotionally expressive than boys (Brody, 2000).

Do these gender differences carry through to adulthood? Basically, yes. Women display more emotional awareness than men (Feldman Barrett & others, 2000). They tend to be more sensitive and responsive to the emotional exchanges in a relationship, often playing the role of the "emotion specialist" (Gottman, 1994).

So emotions aside, what can we conclude? Like so many stereotypes, the gender stereotypes of emotions are not completely accurate. Men and women differ less in their *experience* of emotion than they do in their *expression* of those emotions. Women *are* the more emotional sex in terms of the ease with which they express their emotions, think about emotions, and recall emotional experiences (Feldman Barrett & others, 2000). In this chapter, we'll explore the implications of these gender differences for relationships.

Critical Thinking Questions

- How are emotionally expressive males generally regarded in your social group? Emotionally expressive females? Does it make you uncomfortable when gender display rules are violated by either sex? Why?

- What kinds of consequences might occur if gender display rules were violated in a business environment? On a sports team? In a classroom?

CRITICAL THINKING 10.2

"His" and "Her" Brains?

On average, men and women are very similar. But as we discuss in this chapter, researchers have consistently found differences in a few specific cognitive abilities. Some researchers, such as Canadian psychologist Doreen Kimura (1999), believe that these consistent differences are due to male–female differences in brain organization.

"Taken together," Kimura (1992) wrote, "the evidence suggests that men's and women's brains are organized along very different lines from very early in life." How early? Kimura believes that the divergence begins prenatally, when male and female fetuses are exposed to different levels of sex hormones. Other researchers share her view (see Collaer & Hines, 1995).

The mass media have seized on the notion of sex differences in the human brain. The *Newsweek* cover reproduced here is just one example of the attention this issue has received in the popular press. Are there significant differences between male and female brain structure? And if so, do they demonstrate that "men and women think differently," as the headlines proclaim? Before we address those questions, let's consider just a few examples of what researchers have actually discovered.

- Men and women were found to use different parts of their brain when they read nonsense words and determined

Sex Differences and the Brain Subtle gender differences in brain function and structure make headlines. This headline implies that new discoveries about the brain will explain "why men and women think differently." How valid is this conclusion?

whether or not they rhymed (Shaywitz & others, 1995).

- The functions of the left and right cerebral hemispheres appear to be more integrated and symmetrical in women. Women tend to process information in both cerebral hemispheres. In men, the left and right hemispheres are more

asymmetrical and more highly specialized for different tasks (Collaer & Hines, 1995; Springer & Deutsch, 1998).

- Some researchers have reported sex differences in the shape or number of neuronal fibers making up the *corpus callosum,* the structure that connects the left and right cerebral hemispheres (see Breedlove, 1994; Springer & Deutsch, 1998).

- Following comparable injuries to specific brain areas, men and women differ in the incidence of *aphasia*—speech and language disorders (Breedlove, 1994; Kimura, 1992). After a left-hemisphere stroke, men have a higher incidence of aphasia than do women, which suggests to some researchers that women's language functions are less dependent on the left hemisphere.

Do such findings "explain" differences in cognitive abilities between the sexes? Do differences in brain structures demonstrate that men and women "think differently"? Before you swallow the headlines hook, line, and sinker, a more critical examination of the evidence is in order. Consider some additional points.

1. Studies showing anatomical and functional differences are typically based on very small samples.
For example, the finding that men and

Sexual Attitudes and Behaviors

Do men and women differ in their sexual attitudes, preferences, and behaviors? Psychologists Mary Beth Oliver and Janet Hyde (1993) conducted a meta-analysis to investigate that question. They combined and reanalyzed the results of over 170 previous studies that collectively involved more than 100,000 participants. Comparing males and females on a wide range of sexual attitudes and behaviors, Oliver and Hyde found that men and women were very similar on many dimensions. For example, there were no significant differences between men and women on measures of sexual satisfaction or incidence of oral sex.

In several areas, the data showed that certain male–female differences had become much less pronounced over the past few decades. In the 1960s, for example, men and women differed significantly on attitudes toward premarital sex. During the 1980s, this difference narrowed, as both men and women became more accepting of premarital sex.

What differences did emerge? Oliver and Hyde's (1993) analysis found that men had more permissive sexual attitudes than women, including much greater women used different parts of their brain in a rhyming task involved just 19 men and 19 women (Shaywitz & others, 1995).

Perhaps the small sample sizes contribute to the inconsistent and contradictory findings in studies comparing male and female brains. For example, the difference in the corpus callosum is the most frequently reported sex difference. However, as psychologist Marc Breedlove (1994) noted, "The literature concerning the corpus callosum and possible sex differences in the corpus callosum in humans is filled with contradictory findings."

2. There are far more similarities than differences between male and female brains.

Even when sex differences are found, there is often a great deal of overlap between men and women. For example, in the rhyming task cited, 8 of the 19 women displayed the *male* pattern of brain function rather than the female pattern (Shaywitz & others, 1995).

3. There is considerable individual variation in brain structure and function.

The average range of difference *within* each sex is larger than the average difference *between* the sexes. That is, some individual females are found to be more similar to the average male pattern than

to the average female pattern, and vice versa.

4. Other than a slight sex difference in weight, none of the sex differences in brain structure have been detected at birth or in the fetal brain (Breedlove, 1994).

As we have repeatedly noted in this text, the brain's structure changes in response to experience (see Chapter 2). Therefore, it is entirely possible that brain differences in men and women could be due to different environmental and learning experiences (Breedlove, 1997).

5. Sex differences grab headlines.

Similarities in male and female brains are much less likely to receive attention, even in scientific journals.

Finally, just for the sake of argument, let's assume that a reliable sex difference in brain structure is found. For example, suppose the corpus callosum is consistently larger in one sex than in the other. What exactly does this mean? No one knows what the functional significance of such subtle differences in the corpus callosum—or in any other brain structure—might be. As we stressed in Chapter 2, researchers are only beginning to unravel the incredibly complex and interrelated organization of the human brain. Even in animals whose brains have been studied for many years, researchers

are still uncertain about the exact function of many brain areas (Gorski, 1995).

Undoubtedly, researchers will continue to uncover differences between male and female brains. As you encounter headlines proclaiming the significance of sex differences in the brain, remember these three key points. First, even the best-substantiated differences are small and inconsistent. Second, their meaning and practical significance are unclear. And third, the results are open to many different interpretations.

One thing *is* known with certainty, however. Male and female brains are *much* more alike than they are dissimilar. Given that, how well justified do you consider the conclusion that subtle brain differences prove that "men and women think differently"?

Critical Thinking Questions

- Why are sweeping claims about fundamental sex differences in the human brain misleading?

- Why is the notion that gender differences might be due to brain differences so appealing to many people?

---

acceptance of casual sex. Men also tended to have more sexual partners than women and experienced their first intercourse at an earlier average age. The most dramatic difference was the incidence of masturbation, with men reporting a higher incidence than women. Later in the chapter, we'll look at other patterns in the sexual behaviors and attitudes of men and women.

So there you have it. Men and women are *not* dramatically different. Women tend to be more nurturant, are much better at verbal, reading, and writing skills, and tend to be less sexually permissive. Men tend to be more assertive, are better at certain spatial skills, hold a slight (but shrinking) advantage on math skills, are more accepting of casual sex, and masturbate more often. In the chapter Application, we'll look at gender differences in communication style.

Even though men and women are more similar than dissimilar, there is a vast difference between growing up female and growing up male in most societies, including American society. In the next section, we'll look at how each of us learns to identify ourself as either male or female.

Gender-Role Development

Blue Bears and Pink Bunnies

Key Theme

■ Gender plays an important role in most cultures; girls and boys are treated differently from birth.

Key Questions

■ What gender differences develop during childhood?

■ How do social learning theory and gender schema theory explain the development of gender roles?

FAMILY CIRCUS

12-15
©1998 Bil Keane, Inc.
Dist. by Cowles Synd., Inc.

"That's the DOLL aisle, Daddy. Somebody might see us!"

Being male or female *does* make a vast difference in our society. Put simply, males and females *are* treated differently. Within moments after birth, the newborn baby is "color coded" by gender. When our daughter was born, she was immediately wrapped in a pink blanket with bunnies, just like the other female infants in the nursery. The male infants were also color coded by gender—they had blue blankets with little bears. That, of course, is just the beginning.

When brand-new parents call family and friends to announce the birth of a new baby, what's the first question they are asked? In the overwhelming number of cases, the first question is "Is it a boy or a girl?" Given the importance that gender plays in most cultures, that's not a surprising finding. Infant boys and girls are virtually indistinguishable—except for their clothes, toys, and the furnishings in their rooms. If it weren't for the ruffled bonnet and pink booties, you wouldn't be able to tell that the infant in the grocery cart ahead of you was a girl from its size, appearance, or behavior.

Perhaps that's why the color coding that starts at birth continues throughout infancy and toddlerhood. In mainstream U.S. culture, girls are dressed in pink and other pastel colors, boys in blue and red. Even disposable diapers come in blue for infant boys and pink for infant girls. Our friends Bill and Marcia described their efforts to raise their young daughter and infant son in a "gender-neutral, nonsexist environment." But, Marcia confessed, "I don't think I'm brave enough to dress Andrew in pink!"

Logically, of course, there is no reason why parents can't dress their newborn boys in pink overalls. The fact that they don't illustrates the pervasiveness and force of cultural and social expectations for appropriate male and female attire, attributes, and behavior.

When one-year-old infants are dressed identically, adults usually cannot tell male and female infants apart. However, in a series of studies, researcher T. G. R. Bower (1989) found that other one-year-olds could detect the difference. When one-year-old toddlers played with unfamiliar peers dressed in unisex clothes, the toddlers played more with others of the same sex. And when watching videotapes

Pink Bikes, Red Bikes Little boys and little girls clearly have a lot in common. All of these children are wearing blue jeans, and they all enjoy bicycling with their friends. Nevertheless, the girl's bike is pink with white tires, and the boy's bike is red with black tires. Why?

BABY BLUES

of other toddlers, one-year-old girls stared more intently at films of other girls and one-year-old boys looked more intently at films of other boys, no matter how the babies in the tapes were dressed.

One-year-olds, of course, are unlikely to understand the concepts of "male" and "female." However, as research shows, one-year-olds are already sensitive to subtle gender differences in behavior and mannerisms (Poulin-Dubois & others, 1994). Clearly, then, gender awareness emerges at a very early age (Beal, 1994).

Gender Differences in Childhood Behavior
Batman Versus Barbie

Roughly between the ages of two and three, children can identify themselves and other children as boys or girls, although the details are still a bit fuzzy to them (Fagot & others, 1992). Preschoolers don't yet understand that sex is determined by physical characteristics. This is not surprising, considering that the biologically defining sex characteristics—the genitals—are hidden from view most of the time. Instead, young children identify the sexes in terms of external attributes, such as hairstyle, clothing, and activities.

A humorous story told by gender researcher Sandra Bem illustrates this point. Bem (1989) describes going along with her preschool son Jeremy's desire to wear barrettes to nursery school. Another little boy at the school repeatedly insisted that Jeremy "must be a girl, because only girls wear barrettes." So, Jeremy attempted to prove that he really was a boy by dropping his pants. The other little boy was not convinced. "Everybody has a penis, only girls wear barrettes," he countered.

From about the age of 18 months to the age of 2 years, sex differences in behavior begin to emerge. These differences become more pronounced throughout early childhood. Toddler girls play more with soft toys and dolls, and ask for help from adults more than toddler boys do. Toddler boys play more with blocks and transportation toys, such as trucks and wagons. They also play more actively than do girls (see Stern & Karraker, 1989).

Roughly between the ages of two and three, preschoolers start acquiring gender-role stereotypes for toys, clothing, household objects, games, and work (Poulin-Dubois & others, 1994). From the age of about three on, there are consistent gender differences in preferred toys and play activities. Boys play more with balls, blocks, and toy vehicles. Girls play more with dolls and domestic toys and engage in more dressing up and art activities (Turner & Gervai, 1995). By the age of three, children have developed a clear preference for toys that are associated with their own sex. This tendency continues throughout childhood.

Separate Worlds? In childhood, boys tend to play in groups and prefer competitive games. In contrast, girls tend to establish close relationships with one or two other girls and to cement their friendship by sharing thoughts and feelings. How might such gender differences affect intimate relationships in adolescence and adulthood?

Baby Blues Partnership. Reprinted with special permission of King Features Syndicate.

social learning theory of gender-role development
The theory that gender roles are acquired through the basic processes of learning, including reinforcement, punishment, and modeling.

gender schema theory
The theory that gender-role development is influenced by the formation of schemas, or mental representations, of masculinity and femininity.

Children also develop a strong preference for playing with members of their own sex—girls with girls and boys with boys (Egan & Perry, 2001; Thorne, 1993). It's not uncommon to hear boys refer to girls as "icky" and girls refer to boys as "mean" or "rough." And, in fact, preschool boys *do* play more roughly than girls, cover more territory, and play in larger groups. Throughout the remainder of childhood, boys and girls play primarily with members of their own sex (Powlishta, 1995a, 1995b).

According to psychologist Carole Beal (1994), boys and girls almost seem to create separate "social worlds," each with its own style of interaction. They also learn particular ways of interacting that work well with peers of the same sex. For example, boys learn to assert themselves within a group of male friends. Girls tend to establish very close bonds with one or two friends. Girls learn to maintain their close friendships through compromise, conciliation, and verbal conflict resolution. As we'll discuss in the chapter's Application, these gender differences in styles of social interaction persist into adulthood.

Children are far more rigid than adults in their beliefs in gender-role stereotypes. Children's strong adherence to gender stereotypes may be a necessary step in developing a gender identity (Powlishta, 1995b; Stangor & Ruble, 1987). Boys are far more rigid than girls in their preferences for toys associated with their own sex. Their attitudes about the sexes are also more rigid than are those held by girls. As girls grow older, they become even more flexible in their views of sex-appropriate activities and attributes, but boys become even less flexible (Katz & Ksansnak, 1994).

Girls' more flexible attitude toward gender roles may reflect society's greater tolerance of girls who cross gender lines in attire and behavior. A girl who plays with boys, or who plays with boys' toys, may develop the grudging respect of both sexes. But a boy who plays with girls or with girls' toys may be ostracized by both sexes. Girls are often proud to be labeled a "tomboy," but for boys, being called a "sissy" is the ultimate insult (Thorne, 1993). One explanation may be that children of both sexes tend to value the male role more highly than the female role.

As we've seen, there are very few significant differences between the sexes in either personality traits or intellectual abilities. Yet in many ways, children's behavior mirrors the gender-role stereotypes that are predominant in our culture.

Explaining Gender Roles
Two Contemporary Theories

Many theories have been proposed to explain the differing patterns of male and female behavior in our culture and in other cultures. Gender theories have included findings and opinions from anthropology, sociology, neuroscience, medicine, philosophy, political science, economics, and religion. (Let's face it, you probably have a few opinions on the issue yourself.) We won't even attempt to cover the full range of ideas. Instead, we'll describe two of the most influential psychological theories: social learning theory and gender schema theory. In Chapter 11, on personality, we will discuss Freud's ideas on the development of gender roles.

Social Learning Theory: Learning Gender Roles

Based on the principles of learning, **social learning theory** contends that gender roles are learned through *reinforcement, punishment,* and *modeling.* From a very young age, children are reinforced or rewarded when they display gender-appropriate behavior and punished when they do not. For example, psychologists Beverly Fagot and Richard Hagan (1991) observed mothers and fathers interacting with their children in their homes. They found that 18-month-old boys received more positive reactions from their parents for playing with male-typed toys and for exhibiting aggressive or assertive behavior. In contrast, 18-month-old girls received more positive responses for attempts to communicate with their parents, while boys received more negative reactions for such attempts.

To what degree do such parental behaviors influence the development of gender differences? The effect is not as great as you might think. Psychologists David Lytton and David M. Romney (1991) conducted a meta-analysis of nearly 200 studies of parents' different treatment of boys and girls. They found that the actual effects of parental socialization in many areas of gender differences were relatively small. Yes, parents *do* tend to reinforce and encourage gender-appropriate play. But for the most part, parents treat their male and female children rather similarly.

If parents have only a minimal effect, how do children acquire their understanding of gender differences? Children are exposed to many other sources of information about gender roles, including television, books, and observation of same-sex adult role models. Hence, children also learn gender differences through *modeling*: They observe and then imitate the sex-typed behavior of significant adults and older children (Best & Williams, 1997). By observing and imitating such models—whether it's Mom cooking, Dad fixing things around the house, or a male superhero rescuing a helpless female on television—children come to understand that certain activities and attributes are considered more appropriate for one sex than for the other.

"Just One of the Guys" Today, girls receive more encouragement to compete in sports, including such previously male-dominated sports as soccer, basketball, and baseball, than they did just a decade or two ago. A girl who successfully competes in a traditionally male game may earn the respect of both sexes.

Gender Schema Theory: Constructing Gender Categories

Gender schema theory, developed by **Sandra Bem,** incorporates some aspects of social learning theory. However, Bem (1981) approaches gender-role development from a more strongly cognitive perspective. In contrast to the relatively passive role played by children in social learning theory, **gender schema theory** contends that children *actively* develop mental categories (or *schemas*) for masculinity and femininity (Martin & Halverson, 1981). That is, children actively organize information about other people and appropriate behavior, activities, and attributes into gender categories. Saying that "trucks are for boys and dolls are for girls" is an example of a gender schema.

According to gender schema theory, children, like many adults, look at the world through "gender lenses" (Bem, 1987). Gender schemas influence how people pay attention to, perceive, interpret, and remember gender-relevant behavior. Gender schemas also seem to lead children to perceive members of their own sex more favorably than members of the opposite sex (Powlishta, 1995b).

Like schemas in general (see Chapter 6), children's gender schemas do seem to influence what they notice and remember. For example, five-year-olds were shown pictures of children engaged in activities that violated common gender stereotypes, such as girls playing with trucks and boys playing with dolls (Martin & Halverson, 1981, 1983). A few days later, the five-year-olds "remembered" that the *boys* had been playing with the trucks and the *girls* with the dolls!

Children also readily assimilate new information into their existing gender schemas. In a classic study, four- to nine-year-olds were given boxes of gender-neutral gadgets, such as hole punches (Bradbard & others, 1986). But some gadgets were labeled as "girl toys" and some as "boy toys." The boys played more with the "boy" gadgets, and the girls played more with the "girl" gadgets. A week later, the children easily remembered which gadgets went with each sex. They also remembered more information about the gadgets that were associated with their own sex. Simply labeling the objects as belonging to boys or to girls had powerful consequences for the children's behavior and memory—evidence of the importance of gender schemas in learning and remembering new information.

Gender schemas also include a broad range of qualities and attributes that are less concrete, such as associating "gentleness" with females and "toughness" with males. Consider a study by Beverly Fagot and her colleagues (1992). Preschoolers were first shown a

You've Come a Long Way, Baby? Children's books continue to reinforce gender stereotypes, sometimes in subtle ways. In this picture book for preschoolers, a little girl follows her big brother's lead. The boy is shown actively digging in the mud, happily getting dirty with his dog, bat and ball nearby. In contrast, the little girl, dressed in pink, stays clean as she feeds and nurtures her kitten.

Who wants to sleep, anyway? Not us! We want to be busy, busy, busy!

picture of a woman with a small girl and a picture of a man with a small boy. Then, the preschoolers were asked to match drawings of various items to either picture: "Does this belong to the mommy and the little girl or to the daddy and the little boy?"

Some of the drawings were of objects, such as hammers and brooms, that are conventionally associated with one sex rather than with the other. These represented realistic associations that the children might have learned through observation. But other images were only *metaphorically* associated with one sex rather than with the other, such as cats (female) or bears (male).

Fagot and her colleagues (1992) found that the young children made both the concrete *and* the metaphoric associations to the appropriate sex. Children consistently matched the fierce-looking bear with males and the fluffy cat with females. Yet, as the researchers pointed out, "Few men keep bears, and cats do not belong only to women." Thus, beyond the concrete associations the children might have learned through reinforcement or observation, even preschoolers seemed to be aware of the *underlying meanings* of gender stereotypes.

Given the gender-schematized world we grow up in, it's not surprising that gender stereotypes remain so pervasive and influential.

10.1 R·E·V·I·E·W

C·O·N·C·E·P·T

Aspects of Gender and Sexuality

Decide which term applies to each of the following examples. Choose from: gender schema theory, sex, gender-role stereotypes, social learning theory.

1. When John was born, the doctor saw his penis and said, "Mrs. McGillicuddy, it's a boy." _____

2. Michael thinks that women are more nurturing, patient, and emotional than men and that men have greater mechanical aptitude and are more aggressive, logical, and rational than women. His expectations reflect _____.

3. Whenever Boris picked up a doll, he was scolded. Whenever he tried to throw a football to his father, his father beamed and praised him. As Boris grew up, he ignored dolls and took every opportunity to get involved in sports. _____

4. When Sarah first met Greg and Martha, Greg was carrying a doll and Martha was wearing a toy tool belt. The second time Sarah saw Greg, she asked, "Where's your tool belt?" _____

Human Sexuality

Key Theme

■ Multiple factors are involved in understanding human sexuality.

Key Questions

■ What are the four stages of human sexual response?
■ How does sexual motivation differ among animal species?
■ What biological factors are involved in sexual motivation?

On the one hand, sexual feelings and relationships are very private and deeply personal. On the other hand, sexual behavior is very much in the public spotlight. Advertising and entertainment emphasize sexual themes. Sex-related issues and topics are regularly reported in the news media. And daytime talk shows compete for guests who engage in extreme and unusual sexual practices. Like it or not, virtually every aspect of human sexuality is a public topic in American society today.

Whether the media-manufactured images of sex in the United States are accurate, however, is a very different matter. From the standpoint of psychology, an accurate understanding of sexuality is essential to developing a comprehensive picture of behavior. After all, sexual feelings and relationships are an important part of being human.

As you'll see throughout the remainder of this chapter, the scientific study of sexuality is multidimensional. Biological, psychological, social, and cultural factors must all be taken into account to understand human sexuality. By the end of the chapter, you'll have discovered just how well the media images of sex in the United States stack up against the actual data.

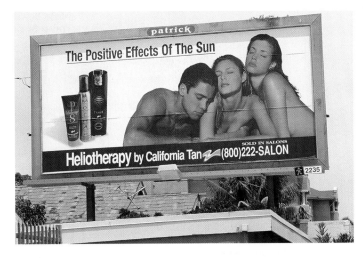

Media Images of Sex and Sexuality
Sexual themes and images are often used to sell products and movies and to boost TV ratings. How accurate are media images of human sexuality?

First Things First
The Stages of Human Sexual Response

The human sexual response cycle was first mapped by sex research pioneers **William Masters** and **Virginia Johnson** during the 1950s and 1960s. Until the 1950s, information about sexual response had been gathered by observing the behavior of different animal species. Masters and Johnson felt that a more direct approach was needed to further the understanding of human sexual anatomy and physiology. Thus, in the name of science, Masters and Johnson observed hundreds of people engage in more than 10,000 episodes of sexual activity in their laboratory. Their findings, published in 1966, indicated that the human sexual response could be described as a cycle with four stages.

As you read the descriptions of these stages, keep in mind that the transitions between stages are not as precise or abrupt as the descriptions might lead you to believe. Moreover, the duration of time spent in any particular stage can vary on different occasions of sexual interaction.

Stage 1: Excitement

The *excitement phase* marks the beginning of sexual arousal. Sexual arousal can occur in response to sexual fantasies or other sexually arousing stimuli, physical contact with another person, or masturbation. In both sexes, the excitement stage is accompanied by a variety of bodily changes in anticipation of sexual interaction. There is a rapid rise in pulse rate and blood pressure. The rate of breathing increases. Blood shifts to the genitals, producing an erect penis in the male and swelling of the clitoris in the female. The female's vaginal lips expand and open up, and her vagina becomes lubricated in preparation for intercourse. Her nipples and breasts may also become enlarged, and the nipples become erect and more sensitive.

Stage 2: Plateau

In the second phase, the *plateau phase,* physical arousal builds as pulse and breathing rates continue to increase. The penis becomes fully erect and sometimes secretes a few drops of fluid, which may contain active sperm. The testes increase in size. The clitoris withdraws under the clitoral hood but remains very sensitive to stimulation. The vaginal entrance tightens, putting pressure on the penis during intercourse. Vaginal lubrication continues. During the excitement and plateau stages, the degree of arousal may fluctuate up and down (Masters & others, 1995). During the plateau stage, the firmness of the male's erection may increase and decrease, and so may the female's degree of vaginal lubrication.

Pioneers of Sex Research: William Masters (1915–2001) and Virginia Johnson (b. 1925)
Masters and Johnson broke new ground with their scientific study of sexual behavior in the 1960s. Along with documenting and describing the human sexual response, they also developed many innovative techniques that are still used in sex therapy.

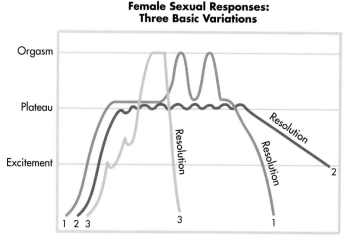

Female Sexual Responses: Three Basic Variations

Typical Male Sexual Response

FIGURE 10.3 The Male and Female Sexual Response Cycles The top figure depicts the three basic variations of the female sexual response. Pattern 1 shows multiple orgasms. Pattern 2 shows sexual arousal that reaches the plateau stage but not orgasm, followed by a slow resolution. Pattern 3 depicts brief reductions in arousal during the excitement stage, followed by rapid orgasm and resolution. The bottom figure depicts the most typical male sexual response, in which orgasm is followed by a refractory period.

SOURCE: Masters & Johnson (1966).

Stage 3: Orgasm

Orgasm is the third and shortest phase of the sexual response cycle. During orgasm, blood pressure and heart rate reach their peak. The muscles in the vaginal walls and the uterus contract rhythmically, as do the muscles in and around the penis as the male ejaculates. Other muscles may contract as well, such as those in the face, arms, and legs. Both men and women describe the subjective experience of orgasm in similar—and very positive—terms.

The vast majority of men experience one intense orgasm. But many women are capable of experiencing multiple orgasms. If sexual stimulation continues following orgasm, women may experience additional orgasms within a short period of time.

Stage 4: Resolution

Following orgasm, both sexes tend to experience a warm physical "glow" and a sense of well-being. Arousal slowly subsides and returns to normal levels in the *resolution phase*. The male experiences a *refractory period,* during which he is incapable of having another erection or orgasm. The duration of the male's refractory period varies. For one man it may last a matter of minutes, for another several hours. As men age, the duration of the refractory period tends to increase.

So, there you have it—the clinical, scientific description of the physiological changes that occur before, during, and after orgasm. Although it is simplified somewhat, Figure 10.3 depicts the basic patterns of sexual response for men and women. Somehow it lacks the lusty appeal of an erotic passage from a Danielle Steele best-seller or D. H. Lawrence's (1928) classic novel, *Lady Chatterley's Lover.* Nonetheless, the early work of Masters and Johnson remains a landmark in the study of human sexuality.

What Motivates Sexual Behavior?

Psychologists consider the drive to have sex a basic human motive. But what exactly motivates that drive? Obviously, there are differences between sex and other basic motives, such as hunger. Engaging in sexual intercourse is essential to the survival of the human species, but it is not essential to the survival of any specific person. In other words, you'll die if you don't eat, but you won't die if you don't have sex (you may just *think* you will).

In most animals, sexual behavior is biologically determined and triggered by hormonal changes in the female. During the cyclical period known as *estrus,* a female animal is fertile and receptive to male sexual advances. Roughly translated, the Greek word *estrus* means "frantic desire." Indeed, the female animal will often actively signal her willingness to engage in sexual activity—as the owner of any unneutered female cat or dog that's "in heat" can testify. In many, but not all, species, sexual activity only takes place when the female is in estrus (Rissman, 1995).

As you go up the evolutionary scale, moving from relatively simple to more sophisticated animals, sexual behavior becomes less biologically determined and more subject to learning and environmental influences. Sexual behavior also becomes less limited to the goal of reproduction. For example, in some primate species, such as monkeys and apes, sexual activity can occur at any time, not just when the female is fertile. In these species, sexual interaction serves important social functions, defining and cementing relationships among the members of the primate group.

One rare species of chimplike apes, the bonobos of the Democratic Republic of the Congo, exhibits a surprising variety of sexual behaviors (de Waal & Lanting, 1998). Although most animals *copulate,* or have sex, with the male mounting the female from behind, bonobos often copulate face to face. Bonobos also engage in oral sex and intense tongue kissing. And bonobos seem to like variety. Along with having frequent heterosexual activity, whether the female is fertile or not, bonobos also engage in homosexual and group sex.

Emory University psychology professor Frans de Waal (1995), who has extensively studied bonobos, observes that their frequent and varied sexual behavior seems to serve important social functions. Sexual behavior is not limited to fulfilling the purpose of reproduction. Among the bonobos, sexual interaction is used to increase group cohesion, avoid conflict, and decrease tension that might be caused by competition for food. According to de Waal (1995), the bonobos' motto seems to be "Make love, not war."

In humans, of course, sexual behavior is not limited to a female's fertile period. Nor is the motivational goal of sex limited to reproduction. Although a woman's fertility is regulated by monthly hormonal cycles, these hormonal changes seem to have little effect on a female's sexual motivation (Davidson & Myers, 1988). Even when a woman's ovaries, which produce the female sex hormone *estrogen,* are surgically removed or stop functioning during menopause, there is little or no drop in sexual interest. In many nonhuman female mammals, however, removal of the ovaries results in a complete loss of interest in sexual activity. If injections of estrogen and other female sex hormones are given, the female animals' sexual interest returns.

In male animals, removal of the testes (castration) typically causes a steep drop in sexual activity and interest, although the decline is more gradual in sexually experienced animals. Castration causes a significant decrease in levels of *testosterone,* the hormone responsible for male sexual development. When human males experience lowered levels of testosterone because of illness or castration, a similar drop in sexual interest tends to occur, although the effects vary among individuals. Some men continue to lead a normal sex life for years, but others quickly lose all interest in sexual activity. In castrated men who experience a loss of sexual interest, injections of testosterone restore the sexual drive.

Testosterone is also involved in female sexual motivation (Davis, 2000). Most of the testosterone in a woman's body is produced by her adrenal glands. If these glands are removed or malfunction, causing testosterone levels to become abnormally low, sexual interest often wanes. When supplemental testosterone is administered, the woman's sex drive returns. Thus, in *both* men and women, sexual motivation is biologically influenced by the levels of the hormone testosterone in the body.

Of course, sexual behavior is greatly influenced by many cultural and social factors. We consider one aspect of sexual behavior in Culture and Human Behavior Box 10.3.

The Bonobos of the Congo Bonobos demonstrate a wide variety of sexual interactions, including face-to-face copulation, kissing, and sexual interaction among same-sex pairs (de Waal & Lanting, 1998). Sexual behavior is not limited to reproduction; it seems to play an important role in maintaining peaceful relations among members of the bonobo group. As Frans de Waal (1995) wrote, "For these animals, sexual behavior is indistinguishable from social behavior."

CULTURE AND HUMAN BEHAVIOR 10.3

Evolution and Mate Preferences

Did the cartoon make you laugh—or at least smile? If it did, it's because you recognized a cultural pattern—the belief that men seek a beautiful, youthful partner, while women are more likely to value financial security and wealth. Cartoons and jokes aside, is there any merit to this observation? *Do* men and women differ in what they look for in a mate?

To investigate mate preferences, psychologist David Buss (1989, 1994) coordinated a large-scale survey of more than 10,000 people in 37 different cultures.

Across all cultures, Buss found, men were more likely than women to value youth and physical attractiveness in a potential mate. In contrast, women were more likely than men to value financial security, access to material resources, high status and education, and good financial prospects. Buss, an evolutionary psychologist, interprets these gender differences as reflecting the different "mating strategies" of men and women.

According to evolutionary psychology, mating behavior is adaptive to the degree that it furthers the reproductive success of transmitting one's genes to the next generation and beyond. And when it comes to reproductive success, Buss (1995a) contends that men and women face very different "adaptive problems" in selecting a mate.

According to Buss (1995b, 1996), the adaptive problem for men is to identify and mate with women who are fertile and likely to be successful at bearing their children. Thus, men are more likely to place a high value on youth, because it is associated with fertility and because younger women have a greater number of child-bearing years ahead of them than older women. And, because men value physical attractiveness it signals that the woman is probably physically healthy and has high-quality genes.

Buss sees the adaptive problem for women as very different. Women also seek "good" genes, and thus they value men who are healthy and attractive. But they have a more pressing need: making sure that the children they do bear survive to

BIZARRO

ONE SECOND BEFORE THE BLIND DATE

carry their genes into future generations. Pregnancy, lactation, and caring for infants, says Buss, leaves women unable to acquire the resources needed to protect and feed themselves and their children. Thus, women look for a mate who will be a "good provider." They seek men who possess the resources that the women and their offspring will need to survive.

In most cultures, Buss (1995a) points out, men of high status and wealth are able to marry younger and more attractive women than poor, low-status men are. In other words, older successful men, whether they are tribal chiefs, corporate CEOs, or aging rock superstars, have the greatest access to young, attractive women—the so-called "trophy wife." On the other side of the coin, physically attractive women can, and often do, marry men with more resources and higher status than unattractive women.

Not surprisingly, this evolutionary explanation of sex differences is controversial. Some psychologists argue that it is overly deterministic and does not sufficiently acknowledge the role of culture, gender-role socialization, and other social factors (Caporael & Brewer, 1995; Hyde, 1996; Pratto, 1996).

Other psychologists interpret Buss's data in a different way. Tim Kasser and Yadika Sharma (1999) analyzed the mate preference data in terms of women's reproductive freedom and educational opportunity in each culture. They found that women who live in cultures that are low in both female reproductive freedom and educational equality between the sexes placed a higher value on a prospective mate's resources.

According to Kasser and Sharma (1999), "When a female is provided with opportunities to fend for herself, she can become less concerned with finding a mate who will provide resources for her, but when she has few opportunities to educate herself or control her own fertility, she will be more concerned with finding a mate who can provide her with the resources needed to support her and her children."

For his part, Buss (1996) is careful to point out that this theory does *not* claim that personal preferences have no effect on mate preferences. In fact, his extensive survey also found that men and women in all 37 cultures agreed that the *most* important factor in choosing a mate was mutual attraction and love. And, here's a finding that will probably be reassuring to those singles who have neither fabulous wealth nor heart-stopping beauty: Both sexes rated kindness, intelligence, emotional stability, health, and a pleasing personality as more important than a prospective mate's financial resources or good looks.

Finally, Buss and other evolutionary psychologists reject the idea that people, cultures, or societies are powerless to overcome tendencies that evolved over hundreds of thousands of years. Buss also flatly states that explaining some of the reasons that might underlie sexual inequality does *not* mean that sexual inequality is natural, correct, or justified. Rather, evolutionary psychologists believe that we must understand the conditions that foster sexual inequality in order to overcome or change those conditions (Smuts, 1996).

BIZARRO © by Dan Piraro. Reprinted with permission of Universal Press Syndicate.

Sexual Orientation
The Elusive Search for an Explanation

Key Theme
- Sexual orientation refers to whether a person is attracted to members of the opposite sex, the same sex, or both sexes.

Key Questions
- Why is sexual orientation sometimes difficult to identify?
- What factors have been associated with sexual orientation?

Given that biological factors seem to play an important role in motivating sexual desire, it seems only reasonable to ask whether biological factors also play a role in sexual orientation. **Sexual orientation** refers to whether a person is sexually aroused by members of the same sex, the opposite sex, or both sexes. A *heterosexual* person is sexually attracted to individuals of the other sex, a *homosexual* person to individuals of the same sex, and a *bisexual* person to individuals of both sexes. Technically, the term *homosexual* can be applied to either males or females. However, female homosexuals are usually called *lesbians*. Male homosexuals typically use the term *gay* to describe their sexual orientation.

Sexual orientation is not nearly as cut and dried as many people believe. Some people *are* exclusively heterosexual or homosexual, but others are less easy to categorize. Many people who consider themselves heterosexual have had a homosexual experience at some point in their lives (Seidman & Rieder, 1994). In the same vein, many homosexuals have had heterosexual experiences. Other people, like our friend Richard in the chapter's Prologue, consider themselves to be homosexual but have had heterosexual relationships. The key point is that there is not always a perfect correspondence between a particular person's sexual identity, sexual desires, and sexual behaviors (Laumann & others, 1994).

Determining the number of people who are homosexual or heterosexual is problematic for several reasons (Rogers & Turner, 1991). First, survey results vary depending on how the researchers define the terms *homosexual, heterosexual,* and *bisexual.* Second, gays and lesbians are not distributed evenly throughout the population. In rural areas and small towns, gays, lesbians, and bisexuals make up about 1 percent of the population. But in the largest U.S. cities, approximately one of eight people (or 12 percent) consider themselves gay, lesbian, or bisexual (Michael & others, 1994). Thus, estimates of the size of the gay and lesbian population can vary, depending on:

- How researchers structure survey questions
- How they define the criteria for inclusion in gay, lesbian, or bisexual categories
- Where the survey is conducted
- How survey participants are selected

More important than the exact number of gays and lesbians is the recognition that gays and lesbians constitute a significant segment of the adult population in the United States. According to the most reasonable estimates, it's safe to say that between 7 million and 15 million American men and women are gay or lesbian (Patterson, 1995c).

What Determines Sexual Orientation?

Despite considerable research on this question, psychologists and other researchers cannot say with certainty why people become homosexual or bisexual. For that matter, psychologists don't know exactly why people become *heterosexual* either. Still, research on sexual orientation has pointed toward several general conclusions, especially with regard to homosexuality.

sexual orientation
The direction of a person's emotional and erotic attraction toward members of the opposite sex, the same sex, or both sexes.

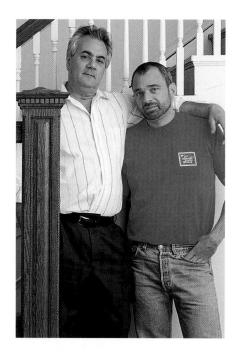

U.S. Congressman Barney Frank and Herb Moses Frank and Moses shared a home for many years before separating. Frank realized he was gay in early adolescence. Was heterosexuality ever an option for him? As Frank (1996) explained, "I wished it was. But it wasn't. I can't imagine that anybody believes that a 13-year-old in 1953 thinks, 'Boy, it would really be great to be part of this minority that everybody hates and to have a really restricted life.' You can't make yourself a different person. I am who I am. I have no idea why."

Evidence from twin studies suggests that genetics plays a role in determining a homosexual orientation. For example, psychologists Michael Bailey and Richard Pillard (1991) compared the incidence of male homosexuality among pairs of identical twins (who have identical genes), fraternal twins (who are genetically as similar as any two nontwin siblings), and adoptive brothers (who have no common genetic heritage but shared the same upbringing). The researchers found that the closer the degree of genetic relationship, the more likely it was that when one brother was homosexual, the other brother would also be homosexual. Specifically, both brothers were homosexual in 52 percent of the identical twins, 22 percent of the fraternal twins, and 11 percent of the adoptive brothers.

Bailey and his colleagues (1993) discovered very similar results in twin studies of lesbians. In 48 percent of identical twins and 16 percent of fraternal twins, when one sister was lesbian, so was the other sister, compared with only 6 percent of adoptive sisters. Although intriguing, such genetic studies are subject to criticisms about methodology and other issues (Byne, 1994; Byne & Parsons, 1993). Furthermore, since the identical twins were both homosexual in only half of the twin pairs, it's clear that genetic predisposition alone cannot explain sexual orientation. Nevertheless, these studies and others support the notion that sexual orientation is at least partly influenced by genetics (Gladue, 1994).

Another biological factor that has been investigated is differences in brain structure between heterosexuals and homosexuals (LeVay & Hamer, 1994). Neurobiologist Simon LeVay (1991) discovered a small but significant difference between male heterosexuals and male homosexuals in a tiny cluster of neurons in the *hypothalamus,* which is known to be involved in sexual behavior. In male homosexuals and heterosexual women, the cluster was only half the size of the cluster in heterosexual men.

LeVay speculates that this tiny structure may be involved in determining sexual orientation (LeVay & Hamer, 1994). However, LeVay also carefully points out that there is no way of knowing whether this difference in brain structure *causes* homosexual behavior in men. Conceivably, it might be the other way around—homosexual behavior might cause the difference in brain structure.

In general, the only conclusion we can draw from these studies is that some biological factors are *correlated* with a homosexual orientation (Byne, 1994). As we've stressed, correlation does not necessarily indicate causality, only that two factors *seem* to occur together. So stronger conclusions about the role of genetic and biological factors in determining sexual orientation await more definitive research findings (Baumrind, 1995; Gladue, 1994).

What about early life experiences? Is homosexuality due to abnormal parenting or early homosexual experiences? Alan Bell and his colleagues (1981) conducted an early comprehensive study investigating these and other popular beliefs regarding the causes of homosexual orientation. On the basis of in-depth interviews of almost 1,000 homosexual men and women, and a comparison group of about 500 heterosexual men and women, they came to the following conclusions:

- Homosexuality is *not* due to an unpleasant early heterosexual experience, such as being sexually abused during childhood by a member of the opposite sex.

- Homosexuality is *not* the result of an abnormal relationship between the parents and the child, such as having a father who is an inadequate male role model or having an overly dominant mother.

Bell and his colleagues (1981) also found that sexual orientation was determined before adolescence and long before the beginning of sexual activity. Gay men and lesbians typically became aware of homosexual feelings about three years before they engaged in any such sexual activity. In this regard, the pattern was very similar to that of heterosexual children, in whom heterosexual feelings are aroused long before the child expresses them in some form of sexual behavior.

Several researchers now believe that sexual orientation is established as early as age six (Strickland, 1995). Do children who later grow up to be homosexuals differ from children who later grow up to be heterosexuals? In at least one respect, there seems to be a difference.

Earlier in the chapter, we described the typical patterns of gender-role development in childhood. We noted that boys and girls differ in their choice of toys, playmates, and play activities. Evidence suggests that male and female homosexuals are less likely to have followed the typical pattern of gender-specific behaviors in childhood (Bailey & others, 2000; Bailey & Zucker, 1995). Compared to heterosexual men, gay men recall engaging in more cross-sex-typed behavior during childhood. For example, they remembered playing more with girls than with other boys, preferring girls' toys over boys' toys, and disliking rough-and-tumble play. Lesbians are also more likely to recall cross-gender behavior in childhood, but to a lesser degree than gay men.

A potential problem with such *retrospective studies* is that the participants may be biased in their recall of childhood events. One way to avoid that problem is by conducting a prospective study. A *prospective study* involves systematically observing a group of people over time to discover what factors are associated with the development of a particular trait, characteristic, or behavior.

One influential prospective study was conducted by Richard Green (1985, 1987). Green followed the development of sexual orientation in two groups of boys. The first group of boys had been referred to a mental health clinic because of their "feminine" behavior. He compared the development of these boys to a matched control group of boys who displayed typically "masculine" behavior in childhood. When all the boys were in their late teens, Green compared the two groups. He found that approximately 75 percent of the previously feminine boys were either bisexual or homosexual, as compared to only 4 percent of the control group.

As researchers J. Michael Bailey and Kenneth J. Zucker (1995) summarized, "There is clear evidence of a relation between patterns of childhood sex-typed behavior and later sexual orientation." However, these researchers and others note that this conclusion is more applicable to the development of sexual orientation in males than in females (L. Diamond, 1998).

Once sexual orientation is established, whether heterosexual or homosexual, it is highly resistant to change (American Psychiatric Association, 1994). The vast majority of homosexuals would be unable to change their orientation even if they wished to, just as the majority of heterosexuals would be unable to change their orientation if *they* wished to. Thus, it's a mistake to assume that homosexuals have deliberately chosen their sexual orientation any more than heterosexuals have. Indeed, when Richard was in high school, he would gladly have "chosen" to be heterosexual if the matter had been that simple.

It seems clear that no single factor determines whether people identify themselves as homosexual, heterosexual, or bisexual (Golombok & Tasker, 1996). Psychological, biological, social, and cultural factors are undoubtedly involved in determining sexual orientation. However, researchers are still unable to pinpoint exactly what those factors are and how they interact. As psychologist Bonnie Strickland (1995) has pointed out, "Sexual identity and orientation appear to be shaped by a complexity of biological, psychological, and social events. Gender identity and sexual orientation, at least for most people, especially gay men, occur early, are relatively fixed, and are difficult to change." As Richard learned, changing his sexual orientation was simply not possible.

Homosexuality is no longer considered a sexual disorder by clinical psychologists or psychiatrists (American Psychiatric Association, 1994). Many research studies have also found that homosexuals who are comfortable with their sexual orientation are just as well adjusted as are heterosexuals (see Strickland, 1995).

Lesbian Parents Are the children of gay or lesbian parents likely to become homosexual themselves? Apparently the children of homosexual parents are no more likely to be gay or lesbian in adulthood than are children raised by heterosexual parents (Bailey & others, 1995; Golombok & Tasker, 1996). Research studies to date show few differences among the children of gay, lesbian, or heterosexual parents (Strickland, 1995).

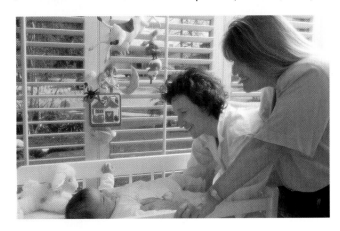

Like heterosexuals, gays and lesbians can be found in every occupation and at every socioeconomic level in our society. And, like heterosexuals, many gays and lesbians are involved in long-term, committed, and caring relationships (Kurdek, 1995; Patterson, 1995b). Children who are raised by gay or lesbian parents are as well adjusted as children who are raised by heterosexual parents (Flaks & others, 1995; Patterson, 1992, 1995c). Furthermore, children who are raised by gay or lesbian parents are no more likely to be gay or lesbian in adulthood than are children who are raised by heterosexual parents (Bailey & others, 1995; Golombok & Tasker, 1996).

10.2 R·E·V·I·E·W

C·O·N·C·E·P·T

Elements of Human Sexuality and Sexual Orientation

1. Malcolm is a 24-year-old heterosexual. His 20-year-old brother, Morris, is homosexual. The brothers differ in their
   a. gender roles.
   b. gender identity.
   c. sexual orientation.
   d. gender schemas.

2. Because of testicular cancer, 25-year-old Arnie had to have his testicles removed. Research suggests that
   a. he will very likely become homosexual.
   b. he may experience a decreased interest in sexual activity.
   c. he is very unlikely to experience any change in his sexual interest.
   d. injections of testosterone will have absolutely no effect on his sex drive.

3. What conclusions can be drawn concerning biological factors and homosexuality?
   a. Biological differences in the hypothalamus cause homosexuality.
   b. Sexual orientation is completely determined by genetics.
   c. Homosexuality is caused by insufficient amounts of testosterone.
   d. Some biological factors are correlated with homosexual orientation.

4. Maxwell is a homosexual. It is likely that
   a. he experienced some early childhood sexual abuse by a female.
   b. his first sexual experience occurred in childhood with a male.
   c. his mother was overly domineering and his father was ineffectual and provided him with a poor masculine role model.
   d. his sexual orientation was determined before adolescence and before any sexual activity occurred.

Sexual Behavior over the Lifespan

Key Theme
■ Sexual development begins in infancy and childhood, although sexual maturation does not take place until adolescence.

Key Questions
■ How is sexuality expressed during childhood?
■ What takes place during puberty, and how does the timing of puberty affect behavior?
■ What characterizes the sexual relationships that develop in adolescence?

Perhaps because sexual behavior tends to be a private matter, it's understandable that people (psychologists included) are curious about what other people do—and don't do—sexually. The mass media tend to offer overheated images of people's sexual activity. If you believe the not-so-subtle media messages, everyone (except you) has such an active, steamy, and varied sex life that you can't help wondering how anyone (except you) ever finds the time to get their laundry done.

So, to prevent unnecessary despondency, let's deal with the "everybody's-sex-life-is-better-than-mine" issue at the beginning of this section. *Are* the media images accurate? Here's what sexual behavior expert Robert T. Michael and his colleagues (1994) have to say about the matter:

> The public image of sex in America bears virtually no relationship to the truth. The public image consists of myths, and they are not harmless, for they elicit unrealistic and at worst dangerous misconceptions about what people do sexually. These resulting false expectations can badly affect self-esteem, marriages, relationships, even physical health.

Possibly you recall Michael's name from Chapter 1. Michael, along with co-researcher Edward O. Laumann and their colleagues at the University of Chicago, conducted the *National Health and Social Life Survey (NHSLS)*—a state-of-the-art, scientifically constructed national survey of adult sexual behavior in the United States (Laumann & others, 1994; Laumann & Michael, 2001). In Chapter 1, we described how participants were randomly selected and how the research was conducted. Throughout this section, we'll rely on this landmark survey for help in accurately answering the "Who's doing what, when, how often, and with whom" questions about human sexuality.

As with other kinds of behavior, patterns of sexual behavior vary over the lifespan. So before we focus on the specifics of adolescent and adult sexuality, we'll start by looking at the emergence of sexuality during infancy and childhood.

Sexuality During Infancy and Childhood
Discovering the Basics

Sexuality does not just magically appear with the onset of puberty during adolescence. Rather, the capacity of the human body to show reflexive sexual responses is present at birth. For example, female newborns can reflexively experience vaginal lubrication, and newborn males can reflexively experience firm erections. Ultrasound studies have shown that male embryos in the womb can experience erections.

Infants commonly show reflexive signs of sexual activation while nursing or being bathed or diapered. Infants as young as three or four months of age will smile or coo as they engage in *genital play,* fondling their own genitals in a very elementary form of masturbation. By the first birthday, genital play is a common occurrence, especially when the baby is being bathed.

Signs of sexual activation or genital play should not cause alarm in parents, because such behaviors reflect completely *normal* developmental patterns. It's equally important to stress that infants or young children are *not* experiencing sexual arousal or expressing a desire for erotic contact. Rather, they have simply discovered, quite naturally, that such stimulation feels good.

During early childhood, roughly from age two to age six, children often become increasingly curious about their own body and its functions. Small children commonly explore their body parts while dressing or in the bathtub (W. Friedrich & others, 1998). Young children also become keenly attuned to parental attitudes, especially negative attitudes, concerning nudity, genital touching, and genital exploration. Gradually, young children begin to notice the anatomical differences between males and females.

Although some parents are psychologically uncomfortable with their children's emerging interest in their own bodies, human sexuality experts encourage parents to relax about such matters. For example, there's really no reason to become frantic because your four-year-old walks in when you're just stepping out of the shower. One study found that childhood exposure to occasional instances of parental nudity, such as when the parents were getting dressed, was not associated with later sexual problems (Lewis & Janda, 1988).

Just Friends? Interest in and affection for the opposite sex often begins in the early stages of adolescence. Because girls mature earlier than boys, they may be taller and heavier than boys of the same age.

The sexual behaviors that are most common among two- to five-year-olds are touching their own genitals, looking at people when they are nude or undressing, and touching or trying to touch adult women's breasts (W. Friedrich & others, 1998). Such overt sexual behaviors tend to drop off sharply after age five. However, awareness of sexual matters expands during middle and late childhood. With each advancing year from about the age of five onward, children tend to show increased interest in exploring sexual topics (Goldman & Goldman, 1982). By about age eight, most children are aware that certain behaviors produce erotic feelings. Sexual curiosity is on the rise during the late childhood years, setting the stage for the attainment of sexual maturity during adolescence.

Sexuality During Adolescence

Nature seems to have a warped sense of humor when it comes to **puberty,** the physical process of attaining sexual maturation and reproductive capacity that begins during the early adolescent years. First, as you may well remember, physical development during adolescence sometimes proceeds unevenly. Feet and hands get bigger before legs and arms do. The torso typically develops last, so shirts and blouses sometimes don't fit quite right. And the left and right sides of the body can grow at different rates. The resulting lopsided effect can be quite distressing: One ear, foot, testicle, or breast may be noticeably larger than the other. Thankfully, such asymmetries tend to even out by the end of adolescence.

Second, nature's timetable seems to be quite whimsical. While one adolescent boy has a baritone voice, is shaving, and looks as though he's ready to enlist in the Marines, another still sings soprano with the church choir and has less facial hair than the average cantaloupe. And because her best friend has been wearing a bra for almost a year, a female adolescent shuns her undershirts and hounds her mother for a "training" bra. Finally, nature literally gives girls a head start on puberty, which seems grossly unfair if you happen to be a sixth-grade boy who dwells much closer to ground level than your taller female classmates.

Physical and Sexual Development

Although nature's game plan for physical change during adolescence may seem haphazard, puberty actually tends to follow a predictable sequence for each sex. These changes are summarized in Table 10.2. Basically, the physical changes of puberty fall into two categories.

Internally, puberty involves the development of the **primary sex characteristics,** which are the sex organs that are directly involved in reproduction. For example, the female's uterus and the male's testes enlarge in puberty. Externally, development of the **secondary sex characteristics,** which are not directly involved in reproduction, signal increasing sexual maturity. Secondary sex characteristics include changes in height, weight, and body shape, the appearance of body hair and voice changes; and, in girls, breast development.

As you can see in Table 10.2, females are typically about two years ahead of males in terms of physical and sexual maturation. For example, the period of marked acceleration in weight and height gains, called the **adolescent growth spurt,** occurs about two years earlier in females than in males. Much to the chagrin of many sixth- and seventh-grade boys, it's not uncommon for their female classmates to be both heavier and taller than they are.

The statistical averages in Table 10.2 are informative, but—because they are only averages—they cannot convey the normal range of individual variation in the timing of pubertal events (Brooks-Gunn & Reiter, 1990). For example, a female's first menstrual period, termed **menarche,** typically occurs around age 12 or 13, but menarche may take place as early as age 9 or 10 or as late as age 16 or 17. For boys, the testicles typically begin enlarging around age 11 or 12, but the process can begin before age 9 or after age 14. Thus, it's

Girls Get a Head Start These two eighth-graders are the same age! In terms of the progress of sexual and physical maturation, girls are usually about two years ahead of boys.

Table **10.2**

The Typical Sequence of Puberty

Girls	Average Age	Boys	Average Age
Ovaries increase production of estrogen and progesterone	9	Testes increase production of testosterone	10
Internal sex organs begin to grow larger	9½	External sex organs begin to grow larger	11
Breast development begins	10	Production of sperm and first ejaculation	13
Peak height spurt	12	Peak height spurt	14
Peak muscle and organ growth, including widening of hips	12½	Peak muscle and organ growth, including broadening of shoulders	14½
Menarche (first menstrual period)	12½	Voice lowers	15
First ovulation (release of fertile egg)	13½	Facial hair appears	16

SOURCE: Based on data in Brooks-Gunn & Reiter (1990).

entirely possible for some adolescents to have already completed physical and sexual maturation before their classmates have even begun puberty. Yet they would all be considered well within the normal age range for puberty.

What determines when puberty will begin? Both genetics and environmental factors play a role in the timing of puberty. Girls often experience menarche at about the same age as their mothers did (Brooks-Gunn & Reiter, 1990). And, not surprisingly, the timing of pubertal changes tends to be closer for identical twins than for nontwin siblings.

Environmental factors, such as nutrition and health, also influence the onset of puberty. Generally, well-nourished and healthy children begin puberty earlier than do children who have experienced serious health problems or inadequate nutrition. As living standards and health care have improved, the average age of puberty has steadily decreased in the United States over the last century. For example, 150 years ago the average age of menarche in the United States was 16. Today it is about 12½ (Beal, 1994; Hamburg & Takanishi, 1989). In recent years, however, the trend toward earlier puberty seems to have slowed.

Body size and degree of physical activity are also related to the timing of puberty. In general, heavy children begin puberty earlier than do lean children. Girls who are involved in physically demanding athletic activities, such as gymnastics, figure skating, dancing, and competitive running, can experience delays in menarche of up to two years beyond the average age (Brooks-Gunn, 1988).

The Timing of Changes: Early Versus Late Maturation

Adolescents tend to be keenly aware of the physical changes they are experiencing as well as of the *timing* of those changes compared with their peer group. Most adolescents are "on time," meaning that the maturational changes are occurring at roughly the same time for them as for others in their peer group. But some adolescents are "off time," experiencing maturation earlier or later than the majority of their peers.

Being off time has different consequences for boys and for girls. For boys, early maturation is generally a plus. Compared with late-maturing boys, early-maturing boys tend to have the advantage in terms of popularity, social maturity, academic achievement, and athletics. However, early-maturing girls tend to be more likely than late-maturing girls to have negative feelings about their body image and pubertal changes, such as menarche. Compared to late-maturing girls,

puberty
The stage of adolescence in which an individual reaches sexual maturity and becomes physiologically capable of sexual reproduction.

primary sex characteristics
Sexual organs that are directly involved in reproduction, such as the uterus, ovaries, penis, and testicles.

secondary sex characteristics
Sexual characteristics that develop during puberty and are not directly involved in reproduction but differentiate between the sexes, such as male facial hair and female breast development.

adolescent growth spurt
The period of accelerated growth during puberty, involving rapid increases in height and weight.

menarche (meh-NAR-kee)
A female's first menstrual period, which occurs during puberty.

early-maturing girls are less likely to have received factual information concerning development. They may also feel embarrassed by unwanted attention from older males (Brooks-Gunn & Reiter, 1990). The positive or negative effects associated with early or late maturation are largely temporary. Eventually, of course, the late maturers catch up with the early maturers. By late adolescence, the individual physical differences in maturation that seemed so noticeable in the sixth or seventh grade have mostly evened out.

The Emergence of Sexual Relationships

Romantic and sexual relationships become increasingly important throughout the adolescent years. During early and middle adolescence, the physical changes of puberty prime the adolescent's interest in sexuality. But social and cultural factors also influence when, why, and how an adolescent initiates sexual behaviors (Brooks-Gunn & Furstenberg, 1989; Katchadourian, 1990). The beginning of dating, for example, coincides more strongly with social expectations and norms, such as when friends begin to date, than with an adolescent's degree of physical maturation.

Generally, age is a good predictor of when teenagers typically begin various sexual behaviors. With increasing age, there is a corresponding increase in the number of adolescents who have engaged in such sexual activities as kissing or petting (Buhrmester & Furman, 1987; Katchadourian, 1990). The number of adolescents who have experienced sexual intercourse also corresponds closely to age (Joyner & Laumann, 2001). Between the ages of 15 and 18, there is a sharp increase in the cumulative percentages of those who have had intercourse. Although the figure varies somewhat by race and gender, by age 19 approximately 70 percent of females and 80 percent of males have lost their virginity.

It's often assumed that parents play a key role in the sexual socialization of their adolescent children, but there is usually little direct communication between parents and children regarding sexual matters (Katchadourian, 1990). Fathers, in particular, are not very likely to be involved in the sexual education of their children. When parents do respond to their children's questions about sexuality and reproduction, it is usually on a single occasion rather than as part of a continuing discussion about sexuality.

It's not very surprising, then, that an adolescent's peer group gradually replaces his or her family as a source of sexual information (and misinformation), attitudes, and values (Katchadourian, 1990). For example, one study found that adolescents were just as likely to consult parents as peers about contraceptives. But on questions about sexual behavior, such as masturbation or homosexuality, peers were identified as the preferred source of information twice as often as parents (Coles & Stokes, 1985).

Looking for Mr. or Ms. Right Although people today are marrying at a later average age than they did in previous generations, most young adults are involved in an intimate, long-term relationship by the time they reach their late twenties. People are most likely to form an intimate relationship with someone who is similar to them and who is part of their existing social network (Michael & others, 1994).

Sexuality in Early and Middle Adulthood

Key Theme

■ Intimate, committed relationships are typically established during early adulthood, but they remain important throughout the lifespan.

Key Questions

■ What characterizes the sexual behavior patterns of adulthood?
■ What are some important aspects of sexual relationships in late adulthood?

For most Americans, the onset of adulthood marks a commitment to the task of establishing long-term, intimate relationships. During their twenties, most men and women develop an intimate relationship with another adult. By the age of 30, most Americans are part of a couple—either married or living with someone (Laumann & Youm, 2001).

focus on Neuroscience

Feelings of euphoria are just one of the many sensations, thoughts, and emotions that accompany moments of impassioned, romantic love. As is shown in the fMRI scan, romantic love also produces a unique pattern of activation in the brain.

Romantic Love and the Brain When it comes to love, it's been said that the brain is the most erotic organ in your body. Indeed, being head over heels in love is an emotionally intoxicating brain state. Do the overpowering feelings of romantic love involve a unique pattern of brain activity?

Using functional magnetic resonance imaging (fMRI) to detect brain activity, researchers Andreas Bartels and Semir Zeki (2000) investigated that idea with 17 love-struck young adults, all professing to be "truly, deeply, madly in love" with their romantic partner. Each participant was scanned several times while gazing at a photo of the romantic partner. Alternating with the "love" scans were "friendship" scans taken while the participant looked at a photo of a good friend who was of the same sex as the loved one.

Bartels and Zeki's (2000) results suggest that romantic love activates brain areas that are involved in other positive emotions, such as happiness, but in a way that represents a unique pattern. Shown here is a side-to-side fMRI brain scan depicting some of the brain areas activated by romantic love. Compared to looking at a photo of a close friend, looking at a photo of one's romantic partner produced heightened activity in four brain areas associated with emotion, including the *anterior cingulate cortex* (not shown), *caudate nucleus* (C), *putamen* (P), and *insula* (I).

Given the complexity of the sentiment of romantic love, the researchers were surprised that the brain areas activated were so small and limited to so few regions. (Perhaps this lack of extensive brain activation explains why love-struck individuals are sometimes oblivious to everything except the object of their infatuation.) Nonetheless, the four activated brain areas offer some insight into the intoxicating effects of romantic love. Why? Because these are the same brain areas that are activated in response to euphoria-producing drugs, such as opiates and cocaine. Clearly, there seem to be some close neural links between romantic love and euphoric states.

The NHSLS generated a mountain of data on the sexual practices of American adults between the ages of 18 and 59 (Laumann & Michael, 2001). Our discussion is necessarily brief. We'll confine it to the NHSLS findings on several key questions about the sexual practices of American adults. In doing so, we hope to dispel some of the media-manufactured myths about adult sexual behavior.

How Many Sex Partners Do People Have?

The notion that people today, especially younger people, have more sex partners than people did 20 or 30 years ago is fundamentally accurate. Among people aged 30 to 50, about half have had five or more sexual partners. In contrast, only about a third of those over age 50 have had five or more sexual partners (Laumann & others, 1994).

Why the difference between age groups in the number of sexual partners? The vast majority of adults in the 50-to-59 age range had their first sexual experience in the context of marriage. In contrast, only about a third of today's young adults had their first sexual experience in the context of marriage (Michael & others, 1994). Young adults today tend to become sexually active at an earlier age and are marrying at a later average age. Hence, younger people today tend to have more sexual partners than members of older generations.

Table | 10.3

Number of Sex Partners During the Previous Year

	0	1	2–4	5+
Total	12%	71%	14%	3%
By Gender				
Men	10	67	18	5
Women	14	75	10	2
By Age				
18–24	11	57	24	9
25–29	6	72	17	6
30–34	9	73	16	2
35–39	10	77	11	2
40–44	11	75	13	1
45–49	15	75	9	1
50–54	15	79	5	0
55–59	32	65	4	0

SOURCE: Adapted from data in Michael & others (1994), Table 6, pp. 102–103.

In this table, you can see that regardless of age or gender, about 80 percent of the people reported having had one or no sexual partners during the previous year.

Intimacy, Love, and Sexuality in Adulthood
Forming a long-term, committed relationship with another person is a key task of early adulthood. For many couples, the bonds of love and intimacy established in early adulthood last a lifetime.

Now consider a slightly different issue, the number of sexual partners in the past year. The majority of people—about 80 percent—had either *one* sexual partner or *none* in the previous year (see Table 10.3). Why so few sexual partners in the last year? In a word, marriage. Marriage continues to be a cornerstone of American society as well as a major developmental milestone for most people on the trek through adulthood. As people become adults, they experience considerable social pressure to find a partner and marry. Doing so confers numerous benefits, not the least of which is the social, legal, and moral acceptance of the sexual partnership.

By the age of 30, about 90 percent of Americans have married. Regardless of age or number of previous partners, once most couples marry or start cohabiting, they feel strongly committed to being faithful to each other. As Michael and his colleagues (1994) explained:

> Marriage regulates sexual behavior with remarkable precision. No matter what they did before they wed, no matter how many partners they had, the sexual lives of married people are similar. Despite the popular myth that there is a great deal of adultery in marriage, our data and other reliable studies do not find it. Instead, the vast majority are faithful while the marriage is intact.

How Often Do People Have Sex?

Perhaps the widest disparity between the media images and the NHSLS results involves the issue of how often people have sex. Put simply, the media images that frequent, frolicking sex is "normal" do not reflect what is going on in U.S. bedrooms.

Here's what the NHSLS found. One-third of American adults have sex with a partner two or more times per week; one-third have sex a few times per month; and one-third have sex a few times a year or not at all. When the data are combined for all adults between ages 18 and 59, men have sex an average of about seven times per month, and women have sex an average of about six times per month (Laumann & others, 1994; Laumann & Youm, 2001). So, any way you look at it, the most frequent activity in America's bedrooms is sleep, not sex.

Which Americans have the most active sex lives? Those young, attractive, footloose, swinging singles, right? Wrong. The fact is that married or cohabiting couples have the most active sex lives (Laumann & Youm, 2001). If you think about it, this finding makes sense. Sexual activity is strongly regulated by the availability of a sex partner. Being a member of a stable couple is the social arrangement most likely to produce a readily accessible sexual partner.

Are people happy with their sex lives? The vast majority of the NHSLS respondents—about 85 percent—reported that they were physically and emotionally satisfied with their sexual relationships (Laumann & others, 1994). A higher proportion of married men and women than of single or cohabiting men and women reported being extremely emotionally satisfied with their sexual relationships (Waite & Joyner, 2001). Part of the explanation for this high percentage is that in today's society there is considerably less social pressure to endure an unhappy marriage "until death do you part" than there used to be. Hence, those who are sexually dissatisfied with their relationship are likely to separate or get divorced—and try again with someone else. The net result is that most Americans are happily married or cohabiting.

What Do People *Actually* Do When They Have Sex?

Vaginal intercourse is nearly universal as the most widely practiced sexual activity among heterosexual couples (Laumann & others, 1994). What about other practices? More than two-thirds of Americans have either given or received *oral sex* at some point in their lives. Fewer men (26 percent) and women (20 percent) have ever engaged in *anal* sex (that is, a penis inserted in the partner's anus).

What Would People *Like* to Do Sexually?

Given that most Americans seem to be having pretty traditional sex, you may be wondering whether they'd like to be a little more adventurous. After all, researchers have found that people do have sexual fantasies about a wide range of activities (see In Focus Box 10.4 on page 438). So what do most people find appealing, and is that any different from what they actually do?

Although the list of potential sexual practices is varied, people prefer to stick with the tried and true. In descending order for both sexes, the most preferred sexual activities are (1) having vaginal intercourse; (2) watching the partner undress; (3) receiving oral sex; and (4) giving oral sex.

In some ways, the flip side of the coin is more revealing. What do people find *un*appealing? Regardless of age, at least 90 percent of women found no appeal in (1) being forced to do something sexual; (2) forcing someone to do something sexual; (3) receiving anal intercourse; (4) having a same-gender sex partner; and (5) having sex with a stranger. With the exception of sex with a stranger, at least 90 percent of men also found these sexual practices unappealing. Other sexual practices that the majority of people do not find appealing include having group sex, using a vibrator or dildo (an object used as a substitute for an erect penis), and watching other people engage in sexual activity (Michael & others, 1994).

In real life, the unheralded, seldom discussed world of married sex is actually the one that satisfies people the most. It may not be an exciting picture of sex in America, but if we look at the social forces that push us toward married life, it is an understandable, if not predicted, picture.

Robert T. Michael (1994)

Sexuality in Late Adulthood

The notion that sexual interest and potency disappear the day you become eligible for Medicare is a far cry from reality. In a recent survey of older Americans, nearly half reported that they engage in sexual activity at least once a month. The survey also found that about 40 percent of the respondents wanted to have sex more often than they currently do (National Council on Aging, 1998).

Even though there does not appear to be an upper age limit to sexuality, aging does have some effects on sexual behavior. Older men and women take longer to become sexually aroused and achieve orgasm. For women, vaginal lubrication typically occurs more slowly,

Sexuality in Late Adulthood Sexual interest and activity are important dimensions of the lives of many senior adults. In a recent survey of older Americans, nearly half reported that they engage in sexual activity at least once a month. The survey also found that more than 70 percent of sexually active seniors said they were as satisfied or more satisfied with their sex lives compared to when they were in their forties (National Council on Aging, 1998, 2000).

Everything You Wanted to Know About Sexual Fantasies

The brain is the most erotic organ in the human body. After all, the brain plays a pivotal role in the expression of human sexuality. What people think about and imagine influences how they behave sexually. And, in turn, people's sexual behavior can influence the content of their *sexual fantasies*—erotic or sexually arousing mental images (Leitenberg & Henning, 1995). In the realm of human sexuality, the mind–body connection is definitely a two-way street.

We experience sexual fantasies in the private theater of our own minds, but psychologists have discovered that sexual fantasies are a nearly universal human phenomenon. Using checklists and questionnaires, researchers have been able to answer various questions about people's sexual fantasies. In this box, with the help of an excellent research summary by University of Vermont psychologists Harold Leitenberg and Kris Henning (1995), we tackle some of the most intriguing questions about this private human experience.

When and How Often Do People Have Sexual Fantasies?

Sexual fantasies tend to begin during the adolescent years, and almost all adult men and women (95 percent) report having had sexual daydreams. It is very common for both men and women occasionally to engage in sexual fantasies during intercourse. But compared to women, men report a higher incidence of sexual fantasies during masturbation and nonsexual activities. In short, men tend to think about sex more often than do women.

What Do People Have Sexual Fantasies About?

If you accept the notion that any fantasy, sexual or not, is based to some degree on life experiences, the three most common types of sexual fantasies that men and women have won't surprise you. They are (1) reliving an exciting sexual experience; (2) imagining that you are having sex with your current partner; and (3) imagining that you are having sex with a different partner.

Do Male and Female Sexual Fantasies Differ?

There are some well-substantiated differences. First, men tend to fantasize themselves in active roles—that is, doing something sexual to their partner. In contrast, women tend to imagine themselves in sexually passive roles—that is, having something sexual done to them.

Second, men tend to have sexual fantasies with more explicit imagery, often involving specific sexual positions or anatomical details. Women are more likely to imagine romantic themes, including warm, loving feelings about their partner and details about the romantic ambiance of the scene.

Third, men are more likely to imagine having sex with multiple partners. As Leitenberg and Henning (1995) put it, "Fantasizing about having sex with multiple partners at the same time appears to be more consonant with the male stereotype of being a 'superstud' than with the female stereotype of wanting a close, loving, monogamous relationship."

Are Sexual Fantasies Psychologically Unhealthy? Are They a Sign of Sexual Frustration or Dissatisfaction?

In a word, no. The people who engage in sexual fantasies most often tend to exhibit the *least* number of sexual problems and the *lowest* level of sexual dissatisfaction.

Nonetheless, some people are troubled by their sexual fantasies. About 25 percent of people experience some degree of guilt over having sexual fantasies. This guilt is usually due to the belief that their sexual fantasies are immoral, are harmful to their relationships, or indicate that something is wrong with them.

What About Sexual Fantasies of "Dominance" or "Submission"?

Men are more likely to fantasize dominance themes (forcing someone to do something sexual), whereas women are more likely to report submission themes (being forced to do something sexual). However, it's important to stress that while a woman might find submission fantasies sexually arousing, this does *not* indicate a desire to *actually* be forced into

sexual submission, much less assaulted or raped (Bond & Mosher, 1986; Kanin, 1982). As we note in the chapter, almost no women or men find appealing the idea of actually being forced to do something sexual or actually forcing someone to do something sexual (Michael & others, 1994). Unlike fantasy women, when real women say "no," they *mean* "no."

Isn't This a Contradiction?

Not really. First, any kind of fantasy, whether it's sexual or not, allows us to imagine possibilities that may have little probability of occurring. Fantasy provides you with your own internal, private, improvisational theater. As the lead character, director, and set designer, you control the plot, action, and dialogue without taking any *real* risks.

Given that, let's go back to the issue of female submission fantasies. The typical female submission fantasy is *not* one of being brutally forced to do something against the woman's will. Instead, as researchers Susan Bond and Donald Mosher (1986) pointed out, the typical female submission fantasy is one of an attractive man being overwhelmed by the woman's irresistible charms as she puts up a minimal effort to resist his sexual advances. Does this fantasy sound the least bit familiar? It should. It is a standard sexual fantasy that has been played out in many romantic novels and movies. Such fantasies have *nothing* in common with mental or actual scenes of nonconsensual sex, unwanted sexual advances, or brutal rape.

sometimes necessitating the use of lubricants during intercourse. For men, erections tend to be less firm, and longer refractory periods follow orgasm. Despite these physical changes, the majority of sexually active senior adults report a high level of sexual enjoyment (Brecher, 1984).

For older women, probably the biggest obstacle to enjoying sexual relations throughout old age is the lack of a sexual partner. At age 60, there are 89 men for every 100 women. By age 75, the ratio is down to 68 men per 100 women (U.S. Census Bureau, 2001). Thus, the number of people with no sexual partner steadily climbs as people get older (Michael & others, 1994).

Many people who have lost their spouse through death or divorce continue to date as they grow older. Older men date more often than older women, mostly because they have a larger pool of potential dating partners. Dating serves a different function in late adulthood than in early adulthood. For young adults, dating is part of the process of selecting a mate. For older adults, dating fills the need for companionship and sexual intimacy. Many older adults have a serious relationship with a single, special dating partner but have no intention of remarrying (Bulcroft & Bulcroft, 1991). In late adulthood, dating helps prevent loneliness and can meet the need for physical and emotional intimacy that continues throughout the lifespan.

Sexual Disorders and Problems

Key Theme
▪ Sexual dysfunctions are consistent disturbances in desire, arousal, or orgasm that cause psychological distress.

Key Questions
▪ How prevalent are sexual problems, and who is most likely to experience them?
▪ What are the paraphilias and gender identity disorder?
▪ What are sexually transmitted diseases, and what characterizes the AIDS epidemic today?

Almost everyone experiences an occasional glitch in responding sexually, such as failing to feel sexually aroused on a particular occasion. What can cause this to happen? There are a number of rather ordinary reasons. You might be feeling tired or grumpy with your sexual partner. Anxiety, including anxiety over your sexual performance, can also interfere with sexual functioning. Drinking too much alcohol can disrupt the ability to achieve sexual arousal or orgasm. And, of course, it's possible that your well-intentioned partner is doing something that you don't find sexually stimulating, as in "Let's just skip the whipped cream next time, okay?"

For most people, such disruptions in sexual response are temporary. In contrast, some people experience persistent sexual problems, or sexual dysfunctions. **Sexual dysfunctions** are consistent disturbances in sexual desire, arousal, or orgasm that cause psychological distress and interpersonal difficulties (American Psychiatric Association, 2000a).

How Common Are Sexual Problems?

Until very recently, researchers did not have reliable data on the prevalence of many sexual dysfunctions. This situation changed, however, with the publication of additional results from the National Health and Social Life Survey—the same survey that provided information about the sexual practices of Americans. After

sexual dysfunction
A consistent disturbance in sexual desire, arousal, or orgasm that causes psychological distress and interpersonal difficulties.

analyzing the data, Edward Laumann and his colleagues (1999, 2001) found that the incidence of sexual dysfunction among adult Americans was much higher than previously believed: 43 percent of women and 31 percent of men suffered from sexual problems.

For women, the most common sexual problems were low sexual desire and arousal problems, including the inability to achieve orgasm. For men, the most common sexual problems were premature ejaculation and problems achieving or maintaining an erection. Overall, married and college-educated men and women had a much lower incidence of sexual problems than unmarried people or people with less education.

One interesting finding was that sexual problems were most common among young women and men older than age 50. The older men tended to report sexual problems related to the aging process: erection difficulties and lack of interest in sex. But what about the younger women? According to Laumann and his colleagues (1999), "Since young women are more likely to be single, their sexual activities involve higher rates of partner turnover as well as periodic spells of sexual inactivity. This instability, coupled with inexperience, generates stressful sexual encounters, providing the basis for sexual pain and anxiety."

The researchers also note that in women, sexual problems *declined* with age, except for problems with lubrication, which tended to increase after age 50. Finally, Laumann and his colleagues (2001) found that stress and emotional problems were associated with sexual difficulties. And, especially for women, sexual problems tended to produce unhappiness and emotional distress.

Categories of Sexual Dysfunctions

Either men or women can experience psychological distress or interpersonal difficulties caused by having little or no sexual desire, a condition called **hypoactive sexual desire disorder.** Keep in mind that the frequency with which people want to have sex varies over the lifespan and according to personal preference. In some instances, what seems like "low desire" in one partner may actually reflect "high desire" in the other partner. More extreme is **sexual aversion disorder,** in which a person actively avoids genital contact with a sexual partner because of extreme anxiety, fear, or disgust over sexual contact. Both men and women can experience chronic genital pain before, during, or after intercourse, a condition called **dyspareunia.**

Some sexual dysfunctions can be experienced by men only or women only. When a man experiences a recurrent inability to achieve or maintain an erection, it's called **male erectile disorder.** At the opposite extreme, an erect male may experience recurring delays or a complete absence of the ability to achieve orgasm through intercourse, a condition called **male orgasmic disorder.** Although the man may not be able to achieve orgasm during intercourse, he may be able to do so through other means, such as by being manually or orally stimulated by his partner. A man may experience considerable stress over recurrent episodes of **premature ejaculation,** in which he reaches sexual climax too soon, often immediately before or shortly after penetration.

When a female experiences distress over consistent delays in achieving orgasm or the complete inability to achieve orgasm, it's called **female orgasmic disorder.** Women can also experience a condition called **vaginismus**—the persistent, involuntary contraction of the vaginal muscles, resulting in uncomfortable or painful intercourse. In severe cases, the vaginal muscle spasms may be so severe as to prevent penetration (American Psychiatric Association, 2000a).

What causes such sexual dysfunctions? Some sexual dysfunctions, such as male erectile disorder, may be the result of a physical or medical condition. In the case of male erectile disorder, two of the most prominent causes are diabetes and alcoholism. Other sexual dysfunctions, such as premature ejaculation and vagin-

hypoactive sexual desire disorder
A sexual dysfunction characterized by little or no sexual desire.

sexual aversion disorder
A sexual dysfunction characterized by active avoidance of genital sexual contact because of extreme anxiety, fear, or disgust.

dyspareunia
A sexual dysfunction characterized by genital pain before, during, or after intercourse.

male erectile disorder
In males, sexual dysfunction characterized by a recurring inability to achieve or maintain an erect penis.

male orgasmic disorder
In males, sexual dysfunction characterized by delayed orgasm during intercourse or the inability to achieve orgasm during intercourse.

premature ejaculation
In males, sexual dysfunction characterized by orgasm occurring before it is desired, often immediately or shortly after sexual stimulation or penetration.

female orgasmic disorder
In females, sexual dysfunction characterized by consistent delays in achieving orgasm or the inability to achieve orgasm.

vaginismus
Sexual dysfunction characterized by persistent, involuntary contractions or spasms of the vaginal muscles, which result in uncomfortable or painful intercourse.

ismus, are more often the result of psychological factors than organic factors. Such psychological factors might include anxiety about sex or the association of pain with early sexual experiences. Fortunately, many sexual dysfunctions can be successfully treated by psychologists and physicians who have received specialized training in sex therapy.

The Paraphilias
Unusual Sexual Fantasies, Urges, or Behaviors

When a person's sexual gratification is highly or completely dependent on fantasies, urges, or behaviors that fall outside the socially accepted range of sexual behavior, the person is said to have a **paraphilia.** Such fantasies, urges, and behaviors may involve suffering or humiliation, children, another nonconsenting adult, or nonhuman objects (American Psychiatric Association, 2000). In general, the paraphilias are much more common among men than among women.

Exactly what kinds of fantasies, urges, or behaviors are we talking about? Here are brief descriptions of the most common paraphilias:

- *Exhibitionism*—sexual arousal achieved by exposing one's genitals to shocked strangers
- *Frotteurism*—sexual arousal from touching and rubbing against a nonconsenting person, usually in a crowded public situation, such as a crowded bus or subway car
- *Fetishism*—sexual arousal in response to inanimate objects (e.g., female undergarments, shoes, leather) or body parts that are not typically associated with sexual arousal (e.g., feet, hair, legs)
- *Transvestic fetishism*—in heterosexual males, sexual arousal from cross-dressing in women's clothes
- *Pedophilia*—sexual fantasies, urges, or behavior involving sexual activity with a prepubescent child (generally age 13 or younger)
- *Voyeurism*—sexual arousal from observing an unsuspecting person who is disrobing, naked, or engaged in sexual activity
- *Sexual sadism*—sexual arousal achieved through intentionally inflicting psychological or physical suffering on another person
- *Sexual masochism*—sexual arousal in response to actually being humiliated, beaten, bound, or otherwise made to suffer

Unlike the person with a sexual dysfunction, the person who has a paraphilia is often not psychologically distressed by it. Rather, these individuals typically come to the attention of mental health professionals only when their behavior has created a conflict with their sexual partner, has been discovered by a family member or coworker, or has resulted in arrest (American Psychiatric Association, 2000). Some paraphilias, such as pedophilia and voyeurism, are illegal.

What causes a particular paraphilia to develop? Theories involving biological and psychological causes exist, but there are no solid answers. The exact causes of paraphilias remain obscure.

Gender Identity Disorder
Feeling Trapped in the Wrong Body

As we noted at the beginning of the chapter, our sense of being male or female is referred to as our *gender identity*. When a person expresses persistent discomfort about his or her assigned gender, and repeatedly expresses a desire to be a member of the opposite sex, the person is said to have **gender identity disorder** (formerly called *transsexualism*).

paraphilia
(pair-uh-FILL-ee-uh) Any of several forms of nontraditional sexual behavior in which a person's sexual gratification depends on an unusual sexual experience, object, or fantasy.

gender identity disorder
A persistent discomfort about one's assigned gender along with the desire to be a member of the opposite sex.

Self-Portrait by Photographer Loren Cameron Not all transsexuals feel that the desire to change sex is an illness, and some protest labeling transsexualism as a psychological disorder (Stryker, 1996). Loren Cameron, shown here, documented his own transformation from female to male. One of his goals was to communicate his sense of pride and satisfaction about his transformation: "It takes a lot of guts to acknowledge how uncomfortable you are before the transition, and to willfully accept the challenge of re-creating yourself."

When it occurs in children, gender identity disorder is marked by an intense preoccupation with the play activities, games, and toys traditionally associated with the opposite sex. Rather than playing with same-sex playmates, the child expresses a strong desire to play with and dress like opposite-sex playmates. A boy may repeatedly voice the desire to be a girl, even insisting that he will grow up to be a woman. During the teenage years, he may exhibit other kinds of cross-gender behaviors, such as shaving his legs.

Adults with gender identity disorder are extremely uncomfortable about being regarded as a member of their assigned gender. In private, they may cross-dress and display mannerisms typical of the opposite sex. Some may do so publicly as well (American Psychiatric Association, 2000a). Often, they resort to hormone treatments or surgical interventions, such as the surgical reduction of the Adam's apple in males, to appear more like the opposite sex. In some cases, they undergo *sex-reassignment surgery,* in which the existing genitalia are removed and the genitals of the opposite sex are surgically constructed. Although male-to-female surgery can result in a functional and authentic-looking vagina, the female-to-male surgery results in an artificial penis that cannot spontaneously become erect. Nonetheless, with an inflatable penile implant, artificial erections are often possible, although ejaculation cannot occur.

Sexually Transmitted Diseases

No discussion of human sexuality would be complete without noting the dangers of **sexually transmitted diseases,** abbreviated **STDs.** An estimated 12 million cases of STDs are diagnosed annually in the United States. About two-thirds, or roughly 8 million, of those cases are among people under the age of 25 (Centers for Disease Control and Prevention, 1998d).

Transmitted primarily through sexual contact, STDs include bacterial, viral, and parasitic infections (see Table 10.4). Bacterial STDs include *gonorrhea, syphilis,* and *chlamydia. Pubic lice* is an example of a parasitic STD. Both bacterial and parasitic STDs can be cured with appropriate treatments, such as antibiotic medications or antiparasitic shampoos. In contrast, viral sexually transmitted diseases, such as *herpes* and *AIDS,* cannot be cured. However, their symptoms can often be reduced with treatment.

Left untreated, many STDs can eventually create significant health problems. This is especially troubling because it is completely possible for a person to be unaware that he or she is infected with an STD. For example, *chlamydia* often does not produce symptoms but can still damage reproductive organs if left untreated. Equally troubling is the fact that an infected person can unknowingly pass on an STD to sexual partners.

The AIDS Epidemic

AIDS, or **acquired immune deficiency syndrome,** is a disease caused when the *human immunodeficiency virus* (HIV) enters the bloodstream through the exchange of infected bodily fluids, primarily semen, blood, and blood products. Once a person is infected, the HIV virus can exist in his or her body for a decade or

sexually transmitted diseases (STDs)
Any of several infectious diseases that are transmitted primarily through sexual intercourse or other intimate sexual contact.

AIDS (acquired immune deficiency syndrome)
A disease caused by the exchange of bodily fluids (semen, blood, or blood products) containing the human immunodeficiency virus (HIV), which attacks and weakens the immune system.

Table | 10.4

Summary of Major Sexually Transmitted Diseases

STD	Symptoms
Bacterial	
Gonorrhea	*Men:* yellowish penile discharge; burning or painful urination
	Women: often no early symptoms; vaginal discharge; burning or painful urination
Syphilis	Painless chancre, or sore; swollen lymph nodes
Chlamydia	*Men:* many are symptom-free; burning or painful urination
	Women: most are symptom-free; painful urination and vaginal discharge
Parasitic	
Pubic lice	Intense itching in pubic area
Viral	
Genital herpes	Painful blisters on or inside the genitals; sometimes accompanied by fever, swollen lymph nodes, bodily aches and pains
AIDS (acquired immune deficiency syndrome)	Initial HIV infection may be accompanied by mild flulike symptoms; HIV virus can be dormant for years; AIDS is characterized by severe weight loss and increased susceptibility to other diseases and infections

longer without causing any apparent symptoms. In other words, the infected person can look and feel perfectly healthy. Nonetheless, the person is an HIV carrier and can infect others.

When the virus becomes active, it selectively attacks a key component of the body's immune system: the *helper T cells.* As you'll see in Chapter 13, on stress and health, helper T cells mobilize other immune system cells to fight off diseases and infections. As the HIV virus weakens the immune system, the person becomes greatly susceptible to other diseases, including cancer, pneumonia, and encephalitis (inflammation of the brain and spinal cord). Eventually, the immune system becomes so weakened that the person succumbs to some opportunistic infection that overwhelms the body (Kalichman, 1998).

Increasing AIDS Awareness Benefits, concerts, and fundraising events, such as the annual Boston to New York AIDS ride, have increased public awareness of the AIDS epidemic.

Gay men, intravenous drug users who share contaminated needles, and people with multiple sex partners are the groups most at risk of becoming infected by HIV in the United States. Other risk factors include being infected with another sexually transmitted disease. Some STDs cause genital sores that can make it easier for the HIV virus to enter the body. But even if no visible lesions are present, infection with another STD can increase the risk of HIV transmission because the STD stimulates an immune response in the genital area that makes infection more likely (Centers for Disease Control and Prevention, 1998a, 1998f).

No one is immune to HIV. Among the various methods of HIV infection, heterosexual transmission is the fastest-growing category. Heterosexual contact now accounts for approximately 10 percent of the AIDS cases in the United States. Some women are infected by HIV through injection drug use, but most women are infected through sexual contact with HIV-positive men.

Cases of AIDS among U.S. women have been steadily rising. In 1985, women made up only about 7 percent of those stricken with AIDS. By 1997, that proportion had more than tripled to 22 percent. And while the HIV infection rate has decreased among men in the last few years, it has increased among women. AIDS is now the fourth leading cause of death among women aged 25 to 44. Among women, African-American and Hispanic women account for about three-quarters of the AIDS cases reported (Centers for Disease Control and Prevention, 1998b, 1998c, 1998e).

Young women under the age of 25, including young adolescent women, are at a higher risk for HIV infection as well as infection by other STDs than are older women. The reason? Younger women tend to have more sexual partners, are more likely to engage in risky behaviors, and may be less able to negotiate safer sexual practices with their partners than older women (Centers for Disease Control and Prevention, 1998d).

Although there is no cure for AIDS yet, there is considerable reason for hope. Among the first compounds found to be effective against HIV was the drug *AZT*. By disrupting an early stage of the HIV life cycle, AZT and similar compounds slow the progression of the disease. Newer antiviral drugs, called *protease inhibitors,* interfere with the last stage of HIV's reproductive cycle.

Combinations of three or more anti-AIDS drugs, called "drug cocktails," have improved both the quality and duration of life for those infected with HIV. However, the combination drug treatments have many side effects, are complicated to administer, and are expensive. HIV patients may take up to 20 pills a day according to a complicated dosing schedule, and the cost typically exceeds $1,000 per month.

Because of new drug treatments, the death rate from AIDS has sharply decreased in the United States and other industrialized countries. However, the story is very different in the developing world, where the costly drug-treatment programs are not available. In some areas of Africa, infection rates are extremely high. In the African nations of Botswana and Zimbabwe, for example, approximately 25 percent of the adults are infected with HIV. HIV infection rates are also increasing dramatically in Asia and eastern Europe. Worldwide, more than 30 million people are currently living with HIV and AIDS (World Health Organization, 1998).

There are steps that any person can and should take to reduce the likelihood of getting a sexually transmitted disease, such as using condoms and spermicides. Equally important is not engaging in high-risk sexual activity, such as anal sex, with new sexual partners. Unfortunately, despite widespread public awareness of the dangers, engaging in risky, unprotected sexual behavior remains common (Centers for Disease Control and Prevention, 1999; Fisher & others, 1995).

10.3 R·E·V·I·E·W

CONCEPT

Sexual Development and Sexual Behavior

Indicate whether each of the following statements is true or false. If a statement is false, correct it.

_____ 1. According to NHSLS data, single adults aged 20 to 25 have the most satisfying sex lives.

_____ 2. Breast development in girls and facial hair in boys are examples of primary sex characteristics.

_____ 3. A girl's first menstrual period is called menarche.

_____ 4. Sexual problems are most common among young adult women and men over the age of 50.

_____ 5. Paraphilias are more common among women than men.

_____ 6. According to NHSLS data, about 80 percent of U.S. adults had one or no sexual partner in the past year.

_____ 7. Early maturation tends to be psychologically advantageous for girls but not for boys.

_____ 8. On the average, the adolescent growth spurt occurs at age 12 in boys and age 10 in girls.

Summing Up
Gender and Sexuality

From birth, each of us is profoundly influenced by the biological, social, cultural, and psychological forces that shape our gender identity and expression of sexuality. As you've seen in this chapter, a person's gender identity is firmly entrenched by late childhood and adolescence.

Throughout adulthood, the expression of sexuality centers on stable interpersonal relationships that are based not only on physical intimacy but also on emotional and psychological intimacy. Even in old age, the need for physical, emotional, and psychological intimacy remains strong.

Over the course of life, much of who we are is defined by our gender and sexual identity. Often without our awareness, that identity shapes the activities we are drawn to, the relationships we form, and how we react in many situations. Most people develop a conventional sense of gender identity and sexual orientation and form sexual relationships that follow the predominant patterns endorsed by society. But other people, like our friend Richard, are faced with the challenge of accepting themselves in a society that is often not very tolerant of sexual difference.

We hope that in reading this chapter, you've developed not only a greater appreciation of your own gender and sexual identity but also a better understanding of people whose gender identity or sexual orientation is different from your own. In the chapter Application, we'll provide suggestions for overcoming gender differences that can interfere with the resolution of conflicts in intimate relationships.

"What's bothering you?"

"Me? Nothing. Why do you ask?"

"You've got that look on your face."

"What look?!"

"You know—that I'm-mad-as-hell-and-don't-talk-to-me look."

"Just leave me alone, okay? What do you want to start a fight for?"

"Who's starting a fight? I'm *not* trying to start a fight. I just want to know what's wrong."

"Did I say there was anything wrong? There's nothing wrong. Can't I just sit here and read the paper without being hassled to death?"

"I'm not trying to hassle you! I'm just trying to figure out what you're . . ."

"Did you hear what I said? Just leave me alone!"

"Yeah, but if you're mad about something, then maybe we should . . ."

"Damn it! You just keep badgering me! *Just leave me alone!*" (Throws paper aside, gets up, and storms out, slamming door.)

Can you identify which is the male and which is the female speaker in this exchange? That's probably not a tough question. As we noted earlier in the chapter, women tend to be more comfortable about expressing their emotions than men. Beyond this basic difference, researchers have found that men and women communicate very differently, especially when they are trying to deal with problems, emotional issues, and interpersonal conflicts (Brehm, 1992; Kalbfleisch & Cody, 1995; Tannen, 1990). In this Application, we will look at some of those communication differences and consider how couples can learn to overcome them.

Conflict in Intimate Relationships

Being able to handle interpersonal conflict is important in any relationship, but especially in marriage. The demands and hassles of sharing and maintaining a household make occasional conflict in marriage virtually inevitable (Stafford & Dainton, 1994). Despite what many people think, the happiest marriages are not conflict-free. Instead, as psychologist John Gottman (1994) has discovered, conflict plays a key role in marital happiness and stability.

Gottman has intensively studied hundreds of married couples over the last 20 years (Gottman & Levenson, 1992; Levenson & others, 1994). He's found that a couple's relationship grows only if the couple successfully reconciles the inevitable differences that occur. As Gottman (1994) explains, "A certain amount of conflict is needed to help couples weed out actions and ways of dealing with each other that can harm the marriage in the long run."

Gottman and his colleagues have also found that men and women react differently to conflict, particularly to conflicts that involve strong emotions (Levenson & others, 1994). Men have typically learned to suppress and contain their emotions. In contrast, women tend to be more comfortable expressing their emotions. In general, women are more comfortable than men when it comes to dealing with emotional issues in intimate relationships.

According to Gottman (1994), women often become the "emotion managers" and "care-takers of intimacy" in close relationships. They tend to be more sensitive to problems that are developing in the relationship and more willing to talk about them. But when problems need to be resolved, Gottman has found, male and female patterns of reacting to and handling conflict often sabotage a couple's best efforts to resolve their differences.

What goes wrong when a couple tries to resolve their differences? First, consider the two types of responses that Gottman has found to occur during emotional conflicts: flooding and stonewalling. *Flooding* means feeling overwhelmed (or "flooded") by your own emotions—feeling upset and out of control. When flooded, people experience high levels of physiological arousal. Heart rate and blood pressure skyrocket.

As an argument or conflict heats up, both men and women can become flooded by their emotions. That said, which sex do you think is *more* likely to become flooded? Men are. In his lab, Gottman has found that during marital conflict a husband's heart rate and blood pressure increase faster, elevate higher, and stay elevated longer than his wife's (Gottman & Levenson, 1992). Not only is this high level of physiological arousal extremely unpleasant, it also makes it very difficult for a man to listen to his partner's words. Hence, because men physiologically react so strongly to conflict, they tend to be less willing to engage in it.

When flooded, what do men typically do? They go into the *stonewalling* mode—they withdraw to contain their uncomfortable emotions (Levenson & others, 1994). Women also stonewall, of course, but men are much more likely to resort to this strategy (Christensen & Heavey, 1993).

Now a vicious circle begins. Although stonewalling protects *him* from overwhelming stress and emotion, it creates enormous stress in *her*. She's accustomed to working through emotional problems. And she tends to experience his stonewalling as disapproval and rejection—and sometimes as the ultimate power play (Tannen, 1990). So how does she react to his stonewalling? Frustrated and angry, she now reacts by *flooding*.

When a woman experiences flooding, rather than withdrawing, she intensifies the expression of her emotions. This raises the temperature of the argument to a higher level and creates even more stress in the male, further increasing his

BLONDIE

urge to withdraw from the situation. In short, this is a very volatile scene. Each partner is exaggerating the frustration and emotional discomfort of the other. Especially in unhappily married couples, Gottman has found that even minor disagreements can quickly escalate in this way, ending up as a no-holds-barred, extremely unpleasant fight.

Breaking the Vicious Circle of Flooding–Stonewalling–Flooding

In his book *Why Marriages Succeed or Fail . . . and How You Can Make Yours Last,* Gottman (1994) offers many thoughtful and concrete suggestions for handling conflicts in a healthier manner. We'll summarize five of these suggestions, which are based on extensive research by Gottman and other psychologists.

1. Be aware of gender differences.

The first step in breaking the vicious circle of flooding–stonewalling–flooding is to be *aware* of the gender differences in handling emotion. To men, stonewalling is a protective strategy. It represents an attempt to contain disturbing emotions before they become overwhelming and out of control. When women look at men's stonewalling in these terms, they're less likely to interpret it as rejection and as a refusal to try to resolve differences.

For their part, men need to remember that women tend to view stonewalling as rejection, disapproval, and abandonment. Rather than abruptly stonewalling and withdrawing, men need to explain their withdrawal. The explanation can be as simple as saying, "Look, I need to be alone for a while so I can calm down and think about what you're saying. When I come back, we will keep talking." For their part, women need to accept men's need to temporarily withdraw from the situation.

2. Call a time-out.

Gottman (1994) advises that whenever either partner begins to feel overwhelmed or in danger of flooding, he or she should call a *time-out*—a 20- to 30-minute intermission with an agreement to continue the discussion after the break. Remember, it takes at least 20 minutes for physiological arousal to subside completely. Because men are more likely to become emotionally flooded, calming down is especially important for them.

When a man agrees to continue the discussion later and explains why he needs the time-out, his partner is less likely to feel angered and threatened by his withdrawal. As simple as the time-out strategy is, it can promote more constructive and rational discussions, increasing the likelihood that a mutually acceptable solution to the problem will be found.

3. Focus on constructive thoughts.

It is critical that you listen to what you're saying to yourself *during* the time-out. Rather than rehearsing hateful or vengeful comments, use the time out to focus on calming thoughts about the immediate situation and on positive thoughts about your mate. For example, rather than saying to yourself, "He/she is such a (fill in with an insult)," try saying to yourself, "Calm down and get a grip on things. This *is* basically a good marriage and I *do* love her/him." The important point here is to spend the time-out thinking about ways to *resolve* the conflict, not about ways to mount a more effective counterattack when the battle resumes.

4. Resolve the problem together.

Men need to make a conscious effort to embrace, rather than avoid, the problem at hand. As Gottman (1994) wrote, "The most important advice I can give to men who want their marriages to work is to try *not* to avoid conflict. Sidestepping a problem won't make it go away." In other words, guys, you need to remember that your partner *really* cares about your relationship. That's why she keeps confronting you—so the two of you can resolve the problem *together.*

5. Keep the focus on maintaining the relationship.

Although women should not avoid raising issues that are in need of resolution, they should try to do it calmly, avoiding personal attacks. Gottman advises that issues be framed in the context of maintaining a loving relationship. As Gottman (1994) put it, "It will be much easier for him to stay engaged if you let him know that talking together about what's bothering you is a way to keep the love between you alive."

Chapter Review
Gender and Sexuality

Key Points

Introduction: Gender and Sexuality

■ Gender and sexuality are important components of everyone's life. The term **sex** refers to the biologically determined physical characteristics that define a person as male or female. **Gender** refers to the cultural, social, and psychological meanings that are associated with masculinity and femininity. **Gender roles** are the behaviors, attitudes, and personality traits designated as either masculine or feminine in a given culture. **Gender identity** refers to the psychological sense of being male or female, while **sexual orientation** refers to the direction of a person's emotional and erotic attraction.

Gender Stereotypes and Gender Roles

■ According to **gender-role stereotypes,** men and women are polar opposites. Research shows that men are more assertive than women and women are more nurturant than men but that men and women are otherwise similar in their personality characteristics.

■ On average, women outscore men on tests of verbal fluency, spelling, reading comprehension, and writing. Men outscore women on mental rotation tasks. Average math scores of men and women are very similar, but more men score in the very highest range.

■ Men and women are largely similar in their sexual attitudes and behaviors. Men have a higher incidence of masturbation and are more accepting of casual sex than are women.

Gender-Role Development: *Blue Bears and Pink Bunnies*

■ Gender plays an important role in our culture. From birth, boys and girls are treated differently. During childhood, boys and girls develop different toy preferences and play with members of their own sex. Girls tend to be less rigid than boys in adhering to gender stereotypes.

■ Two contemporary theories that explain gender-role development are social learning theory and gender schema theory. **Social learning theory** is based on the principles of learning. Through reinforcement, punishment, and modeling, children learn the appropriate behaviors for each gender.

■ **Gender schema theory** is based on the idea that children actively develop mental categories for each gender. Children's gender schemas influence what they learn and remember. At a young age, children develop an awareness of the underlying meaning of gender categories.

Human Sexuality

■ The four stages of human sexual response are excitement, plateau, orgasm, and resolution. Women are capable of multiple orgasms. Men experience a refractory period following orgasm.

■ In nonhuman animals, sexual behavior is biologically determined and typically triggered by hormonal changes in the female. In higher animals, sexual behavior is more strongly influenced by learning and environmental factors and less influenced by biological factors.

■ **Sexual orientation** is not as easily categorized as many people think. More people have had some same-sex sexual experience than identify themselves as exclusively homosexual. Although psychologists do not know exactly what determines sexual orientation, genetics and differences in brain structure may be involved. Cross-gender play patterns in childhood seem to be related to a later homosexual orientation. Sexual orientation develops at a fairly early age and is difficult to change. In itself, homosexuality is not considered a psychological disorder.

Sexual Behavior over the Lifespan

■ Sexual behavior varies over the lifespan. Infants experience reflexive sexual responses. During early and middle childhood, children become increasingly aware of their own bodies and curious about sexual matters.

■ During **puberty,** adolescents reach sexual maturation. Puberty involves the development of **primary** and **secondary sex characteristics,** the **adolescent growth spurt,** and, in females, **menarche.** Although the sequence of pubertal changes is relatively predictable, the timing of puberty varies from child to child. The consequences of early and late maturation tend to be different for boys and girls.

■ Sexual and romantic relationships become increasingly important in adolescence. By the end of adolescence, most males and females have had sexual intercourse.

■ Most adults are involved in an intimate relationship by the age of 30. Young adults today tend to have more sexual partners than previous generations. Married people tend to have the most active sex lives and are the most satisfied with their sex lives. Vaginal intercourse is the most preferred sexual activity.

■ In late adulthood, people experience physical changes that affect sexual response, but satisfying sexual relationships can continue throughout the lifespan.

Sexual Disorders and Problems

■ A **sexual dysfunction** is a consistent disturbance in sexual response that causes psychological distress. Recent research reveals that sexual problems are relatively common in the United States. Either sex can experience **hypoactive sexual desire disorder, sexual aversion disorder,** or **dyspareunia.** Men can experience **male erectile disorder, male orgasmic disorder,** or **premature ejaculation.** Women can experience **female orgasmic disorder** or **vaginismus.** Sexual dysfunction may be caused by physical or psychological factors.

■ The **paraphilias** are unusual sexual fantasies, urges, or behaviors. They may involve nonhuman objects, suffering or humiliation, children, or another nonconsenting adult. Some paraphilias, such as pedophilia and voyeurism, are illegal.

■ In **gender identity disorder,** people are uncomfortable with their assigned gender and wish to be a member of the opposite sex. In some instances, the person undergoes sex-reassignment surgery.

■ **Sexually transmitted diseases (STDs)** may be bacterial, viral, or parasitic. Some STDs have vague or nonexistent symptoms and can be unknowingly transmitted to a sex partner. Left untreated, some STDs can cause severe health problems.

■ **AIDS** is caused by the HIV virus, which is transmitted through the exchange of infected bodily fluids, such as semen and blood. After being infected, a person may not develop AIDS for several years but can still infect others. When the virus becomes active, it attacks the immune system. No one is immune to HIV, but gay men, intravenous drug users and their partners, and people with multiple sex partners are most at risk to contract HIV. Infection rates are very high and rising in many areas of the world. Choosing sex partners carefully and avoiding high-risk sexual behavior are two ways people can help protect themselves against AIDS and other STDs.

Key Terms

sex, p. 411

gender, p. 411

gender roles, p. 411

gender identity, p. 411

sexual orientation, pp. 411, 427

gender-role stereotypes, p. 412

social learning theory of gender-role development, p. 420

gender schema theory, p. 421

puberty, p. 432

primary sex characteristics, p. 432

secondary sex characteristics, p. 432

adolescent growth spurt, p. 432

menarche, p. 432

sexual dysfunction, p. 439

hypoactive sexual desire disorder, p. 440

sexual aversion disorder, p. 440

dyspareunia, p. 440

male erectile disorder, p. 440

male orgasmic disorder, p. 440

premature ejaculation, p. 440

female orgasmic disorder, 440

vaginismus, p. 440

paraphilia, p. 441

gender identity disorder, p. 441

sexually transmitted diseases (STDs), p. 442

AIDS (acquired immune deficiency syndrome), p. 442

Key People

Sandra Lipsitz Bem (b. 1944) American psychologist who has conducted extensive research on sex roles and gender identity; proposed gender schema theory to explain gender-role development. (p. 421)

Virginia E. Johnson (b. 1925) American behavioral scientist who, along with William H. Masters, conducted pioneering research in the field of human sexuality and sex therapy. (p. 423)

William H. Masters (1915–2001) American physician who, along with Virginia E. Johnson, conducted pioneering research in the field of human sexuality and sex therapy. (p. 423)

Concept Review Answers

10.1   page 422

1. sex
2. gender-role stereotypes
3. social learning theory
4. gender schema theory

10.2   page 430

1. c   2. b   3. d   4. d

10.3   page 445

1. False. Married adults tend to have the most satisfying sex lives.

2. False. Breast development in girls and facial hair in boys are examples of secondary sex characteristics.
3. True
4. True
5. False. Paraphilias are more common in men.
6. True
7. False. Early maturation tends to be psychologically advantageous for boys but not for girls.
8. False. On the average, the adolescent growth spurt occurs at age 14 in boys and age 12 in girls.

Two Generations

Personality

Prologue

The Secret Twin

The twins, Kenneth and Julian, were born a few years after the turn of the century. At first, their parents, Gertrude and Henry, thought they were identical, because the twins looked exactly alike. Both had dark hair and deep brown eyes. Kenneth's son, your author Don, would later inherit these qualities.

But Gertrude and Henry quickly learned to tell the twins apart. Kenneth was slightly larger than Julian, and, even as infants, their personalities were distinctly different. In the photographs of Kenneth and Julian as children, Julian smiles broadly, almost merrily, his head cocked slightly. But Kenneth always looks straight at the camera, his expression thoughtful, serious, more intense.

We don't know much about Julian's childhood. Kenneth kept Julian's existence a closely guarded secret for more than 50 years. In fact it was only a few years before his own death that Kenneth revealed that he had once had a twin brother named Julian.

Still, it's possible to get glimpses of Julian's early life from the letters the boys wrote home from summer camp in 1919 and 1920. Kenneth's letters to his mother were affectionate and respectful, telling her about their daily activities and reassuring her that he would look after his twin brother. "I reminded Julian about the boats and I will watch him <u>good</u>," Kenneth wrote in one letter. Julian's letters were equally affectionate, but shorter and filled with misspelled words. Julian's letters also revealed glimpses of his impulsive nature. He repeatedly promised his mother, "I will not go out in the boats alone again."

Julian's impulsive nature was to have a significant impact on his life. When he was 12 years old, Julian darted in front of a car and was seriously injured, sustaining a concussion. In retrospect, Kenneth believed that that was when Julian's problems began. Perhaps it was, because soon after the accident Julian first got into serious trouble: He was caught stealing money from the "poor box" at church.

Although Kenneth claimed that Julian had always been the smarter twin, Julian fell behind in high school and graduated a year later than Kenneth. After high school, Kenneth left the quiet farming community of Grinnell, Iowa, and moved to Minneapolis. He quickly became self-sufficient, taking a job managing newspaper carriers. Julian stayed in Grinnell and became apprenticed to learn typesetting. Given Julian's propensity for adventure, it's not surprising that he found typesetting monotonous. In the spring of 1928, Julian left Iowa, heading east to look for more interesting possibilities.

The Twins Julian *(left)* and Kenneth *(right),* with their father Henry, when they were about 10 years old. As boys, Kenneth and Julian were inseparable.

He found them in Tennessee. A few months after Julian left Iowa, Henry received word that Julian had been arrested for armed robbery and sentenced to 15 years in a Tennessee state prison. Though Kenneth was only 22 years old, Henry gave him a large sum of money and the family car and sent him to try to get Julian released.

Kenneth's conversation with the judge in Knoxville was the first of many times that he would deal with the judicial system on someone else's behalf. After much negotiation, the judge agreed: If Julian promised to leave Tennessee and never return, and Kenneth paid the cash "fines," Julian would be released from prison.

When Julian walked through the prison gates the next morning, Kenneth stood waiting with a fresh suit of clothes. "Mother and Father want you to come back to Grinnell," he told Julian. But Julian would not hear of it, saying that instead he wanted to go to California to make his fortune.

"I can't let you do that, Julian," Kenneth said, looking hard at his twin brother.

"You can't stop me, brother," Julian responded, with a cocky smile. Reluctantly, Kenneth kept just enough money to buy himself a train ticket back to Iowa. He gave Julian the rest of the money and the family car.

Julian got as far as Phoenix, Arizona, before he met his destiny. In broad daylight, he robbed a drugstore at gunpoint. As he backed out of the store, a policeman spotted him. A gun battle followed, and Julian was shot twice. Somehow he managed to escape and holed up in a hotel room. Alone and untended, Julian died two days later from the bullet wounds. Once again, Kenneth was sent to retrieve his twin brother.

On a bitterly cold November morning in 1928, Julian's immediate family laid him to rest in the family plot in Grinnell. On the one hand, Kenneth felt largely responsible for Julian's misguided life. "I should have tried harder to help Julian," Kenneth later reflected. On the other hand, Julian had disgraced the family. From the day Julian was buried, the family never spoke of him again, not even in private.

Kenneth took it upon himself to atone for the failings of his twin brother. In the fall of 1929, Kenneth entered law school in Tennessee—the same state from which he had secured Julian's release from prison. Three years later, at the height of the Great Depression, Kenneth established himself as a lawyer in Sioux City, Iowa, where he would practice law for more than 50 years.

As an attorney, Kenneth Hockenbury was known for his integrity, his intensity in the courtroom, and his willingness to take cases regardless of the client's ability to pay. "Someone must defend the poor," he said repeatedly. In lieu of money, he often accepted labor from a working man or produce from farmers.

Sixty years after Julian's death, Kenneth died. But unlike the sparse gathering that had attended Julian's burial, scores of people came to pay their last respects to Kenneth Hockenbury. "Your father helped me so much," stranger after stranger told Don at Kenneth's funeral. Without question, Kenneth had devoted his life to helping others.

Why did Kenneth and Julian turn out so differently? Two boys, born on the same day into the same middle-class family. Kenneth the conscientious, serious one; Julian the laughing boy with mischief in his eyes. How can we explain the fundamental differences in their personalities?

No doubt your family, too, is made up of people with very different personalities. By the end of this chapter, you'll have a much greater appreciation for how psychologists explain such personality differences.

Introduction

What Is Personality?

■ Personality is defined as an individual's unique and relatively consistent patterns of thinking, feeling, and behaving.

Key Question

■ What are the four major theoretical perspectives on personality?

That you already have an intuitive understanding of the word *personality* is easy to demonstrate. Just from reading this chapter's Prologue, you could easily describe different aspects of Kenneth's and Julian's personalities. Indeed, we frequently toss around the word *personality* in everyday conversations. "He's very competent, but he has an abrasive personality." "She's got such a delightful personality, you can't help liking her."

Your intuitive understanding of personality is probably very similar to the way that psychologists define the concept. **Personality** is defined as an individual's unique and relatively consistent patterns of thinking, feeling, and behaving. A **personality theory** is an attempt to describe and explain how people are similar, how they are different, and why every individual is unique. In short, a personality theory ambitiously tries to explain the *whole person*. At the outset, it's important to stress that no single theory can adequately explain *all* aspects of human personality. Every personality theory has its unique strengths and weaknesses.

Personality theories often reflect the work of a single individual or of a few closely associated individuals. Thus, it's not surprising that many personality theories bear the distinct personal stamp of their creators to a much greater degree than do other kinds of psychological theories. Consequently, we've tried to let the personality theorists speak for themselves. Throughout this chapter, you'll encounter carefully chosen quotations from the theorists' own writings. These quotations will give you brief glimpses into the minds of some of the most influential thinkers in psychology.

There are many personality theories, but they can be roughly grouped under four basic perspectives: the psychoanalytic, humanistic, social cognitive, and trait perspectives. In a nutshell, here's what each perspective emphasizes:

■ The *psychoanalytic perspective* emphasizes the importance of unconscious processes and the influence of early childhood experience.

■ The *humanistic perspective* represents an optimistic look at human nature, emphasizing the self and the fulfillment of a person's unique potential.

■ The *social cognitive perspective* emphasizes learning and conscious cognitive processes, including the importance of beliefs about the self, goal setting, and self-regulation.

■ The *trait perspective* emphasizes the description and measurement of specific personality differences among individuals.

After looking at some of the major personality theories that reflect each perspective, we'll consider a closely related topic—how personality is measured and evaluated. And yes, we'll talk about the famous inkblots. But for the inkblots to make sense, we need to trace the evolution of modern personality theories. We'll begin with the tale of a bearded, cigar-smoking gentleman from Vienna of whom you just may have heard—Sigmund Freud.

Explaining Personality Some people are outgoing, expressive, and fun-loving, like the mother-daughter pair in this picture. Other people consistently display the opposite qualities. Are such personality differences due to early childhood experiences? Genetics? Social environment? Personality theories reflect attempts to account for the individual differences that make each one of us unique.

personality
An individual's unique and relatively consistent patterns of thinking, feeling, and behaving.

personality theory
A theory that attempts to describe and explain individual similarities and differences.

The Psychoanalytic Perspective on Personality

Key Theme

- Freud's psychoanalysis stresses the importance of unconscious forces, sexual and aggressive instincts, and early childhood experience.

Key Questions

- What were the key influences on Sigmund Freud's thinking?
- How are unconscious influences revealed?
- What are the three basic structures of personality, and what are the defense mechanisms?

Freud the Outsider Sigmund Freud (1856–1939) is shown with his wife, Martha, and youngest child, Anna, at their Vienna home in 1898. Freud always considered himself to be an outsider. First, he was a Jew at a time when anti-Semitism was strong in Europe. Second, Freud's belief that expressions of sexuality are reflected in the behavior of infants and young children was unconventional and shocking to many. To some degree, however, Freud enjoyed his role as the isolated scientist—it served him well in trying to set himself, and his ideas on personality, apart from other researchers.

Sigmund Freud, one of the most influential figures of the twentieth century, was the founder of psychoanalysis. **Psychoanalysis** is the theory of personality that stresses the influence of unconscious mental processes, the importance of sexual and aggressive instincts, and the enduring effects of early childhood experience on personality. Because so many of Freud's ideas have become part of our common culture, it is difficult to imagine just how radical a figure he appeared to his contemporaries. The following biographical sketch highlights some of the important influences that shaped Freud's ideas and theory.

The Life of Sigmund Freud

Sigmund Freud was born in 1856 in what is today Pribôr, the Czech Republic. When he was four years old, his family moved to Vienna, where he lived until the last year of his life. Sigmund was the firstborn child of Jakob and Amalia Freud. By the time he was 10 years old, there were six more siblings in the household. Of the seven children, Sigmund was his mother's favorite. As Freud later wrote, "A man who has been the indisputable favorite of his mother keeps for life the feeling of being a conqueror, that confidence of success that often induces real success" (Jones, 1953).

Freud was extremely bright and intensely ambitious. He studied medicine, became a physician, and then proved himself an outstanding physiological researcher. Early in his career, Freud was among the first investigators of a new drug that had anesthetic and mood-altering properties—cocaine. However, one of Freud's colleagues received credit for the discovery of the anesthetic properties of cocaine, a matter that left Freud bitter. Adding to his disappointment, Freud's enthusiasm for the medical potential of cocaine quickly faded when he recognized that the drug was addictive (Fancher, 1973).

Prospects for an academic career in scientific research were very poor, especially for a Jew in Vienna, which was intensely anti-Semitic at that time. So when he married Martha Bernays in 1886, Freud reluctantly gave up physiological research for a private practice in neurology. The income from private practice would be needed: Sigmund and Martha had six children. One of Freud's daughters, Anna Freud, was later to become an important psychoanalytic theorist in her own right.

psychoanalysis
Sigmund Freud's theory of personality, which emphasizes unconscious determinants of behavior, sexual and aggressive instinctual drives, and the enduring effects of early childhood experiences on later personality development.

free association
A psychoanalytic technique in which the patient spontaneously reports all thoughts, feelings, and mental images as they come to mind.

Influences in the Development of Freud's Ideas

Freud's theory evolved gradually during his first 20 years of private practice. He based his theory on observations of his patients as well as on self-analysis. An early influence on Freud was Joseph Breuer, a highly respected physician. Breuer described to Freud the striking case of a young woman with an array of puzzling psychological and physical symptoms. Breuer found that if he first hypnotized this patient, then asked her to talk freely about a given symptom, forgotten memories of traumatic events emerged. After she freely expressed the pent-up emotions associated with the event, her symptom disappeared. Breuer called this phenomenon *catharsis* (Freud, 1925).

At first, Freud embraced Breuer's technique, but he found that not all of his patients could be hypnotized. Eventually, Freud dropped the use of hypnosis and developed his own technique of **free association** to help his patients uncover forgotten memories. Freud's patients would spontaneously report their uncensored thoughts, mental images, and feelings as they came to mind. From these "free associations," the thread that led to the crucial long-forgotten memories could be unraveled. Breuer and Freud described several of their case studies in their landmark book, *Studies on Hysteria*. Its publication in 1895 marked the beginning of psychoanalysis.

In 1900, Freud published what many consider his most important work, *The Interpretation of Dreams*. By the early 1900s, Freud had developed the basic tenets of his psychoanalytic theory and was no longer the isolated scientist. He was gaining international recognition and developing a following.

In 1904, Freud published what was to become one of his most popular books, *The Psychopathology of Everyday Life*. He described how unconscious thoughts, feelings, and wishes are often reflected in acts of forgetting, inadvertent slips of the tongue, accidents, and errors. By 1909, Freud's influence was also felt in the United States, when he and other psychoanalysts were invited to lecture at Clark University in Massachusetts. For the next 30 years, Freud continued to refine his theory, publishing many books, articles, and lectures.

The last two decades of Freud's life were filled with many personal tragedies. The terrible devastation of World War I weighed heavily on his mind. In 1920, one of his daughters died. In the early 1920s, Freud developed cancer of the jaw, a condition for which he would ultimately undergo more than 30 operations. And during the late 1920s and early 1930s, the Nazis were steadily gaining power in Germany.

Given the climate of the times, it's not surprising that Freud came to focus on humanity's destructive tendencies. For years he had asserted that sexuality was the fundamental human motive, but now he added aggression as a second powerful human instinct. During this period, Freud wrote *Civilization and Its Discontents* (1930), in which he applied his psychoanalytic perspective to civilization as a whole. The central theme of the book is that human nature and civilization are in basic conflict—a conflict that cannot be resolved.

Freud's extreme pessimism was undoubtedly a reflection of the destruction he saw all around him. By 1933, Adolf Hitler had seized power in Germany. Freud's books were banned and publicly burned in Berlin. Five years later, the Nazis marched into Austria, seizing control of Freud's homeland. Although Freud's life was clearly threatened, it was only after his youngest daughter, Anna, had been detained and questioned by the Gestapo that Freud reluctantly agreed to leave Vienna. Under great duress, Freud moved his family to the safety of England. A year later, his cancer returned. In 1939, Freud died in London at the age of 83 (Gay, 1988).

This brief sketch cannot do justice to the richness of Freud's life and the influence of his culture and society on his ideas. Today, Freud's legacy continues to influence psychology, philosophy, literature, and art (Gay, 1999).

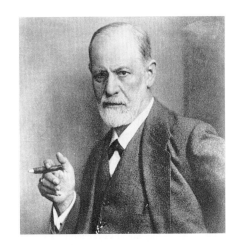

Freud the Leader In 1909, Freud visited the United States to lecture on his ideas at Clark University in Massachusetts. A year later, Freud and his many followers founded the International Psychoanalytic Association.

Freud the Exile In the spring of 1938, Freud fled Nazi persecution for the safety of London on the eve of World War II. Four of Freud's sisters who remained behind later died in the Nazi extermination camps. He is shown arriving in England, his eldest daughter, Mathilde, at his side. Freud died in London on September 23, 1939.

unconscious

In Freud's theory, a term used to describe thoughts, feelings, wishes, and drives that are operating below the level of conscious awareness.

id

Latin for *the it*; in Freud's theory, the completely unconscious, irrational component of personality that seeks immediate satisfaction of instinctual urges and drives; ruled by the pleasure principle.

Eros

In Freud's theory, the self-preservation or life instinct, reflected in the expression of basic biological urges that perpetuate the existence of the individual and the species.

libido

In Freud's theory, the psychological and emotional energy associated with expressions of sexuality; the sex drive.

Thanatos

In Freud's theory, the death instinct, reflected in aggressive, destructive, and self-destructive actions.

pleasure principle

In Freud's theory, the motive to obtain pleasure and avoid tension or discomfort; the most fundamental human motive and the guiding principle of the id.

Freud's Dynamic Theory of Personality

Freud (1940) saw personality and behavior as the result of a constant interplay between conflicting psychological forces. These psychological forces operate at three different levels of awareness: the conscious, the preconscious, and the unconscious. All the thoughts, feelings, and sensations that you're aware of at this particular moment represent the *conscious* level. The *preconscious* contains information of which you're not currently aware but is easily capable of entering your consciousness, such as childhood memories or your Social Security number.

However, the conscious and preconscious are merely the visible tip of the iceberg of the mind. The bulk of this psychological iceberg is made up of the **unconscious,** which lies submerged below the waterline of the preconscious and conscious (see Figure 11.1). You're not directly aware of these submerged thoughts, feelings, wishes, and drives, but the unconscious exerts an enormous influence on your conscious thoughts and behavior.

Although it is not directly accessible, Freud (1904) believed that unconscious material often seeps through to the conscious level in distorted, disguised, or symbolic forms. Like a detective searching for clues, Freud carefully analyzed his patients' reports of dreams and free associations for evidence of unconscious wishes, fantasies, and conflicts. Dream analysis was particularly important to Freud. "The interpretation of dreams is the royal road to a knowledge of the unconscious activities of the mind," he wrote in *The Interpretation of Dreams* (1900). Beneath the surface images, or *manifest content,* of a dream lies its *latent content*—the true, hidden, unconscious meaning of the dream symbols (see Chapter 4).

Freud (1904, 1933) believed that the unconscious can also be revealed in unintentional actions, such as accidents, mistakes, instances of forgetting, and inadvertent slips of the tongue, which are often referred to as "Freudian slips."

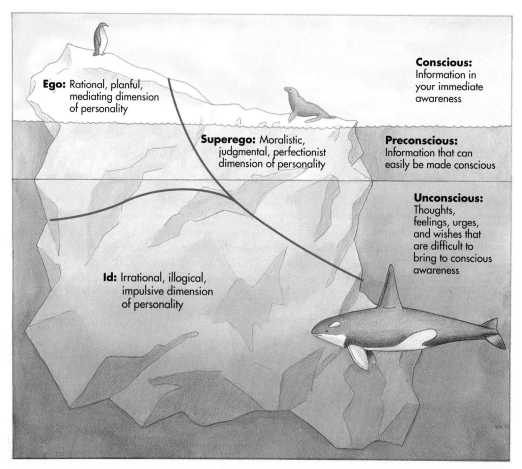

FIGURE 11.1 Levels of Awareness and the Structure of Personality Freud believed that personality is composed of three psychological processes—the id, the ego, and the superego—that operate at different levels of awareness. If you think of personality as being like an iceberg, the bulk of this psychological iceberg is represented by the irrational, impulsive id, which lies beneath the waterline of consciousness. Unlike the entirely unconscious id, the rational ego and the moralistic superego are at least partially conscious.

For example, suppose you forget to set your alarm clock, oversleep, and miss an important exam. Forgetting to set your alarm may reflect your possibly not-so-unconscious desire to avoid taking the exam. But it might also symbolize a deep unconscious conflict about academic success or your career choice. According to Freud, seemingly accidental or unintentional actions are not accidental at all, but are determined by unconscious motives.

The Structure of Personality

According to Freud (1933), each person possesses a certain amount of psychological energy. This psychological energy evolves to form the three basic structures of personality—the id, the ego, and the superego (see Figure 11.1). Understand that these are not separate identities or brain structures. Rather, they are distinct psychological processes.

The **id,** the most primitive part of the personality, is entirely unconscious and present at birth. The id is completely immune to logic, values, morality, danger, and the demands of the external world. It is the original source of psychological energy, parts of which will later evolve into the ego and superego (Freud, 1933, 1940).

The id's reservoir of psychological energy is derived from two conflicting instinctual drives: the life instinct and the death instinct. The *life instinct,* which Freud called **Eros,** consists of biological urges that perpetuate the existence of the individual and the species—hunger, thirst, physical comfort, and, most important, sexuality. Freud (1915c) used the word **libido** to refer specifically to sexual energy or motivation. The *death instinct,* which Freud (1940) called **Thanatos,** is destructive energy that is reflected in aggressive, reckless, and life-threatening behaviors, including self-destructive actions.

Together, the life and death instincts represent the sheer, raw, conflicting psychological forces that fill the id with a reservoir of dammed-up energy, energy that must be released. But because the id resides completely in the unconscious, we're largely unaware of these psychological forces. The id is rather difficult to describe in words. "We come nearer to the id with images," Freud (1933) wrote, "and call it a chaos, a cauldron of seething excitement."

The id is ruled by the **pleasure principle**—the relentless drive toward immediate satisfaction of the instinctual urges, especially sexual urges (Freud, 1920). Thus, the id strives to increase pleasure, reduce tension, and avoid pain. Even though it operates unconsciously, Freud saw the pleasure principle as the most fundamental human motive.

Equipped only with the id, the newborn infant is completely driven by the pleasure principle. When cold, wet, hungry, or uncomfortable, the newborn wants his needs addressed immediately. As the infant gains experience with the external world, however, he learns that his caretakers can't or won't always immediately satisfy those needs.

Appealing to the Id How would Freud explain the appeal of this billboard? In Freud's theory, the id is ruled by the pleasure principle—the instinctual drive to increase pleasure, reduce tension, and avoid pain. Advertisements like this one, which encourage us to be hedonistic, appeal to the pleasure principle.

cathy®   **by Cathy Guisewite**

Establishing the Superego "Don't take something without permission" is just one of the many rules and values we learn as children from parents and other authorities. The internalization of such values is what Freud called the superego—the inner voice that is our conscience. When we fail to live up to its moral ideals, the superego imposes feelings of guilt, shame, and inferiority.

Thus, a new dimension of personality develops from part of the id's psychological energy—the **ego.** Partly conscious, the ego represents the organized, rational, and planning dimensions of personality (Freud, 1933). As the mediator between the id's instinctual demands and the restrictions of the outer world, the ego operates on the reality principle. The **reality principle** is the capacity to postpone gratification until the appropriate time or circumstances exist in the external world (Freud, 1940).

As the young child gains experience, she gradually learns acceptable ways to satisfy her desires and instincts, such as finishing her dinner to get a cookie, saying "please," and waiting her turn rather than pushing another child off a playground swing. Hence, the ego is the pragmatic part of the personality that learns various compromises to reduce the tension of the id's instinctual urges. If the ego can't identify an acceptable compromise to satisfy an instinctual urge, such as a sexual urge, it can *repress* the impulse, or remove it from conscious awareness (Freud, 1915a).

In early childhood, the ego must deal with external parental demands and limitations. Implicit in those demands are the parents' values and morals, their ideas of the right and wrong ways to think, act, and feel. Eventually, the child encounters other advocates of society's values, such as teachers and religious and legal authorities (Freud, 1926). Gradually, these social values move from being externally imposed demands to being *internalized* rules and values.

By about age five or six, the young child has developed an internal, parental voice that is partly conscious—the **superego.** As the internal representation of parental and societal values, the superego evaluates the acceptability of behavior and thoughts, then praises or admonishes. Put simply, your superego represents your conscience, issuing demands "like a strict father with a child" (Freud, 1926). It judges your own behavior as right or wrong, good or bad, acceptable or unacceptable. And, should you fail to live up to these morals, the superego can be harshly punitive, imposing feelings of inferiority, guilt, shame, self-doubt, and anxiety. If we apply Freud's terminology to the twins described in the chapter Prologue, Kenneth's superego was clearly stronger than Julian's.

The Ego Defense Mechanisms: Unconscious Self-Deceptions

The ego has a difficult task. It must be strong, flexible, and resourceful to successfully mediate conflicts among the instinctual demands of the id, the moral authority of the superego, and external restrictions. According to Freud (1923), everyone experiences an ongoing daily battle among these three warring personality processes.

Let's try to illustrate what Freud meant. Imagine lying in bed on a dark, cold morning. You've promised to meet a friend on the running path in 20 minutes. On the one hand, your id starts to whine, "I really want to go back to sleep. I'm tired, and it's dark and cold outside!" Your superego, on the other hand, is scolding away: "Hey, you lazy slob! Get out of bed. Believe me, the cold air will be nothing compared to the guilt trip I'm going to lay on you if you don't keep your promise!" Your ego must deal with these two warring factions, either by giving in to one side or the other or by finding a compromise that satisfies both id and superego (Freud, 1926).

When the demands of the id or superego threaten to overwhelm the ego, *anxiety* results (Freud, 1915b). If instinctual id impulses overpower the ego, a person may act impulsively and perhaps destructively. Using Freud's terminology, you could say that Julian's id was out of control when he stole from the church and

ego
Latin for *I*; in Freud's theory, the partly conscious rational component of personality that regulates thoughts and behavior and is most in touch with the demands of the external world.

reality principle
In Freud's theory, the awareness of environmental demands and the capacity to accommodate them by postponing gratification until the appropriate time or circumstances exist.

superego
In Freud's theory, the partly conscious, self-evaluative, moralistic component of personality that is formed through the internalization of parental and societal rules.

tried to rob the drugstore. In contrast, if superego demands overwhelm the ego, an individual may suffer from guilt, self-reproach, or even suicidal impulses for failing to live up to the superego's moral standards (Freud, 1936). Using Freudian terminology again, it is probably safe to say that Kenneth's feelings of guilt over Julian were inspired by his superego.

If a realistic solution or compromise is not possible, the ego may temporarily reduce anxiety by *distorting* thoughts or perceptions of reality through processes that Freud called **ego defense mechanisms** (A. Freud, 1946; Freud, 1915c). By resorting to these largely unconscious self-deceptions, the ego can maintain an integrated sense of self while searching for a more acceptable and realistic solution to a conflict between the id and superego.

The most fundamental ego defense mechanism is **repression** (Freud, 1915a, 1936). To some degree, repression occurs in every ego defense mechanism. In simple terms, repression is unconscious forgetting. Unbeknownst to the person, anxiety-producing thoughts, feelings, or impulses are pushed out of conscious awareness into the unconscious.

What kinds of information are likely to be repressed? Common examples include traumatic events, past failures, embarrassments, disappointments, the names of disliked people, episodes of physical pain or illness, and unacceptable urges. So if you "forget" a meeting, a deadline, or a dental appointment that you'd prefer to avoid, you may be experiencing a minor instance of repression.

Repression, however, is not an all-or-nothing psychological process. As Freud (1939) explained, "The repressed material retains its impetus to penetrate into consciousness." In other words, if you encounter a situation that is very similar to one you've repressed, bits and pieces of memories of the previous situation may begin to resurface. In such instances, the ego may employ other defense mechanisms that allow the urge or information to remain partially conscious.

This is what occurs with the ego defense mechanism of displacement. **Displacement** occurs when emotional impulses are redirected to a substitute object or person, usually one less threatening or dangerous than the original source of conflict (A. Freud, 1946). For example, an employee angered by his supervisor's unfair treatment may displace his hostility onto other drivers while driving home. He consciously experiences anger but directs it toward someone other than its true target, which remains unconscious.

Freud (1930) believed that a special form of displacement, called *sublimation,* is largely responsible for the productive and creative contributions of people and even of whole societies. **Sublimation** involves displacing sexual urges toward "an aim other than, and remote from, that of sexual gratification" (Freud, 1914). In effect, sublimation channels sexual urges into productive, socially acceptable, nonsexual activities.

A humorous example of sublimation was provided by a married student in one of our classes. After the young woman had surgery, she was told to abstain from sexual intercourse for six weeks. As she explained in class, "It's amazing what got done around the house. Mark put flower boxes outside the windows, waxed the cars, trimmed the hedges, painted the house inside and out, and he even replaced the kitchen floor!" No doubt Freud would see this flurry of activity as the sublimation of sexual energy, or libido.

ego defense mechanisms
In psychoanalytic theory, largely unconscious distortions of thought or perception that act to reduce anxiety.

repression
In psychoanalytic theory, the unconscious exclusion of anxiety-provoking thoughts, feelings, and memories from conscious awareness; the most fundamental ego defense mechanism.

displacement
In psychoanalytic theory, the ego defense mechanism that involves unconsciously shifting the target of an emotional urge to a substitute target that is less threatening or dangerous.

sublimation
In psychoanalytic theory, an ego defense mechanism that involves redirecting sexual urges toward productive, socially acceptable, nonsexual activities; a form of displacement.

Sublimation In Freud's view, creative or productive behaviors represent the rechanneling of sexual energy, or *libido*—an ego defense mechanism he termed *sublimation.* Freud believed that civilization's greatest achievements are the result of the sublimation of instinctual energy into socially acceptable activities. Later personality theorists criticized Freud's refusal to consider creativity a drive in its own right.

"Look, call it denial if you like, but I think what goes on in my personal life is none of my own damn business."

Table 11.1

The Major Ego Defense Mechanisms

Defense	Description	Example
Repression	The complete exclusion from consciousness of anxiety-producing thoughts, feelings, or impulses; most basic defense mechanism.	Three years after being hospitalized for back surgery, the person can remember only vague details about the event.
Displacement	Emotional impulses are redirected toward a substitute person or object, usually one less threatening or dangerous than the original source of conflict.	Angered by a neighbor's hateful comment, a mother spanks her daughter for accidentally spilling her milk.
Sublimation	A form of displacement in which sexual urges are rechanneled into productive, nonsexual activities.	A graduate student works on her thesis 14 hours a day while her husband is on an extended business trip.
Rationalization	Justifying one's actions or feelings with socially acceptable explanations rather than consciously acknowledging one's true motives or desires.	After being rejected by a prestigious university, a student explains that he is glad, because he would be happier at a smaller, less competitive college.
Projection	The attribution of one's own unacceptable urges or qualities to others.	A married woman who is sexually attracted to a co-worker accuses him of flirting with her.
Reaction formation	Thinking or behaving in a way that is the extreme opposite of unacceptable urges or impulses.	Threatened by their awakening sexual attraction to girls, adolescent boys often go out of their way to tease and torment adolescent girls.
Denial	The failure to recognize or acknowledge the existence of anxiety-provoking information.	An alcoholic fails to acknowledge that he is addicted to a drug.
Undoing	A form of unconscious repentance that involves neutralizing or atoning for an unacceptable action or thought with a second action or thought.	A woman who gets a tax refund by cheating on her taxes makes a larger than usual donation to the church collection on the following Sunday.
Regression	Retreating to a behavior pattern characteristic of an earlier stage of development.	After her parents' bitter divorce, a 10-year-old girl refuses to sleep alone in her room, crawling into bed with her mother.

The major defense mechanisms are summarized in Table 11.1. In Freud's view, the drawback to using any defense mechanism is that maintaining these self-deceptions requires psychological energy. As Freud (1936) pointed out regarding the most basic defense mechanism, repression does not take place "on a single occasion," but rather demands "a continuous expenditure of effort." Such effort depletes psychological energy that is needed to cope effectively with the demands of daily life.

The use of defense mechanisms is very common. Many psychologically healthy people temporarily use ego defense mechanisms to deal with stressful events. When ego defense mechanisms are used in limited areas and on a short-term basis, psychological energy is not seriously depleted. Ideally, we strive to maintain realistic perceptions of the world and our motives and search for workable solutions to conflicts and problems. Using ego defense mechanisms is often a way of buying time while we consciously or unconsciously wrestle with more realistic solutions for whatever is troubling us. But when defense mechanisms delay or interfere with our use of more constructive coping strategies, they can be counterproductive.

Personality Development
The Psychosexual Stages

Key Theme
- The psychosexual stages are age-related developmental periods, and each stage represents a different focus of the id's sexual energies.

Key Questions
- What are the five psychosexual stages, and what are the core conflicts of each stage?
- What is the consequence of fixation?
- What role does the Oedipus complex play in personality development?

According to Freud (1905), people progress through five psychosexual stages of development. The foundations of adult personality are established during the first five years of life, as the child progresses through the *oral, anal,* and *phallic* psychosexual stages. The *latency stage* occurs during late childhood, and the fifth and final stage, the *genital stage,* begins in adolescence.

Each psychosexual stage represents a different focus of the id's sexual energies. Freud (1940) contended that "sexual life does not begin only at puberty, but starts with clear manifestations after birth." This statement is often misinterpreted. Freud was *not* saying that an infant experiences sexual urges in the same way as an adult. Instead, Freud believed that the infant or young child expresses primitive sexual urges by seeking sensual pleasure from different areas of the body. Thus, the **psychosexual stages** are age-related developmental periods in which sexual impulses are focused on different bodily zones and are expressed through activities associated with these areas.

Over the first five years of life, the expression of primitive sexual urges progresses from one bodily zone to another in a distinct order: the mouth, the anus, and the genitals. The first year of life is characterized as the *oral stage.* During this time the infant derives pleasure through the oral activities of sucking, chewing, and biting. During the next two years, pleasure is derived through elimination and acquiring control over elimination—the *anal stage.* In the *phallic stage,* pleasure seeking is focused on the genitals.

Fixation: Unresolved Developmental Conflicts

At each psychosexual stage, Freud (1905) believed that the infant or young child is faced with a developmental conflict that must be successfully resolved in order to move on to the next stage. The heart of this conflict is the degree to which parents either frustrate or overindulge the child's expression of pleasurable feelings. Hence, Freud (1940) believed that parental attitudes and the timing of specific child-rearing events, such as weaning or toilet training, leave a lasting influence on personality development.

If frustrated, the child will be left with feelings of unmet needs characteristic of that stage. If overindulged, the child may be reluctant to move on to the next stage. In either case, the result of an unresolved developmental conflict is *fixation* at a particular stage. The person continues to seek pleasure through behaviors that are similar to those associated with that psychosexual stage. For example, the adult who constantly chews gum, smokes, or bites her fingernails may have unresolved oral psychosexual conflicts.

The Oedipus Complex: A Psychosexual Drama

The most critical conflict that the child must successfully resolve for healthy personality and sexual development occurs during the phallic stage (Freud, 1923, 1940). As the child becomes more aware of pleasure derived from the genital area,

"He has a few things to work through, but we're good together."

psychosexual stages
In Freud's theory, age-related developmental periods in which the child's sexual urges are expressed through different areas of the body and the activities associated with those areas.

Oedipus complex
In Freud's theory, a child's unconscious sexual desire for the opposite-sex parent, usually accompanied by hostile feelings toward the same-sex parent.

identification
In psychoanalytic theory, an ego defense mechanism that involves reducing anxiety by modeling the behavior and characteristics of another person.

Competing with Mom for Dad? According to Freud, the child identifies with the same-sex parent as a way of resolving sexual attraction toward the opposite-sex parent—the Oedipus complex. Freud believed that imitating the same-sex parent also plays an important role in the development of gender identity and, ultimately, of healthy sexual maturity.

*I*t often happens that a young man falls in love seriously for the first time with a mature woman, or a girl with an elderly man in a position of authority; this is a clear echo of the [earlier] phase of development that we have been discussing, since these figures are able to re-animate pictures of their mother or father.

Sigmund Freud (1905)

Freud believed that the child develops a sexual attraction to the opposite-sex parent and hostility toward the same-sex parent. This is the famous **Oedipus complex,** named after the hero of a Greek myth. Abandoned at birth, Oedipus does not know the identity of his parents. As an adult, Oedipus unknowingly kills his father and marries his mother.

Outward manifestations of the Oedipus complex can include the child's possessiveness of the opposite-sex parent, such as the little boy who defiantly says, "Don't kiss my mommy, Daddy!" or the little girl who competitively proclaims, "When I grow up, I'm going to marry Daddy!" According to Freud, this attraction to the opposite-sex parent plays out as a sexual drama in the child's mind, a drama with different plot twists for boys and for girls.

For boys, the Oedipus complex unfolds as a confrontation with the father for the affections of the mother. The little boy feels hostility and jealousy toward his father, but he realizes that his father is more physically powerful. The boy experiences *castration anxiety,* or the fear that his father will punish him by castrating him (Freud, 1933).

To resolve the Oedipus complex and these anxieties, the little boy ultimately joins forces with his former enemy by resorting to the defense mechanism of **identification.** That is, he imitates and internalizes his father's values, attitudes, and mannerisms. There is, however, one strict limitation in identifying with the father. Only the father can enjoy the sexual affections of the mother. This limitation becomes internalized as a taboo against incestuous urges in the boy's developing superego, a taboo that is enforced by the superego's use of guilt and societal restrictions (Freud, 1905, 1923).

Girls also ultimately resolve the Oedipus complex by identifying with the same-sex parent and developing a strong superego taboo against incestuous urges. But the underlying sexual drama in girls follows different themes. The little girl discovers that little boys have a penis and that she does not. She feels a sense of deprivation and loss that Freud termed *penis envy.*

According to Freud (1940), the little girl blames her mother for "sending her into the world so insufficiently equipped." Thus, she develops contempt for and resentment toward her mother. However, in her attempt to take her mother's place with her father, she also *identifies* with her mother. Like the little boy, the little girl internalizes the attributes of the same-sex parent.

Freud's views on female sexuality, particularly the concept of penis envy, are among his most severely criticized ideas. Perhaps recognizing that his explanation of female psychosexual development rested on shaky ground, Freud (1926) admitted, "We know less about the sexual life of little girls than of boys. But we need not feel ashamed of this distinction. After all, the sexual life of adult women is a 'dark continent' for psychology."

The Latency and Genital Stages

Freud felt that because of the intense anxiety associated with the Oedipus complex, the sexual urges of boys and girls become repressed during the *latency stage* in late childhood. Outwardly, children in the latency stage express a strong desire to associate with same-sex peers, a preference that strengthens the child's sexual identity.

The final resolution of the Oedipus complex occurs in adolescence, during the *genital stage.* As incestuous urges start to resurface, they are prohibited by the moral ideals of the superego as well as by societal restrictions. Thus, the person

Table 11.2

Freud's Psychosexual Stages

Age	Stage	Description
Birth to age 1	**Oral**	The mouth is the primary focus of pleasurable and gratifying sensations, which the infant achieves via feeding and exploring objects with his mouth.
Ages 1 to 3	**Anal**	The anus is the primary focus of pleasurable sensations, which the young child derives in developing control over elimination via toilet training.
Ages 3 to 6	**Phallic**	The genitals are the primary focus of pleasurable sensations, which the child derives through sexual curiosity, masturbation, and sexual attraction to the opposite-sex parent.
Ages 7 to 11	**Latency**	Sexual impulses become repressed and dormant as the child develops same-sex friendships with peers and focuses on school, sports, and other activities.
Adolescence	**Genital**	As the adolescent reaches physical sexual maturity, the genitals become the primary focus of pleasurable sensations, which the person seeks to satisfy in heterosexual relationships.

directs sexual urges toward socially acceptable substitutes, who often resemble the person's opposite-sex parent (Freud, 1905).

In Freud's theory, a healthy personality and sense of sexuality result when conflicts are successfully resolved at each stage of psychosexual development (summarized in Table 11.2). Successfully negotiating the conflicts at each psychosexual stage results in the person's capacity to love and in expressions of productive living through one's life's work, child rearing, and other accomplishments.

11.1 R·E·V·I·E·W

CONCEPT

Freud's Psychoanalytic Theory

1. The id is guided by the _____, and the ego is guided by the _____.
   a. manifest content; latent content
   b. reality principle; pleasure principle
   c. latent content; manifest content
   d. pleasure principle; reality principle

2. Freud developed the method of _____ to help his patients uncover forgotten memories.
   a. hypnosis   c. free association
   b. catharsis   d. Thanatos

3. The structure of personality that evaluates the morality of behavior is called the _____.
   a. ego   c. libido
   b. superego   d. repression

4. Eight-year-old Johnny wants to be a truck driver when he grows up, just like his dad. Johnny's

acceptance of his father's attitudes and values indicates the process of _____.
   a. fixation   c. denial
   b. identification   d. projection

5. Every time four-year-old Felix touches his genitals, his parents call him a "dirty little boy" and slap his hands. According to Freud, Felix's frustration may result in an unresolved developmental conflict called _____.
   a. fixation   c. sublimation
   b. identification   d. denial

6. Seven-year-old Carolyn prefers to play with girls and does not like playing with boys very much. Carolyn is probably in the _____ stage of sexual development.
   a. anal   b. phallic   c. latency   d. genital

collective unconscious

In Jung's theory, the hypothesized part of the unconscious mind that is inherited from previous generations and that contains universally shared ancestral experiences and ideas.

archetypes

In Jung's theory, the inherited mental images of universal human instincts, themes, and preoccupations that are the main components of the collective unconscious.

The Neo-Freudians
Freud's Descendants and Dissenters

Key Theme

- The neo-Freudians followed Freud in stressing the importance of the unconscious and early childhood, but they developed their own personality theories.

Key Questions

- How did the neo-Freudians generally depart from Freud's ideas?
- What were the key ideas of Jung, Horney, and Adler?
- What are three key criticisms of Freud's theory and of the psychoanalytic perspective?

Freud's ideas were always controversial. But by the early 1900s, he had attracted a number of followers, many of whom went to Vienna to study with him. Although these early followers developed their own personality theories, they still recognized the importance of many of Freud's basic notions, such as the influence of unconscious processes and early childhood experiences. In effect, they kept the foundations that Freud had established but offered new explanations for personality processes. Hence, these theorists are often called *neo-Freudians* (the prefix *neo* means "new"). The neo-Freudians and their theories are considered part of the psychoanalytic perspective on personality.

In general, the neo-Freudians disagreed with Freud on three key points. First, they took issue with Freud's belief that behavior was primarily motivated by sexual urges. Second, they disagreed with Freud's contention that personality is fundamentally determined by early childhood experiences. Instead, the neo-Freudians believed that personality can also be influenced by experiences throughout the lifespan. Third, the neo-Freudian theorists departed from Freud's generally pessimistic view of human nature and society.

In Chapter 9, on lifespan development, we described the psychosocial theory of one famous neo-Freudian, Erik Erikson. In this chapter, we'll look at the basic ideas of three other important neo-Freudians: Carl Jung, Karen Horney, and Alfred Adler.

Carl Jung: Archetypes and the Collective Unconscious

Born in a small town in Switzerland, **Carl Jung** (1875–1961) was fascinated by the myths, folktales, and religions of his own and other cultures. After studying medicine, Jung was drawn to the relatively new field of psychiatry because he believed it could provide deeper insights into the human mind (Jung, 1963).

Intrigued by Freud's ideas, Jung began a correspondence with him. At their first meeting, the two men were so compatible that they talked for 13 hours nonstop. Freud felt that his young disciple was so promising that he called him his "adopted son" and his "crown prince." It would be Jung, Freud decided, who would succeed him and lead the international psychoanalytic movement. However, Jung was too independent to relish his role as Freud's unquestioning disciple. As Jung continued to put forth his own ideas, his close friendship with Freud ultimately ended in bitterness.

Jung rejected Freud's belief that human behavior is fueled by the instinctual drives of sex and aggression. Instead, Jung believed that people are motivated by a more general psychological energy that pushes them to achieve psychological growth, self-realization, and psychic wholeness and harmony. Jung (1963) also believed that personality continues to develop in significant ways throughout the lifespan.

In studying different cultures, Jung was struck by the universality of many images and themes, which also surfaced in his patients' dreams and preoccupa-

What we properly call instincts are physiological urges, and are perceived by the senses. But at the same time, they also manifest themselves in fantasies and often reveal their presence only by symbolic images. These manifestations are what I call the archetypes. They are without known origin; and they reproduce themselves in any time or in any part of the world.

Carl Jung (1964)

tions. These observations led to some of Jung's most intriguing ideas, the notions of the collective unconscious and archetypes.

Jung (1936) believed that the deepest part of the individual psyche is the **collective unconscious,** which is shared by all people and reflects humanity's collective evolutionary history. He described the collective unconscious as containing "the whole spiritual heritage of mankind's evolution, born anew in the brain structure of every individual" (Jung, 1931).

Archetypes in Popular Culture According to Jung, archetypal images are often found in popular myths, novels, and even films. Consider the classic film *The Wizard of Oz*. The motherless child, Dorothy, is on a quest for self-knowledge and selfhood, symbolized by the circular Emerald City. She is accompanied by her symbolic helpers, the Cowardly Lion (seeking courage), the Tin Woodsman (seeking love), and the Scarecrow (seeking wisdom).

Contained in the collective unconscious are the **archetypes,** the mental images of universal human instincts, themes, and preoccupations (Jung, 1964). Common archetype themes that are expressed in virtually every culture are the hero, the powerful father, the nurturing mother, the witch, the wise old man, the innocent child, and death and rebirth.

Two important archetypes that Jung (1951) described are the *anima* and the *animus*—the representations of feminine and masculine qualities. Jung believed that every man has a "feminine" side, represented by his anima, and that every woman has a "masculine" side, represented by her animus. To achieve psychological harmony, Jung believed, it is important for men to recognize and accept their feminine aspects and for women to recognize and accept the masculine side of their nature.

Not surprisingly, Jung's concepts of the collective unconscious and shared archetypes have been criticized as being unscientific or mystical. As far as we know, individual experiences cannot be genetically passed down from one generation to the next. Regardless, Jung's ideas make more sense if you think of the collective unconscious as reflecting shared human experiences. The archetypes, then, can be thought of as symbols that represent the common, universal themes of the human life cycle. These universal themes include birth, achieving a sense of self, parenthood, the spiritual search, and death.

Although Jung's theory never became as influential as Freud's, some of his ideas have gained wide acceptance. For example, Jung (1923) was the first to describe two basic personality types: *introverts,* who focus their attention inward, and *extraverts,* who turn their attention and energy toward the outside world. We will encounter these two basic personality dimensions again, when we look at trait theories later in this chapter. Finally, Jung's emphasis on the drive toward psychological growth and self-realization anticipated some of the basic ideas of the humanistic perspective on personality, which we'll look at shortly.

The Mandala To Jung (1974), the mandala was the archetypal symbol of the self and psychic wholeness. Mandala images are found in cultures throughout the world. Shown here are a ceremonial buffalo robe of the Plains Indians *(left),* and the Bhavacakra, or Buddhist Wheel of Life, from Tibet *(right).* Mandalas are also common in the Christian religious tradition. For example, stained glass windows in cathedrals often include mandala patterns.

Karen Horney: Basic Anxiety and "Womb Envy"

Trained as a Freudian psychoanalyst, **Karen Horney** (pronounced HORN-eye) (1885–1952) emigrated from Germany to the United States during the Great Depression in the 1930s. Horney noticed distinct differences between her American and her German patients. Whereas Freud traced psychological

*M*an, [Freud] postulated, is doomed to suffer or destroy. . . . My own belief is that man has the capacity as well as the desire to develop his potentialities and become a decent human being, and that these deteriorate if his relationship to others and hence to himself is, and continues to be, disturbed. I believe that man can change and go on changing as long as he lives.

Karen Horney (1945)

*T*o be a human being means to have inferiority feelings. One recognizes one's own powerlessness in the face of nature. One sees death as the irrefutable consequence of existence. But in the mentally healthy person this inferiority feeling acts as a motive for productivity, as a motive for attempting to overcome obstacles, to maintain oneself in life.

Alfred Adler (1933)

problems to sexual conflicts, Horney found that her American patients were much more worried about their jobs and economic problems than their sex lives. Thus, Horney came to stress the importance of cultural and social factors in personality development—matters that Freud had largely ignored (Horney, 1945).

Horney also stressed the importance of social relationships, especially the parent–child relationship, in the development of personality. She believed that disturbances in human relationships, not sexual conflicts, were the cause of psychological problems. Such problems arise from the attempt to deal with *basic anxiety,* which Horney (1945) described as "the feeling a child has of being isolated and helpless in a potentially hostile world."

Horney (1945) described three patterns of behavior that the individual uses to defend against basic anxiety: moving toward, against, or away from other people. Those who move *toward* other people have an excessive need for approval and affection. Those who move *against* others have an excessive need for power, especially power over other people. They are often competitive, critical, and domineering, and they need to feel superior to others. Finally, those who move *away from* other people have an excessive need for independence and self-sufficiency, which often makes them aloof and detached from others.

Horney contended that people with a healthy personality are *flexible* in balancing these different needs, for there are times when each behavior pattern is appropriate. As Horney (1945) wrote, "One should be capable of giving in to others, of fighting, and keeping to oneself. The three can complement each other and make for a harmonious whole." But when one pattern becomes the predominant way of dealing with other people and the world, psychological conflict and problems can result.

Horney also sharply disagreed with Freud's interpretation of female development, especially his notion that women suffer from penis envy. What women envy in men, Horney (1926) claimed, is not their penis, but their superior status in society. In fact, Horney contended that men often suffer *womb envy,* envying women's capacity to bear children. Neatly standing Freud's view of feminine psychology on its head, Horney argued that *men* compensate for their relatively minor role in reproduction by constantly striving to make creative achievements in their work (Gilman, 2001). As Horney (1945) wrote, "Is not the tremendous strength in men of the impulse to creative work in every field precisely due to their feelings of playing a relatively small part in the creation of living beings, which constantly impels them to an overcompensation in achievement?"

Horney shared Jung's belief that people are not doomed to psychological conflict and problems. Also like Jung, Horney contended that the drive to grow psychologically and achieve one's potential are basic human motives.

Alfred Adler: Feelings of Inferiority and Striving for Superiority

Born in Vienna, **Alfred Adler** (1870–1937) was an extremely sickly child. Yet through determination and hard work, he overcame his physical weaknesses. After studying medicine, he became associated with Freud. But from the beginning of Adler's interest in psychoanalysis, he disagreed with Freud on several issues. In particular, Adler placed much more emphasis on the importance of conscious thought processes and social urges. Eventually, Adler broke away from Freud to establish his own theory of personality.

Adler (1933b) believed that the most fundamental human motive is *striving for superiority*—the desire to improve oneself, master challenges, and move toward self-perfection and self-realization. Striving toward superiority arises from universal *feelings of inferiority* that are experienced during infancy and childhood, when the child is helpless and dependent on others. These feelings motivate people to *compensate* for their real or imagined weaknesses by emphasizing their talents and abilities and by working hard to improve themselves. Hence, Adler (1933a) saw the universal human feelings of inferiority as ultimately constructive and valuable.

However, when people are unable to compensate for specific weaknesses or when their feelings of inferiority are excessive, they can develop an *inferiority complex*—a general sense of inadequacy, weakness, and helplessness. People with an inferiority complex are often unable to strive for mastery and self-improvement.

At the other extreme, people can *overcompensate* for their feelings of inferiority and develop a *superiority complex*. Behaviors caused by a superiority complex might include exaggerating one's accomplishments and importance in an effort to cover up weaknesses and denying the reality of one's limitations (Adler, 1954).

Although we've only been able to touch on the highlights of the work of Jung, Horney, and Adler, their theories provide a wealth of insights and ideas about human behavior and personality. The neo-Freudians, like Freud, have their own followings among therapists and personality theorists.

11.2 R·E·V·I·E·W

CONCEPT

Psychoanalytic Theorists

Which psychoanalytic theorist made each of the following statements?

1. _____ "The interpretation of dreams is the royal road to a knowledge of the unconscious activities of the mind."

2. _____ "My own belief is that man has the capacity as well as the desire to develop his potentialities and become a decent human being, and that these deteriorate if his relationship to others and hence to himself is, and continues to be, disturbed."

3. _____ "To be human means to have inferiority feelings."

4. _____ "The whole spiritual heritage of mankind's evolution [is] born anew in the brain structure of every individual."

5. _____ "Sexual life does not begin only at puberty, but starts with clear manifestations after birth."

6. _____ "One should be capable of giving in to others, of fighting, and of keeping to oneself. The three can complement each other and make for a harmonious whole."

Evaluating Freud and the Psychoanalytic Perspective on Personality

Like it or not, Sigmund Freud's ideas have had a profound and lasting impact on our culture and on our understanding of human nature. Today, opinions on Freud span the entire spectrum. Some see him as a genius who discovered brilliant, lasting insights into human nature. Others contend that Freud was a deeply neurotic, driven man who successfully foisted his twisted personal view of human nature onto an unsuspecting public (Crews, 1984, 1996).

The truth, as you might suspect, lies somewhere in between. Although Freud has had an enormous impact on psychology and on society, there are several valid criticisms of Freud's theory and, more generally, of the psychoanalytic perspective. We'll discuss three of the most important problems next.

A Century of Influence One indicator of Freud's influence is that he appeared on the cover of *Time* magazine four different times— in 1924, just before his death in 1939, in 1993, and again in 1999. The 1999 cover shown here with the caricature of Freud psychoanalyzing Albert Einstein was a special issue of *Time* commemorating the 100 greatest scientists and thinkers of the twentieth century.

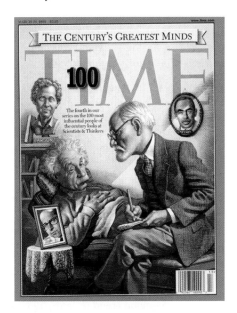

For good or ill, Sigmund Freud, more than any other explorer of the psyche, has shaped the mind of the 20th century. The very fierceness and persistence of his detractors are a wry tribute to the staying power of Freud's ideas.

Peter Gay (1999)

Step by step, we are learning that Freud has been the most overrated figure in the entire history of science and medicine—one who wrought immense harm through the propagation of false etiologies, mistaken diagnoses, and fruitless lines of inquiry.

Frederick Crews (1995)

Freud has fundamentally altered the way we think. He has changed our intellectual manners, often without being aware of it. For most of us Freud has become a habit of mind. . . . He is the major source of our modern inclination to look for meanings beneath the surface of behavior—to be always on the alert for the "real" (and presumably hidden) significance of our actions.

Paul Robinson (1993)

The great question that has never been answered, and which I have not yet been able to answer, despite my thirty years of research into the feminine soul, is "What do women want?"

Sigmund Freud (E. Jones, 1955)

Inadequacy of Evidence

Freud's theory relies wholly on data derived from his relatively small number of patients and from self-analysis. Most of Freud's patients were relatively well-to-do, well-educated members of the middle and upper classes in Vienna at the turn of the twentieth century. Freud (1916, 1919, 1939) also analyzed the lives of famous historical figures, such as Leonardo da Vinci, and looked to myth, religion, literature, and evolutionary prehistory for confirmation of his ideas. Any way you look at it, this is a rather small and skewed sample from which to draw sweeping generalizations about human nature.

Furthermore, it is impossible to objectively assess Freud's "data." Freud did not take notes during his private therapy sessions. And, of course, when he did report a case in detail, it is still Freud's interpretation of the case that is recorded. For Freud, proof of the validity of his ideas depended on his uncovering similar patterns in different patients. So the critical question is this: Was Freud imposing his own ideas onto his patients, seeing only what he expected to see? Some critics think so (e.g., Crews, 1996; Masson, 1984a, 1984b; P. Robinson, 1993).

Lack of Testability

Many psychoanalytic concepts are so vague and ambiguous that they are impossible to objectively measure or confirm (Crews, 1996). For example, how might you go about proving the existence of the id or the superego? Or how could you operationally define and measure the effects of the pleasure principle, the life instinct, or the Oedipus complex?

Psychoanalytic "proof" often has a "heads I win, tails you lose" style to it. In other words, psychoanalytic concepts are often impossible to *dis*prove, because even seemingly contradictory information can be used to support Freud's theory. For example, if your memory of childhood doesn't jibe with Freud's description of the psychosexual stages or the Oedipus complex, well, that's because you've repressed it. Freud himself was not immune to this form of reasoning (P. Robinson, 1993). When one of Freud's patients reported dreams that didn't seem to reveal a hidden wish, Freud interpreted the dreams as betraying the patient's hidden wish to disprove Freud's dream theory!

As Freud acknowledged, psychoanalysis is better at explaining *past* behavior than at predicting future behavior (Gay, 1989). Indeed, psychoanalytic interpretations are so flexible that a given behavior can be explained by any number of completely different motives. For example, a man who is extremely affectionate toward his wife might be exhibiting displacement of a repressed incestuous urge (he is displacing his repressed affection for his mother onto his wife), reaction formation (he actually hates his wife intensely, so he compensates by being overly affectionate), or fixation at the oral stage (he is overly dependent on his wife).

Nonetheless, several key psychoanalytic ideas *have* been substantiated by empirical research (Westen, 1990, 1998). Among these are the ideas that (1) much of mental life is unconscious; (2) early childhood experiences have a critical influence on interpersonal relationships and psychological adjustment; and (3) people differ significantly in the degree to which they are able to regulate their impulses, emotions, and thoughts toward adaptive and socially acceptable ends.

Sexism

Many people feel that Freud's theories reflect a sexist view of women. Because penis envy produces feelings of shame and inferiority, Freud (1925) claimed, women are more vain, masochistic, and jealous than men. He also believed that women are more influenced by their emotions and have a lesser ethical and moral sense than men.

As Horney and other female psychoanalysts have pointed out, Freud's theory uses male psychology as a prototype. Women are essentially viewed as a deviation from the norm of masculinity (Horney, 1926; Thompson, 1950). Perhaps, Horney suggested, psychoanalysis would have evolved an entirely different view of women if it were not dominated by the male point of view.

To Freud's credit, women were quite active in the early psychoanalytic movement. Several female analysts became close colleagues of Freud (Freeman & Strean, 1987; Roazen, 1999, 2000). And it was Freud's daughter Anna, rather than any of his sons, who followed in his footsteps as an eminent psychoanalyst. Ultimately, Anna Freud became her father's successor as leader of the international psychoanalytic movement.

The weaknesses in Freud's theory and in the psychoanalytic approach to personality are not minor problems. All the same, Freud made some extremely significant contributions to modern psychological thinking. Most important, he drew attention to the existence and influence of mental processes that occur outside conscious awareness, an idea that continues to be actively investigated by today's psychological researchers (see Kihlstrom & others, 1992; Underwood, 1996; Westen, 1998).

Anna Freud (1895–1982) Freud's youngest daughter, Anna, became his chief disciple and the founder of a psychoanalytic school in her own right. Expanding on her father's theory, she applied psychoanalysis to therapy with children. She is shown here addressing a debate on psychoanalysis at the Sorbonne University in Paris in 1950.

The Humanistic Perspective on Personality

Key Theme
- The humanistic perspective emphasizes free will, self-awareness, and psychological growth.

Key Questions
- What role do the self-concept, actualizing tendency, and unconditional positive regard play in Rogers's personality theory?
- What are key strengths and weaknesses of the humanistic perspective?

By the 1950s, the field of personality was dominated by two completely different perspectives: Freudian psychoanalysis and B. F. Skinner's brand of behaviorism (see Chapter 5). Whereas Freud's theory of personality proposed elaborate and complex internal states, Skinner's ideas on personality went to the opposite extreme.

Skinner (1953, 1954) saw the very concept of personality as unnecessary in a scientific understanding of behavior. It was unscientific, he maintained, to focus on a person's inner mental states, which cannot be directly observed or measured. Instead, Skinner believed that psychologists should focus on observable behaviors and on the environmental factors that shape and maintain those behaviors (see Rogers & Skinner, 1956). As Skinner (1971) wrote, "A person does not act upon the world, the world acts upon him."

The Emergence of the "Third Force"

Another group of psychologists had a fundamentally different view of human nature. In opposition to both psychoanalysis and behaviorism, they championed a "third force" in psychology, which they called humanistic psychology. **Humanistic psychology** is a view of personality that emphasizes human potential and such uniquely human characteristics as self-awareness and free will (Cain, 2002).

humanistic psychology
The theoretical viewpoint on personality that generally emphasizes the inherent goodness of people, human potential, self-actualization, the self-concept, and healthy personality development.

actualizing tendency
In Rogers's theory, the innate drive to maintain and enhance the human organism.

In contrast to Freud's pessimistic view of people as being motivated by unconscious sexual and destructive instincts, the humanistic psychologists saw people as being innately good. Humanistic psychologists also differed from psychoanalytic theorists by their focus on the *healthy* personality. They questioned how personality theories that were based largely on the characteristics of psychologically troubled people—such as psychoanalytic theories—could accurately portray normal personality functioning.

In contrast to the behaviorist view that human and animal behavior is due largely to environmental reinforcement and punishment, the humanistic psychologists believed that people are motivated by the need to grow psychologically. They also doubted that laboratory research with rats and pigeons accurately reflected the essence of human nature, as the behaviorists claimed. Instead, humanistic psychologists contended that the most important factor in personality is the individual's *conscious, subjective perception of his or her self* (Purkey & Stanley, 2002).

The two most important contributors to the humanistic perspective were Carl Rogers and Abraham Maslow. In Chapter 8, on motivation, we discussed **Abraham Maslow**'s (1908–1970) famous *hierarchy of needs.* Maslow's (1970) research identified several qualities of *self-actualized* people, summarized in Figure 11.2. As you'll see in this section, Rogers also placed considerable importance on the tendency of human beings to strive to fulfill their potential and capabilities.

FIGURE 11.2 Maslow's Characteristics of Self-Actualized People Maslow (1970) proposed that human motives are arranged in a hierarchy of needs. Gratification of each need in the hierarchy is required before the next level of motives is activated. At the very top of the hierarchy is the need for self-actualization—the drive toward self-expression, growth, creativity, and the fulfillment of one's potential. From his investigations of psychologically healthy people, Maslow identified attributes that characterize self-actualizers, which are summarized here. Maslow also found that very few people seem to achieve self-actualization as he defined it.

Pyramid (top to bottom):
- Self-actualization
- Esteem needs
- Belongingness and love needs
- Safety needs
- Physiological needs

Self-actualized people:
- Realistically perceive themselves, others, and external reality.
- Are spontaneous, natural, and open in their behavior and thoughts.
- Easily accept themselves and others as they are.
- Focus on problems outside the self.
- Have a strong need for privacy and independence.
- Continue to enjoy and appreciate positive aspects of everyday life.
- Tend to be creative.

Carl Rogers
On Becoming a Person

Carl Rogers (1902–1987) grew up in a large, close-knit family in Oak Park, Illinois, a suburb of Chicago. His parents were highly religious and instilled a moral and ethical atmosphere in the home, which no doubt influenced Rogers's early decision to become a minister. After studying theology, Rogers decided that the ministry was not for him. Instead, he turned to the study of psychology, ultimately enjoying a long, productive, and distinguished career as a psychotherapist, writer, and university professor.

Like Freud, Rogers developed his personality theory from his clinical experiences with his patients. Rogers referred to his patients as "clients" to emphasize their active and voluntary participation in therapy. In marked contrast to Freud, Rogers was continually impressed by his clients' drive to grow and develop their potential.

These observations convinced Rogers that the most basic human motive is the **actualizing tendency**—the innate drive to maintain and enhance the human organism. According to Rogers, all other human motives, whether biological or social, are secondary. He compared the actualizing tendency to a child's drive to learn to walk despite early frustration and falls—and even to a lowly potato's struggling efforts to send out roots and thrive in a less than ideal environment. To get a taste of the vastly different views of Rogers and Freud, read Critical Thinking Box 11.1.

At bottom, each person is asking, "Who am I, really? How can I get in touch with this real self, underlying all my surface behavior? How can I become myself?"

Carl Rogers (1961)

CRITICAL THINKING 11.1

Freud Versus Rogers on Human Nature

Freud's view of human nature was deeply pessimistic. He believed that the human aggressive instinct was innate, persistent, and pervasive. Were it not for internal superego restraints and external societal restraints, civilization as we know it would collapse: The destructive instincts of humans would be unleashed. As Freud (1930) wrote in *Civilization and Its Discontents:*

> Men are not gentle creatures who want to be loved, and who at the most can defend themselves if they are attacked; they are, on the contrary, creatures among whose instinctual endowments is to be reckoned a powerful share of aggressiveness. As a result, their neighbor is for them not only a potential helper or sexual object, but also someone who tempts them to satisfy their aggressiveness on him, to exploit his capacity for work without compensation, to use him sexually without his consent, to seize his possessions, to humiliate him, to cause him pain, to torture and to kill him. *Man is a wolf to man.* Who, in the face of all his experience of life and of history, will have the courage to dispute this assertion?

In Freud's view, then, the essence of human nature is destructive. Control of these destructive instincts is necessary. Yet societal, cultural, religious, and moral restraints also make people frustrated, neurotic, and unhappy. Why? Because the strivings of the id toward instinctual satisfaction *must* be frustrated if civilization and the human race are to survive. Hence, as the title of Freud's book emphasizes, civilization is inevitably accompanied by human "discontent."

A pretty gloomy picture, isn't it? Yet if you watch the evening news or read the newspaper, you may find it hard to disagree with Freud's negative image of human nature. People *are* often exceedingly cruel and selfish, committing horrifying acts of brutality against strangers and even against loved ones.

However, you might argue that people can also be extraordinarily kind, self-sacrificing, and loving toward others. Freud would agree with this observation. Yet according to his theory, "good" or "moral" behavior does not disprove the essentially destructive nature of people. Instead, he explains good or moral be-

Are People Innately Good ... or Innately Evil? These volunteers are members of Doctors Without Borders, an international group of medical workers that won the Nobel Peace Prize for its work in helping the victims of violence and disasters all over the world. Here, they carry a wounded survivor of a brutal massacre to safety in a refugee camp. On the one hand, killings motivated by political or ethnic hatred seem to support Freud's contentions about human nature. On the other hand, the selfless behavior of those who help others, often at a considerable cost to themselves, seems to support Rogers's view. Which viewpoint do you think more accurately describes the essence of human nature?

havior in terms of superego control, sublimation of the instincts, displacement, and so forth.

But is this truly the essence of human nature? Carl Rogers disagreed strongly. "I do not discover man to be well characterized in his basic nature by such terms as *fundamentally hostile, antisocial, destructive, evil,*" Rogers (1957a) wrote. Instead, Rogers believed that people are more accurately described as *"positive, forward-moving, constructive, realistic, trustworthy."*

If this is so, how can Rogers account for the evil and cruelty in the world? Rogers didn't deny that people can behave destructively and cruelly. Yet throughout his life, Rogers insisted that people are innately good. Rogers (1981) explained the existence of evil in this way:

> My experience leads me to believe that it is cultural factors which are the major factor in our evil behaviors. The

rough manner of childbirth, the infant's mixed experience with the parents, the constricting, destructive influence of our educational system, the injustice of our distribution of wealth, our cultivated prejudices against individuals who are different— all these elements and many others warp the human organism in directions which are antisocial.

In sharp contrast to Freud, Rogers (1964) said we should *trust* the human organism, because the human who is truly free to choose will naturally gravitate toward behavior that serves to perpetuate the human race and improve society as a whole:

> I dare to believe that when the human being is inwardly free to choose whatever he deeply values, he tends to value those objects, experiences, and goals that will make for his own survival, growth, and development, and for the survival and development of others. . . . The psychologically mature person as I have described him has, I believe, the qualities which would cause him to value those experiences which would make for the survival and enhancement of the human race.

Two great thinkers, two diametrically opposing views of human nature. Now it's your turn to critically evaluate their views.

Critical Thinking Questions

- Are people inherently driven by aggressive instincts, as Freud claimed? Must the destructive urges of the id be restrained by parents, culture, religion, and society if civilization is to continue? Would an environment in which individuals were unrestrained inevitably lead to an unleashing of destructive instincts?

- Or are people naturally good, as Rogers claimed? If people existed in a truly free and nurturing environment, would they invariably make constructive choices that would benefit both themselves and society as a whole?

The Self-Concept

Rogers (1959) was struck by how frequently his clients in therapy said, "I'm not really sure who I am" or "I just don't feel like myself." This observation helped form the cornerstone of Rogers's personality theory: the idea of the self-concept. The **self-concept** is the set of perceptions and beliefs that you have about yourself, including your nature, your personal qualities, and your typical behavior.

According to Rogers (1980), people are motivated to act in accordance with their self-concept. So strong is the need to maintain a consistent self-concept that people will deny or distort experiences that contradict their self-concept. For example, if a person who thinks that he is not intelligent were to receive a high grade on a test, he probably would explain it away as an easy test or luck.

The self-concept begins evolving early in life. Because they are motivated by the actualizing tendency, infants and young children naturally gravitate toward self-enhancing experiences. But as children develop a greater sense of self-awareness, there is an increasing need for positive regard. *Positive regard* is the sense of being loved and valued by other people, especially one's parents.

Rogers (1959) maintained that most parents provide their children with **conditional positive regard**—the sense that the child is valued and loved only when she behaves in a way that is acceptable to others. The problem with conditional positive regard is that it causes the child to learn to deny or distort her genuine feelings. For example, if little Amy's parents scold and reject her when she expresses angry feelings, her strong need for positive regard will cause her to deny her anger, even when it's justified or appropriate. Eventually, Amy's self-concept will become so distorted that genuine feelings of anger are denied, because they are inconsistent with her self-concept as "a good girl who never gets angry." Because of the fear of losing positive regard, she cuts herself off from her true feelings.

Like Freud, Rogers believed that feelings and experiences could be driven from consciousness by being denied or distorted. But Rogers believed that feelings become denied or distorted not because they are threatening, but because they contradict the self-concept. In this case, people are in a state of *incongruence:* Their self-concept conflicts with their actual experience (Rogers, 1959). Such a person is continually defending against genuine feelings and experiences that are inconsistent with his self-concept. As this process continues over time, a person progressively becomes more "out of touch" with his true feelings and his essential self, often experiencing psychological problems as a result.

How is incongruence to be avoided? In the ideal situation, a child experiences a great deal of unconditional positive regard. **Unconditional positive regard** refers to the child's sense of being unconditionally loved and valued, even if she doesn't conform to the standards and expectations of others. In this way, the child's actualizing tendency is allowed its fullest expression. Rogers believed that parents should provide unconditional acceptance and love of their children, whatever the children's behavior.

Note, however, that Rogers did *not* advocate permissive parenting. He thought that parents were responsible for controlling their children's behavior and for teaching them acceptable standards of behavior. Rogers maintained that parents can discipline their child without undermining the child's sense of self-worth.

Unconditional Positive Regard Rogers contended that healthy personality development is the result of being unconditionally valued and loved as a person. He advocated that parents and teachers should control a child's inappropriate behavior without rejecting the child himself. Such a style of discipline teaches acceptable behaviors without diminishing the child's sense of self-worth.

"To this day, I can hear my mother's voice—harsh, accusing. 'Lost your mittens? You naughty kittens! Then you shall have no pie!'"

For example, parents can disapprove of a child's specific *behavior* without completely rejecting the *child herself.* The goal is that each child should experience a strong sense of positive regard, even if she doesn't eat her green beans, screams when you shampoo her hair, or throws a tantrum when you invite your boss over for dinner. In effect, the parent's message should be, "I do not value your behavior right now, but I still love and value *you.*" In this way, according to Rogers, the child's essential sense of self-worth can remain intact.

The Fully Functioning Person

Rogers (1957b) believed that it is through consistent experiences of unconditional positive regard that one becomes a psychologically healthy, fully functioning person. The *fully functioning person* has a flexible, constantly evolving self-concept. She is realistic, open to new experiences, and capable of changing in response to new experiences.

Rather than defending against or distorting her own thoughts or feelings, the person experiences *congruence:* Her sense of self is consistent with her emotions and experiences. The actualizing tendency is fully operational in her, and she makes conscious choices that move her in the direction of greater growth and fulfillment of potential. Rogers (1957b, 1964) believed that the fully functioning person is likely to be creative and spontaneous, and to enjoy harmonious relationships with others.

Evaluating the Humanistic Perspective on Personality

Humanistic psychology has been extremely influential in psychotherapy, which we'll discuss more fully in Chapter 15. Beyond psychotherapy, humanistic theories have also had a significant impact in such diverse areas as education, parenting, and even business management practices (see Rogers, 1977, 1980). But the humanistic perspective has been criticized on two particular points.

First, humanistic theories are hard to validate or test scientifically. Humanistic theories tend to be based on philosophical assumptions or clinical observations, rather than on empirical research. For example, concepts like the self-concept, unconditional positive regard, and the actualizing tendency are very difficult to define or measure objectively.

Second, many psychologists believe that humanistic psychology's view of human nature is *too* optimistic. For example, if self-actualization is a universal human motive, why are self-actualized people so hard to find? And, critics claim, humanistic psychologists have minimized the darker, more destructive side of human nature. Can we really account for all the evil in the world by ascribing it to upbringing, society, or culture?

Rogers disagreed with the accusation that his view of human nature was hopelessly naive. "I am quite aware that out of defensiveness and inner fear individuals can and do behave in ways which are incredibly cruel, horribly destructive, immature, regressive, antisocial, and hurtful," Rogers (1961) wrote. "Yet one of the most refreshing and invigorating parts of my experience is to work with such individuals and to discover the strongly positive directional tendencies which exist in them, as in all of us, at the deepest levels."

The influence of humanistic psychology has waned since the 1960s and early 1970s (Cain & Seeman, 2002b). Nevertheless, it has made lasting contributions, especially in the realms of psychotherapy, counseling, education, and parenting (K. Schneider, 1998). The humanistic perspective has also promoted the scientific study of such topics as the healthy personality and creativity (e.g., Harrington & others, 1987). Finally, the importance of subjective experience and the self-concept has become widely accepted in different areas of psychology (Markus & Cross, 1990; Markus & Kitayama, 1994).

self-concept
The set of perceptions and beliefs that you hold about yourself.

conditional positive regard
In Rogers's theory, the sense that you will be valued and loved only if you behave in a way that is acceptable to others; conditional love or acceptance.

unconditional positive regard
In Rogers's theory, the sense that you will be valued and loved even if you don't conform to the standards and expectations of others; unconditional love or acceptance.

social cognitive theory
Bandura's theory of personality, which emphasizes the importance of observational learning, conscious cognitive processes, social experiences, self-efficacy beliefs, and reciprocal determinism.

reciprocal determinism
A model proposed by psychologist Albert Bandura that explains human functioning and personality as caused by the interaction of behavioral, cognitive, and environmental factors.

self-efficacy
The beliefs that people have about their ability to meet the demands of a specific situation; feelings of self-confidence or self-doubt.

The Social Cognitive Perspective on Personality

Key Theme

- The social cognitive perspective stresses conscious thought processes, self-regulation, and the importance of situational influences.

Key Questions

- What is the principle of reciprocal determination?
- What is the role of self-efficacy beliefs in personality?
- What are key strengths and weaknesses of the social cognitive perspective?

Have you ever noticed how different your behavior and sense of self can be in different situations? Consider this example: You feel pretty confident as you enter your English composition class. After all, you're pulling an A, and your prof nods approvingly every time you participate in the class discussion, which you do frequently. In contrast, your college algebra class is a disaster. You're worried about passing the course, and you feel so shaky about your skills that you're afraid to even ask a question, much less participate in class. Even a casual observer would notice how differently you behave in the two different situations—speaking freely and confidently in one class, and staring at your desk in hopes that your instructor won't notice you in the other.

The idea that a person's conscious thought processes in different situations strongly influence his or her actions is one important characteristic of the *social cognitive perspective* on personality (Cervone, 1997). According to the social cognitive perspective, people actively process information from their social experiences. This information influences their goals, expectations, beliefs, and behavior, as well as the specific environments they choose.

The social cognitive perspective differs from psychoanalytic and humanistic perspectives in several ways (Meichenbaum, 1995). First, rather than basing their approach on self-analysis or insights derived from psychotherapy, social cognitive personality theorists rely heavily on experimental findings. Second, the social cognitive perspective emphasizes conscious, self-regulated behavior rather than unconscious mental influences and instinctual drives. And third, as in our English-versus-algebra-class example, the social cognitive approach emphasizes that our sense of self can vary, depending on our thoughts, feelings, and behaviors in a given situation.

Albert Bandura and Social Cognitive Theory

Although several contemporary personality theorists have embraced the social cognitive approach to explaining personality, probably the most influential is **Albert Bandura**. We examined Bandura's now-classic research on *observational learning* in Chapter 5. In Chapter 8, we encountered Bandura's more recent research on self-efficacy. Here, you'll see how Bandura's ideas on both these topics are reflected in his personality theory, called social cognitive theory. **Social cognitive theory** emphasizes the social origins of thoughts and actions but also stresses active cognitive processes and the human capacity for *self*-regulation (Bandura, 2001).

As Bandura's early research demonstrated, we learn many behaviors by observing, and then imitating, the behavior of other people. But, as Bandura (1997) has pointed out, we don't merely observe people's actions. We also observe the *consequences* that follow people's actions, the *rules* and *standards* that apply to behavior in specific situations, and the ways in which people *regulate their own behavior*. Thus, environmental influences are important, but conscious, self-

The capacity to exercise control over the nature and quality of life is the essence of humanness. Unless people believe they can produce desired results and forestall detrimental ones by their actions, they have little incentive to act or persevere in the face of difficulties.

Albert Bandura (2001)

generated goals and standards also exert considerable control over thoughts, feelings, and actions (Bandura, 2001).

For example, consider your own goal of getting a college education. No doubt many social and environmental factors influenced your decision. In turn, your conscious decision to attend college determines many aspects of your current behavior, thoughts, and emotions. And your goal of attending college classes determines which environments you choose.

Bandura (1986, 1997) explains human behavior and personality as being caused by the interaction of behavioral, cognitive, and environmental factors. He calls this process **reciprocal determinism** (see Figure 11.3). According to this principle, each factor both influences the other factors and is influenced by the other factors. Thus, in Bandura's view, our environment influences our thoughts and actions, our thoughts influence our actions and the environments we choose, our actions influence our thoughts and the environments we choose, and so on in a circular fashion.

Beliefs of Self-Efficacy: Anybody Here Know How to Fix a Light Switch?

Collectively, a person's cognitive skills, abilities, and attitudes represent the person's *self-system*. According to Bandura (2001), it is our self-system that guides how we perceive, evaluate, and control our behavior in different situations. Bandura (1997) has found that the most critical elements influencing the self-system are our beliefs of self-efficacy. **Self-efficacy** refers to the degree to which you are subjectively convinced of your own capabilities and effectiveness in meeting the demands of a particular situation.

For example, your authors, Don and Sandy, are at opposite ends of the spectrum in their beliefs of self-efficacy when it comes to repairs around the house. Don thinks he can fix anything, whether he really can or not. Sandy likes to describe herself as "mechanically challenged." When a light switch recently broke in our house, it was obvious that Sandy had very little faith in her ability to fix or replace it: she instantly hollered for help. As Don was investigating the matter, he casually asked Sandy whether *she* could replace the light switch.

"Me? You must be kidding," Sandy immediately responded. "It would never occur to me to even *try* to replace a light switch."

Bandura would be quick to point out how Sandy's weak belief of self-efficacy about electrical repairs guides her behavior—it would prevent her from even attempting to fix a light switch on her own. When Don reassured Sandy that the directions were right on the light-switch package and that it was a very simple task, Sandy still expressed strong self-doubt about her abilities. "I'd probably blow up the house or burn it down or black out the whole neighborhood," she said.

Albert Bandura would, no doubt, smile at how readily Sandy's remark was an everyday confirmation of his research finding that our beliefs of self-efficacy help shape our imagination of future consequences (Bandura, 1992; Ozer & Bandura, 1990). In Sandy's case, her weak belief of self-efficacy contributed to her imagination of dire future consequences should she attempt this task.

Bandura's concept of self-efficacy makes it easier to understand why people often fail to perform optimally at certain tasks, even though they possess the necessary skills. Sandy has made presentations in front of hundreds of people, knows how to slab a geode with a diamond saw, can easily navigate Chicago's rush-hour traffic, and once single-handedly landed an eight-pound northern pike. In all these situations, she has strong feelings of self-efficacy. But hand her a package containing a light switch and she's intimidated.

Hence, our self-system is very flexible. How we regard ourselves and our abilities varies depending on the situations or tasks we're facing. In turn, our beliefs influence the tasks we are willing to try and how persistent we'll be in the face of obstacles (Bandura, 1996).

FIGURE 11.3 Reciprocal Determinism
SOURCE: Bandura (1997).

*M*astery experiences are the most influential source of efficacy information because they provide the most authentic evidence of whether one can muster whatever it takes to succeed. Successes build a robust belief in one's personal efficacy. Failures undermine it, especially if failures occur before a sense of efficacy is firmly established.

Albert Bandura (1997)

Self-Efficacy We acquire a strong sense of self-efficacy by meeting challenges and mastering new skills specific to a particular situation. With her mother showing her how to ride her new bike, this three-year-old is well on her way to developing a strong sense of self-efficacy in this domain. Self-efficacy beliefs begin to develop in early childhood but continue to evolve throughout the lifespan as we encounter new and different challenges.

CRITICAL THINKING 11.2

Freud Versus Bandura on Human Aggression

Freud viewed aggression as a universal, unconscious human instinct that must be controlled by the internal restraints of the superego and the external restraints of culture, society, and morality. In Freud's eyes, aggressive instincts were part of the irrational, impulsive, and unconscious id.

Social cognitive theorists, however, discount the importance of unconscious instincts or motives. Instead, they emphasize that behavior is driven by conscious goals and motives. Not surprisingly, Albert Bandura has taken issue with Freud's explanation of war and cruelty as being caused by the failure of the rational ego, the superego's restraints, and society's laws to control the id's destructive impulses (see Critical Thinking Box 11.1). Bandura (1986) has noted that some of the most horrifying examples of human cruelty have involved conscious, *rational* behavior:

> People frequently engage in destructive activities, not because of reduced self-control, but because their cognitive skills and self-control are too well enlisted through moral justification and self-exonerative devices in the service of destructive causes. The infamous extermination procedures of Nazi con-

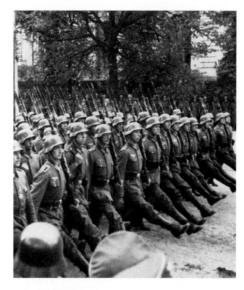

Irrational Id or Rational Choice? Nazi soldiers goose step in perfect formation down a city street during a victory parade after invading Poland in 1939. Bandura argues that many of the worst horrors of the twentieth century, such as the Nazi extermination camps, were not the result of unrestrained aggressive emotional impulses. Rather, he contends that they reflect deliberate choices and actions.

centration camps were perfected in laboratories using human victims. In the Nazi value system, where the enslavement and execution of Jewish people were viewed as meritorious acts of patriotism, camp commandants proudly compared execution rates as if they were industrial production figures. This monstrous death industry required a methodical program of research and efficient and dedicated management. The massive threats to human welfare are generally brought about by deliberate acts of principle, rather than unrestrained acts of impulse.

Given Freud and Bandura's differing views, what do you think?

Critical Thinking Questions

- Are acts of violent, aggressive, and cruel behavior the result of unconscious forces that are out of control, as Freud contended?

- Or are acts of aggression and cruelty the result of conscious, deliberate motives, as Bandura maintains?

With the light switch, Don insisted on proving to Sandy that she was capable of changing it. "Well, maybe if I watched you install one, I might be willing to try it," Sandy finally offered. Sandy's suggestion illustrates how we acquire new behaviors and strengthen our beliefs of self-efficacy in particular situations—through observational learning and *mastery experiences* (Bandura, 1990, 1997). When we perform a task successfully, our sense of self-efficacy becomes stronger. When we fail to deal effectively with a particular task or situation, our sense of self-efficacy is undermined.

From very early in life, children develop feelings of self-efficacy from their experiences in dealing with different tasks and situations, such as athletic, social, and academic activities (Bandura, 1989b). As Bandura (1992) has pointed out, developing self-efficacy begins in childhood, but it continues as a lifelong process. Each stage of the lifespan presents new challenges. And just for the record, Sandy *did* successfully replace the broken light switch. Now, about that dripping faucet . . .

Evaluating the Social Cognitive Perspective on Personality

A key strength of the social cognitive perspective on personality is its grounding in empirical, laboratory research. The social cognitive perspective is built on research in learning, cognitive psychology, and social psychology, rather than on clinical impressions. And, unlike vague psychoanalytic and humanistic concepts, the concepts of social cognitive theory are scientifically testable—that is, they can be operationally defined and measured. For example, psychologists can study beliefs of self-efficacy by comparing subjects who are low in self-efficacy in a given situation with subjects who are high in self-efficacy (e.g., Ozer & Bandura, 1990). Not surprisingly, then, the social cognitive perspective has had a major impact on the study of personality.

However, some psychologists feel that the social cognitive approach to personality applies *best* to laboratory research. In the typical laboratory study, the relationships among a limited number of very specific variables are studied. In everyday life, situations are far more complex, with multiple factors converging to affect behavior and personality. Thus, an argument can be made that clinical data, rather than laboratory data, may be more reflective of human personality.

The social cognitive perspective also ignores unconscious influences, emotions, or conflicts. Some psychologists argue that the social cognitive theory focuses on very limited areas of personality—learning, the effects of situations, and the effects of beliefs about the self. Thus, it seems to lack the richness of psychoanalytic and humanistic theories, which strive to explain the *whole* person, including the unconscious, irrational, and emotional aspects of personality (Westen, 1990).

Nevertheless, by emphasizing the reciprocal interaction of mental, behavioral, and situational factors, the social cognitive perspective recognizes the complex combination of factors that influences our everyday behavior. By emphasizing the important role of learning, especially observational learning, the social cognitive perspective offers a developmental explanation of human functioning that persists throughout one's lifetime. Finally, by emphasizing the self-regulation of behavior, the social cognitive perspective places most of the responsibility for our behavior—and for the consequences we experience—squarely on our own shoulders.

11.3 R·E·V·I·E·W

C·O·N·C·E·P·T

Humanistic and Social Cognitive Perspectives

Determine whether each of the following statements is true or false. If a statement is false, rewrite it to correct it.

_____ 1. According to Carl Rogers, children's impulses are innately good, and they should never be disciplined.

_____ 2. Carl Rogers strongly advocated the use of conditional positive regard to enhance the psychological well-being of others.

_____ 3. Unlike Freud, Rogers advocated that people should be given greater freedom to choose the values and experiences that are important to them.

_____ 4. The humanistic perspective on personality has been criticized for being too optimistic about human nature.

_____ 5. According to social cognitive theory, people's behavior is determined solely by environmental influences.

_____ 6. Self-efficacy beliefs can vary from one situation to another.

_____ 7. Unlike Freud, Bandura contends that destructive behaviors often reflect conscious, deliberate choices rather than unrestrained aggressive impulses.

trait
A relatively stable, enduring predisposition to consistently behave in a certain way.

trait theory
A theory of personality that focuses on identifying, describing, and measuring individual differences.

surface traits
Personality characteristics or attributes that can easily be inferred from observable behavior.

source traits
The most fundamental dimensions of personality; the broad, basic traits that are hypothesized to be universal and relatively few in number.

The Trait Perspective on Personality

Key Theme
- Trait theories of personality focus on identifying, describing, and measuring individual differences.

Key Questions
- What are traits, and how do surface and source traits differ?
- What are three influential trait theories, and how might heredity affect personality?
- What are key strengths and weaknesses of trait theories of personality?

Suppose we asked you to describe the personality of a close friend. How would you begin? Would you describe her personality in terms of her unconscious conflicts, the congruence of her self-concept, or her level of self-efficacy? Probably not. Instead, you'd probably generate a list of her personal characteristics, such as "outgoing," "cheerful," and "generous." This rather commonsense approach to personality is shared by the trait theories.

The trait approach to personality is very different from the theories we have encountered thus far. The psychoanalytic, humanistic, and social cognitive theories emphasize the *similarities* among people. They focus on discovering the universal processes of motivation and development that explain human personality (Revelle, 1995). Although these theories do deal with individual differences, they do so only indirectly. In contrast, the trait approach to personality *focuses primarily on describing individual differences* (Funder, 2001).

Trait theorists view the person as being a unique combination of personality characteristics or attributes, called *traits*. A **trait** is formally defined as a relatively stable, enduring predisposition to behave in a certain way. A **trait theory** of personality, then, is one that focuses on identifying, describing, and measuring individual differences. Think back to our description of the twins, Kenneth and Julian, in the chapter Prologue. You can probably readily identify some of their personality traits. For example, Julian was described as impulsive, cocky, and adventurous, while Kenneth was serious, intense, and responsible.

People possess traits to different degrees. For example, a person might be extremely shy, somewhat shy, or not shy at all. Hence, a trait is typically described in terms of a range from one extreme to its opposite. Most people fall in the middle of the range (average shyness), while fewer people fall at opposite poles (extremely shy or extremely outgoing).

Surface Traits and Source Traits

Most of the terms that we use to describe people are **surface traits**—traits that lie on "the surface" and can be easily inferred from observable behaviors. Examples of surface traits include attributes like "happy," "exuberant," "spacey," and "gloomy." The list of potential surface traits is extremely long. Personality researcher Gordon Allport combed through an English-language dictionary and discovered more than 4,000 words that described specific personality traits (Allport & Odbert, 1936).

Source traits are thought to be more fundamental than surface traits. As the most basic dimension of personality, a source trait can potentially give rise to a vast number of surface traits. Trait theorists believe that there are relatively few source traits (Goldberg, 1993). Thus, one goal of trait theorists has been to identify the most basic set of universal source traits that can be used to describe all individual differences (Pervin, 1994).

Raymond Cattell (1905–1998) Cattell was a strong advocate of the trait approach to personality. His research led to the development of the Sixteen Personality Factor Questionnaire, one of the most widely used psychological tests for assessing personality.

Two Representative Trait Theories
Raymond Cattell and Hans Eysenck

How many source traits are there? Not surprisingly, trait theorists differ in their answers. For example, pioneer trait theorist **Raymond Cattell** reduced Allport's list of 4,000 terms to about 171 characteristics by eliminating terms that seemed to be redundant or uncommon (see John, 1990). Cattell collected data on a large sample of people, who were rated on each of the 171 terms. He then used a statistical technique called *factor analysis* to identify the traits that were most closely related to one another. After further research, Cattell eventually reduced his list to 16 key personality factors, which are described in Table 11.3.

Cattell (1994) believed that these 16 personality factors represent the essential source traits of human personality. To measure these traits, Cattell developed what has become one of the most widely used personality tests, the *Sixteen Personality Factor Questionnaire* (abbreviated *16PF*). We'll discuss the 16PF in more detail later in the chapter.

An even simpler model of universal source traits was proposed by **Hans Eysenck**, a British psychologist. Eysenck's methods were similar to Cattell's, but his conception of personality includes just three dimensions. The first dimension is introversion–extraversion, which is the degree to which a person directs his energies outward toward the environment and other people versus inward toward his inner and self-focused experiences. A person who is high on the dimension of *introversion* might be quiet, solitary, and reserved, avoiding new experiences. A person high on the *extraversion* scale would be outgoing and sociable, enjoying new experiences and stimulating environments.

Eysenck's second major dimension is neuroticism–emotional stability. *Neuroticism* refers to a person's predisposition to become emotionally upset, while *stability* reflects a person's predisposition to be emotionally even. Surface traits associated with neuroticism are anxiety, tension, depression, and guilt. At the opposite end, emotional stability is associated with the surface traits of being calm, relaxed, and even-tempered.

Eysenck believed that by combining these two dimensions people can be classified into four basic types: introverted-neurotic; introverted-stable; extraverted-neurotic; and extraverted-stable. Each basic type is associated with a different combination of surface traits, as shown in Figure 11.4.

In later research, Eysenck identified a third personality dimension, called *psychoticism* (Eysenck, 1990; Eysenck & Eysenck, 1975). A person high on this trait is antisocial, cold, hostile, and unconcerned about others. A person who is low on psychoticism is warm and caring toward others. In the chapter Prologue, Julian might be described as above average on psychoticism, while Kenneth was extremely low on this trait.

Table | **11.3**

Cattell's 16 Personality Factors

1. Reserved, unsociable	⟷	Outgoing, sociable
2. Less intelligent, concrete	⟷	More intelligent, abstract
3. Affected by feelings	⟷	Emotionally stable
4. Submissive, humble	⟷	Dominant, assertive
5. Serious	⟷	Happy-go-lucky
6. Expedient	⟷	Conscientious
7. Timid	⟷	Venturesome
8. Tough-minded	⟷	Sensitive
9. Trusting	⟷	Suspicious
10. Practical	⟷	Imaginative
11. Forthright	⟷	Shrewd, calculating
12. Self-assured	⟷	Apprehensive
13. Conservative	⟷	Experimenting
14. Group-dependent	⟷	Self-sufficient
15. Undisciplined	⟷	Controlled
16. Relaxed	⟷	Tense

SOURCE: Adapted from Cattell (1973).

Raymond Cattell believed that personality could be described in terms of 16 source traits, or basic personality factors. Each factor represents a dimension that ranges between two extremes.

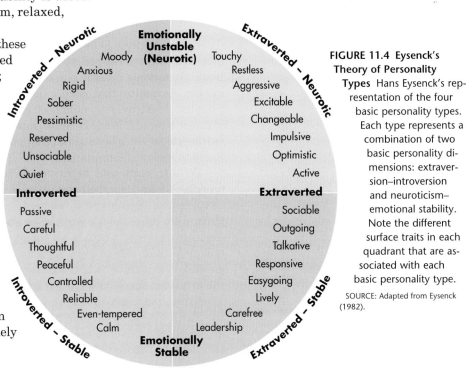

FIGURE 11.4 Eysenck's Theory of Personality Types Hans Eysenck's representation of the four basic personality types. Each type represents a combination of two basic personality dimensions: extraversion–introversion and neuroticism–emotional stability. Note the different surface traits in each quadrant that are associated with each basic personality type.

SOURCE: Adapted from Eysenck (1982).

focus on Neuroscience

(a) Extraversion correlating with brain reactivity to positive pictures

(b) Neuroticism correlating with brain reactivity to negative pictures

Personality Traits and Patterns of Brain Activity People who rate high on the personality trait of extraversion tend to be upbeat, optimistic, and sociable. They also report experiencing more positive emotions on a daily basis than less extraverted people. In contrast, people who rate high on neuroticism tend to be anxious, worried, and socially insecure. And they report more negative emotions in everyday life than less neurotic people. Could these personality traits also influence how the brain responds to emotional situations?

To investigate this idea, psychologist Turhan Canli and his colleagues (2001) gave 14 healthy female volunteers a personality test to determine their level of extraversion or neuroticism. Then, each woman was placed in a functional magnetic resonance imaging (fMRI) scanner to record her brain's reaction to positive images (e.g., a happy couple, puppies, ice cream, sunsets) or negative images (e.g., angry or crying people, spiders, guns, or a cemetery).

The fMRI results show that the women who scored high on extraversion had greater brain reactivity to positive images than did the women who scored low on extraversion. In image (a), red loca-

tions show significant positive correlations between extraversion and reactions to positive images. For the extraverted women, brain activity in response to the positive images was most strongly correlated with brain areas that control emotion, including the frontal cortex and the amygdala.

In contrast, the women who scored high on neuroticism had more brain activation in response to negative images, but in fewer brain areas that control emotions. In image (b), blue locations show significant positive correlations between neuroticism and reactions to negative images. These areas of activation were mostly in the left frontal and temporal cortical areas.

What this study shows is that specific personality traits can produce individual differences in the brain's reaction to emotional stimuli. According to researcher John Gabrieli (2001), "Depending on personality traits, people's brains seem to amplify some aspects of experience over others. All of the participants in this study saw very positive and very negative scenes, but people's brain reactions were very different. One group saw the cup as being very full while the other group saw it as very empty."

---

five-factor model of personality
A trait theory of personality that identifies five basic source traits (extraversion, neuroticism, agreeableness, conscientiousness, and openness to experience) as the fundamental building blocks of personality.

Eysenck (1990) believed that individual differences in personality are due to biological differences among people. For example, Eysenck proposed that an introvert's nervous system is more easily aroused than is an extravert's nervous system. Assuming that people tend to seek out an optimal level of arousal (see Chapter 8), extraverts would seek stimulation from their environment more than introverts would. And, because introverts would be more uncomfortable than extraverts in a highly stimulating environment, introverts would be much less likely to seek out stimulation.

Do introverts and extraverts actually prefer different environments? Researchers John Campbell and Charles Hawley (1982) found that extraverted students tended to study in a relatively noisy, open area of a college library, where there were ample opportunities for socializing with other students. Introverted students preferred to study in a quiet section of the library, where individual carrels and small tables were separated by tall bookshelves. As Eysenck's theory predicts, the introverts preferred study areas that minimized stimulation, while the extraverts preferred studying in an area that provided stimulation.

Brain imaging studies are providing a different line of evidence supporting Eysenck's idea that personality traits reflect biological differences. As discussed in the Focus on Neuroscience, personality traits like extraversion and neuroticism may be associated with distinct patterns of brain activity.

Sixteen Are Too Many, Three Are Too Few
The Five-Factor Model

Many trait theorists felt that Cattell's trait model was too complex and that his 16 personality factors could be reduced to a smaller, more basic set of traits. Yet Eysenck's three-dimensional trait theory seemed too limited, failing to capture other important dimensions of human personality (see Block, 1995).

Today, the consensus among many trait researchers is that the essential building blocks of personality can be described in terms of five basic personality dimensions, which are sometimes called "the Big Five" (Funder, 2001; Goldberg, 1993). According to the **five-factor model of personality,** these five dimensions represent the structural organization of personality traits (McCrae & Costa, 1996).

What are the Big Five? Different trait researchers describe the five basic traits somewhat differently (Johnson & Ostendorf, 1993; Zuckerman & others, 1993). However, the most commonly accepted five factors are: extraversion, neuroticism, agreeableness, conscientiousness, and openness to experience. Table 11.4 describes the Big Five traits, as defined by personality theorists Robert McCrae and Paul Costa, Jr. Note that factor 1, neuroticism, and factor 2, extraversion, are essentially the same as Eysenck's first two personality dimensions.

The five-factor structure of personality has been found in a variety of cultures, including Israel, Portugal, Japan, Korea, and China (McCrae & Costa, 1997). In Canada, Finland, and Poland, as well as other European countries, people describe personality in much the same way, using terms that are generally consistent with the five-factor model (Paunonen & others, 1992). The same five basic trait dimensions were found in Spanish-speaking subjects, whether they were bilingual college students in the United States or Spain (Benet-Martínez & John, 1998). Similar findings seen among Filipinos provide evidence of the Big Five in a non-Western culture (Church & Katigbak, 1989). Based on extensive evidence, personality theorists Robert McCrae and Paul Costa (1997) note that "the structure of individual differences in personality is uniform across several cultures and may in fact be universal."

How can we account for the seeming universality of the five-factor structure? Psychologist David Buss (1991, 1995a) has one intriguing explanation. Buss thinks we should look at the utility of these factors from an evolutionary perspective. He believes that the Big Five traits reflect the personality dimensions that are the most important in the "social landscape" to which humans have had to adapt. Being able to identify who has social power (extraversion), who is likely to share resources (agreeableness), and who is trustworthy (conscientiousness) enhances our likelihood of survival.

Research has shown that traits are remarkably stable over time (Costa & McCrae, 1994; McCrae, 1993). A young adult who is very extraverted, emotionally stable, and relatively open to new experiences is likely to grow into an older adult who could be described in much the same way (McCrae & Costa, 1990). Kenneth's conscientiousness and his willingness to help others were consistent themes throughout his long life. Likewise, Julian's lack of self-control and impulsiveness seemed to be traits that were consistent from childhood to adulthood.

Traits are also generally consistent across different situations. However, situational influences may affect the expression of personality traits. Situations in which your behavior is limited by social "rules" or expectations may limit the expression of your personality characteristics. For the majority of people, behavior is most

Table 11.4

The Five-Factor Model of Personality

Low ⟵——————⟶ High

Factor 1: Neuroticism

Calm	Worrying
Even-tempered, unemotional	Temperamental, emotional
Hardy	Vulnerable

Factor 2: Extraversion

Reserved	Affectionate
Loner	Joiner
Quiet	Talkative

Factor 3: Openness to Experience

Down-to-earth	Imaginative
Conventional, uncreative	Original, creative
Prefer routine	Prefer variety

Factor 4: Agreeableness

Antagonistic	Acquiescent
Ruthless	Softhearted
Suspicious	Trusting

Factor 5: Conscientiousness

Lazy	Hardworking
Aimless	Ambitious
Quitting	Persevering

SOURCE: Adapted from McCrae & Costa (1990).

This table shows the five major factors, or source traits, of personality, according to Big Five theorists Robert McCrae and Paul Costa, Jr. Note that each factor represents a dimension, or range, between two extremes. Listed below each major personality dimension are surface traits that are associated with that dimension.

The Continuity of Traits over the Lifespan Kenneth's conscientiousness was a trait that was evident throughout his life. Because he was too old to join the military when the United States entered World War II, Kenneth volunteered his legal expertise to the American Red Cross, providing them with legal services for the western half of the United States.

behavioral genetics
An interdisciplinary field that studies the effects of genes and heredity on behavior.

*B*ehavioral genetics has documented, without a shadow of a remaining doubt, that personality is to some degree genetically influenced: Identical twins reared apart have similar traits. The *tabula rasa* view of personality as a blank slate at birth that is written upon by experience, for many years a basic assumption of theories of all stripes, is wrong.

David C. Funder (2001)

likely to reflect personality traits when they're in familiar, informal, or private situations that don't involve a lot of social rules or expectations (A. H. Buss, 1989).

Keep in mind, however, that human behavior is the result of a complex *interaction* between traits and situations. People *do* respond, sometimes dramatically, to the demands of a particular situation. But the situations that people choose, and the characteristic way in which they respond to similar situations, are likely to be consistent with their individual personality dispositions (Mischel, 1990; Mischel & Shoda, 1995).

Personality Traits and Behavioral Genetics
Just a Chip off the Old Block?

Do personality traits run in families? Are personality traits determined by genetics? Many trait theorists, such as Raymond Cattell and Hans Eysenck, believed that traits are at least partially genetic in origin. For example, our daughter Laura has always been outgoing and sociable, traits that she shares with both her parents. But is she outgoing because she inherited that trait from us? Or is she outgoing because we modeled and reinforced outgoing behavior? Is it even possible to sort out the relative influence that genetics and environmental experiences have on personality traits?

The field of **behavioral genetics** studies the effects of genes and heredity on behavior. Most behavioral genetics studies on humans involve measuring similarities and differences among members of a large group of people who are genetically related to different degrees. The basic research strategy is to compare the degree of difference among subjects to their degree of genetic relatedness. If a trait is genetically influenced, then the more closely two people are genetically related, the more you would expect them to be similar on that trait (see Chapter 7).

Such studies may involve comparisons between identical twins and fraternal twins or comparisons between twins reared apart and identical twins reared together (see In Focus Box 11.3). Adoption studies, in which adopted children are compared to their biological and adoptive families, are also used in behavioral genetics.

Evidence gathered from twin studies and adoption studies shows that certain personality traits *are* substantially influenced by genetics. The evidence for genetic influence is particularly strong for extraversion and neuroticism, two of the Big Five personality traits (Plomin, 1990; Plomin & others, 1994). Twin studies have also found that openness to experience and conscientiousness, two other Big Five traits, are influenced by genetics, although to a lesser degree than extraversion and neuroticism (Bergeman & others, 1993). Thus, heredity seems to play a significant role in four of the Big Five personality traits: extraversion, neuroticism, openness to experience, and conscientiousness (Bouchard, 1994).

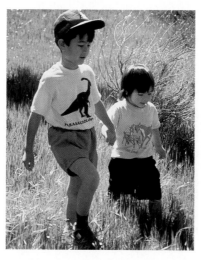

Why Are Siblings So Different? Although two children may grow up in the same home, they experience the home environment in very different ways. Of course, sibling relationships are themselves an important environmental influence in personality development.

So is personality completely determined by genetics? Not at all. As behavioral geneticists Robert Plomin and Richard Rende (1991) explain, "The same data that point to significant genetic influence provide the best available evidence for the importance of nongenetic factors.... Behavioral variability is due at least as much to environment as to heredity." In other words, the influence of environmental factors on personality traits is at least equal to the influence of genetic factors. Some additional evidence that underscores this point is that identical twins are most alike in early life. As the twins grow up, leave home, and encounter different experiences and environments, their personalities become more different (McCartney & others, 1990).

IN FOCUS 11.3

Explaining Those Amazing Identical-Twin Similarities

As part of the ongoing "Minnesota Study of Twins Reared Apart" at the University of Minnesota, researchers David Lykken, Thomas Bouchard, and their colleagues (1992) have been studying a very unusual group of people: over 100 pairs of identical and fraternal twins who were separated at birth or in early childhood and raised in different homes. Shortly after the study began in 1980, the researchers were struck by some of the amazing similarities between identical twins—similarities in occupations, hobbies, personality traits, habits, and sometimes even their life histories—despite the fact that the twins had been separated for many years.

One of the most famous cases is that of the "Jim twins," who had been separated for close to 40 years. Like many of the other reunited twins, the two Jims had similar heights, postures, and voice and speech patterns. More strikingly, both Jims had married and divorced women named Linda, and then married women named Betty. One Jim named his son James Allan, while the other Jim named his son James Alan. Both Jims bit their nails, chain-smoked Salems, and enjoyed working in their basement workshops. And both Jims had vacationed at the same Florida beach, driving there in the same model Chevrolet (Lykken & others, 1992).

Granted, such similarities could simply be due to coincidence (see Wyatt & others, 1984). Linda, Betty, James, and Alan are not exactly rare names in the United States. And literally thousands of people buy the same model car every year, just as thousands of people vacation in Florida. Besides, if you look closely at any two people of the same age, sex, and culture, there are bound to be similarities. It's probably a safe bet, for example, that you enjoy eating pizza and often wear jeans and T-shirts.

But it's difficult to dismiss as mere coincidences all the striking similarities between identical twins in the Minnesota study. Lykken and his colleagues (1992)

Identical Twins As well as sharing common genes, many identical twins share common interests—like professional baseball players Jose (left) and Ozzie Conseco, shown here at the Bears and Eagles Riverfront Stadium in Newark, New Jersey. Because the Conseco twins were reared together, it would be difficult to disentangle the relative importance of genetic and environmental influences on their choice of an identical career.

have pointed out numerous quirky similarities that occurred in the identical twins they studied but did not occur in the fraternal-twin pairs. For example, in the entire sample of twins, there were only two subjects who had been married five times; two subjects who habitually wore seven rings; and two who left love notes around the house for their wives. In each case, the two were identical twins. And only two subjects independently (and correctly) diagnosed a problem with researcher Bouchard's car—a faulty wheel bearing. Again, the two were members of an identical-twin pair. While Lykken and his colleagues acknowledge that some identical-twin similarities are probably due to coincidence, such as the Jim twins marrying women with the same first names, others are probably genetically influenced.

So does this mean that there's a gene for getting married five times or wearing seven rings? Not exactly. Although some physical characteristics and diseases are

influenced by a single gene, complex psychological characteristics, such as your personality, are influenced by a large number of genes acting in combination (Plomin, 1990). Unlike fraternal twins and regular siblings, identical twins share the same specific *configuration* of interacting genes. Lykken and his colleagues suggest that many complex psychological traits, including the strikingly similar idiosyncrasies of identical twins, may result from a unique configuration of interacting genes.

Lykken and his colleagues call certain traits *emergenic traits* because they appear (or *emerge*) only out a unique configuration of many interacting genes. Although they are genetically influenced, emergenic traits do not run in families. To illustrate the idea of emergenic traits, consider the couple of average intelligence who give birth to an extraordinarily gifted child. By all predictions, this couple's offspring should have normal, average intelligence. But because of the unique configuration of the child's genes acting in combination, extraordinary giftedness emerges (Lykken & others, 1992).

David Lykken compares emergenic traits to a winning poker hand. All the members of the family are drawing from the same "deck," or pool of genes. But one member may come up with the special configuration of cards that produces a royal flush—the unique combination of genes that produces a genius or an Olympic athlete. History is filled with cases of people with exceptional talents and abilities in varied fields who grew up in average families.

Finally, it's important to point out there were many differences, as well as similarities, between the identical twins in the Minnesota study. For example, one twin was prone to depression, while the other was not; one twin was an alcoholic, while the other did not drink. So, even with identical twins, it's important to remember that personality is only *partly* determined by genetics.

Evaluating the Trait Perspective on Personality

Although psychologists continue to disagree on how many basic traits exist, they do generally agree that people can be described and compared in terms of basic personality traits. But like the other personality theories, the trait approach has its weaknesses (Block, 1995).

One criticism is that trait theories don't really explain human personality (Pervin, 1994). Instead, they simply label general predispositions to behave in a certain way. Second, trait theorists don't attempt to explain how or why individual differences develop. After all, saying that trait differences are due partly to genetics and partly to environmental influences doesn't say much.

A third criticism is that trait approaches generally fail to address other important personality issues, such as the basic motives that drive human personality, the role of unconscious mental processes, how beliefs about the self influence personality, or how psychological change and growth occur (McAdams, 1992). Conspicuously absent are the grand conclusions about the essence of human nature that characterize the psychoanalytic and humanistic theories. So, although trait theories are useful in describing individual differences and predicting behavior, there are limitations to their usefulness.

As you've seen, each of the major perspectives on personality has contributed to our understanding of human personality. The four perspectives are summarized in Table 11.5. For a critical look at a distinctly different approach to understanding personality, read Science Versus Pseudoscience Box 11.4, Is Your Personality Written in the Stars?

Our discussion of personality would not be complete without a description of how personality is formally evaluated and measured. In the next section, we'll briefly survey the tests that are used in personality assessment.

Table | 11.5

The Major Personality Perspectives

Perspective	Key Theorists	Key Themes and Ideas
Psychoanalytic	Sigmund Freud	Influence of unconscious psychological processes; importance of sexual and aggressive instincts; lasting effects of early childhood experiences
	Carl Jung	The collective unconscious, archetypes, and psychological harmony
	Karen Horney	Importance of parent–child relationship; defending against basic anxiety; womb envy
	Alfred Adler	Striving for superiority, compensating for feelings of inferiority
Humanistic	Carl Rogers	Emphasis on the self-concept, psychological growth, free will, and inherent goodness
	Abraham Maslow	Behavior as motivated by hierarchy of needs and striving of self-actualization
Social cognitive	Albert Bandura	Reciprocal interaction of behavioral, cognitive, and environmental factors; emphasis on conscious thoughts, self-efficacy beliefs, and self-regulation,
Trait	Raymond Cattell	Emphasis on measuring and describing individual differences; 16 source traits of personality
	Hans Eysenck	Three basic dimensions of personality: introversion–extraversion, neuroticism–emotional stability, and psychoticism
	Robert McCrae, Paul Costa, Jr.	Five-factor model: five basic dimensions of personality: neuroticism, extraversion, openness to experience, agreeableness, conscientiousness

SCIENCE VERSUS PSEUDOSCIENCE 11.4

Is Your Personality Written in the Stars?

Pseudoscientific explanations for personality, such as astrology, existed long before any of the personality theories described in this chapter came into being. The history of astrology can be traced back over 4,000 years (Dean & others, 1996). Astrology's basic premise is that the positions of the planets and stars at the time and place of your birth determine your personality and destiny. Originally, astrology was based on the theory that the earth was the center of the solar system, with the stars, the planets, and the sun revolving around the earth (Crowe, 1990). This theory was scientifically refuted in the early 1600s by Galileo, the Italian astronomer who invented the telescope.

Today, belief in astrological interpretations and predictions remains widespread. Surveys of college students have found that over 30 percent believe in astrology (Clarke, 1991; Duncan & others, 1992). Every year, about 40 million Americans seek astrological guidance from one of the approximately 200,000 practicing astrologers (Glick & others, 1989). About 1,200 North American newspapers carry astrology columns, yet another testament to astrology's widespread popularity (Kurtz & Fraknoi, 1986).

Just how valid is astrology in assessing personality? Can the claims of astrologers be scientifically tested? As it turns out, there is no shortage of scientific investigations of the abilities of astrologers to assess personality characteristics. Let's consider Shawn Carlson's (1985) carefully designed study.

Carlson's (1985) study involved 30 American and European astrologers who were considered by their peers in the astrological community to be among the best. A panel of astrological advisers was also involved in helping Carlson design his study. All the participating astrologers agreed beforehand that Carlson's study was a "fair test" of astrological claims.

In the first part of Carlson's study, the astrologers developed astrological pro-

Non-Sequitur

files for 177 subjects based on each person's time, date, and place of birth. Each subject was later shown three astrological profiles—one that was based on the person's time and place of birth and two randomly chosen astrological profiles of other subjects in the study. The question was simple: Could the subject pick out his or her own personality profile from the three astrological profiles? If the subjects did no better than merely guessing, you would expect them to be correct about one-third of the time.

In the second part of Carlson's study, 116 of the subjects completed the California Personality Inventory (CPI). The CPI is one of the most widely used personality inventories and has been shown to be scientifically valid in hundreds of studies (Kramer & Conoley, 1992). All the astrologers in the study were familiar with reading CPI profiles. The astrologers were given a subject's astrological profile and three CPI profiles. All the astrologer had to do was match the person's astrological profile with the same person's CPI profile.

Carlson also presented the subjects with three CPI profiles. One was their own and two were randomly chosen. All the subjects had to do was identify which CPI profile they thought was theirs. If the astrologers or the subjects did no better than merely guessing, you would expect them to be correct only one-third of the time.

The results of Carlson's study? When presented with three astrological profiles, the subjects were correct only 33 percent of the time, meaning that they did *no better than chance* at identifying their own astrological profiles. Interestingly, the subjects were *also* unable to select their own CPI profiles at a rate better than chance! In other words, Carlson's findings cast doubt on the ability of people to subjectively evaluate the accuracy of *any* kind of personality description.

How did the astrologers do when they tried to match a subject's astrological profile with his or her CPI profile? The astrologers were correct only 34 percent of the time—they performed no better than someone merely guessing. Carlson (1985) summarized the results of his study in this way:

> Great pains were taken to insure that the experiment was unbiased and to make sure that astrology was given every reasonable chance to succeed. It failed. . . . Despite the fact that the astrologers approved the design and predicted 50 percent as the "minimum" effect they would expect to see, astrology failed to perform at a level better than chance.

Carlson's findings are not isolated, by any means (see Dean & others, 1996; French & others, 1991). In a thoughtful review of scientific research on astrology, University of Hawaii researcher Richard Crowe (1990) concluded: "Popular and serious astrology have absolutely no reliable basis in scientific fact. Statistically, astrology does not stand up to any valid test that can be applied."

psychological test
A test that assesses a person's abilities aptitudes, interests, or personality, based on a systematically obtained sample of behavior.

projective test
A type of personality test that involves a person's interpreting an ambiguous image; used to assess unconscious motives, conflicts, psychological defenses, and personality traits.

Rorschach Inkblot Test
A projective test using inkblots, developed by Swiss psychiatrist Hermann Rorschach in 1921.

graphology
A pseudoscience that claims to assess personality, social, and occupational attributes based on a person's distinctive handwriting, doodles, and drawing style.

Assessing Personality
Psychological Tests

Key Theme

■ Tests to measure and evaluate personality fall into two basic categories: projective tests and self-report inventories.

Key Questions

■ What are the most widely used personality tests, and how are they administered and interpreted?
■ What are the strengths and weaknesses of projective tests and self-report inventories?

When we discussed intelligence tests in Chapter 7, we described what makes a good psychological test. Beyond intelligence tests, there are literally hundreds of **psychological tests** that can be used to assess abilities, aptitudes, interests, and personality (see Plake & Impara, 2001). Any psychological test is useful insofar as it archieves two basic goals:

1. It accurately and consistently reflects a person's characteristics on some dimension.

2. It predicts a person's future psychological functioning or behavior.

In this section, we'll look at the very different approaches used in the two basic types of personality tests—projective tests and self-report inventories. After looking at some of the most commonly used tests in each category, we'll evaluate the strengths and weaknesses of each approach.

Projective Tests
Like Seeing Things in the Clouds

Projective tests developed out of psychoanalytic approaches to personality. In the most commonly used projective tests, a person is presented with a vague image, such as an inkblot or an ambiguous scene, then asked to describe what she "sees" in the image. The person's response is thought to be a projection of her unconscious conflicts, motives, psychological defenses, and personality traits. Notice that this idea is related to the defense mechanism of *projection,* which was described in Table 11.1. The first projective test was the famous **Rorschach Inkblot Test,** published by Swiss psychiatrist Hermann Rorschach in 1921 (Hertz, 1992). The Rorschach test consists of 10 cards, 5 that show black-and-white inkblots and 5 that depict colored inkblots. One card at a time, the person describes whatever he sees in the inkblot. The examiner records the person's responses verbatim and also observes his behavior, gestures, and reactions.

Numerous scoring systems exist for the Rorschach. Interpretation is based on such criteria as whether the person reports seeing animate or inanimate objects, human or animal figures, and movement, and whether the person deals with the whole blot or just fragments of it (Exner, 1993).

The Rorschach Inkblot Test Because he died the year after his inkblot test was published, Hermann Rorschach (1884–1922) never knew how popular his projective test would become. The Rorschach Inkblot Test is sometimes used to "break the ice" in clinical interviews.

SCIENCE VERSUS PSEUDOSCIENCE 11.5

Graphology: The "Write" Way to Assess Personality?

Does the way that you shape your *d*'s, dot your *i*'s, and cross your *t*'s reveal your true inner nature? That's the basic premise of **graphology,** a pseudoscience that claims that your handwriting reveals your temperament, personality traits, intelligence, and reasoning ability. If that weren't enough, graphologists also claim that they can accurately evaluate a job applicant's honesty, reliability, leadership potential, ability to work with others, and so forth (B. Beyerstein & D. Beyerstein, 1992).

Handwriting analysis is very popular throughout North America and Europe. In the United States alone, there are over 30 graphology societies, each promoting its own specific methods of analyzing handwriting (Beyerstein, 1996). Many different types of agencies and institutions use graphology. For example, the FBI and the U.S. State Department have consulted graphologists to assess the handwriting of people who mail death threats to government officials (Scanlon & Mauro, 1992).

Graphology is especially popular in the business world. Thousands of American companies, including Sears, U.S. Steel, and Bendix, have used graphology to assist in hiring new employees (Basil, 1991; Taylor & Sackheim, 1988). The use of graphology in hiring and promotions is even more widespread in Europe. According to one estimate, over 80 percent of European companies use graphology in personnel matters (Greasley, 2000).

When subjected to scientific evaluation, how does graphology fare? Consider a study by Anthony Edwards and Peter Armitage (1992) that investigated graphologists' ability to distinguish between people in three different groups:

- Successful versus unsuccessful secretaries
- Successful business entrepreneurs versus librarians and bank clerks
- Actors and actresses versus monks and nuns

In designing their study, Edwards and Armitage enlisted the help of leading graphologists and incorporated their suggestions into the study design. The graphologists preapproved the study's format and indicated that they felt it was a fair test of graphology. The grapholo-

DILBERT

DILBERT Reprinted with permission of United Features Syndicate, Inc.

gists also predicted they would have a high degree of success in discriminating between the people in each group. One graphologist stated that the graphologists would have close to a 100 percent success rate. Remember that prediction.

The three groups—successful/unsuccessful secretaries, entrepreneurs/librarians, and actors/monks—represented a combined total of 170 participants. As requested by the graphologists, each participant indicated their age, sex, and hand preference. Each person also produced 20 lines of spontaneous handwriting on a neutral topic.

Four leading graphologists independently evaluated the handwriting samples. For each group, the graphologists tried to assign each handwriting sample to one category or the other. Two control measures were built into the study: (1) the handwriting samples were also analyzed by four ordinary people with *no* formal training in graphology or psychology; and (2) a *typewritten* transcript of the handwriting samples was evaluated by four psychologists. The psychologists made their evaluations on the basis of the *content* of the transcripts rather than on the handwriting itself.

In the accompanying table, you can see how well the graphologists fared as com-

pared to the untrained evaluators and the psychologists. Clearly, the graphologists fell far short of the nearly perfect accuracy they predicted they would demonstrate. In fact, in one case, the *untrained* assessors actually *outperformed* the graphologists— they were slightly better at identifying successful versus unsuccessful secretaries.

Overall, the completely inexperienced judges achieved a success rate of 59 percent correct. The professional graphologists achieved a slightly better success rate of 65 percent. Obviously, this is not a great difference.

Hundreds of other studies have cast similar doubts on the ability of graphology to identify personality characteristics and to predict job performance from handwriting samples (see Dean, 1992; Furnham, 1991; Neter & Ben-Shakhar, 1989). In a global review of the evidence, psychologist Barry Beyerstein (1996) wrote that "Graphologists have unequivocally failed to demonstrate the validity or reliability of their art for predicting work performance, aptitudes, or personality.... If graphology cannot legitimately claim to be a scientific means of measuring human talents and leanings, what is it really? In short, it is a pseudoscience."

Success Rates by Type of Assessor

Group Assessed	Graphologists	Untrained Assessors	Psychologists
Good/bad secretaries	67%	70%	56%
Entrepreneurs/librarians	63%	53%	52%
Actors/monks	67%	58%	53%
Overall success rate	65%	59%	54%

The Thematic Apperception Test Developed by psychologist Henry Murray, the TAT involves creating a story about an ambiguous scene, like the one shown on the card this young man is holding. The person is thought to project his own motives, conflicts, and other personality characteristics into the story he creates. According to Murray (1943), "Before he knows it, he has said things about an invented character that apply to himself, things which he would have been reluctant to confess in response to a direct question."

A more structured projective test is the **Thematic Apperception Test,** abbreviated **TAT,** which we discussed in Chapter 8. In the TAT, the person looks at a series of cards, each depicting an ambiguous scene. The person is asked to create a story about the scene, including what the characters are feeling and how the story turns out. The stories are scored for the motives, needs, anxieties, and conflicts of the main character, and how conflicts are resolved (Bellak, 1993). As with the Rorschach, interpreting the TAT involves the subjective judgment of the examiner.

Strengths and Weaknesses of Projective Tests

Although sometimes used in research, projective tests are mainly used to help assess emotionally disturbed individuals. According to many clinicians, the primary strength of projective tests is that they provide a wealth of qualitative information about an individual's psychological functioning, information that can be explored further in psychotherapy.

However, there are several drawbacks to projective tests. First, the testing situation or the examiner's behavior can influence a person's responses. Second, the scoring of projective tests is highly subjective, requiring the examiner to make numerous judgments about the person's responses. Consequently, two examiners may test the same individual and arrive at different conclusions. Third, projective tests often fail to produce consistent results. If the same person takes a projective test on two separate occasions, very different results may be found. Finally, projective tests are poor at predicting future behavior.

The bottom line? Despite their widespread use, hundreds of studies of projective tests seriously question their *validity* (that the tests measure what they purport to measure) and their *reliability* (the consistency of test results) (see Lilienfeld & others, 2000, 2001). Nonetheless, projective tests remain very popular, especially among clinical psychologists (Butcher & Rouse, 1996).

Self-Report Inventories
Does Anyone Have an Eraser?

Self-report inventories typically use a paper-and-pencil format and take a direct, structured approach to assessing personality. People answer specific questions or rate themselves on various dimensions of behavior or psychological functioning. Often called *objective personality tests,* self-report inventories contain items that have been shown by previous research to differentiate between people on a particular personality characteristic. Unlike projective tests, self-report inventories are objectively scored by comparing a person's answers to standardized norms collected on large groups of people.

The most widely used self-report inventory is the **Minnesota Multiphasic Personality Inventory (MMPI)** (Butcher & Rouse, 1996). First published in the 1940s and revised in the 1980s, the current version is referred to as the *MMPI-2.* The MMPI consists of over 500 statements. The person responds to each statement with "True," "False," or "Cannot say." Topics include social, political, religious, and sexual attitudes, physical and psychological health, interpersonal relationships, and abnormal thoughts and behaviors (Graham, 1993). Sample MMPI items are shown in Table 11.6.

The MMPI is widely used by clinical psychologists and psychiatrists to assess patients. It is also used to evaluate the mental health of candidates for such occupations

Table **11.6**

Simulated MMPI-2 Items

Most people will use somewhat unfair means to gain profit or an advantage rather than lose it.

I am often very tense on the job.

The things that run through my head sometimes are horrible.

Sometimes there is a feeling like something is pressing in on my head.

Sometimes I think so fast I can't keep up.

I am worried about sex.

I believe I am being plotted against.

I wish I could do over some of the things I have done.

SOURCE: MMPI-2®.

as police officers, doctors, nurses, and professional pilots. What keeps people from simply answering items in a way that makes them look psychologically healthy? Like many other self-report inventories, the MMPI has special scales to detect whether a person is answering honestly and consistently (Butcher, 1999). For example, if someone responds "True" to items such as "I *never* put off until tomorrow what I should do today" and "I *always* pick up after myself," it's probably a safe bet that the person is inadvertently or intentionally distorting his or her other responses.

The MMPI was originally designed to assess mental health and detect psychological symptoms. In contrast, the California Personality Inventory and the Sixteen Personality Factor Questionnaire are personality inventories that were designed to assess normal populations. Of the 462 true–false items on the **California Personality Inventory (CPI),** nearly half are drawn from the MMPI. The CPI provides measures on such characteristics as interpersonal effectiveness, self-control, independence, and empathy. Profiles generated by the CPI are used to predict such things as high school and college grades, delinquency, and job performance (Gough, 1989).

The **Sixteen Personality Factor Questionnaire (16PF),** originally developed by Raymond Cattell, is based on Cattell's trait theory. The 16PF uses a forced-choice format in which the person must respond to each item by choosing one of three alternatives. Just as the test's name implies, the results generate a profile on Cattell's 16 personality factors. Each personality factor is represented as a range, with a person's score falling somewhere along the continuum between the two extremes (see Figure 11.5). The 16PF is widely used for career counseling, marital counseling, and evaluating employees and executives (Karson & O'Dell, 1989).

(a)

EXAMPLE QUESTIONS

1. I often like to watch team games.
   a. true
   b. ?
   c. false
2. I prefer friends who are:
   a. quiet
   b. ?
   c. lively
3. Adult is to child as cat is to:
   a. kitten
   b. dog
   c. baby

Note: The person taking the test is instructed to answer "b.?" only when neither *a* nor *c* is a better choice for him or her.

(b)

Airline pilots — Writers

FIGURE 11.5 The 16PF: Example Questions and Profiles The 16PF, developed by Raymond Cattell, is a self-report inventory that contains 185 items. When scored, the 16PF generates a personality profile. In the example shown, personality profiles of airline pilots and writers are compared. Cattell (1973) found that pilots are more controlled, more relaxed, more self-assured, and less sensitive than writers.

SOURCE: Cattell & others (1993).

Strengths and Weaknesses of Self-Report Inventories

The two most important strengths of self-report inventories are their *standardization* and their *use of established norms* (see Chapter 7). Each person receives the same instructions and responds to the same items. The results of self-report inventories are objectively scored and compared to norms established by previous research. In fact, the MMPI, the CPI, and the 16PF can all be scored by computer.

As a general rule, the reliability and validity of self-report inventories are far greater than those of projective tests. Literally thousands of studies have demonstrated that the MMPI, the CPI, and the 16PF provide accurate, consistent results that can be used to generally predict behavior (Anastasi & Urbina, 1997).

However, self-report inventories also have their weaknesses. First, despite the inclusion of items designed to detect deliberate deception, there is considerable evidence that people can still successfully fake responses and answer in socially desirable ways (Anastasi & Urbina, 1997). Second, some people are prone to responding in a set way. They may consistently pick the first alternative or answer "True" whether the item is true for them or not. And some tests, such as the MMPI and CPI, include hundreds of items. Taking these tests can

Thematic Apperception Test (TAT)
A projective personality test that involves creating stories about each of a series of ambiguous scenes.

self-report inventory
A type of psychological test in which a person's responses to standardized questions are compared to established norms.

Minnesota Multiphasic Personality Inventory (MMPI)
A self-report inventory that assesses personality characteristics and psychological disorders; used to assess both normal and disturbed populations.

California Personality Inventory (CPI)
A self-report inventory that assesses personality characteristics in normal populations.

Sixteen Personality Factor Questionnaire (16PF)
A self-report inventory developed by Raymond Cattell that generates a personality profile with ratings on 16 trait dimensions.

become quite tedious, and people may lose interest in carefully choosing the most appropriate response.

Third, people are not always accurate judges of their own behavior, attitudes, or attributes. And some people defensively deny their true feelings, needs, and attitudes, even to themselves (Shedler & others, 1993). For example, a person might indicate that she enjoys parties, even though she actually avoids social gatherings whenever possible.

To sum up, personality tests are generally useful strategies that can provide insights about the psychological makeup of people. But no personality test, by itself, is likely to provide a definitive description of a given individual. In practice, psychologists and other professionals usually combine personality test results with behavioral observations and background information, including interviews with family members, co-workers, or other significant people in the person's life.

Finally, people can and often do change over time, especially when their life circumstances undergo a significant change. Hence, projective tests and self-report inventories provide a barometer of personality and psychological functioning only at the time of the test.

11.4 R·E·V·I·E·W

C·O·N·C·E·P·T

Trait Theories and Personality Assessment

1. Trait theories focus on:
   a. individual differences
   b. individual similarities
   c. stages of personality development
   d. universal processes of motivation

2. Surface traits are to source traits as:
   a. aggression is to violent behavior
   b. friendly is to extraversion
   c. conscientiousness is to personality
   d. relaxed is to tense

3. Personality differences among siblings are primarily due to:
   a. shared experiences   c. birth order
   b. genetic differences   d. nonshared experiences

4. Dana took the same personality test twice within three months. She obtained very different results each time. Which test did she most likely take?
   a. MMPI   c. 16PF
   b. TAT   d. CPI

5. A key strength of the MMPI and the 16PF is:
   a. they provide a wealth of qualitative information about the individual
   b. they are unstructured
   c. they are standardized
   d. that scoring relies on the examiner's expertise and clinical judgment

Summing Up
Personality

Over the course of this chapter, you've encountered firsthand some of the most influential contributors to modern psychological thought. Their ideas continue to engage today's researchers (see Bandura, 1997; Freiberg, 1996; Mischel & Shoda, 1995; Wiggins, 1996). As you'll see in Chapter 15, the major personality perspectives provide the basis for many forms of psychotherapy.

Clearly, the psychoanalytic, humanistic, social cognitive, and trait perspectives each provide a fundamentally different way of conceptualizing personality. That each perspective has strengths and weaknesses underscores the point that no single perspective can explain all aspects of human personality. Indeed, no one personality theory could explain why Kenneth and Julian were so different. And, given the complex factors involved in human personality, it's doubtful that any single theory ever will capture the essence of human personality. Even so, each perspective has made important and lasting contributions to the understanding of human personality.

possible selves
The aspect of the self-concept that includes images of the selves that you hope, fear, or expect to become in the future.

Some psychologists believe that a person's self-concept is not a singular mental self-image, as Carl Rogers proposed, but a *multifaceted system* of related images and ideas (Hermans, 1996; Markus & Kunda, 1986). This collection of related images about yourself reflects your goals, values, emotions, and relationships (Markus & Cross, 1990; Markus & Wurf, 1987).

According to psychologist Hazel Markus and her colleagues, an important aspect of your self-concept has to do with the images of the selves that you *might* become—your **possible selves.** Possible selves are highly personalized, vivid, futuristic images of the self that reflect hopes, fears, and fantasies. As Markus and co-researcher Paula Nurius (1986) wrote, "The possible selves that are hoped for might include the successful self, the creative self, the rich self, the thin self, or the loved and admired self, whereas the dreaded possible selves could be the alone self, the depressed self, the incompetent self, the alcoholic self, the unemployed self, or the bag lady self."

The Influence of Hoped-For and Dreaded Possible Selves

Possible selves are more than just idle daydreams or wishful fantasies. In fact, possible selves influence our behavior in important ways (Markus & Nurius, 1986; Oyserman & others, 1995). We're often not aware of the possible selves that we have incorporated into our self-concepts. Nevertheless, they can serve as powerful forces that either activate or stall our efforts to reach important goals. Your incentive, drive, and motivation are greatly influenced by your possible selves, and so are your decisions and choices about future behavior.

Imagine that you harbor a hoped-for possible self of becoming a professional musician. You would probably practice with greater regularity and intensity than someone who does not hold a vivid mental picture of performing solo at Carnegie Hall or being named Performer of the Year at the American Country Music Awards.

Dreaded possible selves can also influence behavior, whether they are realistic or not. Consider Don's father, Kenneth. Although never wealthy, Kenneth was financially secure throughout his long life. Yet Kenneth had lived through the Great Depression and witnessed firsthand the financial devastation that occurred in the lives of countless people. Kenneth seems to have harbored a dreaded possible self of becoming penniless. When Kenneth died, the family found a $100 bill tucked safely under his mattress.

A positive possible self, even if it is not very realistic, can protect an individual's self-esteem in the face of failure (Markus & Nurius, 1986). A high school girl who thinks she is unpopular with her classmates may console herself with visions of a possible self as a famous scientist who snubs her intellectually inferior classmates at her 10-year class reunion. As Hazel Markus and Paul Nurius (1986) explained:

> Positive possible selves can be exceedingly liberating because they foster hope that the present self is not immutable. At the same time, negative possible selves can be powerfully imprisoning because their [emotional impact] and expectations may stifle attempts to change or develop.

Possible Selves, Self-Efficacy Beliefs, and Motivation

Self-efficacy beliefs are closely connected to the idea of possible selves. Performing virtually any task involves the construction of a possible self that is capable and competent of performing the action required (Ruvolo & Markus, 1992).

Thus, people who vividly imagine possible selves as "successful because of hard work" persist longer and expend more effort on tasks than do people who imagine themselves as "unsuccessful despite hard work" (Ruvolo & Markus, 1992). The motivation to achieve academically increases when your possible selves include a future self who is successful because of academic achievement (Oyserman & others, 1995).

Applying the Research: Assessing Your Possible Selves

How can you apply these research findings to *your* life? First, it's important to stress again that we're often unaware of how the possible selves we've mentally constructed influence our beliefs, actions, and self-evaluations. Thus, the first step is to consciously assess the role that your possible selves play in your life (Oyserman & others, 1995).

Take a few moments and jot down the "possible selves" that are active in your working self-concept. To help you in this task, write three responses to each of the following questions:

1. Next year, I expect to be . . .

2. Next year, I am afraid that I will be . . .

3. Next year, I want to avoid becoming . . .

After focusing on the short-term future, take these same questions and extend them to 5 years from now or even 10 years from now. Most likely, certain themes and goals will consistently emerge. Now the critical questions:

- How are your possible selves affecting your *current* motivation, goals, feelings, and decisions?

- Are your possible selves even remotely plausible?

- Are they pessimistic and limiting?

- Are they unrealistically optimistic?

Finally, ask yourself honestly: What realistic strategies are you using to try to become like the self that you want to become? To avoid becoming the selves that you dread?

These questions should help you gain some insight into whether your possible selves are influencing your behavior in productive, constructive ways. If they are not, now is an excellent time to think about replacing or modifying the possible selves that operate most powerfully in your own self-concept. Why is this so important? Because to a large extent, who we become is guided by who we *imagine* we'll become. Just imagine the possibilities of who *you* could become!

Chapter Review

Personality

Key Points

Introduction: What Is Personality?

- **Personality** is defined as an individual's unique and relatively consistent patterns of thinking, feeling, and behaving. **Personality theories** attempt to explain how people are similar, why they are different, and why every individual is unique.

- The four major theoretical perspectives on personality are the psychoanalytic, humanistic, social cognitive, and trait perspectives.

The Psychoanalytic Perspective on Personality

- **Psychoanalysis** was founded by Sigmund Freud. It stresses the unconscious, the importance of sex and aggression, and the influence of early childhood experience. Freud's theory was extremely controversial throughout his lifetime and remains so today.

- Freud believed that behavior is strongly influenced by the unconscious. The contents of the **unconscious** can surface in disguised form in **free associations,** dreams, slips of the tongue, and seeming accidents.

- Personality consists of three psychological processes: id, ego, and superego. The **id** is fueled by instinctual energy and ruled by the **pleasure principle.** The two instinctual drives are **Eros,** the life instinct, and **Thanatos,** the death instinct. **Libido** is the psychological and emotional energy associated with the sex drive. The **ego** is partly conscious and is ruled by the **reality principle.** The **superego** is partly conscious and represents internalized moral values and rules.

- Anxiety results when the demands of the id or the superego threaten to overwhelm the ego. **Ego defense mechanisms** reduce anxiety by distorting either thoughts or reality. **Repression** is involved in all ego defense mechanisms. **Displacement** is another defense mechanism involving the unconscious shifting of emotional impulses to a less threatening substitute target. **Sublimation** is a special form of displacement.

- The **psychosexual stages** are age-related developmental periods in which sexual impulses are expressed through different bodily zones and activities associated with these areas. The foundations of adult personality are established during the first five years of life by the child's progression through the oral, anal, and phallic stages. One result of the **Oedipus complex** is that children come to join forces with the same-sex parent, a process Freud called **identification.** Fixation at a particular stage may result if the developmental conflicts are not successfully resolved. The latency and genital stages occur during late childhood and adolescence.

- The neo-Freudians believed in the importance of the unconscious and early childhood experience but disagreed with other aspects of Freud's theory. Carl Jung emphasized psychological growth and proposed the existence of the **collective unconscious** and **archetypes.** Karen Horney emphasized the role of social relationships in protecting against basic anxiety. Horney objected to Freud's views on female development, particularly his idea of penis envy. Alfred Adler believed that the most fundamental human motive was to strive for superiority.

- Freud's theory has been criticized for resting on insufficient evidence, being difficult to test, and being sexist.

The Humanistic Perspective on Personality

- **Humanistic psychology** was championed as the "third force" in psychology. It emphasized human potential, psychological growth, self-awareness, and free will. Important humanistic theorists were Carl Rogers and Abraham Maslow.

- Rogers believed that the most basic human motive is the **actualizing tendency.** He viewed the **self-concept** as the most important aspect of personality. **Conditional positive regard** by parents or other caregivers causes a person to deny or distort aspects of experience, leading to a state of incongruence with regard to the self-concept. In contrast, **unconditional positive regard** leads to a state of congruence. The fully functioning person experiences congruence, the actualizing tendency, and psychological growth.

- The humanistic perspective on personality has been criticized for being difficult to validate or test scientifically and for being too optimistic.

The Social Cognitive Perspective on Personality

- Albert Bandura's **social cognitive theory** stresses the role of conscious thought processes, goals, and self-regulation. **Reciprocal determinism** emphasizes the interaction of behavioral, cognitive, and environmental factors in behavior and personality.

- **Self-efficacy** beliefs influence behavior, performance, motivation, and persistence.

- Social cognitive theories emphasize the interaction of multiple factors in determining personality and behavior. Although a key strength of this perspective is its grounding in empirical research, it has been criticized for its limited view of human personality, which ignores unconscious conflicts and emotions.

The Trait Perspective on Personality

- **Trait theories** focus on measuring and describing individual differences, or **traits. Surface traits** can be easily inferred from observable behaviors. **Source traits** are thought to represent the basic, fundamental dimensions of personality.

- Raymond Cattell believed that there are 16 basic personality factors. Hans Eysenck proposed that there are three basic personality dimensions. Eysenck believed that the extraversion–introversion dimension may reflect psychological differences.

- According to the **five-factor model,** there are five basic personality dimensions: extraversion, neuroticism, agreeableness, conscientiousness, and openness to experience.

- Traits are generally stable over time and across situations, although situations do influence how and whether traits are expressed.

- **Behavioral genetics** research uses twin and adoption studies to measure the relative influence of genetics and environment. Extraversion, neuroticism, openness to experience, and conscientiousness seem to have a significant genetic component.

- The trait perspective is useful in describing individual differences and in predicting behavior. Trait theories have been criticized for their failure to explain human personality and the development of individual differences.

Assessing Personality: *Psychological Tests*

- Successful **psychological tests** accurately reflect personal characteristics on some dimension and predict future psychological functioning or behavior. The two basic types of personality tests are projective tests and self-report inventories. **Projective tests** developed out of the psychoanalytic approach and include the **Rorschach Inkblot Test** and the **Thematic Apperception Test.**

- Projective tests provide qualitative information about an individual. They have some weaknesses: Responses may be affected by the examiner or the situation; scoring is very subjective; results may be inconsistent; and they do not predict behavior well.

- **Self-report inventories** are objectively scored and differentiate among people on particular personality characteristics. Self-report inventories include the **MMPI, CPI,** and **16PF.** The reliability, validity, and predictive value of self-report inventories are high. However, people do not always respond honestly or accurately to items in self-report inventories. Psychological tests provide one measure of personality at a particular point in time.

Key Terms

personality, p. 453

personality theory, p. 453

psychoanalysis, p. 454

free association, p. 455

unconscious, p. 456

id, p. 457

Eros, p. 457

libido, p. 457

Thanatos, p. 457

pleasure principle, p. 457

ego, p. 458

reality principle, p. 458

superego, p. 458

ego defense mechanisms, p. 459

repression, p. 459

displacement, p. 459

sublimation, p. 459

psychosexual stages, p. 461

Oedipus complex, p. 462

identification, p. 462

collective unconscious, p. 465

archetypes, p. 465

humanistic psychology, p. 469

actualizing tendency, p. 470

self-concept, p. 472

conditional positive regard, p. 472

unconditional positive regard, p. 472

social cognitive theory, p. 474

reciprocal determinism, p. 475

self-efficacy, p. 475

trait, p. 478

trait theory, p. 478

surface traits, p. 478

source traits, p. 478

five-factor model of personality, p. 481

behavioral genetics, p. 482

psychological test, p. 486

projective test, p. 486

Rorschach Inkblot Test, p. 486

graphology, p. 487

Thematic Apperception Test (TAT), p. 488

self-report inventory, p. 488

Minnesota Multiphasic Personality Inventory (MMPI), p. 488

California Personality Inventory (CPI), p. 489

Sixteen Personality Factor Questionnaire (16PF), p. 489

possible selves, p. 491

Key People

Alfred Adler (1870–1937)   Austrian physician who broke with Sigmund Freud and developed his own psychoanalytic theory of personality, which emphasized social factors and the motivation toward self-improvement and self-realization; key ideas include the inferiority complex and the superiority complex. (p. 466)

Albert Bandura (b. 1925)   Contemporary American psychologist who is best known for his research on observational learning and his social cognitive theory of personality; key ideas include self-efficacy beliefs and reciprocal determinism. (p. 474)

Raymond Cattell (1905–1998)   British-born American psychologist who developed a trait theory that identifies 16 essential source traits or personality factors; also developed the widely used self-report personality test, the Sixteen Personality Factor Questionnaire (16PF). (p. 479)

Hans Eysenck (1916–1997)   German-born British psychologist who developed a trait theory of personality that identifies the three basic dimensions of personality as neuroticism, extraversion, and psychoticism. (p. 479)

Sigmund Freud (1856–1939)   Austrian neurologist who founded psychoanalysis, which is both a comprehensive theory of personality and a form of psychotherapy; emphasized the role of unconscious determinants of behavior and early childhood experiences in the development of personality and psychological problems; key ideas include id, ego, and superego; the psychosexual stages of development; and the ego defense mechanisms. (p. 454)

Karen Horney (1885–1952)   German-born American psychoanalyst who emphasized the role of social relationships and culture in personality; sharply disagreed with Freud's characterization of female psychological development, especially his notion that women suffer from penis envy; key ideas include basic anxiety. (p. 465)

Carl G. Jung (1875–1961)   Swiss psychiatrist who broke with Sigmund Freud to develop his own psychoanalytic theory of personality, which stressed striving toward psychological harmony; key ideas include the collective unconscious and archetypes. (p. 464)

Abraham Maslow (1908–1970)   American psychologist who was one of the founders of humanistic psychology and emphasized the study of healthy personality development; developed a hierarchical theory of motivation based on the idea that people will strive for self-actualization, the highest motive, only after more basic needs have been met; key ideas include the hierarchy of needs and self-actualization. (p. 470)

Carl Rogers (1902–1987)   American psychologist who was one of the founders of humanistic psychology; developed a theory of personality and form of psychotherapy that emphasized the inherent worth of people, the innate tendency to strive toward one's potential, and the importance of the self-concept in personality development; key ideas include the actualizing tendency and unconditional positive regard. (p. 470)

Concept Review Answers

11.1   page 463

1. d.   *2.* c   *3.* b   *4.* b   *5.* a   *6.* c

11.2   page 467

1. Freud   *3.* Adler   *5.* Freud
2. Horney   *4.* Jung   *6.* Horney

11.3   page 477

1. False. Rogers believed it is parents' responsibility to guide and control their children's behavior.

2. False. Rogers advocated the use of unconditional positive regard.

3. True

4. True

5. False. Social cognitive theory holds that human behavior is determined by the interaction of environmental, cognitive, and behavioral factors.

6. True

7. True

11.4 page 490

1. a   *2.* b   *3.* d   *4.* b   *5.* c

Web Companion   Review Activities

You can find additional review activities at **www.worthpublishers.com/hockenbury**
The Psychology 3e Web Companion has a self-scoring practice quiz, flashcards, two interactive crossword puzzles, and other activities to help you master the material in this chapter.

Push to Walk

Social Psychology

Prologue

The "Homeless" Man

Remember Erv and Fern, Sandy's parents, from Chapter 5? A few years ago, Fern and Erv got two free plane tickets when they were bumped from an overbooked flight. They decided to use their free plane tickets to visit a city they had always wanted to see—San Francisco. Even though Fern was excited about the trip, she was also anxious about visiting the earthquake zone. Erv wasn't especially worried about earthquakes, but he was worried about whether his old army buddy could still beat him at poker. Mostly, they both wanted to see the famous sights, eat seafood, wander through shops, and explore used bookstores, which is Erv's favorite hobby.

As it turned out, Fern and Erv were both quite taken by the beauty and charm of San Francisco. But they were also disturbed by the number of homeless people they saw on the city streets, sleeping in the doorways of expensive shops and restaurants. This was especially disturbing to Fern, who has a heart of gold and is known among her family and friends for her willingness to help others, even complete strangers.

On the third morning of their San Francisco visit, Erv and Fern were walking along one of the hilly San Francisco streets near the downtown area. That's when Fern saw a scruffy-looking man in faded jeans sitting on some steps, holding a cup. Surely this was one of San Francisco's less fortunate, Fern thought to herself. Without a moment's hesitation, Fern rummaged through her purse, walked over to the man, and dropped a handful of quarters in his cup.

"Hey, lady! What the hell d'ya think you're doing!?!" the man exclaimed, jumping up.

"Oh, my! Aren't you homeless!?" Fern asked, mortified and turning bright red with embarrassment.

"Lady, this *is* my home," the man snapped, motioning with his thumb to the house behind him. "I live here! And that's my cup of coffee you just ruined!"

Fortunately, the "homeless" man also had a sense of humor. After fishing Fern's quarters out of his coffee, he chatted with the out-of-towners, enlightening them on the extraordinary cost of real estate near downtown San Francisco. As they parted, the not-so-homeless man ended up recommending a couple of his favorite seafood restaurants to Erv and Fern.

Like Fern, we all try to make sense out of our social environment. We constantly make judgments about the traits, motives, and goals of other people. And, like Fern, sometimes we make mistakes! In this chapter, we will look at how we interpret our social environment, including how we form impressions of other people. We'll explore how our behavior, including our willingness to help others, is influenced by the social environment and other people. In the process, we'll come back to Erv and Fern's incident with the "homeless" man to illustrate several important concepts.

Introduction What Is Social Psychology?

Why did Fern think the man on the steps was homeless? How did the "homeless" man initially interpret Fern's efforts to help him? And in contrast to Fern, not everyone who feels compassion toward homeless people acts in accordance with that attitude. Why did Fern do so?

These are the kinds of issues social psychologists study. **Social psychology** is the scientific study of how individuals think, feel, and behave in social situations. In this chapter, we focus on two basic areas of social psychology. We'll begin by exploring different dimensions of social cognition. **Social cognition** refers to how we form impressions of other people, how we interpret the meaning of other people's behavior, and how our behavior is affected by our attitudes (Fiske, 1993). Later in the chapter, we'll look at **social influence,** which focuses on how our behavior is affected by situational factors and other people. The study of social influence includes such questions as why we conform to group norms, what compels us to obey an authority figure, and under what circumstances people will help a stranger.

Person Perception
Forming Impressions of Other People

Key Theme
- *Person perception* refers to the mental processes we use to form judgments about other people.

Key Questions
- What four principles are followed in the person perception process?
- How do social categorization, implicit personality theory, and physical attractiveness affect person perception?

Consider the following scenario. You're attending a college in the middle of a big city and commute from your apartment to the campus via the subway. Today you stayed a bit later than usual on campus, so the rush hour is pretty much over. As a seasoned subway rider, you know you're safer when the subway is full of commuters. So as you step off the platform into the subway car, you're feeling just a bit anxious. The car is more than half full. If you want to sit down, you'll have to share a seat with some other passenger. You quickly survey your fellow passengers. In a matter of seconds, you must decide which stranger you'll share your ride home with, elbow to elbow, thigh to thigh. How will you decide?

Even if you've never ridden on a subway, it doesn't matter. You could just as easily imagine choosing a seat on a bus or in a crowded movie theater. What these situations have in common is a task that most of us confront almost every day. On the basis of very limited information, we must quickly draw conclusions about the nature of people who are complete strangers to us. We also have to make some rough predictions as to how these strangers are likely to behave. How do we arrive at these conclusions?

social psychology
The branch of psychology that studies how people think, feel, and behave in social situations.

social cognition
The study of the mental processes people use to make sense out of their social environment.

social influence
The study of the effects of situational factors and other people on an individual's behavior.

person perception
The mental processes we use to form judgments and draw conclusions about the characteristics and motives of others.

social norms
The "rules," or expectations, for appropriate behavior in a particular social situation.

Person perception refers to the mental processes we use to form judgments and draw conclusions about the characteristics of others. Person perception is an active and subjective process that always occurs in some *interpersonal context* (Jones, 1990). Every interpersonal context has three key components:

- The characteristics of the individual you are attempting to size up
- Your own characteristics as the perceiver
- The specific situation in which the process occurs

Each component influences the conclusions you reach about other people. As a psychological process, person perception follows some basic principles (see Fiske, 1993; Fiske & Neuberg, 1990; Jones, 1990). We'll illustrate these basic principles using the subway scenario.

Principle 1. Your reactions to others are determined by your perceptions of them, not by who or what they really are. Put simply, you treat others according to how you perceive them to be. So, as you step inside the subway car, you quickly choose not to sit next to the big, burly man with a scowl on his face. Why? Because *you* perceive Mr. Burly-Surly as potentially threatening. This guy's picture is probably on the FBI bulletin board at the post office for being an axe murderer, you think. Of course, he could just as easily be a burly florist who's surly because he's getting home late. It doesn't matter. Your behavior toward him is determined by your subjective perception of him.

Principle 2. Your goals in a particular situation determine the amount and kind of information you collect about others. Your goal in this situation is simple: You want to share a subway seat with someone who will basically leave you alone. Hence, you focus your attention on the characteristics of other people that seem to be relevant to your goal, ignoring details that are unrelated to it (Hilton & Darley, 1991; Swann, 1984). After all, you're not looking for a date for Saturday night, a plumber, or a lab partner for your biology class. If you were, you'd focus on very different aspects of the other people in the situation.

Principle 3. In every situation, you evaluate people partly in terms of how you expect them to act in that situation. Whether you're in a classroom, restaurant, or public restroom, your behavior is governed by **social norms**—the "rules," or expectations, for appropriate behavior in that social situation. Riding a subway is no exception to this principle (Milgram, 1992). For example, you don't sit next to someone else when empty seats are available, you don't try to borrow your seatmate's newspaper, and you avoid eye contact with others.

These "subway rules" aren't posted anywhere, of course. Nevertheless, violating these social norms will draw attention from others and probably make them uneasy. So as you size up your fellow subway passengers, you're partly evaluating their behavior in terms of how people-riding-the-subway-at-night-in-a-big-city should behave.

How Do We Form Impressions of Other People? Deciding where to sit in a subway car or on the bus involves making some quick decisions about other people. What kinds of factors do you consider when you make judgments about others?

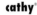

Principle 4. Your self-perception also influences how you perceive others and how you act on your perceptions. Your decision about where to sit is also influenced by how you perceive your *self.* For example, if you think of yourself as looking a bit threatening (even though you're really a mild-mannered biology major), you may choose to sit next to the 20-something guy with a briefcase rather than the anxious-looking middle-aged woman who's clutching her purse with both hands.

In combination, these four basic principles underscore the fact that person perception is not a one-way process in which we objectively survey other people and then logically evaluate their characteristics. Instead, the context, our self-perceptions, and the perceptions we have of others all interact. Each component plays a role in the judgments we form of others (Jones, 1990).

Social Categorization
Using Mental Shortcuts in Person Perception

Social categorization is the mental process of classifying people into groups on the basis of common characteristics. Much of this mental work is automatic and spontaneous, and it often occurs outside your conscious awareness (Bargh & others, 1996; Macrae & others, 1994).

When you have limited time to form your impressions and limited information about a person, such as another passenger in the subway car, you tend to rely on very broad social categories, such as the other person's gender, race, age, and occupation (Fiske, 1993; Fiske & Neuberg, 1990). You glance at a person and quickly categorize him as, for example, "Asian male, 20-something, probably a college student."

Using social categories has disadvantages and advantages. On the one hand, relegating someone to a social category on the basis of superficial information ignores that person's unique qualities. In effect, you're jumping to conclusions about a person based on very limited information. Sometimes these conclusions are wrong, as Fern was when she categorized the man with a cup in his hand as "homeless."

On the other hand, relying on social categories is a natural, adaptive cognitive process. After all, social categories provide us with considerable basic information about other people. Using social categories allows us to mentally organize and remember information about others more efficiently and effectively (Fiske, 1993; Macrae & others, 1994).

When it's important to your goals to perceive another person as accurately as possible, you're less likely to rely on automatic categorization (Fiske & Neuberg, 1990; Fiske & Taylor, 1991). Instead, you go into mental high gear, consciously and deliberately exerting mental effort to understand the other person better and to form a more accurate impression (Fiske, 1993). You might also check the impressions that you form by seeking additional information, such as calling a job applicant's previous employers.

Implicit Personality Theories
He's *Not* That Kind of Person!

Closely related to social categories are implicit personality theories. An **implicit personality theory** is a network of assumptions or beliefs about the relationships among various types of people, traits, and behaviors. Through previous social experiences, we form cognitive schemas about the traits and behaviors associated with different "types" of people. When we perceive someone to be a particular "type," we often assume that the person will display these traits and behaviors (Sedikides & Anderson, 1994).

Using Social Categories We often use superficial cues such as clothing and context to assign people to social categories and draw conclusions about their behavior. For example, you might characterize some people in this crowd as belonging to the category of "businessmen" because they are wearing suits and ties—and conclude that they are on their way to or from work. What other sorts of social categories are evident here?

social categorization
The mental process of categorizing people into groups (or *categories*) on the basis of their shared characteristics.

implicit personality theory
A network of assumptions or beliefs about the relationships among various types of people, traits, and behaviors.

For example, your choice of a seatmate on the subway might well reflect some of your own implicit personality theories. You might feel comfortable sitting next to the silver-haired man who's reading the *Wall Street Journal*, wearing an expensive suit, and carrying a leather briefcase. Why? Because these superficial characteristics lead you to assume that he's a particular type of person—a conservative businessman. And on the basis of your implicit personality theory for a "conservative businessman," you conclude that he's a "law-abiding citizen" who is not likely to try to pick your pocket or whip out a gun and start shooting.

Like social categories, implicit personality theories can be useful as mental shortcuts in perceiving other people. But just like social categories, implicit personality theories are not always accurate. In some instances, they can even be dangerously misleading.

Consider a man named John, whom Sandy met when she was a research associate at a University of Chicago research institute. John was a divorced, slightly overweight, middle-aged businessman who had built up a successful contracting and remodeling business. He lived in a quiet suburban neighborhood, where he was well-liked. Every year John threw a block party for his neighbors, and he often helped them with minor home repairs. He was involved in local politics and civic organizations. And John regularly volunteered at a nearby hospital, where, dressed as Pogo the clown, he would perform magic tricks and pass out candy to sick and injured children.

Sounds like the kind of person you wouldn't mind knowing, doesn't he? Sandy met John under somewhat different circumstances. When John came to see the psychiatrist with whom Sandy worked, he was shackled in leg irons and handcuffs and flanked by three police officers. The psychiatrist had been appointed by the courts to evaluate John's mental condition. Outside the clinic, a squadron of police had sealed off every possible escape route from the area. Stationed on the roofs of the nearby buildings were police sharpshooters.

Why were so many police guarding a guy who dressed up as a clown and entertained sick children? Because this man was John Wayne Gacy, "the undisputed champion of American serial killers," as *Newsweek* described him (Holmes, 1994). Gacy was subsequently convicted of murdering 33 boys and young men, most of whom he had buried in a crawl space under his suburban home. After years of legal appeals, Gacy was executed in 1994.

One reason Gacy had escaped detection for so many years was that he contradicted the implicit personality theory most people have for a serial killer. Indeed, most of us find it difficult to believe that a ruthless murderer would also be well-liked by his neighbors and successful in business—or that he would be someone who compassionately visited sick children in the hospital.

Although they can lead us to inaccurate conclusions, implicit personality theories represent another important social cognition strategy in our efforts to make sense out of other people (Fiske & Neuberg, 1990). Like social categories, implicit personality theories simplify information processing about other people and provide a mental framework that helps us organize observations, memories, and beliefs about people (Macrae & others, 1994).

Physical Attractiveness
Can You Judge a Book by Its Cover?

As the subway scenario illustrates, physical appearance cues play a pivotal role in person perception (Jones, 1990). Physical attractiveness is particularly influential. Of course, we pay lip service to the idea that physical attractiveness is less important than a person's behavior, personality traits, and abilities. That's the point of such common sayings as "Beauty is only skin deep" and "You can't judge a book by its cover."

Pogo the Clown Dressed as Pogo the clown, John would visit sick children in the hospital to cheer them up. He was also a successful building contractor and active in local politics. Given this information, what sorts of personal qualities would you expect him to display?

What Is Beautiful Is Good We are culturally conditioned to associate beauty with goodness and evil with ugliness—an implicit personality theory that has been dubbed the "what is beautiful is good" myth. One example of this cultural conditioning is the classic Disney film *Snow White.* In the scene shown, the wicked stepmother, complete with a wart on her nose, offers the poisoned apple to the innocent and virtuous heroine, Snow White. (The Walt Disney Co.)

focus on **Neuroscience**

Eye Contact

Non–Eye Contact

Brain Reward When Making Eye Contact with Attractive People How does physical attractiveness contribute to social success? A study by neuroscientist Knut Kampe and his colleagues (2001) at University College London may offer some insights. In their functional magnetic resonance imaging (fMRI) study, participants were scanned while they looked at color photographs of 40 different faces, some looking directly at the viewer (eye-contact) and some glancing away (non–eye-contact). After the fMRI scanning session, participants rated the attractiveness of the faces they had seen.

The results showed that when we make direct eye contact with a physically attractive person, a brain area called the *ventral striatum* is activated (see fMRI scan). When the attractive person's eye gaze is shifted away from the viewer, activity in the ventral striatum decreases. What makes this so interesting is that the ventral striatum is a brain area that predicts reward (Schultz & others, 1997). Neural activity in the ventral striatum increases when an unexpected reward, such as food or water, suddenly appears. Conversely, activity in the ventral striatum decreases when an expected reward fails to appear.

As Knut Kampe (2001) explains, "What we've shown is that when we make eye contact with an attractive person, the brain area that predicts reward starts firing. If we see an attractive person but cannot make eye contact with that person, the activity in this region goes down, signaling disappointment. This is the first study to show that the brain's ventral striatum processes rewards in the context of human social interaction."

But from childhood on, we are bombarded with images that suggest an entirely different cultural message. In fairy tales, cartoons, movies, and even computer games, the heroes are handsome and the heroines beautiful. The bad guys, wicked witches, and evil stepmothers are ugly. The implicit cultural message in these social schemas is "what is beautiful is good" (Eagly & others, 1991).

As a result of such cultural conditioning, most people do associate physical attractiveness with a wide range of other desirable characteristics (Eagly & others, 1991; Feingold, 1992). For example, good-looking people are perceived as being more intelligent, happier, and better adjusted than other people. They're also seen as being more socially competent and—surprise!—sexier than less attractive people. However, very good-looking people are also perceived as being more vain and less modest than unattractive people.

Are attractive people *really* better adjusted, smarter, or more assertive than unattractive people? After analyzing dozens of studies, psychologist Alan Feingold (1992) found that there were actually very *few* personality differences between beautiful people and their plainer counterparts. Overall, attractive people tend to be less lonely, more popular, and less anxious in social situations—all characteristics related to the advantage that their physical attractiveness seems to confer on them in social situations. In the Focus on Neuroscience above, we explore one possible explanation for why physically attractive people enjoy greater social success than average-looking people.

Physical attractiveness is *not* correlated with intelligence, mental health, or even self-esteem, however (Feingold, 1992). Good-looking people are also well aware of the effect their looks have on other people's judgments of them. Thus, they're more likely than unattractive people to attribute other people's approval of their accomplishments to their looks rather than to their effort or talent (Major & others, 1984).

Attribution
Explaining Behavior

Key Theme

▪ *Attribution* refers to the process of explaining your own behavior and the behavior of other people.

Key Questions

▪ What are the fundamental attribution error, the actor–observer discrepancy, and the self-serving bias?
▪ How do attributional biases affect our judgments about the causes of behavior?
▪ How does culture affect attributional processes?

As you're studying in the college library, the activities of two workers catch your attention. The two men are trying to lift and move a large file cabinet. "Okay, let's lift it and tip it this way," one guy says with considerable authority. In unison, they heave and tip the file cabinet. When they do, all four file drawers come flying out, bonking the first guy on the head. As the file cabinet goes crashing to the floor, you bite your lip to keep from laughing and think to yourself, "Yeah, they're obviously a pair of 40-watt bulbs."

Why did you arrive at that conclusion? After all, it's completely possible that the workers were not dimwits. Maybe the lock on the file drawers broke. Or maybe there was some other explanation for their mishap.

Attribution is the process of inferring the cause of someone's behavior, including your own. Psychologists also use the word *attribution* to refer to the explanation you make for a particular behavior. The attributions you make have a strong influence on your thoughts and feelings about other people.

If your attribution for the file cabinet incident was that the workers were not very bright, you demonstrated a pattern that occurs consistently in explaining the behavior of other people. *We tend to spontaneously attribute the behavior of others to internal, personal characteristics, while ignoring or underestimating the effects of external, situational factors.* This bias is so common in individualistic cultures that it's called the **fundamental attribution error** (Ross, 1977). Even though it's entirely possible that situational forces are behind another person's behavior, we tend to automatically assume that the cause is an internal, personal characteristic (Van Boven & others, 1999).

The fundamental attribution error plays a role in a common explanatory pattern called **blaming the victim.** The innocent victim of a crime, disaster, or serious illness is blamed for having somehow caused the misfortune or for not having taken steps to prevent it. For example, many people blame the poor for their dire straits, the sick for bringing on their illnesses, and battered women and rape survivors for somehow "provoking" their attackers. Hindsight makes it seem as if the victim should have been able to predict and prevent what was going to happen (Carli & Leonard, 1989).

Along with the fundamental attribution error, a second bias contributes to unfairly blaming the victim of misfortune. People have a strong need to believe that the world is fair—that "we get what we deserve and deserve what we get." Social psychologist Melvin Lerner (1980) calls this the **just-world hypothesis.** Blaming the victim reflects the belief that, because the world is just, the victim must have done *something* to deserve his or her fate.

Why do we have a psychological need to believe in a just world? Well, if you believe the world is unfair, then no one—including you—is safe from tragic twists of fate and chance, no matter how virtuous, careful, or conscientious you may be (Thornton, 1992). Hence, blaming the victim and believing the just-world hypothesis provide a way to psychologically defend yourself against the threatening thought, "It could just as easily have been me."

attribution
The mental process of inferring the causes of people's behavior, including one's own. Also refers to the explanation made for a particular behavior.

fundamental attribution error
The tendency to attribute the behavior of others to internal, personal characteristics, while ignoring or underestimating the effects of external, situational factors; an attributional bias that is common in individualistic cultures.

blaming the victim
The tendency to blame an innocent victim of misfortune for having somehow caused the problem or for not having taken steps to avoid or prevent it.

just-world hypothesis
The assumption that the world is fair and that therefore people get what they deserve and deserve what they get.

Blaming the Victim This couple's home was destroyed by a wildfire in Alaska. Why do people often "blame the victim" after natural disasters, accidents, and crimes?

CULTURE AND HUMAN BEHAVIOR 12.1

Explaining Failure and Murder: Culture and Attributional Biases

Although the self-serving bias is common in individualistic cultures such as Australia and the United States, it is far from universal. In collectivistic cultures, such as Asian cultures, an opposite attributional bias is often demonstrated (Bond, 1994; Moghaddam & others, 1993). Called the *self-effacing bias* or *modesty bias,* it involves blaming failure on internal, personal factors, while attributing success to external, situational factors.

For example, compared to American students, Japanese and Chinese students are more likely to attribute academic failure to personal factors, such as lack of effort, instead of situational factors (Dornbusch & others, 1996). Thus, a Japanese student who does poorly on an exam is likely to say, "I didn't study hard enough." When Japanese or Chinese students perform poorly in school, they are expected to study harder and longer (Stevenson & Stigler, 1992). In contrast, Japanese and Chinese students tend to attribute academic *success* to *situational* factors. For example, they might say, "The exam was very easy" or "There was very little competition this year" (Stevenson & others, 1986).

Psychologists Hazel Markus and Shinobu Kitayama (1991) believe that the self-effacing bias reflects the emphasis

that interdependent cultures place on fitting in with other members of the group. As the Japanese proverb goes, "The nail that sticks up gets pounded down." In collectivistic cultures, self-esteem does not rest on doing better than others in the group. Rather, standing out from the group is likely to produce psychological discomfort and tension.

Cross-cultural differences are also evident with the fundamental attribution error. In general, members of collectivistic cultures are less likely to commit the fundamental attribution error than are members of individualistic cultures (M. Bond & Smith, 1996; Choi & others, 1999). That is, collectivists are more likely to attribute the causes of another person's behavior to external, situational factors rather than to internal, personal factors—the exact *opposite* of the attributional bias that is demonstrated in individualistic cultures.

To test this idea in a naturally occurring context, psychologists Michael Morris and Kaiping Peng (1994) compared articles reporting the same mass murders in Chinese-language and English-language newspapers. In one case, the murderer was a Chinese graduate student attending a U.S. university. In the other case, the mur-

Haughtiness invites ruin; humility receives benefits.

Chinese proverb

derer was a U.S. postal worker. Regardless of whether the murderer was American or Chinese, the news accounts were fundamentally different depending on whether the *reporter* was American or Chinese.

The American reporters were more likely to explain the killings by making personal, internal attributions. For example, American reporters emphasized the murderers' personality traits, such as the graduate student's "bad temper" and the postal worker's "history of being mentally unstable."

In contrast, the Chinese reporters emphasized situational factors, such as the fact that the postal worker had recently been fired from his job and the fact that the graduate student had failed to receive an academic award. The Chinese reporters also cited social pressures and problems in U.S. society to account for the actions of the killers.

Clearly, then, how we account for our successes and failures, as well as how we account for the actions of others, is yet another example of how human behavior is influenced by cultural conditioning.

The Actor–Observer Discrepancy

You're a Klutz, but *I* Slipped on Some Ice!

There is an interesting exception to the fundamental attribution error. When it comes to explaining our *own* behavior, we tend to be biased in the opposite direction. We're more likely to use an *external, situational* attribution than an *internal, personal* attribution. This common attributional bias is called the **actor–observer discrepancy** because there is a discrepancy between the attributions you make when you are the *actor* in a given situation and those you make when you are the *observer* of other people's behavior (Jones & Nisbett, 1971).

Once you become aware of the actor–observer discrepancy, it's almost embarrassing to admit how often you succumb to it. He dropped the file cabinet because he is a dimwit; you dropped the file cabinet because you didn't have room to tip it the other way. Some jerk pulled out in front of your car because she's a reckless, inconsiderate moron; you pulled out in front of her car because your view was blocked by a school bus. And so on.

How can we explain the strong tendency to commit the actor–observer discrepancy? One possible explanation is that we simply have more information about the potential causes of our own behavior than we do about the causes of other people's behavior. When you observe another driver turn directly into the path of your car, that's typically all the information you have on which to judge that behavior.

actor–observer discrepancy
The tendency to attribute one's own behavior to external, situational causes, while attributing the behavior of others to internal, personal causes; especially likely to occur with regard to behaviors that lead to negative outcomes.

But when *you* pull in front of another car, you perceive your own behavior in the context of the many situational factors that influenced your action. You're aware of such factors as visibility and road conditions. You also know what motivated your behavior and how differently you have behaved in similar situations in the past. Thus, you are much more aware of the extent to which *your* behavior has been influenced by situational factors (Fiske & Taylor, 1991; Jones, 1990).

Not surprisingly, then, we're less susceptible to the actor–observer discrepancy with people whom we know well. Because we possess more information about the behavior of our friends and relatives in different situations, we're more aware of the possible situational influences on their behavior (Aron & others, 1992). We're also better at seeing situations from their point of view.

The Self-Serving Bias
Using Explanations That Meet Our Needs

If you've ever listened to other students react to their grades on an important exam, you've seen the **self-serving bias** in action (Whitley & Frieze, 1985). When students do well on a test, they tend to congratulate themselves and to attribute their success to how hard they studied, their intelligence, and so forth—all *internal* attributions. But when a student blows a test big time, the *external* attributions fly left and right: "They were all trick questions!" "I couldn't concentrate because the guy behind me kept coughing."

In a wide range of situations, people tend to credit themselves for their success and to blame their failures on external circumstances (Schlenker & Weigold, 1992; Schlenker & others, 1990). Psychologists explain the self-serving bias as resulting from an attempt to save face and protect self-esteem in the face of failure (Banaji & Prentice, 1994; Dunning & others, 1995).

Although common in many societies, the self-serving bias is far from universal, as cross-cultural psychologists have discovered. We discuss this finding in Culture and Human Behavior Box 12.1. The various attributional biases are summarized in Table 12.1.

Table | **12.1**

Some Common Attributional Biases

Bias	Description
Fundamental attribution error	We tend to explain the behavior of other people by attributing their behavior to internal, personal characteristics, while underestimating or ignoring the effects of external, situational factors.
Actor–observer discrepancy	When we are the *actor,* we tend to attribute our own behavior to external causes. When we are the *observer* of someone else's behavior, we tend to attribute their behavior to internal causes.
Blaming the victim	When we're unable to help the victims of misfortune, we tend to blame them for causing their own misfortune or for not taking steps to prevent or avoid it. Partly due to the *just-world hypothesis.*
Self-serving bias	We have a tendency to take credit for our *successes* by attributing them to internal, personal causes, along with a tendency to distance ourselves from our *failures* by attributing them to external, situational causes. Most common in individualistic cultures.
Self-effacing (or modesty) bias	We tend to blame ourselves for our *failures,* attributing them to internal, personal causes, while downplaying our *successes* by attributing them to external, situational causes. Most common in collectivistic cultures.

self-serving bias
The tendency to attribute successful outcomes of one's own behavior to internal causes and unsuccessful outcomes to external, situational causes.

12.1 R·E·V·I·E·W

Person Perception and Attribution

Match each of the following concepts with one of the examples below.

- a. fundamental attribution error
- b. self-serving bias
- c. self-effacing bias
- d. implicit personality theory
- e. social categorization

_____ *1.* Dr. Nobuaki, a brilliant young professor who has just joined the faculty, was asked to give a talk about her research to her new colleagues. She began her presentation by saying, "I am very poorly prepared, and my research is not very important. Thank you for being patient with me."

_____ *2.* When Fern saw the man sitting on the steps in San Francisco holding a cup, she thought he was a homeless person.

_____ *3.* Your next-door neighbor is a shy, boring, and mild-mannered Latin teacher. When you sign up for a sky-diving class, you are astonished to discover that he is one of the instructors.

_____ *4.* At the very beginning of the marathon, the top three female runners collided and were all forced to drop out because of their extensive injuries. Christine, the surprise winner of the marathon, told a local sports reporter that her win was due to her hard work, running technique, and self-discipline.

_____ *5.* You're sitting in a nice restaurant looking over the menu. From behind you, you hear a loud crash as a tray full of dishes hits the floor. As you watch the waiter scrambling to clean up the mess, you think, "What a klutz!"

The Social Psychology of Attitudes

Key Theme

■ An attitude is a learned tendency to evaluate objects, people, or issues in a particular way.

Key Questions

■ What are the three components of an attitude?
■ Under what conditions are attitudes most likely to determine behavior?
■ What is cognitive dissonance?

Are the Democrats or the Republicans better at leading the United States? What's your favorite kind of music? How do you feel about gun control? Abortion rights? Smoking in public places? Gays in the military?

On these and many other subjects, you've probably formed an attitude. Psychologists formally define an **attitude** as a learned tendency to evaluate some object, person, or issue in a particular way (Olson & Zanna, 1993; Zimbardo & Leippe, 1991). Attitudes are typically positive or negative, but they can also be *ambivalent,* as when you have mixed feelings about an issue or person.

As shown in Figure 12.1, attitudes can include three components (Eagly & Chaiken, 1998). First, an attitude may have a *cognitive component:* your thoughts and conclusions about a given topic or object. For example, a person who strongly favors gun control might say, "In my opinion, the easy access to guns is contributing to violence in the schools." Second, an attitude may have an emotional or *affective component:* "I'm really scared and upset by the number of handguns that are floating around." Finally, an attitude may have a *behavioral component,* in which your attitude is reflected in your actions. For instance, "I've started a petition drive for stricter gun control laws in my state."

attitude
A learned tendency to evaluate some object, person, or issue in a particular way; such evaluations may be positive, negative, or ambivalent.

The Effect of Attitudes on Behavior

You may take it for granted that your attitudes tend to guide your behavior. But social psychologists have consistently found that people don't always act in accordance with their attitudes (see Eagly, 1992; Eagly & Chaiken, 1993). For example, you might disapprove of cheating, yet find yourself sneaking a peek at a classmate's exam paper when the opportunity presents itself. Or you might favor a certain political candidate, yet not vote on election day.

Under what conditions are your attitudes most likely to influence or determine your behavior? Social psychologists have found that you're most likely to behave in accordance with your attitudes when any of the following conditions exist:

- Attitudes are extreme or are frequently expressed (Ajzen, 2001).

- Attitudes have been formed through direct experience (Fazio, 1990). For example, suppose you once escaped serious injury in an auto accident because you were wearing your seatbelt. You'd probably strongly favor seatbelt use, might actively support a mandatory seatbelt law in your state, and would always buckle up whenever you get in a car.

- You are very knowledgeable about the subject (Wood & others, 1995).

- You have a vested interest in the subject (Crano, 1995). If you personally stand to gain or lose something on a specific issue, you're more likely to act in accordance with your attitudes.

- You anticipate a favorable outcome or response from others for doing so (Ajzen, 1991).

What we've discussed thus far meshes nicely with common sense. People tend to act in accordance with their attitudes when they feel strongly about an issue, have a personal stake in the issue, and anticipate a positive outcome in a particular situation. In short, your attitudes do influence your behavior in many instances. Now, let's consider the opposite question. Can your behavior influence your attitudes?

Cognitive Component: Beliefs, thoughts, ideas about the attitude object

"The easy availability of fast food discourages people from eating healthy food, like fresh fruits and vegetables."

Attitude: Jill has a negative attitude toward fast-food restaurants.

Behavioral Component: Predispositon to act in a particular way

"When a big hamburger chain tried to build a new restaurant in my neighborhood, I organized a petition drive to oppose it."

Emotional Component: Feelings and emotions about the attitude object

"Fast food is disgusting. I hate their greasy fries and their fake milkshakes. Not to mention their smarmy ad campaigns!"

FIGURE 12.1 The Components of Attitudes An attitude is a positive or negative evaluation of an object, person, or idea. An attitude may have cognitive, emotional, and behavioral components.

The Effect of Behavior on Attitudes
Fried Grasshoppers for Lunch?!

Suppose you have volunteered to participate in a psychology experiment. When you arrive at the lab, you're asked to indicate your degree of preference for a variety of foods, including fried grasshoppers, which you rank pretty low on the list. During the experiment, the experimenter instructs you to eat some fried grasshoppers. You manage to swallow three of the crispy critters. At the end of the experiment, your attitudes toward grasshoppers as a food source are surveyed again.

Later in the day, you talk to a friend who also participated in the experiment. You mention how friendly and polite you thought the experimenter was. As it turns out, your friend had a very different experience. He thought the experimenter was an arrogant, rude jerk.

Here's the critical question: Whose attitude toward eating fried grasshoppers is more likely to change in a positive direction—yours or your friend's? Circle your answer below.

A. You, who encountered a friendly experimenter

B. Your friend, who encountered a rude experimenter

The correct answer is obvious, right? If you're like most people, you probably predicted A as the correct answer. Well, before you pat yourself on the back for your keen psychological insight, the correct answer is B!

At first glance, the correct answer seems to go against the grain of common sense. So how can we explain this outcome? To begin with, our fried grasshoppers scenario represents the basic design of a classic experiment by psychologist Philip Zimbardo and his colleagues (1965). Zimbardo's experiment and other similar ones underscore the power of cognitive dissonance (see Festinger, 1962). **Cognitive dissonance** is an unpleasant state of psychological tension (*dissonance*) that occurs when there's an inconsistency between two thoughts or perceptions (*cognitions*). This state of dissonance is so unpleasant that we are strongly motivated to reduce it (Festinger, 1957).

Cognitive dissonance commonly occurs in situations in which you become uncomfortably aware that your behavior and your attitudes are in conflict. In these situations, you are simultaneously holding two conflicting cognitions: your original attitude versus the realization that you have behaved in a way that contradicts that attitude. If you can easily rationalize your behavior to make it consistent with your attitude, then any dissonance you might experience can be quickly and easily resolved. But when your behavior *cannot* be easily justified, how can you resolve the contradiction and eliminate the unpleasant state of dissonance? Since you can't go back and change the behavior, *you change your attitude to make it consistent with your behavior.*

Let's take another look at the results of the grasshopper study, this time from the perspective of cognitive dissonance theory. Your attitude toward eating grasshoppers did *not* change, because you could easily rationalize the conflict between your attitude ("Eating grasshoppers is disgusting") and your behavior (eating three grasshoppers). You probably justified your behavior by saying something like, "I ate the grasshoppers because the experimenter was such a nice guy and I wanted to help him out."

However, your friend, who encountered the rude experimenter, can't easily explain the contradiction between disliking grasshoppers and voluntarily eating them. Thus, he experiences an uncomfortable state of cognitive dissonance. Since he can't go back and change his behavior, he is left with only one part of the equation that can be changed—his attitude (see Figure 12.2). "You know, eating those

FIGURE 12.2 How Cognitive Dissonance Leads to Attitude Change When your behavior conflicts with your attitudes, an uncomfortable state of tension is produced. However, if you can rationalize or explain your behavior, the conflict (and the tension) is eliminated or avoided. If you *can't* explain your behavior, you may change your attitude so that it is in harmony with your behavior.

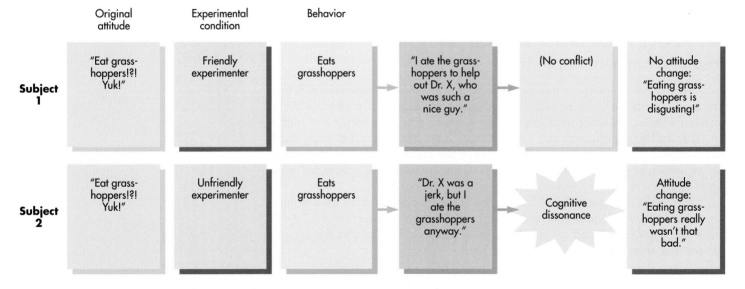

grasshoppers wasn't *that* bad," your friend comments. "In fact, they were kind of crunchy." Notice how his change in attitude reduces the dissonance between his previous attitude and his behavior.

Attitude change due to cognitive dissonance is quite common in everyday life. For example, consider the person who impulsively buys a new leather coat that she really can't afford. "It was too good a bargain to pass up," she rationalizes.

Cognitive dissonance can also change the strength of an attitude to make it consistent with some behavior that has already been performed. For example, people tend to be much more favorably inclined toward a given political candidate *after* they have voted for him or her than just before (Frenkel & Doob, 1976; Regan & Kilduff, 1988).

A similar example of cognitive dissonance in action involves choosing between two basically equal alternatives, especially if the decision is important and difficult to undo (Festinger, 1962). Suppose you had to choose between two colleges or two jobs. Each choice has desirable and undesirable features, creating dissonance. But once you actually make the choice, you immediately bring your attitudes more closely into line with that commitment, reducing cognitive dissonance. In other words, after you make the choice, you emphasize the negative features of the choice you've rejected, which is commonly called a "sour grapes" rationalization. You also emphasize the positive features of the choice to which you have committed yourself—a "sweet lemons" rationalization.

cognitive dissonance
An unpleasant state of psychological tension or arousal (*dissonance*) that occurs when two thoughts or perceptions (*cognitions*) are inconsistent; typically results from the awareness that attitudes and behavior are in conflict.

prejudice
A negative attitude toward people who belong to a specific social group.

Understanding Prejudice

Key Theme
- **Prejudice refers to a negative attitude toward people who belong to a specific social group, while stereotypes are clusters of characteristics that are attributed to people who belong to specific social categories.**

Key Questions
- **What is the function of stereotypes, and how do they relate to prejudice?**
- **What are in-groups and out-groups, and how do they influence social judgments?**
- **What is ethnocentrism?**

In this section, you'll see how person perception, attribution, and attitudes come together in explaining **prejudice**—a negative attitude toward people who belong to a specific social group. Prejudice is not limited to negative attitudes toward specific racial, ethnic, or religious groups. Other kinds of social groups can also be the target of prejudice, such as homosexuals, people with disabilities, women, and elderly people. Historically, some groups have suffered more than others from the effects of prejudice, especially people of color and *indigenous populations* (people who are native to a particular area that has come to be dominated by people of another ethnic group or race).

Much of the psychological research on prejudice has focused on relations between white Americans and African-Americans. Increasingly, however, prejudice has become an "intergroup" affair, as mutual distrust and dislike have taken hold among many different majority *and* minority groups (Mackie & Hamilton, 1993; National Conference of Christians and Jews, 1994).

Prejudice is ultimately based on the exaggerated notion that members of other social groups are very different

Combating Prejudice and Stereotyping
The attacks on the United States by members of a radical Islamic terrorist group in September 2001 brought an increased awareness of religious differences among ethnic groups. But along with outbreaks of anger against members of certain religious groups, there were also many attempts to reach across racial, ethnic, and religious divisions to find a new sense of national unity. Here, clergy of different faiths join hands and sing during an Inter-Faith Prayer Service in Detroit, Michigan, one of hundreds that took place in cities across the country in the days and weeks following the attacks on the World Trade Center and the Pentagon.

from members of our own social group. So as you read this discussion, it's important for you to keep two well-established points in mind. First, *racial and ethnic groups are far more alike than they are different* (Jones, 1991). And second, any differences that may exist *between* members of different racial and ethnic groups are far smaller than differences *among* various members of the same group.

From Stereotypes to Prejudice: In-Groups and Out-Groups

As we noted earlier, using social categories to organize information about other people seems to be a natural cognitive tendency. Many social categories can be defined by relatively objective characteristics, such as age, language, religion, and skin color. A specific kind of social category is a **stereotype**—a cluster of characteristics that are attributed to members of a specific social group or category

The Power of Stereotypes American movies have made the image of the cowboy almost universally recognizable. What kinds of qualities are associated with the stereotype of the cowboy? How might that stereotype be an inaccurate portrayal of a person working on a cattle ranch today?

(Fiske, 1998; Hilton & von Hippel, 1996). In other words, stereotypes are based on the assumption that people have certain characteristics *because* of their membership in a particular group.

Stereotypes typically include qualities that are unrelated to the objective criteria that define a given category (Taylor & Porter, 1994). For example, we can objectively sort people into different categories by age. But our stereotypes for different age groups may include many qualities that have little to do with "number of years since birth." Associations of "reckless and irresponsible" with teenagers, "forgetful and incompetent" with elderly people, and "boring and stodgy" with middle-aged adults are examples of associating unrelated qualities with age groups—that is, stereotyping.

Like other social categories, stereotypes simplify social information so that we can sort out, process, and remember information about other people more easily (Macrae & others, 1994). And like our use of other social categories, our tendency to stereotype social groups seems to be a natural cognitive process. Some social psychologists believe that the use of stereotypes is an inescapable fact of social cognition (Lee & others, 1995; Taylor & Porter, 1994). However, relying on stereotypes can have some very negative consequences, as you'll see in the next few sections.

The Problem of Stereotyped Thinking

Although forming and using stereotypes may be a "natural" way of categorizing others, stereotypes can easily be misused. And relying on stereotypes can cause numerous problems (Stangor, 1995). Stereotypes often determine what people do *not* see as well as what people do see. Attributing a stereotypic cause for an outcome or event can blind us to the true causes of events (Sanbonmatsu & others, 1994). For example, a teacher might assume that a girl's poor math grades are due to her gender rather than to a lack of preparation or encouragement. (We discussed the myth that "boys are better at math than girls" in Chapter 10, on gender and sexuality.)

Once they are formed, stereotypes are hard to shake. One reason for this is that stereotypes are not always completely false (Ottati & Lee, 1995). Sometimes they have a kernel of truth, making them easy to confirm, especially when you see only what you expect to see (Judd & Park, 1993; Swim, 1994). However, there's a vast difference between a kernel and the cornfield. When stereotypic beliefs become expectations that are applied to *all* members of a given group, stereotypes can be both misleading and damaging (Stangor & Lange, 1994).

Consider the stereotype that men are more assertive than women and that women are more nurturant than men. As noted in Chapter 10, this stereotype does have some truth to it, but only in terms of the *average* difference between men and women (see Eagly, 1995b; Swim, 1994). Thus, it would be inappropriate to automatically apply this stereotype to *every* individual man and woman. Doing so would be an example of prejudice.

Equally important, when confronted by evidence that contradicts a stereotype, people tend to discount that information in a variety of ways (Seta & Seta, 1993; Weisz & Jones, 1993). For example, suppose you are firmly convinced that all "Zeegs" are dishonest, sly, and untrustworthy. One day you absentmindedly leave your wallet on a store's checkout counter. As you walk into the parking lot, you hear a voice calling, "Hey, you forgot your wallet!" It's a Zeeg running after you and waving your wallet in the air. "I was behind you in line and thought you might need this," the Zeeg smiles, handing you your wallet.

Will this experience change your stereotype of Zeegs as dishonest, sly, and untrustworthy? Probably not. It's more likely that you'll conclude that this individual Zeeg is an *exception* to the stereotype. If you run into more than one honest Zeeg, you may create a mental subgroup for individuals who belong to the larger group but depart from the stereotype in some way (Stangor & Lange, 1994). By creating a subcategory of "honest, hardworking Zeegs," you can still maintain your more general stereotype of Zeegs as dishonest, sly, and untrustworthy.

Creating special cases, or exceptions, allows people to maintain stereotypes in the face of contradictory evidence. Typical of this exception-that-proves-the-rule approach is the person who says, "Hey, I'm not prejudiced! Why, some of my best friends are Zeegs."

Stereotypes are closely related to another tendency in person perception. People have a strong tendency to perceive others in terms of two very basic social categories: "us" and "them." More precisely, the **in-group** ("us") refers to the group or groups to which we belong, and **out-groups** ("them") refer to groups of which we are not a member. As you'll see, we're more likely to resort to negatively biased stereotypes to describe members of out-groups than to describe fellow members of our in-group (Hewstone & others, 2002).

In-groups and out-groups aren't necessarily limited to racial, ethnic, or religious boundaries. Sometimes, it seems, virtually any characteristic can be used to make in-group and out-group distinctions: Cubs versus White Sox fans, Northsiders versus Southsiders, math majors versus English majors, and so forth.

The Out-Group Homogeneity Effect: They All Look Alike to Me

Two important patterns characterize our views of in-groups versus out-groups. First, when we describe the members of our *in-group,* we typically see them as being quite varied, despite having enough features in common to belong to the same group. In other words, we notice the diversity within our own group.

Second, we tend to see members of the *out-group* as much more similar to one another, even in areas that have little to do with the criteria for group membership (Hilton & von Hippel, 1996; Stangor & Lange, 1994). This tendency is called the **out-group homogeneity effect.** (The word *homogeneity* means "similarity" or "uniformity.")

For example, what qualities do you associate with the category of "engineering major"? If you're *not* an engineering major, you're likely to see engineering majors as a rather similar crew: male, logical, analytical, conservative, and so forth. However, if you *are* an engineering major, you're much more likely to see your in-group as quite *heterogeneous,* or varied (Park & others, 1992). You might even come up with several subgroups, such as studious engineering majors, party-animal engineering majors, and electrical engineering majors versus chemical engineering majors.

---

stereotype
A cluster of characteristics that are associated with all members of a specific social group, often including qualities that are unrelated to the objective criteria that define the group.

in-group
A social group to which one belongs.

out-group
A social group to which one does not belong.

out-group homogeneity effect
The tendency to see members of out-groups as very similar to one another.

in-group bias
The tendency to judge the behavior of in-group members favorably and out-group members unfavorably.

ethnocentrism
The belief that one's own culture or ethnic group is superior to all others and the related tendency to use one's own culture as a standard by which to judge other cultures.

In-Group Bias: *We're* Tactful—*They're* Sneaky

In-group bias is our tendency to make favorable, positive attributions for behaviors by members of our in-group and unfavorable, negative attributions for behaviors by members of out-groups (Hewstone & others, 2002). We succeeded because we worked hard; they succeeded because they lucked out. We failed because of circumstances beyond our control; they failed because they're stupid and incompetent. We're thrifty; they're stingy. And so on.

One form of in-group bias is called **ethnocentrism**—the belief that one's culture or ethnic group is superior to others. You're engaging in ethnocentrism when you use your culture or ethnic group as the yardstick by which you judge other cultures or ethnic groups. Not surprisingly, ethnocentric thinking contributes to the formation of negative stereotypes about other cultures whose customs differ from our own (Smith, 1993; Triandis, 1994).

The Emotional Basis of Prejudice: The Perception of Threat

Stereotypes and in-group/out-group bias form the *cognitive* basis for prejudicial attitudes (Hilton & von Hippel, 1996). But, as with many attitudes, prejudice also has a strong *emotional* component. In the case of prejudice, the emotions are intensely negative—hatred, contempt, fear, loathing. *Behaviorally,* prejudice can be displayed in the form of *discrimination*—behaviors ranging from privately sneering at to physically attacking members of the out-group.

Intense prejudice is part of what allowed Nazi soldiers to systematically slaughter over 6 million Jews during World War II. Unfortunately, there is no shortage of ethnic hatred in today's world, either. In the name of the in-group, prejudice justifies "ethnic cleansing," or *genocide*. Former neighbors turn on one another and try to obliterate all members of the out-group. Whether it's the Middle East, Asia, Africa, Europe, or the Americas, discrimination and violence occur against men, women, and children *just because they are members of a particular out-group.*

How can we account for the extreme emotions that often characterize prejudice against out-group members? One theory holds that prejudice and intergroup hostility increase when different groups are competing for scarce resources, whether jobs, acreage, oil, water, or political power (Bobo, 1988a, 1988b). Prejudice and intergroup hostility are also likely to increase during times of social change (Brewer, 1994; Staub, 1996).

However, prejudice often exists in the absence of direct competition for resources, changing social conditions, or even contact with members of a particular out-group. What accounts for prejudice in such situations? Increasingly, social psychologists are examining the *emotional* basis of prejudice (see Mackie & Hamilton, 1993; Smith, 1993). Research by psychologist Victoria Esses and her colleagues (1993) has demonstrated that people are often prejudiced against groups that are perceived as threatening important in-group norms and values.

For example, a person might be extremely prejudiced against gays and lesbians even though he is not competing with them for jobs or other resources. Instead, his prejudice is fueled by his perception that homosexual behavior threatens his in-group's cherished norms and values, such as a strong commitment to traditional sex roles and family structure (Haddock & others, 1993).

HAGAR

Overcoming Prejudice

Key Theme

- Prejudice can be overcome when rival groups cooperate to achieve a common goal.

Key Questions

- How has this finding been applied in the educational system?
- What other conditions are essential to reducing tension between groups?
- How can prejudice be overcome at the individual level?

At one point, it was believed that simply bringing members of different groups into contact with one another would inevitably reduce prejudice among groups. This is referred to as the *contact theory.* As members of different groups got to know one another as individuals, the theory went, negative stereotypes would be disproved. In time, positive attitudes would naturally replace negative attitudes.

Unfortunately, experience demonstrated that mere contact would not reduce prejudice. Under some circumstances, in fact, contact between different groups can *increase* prejudice by confirming negative stereotypes or failing to meet positive expectations (Amir, 1994; Desforges & others, 1991). And when people mingle with members of out-groups whose behavior and attitudes are unfamiliar or difficult to explain, they can become puzzled, upset, or disturbed (Fiske & Ruscher, 1993).

How can prejudice be combated at the group level? A classic series of studies headed by psychologist **Muzafer Sherif** helped clarify the conditions that produce intergroup conflict *and* harmony. Sherif and his colleagues (1961) studied a group of 11-year-old boys in an unlikely setting for a scientific experiment: a summer camp located at Robbers Cave State Park in Oklahoma. Pretending to be camp counselors and staff, the researchers observed the boys' behavior under carefully orchestrated conditions.

The Robbers Cave Experiment

The boys were randomly assigned to two groups. The groups arrived at camp in separate buses and were headquartered in different areas of the camp. One group of boys dubbed themselves the Eagles, the other the Rattlers. After a week of separation, the researchers arranged for the groups to meet in a series of competitive games. A fierce rivalry quickly developed, demonstrating the ease with which mutually hostile groups could be created.

The rivalry became increasingly bitter. The Eagles burned the Rattlers' flag. In response, the Rattlers trashed the Eagles' cabin. Somewhat alarmed, the researchers tried to diminish the hostility by bringing the two groups together under peaceful circumstances and on an equal basis—having them go to the movies together, eat in the same dining hall, and so forth. But contact alone did not mitigate the hostility. If anything, these situations only served as opportunities for the rival groups to berate and attack each other. For example, when the Rattlers and Eagles ate together in the same dining hall, a massive food fight erupted!

How could harmony between the groups be established? Sherif and his fellow researchers created a series of situations in which the two groups would need to *cooperate to achieve a common goal.* For example, the researchers secretly sabotaged the water supply. Working together, the Eagles and the Rattlers managed to fix it. On another occasion, the researchers sabotaged a truck that was to bring

Creating Conflict Between Groups Psychologist Muzafer Sherif and his colleagues demonstrated how easily hostility and distrust could be created between two groups. Competitive situations, like this tug-of-war, increased tension between the Rattlers and the Eagles.

Overcoming Group Conflict To decrease hostility between the Rattlers and the Eagles at Robbers Cave, the researchers created situations that required the joint efforts of both groups to achieve a common goal, such as fixing the water supply. These cooperative tasks helped the boys recognize their common interests and become friends.

food to the campers. The hungry campers overcame their differences to join forces and restart the truck. After a series of such joint efforts, the rivalry diminished and the groups became good friends (Sherif, 1956; Sherif & others, 1961).

Sherif successfully demonstrated how hostility between groups could be created and, more important, how that hostility could be overcome. However, other researchers questioned whether these results would apply to other intergroup situations. After all, these boys were very homogeneous: white, middle class, Protestant, and carefully selected for being healthy and well-adjusted (Fiske & Ruscher, 1993; Sherif, 1966). In other words, there were no *intrinsic* differences between the Rattlers and the Eagles; there was only the artificial distinction created by the researchers.

The Jigsaw Classroom: Promoting Cooperation

Social psychologist Elliot Aronson (1990, 1992) tried adapting the results of the Robbers Cave experiments to a very different group situation—a newly integrated elementary school. Realizing that mere contact between black and white children was not dissipating tension and prejudice, Aronson reasoned that perhaps the competitive schoolroom atmosphere was partly at fault. Perhaps tension between racial groups might decrease if cooperation replaced competition.

Aronson and his colleagues tried a teaching technique that stressed cooperative, rather than competitive, learning situations (see Aronson, 1990; Aronson & Bridgeman, 1979). Dubbed the *jigsaw classroom technique,* this approach brought together students in small, ethnically diverse groups to work on a mutual project. Like the pieces of a jigsaw puzzle, each student had a unique contribution to make toward the success of the group. Each student became an expert on one aspect of the overall project and had to teach it to the other members of the group. Thus, interdependence and cooperation replaced competition.

The results? Children in the jigsaw classrooms benefited. They had higher self-esteem and a greater liking for children in other ethnic groups than did children in traditional classrooms. They also demonstrated a lessening of negative stereotypes and prejudice and a reduction in intergroup hostility (see Aronson, 1987, 1995; Aronson & Bridgeman, 1979). As Aronson (1999) points out, "Cooperation changes our tendency to categorize the out-group from 'those people' to 'us people.' "

Combating Prejudice at the Individual Level

Many people today agree that prejudice and racism are wrong (see National Conference of Christians and Jews, 1994). However, some psychologists believe that blatant racism has been replaced by a more subtle form of racism (Hewstone & others, 2002).

Sometimes people who are not *consciously* prejudiced against particular groups nevertheless react in prejudiced ways (Devine & Monteith, 1993; Devine & others, 1991). For example, a white person who is low in racial prejudice might still momentarily hesitate to invite an African-American colleague to her home (Monteith & others, 1993). Or a man who consciously strives to be nonsexist might be reluctant to consult a female surgeon or feel uncomfortable when he boards a flight and discovers that the pilot is a woman.

Psychologist Patricia Devine and her colleagues (2000) argue that prejudice reduction at the individual level is a three-step process. First, individuals must decide that prejudiced responses are wrong and consciously reject prejudice and stereotyped thinking (Hilton & von Hippel, 1996). Second, they must internalize their nonprejudiced beliefs so that those beliefs become an integral part of their personal self-concept. Third, individuals must learn to inhibit automatic prejudicial reactions and deliberately replace them with nonprejudiced responses that are based on their personal standards.

As Devine's research supports, the first step in overcoming prejudice is to become aware of the biases that allow it to flourish, such as in-group bias and the out-group homogeneity effect. So the next time you find yourself saying, "Oh, those zebras, they're all alike—not like us giraffes," stop and think. Stereotyping may be a "natural" cognitive process, but we don't necessarily have to fall victim to the biases that stereotypes foster. Nor should we act on those biases. Rather, it's important that we make a concerted effort to see each person as he or she really is—a unique individual.

12.2 R·E·V·I·E·W

C·O·N·C·E·P·T

The Psychology of Attitudes and Prejudice

Which of the following concepts is being illustrated in each of the examples below: cognitive dissonance, stereotyping, in-group bias, ethnocentrism, out-group homogeneity?

1. Henry's classmate in college was from Sardinia, and he loved to eat sardines for lunch. Henry now believes that the diet of all Sardinians is centered on sardines, and he has little doubt about why the island is called Sardinia. _____

2. A group of employees in the marketing department went out to lunch. They started to complain about the people who worked in accounting. One of them said, "Oh, well, you know those number crunchers are all alike. They just aren't very creative." _____

3. A group of students from Northern State College was watching the antics of a group of students from Western State College at a football game. "Look at how rowdy those guys are. That's disgusting!" one Northern State student observed. A half-hour later,

the same student said, "I love going to our football games because everybody's so friendly and laid back. We really know how to let loose and have a good time." _____

4. Georgia thinks that track is a great all-around sport and desperately wants to make the track team. For the first few weeks, she trains hard every day. Gradually, however, she starts missing practice sessions, and on the day of the tryouts she oversleeps, performs poorly, and gets cut in the first round. Georgia says, "Track is so-o-o boring. I'd much rather be on the softball team." _____

5. In an introductory anthropology class, students begin to groan and laugh as they watch a film showing members of a remote tribe eating head lice, grubs, and iguanas. "How repulsive," remarked one gum-chewing student. "Those poor savages are really ignorant and uncivilized," another student agreed, as he put a pinch of chewing tobacco in his mouth. _____

Conformity
Following the Crowd

Key Theme

■ Social influence involves the study of how behavior is influenced by other people and by the social environment.

Key Questions

■ What factors influence the degree to which people will conform?
■ Why do people conform?
■ How does culture affect conformity?

As we noted earlier in this chapter, **social influence** is the psychological study of how our behavior is influenced by the social environment and other people. For example, if you typically contribute to class discussions, you've probably felt the power of social influence in classes where nobody else said a word. No doubt you found yourself feeling at least slightly uncomfortable every time you ventured a comment or question.

social influence
The study of the effects of situational factors and other people on an individual's behavior.

conformity
The tendency to adjust one's behavior, attitudes, or beliefs to group norms in response to real or imagined group pressure.

normative social influence
Behavior that is motivated by the desire to gain social acceptance and approval.

informational social influence
Behavior that is motivated by the desire to be correct.

If you changed your behavior to mesh with that of your classmates, you demonstrated conformity. **Conformity** occurs when we change our behavior, attitudes, or beliefs in response to real or imagined group pressure (Kiesler & Kiesler, 1969). However, the fact that we act or present ourselves in the same way as other people doesn't necessarily mean that we're conforming to group standards. As social psychologist David Myers (1999) explained, "Conformity is not just acting as other people act, it is being affected by how they act. It is acting differently from the way you would act alone."

So if everyone in the concert hall rises to give the musician a standing ovation and you do the same because you thought the performance was fantastic, your behavior does not reflect conformity, even though you're behaving just like everyone else in the concert hall. But if you thought the performance was just so-so, and you stand up and applaud anyway, you're displaying conformity. Notice, you may still *privately* think it was just an average performance, but your *public* behavior conforms to that of the larger group.

At other times we may alter *both* our private beliefs and our outward behavior. As the prevailing group norms change over time, group pressure can influence our perceptions and opinions as well as our behaviors. Clothing fashions and hairstyles are large-scale examples of conformity to norms that shift over time. Men who wore earrings and women adorned with multiple earrings would have drawn stares just a few years ago. Now, pierced eyebrows, noses, cheeks, and tongues (not to mention more delicate body parts) are relatively common.

Group Pressure to Conform
The Work of Solomon Asch

There's no question that all of us conform to group norms to some degree. The more critical issue is *how far* we'll go to adjust our perceptions and opinions so that they're in sync with the majority opinion—an issue that intrigued psychologist **Solomon Asch.** Asch (1951) posed a straightforward question: Would people still conform to the group if the group opinion was clearly wrong?

To study this question experimentally, Asch (1955) chose a simple, objective task with an obvious answer (see Figure 12.3). A group of people sat at a table and looked at a series of cards. On one side of each card was a standard line. On the other side were three comparison lines. All each person had to do was publicly indicate which comparison line was the same length as the standard line.

Asch's experiment had a hidden catch. All the people sitting around the table were actually in cahoots with the experimenter, except for one—the real subject. Had you been the real subject in Asch's (1956) experiment, here's what you would have experienced. The first card is shown, and the five people ahead of you respond, one at a time, with the obvious answer: "Line B." Now it's your turn, and you respond the same. The second card is put up. Again, the answer is obvious and the group is unanimous. So far, so good.

Then the third card is shown, and the correct answer is just as obvious: Line C. But the first person confidently says, "Line A." And so does everyone else, one by one. Now it's your turn. To you it's clear that the correct answer is line C. But the five people ahead of you have already publicly chosen line A. How do you respond? You hesitate. Do you go with the flow or with what you know?

The real subject was faced with the uncomfortable situation of disagreeing with a unanimous majority on 12 of 18 trials in Asch's experiment. Notice, there was *no* direct pressure to conform—just the implicit, unspoken pressure of answering differently from the rest of the group.

FIGURE 12.3 Sample Line Judgment Task Used in the Asch Conformity Studies In Asch's classic studies on conformity, subjects were asked to pick the comparison line that matched the standard line.

SOURCE: Asch (1957).

Standard line

A B C
Comparison lines

Over a hundred subjects experienced Asch's experimental dilemma. Not surprisingly, participants differed in their degree of conformity. Nonetheless, the majority of Asch's subjects (76 percent) conformed with the group judgment on at least one of the critical trials. When the data for all subjects were combined, the subjects followed the majority and gave the wrong answer on *37 percent* of the critical trials (Asch, 1955, 1957). In comparison, a control group of subjects who responded alone instead of in a group accurately chose the matching line 99 percent of the time.

Although the majority opinion clearly exerted a strong influence, it's also important to stress the flip side of Asch's results. On almost two-thirds of the trials in which the majority named the wrong line, the subjects stuck to their guns and gave the correct answer, despite being in the minority (see Friend & others, 1990).

Adolescents and Conformity The adolescent uniform: T-shirts, jeans, and athletic shoes. Think back to your own adolescent years. Do you remember how important it was to you to fit in with other adolescents, especially those in your peer group? Conformity to group norms peaks during early adolescence.

Factors Influencing Conformity

The basic model of Asch's classic experiment has been used in hundreds of studies exploring the dynamics of conformity (R. Bond & Smith, 1996; Tanford & Penrod, 1984). Why do we sometimes find ourselves conforming to the larger group? There are two basic reasons.

First is our desire to be liked and accepted by the group, which is referred to as **normative social influence.** If you've ever been ridiculed and rejected for going against the grain of a unanimous group, you've had firsthand experience with the pressure of normative social influence. Second is our desire to be right. When we're uncertain or doubt our own judgment, we may look to the group as a source of accurate information, which is called **informational social influence.**

Asch and other researchers identified several conditions that promote conformity, which are summarized in Table 12.2. But Asch also discovered that conformity *decreased* under certain circumstances. For example, having an ally seemed to counteract the social influence of the majority. Subjects were more likely to go against the majority view if just one other participant did so. Other researchers have found that any dissent increases resistance to the majority opinion, even if the other person's dissenting opinion is wrong (Allen & Levine, 1969). Conformity also lessens even if the other dissenter's competence is questionable, as in the case of a dissenter who wore thick glasses and complained that he could not see the lines very well (Allen & Levine, 1971).

Culture and Conformity

Asch's original studies were conducted in the 1950s using U.S. college students as the experimental participants. Would participants today be less likely to conform to the majority's opinion? In general, levels of conformity *have* steadily declined since Asch's original studies in the 1950s (R. Bond & Smith, 1996).

One possible explanation for this finding is that the cultural climate of American society was fundamentally different in the 1950s. The 1950s was an era in which conformity was socially expected. Deviation from the group, especially deviation that appeared the least bit anti-American, was treated with suspicion. So perhaps it's not that surprising that college students during the 1950s were more "conformist" than students during more recent decades.

Do patterns of conformity differ in other cultures? British psychologists Rod Bond and Peter Smith (1996) found in a wide-ranging meta-analysis that

Table | **12.2**

Factors That Promote Conformity

You're more likely to conform to group norms when:

- You are facing a unanimous majority of four or five people
- You must give your response in front of the group
- You have not already expressed commitment to a different idea or opinion
- You find the task is ambiguous or difficult
- You doubt your abilities or knowledge in the situation
- You are strongly attracted to a group and want to be a member of it

SOURCES: Asch (1955); Campbell & Fairey (1989); Deutsch & Gerard (1955); Gerard & others (1968); Tanford & Penrod (1984).

obedience

The performance of an action in response to the direct orders of an authority or person of higher status.

conformity is generally higher in collectivistic cultures than in individualistic cultures. Because individualistic cultures tend to emphasize independence, self-expression, and standing out from the crowd, the whole notion of conformity tends to carry a negative connotation.

In collectivistic cultures, however, publicly conforming while privately disagreeing tends to be regarded as socially appropriate tact or sensitivity. Publicly challenging the judgments of others, particularly the judgment of members of one's in-group, would be considered rude, tactless, and insensitive to the feelings of others. Thus, conformity in collectivistic cultures does not seem to carry the same negative connotation that it does in individualistic cultures.

Obedience
Just Following Orders

Key Theme
- Stanley Milgram conducted several controversial studies on obedience, which is behaving in direct response to the orders of an authority.

Key Questions
- What were the results of Milgram's original obedience experiments?
- What experimental factors were shown to increase the level of obedience?
- What experimental factors were shown to decrease the level of obedience?

Stanley Milgram was one of the most creative and innovative researchers that social psychology has known (Blass, 1992; Miller, 1986; Zimbardo, 1992). Sadly, Milgram died of a heart attack at the age of 51. Though Milgram made many contributions to social psychology, he is best known for his experimental investigations of obedience. **Obedience** is the performance of an action in response to the direct orders of an authority or person of higher status, such as a teacher or a supervisor.

Milgram's experimental studies of obedience grew out of his interest in the conformity research and, even more directly, from the influence of Solomon Asch himself (Blass, 1992). Milgram was Asch's teaching assistant when Asch spent a year at Harvard as a visiting professor. For his doctoral dissertation, Milgram (1960, 1961) used Asch's experimental design to conduct the first cross-cultural investigations of conformity, comparing French and Norwegian subjects.

Milgram was intrigued by Asch's discovery of how easily people could be swayed by group pressure. But Milgram wanted to investigate behavior that had greater personal significance than simply judging the lengths of lines on a card (Milgram, 1963, 1980). Thus, Milgram posed what he saw as the most critical question: Could a person be pressured by others into committing an immoral act, some action that violated his or her own conscience, such as hurting a stranger? In his efforts to answer that question, Milgram embarked on one of the most systematic and controversial investigations in the history of psychology: to determine how and why people obey the destructive dictates of an authority figure.

Social Psychologist Stanley Milgram (1933–1984) Milgram is best known for his obedience studies, but his creative research skills went far beyond the topic of obedience. To study social norms, for example, Milgram sent his students out into New York City to intrude into waiting lines or ask subway passengers to give up their seats. Milgram often capitalized on the "texture of everyday life" to "examine the way in which the social world impinges on individual action and experience" (Milgram, 1974a).

Milgram's Original Obedience Experiment

Milgram was only 28 years old when he conducted his first obedience experiments. At the time, he was a new faculty member at Yale University in New Haven, Connecticut. He recruited participants through direct-mail solicitations and ads in the local paper. Collectively, Milgram's subjects represented a wide range of occupational and educational backgrounds. Postal workers, high school teachers, white-collar workers, engineers, and laborers participated in the study.

Outwardly, it appeared that two subjects showed up at Yale University to participate in each session of the psychology experiment, but the second subject was actually an accomplice working with Milgram. The role of the experimenter, complete with white lab coat, was played by a high school biology teacher. When both subjects arrived, the experimenter greeted them and gave them a plausible explanation of the study's purpose: to examine the effects of punishment on learning.

Both subjects drew slips of paper to determine who would be the "teacher" and who the "learner." However, the drawing was rigged so that the real subject was always the teacher and the accomplice was always the learner. The learner was actually a mild-mannered, 47-year-old accountant who had been carefully rehearsed for his part in the drama. Assigned to the role of the teacher, the real subject would be responsible for "punishing" the learner's mistakes by administering electric shocks.

Immediately after the drawing, the teacher and learner were taken to another room, where the learner was strapped into an "electric chair." The teacher was then taken to a different room, from which he could hear but not see the learner. Speaking into a microphone, the teacher tested the learner on a simple word-pair memory task. In the other room, the learner pressed one of four switches to indicate with which alternative the word had previously been paired. The learner's response was registered in an answer box positioned on top of the "shock generator" in front of the teacher. Each time the learner answered incorrectly, the teacher was to deliver an electric shock.

Milgram's (1963) meticulous attention to details greatly enhanced the realism of the situation. The front panel of the bogus shock generator had been engraved by professional industrial engravers. Each of the 30 switches, which progressed from 15 to 450 volts, was clearly labeled with its electrical voltage, and each group of switches was also labeled. At the lowest levels, the labels read "Slight Shock" and "Mild Shock." At higher voltages, the label was "Severe Shock." At the highest voltage level, an ominous label simply read "XXX." Whenever the teacher pressed a shock switch, the red light above the switch went on, a buzzing and clicking sound was heard, and the needle on the voltage meter swung to the right. Very convincing details.

Just in case there was any lingering doubt in the teacher's mind about the legitimacy of the shock generator, the *teacher* was given a sample jolt using the switch marked 45 volts. In fact, this sample shock was the only real shock given during the course of the staged experiment.

The first time the learner answered incorrectly, the teacher was to deliver an electric shock at the 15-volt level. With each subsequent error, the teacher was told to progress to the next level on the shock generator. The teacher was also told to announce the voltage level to the learner before delivering the shock.

The "Electric Chair" With the help of the real subject, who has been assigned the role of "teacher," the experimenter straps the "learner" into the electric chair. Unbeknownst to the real subject, the learner was actually a 47-year-old accountant who had been carefully rehearsed for his part in the drama. The experimenter told both subjects, "Although the shocks can be extremely painful, they cause no permanent tissue damage."

Milgram's "Shock Generator" Machine A young Stanley Milgram sits next to his "shock generator." Milgram went to great lengths to make the shock generator look as authentic as possible. Do you think you would have been fooled into believing that this was a real shock generator?

Table | **12.3**

> **The Learner's Schedule of Protests in Milgram's Obedience Experiment**
>
> 120 volts → Ugh! Hey, *this* really hurts.
>
> 150 volts → Ugh!!! Experimenter! That's all. Get me out of here. I told you I had heart trouble. My heart's starting to bother me now. Get me out of here, please. My heart's starting to bother me. I refuse to go on. Let me out.
>
> 210 volts → Ugh!! Experimenter! Get me out of here. I've had enough. I *won't* be in the experiment any more.
>
> 270 volts → (*Agonized scream.*) Let me out of here. Let me out of here. Let me out of here. Let me out. Do you hear? Let me out of here.
>
> 300 volts → (*Agonized scream.*) I absolutely refuse to answer any more. Get me out of here. You can't hold me here. Get me out. Get me out of here.
>
> 315 volts → (*Intensely agonized scream.*) I told you I refuse to answer. I'm no longer part of this experiment.
>
> 330 volts → (*Intense and prolonged agonized scream.*) Let me out of here. Let me out of here. My heart's bothering me. Let me out, I tell you. (*Hysterically*) Let me out of here. Let me out of here. You have no right to hold me here. Let me out! Let me out! Let me out! Let me out of here! Let me out! Let me out!
>
> SOURCE: Milgram (1974a), pp. 56–57.

This table shows examples of the learner's protests at different voltage levels. If the teacher administered shocks beyond the 330-volt level, the learner's agonized screams were replaced with an ominous silence.

The individual who is commanded by a legitimate authority ordinarily obeys. Obedience comes easily and often. It is a ubiquitous and indispensable feature of social life.

Stanley Milgram (1963)

At predetermined voltage levels, the learner vocalized first his discomfort, then his pain, and, finally, agonized screams. Some of the learner's vocalizations at the different voltage levels are shown in Table 12.3. After 330 volts, the learner's script called for him to fall silent. If the teacher protested that he wished to stop or that he was worried about the learner's safety, the experimenter would say, "The experiment requires that you continue" or "You have no other choice, you *must* continue."

According to the script, the experiment would be halted when the teacher–subject refused to obey the experimenter's orders to continue. Alternatively, if the teacher–subject obeyed the experimenter, the experiment would be halted once the teacher had progressed all the way to the maximum shock level of 450 volts.

Either way, after the experiment the teacher was interviewed and it was explained that the learner had not actually received dangerous electric shocks. To underscore this point, a "friendly reconciliation" was arranged between the teacher and the learner, and the true purpose of the study was explained to the subject.

The Results of Milgram's Original Experiment

Can you predict how Milgram's subjects behaved? Of the 40 subjects, how many obeyed the experimenter and went to the full 450-volt level? On a more personal level, how do you think *you* would have behaved had you had been one of Milgram's subjects?

Milgram himself asked psychiatrists, college students, and middle-class adults to predict how subjects would behave (see Milgram, 1974a). All three groups predicted that *all* of Milgram's subjects would refuse to obey at some point. They predicted that most subjects would refuse at the 150-volt level, the point at which the learner first protested. They also believed that only a few rare individuals would go as far as the 300-volt level. Finally, *none* of those surveyed thought that any of Milgram's subjects would go to the full 450 volts.

As it turned out, they were all wrong. *Two-thirds of Milgram's subjects—26 of the 40—went to the full 450-volt level.* And of those who defied the experimenter, *not one stopped before the 300-volt level*. The actual results of Milgram's original obedience study are shown in Figure 12.4.

Surprised? Milgram himself was stunned by the results, never expecting that the majority of subjects would administer the maximum voltage. Were his results a fluke? Did Milgram inadvertently assemble a sadistic group of New Haven residents who were all too willing to inflict extremely painful, even life-threatening, shocks on a complete stranger?

The answer to both these questions is no. Milgram's obedience study has been repeated many times in the United States and other countries (see Blass, 2000). And, in fact, Milgram (1974a) replicated his own study on numerous occasions, using variations of his basic experimental procedure. In one replication, for instance, Milgram's subjects were 40 women. Were female subjects any less likely to inflict pain on a stranger? Not at all. The results were identical.

Were Milgram's subjects heartless, cold, and callous people? Or did they see through his elaborate experimental hoax, as some critics have suggested (Orne & Holland, 1968)? Was it possible that the subjects did not believe that they were really harming the learner?

Again, the answer seems to be no. Milgram's subjects seemed totally convinced that the situation was authentic. And they did not behave in a cold-blooded, unfeeling way. Far from it. As the experiment progressed, many subjects showed signs of extreme tension and conflict. In describing the reaction of one subject, Milgram (1963) wrote, "I observed a mature and initially poised businessman enter the laboratory smiling and confident. Within 20 minutes he was reduced to a twitching, stuttering wreck, who was rapidly approaching a point of nervous collapse."

Making Sense of Milgram's Findings
Multiple Influences

On the one hand, Milgram's subjects appeared genuinely upset about hurting another person. On the other hand, the majority of them continued to administer stronger and stronger shocks, obediently following the experimenter's commands. How can we explain their willingness to obey?

Milgram, along with other researchers, identified several aspects of the experimental situation that had a strong impact on the subjects (see Blass, 1992, 2000; Milgram, 1965). Here are some of the forces that influenced subjects to continue obeying the experimenter's orders:

■ *A previously well-established mental framework to obey.* Having volunteered to participate in a psychology experiment, Milgram's subjects arrived at the lab with the mental expectation that they would obediently follow the directions of the person in charge—the experimenter. They also accepted compensation on their arrival, which may have increased their sense of having made a commitment to cooperate with the experimenter.

■ *The situation, or context, in which the obedience occurred.* The subjects were familiar with the basic nature of scientific investigation, believed that scientific research was worthwhile, and were told that the goal of the experiment was to "advance the scientific understanding of learning and memory" (Milgram, 1974a). All these factors predisposed the subjects to trust and respect the experimenter's authority (Darley, 1992). Even when subjects protested, they were polite and respectful. Milgram (1974a) suggested that subjects were afraid that defying the experimenter's orders would make them appear arrogant, rude, disrespectful, or uncooperative.

■ *The gradual, repetitive escalation of the task.* At the beginning of the experiment, the subject administered a very low level of shock—

FIGURE 12.4 The Results of Milgram's Original Study Contrary to what psychiatrists, college students, and middle-class adults predicted, the majority of Milgram's subjects did not refuse to obey by the 150-volt level of shock. As this chart shows, 5 of Milgram's 40 subjects (13 percent) refused to continue after administering 300 volts to the learner. Twenty-six of the 40 subjects (65 percent) remained obedient to the end, administering the full 450 volts to the learner.

SOURCE: Milgram (1974a), p. 35.

Shock Level	Switch Labels and Voltage Levels	Number of Subjects Who Refused to Administer a Higher Voltage Level
	Slight Shock	
1	15	
2	30	
3	45	
4	60	
	Moderate Shock	
5	75	
6	90	
7	105	
8	120	
9	135	
10	150	
11	165	
12	180	
	Very Strong Shock	
13	195	
14	210	
15	225	
16	240	
	Intense Shock	
17	255	
18	270	
19	285	
20	300	
	Extreme Intensity Shock	
21	315	5
22	330	
23	345	4
24	360	2
	Danger: Severe Shock	1
25	375	1
26	390	
27	405	1
28	420	
	XXX	
29	435	
30	450	

26

15 volts. Subjects could easily justify using such low levels of electric shock in the service of science. The shocks, like the learner's protests, escalated only gradually. Each additional shock was only 15 volts stronger than the preceding one.

■ ***The experimenter's behavior and reassurances.*** Many subjects asked the experimenter who was responsible for what might happen to the learner. In every case, the teacher was reassured that the *experimenter* was responsible for the learner's well-being. Thus, the subjects could believe that they were not responsible for the consequences of their actions. They could tell themselves that their behavior must be appropriate if the experimenter approved of it.

■ ***The physical and psychological separation from the learner.*** Several "buffers" distanced the subject from the pain that he was inflicting on the learner. First, the learner was in a separate room and not visible. Only his voice could be heard. Second, punishment was depersonalized: The subject simply pushed a switch on the shock generator. Finally, the learner never appealed directly to the teacher to stop shocking him. The learner's pleas were always directed toward the *experimenter,* as in "Experimenter! Get me out of here!" Undoubtedly, this contributed to the subject's sense that the experimenter, rather than the subject, was ultimately in control of the situation, including the teacher's behavior.

Conditions That Undermine Obedience
Variations on a Theme

In a lengthy series of experiments, Milgram systematically varied the basic obedience paradigm. To give you some sense of the enormity of Milgram's undertaking, approximately *1,000* subjects, each tested individually, experienced some variation of Milgram's obedience experiment. Thus, Milgram's obedience research represents one of the largest and most integrated research programs in social psychology (Blass, 2000).

By varying his experiments, Milgram identified several conditions that decreased the likelihood of destructive obedience, which are summarized in Figure 12.5. For example, willingness to obey diminished sharply when the buffers that separated the teacher from the learner were lessened or removed, such as when both of them were put in the same room.

The proximity of the experimenter was another critical element. If the experimenter left the room and spoke to the subject over the telephone instead of face to face, complete obedience dropped to 23 percent. Interestingly, several subjects in this condition found an easy way to reconcile the demands of their conscience with the demands of authority: They simply lied to the experimenter! Over the phone, they assured the experimenter that they were increasing the shock level as ordered—all the while continuing to administer the *lowest* possible shock.

FIGURE 12.5 Factors That Decrease Destructive Obedience By systematically varying his basic experimental design, Milgram identified several factors that diminish the likelihood of destructive obedience. In this graph, you can see the percentage of subjects who administered the maximum shock in different experimental variations.

SOURCE: Adapted from data reported in Milgram (1974a).

Experimental Variations

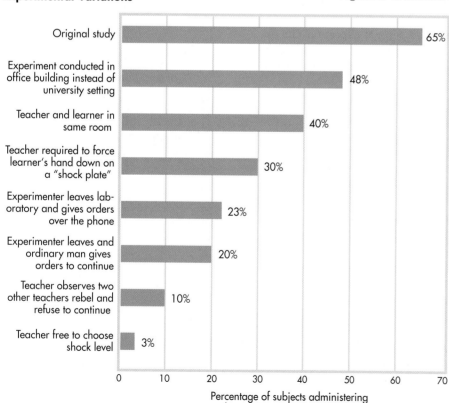

Percentage of subjects administering the maximum shock (450 volts)

CRITICAL THINKING 12.2

Were Milgram's Obedience Experiments Ethical?

Less than a year after the initial publication of Stanley Milgram's obedience studies, psychologist Diana Baumrind (1964) attacked the experiments for the emotional stress, tension, and loss of dignity experienced by Milgram's subjects. To Baumrind, Milgram's experiment was a violation of the trust that a naive subject is likely to place in a researcher. As Baumrind wrote:

> The subject's personal responsibility for his actions is not erased because the experimenter reveals to him the means which he used to stimulate these actions. The subject realizes that he would have hurt the victim if the current were on. The realization that he has also made a fool of himself by accepting the experimental set results in additional loss of self-esteem.

In his response to Baumrind, Milgram (1964) noted that he did not set out to create stress in his subjects and that he and other experts had assumed that few people would proceed beyond a very low level of shock. What was disturbing to people, Milgram suggested, were not so much his methods but his results:

> Is not Baumrind's criticism based as much on the unanticipated findings as on the method? The findings were that some subjects performed in what appeared to be a shockingly immoral way. If, instead, every one of the subjects had

The Ethics of Deception In the experimental variation shown, the teacher was ordered to hold the learner's hand down on a "shock plate." Some 30 percent of subjects were completely obedient. Was the extreme deception used in Milgram's experiments justified?

broken off at "slight shock," or the first sign of the learner's discomfort, the results would have been pleasant, and reassuring, and who would protest?

Although Baumrind believed that the subjects were likely to experience serious aftereffects from the experiment, Milgram (1964, 1974b) pointed out that this was not the case. In a follow-up questionnaire, 84 percent of the participants in Milgram's experiment stated that they were glad to have taken part in the experiment. Only 1.3 percent said that they were "sorry to have been in the experiment." An additional follow-up examination by a psychiatrist a year after the experiment found no signs of harm or traumatic reaction.

Still, the debate over Milgram's studies sensitized psychologists and other social scientists to the ethical issues involved in research with human subjects (Fisher & Fyrberg, 1994). The controversy helped lead to the establishment of ethical safeguards by the American Psychological Association and the federal government regarding experiments involving human subjects (Blass, 1992).

Critical Thinking Questions

- Was the extreme deception used in Milgram's studies unethical?

- Did Milgram's dramatic and unexpected results justify the emotional distress experienced by the participants in his studies?

- Could Milgram have reached the same conclusions using less deceptive research methods?

- Under what conditions is such experimental deception justified?

If Milgram's findings seem to cast an unfavorable light on human nature, there are two reasons to take heart. First, when teachers were allowed to act as their own authority and freely choose the shock level, 95 percent of them did not venture beyond 150 volts—the first point at which the learner protested. Clearly, Milgram's subjects were not responding to their own aggressive or sadistic impulses, but rather to orders from an authority figure.

Second, Milgram found that people were more likely to muster up the courage to defy an authority when they saw others do so. When Milgram's subjects observed what they thought were two other subjects disobeying the experimenter, the real subjects followed their lead 90 percent of the time and refused to continue. Like the subjects in Asch's experiment, Milgram's subjects were more likely to stand by their convictions when they were not alone in expressing them.

Despite these encouraging notes, the overall results of Milgram's obedience research painted a bleak picture of human nature. Not surprisingly, the obedience studies were highly publicized—and extremely controversial. Many people were upset by his findings, but his methods drew fire as well. Critical Thinking Box 12.2 describes this controversy.

Asch, Milgram, and the Real World
Implications of the Classic Social Influence Studies

Conformity and obedience were more than just academic issues to Asch and Milgram. Like countless others, Asch and Milgram struggled to make sense of all-too-real human atrocities. In particular, both were haunted by the systematic slaughter of 6 million European Jews by the Nazis during World War II. The Holocaust also involved killing tens of thousands of others whom the Nazis deemed unfit to live: Gypsies, homosexuals, political dissidents, people with disabilities, and people with mental illness. Unfortunately, it is all too easy to identify other examples of destructive conformity and obedience that have resulted in the brutal sacrifice of innocent people.

There are, of course, enormous differences between a carefully controlled laboratory demonstration of conformity and obedience, and the multitude of complex factors operating in concentration camps, wartime massacres, and religious cults. Nevertheless, the scientific study of conformity and obedience has produced some important insights.

The first is the degree to which our behavior is influenced by situational factors. Being at odds with the majority or with authority figures is very uncomfortable for most people—enough so that our judgment and perceptions can be distorted and we may act in ways that violate our conscience.

More important, perhaps, is the insight that each of us *does* have the capacity to resist group or authority pressure (Rochat & others, 2000). Because the central findings of these studies are so dramatic, it's easy to overlook the fact that some subjects refused to conform or obey despite considerable social and situational pressure. Consider the response of a subject in one of Milgram's later studies (Milgram, 1974a). A 32-year-old industrial engineer named Jan Rensaleer protested when he was commanded to continue at the 255-volt level:

EXPERIMENTER: *It is absolutely essential that you continue.*

MR. RENSALEER: *Well, I won't—not with the man screaming to get out.*

EXPERIMENTER: *You have no other choice.*

MR. RENSALEER: *I* do *have a choice.* (Incredulous and indignant) *Why don't I have a choice? I came here on my own free will. I thought I could help in a research project. But if I have to hurt somebody to do that, or if I was in his place, too, I wouldn't stay there. I can't continue. I'm very sorry. I think I've gone too far already, probably.*

Like some other subjects in the obedience and conformity studies, Rensaleer effectively resisted the situational and social pressures pushing him in a different direction. In real-life situations, people like Raoul Wallenberg, a Swedish diplomat, have done the same. During World War II, Wallenberg supplied Swedish passports to more than 20,000 Hungarian Jews, saving them from being deported to the Nazi death camps. When the Soviet army entered Budapest, Wallenberg was arrested, and he ultimately died in a Soviet prison.

How are such people different from those who conform or obey? Unfortunately, there's no satisfying answer to that question. No specific personality trait consistently predicts conformity or obedience in experimental situations such as those Asch and Milgram created (see Blass, 1991; Burger, 1992). In other words, the social influences that Asch and Milgram created in their experimental situations can be compelling even to people who are normally quite independent.

Finally, we need to emphasize that conformity and obedience are not completely bad in and of themselves. Quite the contrary. Conformity and obedience are necessary for an orderly society, which is why such behaviors were instilled in all of us as children. The critical issue is not

Destructive Obedience and Prejudice Blind obedience to authority combined with ethnic prejudice in Germany during World War II led to the slaughter of millions of Jews in concentration camps (Saltzman, 2000)—see top photo. When questioned after the war, Nazi officials and soldiers claimed that they were "just following orders." As the twentieth century drew to a close, history seemed to repeat itself in the Baltic Republics as prejudice and ethnic hatred boiled over in Bosnia, Croatia, and Kosovo. In the photo at the bottom, mourners sit among the coffins bearing the bodies of ethnic Albanians who had been killed by Serb forces and dumped into mass graves in Kosovo.

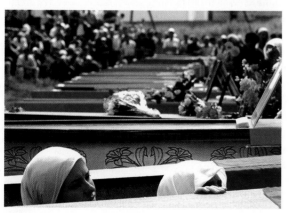

so much whether people conform or obey, because we all do so every day of our lives. Rather, the critical issue is whether the norms we conform to, or the orders we obey, reflect values that respect the rights, well-being, and dignity of others.

In the next section, we'll look at another dimension of social influence: the factors that influence whether we will help another person.

Helping Behavior
Coming to the Aid of Strangers

Key Theme
- Prosocial behavior describes any behavior that helps another person, including altruistic acts.

Key Questions
- What factors increase the likelihood that people will help a stranger?
- What factors decrease the likelihood that people will help a stranger?
- How can the lack of bystander response in the Genovese murder case be explained in light of psychological research on helping behavior?

Kitty Genovese

The Murder Scene At the end of the sidewalk you can see the railroad station where Genovese parked her car. Along the sidewalk are entrances to shops as well as stairways leading to apartments above the shops. After Genovese staggered to the entrance of her apartment, her attacker returned and stabbed her to death.

It was about 3:20 A.M. on Friday, March 13, 1964, when 28-year-old Kitty Genovese returned home from her job managing a bar. Like other residents in her middle-class New York City neighborhood, she parked her car at an adjacent railroad station. Her apartment entrance was only 100 feet away.

As she got out of her car, she noticed a man at the end of the parking lot. When the man moved in her direction, she began walking toward a nearby police call box, which was under a streetlight in front of a bookstore. On the opposite side of the street was a 10-story apartment building. As she neared the streetlight, the man grabbed her and she screamed. Across the street, lights went on in the apartment building. "Oh, my God! He stabbed me! Please help me! Please help me!" she screamed.

"Let that girl alone!" a man yelled from one of the upper apartment windows. The attacker looked up, then walked off, leaving Kitty on the ground, bleeding. The street became quiet. Minutes passed. One by one, lights went off. Struggling to her feet, Kitty made her way toward her apartment. As she rounded the corner of the building moments later, her assailant returned, stabbing her again. "I'm dying! I'm dying!" she screamed.

Again, lights went on. Windows opened and people looked out. This time, the assailant got in his car and drove off. It was now 3:35 A.M. Fifteen minutes had passed since Kitty's first screams for help. A New York City bus passed by. Staggering, then crawling, Kitty moved toward the entrance of her apartment. She never made it. Her attacker returned, searching the apartment entrance doors. At the second apartment entrance, he found her, slumped at the foot of the steps. This time, he stabbed her to death.

It was 3:50 A.M. when someone first called the police. The police took just two minutes to arrive at the scene. About half an hour later, an ambulance carried Kitty Genovese's body away. Only then did people come out of their apartments to talk to the police.

Over the next two weeks, police investigators learned that a total of 38 people had witnessed Kitty's murder—a murder that involved three separate attacks over a period of 35 minutes. Why didn't anyone try to help her? Or call the police when she first screamed for help?

When *The New York Times* interviewed various experts, they seemed baffled, although one expert said it was a "typical" reaction (Mohr, 1964). If there was a common theme in their explanations, it seemed to be "apathy." The occurrence

Prosocial Behavior in Action Everyday life is filled with countless acts of prosocial behavior. Many people volunteer their time and energy to help others, like these teenagers serving Christmas dinner at a church soup kitchen in Minneapolis.

Bystander Intervention In the situation shown here, bystanders are coming to the aid of a stranger injured in a car accident on a New York City street. What factors in this situation may have influenced their decision to help the accident victim?

was simply representative of the alienation and depersonalization of life in a big city, people said (see Rosenthal, 1964a, 1964b).

Not everyone bought this pat explanation. In the first place, it wasn't true. As social psychologists **Bibb Latané** and **John Darley** (1970) later pointed out in their landmark book, *The Unresponsive Bystander: Why Doesn't He Help?*:

> People often help others, even at great personal risk to themselves. For every "apathy" story, one of outright heroism could be cited. . . . It is a mistake to get trapped by the wave of publicity and discussion surrounding incidents in which help was not forthcoming into believing that help never comes. People sometimes help and sometimes don't. What determines when help will be given?

That's the critical question, of course. When do people help others? And *why* do people help others?

When we help another person with no expectation of personal reward or benefit, we're displaying **altruism** (Piliavin & others, 1981). An altruistic act is fundamentally selfless—the individual is motivated purely by the desire to help someone in need. Everyday life is filled with little acts of altruistic kindness, such as Fern giving the "homeless" man a handful of quarters or the stranger who thoughtfully holds a door open for you as you juggle an armful of packages.

Altruistic actions fall under the broader heading of **prosocial behavior,** which describes any behavior that helps another person, whatever the underlying motive. Note that prosocial behaviors are not necessarily altruistic. Sometimes we help others out of guilt (Baumeister & others, 1994; McGuire, 1994). And sometimes we help others in order to gain something, such as recognition, rewards, increased self-esteem, or having the favor returned (Staub, 1978).

Factors That *Increase* the Likelihood of Bystanders Helping

Kitty Genovese's death triggered hundreds of investigations into the conditions under which people will help others (Dovidio, 1984). Those studies began in the 1960s with the pioneering efforts of Latané and Darley, who conducted a series of ingenious experiments in which people appeared to need help. Often, these studies were conducted using locations in and around New York City as a kind of open-air laboratory.

Other researchers joined the effort to understand what factors influence a person's decision to help another (see Eisenberg, 1991; Piliavin & Charng, 1990). Some of the most significant factors that have been found to increase the likelihood of helping behavior are noted below.

■ *The "feel good, do good" effect.* People who feel good, successful, happy, or fortunate are more likely to help others (see Salovey & others, 1991; Schaller & Cialdini, 1990). Those good feelings can be due to virtually any positive event, such as receiving a gift, succeeding at a task, listening to pleasant music, finding a small amount of money, or even just enjoying a warm, sunny day.

■ *Feeling guilty.* We tend to be more helpful when we're feeling guilty. For example, after telling a lie or inadvertently causing an accident, people were more likely to help others (Baumeister & others, 1994; Cialdini & others, 1973; Regan & others, 1972).

■ *Seeing others who are willing to help.* Whether it's donating blood, helping a stranded motorist change a flat tire, or dropping money in the Salvation Army kettle during the holiday season, we're more likely to help if we observe others do the same (Bryan & Test, 1967; Sarason & others, 1991).

- **Perceiving the other person as deserving help.** We're more likely to help people who are in need of help through no fault of their own. For example, people are twice as likely to give some change to a stranger if they believe the stranger's wallet has been stolen than if they believe the stranger has simply spent all his money (Latané & Darley, 1970).

- **Knowing how to help.** Research has confirmed that simply knowing what to do contributes greatly to the decision to help someone else (e.g., Clark & Word, 1974; Huston & others, 1981).

- **A personalized relationship.** When people have any sort of personal relationship with another person, they're more likely to help that person. Even minimal social interaction with each other, such as making eye contact or engaging in small talk, increases the likelihood that one person will help the other (Howard & Crano, 1974; Solomon & others, 1981).

Factors That *Decrease* the Likelihood of Bystanders Helping

It's equally important to consider influences that decrease the likelihood of helping behavior. As we look at some of the key findings, we'll also note how each factor might have played a role in the death of Kitty Genovese.

- **The presence of other people.** People are much more likely to help when they are alone (Latané & Nida, 1981). If other people are present, helping behavior declines—a phenomenon called the **bystander effect.**

How can we account for this surprising finding? There seem to be two major reasons for the bystander effect (see Dovidio, 1984; Latané & Darley, 1970). First, the presence of other people creates a **diffusion of responsibility.** The responsibility to intervene is *shared* (or *diffused*) among all the onlookers. Because no one person feels all the pressure to respond, each bystander becomes less likely to help.

Ironically, the sheer number of bystanders seemed to be the most significant factor working against Kitty Genovese. Remember that when she first screamed, a man yelled down, "Let that girl alone!" With that, each observer instantly knew that he or she was not the only one watching the events on the street below. Hence, no single individual felt the full responsibility to help. Instead, there was a diffusion of responsibility among all the bystanders so that each individual's share of responsibility was small indeed (Latané & Darley, 1970).

Second, the bystander effect seems to occur because each of us is motivated to some extent by the desire to behave in a socially acceptable way (*normative social influence*) and to appear correct (*informational social influence*). Thus, we often rely on the reactions of others to help us define a situation and guide our response to it. In the case of Kitty Genovese, the lack of intervention by any of the witnesses may have signaled the others that intervention was not appropriate, wanted, or needed.

- **Being in a big city or a very small town.** Kitty Genovese was attacked late at night in one of the biggest cities in the world, New York. Are people less likely to help strangers in big cities? Researcher Nancy Steblay (1987) has confirmed that this common belief is true—but with a twist. People are less likely to help a stranger in very big cities (300,000 people or more) *or* in very small towns (5,000 people or less). Either extreme—very big or very small—seems to work against helping a stranger.

altruism
Helping another person with no expectation of personal reward or benefit.

prosocial behavior
Any behavior that helps another, whether the underlying motive is self-serving or selfless.

bystander effect
The phenomenon in which the greater the number of people present, the less likely each individual is to help someone in distress.

diffusion of responsibility
The phenomenon in which the presence of other people makes it less likely that any individual will help someone in distress because the obligation to intervene is shared among all the onlookers.

The Bystander Effect In contrast to the situation shown in the photograph on page 526, the people in this situation are obviously trying to ignore the heated argument between the man and the woman, even though the man has the woman pinned against a wall. What factors in this situation make it less likely that bystanders will intervene and try to help a stranger?

■ *Vague or ambiguous situations.* When situations are ambiguous and people are not certain that help is needed, they're less likely to offer help (Solomon & others, 1978). The ambiguity of the situation may also have worked against Kitty Genovese. The people in the apartment building saw a man and a woman struggling on the street below but had no way of knowing whether the two were acquainted. "We thought it was a lovers' quarrel," some of the witnesses later said (Gansberg, 1964). Researchers have found that people are especially reluctant to intervene when the situation appears to be a domestic dispute or a "lovers' quarrel," because they are not certain that assistance is wanted (Shotland & Straw, 1976).

■ *When the personal costs for helping outweigh the benefits.* As a general rule, we tend to weigh the costs as well as the benefits of helping in deciding whether to act. If the potential costs outweigh the benefits, it's less likely that people will help (Dovidio & others, 1991; Hedge & Yousif, 1992). The witnesses in the Genovese case may have felt that the benefits of helping Genovese were outweighed by the potential hassles and danger of becoming involved in the situation.

On a small yet universal scale, the murder of Kitty Genovese dramatically underscores the power of situational and social influences on our behavior. Although social psychological research has provided insights about the factors that influenced the behavior of those who witnessed the Genovese murder, it should not be construed as a justification for the inaction of the bystanders. After all, Kitty Genovese's death probably could have been prevented by a single phone call. Like the topics of conformity and obedience, the research on helping behavior has important implications as we go about negotiating daily life. If we understand the factors that decrease helping behavior, we can recognize and overcome those obstacles when we encounter someone who needs assistance. If *you* had been Kitty Genovese, how would *you* have hoped other people would react?

12.3 R·E·V·I·E·W

C·O·N·C·E·P·T

Factors Influencing Conformity, Obedience, and Helping Behavior

1. Although Gary prefers to dress casually, he wears a suit and tie to work because he wants to fit in with the other sales representatives. Gary's behavior is best explained as a matter of:

a. informational social influence
b. obedience
c. normative social influence
d. collectivistic culture

2. According to Stanley Milgram, which of the following statements helps explain the teachers' willingness to deliver progressively stronger shocks to the learner in the original obedience experiment?

a. The teachers were selected on the basis of their willingness to inflict pain in the name of scientific research.
b. The experimenter warned the teachers that they would be severely punished if they disobeyed his orders.
c. The teachers were physically and psychologically separated from the learner.
d. The average person is willing to blame an authority figure for his or her own behavior.

3. Conformity and obedience research suggests that:

a. people are innately predisposed to be cruel and aggressive
b. people are much less likely to conform or obey if they observe someone else who is defiant in the situation
c. only on rare occasions does someone resist group or authority pressure
d. extroverted people are most likely to resist group or authority pressure

4. Dan drives home from work elated because he had just received an unexpected promotion and a big raise in salary. As he pulls into his driveway, he notices his elderly neighbor struggling to clear the snow from the sidewalk in front of her home. How does Dan respond?

a. Dan is unlikely to help her, because he lives in a very small town.
b. Dan is likely to help her, because of the "feel good, do good" effect.
c. Dan is unlikely to help her, because of the just-world effect.
d. Dan is likely to help her, because of the diffusion of responsibility effect.

The Influence of Groups on Individual Behavior

social loafing
The tendency to expend less effort on a task when it is a group effort.

Key Theme
- Individual behavior can be strongly influenced by the presence of others.

Key Questions
- What are social loafing and social striving?
- What are social facilitation and deindividuation?

In our discussions of conformity, obedience, and altruism, we have touched on a variety of ways in which the presence of other people influences an individual's thoughts and behavior. In this section, we'll focus directly on how the behavior of individuals can be affected by being part of a group. As you'll see, the diffusion of responsibility that can occur when a group of people observe someone who needs help also contributes to other aspects of group behavior.

Social Loafing

When Individual Effort Is "Lost in the Crowd"

The performance and motivation of individuals who are part of a group can be influenced by many different factors (Guzzo & Dickson, 1996; Stanne & others, 1999). Whether it's cheering, clapping, or rope pulling, people tend to expend less effort on collective tasks than they do when performing the same task alone, a phenomenon called **social loafing.** Social loafing is especially pronounced when it's difficult or impossible to assess each individual's contribution to the collective effort. As a general rule, the greater the number of people involved in a collective effort, the lower each individual's output (Karau & Williams, 1993).

Is social loafing inevitable in any group task? Not at all. Psychologists Steven Karau and Kipling Williams (1993) conducted a meta-analysis of more than 70 social loafing studies. Collectively, the studies indicate that social loafing is reduced or eliminated when (1) the group is composed of people we know, (2) we are members of a highly valued group, or (3) the task is meaningful or unique. Interestingly, some gender differences also surfaced. Women are generally less likely to engage in social loafing than are men. And when the group size increases, the degree of social loafing increases for men, but not for women.

Why does social loafing occur? Like the diffusion of responsibility that occurs when a group witnesses someone who needs help, a similar diffusion of responsibility seems to occur among group members working on a collective task. The responsibility for attaining the group goal is spread across all the group members, resulting in reduced effort by each individual group member (Latané, 1981). Social loafing can also occur because people expect other group members to slack off. To keep the situation equitable, people reduce their efforts to match the level of effort they expect other group members to display (Jackson & Harkins, 1985).

Cultural Variations: Social Striving

Social loafing is a common phenomenon in individualistic cultures. However, cross-cultural psychologists have found that social loafing is not only absent, but *reversed* in many collectivistic cultures, including in China, Israel, and Japan (M. Bond & Smith, 1996). That is, individuals worked *harder* when they were in groups than when they

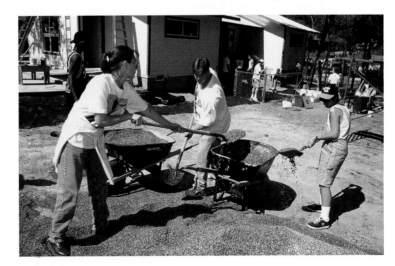

Social Loafing These teenagers, hard at work at a Habitat for Humanity building project in Austin, Texas, demonstrate that social loafing does not always take place. When people know the other members of their group, social loafing is less likely to occur. What other factors make social loafing less likely?

social facilitation
The tendency for the presence of other people to enhance individual performance.

deindividuation
The reduction of self-awareness and inhibitions that can occur when a person is part of a group whose members feel anonymous.

were alone—a pattern referred to as *social striving*. In the China and Israel studies, those participants who most highly endorsed collectivistic values were most likely to demonstrate increased performance and productivity in groups (M. Bond & Smith, 1996).

Why is social loafing less pronounced or even absent in collectivistic cultures? In collectivistic cultures, group success tends to be more highly valued than individual success. The contributions made by individuals to group success are also more highly valued than they are in individualistic cultures. Finally, the social norms in collectivistic cultures encourage a sense of social responsibility and hard work within groups (Karau & Williams, 1993).

Social Facilitation
Individual Performance in the Presence of Others

When your individual efforts go undetected and are "lost in the crowd," individual performance may drop. But what if your individual efforts are *not* lost in the crowd, but instead are the focus of the crowd's attention? Would your performance then be the same in the presence of others as it would be if you were working alone?

Partly, it depends on the complexity of the task that you're trying to perform. When a task is relatively simple or well rehearsed, the presence of other people tends to enhance individual performance, a pattern called **social facilitation.** So when others are watching you perform simple multiplication tables, your individual performance tends to improve. However, if the task is complex or poorly learned, such as a complex memory task, the opposite effect can occur: The presence of other people is likely to *hinder* performance (Allport, 1920, 1924; Travis, 1925).

How can this be explained? Several factors are involved (Geen, 1991, 1995). The presence of others tends to increase our level of arousal and motivation, possibly because of concerns over being favorably or unfavorably evaluated by others. When a task is simple or well learned, increased motivation, spurred on by the anticipation of being positively evaluated, seems to work to our benefit. Under these conditions, social facilitation often occurs: Individual performance is *better* in the presence of others. Hence, a well-trained athlete is likely to perform better when others are present than when alone (Guerin, 1986).

However, when the task is complex or poorly learned, arousal coupled with apprehension about being negatively evaluated tends to work against us. Under these conditions, the presence of others can diminish an individual's performance. For example, the apprehensive actor who is not as well rehearsed as he should be may end up missing cues and flubbing lines in front of the opening-night audience.

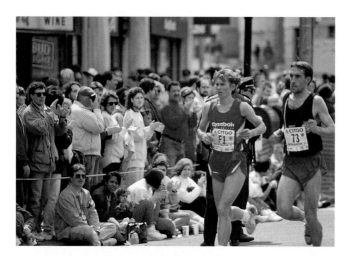

Social Facilitation As the crowd watches and applauds their performance, these professional runners are likely to turn in some of their best running times. When does the presence of other people facilitate the performance of a task? When does it work against us?

Deindividuation
When Group Members Feel Anonymous

What happens when you combine the increased arousal due to the presence of others with the diffusion of responsibility that characterizes social loafing and the bystander effect? In combination, increased arousal and a diminished sense of responsibility can lead to deindividuation. **Deindividuation** refers to the reduction of self-awareness and inhibitions that can occur when a person is part of a group whose members feel anonymous.

Under these conditions, people may do things that they wouldn't do if they were alone or identifiable. In this way, deindividuation can lead to irresponsible or antisocial behaviors. For example, deindividuation can help explain adolescent acts of vandalism on Halloween. Succumbing to the feeling of anonymity provided by darkness and Halloween masks, groups of otherwise law-abiding teenagers may commit minor acts of vandalism, such as smashing pumpkins, stealing Halloween decorations, and damaging mailboxes.

Much more serious consequences can result from the deindividuation that occurs in a mob or during a riot. The large crowd of people and general social chaos heighten both arousal and the sense of anonymity. This volatile combination can lead to mobs of rioting people who smash windows, steal, and injure innocent bystanders.

Similarly, onlookers are more likely to taunt someone who is threatening a suicidal jump when the incident occurs at night. The darkness of the night adds to the sense of anonymity felt by members of the crowd, who sometimes collectively start chanting, "Jump! Jump! Jump!" Not surprisingly, people are much *less* likely to urge on the would-be jumper when they are in small groups or during the day, when there is less of a sense of anonymity (Mann, 1981).

How can deindividuation be counteracted? An important element of deindividuation is the reduced sense of self-awareness (Diener, 1980). Thus, one way to counteract deindividuation is to heighten self-awareness. For example, when a mirror was placed above a bowl of Halloween candy, unattended trick-or-treaters were less likely to take more candy than they were told they could take (Beaman & others, 1979). Simply seeing their own faces in the mirror increased personal self-awareness and reduced impulsive, dishonest actions. In contrast, trick-or-treaters who did not see their faces in a mirror were more likely to take more candy than they were supposed to.

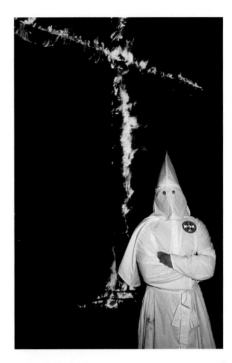

Deindividuation: Anonymity and Reduced Self-Awareness The hood and mask of the Ku Klux Klan uniform heighten the sense of anonymity felt by Klan members. So does the darkness of night at this cross burning. Such factors add to the likelihood that people will commit antisocial acts that they would not commit if their identities were known.

12.4 R·E·V·I·E·W

C·O·N·C·E·P·T

Influence of Groups on Individual Behavior

Match each example with the correct concept.

a. social loafing   c. social facilitation
b. social striving   d. deindividuation

_____ 1. Nina's best running time during practice was 5 minutes and 12 seconds for one mile. During the actual race, however, her time improved to 4 minutes and 42 seconds for one mile.

_____ 2. A team of workers in a car factory in Thailand is much more productive than are the individual team members when they work alone.

_____ 3. In a social psychology experiment, university students picked up less litter per person when they were members of a large group than when they worked alone.

_____ 4. When the Slammers won the play-offs on Friday night, the excitement and chaos following the game turned into a riot, and several stores were looted.

Summing Up
Social Psychology

We began this chapter with a Prologue about Fern's attempt to help a stranger in a strange city. As it turned out, Fern's social perceptions of the stranger were inaccurate: He was not a homeless person living on the streets of San Francisco. As simple as this incident was, it introduced a theme that was repeatedly echoed throughout our subsequent discussions of person perception, attribution, and

persuasion
The deliberate attempt to influence the attitudes or behavior of another person in a situation in which that person has some freedom of choice.

attitudes. Our subjective impressions, whether accurate or not, play a pivotal role in how we perceive and think about other people.

A different theme emerged in our later discussions of conformity, obedience, helping behavior, and the influence of groups. Social and situational factors, especially the behavior of others in the same situation, can have powerful effects on how we act at a given moment. But like Fern, each of us has the freedom to choose how we respond in a given situation. When we're aware of the social forces that influence us, it can be easier for us to choose wisely.

In the final analysis, we are social animals who often influence one another's thoughts, perceptions, and actions, sometimes in profound ways. In the chapter Application, we'll look at some of the ways in which social psychological insights have been applied by professional persuaders—and how you can counteract attempts to persuade you.

APPLICATION **The Persuasion Game**

Our daughter, Laura, was three-and-a-half years old, happily munching her Cheerios and doodling pictures in the butter on her bread. Don sat across from her at the kitchen table, reading a draft of this chapter. "Don't play with your food, Laura," Don said without looking up.

"Okay, Daddy," she chirped. "Daddy, are you in a happy mood?"

Don paused. "Yes, I'm in a happy mood, Laura," he said thoughtfully. "Are you in a happy mood?"

"Yes, Daddy," Laura replied as she made the banana peel dance around her placemat. "Daddy, will you get me a Mermaid Barbie doll for my birthday?"

Ah, so young and so clever! From very early in life, we learn the basics of **persuasion**—the deliberate attempt to influence the attitudes or behavior of another person in a situation in which that person has some freedom of choice. Clearly, Laura had figured out one basic rule: She's more likely to persuade Mom or Dad when they're in "a happy mood."

Professional persuaders often manipulate people's attitudes and behavior using techniques based on two fundamental social norms: the rule of reciprocity and the rule of commitment (Cody & Seiter, 2001). Here we'll provide you with some practical suggestions to avoid being taken in by persuasion techniques.

The Rule of Reciprocity

The *rule of reciprocity* is a simple but powerful social norm (Cialdini & Trost, 1998). If someone gives you something or does you a favor, you feel obligated to return the favor. That's why encyclopedia

salespeople offer you a "free" dictionary for listening to their spiel and department stores that sell expensive cosmetics offer "free" makeovers. Technically, you are under "no obligation" to buy anything. Nonetheless, the tactic often creates an uncomfortable sense of obligation, so you *do* feel pressured to reciprocate by buying the product (Cialdini, 2000).

One strategy that uses the rule of reciprocity is called the *door-in-the-face technique* (Dillard, 1991; Perloff, 1993). First, the persuader makes a large request that you're certain to refuse. For example, Joe asks to borrow $500. You figuratively "slam the door in his face" by quickly turning him down. But then Joe, apologetic, appears to back off and makes a much smaller request—to borrow $20. From your perspective, it appears that Joe has made a concession to you and is trying to be reasonable. This puts you in the position of reciprocating with a concession of your own. "Well, I can't lend you $500," you grumble, "but I guess I could lend you 20 bucks." Of course, the persuader's real goal was to persuade you to comply with the second, smaller request.

The rule of reciprocity is also operating in the *that's-not-all technique* (Zimbardo & Leippe, 1991). First, the persuader makes an offer. But before you can accept or reject it, the persuader appears to throw in something extra to make the deal even more attractive to you. So as you're standing there mulling over the price of the more expensive DVD player, the salesperson says, "Listen, I'm offering you a great price but that's not all I'll do—I'll throw in some headphones at no charge." From your perspective, it appears as though

the salesperson has just done you a favor by making a concession you did not ask for. This creates a sense of obligation for you to reciprocate by buying the "better" package.

The Rule of Commitment

Another powerful social norm is the *rule of commitment*. Once you make a public commitment, there is psychological and interpersonal pressure on you to behave consistently with your earlier commitment. The *foot-in-the-door technique* is one strategy that capitalizes on the rule of commitment (Cialdini, 2000; Perloff, 1993). Here's how it works.

First, the persuader makes a small request that you're likely to agree to. For example, she might ask you to wear a lapel pin publicizing a fundraising drive for a charity (Pratkanis & Aronson, 1992). By agreeing to wear the lapel pin, you've made a *commitment* to the fundraising effort. At that point, she has gotten her "foot in the door." Later, the persuader asks you to comply with a second, larger request, such as donating money to the charity. Because of your earlier commitment, you feel psychologically pressured to behave consistently by now agreeing to the larger commitment (Gorassini & Olson, 1995).

The rule of commitment is also operating in the *low-ball technique*. First, the persuader gets you to make a commitment by deliberately understating the cost of the product you want. He's thrown you a "low ball," one that is simply too good to turn down. In reality, the persuader has no intention of honoring the artificially low price.

Here's an example of the low-ball technique in action: You've negotiated an excellent price (the "low ball") on a used car and filled out the sales contract. The car salesman shakes your hand and beams, then takes your paperwork into his manager's office for approval. Ten minutes pass—enough time for you to convince yourself that you've made the right decision and solidify your commitment to it.

At that point, the salesman comes back from his manager's office looking dejected. "I'm terribly sorry," the car salesman says. "My manager won't let me sell the car at that price because we'd lose too much money on the deal. I told him I would even take a lower commission, but he won't budge."

Notice what has happened. The attractive low-ball price that originally prompted you to make the commitment has been pulled out from under your feet. What typically happens? Despite the loss of the original inducement to make the purchase—the low-ball price—people often feel compelled to keep their commitment to make the purchase even though it is at a higher price (Cialdini, 2000).

Defending Against Persuasion Techniques

How can you reduce the likelihood that you'll be manipulated into making a decision that is not in your best interest? Here are three practical suggestions.

1. Sleep on it.

Persuasive transactions typically occur quickly. Part of this is our own doing. We've finally decided to go look at a new computer, automobile, or whatever, so we're psychologically primed to buy the product. The persuader uses this psychological momentum to help coax you into signing on the dotted line right then and there. It's only later, of course, that you sometimes have second thoughts. So when you think you've got the deal you want, tell the persuader that you always sleep on important decisions before making a final commitment.

The sleep-on-it rule often provides an opportunity to discover whether the persuader is deliberately trying to pressure or manipulate you. If the persuader responds to your sleep-on-it suggestion by saying something like, "This offer is good for today only," then it's likely that he or she is afraid that your commitment to the deal will crumble if you think about it too carefully or look elsewhere.

2. Play devil's advocate.

List all of the reasons why you should *not* buy the product or make a particular commitment (Pratkanis & Aronson, 1992). Arguing *against* the decision will help activate your critical thinking skills. It's also helpful to discuss important decisions with a friend, who might be able to point out disadvantages that you have overlooked.

3. Pay attention to your gut feelings.

Learn to trust your gut feelings when something doesn't feel quite right. If you feel that you're being psychologically pressured or cornered, you probably are. As a general rule, if you feel any sense of hesitation, lean toward the conservative side and do nothing. If you take the time to think things over, you'll probably be able to identify the source of your reluctance.

Chapter Review Social Psychology

Key Points

Introduction: What Is Social Psychology?

- **Social psychology** is the scientific study of how individuals think, feel, and behave in social situations. **Social cognition** and **social influence** are two important areas of research in social psychology.

Person Perception: *Forming Impressions of Other People*

- **Person perception** is an active and subjective process that occurs in an interpersonal context. The interpersonal context includes the characteristics of the individual you are judging, your own characteristics, and the situation.

- Person perception is influenced by subjective perceptions, personal goals, **social norms,** and self-perception.

- People often rely on social categories when they evaluate others. **Social categorization** may be automatic or deliberate. Using social categories is cognitively efficient but can lead to inaccurate conclusions.

- Because we expect certain traits and behaviors to go together, we often form and rely on implicit personality theories in person perception. Implicit personality theories provide a mental framework that organizes observations, memories, and beliefs about other people.

- One common **implicit personality theory** is "what is beautiful is good." Although people tend to associate physical attractiveness with many desirable characteristics, there are few personality differences between attractive and less attractive people.

Attribution: *Explaining Behavior*

- The **attribution** process refers to how we infer the cause of our own or another person's behavior. Attributions can strongly influence our opinions of other people, but the attribution process is susceptible to many biases.

- Three important attributional biases are the **fundamental attribution error,** the **actor–observer discrepancy,** and the **self-serving bias.** The **just-world hypothesis,** along with the fundamental attribution error, contributes to **blaming the victim** of a tragedy. In some collectivistic cultures, people display the modesty, or self-effacing, bias and are less prone to making the fundamental attribution error than are people in individualistic cultures.

The Social Psychology of Attitudes

- An **attitude** is a learned tendency to evaluate an object, person, or issue in a particular way. This evaluation is usually positive or negative, but may be ambivalent. Attitudes can have cognitive, emotional, and behavioral components.

- Attitudes are likely to determine behaviors when they are extreme or expressed frequently, when they have been formed through direct experience, when people are very knowledgeable about the attitude object, when people have a vested interest in the subject of the attitude, and when people expect a favorable outcome from acting in accordance with their attitude.

- When behavior conflicts with attitudes, **cognitive dissonance** may occur, and people may change their attitudes to conform to their behavior.

Understanding Prejudice

- **Prejudice** refers to a negative attitude toward people who belong to a specific social group.

- **Stereotypes** are social categories about members of particular social groups. Relying on stereotypes can have many negative consequences. Stereotyped thinking can distort perception and cause us to inaccurately prejudge individuals. Once formed, stereotypes resist change.

- Judgments of others are also influenced by whether they are members of the **in-group** or an **out-group.** We're more likely to use negative stereotypes to evaluate members of out-groups. The **out-group homogeneity effect, in-group bias,** and **ethnocentrism** are three forms of bias that can result from in-group/out-group thinking.

- Stereotypes form the cognitive basis for prejudicial attitudes. Prejudice also has an emotional component, which often occurs in response to the belief that an out-group somehow threatens the in-group's values or norms.

- Mere contact between members of different groups is not enough to dissolve prejudicial attitudes. Muzafer Sherif demonstrated that intergroup conflict can be decreased when groups engage in a cooperative effort. Cooperative learning is one way of reducing prejudice in classrooms.

- People are sometimes not aware of their prejudiced attitudes. On an individual level, prejudice can be reduced by consciously rejecting prejudiced attitudes, internalizing nonprejudiced beliefs, and deliberately inhibiting prejudicial reactions while replacing them with nonprejudiced responses.

Conformity: *Following the Crowd*

- **Social influence** is the psychological study of how behavior is influenced by the social environment and other people. **Conformity** occurs when people change their behavior, attitudes, or beliefs in response to real or imagined group pressure. Sometimes people conform publicly but not privately; at other times, both private beliefs and outward behavior are changed to conform to group norms or pressure.

- Research by Solomon Asch demonstrated the degree to which people will conform to a majority view and the conditions under which conformity is most likely. **Normative and informational social influence** both contribute to conformity.

- Conformity is generally higher in collectivistic cultures than in individualistic cultures. Conformity to group norms is viewed less negatively in many collectivistic cultures than it is in individualistic cultures.

Obedience: *Just Following Orders*

- **Obedience** was studied most extensively by Stanley Milgram. In Milgram's original obedience experiment, the subject (the "teacher") thought he was delivering ever-increasing levels of electric shock to another person (the "learner"). In contrast to predictions, most of the subjects obeyed the experimenter and progressed to the maximum shock level.

- Milgram identified several powerful aspects of the original experimental situation that influenced subjects to obey the experimenter and continue delivering electric shocks. In later experiments, Milgram also identified several situational factors that made people less likely to obey.

- Asch's research on conformity and Milgram's research on obedience demonstrate the degree to which behavior is influenced by situational factors.

Helping Behavior: *Coming to the Aid of Strangers*

- The scientific study of helping behavior—**altruism** and **prosocial behavior**—was spurred by the murder of Kitty Genovese in front of 38 witnesses. Although no one intervened to save Genovese, sometimes people do help others.

- Bibb Latané and John Darley developed a model to explain the circumstances under which people will help a stranger. Several factors have been identified that affect the likelihood of bystander intervention. **Diffusion of responsibility** is the most important factor that explains the **bystander effect.**

The Influence of Groups on Individual Behavior

- Individual behavior can be strongly influenced by the presence of others. In **social loafing,** people expend less effort when working as a group on a collective task than when working alone on the same task. Social loafing is less likely when we know the other people in a group, when we are members of a highly valued group, or when a task is meaningful or unique.

- Social loafing is reduced or reversed in some collectivistic cultures. Instead, individuals expend more effort when they are working in a group on a collective task, a phenomenon known as social striving.

- Under some conditions, the presence of others enhances individual performance, a phenomenon called social facilitation. **Social facilitation** is most likely when a task is simple or well rehearsed. Performance decreases when a task is complex or poorly learned.

- **Deindividuation** can occur when increased arousal due to the presence of others is combined with diffusion of responsibility and anonymity. Deindividuation can lead to antisocial behaviors, but it can be reduced if self-awareness is heightened.

Key Terms

social psychology, p. 498

social cognition, p. 498

social influence, pp. 498, 515

person perception, p. 499

social norms, p. 499

social categorization, p. 500

implicit personality theory, p. 500

attribution, p. 503

fundamental attribution error, p. 503

blaming the victim, p. 503

just-world hypothesis, p. 503

actor–observer discrepancy, p. 504

self-serving bias, p. 505

attitude, p. 506

cognitive dissonance, p. 508

prejudice, p. 509

stereotype, p. 510

in-group, p. 511

out-group, p. 511

out-group homogeneity effect, p. 511

in-group bias, p. 512

ethnocentrism, p. 512

conformity, p. 516

normative social influence, p. 517

informational social influence, p. 517

obedience, p. 518

altruism, p. 526

prosocial behavior, p. 526

bystander effect, p. 527

diffusion of responsibility, p. 527

social loafing, p. 529

social facilitation, p. 530

deindividuation, p. 530

persuasion, p. 530

Key People

Solomon Asch (1907–1996)   American social psychologist who is best known for his pioneering studies of conformity. (p. 516)

John M. Darley (b. 1938)   Contemporary American social psychologist who, along with co-researcher Bibb Latané, is best known for his pioneering studies of bystander intervention in emergency situations. (p. 526)

Bibb Latané (b. 1937)   Contemporary American social psychologist who, along with co-researcher John Darley, is best

known for his pioneering studies of bystander intervention in emergency situations. (p. 526)

Stanley Milgram (1933–1984)   American social psychologist who is best known for his controversial series of studies investigating destructive obedience to an authority. (p. 518)

Muzafer Sherif (1906–1988)   American social psychologist who is best known for his Robbers Cave experiments to study prejudice, conflict resolution, and group processes. (p. 513)

Concept Review Answers

12.1   page 506

1. c   *2.* e   *3.* d   *4.* b   *5.* a

12.2   page 515

1. stereotyping   *4.* cognitive dissonance

2. out-group homogeneity   *5.* ethnocentrism

3. in-group bias

12.3   page 528

1. c   *2.* c   *3.* b   *4.* b

12.4   page 531

1. c   *2.* b   *3.* a   *4.* d

Web Companion   Review Activities

You can find additional review activities at: **www.worthpublishers.com/hockenbury** The Psychology 3e Web Companion has a self-scoring practice quiz, flashcards, two interactive crossword puzzles, and other activities to help you master the material in this chapter.

Buy One Get One Free

chapter 13

Stress, Health, and Coping

Prologue

Katie's Story

In her high-rise apartment at 1 West Street, our 20-year-old niece Katie was fixing herself some eggs for breakfast on a beautiful, crystal-clear New York morning. In the background, Katie could hear the muted sound of sirens down on the streets below, but she thought nothing of it. The phone rang. It was Lydia, her roommate, calling from her job in mid-Manhattan. "Katie, you're not going to believe this. A plane hit the World Trade Center. Go up on the roof and take a look!"

Katie hung up the phone and scurried up the fire escape stairwell, joining other residents already gathered on the roof. Down below, sirens were blaring and she could see emergency vehicles, fire engines, and people racing from all directions toward the World Trade Center, just a few blocks away. There was a gaping hole in the north tower. Black, billowing smoke was gushing out, drifting upward, and filling the sky. She thought she could see the flames. *What a freaky accident.*

After watching and talking with some of the other residents for a few minutes, Katie was ready to go back downstairs and get ready for her dance lesson. "Look at that plane!" one of the people suddenly yelled. Just as Katie turned to look, a massive jet roared overhead and slammed into the World Trade Center's south tower, exploding into a huge fireball.

People screaming. Panic. Pushing and shoving at the stairwell door. *Get back to the apartment.* The television. Live views of the burning towers. Newscaster shouting: "Terrorist attack! New York is being attacked!" The TV went dead. *Don't panic. What am I going to do? Are we being bombed?*

Two thousand miles away. A sunny Colorado morning. Phone ringing. Judy was sound asleep. Ringing. Answer the phone. "Katie? What's wrong? Is someone in your apartment? Calm down, I can't understand . . ."

"Mom, New York is being attacked! I don't know what to do! What should I do?" Katie sobbed uncontrollably.

As Katie tried to explain to Judy what was happening, Judy held the portable phone to her ear as she stood up and fumbled for the remote control, flipping on the bedroom television. Pandemonium. Bizarre scenes of chaos in New York. *Oh my God, New York is being attacked . . . Katie's only a couple of blocks from the World Trade Center . . .*

"Katie, breathe. Calm down. It's chaos out on the street, Katie, it's horrible. Don't go out there! Just stay in your apartment. Don't leave, Katie! You'll be safe in your apartment. Katie, I want you to . . ." The phone connection went dead. Desperately, Judy dialed and redialed Katie's number, only to hear a busy signal. She tried Katie's cell phone. Nothing. *Katie has to get out of there . . .*

Katie dropped the phone. *Worthless.* Lights flickered off, then on. Pounding on the door. "Evacuate the building! Get out!" a man's voice shouted. "Get out now! Use the stairwell!" *Gotta get out of here. Get out.*

Putting on her shoes and pulling a T-shirt over her pajamas, Katie grabbed her cell phone and raced out of her apartment toward the crowded stairwell. As she emerged on the street, it was mass confusion. *Cross the street.* She joined a throng of people gathering in Battery Park. *Stay calm.* As the crowd watched the burning towers, people shouted out more news. *Pentagon has been hit. White House is on fire. More planes in the air. President on Air Force One.*

Shaking, she couldn't take her eyes off the burning towers. *What's falling?* Figures falling from the windows of the Trade Center, a hundred stories high. *On fire. That person was on fire. Oh my God, they're jumping out of the building! Don't look!* Watching the firefighters, EMT workers, media people swarming at the base of the site. *This is not real. It's a movie. It's not real.*

Suddenly, unbelievably, the south tower crumbled. Screaming. *It's collapsing! It's coming down.* A vast ball of smoke formed, like an atomic mushroom cloud. Like everyone else in the park, Katie turned and started running blindly. Behind her, a huge cloud of black smoke, ash, and debris followed, howling down West Street like a tornado.

Running. Cops shouting. "Go north! Don't go back! Get out of here!" *Don't go north. The ferry.* Choking on the smoke and dust, Katie covered her face with her T-shirt and stumbled down the street, moving toward the river. *I'm going to choke . . . can't breathe.* She saw a group of people near the Staten Island ferry. *Get on the ferry, get out of Manhattan.* Another explosion. Panic. More people running.

Dazed and disoriented, Katie is still not certain how she ended up on a boat—a commuter ferry taking people to Atlantic Highlands, New Jersey. *On the boat at last. I'm safe.* Covered with soot. Filthy. Standing in her pajamas amid stunned Wall Street workers in their suits and ties. Call anyone. Trying to call people. *Cell phone dead.* "Here, Miss, use mine, it's working." Call anyone. Crying. *They're dead. Those firemen, the EMT workers at the base of the towers. Dead. They're all dead.* From the boat, she got a call through to her dance teacher, Pam, who lived in New Jersey. Pam would come and get her. She could stay with Pam.

In Colorado, Judy was crying, frantic. What had happened to Katie? She tried to help the boys, Jordon and Zak, get ready for school. She called her ex-husband, who told her not to worry. Katie would be fine, he said. She called your author Sandy and left a frantic phone message. *Where was Katie? Was she dead?* It was not for many hours—later that Tuesday afternoon—that Judy finally heard Katie's voice and knew that she was alive.

Katie survived, but the next few weeks were difficult ones. She had no money, no clothes, none of her possessions. When she got off the ferry in Atlantic Highlands, government workers wearing masks and special yellow protective clothing made her throw her shoes away. "They're filled with asbestos," one worker said. "I don't care if they're new."

Like the other residents in her area near the World Trade Center, Katie wasn't allowed back into her apartment for many days. Her dance teacher, Pam, lent her money to buy new clothes. Late on Tuesday afternoon, she called her workplace, an upscale retail store. The manager wanted her back at work the next day. "Show up or lose your job," the manager said. When Katie did show up, the manager chewed her out because her blouse was wrinkled. Taking the train every day from New Jersey, she saw the same cars parked in the lot, day after day. It suddenly dawned on her. The owners of the cars were commuters. *They're dead. Dead.*

For the first few weeks, Katie was fine, almost lighthearted. Everyone was pulling together. "It was really beautiful," she said. "New Yorkers were helping each other." But there were constant reminders, new fears. In the week following the attack, there were more than 70 bomb scares in the area where she worked. She went out with some friends one night, downtown, everyone wearing face masks because of the dust. It was like living in the twilight zone.

Two weeks after the attacks, the nightmares started. Katie felt panicky on buses, trains, subways. She had to will herself to stay in her seat. On one crowded bus, her fear became overwhelming. Shaking uncontrollably, she got off the bus. "I couldn't help it. I was afraid I would start screaming."

The reminders were everywhere—the fire station shrines, signs for the subway stop that didn't exist anymore. Photographs and notes and flowers on fences, walls. People still missing. And then there were the mental images . . . the images of people jumping, falling, the faces of the rescue workers, the plane ripping through the building. Then it was the men in the white coats and masks at NBC, anthrax right next door to the store where she worked.

Judy kept calling her every day, telling her, "Katie, come home. I want you to get out of New York, it's not safe." Her older brother, Josh, called repeatedly from Miami and said the same thing. "Kate, you can dance in Los Angeles. Or Denver. Or Miami. Please, Katie, get out of there."

But like millions of other New Yorkers, Katie regained her equilibrium. After pleading with the National Guardsmen patrolling the area, Katie and Lydia were allowed to get their belongings out of their apartment. They loaded as much as they could into a shopping cart, dragging and pushing the cart some 30 blocks north to a friend's home. They found a new apartment.

The best thing that Katie did, she said, was go back to her daily dance class. In that two hours a day, Katie began to feel right again, doing what she loved, surrounded by the people she loved. The nightmares slowly receded, although the memories never will.

"Are things back to normal?" Katie said. "No, things will never be normal again, not in a hundred years. But it's okay. I'm fine. And I'm not going to leave New York. This is where I am, this is where I live, this is where I can dance."

Introduction

What Is Stress?

Key Theme

- When events are perceived as exceeding your ability to cope with them, you experience an unpleasant emotional and physical state—stress.

Key Questions

- What is health psychology, and what is the biopsychosocial model?
- How do life events, daily hassles, and conflict contribute to stress?
- What are some social and cultural sources of stress?

How Do You Define Stress? From a ripped grocery bag to the threat of unemployment, stressors come in all sizes. Any event can produce stress—if you think you don't have the resources to cope with it.

stress
A negative emotional state occurring in response to events that are perceived as taxing or exceeding a person's resources or ability to cope.

health psychology
The branch of psychology that studies how biological, behavioral, and social factors influence health, illness, medical treatment, and health-related behaviors.

biopsychosocial model
The belief that physical health and illness are determined by the complex interaction of biological, psychological, and social factors.

stressors
Events or situations that are perceived as harmful, threatening, or challenging.

When you think of the causes of psychological stress, your initial tendency is probably to think of events and issues directly related to yourself, such as school, work, or family pressures. And, indeed, we don't want to minimize those events as stressors. If you're like most of our students, you probably have ample first-hand experience with the stress of juggling the demands of college, work, and family responsibilities. Those pressures represent very real and personal concerns for many of us as we negotiate the challenges of daily life.

But as the terrorist attacks of September 11th unfolded, our entire nation was thrown into an extraordinary state of shared psychological stress as we watched, minute by minute, reeling in disbelief. It is impossible, of course, to convey the sense of agony, grief, and despair experienced by the thousands of people who lost loved ones as a result of the terrorist attacks on September 11th. It is equally impossible to convey the sense of relief that thousands of other people felt when they eventually learned that their loved ones—like our niece Katie—had survived the attack.

Both the extraordinary events of September 11th and the ordinary events of daily life can provide us with insights about how stress affects us and, equally important, how we cope with stress. What exactly is *stress?* It's one of those words that is frequently used but is hard to define precisely. Early stress researchers, who mostly studied animals, defined stress in terms of the physiological response to harmful or threatening events (e.g., Selye, 1956). However, people are far more complex than animals in their response to potentially stressful events. Two people may respond very differently to the same potentially stressful event.

Since the 1960s, psychologists have been actively studying the human response to stress, including the effects of stress on health and how people cope with stressful events. As research findings have accumulated, it has become clear that psychological and social factors, as well as biological factors, are involved in the stress experience and its effects.

Today, **stress** is widely defined as a negative emotional state occurring in response to events that are perceived as taxing or exceeding a person's resources or ability to cope. This definition emphasizes the important role played by a person's perception or appraisal of events in the experience of stress. Whether we experience stress depends largely on our *cognitive appraisal* of an event and the resources we have to deal with the event (Lazarus & Folkman, 1984; Tomaka & others, 1993).

If we think that we have adequate resources to deal with a situation, it will probably create little or no stress in our lives. But if we perceive our resources as being inadequate to deal with a situation we see as threatening, challenging, or even harmful, we'll experience the effects of stress. If our coping efforts are effective, stress will decrease. If they are ineffective, stress will increase.

The study of stress is a key topic in **health psychology,** one of the most rapidly growing specialty areas in psychology. Health psychology is also sometimes referred to as *behavioral medicine* or *medical psychology.* Health psychologists are interested in how biological, psychological, and social factors influence health, illness, and treatment. Along with developing strategies to foster emotional and physical well-being, they investigate issues such as the following:

- How to promote health-enhancing behaviors
- How people respond to being ill
- How people respond in the patient–health practitioner relationship
- Why some people don't follow medical advice

Health psychologists work with many different health care professionals, including physicians, dentists, nurses, social workers, and occupational and physical therapists. In their research and clinical practice, health psychologists are guided by the **biopsychosocial model.** According to this model, health and illness are determined by the complex interaction of biological factors (e.g., genetic predispositions), psychological and behavioral factors (e.g., health beliefs and attitudes, lifestyle, stress), and social conditions (e.g., family relationships, social support, cultural influences). Throughout this chapter, we'll look closely at the roles that different biological, psychological, and social factors play in our experience of stress.

Sources of Stress

Life is filled with potential **stressors**—events or situations that produce stress. Virtually any event or situation can be a source of stress if you question your ability or resources to deal effectively with it (Lazarus & Folkman, 1984). In this section, we'll survey some of the most important and common sources of stress.

Life Events and Change: Is *Any* Change Stressful?

Early stress researchers Thomas Holmes and Richard Rahe (1967) believed that any change that required you to adjust your behavior and lifestyle would cause stress. In an attempt to measure the amount of stress people experienced, they developed the *Social Readjustment Rating Scale.* The scale included 43 life events that are likely to require some level of adaptation. Each life event was assigned a numerical rating that estimates its relative impact in terms of *life change units.* Sample items from the original Social Readjustment Rating Scale are shown in Table 13.1.

Life event ratings range from 100 life change units for the most stress-producing to 11 life change units for the least stress-producing events. Cross-cultural studies have shown that people in many different cultures tend to rank the magnitude of stressful events in a similar way (McAndrew & others, 1998). Notice that some of the life events are generally considered to be positive events, such as a vacation. According to the life events approach, *any* change, whether positive or negative, is inherently stress-producing.

To measure their level of stress, people simply check off the life events they have experienced in the past year and total the life change units. Holmes and Rahe found that people who had accumulated more than 150 life change units within a year had an increased rate of physical or psychological illness (Holmes & Masuda, 1974; Rahe, 1972).

Despite its initial popularity, several problems with the life events approach have been noted. First, the link between scores on the Social Readjustment Rating Scale and the development of physical and psychological problems is relatively weak. In general, scores on the Social Readjustment Rating Scale are *not* very good predictors of poor physical or mental health. Instead, researchers have found that most people weather major life events without developing serious physical or psychological problems (Coyne & Downey, 1991; Kessler & others, 1985).

Table | **13.1**

The Social Readjustment Rating Scale: Sample Items

Life Event	Life Change Units
Death of spouse	100
Divorce	73
Marital separation	65
Death of close family member	63
Major personal injury or illness	53
Marriage	50
Fired at work	47
Retirement	45
Pregnancy	40
Change in financial state	38
Death of close friend	37
Change to different line of work	36
Mortgage or loan for major purchase	31
Foreclosure on mortgage or loan	30
Change in work responsibilities	29
Outstanding personal achievement	28
Begin or end school	26
Trouble with boss	23
Change in work hours or conditions	20
Change in residence	20
Change in social activities	18
Change in sleeping habits	16
Vacation	13
Christmas	12
Minor violations of the law	11

SOURCE: Holmes & Rahe (1967).

The Social Readjustment Rating Scale, developed by Thomas Holmes and Richard Rahe (1967), was an early attempt to quantify the amount of stress experienced by people in a wide range of situations. Holmes and Rahe reasoned that any life event that required some sort of adaptation or change would create stress, whether the life event was pleasant or unpleasant.

Major Life Events and Stress Would a welcome pregnancy or losing your home in a fire both produce damaging levels of stress? According to the life events approach, any event that required you to change or adjust your lifestyle would produce significant stress—whether the event was positive or negative, planned or unexpected. How was the life events approach modified by later research?

Second, the Social Readjustment Rating Scale does not take into account a person's subjective appraisal of an event, response to that event, or ability to cope with the event (Lazarus, 1999). Instead, the number of life change units on the scale is preassigned, reflecting the assumption that a given life event will have the same impact on virtually everyone. But clearly, the stress-producing potential of an event might vary widely from one person to another. For instance, if you are in a marriage that is filled with conflict, tension, and unhappiness, getting divorced (73 life change units) might be significantly less stressful than remaining married.

Third, the life events approach assumes that change in itself, whether good or bad, produces stress. However, researchers have found that negative life events have the greatest adverse effects on health, especially when they're unexpected and uncontrollable (Dohrenwend & others, 1993). In contrast, positive or desirable events are much *less* likely to affect your health adversely. Today, most researchers agree that undesirable events are significant sources of stress but that change in itself is not necessarily stressful.

Nonetheless, the Social Readjustment Rating Scale is still often used in stress research (e.g., Toews & others, 1997; York & others, 1998). And efforts have recently been made to revise and update the scale so that it more fully takes into account the influences of gender, age, marital status, and other characteristics (C. Hobson & others, 1998; M. Miller & Rahe, 1997).

Daily Hassles: That's *Not* What I Ordered!

What made you feel "stressed out" in the last week? Chances are it was not a major life event. Instead, it was probably some unexpected but minor annoyance, such as splotching ketchup on your new white T-shirt, misplacing your keys, or discovering that you've been standing in the wrong line.

Stress researcher **Richard Lazarus** and his colleagues suspected that such ordinary irritations in daily life might be an important source of stress. To explore this idea, they developed a scale measuring **daily hassles**—everyday occurrences that annoy and upset people (DeLongis & others, 1982; Kanner & others, 1981). The *Daily Hassles Scale* measures the occurrence of everyday annoyances, such as losing something, getting stuck in traffic, and even being inconvenienced by lousy weather.

Are there gender differences in the frequency of daily hassles? One study measured the daily hassles experienced by married couples (Almeida & Kessler, 1998). The women experienced both more daily hassles and higher levels of psychological stress than their husbands did. For men, the most common sources of daily stress were financial and job-related problems. For women, family demands and interpersonal conflict were the most frequent causes of stress.

What about the hassle of bad hair days? Are only women affected by them? Although it is commonly believed that men are not affected by their appearance, Yale psychologist Marianne LaFrance (2000) found that bad hair days intensify feelings of social insecurity, self-consciousness, and self-criticism for both women and men. According to LaFrance, "Individuals perceive their capabilities to be significantly lower than others when experiencing bad hair." In response to unruly hair or, worse yet, a horrible haircut, women tend to feel embarrassed or

Richard Lazarus Psychologist Richard Lazarus (b. 1922) has made several influential contributions to the study of stress and coping. His definition of stress emphasizes the importance of cognitive appraisal in the stress response. He also demonstrated the significance of everyday hassles in producing stress.

daily hassles
Everyday minor events that annoy and upset people.

self-conscious. In contrast, men tend to feel less confident and more unsociable.

How important are daily hassles in producing stress? The frequency of daily hassles is linked to both psychological distress and physical symptoms, such as headaches and backaches (DeLongis & others, 1988). In fact, the number of daily hassles people experience is a better predictor of physical illness and symptoms than is the number of major life events experienced (Burks & Martin, 1985).

Why do daily hassles take such a toll? One explanation is that such minor stressors are *cumulative* (Repetti, 1993). Each hassle may be relatively unimportant in itself, but after a day filled with minor hassles, the effects add up. People feel drained, grumpy, and stressed out. Daily hassles also contribute to the stress produced by major life events. Any major life change, whether positive or negative, can create a ripple effect, generating a host of new daily hassles (Pillow & others, 1996).

For example, like many other New Yorkers, Katie had to contend with a host of daily hassles after the terrorist attacks. She had no place to live, could not get access to her clothing or other possessions, and was unable to get money from the Red Cross because her roommate's father's name was on the lease. Transportation to and around New York was frequently de-

Daily Hassles Life's little hassles and irritants can be a significant source of stress—especially when they pile up. Traffic jams, slow-moving lines when you're in a hurry, and computer crashes are just a few examples of daily hassles. What daily hassles have you experienced in the past week?

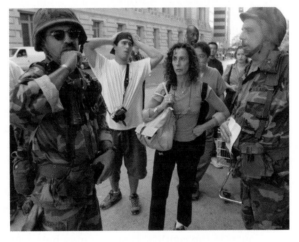

Major Life Events, Daily Hassles, and Stress After the collapse of the two World Trade Center towers, people who lived in nearby apartments were evacuated. More than a week after the disaster, these lower Manhattan residents are waiting to be escorted by members of the National Guard to retrieve some of their possessions. Even after people were allowed to return to their homes, they had to deal with damaged apartments, air filled with smoke and dust, and a lack of basic services, like telephone service. The daily hassles created by major disasters add to the level of stress felt by those affected.

layed, and she had a persistent cough from all of the soot and fumes she had inhaled. She hated her job in the upscale clothing store, because selling overpriced leather jackets to "Fifth Avenue matrons," as she called them, seemed so inconsequential after the tragedies she had witnessed. Eventually, she quit working at the store and took on two waitressing jobs to help finance her dance lessons, pay for her new apartment, and save for college.

Conflict: Torn Between Two Choices

Another common source of stress is **conflict**—feeling pulled between two opposing desires, motives, or goals (Mellers, 2000). There are three basic types of conflict, each with a different potential to produce stress. These conflicts are described in terms of *approach* and *avoidance*. An individual is motivated to *approach* desirable or pleasant outcomes and to *avoid* undesirable or unpleasant outcomes.

An *approach–approach conflict* represents a win–win situation—you're faced with a choice between two equally appealing outcomes. As a rule, approach–approach conflicts are usually easy to resolve and don't produce much stress. More stressful are *avoidance–avoidance conflicts*—choosing between two unappealing

conflict
A situation in which a person feels pulled between two or more opposing desires, motives, or goals.

CATHY

or undesirable outcomes. A common response is to avoid both outcomes by delaying the decision (Tversky & Shafir, 1992).

Most stressful are *approach–avoidance conflicts.* Here, a goal has both desirable and undesirable aspects. When faced with an approach–avoidance conflict, people often *vacillate,* unable to decide whether to approach or avoid the goal. From a distance, the desirable aspects of the goal can exert a strong pull. But as you move toward or approach the goal, the negative aspects loom more vividly in your mind, and you pull back (Epstein, 1982). Not surprisingly, people facing approach–avoidance conflicts often find themselves "stuck"—unable to resolve the conflict but unable to stop thinking about it, either (Emmons & King, 1988). The result is a significant increase in feelings of stress and anxiety.

How can you get "unstuck"? There are several things you can do to resolve an approach–avoidance conflict. First, accept the reality that very few of life's major decisions are likely to be simple, with one alternative standing head and shoulders above the others. Second, see if you can adopt a *partial approach strategy,* in which you test the waters but leave yourself an "out" before making a final decision or commitment.

Third, get as much information as you can about each option. Try to analyze objectively the pros and cons of every option. (We described this strategy of decision making in Chapter 7.) Finally, discuss the issue with a friend or someone outside the conflict. Doing so may help you see other possible rewards or pitfalls that your own analysis might have missed.

Social and Cultural Sources of Stress

Social conditions can also be an important source of stress. Racism and discrimination, whether real or suspected, can create stress (Contrada & others, 2000). Crowding, crime, unemployment, poverty, inadequate health care, and substandard housing are all associated with increased stress (Graig, 1993; Pearlin, 1993). When people live in an environment that is inherently stressful, they often experience ongoing, or *chronic,* stress (Krantz & McCeney, 2002).

People in the lowest socioeconomic levels of society tend to have the highest levels of psychological distress, illness, and death (Cohen & Williamson, 1988). In a poverty-stricken neighborhood, people are likely to be exposed to more negative life events and to have fewer resources available to cope with those events. Daily hassles are also more common.

Stress can also result when cultures clash (Berry, 1994). For refugees, immigrants, and their children, adapting to a new culture can be extremely stress producing (Shuval, 1993). In Culture and Human Behavior Box 13.1, we describe the stress that can result from adapting to a different culture.

acculturative stress
(ah-KUL-chur-uh-tiv) The stress that results from the pressure of adapting to a new culture.

CULTURE AND HUMAN BEHAVIOR 13.1

The Stress of Adapting to a New Culture

Refugees and immigrants are often unprepared for the dramatically different values, language, food, customs, and climate that await them in their new land. Coping with a new culture can be extremely stress-producing (Johnson & others, 1995). The process of changing one's values and customs as a result of contact with another culture is referred to as *acculturation*. Thus, the term **acculturative stress** describes the stress that results from the pressure of adapting to a new culture (Williams & Berry, 1991).

Many factors can influence the degree of acculturative stress that a person experiences. For example, when the new society is one that accepts ethnic and cultural diversity, acculturative stress is reduced (Shuval, 1993). The ease of transition is also enhanced when the person has some familiarity with the new language and customs, advanced education, and social support from friends, family members, and cultural associations (Berry, 1994).

Cross-cultural psychologist John Berry has found that a person's attitudes are important in determining how much acculturative stress is experienced. When people encounter a new cultural environment, they are faced with two fundamental questions: (1) Should I seek positive relations with the dominant society? (2) Is my original cultural identity of value to me, and should I try to maintain it?

The answers to these questions result in one of four possible patterns of acculturation: integration, assimilation, separation, or marginalization (see the diagram). Each pattern represents a different way of coping with the stress of

	Question 1: Should I seek positive relations with the dominant society?	
Question 2: Is my original cultural identity of value to me, and should I try to maintain it?	**Yes**	**No**
Yes	Integration	Separation
No	Assimilation	Marginalization

Patterns of Adapting to a New Culture According to cross-cultural psychologist John Berry (1994), there are four basic patterns of adapting to a new culture. Which pattern is followed depends on how the person responds to the two key questions shown.

adapting to a new culture (Berry, 1994, 1997). Let's briefly describe each pattern.

Integrated individuals continue to value their original cultural customs but also seek to become part of the dominant society. Ideally, the integrated individual feels comfortable in both her culture of origin and the culture of the dominant society, moving easily from one to the other (LaFromboise & others, 1993). The successfully integrated individual's level of acculturative stress will be low (Ward & Rana-Deuba, 1999).

Assimilated individuals give up their old cultural identity and try to become part of the new society. They may adopt the new clothing, religion, and social values of the new environment and abandon their old customs and language.

Assimilation usually involves a moderate level of stress, partly because it involves a psychological loss—one's previous cultural identity. People who follow this pattern also face the possibility of being

rejected either by members of the majority culture or by members of their original culture (LaFromboise & others, 1993). The process of learning new behaviors and suppressing old behaviors can also be moderately stressful.

Individuals who follow the pattern of *separation* maintain their cultural identity and avoid contact with the new culture. They may refuse to learn the new language, live in a neighborhood that is primarily populated by others of the same ethnic background, and socialize only with members of their own ethnic group.

In some instances, such withdrawal from the larger society is self-imposed. However, separation can also be the result of discrimination by the dominant society, as when people of a particular ethnic group are discouraged from fully participating in the dominant society. Not surprisingly, the level of acculturative stress associated with separation is likely to be very high.

Finally, the *marginalized* person lacks cultural and psychological contact with *both* his traditional cultural group and the culture of his new society. By taking the path of marginalization, he has lost the important features of his traditional culture, but has not replaced them with a new cultural identity.

Marginalized individuals are likely to experience the greatest degree of acculturative stress, feeling as if they don't really belong anywhere. Essentially, they are stuck in an unresolved conflict between the traditional culture and the new social environment. They are also likely to experience feelings of alienation and a loss of identity (Berry & Kim, 1988).

Acculturative Stress As this Sikh family crossing a busy street in Chicago has discovered, adapting to a new culture can be a stressful process. What factors can make the transition less stressful? How can the acculturation process be eased?

fight-or-flight response
A rapidly occurring chain of internal physical reactions that prepare people either to fight or take flight from an immediate threat.

FIGURE 13.1 Disrupted Sleep: One Indicator of Stress In the weeks immediately following the September 11th terrorist attacks, the psychological stress of those events was evident in the increased sleep disruptions experienced by millions of Americans. Almost a year after the attack, hundreds of the firefighters and emergency medical workers who responded to the situation continued to experience sleep disruptions as the psychological stress lingered.

SOURCE: National Sleep Foundation (2002).

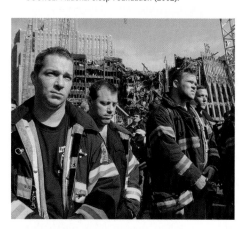

Had difficulty falling asleep

| 2001 until September 11 | 25% |
| Following September 11, 2001 | 44% |

Had frequent awakenings

| 2001 until September 11 | 38% |
| Following September 11, 2001 | 49% |

Wake up early and can't get back to sleep

| 2001 until September 11 | 25% |
| Following September 11, 2001 | 39% |

Wake unrefreshed

| 2001 until September 11 | 40% |
| Following September 11, 2001 | 50% |

Percent of American Adults Who Have Had Sleep Problems Prior to and Following September 11

Physical Effects of Stress
The Mind–Body Connection

Key Theme
- The effects of stress on physical health were demonstrated in research by Walter Cannon and Hans Selye.

Key Questions
- What endocrine pathways are involved in the fight-or-flight response and the general adaptation syndrome?
- What is psychoneuroimmunology, and how does the immune system interact with the nervous system?
- What kinds of stressors affect immune system functioning?

From headaches to heart attacks, stress contributes to a wide range of disorders, especially when it is long-term or chronic (Krantz & McCeney, 2002). Basically, stress appears to undermine physical well-being in two ways: indirectly and directly.

First, stress can *indirectly* affect a person's health by prompting behaviors that jeopardize physical well-being, such as not eating or sleeping properly (see Figure 13.1). Many studies have shown that people under chronic stress are more likely to use alcohol, coffee, and cigarettes than are people under less stress (Baer & others, 1987; Cohen & Williamson, 1988). High levels of stress can also interfere with cognitive abilities, such as attention, concentration, and memory (Mandler, 1993). In turn, such cognitive disruptions can increase the likelihood of accidents and injuries (Holt, 1993).

Second, stress can *directly* affect physical health by altering body functions, leading to symptoms, illness, or disease (Kiecolt-Glaser & others, 2002). Here's a very common example: When people are under a great deal of stress, their neck and head muscles can contract and tighten, resulting in stress-induced tension headaches. But exactly how do stressful events influence bodily processes, such as muscle contractions?

Stress and the Endocrine System

To explain the connection between stress and health, researchers have focused on how the nervous system, including the brain, interacts with two other important body systems: the endocrine and immune systems. We'll first consider the role of the endocrine system in our response to stressful events and then look at the connections between stress and the immune system.

Walter Cannon: Stress and the Fight-or-Flight Response

Any kind of immediate threat to your well-being is a stress-producing experience that triggers a cascade of changes in your body. As we've noted in previous chapters, this rapidly occurring chain of internal physical reactions is called the **fight-or-flight response.** Collectively, these changes prepare us either to fight or to take flight from an immediate threat.

The fight-or-flight response was first described by American physiologist **Walter Cannon,** one of the earliest contributors to stress research. Cannon (1932) found that the fight-or-flight response involved both the sympathetic nervous system and the endocrine system (see Chapter 2).

With the perception of a threat, the hypothalamus and lower brain structures activate the sympathetic nervous system (see left side of Figure 13.2). The sympathetic nervous system stimulates the adrenal medulla to secrete hormones called **catecholamines,** including *adrenaline* and *noradrenaline*. Circulating through the blood, catecholamines trigger the rapid and intense bodily changes associated with the fight-or-flight response. Once the threat is removed, the high level of bodily arousal subsides gradually, usually within about 20 to 60 minutes.

As a short-term reaction, the fight-or-flight response helps ensure survival by swiftly mobilizing internal physical resources to defensively attack or flee an immediate threat. Without question, the fight-or-flight response is very useful if you're suddenly faced with a life-threatening situation, such as a guy pointing a gun at you in a deserted parking lot. However, when exposure to an unavoidable threat is prolonged, the intense arousal of the fight-or-flight response can also become prolonged. Under these conditions, Cannon believed, the fight-or-flight response could prove harmful to physical health.

Walter B. Cannon (1875–1945) Cannon made many lasting contributions to psychology, including an influential theory of emotion, which we discussed in Chapter 8. During World War I, Cannon's research on the effects of stress and trauma led him to recognize the central role of the adrenal glands in mobilizing the body's resources in response to threatening circumstances—the essence of the *fight-or-flight response.* Cannon also coined the term *homeostasis,* which is the tendency of the body to maintain a steady internal state.

FIGURE 13.2 Endocrine System Pathways in Stress Two different endocrine system pathways are involved in the response to stress. Walter Cannon identified the endocrine pathway shown on the left side of this diagram. This is the pathway involved in the fight-or-flight response to immediate threats. Hans Selye identified the endocrine pathway shown on the right. This second endocrine pathway plays an important role in dealing with prolonged or chronic stressors.

Hans Selye: Stress and the General Adaptation Syndrome

Does the man in the photograph on the next page look like someone who had met and conquered stress? **Hans Selye** was the Canadian endocrinologist whose pioneering scientific investigations confirmed Cannon's suggestion that prolonged stress could be physically harmful. Most of Selye's pioneering research was done with rats that were exposed to prolonged stressors, such as electric shock, extreme heat or cold, or forced exercise. Regardless of the condition that Selye used to produce prolonged stress, he found the same pattern of physical changes in the rats.

catecholamines
(*cat*-eh-COLE-uh-meens) Hormones secreted by the adrenal medulla that cause rapid physiological arousal; include adrenaline and noradrenaline.

A Pioneer in Stress Research With his tie off and his feet up, Canadian endocrinologist Hans Selye (1907–1982) looks the very picture of relaxation. Selye's research at the University of Montreal documented the physical effects of exposure to prolonged stress. His popular book *The Stress of Life* (1956) helped make stress a household word.

First, the adrenal glands became enlarged. Second, stomach ulcers and loss of weight occurred. And third, there was shrinkage of the thymus gland and lymph glands, two key components of the immune system. Selye believed that these distinct physical changes represented the essential effects of stress—the body's response to any demand placed on it.

Selye discovered that if the bodily "wear and tear" of the stress-producing event continued, the effects became evident in three progressive stages. He called these stages the **general adaptation syndrome.** During the initial *alarm stage,* intense arousal occurs as the body mobilizes internal physical resources to meet the demands of the stress-producing event. Selye (1976) found that the rapidly occurring changes during the alarm stage result from the release of catecholamines by the adrenal medulla, as Cannon had previously described.

In the *resistance stage,* the body actively tries to resist or adjust to the continuing stressful situation. The intense arousal of the alarm stage diminishes, but physiological arousal remains above normal and resistance to new stressors is impaired.

focus on **Neuroscience**

Received opiate painkiller

Received placebo

Mind, Body, and the Mysterious Placebo Effect The *placebo effect* is perhaps one of the most dramatic examples of how the mind influences the body. A *placebo* is an inactive substance with no known effects, like a sugar pill or an injection of sterile water. Placebos are often used in biomedical research to help gauge the effectiveness of an actual medication or treatment. But after being given a placebo, many research participants, including those suffering from pain or diseases, experience benefits from the placebo treatment. How can this be explained?

In Chapter 2 we noted that one possible way that placebos might reduce pain is by activating the brain's own natural painkillers—the *endorphins*. The endorphins are structurally similar to opiate painkillers, like morphine. One reason for believing this is that a drug called *naloxone,* which blocks the brain's endorphin response, also blocks the painkilling effects of placebos (Fields & Levine, 1984). Might placebos reduce pain by activating the brain's natural opioid network?

A brain-imaging study by Swedish neuroscientist Predrag Petrovic and his colleagues (2002) tackled this question. In the study, painfully hot metal was placed on the back of each volunteer's hand. Each volunteer was then given an injection of either an actual opioid painkiller or a saline solution placebo. About 30 seconds later, positron emission tomography (PET) was used to scan the participants' brain activity.

Both the volunteers who received the painkilling drug *and* the volunteers who received the placebo treatment reported that the injection provided pain relief. In the two PET scans shown here, you can see that the genuine painkilling drug (left) and the placebo (right) activated the same brain area, called the *anterior cingulate cortex* (marked by the cross). The anterior cingulate cortex is known to contain many opioid receptors. Interestingly, the level of brain activity was directly correlated with the participants' subjective perception of pain relief. The right PET scan shows the brain activity of those participants who had strong placebo responses.

Although questions remain about exactly how placebos can produce their effects, the PET scan study by Petrovic and his colleagues (2002) vividly substantiates the mind–body interaction. Clearly, "higher" mental processes—such as cognitive expectations, learned associations, and emotional responses—can have a profound effect on the perception of pain. Other studies have shown that placebos produce measurable effects on other types of brain processes, including those of people experiencing Parkinson's disease or major depression (Fuente-Fernandez & others, 2001; Leuchter & others, 2002).

general adaptation syndrome
Selye's term for the three-stage progression of physical changes that occur when an organism is exposed to intense and prolonged stress. The three stages are alarm, resistance, and exhaustion.

corticosteroids
Hormones released by the adrenal cortex that play a key role in the body's response to long-term stressors.

immune system
Body system that produces specialized white blood cells that protect the body from viruses, bacteria, and tumor cells.

lymphocytes
Specialized white blood cells that are responsible for immune defenses.

If the stress-producing event persists, the *exhaustion stage* may occur. In this third stage, the symptoms of the alarm stage reappear, only now irreversibly. As the body's energy reserves become depleted, adaptation begins to break down, leading to exhaustion, physical disorders, and, potentially, death.

Selye (1956, 1976) found that prolonged stress activates a second endocrine pathway (see Figure 13.2) that involves the hypothalamus, the pituitary gland, and the adrenal cortex. In response to a stressor, the hypothalamus signals the pituitary gland to secrete a hormone called *adrenocorticotropic hormone,* abbreviated *ACTH.* In turn, ACTH stimulates the adrenal cortex to release stress-related hormones called **corticosteroids,** the most important of which is *cortisol.*

In the short run, the corticosteroids provide several benefits, helping protect the body against the harm caused by stressors. For example, corticosteroids reduce inflammation of body tissues and enhance muscle tone in the heart and blood vessels. However, unlike the effects of catecholamines, which tend to diminish rather quickly, corticosteroids have long-lasting effects. If a stressor is prolonged, continued high levels of corticosteroids can weaken important body systems, lowering immunity and increasing susceptibility to physical symptoms and illness. Chronic stress can also lead to depression and other psychological problems (Nemeroff, 1998).

Selye's pioneering studies are widely regarded as the cornerstone of modern stress research. His description of the general adaptation syndrome firmly established some of the critical biological links between stress-producing events and their potential impact on physical health. But as you'll see in the next section, the endocrine system is only part of the equation in the mind–body connection between stress and health.

Stress and the Immune System

Stress can diminish the effectiveness of the immune system. The **immune system** is your body's surveillance system. It detects and battles foreign invaders, such as bacteria, viruses, and tumor cells. Your immune system comprises several organs, including bone marrow, the spleen, the thymus, and lymph nodes (see Figure 13.3). The most important elements of the immune system are **lymphocytes**—the specialized white blood cells that fight bacteria, viruses, and other foreign invaders. Lymphocytes are initially manufactured in the bone marrow. From the bone marrow, they migrate to other immune system organs, such as the thymus and spleen, where they develop more fully and are stored until needed.

Until the 1970s, the immune system was thought to be completely independent of other body systems. Many scientists believed that the nervous system, the endocrine system, and psychological processes had no impact on immune system functioning. As you'll see in this section, the scientific view of the immune system has changed dramatically in the last few decades.

FIGURE 13.3 The Immune System Your immune system battles bacteria, viruses, and other foreign invaders that try to set up housekeeping in your body. The specialized white blood cells that fight infection are manufactured in the bone marrow and are stored in the thymus, spleen, and lymph nodes until needed.

Thymus — Lymph nodes — Spleen — Lymph nodes — Lymphatic vessels — Bone marrow — Lymph nodes

Lymphocytes in Action In this color-enhanced photo, you can see white blood cells, or lymphocytes, attacking and ingesting the beadlike chain of streptococcus bacteria, which can cause diseases such as pneumonia and scarlet fever.

Ader and Cohen: Conditioning the Immune System

The notion that the immune system operated independently was challenged in the mid-1970s, when psychologist **Robert Ader** teamed up with immunologist Nicholas Cohen. As Ader (1993) recalled, "You have to understand that as a

Conditioning the Immune System
Psychologist Robert Ader (*left*) teamed with immunologist Nicholas Cohen (*right*) and demonstrated that immune system responses could be classically conditioned. Ader and Cohen's groundbreaking research helped lead to the new field of psychoneuroimmunology—the study of the connections among psychological processes, the nervous system, and the immune system.

psychoneuroimmunology
An interdisciplinary field that studies the interconnections among psychological processes, nervous and endocrine system functions, and the immune system.

psychologist, I was not aware of the general position of immunology that there were no connections between the brain and the immune system." In their landmark study, Ader and Cohen (1975) demonstrated that immune system functions could be influenced by the brain. They did so by showing that the immune system response in rats could be classically conditioned.

Using the same basic procedure that Pavlov used to condition dogs to salivate in response to the sound of a bell (see Chapter 5), Ader and Cohen (1975) paired saccharin-flavored water with a drug (cyclophosphamide) that suppressed immune system functioning. After being paired with the drug, the saccharin-flavored water *alone* suppressed the rat's immune system. As Ader (1993) explained, "In effect, we had demonstrated that learning processes could influence immune responses. The experiment was a direct and rather dramatic demonstration of a relationship between nervous system function and immune function."

Ader and Cohen's study was important for two reasons. First, it challenged the prevailing scientific view that the immune system operated independently of the brain and psychological processes. Since the publication of Ader and Cohen's research, hundreds of other studies have demonstrated that immune system responses can be conditioned to various stimuli (see Ader & Cohen, 1991, 1993).

Second, Ader and Cohen's study triggered interest in other possible influences on the immune system, including the effects of stress and emotional states. By stimulating diverse lines of research, Ader and Cohen's study helped establish a new interdisciplinary field, called psychoneuroimmunology (Ader, 2001). **Psychoneuroimmunology** is the scientific study of the interconnections among psychological processes (*psycho-*), the nervous and endocrine systems (*-neuro-*), and the immune system (*-immunology*).

In the last decade, researchers in psychoneuroimmunology have made many important discoveries (see Vitkovic, 1995). First, they discovered that the central nervous system and the immune system are *directly* linked. Sympathetic nervous system fibers go into virtually every organ of the immune system, where they directly influence the production and functioning of lymphocytes.

Second, the surfaces of lymphocytes contain receptor sites for neurotransmitters and hormones, including catecholamines and cortisol. Thus, rather than operating independently, the activities of lymphocytes and the immune system are directly influenced by neurotransmitters, hormones, and other chemical messengers from the nervous and endocrine systems.

Third, psychoneuroimmunologists have discovered that lymphocytes themselves *produce* neurotransmitters and hormones. These neurotransmitters and hormones, in turn, influence the nervous and endocrine systems. In other words, there is ongoing interaction and communication among the nervous system, the endocrine system, and the immune system. Each system influences *and* is influenced by the other systems (Ader, 2001).

Stressors That Can Influence the Immune System

When researchers began studying how stress affects the immune system, they initially focused on extremely stressful events (see Kiecolt-Glaser & Glaser, 1993). For example, researchers looked at how the immune system was affected by such intense stressors as the reentry and splashdown of returning *Skylab* astronauts, being forced to stay awake for days, and fasting for a week (Kimzey, 1975; Leach & Rambaut, 1974; Palmblad & others, 1979). Each of these highly stressful events, it turned out, was associated with reduced immune system functioning.

Could immune system functioning also be affected by more common negative life events, such as the death of a spouse, divorce, or marital separation? In a word, yes. Researchers consistently found that the stress caused by the end or disruption of important interpersonal relationships impairs immune function, putting people at greater risk for health problems (Kiecolt-Glaser, 1999; Kiecolt-Glaser & Newton, 2001). And perhaps not surprisingly, chronic stressors that continue for years, such as caring for a family member with Alzheimer's disease, also diminish immune system functioning (see Kiecolt-Glaser & others, 2002).

What about the ordinary stressors of life, such as the pressure of exams? Do they affect immune system functioning? Since 1982, psychologist **Janice Kiecolt-Glaser** and her husband, immunologist Ronald Glaser, have collected immunological and psychological data from medical students. Several times each academic year, the medical students face three-day examination periods. Kiecolt-Glaser and Glaser (1991, 1993) have consistently found that even the rather commonplace stress of exams adversely affects the immune system.

Ron Glaser and Janice Kiecolt-Glaser Two of the leading researchers in psychoneuroimmunology are psychologist Janice Kiecolt-Glaser and her husband, immunologist Ron Glaser. Their research has shown that the effectiveness of the immune system can be lowered by many common stressors—from marital arguments to caring for sick relatives.

What are the practical implications of reduced immune system functioning? One consistent finding is that psychological stress can increase the length of time it takes for a wound to heal. In one study, dental students volunteered to receive two small puncture wounds on the roof of their mouths (Marucha & others, 1998). To compare the impact of stress on wound healing, the students received the first wound when they were on summer vacation and the second wound three days before their first major exam during the fall term. The results? The wounds inflicted before the major test healed an average of 40 percent more slowly—an extra three days—than the wounds inflicted on the same volunteers during summer vacation. Other studies have shown similar findings (see Kiecolt-Glaser & Glaser, 2001).

Taken together, the research evidence suggests that a wide variety of stressors are associated with diminished immune system functioning, putting us at greater risk for health problems and slower recovery times (Kiecolt-Glaser & others, 1998, 2002). In Focus Box 13.2 on the next page describes another compelling study demonstrating the relationship between stress and a health risk to which we are all frequently exposed: the common cold virus.

While stress-related decreases in immune system functioning may heighten our susceptibility to health problems, exposure to stressors does not automatically translate into poorer health. Your physical health is affected by the interaction of many factors, such as your unique genetic makeup, nutrition, exercise, personal habits, and access to medical care. Also required, of course, is exposure to bacteria, viruses, and other disease-causing agents.

It's also important to keep in mind that the stress-induced decreases in immune system functioning that have been demonstrated experimentally are often small. As psychoneuroimmunology researchers are careful to note, these small decreases in immune function may not translate into an added health risk for most people. As Kiecolt-Glaser and Glaser (1993) have explained:

Can Exams Be Hazardous to Your Health? From studies of medical students, Kiecolt-Glaser and Glaser have shown that the common student stressor of taking exams can lower the effectiveness of the immune system.

> Our best understanding at this point is that the people most likely to become ill in response to stress are probably those whose immune systems are already compromised to some extent, either by a disease like AIDS or by a natural process like aging. These people start out with poorer immunological defenses, so that small changes associated with stress could have more important consequences. But even young, generally healthy people may find themselves getting sick more often if they are subject to severe or ongoing, long-term stress.

Finally, the simple fact is that some people are more vulnerable to the negative effects of stress than others (Adler & Matthews, 1994). Why? As you'll see in the next section, researchers have found that a wide variety of psychological factors can influence people's reactions to stressors.

Stress and the Common Cold

Does stress increase your susceptibility to the common cold? That's certainly what many people believe. But if you think critically about the matter, other explanations are possible. For example, it may be that high-stressed people interact with more people than low-stressed people. In turn, this would mean that high-stressed people have more opportunities for exposure to cold viruses. Or it could be that stressed-out people engage in more health-compromising behaviors, such as smoking, eating poorly, not exercising, and not getting enough sleep.

Psychologist Sheldon Cohen and his colleagues (1991, 1993) tackled such issues in a carefully controlled experiment. More than 400 healthy volunteers underwent a thorough medical examination and completed questionnaires assessing their stress levels and health behaviors. The participants were then given nasal drops containing either a cold virus or salt water. For two days before and seven days after receiving the drops, the participants were quarantined together in apartments. Each day during the study, the participants were medically examined for any signs or symptoms of a cold. Blood samples were also monitored for evidence of infection.

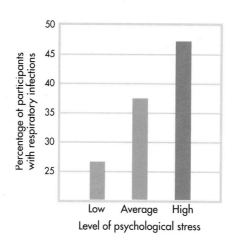

The results? Of the people exposed to cold virus, one factor stood out in determining the rate of infection: the level of stress. The researchers found an almost perfect relationship between the level of stress and the rate of respiratory infection and colds. Put simply, the higher the psychological stress score, the higher the rate of respiratory infection and colds.

Could it be that other factors, such as health-compromising behaviors, were underlying the stress–illness connection? Not at all. The stress–illness effect held even when the researchers took into account the number of participants housed together, whether roommates were also infectious, and the participants' age, sex, smoking, alcohol consumption, exercise, diet, and quality of sleep. In other words, *none* of these factors could account for the relationship between stress and increased susceptibility to infection (Cohen & others, 1991, 1993).

In a later study, Cohen and his colleagues (1998) found that particular kinds of life stresses seemed to be most highly associated with susceptibility to infection. People who experienced *chronic* stressors that lasted more than a month were more than twice as likely to develop colds than people who were not under chronic stress. The longer the duration of the stressor, the greater was the risk for colds. Unemployment, problems at work, and interpersonal conflict were among the chronic stressors that were associated with increased susceptibility to disease.

So how does stress increase our susceptibility to colds and infections? Basically, stress reduces the effectiveness of the immune system and its ability to fight off viruses, bacteria, and other foreign invaders (see Kiecolt-Glaser & Glaser, 1991, 1993).

13.1 R·E·V·I·E·W

CONCEPT

Sources and Effects of Stress

Indicate whether each of the following items is true or false. Rewrite each false statement to correct it.

_____ **1.** According to the biopsychosocial model, physical well-being is wholly determined by stress and social adjustment.

_____ **2.** In the past year, Andrea has gotten divorced, changed jobs, moved three times, and lost her closest friend in an auto accident. Because of the number of stress-producing life events Andrea has experienced, she is certain to develop a major illness in the next six months.

_____ **3.** The level of stress due to daily hassles is measured by the Social Readjustment Rating Scale.

_____ **4.** During periods of prolonged stress, the adrenal medulla secretes stress-related hormones called catecholamines.

_____ **5.** Shelley's manager has just unexpectedly informed her that she is being laid off, effective immediately. Shelley is probably experiencing the "exhaustion" stage of the general adaptation syndrome.

_____ **6.** The study of interconnections among the nervous system, immune system, endocrine system, and psychological factors is called *psychoneuroimmunology.*

Individual Factors That Influence the Response to Stress

Key Theme

- Psychologists have identified several psychological factors that can modify an individual's response to stress and affect physical health.

Key Questions

- How do feelings of control, explanatory style, and negative emotions influence stress and health?
- What is Type A behavior, and what role does hostility play in the relationship between Type A behavior and health?

People vary a great deal in the way they respond to a distressing event, whether it's a parking ticket or a pink slip. In part, individual differences in reacting to stressors result from how people appraise an event and their resources for coping with the event. However, psychologists and other researchers have identified several different factors that influence an individual's response to stressful events. In this section, we'll take a look at some of the most important psychological and social factors that seem to affect an individual's response to stress.

Psychological Factors

It's easy to demonstrate the importance of psychological factors in the response to stressors. Sit in any airport waiting room during a busy holiday travel season and observe how differently people react to news of flight cancellations or delays. Some people take the news calmly, while others become enraged and indignant. Psychologists have confirmed what common sense suggests: Psychological processes play a key role in determining the level of stress experienced.

Personal Control

Who is more likely to experience more stress, a person who has some control over a stressful experience or a person who has no control? Psychological research has consistently shown that having a sense of control over a stressful situation reduces the impact of stressors and decreases feelings of anxiety and depression (Taylor & others, 1991; Thompson & Spacapan, 1991). Those who can control a stress-producing event often show no more psychological distress or physical arousal than people who are not exposed to the stressor.

Psychologists Judith Rodin and Ellen Langer (1977) demonstrated the importance of a sense of control in a classic series of studies with nursing home residents. One group of residents—the "high-control" group—was given the opportunity to make choices about their daily activities and to exercise control over their environment. For example, the residents were allowed to determine where they would receive visitors and when they would attend a movie screening. In contrast, the "low-control" group had little control over their daily activities. Decisions were made for them by the nursing home staff.

Rodin and Langer found that having a sense of control over their environment had powerful effects on the nursing home residents. Eighteen months later, the high-control residents were more active, alert, sociable,

Uncontrollable Stressors There was nothing this man could do to protect his apartment, which faced the World Trade Center towers. A month after the terrorist attacks, he surveys his damaged possessions and sorts through the wreckage that was once his home. Psychological research has shown that stressors that are experienced as beyond your control can be especially damaging to physical and mental health.

and healthier than the low-control residents. Members of the high-control group were also more likely to be alive: twice as many of the low-control residents had died (Langer & Rodin, 1976; Rodin & Langer, 1977).

How does a sense of control affect health? If you feel that you can control a stressor by taking steps to minimize or avoid it, you will experience less stress, both subjectively and physiologically (Thompson & Spacapan, 1991). Having a sense of personal control also works to our benefit by enhancing positive emotions, such as self-confidence and feelings of self-efficacy, autonomy, and self-reliance (Burger, 1992). In contrast, feeling a lack of control over events produces all the hallmarks of the stress response. Levels of catecholamines and corticosteroids increase, and the effectiveness of immune system functioning decreases (see Maier & Watkins, 2000; Rodin, 1986).

However, the perception of personal control in a stressful situation must be *realistic* to be adaptive (Helgeson, 1992; Taylor & others, 1991). Studies of people with chronic diseases, like heart disease and arthritis, have shown that unrealistic perceptions of personal control contribute to stress and poor adjustment (Affleck & others, 1987a, 1987b). But, even in low-control situations, there is often some aspect of the overall situation that people can realistically influence.

For example, Suzanne Thompson and her colleagues (1993) found that the best-adjusted cancer patients accepted the fact that they could not actually control the course of their disease. Rather, they focused on what they realistically could do to control the *consequences* of the disease. They exercised control by managing their emotions, seeking medical information, improving their personal relationships, and changing their diet. In this way, they lowered their subjective level of stress and increased their sense of personal well-being.

Explanatory Style: Optimism Versus Pessimism

We all experience defeat, rejection, or failure at some point in our lives. Yet despite repeated failures, rejections, or defeats, some people persist in their efforts. In contrast, some people give up in the face of failure and setbacks—the essence of *learned helplessness,* which we discussed in chapter 5. What distinguishes between those who persist and those who give up?

According to psychologist **Martin Seligman** (1990, 1992), how people characteristically explain their failures and defeats makes the difference. People who have an **optimistic explanatory style** tend to use *external, unstable,* and *specific* explanations for negative events. In contrast, people who have a **pessimistic explanatory style** use *internal, stable,* and *global* explanations for negative events. Pessimists are also inclined to believe that no amount of personal effort will improve their situation. Not surprisingly, pessimists tend to experience more stress than optimists.

Let's look at these two explanatory styles in action. Optimistic Olive sees an attractive guy at a party and starts across the room to introduce herself and strike up a conversation. As she approaches him, the guy glances at her, then abruptly turns away. Hurt by the obvious snub, Optimistic Olive retreats to the buffet table. Munching on some fried zucchini, she mulls the matter over in her mind. At the same party, Pessimistic Pete sees an attractive female across the room and approaches her. He, too, gets a cold shoulder and retreats to the chips and clam dip. Standing at opposite ends of the buffet table, here is what each of them is thinking:

Optimistic Olive: *What's his problem? (External explanation: The optimist blames other people or external circumstances.)*

Pessimistic Pete: *I must have said the wrong thing. She probably saw me stick my elbow in the clam dip before I walked over. (Internal explanation: The pessimist blames self.)*

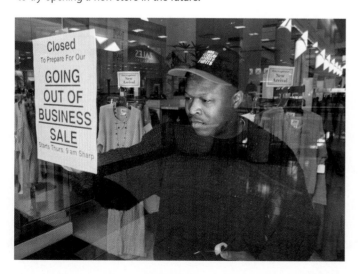

How Do You Explain Your Setbacks and Failures? Everyone experiences setbacks, rejection, and failure at some point. The way you explain your setbacks has a significant impact on motivation and on mental and physical health. If the owner of this store blames his business failure on temporary and external factors, such as a short-lived downturn in the economy, he might be more likely to try opening a new store in the future.

OPTIMISTIC OLIVE: *I'm really not looking my best tonight. I've just got to get more sleep.* (Unstable, temporary *explanation*)

PESSIMISTIC PETE: *Let's face it, I'm a pretty boring guy and really not very good-looking.* (Stable, permanent *explanation*)

OPTIMISTIC OLIVE: *He looks pretty preoccupied. Maybe he's waiting for his girlfriend to arrive. Or his boyfriend! Ha!* (Specific *explanations*)

PESSIMISTIC PETE: *Women never give me a second look, probably because I dress like a nerd and I never know what to say to them.* (Global, pervasive *explanation*)

OPTIMISTIC OLIVE: *Whoa! Who's that hunk over there?! Okay, Olive, turn on the charm! Here goes!* (Perseverance *after a rejection*)

PESSIMISTIC PETE: *Maybe I'll just hold down this corner of the buffet table . . . or go home and soak up some TV.* (Passivity *and* withdrawal *after a rejection*)

> **optimistic explanatory style**
> Accounting for negative events or situations with external, unstable, and specific explanations.

> **pessimistic explanatory style**
> Accounting for negative events or situations with internal, stable, and global explanations.

Most people, of course, are neither as completely optimistic as Olive nor as totally pessimistic as Pete. Instead, they fall somewhere along the spectrum of optimism and pessimism, and their explanatory style may vary somewhat in different situations (Peterson & Bossio, 1993). Even so, a person's characteristic explanatory style, particularly for negative events, is relatively stable across the lifespan (Burns & Seligman, 1989).

Like personal control, explanatory style is related to health consequences (Gilham & others, 2001). One study showed that explanatory style in early adulthood predicted physical health status decades later. On the basis of interviews conducted at age 25, explanatory style was evaluated for a large group of Harvard graduates. At the time of the interviews, all the young men were in excellent physical and mental health. Thirty-five years later, however, those who had an optimistic explanatory style were significantly healthier than those with a pessimistic explanatory style. They also were more likely to be alive (Peterson & others, 1988).

Other studies have shown that a pessimistic explanatory style is associated with poorer physical health, including increased occurrences of infectious disease (Peterson & Bossio, 2001). A recent study of first-year law school students confirmed the benefits of optimism (Segerstrom & others, 1998). Students who had an optimistic, confident, and generally positive outlook experienced fewer negative moods than students who were more pessimistic. And, in terms of their immune system measures, the optimistic students had significantly higher levels of lymphocytes, T cells, and helper T cells than the pessimistic students.

Chronic Negative Emotions: The Hazards of Being Grouchy

Everyone experiences an occasional bad mood. However, some people almost always seem to be unhappy campers—they frequently experience bad moods and negative emotions (Marshall & others, 1992; Watson & Pennebaker, 1989). Are people who are prone to chronic negative emotions more likely to suffer health problems?

Howard S. Friedman and Stephanie Booth-Kewley (1987) set out to answer this question. After systematically analyzing more than 100 studies investigating the potential links between personality factors and disease, they concluded that people who are habitually anxious, depressed, angry, or hostile *are* more likely to develop a chronic disease such as arthritis or heart disease.

Calvin and Hobbes   by Bill Watterson

Type A behavior pattern
A behavioral and emotional style characterized by a sense of time urgency, hostility, and competitiveness.

How might chronic negative emotions predispose people to develop disease? Not surprisingly, tense, angry, and unhappy people experience more stress than do happier people. They also report more frequent and more intense daily hassles than people who are generally in a positive mood (Bolger & Schilling, 1991; Bolger & Zuckerman, 1995). And they react much more intensely, and with far greater distress, to stressful events (Marco & Suls, 1993).

Of course, everyone occasionally experiences bad moods. Are transient negative moods also associated with health risks? One series of studies investigated the relationship between daily mood and immune system functioning (Stone & others, 1987, 1994). For three months, participants recorded their mood every day. On the days on which they experienced negative events and moods, the effectiveness of their immune system dipped. But their immune system improved on the days on which they experienced positive events and good moods.

Type A Behavior and Hostility

The concept of Type A behavior originated about 30 years ago, when two cardiologists, Meyer Friedman and Ray Rosenman, noticed that many of their patients shared certain traits. The original formulation of the **Type A behavior pattern** included a cluster of three characteristics: (1) an exaggerated sense of time urgency, often trying to do more and more in less and less time; (2) a general sense of hostility, frequently displaying anger and irritation; and (3) intense ambition and competitiveness. In contrast, people who were more relaxed and laid back were classified as displaying the *Type B behavior pattern* (Janisse & Dyck, 1988; Rosenman & Chesney, 1982).

Friedman and Rosenman (1974) interviewed and classified more than 3,000 middle-aged, healthy men as either Type A or Type B. They tracked the health of these men for eight years and found that Type A men were twice as likely to develop heart disease as Type B men. This held true even when the Type A men did not display other known risk factors for heart disease, such as smoking, high blood pressure, and elevated levels of cholesterol in their blood. The conclusion seemed clear: The Type A behavior pattern was a significant risk factor for heart disease.

Although early results linking the Type A behavior pattern to heart disease were impressive, studies soon began to appear in which Type A behavior did *not* reliably predict the development of heart disease (see Krantz & McCeney, 2002). These findings led researchers to question whether the different components of the Type A behavior pattern were equally hazardous to health. After all, many people thrive on hard work, especially when they enjoy their jobs. And high achievers don't necessarily suffer from health problems (Robbins & others, 1991).

The Type A Behavior Pattern The original formulation of the Type A behavior pattern included hostility, ambition, and a sense of time urgency. Type A people always seem to be in a hurry, hate wasting time, and often try to do two or more things at once. Do you think any of the people in this photograph might qualify as Type A?

When researchers focused on the association between heart disease and each separate component of the Type A behavior pattern—time urgency, achievement striving, and hostility—an important distinction began to emerge. Feeling a sense of time urgency and being competitive or achievement-oriented did *not* seem to be associated with the development of heart disease. Instead, the critical component that emerged as the strongest predictor of cardiac disease was hostility (Miller & others, 1996). *Hostility* refers to the tendency to feel anger, annoyance, resentment, and contempt and to hold negative beliefs about human nature in general. Hostile people are also prone to believing that the disagreeable behavior of others is intentionally directed against them. Thus, hostile people tend to be suspicious, mistrustful, cynical, and pessimistic (Barefoot, 1992).

Hostile men and women are much more likely than other people to develop heart disease. In one study that covered a 25-year span, hostile men were five times as likely to develop heart disease and nearly seven times as likely to die as nonhostile men (Barefoot & others, 1983). The results of this prospective study are shown in Figure 13.4. Subsequent research has found that high hostility levels increase the likelihood of dying from *all* natural causes, including cancer (Miller & others, 1996).

How does hostility predispose people to heart disease and other health problems? First, hostile Type A's tend to react more intensely to a stressor than other people do (Lyness, 1993). They experience greater increases in blood pressure, heart rate, and the production of stress-related hormones. Because of their attitudes and behavior, hostile men and women also tend to *create* more stress in their own lives. They experience more frequent, and more severe, negative life events and daily hassles than other people (Smith, 1992).

In general, the research evidence demonstrating the role of personality factors in the development of stress-related diseases is impressive. However, it's important to keep in mind that personality characteristics are just some of the risk factors involved in the overall picture of health and disease (Adler & Matthews, 1994; Cohen & Herbert, 1996). We look at this issue in more detail in Critical Thinking Box 13.3.

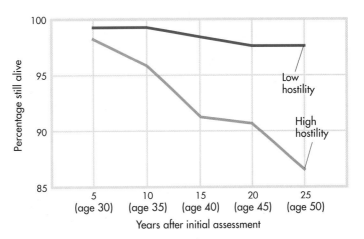

FIGURE 13.4 Hostility and Mortality Beginning when they were in medical school, more than 250 doctors were monitored for their health status for 25 years. In this prospective study, those who had scored high in hostility in medical school were seven times more likely to die by age 50 than were those who had scored low in hostility.

SOURCE: Based on Barefoot & others (1983), p. 61.

13.2 R·E·V·I·E·W

C·O·N·C·E·P·T

Psychological Factors and Stress

Identify the psychological characteristic that is best illustrated by each of the examples below. Choose from the following:

  a. high level of personal control
  b. optimistic explanatory style
  c. Type A behavior pattern
  d. Type B behavior pattern
  e. pessimistic explanatory style
  f. chronic negative emotions

_____ *1.* No matter what happens to her, Lucy is dissatisfied and grumpy. She constantly complains about her health, her job, and how awful her life is. She dislikes most of the people she meets.

_____ *2.* Cheryl was despondent when she received a low grade on her algebra test. She said, "I never do well on exams because I'm not very smart. I might as well drop out of school now before I flunk out."

_____ *3.* In order to deal with the high levels of stress associated with returning to college full-time, Pat selected her courses carefully, arranged her work and study schedules to make the best use of her time, and scheduled time for daily exercise and social activities.

_____ *4.* Richard is a very competitive, ambitious stockbroker who is easily irritated by small inconveniences. If he thinks that someone or something is wasting his time, he blows up and becomes completely enraged.

_____ *5.* Max flubbed an easy free throw in the big basketball game but told his coach, "My game was off today because I'm still getting over the flu and I pulled a muscle in practice yesterday. I'll do better in next week's game."

CRITICAL THINKING 13.3

Do Personality Factors Cause Disease?

- You overhear a co-worker saying, "I'm not surprised he had a heart attack—the guy is a workaholic!"

- An acquaintance casually remarks, "She's been so depressed since her divorce. No wonder she got cancer."

- A tabloid headline hails, "New Scientific Findings: Use Your Mind to Cure Cancer!"

Statements like these make health psychologists, physicians, and psychoneuroimmunologists extremely uneasy. Why? Throughout this chapter, we've presented scientific evidence that emotional states can affect the functioning of the endocrine system and the immune system. Both systems play a significant role in the development of various physical disorders. We've also shown that personality factors, such as hostility and pessimism, are associated with an increased likelihood of developing poor health. But saying that "emotions affect the immune system" is a far cry from making such claims as "a positive attitude can cure cancer."

Psychologists and other scientists are cautious in the statements they make about the connections between personality and health for several reasons. First, many studies investigating the role of psychological factors in disease are *correlational*. That is, researchers have statistical evidence that two factors happen together so often that the presence of one factor reliably predicts the occurrence of the other. However, correlation does not necessarily indicate causality—it indi-

"What do you mean, I have an ulcer? I give ulcers, I don't get them!"

cates only that two factors occur together. It's completely possible that some third, unidentified factor may have caused the other two factors to occur.

Second, personality factors might indirectly lead to disease via poor health habits. Low control, pessimism, chronic negative emotions, and hostility are each associated with poor health habits (Herbert & Cohen, 1993; Peterson, 2000). In turn, poor health habits are associated with higher rates of illness. That's why psychologists who study the role of personality factors in disease are typically careful to measure and consider the possible influence of the participants' health practices.

Third, it may be that the disease influences a person's emotions, rather than the other way around. After being diag-

nosed with advanced cancer or heart disease, most people would probably find it difficult to feel cheerful, optimistic, or in control of their lives.

One way researchers try to disentangle the relationship between personality and health is to conduct carefully controlled prospective studies. A *prospective study* starts by assessing an initially healthy group of participants on variables thought to be risk factors, such as certain personality traits. Then the researchers track the health, personal habits, health habits, and other important dimensions of the participants' lives over a period of months, years, or decades. In analyzing the results, researchers can determine the extent to which each risk factor contributed to the health or illness of the participants. Thus, prospective studies provide more compelling evidence than do correlational studies that are based on people who are already in poor health.

Critical Thinking Questions

- Given that health professionals frequently advise people to change their health-related behaviors to improve physical health, should they also advise people to change their psychological attitudes, traits, and emotions? Why or why not?

- What are the advantages and disadvantages of prospective studies?

Social Factors: A Little Help from Your Friends

Key Theme

- Social support refers to the resources provided by other people.

Key Questions

- How has social support been shown to benefit health?
- How can relationships and social connections sometimes increase stress?
- What gender differences have been found in social support and its effects?

Psychologists have become increasingly aware of the importance that close relationships play in our ability to deal with stressors and, ultimately, in our physical health. Consider the following research evidence:

■ Patients with advanced breast cancer who attended weekly support group sessions survived twice as long as a matched group of patients with equally advanced cancer who did not attend support groups. Both groups of women received comparable medical treatment. The added survival time for those who attended support group sessions was longer than that which could have been provided by any known medical treatment (Spiegel, 1993b; Spiegel & others, 1989).

■ After monitoring the health of 2,800 people for seven years, researchers found that people who had no one to talk to about their problems were three times as likely to die after being hospitalized for a heart attack than were those who had at least one person to provide such support (Berkman & others, 1992).

■ The health of nearly 7,000 adults was tracked for nine years. Those who had few social connections were twice as likely to die from all causes than were those who had numerous social contacts, even when risk factors such as cigarette smoking, obesity, and elevated cholesterol levels were taken into account (Berkman, 1995; Berkman & Syme, 1979).

■ In a study begun in the 1950s, college students rated their parents' level of love and caring. More than 40 years later, 87 percent of those who had rated their parents as being "low" in love and caring had been diagnosed with a serious physical disease. In contrast, only 25 percent of those who had rated their parents as being "high" in love and caring had been diagnosed with a serious physical disease (Russek & Schwartz, 1997).

These are just a few of the hundreds of studies conducted in the last few years exploring how interpersonal relationships influence our health and ability to tolerate stress. To investigate the role played by personal relationships in stress and health, psychologists measure the level of **social support**—the resources provided by other people in times of need (Hobfoll & Stephens, 1990). Repeatedly, researchers have found that socially isolated people have poorer health and higher death rates than people who have many social contacts or relationships (Uchino & others, 1996). In fact, social isolation seems to be just as potent a health risk as smoking, high blood cholesterol, obesity, and physical inactivity (Cohen & others, 2000).

How Social Support Benefits Health

Social support may benefit our health and improve our ability to cope with stressors in several ways (Cohen & others, 2000). First, the social support of friends and relatives can modify our appraisal of a stressor's significance, including the degree to which we perceive it as threatening or harmful. Simply knowing that support and assistance are readily available may make the situation seem less threatening.

Second, the presence of supportive others seems to decrease the intensity of physical reactions to a stressor. Thus, when faced with a painful medical procedure or some other stressful situation, many people find the presence of a supportive friend to be calming.

Third, social support can influence our health by making us less likely to experience negative emotions (Cohen & Herbert, 1996). Given the well-established link between chronic negative emotions and poor health, a strong social support network can promote positive moods and emotions, enhance self-esteem, and increase feelings of personal control. In contrast, loneliness and depression are unpleasant emotional states that increase levels of stress hormones and adversely affect immune system functioning (Weisse, 1992).

The flip side of the coin is that relationships with others can also be a significant *source* of stress. In fact, negative interactions with other people are often more effective at creating psychological distress than positive interactions are at improving well-being (Lepore, 1993; Rook, 1992). And, although married people tend

The Health Benefits of Companionship
This married couple in their seventies are enjoying an afternoon of cross-country skiing. Numerous research studies have shown that married people and couples live longer than people who are single, divorced, or widowed (Burman & Margolin, 1992). How do close relationships benefit health?

social support
The resources provided by other people in times of need.

The Social Support of Friends Hundreds of studies have documented the beneficial effects of social support, whether it is emotional support or tangible support. By listening to us when we're upset, helping us move, or simply being there when we need them, friends help us handle problems and cope with stress.

Pets and Social Support Pets can be an important source of companionship, especially for people with limited social contacts. Can the social support of pets help buffer the negative effects of stress? In a study of elderly individuals, pet owners reported feeling less stress and were less likely to go to the doctor than were people without pets (Siegel, 1990). Another study showed that a companion pet helped reduce the effects of stress in caregivers to people with Alzheimer's disease (Fritz & others, 1996).

to be healthier than unmarried people overall, marital conflict has been shown to have adverse effects on physical health, especially for women (Kiecolt-Glaser & Newton, 2001).

Clearly, the quality of interpersonal relationships is an important determinant of whether those relationships help or hinder our ability to cope with stressful events (Feeney & Kirkpatrick, 1996). When other people are perceived as being judgmental, their presence may increase the individual's physical reaction to a stressor. In a clever study, psychologist Karen Allen and her colleagues (1991) demonstrated that the presence of a favorite dog was more effective than the presence of a friend in lowering reactivity to a stressor. Why? Perhaps because the dog was perceived as being nonjudgmental, nonevaluative, and unconditionally supportive. Unfortunately, the same is not always true of friends, family members, and spouses.

Stress may also increase when well-meaning friends or family members offer unwanted or inappropriate social support. The chapter Application offers some suggestions on how to provide helpful social support and avoid inappropriate support behaviors.

Gender Differences in the Effects of Social Support

Women may be particularly vulnerable to some of the problematic aspects of social support, for a couple of reasons. First, women are more likely than men to serve as providers of support, which can be a very stressful role (Hobfoll & Vaux, 1993; Shumaker & Hill, 1991). Consider the differences found in one study. When middle-aged male patients were discharged from the hospital after a heart attack, they went home and their wives took care of them. But when middle-aged female heart attack patients were discharged from the hospital, they went home and fell back into the routine of caring for their husbands (Coyne & others, 1990).

Second, women may be more likely to suffer from the *stress contagion effect,* becoming upset about negative life events that happen to other people whom they care about (Belle, 1991). Since women tend to have larger and more intimate social networks than men, they have more opportunities to become distressed by what happens to people who are close to them. And women are more likely than men to be upset about negative events that happen to their relatives and friends. For example, when your author's sister Judy was unable to reach Katie by phone on the morning of September 11th, she quickly called two family members for advice and comfort: your author Sandy in Tulsa and her mother, Fern, in Chicago. Like Judy, there was nothing Sandy or Fern could do to help Katie escape the maelstrom of lower Manhattan. And, like Judy, they became increasingly upset and worried as they watched the events of the day unfold from hundreds of miles away. Nevertheless, when stressful events strike, women tend to reach out to one another (Taylor & others, 2000).

In contrast, men are more likely to be distressed only by negative events that happen to their immediate family—their wives and children (Wethington & others, 1987). Men tend to rely heavily on a close relationship with their spouse, placing less importance on relationships with other people. Women, in contrast, are more likely to list close friends along with their spouse as confidants (Shumaker & Hill, 1991). Because men tend to have a much smaller network of intimate others, they may be particularly vulnerable to social isolation, especially if their spouse dies. Thus, it's not surprising that the health benefits of being married are more pronounced for men than for women (Kiecolt-Glaser & Newton, 2001).

In summary, it should be clear that having a strong network of social support is generally advantageous to your ability to cope with stressors and to maintain health. This is especially true when you are fundamentally satisfied with both the quality and the quantity of your relationships.

Coping
How People Deal with Stress

coping
Behavioral and cognitive responses used to deal with stressors; involves efforts to change circumstances, or your interpretation of circumstances, to make them more favorable and less threatening.

Key Theme

▪ Coping refers to the ways in which we try to change circumstances, or our interpretation of circumstances, to make them less threatening.

Key Questions

▪ What are the two basic forms of coping, and when is each form typically used?

▪ What are some of the most common coping strategies?

▪ How does culture affect coping style?

Think about some of the stressful periods that have occurred in your life. What kinds of strategies did you use to deal with those distressing events? Which strategies seemed to work best? Did any of the strategies end up working against your ability to reduce the stressor? If you had to deal with the same events again today, would you do anything differently?

Katie survived a terrorist attack on her neighborhood by being resourceful, and, as she would be the first to admit, through sheer good luck. But how did she survive the months following? Along with having a good support system—friends, relatives, and a dance teacher who could offer her help—she used a number of different strategies to help her to cope with the stress that she continued to experience.

Two Ways of Coping
Problem-Focused and Emotion-Focused Coping

The strategies that you use to deal with distressing events are examples of coping. **Coping** refers to the ways in which we try to change circumstances, or our interpretation of circumstances, to make them more favorable and less threatening (Folkman & Lazarus, 1991; Lazarus, 1999, 2000).

Coping tends to be a dynamic, ongoing process. We may switch our coping strategies as we appraise the changing demands of a stressful situation and our available resources at any given moment. We also evaluate whether our efforts have made a stressful situation better or worse, and adjust our coping strategies accordingly.

Ways of Coping Like the stress response itself, adaptive coping is a dynamic and complex process. Imagine that you had lost your home and most of your possessions in a fire. What kinds of coping strategies might prove most helpful?

Gender Differences in Responding to Stress: "Tend-and-Befriend" or "Fight-or-Flight"?

It was in 1932 that Walter Cannon detailed the physiological chain of events called the "fight-or-flight" response, which we described earlier in this chapter. Faced with a threat or other stressor, our body automatically gears up to defensively fight or flee the situation. Ever since Cannon's landmark description, the fight-or-flight response has been regarded as the central mechanism in the stress response. *Physiologically,* both sexes show the same hormonal and sympathetic nervous system activation that Walter Cannon detailed. Yet *behaviorally,* men and women react very differently.

To illustrate, consider this finding: When fathers come home after a stressful day at work, they tend to withdraw from their families, wanting to be left alone—an example of the "flight" response. If their workday was filled with a lot of interpersonal conflicts, they tend to initiate conflicts with family members—evidence of the "fight" response. In contrast, when mothers experience high levels of stress at work, they come home and are *more* nurturing toward their children (Repetti, 1989; Repetti & Wood, 1997).

As we have noted in this chapter, women tend to be much more involved in their social networks than men. And, as compared to men, women are much more likely to seek out and use social support when they are under stress (Belle, 1991; Glynn & others, 1999). Throughout their lives, women tend to mobilize social support—especially from other women—in times of stress (Taylor & others, 2000). We saw this pattern in our chapter Prologue. Just as Katie called her mother, Judy, when her neighborhood came under attack, Judy called her sister and her *own* mother when she feared that her daughter's life was in danger.

Why the gender difference in coping with stress? Health psychologists Shelley Taylor, Laura Klein, and their colleagues (2000) believe that evolutionary theory offers some insight. According to the evolu-

"I'm somewhere between O. and K."

tionary perspective, the most adaptive response in virtually any situation is one that promotes the survival of both the individual *and* the individual's offspring. Given that premise, neither fighting nor fleeing is likely to have been an adaptive response for females, especially females who were pregnant, nursing, or caring for their offspring. According to Taylor and her colleagues (2000), "Stress responses that enabled the female to simultaneously protect herself and her offspring are likely to have resulted in more surviving offspring." Rather than fighting or fleeing, they argue, women developed a *tend-and-befriend* behavioral response to stress.

What is the "tend-and-befriend" pattern of responding? *Tending* refers to "quieting and caring for offspring and blending into the environment," Taylor and her colleagues (2000) write. That is, rather than confronting or running from the threat, females take cover and protect their young. Evidence supporting this behavior pattern includes studies of nonhuman animals showing that many female animals adopt a "tending" strategy when faced by a threat (Francis & others, 1999; Liu & others, 1997).

The "befriending" side of the equation refers to the fact that, as compared to men, women seek out and use social support in all types of stressful situations,

including conflicts at work, relationship and health problems, and concern about the well-being of family members. Taylor and her colleagues (2000) describe *befriending* as "the creation of networks of associations that provide resources and protection for the female and her offspring under conditions of stress."

But that still leaves us with the question of why females respond with "tend-and-befriend" rather than "fight-or-flight." Remember, both males and females show the same neuroendocrine responses to an acute stressor—the sympathetic nervous system activates, stress hormones pour into the bloodstream, and, as those hormones reach different organs, the body kicks into high gear. So why do women tend and befriend, rather than fight or flee, as men do? Taylor (2000) points to the effects of another hormone, *oxytocin*. Higher in females than in males, oxytocin is associated with maternal behaviors in all female mammals, including humans. It also tends to have a calming effect on male and female animals.

Taylor speculates that oxytocin might simultaneously help calm stressed females and promote affiliative behavior. Supporting this speculation is research showing that oxytocin increases affiliative behaviors and reduces stress in many mammals (Carter & DeVries, 1999; Light & others, 2000).

In humans, oxytocin is highest in nursing mothers. Pleasant physical contact, such as hugging, cuddling, and touching, stimulates the release of oxytocin. In the laboratory, higher oxytocin levels in female research volunteers were associated with reduced cortisol responses to stress and faster recovery following an acute stressor (Taylor & others, 2000). In combination, all of these oxytocin-related changes seem to help turn down the physiological intensity of the fight-or-flight response for women. And perhaps, Taylor and her colleagues suggest, they also promote the tend-and-befriend response.

When coping is effective, we adapt to the situation and stress is reduced. Unfortunately, coping efforts do not always help us adapt. Maladaptive coping can involve thoughts and behaviors that intensify or prolong distress or that produce self-defeating outcomes (Bolger & Zuckerman, 1995). The rejected lover who continually dwells on her former companion, passing up opportunities to form new relationships and letting her studies slide, is demonstrating maladaptive coping.

Adaptive coping responses serve many functions. Most important, adaptive coping involves realistically evaluating the situation and determining what can be done to minimize the impact of the stressor. But adaptive coping also involves dealing with the emotional aspects of the situation. In other words, adaptive coping often includes developing emotional tolerance for negative life events, maintaining self-esteem, and keeping emotions in balance. Finally, adaptive coping efforts are directed toward preserving important relationships during stressful experiences (Lazarus, 1993; R. Lazarus & Folkman, 1984).

Psychologists Richard Lazarus and Susan Folkman (1984) have described two basic types of coping, each of which serves a different purpose. **Problem-focused coping** is aimed at managing or changing a threatening or harmful stressor. If we think there's nothing that can be done to alter a situation, we tend to rely on **emotion-focused coping:** We direct our efforts toward relieving or regulating the emotional impact of the stressful situation. Although emotion-focused coping doesn't change the problem, it can help you feel better about the situation.

People are flexible in the coping styles they adopt, often relying on different coping strategies for different stressors. Table 13.2 shows some of the coping behaviors of people in the United States immediately after the September 11th terrorist attacks.

Problem-Focused Coping Strategies: Changing the Stressor

Problem-focused coping strategies represent actions that have the goal of changing or eliminating the stressor. When people use aggressive or risky efforts to change the situation, they are engaging in *confrontive coping*. Ideally, confrontive coping is direct and assertive without being hostile. When it is hostile or aggressive, confrontive coping may well generate negative emotions in the people being confronted, damaging future relations with them (Folkman & Lazarus, 1991).

In contrast, *planful problem solving* involves efforts to rationally analyze the situation, identify potential solutions, and then implement them. In effect, you take the attitude that the stressor represents a problem to be solved. Once you assume that mental stance, you follow the basic steps of problem solving (see Chapter 7).

problem-focused coping
Coping efforts primarily aimed at directly changing or managing a threatening or harmful stressor.

emotion-focused coping
Coping efforts primarily aimed at relieving or regulating the emotional impact of a stressful situation.

Problem-Focused Coping People rely on different coping strategies at different times in dealing with the same stressor. After dealing with the emotional impact of losing their home to a wildfire, this California family is engaged in problem-focused coping as they help clear the site before rebuilding.

Table | **13.2**

Coping Behaviors the Week After September 11, 2001				
How much have you:	**A lot**	**A medium amount**	**A little bit**	**Not at all**
Talked with someone about your thoughts and feelings about what happened?	57%	30%	12%	1%
Turned to prayer, religion, or spiritual feelings?	44	31	15	10
Participated in a public or group activity in recognition of what happened?	11	23	26	40
Avoided activities such as watching TV because they remind you of what happened?	5	14	20	61

SOURCE: Schuster & others (2001).

Interviews with randomly selected Americans in the days immediately following the September 11, 2001, terrorist attacks revealed some of the strategies that people used to cope with the horrifying events. As you can see, seeking social support was an important coping strategy. The same survey also found that 36% of the respondents had given blood, donated money, or performed volunteer services to aid those directly affected by the attacks.

Emotion-Focused Coping Strategies: Changing Your Reaction to the Stressor

When the stressor is one over which we can exert little or no control, we often focus on dimensions of the situation that we *can* control—the emotional impact of the stressor on us (Thompson & others, 1994). All the different forms of emotion-focused coping share the goal of reducing or regulating the emotional impact of a stressor. For ways of reducing the physical effects of stress, look at In Focus Box 13.5.

When you shift your attention away from the stressor and toward other activities, you're engaging in the emotion-focused coping strategy called *escape–avoidance.* As the name implies, the basic goal is to escape or avoid the stressor and neutralize distressing emotions. Examples of using escape–avoidance to deal with a stressful situation might include escaping into fantasy (also called wishful thinking), exercising, or immersing yourself in your work, studies, or hobbies. Katie, for example, found that her daily dance classes were a way of forgetting the anxieties of life in New York after September 11th. Maladaptive forms of escape–avoidance include excessive sleeping and the use of drugs or alcohol (Grunberg & others, 1999).

By focusing your attention on something other than the stressor, escape–avoidance tactics provide emotional relief in the short run. Thus, avoidance strategies can be helpful when facing a stressor that is brief and has limited consequences. But avoidance strategies such as wishful thinking tend to be counter-

Minimizing the Physical Effects of Stress

Sometimes stressful situations persist despite our best efforts to resolve them. Knowing that chronic stress can jeopardize your health, what can you do to minimize the adverse impact of stress on your physical well-being? Here are three simple suggestions that you should find helpful.

Suggestion 1: Exercise Regularly

Regular exercise, particularly aerobic exercise like walking, swimming, or running, is one of the best ways to reduce the impact of stress. Simply walking briskly for 20 minutes four or five times a week will improve your physical health and help you cope with stress. Compared to sofa slugs, physically fit people are less physiologically reactive to stressors and produce lower levels of stress hormones (Rejeski & others, 1991, 1992). Psychologically, regular exercise reduces anxiety and depressed feelings and increases self-confidence and self-esteem (Sacks, 1993).

Suggestion 2: Avoid or Minimize the Use of Stimulants

In dealing with a stressful situation, people often turn to stimulants such as coffee or tea to keep them going. And most smokers react to stress by increasing their smoking (Epstein & Jennings, 1985). However, common stimulants like

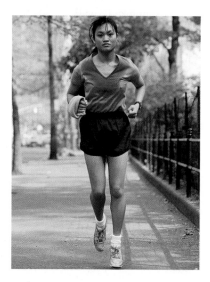

Managing Stress We all experience stressful periods in our lives. How does exercise help people cope with stress?

caffeine and nicotine actually increase the physiological effects of stress by raising heart rate and blood pressure (Lovallo & others, 1996). In effect, users of stimulant drugs are already primed to respond with greater reactivity, exaggerating the physiological consequences of stress.

The best advice? Avoid stimulant drugs altogether. The next best advice? Make a conscious effort to monitor your use of

stimulants, especially when you're under stress. You'll find it easier to deal with stressors when your nervous system is not already in high gear because of caffeine, nicotine, or other stimulants.

Suggestion 3: Regularly Practice a Relaxation Technique

You can significantly reduce stress-related symptoms by regularly using any one of a variety of relaxation techniques (Benson, 1993). One effective relaxation technique is *meditation,* which involves focusing your attention on an object, word, or phrase. We provided you with instructions for a simple meditation technique in Chapter 4.

Another effective technique is *progressive muscle relaxation.* This technique involves systematically tensing and then relaxing the major muscle groups of your body while lying down or sitting in a comfortable chair. You begin by tensing your facial and jaw muscles, paying careful attention to the feeling of muscle tightness. Then, take a deep breath, hold it for a few seconds, and exhale slowly as you relax your facial and jaw muscles as completely as possible. Notice the difference between the sensations of tension and the warm feelings of relaxation. Progressively work your way down your body, tensing and then relaxing muscle groups.

productive when the stressor is severe or long-lasting, like a serious or chronic disease (Stanton & Snider, 1993). Escape–avoidance strategies are also associated with increased psychological distress in facing other types of stressors, such as adjusting to college (Aspinwall & Taylor, 1992).

In the long run, escape–avoidance tactics are associated with poor adjustment and symptoms of depression and anxiety (Stanton & Snider, 1993). That's not surprising if you think about it. After all, the problem *is* still there. And if the problem is one that needs to be dealt with promptly, such as a pressing medical concern, the delays caused by escape–avoidance strategies can make the stressful situation worse.

Seeking social support is the coping strategy that involves turning to friends, relatives, or other people for emotional, tangible, or informational support. As we discussed earlier in the chapter, having a strong network of social support can help buffer the impact of stressors. Confiding in a trusted friend gives you an opportunity to vent your emotions and better understand the stressful situation (Lepore & others, 1996).

When you acknowledge the stressor but attempt to minimize or eliminate its emotional impact, you're engaging in the coping strategy called *distancing*. A relatively common example of distancing occurs when people try to change the meaning of the stressor by claiming that it's "no big deal" or "not that important." Making jokes about the stressful situation is another form of distancing. Sometimes people emotionally distance themselves from a stressor by discussing it in a detached, depersonalized, or intellectual way. Among Katie's circle of young friends, distancing was common. They joked about the soot, the dust, the National Guard troops guarding the subway stations. They made light of the face masks they wore when they went downtown and generally tried to play down the magnitude of the events that they had all experienced.

In certain high-stress occupations, distancing can help workers cope with painful human problems. Clinical psychologists, social workers, rescue workers, police officers, and medical personnel often use distancing to some degree to help them deal with distressing situations without falling apart emotionally themselves.

In contrast to distancing, *denial* is a refusal to acknowledge that the problem even exists. Like escape–avoidance strategies, denial can compound problems in situations that require immediate attention.

Perhaps the most constructive emotion-focused coping strategy is *positive reappraisal*. When we use positive reappraisal, we not only try to minimize the negative emotional aspects of the situation, but we also try to create positive meaning by focusing on personal growth. People sometimes use positive reappraisal to help them make sense of a stressful experience, especially when they have experienced a tragedy, disaster, or catastrophic loss. People who can find some sense of personal meaning in the stressful event—sometimes through their religious faith—tend to cope better with loss than those who see it as senseless (Meichenbaum & Fitzpatrick, 1993; Wortman & others, 1992).

Katie, too, was able to creatively transform the meaning of her experience. She is applying to a competitive college dance program, and, as part of her application, she needs to choreograph and perform an original dance in an audition. She's using her experiences on that September morning as the inspiration, and the centerpiece, of her dance. There is sadness, fear, hope, and renewal in her dance—all of the elements that she experienced on that fateful day. Her ability to express her feelings artistically has helped her come to terms with her experience.

Most people use multiple coping strategies in stressful situations, often combining problem-focused and emotion-focused forms of coping (Dunkel-Schetter & others, 1992; Lazarus, 1993). Different coping strategies may be used at different stages of dealing with a stressor. In the initial stages of a stressful experience, we often rely on emotion-focused strategies to help us step back emotionally from a problem. Once we've regained our emotional equilibrium, we may use problem-focused coping strategies to identify potential solutions.

Transcending Personal Tragedy Some people cope with tragedy by channeling their energies into helping others with similar problems. Actor Christopher Reeve has been paralyzed from the neck down since he suffered a spinal cord injury in a horseback-riding accident. Reeve has become an active advocate for those with spinal cord injuries.

Katie's Dance

13.3 R·E·V·I·E·W

C·O·N·C·E·P·T

Coping Strategies

Identify the coping strategy that is being illustrated in each of the scenarios below. Choose from:

- a. confrontive coping
- b. planful problem solving
- c. escape–avoidance
- d. seeking social support
- e. distancing
- f. denial
- g. positive reappraisal

_____ *1.* In trying to contend with her stormy marriage, Bailey often seeks the advice of her best friend, Paula.

_____ *2.* Lionel was disappointed that he did not get the job, but he concluded that the knowledge he gained from the application and interview process was very beneficial.

_____ *3.* Whenever Dr. Mathau has a particularly hectic and stressful shift in the emergency room, she finds herself making jokes and facetious remarks to the other staff members.

_____ *4.* Phil's job as a public defender is filled with long days and little thanks. To take his mind off his job, Phil jogs every day.

_____ *5.* Faced with low productivity and mounting financial losses, the factory manager bluntly told all his workers, "You people had better start getting more work done in less time, or you will be looking for jobs elsewhere."

_____ *6.* Because of unavoidable personal problems, Martin did very poorly on his last two tests and was very concerned about his GPA. Martin decided to talk with his professor about the possibility of writing an extra paper or taking a makeup exam.

_____ *7.* Although she failed her midterm exam and got a D on her term paper, Sheila insists that she is going to get a B in her economics course.

Culture and Coping Strategies

Culture seems to play an important role in the choice of coping strategies. Americans and other members of individualistic cultures tend to emphasize personal autonomy and personal responsibility in dealing with problems. Thus, they are *less* likely to seek social support in stressful situations than are members of collectivistic cultures, such as Asian cultures (Marsella & Dash-Scheuer, 1988). Members of collectivistic cultures tend to be more oriented toward their social group, family, or community and toward seeking help with their problems.

Individualists also tend to emphasize the importance and value of exerting control over their circumstances, especially circumstances that are threatening or stressful. Thus, they favor problem-focused strategies, such as confrontive coping and planful problem solving. These strategies involve directly changing the situation to achieve a better fit with their wishes or goals (Markus & Kitayama, 1991).

In collectivistic cultures, however, a greater emphasis is placed on controlling your personal reactions to a stressful situation rather than trying to control the situation itself. This emotion-focused coping style emphasizes gaining control over inner feelings by accepting and accommodating yourself to existing realities (Thompson & others, 1994).

For example, the Japanese emphasize accepting difficult situations with maturity, serenity, and flexibility (Weisz & others, 1984). Common sayings in Japan are "The true tolerance is to tolerate the intolerable" and "Flexibility can control rigidity" (Azuma, 1984). Along with controlling inner feelings, many Asian cultures also stress the goal of controlling the outward expression of emotions, however distressing the situation (Johnson & others, 1995).

These cultural differences in coping underscore the point that there is no formula for effective coping in all situations. That we use multiple coping strategies throughout almost every stressful situation reflects our efforts to identify what will work best at a given moment in time. To the extent that any coping strategy helps us identify realistic alternatives, manage our emotions, and maintain important relationships, it is adaptive and effective.

Summing Up

Stress, Health, and Coping

From national tragedies and major life events to the minor hassles and annoyances of daily life, stressors come in all sizes and shapes. Any way you look at it, stress is an unavoidable part of life. Stress that is prolonged or intense can adversely affect both our physical and psychological well-being. Fortunately, most of the time people deal effectively with the stresses in their lives. And as Katie's story demonstrates, the effects of even the most intense stressors can be minimized if we cope with them effectively.

Ultimately, the level of stress that we experience is due to a complex interaction of psychological, biological, and social factors. We hope that reading this chapter has given you a better understanding of how stress affects your life and of how you can reduce its impact on your physical and psychological well-being. In the chapter Application, we'll suggest some ways that you can help other people cope with stressful circumstances.

APPLICATION **Providing Effective Social Support**

A close friend turns to you for help in a time of crisis or personal tragedy. What should you do or say? As we've noted in this chapter, appropriate social support can help people weather crises and can significantly reduce the amount of distress that they feel. Inappropriate support, in contrast, may only make matters worse.

Researchers generally agree that there are three broad categories of social support: emotional, tangible, and informational. Each provides different beneficial functions (Peirce & others, 1996; Taylor & Aspinwall, 1993).

Emotional support includes expressions of concern, empathy, and positive regard. *Tangible support* involves direct assistance, such as providing transportation, lending money, or helping with meals, child care, or household tasks. When people offer helpful suggestions, advice, or possible resources, they are providing *informational support.*

It's possible that all three kinds of social support might be provided by the same person, such as a relative, spouse, or very close friend. More commonly, we turn to different people for different kinds of support.

Research by psychologist Stevan Hobfoll and his colleagues (1992) has identified several support behaviors that are typically perceived as helpful by people under stress. In a nutshell, you're most likely to be perceived as helpful if you:

- Are a good listener and show concern and interest.

- Ask questions that encourage the person under stress to express his or her feelings and emotions.

- Express understanding about why the person is upset.

- Express affection for the person, whether with a warm hug or simply a pat on the arm.

- Are willing to invest time and attention in helping.

- Can help the person with practical tasks, such as housework, transportation, or responsibilities at work or school.

Just as important is knowing what *not* to do or say. Here are several behaviors that, however well intentioned, are often perceived as unhelpful:

- Giving advice that the person under stress has not requested.

- Telling the person, "I know exactly how you feel"—it's a mistake to think that you have experienced distress identical to what the other person is experiencing.

- Talking about yourself or your own problems.

- Minimizing the importance of the person's problem by saying things like, "Hey, don't make such a big deal out of it; it could be a lot worse" or "Don't worry, everything will turn out okay."

- Pretending to be cheerful.

- Offering your philosophical or religious interpretation of the stressful event by saying things like, "It's just fate," "It's God's will," or "It's your karma."

Finally, remember that although social support is helpful, it is *not* a substitute for counseling or psychotherapy. If a friend seems overwhelmed by problems or emotions, or is having serious difficulty handling the demands of everyday life, you should encourage him or her to seek professional help. Most college campuses have a counseling center or a health clinic that can provide referrals to qualified mental health workers. Sliding fee schedules, based on ability to pay, are usually available. Thus, you can assure the person that cost need not be an obstacle to getting help—or an additional source of stress!

Chapter Review
Stress, Health, and Coping

Key Points

Introduction: What Is Stress?

■ **Stress** can be defined as a negative emotional state that occurs in response to events that are appraised as taxing or exceeding a person's resources.

■ **Health psychologists** study stress and other psychological factors that influence health, illness, and treatment. Health psychologists are guided by the **biopsychosocial model.**

■ **Stressors** are events or situations that produce stress. According to the life events approach, any event that requires adaptation produces stress. The Social Readjustment Rating Scale is one way to measure the impact of life events. The life events approach does not take into account a person's subjective appraisal of an event. It also assumes that any change, whether good or bad, produces stress.

■ **Daily hassles** are a significant source of stress and also contribute to the stress produced by major life events.

■ Stress can also be caused by approach–approach, avoidance–avoidance, or approach–avoidance **conflicts.** Approach–avoidance conflicts tend to create the most stress.

■ Social factors, such as unemployment, crime, and racism, can be significant sources of stress, often producing chronic stress. Stress can also result when people encounter different cultural values.

Physical Effects of Stress: *The Mind–Body Connection*

■ Stress can affect health indirectly, by influencing health-related behaviors, and directly, by influencing the body's functioning.

■ Walter Cannon identified the endocrine pathway involved in the **fight-or-flight response.** This endocrine pathway includes the sympathetic nervous system, the adrenal medulla, and the release of **catecholamines.**

■ In studying the physical effects of prolonged stressors, Hans Selye identified the three-stage **general adaptation syndrome,** which includes the alarm, resistance, and exhaustion stages. Selye found that prolonged stress involves a second endocrine pathway, which includes the hypothalamus, the pituitary gland, the adrenal cortex, and the release of **corticosteroids.**

■ Stress affects **immune system** functioning. The most important elements of the immune system are **lymphocytes.** Ader and Cohen's discovery that the immune system could be classically conditioned helped launch the new field of **psychoneuroimmunology.** Subsequent research has discovered that the nervous, endocrine, and immune systems are directly linked and continually influence one another.

■ Stressors that affect immune system functioning include both unusual and common life events, along with everyday pressures. Although stress may increase susceptibility to infection and illness, many other factors are involved in physical health.

Individual Factors That Influence the Response to Stress

■ The impact of stressors is reduced when people feel a sense of control over the stressful situation. Feelings of control have both physical and psychological benefits.

■ The way people explain negative events often determines whether they will persist or give up after failure. People with an **optimistic explanatory style** use external, unstable, and specific explanations for negative events. People with a **pessimistic explanatory style** use internal, stable, and global explanations for negative events. A pessimistic explanatory style contributes to stress and undermines health.

■ Chronic negative emotions are related to the development of some chronic diseases. People who frequently experience negative emotions experience more stress than other people. Transient negative moods have also been shown to decrease immune system functioning.

■ The **Type A behavior pattern** can predict the development of heart disease. The most critical health-compromising component of Type A behavior is hostility. Hostile people react more intensely to stressors and experience stress more frequently than do nonhostile people.

■ Social isolation contributes to poor health. **Social support** improves the ability to deal with stressors by modifying the appraisal of a stressor, decreasing the physical reaction to a stressor, and making people less likely to experience negative emotions. When the quality of relationships is poor, or when social support is inappropriate or unwanted, relationships may increase stress.

■ Women are more likely than men to be the providers of social support and tend to be more vulnerable to the stress contagion effect. Men are less likely to be upset by negative events that happen to people outside their immediate family.

Coping: *How People Deal with Stress*

■ **Coping** refers to the way in which people try to change either their circumstances or their interpretations of circumstances in order to make them more favorable and less threatening. Coping may be maladaptive or adaptive.

■ When people think that something can be done to change a situation, they tend to use **problem-focused coping** strategies, which involve changing a harmful stressor.

■ When people think that a situation cannot be changed, they tend to rely on **emotion-focused coping** strategies, which involve changing their emotional reactions to the stressor.

■ Problem-focused coping strategies include confrontive coping and planful problem solving.

■ Emotion-focused coping strategies include escape–avoidance, seeking social support, distancing, denial, and positive reappraisal. People usually rely on multiple coping strategies in stressful situations.

■ Culture affects the choice of coping strategies. People in individualistic cultures tend to favor problem-focused strategies. People in collectivistic cultures are more likely to seek social support, and they emphasize emotion-focused coping strategies more.

Key Terms

stress, p. 540

health psychology, p. 540

biopsychosocial model, p. 541

stressors, p. 541

daily hassles, p. 542

conflict, p. 543

acculturative stress, p. 545

fight-or-flight response, p. 546

catecholamines, p. 547

general adaptation syndrome, p. 548

corticosteroids, p. 549

immune system, p. 549

lymphocytes, p. 549

psychoneuroimmunology, p. 550

optimistic explanatory style, p. 554

pessimistic explanatory style, p. 554

Type A behavior pattern, p. 556

social support, p. 559

coping, p. 561

problem-focused coping, p. 563

emotion-focused coping, p. 563

Key People

Robert Ader (b. 1932) American psychologist who, with immunologist Nicholas Cohen, first demonstrated that immune system responses could be classically conditioned; helped establish the new interdisciplinary field of psychoneuroimmunology. (p. 549)

Walter B. Cannon (1871–1945) American physiologist who made several important contributions to psychology, especially in the study of emotions. Described the fight-or-flight response, which involves the sympathetic nervous system and the endocrine system (also see Chapter 8). (p. 546)

Janice Kiecolt-Glaser (b. 1951) American psychologist who, with immunologist Ronald Glaser, has conducted extensive research on the effects of stress on the immune system. (p. 551)

Richard Lazarus (b. 1922) American psychologist who helped promote the cognitive perspective in the study of emotion and stress; developed the cognitive appraisal model of stress and coping with co-researcher Susan Folkman (also see Chapter 8). (p. 542)

Martin Seligman (b. 1942) American psychologist who conducted research on explanatory style and the role it plays in stress, health, and illness. (p. 554)

Hans Selye (1907–1982) Canadian endocrinologist who was a pioneer in stress research; defined stress as "the nonspecific response of the body to any demand placed on it" and described a three-stage response to prolonged stress that he termed the *general adaptation syndrome*. (p. 547)

Concept Review Answers

13.1   page 552

1. False. The biopsychosocial model holds that health and illness are determined by the interaction of biological, psychological, and social factors.
2. False. Exposure to life events is only one of many factors that influence health and illness.
3. False. The Social Readjustment Rating Scale measures stress due to life events.
4. False. During periods of prolonged stress, the adrenal cortex secretes corticosteroids.

5. False. Shelley is probably experiencing the "alarm" stage of the general adaptation syndrome.
6. True.

13.2   page 557

1. f   2. e   3. a   4. c   5. b

13.3   page 566

1. d   3. e   5. a   7. f
2. g   4. c   6. b

Life Walk

Psychological Disorders

Prologue

Behind the Steel Door

I had just turned 13 when my dad was hospitalized. At the time, I didn't realize just how sick he was. He nearly died before a diseased kidney was removed, saving his life. As my junior high was only three blocks from the hospital, I visited him every day after school before going to my paper route. It was one of those visits that defined the course of my life.

Lost in my thoughts as I walked through the maze of dim hospital hallways, I took a wrong turn. When I got near the end of the hallway, I realized it was a dead end and started to turn around. That's when her voice pierced the silence, screaming in agony.

"*Help me!* Fire! Fire! Fire! *Please* help me!"

At first I was confused about the direction from which the voice was coming. Then I saw a panic-stricken face against the small window of a steel door. I ran to the door and tried to open it, but it was locked.

"Help me, *somebody!* Fire! Fire! Fire!" she screamed again.

"I'll get help!" I yelled back to her, but she didn't seem to see or hear me. My heart racing, I ran back down the dim hallway to a nurses' station.

"There's a woman who needs help! There's a fire!" I quickly explained to a nurse.

But instead of summoning help, the nurse looked at me with what can only be described as disdain. "Which hallway?" she said flatly, and I pointed in the direction from which I had come. "That's the psychiatric ward down there," she explained. "Those people are crazy."

I stared at her for a moment, feeling confused. *Crazy?* "But she needs help," I finally blurted out.

"That's why she's on the psychiatric ward," the nurse replied calmly. "Which room are you trying to find?"

I didn't answer her. Instead, I walked back down the hallway. I took a deep breath and tried to slow my heart down. As I approached the steel door, the woman was still there, screaming. Standing at the door, I watched her through the wire-reinforced glass. She was completely oblivious to my presence.

"There's fire! I see fire! Fire! Fire! *Fire!*"

She was probably about 25 years old. Her faced looked gaunt, dirty, her hair stringy and unkempt. I remember the dark circles under her deep-set eyes, her pupils dilated with sheer, raw panic.

"Listen to me, there's *no* fire," I said loudly, tapping on the glass, trying to get her attention.

"Help me, *please,*" she sobbed, laying her cheek against the glass.

"My name is Don," I said, tapping on the glass again. "Listen to me, there's no fire."

That's when the attendants came, dressed in white hospital garb. The young woman slapped at their hands as they tried to pull her away from the door. I quickly got next to the glass, trying to see what was happening. *Don't hurt her!* For just an instant I saw her face again, and she looked directly into my eyes.

"It's okay, there's *no* fire!" I yelled, then she was gone.

I stood by the steel door, my mind racing. *What was wrong with her? Where did they take her? Why did she think there was a fire? Did she really see flames?*

When I finally got to my father's hospital room, we talked the entire time about the woman. As a lawyer, my dad had occasionally intervened on behalf of people who had been jailed because they were mentally unstable. "Being mentally ill is not a crime," he explained. "These people need help, not incarceration." When he realized that one of his clients had a mental disorder, he would immediately petition a judge to move the person to a psychiatric ward where the person would be safer and could receive treatment.

Although my dad knew something about mental disorders, he wasn't able to answer the most important questions that I wanted answered: What was wrong with the woman? And what caused her to be that way? "If you'd like," my dad finally said, "I can arrange for you to talk to a psychiatrist that I know. He can probably answer your questions about that better than I can."

A few weeks later, I spent about 30 minutes with the psychiatrist. In very general terms, he talked to me about mental disorders and their treatment. He also explained how psychiatrists usually take a medical approach, typically prescribing different kinds of medication. In contrast, clinical psychologists use different kinds of psychotherapy to help people with psychological disorders. It was at that moment that I knew I wanted to be a clinical psychologist and help people like the woman I had seen.

I never saw that young woman again, nor did I ever find out what happened to her. But I will never forget her face or the sound of her terrified voice. Since that fateful day, I've spent many years of my life working on psychiatric wards, often trying to help people who were just as confused as that young woman.

In this chapter, we'll look at the symptoms that characterize some of the most common psychological disorders, including the one that was being experienced by the young woman I saw that day. As we do, you'll come to better understand how the symptoms of a psychological disorder can seriously impair a person's ability to function. We'll also talk about what researchers have learned about some of the underlying causes of psychological disorders. As you'll see, biological, psychological, and social factors have been implicated as contributing to many psychological disorders.

Introduction

Understanding Psychological Disorders

Key Theme

- Understanding psychological disorders includes considerations of their origins, symptoms, and development, as well as how behavior relates to cultural and social norms.

Key Questions

- What is a psychological disorder, and what differentiates abnormal behavior from normal behavior?
- What is DSM-IV-TR, and how was it developed?
- How prevalent are psychological disorders?

Does the *Far Side* cartoon make you smile? The cartoon is humorous, but it's actually intended to make some serious points. It reflects several common misconceptions about psychological disorders that we hope will be dispelled by this chapter.

First, there's the belief that "crazy" behavior is very different from "normal" behavior. Granted, sometimes it is, like the behavior of the young woman who was screaming "Fire!" when there was no fire. But as you'll see throughout this chapter, the line that divides "normal" and "crazy" behavior is often not as sharply defined as most people think. In many instances, the difference between normal and abnormal behavior is a matter of degree. For example, as you leave your apartment or house, it's normal to check or even double-check that the door is securely locked. However, if you feel compelled to go back and check the lock 50 times, it would be considered abnormal behavior.

The dividing line between normal and abnormal behavior is also often determined by the social or cultural context in which a particular behavior occurs (Foulks, 1991). For example, among traditional Hindus in India, certain dietary restrictions are followed as part of the mourning process. It would be a serious breach of social norms if an Indian widow ate fish, meat, onions, garlic, or any other "hot" foods within six months of her husband's death (see Shweder & others, 1990b). An American Catholic widow would consider such restrictions absurd. In a similar way, hearing "voices" or talking to disembodied "spirits" is accepted in some cultures but is evidence of serious disturbance in the United States (Mulhern, 1991).

Second, when we encounter people whose behavior strikes us as weird, unpredictable, or baffling, it's easy to simply dismiss them as "just plain nuts," as in the *Far Side* cartoon, or as "crazy," like the nurse's insensitive response in the Prologue. Although convenient, such a response is too simplistic. It could also be wrong. Sometimes, unconventional people are labeled as crazy when they're actually just creatively challenging the conventional wisdom with new ideas.

Even if a person's responses are seriously disturbed, labeling that person as "crazy" or "just plain nuts" tells us nothing meaningful. What are the person's specific symptoms? What might be the cause of the symptoms? How did they develop? How long can they be expected to last? And how might the person be helped? The area of psychology and medicine that focuses on these questions is called **psychopathology**—the scientific study of the origins, symptoms, and development of psychological disorders. In this chapter and the next, we'll take a closer look at psychological disorders and their treatment.

The *Far Side* cartoon reflects a third troubling issue. There is still a strong social stigma attached to suffering from a mental disorder (Hinshaw & Cicchetti, 2000). Imagine sitting next to a guy on a plane who grimaces and twitches his head and neck every 10 minutes or so. "Are you okay?" you finally ask. The guy jerks his head around to look at you and explains, "I'm taking medication for a pinched nerve that's causing muscle spasms in my neck, but I don't think the medication is working very well." How would you respond to your seatmate? Now imagine the same scene, only the guy jerks his head around and says, "I'm taking medication for schizophrenia and sometimes it makes me grimace and jerk uncontrollably." *Now* what would you think, and how would you react to your fellow passenger?

The important point here is that most of us regard mental and physical disorders very differently. When we are troubled with physical symptoms, we typically seek medical help. And if we're under medical care for a physical problem, we're usually not reluctant to discuss the fact with friends or acquaintances. But at least partly because of the social stigma that can be associated with psychological disorders, people are often reluctant to seek the help of mental health professionals (see Kessler & others, 1994; Sirey & others, 2001). Many people who are under the care of a mental health professional for serious psychological problems hide the fact, telling only their closest friends—and understandably so. Being labeled "crazy" carries all kinds of implications, most of which reflect negative stereotypes about people with mental problems (see Corrigan, 1998).

The entertainment industry and the news media are major sources of misinformation about mental illness (National Stigma Clearinghouse, 1993). Portrayals of people with psychological disorders in television shows, movies, novels, and even the Sunday comics foster negative stereotypes and myths about psychological problems (Gerbner, 1993). We discuss this issue in more detail in Critical Thinking Box 14.1.

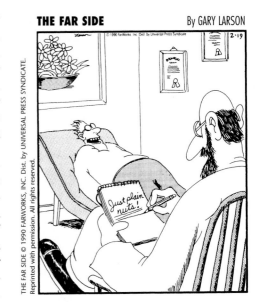

psychopathology
The scientific study of the origins, symptoms, and development of psychological disorders.

CRITICAL THINKING 14.1

Are People with a Mental Illness as Violent as the Media Portrays Them?

A recent children's show on public television presented a retelling of the classic novel *Tom Sawyer* by Mark Twain. However, unlike the original story, the name of the chief villain had been changed: Twain's "Indian Joe" was renamed "Crazy Joe."

As this example illustrates, writers for television are well aware that it is no longer considered acceptable to portray negative stereotypes of particular racial or ethnic groups, including Native Americans. Unfortunately, it also illustrates that another stigmatized group is still fair game: the mentally ill.

In analyzing U.S. television programming, researcher George Gerbner (1993) found that people with mental disorders are the most stigmatized group portrayed on television. People with mental disorders are depicted in two highly negative, stereotypical ways. One stereotype is that of the mentally disturbed person as a helpless victim. The other stereotype is that of the mentally disordered person as an evil villain who is unpredictable, dangerous, and violent.

Gerbner found that although 5 percent of "normal" television characters are murderers, 20 percent of "mentally ill" characters are killers. About 40 percent of normal characters are violent, but 70 percent of characters labeled as mentally ill are violent. This media stereotype reflects and reinforces the widespread belief among Americans that people with mental illness are violent and threatening (Link & Stueve, 1998; Monahan, 1992). Further reinforcing that belief is selective media reporting that sensationalizes violent acts by people with mental disorders (Angermeyer & Matschinger, 1996).

Are people with mental disorders more violent than other people? A study by psychologist Henry Steadman and his colleagues (1998) monitored the behavior of more than 1,000 former mental patients in the year after they were discharged from psychiatric facilities. As a control group, they also monitored the behavior of a matched group of people who were not former mental patients but were living in the same neighborhood.

The researchers found that, overall, the former mental patients did *not* have

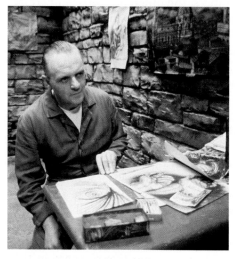

Hollywood Versus Reality The basic plot of a deranged, evil killer on the loose is standard fare in many television dramas and movie thrillers, such as *Copycat* and *Seven* (W. Wilson, 1999). In *The Silence of the Lambs*, Anthony Hopkins won an Oscar for his chilling portrayal of "Hannibal the Cannibal," a psychopathic murderer who helps catch another psychopathic killer. Such media depictions foster the stereotype that people with a mental illness are prone to violence. Does research on this issue support that conclusion?

a higher rate of violence than the comparison group. Former mental patients who demonstrated symptoms of substance abuse were the most likely to engage in violent behavior. However, the same was also true of the control group. In other words, substance abuse was associated with more violent behavior in *all* the participants, whether they had had a mental disorder or not. The study also found that the violent behavior that did occur was most frequently aimed at friends and family members, not at strangers.

Other research has found that people with severe mental disorders who are experiencing extreme psychological symptoms, such as bizarre delusional ideas and hallucinated voices, do have a *slightly* higher level of violent and illegal behavior than do "normal" people (Link & others, 1992). However, the person with a mental

disorder who is not suffering from such symptoms is no more likely than the average person to be involved in violent or illegal behavior. Other factors, such as living in impoverished neighborhoods and abusing drugs or alcohol, are stronger predictors of violence (Eronen & others, 1998; Silver & others, 1999).

Clearly, the incidence of violent behavior among current or former mental patients is grossly exaggerated in media portrayals. In 1999, the U.S. Department of Health and Human Services published a comprehensive report titled *Mental Health: A Report of the Surgeon General*. The report emphasized that fear of violence from people with a mental disorder contributes to the stigma of mental illness. The report also emphasized that such fears are largely unfounded. In reviewing the research, the report summarized it this way: "The overall contribution of mental disorders to the total level of violence in society is exceptionally small. In fact, there is very little risk of violence or harm to a stranger from casual contact with an individual who has a mental disorder."

Critical Thinking Questions

- Can you think of any reasons why people with psychological disorders are more likely to be depicted as villains than members of other social groups?

- Can you think of any television shows or movies in which characters with a severe psychological disorder were shown in a sympathetic light? If so, are such depictions more or less common than depictions of people with a mental illness as dangerous or violent?

- What evidence could you cite to challenge the notion that people with mental illnesses are dangerous?

What Is a Psychological Disorder?

Up to this point, we've used the terms *psychological disorder* and *mental disorder* interchangeably. And, indeed, the terms mean much the same thing. Psychologists generally prefer the term *psychological disorder,* whereas psychiatrists tend to prefer the term *mental disorder.* Both terms are widely used in the research literature. But what exactly are we talking about when we say that someone has a psychological or mental disorder?

A **psychological disorder** or **mental disorder** can be defined as a pattern of behavioral or psychological symptoms that causes significant personal distress, impairs the ability to function in one or more important areas of life, or both (DSM-IV-TR, 2000). An important qualification is that the pattern of behavioral or psychological symptoms must represent a serious departure from the prevailing social and cultural norms. Hence, the behavior of a traditional Hindu woman who refuses to eat onions, garlic, or other "hot" foods following the death of her husband is perfectly normal because that norm is part of the Hindu culture (see Triandis, 1994).

What determines whether a given pattern of symptoms or behaviors qualifies as a psychological disorder? Throughout this chapter, you'll notice numerous references to DSM-IV-TR. **DSM-IV-TR** stands for the *Diagnostic and Statistical Manual of Mental Disorders, Fourth Edition, Text Revision,* which was published by the American Psychiatric Association in 2000. Just for your information, the original DSM-IV was published in 1994. The updated "text revision" of DSM-IV was published in 2000 to incorporate new research and information.

DSM-IV-TR is a book that describes approximately 250 specific psychological disorders. It includes the symptoms, the exact criteria that must be met to make a diagnosis, and the typical course for each mental disorder. An example of the diagnostic criteria for one mental disorder is shown in Figure 14.1. DSM-IV-TR provides mental health professionals with (1) a common language for labeling mental disorders and (2) comprehensive guidelines for diagnosing mental disorders.

It's important to understand that DSM-IV-TR was not written by a single person or even a single organization. Rather, DSM-IV-TR represents the *consensus* of a wide range of mental health professionals and organizations. In developing DSM-IV-TR, teams of mental health professionals conducted extensive reviews of the research findings for each category of mental disorder. More than 1,000 mental health experts, mostly psychiatrists and clinical psychologists, participated in the development of DSM-IV-TR. More than 60 professional organizations, including the American Psychological Association and the American Psychological Society, reviewed early drafts of DSM-IV-TR. Despite these efforts, the *Diagnostic and Statistical Manual of Mental Disorders* has its critics as well as those who would suggest fundamental changes (e.g., Dell, 2001; Tsuang & others, 2000; Widiger & Clark, 2000). Nevertheless, DSM-IV-TR is still the most comprehensive and authoritative set of guidelines available for diagnosing psychological disorders. Thus, we'll refer to it often in this chapter.

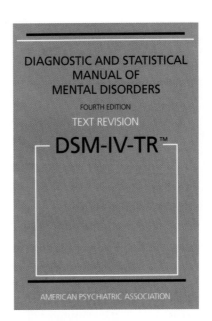

FIGURE 14.1 Sample DSM-IV-TR Diagnostic Criteria Each of the more than 250 psychological disorders described in DSM-IV-TR has specific criteria that must be met in order for a person to be diagnosed with that disorder. Shown here are the DSM-IV-TR criteria for antisocial personality disorder, which is also referred to as *psychopathy, sociopathy,* or *dyssocial personality disorder.* The number 301.7 identifies the specific disorder according to an international code developed by the World Health Organization. The code helps researchers make statistical comparisons of the prevalence of mental disorders in different countries and cultures.

SOURCE: DSM-IV-TR (2000), p. 706.

Diagnostic criteria for 301.7 Antisocial Personality Disorder

A. There is a pervasive pattern of disregard for and violation of the rights of others occurring since age 15 years, as indicated by three (or more) of the following:

  (1) failure to conform to social norms with respect to lawful behaviors as indicated by repeatedly performing acts that are grounds for arrest
  (2) deceitfulness, as indicated by repeated lying, use of aliases, or conning others for personal profit or pleasure
  (3) impulsivity or failure to plan ahead
  (4) irritability and aggressiveness, as indicated by repeated physical fights or assaults
  (5) reckless disregard for safety of self or others
  (6) consistent irresponsibility, as indicated by repeated failure to sustain consistent work behavior or honor financial obligations
  (7) lack of remorse, as indicated by being indifferent to or rationalizing having hurt, mistreated, or stolen from another

B. The individual is at least age 18 years.
C. There is evidence of Conduct Disorder with onset before age 15 years.
D. The occurrence of antisocial behavior is not exclusively during the course of Schizophrenia or a Manic Episode.

psychological disorder or **mental disorder**
A pattern of behavioral and psychological symptoms that causes significant personal distress, impairs the ability to function in one or more important areas of daily life, or both.

DSM-IV-TR
Abbreviation for the *Diagnostic and Statistical Manual of Mental Disorders,* Fourth Edition, Text Revision; the book published by the American Psychiatric Association that describes the specific symptoms and diagnostic guidelines for different psychological disorders.

How Prevalent Are Psychological Disorders? Psychological disorders are far more common than most people think. A recent survey found that one in three American adults had experienced the symptoms of a psychological disorder within the previous year. However, many people who experience such symptoms do not seek help.

The Prevalence of Psychological Disorders
A Fifty-Fifty Chance?

Just how common are psychological disorders? In 1994, the most comprehensive survey to date on the mental health of U.S. adults was published (Kessler & others, 1994). Called the *National Comorbidity Survey (NCS)*, it surveyed a representative sample of Americans aged 15 to 54. NCS participants were asked about the symptoms of psychological disorders that they had experienced (1) at any point in their lives and (2) within the previous 12 months.

The NCS results were surprising. First, the researchers found that the prevalence of psychological disorders was much higher than previously thought. Almost one in two adults—48 percent—had experienced the symptoms of a psychological disorder at same point in their lifetime. The proportion of people who had experienced the symptoms of a psychological disorder in the previous 12 months was 30 percent, or roughly one in three.

Another striking finding was that 80 percent of those who had suffered from the symptoms of a mental disorder in the previous year had *not* sought any type of treatment or help for their symptoms. Although that finding may surprise you, it's consistent with previous research (Narrow & others, 1993).

There are two ways to look at this finding. On the one hand, it's clear that many people who could benefit from mental health treatment do not seek it. This may reflect a lack of awareness about psychological disorders or the fact that a stigma still exists when it comes to seeking treatment for psychological symptoms. It could also be that people lack access to mental health services or lack the financial resources to pay for treatment (U.S. Department of Health and Human Services, 1999).

On the other hand, even though the incidence of mental disorders is much higher than previously believed, *most* people seem to weather the symptoms without becoming completely debilitated and without professional intervention. As NCS director Ronald Kessler (1994) explained, "Really serious conditions that demanded immediate treatment affected 3% to 5% of our sample. These people typically had developed several mental disorders over time, not just one disorder that suddenly appeared."

The NCS also found that the prevalence of certain mental disorders differed for men and women. As you can see in Figure 14.2, women had a higher prevalence of anxiety and depression, and men had a higher prevalence of substance abuse disorders and antisocial personality disorder (Kessler & others, 1994). In trying to explain these gender differences, researchers are investigating differences in exposure to negative life events, willingness to seek help, genetics, and coping styles (Nolen-Hoeksema, 2001; Nolen-Hoeksema & others, 1999; Seeman, 1995).

For the remainder of this chapter, we'll focus on the mental disorders in five DSM-IV-TR categories: anxiety disorders, mood disorders, dissociative disorders, personality disorders, and schizophrenia. The psychological disorders in these five categories are some of the most common disorders encountered by mental health professionals. They're also the ones that our students ask us about most often. And to help you distinguish between normal and maladaptive behaviors, we'll start the discussion of each mental disorder category by describing behavior that falls within the normal range of psychological functioning, such as normal mood variations or feelings of anxiety.

Table 14.1 describes other categories of mental disorders contained in DSM-IV-TR. Some of these disorders have been discussed in previous chapters. In the chapter Application, we'll look at what you can do to help prevent one of the most disturbing consequences of psychological problems—suicide.

FIGURE 14.2 Gender Differences in the Lifetime Prevalence of Selected Psychological Disorders in the National Comorbidity Survey

SOURCE: Adapted from Kessler & others (1994), p. 12.

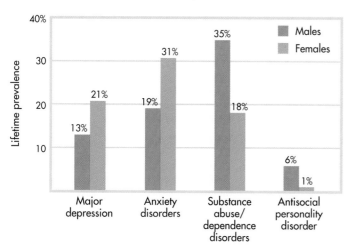

Table | **14.1**

Some Key Diagnostic Categories in DSM-IV-TR

Diagnostic Category	Core Features	Examples of Specific Disorders
Infancy, childhood, or adolescent disorders	Includes a wide range of developmental, behavioral, learning, and communication disorders that are usually first diagnosed in infancy, childhood, or adolescence. Symptoms of a particular disorder may vary depending on a child's age and development level.	**Autistic disorder:** Onset of symptoms prior to age of 3. Characterized by severely impaired social and communication skills, including delayed or a complete lack of language development. Symptoms often include repetitive behaviors, such as body rocking, and abnormal interests, such as intense preoccupation with mechanical toys. **Tourette's disorder:** Onset prior to age of 18. Characterized by motor tics, such as recurring spasmodic movements of the head or arms, and vocal tics, such as recurring and sudden clicking, grunting, or snorting sounds. Sometimes involves uncontrollable utterances of profane or obscene words.
Substance-related disorders (see Chapter 4)	Occurrence of adverse social, behavioral, psychological, and physical effects from seeking or using substances such as alcohol, amphetamines, cocaine, marijuana, hallucinogens, and other drugs.	**Substance abuse:** A recurring pattern of impaired ability to function at work, school, or home due to repeated substance use. **Substance dependence:** A maladaptive pattern of substance use usually resulting in drug tolerance, withdrawal symptoms when the drug is discontinued, and compulsive drug-taking behavior that seriously impairs occupational and social functioning.
Somatoform disorders	Persistent, recurring complaints of bodily (or *somatic*) symptoms that have no physical or medical basis.	**Body dysmorphic disorder:** Exaggerated concern and preoccupation about minor or imagined defects in appearance. **Hypochondriasis:** Preoccupation with imagined diseases based on the person's misinterpretation of bodily symptoms or functions.
Sexual and gender identity disorders (see Chapter 10)	Difficulty in the expression of normal sexuality, including confusion about gender identity, decreased sexual desire or arousal, difficulty having or in timing of orgasm, pain or discomfort during sex, or the use of inappropriate objects to produce sexual arousal.	**Fetishism:** Recurrent, intense, sexually arousing fantasies, urges, or behaviors, usually involving nonliving objects, such as female undergarments, shoes, boots, or other articles of clothing. **Gender identity disorder:** The strong and persistent desire to be the other sex.
Eating disorders (see Chapter 8)	Disturbances in eating behavior that involve obsessive concerns about becoming overweight, a distorted body image, and the inability to maintain a healthy body weight	**Anorexia nervosa:** Severe restriction of eating and the failure to maintain a normal body weight due to the intense fear of gaining weight. **Bulimia nervosa:** Repeated episodes of binge eating followed by self-induced vomiting, misuse of laxatives, fasting, or excessive exercise.
Sleep disorders (see Chapter 4)	Disruptions in the amount, quality, or timing of sleep. Includes difficulty initiating or maintaining sleep, excessive sleepiness, or abnormal behavioral or psychological events during sleep or sleep–wake transitions.	**Narcolepsy:** Recurrent episodes of unintended sleep in inappropriate situations, such as while driving a car or attending a meeting. **Sleep terror disorder:** Repeated episodes of abruptly awakening from sleep, usually beginning with a panicky scream or cry. Intense fear, rapid heartbeat and breathing, sweating, and other signs of autonomic arousal are evident.
Impulse-control disorders	Inability to resist an impulse, urge, or temptation to perform an act that is harmful to the self or others.	**Kleptomania:** The impulse to steal objects not needed for personal use or monetary value. **Pyromania:** The urge to set fires for pleasure, gratification, or relief of tension.

SOURCE: DSM-IV-TR (2000).

Anxiety Disorders
Intense Apprehension and Worry

Key Theme
- The main symptom of anxiety disorders is intense anxiety that disrupts normal functioning.

Key Questions
- How does pathological anxiety differ from normal anxiety?
- What characterizes generalized anxiety disorder and panic disorder?
- What are the phobias, and how have they been explained?

anxiety
An unpleasant emotional state characterized by physical arousal and feelings of tension, apprehension, and worry.

anxiety disorders
A category of psychological disorders in which extreme anxiety is the main diagnostic feature and causes significant disruptions in the person's cognitive, behavioral, or interpersonal functioning.

generalized anxiety disorder
An anxiety disorder characterized by excessive, global, and persistent symptoms of anxiety; also called *free-floating anxiety.*

panic attack
A sudden episode of extreme anxiety that rapidly escalates in intensity.

panic disorder
An anxiety disorder in which the person experiences frequent and unexpected panic attacks.

Anxiety is a familiar emotion to all of us—that feeling of tension, apprehension, and worry that often hits during personal crises and everyday conflicts. Although it is unpleasant, anxiety is sometimes helpful. Think of anxiety as your personal, internal alarm system that tells you that something is not quite right. When it alerts you to a realistic threat, anxiety is adaptive and normal. For example, anxiety about your grades may motivate you to study harder.

Anxiety has both physical and mental effects. As your internal alarm system, anxiety puts you on *physical alert,* preparing you to defensively "fight" or "flee" potential dangers. Anxiety also puts you on *mental alert,* making you focus your attention squarely on the threatening situation. You become extremely vigilant, scanning the environment for potential threats. When the threat has passed, your alarm system shuts off and you calm down. But even if the problem persists, you can put your anxious thoughts aside temporarily and attend to other matters (Noyes & Hoehn-Saric, 1998).

In the **anxiety disorders,** however, the anxiety is *maladaptive,* disrupting everyday activities, moods, and thought processes. It's as if you're dealing with a faulty car alarm that activates at the slightest touch and has a broken "off" switch.

Three features distinguish normal anxiety from pathological anxiety. First, pathological anxiety is *irrational.* The anxiety is provoked by perceived threats that are exaggerated or nonexistent, and the anxiety response is out of proportion to the actual importance of the situation. Second, pathological anxiety is *uncontrollable.* The person can't shut off the alarm reaction, even when he or she knows it's unrealistic. And third, pathological anxiety is *disruptive.* It interferes with relationships, job or academic performance, or everyday activities (Mendlowicz & Stein, 2000). In short, pathological anxiety is unreasonably intense, frequent, persistent, and disruptive.

As a symptom, anxiety occurs in many different mental disorders. In the anxiety disorders, however, anxiety is the *main* symptom, although it is manifested differently in each of the disorders.

Generalized Anxiety Disorder
Worrying About Anything and Everything

Global, persistent, chronic, and excessive apprehension is the main feature of **generalized anxiety disorder,** abbreviated **GAD.** People with this disorder are constantly tense and anxious, and their anxiety is pervasive. They feel anxious about a wide range of life circumstances, sometimes with little or no apparent justification. The more issues about which a person worries excessively, the more likely it is that he or she suffers from generalized anxiety disorder (DSM-IV-TR, 2000).

Normally, anxiety quickly dissipates when a threatening situation is resolved. In generalized anxiety disorder, however, when one source of worry is removed, another quickly moves in to take its place. The anxiety can be attached to virtually any object or to none at all. Because of this, generalized anxiety disorder is sometimes referred to as *free-floating anxiety.*

Panic Attacks and Panic Disorders
Sudden Episodes of Extreme Anxiety

Generalized anxiety disorder is like the dull ache of a sore tooth—a constant, ongoing sense of uneasiness, distress, and apprehension. In contrast, a **panic attack** is a sudden episode of extreme anxiety that rapidly escalates in intensity. The most common symptoms of a panic attack are a pounding heart, rapid breathing, breathlessness, and a choking sensation. The person may also sweat, tremble, and experience lightheadedness, chills, or hot flashes. Accompanying the intense, escalating surge of physical arousal are feelings of terror and the belief that one is about to die, go crazy, or completely lose control. A panic attack typically peaks within 10 minutes of onset and then gradually subsides. Nevertheless, the physical symptoms of a panic attack are so severe and frightening that it's not unusual for people to rush to an emergency room, convinced that they are having a heart attack, stroke, or seizure (Shulman & others, 1994).

When panic attacks occur *frequently* and *unexpectedly*, the person is said to be suffering from **panic disorder.** In this disorder, the frequency of panic attacks is highly variable and quite unpredictable. One person may have panic attacks several times a month. Another person may go for months without an attack and then experience panic attacks for several days in a row. Understandably, people with panic disorder are quite apprehensive about when and where the next panic attack will hit (Barlow, 1991; McNally, 1994).

Sometimes the first panic attack occurs after a stressful experience, such as an injury or illness, or during a stressful period of life, such as while changing jobs or during a period of marital conflict (Craske & others, 1990). In other cases, however, the first panic attack seems to come from nowhere. In a survey of panic disorder patients, 40 percent could not identify any stressful event or negative life experience that might have precipitated the initial panic attack (Shulman & others, 1994).

Explaining Panic Disorder

Both biological and psychological causes seem to be implicated in panic disorder. On the biological side, family and twin studies have found that panic disorder tends to run in families (Hettema & others, 2001). This finding suggests that some individuals may inherit a greater vulnerability to develop panic disorder. However, many panic disorder patients do not have relatives with the disorder (DSM-IV-TR, 2000). So genetics alone does not provide a complete explanation.

Psychologically, people with panic disorder are usually sensitive to the signs of physical arousal (Antony & others, 1992; Ehlers & Breuer, 1992). The fluttering heartbeat or momentary dizziness that the average person barely notices signals disaster to the panic-prone. For example, when normal subjects and panic disorder patients are given a substance, like caffeine, that triggers psychological arousal, only the panic disorder patients react with a full-blown panic attack (Margraf & Ehlers, 1989). Why?

According to the *cognitive-behavioral theory of panic disorder,* people with panic disorder tend to misinterpret the physical signs of arousal as catastrophic and dangerous (Rapee & others, 1992; Zinbarg & others, 1992). When their heart starts to pound and their breathing escalates, they interpret their physical symptoms as frightening or dangerous. This interpretation adds to their physiological arousal and, in a vicious cycle, intensifies the symptoms.

After a frightening initial attack, the person becomes extremely apprehensive about suffering another panic attack. In turn, he becomes even more keenly attuned to physical changes that might signal the onset of another frightening attack. Ironically, this sensitivity simply increases the likelihood that another panic attack will occur.

Panic Attack! The rapidly escalating physical arousal of a panic attack results in a constellation of frightening symptoms: pounding heart, breathlessness, sweating, trembling, and choking sensations. In panic disorder, panic attacks are frequent and unpredictable, often seeming to happen for no apparent reason. How do psychologists explain the development of panic disorder?

The result? After a series of panic attacks, the person becomes behaviorally conditioned to respond with fear to the physical symptoms of arousal (Bouton & others, 2001). Once established, such a conditioned response, combined with catastrophic thoughts, can act as a springboard for repeated panic attacks, leading to panic disorder.

The Influence of Culture on Panic Attacks

Syndromes resembling panic disorder have been reported in many cultures (Amering & Katschnig, 1990; Guarnaccia, 1997). The most common symptoms are the sudden onset of heart palpations, dizziness or faintness, and intense terror. However, other symptoms of panic and the circumstances that trigger panic attacks are influenced by culture (DSM-IV-TR, 2000).

For example, the Spanish phrase *ataque de nervios* literally means "attack of nerves." It's a disorder reported in many Latin American cultures, in Puerto Rico and among Latinos in the United States. *Ataque de nervios* has many symptoms in common with panic disorder—heart palpitations, dizziness, and the fear of dying, going crazy, or losing control. However, the person experiencing *ataque de nervios* also becomes hysterical; may scream, swear, strike out at others; and break things (Salmán & others, 1997). *Ataque de nervios* typically follows a severe stressor, especially one involving a family member. Funerals, accidents, or family conflicts often trigger such attacks (Guarnaccia, 1993). Because *ataque de nervios* tends to elicit immediate social support from others, it seems to be a culturally shaped, acceptable way to respond to severe stress (Liebowitz & others, 1994).

The Phobias

Fear and Loathing

A **phobia** is an intense, irrational fear that is triggered by a specific object or situation. Encountering the feared situation or object can provoke a full-fledged panic attack in some people. People with **specific phobia,** formerly called *simple phobia,* are terrified of a particular object or situation and go to great lengths to avoid that object or situation, even though they know that the fear is irrational.

In the general population, *mild* phobias are extremely common. Many people are fearful of certain animals, such as dogs or snakes, or mildly uncomfortable in particular situations, such as flying in a plane or riding in an elevator. In comparison, the person with a phobia experiences incapacitating terror and anxiety. To be diagnosed as having a psychological disorder, a person must exhibit fear and avoidance that significantly interfere with daily life.

About 10 percent of the general population will experience a specific phobia at some point in their lives (Kessler & others, 1994). More than twice as many women as men suffer from specific phobia. Occasionally, people have unusual phobias, such as the elderly woman that Don knew who was terrified of household cleaning supplies (see Table 14.2). Generally, the objects or situations that produce specific phobias tend to fall into four categories:

- *Fear of particular situations,* such as flying, driving, tunnels, bridges, elevators, crowds, or enclosed places
- *Fear of features of the natural environment,* such as heights, water, thunderstorms, or lightning
- *Fear of injury or blood,* including the fear of injections, needles, and medical or dental procedures
- *Fear of animals and insects,* such as snakes, spiders, dogs, cats, slugs, or bats

Table **14.2**

Some Unusual Phobias

Amathophobia	Fear of dust
Anemophobia	Fear of wind
Aphephobia	Fear of being touched by another person
Bibliophobia	Fear of books
Catotrophobia	Fear of breaking a mirror
Ergophobia	Fear of work or responsibility
Erythrophobia	Fear of red objects
Gamophobia	Fear of marriage
Hypertrichophobia	Fear of growing excessive amounts of body hair
Levophobia	Fear of things being on the left side of your body
Phobophobia	Fear of acquiring a phobia
Phonophobia	Fear of the sound of your own voice
Triskaidekaphobia	Fear of the number thirteen

Agoraphobia: Fear of Panic Attacks in Public Places

One type of phobia deserves special mention—agoraphobia. Compared to the specific phobias, agoraphobia is both more disabling and more complex. Literally, *agoraphobia* means "fear of the marketplace." But rather than fearing public places per se, a person with **agoraphobia** fears having a panic attack in a public place from which it might be difficult to escape or get help (McNally & Luoro, 1992). Consequently, people with agoraphobia avoid (1) situations that they think might provoke a panic attack and (2) situations in which they would be unable to escape or get help if they *did* suffer a panic attack.

What kinds of situations are we talking about? Crowds, standing in line, stores or elevators, public transportation, and traveling in a car may all be avoided because of the fear of suffering a panic attack and being unable to escape the situation. Consequently, many people with agoraphobia become prisoners in their own homes, unable to go beyond the front door. Not surprisingly, then, agoraphobia is the phobia for which people most often seek professional help.

Here's an example to help you understand the distinction between the fear and avoidance in specific phobia as compared to that of agoraphobia. A group of people were seeking treatment to overcome their fear of flying (McNally & Louro, 1992). Half had a diagnosis of specific phobia, and half had been diagnosed with agoraphobia. Those with specific phobia avoided flying because they were afraid that the plane would crash. In contrast, those with agoraphobia were *not* worried about dying in a plane crash. Instead, they were afraid that they might have a panic attack during a flight and be trapped on the plane.

Social Phobia: Fear of Social Situations

A second type of phobia also deserves additional comment—**social phobia.** Also called **social anxiety disorder,** social phobia is more prevalent among women than men (Yonkers & others, 2001). Social phobia goes well beyond the shyness that everyone sometimes feels at social gatherings. Rather, the person with social phobia is paralyzed by fear of social situations, especially if the situation involves performing even routine behaviors in front of others. Eating a meal in public, making small talk at a party, or even using a public restroom can be agonizing for the person with social phobia.

The core of social phobia seems to be an irrational fear of being embarrassed, judged, or critically evaluated by others (Woody, 1996). People with social phobia recognize that their fear is excessive and unreasonable, but they still approach social situations with tremendous anxiety (Ross, 1993). In severe cases, they may even suffer a panic attack in social situations. When the fear of being embarrassed or failing in public significantly interferes with daily life, it qualifies as social phobia (DSM-IV-TR, 2000).

Because of their avoidance of social situations, people with social phobia often have very low self-esteem, poor social skills, and few friends. Their fear of evaluation or criticism by others may lead to occupational or academic underachievement. In classroom situations, they may suffer from intense test anxiety or be afraid to ask questions or make comments (J. R. T. Davidson, 1993; Ross, 1993).

As with panic attacks, cultural influences can add some novel twists to social phobia. Consider the Japanese disorder called *taijin kyofusho. Taijin kyofusho* usually affects young Japanese males. It has several features in common with social phobia, including extreme social anxiety and avoidance of social situations. However, the person with *taijin kyofusho* is not worried about being embarrassed in public. Rather, reflecting the cultural emphasis of concern for others, the person with *taijin kyofusho* fears that his appearance or smell, facial expression, or body language will offend, insult, or embarrass other people (Iwamasa, 1997).

phobia
An irrational fear triggered by a specific object or situation.

specific phobia
An anxiety disorder characterized by an extreme and irrational fear of a specific object or situation that interferes with the ability to function in daily life; formerly called *simple phobia.*

agoraphobia
An anxiety disorder involving the extreme and irrational fear of experiencing a panic attack in a public situation and being unable to escape or get help.

social phobia or **social anxiety disorder**
An anxiety disorder involving the extreme and irrational fear of being embarrassed, judged, or scrutinized by others in social situations.

Social Phobia Social phobia is far more debilitating than everyday shyness. This pleasant scene shows a happy bride dancing with her mother as the wedding guests look on. For those who suffer from social phobia, dancing in public would be impossible, and even attending the wedding as a guest might cause overwhelming anxiety.

Yuck! It's hard to suppress a shudder of disgust at the sight of a slug sliming its way across the sidewalk . . . or a cockroach scuttling across the kitchen floor. Are such responses instinctive? Why are people more likely to develop phobias for slugs, maggots, and cockroaches than for mosquitoes or grasshoppers?

Explaining Phobias: Learning Theories

The development of some phobias can be explained in terms of basic learning principles. *Classical conditioning* may well be involved in the development of a specific phobia that can be traced back to some sort of traumatic event. In Chapter 5, on learning, we saw how psychologist John Watson classically conditioned "Little Albert" to fear a tame lab rat that had been paired with loud noise. Following the conditioning, the infant's fear generalized to other furry objects. In much the same way, our neighbor Michelle has been extremely phobic of dogs ever since she was bitten by a German shepherd when she was four years old. In effect, Michelle developed a *conditioned response* (fear) to a *conditioned stimulus* (the German shepherd) that has *generalized* to similar stimuli—any dog.

Operant conditioning can also be involved in the avoidance behavior that characterizes phobias. In Michelle's case, she quickly learned that she could reduce her anxiety and fear by avoiding dogs altogether. To use operant conditioning terms, her *operant response* of avoiding dogs is *negatively reinforced* by the relief from anxiety and fear that she experiences.

Observational learning can also be involved in the development of phobias. Some people learn to be phobic of certain objects or situations by observing the fearful reactions of someone else who acts as a *model* in the situation. The child who observes a parent react with sheer panic to the sight of a spider or mouse may imitate the same behavioral response. People can also develop phobias from observing vivid media accounts of disasters, such as people who become afraid to fly after watching graphic TV coverage of a plane crash.

We also noted in Chapter 5 that humans seem *biologically prepared* to acquire fears of certain animals or situations, such as snakes or heights, that were survival threats in human evolutionary history (McNally, 1987). People also seem to be predisposed to develop phobias toward creatures that arouse disgust, like slugs, maggots, or cockroaches (Webb & Davey, 1993). Instinctively, it seems, many people find such creatures repulsive, possibly because they are associated with disease, infection, or filth. Such phobias may reflect a fear of contamination or infection that is also based on human evolutionary history (Davey, 1993; Ware & others, 1994).

Posttraumatic Stress Disorder
Reexperiencing the Trauma

A Half-Century of Psychological Pain The symptoms of posttraumatic stress disorder can apparently last a lifetime. More than 50 years after the close of World War II, thousands of veterans, now in their seventies and eighties, still suffer from nightmares, anxiety, and other PTSD symptoms (Lee & others, 1995). Some experts estimate that as many as 200,000 World War II veterans may continue to suffer from the symptoms of posttraumatic stress disorder.

Key Theme
- **Extreme anxiety and intrusive thoughts are symptoms of both posttraumatic stress disorder (PTSD) and obsessive–compulsive disorder.**

Key Questions
- **What is PTSD, and what causes it?**
- **What is obsessive–compulsive disorder?**
- **What are the most common types of obsessions and compulsions?**

Posttraumatic stress disorder, abbreviated **PTSD,** is a long-lasting anxiety disorder that develops in response to an extreme physical or psychological trauma. Extreme traumas are events that produce intense feelings of horror and helplessness, such as a serious physical injury or threat of injury to yourself or to loved ones.

Originally, posttraumatic stress disorder was primarily associated with direct experiences of military combat. However, it's now known that PTSD can also develop in survivors of other sorts of extreme traumas, such as natural disasters, physical or sexual assault, random shooting sprees, or terrorist attacks (Allodi, 1994; North & others, 1994; Sharan & others, 1996). Rescue workers, relief workers, and emergency service personnel can also develop PTSD symptoms (Eriksson & others, 2001). Simply *witnessing* the injury or death of others can be sufficiently traumatic for PTSD to occur (Davis & Breslau, 1994).

In any given year, it's estimated that more than 5 million American adults experience PTSD. There is also a significant gender difference—more than twice as many women as men experience PTSD after exposure to trauma (J. R. Davidson, 2001; Fullerton & others, 2001). And, children can experience the symptoms of PTSD, both during childhood and later, upon reaching adulthood (Margolin & Gordis, 2000; Widom, 1999).

Three core symptoms characterize posttraumatic stress disorder (DSM-IV-TR, 2000). First, the person *frequently recalls the event,* replaying it in her mind. Such recollections are often *intrusive,* meaning that they are unwanted and interfere with normal thoughts. Second, the person *avoids stimuli or situations* that tend to trigger memories of the experience and undergoes a general *numbing of emotional responsiveness.* Third, the person experiences the *increased physical arousal* associated with anxiety. He may be easily startled, experience sleep disturbances, have problems concentrating and remembering, and be prone to irritability or angry outbursts (Tucker & Trautman, 2000).

Not surprisingly, PTSD seriously interferes with the ability to function in daily life. Along with their PTSD symptoms, people often experience depression and feelings of guilt over surviving the trauma when close friends or relatives did not. Substance abuse is also relatively common, often because people are trying to ease their emotional distress by medicating themselves (Bonin & others, 2000; Stewart, 1996). Many individuals with PTSD also display other psychological disorders, such as depression, panic disorder, or generalized anxiety disorder (North & others, 1994; Tomb, 1994).

Posttraumatic stress disorder is somewhat unusual in that the source of the disorder is the traumatic event itself, rather than a cause that lies within the individual. Even well-adjusted and psychologically healthy people may develop PTSD when exposed to an extremely traumatic event (Sutker & others, 1994). However, it's also important to point out that no stressor, no matter how extreme, produces posttraumatic stress disorder in everyone.

So why is it that some people develop PTSD while others don't? Several factors influence the likelihood of developing posttraumatic stress disorder. First, people with a personal or family history of psychological disorders are more likely to develop PTSD when exposed to an extreme trauma. Second, the magnitude of the trauma plays an important role. More extreme stressors are more likely to produce PTSD. Finally, when people undergo *multiple* traumas, the incidence of PTSD can be quite high (Tomb, 1994).

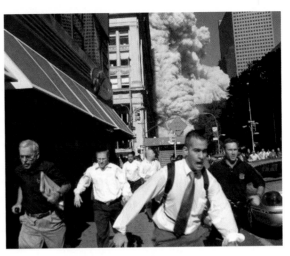

The Aftermath of Terror Because of the magnitude of the disaster, some experts predict that the terrorist attack on the World Trade Center towers in lower Manhattan may produce an "epidemic" of posttraumatic stress disorder—not only among the thousands of people who were directly exposed to the trauma but also among the millions who were indirectly affected (Daw, 2001). Terrorist attacks, because of their suddenness and intensity, are particularly likely to produce posttraumatic stress disorder in observers, survivors, and rescue workers. For example, four years after the Oklahoma City bombing, more than a third of the survivors suffered from posttraumatic stress disorder. Almost all of the survivors had some PTSD symptoms, such as flashbacks, nightmares, intrusive thoughts, and anxiety (North & others, 1999).

Obsessive–Compulsive Disorder

Checking It Again . . . and Again

When you leave your home, you probably check to make sure all the doors are locked. Sometimes, you may even double- or triple-check just to be on the safe side. But once you're confident that the door is locked, you don't think about it again.

Now imagine you've checked the door *20* times. Yet you're still not quite sure that the door is really locked. You know the feeling is irrational, but you feel compelled to check again and again. Imagine you've *also* had to repeatedly check that the coffeepot was unplugged, that the stove was turned off, and so forth. Finally, imagine that you only got two blocks away from home before you felt compelled to turn back and check *again*—because you still were not certain.

Sound agonizing? This is the psychological world of the person who suffers from one form of obsessive–compulsive disorder. **Obsessive–compulsive disorder** is an anxiety disorder in which a person's life is dominated by repetitive thoughts (*obsessions*) and behaviors (*compulsions*).

Obsessions are repeated, intrusive, uncontrollable thoughts or mental images that cause the person great anxiety and distress. Obsessions are not the same as everyday worries. Normal worries typically have some sort of factual basis, even if they're somewhat exaggerated (Freeston & others, 1994). In contrast, obsessions have little or no basis in reality and are often extremely far-fetched.

posttraumatic stress disorder (PTSD)
An anxiety disorder in which chronic and persistent symptoms of anxiety develop in response to an extreme physical or psychological trauma.

obsessive–compulsive disorder
An anxiety disorder in which the symptoms of anxiety are triggered by intrusive, repetitive thoughts and urges to perform certain actions.

obsessions
Repeated, intrusive, and uncontrollable irrational thoughts or mental images that cause extreme anxiety and distress.

A **compulsion** is a repetitive behavior that a person feels driven to perform. Typically, compulsions are ritual behaviors that must be carried out in a certain pattern or sequence. Compulsions may be *overt physical behaviors,* such as repeatedly washing your hands. Or they may be *covert mental behaviors,* such as counting or reciting certain phrases to yourself. When the person tries to resist performing the ritual, unbearable tension, anxiety, and distress result. The most common obsessions and compulsions are described in Table 14.3.

Note that the clinical meanings of *obsessive* and *compulsive* are very different from the meanings intended when people use these words in casual conversation. For example, we may say that someone is "obsessed" with her job, when we mean that she is excessively preoccupied with it. And we may call someone a "compulsive tennis player" when we mean that he really seems to enjoy that activity.

Table | 14.3

The Most Common Obsessions and Compulsions

Obsession	Description	Examples
Contamination	Irrational fear of contamination by dirt, germs, or other toxic substances. Typically accompanied by cleaning or washing compulsion.	Exaggerated fear that shoes, clothing, or visitors will contaminate your home with germs. Exaggerated worry that you will be contaminated by contact with an unclean object.
Pathological doubt	Feeling of uncertainty about having accomplished a simple task. Recurring fear that you have inadvertently harmed someone or violated a law. Typically accompanied by checking compulsion.	Recurring worry that you did not lock doors or shut off appliances, despite having checked them multiple times. While driving, fear that you might have inadvertently hit and killed someone.
Violent or sexual thoughts	Fear that you have harmed or will harm another person or will engage in some sort of unacceptable sexual behavior. Or the fear that you have done or will do something socially unacceptable. May take the form of intrusive mental images or impulses.	Recurring mental images of attacking a family member, although you feel no hostility toward him or her. Recurring worry that you will start screaming obscenities in the middle of class.

Compulsion	Description	Examples
Washing	Urge to repeatedly wash yourself or clean your surroundings. Cleaning or washing may involve an elaborate, lengthy ritual. Often linked with contamination obsession, but may also be a compulsive ritual that is intended to prevent some sort of unrelated catastrophe.	Strict two-hour showering ritual that requires you to perform each step in a precise order or you must restart. Disinfecting everything in your home that has been touched by a visitor, including doorknobs, floor, furniture, and faucets.
Checking	Checking over and over again to make sure that a simple task has been accomplished. Typically occurs in association with pathological doubt. Checking rituals may take hours.	Checking doors, windows, and appliances multiple times yet still feeling uncertain. Checking and rechecking work to make sure you have not made an error. Retracing your route to make sure that you did not inadvertently hit someone while driving.
Counting	Need to engage in certain behaviors a specific number of times or to count to a certain number before performing some action or task.	Having to count to 10 every time a bite of food is taken. Must circle every tree in the front yard 16 times before leaving home.
Symmetry and precision	Need to have things or actions be perfectly symmetrical. Need to have objects in an exact order or position. Need to do or undo certain actions in an exact fashion.	Entering and reentering a doorway until you walk through exactly in the middle. Precise placement of every item on desk coupled with extreme distress when things are "out of order." Rigid step-by-step ritual for getting dressed, brushing teeth, leaving house, or starting car.

SOURCE: Based on Rasmussen & Eisen (1992), Table 1, p. 745.

As this table shows, obsessions and compulsions tend to fall into a limited number of categories. About three-fourths of obsessive–compulsive patients suffer from multiple obsessions, and slightly more than half report more than one type of compulsion (Rasmussen & Eisen, 1992).

In contrast, the true obsessive–compulsive does *not* find any satisfaction in his obsessions or compulsions. Instead, the obsessions and compulsions he experiences are very distressing and anxiety-provoking (De Silva & Rachman, 1992). The obsessive–compulsive does not repeatedly wash his hands because he enjoys being clean. Rather, he washes his hands because to *not* do so would cause extreme, unbearable anxiety.

People may experience either obsessions or compulsions. More commonly, obsessions and compulsions are *both* present. Often, the obsessions and compulsions are linked in some way. For example, a man who was obsessed with the idea that he might have lost an important document felt compelled to pick up every scrap of paper he saw on the street and in other public places.

Other compulsions bear little logical relationship to the feared consequences. For instance, a woman believed that if she didn't get dressed according to a strict pattern, her husband would die in an automobile accident. In all cases, people with obsessive–compulsive disorder feel that something terrible will happen if the compulsive action is left undone.

Interestingly, obsessions and compulsions take a similar shape in different cultures around the world, whether it's Sweden, China, England, the Sudan, India, or Nigeria. Most common are fears of contamination, compulsive washing or cleaning, checking, and repeating actions (Rapoport, 1989; Rasmussen & Eisen, 1992).

However, the *content* of the obsessions and compulsions tends to mirror the particular culture's concerns and beliefs. In the United States, compulsive washers are typically preoccupied with obsessional fears of germs and infection. But in rural Nigeria and rural India, compulsive washers are more likely to have obsessional concerns about religious purity (Rapoport, 1989).

compulsions
Repetitive behaviors or mental acts that are performed to prevent or reduce anxiety.

Explaining Obsessive–Compulsive Disorder

Although researchers are far from fully understanding the causes of obsessive–compulsive disorder, biological factors seem to be involved. For example, a deficiency in the neurotransmitter serotonin has been implicated in obsessive–compulsive disorder. When treated with drugs that increase the availability of serotonin in the brain, many obsessive–compulsive patients experience a marked decrease in symptoms.

In addition, obsessive–compulsive disorder has been linked with dysfunction in specific brain areas, such as the frontal lobes, which play a key role in our ability to think and plan ahead. Another brain area that has been implicated is the *caudate nucleus,* which is involved in regulating movements (Schwartz & others, 1996). Dysfunctions in these brain areas might help account for the overwhelming sense of doubt and lack of control over thoughts and actions that are experienced in obsessive–compulsive disorder (Rapoport, 1991).

The anxiety disorders are summarized in Table 14.4.

Brain Activity in Obsessive–Compulsive Disorder These PET scans show the change in activity in a brain area called the *caudate nucleus* before (*left*) and after (*right*) therapy for obsessive–compulsive disorder (Schwartz & others, 1996). The caudate nucleus is involved in initiating and controlling movement. In obsessive–compulsive disorder, the caudate nucleus is overactive, as indicated by the bright yellow in the left PET scan. After psychotherapy, the obsessions and compulsions cease, and the caudate nucleus becomes less active (*right*).

Table | **14.4**

The Anxiety Disorders

General Anxiety Disorder (GAD)
- Persistent, chronic, unreasonable worry and anxiety
- General symptoms of anxiety, including persistent physical arousal

Panic Disorder
- Frequent and unexpected panic attacks, with no specific or identifiable trigger

Phobias
- Intense anxiety or panic attack triggered by a specific object or situation
- Persistent avoidance of feared object or situation

Posttraumatic Stress Disorder (PTSD)
- Anxiety triggered by memories of a traumatic experience

Obsessive–Compulsive Disorder (OCD)
- Anxiety caused by uncontrollable, persistent, recurring thoughts (obsessions) and/or
- Anxiety caused by uncontrollable, persistent urges to perform certain actions (compulsions)

14.1 R·E·V·I·E·W

Anxiety Disorders

Match each example below with one of the following anxiety disorders: generalized anxiety disorder, panic disorder, specific phobia, posttraumatic stress disorder, obsessive–compulsive disorder, social phobia.

1. Thuan, a Vietnamese refugee, cannot stop thinking about the horrors he experienced while fleeing his country by boat. He sleeps poorly and is often awakened by terrifying nightmares. _____

2. Alayna worries about everything and can never relax. She is very jumpy, has trouble sleeping at night, and has a poor appetite. For the last few months, her anxiety has become so extreme that she is unable to concentrate at work and she is in danger of losing her job. _____

3. Ever since going through a very painful divorce, Kayla has experienced a number of terrifying "spells" that seem to come out of nowhere. Her heart suddenly starts to pound, she begins to sweat and tremble, and she has trouble breathing. _____

4. Carl cannot bear to be in small enclosed places, such as elevators, and goes to great lengths to avoid them. Recently he turned down a high-paying job with an air-conditioning repair company because it involved working in crawl spaces. _____

5. Harry disinfects his shoes, clothing, floor, and door-knobs with bleach several times a day. Nevertheless, he is tormented by worries that his apartment may be contaminated by germs from outside. He doesn't allow anyone to come into his apartment for fear they will contaminate his furniture and belongings. _____

6. Kathy is so painfully shy that she dropped out of college rather than take a public-speaking class. Although she is very bright and hardworking, she is unemployed because she cannot bring herself to go to a job interview. _____

Mood Disorders
Emotions Gone Awry

Key Theme
- Disturbed emotions cause psychological distress and impair daily functioning in the mood disorders, which include major depression and bipolar disorder.

Key Questions
- What are the symptoms and course of major depression, dysthymic disorder, bipolar disorder, and cyclothymic disorder?
- How prevalent are mood disorders?
- What factors contribute to the development of mood disorders?

mood disorders
A category of mental disorders in which significant and chronic disruption in mood is the predominant symptom, causing impaired cognitive, behavioral, and physical functioning.

major depression
A mood disorder characterized by extreme and persistent feelings of despondency, worthlessness, and hopelessness, causing impaired emotional, cognitive, behavioral, and physical functioning.

Let's face it, we all have our ups and downs. When things are going well, we feel cheerful and optimistic. When events take a more negative turn, our mood can sour: We feel miserable and pessimistic. Either way, the intensity and duration of our moods are usually in proportion to the events going on in our lives. That's completely normal.

In the mood disorders, however, emotions violate the criteria of normal moods. In quality, intensity, and duration, a person's emotional state does not seem to reflect what's going on in his or her life. A person may feel a pervasive sadness despite the best of circumstances. Or a person may be extremely energetic and overconfident with no apparent justification. These mood changes persist much longer than the normal fluctuations in moods that we all experience.

DSM-IV-TR formally defines a **mood disorder** as a serious, persistent disturbance in a person's emotions that causes psychological discomfort, impairs the ability to function, or both. In this section, we'll look at the two most important mood disorders: major depression and bipolar disorder.

Major Depression
"Like Some Poisonous Fogbank"

The intense psychological pain of **major depression** is hard to convey to those who have never experienced it. In his book *Darkness Visible,* best-selling author William Styron (1990) described his struggle with major depression in this way:

> All sense of hope had vanished, along with the idea of a futurity; my brain, in thrall to its outlaw hormones, had become less an organ of thought than an instrument registering, minute by minute, varying degrees of its own suffering. The mornings themselves were becoming bad now as I wandered about lethargic, following my synthetic sleep, but afternoons were still the worst, beginning at about three o'clock, when I'd feel the horror, like some poisonous fogbank, roll in upon my mind, forcing me into bed. There I would lie for as long as six hours, stuporous and virtually paralyzed, gazing at the ceiling . . .

Author William Styron The recipient of the Pulitzer Prize and other awards, Styron wrote best-selling novels, including *Sophie's Choice, The Confessions of Nat Turner,* and *Lie Down in Darkness.* Despite his enormous success as a writer, Styron was gripped by the "smothering confinement" of major depression, which he vividly describes in *Darkness Visible.* Styron survived that first bout of major depression only to be confronted with it again in 2000. This second bout of major depression was much more severe than his first episode and lasted for many months before Styron recovered.

The Symptoms of Major Depression

The Styron passage gives you a feeling for how the symptoms of depression affect the whole individual—emotionally, behaviorally, cognitively, and physically (Figure 14.3). *Emotionally,* the person feels an overwhelming sadness. Often, the sadness is accompanied by feelings of guilt, worthlessness, inadequacy, emptiness, and hopelessness. Even if surrounded by close friends and loving family members, the person feels alone and disconnected from others.

Behaviorally, the depressed person's feelings are reflected in dejected and spiritless facial expressions. Crying spells may occur for no apparent reason. Speech, movements, and gestures seem awkward and slower than usual. Compared with nondepressed people, the depressed person speaks more slowly and takes longer to respond to the comments of others. Depressed people make less eye contact with others and smile less often than people who are not depressed. Frequently, depressed people withdraw from activities that they once enjoyed.

> *Many of the artifacts of my house had become potential devices for my own destruction: the attic rafters (and an outside maple or two) a means to hang myself, the garage a place to inhale carbon monoxide, the bathtub a vessel to receive the flow from my opened arteries. The kitchen knives in their drawers had but one purpose for me.*
>
> **William Styron** (1990)

Emotional symptoms
- Feelings of sadness, hopelessness, helplessness, guilt, emptiness, or worthlessness
- Feeling emotionally disconnected from others
- Turning away from other people

Behavioral symptoms
- Dejected facial expression
- Makes less eye contact; eyes downcast
- Smiles less often
- Slowed movements, speech, and gestures
- Tearfulness or spontaneous episodes of crying
- Loss of interest or pleasure in usual activities, including sex
- Withdrawal from social activities

Cognitive symptoms
- Difficulty thinking, concentrating, and remembering
- Global negativity and pessimism
- Suicidal thoughts or preoccupation with death

Physical symptoms
- Changes in appetite resulting in significant weight loss or gain
- Insomnia, early morning awakening, or oversleeping
- Vague but chronic aches and pains
- Diminished sexual interest
- Loss of physical and mental energy
- Global feelings of anxiety
- Restlessness, fidgety activity

FIGURE 14.3 The Symptoms of Depression The experience of major depression can permeate every aspect of life. This figure shows some of the most common emotional, behavioral, cognitive, and physical symptoms of that disorder.

dysthymic disorder
(dis-THY-mick) A mood disorder involving chronic, low-grade feelings of depression that produce subjective discomfort but do not seriously impair the ability to function.

seasonal affective disorder (SAD)
A mood disorder in which episodes of depression typically recur during the fall and winter and remit during the spring and summer.

Kurt Cobain and Major Depression As leader of the alternative rock band Nirvana, Kurt Cobain seemed to have everything: fame, artistic recognition, wealth, and adulation from both fans and music critics. But Cobain also had a history of troubling episodes of deep depression and had attempted suicide several times. Like other people gripped by depression, Cobain focused on the negative during his dark episodes, which was sometimes reflected in his musical lyrics. Just before the release of *In Utero*, the group's last album, Cobain yanked a song he had written titled "I Hate Myself and I Want to Die." Not long after the release of that album, Cobain committed suicide by shooting himself in the head with a shotgun. In his suicide note, Cobain described himself as a "miserable, self-destructive death rocker."

Cognitively, memory is often impaired (Burt & others, 1995). Thought processes feel dull and sluggish, and the person may have problems concentrating. It becomes increasingly difficult or impossible to complete what were once routine tasks, such as studying, balancing a checkbook, or making dinner. Because the depressed person is often gripped by a paralyzing indecisiveness, making even simple decisions may seem impossible.

Self-esteem plummets as thoughts become globally pessimistic and negative about the self, the world, and the future (Beck & others, 1993). Often, this pervasive negativity and pessimism are manifested in suicidal thoughts or a preoccupation with death. Suicide is always a potential risk in major depression. Approximately 10 percent of those suffering major depression attempt suicide (Zweig & Hinrichsen, 1993).

Physically, major depression is characterized by a general loss of mental and physical energy, along with vague physical aches and pains. Some depressed people experience a sense of physical restlessness and anxiety, demonstrated by fidgeting or aimless pacing. And, in fact, the physical symptoms of anxiety often accompany depression (Zimmerman & others, 2001).

Along with a general loss of energy, motivation and drive diminish. Appetite and eating patterns are disturbed. People with depression often lose weight because they lose all interest in food. Less commonly, people may eat excessively and gain weight. Sexual interest also diminishes.

Abnormal sleep patterns are another hallmark of major depression. The amount of time spent in nondreaming, deeply relaxed sleep is greatly reduced or absent (see Chapter 4). Rather than the usual 90-minute cycles of dreaming, the person experiences sporadic REM periods of varying lengths. Spontaneous awakenings occur repeatedly during the night. Very commonly, the depressed person awakens at 3:00 or 4:00 A.M., then cannot get back to sleep, despite feeling exhausted. Less commonly, some depressed people sleep excessively, sometimes as much as 18 hours a day.

To be diagnosed with major depression, a person must display most of the symptoms described for two weeks or longer (DSM-IV-TR, 2000). In many cases, there doesn't seem to be any external reason for the persistent feeling of depression. In other cases, a person's downward emotional spiral has been triggered by some negative event or stressful situation (see Frank & others, 1994).

One significant negative event deserves special mention: the death of a loved one. If a family member or close friend dies, it is completely normal to feel despondent and sad for several months as part of the mourning or bereavement process (Zisook & Shuchter, 1993). Even so, most people resume attending to the routine duties of life within a few weeks. Privately, they may still feel a strong sense of loss, but they function adequately, if not optimally. As a general rule, if a person's ability to function after the death of a loved one is still seriously impaired after two months, major depression is suspected (DSM-IV-TR, 2000).

Dysthymic Disorder

In contrast to major depression, which significantly impairs a person's ability to function, some people experience a less severe form of depression called dysthymic disorder. Briefly, **dysthymic disorder** is chronic, low-grade depression. It's characterized by many of the symptoms of depression, but the symptoms are less intense. Usually, dysthymic disorder develops in response to some stressful event or trauma. Rather than improving over time, however, the negative mood persists indefinitely. Although the person functions adequately, she has a chronic case of "the blues" that can continue for years.

Some people with dysthymic disorder experience *double depression*—they experience one or more episodes of major depression on top of their ongoing dysthymic disorder. As the person recovers from the episode of major depression, he returns to the less intense depressed symptoms of dysthymic disorder.

The Prevalence and Course of Major Depression

Major depression is often called "the common cold" of psychological disorders, and for a good reason: Depression is the most common of all the psychological disorders (Gotlib, 1992; Kessler & others, 1994). In any given year, about 12 million Americans are affected by major depression. Women are about twice as likely as men to be diagnosed with major depression. If you're female, the lifetime odds are approximately 1 in 4 that you'll experience major depression. If you're male, the lifetime odds are about 1 in 8 (Kessler & others, 1994).

Why the striking gender difference in the prevalence of major depression? Research by psychologist Susan Nolen-Hoeksema (2001) suggests that women are more vulnerable to depression because they experience a greater degree of chronic stress in daily life combined with a lesser sense of personal control than men. Women are also more prone to ruminate about their problems, adding to the sense of low mastery and chronic strain in their lives. The interaction of these factors creates a vicious circle that intensifies and perpetuates depressed feelings in women (Nolen-Hoeksema & others, 1999).

Most people who experience major depression try to cope with the symptoms without seeking professional help (Kessler & others, 1994). Left untreated, the symptoms of major depression can easily last six months or longer. In about 10 percent of people experiencing major depression, the symptoms become chronic, meaning they last for two years or longer (Coryell, Akiskal, & others, 1994; Hornig-Rohan & Amsterdam, 1994).

When depression is not treated, it may become a recurring mental disorder that becomes progressively more severe. More than half of all people who have been through one episode of major depression can expect a relapse, usually within two years. With each recurrence, the symptoms tend to increase in severity and the time between major depression episodes decreases (Coryell, Winokur, & others, 1994; Wells & others, 1992).

Finally, for millions of people with **seasonal affective disorder (SAD),** repeated episodes of depression are as predictable as the changing seasons, especially the onset of autumn and winter (Faedda & others, 1993). In the most common form of seasonal affective disorder, episodes of depression recur in the fall and winter months, when there is the least amount of sunlight. Seasonal affective disorder is more common among women and among people who live in the northern latitudes (Rosenthal, 1998).

Bipolar Disorder
An Emotional Roller Coaster

It was about 6:30 A.M. when your author Don arrived for work at 2 Specialty—the hospital psychiatric ward. A few patients sat sipping their morning coffee or looking at the newspaper. As Don walked toward the nurses' station, a tall, overweight young man with black curly hair *zoomed* across the ward and intercepted him.

"Hi! My name's Kelly! What's yours?" he enthusiastically boomed, vigorously shaking hands. Before Don could respond, Kelly moved on to new topics. Within the next 90 seconds, Don heard about (1) Kelly's plans to make millions of dollars organizing garage sales for other people; (2) several songs that Kelly had written that were all going to skyrocket to the top of the music charts; (3) Kelly's many inventions; and (4) a variety of movie stars, rock stars, and professional athletes, all of whom were Kelly's close friends.

Kelly spoke so rapidly that his words often got tangled up with each other. His arms and legs looked as if they were about to get tangled up, too—Kelly was in constant motion. His grinning, rapid-free speech was punctuated with grand, sweeping gestures and exaggerated facial expressions. Before Don could get a word in edgewise, Kelly vigorously shook his hand again and *zoomed* to the other side of the psychiatric ward to intercept another unfamiliar face.

S tress experiences and stress reactivity contribute directly to women's greater rates of depression compared with men. The more stress women suffer, the more hyper-responsive they may be to stress, both biologically and psychologically.

Susan Nolen-Hoeksema (2001)

Carrie Fisher and Bipolar Disorder Best known for her role as Princess Leia in the *Star Wars* movie trilogy, Carrie Fisher was first diagnosed with bipolar disorder when she was 24 years old. She struggled with drug addiction for several years before finally accepting her diagnosis. "Maybe I was taking drugs to keep the monster in the box," Fisher (2001) speculates, referring to her bouts of uncontrollable mania. Today, Fisher takes lithium and other medications to maintain an even keel but still sometimes feels tempted to forgo her medications to "ride the white lightning again." A successful actress in the 1980s, Fisher today focuses on her writing. She has written novels and screenplays, and she works behind the scenes as a Hollywood script doctor. Other famous people with bipolar disorder include media mogul Ted Turner, actress Patty Duke, and rock musicians Peter Gabriel and Axl Rose.

bipolar disorder

A mood disorder involving periods of incapacitating depression alternating with periods of extreme euphoria and excitement; formerly called *manic depression.*

manic episode

A sudden, rapidly escalating emotional state characterized by extreme euphoria, excitement, physical energy, and rapid thoughts and speech.

cyclothymic disorder

(sī-klo-THY-mick) A mood disorder characterized by moderate but frequent mood swings that are not severe enough to qualify as bipolar disorder.

Brain Activity During the Extremes of Bipolar Disorder These PET scans record the brain activity of an individual with bipolar disorder as he cycled rapidly from depression to mania and back to depression over a 10-day period. In the top and bottom PET scans, the blue and green colors clearly show the sharp reduction in overall brain activity that coincided with the episodes of depression. In the center PET scans, the bright red, orange, and yellow colors indicate high levels of activity in diverse brain regions during the intervening episodes of mania.

SOURCE: Lewis Baxter and Michael E. Phelps, UCLA School of Medicine.

The Symptoms of Bipolar Disorder

Kelly displayed classic symptoms of the mental disorder that used to be called *manic depression* and is today called **bipolar disorder.** In contrast to major depression, bipolar disorder almost always involves abnormal moods at *both* ends of the emotional spectrum. In most cases of bipolar disorder, the person experiences extreme mood swings. Episodes of incapacitating depression alternate with shorter periods of extreme euphoria, called **manic episodes.** For most people with bipolar disorder, a manic episode immediately precedes or follows a bout with major depression. However, a small percentage of people with bipolar disorder experience only manic episodes (DSM-IV-TR, 2000).

Manic episodes typically begin suddenly, and symptoms escalate rapidly. During a manic episode, people are uncharacteristically euphoric, expansive, and excited for several days or longer. Although they sleep very little, they have boundless energy. To the unfamiliar observer, people experiencing a manic episode may simply seem overly enthusiastic. But to those who know them, the unbridled enthusiasm and unlimited energy are clearly excessive and out of character.

Typically, the person in the midst of a manic episode does not recognize what is happening to him. As a result, he often resists the efforts of others to help. This was certainly true in the case of Kelly. It took four police officers and three of Kelly's fraternity buddies to corral Kelly and bring him to the psychiatric ward at 2:00 A.M.

A person experiencing a manic episode has a wildly inflated sense of self-esteem. He exudes supreme self-confidence. Often, he has grandiose plans for obtaining wealth, power, and fame (Mondimore, 1993). Sometimes the grandiose ideas represent *delusional,* or false, beliefs. Kelly's belief that various celebrities were his close personal friends was delusional.

Frenzied, goal-directed behavior abounds during a manic episode. Multiple activities, business ventures, shopping sprees, social interactions, or other tasks are initiated, often simultaneously. To an outside observer, the behavior seems disorganized and bizarre. But the manic person believes that he or she is simply seizing golden opportunities. For example, Kelly believed he had invented a new kind of fishing pole that would "revolutionize" game fishing. The hospital staff finally suspended Kelly's telephone privileges after a fishing-rod manufacturer called to confirm his order of 10,000 fishing rods.

Kelly's fast-forward speech was loud and virtually impossible to interrupt. During a manic episode, words are spoken so rapidly, they're often slurred as the person tries to keep up with his own thought processes. The manic person feels as if his thoughts are racing along at Warp Factor 10. Attention is easily distracted by virtually anything, triggering a *flight of ideas,* in which thoughts rapidly and loosely shift from topic to topic.

Not surprisingly, the ability to function during a manic episode is severely impaired. Hospitalization is usually required, partly to protect people from the potential consequences of their own poor judgment and inappropriate behaviors. Bolstered by their supreme self-confidence, they do inappropriate things, such as tell their boss to shove it or show up in the university president's office demanding immediate policy changes, both of which Kelly did. During manic episodes, people can also run up a mountain of bills, disappear for weeks at a time, become sexually promiscuous, or commit illegal acts. Very commonly, the person becomes agitated or verbally abusive when others question his grandiose claims (Hendrix, 1993).

Some people experience a milder but chronic form of bipolar disorder called cyclothymic disorder. In **cyclothymic disorder,** people experience moderate but frequent mood swings for two years or longer. These mood swings are not severe enough to qualify as either bipolar disorder or major depression. Often, people with cyclothymic disorder are perceived as being extremely moody, unpredictable, and inconsistent.

The Prevalence and Course of Bipolar Disorder

As in Kelly's case, the onset of bipolar disorder typically occurs in the person's early twenties. The extreme mood swings of bipolar disorder tend to start and stop much more abruptly than the mood changes of major depression. And whereas an episode of major depression can easily last for six months or longer, the manic and depressive episodes of bipolar disorder tend to be much shorter—lasting anywhere from a few days to a couple of months (Winokur & others, 1993).

Annually, about 2 million Americans suffer from bipolar disorder. Unlike major depression, there are no differences between the sexes in the rate at which bipolar disorder occurs. For both men and women, the lifetime risk of developing bipolar disorder is about 1 percent (Kessler & others, 1994; Leibenluft, 1996).

In the vast majority of cases, bipolar disorder is a recurring mental disorder (Gitlin & others, 1995). A small percentage of people with bipolar disorder display *rapid cycling,* experiencing four or more manic or depressive episodes every year (Maj & others, 1994). More commonly, bipolar disorder tends to recur every couple of years. Often, bipolar disorder recurs when the individual stops taking *lithium,* a medication that helps control the disorder.

Explaining Mood Disorders

Multiple factors appear to be involved in the development of the mood disorders. In this section, we'll briefly consider three key factors that have been implicated: genetics, brain chemistry, and stressful events.

Genetics and Mood Disorders

Thus far, researchers have not been able to directly identify a specific gene or combination of genes that causes mood disorders. However, there is ample indirect evidence from family, twin, and adoption studies that some people inherit a *genetic predisposition,* or a greater vulnerability, to develop a mood disorder.

For example, researchers have consistently found that both major depression and bipolar disorder tend to run in families. If a person has a mood disorder, that person's immediate relatives—children, siblings, and parents—are up to three times more likely than the general population to have a mood disorder (A. Schwartz & R. M. Schwartz, 1993).

Twin studies have shown that if one identical twin has major depression or bipolar disorder, the other twin has about a 70 percent chance of also developing the disorder (Torrey & others, 1994). The same 70 percent shared risk rate has been found in studies of identical twins who were adopted and raised apart (Klein & Wender, 1993). These findings strongly suggest that shared genetics rather than shared environmental experiences account for the high rate of similarity of mood disorders in identical twins.

Neurotransmitters and Mood Disorders

A great deal of indirect evidence implicates at least two important neurotransmitters, serotonin and norepinephrine, in major depression. Since the 1960s, several medications, called *antidepressants,* have been developed to treat major depression. In one way or another, the antidepressants seem to lift the symptoms of depression by increasing the availability of norepinephrine and serotonin in the brain.

In general, the antidepressants are highly effective. The symptoms of major depression are alleviated in about 80 percent of the people for whom antidepressants are prescribed (Sargent, 1993). Evidence has also been accumulating that continued use of antidepressants can prevent recurrences of major depression (Fava & Kaji, 1994).

Creativity and Mood Disorders Mood disorders occur more frequently among creative writers and artists than among the general population, leading some researchers to propose a biochemical or genetic link between mood disorders and the artistic temperament (Jamison, 1993). Writer Mark Twain, novelist Ernest Hemingway, and poet Sylvia Plath all suffered from severe bouts of depression throughout their lives. Both Plath and Hemingway committed suicide, as did Hemingway's father, brother, and sister. In 1996, Hemingway's granddaughter, actress Margaux Hemingway, also committed suicide just one day before the 35th anniversary of her famous grandfather's death.

CRITICAL THINKING 14.2

Does Smoking Cause Depression and Other Psychological Disorders?

Are people with a mental disorder more likely to smoke than other people? Researcher Karen Lasser and her colleagues (2000) assessed smoking rates in American adults with and without psychological disorders. Lasser found that people with mental illness are nearly twice as likely to smoke cigarettes as people with no mental illness. Here are some of the specific findings from Lasser's study:

- Forty-one percent of individuals with a current mental disorder are smokers, as compared to 22 percent of people who have never been diagnosed with a mental disorder.

- People with a mental illness are more likely to be heavy smokers, consuming a pack of cigarettes per day or more.

- People who have been diagnosed with multiple mental disorders have higher rates of smoking and smoke more heavily than people with fewer mental disorders (see accompanying figure).

- Forty-four percent of all cigarettes smoked in the United States are consumed by people with one or more mental disorders.

What can account for the correlation between smoking and psychological disorders? Subjectively, smokers often report that they experience better attention and concentration, increased energy, lower anxiety, and greater calm after smoking, effects that are probably due to the nicotine in tobacco. So, one possible explanation is that people with a mental illness smoke as a form of self-medication. Notice that this explanation assumes that mental illness *causes* people to smoke.

Nicotine, of course, is a powerful psychoactive drug. It triggers the release of *dopamine* and stimulates key brain structures involved in producing rewarding sensations, including the *thalamus,* the *amygdala,* and the *nucleus accumbens* (Salokangas & others, 2000; Stein & others, 1998). Nicotine receptors on different neurons also regulate the re-

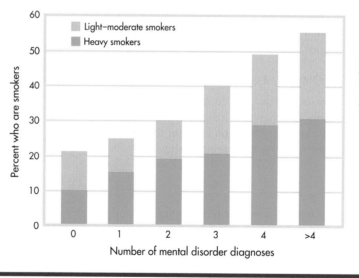

Smoking Rates Compared to the Number of Lifetime Mental Disorder Diagnoses

SOURCE: Lasser & others (2000).

Are neurotransmitters also involved in bipolar disorder? Since the 1960s, the drug lithium has been used to treat bipolar disorder and to prevent its recurrence. It was known that lithium was effective in alleviating symptoms of both mania and depression, but researchers had no idea *how* lithium worked until very recently. In 1998, it was discovered that lithium appears to regulate the availability of a neurotransmitter called *glutamate* (Dixon & Hokin, 1998). Glutamate functions as an excitatory neurotransmitter in many areas of the brain. Apparently, lithium stabilizes the availability of glutamate within a narrow, normal range, eliminating both the excesses that may cause mania and the deficits that may cause depression.

In the next chapter, we'll look more closely at antidepressants, lithium, and other treatments for psychological disorders. For now, simply understand that the effectiveness of these medications provides some of the most compelling evidence that mood disorders involve a disruption in the delicate balance of brain chemistry.

Stress and Mood Disorders

Major depression is often triggered by traumatic and stressful events (Brown & others, 1994). Exposure to recent stressful events is one of the best predictors of

N. accumbens   Amygdala   Thalamus

Nicotine's Effects in the Brain After cigarette smokers were injected with up to 2 milligrams of nicotine, researchers used functional magnetic resonance imaging to track the brain areas activated, which included the *nucleus accumbens,* the *amygdala,* and the *thalamus.* Previous research has shown that these brain structures produce the reinforcing, mood-elevating properties of other abused drugs, including cocaine, amphetamines, and opiates (Stein & others, 1998).

lease of other important neurotransmitters, including *serotonin, acetylcholine, GABA,* and *glutamate* (Quattrocki & others, 2000). In other words, nicotine affects multiple brain structures and alters the release of many different neurotransmitters. These same brain areas and neurotransmitters are also directly involved in many different mental disorders.

Although the idea that mental illness causes smoking seems to make sense, some researchers now believe that the arrow of causation points in the *opposite* direction. In the past decade, many studies have suggested that smoking triggers the onset of symptoms in people who are probably already vulnerable to the development of a mental disorder, especially major depression. Consider just a few studies:

- The lifetime prevalence of developing major depression is strongly linked to the number of cigarettes consumed (Breslau & others, 1993, 1998; Kendler & others, 1993b). People who smoke a pack of cigarettes or more per day have a 50 percent chance of experiencing major depression, while nonsmokers have about a 17 percent chance.

- Three separate studies focusing on adolescents found that cigarette smoking predicted the onset of depressive symptoms, rather than the other way around (Goodman & Capitman, 2000; Windle & Windle, 2001; Wu & Anthony, 1999).

- In a study of patients with bipolar disorder, the prevalence and severity of cigarette smoking predicted the severity of psychotic symptoms during manic episodes (Corvin & others, 2001).

- In a study of people with schizophrenia, 90 percent of the patients had started smoking *before* their illness began (Kelly & McCreadie, 1999). This suggests that in vulnerable people, smoking may precipitate a person's initial schizophrenic episode.

Further research may help disentangle the complex interaction between smoking and mental disorders, but one fact is known. Mentally ill cigarette smokers, like other smokers, are at much greater risk of premature disability and death. So along with the psychological and personal suffering that accompanies almost all psychological disorders, the mentally ill carry the additional burden of consuming nearly half of all the cigarettes smoked in the United States.

Critical Thinking Questions

- Is the evidence sufficient to conclude that there is a causal relationship between cigarette smoking and the onset of mental illness symptoms? Why or why not?

- Should tobacco companies be required to contribute part of their profits to the cost of mental health treatment and research?

episodes of major depression. This is especially true for people who have experienced previous episodes of depression and who have a family history of mood disorders (Kendler & others, 1993a).

But even in people with no family or personal history of mood disorders, chronic stress alone can produce major depression. For example, one study looked at older adults who were caring for spouses whose mental abilities were progressively deteriorating. Almost none of these older adult caregivers had a family history of mood disorders or prior episodes of depression. Nevertheless, 30 percent of them experienced a depressive disorder while caring for their spouses over the course of several years. During the same time period, depression occurred in only 1 percent of those in a matched control group (Dura & others, 1990). There is some evidence that stressful life events also play a role in the course of bipolar disorder (Johnson & Roberts, 1995).

One intriguing finding is that cigarette smoking is closely related to mood disorders, especially the onset of major depression. Research has shown that people who smoke a pack or more of cigarettes per day have a 50 percent lifetime risk of developing major depression (Breslau & others, 1993, 1998). Critical Thinking Box 14.2 explores the connection between cigarette smoking and mental disorders in more detail.

Table | **14.5**

The Mood Disorders

Major Depression

• Loss of interest or pleasure in almost all activities

• Despondent mood; feelings of emptiness, worthlessness, or excessive guilt

• Preoccupation with death or suicidal thoughts

• Difficulty sleeping or excessive sleeping

• Diminished ability to think, concentrate, or make decisions

• Diminished appetite and significant weight loss

Dysthymic Disorder

• Chronic, low-grade depressed feelings that are not severe enough to qualify as major depression

Bipolar Disorder

• One or more manic episodes characterized by euphoria, high energy, grandiose ideas, flight of ideas, inappropriate self-confidence, and decreased need for sleep

• Usually, one or more episodes of major depression

• Possible rapid alternation between symptoms of mania and major depression

Cyclothymic Disorder

• Moderate, recurring mood swings that are not severe enough to qualify as major depression or bipolar disease

---

In summary, considerable evidence points to the role of genetic factors, biochemical factors, and stressful life events in the development of mood disorders. However, exactly how these factors interact to cause mood disorders is still being investigated. Table 14.5 summarizes the symptoms of mood disorders.

14.2   R·E·V·I·E·W

C·O·N·C·E·P·T

Mood Disorders

1. Since moving to Fairbanks, Alaska, five years ago, Joan has experienced episodes of depression during the fall and winter months. Joan is experiencing:

a. bipolar disorder

b. cyclothymic disorder

c. selective Alaskan depression (SAD)

d. seasonal affective disorder (SAD)

2. For as long as she can remember, Mary has felt negative about life. Although good things occasionally happen in Mary's life, they have little impact on her gloomy mood. Mary functions adequately, but she has few friends because she is so pessimistic. Mary probably suffers from:

a. situational aetiology disorder (SAD)

b. dysthymic disorder

c. bipolar disorder

d. cyclothymic disorder

3. After weeks of feeling dejected, despondent, and dissatisfied with his life, Fred has suddenly become euphoric and energetic. He talks constantly about his far-fetched plans for making huge amounts of money. Fred most likely has:

a. bipolar disorder

b. dysthymic disorder

c. seasonal affective disorder (SAD)

d. major depression

4. Bianca, a 19-year-old college student, has missed almost all her classes during the last month. She sleeps 14 hours a day, has withdrawn from friends and family, feels worthless, and cries for no apparent reason. Bianca is most likely suffering from:

a. major depression   c. bipolar disorder

b. dysthymic disorder   d. cylothymic disorder

5. Mark is very unpredictable. One week he is a recluse, the next week he is energetic and initiating activities with others. Even though his mood swings occur regularly, they are not severe enough to qualify as bipolar disorder. Mark's consistent moodiness may well be a symptom of:

a. personality oscillating disorder (POD)

b. dysthymic disorder

c. cyclothymic disorder

d. shifting affective dementia (SAD)

Personality Disorders
Maladaptive Traits

Key Theme

- The personality disorders are characterized by inflexible, maladaptive patterns of thoughts, emotions, behavior, and interpersonal functioning.

Key Questions

- What personality disorders have been identified, and how are they grouped into categories?
- What characteristics and behavioral patterns are associated with the paranoid, antisocial, and borderline personality disorders?

Like every other person, you have your own unique *personality*—your consistent and enduring patterns of thinking, feeling, and behaving that characterize you as an individual. As we described in Chapter 11, your personality can be described as a specific collection of personality traits. Your *personality traits* are relatively stable predispositions to behave or react in certain ways. In other words, your personality traits reflect different dimensions of your personality.

By definition, personality traits are consistent over time and across situations. But that's not to say that personality traits are etched in stone. Rather, the psychologically well-adjusted person possesses a fair degree of flexibility and adaptiveness. Based on our experiences with others, we are able to modify how we display our personality traits so that we can think, feel, and behave in ways that are more effective.

In contrast, someone with a **personality disorder** has personality traits that are *inflexible* and *maladaptive* across a broad range of situations. Personality disorders usually become evident during adolescence or early adulthood, although the person may not recognize that they have a personality disorder. These maladaptive patterns of emotions, thought processes, and behavior are not due to temporary factors, such as stressful life events. Rather, these maladaptive personality traits tend to be very stable over time. They also deviate markedly from the social and behavioral expectations of the individual's culture.

Despite the fact that the maladaptive personality traits consistently cause personal or social turmoil, the person may not consider his personality characteristics as being problematic. In other words, he is unable to see that his inflexible style of thinking and behaving is at the root of his personal and social difficulties. Consequently, people with personality disorders often don't seek help because they don't think they have a problem.

What kinds of maladaptive personality patterns are we discussing? DSM-IV-TR identifies ten personality disorders, which are grouped in three basic clusters. The *odd, eccentric cluster* includes *paranoid, schizoid,* and *schizotypal* personality disorders. The *dramatic, emotional,* or *erratic cluster* consists of *antisocial, borderline, histrionic,* and *narcissistic* personality disorders. And the *anxious, fearful cluster* includes people who display an *avoidant, dependent,* or *obsessive–compulsive* personality disorder. You need to be familiar with the key features of each personality disorder, which are summarized in Table 14.6.

Personality disorders are evident in up to 15% of the general population (Links, 1996; Kessler & others, 1994). The salient features of the different personality disorders overlap to some degree, so it is possible for a person to display the characteristics of more than one personality disorder. Not surprisingly, considerable disagreement exists about the best way to categorize and identify personality disorders (Costello, 1996; Paris, 1997). In the remainder of this section, we'll take a more detailed look at three relatively common personality disorders: paranoid personality disorder, antisocial personality disorder, and borderline personality disorder.

personality disorder
Inflexible, maladaptive patterns of thoughts, emotions, behavior, and interpersonal functioning that are stable over time and across situations, and deviate from the expectations of the individual's culture.

Table **14.6**

Personality Disorders

Odd, Eccentric Cluster	Dramatic, Emotional, Erratic Cluster	Anxious, Fearful Cluster
Paranoid Personality Disorder • Pervasive but unwarranted distrust and suspiciousness; assumes that other people intend to deceive, exploit, or harm them.	**Antisocial Personality Disorder** • Blatantly disregards or violates the rights of others; impulsive, irresponsible, deceitful, manipulative, and lacks guilt or remorse.	**Avoidant Personality Disorder** • Extreme social inhibition due to feelings of inadequacy, and hypersensitivity to criticism, rejection, or disapproval.
Schizoid Personality Disorder • Pervasive detachment from social relationships; emotionally cold and flat; indifferent to praise or criticism from others.	**Borderline Personality Disorder** • Erratic, unstable relationships, emotions, and self-image; impulsive; desperate efforts to avoid real or imagined abandonment; feelings of emptiness; self-destructive tendencies.	**Dependent Personality Disorder** • Excessive need to be taken care of, leading to submissive, clinging behavior, fears of separation, and the inability to assume responsibility.
Schizotypal Personality Disorder • Odd thoughts, speech, emotional reactions, mannerisms, and appearance; impaired social and interpersonal functioning; often superstitious.	**Histrionic Personality Disorder** • Exaggerated, overly dramatic expression of emotions and attention-seeking behavior that often includes sexually seductive or provocative behaviors.	**Obsessive–Compulsive Personality Disorder** • Rigid preoccupation with orderliness, personal control, rules, or schedules that interfere with completing tasks; unreasonable perfectionism.
	Narcissistic Personality Disorder • Grandiose sense of self-importance; exaggerates abilities and accomplishments; excessive need for admiration; boastful, pretentious.	

SOURCE: Adapted from DSM-IV-TR (2000).

Paranoid Personality Disorder
Pervasive Distrust and Suspiciousness

Pervasive mistrust and suspiciousness of others are the defining features of the **paranoid personality disorder.** About 3 percent of the general population display this disorder, which occurs most frequently in men (Bernstein & others, 1995).

Individuals with paranoid personality disorder are constantly on guard. Why? Because they think that other people are out to exploit, harm, or dupe them. Here's how a man with paranoid personality disorder is likely to perceive others: In a restaurant, if a waitress miscalculates the total on his check, she was trying to rip him off. If a neighbor's trash blows into his yard, he's sure that the neighbor dumped it there on purpose.

People with paranoid personality disorder are just as distrustful of people who are close to them, even when there is no evidence to support their suspicious beliefs. Not surprisingly, people with paranoid personality disorder are very reluctant to form close attachments or confide in others. Doing so, they believe, leaves them vulnerable, because the other person could use that information against them. In routine social situations, they often misinterpret the innocent comments or actions of others. Playful teasing from a co-worker is seen as a deliberate insult, an attack on their character or reputation (DSM-IV-TR, 2000).

Getting along with the person with a paranoid personality disorder is like trying to walk on eggshells. Inappropriate outbursts of anger can occur when the person feels as though he has been wronged by some kind of slight, insult, or injustice—which happens frequently. Even a minor criticism or constructive suggestion can trigger a hostile reaction.

They also have a strong tendency to blame others for their own shortcomings. They are often harshly critical of what they perceive as the shortcomings of colleagues, friends, or family members. Though they may superficially present themselves as being objective and unemotional, their underlying hostility is evident in sarcastic comments and put-downs. If another person responds in kind, it only confirms their belief that other people are out to attack them.

paranoid personality disorder
A personality disorder characterized by a pervasive distrust and suspiciousness of the motives of others without sufficient basis.

Pathological jealousy commonly characterizes the intimate relationships of the person with a paranoid personality disorder. Although his spouse or sexual partner may have never given any indication of unfaithfulness, the person still suspects and accuses his mate of harboring feelings of infidelity. When his partner is 10 minutes late, makes casual social conversation with other people, or inadvertently rushes out of the house without her wedding ring, the individual with paranoid personality disorder seizes upon this as "evidence" of the intent to be unfaithful. The goal of this pathological jealousy is to dominate and maintain complete control of his partner. In doing so, he thinks he can keep his partner from betraying him and hurting him emotionally.

Unfortunately, there's not a great deal of research on what causes paranoid personality disorder (Bernstein & others, 1995). However, the disorder also tends to co-occur with schizotypal and avoidant personality disorders (Thompson-Pope & Turkat, 1993).

Antisocial Personality Disorder
Violating the Rights of Others

Often referred to as a *psychopath* or *sociopath,* the individual with **antisocial personality disorder** has the ability to lie, cheat, steal, and otherwise manipulate and harm other people. And, when caught, the person shows little or no remorse for having caused pain, damage, or loss to others (Lykken, 1995). It's as though the person has no conscience or sense of guilt. This pattern of blatantly disregarding and violating the rights of others is the central feature of antisocial personality disorder (DSM-IV-TR, 2000). In the general population, approximately 6 percent of men and 1 percent of women display the characteristics of antisocial personality disorder (Kessler & others, 1994).

Evidence of this maladaptive personality pattern is often seen in childhood or the early adolescent years when the child has repeated run-ins with the law or school authorities. Destroying property, setting fires, harming other people, cruelty to animals, and theft are just a few of the reasons that the child repeatedly comes to the attention of authorities. Such behavior is typically diagnosed as *conduct disorder* during childhood and adolescence. This habitual failure to conform to social norms and rules often becomes the person's predominant life theme, which continues into adulthood (Myers & others, 1998).

Deceiving and manipulating others for their own personal gain is another hallmark of the individual with antisocial personality disorder. With an uncanny ability to look you directly in the eye and speak with complete confidence and sincerity, the person will lie in order to gain money, sex, or whatever their goal may be. When confronted with their actions, the person responds with indifference or offers some superficial rationalization to justify their behavior. Often, they are contemptuous about the feelings or rights of others, blaming the victim for his or her stupidity.

Because they are consistently irresponsible, the individual with antisocial personality disorder often fails to hold a job or meet financial obligations. Losing or quitting one job after another, defaulting on loans, and failing to pay child support payments are common occurrences. Their past is often checkered with a string of arrests and jail sentences. High rates of alcoholism and other forms of substance abuse are also strongly associated with antisocial personality disorder (Morgenstern & others, 1997; Robins, 1998). However, by middle to late adulthood, the antisocial tendencies of such individuals tend to diminish (Black & others, 1997).

Borderline Personality Disorder
Chaos and Emptiness

Of all the personality disorders, the chaotic disorder called **borderline personality disorder** is the most commonly diagnosed (Trull, 1995). Of the estimated 10 million Americans with borderline personality disorder, about 75 percent are

antisocial personality disorder
A personality disorder characterized by a pervasive pattern of disregarding and violating the rights of others; such individuals are also often referred to as being a *psychopath* or *sociopath.*

borderline personality disorder
A personality disorder characterized by instability of interpersonal relationships, self-image, and emotions, and marked impulsivity.

The Dangers of Antisocial Personality Disorder The man in the white sweater with glasses is Henry Louis Wallace. As a disc jockey in Barnwell, South Carolina, Wallace referred to himself as "Night Rider" while on the air late at night. With his silky smooth voice, sincere demeanor, and apparent concern for others, Wallace had no problem finding women to date. He was suspected of murdering at least ten women who had become involved with him. In 1997, Wallace received nine death sentences, one for each of the women he was found guilty of murdering.

women (Kreisman & Straus, 1991). Borderline personality disorder is primarily characterized by chronic instability in emotions, self-image, and relationships. Moods are uncontrollable, intense, and fluctuate quickly. The person unpredictably swings from one mood extreme to another. Angry, sarcastic outbursts are common (DSM-IV-TR, 2000).

The person with borderline personality disorder often has a pervasive feeling of emptiness and is desperately afraid of abandonment. Her sense of self is unstable and just as chaotic as her external world. Partly because her identity is so fragile, she constantly seeks reassurance and definition from others, and then erupts in anger when it is not forthcoming.

Relationships careen out of control as the person shifts from inappropriately idealizing the newfound lover or friend to complete contempt or hostility. This is someone who sees herself, and everyone else, in absolutes: perfect or worthless, ecstatic or miserable (Mason & Kreger, 1998).

Borderline personality disorder is also characterized by self-destructiveness (Morgenstern & others, 1997). Self-mutilation, threats of suicide, and suicide attempts are common, especially in response to perceived rejection or abandonment (Moskovitz, 1996). People with borderline personality disorder are also likely to lack control over their impulses, including self-damaging impulses. They may gamble, drive recklessly, abuse drugs, or be sexually promiscuous. Depression, substance abuse, and eating disorders are commonly present.

What causes borderline personality disorder? As with the other personality disorders, multiple factors have been implicated (Zanarini & Frankenburg, 1997). Because people with borderline personality disorder have such intense and chronic fears of abandonment and are terrified of being alone, some researchers believe that a disruption in attachment relationships in early childhood is an important cause (Gunderson, 1997).

Other researchers have noted that many borderline patients report having experienced physical, sexual, or emotional abuse in childhood (Bailey & Shriver, 1999). One study of hospitalized patients found that a disrupted childhood was common in borderline patients, particularly experiences of neglect by both parents (Zanarini & others, 1997).

The Dissociative Disorders
Fragmentation of the Self

Key Theme

- In the dissociative disorders, disruptions in awareness, memory, and identity interfere with the ability to function in everyday life.

Key Questions

- What is dissociation, and how do normal dissociative experiences differ from the symptoms of dissociative disorders?
- What are dissociative amnesia, dissociative fugue, and dissociative identity disorder (DID)?
- What is thought to cause DID, and why are some psychologists skeptical about its existence?

Despite the many changes you've experienced throughout your lifetime, you have a pretty consistent sense of identity. You're aware of your surroundings and can easily recall memories from the recent and distant past. In other words, a normal personality is one in which *awareness, memory,* and *personal identity* are associated and well-integrated.

In contrast, a **dissociative experience** is one in which a person's awareness, memory, and personal identity become separated or divided. While that may sound weird, dissociative experiences are not inherently pathological. Mild dissociative experiences are quite common and completely normal (Kihlstrom & others, 1994; Putnam, 1993). You are probably familiar with some of these common examples of minor dissociative experiences:

- You become so absorbed in a book or movie that you lose all track of time.
- You daydream your way through class, snapping to only when your instructor calls your name for the third time.
- You are so preoccupied with your thoughts while driving that when you get to your destination, you remember next to nothing about the trip.
- You wake up in a strange room on vacation and are momentarily unable to remember where you are or how you got there.

In each of these cases, you've experienced a temporary "break" or "separation" in your memory or awareness—a mild form of dissociation.

In some cultures, dramatic disruptions in an individual's sense of personality identity are perceived as normal. They can even be highly valued (Mulhern, 1991). For example, *spirit possession* is common in many cultures, typically within a religious context (Krippner, 1994). The usual occupant of a human body is displaced by a "spirit" that takes control of the body. The individual often has no memory for events experienced while the spirit is in control. Another phenomenon that occurs in some cultures is a *trance state,* in which the person loses his sense of personal identity or is unaware of his surroundings (Cardeña, 1992).

If spirit possession and trance states sound like bizarre behaviors that only occur in cultures radically different from your own, think again. *Glossolalia,* or "speaking in tongues," is common in some North American Christian churches (Spanos, 1994). Speaking in tongues is another example of a dissociative possession state: The person is temporarily "possessed" by the Holy Spirit, who speaks through the individual in an unknown language. Like trance states and spirit possession, glossolalia is a highly valued experience within a specific cultural and religious context.

As DSM-IV-TR points out, dissociative possession or trance states are *not* considered pathological if (1) they occur within the context of accepted cultural or religious practices; (2) they occur voluntarily; and (3) they don't cause distress or impair functioning. People who frequently experience possession or trance states may even achieve special status within their culture as spiritual leaders or healers (Mulhern, 1991).

Clearly, then, dissociative experiences are not necessarily abnormal. But in the **dissociative disorders,** the dissociative experiences are more extreme and frequent and severely disrupt everyday functioning. Awareness, or recognition of familiar surroundings, may be completely obstructed. Memories of pertinent personal information may be unavailable to consciousness. Identity may be lost, confused, or fragmented (Spiegel & Cardeña, 1991).

The category of dissociative disorders consists of three basic disorders: *dissociative amnesia, dissociative fugue,* and *dissociative identity disorder,* which was previously called *multiple personality disorder.* Until recently, the dissociative disorders were thought to be extremely rare. However, there is increasing evidence that dissociative symptoms and the dissociative disorders are far more common than researchers formerly believed (Saxe & others, 1993).

dissociative experience
A break or disruption in consciousness during which awareness, memory, and personal identity become separated or divided.

dissociative disorders
A category of psychological disorders in which extreme and frequent disruptions of awareness, memory, and personal identity impair the ability to function.

Dissociation and Possession A Candomble priestess in Brazil holds a woman who is "possessed" by a Christian saint during a religious ceremony. Such dissociative trance and possession states are common in religions around the world (Krippner, 1994). When dissociative experiences take place within a religious ritual context, they are not considered abnormal. In fact, such experiences may be highly valued (Mulhern, 1991).

dissociative amnesia
A dissociative disorder involving the partial or total inability to recall important personal information.

dissociative fugue
(fūg) A dissociative disorder involving sudden and unexpected travel away from home, extensive amnesia, and identity confusion.

dissociative identity disorder (DID)
A dissociative disorder involving extensive memory disruptions along with the presence of two or more distinct identities, or "personalities"; formerly called *multiple personality disorder*.

Dissociative Amnesia and Fugue
Forgetting and Wandering

Dissociative amnesia refers to the partial or total inability to recall important information that is not due to a medical condition, such as an illness, an injury, or a drug. Usually the person develops amnesia for personal events and information, rather than for general knowledge or skills. That is, the person may not be able to remember his wife's name but does remember how to read and who Martin Luther King, Jr., was. In most cases, dissociative amnesia is a response to stress, trauma, or an extremely distressing situation, such as combat, marital problems, or physical abuse (Spiegel & Cardeña, 1991).

A closely related disorder is dissociative fugue. In **dissociative fugue,** the person outwardly appears completely normal. However, the person has extensive amnesia and is confused about his identity. While in the fugue state, he suddenly and inexplicably travels away from his home, wandering to other cities or even countries. In some cases, people in a fugue state adopt a completely new identity.

Like dissociative amnesia, dissociative fugues are associated with traumatic events or stressful periods (Loewenstein, 1993). Interestingly, when the person "awakens" from the fugue state, he may remember his past life but have amnesia for what occurred *during* the fugue state (DSM-IV-TR, 2000).

Dissociative Identity Disorder
Multiple Personalities

Among the dissociative disorders, none is more fascinating—or controversial—than dissociative identity disorder, formerly known as *multiple personality disorder*. **Dissociative identity disorder,** abbreviated **DID,** involves extensive memory disruptions for personal information along with the presence of two or more distinct identities, or "personalities," within a single person (DSM-IV-TR, 2000).

Typically, each personality has its own name and is experienced as if it has its own personal history and self-image. These alternate personalities, often called *alters,* may be of widely varying ages and different genders. The number of alternate personalities can range from 2 to over 100, but having 10 to 15 alters is most common (Goff & Simms, 1993).

Alters are not really separate people. Rather, they constitute a "system of mind" (Kluft, 1993). That is, the alters seem to embody different aspects of the individual's personality that, for some reason, cannot be integrated into the primary personality. The alternate personalities hold memories, emotions, and motives that are not admissible to the individual's conscious mind.

At different times, different alters take control of the person's experience, thoughts, and behavior (Kihlstrom, 1992). Typically, the primary personality is unaware of the existence of the alternate personalities. However, the alters may have knowledge of each other's existence and share memories (Kihlstrom & others, 1994). Sometimes the experiences of one alter are accessible to another alter but not vice versa.

Some researchers claim that there are physiological differences among the different personalities within a single individual. Differences in visual functioning, allergies, brain function, and handedness have been reported (Henninger, 1992; Miller & others, 1991). Although these accounts are intriguing, such physiological differences have yet to be convincingly demonstrated under controlled conditions (Miller & Triggiano, 1992).

Symptoms of amnesia and memory problems are present in virtually all cases of DID. There are frequent gaps in memory for both recent and childhood experiences. Commonly, the person with dissociative identity disorder "loses time" and is unable to recall her behavior or whereabouts during specific time periods. In ad-

CRITICAL THINKING 14.3

Is DID a Real Psychological Disorder?

Many psychologists and other mental health professionals are very skeptical about dissociative identity disorder (Hayes & Mitchell, 1994). Much of this skepticism is related to the fact that the number of reported cases of DID has risen dramatically in the last two decades (Merskey, 1992). Other psychologists point out that DID is not unique in this regard. Psychological disorders such as obsessive–compulsive disorder and PTSD have also increased in prevalence, partly because psychologists have become more aware of the symptoms (Davis & Breslau, 1994; Gleaves, 1996).

Nevertheless, some psychologists flatly claim that there is no such thing as multiple personality disorder or dissociative identity disorder. Rather, they suggest, DID patients are consciously or unconsciously "faking" the symptoms, responding to a therapist's suggestions, or mimicking the symptoms of sensational DID cases portrayed in the media. As outspoken skeptic Nicholas Spanos (1994) put it:

Patients learn to construe themselves as possessing multiple selves, learn to present themselves in terms of this construal, and learn to reorganize and elaborate on their personal biography so as to make it congruent with their understanding of what it means to be a multiple.

Although it is certainly possible that some patients may be faking DID symptoms, it seems unlikely that this is the case in all instances of dissociative identity disorder. Psychologists on the other side of this controversy note that many of these patients experience clear-cut DID symptoms before entering treatment or learning about the disorder (Gleaves, 1996). These psychologists suggest that the increase in DID cases is due to (1) greater clinical awareness of the disorder, (2) improved diagnostic descriptions of DID symptoms, and (3) increased screening for dissociative symptoms.

For example, dissociative identity disorder was once thought to be extremely rare or nonexistent in Puerto Rico, the Netherlands, Belgium, and other countries. However, when formal screening programs for dissociative symptoms were established in these countries, cases of DID and other dissociative disorders were uncovered (Boon & Draijer, 1993; Martinez-Taboas, 1991; Vanderlinden & others, 1991). These DID patients were found to have the same core symptoms and characteristics as DID patients in the United States, including a history of childhood abuse or trauma.

What do you think? Is DID a bona fide psychological disorder? If you think so, you're not alone. Many psychologists believe it is (Gleaves, 1996). On the other hand, many psychologists remain skeptical. In any case, since DID became an official DSM diagnostic category in 1980, its clinical picture has become progressively better defined. As research on DID and other dissociative disorders continues, questions about the prevalence and nature of this diagnostic category may well be answered. For now, it remains the most controversial diagnostic category in DSM-IV-TR.

Critical Thinking Questions

- What kinds of evidence might convince skeptics that dissociative identify disorder is a "real" psychological disorder?

- Playing devil's advocate, does it matter if DID is an authentic psychological disorder or not? In other words, if people are experiencing psychological symptoms and distress, is that subjectively "real" enough to require treatment from mental health professionals?

dition to their memory problems, people with DID typically have numerous psychiatric and physical symptoms, along with a chaotic personal history (Saxe & others, 1994). Symptoms of major depression, anxiety, posttraumatic stress disorder, substance abuse, sleep disorders, and self-destructive behavior are also very common. Often, the DID patient has been diagnosed with a variety of other psychological disorders before the DID diagnosis is made (Carlson & others, 1993).

Not all mental health professionals are convinced that dissociative identity disorder is a genuine psychological disorder. In Critical Thinking Box 14.3, we explore this controversy.

Explaining Dissociative Identity Disorder

According to one explanation, dissociative identity disorder represents an extreme form of dissociative coping (Gleaves, 1996). A very high percentage of DID patients report having suffered extreme physical or sexual abuse in childhood— over 90 percent in most surveys (Coons, 1994). According to this explanation, in order to cope with the trauma, the child "dissociates" himself or herself from it, creating alternate personalities to experience the trauma (Irwin, 1994).

Over time, alternate personalities are created to deal with the memories and emotions associated with intolerably painful experiences. Feelings of anger, rage, fear, and guilt that are too powerful for the child to consciously integrate can be

schizophrenia
A mental disorder in which the ability to function is impaired by severely distorted beliefs, perceptions, and thought processes.

positive symptoms
In schizophrenia, symptoms that reflect excesses or distortions of normal functioning, including delusions, hallucinations, and disorganized thoughts and behavior.

negative symptoms
In schizophrenia, symptoms that reflect defects or deficits in normal functioning, including flat affect, alogia, and avolition.

delusion
A falsely held belief that persists in spite of contradictory evidence.

hallucination
A false or distorted perception that seems vividly real to the person experiencing it.

Table | **14.7**

Dissociative Disorders

Dissociative Amnesia
- Inability to remember important personal information, too extensive to be explained by ordinary forgetfulness

Dissociative Fugue
- Sudden, unexpected travel away from home
- Amnesia
- Confusion about personal identity or assumption of new identity

Dissociative Identity Disorder
- Presence of two or more distinct identities, each with consistent patterns of personality traits and behavior
- Behavior that is controlled by two or more distinct, recurring identities
- Amnesia; frequent memory gaps

---

dissociated into these alternate personalities. In effect, dissociation becomes a pathological defense mechanism that the person uses to cope with overwhelming experiences (Spiegel, 1993a).

Although widely accepted among therapists who work with dissociative identity disorder patients, the dissociative coping theory is difficult to test empirically. The main problem is that memories of childhood are notoriously unreliable (Loftus, 1993). Since DID is usually diagnosed in adulthood, it is very difficult, and often impossible, to determine whether the reports of childhood abuse are real or imaginary (Frankel, 1993). Despite the difficulties of objective verification, a few researchers have confirmed memories of childhood abuse with independent evidence, such as medical records and court testimony by family members and social workers (Coons, 1994).

Table 14.7 summarizes the symptoms of the dissociative disorders. In the next section, we look at a mental disorder that some people mistakenly believe is the same as multiple personality disorder. As you'll see, the symptoms of *schizophrenia* are fundamentally different from those that characterize dissociative identity disorder.

Glimpses of Schizophrenia This drawing was made by a young man hospitalized for schizophrenia. At the time the picture was drawn, he was hallucinating and extremely paranoid. The drawing provides glimpses of the distorted perceptions and thoughts that are characteristic of a schizophrenic episode. Notice the smaller face that is superimposed on the larger face, which might represent the hallucinated voices that are often heard in schizophrenic episodes.

Schizophrenia
A Different Reality

Key Theme
- One of the most serious psychological disorders is schizophrenia, which involves severely distorted beliefs, perceptions, and thought processes.

Key Questions
- How do positive and negative symptoms differ, and what are the major symptoms of schizophrenia?
- What are the main subtypes of schizophrenia?
- What factors have been implicated in the development of schizophrenia?

Normally, you've got a pretty good grip on reality. You can easily distinguish between external reality and the different kinds of mental states that you routinely experience, such as dreams or daydreams. But as we negotiate life's many twists and turns, the ability to stay firmly anchored in reality is not a given. Rather, we're engaged in an ongoing process of verifying the accuracy of our thoughts, beliefs, and perceptions.

If any mental disorder demonstrates the potential for losing touch with reality, it's schizophrenia. **Schizophrenia** is a psychological disorder that involves severely distorted beliefs, perceptions, and thought processes. During a schizophrenic episode, people lose their grip on reality, like the woman screaming "Fire!" in the chapter Prologue. They experience an entirely different inner world, one that is often characterized by mental chaos, disorientation, and frustration.

Symptoms of Schizophrenia

The characteristic symptoms of schizophrenia can be described in terms of two broad categories: positive and negative symptoms. **Positive symptoms** reflect an excess or distortion of normal functioning. Positive symptoms include (1) *delusions,* or false beliefs; (2) *hallucinations,* or false perceptions; and (3) severely disorganized thought processes, speech, and behavior. In contrast, **negative symptoms** reflect a restriction or reduction of normal functions, such as greatly reduced motivation, emotional expressiveness, or speech.

According to DSM-IV-TR, schizophrenia is diagnosed when two or more of these characteristic symptoms are actively present for a month or longer. Usually, schizophrenia also involves a longer personal history, typically six months or more, of odd behaviors, beliefs, perceptual experiences, and other less severe signs of mental disturbance.

In the following sections, we'll describe the positive and negative symptoms that characterize schizophrenia. While these are the core symptoms of schizophrenia, keep in mind that there is enormous individual variation in the onset, intensity, and duration of schizophrenic symptoms.

Delusions: False Beliefs

We've all had the experience of firmly believing something that later turned out to be dead wrong. But when faced with evidence that contradicts our belief, we usually change our views, at least eventually. In contrast, a **delusion** is a falsely held belief that persists in spite of contradictory evidence or appeals to reason.

Unlike beliefs that are simply inaccurate or unconventional, schizophrenic delusions are usually bizarre and far-fetched. The person believes that secret agents are poisoning his food or that the next-door neighbors are actually aliens from outer space who are trying to transform him into a remote-controlled robot. Ignoring any evidence to the contrary, the delusional person clings to his erroneous belief. Even if the delusion is a frightening one, he often becomes so preoccupied with the idea that he can't stop thinking or talking about it. Not surprisingly, delusional beliefs typically cause great psychological distress and interfere with social or occupational functioning.

Although the content of delusions can be quite wide-ranging, delusions are almost always centered on the person who is experiencing them. Certain themes also tend to surface consistently. For example, in *delusions of reference,* the delusional person believes that other people are constantly talking about her or that everything that happens is somehow related to her. The basic theme of *delusions of grandeur* is that the person is extremely important, powerful, or wealthy. In *delusions of persecution,* the basic theme is that others are plotting against or trying to harm the person or someone to whom the person is close.

Because people with schizophrenia find their delusions so convincing, the delusions can sometimes provoke inappropriate or bizarre behavior. In some instances, delusional thinking can lead to dangerous behaviors, such as the person who responds to his delusional ideas by hurting himself or attacking others.

Hallucinations: False Perceptions

Among the most disturbing experiences in schizophrenia are hallucinations. **Hallucinations** are false or distorted perceptions that seem vividly real. Schizophrenia-related hallucinations can involve any of the senses (Carter, 1992). The hallucinations of schizophrenia are often ongoing and persistent, such as hallucinated voices that continually tell the person what to do.

As shown in Figure 14.4, the most common hallucinations experienced in schizophrenia are auditory, followed by visual hallucinations. The most frequent form of auditory hallucination is hearing a voice or voices. The content of hallucinations is often tied to the person's delusional beliefs. If she harbors delusions of grandeur, hallucinated voices may reinforce her

focus on **Neuroscience**

The Hallucinating Brain Researcher David Silbersweig and his colleagues (1995) used PET scans to take a "snapshot" of brain activity during schizophrenic hallucinations. The scan shown here was recorded at the exact instant a schizophrenic patient hallucinated disembodied heads yelling orders at him. The bright orange areas reveal activity in the left auditory and visual areas of his brain, but not in the frontal lobe, which normally is involved in organized thought processes.

FIGURE 14.4 Incidence of Different Types of Hallucinations in Schizophrenia Schizophrenia-related hallucinations can occur in any sensory modality. Auditory hallucinations, usually in the form of voices, are the most common type of hallucination that occurs in schizophrenia, followed by visual hallucinations.

SOURCE: Adapted from data in Mueser & others (1990) and Bracha & others (1989).

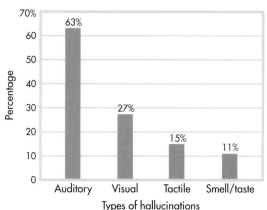

CULTURE AND HUMAN BEHAVIOR 14.4

Travel Advisory: The Jerusalem and Florence Syndromes

Whether it occurs in Baltimore or Beijing, Minneapolis or Moscow, schizophrenia is usually characterized by delusions and hallucinations. However, the *content* of the person's delusions and hallucinations is often influenced by cultural factors, including that culture's dominant religious beliefs. Consider one interesting example: the *Jerusalem syndrome,* which has been described by psychiatrist Yair Bar-El and his colleagues (2000) at Kfar Shaul Mental Health Center in Israel.

Christians, Jews, and Muslims regard the city of Jerusalem as a richly historical and holy city. Annually, about 2 million tourists from around the world visit the city. But for about 100 visitors every year, arriving in the famous holy city is accompanied by a psychotic break that involves religious delusions and hallucinations—the essence of the *Jerusalem syndrome.* About half of these people require psychiatric hospitalization (Fastovsky & others, 2000). The disorder occurs frequently enough that Jerusalem tour guides and hotel personnel are familiar with the symptoms and will notify authorities when they spot someone displaying the symptoms.

Identifying with biblical characters is a common feature of the Jerusalem syndrome. As a general rule, Christians tend to believe that they are Jesus Christ, the Virgin Mary, or John the Baptist. In contrast, Jews tend to gravitate toward a Hebrew hero like Moses, Samson, or King David. And Muslims simply tend to say that they're the Messiah. Most of the time, but not always, the person has a history of serious mental disorders, such as previous episodes of schizophrenia or bipolar disorder.

But in about 10 percent of Jerusalem syndrome cases, the person has *no* history of mental disorders. Instead, the person spontaneously experiences a psychotic episode while in Jerusalem. For example, a Swiss lawyer was on a three-week group tour of Greece, Israel, and Egypt. Everything was fine until the tour

Travel Advisory? Being in the presence of a historic religious site like the Wailing Wall in Jerusalem (top) or an artistic masterpiece, like Michelangelo's statue of David in Florence, Italy (bottom) is an overwhelming emotional experience for many tourists. But in some vulnerable people, such experiences trigger a temporary episode of psychological instability.

visited Jerusalem. On the first night in Jerusalem, the man became nervous and agitated, withdrew from the group, and became obsessed with becoming clean and pure, taking many showers. Then, using the white hotel linen to make a biblical-style, toga-like gown, he marched to one of Jerusalem's holy sites and delivered a rambling "sermon" about how humanity should adopt a more moral and simple way of life. Fortunately, within a matter of days, the syndrome passed and the man's symptoms abated.

What causes the Jerusalem syndrome? One possible explanation is that the disruptions of travel can influence a person's mental state. Time-zone changes, unfamiliar surroundings, exposure to strangers and foreigners, and cultural differences in behavior combined with being on a spiritual pilgrimage to one of the great holy cities of the world can trigger an acute psychotic episode in some people (Bar-El & others, 2000).

Interestingly, there are some parallels between the Jerusalem syndrome and the *Stendhal syndrome,* sometimes called the *Florence syndrome* (Magherini, 1992). Named after the famous French writer Stendhal, this syndrome involves tourists who become emotionally overwhelmed while experiencing the artistic treasures of Florence, Italy. In response to seeing Michelangelo's statue of David, they may faint. Seeing a masterpiece by Raphael can cause a panic attack. Some react with bizarre, emotional outbursts to one of the other great works of art displayed in the city.

The Stendhal syndrome has been studied by Graziella Magherini, who is a clinician on the psychiatric ward of Florence's Santa Maria Nuova Hospital. On average, the Stendhal syndrome occurs about once a month. According to Magherini (1992), "These people were apparently healthy when they left home. But in arriving in Florence, they suddenly lost their equilibrium. The beauty of Florence, while not the cause itself, is a factor." Magherini is careful to note that the great works of art do not directly cause these acute emotional reactions. Rather, the great works of art or the beauty of Florence itself can act as a catalyst to a small number of emotionally vulnerable people.

grandiose ideas by communicating instructions from God, the devil, or angels. If the person harbors delusions of persecution, hallucinated voices or images may be extremely frightening, threatening, or accusing. The content of hallucinations and delusions can also be influenced by culture, as we describe in Culture and Human Behavior Box 14.4.

When a schizophrenic episode is severe, hallucinations can be virtually impossible to distinguish from objective reality. For example, the young woman in the Prologue probably did see vivid images of fire. But when schizophrenic symptoms are less severe, the person may recognize that the hallucination is a product of his own mind. As one young man confided to your author Don, "I know the voices aren't real, but I can't make them stop talking to me." As this young man got better, the hallucinated voices did eventually stop. In some cases of schizophrenia, the auditory hallucinations can last for months or even years (Krausz & Müller-Thomsen, 1993).

Disturbances in Sensation, Thinking, and Speech

People often report that during a schizophrenic episode, sights, sounds, and other sensations feel distorted. One woman described the sensory distortions in this way:

> Looking around the room, I found that things had lost their emotional meaning. They were larger than life, tense, and suspenseful. They were flat, and colored as if in artificial light. I felt my body to be first giant, then minuscule. My arms seemed to be several inches longer than before and did not feel as though they belonged to me. (Anonymous, 1990)

Along with sensory distortions, the person may experience severely disorganized thinking (Braff, 1993). It can be enormously difficult to concentrate, remember, and integrate important information while ignoring irrelevant information (Chen & others, 1994). The person's mind drifts from topic to topic in an unpredictable, illogical manner.

Such disorganized thinking is also often reflected in the person's speech (Barch & Berenbaum, 1996). Ideas, words, and images are sometimes strung together in ways that seem completely nonsensical to the listener. For example, when asked, "How are you today?" a schizophrenic patient responded:

> Yes, sir, it's a good day. Full of rainbows, you know. They go along on their merry way without concern for asphyxiation or impurities. Yes, sir, like unconcerned flappers of the cosmoblue. (Reported in D. Sue & others, 1997)

This response is certainly very odd, but notice that it is not completely unintelligible. If you think carefully about this patient's words, you can see how they reflect ideas that are very loosely related to the question that triggered them. Also notice how he made up a new word—*cosmoblue*—by combining the words *cosmos* and *blue*.

Negative Symptoms: Deficits in Behavior, Emotion, and Motivation

Delusions, hallucinations, and disrupted sensations reflect positive symptoms—excesses or distortions in normal functioning. In contrast, negative symptoms reflect marked deficits or decreases in behavioral or emotional functioning.

One commonly seen negative symptom is referred to as *flat affect,* or *affective flattening.* Regardless of the situation, the person responds in an emotionally "flat" way. She consistently shows a dramatic reduction in emotional responsiveness and a lack of normal facial expressions. Few expressive gestures are made, and the person's speech is slow and monotonous, lacking normal vocal inflections.

A closely related negative symptom is *alogia*—greatly reduced production of speech. In alogia, verbal responses are limited to brief, empty comments. Alogia is also referred to as *poverty of speech.*

Finally, *avolition* refers to the inability to initiate or persist in even simple forms of goal-directed behaviors, such as dressing, bathing, or engaging in social activities. Instead, the person seems to be completely apathetic, sometimes sitting for hours at a time.

Types of Schizophrenia

Figure 14.5 shows the frequency of positive and negative symptoms at the time of hospitalization for schizophrenia. These symptoms are used in diagnosing the particular subtype of schizophrenia. DSM-IV-TR includes three basic subtypes of schizophrenia: *paranoid, catatonic,* and *disorganized* (see Table 14.8).

FIGURE 14.5 Presence of Symptoms in Schizophrenia This graph shows how often specific positive and negative symptoms were present in a study of over 100 individuals at the time they were hospitalized for schizophrenia. Delusions were the most common positive symptom, and avolition, or apathy, was the most common negative symptom.

SOURCE: Based on data reported in Andreasen & Flaum (1991).

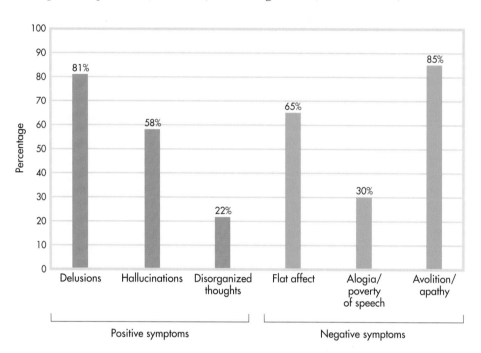

Table 14.8

Types of Schizophrenia

Paranoid Type
- Well-organized delusional beliefs reflecting persecutory or grandiose ideas
- Frequent auditory hallucinations, usually voices
- Little or no disorganized behavior, speech, or flat affect

Catatonic Type
- Highly disturbed movements or actions, such as extreme excitement, bizarre postures or grimaces, or being completely immobile
- Echoing of words spoken by others, or imitation of movements of others

Disorganized Type
- Flat or inappropriate emotional expressions
- Severely disorganized speech and behavior
- Fragmented delusional ideas and hallucinations

Undifferentiated Type
- Display of characteristic symptoms of schizophrenia but not in a way that fits the pattern for paranoid, catatonic, or disorganized type

The *paranoid type* of schizophrenia is characterized by the presence of delusions, hallucinations, or both. However, people with paranoid schizophrenia show virtually no cognitive impairment, disorganized behavior, or negative symptoms. Instead, well-organized delusions of persecution or grandeur are operating. Auditory hallucinations in the form of voices talking about the delusional ideas are also often evident. Convinced that others are plotting against them, these people react with extreme distrust of others. Or they may assume an air of superiority, confident in the delusional belief of their "special powers." The paranoid type is the most common type of schizophrenia.

The *catatonic type* of schizophrenia is marked by highly disturbed movements or actions. These may include bizarre postures or grimaces, extremely agitated behavior, complete immobility, the echoing of words just spoken by another person, or imitation of the movements of others. The people with this form of schizophrenia will resist direction from others and may also assume rigid postures to resist being moved. Catatonic schizophrenia is often characterized by another unusual symptom, called *waxy flexibility*. Like a wax figure, the person can be "molded" into any position and will hold that position indefinitely. The catatonic type of schizophrenia is very rare.

The prominent features of the *disorganized type* of schizophrenia are extremely disorganized behavior, disorganized speech, and flat affect. Delusions and hallucinations are sometimes present, but they are not well organized and integrated, like those that characterize paranoid schizophrenia. Instead, people with the disorganized type experience delusions and hallucinations that contain fragmented, shifting themes. Silliness, laughing, and giggling may occur for no apparent reason. In short, the person's behavior is very peculiar. This type of schizophrenia was formerly called *hebephrenic schizophrenia,* and that term is still sometimes used.

Finally, the label *undifferentiated type* is used when an individual displays some combination of positive and negative symptoms that does not clearly fit the criteria for the paranoid, catatonic, or disorganized types.

The Prevalence and Course of Schizophrenia

Every year, there are about 200,000 new cases of schizophrenia in the United States. The onset of schizophrenia typically occurs during young adulthood (Beratis & others, 1994). Annually, approximately 1 million Americans are treated for schizophrenia. All told, about 1 percent of the U.S. population will experience at least one episode of schizophrenia at some point in life (Regier & others, 1993). Worldwide, no society or culture is immune to this mental disorder. Most cultures correspond very closely to the 1 percent rate of schizophrenia seen in the United States (Gottesman, 1991).

The course of schizophrenia is marked by enormous individual variability. Even so, a few global generalizations are possible (Krausz & Müller-Thomsen, 1993). The good news is that about one-quarter of those who experience an episode of schizophrenia recover completely and never experience another episode. Another one-quarter experience recurrent episodes of schizophrenia, but often with only minimal impairment in the ability to function.

Now the bad news. For the rest of those who have experienced an episode of schizophrenia—one-half of the total—schizophrenia becomes a chronic mental illness, and the ability to function may be severely impaired. The people in this last category face the prospect of repeated hospitalizations and extended treatment. Thus, chronic schizophrenia places a heavy emotional, financial, and psychological burden on people with the disorder, their families, and society.

Explaining Schizophrenia

Schizophrenia is an extremely complex disorder. There is enormous individual variability in the onset, symptoms, duration, and recovery from schizophrenia. So it shouldn't come as a surprise that the causes of schizophrenia seem to be equally complex. In this section, we'll survey some of the factors that have been implicated in the development of schizophrenia.

Genetic Factors: Family, Twin, and Adoption Studies

Studies of families, twins, and adopted individuals have firmly established that genetic factors play a significant role in many cases of schizophrenia. First, family studies have consistently shown that schizophrenia tends to cluster in

focus on **Neuroscience**

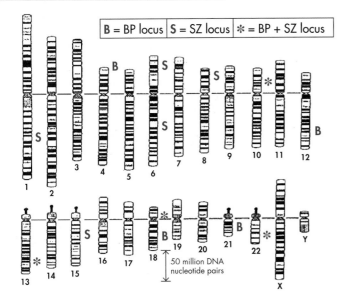

B = BP locus S = SZ locus ∗ = BP + SZ locus

Chromosomal Regions Linked to Schizophrenia and Bipolar Disorder Using family studies, researchers have identified chromosomal regions, called *susceptibility loci,* linked to increased risk of developing schizophrenia or bipolar disorder (Berrettini, 2001). The image shows the susceptibility loci on the 23 human chromosomes for schizophrenia alone (S), for bipolar disorder alone (B), and for bipolar disorder *and* schizophrenia (∗). The identifying symbols are placed to the right of chromosome location.

Why would schizophrenia and bipolar disorder share some of the same susceptibility loci? Although they are very distinct disorders, schizophrenia and bipolar disorder share some common features, including onset during early adulthood, an equal gender risk, and a 1 percent lifetime prevalence rate. It's possible that the shared susceptibility loci may be involved in the shared clinical features of these two disorders. In any case, family studies suggest that these disorders are probably more closely related than previously thought. But as researcher Wade Berrettini (2001) reminds us, "Environmental factors drive gene expression." In other words, the interaction of environmental and genetic factors can increase *or* decrease our susceptibility to any disorder, including mental disorders.

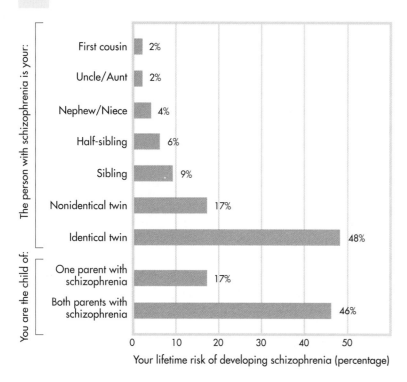

The person with schizophrenia is your:
- First cousin 2%
- Uncle/Aunt 2%
- Nephew/Niece 4%
- Half-sibling 6%
- Sibling 9%
- Nonidentical twin 17%
- Identical twin 48%

You are the child of:
- One parent with schizophrenia 17%
- Both parents with schizophrenia 46%

Your lifetime risk of developing schizophrenia (percentage)

FIGURE 14.6 The Risk of Developing Schizophrenia Among Blood Relatives
The risk percentages shown here reflect the collective results of about 40 studies investigating the likelihood of developing schizophrenia among blood relatives. As you can see, the greatest risk occurs if you have an identical twin who has schizophrenia (48 percent lifetime risk) or if both of your biological parents have schizophrenia (46 percent lifetime risk). However, genetics is just one of a number of factors involved in the development of schizophrenia.

SOURCE: Gottesman (1991), p. 96.

certain families (Kendler & Diehl, 1993; Prescott & Gottesman, 1993). Second, family and twin studies have consistently shown that the more closely related a person is to someone who has schizophrenia, the greater the risk that she will be diagnosed with schizophrenia at some point in her lifetime (see Figure 14.6). Third, adoption studies have consistently shown that if either *biological* parent of an adopted individual had schizophrenia, the adopted individual is at greater risk to develop schizophrenia (Tienari & others, 1994).

Ironically, the strongest evidence that points to genetic involvement in schizophrenia—the almost 50 percent risk rate for a person whose identical twin has schizophrenia—is the same evidence that underscores the importance of environmental factors (Torrey, 1992). If schizophrenia were purely a matter of inherited maladaptive genes, then you would expect a risk rate much closer to 100 percent for monozygotic twins. Obviously, nongenetic factors must play a role in explaining why half of identical twins with a schizophrenic twin do *not* develop schizophrenia.

Paternal Age: Older Fathers and the Risk of Schizophrenia

Despite the fact the family and twin studies point to the role of genetic factors in the risk of developing schizophrenia, no genetic model thus far explains all of the patterns of schizophrenia occurrence within families (Kendler & Diehl, 1993). Adding to the perplexity is the fact that schizophrenia often occurs in individuals with *no* family history of mental disorders.

One explanation for these anomalies is that for each generation, new cases of schizophrenia arise from genetic mutations carried in the sperm of the biological fathers, especially older fathers. As men age, their sperm cells continue to reproduce by dividing. By the time a male is 20, his sperm cells have undergone about 200 divisions; by the time he is 40, about 660 divisions. As the number of divisions increases over time, the sperm cells accumulate genetic mutations that can then be passed on to that man's offspring. Hence, the theory goes, as paternal age increases, the risk of offspring developing schizophrenia also increases.

Researcher Dolores Malaspina and her colleagues (2001) explored this notion by reviewing data on more than 87,000 people born in Jerusalem from 1964 to 1976. Of this group, 658 people had been diagnosed with schizophrenia by 1998. After controlling for various risk factors, the researchers found that paternal age was a strong and significant predictor of the schizophrenia diagnoses. Specifically, Malaspina and her colleagues (2001) found that:

- Men in the 45-to-49 age group who fathered children were twice as likely to have offspring with schizophrenia as compared to fathers age 25 and under.
- Men in the 50+ age range were three times more likely to produce offspring with schizophrenia.
- More than one-quarter of the schizophrenia cases could be attributed to the father's age.
- The mother's age appeared to play *no* role in the development of schizophrenia.

Clearly then, paternal age is a potential risk factor. But although this study points to a higher risk of older fathers producing offspring with schizophrenia, it's important to keep in mind that older paternal age failed to account for three-quarters of the cases of schizophrenia in this study.

Environmental Factors: The Viral Infection Theory

One provocative theory is that schizophrenia might be caused by exposure to an influenza virus or other viral infection during prenatal development or shortly after birth. A virus might seem an unlikely cause of a serious mental disorder, but viruses *can* spread to the brain and spinal cord by traveling along nerves. According to this theory, exposure to a viral infection during prenatal development or early infancy affects the developing brain, producing changes that make the individual more vulnerable to schizophrenia later in life.

There is growing evidence to support the viral infection theory. First, children whose mothers were exposed to a flu virus during the second trimester of pregnancy do show an increased rate of schizophrenia (A. Brown & others, 2000; Huttunen & others, 1994; Venables, 1996). Second, schizophrenia occurs more often in people who were born in the winter and spring months, when upper respiratory infections are most common (Torrey & others, 1993).

For example, Danish researcher Preben Mortensen and his colleagues (1999) used Denmark's national registration system to track the lives and mental health of almost 2 million people over six decades. Like the twin and family research discussed earlier, they found an increased risk for schizophrenia in people who had a mother, father, or sibling with schizophrenia. However, they also found that the risk of schizophrenia was associated with season of birth and place of birth.

More specifically, Mortensen found that the risk of schizophrenia was highest for (1) people living in urban areas and (2) people born during February and March. The lowest risk of schizophrenia was associated with rural areas and being born during August and September. As prominent schizophrenia researcher E. Fuller Torrey (1999) commented, "I think the important finding from this study is that genes are important, but environmental factors are at least as important. And, we probably haven't paid enough attention to them."

Although such findings represent promising leads, it is important to stress again that such evidence is correlational. And some researchers have not found such correlations (Takei & others, 1994).

Abnormal Brain Structures: Loss of Gray Matter

Researchers have found that about half of the people with schizophrenia show some type of brain structure abnormality (Cannon & Marco, 1994). The most consistent finding has been the enlargement of the fluid-filled cavities, called *ventricles,* located deep within the brain (Buckley, 1998). However, researchers aren't certain how enlarged ventricles might be related to schizophrenia. Another difference that has been found is a loss of gray matter tissue (Paillère-Martinot & others, 2001). As we discussed in Chapter 2 (see pp. 71–72), *gray matter* refers to the glial cells, neuron cell bodies, and unmyelinated axons that comprise the quarter-inch-thick cerebral cortex.

To investigate the neurological development of schizophrenia, neuroscientist Paul M. Thompson and his colleagues (2001) undertook a prospective study of brain structure changes in twelve adolescents with early-onset childhood schizophrenia. The six females and six males had all experienced schizophrenic symptoms, including psychotic symptoms, before the age of twelve. The intent of the study was to provide a visual picture of the timing, rates, and anatomical distribution of brain structure changes in adolescents with schizophrenia.

Each of the twelve adolescents was scanned repeatedly with high-resolution MRIs over a five-year period, beginning when the teenagers were about 14. The adolescents were carefully matched with healthy teens of the same gender, age,

Identical Twins but Not Identical Brains
David and Steven Elmore are identical twins, but they differ in one important respect—Steven (*right*) has schizophrenia. Behind each is a CAT scan, which reveals that Steven's brain is slightly smaller, with less area devoted to the cortex at the top of the brain. Steven also has larger fluid-filled ventricles, which are circled in red on his brain scan. As researcher Daniel Weinberger (1995) commented, "The part of the cortex that Steven is missing serves as perhaps the most evolved part of the human brain. It performs complicated tasks such as thinking organized thoughts. This might help explain why paranoid delusions and hallucinations are characteristic of schizophrenia."

focus on **Neuroscience**

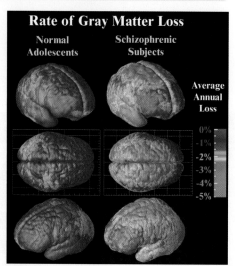

Rate of Gray Matter Loss

Normal Adolescents	Schizophrenic Subjects

Average Annual Loss

0%
-1%
-2%
-3%
-4%
-5%

Schizophrenia: A Wildfire in the Brain In a five-year prospective study, neuroscientist Paul Thompson and his colleagues (2001) used high-resolution brain scans to map brain structure changes in normal adolescents and adolescents with early onset schizophrenia. Thompson found marked differences be-

tween the brain development in normal teens and teens with schizophrenia. As expected, the healthy teenagers showed a gradual, small loss of gray matter—about 1 percent—over the five-year study. This loss is due to the normal pruning of unused brain connections that takes place during adolescence (see page 388, "Brain Changes During Childhood: Pruning Synaptic Connections").

But in sharp contrast to the normal teens, the teenagers with schizophrenia showed a severe loss of gray matter that developed in a specific, wave-like pattern. The loss began in the parietal lobes and, over the five years of the study, progressively spread forward to the temporal and frontal regions. As Thompson (2001) noted, "We were stunned to see a spreading wave of tissue loss that began in a small region of the brain. It moved across the brain like a forest fire, destroying more tissue as the disease progressed."

The brain images show the average rates of gray matter losses over the five-year period. Gray matter tissue loss ranged from about 1 percent (blue) in the normal teens to

more than 5 percent (pink) in the schizophrenic teens. One fascinating finding was that the amount of gray matter loss was directly correlated to the teenage patients' clinical symptoms. Psychotic symptoms increased the most in the participants who lost the greatest quantity of gray matter tissue.

Also, the *pattern* of loss mirrored the progression of neurological and cognitive deficits associated with schizophrenia. For example, more rapid gray matter losses in the *temporal lobes* were associated with more severe *positive* symptoms, such as hallucinations and delusions. More rapid loss of gray matter in the *frontal lobes* was strongly correlated with the severity of *negative* symptoms, including flat affect and poverty of speech. When the participants were 18 to 19 years old and the final brain scans were taken, the patterns of gray matter loss were similar to those found in the brains of adult patients with schizophrenia.

Despite the wealth of information generated by Thompson's study, the critical question remains unanswered: What sparks the cerebral forest fire in the schizophrenic brain?

socioeconomic background, and height. The findings of this important study are featured in the Focus on Neuroscience, Schizophrenia: A Wildfire in the Brain.

Although there is evidence that brain abnormalities are found in schizophrenia, such findings do not prove that brain abnormalities are the sole cause of schizophrenia. First, some people with schizophrenia do *not* show brain structure abnormalities. Second, the evidence is correlational. Researchers are still investigating whether differences in brain structures and activity are the cause or the consequence of schizophrenia. Third, the kinds of brain abnormalities seen in schizophrenia are also seen in other mental disorders. Rather than specifically causing schizophrenia, it's quite possible that brain abnormalities might contribute to mental disorders in general.

Abnormal Brain Chemistry: The Dopamine Hypothesis

According to the **dopamine hypothesis,** schizophrenia is related to excess activity of the neurotransmitter dopamine in the brain (Davis & others, 1991). Two pieces of indirect evidence support this notion. First, antipsychotic drugs, such as Haldol, Thorazine, and Stelazine, *reduce or block dopamine activity in the brain.* These drugs reduce schizophrenic symptoms in many people. Second, drugs that enhance dopamine activity in the brain, such as amphetamines and cocaine, can produce schizophrenia-like symptoms in normal adults or increase symptoms in people who already have schizophrenia (Syvälahti, 1994).

Although the dopamine hypothesis is compelling, there are inconsistencies. Not all individuals who have schizophrenia experience a reduction of symptoms in response to the antipsychotic drugs that reduce dopamine activity in the brain. And for many patients, these drugs reduce some but not all schizophrenic symptoms (Heinrichs, 1993). So although it seems likely that dopamine is somehow involved in schizophrenia, its exact role is far from clear.

dopamine hypothesis
The view that schizophrenia is related to, and may be caused by, excess activity of the neurotransmitter dopamine in the brain.

Psychological Factors: Unhealthy Families

Researchers have investigated such factors as dysfunctional parenting, disturbed family communication styles, and critical or guilt-inducing parental styles as possible contributors to schizophrenia (J. Johnson & others, 2001; Miklowitz, 1994). However, no single psychological factor seems to emerge consistently as causing schizophrenia. Rather, it seems that those who are genetically predisposed to develop schizophrenia may be more vulnerable to the effects of disturbed family environments (Fowles, 1992).

Strong support for this view comes from a landmark study conducted by Finnish psychiatrist Pekka Tienari and his colleagues (1987, 1994). In the Finnish Adoptive Family Study of Schizophrenia, researchers followed about 150 adopted individuals whose biological mothers had schizophrenia. As part of their study, the researchers assessed the adoptive family's degree of psychological adjustment, including the mental health of the adoptive parents. The study also included a control group of about 180 adopted individuals whose biological mothers were *not* schizophrenic.

Tienari and his colleagues (1994) found that adopted children with a schizophrenic biological mother had a much higher rate of schizophrenia than did the children in the control group. However, this was true *only* when the children were raised in a psychologically disturbed adoptive home. As you can see in Figure 14.7, when children with a genetic background of schizophrenia were raised in a psychologically healthy adoptive family, they were *no more likely* than the control-group children to develop schizophrenia.

Although adopted children with no genetic history of schizophrenia were less vulnerable to the psychological stresses of a disturbed family environment, they were by no means completely immune to such influences. As Figure 14.7 shows, one-third of the control-group adoptees developed symptoms of a serious psychological disorder if they were raised in a disturbed family environment.

Tienari's study underscores the complex interaction of genetic and environmental factors. Clearly, children who were genetically at risk to develop schizophrenia benefited from being raised in a healthy psychological environment. Put simply, a healthy psychological environment may counteract a person's inherited vulnerability for schizophrenia. Conversely, a psychologically unhealthy family environment can act as a catalyst for the onset of schizophrenia, especially for those individuals with a genetic history of schizophrenia.

After more than a century of intensive research, schizophrenia remains a baffling disorder. Thus far no single biological, psychological, or social factor has emerged as the causal agent in schizophrenia (Keefe & Harvey, 1994). Nevertheless, researchers are expressing greater confidence that the pieces of the schizophrenia puzzle are beginning to form a more coherent picture.

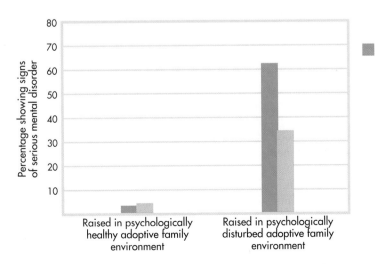

FIGURE 14.7 The Finnish Adoptive Family Study of Schizophrenia In the Finnish Adoptive Family Study, researchers are following two groups of adopted individuals: one group with biological mothers who had schizophrenia and a control group whose biological mothers did not have schizophrenia. This graph shows the strong influence of the adoptive family environment on the development of serious mental disorders.

Even if the exact causes of schizophrenia remain elusive, there is still reason for optimism. In the last few years, new antipsychotic drugs have been developed that are much more effective in treating both the positive and negative symptoms of schizophrenia. In the next chapter, we'll take a detailed look at the different treatments and therapies for schizophrenia and other psychological disorders.

14.3 R·E·V·I·E·W

C·O·N·C·E·P·T

Personality Disorders, Dissociative Disorders, and Schizophrenia

Match each example below with one of the following: dissociative amnesia, dissociative fugue, dissociative identity disorder, paranoid personality disorder, antisocial personality disorder, borderline personality disorder, paranoid schizophrenia, catatonic schizophrenia, disorganized schizophrenia.

1. Jay, a high school physics teacher in New York City, disappeared three days after his wife unexpectedly left him. Six months later, he was discovered tending bar in Miami Beach. Calling himself Martin, he claimed to have no recollection of his past life. _____

2. Bob was fired from yet another job, this time for stealing and forging payroll checks. "They were so stupid at that place, they deserved to lose that money," he bragged to his girlfriend. _____

3. Norma has frequent memory gaps and cannot account for her whereabouts during certain periods of time. While being interviewed by a clinical psychologist, she began speaking in a childlike voice. She claimed that her name was Donna and that she was only six years old. Moments later, she seemed to revert to her adult voice and had no recollection of claiming that her name was Donna. _____

4. After getting the manager to let them into her apartment, Sylvia's parents found her standing motionless near a window and completely unresponsive to their presence. _____

5. Leslie seems charming and vivacious when you first meet her, but you soon discover that she is extremely moody, jealous, and possessive; terrified of being alone; and prone to self-destructive behaviors. _____

6. By the time the neighbors called the police, Dwight had barricaded all the doors and windows of his house because the voices had told him that aliens were coming to kidnap him. _____

Summing Up
Psychological Disorders

In this chapter, we've looked at the symptoms and causes of several psychological disorders. We've seen that some of the symptoms of psychological disorders represent a sharp break from normal experience. The behavior of the young woman in the Prologue was an example of the severely disrupted functioning characteristic of schizophrenia. In contrast, the symptoms of other psychological disorders, such as the mood disorders, differ from normal experience primarily in their degree, intensity, and duration.

Psychologists are only beginning to understand the causes of many psychological disorders. The broad picture that emerges reflects a familiar theme: Biological, psychological, and social factors all contribute to the development of psychological disorders. In the next chapter, we'll look at how psychological disorders are currently treated.

In the chapter Application, we'll explore one of the most serious consequences of psychological problems—suicide. Since people who are contemplating suicide often turn to their friends before they seek help from a mental health professional, we'll also suggest several ways in which you can help a friend who expresses suicidal intentions.

Understanding and Helping to Prevent Suicide

It was a warm October afternoon when Ann made her second attempt. This time she was more determined. She shut the garage door and then methodically sealed the base of the garage door with towels. She moved a reclining lawn chair to the spot where her husband Doug's car was normally parked. Calling Doug at work, she nonchalantly explained that she was going shopping but would be back in a few hours. From the bookcase in the living room, Ann took down her album of wedding photographs and the Bible that her grandmother had given her when she was a little girl. Rummaging through the medicine cabinet, she found the four remaining sleeping pills that her doctor had prescribed and swallowed them.

Ann went back into the garage, sealing the door behind her with more towels. Then she started her car, put it in neutral, and sat down in the lawn chair. She looked at her wedding pictures and began to cry. Setting her wedding album aside, she started reading aloud from her Bible. A short while later, Ann slipped into unconsciousness as the sleeping pills took effect and the garage filled with the car's exhaust fumes.

Who Commits Suicide?

Ann's story is dramatic, but unfortunately, suicide and attempted suicide is all too common. Each year in the United States, approximately 500,000 people require emergency room treatment as a result of attempted suicide (U.S. Public Health Service, 1999). Statistically, the number of people who actually commit suicide each year has decreased by over 10 percent in the last several years (Hoyert & others, 2001). Compared to 31,000 suicide deaths in 1996, there were about 28,000 suicides in 2000 (Minino & Smith, 2001).

Despite this downward trend, the number of people who commit suicide is still unacceptably high. Many people don't realize that almost twice as many Americans die each year from suicide than from homicide. In 2000, suicide was the 11th leading cause of death, while homicide ranked as 14th (Minino & Smith, 2001).

Women outnumber men by 3 to 1 in the number of suicide attempts. However, men outnumber women by better than 4 to 1 in suicide deaths, primarily because men tend to use more lethal methods, such as guns and hanging.

How to Help a Friend The majority of those who attempt suicide communicate their intentions to friends or family members (Shneidman, 1998). When a friend is despondent and desperate, you can help by listening, expressing your understanding and compassion, and, if necessary, referring him or her to a professional counselor or suicide prevention specialist.

Suicide is the third leading cause of death for young people aged 15 to 24. Over the last four decades, the suicide rate for adolescents and young adults has increased by almost 300 percent (U.S. Public Health Service, 1999). Although this trend has received considerable media attention, the suicide rate of adolescents and young adults is still below that of older adults. In fact, the highest suicide rate consistently occurs in the oldest segments of our population— among those age 75 and above (Hoyert & others, 2001).

On average, someone commits suicide in the United States every 18 minutes. It is estimated that each suicide affects the lives of at least six other people.

Donna Hoyert, 2001

What Risk Factors Are Associated with Suicidal Behavior?

Hundreds of studies have identified psychosocial and environmental factors that are associated with an increased risk of suicidal behavior (see Mann & others, 1999; Rosenberg, 1999; Sánchez, 2001).

Some of the factors that increase the risk of suicidal behavior include:

- Recent relationship problems or a lack of significant relationships
- Poor coping and problem-solving skills
- Poor impulse control and impaired judgment
- Rigid thinking or irrational beliefs
- A major psychological disorder, especially depression, bipolar disorder, or schizophrenia
- Alcohol or other substance abuse
- Childhood physical or sexual abuse
- Prior self-destructive behavior or a family history of suicide
- Presence of a firearm in the home

Why Do People Attempt or Commit Suicide?

Fleeting thoughts of suicide are not uncommon. But there is a vast difference between having such occasional thoughts and being genuinely intent on self-destruction. Why do people attempt or commit suicide? In general terms, the suicidal person's view of life has become progressively more pessimistic and negative. At the same time, his view of self-inflicted death as an alternative to life becomes progressively more acceptable and positive (Shneidman, 1998).

Some people choose suicide in order to escape the pain of a chronic illness or the slow, agonizing death of a terminal disease. Others commit suicide because of feelings of hopelessness, depression, guilt, rejection, failure, humiliation, or shame (Lester, 1997). The common denominator is that they see suicide as the only escape from their own unbearably painful emotions. Ann, for example, was deeply despondent over the fact that she had failed to live up to her own expectations of becoming a highly acclaimed, successful painter.

When faced with a dilemma, the average person tends to see a range of possible solutions, accepting the fact that none of the solutions may be ideal. In contrast, the suicidal person's thinking and perceptions have become rigid and constricted. She can see only two ways to solve her problems: a magical resolution or suicide. Because she cannot imagine a realistic way of solving her problems, death seems to be the only logical option (Shneidman, 1998).

How Can You Help Prevent Suicide?

If someone is truly intent on taking his or her own life, it may be impossible to prevent them from doing so. But that does not mean that you can't try to help a friend who is expressing suicidal intentions. People often turn to their friends rather than to mental health professionals. If a friend confides that he or she is feeling hopeless and suicidal, these guidelines may help you help your friend.

It's important to stress, however, that these guidelines are meant only to help you provide "psychological first aid" in a crisis situation. They do *not* qualify you as a suicide prevention expert. Your goal is to help your friend weather the immediate crisis so that he or she can be directed to a mental health professional.

Guideline 1: Actively listen as the person talks and vents her feelings.

The suicidal person often feels isolated or lonely, with few sources of social support. Let the person talk, and try to genuinely empathize with your friend's feelings. An understanding friend who is willing to take the time to listen patiently without passing judgment may provide just the support the person needs to overcome the suicidal feelings. Hearing themselves talk can also help suicidal individuals identify and better understand their own feelings.

Guideline 2: Don't deny or minimize the person's suicidal intentions.

Brushing aside suicidal statements with platitudes like "Don't be silly, you've got everything to live for," or clichés, like "Every cloud has a silver lining," is not a helpful response. This is *not* the time to be glib, patronizing, or superficial. Instead, ask your friend if she wants to talk about her feelings. Try to be matter-of-fact and confirm that she is indeed seriously suicidal, rather than simply exaggerating her frustration or disappointment.

How can you confirm that the person is suicidal? Simply ask her, "Are you really thinking about killing yourself?" Talking about specific suicide plans (how,

when, and where), giving away valued possessions, and putting her affairs in order are some indications that a person's suicidal intentions are serious.

Guideline 3: Identify other potential solutions.

The suicidal person is operating with psychological blinders that prevent him from seeing alternative courses of action or other ways of looking at his problems. How can you remove those blinders? Simply saying, "Here are some options you may not have thought about," is a good starting point. You might list alternative solutions to the person's problems, helping him to understand that other potential solutions do exist, even though none may be perfect (Shneidman, 1998).

So ubiquitous is the impulse to commit suicide that one out of every two Americans has at some time considered, threatened, or actually attempted suicide.

David Lester, 1997

Guideline 4: Ask the person to delay his decision.

Most suicidal people are ambivalent about wanting to die. If your friend did not have mixed feelings about committing suicide, he probably wouldn't be talking to you. If he is still intent on suicide after talking about other alternatives, ask him to *delay* his decision. Even a few days' delay may give the person enough time to psychologically regroup, consider alternatives, or seek help.

Guideline 5: Encourage the person to seek professional help.

If the person is seriously suicidal and may harm herself in the near future, do *not* leave her alone. The most important thing you can do is help to get the person referred to a mental health professional for evaluation and treatment. If you don't feel you can do this alone, find another person to help you.

There are any number of resources you can suggest, including local suicide

hot lines or mental health associations, the college counseling service, and the person's family doctor or religious adviser. You can also suggest calling 1-800-SUICIDE (1-800-784-2433), which will connect you with a crisis center in your area.

Some Final Thoughts

Even if you follow all of these guidelines, there's no guarantee that the person won't attempt or commit suicide. Ann's case illustrates this point. Ann first tried to kill herself with an overdose of sleeping pills, but she was discovered and rushed to a hospital emergency room. Ann went into therapy three times a week with a clinical psychologist. Eventually, it appeared that Ann was regaining her psychological equilibrium.

Nevertheless, a few months later, Ann made the second, much more serious suicide attempt that we described at the beginning of this Application. By all accounts, Ann should have died in the garage on that October afternoon. But she didn't die. Instead, after about 90 minutes, Ann regained consciousness, the garage air thick with the exhaust from her running car. Extremely nauseous and dizzy, her head pounding with excruciating pain, Ann struggled to her feet and opened the garage door. To this day, Ann maintains that angels woke her up and pulled her out of the garage.

After her second suicide attempt, Ann was hospitalized at a psychiatric facility, where she stayed for a month. That was over four years ago. The world looks much different to Ann today. She eventually earned a business degree and now works full time as a hospital administrator.

Ann continues to see her psychologist at least once a month, sometimes more often. "I've got to work at keeping myself mentally healthy," she will tell you without apology or embarrassment. And, most important, Ann has resumed painting her glorious watercolors of flowers and nature scenes. "I may never be famous," she says, smiling, with only a hint of disappointment in her expression, "but at least I'm still here to enjoy painting."

Chapter Review Psychological Disorders

Key Points

Introduction: Understanding Psychological Disorders

- Distinguishing "normal" from "abnormal" behavior involves consideration of many different factors, including cultural norms. **Psychopathology** refers to the scientific study of the origins, symptoms, and development of psychological disorders.

- A **psychological disorder,** or **mental disorder,** is a pattern of behavioral or psychological symptoms that causes significant personal distress and/or impairs the ability to function. The diagnostic criteria for specific psychological disorders are described in **DSM-IV-TR.**

- The prevalence of psychological disorders is much higher than had previously been thought. According to one comprehensive survey, approximately one in two Americans will experience a psychological disorder at some point in their lifetime, and approximately one in three Americans has experienced the symptoms of a psychological disorder in the previous year.

Anxiety Disorders: *Intense Apprehension and Worry*

- In contrast to normal **anxiety, anxiety disorders** consist of irrational and uncontrollable feelings that are unreasonably intense, frequent, persistent, and disruptive.

- **Generalized anxiety disorder (GAD)** and **panic disorder** are characterized by intense anxiety that is not triggered by a specific stimulus. Generalized anxiety disorder involves a constant, persistent state of anxiety. Panic disorder involves sudden episodes of extreme, intense anxiety, which are called **panic attacks.**

- The **phobias** involve intense, irrational fear and avoidance of the feared object or situation. Important forms of phobias include **specific phobia, social phobia (social anxiety disorder),** and **agoraphobia,** which is fear of having a **panic attack** in a public or inescapable situation. Learning theories and evolved biological predispositions have been offered as explanations of the development of phobias.

- **Posttraumatic stress disorder (PTSD)** develops in response to an extreme psychological or physical trauma. Symptoms include frequent intrusive memories of the trauma, avoidance, emotional numbness, and increased physical arousal.

- **Obsessive–compulsive disorder** is an anxiety disorder in which a person's life is dominated by repetitive thoughts **(obsessions)** and actions **(compulsions).** Biological factors that have been implicated in obsessive–compulsive disorder include serotonin deficiency and brain dysfunction.

Mood Disorders: *Emotions Gone Awry*

- **Mood disorders** involve serious, persistent disturbances in emotions that cause psychological discomfort and/or impair the ability to function.

- The symptoms of **major depression** include negative emotions, extreme pessimism, thoughts of suicide, cognitive impairment, lack of motivation, and sleep disruption for a period of two weeks or longer. **Dysthymic disorder** is a milder but chronic form of depression.

- Major depression is the most common psychological disorder. Left untreated, depression may recur and become progressively more severe. **Seasonal affective disorder (SAD)** generally occurs with the onset of the fall and winter months, and is associated with lesser amounts of sunlight.

- **Bipolar disorder** usually involves periods of depression alternating with **manic episodes.** A milder form of bipolar disorder is **cyclothymic disorder.** Bipolar disorder is less common than major depression.

- Genetics, brain chemistry, and stress have all been implicated in mood disorders. The neurotransmitters serotonin and norepinephrine have been implicated in depression. Another neurotransmitter, glutamate, may be involved in bipolar disorder.

Personality Disorders: *Maladaptive Traits*

- **Personality disorders** are characterized by inflexible, maladaptive patterns of thoughts, emotions, behavior, and interpersonal functioning. These traits are stable over time and across situations, and deviate from the social and behavioral expectations of the individual's culture.

- Personality disorders are grouped according to three clusters. Paranoid, schizoid, and schizotypal personality disorders represent the odd, eccentric cluster. The dramatic, emotional, or erratic cluster consists of antisocial, borderline, histrionic, and narcissistic personality disorders. The anxious, fearful cluster is composed of avoidant, dependent, and obsessive–compulsive personality disorders.

- **Paranoid personality disorder** is characterized by a pervasive distrust and suspiciousness of the motives of others. Others are perceived as trying to exploit or deceive the person. Inappropriate outbursts of anger, blaming others for their own inadequacies, and pathological jealousy are common features of this disorder.

- **Antisocial personality disorder** is characterized by a pervasive pattern of disregarding and violating the rights of others. People with this personality disorder habitually deceive and manipulate others for their own gain. A history of substance abuse, arrests, and other irresponsible behaviors are common. Multiple factors seem to be involved in the development of antisocial personality disorder.

- **Borderline personality disorder** is characterized by instability of interpersonal relationships, self-image, and emotions. Mood swings, impulsive actions, self-destructive tendencies, and substance abuse are common features. Factors that seem to contribute to the development of this disorder include parental neglect or abuse during childhood.

The Dissociative Disorders: *Fragmentation of the Self*

■ **Dissociative experiences** involve a disruption in awareness, memory, and personal identity. In the **dissociative disorders,** however, dissociative experiences are extreme, frequent, and disruptive.

■ **Dissociative amnesia** refers to the inability to recall important information that is not due to a medical condition and cannot be explained by ordinary forgetfulness. **Dissociative fugue** involves amnesia and sudden, unexplained travel away from home.

■ **Dissociative identity disorder (DID)** involves memory gaps and the presence of two or more distinct identities. Some psychologists are skeptical of dissociative identity disorder. According to one theory, DID is caused by trauma in childhood and represents an extreme form of coping through dissociation.

Schizophrenia: *A Different Reality*

■ **Schizophrenia** is a psychological disorder that involves severely distorted beliefs, perceptions, and thought processes.

■ The **positive symptoms** of schizophrenia represent excesses in normal functioning. They include **delusions, hallucinations,** and severely disorganized thought processes,

speech, and behavior. **Negative symptoms** reflect deficits or decreases in normal functioning. They include flat affect, alogia, and avolition.

■ Three subtypes of schizophrenia are the paranoid type, the catatonic type, and the disorganized type, each of which is distinguished by a particular combination of symptoms. When symptoms do not match any of these three subtypes, the diagnosis of undifferentiated type is made.

■ The course of schizophrenia is highly variable. Schizophrenia becomes chronic in about one-half of the people who experience a schizophrenic episode. About one-quarter recover completely, and about one-quarter experience recurrent episodes but are able to function with minimal impairment.

■ Family, twin, and adoption studies have shown that genetics contributes to the development of schizophrenia. However, studies of identical twins demonstrate that nongenetic factors play at least an equal role in the development of schizophrenia. The risk of schizophrenia is higher in the offspring of older fathers.

■ Excess dopamine—the **dopamine hypothesis**—and abnormalities in brain structure and function have been identified as factors associated with schizophrenia.

■ Environmental factors that may be involved in schizophrenia include exposure to a virus during prenatal development and a psychologically unhealthy family environment. Adopted children who were genetically at risk to develop schizophrenia were found to be less likely to develop the disorder when raised in a psychologically healthy family.

Key Terms

Concept Review Answers

14.1   page 586

1. posttraumatic stress disorder
2. generalized anxiety disorder
3. panic disorder
4. specific phobia
5. obsessive–compulsive disorder
6. social phobia

14.2   page 594

1. d   2. b   3. a   4. a   5. c

14.3   page 612

1. dissociative fugue
2. antisocial personality disorder
3. dissociative identity disorder
4. catatonic schizophrenia
5. borderline personality disorder
6. paranoid schizophrenia

Web Companion   Review Activities

You can find additional review activities at **www.worthpublishers.com/hockenbury**
The Psychology 3e Web Companion has a self-scoring practice quiz, flashcards, two interactive crossword puzzles, and other activities to help you master the material in this chapter.

Training Ground

Therapies

Prologue

"A Clear Sense of Being Heard . . ."

How would we describe Marcia? She's an extraordinarily kind, intelligent woman. Her thoughtfulness and sensitivity are tempered by a ready laugh and a good sense of humor. She's happily married, has a good job as a feature writer for a large suburban newspaper, and has two young children, who only occasionally drive her crazy. If Marcia has a flaw, it's that she tends to judge herself much too harshly. She's too quick to blame herself when anything goes wrong.

Juggling a full-time career, marriage, and parenting is a challenge for anyone, but Marcia always makes it look easy. The last time we had dinner at Bill and Marcia's home, the meal featured home-grown vegetables, made-from-scratch bread, and fresh seasonings from the herb pots in the kitchen. Outwardly, Marcia appears to have it all. But a few years ago, she began to experience a pervasive sense of dread and unease—feelings that gradually escalated into a full-scale depression. Marcia describes the onset of her feelings in this way:

> Physically I began to feel as if I were fraying around the edges. I had a constant sense of anxiety and a recurring sense of being a failure. My daughter, Maggie, was going through a rather difficult stage. Andy was still a baby. I felt worn out. I started worrying constantly about my children. Are they safe? Are they sick? What's going to happen? Are my kids going to get hurt? I knew that I really didn't have any reason to worry that much, but I did. It finally struck me that my worrying and my anxiety and my feelings of being a failure were not going to go away on their own.

Marcia decided to seek help. She made an appointment with her therapist, a psychiatrist whom Marcia had last seen 10 years earlier, when she had helped Marcia cope with a very difficult time in her life. In some ways, Marcia's experience with her therapist this time was very different from her sessions of 10 years ago, but some aspects of their relationship remained the same. As Marcia explains:

> Since I have seen the same therapist at different times in my life, I can say that her approach has changed a great deal since I first worked with her. She was originally very classically psychoanalytic, saying little, and listening impassively. She concentrated on looking at historic family relationships as the origin of problems in the present.

In the past two years, we have tried quite different techniques: short-term, solution-oriented therapy and a 12-step approach. At her suggestion,

I joined a 12-step support group called Emotions Anonymous, and I now attend a group meeting once a week. My therapist has also "prescribed" books for me that use the 12-step framework. Until we moved to the 12-step framework, I never had a very clear sense of a progression in therapy. I always felt better after a session, but it would not last very long. I now feel more engaged in a process that has a course to run and that will, I hope, give me coping skills and some needed sense of perspective or ability to detach from a given issue or problem.

How has therapy helped me? My feelings before a therapy session may vary greatly, depending on the issue under discussion. However, I always find the sessions cathartic and I invariably feel great relief. I feel a sense of being understood by someone who knows me but who is detached from me. I have a clear sense of being heard, as though my therapist has given me a gift of listening and of allowing me to see myself as the worthwhile and capable person I am. It is as though therapy allows me to see more clearly into a mirror that my problems have obscured.

Over the course of several months, Marcia made progressive gains. Today, Marcia is calmer, more confident, and feels much more in control of her emotions and her life. As Marcia's mental health improved, so did her relationships with her children and her husband.

Psychotherapy has also helped me communicate more clearly. It has enabled me to become more resilient after some emotional conflict. It has had a preventive effect in helping me to ignore or manage situations that might under certain circumstances trigger depression, anxiety, or obsessive worry. And it makes me a better parent and marriage partner.

Therapy's negative effects? I'm poorer; it costs money. And therapy poses the risk of becoming an end in itself. Psychotherapy has the attraction of being a safe harbor from the petty assaults of everyday life. There's always the danger of losing sight of the goal of becoming a healthier and more productive person, and becoming stuck in the therapy process.

Marcia's experience with psychotherapy reflects many of the themes we will touch on in this chapter. We'll look at different forms of therapy that psychologists and other mental health professionals use to help people cope with psychological problems. We'll also consider the growing popularity of self-help groups and how they differ from more structured forms of therapy. Toward the end of the chapter, we'll discuss biomedical approaches to the treatment of psychological disorders. Over the course of the chapter, we'll come back to Marcia's story.

Introduction
Psychotherapy and Biomedical Therapy

Key Theme
- Two forms of therapy are used to treat psychological disorders and personal problems—psychotherapy and the biomedical therapies.

Key Questions
- What is psychotherapy, and what is its basic assumption?
- What is biomedical therapy, and how does it differ from psychotherapy?

People seek help from mental health professionals for a variety of reasons. In Marcia's case, feelings of anxiety and depression were beginning to dominate her life. Although she could still function at work and at home, Marcia found it increasingly difficult to deal with the ordinary tasks of daily life. The intensity of her anxious and depressed feelings finally got to the point where Marcia knew she needed professional help—help that well-meaning friends and family could not provide.

Like Marcia, many people seek help because they are suffering from some form of a *psychological disorder*—troubling thoughts, feelings, or behaviors that cause psychological discomfort or interfere with a person's ability to function. As we saw in Chapter 14, psychological disorders are much more prevalent than most people realize. In any given year, approximately one in three adults experiences the symptoms of a psychological disorder (Kessler & others, 1994).

Seeking Help People enter psychotherapy for many different reasons. Some people seek to overcome severe psychological disorders, while others want to learn how to cope better with everyday challenges or relationship problems. And, for some people, the goal of therapy is to attain greater self-knowledge or personal fulfillment.

Not everyone who seeks professional help is suffering from a psychological disorder. Many people seek help in dealing with troubled relationships, such as an unhappy marriage or parent–child conflicts. And sometimes people need help with life's transitions, such as coping with the death of a loved one, dissolving a marriage, or adjusting to retirement.

In this chapter, we'll look at the two broad forms of therapy that mental health professionals use to help people: *psychotherapy* and *biomedical therapy*. **Psychotherapy** refers to the use of psychological techniques to treat emotional, behavioral, and interpersonal problems. While there are hundreds of different types of psychotherapy, they all share the assumption that psychological factors play a significant role in a person's troubling feelings, behaviors, or relationships.

In contrast to psychotherapy, the **biomedical therapies** involve the use of medication or other medical treatments to treat the symptoms associated with psychological disorders. The biomedical therapies are based on the assumption that the symptoms of many psychological disorders involve biological factors, such as abnormal brain chemistry. As we saw in Chapter 14, the involvement of biological factors in many psychological disorders is well documented. Treating psychological disorders with a combination of psychotherapy and biomedical therapy, especially drug therapy, has become increasingly common (Keller & others, 2000; Kopta & others, 1999).

Currently, only licensed physicians, such as psychiatrists, are legally allowed to prescribe the different forms of biomedical therapy. However, that tradition may be changing (Foxhall, 2001a, 2001b). In recent years, field trials have been conducted in which specially trained clinical psychologists were allowed to prescribe medications to treat psychological disorders. In order to acquire prescription privileges, clinical psychologists would be required to undergo additional training (Ax & Resnick, 2001). Eventually, clinical psychologists may be able to prescribe the same medications that psychiatrists use to treat psychological disorders. Some psychologists, however, oppose the idea of extending prescription privileges to qualified psychologists (DeNelsky, 1996). They argue that clinical psychologists should focus on what they do best: providing psychological interventions and treatments that help people acquire more effective thinking and behavior patterns.

Table 15.1 summarizes the diverse range of mental health professionals who use psychotherapy techniques to help people. Although psychotherapy is usually conducted in a one-to-one relationship between the therapist and the person seeking help, it can also be conducted with groups of people, families, or couples.

psychotherapy
The treatment of emotional, behavioral, and interpersonal problems through the use of psychological techniques designed to encourage understanding of problems and modify troubling feelings, behaviors, or relationships.

biomedical therapies
The use of medications, electroconvulsive therapy, or other medical treatments to treat the symptoms associated with psychological disorders.

Table | **15.1**

Who's Who Among Mental Health Professionals

Clinical psychologist	Holds an academic doctorate (Ph.D., Psy.D., or Ed.D) and is required to be licensed to practice. Has expertise in psychological testing, diagnosis, psychotherapy, research, and prevention of mental and emotional disorders. May work in private practice, hospitals, or community mental health centers.
Psychiatrist	Holds a medical degree (M.D. or D.O.) and is required to be licensed to practice. Has expertise in the diagnosis, treatment, and prevention of mental and emotional disorders. Often has training in psychotherapy. May prescribe medications, electroconvulsive therapy, or other medical procedures.
Psychoanalyst	Usually a psychiatrist or clinical psychologist who has received additional training in the specific techniques of psychoanalysis, the form of psychotherapy originated by Sigmund Freud.
Licensed professional counselor	Holds at least a master's degree in counseling, with extensive supervised training in assessment, counseling, and therapy techniques. May be certified in specialty areas. Most states require licensure or certification.
Psychiatric social worker	Holds a master's degree in social work (M.S.W.). Training includes an internship in a social service agency or mental health center. Most states require certification or licensing. May or may not have training in psychotherapy.
Marriage and family therapist	Usually holds a master's degree, with extensive supervised experience in couple or family therapy. May also have training in individual therapy. Many states require licensing.
Psychiatric nurse	Holds an R.N. degree and has selected psychiatry or mental health nursing as a specialty area. Typically works on a hospital psychiatric unit or in a community mental health center. May or may not have training in psychotherapy.

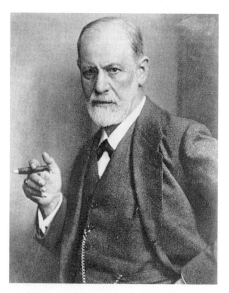

Sigmund Freud and Psychoanalytic Therapy At the beginning of the twentieth century, Sigmund Freud (1856–1939) developed an influential form of psychotherapy called psychoanalysis. Traditional psychoanalysis is not widely practiced today, partly because it is too lengthy and expensive. However, many of the techniques that Freud pioneered, such as free association, dream analysis, and transference, are still commonly used in different forms of psychotherapy.

We'll begin this chapter by surveying some of the most influential approaches in psychotherapy: psychoanalytic, humanistic, behavioral, and cognitive. As you'll see, each approach is based on different assumptions about the underlying causes of psychological problems. And each approach uses different strategies to produce beneficial changes in the way a person thinks, feels, and behaves—the ultimate goal of all forms of psychotherapy. After discussing the effectiveness of psychotherapy, we'll look at the most commonly used biomedical treatments for psychological disorders.

Psychoanalytic Therapy

Key Theme

■ Psychoanalysis is a form of therapy developed by Sigmund Freud and is based on his theory of personality.

Key Questions

■ What are the key assumptions and techniques of psychoanalytic therapy?
■ How do short-term dynamic therapies differ from psychoanalysis, and what is interpersonal therapy?

When cartoonists portray a psychotherapy session, they often draw a person lying on a couch and talking while a bearded gentleman sits behind the patient, passively listening. This stereotype reflects some of the key ingredients of traditional **psychoanalysis,** a form of psychotherapy originally developed by

Sigmund Freud in the early 1900s. Although psychoanalysis was developed a century ago, its assumptions and techniques continue to influence many psychotherapies today.

Sigmund Freud and Psychoanalysis

As a therapy, traditional psychoanalysis is closely tied to Freud's theory of personality. As you may recall from Chapter 11, on personality, Freud stressed that early childhood experiences provide the foundation for later personality development. When early experiences result in unresolved conflicts and frustrated urges, these emotionally charged memories are *repressed,* or pushed out of conscious awareness. Although unconscious, these repressed conflicts continue to influence a person's thoughts and behavior, including the dynamics of his relationships with others.

According to Freud, these conflicts festering in the unconscious are at the core of maladjusted behavior and psychological disorders. To achieve psychological health, Freud believed it is essential to move these conflicts from the unconscious to conscious awareness. Thus, psychoanalysis is designed to help unearth past conflicts so the patient attains *insight* as to the real source of her problems. Central to this process is the intense relationship that gradually forms between the psychoanalyst and the patient. In this relationship, long-standing psychological conflicts are recognized, reexperienced, and ideally, ultimately resolved.

How can unconscious conflicts be uncovered in psychoanalysis? Freud (1904) believed that unconscious material occasionally surfaces in disguised form. Glimpses of unconscious conflicts can be revealed in dreams, memory lapses, inadvertent slips of the tongue, and even in apparent "accidents," such as clumsily spilling coffee all over a colleague whom you secretly envy.

Freud also developed several techniques to coax a patient's unconscious conflicts to awareness. In the famous technique called **free association,** the patient lies on a couch and spontaneously reports all thoughts, mental images, and feelings as they come to mind. Usually the psychoanalyst sits out of view, occasionally asking questions and encouraging the patient to elaborate on his or her feelings.

Free association can reveal several clues about possible unconscious conflicts or repressed memories (Liff, 1992). Along with the general themes that keep resurfacing in the patient's free associations, the psychoanalyst notes the occasional inadvertent comment that seems puzzling or disconnected from other thoughts. Rather than being dismissed, such remarks are explored for their potential meaning.

Even more significant are blocks in free association, an abrupt change in topic, or sudden silences. Such instances may be signs of **resistance**—the patient's unconscious attempts to block the process of revealing repressed memories and conflicts. To the psychoanalyst, resistance is a signal that the patient is uncomfortably close to uncovering psychologically threatening material.

Another technique that Freud made famous is **dream interpretation** (see Chapters 4 and 11). He believed that because psychological defenses are reduced during sleep, frustrated desires, impulses, and motives are expressed symbolically in dreams. According to Freud (1933), we consciously remember the *manifest content,* or actual dream images. But beneath these surface images lies what Freud called the *latent content*—the true, hidden, and unconscious meaning of the dream that is disguised in dream symbols. We'll let Freud (1911) himself describe what he saw as the symbolic meaning of some common dream images:

> There are some symbols which bear a single meaning almost universally: thus the Emperor and Empress (or the King and Queen) stand for the parents, rooms represent women, and their entrances and exits the openings of the body. . . . Sharp weapons, long and stiff objects, such as tree-trunks and sticks, stand for the male genital; while cupboards, boxes, carriages, or ovens may represent the uterus. Symbols such as a staircase or going upstairs represent sexual intercourse. . . .

psychoanalysis
A type of psychotherapy originated by Sigmund Freud in which free association, dream interpretation, and analysis of resistance and transference are used to explore repressed or unconscious impulses, anxieties, and internal conflicts.

free association
A technique used in psychoanalysis in which the patient spontaneously reports all thoughts, feelings, and mental images as they come to mind, as a way of revealing unconscious thoughts and emotions.

resistance
In psychoanalysis, the patient's unconscious attempts to block the revelation of repressed memories and conflicts.

dream interpretation
A technique used in psychoanalysis in which the content of dreams is analyzed for disguised or symbolic wishes, meanings, and motivations.

We ask the dreamer as well to free himself from the impression of the manifest dream, to switch his attention from the dream as a whole to individual parts of its content, and tell us one after another the things that occur to him in connection with these parts, what associations come into his mind when he turns his mental eye on to each of them separately.

Sigmund Freud (1933)

The resistance accompanies the treatment step by step. Every single association, every act of the person under treatment must reckon with the resistance and represents a compromise between the forces that are striving towards recovery and opposing ones.

Sigmund Freud (1912)

Freud's Famous Couch During psychoanalytic sessions, Freud's patients would lie on the couch. Freud himself sat at the head of the couch, out of the patient's view. Freud believed that this arrangement encouraged the patient's free flow of thoughts, feelings, and images. Although some traditional psychoanalysts still have the patient lie on the couch, many psychoanalysts today favor comfortable chairs in which analyst and patient are facing one another.

interpretation
A technique used in psychoanalysis in which the psychoanalyst offers a carefully timed explanation of the patient's dreams, free associations, or behaviors to facilitate the recognition of unconscious conflicts or motivations.

transference
In psychoanalysis, the process by which emotions and desires originally associated with a significant person in the patient's life, such as a parent, are unconsciously transferred to the psychoanalyst.

In helping the patient process dreams and free associations, the psychoanalyst gently guides him toward areas of psychological conflict. The analyst asks questions, encourages the patient to elaborate on thoughts, and occasionally confronts him with patterns of resistance that have emerged. For example, the analyst might say, "Every time you talk about your father, you seem to hesitate and measure your words carefully. What do you think that might mean?"

More directly, the analyst sometimes makes carefully timed **interpretations,** explaining the possible meaning of dreams, free associations, instances of resistance, or the patient's reactions to the psychoanalyst. The timing of such interpretations is important. If an interpretation is offered before the patient is psychologically ready to confront an issue, she may reject the interpretation or respond defensively, increasing resistance (Henry & others, 1994).

One of the most important processes that occurs in the relationship between the patient and the psychoanalyst is called transference. As Freud (1940) explains, **transference** occurs when the patient unconsciously responds to the therapist as though the therapist were a significant person in the patient's life, often a parent:

> The patient sees in his analyst the return—the reincarnation—of some important figure out of his childhood or past, and consequently transfers on to him the feelings and reactions that undoubtedly applied to this model. . . . This transference comprises positive and affectionate as well as negative and hostile attitudes toward the analyst who, as a rule, is put in the place of one or other of the patient's parents, his father or mother.

The psychoanalyst encourages transference by purposely remaining as neutral as possible. In other words, the psychoanalyst does not reveal personal feelings, take sides, make judgments, or actively advise the patient. This therapeutic neutrality is designed to produce "optimal frustration" so that the patient transfers and projects unresolved conflicts onto the psychoanalyst (Eagle & Wolitzky, 1992).

As these transference feelings become more intense, the patient relives unconscious emotional conflicts that have been repressed since childhood. Only now, these conflicts are being relived and played out in the context of the relationship between the psychoanalyst and the patient. For example, the patient might transfer toward the analyst feelings of anger that he repressed in response to a harsh or rejecting parent. At the appropriate time, the analyst offers interpretations to help the patient perceive and understand the transference that is occurring.

All these psychoanalytic techniques are designed to help the patient see how past conflicts influence her current behavior and relationships, including her relationship with the psychoanalyst. Once these kinds of insights are achieved, the psychoanalyst helps the patient work through and resolve long-standing conflicts. As resolutions occur, maladaptive behavior patterns that were previously driven by unconscious conflicts can be replaced with more adaptive emotional and behavioral patterns.

The intensive relationship between the patient and the psychoanalyst takes time to develop. On average, the traditional psychoanalyst sees the patient four or five times a week over the course of four years or longer (Garfield & Bergin, 1994). Freud's patients were on the couch six days a week (Liff, 1992). Obviously, traditional psychoanalysis is a slow, expensive process that few people can afford. For those who have the time and the money, traditional psychoanalysis is still available.

Short-Term Dynamic Therapies

Today, few psychotherapists practice the traditional form of psychoanalysis that lasts for years. The simple fact is that most people entering psychotherapy are not seeking the kind of major personality overhaul that traditional psychoanalysis is designed to produce. Instead, people come to therapy expecting help with specific problems. People also expect therapy to provide beneficial changes in a matter of weeks or months, not years.

Today, there are many different forms of **short-term dynamic therapies** based on traditional psychoanalytic notions (Binder & others, 1995). These short-term dynamic therapies have several features in common (Koss & Shiang, 1994). Therapeutic contact lasts for no more than a few months. The patient's problems are quickly assessed at the beginning of therapy. The therapist and patient agree on specific, concrete, and attainable goals. In the actual sessions, most psychodynamic therapists are more directive than are traditional psychoanalysts, actively engaging the patient in a dialogue.

As in traditional psychoanalysis, the therapist uses interpretations to help the patient recognize hidden feelings and transferences that may be occurring in important relationships in her life (Liff, 1992). Therapy also focuses on helping the patient identify psychological resources that she can use to cope with the current difficulty as well as with future problems (Koss & Shiang, 1994).

One particularly influential short-term psychodynamic therapy is **interpersonal therapy,** abbreviated **IPT.** In contrast to other psychodynamic therapies, interpersonal therapy focuses on *current* relationships and social interactions rather than on past relationships. Originally developed as a brief treatment for depression, interpersonal therapy is based on the assumption that depressive symptoms are caused and maintained by interpersonal problems (Klerman & others, 1984; Weissman & others, 2000).

Interpersonal therapy may be brief or long-term, but it is highly structured (Klerman & Weissman, 1993). In the first phase of treatment, the therapist identifies the interpersonal problem that is causing difficulties in psychological functioning. In the interpersonal therapy model, there are four categories of personal problems: unresolved grief, role disputes, role transitions, and interpersonal deficits. *Unresolved grief* refers to problems dealing with the death of significant others, while *role disputes* refer to repetitive conflicts with significant others, such as the person's partner, family members, friends, or co-workers. *Role transitions* include problems involving major life changes, such as going away to college, becoming a parent, getting married or divorced, or retiring. *Interpersonal deficits* refer to absent or faulty social skills that limit the ability to start or maintain healthy relationships with others (Mallinckrodt, 2001). In the next phases of treatment, the therapist helps the person understand particular interpersonal problem and develop strategies to resolve it.

Although originally developed specifically to treat depression, IPT has also been applied to other psychological disorders, including eating disorders and substance abuse (see Markowitz, 1998). In addition, it is used to help people deal with interpersonal problems, such as marital conflict, parenting issues, and conflicts at work (Weissman & others, 2000; Whisman, 2001).

Were Sigmund Freud alive today, would he be upset by these departures from traditional psychoanalysis? Not at all. In fact, Freud himself treated some of his patients using short-term psychodynamic therapy that sometimes lasted for only one lengthy session. Several of Freud's patients completed psychoanalysis in as little as two months (Magnavita, 1993).

Even though traditional, lengthy psychoanalysis is uncommon today, Freud's basic assumptions and techniques continue to be influential. Although contemporary research has challenged some of Freud's original ideas, modern researchers are also studying the specific factors that seem to influence the effectiveness of basic Freudian techniques, such as interpretation, transference, and the role of insight in reducing psychological symptoms (Henry & others, 1994; Kivlighan & others, 2000). Without question, psychoanalysis has many critics (e.g., Eysenck, 1985, 1994; Macmillan, 2001). Nevertheless, the legacy of Freud's contributions to personality theory and psychotherapy is enormous.

short-term dynamic therapies
Type of psychotherapy that is based on psychoanalytic theory but differs in that it is typically time-limited, has specific goals, and involves an active, rather than neutral, role for the therapist.

interpersonal therapy (IPT)
A brief, psychodynamic psychotherapy that focuses on current relationships and is based on the assumption that symptoms are caused and maintained by interpersonal problems.

BIZARRO

client-centered therapy

A type of psychotherapy developed by humanistic psychologist Carl Rogers in which the therapist is nondirective and reflective, and the client directs the focus of each therapy session; also called *person-centered therapy*.

Humanistic Therapy

Key Theme

■ The most influential humanistic psychotherapy is client-centered therapy, which was developed by Carl Rogers.

Key Questions

■ What are the key assumptions of humanistic therapy, including client-centered therapy?

■ What therapeutic techniques and conditions are important in client-centered therapy?

■ How do client-centered therapy and psychoanalysis differ?

The *humanistic perspective* in psychology emphasizes human potential, self-awareness, and freedom of choice (see Chapter 11). Humanistic psychologists contend that the most important factor in personality is the individual's conscious, subjective perception of his or her self. They see people as being innately good and motivated by the need to grow psychologically. If people are raised in a genuinely accepting atmosphere and given freedom to make choices, they will develop healthy self-concepts and strive to fulfill their unique potential as human beings (Rice & Greenberg, 1992).

Carl Rogers and Client-Centered Therapy

The humanistic perspective has exerted a strong influence on psychotherapy (Cain, 2002; K. Schneider, 1998). Probably the most influential of the humanistic psychotherapies is **client-centered therapy,** also called *person-centered therapy*, developed by **Carl Rogers.** In naming his therapy, Rogers (1951) deliberately used the word *client* rather than *patient*. He believed that the medical term *patient* implied that people in therapy were "sick" and were seeking treatment from an all-knowing authority figure who could "heal" or "cure" them. Instead of stressing the therapist's expertise or perceptions of the patient, client-centered therapy emphasizes the *client's* subjective perception of himself and his environment (Zimring & Raskin, 1992).

Like Freud, Rogers saw the therapeutic relationship as the catalyst that leads to insight and lasting personality change. But Rogers viewed the nature of this relationship very differently from Freud. According to Rogers (1977), the therapist should not exert power by offering carefully timed "interpretations" of the patient's unconscious conflicts. Advocating just the opposite, Rogers believed that the therapist should be *nondirective*. That is, the therapist must not direct the client, make decisions for the client, offer solutions, or pass judgment on the client's thoughts or feelings. Instead, Rogers believed, change in therapy must be chosen and directed by the client (Bozarth & others, 2002). The therapist's role is to create the conditions that allow the client, not the therapist, to direct the focus of therapy.

What are the therapeutic conditions that promote self-awareness, psychological growth, and self-directed change? Rogers (1957c, 1980) believed that three qualities of the therapist are necessary: *genuineness, unconditional positive regard,* and *empathic understanding*. First, *genuineness* means that the therapist honestly and openly shares her thoughts and feelings with the client. By modeling genuineness, the therapist indirectly encourages the client to exercise this capability more fully in himself.

Second, the therapist must value, accept, and care for the client, whatever her problems or behavior. Rogers called this quality *unconditional positive regard*. Rogers believed that people develop psychological problems largely because they have

Carl Rogers (1902–1987) Shown on the far right, Rogers contended that human potential would flourish in an atmosphere of genuineness, unconditional positive regard, and empathic understanding. Rogers filmed many of his therapy sessions as part of a research program to identify the most helpful aspects of client-centered therapy.

consistently experienced only *conditional acceptance*. That is, parents, teachers, and others have communicated this message to the client: "I will accept you only *if* you conform to my expectations." Because acceptance by significant others has been conditional, the person has cut off or denied unacceptable aspects of herself and her experience. As a result, the person's self-concept and worldview become distorted. In turn, these distorted perceptions affect her thoughts and behaviors in unhealthy, unproductive ways.

The therapist who successfully creates a climate of unconditional positive regard fosters the person's natural tendency to move toward self-fulfilling decisions without fear of evaluation or rejection. Rogers (1977) described this important aspect of therapy in this way:

Client-Centered Therapy Rather than "interpreting" the client's thoughts and behavior, the client-centered therapist strives to create a warm, accepting climate that allows the client the freedom to explore troubling issues. The therapist engages in active listening, reflecting both the content and the personal meaning of what the client is saying. In doing so, the therapist helps the client develop a clearer perception and understanding of her own feelings and motives.

> Unconditional positive regard means that when the therapist is experiencing a positive, acceptant attitude toward whatever the client *is* at that moment, therapeutic movement or change is more likely. It involves the therapist's willingness for the client to be whatever feeling is going on at that moment—confusion, resentment, fear, anger, courage, love, or pride. . . . The therapist prizes the client in a total rather than a conditional way.

Third, the therapist must communicate *empathic understanding* by reflecting the content and personal meaning of the feelings being experienced by the client. In effect, the therapist creates a psychological mirror, reflecting the client's thoughts and feelings as they exist in the client's private inner world. The goal is to help the client explore and clarify his feelings, thoughts, and perceptions. In the process, the client begins to see himself, and his problems, more clearly (Egan, 1994).

Empathic understanding requires the therapist to listen *actively* for the personal meaning beneath the surface of what the client is saying (Watson, 2002). To illustrate, consider the following brief excerpt from a client-centered therapy session with an 18-year-old female college student:

CLIENT: My parents really bug me. First it was Arthur they didn't like; now it's Peter. I'm just fed up with all their meddling.

THERAPIST: You really are angry at your folks.

CLIENT: Well, how do you expect me to feel? Here I am with a 3.5 GPA, and providing all sorts of other goodies, and they claim the right to pass judgment on how appropriate my boyfriend is. (Begins to sob.)

THERAPIST: It strikes me that you're not just angry with them. (Pause) Maybe you're worried about disappointing them.

CLIENT: (Crying even more) I've tried all my life to please them. Sure, their approval is important to me. They're really pleased when I get A's, but why do they have to pass judgment on my social life as well? (Excerpt cited in Davison & Neale, 1998)

Notice how the therapist's first response reflects the *content* of what the client has said—her annoyance with her parents. But the therapist's second statement reflects the *personal meaning* of what the client has said—that she's worried about disappointing her parents. By communicating empathic understanding, the therapist helps the client explore and clarify the meaning of her own feelings.

Rogers believed that when the therapeutic atmosphere contains genuineness, unconditional positive regard, and empathic understanding, change is more likely to occur. Such conditions foster feelings of being psychologically safe, accepted, and valued. In this therapeutic atmosphere, change occurs as the person's self-concept and worldview gradually become healthier and less distorted. According to Rogers (1977), "As the client becomes more self-aware, more self-acceptant, less defensive and more open, she finds at last some of the freedom to grow and change in directions natural to the human organism." In effect, the

An empathic way of being with another person has several facets. It means entering the private perceptual world of the other and becoming thoroughly at home in it. It involves being sensitive, moment by moment, to the changing felt meanings which flow in this other person, to the fear or rage or tenderness or confusion of whatever that he or she is experiencing.

Carl Rogers (1990)

Table | **15.2**

Comparing Psychodynamic and Humanistic Therapies

Type of Therapy	Founder	Source of Problems	Treatment Techniques	Goals of Therapy
Psychoanalysis	Sigmund Freud	Repressed, unconscious conflicts stemming from early childhood experiences	Free association, analysis of dream content, interpretation, and transference	To recognize, work through, and resolve long-standing conflicts
Client-centered therapy	Carl Rogers	Conditional acceptance that causes the person to develop a distorted self-concept and worldview	Nondirective therapist who displays unconditional positive regard, genuineness, and empathic understanding	To develop self-awareness, self-acceptance, and self-determination

client is moving in the direction of *self-actualization*—the realization of his or her unique potentials and talents.

A large number of studies have generally supported Rogers's contention that it is important for the therapist to demonstrate genuineness, unconditional positive regard, and empathic understanding (Asay & Lambert, 2002; Greenberg & others, 1994). Such factors promote trust and self-exploration in therapy. However, these conditions, by themselves, may not be sufficient to help clients change (Sachse & Elliott, 2002; Cain & Seeman, 2002a).

The client-centered approach continues to be developed by therapists, teachers, social workers, and counselors (Elliott & Greenberg, 2002). Along with being influential in individual psychotherapy, the client-centered approach has been applied to marital counseling, parenting, education, business, and even community and international relations (K. Schneider, 1998; Zimring & Raskin, 1992). Table 15.2 compares some aspects of psychoanalysis and client-centered therapy.

Behavior Therapy

Key Theme

- Behavior therapy uses learning principles to directly change problem behaviors.

Key Questions

- What are the key assumptions of behavior therapy?
- What therapeutic techniques are based on classical conditioning, and how are they used to treat psychological disorders and problems?
- What therapy treatments are based on operant conditioning, and how are they used to treat psychological disorders and problems?

Behavior Therapy—From Bad Habits to Severe Psychological Disorders Nail biting and cigarette smoking are examples of the kinds of everyday maladaptive behaviors that can be successfully treated with behavior therapy. Behavioral techniques can also be used to treat more severe psychological problems, such as phobias, and to improve functioning in people with severe mental disorders such as schizophrenia and autism.

Psychoanalysis, client-centered therapy, and other insight-oriented therapies maintain that the road to psychologically healthier behavior is through increased self-understanding of motives and conflicts. As insights are acquired through therapy, problem behaviors and feelings presumably will give way to more adaptive behaviors and emotional reactions.

However, gaining insight into the source of problems does not necessarily result in desirable changes in behavior and emotions. Even though you fully understand *why* you are behaving in counterproductive ways, your maladaptive or self-defeating behaviors may continue. For instance, an adult who is extremely anxious about public speaking may understand that he feels that way because he was raised by a critical and demanding parent. But having this insight into the underlying cause of his anxiety may do little, if anything, to reduce his anxiety or change his avoidance of public speaking.

In sharp contrast to the insight-oriented therapies we discussed in the preceding sections, the goal of **behavior therapy,** also called *behavior modification,* is to modify specific problem behaviors, not to change the entire personality. And, rather than focusing on the past, behavior therapists focus on current behaviors.

Behavior therapists assume that maladaptive behaviors are *learned,* just as adaptive behaviors are. Thus, the basic strategy in behavior therapy involves unlearning maladaptive behaviors and learning more adaptive behaviors in their place. Behavior therapists employ techniques that are based on the learning principles of classical conditioning, operant conditioning, and observational learning to modify the problem behavior.

Techniques Based on Classical Conditioning

Just as Pavlov's dogs learned to salivate to a ringing bell that had become associated with food, learned associations can be at the core of some maladaptive behaviors, including strong negative emotional reactions. In the 1920s, psychologist John Watson demonstrated this phenomenon with his famous "Little Albert" study. In Chapter 5, we described how Watson classically conditioned an infant known as Little Albert to fear a tame lab rat by repeatedly pairing the rat with a loud clanging sound. Over time, Albert's conditioned fear generalized to other furry objects, including a fur coat, cotton, and a Santa Claus mask (Watson & Rayner, 1920).

Mary Cover Jones: The First Behavior Therapist

Watson himself never tried to eliminate Little Albert's fears. But Watson's research inspired one of his students, **Mary Cover Jones,** to explore ways of reversing conditioned fears. With Watson acting as a consultant, Jones (1924a) treated a three-year-old named Peter who "seemed almost to be Albert grown a bit older." Like Little Albert, Peter was fearful of various furry objects, including a tame rat, a fur coat, cotton, and wool. Because Peter was especially afraid of a tame rabbit, Jones focused on eliminating the rabbit fear. She used a procedure that has come to be known as **counterconditioning**—the learning of a new conditioned response that is incompatible with a previously learned response.

Jones's procedure was very simple (Jones, 1924b; Watson, 1924). The caged rabbit was brought into Peter's view but kept far enough away to avoid eliciting fear (the original conditioned response). With the rabbit visible at a tolerable distance, Peter sat in a high chair and happily munched his favorite snack, milk and crackers. Peter's favorite food was used because, presumably, the enjoyment of eating would naturally elicit a positive response (the desired conditioned response). Such a positive response would be incompatible with the negative response of fear.

Every day for almost two months, the rabbit was inched closer and closer to Peter as he ate his milk and crackers. As Peter's tolerance for the rabbit's presence gradually increased, he was eventually able to hold the rabbit in his lap, petting it with one hand while happily eating with his other hand (Jones, 1924a, 1924b). Not only was Peter's fear of the rabbit eliminated, but he also stopped being afraid of other furry objects, including the rat, cotton, and fur coat (Watson, 1924).

Along with counterconditioning, Jones (1924a) used social imitation, or *observational learning,* techniques to help eliminate Peter's fear of rabbits (Kornfeld, 1989). As part of the treatment, Peter observed other children petting or holding the tame rabbit. As you can see in Jones's treatment note, Peter imitated the actions of the nonfearful children. For her pioneering efforts in the treatment of children's fears, Jones is widely regarded as the first behavior therapist (Gieser, 1993; Reiss, 1990). For more of the contributions she made to psychology, see In Focus Box 15.1.

behavior therapy
A type of psychotherapy that focuses on directly changing maladaptive behavior patterns by using basic learning principles and techniques; also called *behavior modification.*

counterconditioning
A behavior therapy technique based on classical conditioning that involves modifying behavior by conditioning a new response that is incompatible with a previously learned response.

*T*reatment Note: Laurel, Mary, Arthur, Peter playing together in laboratory. Experimenter put rabbit down on floor. . . . Laurel and Mary stroked the rabbit and chattered away excitedly. Peter walked over, touched the rabbit on the back, exulting, "I touched him on the end."

Mary Cover Jones (1924)

Mary Cover Jones: The First Behavior Therapist

Often called "the mother of behavior therapy" for her pioneering studies on the removal of fears, Mary Cover Jones never identified herself as a behaviorist (Gieser, 1993). She became associated with the famous founder of behaviorism, John Watson, through her friendship with Rosalie Rayner, a college classmate (Jones, 1974). Rayner, you will recall, was Watson's co-researcher in the famous "Little Albert" study. Rayner married Watson shortly after that study.

Impressed by Watson and Rayner's Little Albert study, Jones was intrigued by the possibility of using learning principles to modify behavior. She asked herself, "If fears could be built in by conditioning, as Watson had demonstrated, could they not also be removed by similar procedures?"

In her treatment of three-year-old Peter, described in the text, Jones demonstrated that conditioning could be used to remove fears.

Some 50 years after her landmark study with Peter, Jones (1974) described her motives for the research:

> And so we come to Peter. It has always been of the greatest satisfaction to me that I could be associated with the removal of a fear when I came in contact with this three-year-old in whom a fear

Mary Cover Jones (1896-1987) This photograph, taken around 1919, shows Mary Cover Jones as a college student in her early twenties. Although Jones pioneered the use of behavioral techniques in therapy, she did not consider herself a "behaviorist" and ultimately came to disagree with many of Watson's views.

> of animals was already well-established. I could not have played the role of creating a fear in a child, no matter how important the theoretical implications. When my own children came across the case of Peter in their college textbooks, they too were relieved to find out that I had functioned in this benign capacity

in the psychological experiments with children and children's fears.

After receiving her Ph.D. from Columbia University in 1925, Jones became involved in the Oakland Growth Study, a longitudinal study that followed the lives of some 200 people for over half a century. When Jones began studying them in 1931, the subjects were 10 years of age. She continued the study for 55 years, until 1986. In describing that research, Jones (1975) provided a clear contrast to the assumptions and methods of Watson's early behaviorism:

> I have watched the psychobiological development of our study members as they grew from children to adults now in their 50s. I think of what we have learned as we studied these lives in progress. Participants have provided information on somatic [bodily], environmental, family, attitudinal and behavioral growth and change.
>
> It is my own regret that I did not have so extensive an association with little Peter of the fear study.... Now I would be less satisfied to treat the fears of a three-year-old, or of anyone else without a later follow-up and in isolation from an appreciation of him as a tantalizingly complex person with unique potentials for stability and change....
>
> Behaviorism has come a long way since the days of John B. Watson.

Systematic Desensitization

Mary Cover Jones's pioneering studies in treating children's fears helped set the stage for the later development of a more standardized procedure to treat phobias and other anxiety disorders. Developed by South African psychiatrist Joseph Wolpe in the 1950s, the procedure is called *systematic desensitization* (Wolpe, 1958, 1982). Based on the same premise as counterconditioning, **systematic desensitization** involves learning a new conditioned response (relaxation) that is incompatible with or inhibits the old conditioned response (fear and anxiety).

We'll illustrate the three basic steps of systematic desensitization by describing the behavioral treatment of a common phobia, fear of dentists. Mild to moderate dental anxiety is very common; 80 percent of American adults experience at least mild anxiety about trips to the dentist. But about 5 percent of adults experience such intense fear of going to the dentist that they avoid dental treatment even when it is medically necessary (Getka & Glass, 1992).

Classical conditioning often plays a role in the acquisition of dental fear (Milgrom & others, 1995). In much the same way that Little Albert was classically conditioned to fear a tame lab rat, many people have acquired a conditioned fear of the dentist's office because it has become paired with a painful or traumatic experience (Davey, 1989; De Jongh & others, 1995).

systematic desensitization
A type of behavior therapy in which phobic responses are reduced by pairing relaxation with a series of mental images or real-life situations that the person finds progressively more fear-provoking, based on the principle of counterconditioning.

Three basic steps are involved in systematic desensitization (Morris, 1991). Let's say you're one of the phobic 5 percent of dental patients. First, the behavior therapist teaches you *progressive relaxation,* which involves successively relaxing one muscle group after another until a deep state of relaxation is achieved. Second, the therapist helps you construct a list of specific anxiety-provoking images associated with dental visits. These scenes are arranged in a hierarchy from least anxiety-provoking to most anxiety-provoking (see Figure 15.1). The therapist would also have you create a very relaxing, unrelated *control scene,* such as imagining yourself walking on a beach on a warm, sunny day.

The third step is the actual process of desensitization. After becoming deeply relaxed, you close your eyes and vividly imagine the least threatening scene, the one at the bottom of the hierarchy. After you can maintain complete relaxation while imagining this scene three or four times, you move up to the next scene in your hierarchy. If you start to feel twinges of anxiety or tension, you signal the therapist by raising a finger. The therapist would then guide you back to imagining a previous scene or the relaxing control scene. If necessary, the therapist would help you relax again by using the progressive relaxation technique.

Over several sessions, you gradually work your way up the anxiety hierarchy, imagining each scene while maintaining complete relaxation. Very systematically, desensitization to the feared situations occurs as each imagined scene becomes paired with a conditioned response of relaxation rather than anxiety. Once mastered with mental images, desensitization is often continued, step by step, in the actual feared setting. In an interesting twist, new computer technology is providing another avenue for desensitization, which is discussed in In Focus Box 15.2.

In practice, systematic desensitization is often combined with other techniques. For example, in a behavioral treatment program for dental anxiety conducted by Eric Getka and Carol Glass (1992), participants received relaxation training and systematic desensitization. They then visited an actual dental clinic and practiced their relaxation skills there. *Observational learning* was also incorporated into the program: Participants watched videotapes of patients calmly receiving routine dental care.

The acid test for such a behavioral treatment package is not merely whether fear and anxiety are reduced, but whether treated subjects actually go to a dentist following treatment. Given these criteria, the behavioral treatment was highly effective. Compared with people with dental anxiety in an untreated control group, treated subjects were much more likely to have actually gone to a dentist on their own in the year following treatment (Getka & Glass, 1992).

Degree of Fear	Imagined Scene
100	Holding mouth open, eyes closed, listening to the sound of the dental drill as a cavity is repaired
95	Holding mouth open in preparation for an oral injection
90	Lying back in dental chair, eyes closed, as dentist examines teeth
85	Lying back in dental chair, mouth open, listening to the sounds of dental equipment, as dental technician cleans teeth
80	Lying in dental chair, watching dental technician unwrap sterilized dental tools
75	Being greeted by the dental technician and walking back to dental examination chair
70	Sitting in dentist's waiting room
60	Driving to dentist's office for appointment
50	Looking at the bright yellow reminder postcard on the refrigerator and thinking about dental appointment
40	Listening to a family member talk about her last dental visit
30	Looking at television or magazine advertisements depicting people in a dentist's chair
25	Calling dentist's office to make an appointment
20	Thinking about calling dentist's office to set up an appointment
15	Driving past dentist's office on a workday
10	Driving past dentist's office on a Sunday afternoon

FIGURE 15.1 A Sample Anxiety Hierarchy Used in Systematic Desensitization As part of systematic desensitization, the therapist helps the client develop an anxiety hierarchy. The sample anxiety hierarchy shown here illustrates the kinds of scenes that a person who is fearful of dental treatment might list. Relaxation is paired with each scene, starting with the least threatening scene, until the client can successfully imagine the scene while maintaining complete relaxation.

IN FOCUS 15.2

Using Virtual Reality to Conquer Phobias

Virtual reality (VR) therapy consists of computer-generated scenes that you view using a special motion-sensitive helmet, as shown in the photograph. Move your head in any direction and an electromagnetic sensor in the helmet detects the movement, and the computer-generated scene you see changes accordingly (Kalawsky, 1993). Turning a handgrip lets you move forward or backward to explore your artificial world. You can also use a virtual hand to reach out and touch objects, such as an elevator button or a spider.

VR technology is now being used experimentally as a treatment for some specific phobias, including fear of flying, heights, and spiders (Rothbaum & others, 2000). For example, psychologist Ralph Lamson has used virtual reality as a form of computer-assisted systematic desensitization to help more than 60 patients conquer their fear of heights. Rather than mental images, the person experiences computer-generated images that seem almost real. Once the helmet is donned, patients begin a 40-minute journey that starts in a café and progresses to a narrow wooden plank that leads to a bridge.

Although computer-generated and cartoonlike, the scenes of being high above the ground on the plank or bridge are real enough to trigger the physiological indicators of anxiety. Lamson (1994) explains: "When people look down, their heart rate and blood pressure go up. They may say, 'Oh my God, I can't do this.'"

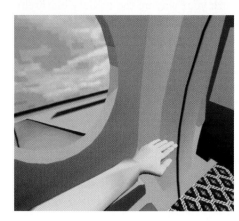

Lamson encourages the person to stay in the same spot until the anxiety diminishes. Once relaxed, the person continues the VR journey. By the time the person makes the return journey back over the plank, heart rate and blood pressure are close to normal.

How effective is VR in helping desensitize people to their fear of heights? After virtual reality therapy, over 90 percent of Lamson's patients successfully rode a glass elevator up to the 15th floor. They also completed self-assigned activities, such as driving across the Golden Gate Bridge and standing on a ladder to clean leaves from roof gutters.

Researcher Barbara Olasov Rothbaum and her colleagues (2000) believe that VR therapy has great potential as a treatment for phobias, especially for patients who have difficulty imagining frightening scenes on their own. VR therapy also has the advantage of providing controlled exposure to fear-provoking situations, such as flying, without the need to leave the therapist's office.

Once experimental, virtual reality therapy has now become an accepted treatment for phobias. Controlled studies have shown that VR treatments of phobias, including fear of flying and claustrophobia, are just as effective as graduated exposure to the actual feared objects or situations (Botella & others, 2000; Rothbaum & others, 2000). Virtual reality treatments are both easier and less expensive than standard treatment. An additional benefit is that the availability of VR may increase the number of phobics who seek treatment. In one survey of people who were phobic of spiders, more than 80 percent preferred virtual reality treatment over graduated exposure to real spiders (Garcia-Palacios & others, 2001).

The Bell and Pad Treatment

Another problem that has been effectively treated by techniques based on classical conditioning is bedwetting by children over the age of six. (Occasional bedwetting by children under the age of six is not considered a clinical problem.) About 3 percent of girls and 7 percent of boys age seven and older have problems with bedwetting. For some individuals, bedwetting may persist into early adolescence (Kaplan & Busner, 1993).

Children who are chronic bedwetters tend to be very deep sleepers. They spend more time in the very relaxed, deep stages of nondreaming sleep than do other children (Anch & others, 1988). Behavior therapy is based on the assumption that bedwetting occurs because the child has not learned to wake up when his bladder is full. The goal of the **bell and pad treatment** is to use classical conditioning to pair arousal with the sensation of a full bladder.

First developed in the 1930s, the bell and pad treatment is a very simple and effective procedure (O'Leary & Wilson, 1987). A special insulated pad is placed under the bottom bedsheet. When the child starts to wet the bed, a loud bell goes

bell and pad treatment
A behavior therapy technique used to treat nighttime bedwetting by conditioning arousal from sleep in response to bodily signals of a full bladder.

aversive conditioning
A relatively ineffective type of behavior therapy that involves repeatedly pairing an aversive stimulus with the occurrence of undesirable behaviors or thoughts.

off, waking the child. After shutting off the alarm, the child uses the bathroom and then changes the sheet. Before going back to bed, he resets the alarm.

Over the course of a few weeks, the child becomes conditioned so that the sensation of a full bladder (the conditioned stimulus) triggers waking arousal (the desired conditioned response). In the process, the child's sleeping cycles are also modified so that the child is not such a heavy sleeper. The bell and pad procedure is effective in about 75 percent of school-age children who have difficulties with bedwetting (Kaplan & Busner, 1993).

Notice that behavior therapists are not inclined to dwell on the "psychological meaning" of bedwetting. Instead, behavior therapists attempt to modify the problem behavior directly.

Aversive Conditioning

It was psychologist John Garcia who first demonstrated how taste aversions could be classically conditioned (see Chapter 5). After rats drank a sweet-flavored water, Garcia injected them with a drug that made them ill. The rats developed a strong taste aversion for the sweet-flavored water, avoiding it altogether (Garcia & others, 1966). In much the same way, **aversive conditioning** attempts to create an unpleasant conditioned response to a harmful stimulus, such as cigarette smoking or alcohol consumption. We'll illustrate how this approach works by describing how your author Don used aversive conditioning as part of a hospital program he conducted to help people quit smoking.

Participants in the stop-smoking program attended daily sessions for a week. Much of the program involved information about the health hazards of smoking, including slides of people with throat, mouth, and lung cancer. At the end of every night's meeting, the participants engaged in a rapid-puffing procedure. They had three minutes to rapidly puff, but not inhale, five cigarettes. Unbeknownst to the participants, the filters of the cigarettes had been coated with a harmless but foul-tasting substance.

Imagine the scene: 40 people in close quarters rapidly puffing five cigarettes that taste absolutely horrible. As the stench of cigarette smoke filled the unventilated room, gruesome slides of cancer victims flashed on the screen. Not surprisingly, this combination of factors left many participants gagging and nauseous.

The goal of this aversive conditioning procedure was to replace the former positive conditioned response to the taste of cigarettes with a response that produced distaste, even nausea. Similar aversive conditioning techniques have been used to treat alcohol addiction, sexual deviance, compulsive gambling, and overeating (see Emmelkamp, 1994; Sandler & Steele, 1991). For example, a medication called *Antabuse* is used in aversion therapy for alcohol addiction. If a person taking Antabuse consumes any amount of alcohol, extreme nausea is induced. For some conditions, such as sexual deviance, mild electric shocks are used rather than nausea-producing drugs.

In general, aversive conditioning is not very effective, and its use has been on the decline in recent years (Emmelkamp, 1994). The problem seems to be that aversive conditioning procedures do not generalize well to situations beyond the specific therapy setting. For example, in the case of the stop-smoking class Don taught, participants could easily counteract the aversive conditioning procedure simply by smoking outside the class. And indeed, at least some of the participants did just that.

The Bell and Pad Treatment for Bedwetting On the bedside table is an electronic device that monitors a moisture-sensitive pad that is placed below the bottom sheet of the bed. If the child wets the bed, a loud buzzer and a bright light are activated, waking the child. Over the course of several weeks, the bell and pad device conditions arousal from sleep in response to the body signals of a full bladder.

Techniques Based on Operant Conditioning

B. F. Skinner's *operant conditioning* model of learning is based on the simple principle that behavior is shaped and maintained by its consequences (see Chapter 5). When a behavior increases as the result of a desirable consequence, *reinforcement* has occurred. When a behavior decreases because it no longer leads to a reinforcer, *extinction* has occurred. And when behavior decreases in response to an unpleasant consequence, *punishment* has occurred.

Behavior therapists have developed a variety of techniques based on the principles of operant conditioning. For example, *shaping,* which involves reinforcing successive approximations of a desired behavior, can be used with extremely impaired patients in whom the desired behaviors do not normally occur. One successful application of shaping was to increase the attention span of hospitalized patients with severe schizophrenia (Silverstein & others, 2001). Shaping has also been effective in teaching patients with autism or severe mental retardation to develop more appropriate behaviors in such areas as speaking, interacting with others, and self-care.

Other applications of operant conditioning involve controlling the consequences that follow desired and undesired behaviors. For example, *positive reinforcement* is used to increase the incidence of desired behaviors, while *extinction,* or nonreinforcement, is used to reduce the occurrence of undesired behaviors.

Let's illustrate how operant techniques are used in therapy by describing a behavioral program to treat a four-year-old girl's sleeping problems (Ronen, 1991). When it came to bedtime, this child was not a happy camper. She would resist going to bed. After finally falling asleep, she would wake up five to seven times a night, screaming and shouting for hours. She would not stop crying unless her parents let her sleep in their bed. If her parents carried her back to her own bed, she would continue to wake up every hour, returning to their bed and crying.

The first step in the treatment program was to identify specific problem behaviors and determine their *baseline rate,* or how often each problem occurred before treatment began. After measuring the baseline rate, the therapist could target each problem behavior individually and objectively measure the child's progress. The parents next identified several very specific behavioral goals for their daughter. These goals included not crying when she was put to bed, not crying if she woke up in the night, not getting into her parents' bed, and staying in her own bed throughout the night.

The parents were taught operant techniques to decrease the undesirable behaviors and increase desirable ones. For example, the parents were taught to *extinguish* the girl's screaming and crying: They were to ignore the behavior rather than continue to reinforce it with parental attention. In contrast, desirable behaviors were to be *positively reinforced* with abundant praise, encouragement, social attention, and other rewards.

At first, positive reinforcers were delivered for small gains in desirable behaviors, such as when the little girl stayed in her bed for a short period of time. As the treatment progressed, rewards were given only for greater behavioral gains, such as sleeping all night. In Figure 15.2, you can see the little girl's progress for specific problem behaviors during the intervention and follow-up phases.

Operant conditioning techniques have been applied to many different kinds of psychological problems, from habit and weight control to helping autistic children learn to speak and behave more adaptively. Techniques based on operant conditioning have also been successfully used to modify the behavior of people who are severely disabled by retardation or mental disorders (O'Leary & Wilson, 1987).

Operant conditioning has also been used to modify the behavior of groups of people in a particular environment, such as a psychiatric ward or group home, in a treatment approach called a **token economy.** A token economy uses conditioned reinforcers called tokens that can be exchanged for tangible rewards. A set of rules specifies the number of tokens that will be earned for specific behaviors and the cost, in tokens, for the rewards. The tokens are conditioned reinforcers, valuable because they can be traded or exchanged for other rewards, such as privileges, activities,

FIGURE 15.2 The Effect of Operant Conditioning Techniques These graphs depict the changes in three specific sleep-related problem behaviors of a four-year-old girl over the course of behavioral therapy. The intervention for each problem behavior was introduced separately over several weeks. As you can see, behavior therapy produced a rapid reduction in the rate of each problem behavior. The green area shows the maintenance of desired behavior changes over a six-month follow-up.

SOURCE: Adapted from Ronen (1991).

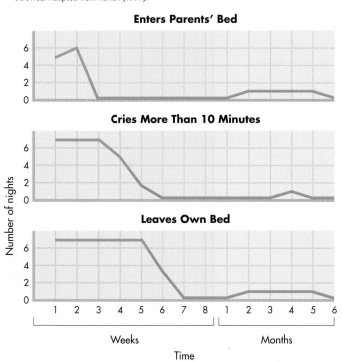

money, or food, depending on the population and the setting. They can be earned for desired behaviors and withheld or taken away for undesirable behaviors. For example, when a token economy is used with schizophrenic patients in a psychiatric hospital, the patients might receive tokens for maintaining personal hygiene, interacting appropriately, or attending therapy sessions. The tokens can be exchanged for reinforcers such as special privileges or desirable items or activities, such as recreational opportunities, grounds passes, candy or other snacks, and so forth.

Token economies have been used in prisons, classrooms, and juvenile corrections institutions, as well as with people diagnosed with psychiatric disorders or mental retardation in hospitals and group homes (Glenn, 1990; Kazdin, 1982). They have been shown to be effective even with severely disturbed patients who have been hospitalized for many years (Paul & Menditto, 1992). However, because token economies were difficult to implement, especially in community-based outpatient clinics, they are not in wide use today (R. Lieberman, 2000).

More recently, a modified version of the token economy has been used with outpatients in a treatment program called *contingency management interventions*. Like the token economy, a contingency management intervention involves carefully specified behaviors, a target group of clients or patients, and the use of vouchers or other conditioned reinforcers that can be exchanged for prizes, cash, or other rewards. Contingency management interventions have proven to be especially effective in the outpatient treatment of substance abuse and dependence in people who were dependent on heroin, cocaine, alcohol, or multiple drugs (Dallery & others, 2001; Petry & others, 2001). Several studies have shown that contingency management interventions are more effective than other methods of treating substance abuse (see Petry & others, 2000). In some cases, the contingency management interventions significantly reduced substance abuse in patients for whom other forms of treatment had failed.

How does a contingency management intervention work in practice? In one study, alcohol-dependent veterans were divided into two groups (Petry & others, 2000). One group received standard treatment alone, while the other group received standard treatment plus contingency management. In the contingency management group, the conditioned reinforcers were chances to win a small, medium, or large prize. After testing negative for alcohol use, completing steps related to their treatment goals, or attending therapy sessions, patients were each allowed to draw a slip of paper from a prize bowl. Winning slips could be exchanged for prizes in the category drawn. Bonus draws were awarded when long-term goals were achieved.

Participants in the contingency management intervention group were much more likely to stay in treatment: 84 percent of them attended the clinic for the full eight weeks, while only 22 percent of participants receiving the standard treatment did so. The bottom line? Over the course of the eight-week study period, more than 60 percent of those in the standard treatment group had relapsed to heavy alcohol use, while only about a quarter of those in the contingency management intervention group suffered a relapse.

Table 15.3 briefly summarizes key points about behavior therapy.

token economy
A form of behavior therapy in which the therapeutic environment is structured to reward desired behaviors with tokens or points that may eventually be exchanged for tangible rewards.

Table | **15.3**

Behavior Therapy

Type of Therapy	Foundation	Source of Problems	Treatment Techniques	Goals of Therapy
Behavior therapy	Based on classical conditioning, operant conditioning, and observational learning	Learned maladaptive behavior patterns	Systematic desensitization, virtual reality, bell and pad treatment, aversive conditioning, reinforcement and extinction, token economy, contingency management interventions, observational learning	To unlearn maladaptive behaviors and learn adaptive behaviors in their place

cognitive therapies
A group of psychotherapies based on the assumption that psychological problems are due to maladaptive patterns of thinking; treatment techniques focus on recognizing and altering these unhealthy thinking patterns.

rational-emotive therapy (RET)
A type of cognitive therapy, developed by psychologist Albert Ellis, that focuses on changing the client's irrational beliefs.

There is nothing either good or bad, but thinking makes it so.

William Shakespeare, *Hamlet*

Albert Ellis (b. 1913) A colorful and sometimes controversial figure, Albert Ellis developed rational-emotive therapy (RET). Rational-emotive therapy promotes psychologically healthier thought processes by disputing irrational beliefs and replacing them with more rational interpretations of events.

Cognitive Therapies

Key Theme
- Cognitive therapies are based on the assumption that psychological problems are due to maladaptive thinking.

Key Questions
- What are rational-emotive therapy and cognitive therapy, and how do they differ?
- What is cognitive-behavioral therapy?

Whereas behavior therapy assumes that faulty learning is at the core of problem behaviors and emotions, the **cognitive therapies** assume that the culprit is *faulty thinking.* The key assumption of the cognitive therapies could be put like this: Most people blame their unhappiness and problems on external events and situations, but the real cause of unhappiness is the way the person *thinks* about the events, not the events themselves. Thus, cognitive therapists zero in on the faulty patterns of thinking that they believe are causing the psychological problems. Once faulty patterns of thinking have been identified, the next step is to *change* them to more adaptive, healthy patterns of thinking. In this section, we'll look at how this change is accomplished in two influential forms of cognitive therapy: Ellis's *rational-emotive therapy* (RET) and Beck's *cognitive therapy* (CT).

Albert Ellis and Rational-Emotive Therapy

Shakespeare said it more eloquently, but psychologist **Albert Ellis** has expressed the same sentiment: "You largely feel the way you think." Ellis was trained as both a clinical psychologist and a psychoanalyst. As a practicing psychoanalyst, Ellis became increasingly disappointed with the psychoanalytic approach to solving human problems. Psychoanalysis simply didn't seem to work: His patients would have insight after insight, yet never get any better.

In the 1950s, Ellis began to take a more active, directive role in his therapy sessions. He developed **rational-emotive therapy,** abbreviated **RET.** RET is based on the assumption that "people are not disturbed by things but rather by their view of things" (Ellis, 1991). The key premise of RET is that people's difficulties are caused by their faulty expectations and irrational beliefs. Rational-emotive therapy focuses on changing the patterns of irrational thinking that are believed to be the primary cause of the client's emotional distress and psychological problems.

Ellis points out that most people mistakenly believe that they become upset and unhappy because of external events. Here's an example: Our friend Carrie was upset one day because an attractive co-worker, who had previously seemed to like her, was giving her the cold shoulder. The more she thought about it, the more upset and depressed she felt. When another friend asked Carrie why she was upset, she explained, "Because David is avoiding me, and I want him to like me."

Ellis (1993) would argue that Carrie's commonsense assessment is completely wrong. It's not David's behavior that's really making Carrie miserable—it's Carrie's *interpretation* of the meaning of David's behavior. In rational-emotive therapy, psychological problems are explained by the "ABC" model, as shown in Figure 15.3. According to this model, when an *Activating event* (**A**) occurs, it is the person's *Beliefs* (**B**) about the event that cause emotional *Consequences* (**C**). Notice how this differs from the commonsense view that it is the event (A) that causes the emotional and behavioral consequences (C).

Identifying the core irrational beliefs that underlie personal distress is the first step in rational-emotive therapy. In Carrie's case, the underlying cause of her distress is the common irrational belief that "everyone must love and accept me, or else I am a worthless person." The second step in rational-emotive therapy is for the therapist to vigorously *dispute and challenge the irrational beliefs.* A rational-emotive therapist might pose very direct questions to Carrie, like these: "Is there any reason David *should* think highly of you? So what if David does dislike you? Isn't that his perfect right? Is it the end of the world if he does dislike you? And even if David absolutely despises you, how does that make you a worthless person?"

Notice how irrational beliefs reflect "musts" and "shoulds" that are absolutes, such as the notion that "I should be competent at everything I do." Other common irrational beliefs are listed in Table 15.4. When these absolute demands are not satisfied, the person who subscribes to such beliefs responds by saying, in effect, "This is terrible, horrible, and I cannot and will not stand it."

The consequences of such thinking are unhealthy negative emotions, like extreme anger, despair, resentment, and feelings of worthlessness. Not only does the person feel miserable, but she also feels that she is unable to control or cope with an upsetting situation. These kinds of irrational cognitive and emotional responses interfere with constructive attempts to change disturbing situations (Ellis & Harper, 1975). According to RET, the result is self-defeating behaviors, anxiety disorders, depression, and other psychological problems.

In challenging a person's irrational beliefs, rational-emotive therapists tend to be very direct and even confrontational (Haaga & Davison, 1991). Rather than trying to establish a warm, supportive atmosphere, rational-emotive therapists rely on logical persuasion and reason to push the client toward recognizing and surrendering his irrational beliefs (Hollon & Beck, 1994). According to Ellis (1991), blunt, harsh language is sometimes needed to push people into helping themselves.

Commonsense View

| A — Activating Event | Causes | C — Consequence |

Example: You're passed over for a promotion at work.

You're miserable and depressed.

Rational-Emotive Therapy's ABC Model

| A — Activating Event | Triggers | B — Beliefs | Causes | C — Consequence |

Example: You're passed over for a promotion at work.

"I must be successful at everything I do or I am a complete failure. I was not successful, so I am a complete failure and a worthless human being."

You're miserable and depressed.

FIGURE 15.3 The "ABC" Model in Rational-Emotive Therapy Common sense tells us that unhappiness and other unpleasant emotions are caused by unpleasant or disturbing events. This view is shown in the top part of the figure. But Albert Ellis (1993) points out that it is really our *beliefs* about the events, not the events themselves, that make us miserable, as diagrammed in the bottom part of the figure.

Table | 15.4

Irrational Beliefs

1. It is a dire necessity for you to be loved or approved by virtually everyone in your community.
2. You must be thoroughly competent, adequate, and achieving in all possible respects if you are to consider yourself worthwhile.
3. Certain people are bad, wicked, or villainous, and they should be severely blamed and punished for their villainy. You should become extremely upset over other people's wrongdoings.
4. It is awful and catastrophic when things are not the way you would very much like them to be.
5. Human unhappiness is externally caused, and you have little or no ability to control your bad feelings and emotions.
6. It is easier to avoid than to face difficulties and responsibilities. Avoiding difficulties whenever possible is more likely to lead to happiness than facing difficulties.
7. You need to rely on someone stronger than yourself.
8. Your past history is an all-important determinant of your present behavior. Because something once strongly affected your life, it should indefinitely have a similar effect.
9. You should become extremely upset over other people's problems.
10. There is a single perfect solution to all human problems, and it is catastrophic if this perfect solution is not found.

SOURCE: Based on Ellis (1991).

According to rational-emotive therapy, unhappiness and psychological problems can often be traced to people's irrational beliefs. Becoming aware of these irrational beliefs is the first step toward replacing them with more rational alternatives. Some of the most common irrational beliefs are listed here.

From the client's perspective, rational-emotive therapy requires considerable effort. First, the person must admit her irrational beliefs and accept the fact that those beliefs are irrational and unhealthy, which is not as easy as it sounds. Old mental habits don't always yield easily. Equally challenging, the client must radically change her way of interpreting and responding to stressful events (Haaga & Davison, 1991).

Carrie would learn in therapy how to replace her irrational beliefs with more rational interpretations of adverse events. For example, she could learn to say to herself, "I would *prefer* that David really like me, and it's *disappointing* that he does not, but it's certainly not the end of the world." The long-term therapeutic goal would be to teach Carrie to recognize and dispute her own irrational beliefs in a wide range of situations.

It's important to note that responding "rationally" to unpleasant situations does not mean denying your feelings (Ellis & Bernard, 1985). Ellis believes that it is perfectly appropriate and rational to feel sad when you are rejected, or regretful when you make a mistake. Other appropriate emotional responses include disappointment, annoyance, frustration, and displeasure.

Appropriate emotions are the consequences of rational beliefs, such as "I would prefer that everyone like me, but that's not likely to happen," or "It would be nice if I never failed at anything, but it's unlikely that I will always succeed in everything I do." Such healthy mental and emotional responses encourage people to work toward constructively changing or coping with difficult situations (Ellis & Harper, 1975). In effect, the person accepts that his absolute demands are unlikely to be met.

Albert Ellis is a colorful figure whose ideas have been extremely influential in psychotherapy (Haaga & Davison, 1993). Rational-emotive therapy is a popular approach in clinical practice, partly because it is straightforward and simple (Arnkoff & Glass, 1992). It has been shown to be generally effective in the treatment of depression, social phobia, and certain anxiety disorders. Rational-emotive therapy is also useful in helping people overcome self-defeating behaviors, such as an excessive need for approval, extreme shyness, and chronic procrastination.

Aaron Beck and Cognitive Therapy

Like Albert Ellis, psychiatrist **Aaron T. Beck** was initially trained as a psychoanalyst. Beck's development of **cognitive therapy,** abbreviated **CT,** grew out of his research on depression (Beck & others, 1979). Seeking to scientifically validate the psychoanalytic assumption that depressed patients "have a need to suffer," Beck began collecting data on the free associations and dreams of his depressed patients. What he found, however, was that his depressed patients did *not* have a need to suffer. In fact, his depressed patients often went to great lengths to avoid being rejected by others.

Instead, Beck discovered that depressed people have an extremely negative view of the past, present, and future (Beck & others, 1979). Rather than realistically evaluating their situation, depressed patients have developed a *negative cognitive bias,* consistently distorting their experiences in a negative way. Their negative perceptions of events and situations are shaped by deep-seated, self-deprecating beliefs, such as "I can't do anything right," "I'm worthless," or "I'm unlovable" (Beck, 1991). Beck's cognitive therapy essentially focuses on correcting the cognitive biases that underlie depression and other psychological disorders.

Beck's CT has much in common with Ellis's rational-emotive therapy. Like Ellis, Beck believes that what people think creates their moods and emotions. And like RET, CT involves helping clients identify faulty thinking and replace unhealthy patterns of thinking with healthier ones.

But in contrast with Ellis's emphasis on "irrational" thinking, Beck believes that depression and other psychological problems are caused by *distorted thinking* and *unrealistic beliefs* (Arnkoff & Glass, 1992; Hollon & Beck, 1994). Rather than logically debating the "irrationality" of a client's beliefs, the CT therapist en-

Aaron Beck (b. 1921) In Aaron Beck's cognitive therapy, called CT, clients learn to identify and change their automatic negative thoughts. Originally developed to treat depression, CT has also been applied to other psychological problems, such as anxiety disorders, phobias, and eating disorders.

courages the client to *empirically test the accuracy of his or her assumptions and beliefs.* Let's look at how this occurs in Beck's CT.

The first step in CT is to help the client learn to recognize and monitor the automatic thoughts that occur without conscious effort or control (Beck, 1991). Because their perceptions are shaped by their negative cognitive biases, depressed people usually have automatic thoughts that reflect very negative interpretations of experiences. Table 15.5 summarizes some of the negative cognitive biases that often operate in depression.

Whether negative or positive, automatic thoughts can control your mood and shape your emotional and behavioral reactions to events (Robins & Hayes, 1993). For example, suppose a classmate seems to snub you in the hall. A psychologically healthy person might automatically think, "Connor must be preoccupied about something. I wonder what's wrong?" Such automatic thoughts are unlikely to provoke a negative emotional reaction.

In contrast, a depressed person is more likely to respond with different automatic thoughts, like these: "Connor is mad at me because of what I said yesterday. Nobody likes me. I always say the wrong thing to people. I'm such a jerk." Not surprisingly, the result of such negative automatic thoughts is a deepened sense of depression, hopelessness, and helplessness.

Once the client has learned how to recognize and monitor his negative automatic thoughts, the therapist moves to the second step of CT. The therapist helps the client learn how to *empirically test* the reality of the automatic thoughts that are so upsetting. For example, if a client reported negative automatic thoughts like those just mentioned, a CT therapist might respond in this way: "Is it *really* true that 'nobody likes you'? What's your evidence for that statement? Surely *somebody* must like you. Didn't Jill invite you to her party last week?" The CT therapist might also assign behavioral tasks to "test" the accuracy of the negative automatic thoughts. To test the belief that "I always say the wrong thing," the therapist might assign the person the task of initiating a conversation with three acquaintances and noting how often he actually said the wrong thing.

cognitive therapy (CT)
A type of cognitive therapy, developed by psychiatrist Aaron T. Beck, that focuses on changing the client's unrealistic beliefs.

According to Aaron Beck, depressed people perceive and interpret experience in very negative terms. They are prone to systematic errors in logic, or cognitive biases, which shape their negative interpretation of events. The table shows the most common cognitive biases in depression.

Table | 15.5

Cognitive Biases in Depression

Cognitive Bias (Error)	Description	Example
Arbitrary inference	Drawing a negative conclusion when there is little or no evidence to support it.	When Joan calls Jim to cancel their lunch date because she has an important meeting at work, Jim concludes that she is probably going out to lunch with another man.
Selective abstraction	Focusing on a single negative detail taken out of context, ignoring the more important aspects of the situation.	During Jacqueline's annual review, her manager praises her job performance but notes that she could be a little more confident when she deals with customers over the phone. Jacqueline leaves her manager's office thinking that he is on the verge of firing her because of her poor telephone skills.
Overgeneralization	Drawing a sweeping, global conclusion based on an isolated incident and applying that conclusion to other unrelated areas of life.	Tony spills coffee on his final exam. He apologizes to his instructor but can't stop thinking about the incident. He concludes that he is a klutz who will never be able to succeed in a professional career.
Magnification and minimization	Grossly overestimating the impact of negative events and grossly underestimating the impact of positive events so that small, bad events are magnified, but good, large events are minimized.	One week after Emily aces all her midterms, she worries about flunking out of college when she gets a B on an in-class quiz.
Personalization	Taking responsibility, blaming oneself, or applying external events to oneself when there is no basis or evidence for making the connection.	Richard becomes extremely upset when his instructor warns the class about plagiarism. He thinks the instructor's warning was aimed at him, and he concludes that the instructor suspects him of plagiarizing parts of his term paper.

SOURCE: Based on Beck & others (1979), p. 14.

Table | 15.6

Comparing Cognitive Therapies

Type of Therapy	Founder	Source of Problems	Treatment Techniques	Goals of Therapy
Rational-emotive therapy (RET)	Albert Ellis	Irrational beliefs	Very distinctive: Identify, logically dispute, and challenge irrational beliefs	Surrender of irrational beliefs and absolutist demands
Cognitive therapy (CT)	Aaron T. Beck	Unrealistic, distorted perceptions and interpretations of events due to cognitive biases	Directive collaboration: Teach client to monitor automatic thoughts; test accuracy of conclusions; correct distorted thinking and perception	Accurate and realistic perception of self, others, and external events

Initially, the CT therapist acts as a model, showing the client how to evaluate the accuracy of automatic thoughts. By modeling techniques for evaluating the accuracy of automatic thoughts, the therapist hopes to eventually teach the client to do the same on her own. The CT therapist also strives to create a therapeutic climate of *collaboration* that encourages the client to contribute to the evaluation of the logic and accuracy of automatic thoughts (Beck & others, 1979; Robins & Hayes, 1993). This approach contrasts with the confrontational approach used by the RET therapist, who directly challenges the client's thoughts and beliefs.

Beck's cognitive therapy has been shown to be very effective in treating depression and other psychological disorders, including anxiety disorders, eating disorders, posttraumatic stress disorder, and relationship problems (Beck, 1993; Chambless & Gillis, 1993; Klinger, 1993; Wilson & Fairburn, 1993). Along with effectively treating depression, cognitive therapy may also help *prevent* depression from recurring, especially if clients learn and then use the skills they have learned in therapy. In one recent study, high-risk patients who had experienced several episodes of depression in the past were much less likely to relapse when they continued cognitive therapy after their depression had lifted (Jarrett & others, 2001). Beck's cognitive therapy techniques have even been adapted to help treat psychotic symptoms, such as the delusions and disorganized thought processes that often characterize schizophrenia (Alford & Correia, 1994; Chadwick & others, 1994).

Table 15.6 summarizes the key characteristics of the two cognitive therapies presented here.

Cognitive-Behavioral Therapy

Although we've presented cognitive and behavioral therapies in separate sections, it's important to note that cognitive and behavioral techniques are often combined in therapy. **Cognitive-behavioral therapy** (abbreviated **CBT**) refers to a group of psychotherapies that incorporate techniques from *both* approaches. CBT is based on the assumption that cognitions, behaviors, and emotional responses are interrelated (Brewin, 1996; Hollon & Beck, 1994). Thus, changes in thought patterns will affect moods and behaviors, and changes in behaviors will affect thoughts and moods. Along with challenging maladaptive beliefs and substituting more adaptive cognitions, the therapist uses behavior modification, shaping, reinforcement, and modeling to teach problem solving and to change unhealthy behavior patterns.

The hallmark of cognitive-behavioral therapy is its pragmatic approach. Therapists design an integrated treatment plan, utilizing the techniques that are most appropriate for specific problems. For example, psychologist Richard A. Brown and his colleagues (2001) used cognitive-behavioral therapy to help people with a history of depression quit smoking. Both smoking behavior and depressive symptoms were targeted in the therapy. Behavioral elements of the treatment program included the following: Participants monitored their smoking behavior, identified

cognitive-behavioral therapy
Therapy that integrates cognitive and behavioral techniques and that is based on the assumption that thoughts, moods, and behaviors are interrelated.

common cues for smoking, and learned how to alter their responses to such cues. Modeling and role-playing were used to help the participants develop better social skills and to help them overcome the urge to smoke in social situations. On the cognitive side, participants monitored their positive and negative thoughts. They were also taught how to identify and combat negative thinking patterns using Ellis's ABC technique and Beck's identification of cognitive distortions. The results showed that heavy smokers and smokers with recurrent depressive episodes were most likely to benefit from the treatment. This study exemplifies the flexible, integrated use of diverse techniques that characterize cognitive-behavioral therapy.

Group and Family Therapy

Key Theme

- Group therapy involves one or more therapists working with several clients simultaneously.

Key Questions

- What are some key advantages of group therapy?
- What is family therapy, and how do its assumptions and techniques differ from those of individual therapy?

Individual psychotherapy offers a personal relationship between a client and a therapist, one that is focused on a single client's problems, thoughts, and emotions. But individual psychotherapy has certain limitations (Feldman & Powell, 1992). The therapist sees the client in isolation, rather than within the context of the client's interactions with others. Hence, the therapist must rely on the client's interpretation of reality and the client's description of relationships with others.

Group Therapy

Group therapy involves one or more therapists working with several people simultaneously. Group therapy may be provided by a therapist in private practice or at a community mental health clinic. Often, group therapy is an important part of the treatment program for hospital inpatients (Kibel, 1993). Groups may be as small as 3 or 4 people or as large as 10 or more people.

Virtually any approach—psychodynamic, client-centered, behavioral, or cognitive—can be used in group therapy (Alonso & Swiller, 1993a). And just about any problem that can be handled individually can be dealt with in group therapy.

Some therapy groups are made up of clients who share the same problem, but others are far more diverse. Regardless, the goals of group therapy are the same as those for individual psychotherapy—resolving psychological problems and promoting more adaptive behaviors. The therapeutic success of group therapy often hinges on the group's collective sense of *cohesion,* or togetherness (Bednar & Kaul, 1994).

Group therapy has a number of advantages over individual psychotherapy (Dies, 1993). First, group therapy is very cost-effective: A single therapist can work simultaneously with several people. Thus, it is less expensive for the client and less time-consuming for the therapist. Second, rather than relying on a client's self-perceptions about how she relates to other people, the therapist can observe her actual interactions with others. Observing the way clients interact with others in a group may provide unique insights into their personalities and behavior patterns (Alonso & Swiller, 1993b; Porter, 1993).

Third, the support and encouragement provided by the other group members may help a person feel less alone and understand that his or her problems are not unique (Alonso & Swiller, 1993a; Ballinger & Yalom, 1995). Fourth, group

group therapy
A form of psychotherapy that involves one or more therapists working simultaneously with a small group of clients.

Self-Help Groups: Helping Yourself by Helping Others

Every month our local newspaper publishes a list of more than 300 self-help and support groups that meet in our area. These groups range from the familiar (Alcoholics Anonymous, Tough-Love) to the obscure (Abused by Religion, Cult Awareness Group, Cross-Dressers of Green County), and from the general (Parents of Adolescents, Effective Black Parenting) to the specific (Multiple Sclerosis—Newly Diagnosed). There are also groups for people dealing with life's transitions and crises, such as divorce, retirement, or bereavement.

What this bewildering array of groups have in common is that all of them are organized and led by nonprofessionals. Typically, such groups are made up of members who have a common problem and meet for the purpose of exchanging psychological support. Some groups are focused on psychological growth and change. Other groups have a more practical emphasis, providing information and advice (Carroll, 1993). The groups either

are free or charge nominal fees to cover the cost of materials.

The format of self-help groups varies enormously. Some groups are quite free-wheeling, but others are highly structured (McFadden & others, 1992). Meetings may follow a prescribed format, and there may be rules regulating contacts among group members outside the meetings. For example, our friend Marcia attends weekly meetings of a self-help group called Emotions Anonymous. In Marcia's group, each person takes a turn speaking for five minutes. Interruptions are not allowed, and other members simply listen without responding to the speaker's comments.

Many self-help groups follow a 12-step approach, patterned after the famous 12-step program of Alcoholics Anonymous (AA). The 12 steps of AA include themes of admitting that you have a problem, seeking help from a "higher power," confessing your shortcomings, repairing your relationships with others, and helping other people who have the same problem.

These 12 steps have been adapted by many different groups to fit their particular problem. Some psychologists criticize the 12-step approach for its emphasis on the idea that people are "powerless" to cope with their problems on their own and must depend on a higher power and on other group members (Kasl, 1992).

Just how helpful are self-help groups? Research has shown that self-help groups can be as effective as therapy provided by a mental health professional, at least for some psychological problems (Christensen & Jacobson, 1994). Given that many people cannot afford professional counseling, self-help groups may be a cost-effective alternative to psychotherapy for some people.

What is not known is *why* self-help groups are effective. Support and encouragement from others are undoubtedly important. So may be the "helper therapy" principle on which all self-help groups are based: People who help other people are themselves helped. But more research is needed to clarify the elements that contribute most to a successful outcome. Research is also needed to identify the kinds of people and problems that are most likely to benefit from a self-help approach (Christensen & Jacobson, 1994).

An Alcoholics Anonymous Meeting Founded in 1935, Alcoholics Anonymous has more than 2 million members worldwide. People from all walks of life attend AA, and many credit AA for turning their lives around. Because AA group members are guaranteed anonymity, their faces cannot be shown in the photograph. Many other kinds of self-help groups are modeled on the AA program.

members may provide each other with helpful, practical advice for solving common problems and can act as models for successfully overcoming difficulties. Finally, working within a group gives people an opportunity to try out new behaviors in a safe, supportive environment (Porter, 1993). For instance, someone who is very shy and submissive can practice more assertive behaviors and receive honest feedback from other group members.

Group therapy is typically conducted by a mental health professional. In contrast, *self-help groups* and *support groups* are typically conducted by nonprofessionals. Self-help groups and support groups have become increasingly popular in the United States. And, like Marcia's therapist in the chapter Prologue, some therapists recommend self-help groups as an adjunct to traditional psychotherapy. As discussed in In Focus Box 15.3, the potential of these groups to promote mental health should not be underestimated.

Family and Couple Therapy

Most forms of psychotherapy, including most group therapies, tend to see a person's problems—and the solutions to those problems—as primarily originating within the individual himself. **Family therapy** operates on a different premise, focusing on the whole family rather than on an individual. The major goal of family therapy is to alter and improve the ongoing interactions among family members (Lebow & Gurman, 1995). Typically, family therapy involves every member of the family, even young children, and may also include important members of the extended family, such as grandparents or in-laws.

Family therapy is based on the assumption that the family is a *system*, an interdependent unit, not just a collection of separate individuals. The family is seen as a dynamic structure in which each member plays a unique role. According to this view, every family has certain unspoken "rules" of interaction and communication. Some of these tacit rules revolve around issues such as which family members exercise power and how, who makes decisions, who keeps the peace, and what kinds of alliances members have formed among themselves. As such issues are explored, unhealthy patterns of family interaction can be identified and replaced with new "rules" that promote the psychological health of the family as a unit.

Family therapy is often used to enhance the effectiveness of individual psychotherapy. For example, patients with schizophrenia are less likely to experience relapses when family members are involved in therapy (Pitschel-Walz & others, 2001). In many cases, the therapist realizes that the individual client's problems reflect conflict and disturbance in the entire family system (Lebow & Gurman, 1995). In order for the client to make significant improvements, the family as a whole must become psychologically healthier. Family therapy is also indicated when there is conflict among family members, such as among parents and adolescent children, or when younger children are being treated for behavior problems, such as truancy or aggressive behavior (Kazdin, 1994b).

Many family therapists also provide *marital* or *couple therapy*. The term *couple therapy* is preferred today because such therapy is conducted with any couple in a committed relationship, whether they are married or unmarried, heterosexual or homosexual (Lebow & Gurman, 1995). As is the case with family therapy, there are many different approaches to couple therapy (J. F. Alexander & others, 1994; Christensen & Heavey, 1999). However, most couple therapies have the goal of improving communication and problem-solving skills and increasing intimacy between the pair.

A current trend in couple therapy is for the therapist to be closely attuned to the cultural and social context within which the couple functions. Therapists are taking greater care not to impose their own expectations on client couples. This is especially important when the couple is from a cultural background that is different from that of the therapist and has different values and expectations about gender roles and about the marital relationship. As you'll see in the next section, psychotherapists have generally become more aware of the importance of culture in the therapist–client relationship.

A Family Therapy Session Family therapists typically work with all the members of a family at the same time, including young children. The family therapist can then directly observe how family members interact, resolve differences, and exert control over one another. As unhealthy patterns of family interactions are identified, they can often be replaced with new patterns that promote the psychological well-being of the family as a whole.

Couple Therapy Couple therapy focuses on helping people who are in a committed relationship. Couple therapy usually emphasizes improving communication, increasing intimacy, and strengthening the relationship bond.

family therapy
A form of psychotherapy that is based on the assumption that the family is a system and that treats the family as a unit.

15.1 R·E·V·I·E·W

Types of Psychotherapy

Match each statement below with one of the following types of psychotherapy: psychoanalytic therapy, behavior therapy, humanistic therapy, cognitive therapy, family therapy.

_____ *1.* Our problems are not the result of what happens to us, but instead are a function of our cognitive interpretations and irrational thinking about what happens to us.

_____ *2.* Maladaptive behavior is learned in the same way as any other behavior. Improvement occurs when the environmental conditions are changed so that adaptive behavior is reinforced and maintained.

_____ *3.* A client's psychological problems often reflect a disturbance or conflict in his or her family. If the client's family becomes psychologically healthier, the client is more likely to improve.

_____ *4.* The therapist's role is to be nondirective and to provide the client with unconditional positive regard and empathic understanding.

_____ *5.* People can regain mental health only by developing insight into their hidden, unconscious conflicts through the techniques of free association, dream interpretation, and transference.

Evaluating the Effectiveness of Psychotherapy

Key Themes

- Decades of research demonstrate that psychotherapy is effective in helping people with psychological disorders.

Key Questions

- What are the common factors that contribute to successful outcomes in psychotherapy?
- What is eclecticism?

Let's start with a simple fact: Most people with psychological symptoms do *not* seek help from mental health professionals (Kessler & others, 1994). This suggests that most people eventually weather their psychological problems without professional intervention. Some people cope with psychological difficulties with the help and support of friends and family. And some people eventually improve simply with the passage of time, a phenomenon called *spontaneous remission* (see Eysenck, 1952, 1994). Does psychotherapy offer significant benefits over simply waiting for the possible "spontaneous remission" of symptoms?

The basic strategy for investigating this issue is to compare people who enter psychotherapy with a carefully selected, matched control group of people who do not receive psychotherapy (Kazdin, 1994a). During the last 30 years, hundreds of such studies have investigated the effectiveness of the major forms of psychotherapy (Chambless & Ollendick, 2001; Nathan & others, 2000). To combine and interpret the results of such large numbers of studies, researchers have used a statistical technique called *meta-analysis* (Lipsey & Wilson, 1993). Meta-analysis involves pooling the results of several studies into a single analysis, essentially creating one large study that can reveal overall trends in the data.

When meta-analysis is used to summarize studies that compare people who receive psychotherapy treatment to no-treatment controls, researchers consistently arrive at the same conclusion: *Psychotherapy is significantly more effective than no treatment.* On the average, the person who completes psychotherapy treatment is better off than about 80 percent of those in the untreated control group (Asay & Lambert, 1999).

The benefits of psychotherapy are usually apparent in a relatively short period of time. As shown in Figure 15.4, approximately 50 percent of people show significant improvement by the eighth weekly session of psychotherapy. By the end of six months of weekly psychotherapy sessions, about 75 percent are significantly improved (Howard & others, 1986; McNeilly & Howard, 1991). The gains that people make as a result of psychotherapy also tend to endure long after the therapy has ended, sometimes for years (Lambert & Bergin, 1994). Even brief forms of psychotherapy tend to produce beneficial and long-lasting changes (Koss & Shiang, 1994).

Brain-imaging technologies are providing another line of evidence demonstrating the power of psychotherapy to effect change. In one study, PET scans were used to measure brain activity before and after 10 weeks of therapy for obsessive–compulsive disorder (Schwartz & others, 1996). The psychotherapy patients who improved showed the same changes in brain function that are associated with effective drug therapy for this disorder (see page 585 in Chapter 14). Similarly, as we'll show you later in this chapter, PET scans of patients with depression show changes in brain functioning toward more normal levels after 12 weeks of interpersonal therapy (Martin & others, 2001). In other words, psychotherapy alone produces distinct physiological changes in the brain—changes that are associated with a reduction in symptoms.

Nevertheless, it's important to note that psychotherapy is *not* a miracle cure. While most people experience significant benefits from psychotherapy, not everyone benefits to the same degree. Some people who enter psychotherapy improve only slightly or not at all.

Is One Form of Psychotherapy Superior?

Given the very different assumptions and techniques used in the major types of psychotherapy, does one type of psychotherapy stand out as more effective than the others? In some cases, one type of psychotherapy is more effective than another in treating a particular problem. For example, cognitive therapy and interpersonal therapy are effective in treating depression (Elkin & others, 1989, 1996). Cognitive and behavioral therapies tend to be more successful than insight-oriented therapies in helping people who are experiencing panic disorder, obsessive–compulsive disorder, and phobias (Chambless & Ollendick, 2001). Insight-oriented therapies are also less effective than other therapies in the treatment of disorders characterized by severe psychotic symptoms, such as schizophrenia (Mueser & Glynn, 1993).

However, when meta-analysis techniques are used to assess the collective results of treatment outcome studies, a surprising but consistent finding emerges: *In general, there is little or no difference in the effectiveness of different psychotherapies.* Despite sometimes dramatic differences in psychotherapy techniques, all of the standard psychotherapies have very similar success rates (Kopta & others, 1999; Nathan & others, 2000).

One important qualification must be made at this point. In this chapter, we've devoted considerable time to explaining four major approaches to therapy: psychoanalytic and psychodynamic therapy; humanistic therapy; behavior therapy; and cognitive and cognitive-behavioral therapies. While distinct, all of these psychotherapy approaches have in common the fact that they are *empirically supported treatments*. In other words, they are based on known psychological principles, have been subjected to controlled scientific trials, and have demonstrated their effectiveness in helping people with psychological problems (Chambless & Ollendick, 2001).

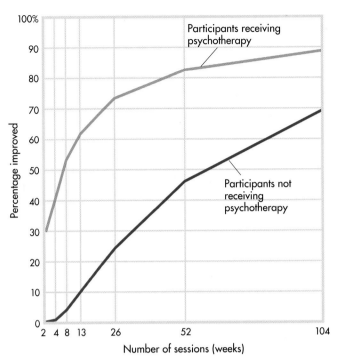

FIGURE 15.4 Psychotherapy Versus No Treatment This graph depicts the rates of improvement for more than 2,000 people in weekly psychotherapy and for 500 people who did not receive psychotherapy. As you can see, after only eight weekly sessions, better than 50 percent of participants receiving psychotherapy were significantly improved. After the same length of time, only 4 percent of participants not receiving psychotherapy showed "spontaneous remission" of symptoms. Clearly, psychotherapy accelerates both the rate and degree of improvement for those experiencing psychological problems.

SOURCE: Adapted from McNeilly & Howard (1991). Reprinted by permission of Guilford Press.

EMDR: Can You Wave Your Fears Away?

In the late 1980s, a psychology graduate student named Francine Shapiro was walking alone in a park, grappling with some troubling thoughts. According to Shapiro, "I noticed that when a disturbing thought entered my mind, my eyes spontaneously started moving back and forth. At the same time, I noticed that my disturbing thought had shifted from consciousness, and when I brought it back to mind, it no longer bothered me as much" (Shapiro & Forrest, 1997). Speculating that her back-and-forth eye movements were simulating the rapid eye movements (REM) of dreaming sleep, Shapiro developed a treatment technique in which patients suffering from traumatic memories visually followed her waving finger while simultaneously holding a mental image of disturbing memories, events, or situations.

Ultimately, Shapiro earned her doctorate in psychology by treating 22 patients with posttraumatic stress disorder (PTSD) with her new therapy, which she dubbed **eye movement desensitization reprocessing,** abbreviated **EMDR.** In two published papers, Shapiro (1989a, 1989b) reported that almost all of her patients experienced significant relief from their symptoms after just *one* EMDR therapy session.

This was the beginning of what was to become one of the fastest-growing—and most lucrative—therapeutic techniques of the last decade (Herbert & others, 2000). How popular is EMDR? Since Shapiro established her EMDR Institute in 1990, more than 40,000 therapists have been trained in EMDR. Close to a million patients have been treated with the new therapy (EMDR Institute, 2001).

Since its launch, the claims, techniques, and jargon of EMDR have undergone some changes. While originally touted as a one-session treatment for the distress associated with traumatic memories in PTSD (Shapiro, 1989a), EMDR therapy today fre-

Eye Movement Desensitization Reprocessing (EMDR) In EMDR therapy, the client visually follows the therapist's moving finger while mentally focusing on a traumatic memory or vivid mental image of a troubling situation. Supposedly, the rhythmic eye movements help the client to "release" and "integrate" the trauma.

quently involves multiple sessions. According to Shapiro (1995), comprehensive EMDR treatment involves eight phases, which combine elements of psychodynamic, behavioral, and cognitive therapies. Along with the eye movements, other forms of "bilateral stimulation" may be used, such as tones in alternating ears or taps on different sides of the body.

Along with posttraumatic stress disorder, EMDR has been used to treat panic disorder and other anxiety disorders, addiction, substance abuse, and sleep disorders. Proponents claim that EMDR is also effective in overcoming depression, phobias, pathological gambling, and self-esteem problems, as well as helping athletes and workers achieve "peak performance" (see EMDR Institute, 2001; Shapiro & Forrest, 1997).

Originally, Shapiro (1989b) contended that the eye movements simulated brain processes during sleep, "releasing" and "integrating" traumatic memories. More

recently, Shapiro (1995) has proposed that EMDR facilitates what she calls "Accelerated Information Processing," in which "dysfunctionally stored information can be properly assimilated through a dynamically activated processing system." Supposedly, EMDR "accelerates a natural information processing" that helps heal the nervous system.

Is EMDR "the breakthrough therapy for overcoming anxiety, stress, and trauma," as is claimed on the cover of Shapiro's 1997 book? Does it represent a "paradigm shift" in psychotherapy, as its founder (Shapiro, 1995) claims? Let's consider the evidence.

Does EMDR Provide Therapeutic Benefits Compared to *No* Treatment?

Yes, numerous studies have shown that patients experience relief from symptoms of anxiety after EMDR. In a meta-analysis of dozens of studies examining EMDR, Canadian psychologists Paul Davidson and Kevin Parker (2001) concluded the following: "When outcomes of EMDR treatment are compared with no treatment, and when outcomes are compared with pretreatment status, clients are better off with EMDR treatment than without." Other researchers have also found that patients benefit from EMDR and that EMDR is more effective than no treatment at all (DeBell & Jones, 1997; Goldstein & others, 2000).

Is EMDR *More* Effective Than Other Standard Therapies?

The alert reader will have noticed that EMDR has many elements in common with other treatment techniques, some of them well-established and based on well-documented psychological principles. For example, *exposure therapy* is one technique that has long been recognized as an effective treatment for PTSD and phobias. **Exposure therapy** is related to systematic

In contrast, one ongoing issue in contemporary psychotherapy is the proliferation of *untested* psychotherapies (Beutler, 2000; Lilienfeld, 1998). The fact that there is little difference in outcome among the empirically supported therapies does *not* mean that any and every form of psychotherapy is equally effective (Herbert & others, 2000). Too often, untested therapy techniques are heavily marketed and promoted, promising miraculous cures with little or no empirical research to back them up. As veteran psychotherapy researcher Arnold Lazarus (2000) writes:

desensitization: The person gradually and repeatedly relives the frightening experience under controlled conditions to help him overcome his fear of the dreaded object or situation and establish more adaptive beliefs and cognitions. Using a combination of behavioral and cognitive techniques, exposure therapy has a high rate of success in the treatment of anxiety disorders (Foa & Meadows, 1997).

Is EMDR more effective than exposure therapy or other cognitive-behavioral treatments? No. When Davidson and Parker (2001) compared the effectiveness of EMDR to other exposure treatments, no difference was found. EMDR was no more effective than standard treatments for anxiety disorders, including PTSD.

Are the Eye Movements Necessary?

Several research studies have compared standard EMDR with other treatments that duplicate all aspects of the treatment *except* the eye movement component. For example, some studies have compared treatment effects between an eye-movement condition (EMDR) and "sham" EMDR, a kind of placebo condition in which the participants fixed their eyes on a bright light that did not move or engaged in finger tapping with alternate hands. All these studies found *no difference* between

"real" EMDR and sham EMDR (DeBell & Jones, 1997; Feske & Goldstein, 1997; Goldstein & others, 2000). In their meta-analysis, Davidson and Parker (2001) agreed with other researchers: There was *no difference* in outcome between treatments that incorporated eye movements and the "sham" EMDR that did not.

So if you remove the eye movements from the EMDR treatment protocol, what is left? Harvard psychologist Richard McNally (1998), an expert in the treatment of anxiety disorders, puts it succinctly: "What is effective in EMDR is not new, and what is new is not effective." Psychologists Gerald Rosen and Jeffrey Lohr (1997) are more blunt:

> Shapiro took existing elements from cognitive-behavior therapies, added the unnecessary ingredient of finger waving, and then took the technique on the road before science could catch up.

Is EMDR a Pseudoscience?

Some psychologists argue that EMDR is just that—a pseudoscience (Lilienfeld, 1996; G. Rosen & others, 1999). Psychologist James D. Herbert and his colleagues (2000) note several ways in which EMDR displays the fundamental characteristics of a pseudoscience, which was discussed in Chapter 1:

EMDR appears to possess the outward form of science but little of its substance. The appearance of science, such as case studies reported in peer reviewed journals, selective publicity of weak tests of effectiveness, [and] scientific-sounding jargon . . . serve to obscure EMDR's lack of scientific substance and have persuaded many of its scientific legitimacy. Although there is little evidence to support the strong claims of EMDR's proponents, this treatment has resulted in a significant financial return.

The case of EMDR highlights an ongoing problem in contemporary psychotherapy. Too often, "revolutionary" new therapies are developed, advertised, and marketed directly to the public—and to therapists—*before* controlled scientific studies of their effectiveness have been conducted (A. Lazarus, 2000). Many of the untested therapies are ineffective or, as in the case of EMDR, no more effective than established therapies. Others are downright dangerous, such as the "rebirthing" technique that resulted in the death of a young girl in Colorado in April 2000. Ten-year-old Candace Newmaker suffocated after being wrapped in a blanket, covered with pillows, and restrained by four adult "therapists" who taunted her when she cried, pleaded for oxygen, and repeatedly told them she could not breathe.

Like many pseudosciences, such fringe therapies rely on anecdotes and testimonials to persuade others of their efficacy. Their proponents often resort to vague, scientific-sounding explanations of their mechanisms rather than established—and testable—scientific principles (Lilienfeld, 1998). James Herbert and his colleagues (2000) argue that new therapeutic techniques should be tested *before* they are put into widespread use, not after. The conditions that new therapies should meet are summarized in the table at left.

The Burden of Proof

Psychologist James D. Herbert and his colleagues (2000) argue that before being put into widespread use, new therapies should provide empirically based answers to the following questions:

- Does the treatment work better than no treatment?
- Does the treatment work better than a placebo?
- Does the treatment work better than standard treatments?
- Does the treatment work through the processes that its proponents claim?

SOURCE: Herbert & others (2000).

In today's world, it seems to me that good marketing lies behind the uncritical acceptance of a spate of ill-founded nostrums. Pretty packages (quite literally in some cases) and advertising hype are widely used to persuade the public (and professionals) to endorse their dubious philosophies and treatments.

We examine the empirical evidence for one highly promoted new therapy in Science Versus Pseudoscience Box 15.4.

eclecticism
(ee-KLEK-tuh-*sizz*-um) The pragmatic and integrated use of techniques from different psychotherapies.

What Factors Contribute to Effective Psychotherapy?

How can we explain the fact that different forms of psychotherapy are basically equivalent in producing positive results? One possible explanation is that the factors that are crucial to producing improvement are present in *all* effective therapies. Researchers have identified a number of common factors that are related to a positive therapy outcome (see Hubble & others, 1999).

First and most important is the quality of the *therapeutic relationship* (Bachelor & Horvath, 1999). In effective psychotherapies, the therapist–client relationship is characterized by mutual respect, trust, and hope. Working in a cooperative alliance, both people are actively trying to achieve the same goals.

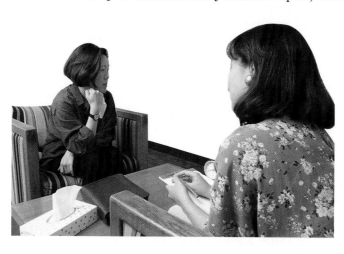

Therapeutic Sensitivity to Cultural Differences A therapist's sensitivity to a client's cultural values can affect the ability to form a good working relationship and, ultimately, the success of psychotherapy. Thus, some clients prefer to see therapists who are from the same cultural background, as is the case with the Korean-American therapist and client shown. In general, therapists have become more attuned to the important role played by culture in effective psychotherapy.

Second, certain *therapist characteristics* are associated with successful therapy. Effective therapists have a caring attitude and the ability to listen empathically. They are genuinely committed to their clients' welfare (Strupp, 1996). Regardless of orientation, effective therapists tend to be warm, sensitive, and responsive people, and they are perceived as sincere and genuine (Beutler & others, 1994).

Effective therapists are also sensitive to the *cultural differences* that may exist between themselves and their clients (Pope-Davis & others, 2001). As described in Culture and Human Behavior Box 15.5, cultural differences can be a barrier to effective psychotherapy. Increasingly, training in cultural sensitivity and multicultural issues is being incorporated into psychological training programs in the United States (G. Hall, 2001).

Third, *client characteristics* are important. If the client is motivated, committed to therapy, and actively involved in the process, a successful outcome is much more likely (Tallman & Bohart, 1999). Emotional and social maturity and the ability to express thoughts and feelings are important. Clients who are optimistic, who expect psychotherapy to help them with their problems, and who don't have a previous history of psychological disorders are more likely to benefit from therapy (Leon & others, 1999). Finally, *external circumstances,* such as a stable living situation and supportive family members, can enhance the effectiveness of therapy.

Notice that none of these factors is specific to any particular brand of psychotherapy. However, this does not mean that differences between psychotherapy techniques are completely irrelevant. Rather, it's important that there be a good "match" between the person seeking help and the specific psychotherapy techniques used. One person may be very comfortable with psychodynamic techniques, such as exploring childhood memories and free association. Another person might be more open to behavioral techniques, like systematic desensitization. For therapy to be optimally effective, the individual should feel comfortable with both the therapist and the therapist's approach to therapy.

Increasingly, such a personalized approach to therapy is being facilitated by the movement of mental health professionals toward **eclecticism**—the pragmatic and integrated use of diverse psychotherapy techniques (Garfield, 1992). Today, therapists iden-

"I UTILIZE THE BEST FROM FREUD, THE BEST FROM JUNG AND THE BEST FROM MY UNCLE MARTY, A VERY SMART FELLOW."

CULTURE AND HUMAN BEHAVIOR 15.5

Cultural Values and Psychotherapy

The goals and techniques of many established approaches to psychotherapy tend to reflect European and North American cultural values. In this box, we'll look at how those cultural values can clash with the values of clients from other cultures, diminishing the effectiveness of psychotherapy.

A Focus on the Individual

In Western psychotherapy, the client is usually encouraged to become more assertive, more self-sufficient, and less dependent on others in making decisions. Problems are assumed to have an internal cause and are expected to be solved by the client alone. Therapy emphasizes meeting the client's individual needs, even if those needs conflict with the demands of significant others. In collectivistic cultures, however, the needs of the individual are much more strongly identified with the needs of the group to which he or she belongs (Triandis, 1996).

For example, traditional Native Americans are less likely than European-Americans to believe that personal problems are due to an internal cause within the individual (Sue & others, 1994). Instead, one person's problems may be seen as a problem for the entire community to resolve. In traditional forms of Native American healing, family members, friends, and other members of the community may be asked to participate in the treatment or healing rituals. One type of therapy, called *network therapy,* is conducted in the person's home and can involve as many as 70 members of the individual's community or tribe (LaFromboise & others, 1993b).

Latino cultures, too, emphasize interdependence over independence. In particular, they stress the value of *familismo*—the importance of the extended family network. Because the sense of family is so central to Latino culture, psychologist Lilian Comas-Diaz (1993) recommends that members of the client's extended family, such as grandparents

Cultural Values Even after immigrating to the United States, many people maintain strong ties with their cultural heritage. Here, Arab-American children attend an Islamic school. Notice that the young female students as well as the teacher are wearing the traditional *chador,* or veil. The traditional beliefs of some cultures, such as the Islamic belief that women should be modest and obedient to their husbands, may conflict with the values inherent in Western psychotherapies.

and in-laws, be actively involved in psychological treatment.

Many collectivistic Asian cultures also emphasize a respect for the needs of others. The Japanese psychotherapy called *Naikan therapy* is a good example of how such cultural values affect the goals of psychotherapy (Reynolds, 1990). According to Naikan therapy, being self-absorbed is the surest path to psychological suffering. Thus, the goal of Naikan therapy is to replace the focus on the self with a sense of gratitude and obligation toward others. Rather than talking about how his own needs were not met by family members, the Naikan client is asked to mediate on how he has failed to meet the needs of others.

The Importance of Insight

Psychodynamic, humanistic, and cognitive therapies all stress the importance of insight or awareness of an individual's thoughts and feelings. But many cultures

do *not* emphasize the importance of exploring painful thoughts and feelings in resolving psychological problems. For example, Asian cultures stress that mental health is enhanced by the avoidance of negative thinking. Hence, a depressed or anxious person in China and many other Asian countries would be encouraged to *avoid* focusing on upsetting thoughts (Sue & others, 1994).

Intimate Disclosure Between Therapist and Client

Many Western psychotherapies are based on the assumption that the clients will disclose their deepest feelings and most private thoughts to their therapists. But in some cultures, intimate details of one's personal life would never be discussed with a stranger. Asians are taught to disclose intimate details only to very close friends. For example, a young Vietnamese student of ours vowed never to return to see a psychologist she had consulted about her struggles with depression. The counselor, she complained, was too "nosy" and asked too many personal questions. In many cultures, people are far more likely to turn to family members or friends than they are to mental health professionals (Nishio & Bilmes, 1993).

The demands for emotional openness may also clash with cultural values. In Asian cultures, people tend to avoid the public expression of emotions and often express thoughts and feelings nonverbally. Native American cultures tend to value the restraint of emotions rather than the open expression of emotions (LaFromboise & others, 1993b).

Recognizing the need for psychotherapists to become more culturally sensitive, the American Psychological Association has recommended formal training in multicultural awareness for all psychologists (Edwards, 1995a; Hall, 1997). The APA (1993) has also published guidelines for psychologists who provide psychological help to culturally diverse populations.

tify themselves as eclectic more often than any other orientation (Kopta & others, 1999). *Eclectic psychotherapists* carefully tailor the therapy approach to the problems and characteristics of the person seeking help. For example, an eclectic therapist might integrate insight-oriented techniques with specific behavioral techniques to help someone suffering from extreme shyness.

15.2 R·E·V·I·E·W

Elements of Effective Psychotherapy

Identify each statement below as true or false. If a statement is false, rewrite it to correct it.

_____ *1.* Meta-analysis is the most effective psychoanalytic technique.

_____ *2.* In general, psychotherapy is no more effective than talking with a friend.

_____ *3.* Behavior therapy is the single most effective therapy available for all psychological disorders.

_____ *4.* Because the principles of effective therapy are universal, cultural differences between clients and therapists have no impact on the effectiveness of psychotherapy.

_____ *5.* Regardless of which form of therapy they practice, the most effective psychotherapists are perceived as warm, genuine, and sincere.

_____ *6.* A client's attitude toward therapy has minimal impact on therapy's effectiveness.

Biomedical Therapies

Key Theme

▓ The biomedical therapies are medical treatments for the symptoms of psychological disorders and include medication and electroconvulsive therapy.

Key Questions

▓ What medications are used to treat the symptoms of schizophrenia, anxiety, bipolar disorder, and depression, and how do they achieve their effects?

▓ What is electroconvulsive therapy, and what are its advantages and disadvantages?

Medical treatments for psychological disorders actually predate modern psychotherapy by hundreds of years. In past centuries, patients were whirled, soothed, drenched, restrained, and isolated—all in an attempt to alleviate symptoms of psychological disorders. Today, such "treatments" seem cruel, inhumane, and useless. Keep in mind, however, that these early treatments were based on the limited medical knowledge of the time. As you'll see in this section, some of the early efforts to treat psychological disorders did eventually evolve into treatments that are widely used today.

For the most part, it was not until the twentieth century that effective biomedical therapies were developed to treat the symptoms of mental disorders. Today, the most common biomedical therapy is the use of *psychoactive medications*—prescription drugs that alter mental functions and alleviate psychological symptoms. Although often used alone, psychoactive medications are increasingly combined with psychotherapy (Keller & others, 2000; Kupfer & Frank, 2001).

Many of the psychoactive medications used today were discovered by accident or in the course of medical research in some other area. Typically, it was only after a medication had been observed to relieve psychological symptoms that sci-

antipsychotic medications (an-ti-sī-KA-tick) Prescription drugs that are used to reduce psychotic symptoms; frequently used in the treatment of schizophrenia; also called *neuroleptics*.

entists began to unravel how the drug worked (Klerman & others, 1994). In the process, researchers have gained important insights about the biological underpinnings of many psychological disorders.

Because they are medical treatments, the biomedical therapies currently must be administered by a psychiatrist or other licensed physician. Family physicians write many of the prescriptions for medications that affect psychological symptoms (Sleek, 1994). But as we noted at the beginning of this chapter, the momentum to allow clinical psychologists to prescribe psychoactive medications is growing, and some psychologists in the U.S. military are already prescribing medications for the treatment of mental disorders.

We'll begin this section by looking at the major categories of psychoactive medications used to treat psychological symptoms. Following that, we'll consider the most controversial biomedical therapy in use today: electroconvulsive shock therapy.

Antipsychotic Medications

For more than 2,000 years, traditional practitioners of medicine in India used an herb derived from the snakeroot plant, a shrub that grows in central Asia. The herbal extract was used to treat diverse medical conditions, including insomnia, epilepsy, and snakebite. But its primary use in traditional Indian medicine was to diminish the psychotic symptoms commonly associated with schizophrenia: hallucinations, delusions, and disordered thought processes (Bhatara & others, 1997). The same plant was used in traditional Japanese medicine to treat anxiety and restlessness (Jilek, 1993). In the 1930s, Indian physicians discovered that the herb was also helpful in the treatment of high blood pressure. They developed a synthetic version of the herb's active ingredient, called *reserpine.*

Reserpine first came to the attention of American researchers as a potential treatment for high blood pressure. But it wasn't until the early 1950s that American researchers became aware of research in India demonstrating the effectiveness of reserpine in treating schizophrenia (Frankenburg, 1994). Almost 2,000 years after reserpine's effectiveness had first been discovered, U.S. clinical trials on reserpine as a treatment of schizophrenia finally began in the 1950s.

It was also during the 1950s that French scientists began investigating the psychoactive properties of another drug, called *chlorpromazine.* Like reserpine, chlorpromazine diminished the psychotic symptoms commonly seen in schizophrenia. Hence, reserpine and chlorpromazine were dubbed **antipsychotic medications.** Because chlorpromazine had fewer side effects than reserpine, it nudged out reserpine as the preferred medication for treating schizophrenia-related symptoms. Today, chlorpromazine is better known by its trade name, *Thorazine,* and is still widely used to treat psychotic symptoms. The antipsychotic drugs are also referred to as *neuroleptic medications* or simply *neuroleptics.*

How do these drugs diminish psychotic symptoms? Reserpine and chlorpromazine act differently on the brain, but both drugs reduce levels of the neurotransmitter called

Historical Treatments for Mental Illness
Top left: Found in Peru, this pre-Columbian skull shows the results of primitive surgery on the brain, called *trephining,* presumably as a treatment to allow evil spirits to leave the body. Bottom left: A "tranquilizing chair" was developed in the early 1800s to restrain and sedate unmanageable patients. Above: An early treatment apparatus called the "circulating swing" involved spinning patients.

The First Herbal Antipsychotic More than 2,000 years before chlorpromazine was synthesized, physicians in India were using an herb derived from *Rauwolfia serpentina,* which is more commonly known as the snakeroot plant. Ancient Hindu medical texts advised the use of the herb to treat *oonmaad,* a Sanskrit term that referred to an abnormal condition of the mind that included disruptions in "wisdom, perception, knowledge, memory, character, creativity, conduct, and behavior" (Bhatara & others, 1997). Today, it is known that the herb has a high affinity for dopamine receptors in the brain.

SOURCE: Woodson & others (1957). Reprinted by permission.

Table | **15.7**

Antipsychotic Drugs

	Generic Name	Trade Name
Typical Antipsychotics	Chlorpromazine	Thorazine
	Fluphenazine	Prolixin
	Trifluoperazine	Stelazine
	Thioridazine	Mellaril
	Thiothixene	Navane
	Haloperidol	Haldol
Atypical Antipsychotics	Clozapine	Clozaril
	Risperidone	Risperdal
	Olanzapine	Zyprexa
	Sertindole	Serlect
	Quetiapine	Seroquel

SOURCE: Adapted from Julien (2001).

FIGURE 15.5 Change in the Number of Patients Hospitalized for Mental Disorders, 1946–1983 When the first antipsychotic drugs came into wide use in the late 1950s, the number of people hospitalized for mental disorders began to drop sharply.

SOURCE: Adapted from Julien (2001).

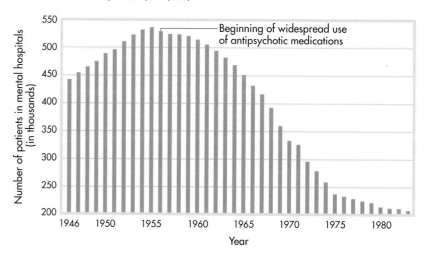

dopamine. Since the development of these early drugs, more than 30 other antipsychotic medications have been developed (see Table 15.7). These antipsychotic medications also act on dopamine receptors in the brain (Klerman & others, 1994).

The first antipsychotics effectively reduced the *positive symptoms* of schizophrenia—hallucinations, delusions, and disordered thinking (see Chapter 14). This therapeutic effect had a revolutionary impact on the number of people hospitalized for schizophrenia. Until the 1950s, patients with schizophrenia were thought to be incurable. These chronic patients formed the bulk of the population on the "back wards" of psychiatric hospitals. With the introduction of the antipsychotic medications, however, the number of patients in mental hospitals decreased dramatically (see Figure 15.5).

Drawbacks of Antipsychotic Medications

Even though the early antipsychotic drugs allowed thousands of patients to be discharged from hospitals, these drugs had a number of drawbacks. First, they didn't actually *cure* schizophrenia. Psychotic symptoms often returned if a person stopped taking the medication.

Second, the early antipsychotic medications were not very effective in eliminating the *negative symptoms* of schizophrenia—social withdrawal, apathy, and lack of emotional expressiveness (Marder & others, 1993). In some cases, the drugs even made negative symptoms worse. Third, the antipsychotics often produced unwanted side effects, such as dry mouth, weight gain, constipation, sleepiness, and poor concentration (Gerlach & Peacock, 1994).

Fourth, the fact that the early antipsychotics *globally* altered brain levels of dopamine turned out to be a double-edged sword. Dopamine pathways in the brain are involved not only in psychotic symptoms, but also in normal motor movements. Consequently, the early antipsychotic medications could produce motor-related side effects—muscle tremors, rigid movements, a shuffling gait, and a masklike facial expression (Barondes, 1993). This collection of side effects occurred so commonly that mental hospital staff members sometimes informally referred to it as the "Thorazine shuffle."

Even more disturbing, the long-term use of antipsychotic medications causes a small percentage of people to develop a potentially irreversible motor disorder called *tardive dyskinesia.* Tardive dyskinesia is characterized by severe, uncontrollable facial tics and grimaces, chewing movements, and other involuntary movements of the lips, jaw, and tongue.

Closely tied to the various side effects of the first antipsychotic drugs is a fifth problem: the "revolving door" pattern of hospitalization, discharge, and rehospitalization. Schizophrenic patients, once stabilized by antipsychotic medication, were released from hospitals into the community. But because of the medication's unpleasant side effects, inadequate medical follow-up, or both, many patients eventually stopped taking the medication. When psychotic symptoms returned, the patients were rehospitalized.

The Atypical Antipsychotics

Recently, a new generation of antipsychotic drugs has given rise to increased optimism about the treatment of schizophrenia. Called **atypical antipsychotic medications,** these drugs act differently on the brain than the older antipsychotic drugs. The first atypical antipsychotics, *clozapine* and *risperidone,* affect levels of the neurotransmitter *serotonin* as well as dopamine in the brain.

The atypical antipsychotics have three important advantages over traditional antipsychotic drugs (Meltzer, 1994, 1995). First, clozapine and risperidone are much less likely to cause the movement-related side effects associated with the older antipsychotic drugs. That's because these new drugs block dopamine brain receptors far more *selectively* than the older antipsychotics do. Rather than blocking dopamine receptors globally throughout the brain, they act on dopamine receptors primarily in the brain areas associated with psychotic symptoms.

Second, clozapine and risperidone are much more effective than the older antipsychotics in treating the negative symptoms of schizophrenia—apathy, social withdrawal, and flat emotions. And third, a significant proportion of patients who have not responded to any of the traditional antipsychotic drugs improve after taking clozapine or risperidone, sometimes dramatically (Kane, 1994; Marder & Meibach, 1994).

However, new drugs bring the potential of new side effects. In a small percentage of patients, clozapine can cause a life-threatening drop in white blood cells. Thus, patients taking clozapine must be monitored with weekly blood tests. Another new drug, *olanzapine,* is structurally similar to clozapine but does not produce this dangerous side effect. The new drugs appear to lessen the incidence of the "revolving door" pattern of hospitalization and rehospitalization. When compared to discharged patients taking conventional drugs, patients taking risperidone or olanzapine were much less likely to relapse and return to the hospital (Rabinowitz & others, 2001).

Along with olanzapine, two other new atypical antipsychotic medications have been released: *sertindole* and *quetiapine.* These new drugs produce greater benefits and far fewer side effects for people suffering from the most severe forms of mental disorder.

Antianxiety Medications

The symptoms of anxiety are well known to almost everyone—feeling tense, jittery, and apprehensive. It's perfectly normal to feel mildly anxious when you're facing a difficult challenge or trying to cope with some crisis. But when anxiety is intense and persistent, it can be disabling, interfering with a person's ability to eat, sleep, and function. At such times, **antianxiety medications** may be prescribed (see Table 15.8).

The best-known antianxiety drugs are the *benzodiazepines,* which include the trade-name drugs *Valium* and *Xanax.* These antianxiety medications calm jittery feelings, relax the muscles, and promote sleep. They take effect rapidly, usually within an hour or

atypical antipsychotic medications
Newer antipsychotic medications that, in contrast to the early antipsychotic drugs, block dopamine receptors in brain regions associated with psychotic symptoms rather than more globally throughout the brain, resulting in fewer side effects.

antianxiety medications
Prescription drugs that are used to alleviate the symptoms of anxiety.

Table | **15.8**

Antianxiety Drugs		
	Generic Name	**Trade Name**
Benzodiazepines	Diazepam	Valium
	Chlordiazepoxide	Librium
	Lorazepam	Ativan
	Triazolam	Halcion
	Alprazolam	Xanax
Non-benzodiazepine	Buspirone	Buspar

SOURCE: Based on Julien (2001).

so. In general, the benzodiazepines produce their effects by increasing the level of *GABA,* a neurotransmitter that inhibits the transmission of nerve impulses in the brain and slows brain activity.

Taken for a week or two, and in therapeutic doses, the benzodiazepines can effectively reduce anxiety levels. However, the benzodiazepines have several potentially dangerous side effects. First, they can reduce coordination, alertness, and reaction time. Second, their effects can be intensified when they are combined with alcohol and many other drugs, including over-the-counter antihistamines. Such a combination can produce severe drug intoxication, even death.

Third, the benzodiazepines are physically addictive if taken in large quantities or over a long period of time (Maxmen & Ward, 1995). If physical dependence occurs, the person must withdraw from the drug gradually, as abrupt withdrawal can produce life-threatening symptoms. Because of their addictive potential, the benzodiazepines are less widely prescribed today than they were 25 years ago.

A newer antianxiety drug with the trade name *Buspar* has fewer side effects. Buspar is not a benzodiazepine, and it does not affect the neurotransmitter GABA. In fact, exactly how Buspar works is unclear, but it is believed to affect brain dopamine and serotonin levels (Mahmood & Sahajwalla, 1999). Regardless, Buspar relieves anxiety while allowing the individual to maintain normal alertness. It does not cause the drowsiness, sedation, and cognitive impairment that are associated with the benzodiazepines. And Buspar seems to have a very low risk of dependency and physical addiction.

However, Buspar has one major drawback: It must be taken for two to three *weeks* before anxiety is reduced. While this reduces Buspar's potential for abuse, it also reduces its effectiveness for treating acute anxiety. For immediate, short-term relief from anxiety, the benzodiazepines are still regarded as the most effective medications currently available (Lickey & Gordon, 1991). But for the long-term treatment of chronic anxiety, such as in panic disorder or generalized anxiety disorder, Buspar may be the most appropriate antianxiety medication.

Lithium

In Chapter 14, on psychological disorders, we described *bipolar disorder,* more commonly known as *manic depression.* The medication most commonly used to treat bipolar disorder is **lithium,** a naturally occurring substance. Lithium counteracts both manic and depressive symptoms in bipolar patients (Barondes, 1993). Its effectiveness in treating bipolar disorder has been well established since the 1960s (Shou, 1993).

The beneficial effects of lithium have been known about for better than a century. Soaking in the famous hot springs in Arkansas or Banff, Canada, has long been suggested to people to help diminish symptoms of depression. The water in those hot springs has a naturally high concentration of lithium. An early version of the soft drink 7-Up included small amounts of lithium (Maxmen & Ward, 1995). Marketed as "lithium soda," the ad campaign claimed that it was the drink that "took the ouch out of the grouch!"

As a treatment for bipolar disorder, lithium stops acute manic episodes over the course of a week or two. Once an acute manic episode is under control, the long-term use of lithium can help prevent relapses into either mania or depression. The majority of patients with bipolar disorder respond well to lithium therapy (Keck & McElroy, 1993; Shou, 1993). However, lithium doesn't help everyone. Some people on lithium therapy experience relapses (Sachs & others, 1994).

Like all other medications, lithium has potential side effects. There is a very narrow difference between the therapeutic dosage level and the toxic dosage level. If the lithium level is too low, manic symptoms persist. If it is too high, lithium poisoning may occur, with symptoms such as vomiting, muscle weakness, and reduced muscle coordination. Consequently, the patient's lithium blood level must be carefully monitored (Shou, 1993).

Lithium Water Lithium salt, a naturally occurring substance, was used in many over-the-counter medicines before it was discovered to be helpful in the treatment of mania. As this late-nineteenth-century ad shows, small amounts of lithium salt were also added to bottled water. An early version of the soft drink 7-Up included small amounts of lithium (Maxmen & Ward, 1995). Marketed as "lithium soda," the ad campaign claimed that it was the drink that took "the ouch out of the grouch!"

How lithium works was a complete mystery until very recently. Lithium's action was especially puzzling because it prevented mood disturbances at both ends of the emotional spectrum—mania *and* depression. It turns out that lithium affects levels of an excitatory neurotransmitter called *glutamate,* which is found in many areas of the brain. Apparently, lithium stabilizes the availability of glutamate within a narrow, normal range, preventing both abnormal highs and abnormal lows (Dixon & Hokin, 1998).

Bipolar disorder can also be treated with an anticonvulsant medicine called *Depakote.* Originally used to prevent epileptic seizures, Depakote seems to be especially helpful in treating those who rapidly cycle through bouts of bipolar disorder several times a year. It's also useful for treating bipolar patients who do not respond to lithium (Jefferson, 1995). Depakote is the first new biomedical treatment for bipolar disorder since lithium was approved in 1970.

Antidepressant Medications

The **antidepressant medications** counteract the classic symptoms of depression—hopelessness, guilt, dejection, suicidal thoughts, difficulty concentrating, and disruptions in sleep, energy, appetite, and sexuality. The first effective antidepressant was accidentally discovered when a new drug for tuberculosis was being tested in the 1950s. Unexpectedly, patients experienced relief from depressive symptoms (Carlson, 1994; Kramer, 1993). Since that discovery, new groups of antidepressant drugs have been developed (see Table 15.9).

The first generation of antidepressants consists of two classes of drugs, called *tricyclics* and *MAO inhibitors*. Tricyclics and MAO inhibitors affect multiple neurotransmitter pathways in the brain (Golden & Gilmore, 1990). Evidence suggests that these drugs alleviate depression by increasing the availability of two key brain neurotransmitters, *norepinephrine* and *serotonin.*

Once again, though, exactly how tricyclics and MAO inhibitors work is unknown. For example, even though brain levels of norepinephrine and serotonin begin to rise within *hours* of taking a tricyclic or MAO inhibitor, it can take up to six *weeks* before depressive symptoms begin to lift (Richelson, 1993).

Tricyclics and MAO inhibitors have been widely used for many years. In about 75 percent of patients with depression, they effectively eliminate depressive symptoms (Fawcett, 1994; Hornig-Rohan & Amsterdam, 1994). But these drugs can also produce numerous side effects. Tricyclic antidepressants can cause weight gain, dizziness, dry mouth and eyes, and sedation. And, because tricyclics affect the cardiovascular system, an overdose can be fatal. As for the MAO inhibitors, they can interact with a chemical found in many foods, including cheese, smoked meats, and red wine. Eating these foods while taking an MAO inhibitor can result in dangerously high blood pressure, leading to stroke or even death.

The search for antidepressants with fewer side effects led to the development of the second generation of antidepressants. Second-generation antidepressants include *trazodone* and *bupropion.* Although chemically different from the tricyclics, the second-generation antidepressants were generally no more effective than the first-generation ones, and they turned out to have many of the same side effects (Kramer, 1993).

In 1987, the picture changed dramatically with the introduction of a third group of antidepressants, the **selective serotonin reuptake inhibitors,** abbreviated **SSRIs.** Rather than acting on multiple neurotransmitter pathways, the SSRIs primarily affect the availability of a single neurotransmitter—

lithium
A naturally occurring substance that is used in the treatment of bipolar disorder.

antidepressant medications
Prescription drugs that are used to reduce the symptoms associated with depression.

selective serotonin reuptake inhibitors (SSRIs)
Class of antidepressant medications that increase the availability of serotonin in the brain and cause fewer side effects than earlier antidepressants; they include Prozac, Paxil, and Zoloft.

Table | **15.9**

Antidepressant Drugs

	Generic Name	Trade Name
First-Generation Antidepressants		
Tricyclic antidepressants	Imipramine	Tofranil
	Desipramine	Norpramin
	Amitriptyline	Elavil
MAO inhibitors	Phenelzine	Nardil
	Tranylcypromine	Parnate
Second-Generation Antidepressants	Trazodone	Desyrel
	Bupropion	Wellbutrin
Selective Serotonin Reuptake Inhibitors (SSRIs)	Fluoxetine	Prozac
	Sertraline	Zoloft
	Paroxetine	Paxil
	Fluvoxamine	Luvox
Dual-Action Antidepressants	Nefazodone	Serzone
	Mirtazapine	Remeron
	Citalopram	Celexa
Dual-Reuptake Inhibitors	Venlafaxine	Effexor

SOURCE: Based on Julien (2001).

focus on **Neuroscience**

Prefrontal cortex

(a)
Baseline—Before Treatment

Prefrontal cortex

(b)
Decrease in activity after 12 weeks
of treatment with Paxil

Prefrontal cortex

(c)
Decrease in activity after 12 weeks of
treatment with interpersonal therapy

Comparing Psychotherapy and Antidepressant Medication Both antidepressant medication and psychotherapy have been used to treat major depression. As we discussed in Chapter 14, major depression is characterized by a variety of physical symptoms, including changes in brain activity (Sackeim, 2001; Thase, 2001). Antidepressants are assumed to work their effect by changing brain chemistry and activity. Does psychotherapy have the same effect?

In a recent study, PET scans were done on people with major depression and compared to a matched group of normal control subjects who were *not* depressed (Brody & others, 2001). Compared with nondepressed adults, depressed individuals showed increased activity in three areas of the brain: the *prefrontal cortex,* the *caudate nucleus,* and the *thalamus.* The day after the first scan, 10 of the individuals started taking the antidepressant Paxil, an SSRI. The remaining 14 individuals in the study started interpersonal therapy (discussed earlier in this chapter), a psychodynamic therapy that has been shown to be effective in the treatment of depression. Twelve weeks after beginning treatment, the participants' depressive symptoms were measured, and all 24 study participants underwent PET scans again.

Following *either* treatment, patients' depressive symptoms improved. And as the PET scans reveal, patients in *both* groups showed a trend toward more normalized brain functioning. Activity declined significantly in brain regions that had shown abnormally high activity before treatment began.

The PET scans shown here depict changes in the prefrontal cortex, one of the regions that showed a significant change toward more normal metabolic levels. Scan (a) shows activity levels in the prefrontal cortex before treatment. Scans (b) and (c) show the metabolic *decrease* in activity following treatment with Paxil (b) or interpersonal therapy (c). In this comparison, note that (b) and (c) show the amount of change from the baseline condition, rather than the actual metabolic level of activity.

As these findings emphasize, *both* psychotherapy and antidepressant medication affect brain chemistry and functioning. In another study, both patients who were treated with interpersonal therapy or with the antidepressant Effexor also showed improvement and similar changes in brain functioning (Martin & others, 2001).

SOURCE: Brody & others (2001).

serotonin. Compared with the earlier antidepressants, the new antidepressants act much more selectively in targeting specific serotonin pathways in the brain. The first SSRI to be released was *fluoxetine,* which is better known by its trade name, *Prozac.* Prozac was quickly followed by its chemical cousins, *Zoloft* and *Paxil.*

Prozac was specifically designed to alleviate depressive symptoms with fewer side effects than earlier antidepressants. It achieved that goal with considerable success. Although no more effective than tricyclics or MAO inhibitors, Prozac and the other SSRI antidepressants tend to produce fewer, and milder, side effects. But no medication is risk-free. Among Prozac's potential side effects are headaches, nervousness, difficulty sleeping, loss of appetite, and sexual dysfunction (Sleek, 1994).

Because of its overall effectiveness and relatively mild side-effects profile, Prozac quickly became very popular. By the early 1990s, an estimated *1 million prescriptions per month* were being written for Prozac. By the late 1990s, Prozac had become the best-selling antidepressant in the world, with annual sales of more than $2 billion.

Since the original SSRIs were released, new antidepressants have been developed, including *Serzone, Remeron,* and *Celexa.* These antidepressants, called *dual-action antidepressants,* also affect serotonin levels, but their mechanism is somewhat different from that of the SSRIs. They are as effective as the SSRIs but have different side effects. *Effexor* is a newer antidepressant best classified as a dual reuptake inhibitor, affecting levels of both serotonin and norepinephrine. Possibly because of its dual action, Effexor seems to be more effective than the SSRIs in alleviating the symptoms of depression (Thase & others, 2001).

Electroconvulsive Therapy

As we have just seen, millions of prescriptions are written for antidepressant medications in the United States every year. In contrast, about 100,000 patients a year receive **electroconvulsive therapy,** or **ECT,** as a medical treatment for severe depression. Also known as *electroshock therapy* or *shock therapy,* electroconvulsive therapy involves using a brief burst of electric current to induce a seizure in the brain, much like an epileptic seizure. Although ECT is most commonly used to treat depression, it is occasionally used to treat mania, catatonia, and other severe mental disorders (Glass, 2001).

Zapping the brain with electric current as a treatment for mental illness may seem a bit far-fetched, but there was a scientific rationale for the development of ECT. Chemically induced seizures were first used as a treatment for mental disorders in the mid-1700s. Although some patients' psychotic symptoms improved, the effects of chemically produced seizures were both dangerous and unpredictable. Given the controversy that still swirls around ECT, it's ironic that ECT was originally developed by two Italian doctors in the 1930s as a safer and more controlled alternative to chemically induced brain seizures. By the 1940s and 1950s, ECT was being widely used in the United States and Europe (Abrams, 1994).

Today, ECT is a relatively simple and quick medical procedure, usually performed in a hospital. The patient lies on a table. Electrodes are placed on one or both of the patient's temples, and the patient is given a short-term, light anesthesia and muscle-relaxing drugs. To ensure adequate airflow, a breathing tube is placed in the patient's mouth.

While the patient is unconscious, a split-second burst of electricity induces a seizure. The seizure lasts for about a minute. Outwardly, the seizure typically produces mild muscle tremors. After the anesthesia wears off and the patient wakes up, confusion and disorientation may be present for a few hours. It is common for the patient to experience a temporary or permanent memory loss for the events leading up to the treatment. To treat major depression, a series of 6 to 10 ECT treatments are usually spaced over a few weeks.

In the short term, ECT is a very effective treatment for severe depression: About 80 percent of depressed patients improve (Glass, 2001). ECT also relieves the symptoms of depression very quickly, typically within days. Because of its rapid therapeutic effects, ECT can be a lifesaving procedure for extremely suicidal or severely depressed patients. Such patients may not survive for the several weeks it takes for antidepressant drugs to alleviate symptoms. In fact, it is not difficult to find former ECT patients who will flatly say that ECT saved their lives.

ECT may also be considered when patients are not helped by antidepressant medications or psychotherapy or when they cannot tolerate the side effects of medications. For some people, such as elderly individuals, ECT may be less dangerous than antidepressant drugs (Maxmen & Ward, 1995). In general, the complication rate from ECT is very low.

Nevertheless, inducing a brain seizure is not a matter to be taken lightly. ECT has potential dangers. Serious cogni-

electroconvulsive therapy (ECT)
A biomedical therapy used primarily in the treatment of depression that involves electrically inducing a brief brain seizure; also called *electroshock therapy* or *shock therapy.*

Electroconvulsive Therapy ECT is still used in the treatment of depression, especially in people who do not respond to antidepressant medication. In modern ECT, the person is given a short-acting anesthetic and muscle relaxants. A mild seizure, which lasts about a minute, is induced by a brief pulse of electricity.

tive impairments can occur, such as extensive amnesia (memory loss) and disturbances in language and verbal abilities. However, fears that ECT might produce brain damage have not been confirmed by research (Devanand & others, 1994).

ECT's biggest drawback is that its antidepressive effects can be short-lived. Relapses within four months are relatively common (Glass, 2001). About half the patients treated for major depression experience a relapse within six months. Today, patients are often treated with long-term antidepressant medication following ECT, which reduces the relapse rate (Sackeim & others, 2001). In cases of severe, recurrent depression, ECT may also be periodically readministered to prevent the return of depressive symptoms (Gagné & others, 2000).

At this point, you may be wondering why ECT is not in wider use. The reason is that ECT is probably the single most controversial medical treatment for psychological disorders (Glass, 2001). Not everyone agrees that ECT is either safe or effective (Breggin, 1991). For example, ECT has been banned in some countries, like Japan, because of concerns about its safety.

Much of the controversy over ECT stems from its use in the 1940s and 1950s. At that time, electroconvulsive therapy was a frightening and overused treatment. Patients were strapped to a table, and the shock was administered while they were fully conscious. The electrically induced seizures produced such violent convulsions that patients sometimes suffered fractured spines and broken bones. ECT was also used indiscriminately and inappropriately, often as a routine treatment for schizophrenia. Patients and others claimed that "shock therapy" was used to punish unruly patients and maintain order in institutions (Breggin, 1979).

In most countries today, ECT is conducted very differently. Because patients are anesthetized during the seizure, the procedure is painless and psychological trauma is minimized. Muscle-relaxing drugs have reduced the once violent, bone-breaking convulsions to mild muscle twitches. In one survey of patients who had received ECT, two-thirds said that going to the dentist was more upsetting than their ECT treatments (see Maxmen & Ward, 1995).

How does ECT work? Despite more than 50 years of research, it's still not known why electrically inducing a convulsion relieves the symptoms of depression (Glass, 2001). Brain-imaging studies suggest that ECT may reduce activity in brain regions involved in depression (Nobler & others, 2001).

15.3 R·E·V·I·E·W

C·O·N·C·E·P·T

Biomedical Therapies

Match each statement below with one of the following terms: atypical antipsychotic medications, antipsychotic medications, antidepressant medications, ECT, antianxiety medications, lithium.

_____ **1.** Controversial biomedical therapy that induces a brief brain seizure.

_____ **2.** Used in the treatment of bipolar disorder.

_____ **3.** Drugs that globally reduce dopamine levels in the brain.

_____ **4.** Drugs that produce their effects by increasing brain levels of GABA.

_____ **5.** Drugs that are effective in reducing positive and negative symptoms of schizophrenia.

_____ **6.** A category of psychoactive drugs that includes SSRIs and MAO inhibitors.

_____ **7.** Medication that stabilizes the availability of the neurotransmitter called glutamate.

Summing Up
Therapies

As we've seen throughout this chapter, a wide range of therapies is available to help people who are troubled by psychological symptoms and disorders. Marcia, discussed in our Prologue, found a combination of individual psychotherapy and a self-help group particularly effective. Some people are helped by one of the biomedical therapies. Often, psychotherapy includes elements from insight, behavioral, and cognitive forms of therapy. Increasingly, people are being helped by a combination of psychotherapy and biomedical therapy, usually one of the psychoactive medications.

As our discussion of the effectiveness of psychotherapy has shown, characteristics of both the therapist and the client are important to the success of psychotherapy. In our chapter Application, we discuss some general ground rules of psychotherapy, dispel some common misunderstandings, and describe the attitudes that should be brought to the therapeutic relationship. The Application will help you understand the nature of the therapeutic relationship and provides information useful to anyone who may be considering entering psychotherapy.

| **APPLICATION** | What to Expect in Psychotherapy |

The cornerstone of psychotherapy is the relationship between the therapist and the person seeking help. But the therapy relationship is different from all other close relationships. On the one hand, the therapist–client relationship is characterized by intimacy and the disclosure of very private, personal experiences. On the other hand, there are distinct boundaries to the therapist–client relationship. To a therapy client, especially one who is undertaking psychotherapy for the first time, the therapy relationship may sometimes seem confusing and contradictory.

The goal of this Application is to help you develop realistic expectations about the therapist–client relationship and the psychotherapy process. These guidelines are very general, but they should help you better understand the special nature of the therapy relationship. In turn, your awareness of these "ground rules" may increase the likelihood that therapy will produce beneficial results for you. Or, if someone you know is in psychotherapy, this Application may help you understand and support the therapeutic process.

1. Therapy is a collaborative effort.
Don't expect your therapist to do all the work for you. If you are going to benefit from psychotherapy, you must actively participate in the therapeutic process. Often, therapy requires effort not only during the therapy sessions, but also *outside* them. Many therapists assign "homework" to be completed between sessions. You may be asked to keep a diary of your thoughts and behaviors, read assigned material, rehearse skills that you've learned in therapy, and so forth. Such exercises are important components of the overall therapy process.

2. Don't expect your therapist to make decisions for you.
One of the most common misunderstandings about psychotherapy is that your therapist is going to tell you how to run your life. Not so. Virtually all forms of therapy are designed to increase a person's sense of responsibility, confidence, and mastery in dealing with life's problems. Your therapist won't make your decisions for you, but he or she *will* help you explore your feelings about important decisions—including ambivalence or fear. Some people find this frustrating because they want the therapist to tell them what to do. But if your therapist made decisions for you, it would only foster dependency and undermine your ability to be responsible for your own life.

3. Your therapist is not a substitute friend.
Unlike friendship, which is characterized by a mutual give-and take, psychotherapy is focused solely on *you*. Rather than thinking of your therapist as a friend, think of him or her as an expert consultant—someone you've hired to help you deal better with your problems. The fact that your therapist is not socially or personally involved with you allows your therapist to respond objectively and honestly. Part of what allows you to trust your therapist and "open up" emotionally is the knowledge that your therapist is ethically and legally bound to safeguard the confidentiality of what you say.

4. Therapeutic intimacy does not include sexual intimacy.
It's very common for clients to have strong feelings of affection, love, and even sexual attraction toward their therapists (Pope & Tabachnick, 1993). After all, the most effective therapists tend to be warm, empathic people who are genuinely caring and supportive (Beutler & others, 1994). However, *it is never ethical or appropriate for a therapist to have any form of sexual contact with a client.* There are *no* exceptions to that statement. Sexual contact between a therapist and a client violates the ethical standards of all mental health professionals.

Lest we make the matter seem completely one-sided, surveys have revealed that many therapists occasionally feel sexually attracted to their clients (Pope & Tabachnick, 1993; Stake & Oliver, 1991). How often does actual sexual contact occur? About 7 percent of male and 2 percent of female therapists admit that they have had sexual contact with clients (Davis & others, 1995; Williams, 1992).

Sexual involvement between client and therapist can be enormously damaging (Pope, 1990). Not only does it destroy the therapist's professional objectivity in the therapist–client relationship, but it also destroys the trust the client has invested in the therapist. When a therapist becomes sexually involved with a client, regardless of who initiated the sexual contact, the client is being exploited.

Just how psychologically devastating can such sexual exploitation be? One survey found that of patients who had had sex with their therapists, 11 percent were hospitalized, 14 percent attempted suicide, and 1 percent killed themselves because of the experience (see M. Beck & others, 1992; Pope & Bouhoutsos, 1986).

Rather than exploiting a client's feelings of sexual attraction, an ethical therapist will help the client understand and work through such feelings. Therapy should ultimately help you develop closer, more loving relationships with other people—but *not* with your therapist.

5. Expect therapy to challenge how you think and act.
As you confront issues that you've never discussed before or even admitted

to yourself, you may find therapy very anxiety-provoking. Moments of psychological discomfort are a normal, even expected, part of the therapy process.

Think of therapy as a psychological magnifying glass. Therapy tends to magnify both your strengths and your weaknesses. Such intense self-scrutiny is not always flattering. Examining how you habitually deal with failure and success, conflict and resolution, disappointment and joy can be disturbing. You may become aware of the psychological games you play or of how you use ego defense mechanisms to distort reality. You may have to acknowledge your own immature, maladaptive, or destructive behavior patterns. Although it can be painful, becoming aware that changes are needed is a necessary step toward developing healthier forms of thinking and behavior.

6. Don't confuse insight with change.
Despite what you've seen in the movies, developing insight into the sources or nature of your psychological problems does not magically resolve them. Nor does insight automatically translate into healthier thoughts and behaviors. Instead, insight allows you to look at and understand your problems in a new light. The opportunity for change occurs when your therapist helps you use these insights to redefine past experiences, resolve psychological conflicts, and explore more adaptive

forms of behavior. Even with the benefit of insight, it takes effort to change how you think, behave, and react to other people.

7. Don't confuse catharsis with change.
Catharsis refers to the emotional release that people experience from the simple act of talking about their problems. Although it usually produces short-term emotional relief, catharsis in itself does not resolve the problem. Even so, catharsis is an important element of psychotherapy. Discussing emotionally charged issues with a therapist can lessen your sense of psychological tension and urgency and help you explore the problem more rationally and objectively.

8. Don't expect change to happen overnight.
Change occurs in psychotherapy at different rates for different people. How quickly change occurs depends on many factors, such as the seriousness of your problems, the degree to which you are psychologically ready to make needed changes, and the therapist's skill in helping you implement those changes. As a general rule, most people make significant progress in a few months of weekly therapy sessions (McNeilly & Howard, 1991). You can help create the climate for change by choosing a therapist whom you feel comfortable working with and by genuinely investing yourself in the therapy process.

Chapter Review

Therapies

Key Points

Introduction: Psychotherapy and Biomedical Therapy
- Psychological disorders can be treated with psychotherapy or biomedical therapy. **Psychotherapy** is based on the assumption that psychological factors play an important role in psychological disorders and symptoms. The **biomedical therapies** are based on the assumption that biological factors play an important role in psychological disorders and symptoms.

Psychoanalytic Therapy
- **Psychoanalysis** is a form of therapy developed by Sigmund Freud and based on his theory of personality. The goal of psychoanalysis is to unearth repressed conflicts and resolve them in therapy.

- Psychoanalytic techniques and processes include **free association, resistance, dream interpretation, interpretation,** and **transference.** Traditional psychoanalysis involves an intensive, long-term relationship between the patient and the psychoanalyst.

- **Short-term dynamic therapies** are based on psychoanalytic ideas but are more problem-focused and of shorter duration than traditional psychoanalysis. Therapists play a more directive role than traditional psychoanalysts, but they still use psychoanalytic techniques to help the patient resolve unconscious conflicts. **Interpersonal therapy (IPT)** is based on the premise that interpersonal problems are the cause of psychological disorders.

Humanistic Therapy

- **Client-centered therapy** was developed by Carl Rogers. Important aspects of client-centered therapy include a client who directs the focus of therapy sessions and a therapist who is genuine, demonstrates unconditional positive regard, and communicates empathic understanding.

- According to Rogers, clients change and grow when their self-concept becomes healthier as a result of these therapeutic conditions.

Behavior Therapy

- **Behavior therapy** assumes that maladaptive behaviors are learned and uses learning principles to directly change problem behaviors.

- Mary Cover Jones was the first behavior therapist, using the procedure of **counterconditioning** to extinguish phobic behavior in a child.

- Classical conditioning principles are involved in the use of **systematic desensitization** to treat phobias, the **bell and pad treatment** to treat bedwetting, and **aversive conditioning** to treat harmful behaviors such as smoking and alcohol addiction.

- Operant conditioning techniques include using positive reinforcement for desired behaviors and extinction for undesired behaviors. The **token economy** represents the application of operant conditioning to modify the behavior of groups of people who live in a hospital or other institution. Contingency management interventions are one application of the token economy, typically used in outpatient treatment.

Cognitive Therapies

- The **cognitive therapies** are based on the assumption that psychological problems are caused by maladaptive patterns of thinking. Treatment focuses on changing unhealthy thinking patterns to healthier ones.

- **Rational-emotive therapy (RET)** was developed by Albert Ellis. RET focuses on changing the irrational thinking that is assumed to be the cause of emotional distress and psychological problems. Therapy involves identifying and challenging core irrational beliefs.

- **Cognitive therapy (CT)** was developed by Aaron T. Beck. CT is based on the assumption that psychological problems are caused by unrealistic and distorted thinking. Therapy involves teaching the client to recognize negative automatic thoughts and cognitive biases, and to empirically test the reality of the upsetting automatic thoughts.

- **Cognitive-behavioral therapy (CBT)** is based on the assumption that thoughts, moods, and behaviors are functionally interrelated. CBT combines cognitive and behavioral techniques in an integrated but flexible treatment plan.

Group and Family Therapy

- **Group therapy** involves one or more therapists working with several people simultaneously. Group therapy has these advantages: It is cost-effective; therapists can observe clients interacting with other group members; clients benefit from the support, encouragement, and practical suggestions provided by other group members; and people can try out new behaviors in a safe, supportive environment.

- **Family therapy** focuses on the family rather than on the individual and is based on the assumption that the family is an interdependent system. Marital or couple therapy focuses on improving communication, problem-solving skills, and intimacy between members of a couple.

Evaluating the Effectiveness of Psychotherapy

- Meta-analysis has been used to combine the findings of many different studies on the effectiveness of psychotherapy. In general, psychotherapy has been shown to be significantly more effective than no treatment.

- Among the standard psychotherapies, no particular form of therapy is superior to the others. However, particular forms of therapy are more effective than others for treating some specific problems.

- Factors identified as crucial to therapy's effectiveness include the quality of the therapeutic relationship; the therapist's characteristics; the therapist's sensitivity to cultural differences; the client's characteristics; and supportive, stable external circumstances.

- Most psychotherapists today identify their orientation as **eclectic,** meaning that they integrate the techniques of more than one form of psychotherapy, tailoring their approach to the individual client's needs.

Biomedical Therapies

- The most common biomedical therapy is psychoactive medication, which must be prescribed by a physician.

- **Antipsychotic medications** include reserpine and chlorpromazine, which alter dopamine levels in the brain. Although chlorpromazine and reserpine reduce positive symptoms of schizophrenia, they have little or no effect on negative symptoms. Serious side effects can include the development of tardive dyskinesia after long-term use.

- The new **atypical antipsychotic medications** include clozapine, risperidone, and olanzapine, which affect both serotonin and dopamine levels in the brain. The atypical antipsychotics have fewer side effects and are more effective in treating both positive and negative symptoms of schizophrenia.

- **Antianxiety medications** include the benzodiazepines. The benzodiazepines are effective in the treatment of anxiety but are potentially addictive and have many side effects. Buspirone (Buspar) is a newer antianxiety medication that is apparently nonaddictive.

- **Lithium** effectively treats bipolar disorder by regulating glutamate levels in the brain. Depakote, an anticonvulsant, is also used to treat bipolar disorder.

- **Antidepressant medications** include the tricyclics, the MAO inhibitors, and the second-generation antidepressants. New antidepressants, including the **selective serotonin reuptake inhibitors (SSRIs),** the dual-action antidepressants, and the dual-reuptake inhibitors, tend to produce fewer side effects than the first- and second-generation antidepressants.

- **Electroconvulsive therapy (ECT),** which involves delivering a brief electric shock to the brain, is used in treating severe depression. The therapeutic effects of ECT tend to be short-lived, lasting no more than a few months. Partly because it is controversial, ECT is used far less frequently than antidepressant medication in the treatment of depression.

Key Terms

psychotherapy, p. 621

biomedical therapies, p. 621

psychoanalysis, p. 622

free association, p. 623

resistance, p. 623

dream interpretation, p. 623

interpretation, p. 624

transference, p. 624

short-term dynamic
therapies, p. 625

interpersonal therapy (IPT),
p. 625

client-centered therapy,
p. 626

behavior therapy, p. 629

counterconditioning, p. 629

systematic desensitization,
p. 630

bell and pad treatment,
p. 632

aversive conditioning,
p. 633

token economy, p. 634

cognitive therapies, p. 636

rational-emotive therapy
(RET), p. 636

cognitive therapies, p. 636

cognitive therapy (CT), p. 638

cognitive-behavioral therapy
(CBT), p. 640

group therapy, p. 641

family therapy, p. 643

eye movement desensitiza-
tion reprocessing (EMDR),
p. 646

exposure therapy, p. 646

eclecticism, p. 648

antipsychotic medications,
p. 651

atypical antipsychotic
medications, p. 653

antianxiety medications,
p. 653

lithium, p. 654

antidepressant medications,
p. 655

selective serotonin reuptake
inhibitors (SSRIs), p. 655

electroconvulsive therapy
(ECT), p. 657

Key People

Aaron T. Beck (b. 1921) American psychiatrist who founded cognitive therapy (CT), a psychotherapy based on the assumption that depression and other psychological problems are caused by biased perceptions, distorted thinking, and inaccurate beliefs. (p. 638)

Albert Ellis (b. 1913) American psychologist who founded the cognitive psychotherapy called rational-emotive therapy (RET), which emphasizes recognizing and changing irrational beliefs. (p. 636)

Sigmund Freud (1856–1939) Austrian physician and founder of psychoanalysis who theorized that psychological symptoms are the result of unconscious and unresolved conflicts stemming from early childhood (also see Chapter 11). (p. 623)

Mary Cover Jones (1896–1987) American psychologist who conducted the first clinical demonstrations of behavior therapy. (p. 629)

Carl Rogers (1902–1987) American psychologist who helped found humanistic psychology and developed client-centered therapy (also see Chapter 11). (p. 626)

Concept Review Answers

15.1   page 644

1. cognitive therapy
2. behavior therapy
3. family therapy
4. humanistic therapy
5. psychoanalytic therapy

5. True
6. False. The client's willingness to change and his or her attitude toward therapy are essential to psychotherapy's success.

15.2   page 650

1. False. Meta-analysis is a statistical technique used to combine and analyze the results of multiple studies on the same topic or issue.
2. False. Psychotherapy is significantly more effective than no treatment.
3. False. In general, there is little or no difference in the effectiveness of the different forms of empirically supported psychotherapy.
4. False. For psychotherapy to be effective, psychotherapists must be sensitive to cultural differences.

15.3   page 658

1. ECT
2. lithium
3. antipsychotic medications
4. antianxiety medications
5. atypical antipsychotic medications
6. antidepressant medications
7. lithium

Statistics: Understanding Data

Marie D. Thomas *California State University, San Marcos*

The Tables Are Turned: A Psychologist Becomes a Research Subject

For 12 months I was a participant in a research project that was designed to compare the effects of "traditional" and "alternative" diet, exercise, and stress-reduction programs (Riegel & others, 1996). Volunteers who were randomly assigned to the *traditional* program were taught to eat a high-fiber, low-fat diet; do regular aerobic exercise; and practice a progressive muscle relaxation technique (described in Chapter 13 on page 564). Participants who were randomly assigned to the *alternative* program received instruction in yoga and in a meditation technique, along with a diet based on body type and tastes. I was randomly assigned to the *no-treatment* control group, which was monitored throughout the year for weight and general health but received no diet, exercise, or stress-reduction intervention.

The participants in the study were drawn from a large medical group. Invitations to participate in the study were sent to 15,000 members of the medical group. Out of that initial pool, 124 volunteers were recruited, and about 40 were randomly selected for each group—the *traditional, alternative,* and *no-treatment control group.* The participants included men and women between the ages of 20 and 56. A total of 88 subjects lasted the full year. The researchers were pleased that so many of us stayed with the project; it isn't easy to get people to commit to a year-long study!

Data collection began even before participants found out the group to which they had been randomly assigned. We were mailed a thick packet of questionnaires covering a wide range of topics. One questionnaire asked about our current health status, use of prescription and over-the-counter medications, use of vitamins, and visits to both physicians and alternative health care practitioners. Another questionnaire focused on self-perceptions of health and well-being. Here we rated our mood, energy level, physical symptoms, and health in general. A lifestyle survey requested information about diet (how often did we eat red meat? how many servings of fruits and vegetables did we consume a day?), exercise (how many times per week did we do aerobic exercise?), and behavior (such as cigarette smoking and consumption of alcoholic beverages). The lifestyle survey also assessed psychological variables such as levels of stress and happiness and how well we felt we were coping.

At our first meeting with the researchers, we handed in the questionnaires and were told which of the three groups we had been assigned to. We returned early the next morning to have our blood pressure and weight measured and to have blood drawn for tests of our levels of cholesterol, triglycerides, and glucose. The two intervention groups also received a weekend of training in their respective programs. In addition to daily practice of the techniques they had been taught, people in the *traditional* and *alternative* groups were expected to maintain a "compliance diary"—a daily record of their exercise, diet, and relaxation/meditation activities. The purpose of this diary was to determine whether health outcomes were better for people who practiced the techniques regularly. At first I was disappointed when I was randomly assigned to the control group, because I was especially interested in learning the alternative techniques. However, I was relieved later when I found out how much detailed record keeping the intervention groups had to do!

The researchers accumulated even more data over the year-long period. Every 3 months, our blood pressure and weight were measured. At 6 and 12 months, the researchers performed blood tests and asked us to fill out questionnaires identical to those we'd completed at the beginning of the project.

The study included many variables. The most important independent variable (the variable that the researcher manipulates) was group assignment: *traditional* program, *alternative* program, or *no-treatment* control. The dependent variables (variables that are not directly manipulated by the researcher but that may change in response to manipulations of the independent variable) included weight, blood pressure, cholesterol level, self-perceptions regarding health, and mood. Since the dependent variables were measured several times, the researchers could study changes in them over the course of the year.

This study can help to answer important questions about the kinds of programs that tend to promote health. But the purpose of describing it here is not just to tell you whether the two intervention programs were effective and whether one worked better than the other. In the next couple of sections, I will use this study to help explain how researchers use statistics to (1) summarize the data they have collected and (2) draw conclusions about the data. The job of assessing what conclusions can be drawn from the research findings is the domain of *inferential statistics,* which I'll discuss later in this appendix. We'll begin by exploring how research findings can be summarized in ways that are brief yet meaningful and easy to understand. For this, researchers use *descriptive statistics.*

descriptive statistics
Statistics used to organize and summarize data in a meaningful way.

frequency distribution
A summary of how often various scores occur in a sample of scores. Score values are arranged in order of magnitude, and the number of times each score occurs is recorded.

histogram
A way of graphically representing a frequency distribution; a type of bar chart that uses vertical bars that touch.

Descriptive Statistics

The study of programs to promote health generated a large amount of data. How did the researchers make sense of such a mass of information? How did they summarize it in meaningful ways? The answer lies in descriptive statistics. **Descriptive statistics** do just what their name suggests—they describe data. There are many ways to describe information. This appendix will examine four of the most common: frequency distributions, measures of central tendency, measures of variability, and measures of relationships. Since I don't have access to all the data that the health-promotion researchers gathered, I'll use hypothetical numbers to illustrate these statistical concepts.

Frequency Distribution

Suppose that at the start of the health-promotion study 30 people in the *traditional* group reported getting the following number of hours of aerobic exercise each week:

2, 5, 0, 1, 2, 2, 7, 0, 6, 2, 3, 1, 4, 5, 2,
1, 1, 3, 2, 1, 0, 4, 2, 3, 0, 1, 2, 3, 4, 1

Even with only 30 cases, it is difficult to make much sense of these data. Researchers need a way to organize such *raw scores* so that the information makes sense at a glance. One way to organize the data is to determine how many participants reported exercising 0 hours per week, how many reported exercising 1 hour, and so on, until all the reported amounts are accounted for. If the data were put into a table, the table would look like Table A.1.

Table | **A.1**

A Frequency Distribution Table

Hours of Aerobic Exercise per Week	Frequency
0	4
1	7
2	8
3	4
4	3
5	2
6	1
7	1
	30

A table like this is one way of presenting a frequency distribution. It shows at a glance that most of the people in our hypothetical group of 30 were not zealous exercisers before they began their traditional health-promotion program. Nearly two-thirds of them (19 people) engaged in vigorous exercise for 2 hours or less each week.

This table is one way of presenting a **frequency distribution**—a summary of how often various scores occur. Categories are set up (in this case, the number of hours of aerobic exercise per week), and occurrences of each category are tallied to give the frequency of each one.

What information can be gathered from this frequency distribution table? We know immediately that most of the participants did aerobic exercise less than 3 hours per week. The number of hours per week peaked at 2 and declined steadily thereafter. According to the table, the most diligent exerciser worked out about an hour per day.

Some frequency distribution tables include an extra column that shows the percentage of cases in each category. For example, what percentage of participants reported 2 hours of aerobic exercise per week? The percentage is calculated by dividing the category frequency (8) by the total number of people (30), which yields about 27 percent.

While a table is good for summarizing data, it is often useful to present a frequency distribution visually, with graphs. One type of graph is the **histogram** (see Figure A.1). A histogram is like a bar chart with two special features: The bars are always vertical, and they always touch. Categories (in our example, the number of hours of aerobic exercise per week) are placed on the

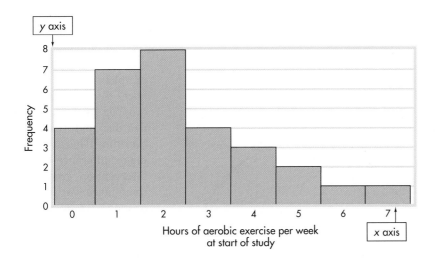

FIGURE A.1 A Histogram This histogram is another way of presenting the data given in Table A.1. Like the table, the histogram shows that most people do, at best, only a moderate amount of aerobic exercise (2 hours or less each week). This is immediately clear from the fact that the highest bars on the chart are on the left, where the hours of exercise are lowest.

FIGURE A.2 A Frequency Polygon (Positive Skew) Like Table A.1 and Figure A.1, this frequency polygon shows at a glance that the number of hours of aerobic exercise weekly is not great for most people. The high points come at 1 and 2 hours, which doesn't amount to much more than 10 or 15 minutes of exercise daily. An asymmetrical distribution like this one, which includes mostly low scores, is said to be positively skewed.

x (horizontal) axis, and the *y* (vertical) axis shows the frequency of each category. The resulting graph looks something like a city skyline, with buildings of different heights.

Another way of graphing the same data is with a **frequency polygon,** shown in Figure A.2. A mark is made above each category at the point representing its frequency. These marks are then connected by straight lines. In our example, the polygon begins before the "0" category and ends at a category of "8," even though both these categories have no cases in them. This is traditionally done so that the polygon is a closed figure.

Frequency polygons are good for showing the shape of a distribution. The polygon in Figure A.2 looks like a mountain, rising sharply over the first two categories, peaking at 2, and slowly diminishing from there. Such a distribution is asymmetrical, or a **skewed distribution,** meaning that if we drew a line through the middle of the *x* axis (halfway between 3 and 4 hours), more scores would be piled up on one side of the line than on the other. More specifically, the polygon in Figure A.2 represents a *positively skewed* distribution, indicating that most people had low scores. A *negatively skewed* distribution would have mostly high scores, with fewer scores at the low end of the distribution. For example, if the traditional diet and exercise intervention worked, the 30 participants should, as a group, be exercising more at the end of the study than they had been at the beginning. Perhaps the distribution of hours of aerobic exercise per week at the end of the study would look something like Figure A.3—a distribution with a slight negative skew.

In contrast to skewed distributions, a **symmetrical distribution** is one in which scores fall equally on both halves of the graph. A special case of a symmetrical distribution, the normal curve, is discussed in a later section.

A useful feature of frequency polygons is that more than one distribution can be graphed on the same set of axes. For example, the end-of-study hours of aerobic exercise per week for the *traditional* and *alternative* groups could be compared on a single graph. Doing so would make it possible to see at a glance whether one group was exercising more than the other after a year of their respective programs.

By the way, Figure A.3 is actually a figment of my imagination. According to the diaries kept by the traditional and alternative program participants, compliance with the exercise portion of the program decreased over time. This does not necessarily mean that these subjects were exercising *less* at the end of the study than at the beginning, but they certainly did not keep up the program as it was taught to them. Compliance with the prescribed diets was steadier than compliance with exercise; compliance by the alternative group dropped between 3 months and 6 months, and then rose steadily over time. There was, however, one major difference between the two intervention groups in terms of compliance. Participants in the alternative group were more likely to be meditating at the end of the study than their traditional-group counterparts were to be practicing progressive relaxation.

FIGURE A.3 A Frequency Polygon (Negative Skew) When more scores fall at the high end of a distribution than at the low end, the distribution is said to be negatively skewed. We would expect a negatively skewed distribution if a health-promotion program worked and encouraged more hours of aerobic exercise. The more effective the program, the greater the skew.

Measures of Central Tendency

Frequency distributions can be used to organize a set of data and tell us how scores are generally distributed. But researchers often want to put this information into a more compact form. They want to be able to summarize a distribution with a single score that is "typical." To do this they use a **measure of central tendency.**

The Mode

The **mode** is the easiest measure of central tendency to calculate. The mode is simply the score or category that occurs most frequently in a set of raw scores or in a frequency distribution. The mode in the frequency distribution shown in Table A.1 is 2; more participants reported exercising 2 hours per week than any other category. In this example, the mode is an accurate representation of central tendency, but this is not always the case. In the distribution 1, 1, 1, 10, 20, 30, the mode is 1, yet half the scores are 10 and above. This type of distortion is the reason measures of central tendency other than the mode are needed.

The Median

Another way of describing central tendency is to determine the **median,** or the score that falls in the middle of a distribution. If the exercise scores were laid out from lowest to highest, they would look like this:

0, 0, 0, 0, 1, 1, 1, 1, 1, 1, 1, 2, 2, 2, 2, 2, 2, 2, 3, 3, 3, 3, 4, 4, 4, 5, 5, 6, 7

↑

What would the middle score be? Since there are 30 scores, look for the point that divides the distribution in half, with 15 scores on each side of this point. The median can be found between the 15th and 16th scores (indicated by the arrow). In this distribution, the answer is easy: A score of 2 is the median as well as the mode.

The Mean

A problem with the mode and the median is that both measures reflect only one score in the distribution. For the mode, the score of importance is the most frequent one; for the median it is the middle score. A better measure of central tendency is usually one that reflects *all* scores. For this reason the most commonly used measure of central tendency is the **mean,** or arithmetic average. You have calculated the mean many times. It is computed by summing a set of scores and then dividing by the number of scores that went into the sum. In our example, adding together the exercise distribution scores gives a total of 70; the number of scores is 30, so 70 divided by 30 gives a mean of 2.33.

Formulas are used to express how a statistic is calculated. The formula for the mean is

$$\bar{X} = \frac{\Sigma X}{N}$$

In this formula, each letter and symbol has a specific meaning:

$\bar{X}$ is the symbol for the mean.

Σ is sigma, the Greek letter for capital S, and it stands for "sum." (Taking a course in statistics is one way to learn the Greek alphabet!)

X represents the scores in the distribution, so the numerator of the equation says, "Sum up all the scores."

N is the total number of scores in the distribution.

frequency polygon
A way of graphically representing a frequency distribution; frequency is marked above each score category on the graph's horizontal axis, and the marks are connected by straight lines.

skewed distribution
An asymmetrical distribution; more scores occur on one side of the distribution than on the other. In a *positively* skewed distribution, most of the scores are low scores; in a *negatively* skewed distribution, most of the scores are high scores.

symmetrical distribution
A distribution in which scores fall equally on both sides of the graph. The normal curve is an example of a symmetrical distribution.

measure of central tendency
A single number that presents some information about the "center" of a frequency distribution.

mode
The most frequently occurring score in a distribution.

median
The score that divides a frequency distribution exactly in half, so that the same number of scores lie on each side of it.

mean
The sum of a set of scores in a distribution divided by the number of scores; the mean is usually the most representative measure of central tendency.

Therefore, the formula says, "The mean equals the sum of all the scores divided by the total number of scores."

Although the mean is usually the most representative measure of central tendency because each score in a distribution enters into its computation, it is particularly susceptible to the effect of extreme scores. Any unusually high or low score will pull the mean in its direction. Suppose, for example, that in our frequency distribution for aerobic exercise one exercise zealot worked out 70 hours per week. The mean number of aerobic exercise hours would jump from 2.33 to 4.43. This new mean is deceptively high, given that most of the scores in the distribution are 2 and below. Because of just that one extreme score, the mean has become less representative of the distribution. Frequency tables and graphs are important tools for helping us identify extreme scores *before* we start computing statistics.

Measures of Variability

In addition to identifying the central tendency in a distribution, researchers may want to know how much the scores in that distribution differ from one another. Are they grouped closely together or widely spread out? To answer this question, we need some **measure of variability.** Figure A.4 shows two distributions with the same mean but with different variability.

A simple way to measure variability is with the **range,** which is computed by subtracting the lowest score in the distribution from the highest score. Let's say that there are 15 women in the traditional diet and exercise group and that their weights at the beginning of the study varied from a low of 95 pounds to a high of 155 pounds. The range of weights in this group would be 155 − 95 = 60 pounds.

As a measure of variability, the range provides a limited amount of information, because it depends on only the two most extreme scores in a distribution (the highest and lowest scores). A more useful measure of variability would give some idea of the average amount of variation in a distribution. But variation from what? The most common way to measure variability is to determine how far scores in a distribution vary from the distribution's mean. We saw earlier that the mean is usually the best way to represent the "center" of the distribution, so the mean seems like an appropriate reference point.

What if we subtract the mean from each score in a distribution to get a general idea of how far each score is from the center? When the mean is subtracted from a score, the result is a *deviation* from the mean. Scores that are above the mean would have positive deviations, and scores that are below the mean would have negative deviations. To get an average deviation, we would need to sum the deviations and divide by the number of deviations that went into the sum. There is a problem with this procedure, however. If deviations from the mean are added together, the sum will be 0, because the negative and positive deviations will cancel each other out. In fact, the real definition of the mean is "the only point in a distribution where all the scores' deviations from it add up to 0."

We need to somehow "get rid of" the negative deviations. In mathematics, such a problem is solved by squaring. If a negative number is squared, it becomes positive. So instead of simply adding up the deviations and dividing by the number of scores (*N*), we first square each deviation, then add together the *squared* deviations and divide by *N*. Finally, we need to compensate for the squaring operation. To do this, we take the square root of the number just calculated. This leaves us with the **standard deviation.** The larger the standard deviation, the more spread out are the scores in a distribution.

Let's look at an example to make this clearer. Table A.2 lists the hypothetical weights of the 15 women in the traditional group at the beginning of the study. The mean, which is the sum of the weights divided by 15, is calculated to be 124

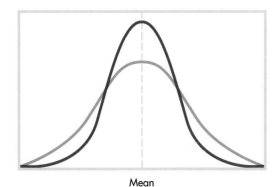

Mean

FIGURE A.4 Distributions with Different Variability Two distributions with the same mean can have very different variability, or spread, as shown in these two curves. Notice how one is more spread out than the other; its scores are distributed more widely.

Table A.2

Calculating the Standard Deviation

Weight	Mean	Weight − Mean	(Weight − Mean) Squared
X	$\overline{X}$	$X - \overline{X}$	$(X - \overline{X})^2$
155	124	31	961
149	124	25	625
142	124	18	324
138	124	14	196
134	124	10	100
131	124	7	49
127	124	3	9
125	124	1	1
120	124	−4	16
115	124	−9	81
112	124	−12	144
110	124	−14	196
105	124	−19	361
102	124	−22	484
95	124	−29	841

Sum (Σ) = 1,860 $\Sigma = 0$ $\Sigma = 4,388$

Mean ($\overline{X}$) = 124

$$SD = \sqrt{\frac{\Sigma(X - \overline{X})^2}{N}} = \sqrt{\frac{4,388}{15}} = 17.10$$

To calculate the standard deviation, you simply add all the scores in a distribution (the left-hand column in this example) and divide by the total number of scores to get the mean. Then you subtract the mean from each score to get a list of deviations from the mean (third column). Next you square each deviation (fourth column), add the squared deviations together, divide by the total number of cases, and take the square root.

measure of variability
A single number that presents information about the spread of scores in a distribution.

range
A measure of variability; the highest score in a distribution minus the lowest score.

standard deviation
A measure of variability; expressed as the square root of the sum of the squared deviations around the mean divided by the number of scores in the distribution.

pounds, as shown at the bottom of the left-hand column. The first step in computing the standard deviation is to subtract the mean from each score, which gives that score's deviation from the mean. These deviations are listed in the third column of the table. The next step is to square each of the deviations (done in the fourth column), then add the squared deviations ($\Sigma = 4,388$) and divided that total by the number of women ($N = 15$). Finally, we take the square root to obtain the standard deviation ($SD = 17.10$). The formula for the standard deviation (SD) incorporates these instructions:

$$SD = \sqrt{\frac{\Sigma(X - \overline{X})^2}{N}}$$

Notice that when scores have large deviations from the mean, the *standard deviation* is also large.

z Scores and the Normal Curve

The mean and the standard deviation provide useful descriptive information about an entire set of scores. But researchers can also describe the relative position of any individual score in a distribution. This is done by locating how far away from the mean the score is in terms of standard deviation units. A statistic called a **z score** gives us this information:

$$z = \frac{X - \overline{X}}{SD}$$

This equation says that to compute a z score, we subtract the mean from the score we are interested in (that is, we calculate its deviation from the mean) and divide this quantity by the standard deviation. A positive z score indicates that the score is above the mean, and a negative z score shows that the score is below the mean. The larger the z score, the farther away from the mean the score is.

Let's take an example from the distribution found in Table A.2. What is the z score of a weight of 149 pounds? To find out, you simply subtract the mean from 149 and divide by the standard deviation.

$$z = \frac{149 - 124}{17.10} = 1.46$$

A z score of +1.46 tells us that a person weighing 149 pounds falls about one and a half standard deviations above the mean. In contrast, a person weighing 115 pounds has a weight below the mean and would have a negative z score. If you calculate this z score you will find it is −.53. This means that a weight of 115 is a little more than one-half a standard deviation below the mean.

Some variables, such as height, weight, and IQ, if graphed for large numbers of people, fall into a characteristic pattern. Figure A.5 shows this pattern, which is called the **standard normal curve** or the **standard normal distribution.** The normal curve is symmetrical (that is, if a line is drawn down its center, one side of the curve is a mirror image of the other side), and the mean, median, and mode fall exactly in the middle. The x axis of Figure A.5 is marked off in standard deviation units, which, conveniently, are also z scores. Notice that most of the cases fall between −1 and +1 *SD*s, with the number of cases sharply tapering off at either end. This pattern is the reason the normal curve is often described as "bell shaped."

The great thing about the normal curve is that we know exactly what percentage of the distribution falls between any two points on the curve. Figure A.5 shows the percentages of cases between major standard deviation units. For example, 34.13 percent of the distribution falls between 0 and +1. That means that 84.13 percent of the distribution falls *below* one standard deviation (the 34.13 percent that is between 0 and +1, plus the 50 percent that falls below 0). A person who obtains a z score of +1 on some normally distributed variable has scored better than 84 percent of the other people in the distribution. If a variable is normally distributed (that is, if it has the standard bell-shaped pattern), a person's z score can tell us exactly where that person stands relative to everyone else in the distribution.

FIGURE A.5 The Standard Normal Curve
The standard normal curve has several characteristics. Most apparent is its symmetrical bell shape. On such a curve, the mean, the median, and the mode all fall at the same point. But not every curve that is shaped roughly like a bell is a standard normal curve. With a normal curve, specific percentages of the distribution fall within each standard deviation unit from the mean. These percentages are shown on the graph.

Correlation

So far, the statistical techniques we've looked at focus on one variable at a time, such as hours of aerobic exercise weekly or weight measured in pounds. Life would be simple if it were influenced by only one variable at a time! The world, however, is a far more complicated place. Accordingly, statistical techniques have been devised that allow us to look at the relationship—the **correlation**—between two variables. This relationship is assessed by a statistic called the **correlation coefficient.**

To compute a correlation coefficient, we need two sets of measurements from the same individuals or from pairs of people who are similar in some way. To take a simple example, let's determine the correlation between height (we'll call this the *x* variable) and weight (the *y* variable). We start by obtaining height and weight measurements for each individual in a group. The idea is to combine all these measurements into one number that expresses something about the relationship between the two variables, height and weight. However, we are immediately confronted with a problem: The two variables are measured in different ways. Height is measured in inches, and weight is measured in pounds. We need some way to place both variables on a single scale.

Think back to our discussion of the normal curve and *z* scores. What do *z* scores do? They take data of any form and put them into a standard scale. Remember, too, that a high score in a distribution always has a positive *z* score, and a low score in a distribution always has a negative *z* score. To compute a correlation coefficient, the data from both variables of interest can be converted to *z* scores. Therefore, each individual will have two *z* scores: one for height (the *x* variable) and one for weight (the *y* variable).

Then, to compute the correlation coefficient, each person's two *z* scores are multiplied together. All these "cross-products" are added up, and this sum is divided by the number of individuals. In other words, a correlation coefficient is the average (or mean) of the *z*-score cross-products of the two variables being studied:

$$\text{correlation coefficient} = \frac{\sum z_x z_y}{N}$$

A correlation coefficient can range from -1 to $+1$. The exact number provides two pieces of information: It tells us about the *magnitude* of the relationship being measured, and it tells us about its *direction*. The magnitude, or degree, of relationship is indicated by the size of the number. A number close to 1 (whether positive or negative) indicates a strong relationship, while a number close to 0 indicates a weak relationship. The sign (+ or −) of the correlation coefficient tells us about the relationship's direction. A *positive* correlation means that as one variable increases in size, the second variable also increases. For example, height and weight are positively correlated: As height increases, weight tends to increase also. In terms of *z* scores, a positive correlation means that high *z* scores on one variable tend to be multiplied by high *z* scores on the other variable and that low *z* scores on one variable tend to be multiplied by low *z* scores on the other. Remember that just as two positive numbers multiplied together result in a positive number, so two negative numbers multiplied together also result in a positive number. When the cross-products are added together, the sum in both cases is positive.

A *negative* correlation, in contrast, means that two variables are *inversely* related. As one variable increases in size, the other variable decreases. For example, professors like to believe that the more hours students study, the fewer errors they will make on exams. In *z*-score language, high *z* scores (which are positive) on one variable (more hours of study) tend to be multiplied by low *z* scores (which are negative) on the other variable (fewer errors on exams), and vice versa, making negative cross-products. When the cross-products are summed and divided by the number of cases, the result is a negative correlation coefficient.

z score
A number, expressed in standard deviation units, that shows a score's deviation from the mean.

standard normal curve or **standard normal distribution**
A symmetrical distribution forming a bell-shaped curve in which the mean, median, and mode are all equal and fall in the exact middle.

correlation
The relationship between two variables.

correlation coefficient
A measure of the magnitude and direction of the relationship (the correlation) between two variables. The closer the correlation coefficient is to +1 or −1, the stronger the relationship is. A *positive* correlation coefficient indicates that as one variable increases, the other tends to increase. A *negative* correlation coefficient indicates that as one variable increases, the other tends to decrease.

FIGURE A.6 Scatter Plot of a Positive Correlation A correlation (or the lack of one) can be clearly shown on a scatter diagram. This one shows a moderately strong positive correlation between subjects' compliance with the yoga component of the alternative health-promotion program and their energy level. The positive direction of the correlation is indicated by the upward-sloping pattern of the dots, from bottom left to top right. This means that if one variable is high, the other tends to be high, too, and vice versa. That the strength of the relationship is only moderate is indicated by the fact that the data points (each indicating an individual subject's score) are not all positioned along a straight diagonal line.

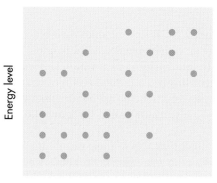

An easy way to show different correlations is with graphs. Plotting two variables together creates a **scatter diagram** or **scatter plot,** like the ones in Figures A.6, A.7, and A.8. These figures show the relationship between complying with some component of the alternative health-promotion program and some other variable related to health. Although the figures describe relationships actually found in the study, I have made up the specific correlations to illustrate key points.

Figure A.6 shows a moderately strong positive relationship between compliance with the yoga part of the alternative program and a person's energy level. You can see this just by looking at the pattern of the data points. They generally form a line running from lower left to upper right. When calculated, this particular correlation coefficient is +.59, which indicates a correlation roughly in the middle between 0 and +1. In other words, people who did more yoga tended to have higher energy levels. The "tended to" part is important. Some people who did not comply well with the yoga routine still had high energy levels, while the reverse was also true. A +1 correlation, or a *perfect* positive correlation, would indicate that frequent yoga sessions were *always* accompanied by high levels of energy, and vice versa. What would a scatter diagram of a perfect +1 correlation look like? It would be a straight diagonal line starting in the lower left-hand corner of the graph and progressing to the upper right-hand corner.

Several other positive correlations were found in this study. Compliance with the alternative diet was positively associated with increases in energy and positive health perceptions. In addition, following the high-fiber, low-fat traditional diet was associated with a higher level of coping and high vitamin intake.

The study also found some negative correlations. Figure A.7 illustrates a *negative* correlation between compliance with the meditation part of the alternative program and cigarette smoking. This correlation coefficient is −.77. Note that the data points fall in the opposite direction from those in Figure A.6, indicating that as the frequency of meditation increased, cigarette smoking decreased. The pattern of points in Figure A.7 is closer to a straight line than is the pattern of points in Figure A.6. A correlation of −.77 shows a relationship of greater magnitude than does a correlation of +.59. But though −.77 is a relatively high correlation, it is not a perfect relationship. A *perfect* negative relationship would be illustrated by a straight diagonal line starting in the upper left-hand corner of the graph and ending at the lower right-hand corner.

Finally, Figure A.8 shows two variables that are not related to each other. The hypothetical correlation coefficient between compliance with the aerobic exercise part of the traditional program and a person's level of coping is +.03, barely above 0. In the scatter diagram, data points fall randomly, with no general direction to them. From a *z*-score point of view, when two variables are not related, the cross-products are mixed—that is, some are positive and some are negative. Sometimes high *z* scores on one variable go with high *z* scores on the other, and

FIGURE A.7 Scatter Plot of a Negative Correlation In general, people who engage in meditation more often tend to smoke less. This negative correlation is indicated by the downward-sloping pattern of dots, from upper left to lower right. Because these dots are clustered somewhat closer together than those in Figure A.6, we can tell at a glance that the relationship here is somewhat stronger.

low z scores on one variable go with low z scores on the other. In both cases, positive cross-products result. In other pairs of scores, high z scores on one variable go with low z scores on the other variable (and vice versa), producing negative cross-products. When the cross-products for the two variables are summed, the positive and negative numbers cancel each other out, resulting in a 0 (or close to 0) correlation.

In addition to describing the relationship between two variables, correlation coefficients are useful for another purpose: prediction. If we know a person's score on one of two related variables, we can predict how he or she will perform on the other variable. For example, in a recent issue of a magazine I found a quiz to rate my risk of heart disease. I assigned myself points depending on my age, HDL ("good") and total cholesterol levels, systolic blood pressure, and other risk factors, such as cigarette smoking and diabetes. My total points (−2) indicated that I had less than a 1 percent risk of developing heart disease in the next five years. How could such a quiz be developed? Each of the factors I rated is correlated to some degree with heart disease. The older you are and the higher your cholesterol and blood pressure, the greater your chance of developing heart disease. Statistical techniques are used to determine the relative importance of each of these factors and to calculate the points that should be assigned to each level of a factor. Combining these factors provides a better prediction than any single factor, because none of the individual risk factors correlate perfectly with the development of heart disease.

One thing a correlation does *not* tell us is *causality*. In other words, the fact that two variables are highly correlated does not mean that one variable directly causes the other. Take the meditation and cigarette-smoking correlation. This negative correlation tells us that people in the study who diligently practiced meditation tended to smoke less than those who seldom meditated. Regular meditation may have had a direct effect on the desire to smoke cigarettes, but it is also possible that one or more other variables affected both meditation and smoking. For example, perhaps participation in the study convinced some people that they needed to change their lifestyles completely. Both compliance with the meditation routine and a decreased level of cigarette smoking may have been "caused" by this change in lifestyle. The only way to determine cause and effect is to conduct an experiment, as you saw in Chapter 1. Can you think of a way to test the hypothesis that regularly practicing meditation causes a reduction in the desire to smoke cigarettes?

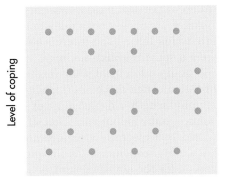

Level of coping (y-axis)

Compliance with
aerobic exercise program

FIGURE A.8 Scatter Plot of No Correlation
You may be surprised to learn that in this study, compliance with the aerobic exercise portion of the traditional program was not related to level of coping. This scatter diagram shows that lack of relationship. The points fall randomly, revealing no general direction or trend and thus indicating the absence of a correlation.

Inferential Statistics

Let's say that the mean number of physical symptoms (like pain) experienced by the participants in each of the three groups was about the same at the beginning of the health-promotion study. A year later, the number of symptoms had decreased in the two intervention groups but had remained stable in the control group. This may or may not be a meaningful result. We would expect the average number of symptoms to be somewhat different for each of the three groups, because each group consisted of different people. And we would expect some fluctuation in level over time, due simply to chance. But are the differences in number of symptoms between the intervention groups and the control group large enough *not* to be due to chance alone? If other researchers conducted the same study with

scatter diagram or **scatter plot**
A graph that represents the relationship between two variables.

inferential statistics
Statistical techniques that allow researchers to determine whether the outcomes in a study are likely to be more than just chance events and whether they can be legitimately generalized to a larger population.

population
A complete set of something—people, nonhuman animals, objects, or events.

sample
A subset of a population.

different participants, would they be likely to get the same general pattern of results? To answer such questions, we turn to inferential statistics. **Inferential statistics** tell us the inferences, or conclusions, that we can legitimately draw from a set of research findings.

Many inferential statistical techniques can be called into service to answer questions such as the ones raised in the preceding paragraph. Each helps determine whether or not a set of findings can plausibly be explained merely by chance and random variation. If the results of a study are more extreme than would be expected by chance alone, we reject the idea that no *real* effect occurred and conclude that the manipulation of the independent variable is the reason for the obtained results. In other words, we say that our results are *statistically significant.*

To see how this works, let's go back to the normal curve for a moment. Remember that we know exactly what percentage of a normal curve falls between any two z scores. If we choose one person at random out of a normal distribution, what is the chance that this person's z score is above $+2$? If you look again at Figure A.5, you will see that 2.28 percent of the curve lies above a z score (or standard deviation unit) of $+2$. Therefore, the chance, or *probability,* that the person we choose will have a z score above $+2$ is .0228 (or 2.28 chances out of 100). That's a pretty small chance. If you study the normal curve, you will see that the majority of cases fall between -2 and $+2$ SDs (95.44 percent of the cases, to be exact), so in choosing a person at random, that person is not likely to fall above a z score of $+2$.

When researchers test for statistical significance, they usually employ statistics other than z scores, and they may use distributions that differ in shape from the normal curve. The logic, however, is the same. They compute some kind of inferential statistic that they compare to the appropriate distribution. This comparison tells them the likelihood of obtaining their results if chance alone is operating.

The problem is that no test exists that will tell us for sure whether our intervention or manipulation "worked"; we always have to deal with probabilities, not certainties. Researchers have developed some conventions to guide them in their decisions about whether or not their study results are statistically significant. Generally, when the probability of obtaining a particular result if random factors alone are operating is less than .05 (5 chances out of 100), the results are considered statistically significant. Researchers who want to be even more sure set their probability value at .01 (1 chance out of 100).

Because researchers deal with probabilities, there is a small but real possibility of *erroneously* concluding that study results are significant. The results of one study, therefore, should never be completely trusted. In order to have greater confidence in a particular effect or result, the study should be repeated, or *replicated.* If the same results are obtained in different studies, then we can draw conclusions about a particular intervention or effect with greater certainty.

One final point about inferential statistics. Are the researchers interested only in the changes that might have occurred in the small groups of people participating in the health-promotion study, or do they really want to know whether the interventions would be effective for people in general? This question focuses on the difference between a population and a sample. A **population** is a complete set of something—people, nonhuman animals, objects, or events. The researchers who designed this study wanted to know whether the interventions they developed would benefit *all* people (or, more precisely, all people between the ages of 20 and 56). Obviously, they could not conduct a study on this entire population. The best they could do was choose some portion of that population to serve as subjects; in other words, they selected a **sample.** The study was conducted on this sample. The researchers analyzed the sample results using inferential statistics to make guesses about what they would find had they studied the entire population. Inferential statistics allow researchers to take the findings they obtain from a sample and apply them to a population.

So what did the health-promotion study find? Did the interventions work? The answer is yes, sort of. The traditional and alternative groups, when combined, improved more than the no-treatment control group. At the end of the study, participants in the two intervention programs had better self-perceptions regarding health, better mood, more energy, and fewer physical symptoms. Compared with the traditional and the no-treatment groups, the alternative group showed greater improvement in health perceptions and a significant decrease in depression and the use of prescription drugs. Interestingly, participation in the treatment groups did not generally result in changes in health risk, such as lowered blood pressure or decreased weight. The researchers believe that little change occurred because the people who volunteered for the study were basically healthy individuals. The study needs to be replicated with a less-healthy sample. In sum, the intervention programs had a greater effect on health perceptions and psychological variables than on physical variables. The researchers concluded that a health-promotion regimen (either traditional or alternative) is helpful. I'm sure other studies will be conducted to explore these issues further!

Endnote

Although I briefly saw other study participants at each three-month data-collection point, I never spoke to anyone. The last measurement session, however, was also a celebration for our year-long participation in the project. Approximately 30 people attended my session, and participants from each of the three groups were present. After our blood was drawn and our blood pressure and weight readings were taken, we were treated to breakfast. Then one of the principal researchers *debriefed* us: She gave us some background on the study and told us what she hoped to learn. At this point, participants were given the opportunity to talk about how the study had affected their lives. It was fascinating to hear members of the intervention groups describe the changes they had made over the past year. One woman said that a year ago she could never imagine getting up early to meditate, yet now she looks forward to awakening each morning at 4:00 A.M. for her first meditation session. Other people described the modifications they had made in their diet and exercise patterns and how much better they felt. Although I did not experience either of the interventions, I know that simply being a subject in the study made me more conscious of what I ate and how much I exercised. This could have been a confounding factor; that is, it could have inadvertently changed my behavior even though I was in the control group. In fact, my weight decreased and my level of "good" cholesterol increased over the course of the year.

We were not paid for our participation in this study, but we received small gifts as tokens of the researchers' appreciation. In addition, we were all given the option of taking any or all of the intervention training at no cost (and some courses in alternative techniques could be quite expensive). The most important thing for me was the satisfaction of participation—the fact that I had stayed with the study for an entire year and, in a small way, had made a contribution to science.

Appendix Review
Statistics: Understanding Data

Key Points

Descriptive Statistics

■ **Descriptive statistics** allow us to organize and summarize data in ways that are brief yet meaningful and easy to understand. One descriptive statistic is a **frequency distribution,** which can be presented in the form of a table, a **histogram, or a frequency polygon.** Some frequency distributions are positively **skewed;** that is, most of the scores in the distribution pile up at the low end. Distributions that are negatively skewed have mostly high scores. **Symmetrical distributions** have equal numbers of scores on both sides of the distribution's midpoint.

■ The **mode,** the **median,** and the **mean** are **measures of central tendency** of a distribution. The mode is the most frequent score. The median is the middle score in the distribution. The mean is the arithmetic average. To calculate the mean, scores are summed and divided by the total number of scores. The mean is usually the best overall representation of central tendency, but it is strongly influenced by extremely high or extremely low scores.

■ The **range** and **standard deviation** are **measures of variability** or spread of a distribution. The range is the highest score in the distribution minus the lowest score. The **standard deviation** is the square root of the average of the squared deviations from the mean.

■ A *z* **score** expresses a single score's deviation from the mean of a distribution in standard deviation units.

■ The **standard normal curve** is a symmetrical distribution forming a bell-shaped curve in which the mean, median, and mode are all equal and fall in the exact middle. The percentage of cases that fall between any two points on the normal curve is known. Over 95 percent of the cases fall between two standard deviations above the mean and two standard deviations below the mean.

■ **Correlation** refers to the relationship between two variables. A **correlation coefficient** is a number that indicates the magnitude and direction of such a relationship. A correlation coefficient may range from -1 to $+1$. The closer the value is to -1 or $+1$, the stronger the relationship is. Correlations close to 0 indicate no relationship. A positive correlation coefficient tells us that as one variable increases in size, the second variable also increases. A negative correlation coefficient indicates that as one variable increases in size, the second variable decreases. A correlation relationship may be presented visually in a **scatter diagram.**

■ Correlations enable us to predict the value of one variable from knowledge of another variable's value. However, a correlational relationship is not necessarily a causal relationship.

Inferential Statistics

■ **Inferential statistics** are used to determine whether the outcomes of a study can be legitimately generalized to a larger population. A **population** is a complete set of something. A **sample** is a subset of a population.

■ Inferential statistics provide information about the probability of a particular result if only chance or random factors are operating. If this probability is small, the findings are said to be statistically significant; that is, they are probably due to the researcher's interventions.

Key Terms

descriptive statistics, p. A-2

frequency distribution, p. A-3

histogram, p. A-3

frequency polygon, p. A-4

skewed distribution, p. A-4

symmetrical distribution, p. A-4

measure of central tendency, p. A-5

mode, p. A-5

median, p. A-5

mean, p. A-5

measure of variability, p. A-6

range, p. A-6

standard deviation, p. A-6

z score, p. A-8

standard normal curve (standard normal distribution), p. A-8

correlation, p. A-9

correlation coefficient, p. A-9

scatter diagram (scatter plot), p. A-10

inferential statistics, p. A-12

population, p. A-12

sample, p. A-12

Industrial/Organizational Psychology

Marie Waung *University of Michigan, Dearborn*

What Is Industrial/Organizational Psychology?

I was at a party recently when the inevitable question was asked of me: "What do you do?" When I answered that I am an industrial/organizational psychologist, the people around me looked puzzled. Finally, one man said with a smile, "Oh, is that like *big* psychology—you know, industrial size?" Another person remarked, "Well, you certainly must be well organized!" While the conversation made for a good icebreaker, it was clear that few people at the party were familiar with I/O psychology, even though I/O psychologists have been conducting research for some 100 years. The general unfamiliarity with the field is unfortunate, since its research and applications touch the lives of almost everyone who works.

Industrial/organizational (I/O) psychology is the branch of psychology that focuses on the study of human behavior at work. The "industrial," or "I," side of I/O psychology focuses on measuring human characteristics and matching these characteristics with the characteristics required in particular jobs. If a good match is made, employees are likely to be more productive. Identifying criteria or standards for job performance and then using these standards to measure job performance also fall within the "I" side of I/O psychology, as does the training of employees. This industrial side of industrial/organizational psychology is sometimes also called **personnel psychology.**

In contrast, the "organizational," or "O," side focuses on the influence that organizations have on behavior. Elements of the social environment of an organization (e.g., norms, roles, group processes) as they impact employee behavior are emphasized. The "O" side of I/O psychology is also called **organizational behavior.** Later we will examine more closely selected topics from both personnel psychology and organizational behavior.

I/O psychologists generally spend their time working within one of the six content areas described below (Muchinsky, 2000):

1. **Selection and placement.** I/O psychologists working in this area spend their time developing assessment techniques to help select from a pool of job applicants those who are most likely to be successful in a given job or organization. If you have applied for a job in the past, were any types of selection devices used? How were you singled out from other job candidates as being most suited for the job?

2. **Training and development.** This area focuses on determining what types of skills need to be enhanced to improve job performance. I/O psychologists who work in this area also spend their time designing training programs and evaluating the effectiveness of those

industrial/organizational (I/O) psychology
The branch of psychology that focuses on the study of human behavior at work.

personnel psychology
A subarea of I/O psychology that focuses on matching people's characteristics to job requirements, accurately measuring job performance, and assessing employee training needs.

organizational behavior
A subarea of I/O psychology that focuses on how the organization and the social environment in which people work affect their attitudes and behaviors.

Designing for People One subarea of industrial/organizational psychology is concerned with the human factors involved in the use of workplace procedures and equipment. For example, this factory's procedure for stitching jacket seams requires the sewing-machine operator to hold her arms away from her body—an unnatural, painful position. The employer, attentive to ergonomics, installed a pulley system with slings that allow the operator to work with her arms relaxed.

organizational development (OD)
A subarea of I/O psychology that focuses on bringing about positive change in an organization, such as increased profitability or improved products.

ergonomics
A subarea of I/O psychology that focuses on the design of equipment and the development of work procedures in accordance with human capabilities and limitations.

programs. Management development programs are training programs that attempt to teach managers with a great deal of technical expertise, but little experience managing people, how to be better managers. These programs, which typically involve simulations, case studies, and role-plays, may focus on topics such as management style, problem solving, and communication.

3. **Performance management.** The first step in performance management involves identifying criteria or standards for determining the degree to which employees are performing their jobs well. I/O psychologists working in this area are generally concerned with how to measure performance accurately and how to best convey performance results to employees. It may come as no surprise to you that employees do not like to be criticized. Supervisors tend to give subordinates higher performance ratings than they deserve and to avoid giving honest feedback to subordinates because they are concerned about damaging their relationships with them. A continuing challenge for I/O psychologists is to find ways to motivate managers to provide employees with honest performance feedback. Candid feedback may improve performance by enabling employees to select the appropriate performance strategies and training schedules as well as to exert the expected level of effort.

4. **Organizational development.** The goal of **organizational development (OD)** is to bring about positive change in an organization, such as greater profitability or improvement in the quality of products. The structure of an organization as well as the social environment may be examined in an attempt to facilitate positive change. An important challenge for those in the field of OD is to help organizations manage workforce diversity and the global nature of contemporary business.

5. **Quality of work life.** The focus of this area is on the factors that contribute to a productive and healthy workforce. For example, I/O psychologists may try to maximize employee satisfaction by redesigning jobs to make them more rewarding. The quality-of-work-life movement, which began in the 1970s, has resulted in a great number of diverse approaches and programs. Adequate and fair compensation, a safe and healthy work environment, the development of human capacities, and constitutionalism (e.g., developing an employee bill of rights) are some of the types of quality-of-work-life programs that have been developed (Walton, 1973).

6. **Ergonomics.** The focus of **ergonomics** is the design of equipment and the development of work procedures in light of human capabilities and limitations. Some of these factors involve strength, size (e.g., human height, girth, arm and leg length), and other physical characteristics. With the increased dependence on technological devices such as computers and automated production equipment, ergonomics is likely to become even more important. The proper design of such devices will enable technology to help people become more productive rather than to frustrate them. These better-designed products might even reduce injuries and deaths. For example, car manufacturers are incorporating windshield displays in some vehicles so that drivers can view the speedometer and radio settings on the windshield, rather than looking down at the dashboard. Similarly, cell phones have been developed that keep the driver's hands free.

Although you now know what I/O psychologists do, you may still have questions about the types of settings in which they work, the training they must have, and their employment outlook. We turn to these topics next.

Work Settings, Type of Training, and Employment Outlook

Many I/O psychologists belong to a division of the American Psychological Association (APA) called the Society for Industrial and Organizational Psychologists (SIOP). The division conducts periodic surveys of its members and, as a result, can supply information on topics such as typical work settings, job duties, and salary levels of I/O psychologists. To work in the field of I/O psychology, a doctorate or a master's degree is generally required. However, some areas closely related to I/O psychology are open to people with bachelor's degrees only. These will be discussed later in this section.

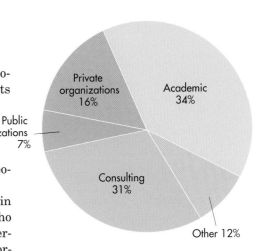

The principal employment settings of I/O psychologists are presented in Figure B.1. Thirty-four percent of I/O psychologists who belong to SIOP and who responded to the latest survey reported working in a university or college; 31 percent worked as consultants to organizations; 16 percent worked in private organizations (such as utility companies, insurance companies, and companies that make consumer products); and 7 percent worked for public organizations (federal, state, and local governments, for example, or the military).

A survey of SIOP members indicated that the median salary in 2000 for those with doctorates was $90,000 and for those with master's degrees, $67,000 (Katkowski & Medsker, 2001). In addition, the job market for I/O psychologists has remained strong over the years; surveys done by the American Psychological Association indicate an unemployment rate of less than 1 percent.

Although it is very difficult for people with bachelor's degrees to find employment in the field of I/O psychology, some related areas are open to them. For example, jobs for personnel, training, and labor-relations specialists and managers are open to those with bachelor's degrees. The purpose of these jobs is to help management make effective use of employees' knowledge, skills, and abilities and to help employees find job satisfaction.

The educational requirements for personnel, training, and labor-relations specialists and managers vary widely. Some employers prefer applicants with majors in human resources, public administration, or industrial relations. Others seek those with backgrounds in technical or business areas, while still others want people with well-rounded liberal arts educations. Given the wide variety of skills required for these jobs, an interdisciplinary background that combines social and behavioral sciences and business is useful. In fact, one study found that managers who majored in the humanities or social sciences in college tended to be better managers than those who majored in business, engineering, or math/science (Howard, 1986). In addition, managers who majored in the humanities or social sciences showed more potential for advancement to higher levels of management than those with other college majors.

Job growth for personnel, training, and labor-relations specialists and managers is expected to be about as fast as average job growth through the year 2008. The job market is likely to remain competitive due to the high number of qualified college graduates and experienced workers (Bureau of Labor Statistics, 2000).

Another I/O-related career in which people with bachelor's degrees may sometimes find employment is that of *management analysts and consultants*. Management analysts and consultants deal with a variety of organizational problems, from helping organizations relocate to helping them restructure. Generally, these analysts collect, review, and analyze information, make recommendations, and help to implement those recommendations. Educational requirements vary for these jobs. Those with bachelor's degrees may work in government agencies in entry-level positions as research associates or junior consultants. Most companies prefer that their full-fledged management consultants have master's degrees.

Growth in the demand for management consultants and analysts is expected to be higher than average job growth through 2008. The reason for this expected

FIGURE B.1 Work Settings of I/O Psychologists Most I/O psychologists work in institutions of higher education. Thirty-four percent of the members of the Society for Industrial and Organizational Psychologists work in colleges and universities. Next come I/O psychologists who work as consultants to organizations (31%). Another substantial percentage (16%) are employed by large private corporations, such as insurance companies and consumer-product manufacturers. Public organizations, such as government agencies, employ less than half as many I/O psychologists as private organizations do (7% versus 16%).

SOURCE: Burnfield & Medsker (1999).

growth is the greater reliance of private companies and government agencies on outside expertise to improve productivity (Bureau of Labor Statistics, 2000).

Employment interviewer is a third I/O-related field open to those with bachelor's degrees. Employment interviewers typically work for personnel supply firms, matching employers with job applicants and job applicants with employers. An employment interviewer needs sales ability, because he or she is expected to attract clients and job applicants to the personnel supply firm. Self-confidence is needed, too, as are strong oral and interpersonal skills.

Demand for employment interviewers is expected to grow at an average rate. Some of the demand is being curtailed by the increased use of computerized job matches and information systems (Bureau of Labor Statistics, 2000).

If you would like to learn more about career opportunities in I/O psychology, visit some of the Web sites listed in Table B.1. For information that every employee should know, turn to In Focus Box B.1.

Table **B.1**

Below is a list of Web sites that relate to working in the field of industrial/organizational psychology.

www.aom.pace.edu	Academy of Management
www.dol.gov	The U.S. Department of Labor Job Information Site
www.shrm.org	The Society for Human Resource Management
www.siop.org	The Society for Industrial and Organizational Psychology

---

IN FOCUS B.1

What Every Employee Should Know

Getting the Boss to Like You

Employees who are good citizens (e.g., who help other employees, volunteer to do extra work, don't complain, and help their supervisors without being asked) are valuable to organizations, and as a result they may be recognized by their supervisors with higher performance evaluations and higher pay raises. In contrast, employees who are viewed as ingratiating (who are "political," seeking only to further their personal interests) do not reap these same benefits. In comparing the concept of being a good citizen with that of being ingratiating, Kenneth Eastman (1994) concluded that even though two employees might behave in similar ways, the motives that supervisors attributed to these behaviors were important to whether an employee was considered a good citizen or ingratiating. On a practical note, employees should become aware of how others, especially their supervisors, are interpreting their behavior (Eastman, 1994). Sincerity, consistency, and loyalty are likely to positively influence supervisors as they evaluate their employees.

Dispute Resolution

Imagine that you have been clearly and repeatedly sexually harassed by your supervisor or a co-worker. To address this problem, you may choose to use either (1) formal administrative and legal channels by filing a complaint with the Equal Employment Opportunity Commission (EEOC) or (2) the organization's system for resolving internal disputes. Organizations cannot forbid employees to use formal, legal channels, but they can encourage employees to use internal complaint procedures. In fact, the vast majority of complaints are handled internally, never reaching the courts or administrative agencies (Miller & Sarat, 1981). Internal complaint procedures should involve a neutral third-party mediator or arbitrator who helps to resolve the issue. Because internal dispute resolution often provides greater flexibility in solving problems, this process may be more likely to result in outcomes that are satisfactory for both parties in the dispute (Bush, 1989). However, it may be difficult for the third-party arbitrator or mediator to be truly neutral. The third party not only works for the organization but also would likely be involved in assisting or representing the organization should the employee file an external complaint (Edelman & others, 1993).

Getting Fired: Your Rights

In the absence of a specific contract, the relationship between employer and employee is an "at-will" one. Employment-at-will means that either the employer or the employee may terminate the relationship at any time, for any reason, without prior warning (Bakaly & Grossman, 1995). However, there are some restrictions on this doctrine. Specifically, employers are prohibited from discharging employees on the basis of legally protected characteristics (e.g., sex, race, religion), for exercising rights guaranteed by law (e.g., filing a discrimination charge against the employer), or for refusing to engage in illegal, immoral, or unethical acts on behalf of the employer. In addition, some discharged employees have been successful in suing the organization on the basis that an implied contract was violated. (You may have noticed that most employee handbooks state clearly that they are not contracts. This is to prevent discharged employees from arguing in court that the handbook was a contract.) Clearly, the power relationship between employer and employee is asymmetrical, with employees being more likely than employers to suffer if the relationship ends.

Personnel Psychology

Industrial or personnel psychology, as you have seen, focuses on the measurement of human knowledge, skills, and abilities; the measurement of job performance; the matching of people and jobs; and the training of workers.

Three major goals of personnel psychologists are: (1) selecting the best applicants for jobs, (2) training employees so that they perform their jobs effectively, and (3) accurately evaluating employee performance. The first step in attaining each of these goals is to perform a job analysis.

job analysis
An assessment of the major responsibilities of a particular job and the human characteristics needed to fill it.

The First Step
Job Analysis

Job analysis is a technique in which the major responsibilities of a job, along with the human characteristics needed to fill it, are determined. Information about the job is usually collected from employees who currently hold the job or from their supervisors. These people may be observed at their work, interviewed, or asked to complete surveys. Figure B.2 presents a job analysis for the position of job analyst itself.

Once a job's requirements are determined and written down in a job analysis, it is easier to achieve the goal of selecting an appropriate person for the position. Selection devices, such as tests and interviews, are used to determine which applicants have the knowledge, skills, and abilities specified in a job analysis. For example, a job analysis might reveal that as a salesperson, a dominant, extraverted personality is important. Applicants' personality traits might therefore be measured to screen for those who have these characteristics.

After appropriate applicants have been selected, the job of training them begins. Here, too, the key is to have a clear view of the job procedures, knowledge, and skills needed for effective job performance—that is, to have a good job analysis. Training program developers might begin by comparing the current work procedures, knowledge, and skills of employees with the information obtained from a job analysis. They would then design training programs to eliminate gaps between what currently exists and what is optimal.

Job analysis is also the first step in the design of performance appraisal systems. Before performance can be measured, expected performance must be defined. Job analysis defines and clarifies what effective performance is so that performance appraisal instruments may be developed.

A Closer Look at Personnel Selection

Have you ever applied for a job and not been hired? If so, you probably wondered what happened. Did you lose the job because of something you said or did in the interview or, perhaps, because of your responses on an application test? In this section, you'll learn about the applicant selection process. While you won't necessarily discover why you weren't picked for a particular job, you will get a better understanding of the selection processes that many companies use. This knowledge may help you to feel better prepared and more relaxed the next time you apply for a job.

The goal in personnel selection is to hire only those applicants who will perform the job effectively. A variety of selection devices are used to choose among applicants. The effectiveness of each device depends, in part, on its appropriate-

JOB ANALYST alternate titles: personnel analyst
Collects, analyzes, and prepares occupational information to facilitate personnel, administration, and management functions of organization; consults with management to determine type, scope, and purpose of study. Studies current organizational occupational data and compiles distribution reports, organization and flow charts, and other background information required for study. Observes jobs and interviews workers and supervisory personnel to determine job and worker requirements. Analyzes occupational data, such as physical, mental, and training requirements of jobs and workers, and develops written summaries, such as job descriptions, job specifications, and lines of career movement. Utilizes developed occupational data to evaluate or improve methods and techniques for recruiting, selecting, promoting, evaluating, and training workers, and administration of related personnel programs. May specialize in classifying positions according to regulated guidelines to meet job classification requirements of civil service system, a specialty known as Position Classifier.

FIGURE B.2 A Sample Job Analysis The job analysis is a crucial tool in personnel psychology. A thorough job analysis is the first step not only in selecting among job applicants but also in training employees for specific positions and in evaluating their performance. This job analysis is for the job of job analyst itself.

SOURCE: *Dictionary of Occupational Titles* (1991).

Bizzaro

selection device validity
The extent to which a personnel selection device is successful in distinguishing between those who will become high performers at a certain job and those who will not.

ness for a particular job. For example, a test of visual acuity may be a good selection device for the job of airline pilot but a poor selection device for the job of sewing-machine operator (some sewing-machine operators are able to sew with their eyes closed!). Personnel psychologists are concerned with the degree to which selection devices are valid. **Selection device validity** refers to the extent to which a selection device is successful in distinguishing between those applicants who will become high performers and those who will not. If a personality measure is used to select salespeople, it is considered valid if those whom it singles out as potential high performers do, indeed, become high performers.

Psychological Tests

Psychological tests are one kind of selection device that employers often use. Such tests are usually classified on the basis of what they measure. Common types of psychological tests are cognitive ability tests, mechanical aptitude tests, motor and sensory ability tests, and personality tests.

Cognitive ability tests measure general intelligence or specific cognitive skills, such as mathematical or verbal ability. Some items from two cognitive ability tests are presented in Figure B.3. *Mechanical ability tests* measure mechanical reasoning and may be used to predict job performance for engineering, carpentry, and assembly work. Figure B.4 presents sample items from the Bennett Test of Mechanical Comprehension. *Motor ability tests* include measures of fine dexterity in fingers and hands (for jobs that require the assembly of products with tiny parts), accuracy and speed of arm and hand movements, and eye–hand coordination. *Sensory ability tests* include measures of visual acuity, color vision, and hearing.

Personality tests may be designed to measure either abnormal or normal personality characteristics. An assessment of abnormal personality characteristics might be appropriate for selecting people for sensitive jobs, such as nuclear power plant operator, police officer, and airline pilot. Recently, tests designed to measure normal personality traits, such as conscientiousness, extraversion, and agreeableness, have become more popular for the selection of employees (e.g., Barrick & Mount, 1991, 1993; Tett & others, 1991).

Because of legal restrictions on the use of polygraph tests in the workplace, honesty tests have also become more widely used in recent years. Honesty tests attempt to assess an applicant's level of honesty by asking about past behaviors involving theft or dishonesty, attitudes about theft and the punishment of it, and perceptions about the prevalence of theft. Honesty tests are used primarily in retail situations—and with good reason. Research indicates that dishonest employees steal $10.37 for every dollar stolen by shoplifters (Washburn, 1997). Furthermore, according to one study (Wimbush & Dalton, 1997), half of employees with access to cash steal from their employers. There are many honesty tests available to employers, with some of them doing a good job of

(a) 1. RESENT/RESERVE — Do these words
    1 have similar meanings
    2 have contradictory meanings
    3 mean neither the same nor opposite
2. Paper sells for 21 cents per pad. What will 4 pads cost?

(b)

For each item find the picture that goes best with the picture in the first box. Draw a dark line from the upper right corner to the lower left corner in the proper box to show the right answer.

FIGURE B.3 Sample Items from Two Cognitive Ability Tests Cognitive ability tests can measure either general intelligence or specific cognitive skills, such as mathematical ability. **(a)** These two items are from the Wonderlic Personnel Test, which is designed to assess general cognitive ability. Employers assume that people who cannot answer most such questions correctly would not be good candidates for jobs that require general knowledge and reasoning skills. **(b)** The chart is from the Non-Verbal Reasoning Test. It assesses reasoning skills apart from the potentially confounding factor of skill with the English language.

SOURCE: Corsini (1957), Wonderlic (1998).

predicting admissions of theft (i.e., comparing honesty test responses with anonymous admissions of theft) and polygraph results (i.e., comparing honesty test responses with polygraph operators' judgments about an individual's truthfulness) (Ones & others, 1993; Snyman & others, 1991).

Work Samples and Situational Exercises

Two other kinds of personnel selection devices are work samples and situational exercises. Work samples are typically used for jobs involving the manipulation of objects, while situational exercises are usually used for jobs involving managerial or professional skills. Work samples provide a high degree of realism in that they require applicants to complete work-related problems. They have been called "high-fidelity simulations" in that they require applicants to complete tasks as if they were on the job (Motowidlo & others, 1997). A high degree of realism is important because it may serve as a realistic job preview (RJP) (Phillips, 1998; Premack & Wanous, 1985). RJPs give applicants a realistic view of the job so that they have more information to help them to decide whether or not to accept the job. This technique may reduce turnover by preventing people who would have quit early on from accepting the job.

One work-sample test for the job of mechanic, for instance, required the applicant to perform tasks such as taking apart and repairing a gearbox and installing pulleys and belts. Successful performance on the work-sample test did, in fact, predict successful performance on the job (Campion, 1972). A common situational exercise is the in-basket test, which requires the applicant to sort through a series of memos, directives, reports, letters, and phone messages in a limited amount of time (Frederickson, 1968). The employer evaluates the way in which the applicant organizes and deals with the items.

Selection Interviews

Although the general interview is one of the most commonly used selection devices, it typically possesses low validity. That is, assessments of applicants in general interviews are not strongly related to the applicants' subsequent job performance (Hunter & Hunter, 1984). The reason for the low validity of interviews is that they are often unstructured. The questions asked may be vague and unrelated to job performance, such as "Tell me about yourself" and "Why do you want this job?" In addition, different questions are sometimes asked of different applicants; as a result, it is difficult to compare their responses, and employers are forced to evaluate them on the basis of different information. Consider how unfair it would be if some students in your class were graded on their exam performances, others on their class attendance, and still others on their physical attractiveness (Berry & Houston, 1993).

In contrast to unstructured interviews, structured ones, if developed and conducted properly, are adequate predictors of job performance. A structured interview should (1) be based on a job analysis, (2) include questions that elicit job-related information about the applicant, (3) ask the same questions of all applicants and in the same order, and (4) be evaluated by a panel of interviewers who record and rate the applicant's responses. When these criteria are met, the interview is likely to be an effective selection tool (Campion & others, 1988).

Which room has more of an echo?

Which would be the better shears for cutting metal?

Which man carries more weight? (If equal, mark C)

Which letter shows the seat where a passenger will get the smoothest ride?

FIGURE B.4 Sample Items from a Mechanical Ability Test Questions such as these from the Bennett Test of Mechanical Comprehension are designed to assess a person's ability to figure out the physical properties of things. Such a test might be used to predict job performance for carpenters or assembly-line workers.

SOURCE: Bennett (1940).

Matching Job and Applicant A job analysis helps to pinpoint the qualities a person must have in order to succeed at a particular job. Not everyone has the special combination of compassion and toughness needed to be an effective physical therapist, for instance.

A situational interview is a type of structured interview in which an applicant is presented with a situation and asked how he or she would respond to it. Situational interviews may be experience-based, with applicants being asked how they have handled past work situations, or they may be based on hypothetical situations. Pulakos and Schmitt (1995) give these examples of each type of interview item:

Experience-based question: Think about a time when you had to motivate an employee to perform a job task that he or she disliked but that you needed the individual to do. How did you handle that situation?

Situational question: Suppose you were working with an employee who you knew greatly disliked performing a particular job task. You were in a situation where you needed this task completed, and this employee was the only one available to assist you. What would you do to motivate the employee to perform the task? (p. 292)

Organizational Behavior

Organizational behavior (OB) focuses on how the organization and social environment in which people work affect their attitudes and behaviors. Job satisfaction is the attitude most thoroughly researched by I/O psychologists. The impact of leadership on attitudes and behaviors is another well-researched OB topic. We will examine both of these topics here.

Job Satisfaction

Lucy and Jane are both engineers who work in the same department of the same company. Lucy is almost always eager to get to work in the morning. She feels that her work is interesting and that she has plenty of opportunities to learn new skills. In contrast, Jane is unhappy because she feels that she doesn't get the recognition she deserves at work. She also complains that the company doesn't give enough vacation time to employees and that it provides inadequate benefits. Jane can't think of many good things about her job. She's even beginning to feel that her job is negatively affecting her personal life.

Fortunately, Lucy is more typical of American workers than Jane is. In a Gallup poll conducted in August 2001, 80 percent of the U.S. workers sampled indicated that they were satisfied with their jobs. Employees tended to be more satisfied with their relations with co-workers and with the physical safety of the work environment. They were less satisfied with levels of on-the-job stress and pay. (For more information on the latest Gallup poll on job satisfaction, visit the Web site www.gallup.com.)

Several approaches have been used to explain differences in job satisfaction. One approach is based on a **discrepancy hypothesis,** which consists of three ideas: (1) that people differ in what they want from a job, (2) that people differ in how they evaluate what they experience at work, and (3) that level of satisfaction is based on the difference between what is desired and what is experienced (Lawler, 1973; Locke, 1976). Lucy and Jane, for instance, may not only want different things from their jobs; they may also make different assessments of the same events at work. Although their supervisor may treat them in the same encouraging manner, Lucy may see the boss's encouragement as supportive while Jane may view it as condescending. As a result, one perceives a discrepancy between desires and experiences, whereas the other does not.

A significant amount of research supports the discrepancy hypothesis. For example, negative discrepancies (getting less than desired) have been related to dissatisfaction. Interestingly, positive discrepancies (getting more than desired) have also been related to dissatisfaction in some cases (Rice & others, 1989). As an example, you might be dissatisfied with a job because it involves more contact with customers than you wanted or expected.

Another hypothesis to explain job satisfaction is the **social influence hypothesis,** which is based on the idea that people interpret their situations in part according to the reactions of others (Salancik & Pfeffer, 1977). For instance, when listening to a comedian, some people will make sure others are laughing before they laugh themselves. Similarly, when evaluating their own job satisfaction, people may be influenced by the attitudes of their co-workers regarding the degree to which the job is satisfying. After hearing Jane complain about the job, Lucy might report a lower level of satisfaction than she would have without Jane's influence. In a laboratory study, people who heard others evaluate a task positively were also likely to evaluate the task positively when they performed it later. Similarly, people who heard others evaluate a task negatively were later likely to evaluate the task negatively (Weiss & Shaw, 1979).

Dispositional factors have also been used to explain differences in job satisfaction. Some researchers believe that "job attitudes may reflect a biologically based trait that predisposes individuals to see positive or negative content in their lives" (Staw & Ross, 1985, p. 471). In other words, some people may be prone to negative perceptions and feelings (such as suspicion, fear, worry, and dissatisfaction), whereas others may be prone to positive ones (such as trust, enthusiasm, and satisfaction). In one study, researchers who examined identical twins raised apart found support for the idea that a tendency toward positive or negative outlooks may be biologically based. They found that sets of twins had similar levels of job satisfaction and concluded that job satisfaction may be explained in part by genetic factors (Arvey & others, 1989).

Discrepancy between desires and experiences, social influence, and inherited dispositions have each been successful in explaining some of the differences in job satisfaction among people. But as is true with most psychological research into human behavior, none of these approaches by itself can completely explain differences in job satisfaction.

Whatever its causes, job satisfaction or the lack of it can affect a person's general level of contentment. Job satisfaction has been found to be related to overall life satisfaction (see, for example, Judge & Watanabe, 1993; Lancer & others, 1989; Weaver, 1978). In general, satisfaction (or dissatisfaction) in one area of life has been found to spill over into others; feelings of happiness or unhappiness tend to pervade all aspects of our lives (Weaver, 1978). This is one reason why high job satisfaction among employees should be a goal of all organizations. In addition to reducing absenteeism and turnover, it contributes to employees' overall level of happiness. Companies might also provide resources to help employees cope with personal problems—again, because of the spillover effect: Happiness in one's personal life is likely to spill over into one's work life.

An interesting line of research examines situations in which job dissatisfaction results in employees actively trying to improve their working conditions. Dissatisfied employees may act creatively by proposing new ways of doing things or making suggestions on how to improve the work situation. Zhou and George (2001) have found that dissatisfied employees are more likely to behave creatively when they are committed to staying with the organization, when they have supportive co-workers or co-workers who provide them with useful feedback, or when they perceive the organization as being supportive of creativity.

discrepancy hypothesis
An approach to explaining job satisfaction that focuses on the discrepancy, if any, between what a person wants from a job and how that person evaluates what is experienced at work.

social influence hypothesis
The view that a person's level of job satisfaction is influenced by the job satisfaction levels of other people.

dispositional factors hypothesis
The view that a person's level of job satisfaction may be due in part to a genetically based disposition toward a positive or negative outlook.

Differences Between Male and Female Managers

My friend Janice has on occasion called me to complain about her supervisor (who happens to be female) and say that she would much rather work for a man than a woman. I also know a number of people who admit to preferring female to male supervisors. Although employees sometimes have strong preferences regarding the gender of their supervisors, research indicates that there are actually few differences between male and female managers.

For example, in one study that examined the conflict-management style of supervisors (Korabik & others, 1993), few personality or behavioral differences were found between male and female managers. However, the gender of the manager influenced how people reacted to the manager. Specifically, female managers who were viewed as dominating were more strongly criticized than males who were viewed as dominating. In addition, female managers who were viewed as obliging received more positive ratings than males who were obliging.

Another study examined the conflict-resolution style of male and female managers at work and at home (Chusmir & Mills, 1989). Again, male and female managers behaved very similarly both at work and at home as they dealt with conflict. Both genders tended to handle conflict more competitively at work than at home and to be more accommodating at home than at work. Interestingly, the rank of the manager in the organizational hierarchy was a strong predictor of how the manager would handle conflict at home as well as at work.

Although male and female managers tend to be similar in personality and behavior, they may tend to talk about their jobs differently and delegate work differently. When male and female managers were interviewed, women were found to talk about how they accomplished their work, whereas men tended to talk about the importance of their work (Statham, 1987). When delegating work, female managers tended to delegate work and then set up checkpoints and time lines to ensure that the work was completed properly. In contrast, male managers tended to delegate and then assume that the work was getting done.

What may be most important to managerial effectiveness is the congruence between managerial style and the preferences and needs of subordinates. For example, an employee who is still learning and developing might welcome a supervisor who is more involved, whereas an employee with a great deal of task experience might prefer to be left to work independently.

Leadership

Leadership is one of the most widely researched topics in I/O psychology, having been investigated in thousands of studies. "Leaders" are those who have the ability to direct groups toward the attainment of goals. According to this definition of leadership, one of the functions of a manager is to lead. Keep in mind, though, that managers act not only as leaders but also as negotiators, disturbance handlers, resource allocators, and decision makers (Mintzberg, 1973). Being a good leader is only one aspect of being a good manager. In Focus Box B.2 discusses the differences between male and female managers.

Leader Effectiveness

What Makes a Leader? Nelson Mandela is an extraordinarily charismatic leader. Not only did he keep his political organization, the African National Congress, functioning during his 27 years of imprisonment, but he also guided South Africa out of its racist apartheid system with a minimum of violence and turmoil.

I/O psychologists have spent a great deal of time trying to determine what makes someone an effective leader. The **trait approach to leader effectiveness,** one of the earliest approaches to the study of leadership, is based on the idea that leaders are born, not made. According to this view, some people possess certain qualities or characteristics that make them natural leaders. Examples are John F. Kennedy, Martin Luther King Jr., Colin Powell, and Bill Clinton. These people presumably share certain characteristics that made them good leaders, and these characteristics would make them good leaders in practically any situation. A large number of traits—such as height, physical attractiveness, dominance, flexibility, and intelligence—have been examined to see whether they determine how effective a leader will be. However, after a substantial amount of research, little connection has been found between personal traits and leader effectiveness (Hollander & Julian, 1970; Stogdill, 1948).

After the failure of the trait approach to identify effective leaders, researchers began to examine the *behaviors* of leaders in the hope of verifying **behavioral**

theories of leader effectiveness. They reasoned that the behaviors of effective and ineffective leaders must differ. One of the most influential studies of leadership behavior was conducted at Ohio State University. The researchers identified two major types of leadership behavior: consideration and initiating structure (Fleishman & Harris, 1962). *Consideration* describes leaders who are deeply concerned about their followers and who spend time building trust, respect, and warmth between themselves and their followers. *Initiating structure* describes leaders who are task-oriented, who structure tasks for their followers and who push for things to get done. Initiating structure has been related to high productivity, but also to low job satisfaction and high personnel turnover. In contrast, consideration has been related to high job satisfaction, but also to low productivity in some situations (Bass, 1981; Locke & Schweiger, 1979).

Additional research on initiating structure and consideration behaviors has led researchers to conclude that the *situation* might have an impact on the effectiveness of a leader's behavior. In some situations, initiating structure might be best; in other situations, consideration might be more effective. The theories that developed from this view are called **situational** (or **contingency**) **theories of leadership.** These theories tend to be complicated, but they seem to do a better job of explaining leader effectiveness than either the trait approach or behavioral theories.

In the last 20 years or so, researchers have once again become interested in leadership traits. In particular, the trait of charisma has received a lot of attention. Typically, charismatic leaders have a high need for power, are extremely self-confident, and believe strongly in a particular cause. Thanks to their compelling personalities and highly developed interpersonal skills, charismatic leaders have extraordinary effects on their followers (House, 1977). For example, a study of U.S. presidents from George Washington to Ronald Reagan revealed that the more charismatic the president, the greater his success with domestic issues (House & others, 1991).

Charismatic leaders are able to change the attitudes and beliefs of their followers and may even be able to evoke strong compliance from them. The followers are motivated by love, enthusiasm, and devotion to their leader. In some cases, compliance to the wishes of a charismatic leader may be so strong that followers are willing to engage in unethical or illegal behavior.

Much of the research on leadership has emphasized the impact of leaders on followers. This ignores the fact that followers also impact leaders. In contrast, the **leader–member exchange model** emphasizes the interaction between supervisor and subordinates (Dansereau & others, 1975; Graen & Cashman, 1975), recognizing that the relationship between leader and followers is unique to each leader–follower dyad—that is, supervisors have unique relationships with each of their subordinates. Supervisors may even create distinct "in-groups" (i.e., subordinates who are treated like partners because they are thought to be motivated and capable) and "out-groups" (subordinates who are viewed as less valuable than in-group members). Some research indicates that in-group members are more likely to be extraverts and to have attitudes similar to those of their supervisors (Phillips & Bedeian, 1994).

The existence of clearly defined in-groups is likely to foster resentment from those who are excluded (Yukl, 1989). Therefore, it is likely that effective leaders manage to develop a special relationship with each subordinate such that subordinates are not treated exactly the same, but each is made to feel valued for his or her unique contributions.

Research on upward influence (i.e., subordinates' influence on supervisors) has examined two types of goals that subordinates try to attain when influencing leaders: organizational goals (e.g., obtaining adequate resources to perform a task) and personal goals (e.g., recognition, approval, pay raises) (Yukl & others, 1995). Upward-influence tactics such as assertiveness and ingratiation have been found to be ineffective, whereas rational persuasion seems to enhance the leader's impression of the persuader's potential for promotion (Thacker & Wayne, 1995).

trait approach to leader effectiveness
An approach to determining what makes an effective leader that focuses on the personal characteristics displayed by successful leaders.

behavioral theories of leader effectiveness
Theories of leader effectiveness that focus on differences in the behaviors of effective and ineffective leaders.

situational (contingency) theories of leadership
Theories that focus on how a particular situation influences a leader's effectiveness.

leader–member exchange model
A model of leadership emphasizing that the quality of the interactions between supervisors and subordinates varies depending on the unique characteristics of both.

Leader Emergence

Research on the emergence of leaders examines who in a group is likely to become the group leader. This topic differs from that of leader effectiveness, because not everyone who emerges as a leader is a good leader. For example, in a discussion with your classmates, you might find that a particular person dominates the conversation and directs the group's efforts. This person is clearly the group's leader, but the effect of his or her behavior on group productivity and satisfaction may be either positive or negative. Using a technique called *leaderless group discussion,* in which a group is given a problem to solve or a topic to discuss, researchers study the group to see who emerges as the leader. Intelligence, aggressiveness, decisiveness, and dominance are personal qualities that have been related to leader emergence (Lord & others, 1986).

Workplace Trends and Issues

In recent years, organizations have become more accepting of telecommuting (i.e., employees working from home) and more concerned with employee work–life balance. In addition, more employers are using the Internet to recruit employees and software to spy on them. Each of these trends has implications for the work of I/O psychologists. Let's take a closer look at each of them.

Telework or Telecommuting: Working at Home As telecommunication technology has become more widespread, so has the number of employees who *telecommute* or work from home. For the individual who is self-motivated and has good communication skills, telecommuting offers the advantages of greater autonomy and flexible time management. On the down side, teleworkers are more likely to work in the evenings and on the weekends (Steward, 2000). Although men and women vary in their reasons for telecommuting, being able to work and provide childcare is a motivating factor for many women (Sullivan & Lewis, 2001).

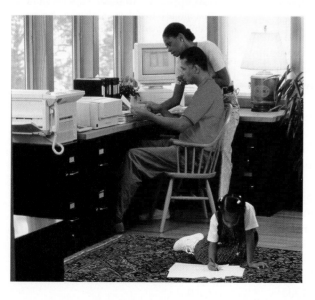

Telecommuting or Telework Organizations such as AT&T, Merrill-Lynch, American Express, Ford Motor Company, and Coca-Cola—along with many others—have telework programs in place (Schilling, 1999). These programs offer such advantages to employees as flexible work schedules, more freedom at work, and less time wasted commuting. From the employer's point of view, telecommuting may reduce costs associated with renting office space and increase the ability to attract and retain talented employees (Howard, 2000; Peltin & Crowder, 2000). However, telework is not for everyone. The characteristics of the position and the employee should be considered.

Telecommuting employees should be self-motivated and flexible, possess a high level of job knowledge and skills, have strong communication and organizational skills, and have a low need for social interaction. They should enjoy responsibility and be trustworthy and reliable (Schilling, 1999). In other words, telecommuters are people who work well with little supervision.

To manage from a distance, supervisors of teleworkers should set measurable performance output, have clear standards to assess performance, give specific performance feedback, and set timetables (Schilling, 1999). Industrial psychologists might develop specialized selection and performance evaluation systems to predict and then measure the performance of teleworkers.

Internet Recruiting Internet job-search services, such as Monster.com and Wetfeet.com, and company Web pages have changed the way in which employees are recruited. For example, in a study reported in HRFocus Newsbriefs (2000), university students were found to spend about four hours on a company's Web site during a job search. In addition to the time spent on company Web pages, job applicants electronically search for articles on prospective employers, post résumés on job boards, and seek career advice.

In a study comparing *Fortune*'s 100 Best Companies with *Fortune*'s 500 Biggest Companies, the 100 Best Companies were found to be more proactive in using their Internet homepages to attract job applicants (Brice & Waung, 2001). These companies were more likely than the 500 Biggest Companies to include corporate mission statements, make references to community outreach programs, and describe policies affecting work–life balance on their Web pages. Given that *Fortune*'s 100 Best Companies tend to be more progressive and proactive, it is no surprise that they have been the first to use the Internet to communicate effectively with job applicants.

Industrial psychologists might examine the usefulness of Internet recruiting. Does this type of recruiting attract better employees? Does it make a positive impression on job applicants? How realistic are the descriptions of jobs and organizations on the Internet compared to other recruitment sources?

Privacy in the Workplace   Employees have fewer rights in the workplace than they may realize. For example, although the federal Wire Tapping Act (Title I of the Electronic Communications Privacy Act of 1986) bars the interception of electronic communications without the consent of at least one of the parties involved in the communication, businesses are exempt from this restriction. That is, communications that are intercepted by an employer in the ordinary course of business are not prohibited (Katz, 1999). To complicate matters, state wire-tapping laws vary and may differ a great deal from the federal Wire Tapping Act. In general, organizations are free to monitor Internet use. Organizations that do so should have clear policies that are communicated to employees regarding such monitoring. Industrial psychologists might examine the impact of such monitoring on employee behavior and morale.

Work–Life Balance   Many employees report that they are seeking a better work–life balance, and some organizations promise to make this possible. These employers believe that policies affecting work–life balance will attract and retain better employees and even impact the bottom line. For example, the SAS Institute has generous policies affecting work–life balance—and resulting low turnover. This is estimated to save the organization $75 million a year (Fishman, 2000). Flexible work schedules, telecommuting, job sharing, sabbaticals, and more vacation and leave time are some of the benefits that many organizations offer to retain employees. Some employers even offer concierge services (e.g., pick-up/delivery of dry cleaning, on-site hair styling) and on-site health clubs to help employees balance personal activities and work. Critics argue that such services tend to be offered by organizations in which long hours are required. Similarly, while cell phones, pagers, and laptop computers might be seen as perks by their recipients, these devices further blur the distinction between home and work, resulting in employees who are constantly "on-call."

In the future, I/O psychologists will continue to have a significant role in the workplace. To keep pace with the changing needs of employees and rapid technological advances, I/O psychologists will continue to adjust the focus of their research and its applications to improve the experiences of people at work.

Appendix Review
Industrial/Organizational Psychology

Key Points

What Is Industrial/Organizational Psychology?

■ **Industrial/organizational (I/O) psychology** is a broad field that examines human behavior in the workplace. I/O psychologists spend their time working in these six content areas: (1) selection and placement, which focuses on developing assessment techniques to select people for jobs; (2) training and development, which focuses on determining what types of skills need to be enhanced and on evaluating the effectiveness of training programs; (3) performance management, which involves identifying performance standards and developing ways to measure performance; (4) **organizational development (OD),** which seeks to bring about positive change in an organization by examining organizational structure and the social systems within the organization; (5) quality of work life, which emphasizes the importance of maintaining a healthy and productive workforce; and (6) **ergonomics,** which focuses on the design of equipment and procedures in light of human capabilities and limitations. The "industrial," or "I," side of I/O psychology is also called **personnel psychology.** In contrast, the "organizational," or "O," side is sometimes called **organizational behavior.**

Work Settings, Type of Training, and Employment Outlook

■ A doctorate or master's degree is required to work as an I/O psychologist. The employment outlook has been good over the years, with consistently less than 1 percent unemployment among I/O psychologists surveyed by the American Psychological Association.

■ I/O psychologists may work in colleges or universities or as consultants to organizations. They may also work for large private corporations or for public institutions, such as government agencies.

■ In certain fields related to I/O psychology, jobs are sometimes available for people with bachelor's degrees. These fields include personnel, training, and labor-relations specialists and managers; management analysts and consultants; and employment interviewers.

Personnel Psychology

■ A first step in the work of personnel psychologists is to perform a **job analysis**—a determination of the major responsibilities of a certain job and the human characteristics needed to fill it. A good job analysis is key to successful personnel selection, effective job-training programs, and accurate evaluation of job performance.

■ Personnel psychologists use many devices to help them with their goal of selecting the best applicants for jobs. These include psychological tests, work samples and situational exercises, and selection interviews. Personnel psychologists are concerned about the **selection device validity**—the extent to which the device succeeds in distinguishing between those applicants who will become high performers and those who will not.

Organizational Behavior

■ One topic extensively studied in the field of organizational behavior is job satisfaction. Researchers have tried to explain different levels of job satisfaction in three ways: the **discrepancy hypothesis,** which focuses on gaps between what a person wants from a job and what he or she actually experiences; the **social influence hypothesis,** which looks at how people interpret their situations in relation to others' reactions; and the **dispositional factors hypothesis,** which links job satisfaction to inherited dispositions. New research examines the situations in which dissatisfied employees are likely to act to improve the workplace.

■ Leadership is also a widely studied topic in the field of organizational behavior. Researchers have tried to explain leadership effectiveness through the **trait approach to leader effectiveness, behavioral theories of leader effectiveness,** and **situational (contingency) theories of leadership.** Of these three approaches, situational theories seem to do the best job. Research also examines how supervisors and subordinates interact (the **leader–member exchange model**), how followers affect leaders' behavior, and how leaders emerge in a group.

Workplace Trends and Issues

■ The workplace of today has been influenced greatly by technological advances. The Internet has affected the ways in which employers seek job candidates and the ways in which job candidates learn about potential employers. It has also affected the social organization of the workplace, allowing some employees to work from home. Technological advances have also made it easier for employers to spy on their employees. Finally, many employees are concerned about work–life balance, and many employers are changing their policies in that area in an attempt to attract and retain good employees.

Key Terms

industrial/organizational (I/O) psychology, p. B-1

personnel psychology, p. B-1

organizational behavior, p. B-1

organizational development (OD), p. B-2

ergonomics, p. B-2

job analysis, p. B-5

selection device validity, p. B-6

discrepancy hypothesis, p. B-8

social influence hypothesis, p. B-9

dispositional factors hypothesis, p. B-9

trait approach to leader effectiveness, p. B-10

behavioral theories of leader effectiveness, p. B-10

situational (contingency) theories of leadership , p. B-11

leader–member exchange model, p. B-11

Web Companion   Review Activities

You can find additional review activities at **www.worthpublishers.com/hockenbury**
The Psychology 3e Web Companion has a self-scoring practice quiz, flashcards, two interactive crossword puzzles, and other activities to help you master the material in this chapter.

glossary

absolute threshold The smallest possible strength of a stimulus that can be detected half the time. (p. 92)

accommodation The process by which the lens changes shape to focus incoming light so that it falls on the retina. (p. 96)

acculturative stress (ah-KUL-chur-uh-tiv) The stress that results from the pressure of adapting to a new culture. (p. 545)

acetylcholine (uh-*seet*-ull-KO-leen) Neurotransmitter that causes muscle contraction and is involved in memory function. (p. 53)

achievement motivation Motivated behavior directed toward excelling, succeeding, or outperforming others at some task. (p. 341)

achievement test A test designed to measure a person's level of knowledge, skill, or accomplishment in a particular area. (p. 300)

action potential A brief electrical impulse by which information is transmitted along the axon of a neuron. (p. 47)

activation–synthesis model of dreaming The theory that brain activity during sleep produces dream images (*activation*), which are combined by the brain into a dream story (*synthesis*). (p. 158)

activity theory of aging The psychosocial theory that life satisfaction in late adulthood is highest when people maintain the level of activity they displayed earlier in life. (p. 400)

actor–observer discrepancy The tendency to attribute one's own behavior to external, situational causes, while attributing the behavior of others to internal, personal causes; especially likely to occur with regard to behaviors that lead to negative outcomes. (p. 504)

actualizing tendency In Rogers's theory, the innate drive to maintain and enhance the human organism. (p. 470)

adaptive theory of sleep The view that the unique sleep patterns of different animals evolved over time to help promote survival and environmental adaptation; also referred to as the *evolutionary theory of sleep*. (p. 149)

adipose tissue Body fat that is the main source of stored, or reserve, energy. (p. 326)

adolescence The transitional stage between late childhood and the beginning of adulthood, during which sexual maturity is reached. (p. 389)

adolescent growth spurt The period of accelerated growth during puberty, involving rapid increases in height and weight. (p. 432)

adrenal cortex The outer portion of the adrenal glands. (p. 61)

adrenal glands Pair of endocrine glands that are involved in the human stress response. (p. 61)

adrenal medulla The inner portion of the adrenal glands; secretes epinephrine and norepinephrine. (p. 61)

afterimage A visual experience that occurs after the original source of stimulation is no longer present. (p. 102)

agoraphobia An anxiety disorder involving the extreme and irrational fear of experiencing a panic attack in a public situation and being unable to escape or get help. (p. 581)

AIDS (acquired immune deficiency syndrome) A disease caused by the exchange of bodily fluids (semen, blood, or blood products) containing the human immunodeficiency virus (HIV), which attacks and weakens the immune system. (p. 442)

algorithm A problem-solving strategy that involves following a specific rule, procedure, or method that inevitably produces the correct solution. (p. 285)

all-or-none law The principle that either a neuron is sufficiently stimulated and an action potential occurs or a neuron is not sufficiently stimulated and an action potential does not occur. (p. 48)

alpha brain waves Brain-wave pattern associated with relaxed wakefulness and drowsiness. (p. 143)

altruism Helping another person with no expectation of personal reward or benefit. (p. 526)

amnesia (am-NEE-zha) Severe memory loss. (p. 270)

amphetamines (am-FET-uh-meens) A class of stimulant drugs that arouse the central nervous system and suppress appetite. (p. 175)

amplitude The intensity or amount of energy of a wave, reflected in the height of the wave; the amplitude of a sound wave determines a sound's loudness. (p. 104)

amygdala (uh-MIG-dull-uh) An almond-shaped cluster of neurons in the brain's temporal lobe that is part of the limbic system and is involved in memory and emotional responses, especially fear. (pp. 76, 348)

animal cognition The study of animal learning, memory, thinking, and language. (p. 296)

anorexia nervosa An eating disorder characterized by excessive weight loss, an irrational fear of gaining weight, and distorted body self-perception. (p. 336)

anterograde amnesia Loss of memory caused by the inability to store new memories; forward-acting amnesia. (p. 271)

anthropomorphism The attribution of human traits, motives, emotions, or behaviors to nonhuman animals or inanimate objects. (p. 355)

antianxiety medications Prescription drugs that are used to alleviate the symptoms of anxiety. (p. 653)

antidepressant medications Prescription drugs that are used to reduce the symptoms associated with depression. (p. 655)

antipsychotic medications (an-ti-sī-KA-tick) Prescription drugs that are used to reduce psychotic symptoms; frequently used in the treatment of schizophrenia; also called *neuroleptics*. (p. 651)

antisocial personality disorder A personality disorder characterized by a pervasive pattern of disregarding and violating the rights of others; such individuals are also often referred to as being a *psychopath* or *sociopath*. (p. 597)

anxiety An unpleasant emotional state characterized by physical arousal and feelings of tension, apprehension, and worry. (p. 578)

anxiety disorders A category of psychological disorders in which extreme anxiety is the main diagnostic feature and causes significant disruptions in the person's cognitive, behavioral, or interpersonal functioning. (p. 578)

aphasia (uh-FAZE-yuh) The partial or complete inability to articulate ideas or understand spoken or written language because of brain injury or damage. (p. 78)

aptitude test A test designed to assess a person's capacity to benefit from education or training. (p. 300)

archetypes In Jung's theory, the inherited mental images of universal human instincts, themes, and preoccupations that are the main components of the collective unconscious. (p. 465)

arousal theory The view that people are motivated to maintain an optimal level of arousal that is neither too high nor too low. (p. 323)

attachment The emotional bond that forms between an infant and caregiver(s), especially his or her parents. (p. 376)

attitude A learned tendency to evaluate some object, person, or issue in a particular way; such evaluations may be positive, negative, or ambivalent. (p. 506)

attribution The mental process of inferring the causes of people's behavior, including one's own. Also refers to the explanation made for a particular behavior. (p. 503)

atypical antipsychotic medications Newer antipsychotic medications that, in contrast to the early antipsychotic drugs, block dopamine receptors in brain regions associated with psychotic symptoms rather than more globally throughout the brain, resulting in fewer side effects. (p. 653)

audition The technical term for the sense of hearing. (p. 104)

authoritarian parenting style Parenting style in which parents are demanding and unresponsive toward their children's needs or wishes. (p. 403)

authoritative parenting style Parenting style in which parents set clear standards for their children's behavior but are also responsive to their children's needs and wishes. (p. 403)

autonomic nervous system (aw-toe-NOM-ick) Subdivision of the peripheral nervous system that regulates involuntary functions. (p. 57)

availability heuristic A strategy in which the likelihood of an event is estimated on the basis of how readily available other instances of the event are in memory. (p. 289)

aversive conditioning A relatively ineffective type of behavior therapy that involves repeatedly pairing an aversive stimulus with the occurrence of undesirable behaviors or thoughts. (p. 633)

axon terminals Branches at the end of the axon that contain tiny pouches, or sacs, called synaptic vesicles. (p. 50)

axon The long, fluid-filled tube that carries a neuron's messages to other body areas. (p. 47)

B

barbiturates (barb-ITCH-yer-ets) A category of depressant drugs that reduce anxiety and produce sleepiness. (p. 173)

basal metabolic rate (BMR) When the body is at rest, the rate at which it uses energy for vital functions, such as heartbeat and respiration. (p. 326)

basic emotions The most fundamental set of emotion categories, which are biologically innate, evolutionarily determined, and culturally universal. (p. 346)

basilar membrane (BAS-uh-ler) The membrane within the cochlea of the ear that contains the hair cells. (p. 106)

behavior modification The application of learning principles to help people develop more effective or adaptive behaviors. (p. 220)

behavior therapy A type of psychotherapy that focuses on directly changing maladaptive behavior patterns by using basic learning principles and techniques; also called *behavior modification*. (p. 629)

behavioral genetics An interdisciplinary field that studies the effects of genes and heredity on behavior. (p. 482)

behavioral theories of leader effectiveness Theories of leader effectiveness that focus on differences in the behaviors of effective and ineffective leaders. (p. B-10)

behaviorism School of psychology and theoretical viewpoint that emphasizes the scientific study of observable behaviors, especially as they pertain to the process of learning. (pp. 8, 192)

bell and pad treatment A behavior therapy technique used to treat nighttime bedwetting by conditioning arousal from sleep in response to bodily signals of a full bladder. (p. 632)

beta brain waves Brain-wave pattern associated with alert wakefulness. (p. 143)

binge-eating disorder A proposed category of eating disorder characterized by recurring episodes of binge eating that are not followed by purging. (p. 336)

binocular cues (by-NOCK-you-ler) Distance or depth cues that require the use of both eyes. (p. 121)

biological preparedness In learning theory, the idea that an organism is innately predisposed to form associations between certain stimuli and responses. (p. 204)

biological psychology Specialized branch of psychology that studies the relationship between behavior and bodily processes and systems; also called *biopsychology*. (p. 44)

biomedical therapies The use of medications, electroconvulsive therapy, or other medical treatments to treat the symptoms associated with psychological disorders. (p. 621)

biopsychosocial model The belief that physical health and illness are determined by the complex interaction of biological, psychological, and social factors. (p. 541)

bipolar cells In the retina, the specialized neurons that connect the rods and cones with the ganglion cells. (p. 99)

bipolar disorder A mood disorder involving periods of incapacitating depression alternating with periods of extreme euphoria and excitement; formerly called *manic depression*. (p. 590)

blaming the victim The tendency to blame an innocent victim of misfortune for having somehow caused the problem or for not having taken steps to avoid or prevent it. (p. 503)

blind spot The point at which the optic nerve leaves the eye, producing a small gap in the field of vision. (p. 98)

body mass index (BMI) A numerical scale indicating adult height in relation to weight; calculated as $(704.5 \times \text{weight in pounds})/(\text{height in inches})^2$. (p. 332)

borderline personality disorder A personality disorder characterized by instability of interpersonal relationships, self-image, and emotions, and marked impulsivity. (p. 597)

bottom-up processing Information processing that emphasizes the importance of the sensory receptors in detecting the basic features of a stimulus in the process of recognizing a whole pattern; analysis that moves from the parts to the whole; also called *data-driven processing*. (p. 115)

brain fingerprinting Technique to detect lies or deception, which uses an electroencephalograph to analyze brain waves; determines whether a stimulus is familiar (i.e., recognized because it is stored in the suspect's memory) or unfamiliar. (p. 349)

brainstem A region of the brain made up of the hindbrain and the midbrain. (p. 69)

brightness constancy The perception that the brightness of an object remains the same even though the lighting conditions change. (p. 125)

brightness The perceived intensity of a color, which corresponds to the amplitude of the light wave. (p. 101)

bulimia nervosa An eating disorder characterized by binges of extreme overeating followed by self-induced vomiting, misuse of laxatives, or other inappropriate methods to purge the excessive food and prevent weight gain. (p. 336)

bystander effect The phenomenon in which the greater the number of people present, the less likely each individual is to help someone in distress. (p. 527)

C

cafeteria diet effect The tendency to eat more when a wide variety of palatable foods is available. (p. 332)

caffeine (kaff-EEN) A stimulant drug found in coffee, tea, cola drinks, chocolate, and many over-the-counter medications. (p. 175)

California Personality Inventory (CPI) A self-report inventory that assesses personality characteristics in normal populations. (p. 489)

Cannon-Bard theory of emotion The theory that emotions arise from the simultaneous activation of the sympathetic nervous system, which causes physical arousal, and the cortex, which causes the subjective experience of emotion. (p. 357)

case study A highly detailed description of a single individual or event. (p. 23)

catecholamines (*cat*-eh-COLE-uh-meens) Hormones secreted by the adrenal medulla that cause rapid physiological arousal; include adrenaline and noradrenaline. (p. 547)

cell body The part of a neuron that contains the nucleus. (p. 46)

central nervous system Division of the nervous system that consists of the brain and spinal cord. (p. 56)

centration In Piaget's theory, the tendency to focus, or *center,* on only one aspect of a situation and ignore other important aspects of the situation. (p. 384)

cerebellum (sare-uh-BELL-um) A large, two-sided hindbrain structure at the back of the brain responsible for muscle coordination and maintaining posture and equilibrium. (p. 70)

cerebral cortex (suh-REE-brull or SARE-uh-brull) The wrinkled outer portion of the forebrain, which contains the most sophisticated brain centers. (p. 71)

cerebral hemispheres The nearly symmetrical left and right halves of the cerebral cortex. (p. 71)

cholecystokinin (CCK) (kola-sis-tow-KINE-in) Hormone secreted primarily by the small intestines that promotes satiation; also found in the brain. (p. 328)

chromosome A long, threadlike structure composed of twisted parallel strands of DNA; found in the nucleus of the cell. (p. 370)

chunking Increasing the amount of information that can be held in short-term memory by grouping related items together into a single unit, or *chunk.* (p. 244)

circadian rhythm (ser-KADE-ee-en) A cycle or rhythm that is roughly 24 hours long; the cyclical daily fluctuations in biological and psychological processes. (p. 138)

classical conditioning The basic learning process that involves repeatedly pairing a neutral stimulus with a response-producing stimulus until the neutral stimulus elicits the same response; also called *respondent conditioning* or *Pavlovian conditioning.* (p. 188)

client-centered therapy A type of psychotherapy developed by humanistic psychologist Carl Rogers in which the therapist is nondirective and reflective, and the client directs the focus of each therapy session; also called *person-centered therapy.* (p. 626)

clustering Organizing items into related groups during recall from long-term memory. (p. 249)

cocaine A stimulant drug derived from the coca tree. (p. 176)

cochlea (COCK-lee-uh) The coiled, fluid-filled inner-ear structure that contains the sensory receptors for sound. (p. 106)

cognition The mental activities involved in acquiring, retaining, and using knowledge. (p. 280)

cognitive dissonance An unpleasant state of psychological tension or arousal (*dissonance*) that occurs when two thoughts or perceptions (*cognitions*) are inconsistent; typically results from the awareness that attitudes and behavior are in conflict. (p. 508)

cognitive map Tolman's term that describes the mental representation of the layout of a familiar environment. (p. 222)

cognitive neuroscience The study of the neural basis of cognitive process that integrates contributions from psychology, neuroscience, and computer science. (p. 66)

cognitive therapies (CBT) A group of psychotherapies based on the assumption that psychological problems are due to maladaptive patterns of thinking; treatment techniques focus on recognizing and altering these unhealthy thinking patterns. (p. 636)

cognitive therapy (CT) A type of cognitive therapy, developed by psychiatrist Aaron T. Beck, that focuses on changing the client's unrealistic beliefs. (p. 638)

cognitive-behavioral therapy Therapy that integrates cognitive and behavioral techniques and that is based on the assumption that thoughts, moods, and behaviors are interrelated. (p. 640)

cognitive-mediational theory of emotion Lazarus's theory that emotions result from the cognitive appraisal of a situation's effect on personal well-being. (p. 359)

collective unconscious In Jung's theory, the hypothesized part of the unconscious mind that is inherited from previous generations and that contains universally shared ancestral experiences and ideas. (p. 465)

collectivistic cultures Cultures that emphasize the needs and goals of the group over the needs and goals of the individual. (p. 13)

color blindness One of several inherited forms of color deficiency or weakness in which an individual cannot distinguish between certain colors. (p. 102)

color The perceptual experience of different wavelengths of light, involving hue, saturation (purity), and brightness (intensity). (p. 101)

competence motivation Motivated behavior directed toward demonstrating competence and exercising control in a situation. (p. 341)

comprehension vocabulary The words that are understood by an infant or child. (p. 381)

compulsions Repetitive behaviors or mental acts that are performed to prevent or reduce anxiety. (p. 584)

concept A mental category of objects or ideas based on properties they share. (p. 283)

concrete operational stage In Piaget's theory, the third stage of cognitive development, which lasts from about age 7 to adolescence; characterized by the ability to think logically about concrete objects and situations. (p. 385)

conditional positive regard In Rogers's theory, the sense that you will be valued and loved only if you behave in a way that is acceptable to others; conditional love or acceptance. (p. 472)

conditioned compensatory response (CCR) A classically conditioned response in which stimuli that reliably precede the administration of a drug elicit a physiological reaction that counteracts, or is opposite to, the drug's effects. (p. 198)

conditioned reinforcer A stimulus or event that has acquired reinforcing value by being associated with a primary reinforcer; also called a *secondary reinforcer.* (p. 210)

conditioned response (CR) The learned, reflexive response to a conditioned stimulus. (p. 189)

conditioned stimulus (CS) A formerly neutral stimulus that acquires the capacity to elicit a reflexive response. (p. 189)

conditioning The process of learning associations between environmental events and behavioral responses. (p. 187)

cones The short, thick, pointed sensory receptors of the eye that detect color and are responsible for color vision and visual acuity. (p. 97)

conflict A situation in which a person feels pulled between two or more opposing desires, motives, or goals. (p. 543)

conformity The tendency to adjust one's behavior, attitudes, or beliefs to group norms in response to real or imagined group pressure. (p. 516)

consciousness Personal awareness of mental activities, internal sensations, and the external environment. (p. 136)

conservation In Piaget's theory, the understanding that two equal quantities remain equal even though the form or appearance is rearranged, as long as nothing is added or subtracted. (p. 384)

context effect The tendency to recover information more easily when the retrieval occurs in the same setting as the original learning of the information. (p. 253)

continuous reinforcement A schedule of reinforcement in which every occurrence of a particular response is reinforced. (p. 218)

control group or **control condition** In an experiment, the group of participants who are exposed to all experimental conditions, except the independent variable or treatment of interest; the group against which the experimental group is compared. (p. 29)

coping Behavioral and cognitive responses used to deal with stressors; involves efforts to change circumstances, or your interpretation of circumstances, to make them more favorable and less threatening. (p. 561)

cornea (CORE-nee-uh) A clear membrane covering the visible part of the eye that helps gather and direct incoming light. (p. 95)

corpus callosum A thick band of nerve fibers that connects the two cerebral hemispheres and acts as a communication link between them. (p. 71)

correlation The relationship between two variables. (p. A-9)

correlation coefficient A numerical indication of the magnitude and direction of the relationship (the correlation) between two variables. The closer the correlation coefficient is to +1 or −1, the stronger the relationship is. A *positive* correlation coefficient indicates that as one variable increases, the other tends to increase. A *negative* correlation coefficient indicates that as one variable increases, the other tends to decrease. (pp. 25, A-9)

correlational study A research strategy that allows the precise calculation of how strongly related two factors are to one another. (p. 25)

cortical localization The notion that different functions are located or localized in different areas of the brain; also referred to as *localization of function*. (p. 64)

cortical localization The notion that different functions are located or localized in different areas of the brain. (p. 78)

corticosteroids Hormones released by the adrenal cortex that play a key role in the body's response to long-term stressors. (p. 549)

corticotropin-releasing hormone (CRH) Hormone manufactured primarily in the hypothalamus that reduces eating behavior and increases metabolism, promoting negative energy balance and weight loss; also spelled *corticotrophin*. (p. 329)

counterconditioning A behavior therapy technique based on classical conditioning that involves modifying behavior by conditioning a new response that is incompatible with a previously learned response. (p. 629)

creativity A group of cognitive processes used to generate useful, original, and novel ideas or solutions to problems. (p. 313)

critical thinking The active process of trying to minimize the influence of preconceptions and biases while rationally evaluating evidence, determining what conclusions can be drawn from the evidence, and considering alternative explanations. (p. 17)

cross-cultural psychology Branch of psychology that studies the effects of culture on behavior and mental processes. (p. 12)

cryptomnesia A memory distortion in which a seemingly "new," or "original," memory is actually based on an unrecalled previous memory. (p. 257)

cued recall A test of long-term memory that involves remembering an item of information in response to a retrieval cue. (p. 252)

culture The attitudes, values, beliefs, and behaviors shared by a group of people and communicated from one generation to another. (p. 12)

cyclothymic disorder (sī-klo-THY-mick) A mood disorder characterized by moderate but frequent mood swings that are not severe enough to qualify as bipolar disorder. (p. 590)

D

daily hassles Everyday minor events that annoy and upset people. (p. 542)

decay theory The view that forgetting is due to normal metabolic processes that occur in the brain over time. (p. 265)

decibel (DESS-uh-bell) The unit of measurement for loudness. (p. 104)

deindividuation The reduction of self-awareness and inhibitions that can occur when a person is part of a group whose members feel anonymous. (p. 530)

delusion A falsely held belief that persists in spite of contradictory evidence. (p. 603)

demand characteristics In a research study, subtle cues or signals expressed by the researcher that communicate the kind of response or behavior that is expected from the participant. (p. 32)

dendrites Multiple short fibers that extend from the neuron's cell body and receive information from other neurons or from sensory receptor cells. (p. 46)

deoxyribonucleic acid (DNA) The chemical basis of heredity; carries the genetic instructions in the cell. (p. 370)

dependent variable The factor that is observed and measured for change in an experiment; thought to be influenced by the independent variable. (p. 28)

depressants A category of psychoactive drugs that depress or inhibit brain activity. (p. 171)

depth perception The use of visual cues to perceive the distance or three-dimensional characteristics of objects. (p. 119)

descriptive methods Scientific procedures that involve systematically observing behavior in order to describe the relationship among behaviors and events. (p. 22)

descriptive statistics Statistics used to organize and summarize data in a meaningful way. (p. A-2)

developmental psychology The branch of psychology that studies how people change over the lifespan. (p. 368)

difference threshold The smallest possible difference between two stimuli that can be detected half the time; also called *just noticeable difference*. (p. 92)

diffusion of responsibility The phenomenon in which the presence of other people makes it less likely that any individual will help someone in distress because the obligation to intervene is shared among all the onlookers. (p. 527)

discrepancy hypothesis An approach to explaining job satisfaction that focuses on the discrepancy, if any, between what a person wants from a job and how that person evaluates what is experienced at work. (p. B-8)

discriminative stimulus A specific stimulus in the presence of which a particular response is more likely to be reinforced, and in the absence of which a particular response is not reinforced. (p. 213)

displacement In psychoanalytic theory, the ego defense mechanism that involves unconsciously shifting the target of an emotional urge to a substitute target that is less threatening or dangerous. (p. 459)

display rules Social and cultural rules that regulate emotional expression, especially facial expressions. (p. 383)

dispositional factors hypothesis The view that a person's level of job satisfaction may be due in part to a genetically based disposition toward a positive or negative outlook. (p. B-9)

dissociation The splitting of consciousness into two or more simultaneous streams of mental activity. (p. 163)

dissociative amnesia A dissociative disorder involving the partial or total inability to recall important personal information. (p. 600)

dissociative anesthetics Class of drugs that reduce sensitivity to pain and produce feelings of detachment and dissociation; includes the club drugs, phencyclidine (PCP), and ketamine. (p. 178)

dissociative disorders A category of psychological disorders in which extreme and frequent disruptions of awareness, memory, and personal identity impair the ability to function. (p. 599)

dissociative experience A break or disruption in consciousness during which awareness, memory, and personal identity become separated or divided. (p. 599)

dissociative fugue (fūg) A dissociative disorder involving sudden and unexpected travel away from home, extensive amnesia, and identity confusion. (p. 600)

dissociative identity disorder (DID) A dissociative disorder involving extensive memory disruptions along with the presence of two or more distinct identities, or "personalities"; formerly called *multiple personality disorder*. (p. 600)

dominant gene In a pair of genes, the gene containing genetic instructions that will be expressed whether paired with another dominant gene or with a recessive gene. (p. 371)

dopamine (DOPE-uh-meen) Neurotransmitter involved in the regulation of bodily movement, thought processes, and rewarding sensations. (p. 53)

dopamine hypothesis The view that schizophrenia is related to, and may be caused by, excess activity of the neurotransmitter dopamine in the brain. (p. 610)

double-blind study Experimental technique in which neither the participants nor the researcher interacting with the participants is aware of the group or condition to which the participants have been assigned. (p. 52)

dream A storylike episode of unfolding mental imagery during sleep. (p. 154)

dream interpretation A technique used in psychoanalysis in which the content of dreams is analyzed for disguised or symbolic wishes, meanings, and motivations. (p. 623)

drive A need or internal motivational state that activates behavior to reduce the need and restore homeostasis. (p. 323)

drive theories The view that behavior is motivated by the desire to reduce internal tension caused by unmet biological needs. (p. 322)

drug abuse Recurrent drug use that results in disruptions in academic, social, or occupational functioning or in legal or psychological problems. (p. 170)

drug rebound effect Withdrawal symptoms that are the opposite of a physically addictive drug's action. (p. 169)

drug tolerance A condition in which increasing amounts of a physically addictive drug are needed to produce the original, desired effect. (p. 169)

DSM-IV-TR Abbreviation for the *Diagnostic and Statistical Manual of Mental Disorders,* Fourth Edition, Text Revision; the book published by the American Psychiatric Association that describes the specific symptoms and diagnostic guidelines for different psychological disorders. (p. 575)

dyspareunia A sexual dysfunction characterized by genital pain before, during, or after intercourse. (p. 440)

dysthymic disorder (dis-THY-mick) A mood disorder involving chronic, low-grade feelings of depression that produce subjective discomfort but do not seriously impair the ability to function. (p. 588)

E

eardrum A tightly stretched membrane at the end of the ear canal that vibrates when hit by sound waves. (p. 105)

eating disorder A category of mental disorders characterized by severe disturbances in eating behavior. (p. 335)

eclecticism (ee-KLEK-tuh-*sizz*-um) The pragmatic and integrated use of techniques from different psychotherapies. (p. 648)

EEG (electroencephalogram) The graphic record of brain activity produced by an electroencephalograph. (p. 142)

ego Latin for *I*; in Freud's theory, the partly conscious rational component of personality that regulates thoughts and behavior and is most in touch with the demands of the external world. (p. 458)

ego defense mechanisms In psychoanalytic theory, largely unconscious distortions of thought or perception that act to reduce anxiety. (p. 459)

egocentrism In Piaget's theory, the inability to take another person's perspective or point of view. (p. 384)

elaborative rehearsal Rehearsal that involves focusing on the meaning of information to help encode and transfer it to long-term memory. (p. 245)

electroconvulsive therapy (ECT) A biomedical therapy used primarily in the treatment of depression that involves electrically inducing a brief brain seizure; also called *electroshock therapy* or *shock therapy.* (p. 657)

electroencephalograph (e-lec-tro-en-SEFF-uh-low-graph) An instrument that uses electrodes placed on the scalp to measure and record the brain's electrical activity. (pp. 65, 142)

embryonic period The second period of prenatal development, extending from the third week through the eighth week. (p. 373)

emotion A complex psychological state that involves subjective experience, a physiological response, and a behavioral or expressive response. (p. 344)

emotional intelligence The capacity to understand and manage your own emotional experiences and to perceive, comprehend, and respond appropriately to the emotional responses of others. (p. 345)

emotion-focused coping Coping efforts primarily aimed at relieving or regulating the emotional impact of a stressful situation. (p. 563)

empirical evidence Evidence that is based upon objective observation, measurement, and/or experimentation. (p. 18)

encoding failure The inability to recall specific information because of insufficient encoding for storage in long-term memory. (p. 262)

encoding specificity principle The principle that when the conditions of information retrieval are similar to the conditions of information encoding, retrieval is more likely to be successful. (p. 252)

encoding The process of transforming information into a form that can be entered into and retained by the memory system. (p. 239)

endocrine system (EN-doe-krin) System of glands located throughout the body that secrete hormones into the bloodstream. (p. 59)

endorphins (en-DORF-ins) Neurotransmitters that regulate pain perceptions. (p. 54)

energy homeostasis The long-term matching of food intake to energy expenditure. (p. 326)

episodic memory Category of long-term memory that includes memories of particular events. (p. 246)

ergonomics A subarea of I/O psychology that focuses on the design of equipment and the development of work procedures in accordance with human capabilities and limitations. (p. B-2)

Eros In Freud's theory, the self-preservation or life instinct, reflected in the expression of basic biological urges that perpetuate the existence of the individual and the species. (p. 457)

ESP (extrasensory perception) Perception of information by some means other than

through the normal processes of sensation. (p. 114)

ethnocentrism The belief that one's own culture or ethnic group is superior to all others and the related tendency to use one's own culture as a standard by which to judge other cultures. (pp. 12, 512)

evolutionary psychology The application of principles of evolution, including natural selection, to explain psychological processes and phenomena. (p. 12)

expectancy effects Changes in a subject's behavior produced by the subject's belief that change should happen; also called *placebo effects.* (p. 32)

experimental group or **experimental condition** In an experiment, the group of participants who are exposed to all experimental conditions, including the independent variable or treatment of interest. (p. 28)

experimental method A method of investigation used to demonstrate cause-and-effect relationships by purposely manipulating a factor thought to produce change in a second factor. (p. 27)

explicit memory Information or knowledge that can be consciously recollected; also called *declarative memory.* (p. 248)

exposure therapy Behavioral therapy for phobias, panic disorder, posttraumatic stress disorder, or related anxiety disorders in which the person is repeatedly exposed to the disturbing object or situation under controlled conditions. (p. 646)

extinction (in classical conditioning) The gradual weakening and apparent disappearance of conditioned behavior. In classical conditioning, extinction occurs when the conditioned stimulus is repeatedly presented without the unconditioned stimulus. (p. 191)

extinction (in operant conditioning) The gradual weakening and disappearance of conditioned behavior. In operant conditioning, extinction occurs when an emitted behavior is no longer followed by a reinforcer. (p. 218)

extrinsic motivation Behavior motivated by external factors or influences, such as rewards, consequences, or social expectations. (p. 340)

eye movement desensitization reprocessing (EMDR) Therapy technique in which the client holds a vivid mental image of a troubling event or situation while rapidly moving his or her eyes back and forth in response to the therapist's waving finger or while the therapist administers some other form of bilateral stimulation, such as sounding tones in alternate ears. (p. 646)

F

facial feedback hypothesis The view that expressing a specific emotion, especially facially, causes the subjective experience of that emotion. (p. 358)

family therapy A form of psychotherapy that is based on the assumption that the family is a system and that treats the family as a unit. (p. 643)

female orgasmic disorder In females, sexual dysfunction characterized by consistent delays in achieving orgasm or the inability to achieve orgasm. (p. 440)

fetal period The third and longest period of prenatal development, extending from the ninth week until birth. (p. 373)

fight-or-flight response A rapidly occurring chain of internal physical reactions that prepare people either to fight or take flight from an immediate threat. (p. 546)

figure–ground relationship A Gestalt principle of perceptual organization that states that we automatically separate the elements of a perception into the feature that clearly stands out (the figure) and its less distinct background (the ground). (p. 117)

five-factor model of personality A trait theory of personality that identifies five basic source traits (extraversion, neuroticism, agreeableness, conscientiousness, and openness to experience) as the fundamental building blocks of personality. (p. 481)

fixed-interval (FI) schedule A reinforcement schedule in which a reinforcer is delivered for the first response that occurs after a fixed-time interval has elapsed. (p. 219)

fixed-ratio (FR) schedule A reinforcement schedule in which a reinforcer is delivered after a fixed number of responses has occurred. (p. 218)

flashbulb memory The recall of very specific images or details surrounding a vivid, rare, or significant personal event. (p. 254)

forebrain The largest and most complex brain region, which contains centers for complex behaviors and mental processes; also called the *cerebrum*. (p. 71)

forgetting The inability to recall information that was previously available. (p. 260)

formal concept A mental category that is formed by learning the rules or features that define it. (p. 282)

formal operational stage In Piaget's theory, the fourth stage of cognitive development, which lasts from adolescence through adulthood; characterized by the ability to think logically about abstract principles and hypothetical situations. (p. 385)

fovea A small area in the center of the retina, composed entirely of cones, where visual information is most sharply focused. (p. 97)

free association A psychoanalytic technique in which the patient spontaneously reports all thoughts, feelings, and mental images as they come to mind, as a way of revealing unconscious thoughts and emotions. (pp. 455, 623)

frequency distribution A summary of how often various scores occur in a sample of scores. Score values are arranged in order of magnitude, and the number of times each score occurs is recorded. (p. A-3)

frequency polygon A way of graphically representing a frequency distribution; frequency is marked above each score category on the graph's horizontal axis, and the marks are connected by straight lines. (p. A-4)

frequency theory The view that the basilar membrane vibrates at the same frequency as the sound wave. (p. 106)

frequency The rate of vibration, or the number of sound waves per second. (p. 104)

frontal lobe The largest lobe of each cerebral hemisphere; processes voluntary muscle movements and is involved in thinking, planning, and emotional control. (p. 73)

functional fixedness The tendency to view objects as functioning only in their usual or customary way. (p. 286)

functional magnetic resonance imaging (fMRI) An imaging technique that uses magnetic fields to map brain activity by measuring changes in the brain's blood supply during different mental activities. (p. 66)

functionalism Early school of psychology that emphasized studying the purpose, or function, of behavior and mental experiences. (p. 6)

fundamental attribution error The tendency to attribute the behavior of others to internal, personal characteristics, while ignoring or underestimating the effects of external, situational factors; an attributional bias that is common in individualistic cultures. (p. 503)

G

***g* factor or general intelligence** The notion of a general intelligence factor that is responsible for a person's overall performance on tests of mental ability. (p. 302)

GABA (gamma-aminobutyric acid) Neurotransmitter that usually communicates an inhibitory message. (p. 53)

ganglion cells In the retina, the specialized neurons that connect to the bipolar cells; the bundled axons of the ganglion cells form the optic nerve. (p. 98)

gate-control theory The theory that pain is a product of both physiological and psychological factors that cause spinal gates to open and relay patterns of intense stimulation to the brain, which perceives them as pain. (p. 112)

gender The cultural, social, and psychological meanings that are associated with masculinity or femininity. (p. 411)

gender identity A person's psychological sense of being male or female. (p. 411)

gender identity disorder A persistent discomfort about one's assigned gender along with the desire to be a member of the opposite sex. (p. 441)

gender roles The behaviors, attitudes, and personality traits that are designated as either masculine or feminine in a given culture. (p. 411)

gender-role stereotypes The beliefs and expectations people hold about the typical characteristics, preferences, and behavior of men and women. (p. 412)

gender schema theory The theory that gender-role development is influenced by the formation of schemas, or mental representations, of masculinity and femininity. (p. 421)

gene The basic unit of heredity that directs the development of a particular characteristic; the individual unit of DNA instructions on a chromosome. (p. 370)

general adaptation syndrome Selye's term for the three-stage progression of physical changes that occur when an organism is exposed to intense and prolonged stress. The three stages are alarm, resistance, and exhaustion. (p. 548)

generalized anxiety disorder An anxiety disorder characterized by excessive, global, and persistent symptoms of anxiety; also called *free-floating anxiety*. (p. 578)

genotype (JEEN-oh-type) The underlying genetic makeup of a particular organism, including the genetic instructions for traits that are not actually displayed. (p. 371)

germinal period The first two weeks of prenatal development. (p. 372)

Gestalt psychology (geh-SHTALT) A school of psychology founded in Germany in the early 1900s that maintained that our sensations are actively processed according to consistent perceptual rules that result in meaningful whole perceptions, or *gestalts*. (p. 116)

glial cells (GLEE-ull) Support cells that assist neurons by providing structural support, nutrition, and removal of cell wastes; manufacture myelin. (p. 45)

glucose Simple sugar that provides energy and is primarily produced by the conversion of carbohydrates and fats; commonly called *blood sugar*. (p. 325)

gonads The endocrine glands that secrete hormones that regulate sexual characteristics and reproductive processes; ovaries in females and testes in males. (p. 61)

graphology A pseudoscience that claims to assess personality, social, and occupational attributes based on a person's distinctive handwriting, doodles, and drawing style. (p. 487)

group therapy A form of psychotherapy that involves one or more therapists working simultaneously with a small group of clients. (p. 641)

gustation Technical name for the sense of taste. (p. 107)

H

hair cells The hairlike sensory receptors for sound, found in the basilar membrane of the cochlea. (p. 106)

hallucination A false or distorted perception that seems vividly real to the person experiencing it. (p. 603)

health psychology The branch of psychology that studies how biological, behavioral, and social factors influence health, illness, medical treatment, and health-related behaviors. (p. 540)

heritability The percentage of variation within a given population that is due to heredity. (p. 307)

heuristic A problem-solving strategy that involves following a general rule of thumb to reduce the number of possible solutions. (p. 285)

hidden observer Hilgard's term for the hidden, or dissociated, stream of mental activity during hypnosis. (p. 163)

hierarchy of needs Maslow's hierarchical division of motivation into levels that progress from basic physical needs to psychological needs to self-fulfillment needs. (p. 339)

hindbrain A region at the base of the brain that contains several structures that regulate basic life functions. (p. 70)

hippocampus A curved forebrain structure that is part of the limbic system and is involved in learning and forming new memories. (p. 75)

histogram A way of graphically representing a frequency distribution; a type of bar chart that uses vertical bars that touch. (p. A-3)

homeostasis (home-ee-oh-STAY-sis) The idea that the body monitors and maintains internal states, such as body temperature and energy supplies, at relatively constant levels; in general, the tendency to reach or maintain equilibrium. (p. 322)

hormones Chemical messengers secreted into the bloodstream by endocrine glands. (p. 59)

hue The property of wavelengths of light known as color; different wavelengths correspond to our subjective experience of different colors. (p. 101)

humanistic psychology School of psychology and theoretical viewpoint on personality that generally emphasizes the inherent goodness of people, human potential, self-actualization, the self-concept, and healthy personality development. (pp. 9, 469)

humanistic theories of motivation The view that emphasizes the importance of psychological and cognitive factors in motivation, especially the notion that people are motivated to realize their personal potential. (p. 324)

hypermnesia (high-perm-NEE-zha) The supposed enhancement of a person's memory for past events through a hypnotic suggestion. (p. 162)

hypnagogic hallucinations (hip-na-GAH-jick) Vivid sensory phenomena that occur during the onset of sleep. (p. 143)

hypnosis (hip-NO-sis) A cooperative social interaction in which the hypnotized person responds to the hypnotist's suggestions with changes in perception, memory, and behavior. (p. 160)

hypoactive sexual desire disorder A sexual dysfunction characterized by little or no sexual desire. (p. 440)

hypothalamus (hi-poe-THAL-uh-muss) A peanut-sized forebrain structure that is part of the limbic system and regulates behaviors related to survival, such as eating, drinking, and sexual activity. (p. 76)

hypothesis (high-POTH-eh-sis) A tentative statement about the relationship between two or more variables. (p. 18)

I

id Latin for *the it*; in Freud's theory, the completely unconscious, irrational component of personality that seeks immediate satisfaction of instinctual urges and drives; ruled by the pleasure principle. (p. 457)

identification In psychoanalytic theory, an ego defense mechanism that involves reducing anxiety by modeling the behavior and characteristics of another person. (p. 462)

identity A person's definition or description of himself or herself, including the values, beliefs, and ideals that guide the individual's behavior. (p. 390)

illusory correlation The mistaken belief that two factors or events are related when they are not. (p. 34)

immune system Body system that produces specialized white blood cells that protect the body from viruses, bacteria, and tumor cells. (p. 549)

implicit memory Information or knowledge that affects behavior or task performance but cannot be consciously recollected; also called *nondeclarative memory*. (p. 248)

implicit personality theory A network of assumptions or beliefs about the relationships among various types of people, traits, and behaviors. (p. 500)

incentive theories The view that behavior is motivated by the pull of external goals, such as rewards. (p. 323)

independent variable The purposely manipulated factor thought to produce change in an experiment; also referred to as the *treatment of interest*. (p. 28)

individualistic cultures Cultures that emphasize the needs and goals of the individual over the needs and goals of the group. (p. 12)

induction A discipline technique that combines parental control with explaining why a behavior is prohibited. (p. 404)

industrial/organizational (I/O) psychology The branch of psychology that focuses on the study of human behavior at work. (p. B-1)

inferential statistics Statistical techniques that allow researchers to determine whether the outcomes in a study are likely to be more than just chance events and whether they can be legitimately generalized to a larger population. (p. A-12)

informational social influence Behavior that is motivated by the desire to be correct. (p. 517)

information-processing model of cognitive development The model that views cognitive development as a process that is continuous over the lifespan and that studies the development of basic mental processes such as attention, memory, and problem solving. (p. 387)

in-group A social group to which one belongs. (p. 511)

in-group bias The tendency to judge the behavior of in-group members favorably and out-group members unfavorably. (p. 512)

inhalants Chemical substances that are inhaled to produce an alteration in consciousness. (p. 174)

inner ear The part of the ear where sound is transduced into neural impulses; consists of the cochlea and semicircular canals. (p. 106)

insight The sudden realization of how a problem can be solved. (p. 286)

insomnia A condition in which a person regularly experiences an inability to fall asleep, to stay asleep, or to feel adequately rested by sleep. (p. 150)

instinct theories The view that certain human behaviors are innate and due to evolutionary programming. (p. 321)

instinctive drift The tendency of an animal to revert to instinctive behaviors that can interfere with the performance of an operantly conditioned response. (p. 226)

insulin Hormone produced by the pancreas that regulates blood levels of glucose and signals the hypothalamus, regulating hunger and eating behavior. (p. 326)

intelligence The global capacity to think rationally, act purposefully, and deal effectively with the environment. (p. 296)

intelligence quotient (IQ) A global measure of intelligence derived by comparing an individual's score with the scores of others in the same age group. (p. 297)

interference theory The theory that forgetting is caused by one memory competing with or replacing another. (p. 262)

interneuron Type of neuron that communicates information from one neuron to the next. (p. 46)

interpersonal engagement Emotion dimension reflecting the degree to which emotions involve a relationship with another person or other people. (p. 347)

interpersonal therapy (IPT) A brief, psychodynamic psychotherapy that focuses on current relationships and is based on the assumption that symptoms are caused and maintained by interpersonal problems. (p. 625)

interpretation   A technique used in psycho-analysis in which the psychoanalyst offers a carefully timed explanation of the patient's dreams, free associations, or behaviors to facilitate to recognition of unconscious conflicts or motivations. (p. 624)

intrinsic motivation   Behavior motivated by the desire to engage in tasks that the person finds inherently satisfying and enjoyable, novel, or optimally challenging; the desire to do something for its own sake. (p. 340)

intuition   Coming to a conclusion or making a judgment without conscious awareness of the thought processes involved. (p. 286)

iridology   (ear-ruh-DOLL-uh-jee) A pseudo-science based on the unproven notion that the physical and psychological functioning of an individual is represented in the markings of the iris. (p. 96)

iris   (EYE-riss) The colored part of the eye, which is the muscle that controls the size of the pupil. (p. 95)

irreversibility   In Piaget's theory, the inability to mentally reverse a sequence of events or logical operations. (p. 384)

J

James-Lange theory of emotion   The theory that emotions arise from the perception of body changes. (p. 356)

job analysis   An assessment of the major responsibilities of a particular job and the human characteristics needed to fill it. (p. B-5)

just-world hypothesis   The assumption that the world is fair and that therefore people get what they deserve and deserve what they get. (p. 503)

K

K complex   Single but large high-voltage spike of brain activity that characterizes stage 2 NREM sleep. (p. 144)

kinesthetic sense   (kin-ess-THET-ick) The technical name for the sense of location and position of body parts in relation to one another. (p. 112)

L

language   A system for combining arbitrary symbols to produce an infinite number of meaningful statements. (p. 292)

latent content   In Freud's psychoanalytic theory, the unconscious wishes, thoughts, and urges that are concealed in the manifest content of a dream. (p. 158)

latent learning   Term coined by Tolman to describe learning that occurs in the absence of reinforcement but is not behaviorally demonstrated until a reinforcer becomes available. (p. 223)

lateralization of function   The notion that specific psychological or cognitive functions are processed primarily on one side of the brain. (p. 78)

law of effect   Learning principle proposed by Thorndike that responses followed by a satisfying effect become strengthened and are more likely to recur in a particular situation, while responses followed by a dissatisfying effect are weakened and less likely to recur in a particular situation. (p. 206)

leader–member exchange model   A model of leadership emphasizing that the quality of the interactions between supervisors and subordinates varies depending on the unique characteristics of both. (p. B-11)

learned helplessness   A phenomenon in which exposure to inescapable and uncontrollable aversive events produces passive behavior. (p. 224)

learning   A process that produces a relatively enduring change in behavior or knowledge as a result of past experience. (p. 186)

lens   A transparent structure located behind the pupil that actively focuses, or bends, light as it enters the eye. (p. 96)

leptin resistance   A condition in which higher-than-normal blood levels of the hormone leptin do not produce the expected physiological response. (p. 334)

leptin   Hormone produced by fat cells that signals the hypothalamus, regulating hunger and eating behavior. (p. 329)

levels-of-processing framework   The view that information that is processed at a deeper (more meaningful) level is more likely to be remembered than information that is processed at a shallow (less meaningful) level. (p. 246)

libido   In Freud's theory, the psychological and emotional energy associated with expressions of sexuality; the sex drive. (p. 457)

limbic system   A group of forebrain structures that form a border around the brainstem and are involved in emotion, motivation, learning, and memory. (p. 75)

linguistic relativity hypothesis   The notion that differences among languages cause differences in the thoughts of their speakers. (p. 295)

lithium   A naturally occurring substance that is used in the treatment of bipolar disorder. (p. 654)

long-term memory   The stage of memory that represents the long-term storage of information. (p. 240)

long-term potentiation   A long-lasting increase in synaptic strength between two neurons. (p. 269)

loudness   The intensity (or amplitude) of a sound wave, measured in decibels. (p. 104)

LSD   A synthetic psychedelic drug. (p. 177)

lymphocytes   Specialized white blood cells that are responsible for immune defenses. (p. 549)

M

magnetic resonance imaging (MRI)   An imaging technique that provides three-dimensional, highly detailed images of the brain using electrical signals generated by the brain in response to magnetic fields. (p. 66)

maintenance rehearsal   The mental or verbal repetition of information in order to maintain it beyond the usual 30-second duration of short-term memory. (p. 243)

major depression   A mood disorder characterized by extreme and persistent feelings of despondency, worthlessness, and hopelessness, causing impaired emotional, cognitive, behavioral, and physical functioning. (p. 587)

male erectile disorder   In males, sexual dysfunction characterized by a recurring inability to achieve or maintain an erect penis. (p. 440)

male orgasmic disorder   In males, sexual dysfunction characterized by delayed orgasm during intercourse or the inability to achieve orgasm during intercourse. (p. 440)

manic episode   A sudden, rapidly escalating emotional state characterized by extreme euphoria, excitement, physical energy, and rapid thoughts and speech. (p. 590)

manifest content   In Freud's psychoanalytic theory, the elements of a dream that are consciously experienced and remembered by the dreamer. (p. 158)

marijuana   A psychoactive drug derived from the hemp plant. (p. 177)

MDMA or **ecstasy**   Synthetic club drug that combines stimulant and mild psychedelic effects. (p. 178)

mean   The sum of a set of scores in a distribution divided by the number of scores; the mean is usually the most representative measure of central tendency. (p. A-5)

measure of central tendency   A single number that presents some information about the "center" of a frequency distribution. (p. A-5)

measure of variability   A single number that presents information about the spread of scores in a distribution. (p. A-6)

median   The score that divides a frequency distribution exactly in half, so that the same number of scores lie on each side of it. (p. A-5)

meditation   Any one of a number of sustained concentration techniques that focus attention and heighten awareness. (p. 166)

medulla   (meh-DOOL-uh) A hindbrain structure that controls vital life functions such as breathing and circulation. (p. 70)

melatonin (mel-ah-TONE-in) A hormone manufactured by the pineal gland that produces sleepiness. (p. 139)

memory consolidation The gradual, physical process of converting new long-term memories to stable, enduring long-term memory codes. (p. 271)

memory trace The brain changes associated with a particular stored memory. (p. 266)

memory The mental processes that enable us to retain and use information over time. (p. 239)

menarche (meh-NAR-kee) A female's first menstrual period, which occurs during puberty. (p. 432)

menopause The natural cessation of menstruation and the end of reproductive capacity in women. (p. 396)

mental age A measurement of intelligence in which an individual's mental level is expressed in terms of the average abilities of a given age group. (p. 297)

mental image A mental representation of objects or events that are not physically present. (p. 281)

mental set The tendency to persist in solving problems with solutions that have worked in the past. (p. 287)

mescaline A psychedelic drug derived from the peyote cactus. (p. 177)

meta-analysis A statistical technique that involves combining and analyzing the results of many research studies on a specific topic in order to identify overall trends. (p. 20)

midbrain The middle and smallest brain region, involved in processing auditory and visual sensory information. (p. 70)

middle ear The part of the ear that amplifies sound waves; consists of three small bones, the hammer, the anvil, and the stirrup. (p. 105)

Minnesota Multiphasic Personality Inventory (MMPI) A self-report inventory that assesses personality characteristics and psychological disorders; used to assess both normal and disturbed populations. (p. 488)

misinformation effect A memory-distortion phenomenon in which a person's existing memories can be altered if the person is exposed to misleading information. (p. 258)

mode The most frequently occurring score in a distribution. (p. A-5)

monocular cues (moe-NOCK-you-ler) Distance or depth cues that can be processed by either eye alone. (p. 119)

mood congruence An encoding specificity phenomenon in which a given mood tends to evoke memories that are consistent with that mood. (p. 254)

mood disorders A category of mental disorders in which significant and chronic disruption in mood is the predominant symptom, causing impaired cognitive, behavioral, and physical functioning. (p. 586)

moon illusion A visual illusion involving the misperception that the moon is larger when it is on the horizon than when it is directly overhead. (p. 126)

moral reasoning The aspect of cognitive development that has to do with how an individual reasons about moral decisions. (p. 392)

motivated forgetting The theory that forgetting occurs because an undesired memory is held back from awareness. (p. 263)

motivation The biological, emotional, cognitive, or social forces that activate and direct behavior. (p. 320)

motor neuron Type of neuron that signals muscles to relax or contract. (p. 46)

Müller-Lyer illusion A famous visual illusion involving the misperception of the identical length of two lines, one with arrows pointed inward, one with arrows pointed outward. (p. 125)

myelin sheath (MY-eh-lin) A white, fatty covering wrapped around the axons of some neurons that increases their communication speed. (p. 47)

N

narcolepsy (NAR-ko-lep-see) A sleep disorder characterized by excessive daytime sleepiness and brief lapses into sleep throughout the day. (p. 153)

natural concept A mental category that is formed as a result of everyday experience. (p. 283)

naturalistic observation The systematic observation and recording of behaviors as they occur in their natural setting. (p. 22)

negative correlation A finding that two factors vary systematically in opposite directions, one increasing as the other decreases. (p. 26)

negative reinforcement A situation in which a response results in the removal, avoidance, or escape from an aversive stimulus, increasing the likelihood that the response will be repeated in similar situations. (p. 209)

negative symptoms In schizophrenia, symptoms that reflect defects or deficits in normal functioning, including flat affect, alogia, and avolition. (p. 603)

neodissociation theory of hypnosis Theory proposed by Ernest Hilgard that explains hypnotic effects as being due to the splitting of consciousness into two simultaneous streams of mental activity, only one of which the hypnotic participant is consciously aware of during hypnosis. (p. 163)

nerves Bundles of neuron axons that carry information in the peripheral nervous system. (p. 55)

nervous system The primary internal communication network of the body; divided into the central nervous system and the peripheral nervous system. (p. 55)

neurogenesis The development of new neurons. (p. 68)

neuron Highly specialized cell that communicates information in electrical and chemical form; a nerve cell. (p. 45)

neuropeptide Y (NPY) Neurotransmitter found in several brain areas, most notably the hypothalamus, that stimulates eating behavior and reduces metabolism, promoting positive energy balance and weight gain. (p. 329)

neuroscience The study of the nervous system, especially the brain. (p. 44)

neurotransmitters Chemical messengers manufactured by a neuron. (p. 50)

nicotine A stimulant drug found in tobacco products. (p. 175)

night terrors A sleep disturbance characterized by an episode of increased physiological arousal, intense fear and panic, frightening hallucinations, and no recall of the episode the next morning; typically occurs during stage 3 or stage 4 NREM sleep; also called *sleep terrors*. (p. 152)

nightmare A frightening or unpleasant anxiety dream that occurs during REM sleep. (p. 157)

norepinephrine (nor-ep-in-EF-rin) Neurotransmitter involved in learning and memory; also a hormone manufactured by adrenal glands. (p. 53)

normal curve or **normal distribution** A bell-shaped distribution of individual differences in a normal population in which most scores cluster around the average score. (p. 301)

normative social influence Behavior that is motivated by the desire to gain social acceptance and approval. (p. 517)

NREM sleep Quiet, typically dreamless sleep in which rapid eye movements are absent; divided into four stages; also called *quiet sleep*. (p. 142)

O

obedience The performance of an action in response to the direct orders of an authority or person of higher status. (p. 518)

obese Condition characterized by excessive body fat and a body mass index equal to or greater than 30.0. (p. 332)

object permanence The understanding that an object continues to exist even when it can no longer be seen. (p. 383)

observational learning Learning that occurs through observing the actions of others. (p. 226)

obsessions Repeated, intrusive, and uncontrollable irrational thoughts or mental images that cause extreme anxiety and distress. (p. 583)

obsessive–compulsive disorder An anxiety disorder in which the symptoms of anxiety are trigged by intrusive, repetitive thoughts and urges to perform certain actions. (p. 583)

occipital lobe (ock-SIP-it-ull) An area at the back of each cerebral hemisphere that is the primary receiving area for visual information. (p. 72)

Oedipus complex In Freud's theory, a child's unconscious sexual desire for the opposite-sex parent, usually accompanied by hostile feelings toward the same-sex parent. (p. 462)

olfaction Technical name for the sense of smell. (p. 107)

olfactory bulb (ole-FACK-toe-ree) The enlarged ending of the olfactory cortex at the front of the brain where the sensation of smell is registered. (p. 108)

operant Skinner's term for an actively emitted (or voluntary) behavior that operates on the environment to produce consequences. (p. 207)

operant chamber or **Skinner box** The experimental apparatus invented by B. F. Skinner to study the relationship between environmental events and active behaviors. (p. 216)

operant conditioning The basic learning process that involves changing the probability of a response being repeated by manipulating the consequences of that response; also called *Skinnerian conditioning.* (p. 207)

operational definition A precise description of how the variables in a study will be manipulated or measured. (p. 18)

opiates (OH-pee-ets) A category of psychoactive drugs that are chemically similar to morphine and have strong pain-relieving properties. (p. 174)

opponent-process theory of color vision The theory that color vision is the product of opposing pairs of color receptors, red/green, blue/yellow, and black/white; when one member of a color pair is stimulated, the other member is inhibited. (p. 102)

optic chiasm (KI-az-em) Point in the brain where the optic nerve fibers from each eye meet and partly cross over to the opposite side of the brain. (p. 99)

optic disk Area of the retina without rods or cones, where the optic nerve exits the back of the eye. (p. 98)

optic nerve The thick nerve that exits from the back of the eye and carries visual information to the visual cortex in the brain. (p. 99)

optimistic explanatory style Accounting for negative events or situations with external, unstable, and specific explanations. (p. 554)

organizational behavior A subarea of I/O psychology that focuses on how the organiza-

tion and the social environment in which people work affect their attitudes and behaviors. (p. B-1)

organizational development (OD) A subarea of I/O psychology that focuses on bringing about positive change in an organization, such as increased profitability or improved products. (p. B-2)

outer ear The part of the ear that collects sound waves; consists of the pinna, the ear canal, and the eardrum. (p. 105)

out-group A social group to which one does not belong. (p. 511)

out-group homogeneity effect The tendency to see members of out-groups as very similar to one another. (p. 511)

P

pain The unpleasant sensation of physical discomfort or suffering that can occur in varying degrees of intensity. (p. 111)

panic attack A sudden episode of extreme anxiety that rapidly escalates in intensity. (p. 579)

panic disorder An anxiety disorder in which the person experiences frequent and unexpected panic attacks. (p. 579)

paranoid personality disorder A personality disorder characterized by a pervasive distrust and suspiciousness of the motives of others without sufficient basis. (p. 596)

paranormal phenomena Alleged abilities or events that fall outside the range of normal experience and established scientific explanations. (p. 34)

paraphilia (pair-uh-FILL-ee-uh) Any of several forms of nontraditional sexual behavior in which a person's sexual gratification depends on an unusual sexual experience, object, or fantasy. (p. 441)

parapsychology The scientific investigation of claims of paranormal phenomena and abilities. (p. 114)

parasomnias (pare-uh-SOM-nee-uz) A category of sleep disorders characterized by arousal or activation during sleep or sleep transitions; includes *sleepwalking, night terrors, sleep bruxism,* and *REM sleep behavior disorder.* (p. 152)

parasympathetic nervous system Branch of the autonomic nervous system that maintains normal bodily functions and conserves the body's physical resources. (p. 59)

parietal lobe (puh-RYE-et-ull) An area on each hemisphere of the cerebral cortex located above the temporal lobe that processes somatic sensations. (p. 72)

partial reinforcement A situation in which the occurrence of a particular response is only sometimes followed by a reinforcer. (p. 218)

partial reinforcement effect The phenomenon by which behaviors that are conditioned

using partial reinforcement are more resistant to extinction than are behaviors that are conditioned using continuous reinforcement. (p. 218)

perception The process of integrating, organizing, and interpreting sensations. (p. 90)

perceptual constancy The tendency to perceive objects, especially familiar objects, as constant and unchanging despite changes in sensory input. (p. 124)

perceptual illusion The misperception of the true characteristics of an object or an image. (p. 125)

perceptual set The influence of prior assumptions and expectations on perceptual interpretations. (p. 129)

peripheral nervous system (per-IF-er-ull) Division of the nervous system that includes all the nerves lying outside the central nervous system. (p. 57)

permissive parenting style Parenting style in which parents are extremely tolerant and not demanding; permissive-indulgent parents are responsive to their children, whereas permissive-indifferent parents are not. (p. 403)

person perception The mental processes we use to form judgments and draw conclusions about the characteristics and motives of others. (p. 499)

personality An individual's unique and relatively consistent patterns of thinking, feeling, and behaving. (p. 453)

personality disorder Inflexible, maladaptive patterns of thoughts, emotions, behavior, and interpersonal functioning that are stable over time and across situations, and deviate from the expectations of the individual's culture. (p. 595)

personality theory A theory that attempts to describe and explain individual similarities and differences. (p. 453)

personnel psychology A subarea of I/O psychology that focuses on matching people's characteristics to job requirements, accurately measuring job performance, and assessing employee training needs. (p. B-1)

persuasion The deliberate attempt to influence the attitudes or behavior of another person in a situation in which that person has some freedom of choice. (p. 532)

pessimistic explanatory style Accounting for negative events or situations with internal, stable, and global explanations. (p. 554)

phenotype (FEEN-oh-type) The observable traits or characteristics of an organism as determined by the interaction of genetics and environmental factors. (p. 371)

pheromones Chemical signals released by an animal that communicate information and affect the behavior of other animals of the same species. (p. 109)

phobia An irrational fear triggered by a specific object or situation. (p. 580)

phrenology (freh-NOL-uh-gee) A discredited pseudoscientific theory of the brain that claimed that personality characteristics, moral character, and intelligence could be determined by examining the bumps on a person's skull. (p. 64)

physical dependence A condition in which a person has physically adapted to a drug so that he or she must take the drug regularly in order to avoid withdrawal symptoms. (p. 169)

pitch The relative highness or lowness of a sound, determined by the frequency of a sound wave. (p. 104)

pituitary gland (pi-TOO-ih-tare-ee) Endocrine gland attached to the base of the brain that secretes hormones that affect the function of other glands as well as hormones that act directly on physical processes. (p. 60)

place theory The view that different frequencies cause larger vibrations at different locations along the basilar membrane. (p. 106)

placebo control group (pluh-SEE-bo) In an experiment, a control group in which the participants are exposed to a fake independent variable, or placebo, the effects of which are compared to a group receiving the actual independent variable, or treatment of interest. (p. 32)

placebo response An individual's psychological and physiological response to what is actually a fake treatment or drug; also called *placebo effect*. (p. 197)

pleasure principle In Freud's theory, the motive to obtain pleasure and avoid tension or discomfort; the most fundamental human motive and the guiding principle of the id. (p. 457)

pons A hindbrain structure that connects the medulla to the two sides of the cerebellum; helps coordinate and integrate movements on each side of the body. (p. 70)

population A complete set of something—people, nonhuman animals, objects, or events. (p. A-12)

positive correlation A finding that two factors vary systematically in the same direction, increasing or decreasing together. (p. 26)

positive incentive value In eating behavior, the anticipated pleasure of consuming a particular food; in general, the expectation of pleasure or satisfaction in performing a particular behavior. (p. 328)

positive reinforcement A situation in which a response is followed by the addition of a reinforcing stimulus, increasing the likelihood that the response will be repeated in similar situations. (p. 208)

positive symptoms In schizophrenia, symptoms that reflect excesses or distortions of normal functioning, including delusions, hallucinations, and disorganized thoughts and behavior. (p. 603)

positron emission tomography (PET scan) An imaging technique that provides color-coded images of brain activity by measuring the amount of a radioactive compound, glucose, or oxygen used in different brain regions. (p. 66)

possible selves The aspect of the self-concept that includes images of the selves that you hope, fear, or expect to become in the future. (p. 491)

posthypnotic amnesia The inability to recall specific information because of a hypnotic suggestion. (p. 162)

posthypnotic suggestion A suggestion made during hypnosis that the person should carry out a specific instruction following the hypnotic session. (p. 162)

posttraumatic stress disorder (PTSD) An anxiety disorder in which chronic and persistent symptoms of anxiety develop in response to an extreme physical or psychological trauma. (p. 582)

prejudice A negative attitude toward people who belong to a specific social group. (p. 509)

premature ejaculation In males, sexual dysfunction characterized by orgasm occurring before it is desired, often immediately or shortly after sexual stimulation or penetration. (p. 440)

prenatal stage The stage of development before birth; divided into the germinal, embryonic, and fetal periods. (p. 372)

preoperational stage In Piaget's theory, the second stage of cognitive development, which lasts from about age 2 to age 7; characterized by increasing use of symbols and prelogical thought processes. (p. 383)

primary reinforcer A stimulus or event that is naturally or inherently reinforcing for a given species, such as food, water, or other biological necessities. (p. 209)

primary sex characteristics Sexual organs that are directly involved in reproduction, such as the uterus, ovaries, penis, and testicles. (p. 432)

proactive interference Forgetting in which an old memory interferes with remembering a new memory; forward-acting memory interference. (p. 262)

problem solving Thinking and behavior directed toward attaining a goal that is not readily available. (p. 284)

problem-focused coping Coping efforts primarily aimed at directly changing or managing a threatening or harmful stressor. (p. 563)

procedural memory Category of long-term memory that includes memories of different skills, operations, and actions. (p. 246)

production vocabulary The words that an infant or child understands and can speak. (p. 381)

projective test A type of personality test that involves a person's interpreting an ambiguous image; used to assess unconscious motives, conflicts, psychological defenses, and personality traits. (p. 486)

proprioceptors (pro-pree-oh-SEP-ters) Sensory receptors, located in the muscles and joints, that provide information about body position and movement. (p. 112)

prosocial behavior Any behavior that helps another, whether the underlying motive is self-serving or selfless. (p. 526)

prototype The most typical instance of a particular concept. (p. 284)

pseudoscience A fake or false science that makes claims based on little or no scientific evidence. (p. 34)

psychedelic drugs A category of psychoactive drugs that create sensory and perceptual distortions, alter mood, and affect judgment. (p. 176)

psychoactive drug A drug that alters consciousness, perception, mood, and behavior. (p. 169)

psychoanalysis Personality theory and form of psychotherapy originated by Sigmund Freud in which free association, dream interpretation, and analysis of resistance and transference are used to explore repressed or unconscious impulses, sexual and aggressive instinctual drives, the enduring effects of early childhood experiences on later personality development, anxieties, and internal conflicts. (pp. 7, 454, 622)

psychological disorder or **mental disorder** A pattern of behavioral and psychological symptoms that causes significant personal distress, impairs the ability to function in one or more important areas of daily life, or both. (p. 575)

psychological test A test that assesses a person's abilities aptitudes, interests, or personality, based on a systematically obtained sample of behavior. (p. 486)

psychology The scientific study of behavior and mental processes. (p. 3)

psychoneuroimmunology An interdisciplinary field that studies the interconnections among psychological processes, nervous and endocrine system functions, and the immune system. (p. 550)

psychopathology The scientific study of the origins, symptoms, and development of psychological disorders. (p. 573)

psychosexual stages In Freud's theory, age-related developmental periods in which the child's sexual urges are expressed through different areas of the body and the activities associated with those areas. (p. 461)

psychotherapy The treatment of emotional, behavioral, and interpersonal problems through the use of psychological techniques designed to encourage understanding of problems and modify troubling feelings, behaviors, or relationships. (p. 621)

puberty The stage of adolescence in which an individual reaches sexual maturity and becomes physiologically capable of sexual reproduction. (p. 432)

punishment The presentation of a stimulus or event following a behavior that acts to decrease the likelihood of the behavior's being repeated. (p. 210)

punishment by application A situation in which an operant is followed by the presentation or addition of an aversive stimulus; also called *positive punishment.* (p. 210)

punishment by removal A situation in which an operant is followed by the removal or subtraction of a reinforcing stimulus; also called *negative punishment.* (p. 212)

pupil The opening in the middle of the iris that changes size to let in different amounts of light. (p. 95)

R

random assignment Assigning participants to experimental conditions in such a way that all participants have an equal chance of being assigned to any of the conditions or groups in the study. (p. 28)

random selection Process in which subjects are selected randomly from a larger group such that every group member has an equal chance of being included in the study. (p. 24)

range A measure of variability; the highest score in a distribution minus the lowest score. (p. A-6)

rational-emotive therapy (RET) A type of cognitive therapy, developed by psychologist Albert Ellis, that focuses on changing the client's irrational beliefs. (p. 636)

reality principle In Freud's theory, the awareness of environmental demands and the capacity to accommodate them by postponing gratification until the appropriate time or circumstances exist. (p. 458)

recall A test of long-term memory that involves retrieving information without the aid of retrieval cues; also called *free recall.* (p. 252)

recessive gene In a pair of genes, the gene containing genetic instructions that will not be expressed unless paired with another recessive gene. (p. 371)

reciprocal determinism A model proposed by psychologist Albert Bandura that explains human functioning and personality as caused by the interaction of behavioral, cognitive, and environmental factors. (p. 475)

recognition A test of long-term memory that involves identifying correct information out of several possible choices. (p. 252)

reinforcement The occurrence of a stimulus or event following a response that increases the likelihood of that response being repeated. (p. 207)

reliability The ability of a test to produce consistent results when administered on repeated occasions under similar conditions. (p. 301)

REM rebound A phenomenon in which a person who is deprived of REM sleep greatly increases the amount of time spent in REM sleep at the first opportunity to sleep uninterrupted. (p. 147)

REM sleep Type of sleep during which rapid eye movements and dreaming usually occur and voluntary muscle activity is suppressed; also called *active sleep* or *paradoxical sleep.* (p. 142)

REM sleep behavior disorder A sleep disorder in which the sleeper acts out his or her dreams. (p. 152)

replicate To repeat or duplicate a scientific study in order to increase confidence in the validity of the original findings. (p. 20)

representative sample A selected segment that very closely parallels the larger population being studied on relevant characteristics. (p. 24)

representativeness heuristic A strategy in which the likelihood of an event is estimated by comparing how similar it is to the prototype of the event. (p. 289)

repression In psychoanalytic theory, the unconscious exclusion of anxiety-provoking thoughts, feelings, and memories from conscious awareness; the most fundamental ego defense mechanism. (pp. 263, 459)

resistance In psychoanalysis, the patient's unconscious attempts to block the revelation of repressed memories and conflicts. (p. 623)

resting potential State in which a neuron is prepared to activate and communicate its message if it receives sufficient stimulation. (p. 48)

restless legs syndrome (RLS) A condition in which unpleasant sensations in the lower legs are accompanied by an irresistible urge to move the legs, temporarily relieving the unpleasant sensation but disrupting sleep. (p. 150)

restorative theory of sleep The view that sleep and dreaming are essential to normal physical and mental functioning. (p. 148)

reticular formation (reh-TICK-you-ler) A network of nerve fibers located in the center of the medulla that helps regulate attention, arousal, and sleep; also called the *reticular activating system.* (p. 70)

retina (RET-in-uh) A thin, light-sensitive membrane located at the back of the eye that contains the sensory receptors for vision. (p. 97)

retrieval The process of recovering information stored in memory so that we are consciously aware of it. (pp. 239, 251)

retrieval cue A clue, prompt, or hint that helps trigger recall of a given piece of information stored in long-term memory. (p. 251)

retrieval cue failure The inability to recall long-term memories because of inadequate or missing retrieval cues. (p. 251)

retroactive interference Forgetting in which a new memory interferes with remembering an old memory; backward-acting memory interference. (p. 262)

retrograde amnesia Loss of memory, especially for episodic information; backward-acting amnesia. (p. 270)

reuptake The process by which neurotransmitter molecules detach from a postsynaptic neuron and are reabsorbed by a presynaptic neuron so they can be recycled and used again. (p. 50)

rods The long, thin, blunt sensory receptors of the eye that are highly sensitive to light, but not to color, and that are primarily responsible for peripheral vision and night vision. (p. 97)

Rorschach Inkblot Test A projective test using inkblots, developed by Swiss psychiatrist Hermann Rorschach in 1921. (p. 486)

rule of falsifiability In order for a claim to be scientifically tested and proved true, there must be identifiable evidence that could prove the claim false. (p. 34)

S

sample A selected segment of the population used to represent the group that is being studied (p. 24); a subset of a population (p. A-12).

satiation (say-she-A-shun) In eating behavior, the feeling of fullness and diminished desire to eat that accompanies eating a meal; in general, to have an appetite or desire fully or excessively satisfied. (p. 328)

saturation The property of color that corresponds to the purity of the light wave. (p. 101)

scatter diagram or **scatter plot** A graph that represents the relationship between two variables. (p. A-10)

schedule of reinforcement The delivery of a reinforcer according to a preset pattern based on the number of responses or the time interval between responses. (p. 218)

schema (SKEE-muh) An organized cluster of information about a particular topic. (p. 255)

schizophrenia A mental disorder in which the ability to function is impaired by severely distorted beliefs, perceptions, and thought processes. (p. 602)

scientific method A set of assumptions, attitudes, and procedures that guide researchers in creating questions to investigate, in generating evidence, and in drawing conclusions. (p. 16)

seasonal affective disorder (SAD) A mood disorder in which episodes of depression typically recur during the fall and winter and remit during the spring and summer. (p. 589)

secondary sex characteristics Sexual characteristics that develop during puberty and are not directly involved in reproduction but differentiate between the sexes, such as male facial hair and female breast development. (p. 432)

selection device validity The extent to which a personnel selection device is successful in distinguishing between those who will become high performers at a certain job and those who will not. (p. B-6)

selective serotonin reuptake inhibitors (SSRIs) Class of antidepressant medications that increase the availability of serotonin in the brain and cause fewer side effects than earlier antidepressants; they include Prozac, Paxil, and Zoloft. (p. 655)

self-actualization Defined by Maslow as "the full use and exploitation of talents, capacities, and potentialities." (p. 339)

self-concept The set of perceptions and beliefs that you hold about yourself. (p. 472)

self-determination theory (SDT) Edward Deci and Richard Ryan's theory that optimal human functioning can occur only if the psychological needs for autonomy, competence, and relatedness are satisfied. (p. 340)

self-efficacy The beliefs that people have about their ability to meet the demands of a specific situation; feelings of self-confidence or self-doubt. (pp. 361, 475)

self-report inventory A type of psychological test in which a person's responses to standardized questions are compared to established norms. (p. 488)

self-serving bias The tendency to attribute successful outcomes of one's own behavior to internal causes and unsuccessful outcomes to external, situational causes. (p. 505)

semantic memory Category of long-term memory that includes memories of general knowledge of facts, names, and concepts. (p. 246)

semantic network model A model that describes units of information in long-term memory as being organized in a complex network of associations. (p. 249)

sensation The process of detecting a physical stimulus, such as light, sound, heat, or pressure. (p. 90)

sensation seeking The degree to which an individual is motivated to experience high levels of sensory and physical arousal associated with varied and novel activities. (p. 324)

sensorimotor stage In Piaget's theory, the first stage of cognitive development, from birth to about age 2; the period during which the infant explores the environment and acquires knowledge through sensing and manipulating objects. (p. 383)

sensory adaptation The decline in sensitivity to a constant stimulus. (p. 92)

sensory memory The stage of memory that registers information from the environment and holds it for a very brief period of time. (p. 240)

sensory neuron Type of neuron that conveys information to the brain from specialized receptor cells in sense organs and internal organs. (p. 46)

sensory receptors Specialized cells unique to each sense organ that respond to a particular form of sensory stimulation. (p. 91)

sensory-specific satiety (sah-TIE-it-tee) The reduced desire to continue consuming a particular food. (p. 328)

serial position effect The tendency to remember items at the beginning and end of a list better than items in the middle. (p. 252)

serotonin (ser-ah-TONE-in) Neurotransmitter involved in sleep and emotions. (p. 53)

set-point theory Theory that proposes that humans and other animals have a natural or optimal body weight, called the *set-point weight,* that the body defends from becoming higher or lower by regulating feelings of hunger and body metabolism. (p. 330)

settling-point models of weight regulation General model of weight regulation suggesting that body weight settles, or stabilizes, around the point at which there is balance between the factors influencing energy intake and energy expenditure. (p. 330)

sex (1) The biological category of male or female as defined by physical differences in genetic composition and in reproductive anatomy and function. (2) The behavioral manifestation of the sexual urge; sexual intercourse. (p. 411)

sex chromosomes Chromosomes designated as X or Y that determine biological sex; the 23rd pair of chromosomes in humans. (p. 371)

sex-linked recessive characteristics Traits determined by recessive genes located on the X chromosome; in males, these characteristics require only one recessive gene to be expressed. (p. 372)

sexual aversion disorder A sexual dysfunction characterized by active avoidance of genital sexual contact because of extreme anxiety, fear, or disgust. (p. 440)

sexual dysfunction A consistent disturbance in sexual desire, arousal, or orgasm that causes psychological distress and interpersonal difficulties. (p. 439)

sexual orientation The direction of a person's emotional and erotic attraction toward members of the opposite sex, the same sex, or both sexes. (pp. 411, 427)

sexually transmitted diseases (STDs) Any of several infectious diseases that are transmitted primarily through sexual intercourse or other intimate sexual contact. (p. 442)

shape constancy The perception of a familiar object as maintaining the same shape regardless of the image produced on the retina. (p. 124)

shaping The operant conditioning procedure of selectively reinforcing successively closer approximations of a goal behavior until the goal behavior is displayed. (p. 216)

short-term dynamic therapies Type of psychotherapy that is based on psychoanalytic theory but differs in that it is typically time-limited, has specific goals, and involves an active, rather than neutral, role for the therapist. (p. 625)

short-term memory or working memory The active stage of memory in which information is stored for about 30 seconds. (p. 240)

situational (contingency) theories of leader effectiveness Theories that focus on how a particular situation influences a leader's effectiveness. (p. B-11)

Sixteen Personality Factor Questionnaire (16PF) A self-report inventory developed by Raymond Cattell that generates a personality profile with ratings on 16 trait dimensions. (p. 489)

size constancy The perception of an object as maintaining the same size despite changing images on the retina. (p. 124)

skewed distribution An asymmetrical distribution; more scores occur on one side of the distribution than on the other. In a *positively* skewed distribution, most of the scores are low scores; in a *negatively* skewed distribution, most of the scores are high scores. (p. A-4)

sleep apnea (APP-nee-uh) A sleep disorder in which the person repeatedly stops breathing during sleep. (p. 151)

sleep disorders Serious disturbances in the normal sleep pattern that interfere with daytime functioning and cause subjective distress. (p. 150)

sleep inertia Feeling of sleepiness on awakening that interferes with the ability to perform mental or physical tasks. (p. 180)

sleep spindles Short bursts of brain activity that characterize stage 2 NREM sleep. (p. 144)

sleep thinking Repetitive, bland, and uncreative ruminations about real-life events during sleep. (p. 153)

sleepwalking A sleep disturbance characterized by an episode of walking or performing other actions during stage 3 or stage 4 NREM sleep; also called *somnambulism.* (p. 151)

social categorization The mental process of categorizing people into groups (or *categories*) on the basis of their shared characteristics. (p. 500)

social cognition The study of the mental processes people use to make sense out of their social environment. (p. 498)

social cognitive theory Bandura's theory of personality, which emphasizes the importance of observational learning, conscious cognitive processes, social experiences, self-efficacy beliefs, and reciprocal determinism. (p. 474)

social facilitation The tendency for the presence of other people to enhance individual performance. (p. 530)

social influence The study of the effects of situational factors and other people on an individual's behavior. (pp. 498, 515)

social influence hypothesis   The view that a person's level of job satisfaction is influenced by the job satisfaction levels of other people. (p. B-9)

social learning theory of gender-role development   The theory that gender roles are acquired through the basic processes of learning, including reinforcement, punishment, and modeling. (p. 420)

social loafing   The tendency to expend less effort on a task when it is a group effort. (p. 529)

social norms   The "rules," or expectations, for appropriate behavior in a particular social situation. (p. 499)

social phobia or **social anxiety disorder**   An anxiety disorder involving the extreme and irrational fear of being embarrassed, judged, or scrutinized by others in social situations. (p. 581)

social psychology   The branch of psychology that studies how people think, feel, and behave in social situations. (p. 498)

social support   The resources provided by other people in times of need. (p. 559)

somatic nervous system   Subdivision of the peripheral nervous system that communicates sensory information to the central nervous system and carries motor messages from the central nervous system to the muscles. (p. 57)

source confusion   A memory distortion that occurs when the true source of the memory is forgotten. (p. 256)

source traits   The most fundamental dimensions of personality; the broad, basic traits that are hypothesized to be universal and relatively few in number. (p. 478)

specific phobia   An anxiety disorder characterized by an extreme and irrational fear of a specific object or situation that interferes with the ability to function in daily life; formerly called *simple phobia*. (p. 580)

spinal reflexes   Simple, automatic behaviors that are processed in the spinal cord. (p. 56)

split-brain operation   A surgical procedure that involves cutting the corpus callosum. (p. 80)

spontaneous recovery   The reappearance of a previously extinguished conditioned response after a period of time without exposure to the conditioned stimulus. (p. 191)

stage model of memory   A model describing memory as consisting of three distinct stages: sensory memory, short-term memory, and long-term memory. (p. 239)

standard deviation   A measure of variability; expressed as the square root of the sum of the squared deviations around the mean divided by the number of scores in the distribution. (p. A-6)

standard normal curve or **standard normal distribution**   A symmetrical distribution forming a bell-shaped curve in which the mean, median, and mode are all equal and fall in the exact middle. (p. A-8)

standardization   The administration of a test to a large, representative sample of people under uniform conditions for the purpose of establishing norms. (p. 300)

state-dependent retrieval   An encoding specificity phenomenon in which information that is learned in a particular drug state is more likely to be recalled while the person is in the same drug state. (p. 253)

statistically significant   A mathematical indication that research results are not very likely to have occurred by chance. (p. 19)

statistics   A branch of mathematics used by researchers to summarize data and draw conclusions based on the data. (p. 19)

stereotype   A cluster of characteristics that are associated with all members of a specific social group, often including qualities that are unrelated to the objective criteria that define the group. (p. 510)

stereotype threat   A psychological predicament in which fear that you will be evaluated in terms of a negative stereotype about a group to which you belong creates anxiety and self-doubt, lowering performance in a particular domain that is important to you. (p. 311)

stimulant-induced psychosis   Schizophrenia-like symptoms that can occur as the result of prolonged amphetamine or cocaine use; also called *amphetamine psychosis* or *cocaine psychosis*. (p. 176)

stimulants   A category of psychoactive drugs that increase brain activity, arouse behavior, and increase mental alertness. (p. 174)

stimulus discrimination   The occurrence of a learned response to a specific stimulus, but not to other, similar stimuli. (p. 190)

stimulus generalization   The occurrence of a learned response not only to the original stimulus, but to other, similar stimuli as well. (p. 190)

stimulus threshold   The minimum level of stimulation required to activate a particular neuron. (p. 47)

storage   The process of retaining information in memory so that it can be used at a later time. (p. 239)

stress   A negative emotional state occurring in response to events that are perceived as taxing or exceeding a person's resources or ability to cope. (p. 540)

stressors   Events or situations that are perceived as harmful, threatening, or challenging. (p. 541)

structural plasticity   A phenomenon in which brain structures physically change in response to environmental influences. (p. 84)

structuralism   Early school of psychology that emphasized studying the most basic components, or structures, of conscious experiences. (p. 5)

sublimation   In psychoanalytic theory, an ego defense mechanism that involves redirecting sexual urges toward productive, socially acceptable, nonsexual activities; a form of displacement. (p. 459)

subliminal perception   The perception of stimuli that are below the threshold of conscious awareness. (p. 93)

substance P   A neurotransmitter that is involved in the transmission of pain messages to the brain. (p. 112)

substantia nigra   (sub-STAN-she-uh NYE-gruh) An area of the midbrain that is involved in motor control and contains a large concentration of dopamine-producing neurons. (p. 70)

superego   In Freud's theory, the partly conscious, self-evaluative, moralistic component of personality that is formed through the internalization of parental and societal rules. (p. 458)

suppression   Motivated forgetting that occurs consciously. (p. 263)

suprachiasmatic nucleus (SCN)   (soup-rah-*kye*-az-MAT-ick) A cluster of neurons in the hypothalamus in the brain that governs the timing of circadian rhythms. (p. 139)

surface traits   Personality characteristics or attributes that can easily be inferred from observable behavior. (p. 478)

survey   A questionnaire or interview designed to investigate the opinions, behaviors, or characteristics of a particular group. (p. 23)

symbolic thought   The ability to use words, images, and symbols to represent the world. (p. 383)

symmetrical distribution   A distribution in which scores fall equally on both sides of the graph. The normal curve is an example of a symmetrical distribution. (p. A-4)

sympathetic nervous system   Branch of the autonomic nervous system that produces rapid physical arousal in response to perceived emergencies or threats. (p. 58)

synapse   (SIN-aps) The point of communication between two neurons. (p. 50)

synaptic gap   (sin-AP-tick) The tiny space between the axon terminal of one neuron and the dendrite of an adjoining neuron. (p. 50)

synaptic transmission   (sin-AP-tick) The process through which neurotransmitters are released by one neuron, cross the synaptic gap, and affect adjoining neurons. (p. 50)

synaptic vesicles   (sin-AP-tick VESS-ick-ulls) Tiny pouches or sacs in the axon terminals that contain chemicals called neurotransmitters. (p. 50)

systematic desensitization   A type of behavior therapy in which phobic responses are reduced by pairing relaxation with a series of mental images or real-life situations that the person finds progressively more fear-provoking, based on the principle of counter-conditioning. (p. 630)

T

taste aversion A classically conditioned dislike for and avoidance of a particular food that develops when an organism becomes ill after eating the food. (p. 202)

taste buds The specialized sensory receptors for taste that are located on the tongue and inside the mouth and throat. (p. 110)

temperament Inborn predispositions to consistently behave and react in a certain way. (p. 376)

temporal lobe An area on each hemisphere of the cerebral cortex near the temples that is the primary receiving area for auditory information. (p. 72)

teratogens Harmful agents or substances that can cause malformations or defects in an embryo or fetus. (p. 373)

thalamus (THAL-uh-muss) A forebrain structure that processes sensory information for all senses, except smell, and relays it to the cerebral cortex. (p. 76)

Thanatos In Freud's theory, the death instinct, reflected in aggressive, destructive, and self-destructive actions. (p. 457)

Thematic Apperception Test (TAT) A projective test developed by Henry Murray and his colleagues that involves creating stories about vague scenes that can be interpreted in a variety of ways. (pp. 341, 488)

theory A tentative explanation that tries to integrate and account for the relationship of various findings and observations. (p. 21)

thinking The manipulation of mental representations of information in order to draw inferences and conclusions. (p. 281)

timbre (TIM-ber) The distinctive quality of a sound, determined by the complexity of the sound wave. (p. 104)

tip-of-the-tongue (TOT) experience A memory phenomenon that involves the sensation of knowing that specific information is stored in long-term memory, but being temporarily unable to retrieve it. (p. 251)

token economy A form of behavior therapy in which the therapeutic environment is structured to reward desired behaviors with tokens or points that may eventually be exchanged for tangible rewards. (p. 634)

top-down processing Information processing that emphasizes the importance of the observer's knowledge, expectations, and other cognitive processes in arriving at meaningful perceptions; analysis that moves from the whole to the parts; also called *conceptually driven processing*. (p. 115)

trait A relatively stable, enduring predisposition to consistently behave in a certain way. (p. 478)

trait approach to leader effectiveness An approach to determining what makes an effective leader that focuses on the personal characteristics displayed by successful leaders. (p. B-10)

trait theory A theory of personality that focuses on identifying, describing, and measuring individual differences. (p. 478)

tranquilizers Depressant drugs that relieve anxiety. (p. 173)

transduction The process by which a form of physical energy is converted into a coded neural signal that can be processed by the nervous system. (p. 91)

transference In psychoanalysis, the process by which emotions and desires originally associated with a significant person in the patient's life, such as a parent, are unconsciously transferred to the psychoanalyst. (p. 624)

trial and error A problem-solving strategy that involves attempting different solutions and eliminating those that do not work. (p. 284)

triarchic theory of intelligence Sternberg's theory that there are three distinct forms of intelligence: analytic, creative, and practical. (p. 304)

trichromatic theory of color vision The theory that the sensation of color results because cones in the retina are especially sensitive to either red light (long wavelengths), green light (medium wavelengths), or blue light (short wavelengths). (p. 102)

two-factor theory of emotion Schachter and Singer's theory that emotion is the interaction of physiological arousal and the cognitive label that we apply to explain the arousal. (p. 358)

Type A behavior pattern A behavioral and emotional style characterized by a sense of time urgency, hostility, and competitiveness. (p. 556)

U

unconditional positive regard In Rogers's theory, the sense that you will be valued and loved even if you don't conform to the standards and expectations of others; unconditional love or acceptance. (p. 472)

unconditioned response (UCR) The unlearned, reflexive response that is elicited by an unconditioned stimulus. (p. 188)

unconditioned stimulus (UCS) The natural stimulus that reflexively elicits a response without the need for prior learning. (p. 188)

unconscious In Freud's theory, a term used to describe thoughts, feelings, wishes, and drives that are operating below the level of conscious awareness. (p. 456)

V

vaginismus Sexual dysfunction characterized by persistent, involuntary contractions or spasms of the vaginal muscles, which result in uncomfortable or painful intercourse. (p. 440)

validity The ability of a test to measure what it is intended to measure. (p. 301)

variable A factor that can vary, or change, in ways that can be observed, measured, and verified. (p. 18)

variable-interval (VI) schedule A reinforcement schedule in which a reinforcer is delivered for the first response that occurs after an average time interval, which varies unpredictably from trial to trial. (p. 220)

variable-ratio (VR) schedule A reinforcement schedule in which a reinforcer is delivered after an average number of responses, which varies unpredictably from trial to trial. (p. 219)

vestibular sense (vess-TIB-you-ler) The technical name for the sense of balance, or equilibrium. (p. 112)

W

wavelength The distance from one wave peak to another. (p. 94)

Weber's law A principle of sensation that holds that the size of the just noticeable difference will vary depending on its relation to the strength of the original stimulus. (p. 92)

weight cycling Repeated cycles of dieting, weight loss, and weight regain; also called *yo-yo dieting*. (p. 335)

withdrawal symptoms Unpleasant physical reactions, combined with intense drug cravings, that occur when a person abstains from a drug on which he or she is physically dependent. (p. 169)

Z

z score A number, expressed in standard deviation units, that shows a score's deviation from the mean. (p. A-8)

Aarts, Henk, & Dijksterhuis, Ap. (2000). Habits as knowledge structures: Automaticity in goal-directed behavior. *Journal of Personality and Social Psychology, 78,* 53–63.

Abramov, Israel, & Gordon, James. (1994). Color appearance: On seeing red—or yellow, or green, or blue. *Annual Review of Psychology, 45,* 451–485.

Abrams, Richard. (1994). The treatment that will not die: Electroconvulsive therapy. *Psychiatric Clinics of North America, 17,* 525–530.

Abramson, Lyn Y.; Seligman, Martin E. P.; & Teasdale, John D. (1978). Learned helplessness in humans: Critique and reformulation. *Journal of Abnormal Psychology, 87,* 49–74.

Adams, James, L. (1979). *Conceptual blockbusting: A guide to better ideas* (2nd ed.). New York: Norton.

Ader, Robert. (1993). Conditioned responses. In Bill Moyers & Betty Sue Flowers (Eds.), *Healing and the mind.* New York: Doubleday.

Ader, Robert. (2000). The placebo effect: If it's all in your head, does that mean you only think you feel better? *Advances in Mind-Body Medicine, 16,* 7–11.

Ader, Robert. (2001). Psychoneuroimmunology. *Current Directions in Psychological Science, 10,* 94–98.

Ader, Robert, & Cohen, Nicholas. (1975). Behaviorally conditioned immunosuppression. *Psychosomatic Medicine, 37,* 333–340.

Ader, Robert, & Cohen, Nicholas. (1991). The influence of conditioning on immune responses. In Robert Ader, David L. Felten, & Nicholas Cohen (Eds.), *Psychoneuroimmunology* (2nd ed.). San Diego, CA: Academic Press.

Ader, Robert, & Cohen, Nicholas. (1993). Psychoneuroimmunology: Conditioning and stress. *Annual Review of Psychology, 44,* 53–85.

Adler, Alfred. (1933a/1979). Advantages and disadvantages of the inferiority feeling. In Heinz L. Ansbacher & Rowena R. Ansbacher (Eds.), *Superiority and social interest: A collection of later writings.* New York: Norton.

Adler, Alfred. (1933b/1979). On the origin of the striving for superiority and of social interest. In Heinz L. Ansbacher & Rowena R. Ansbacher (Eds.), *Superiority and social interest: A collection of later writings.* New York: Norton.

Adler, Alfred. (1954). *Understanding human nature.* New York: Fawcett.

Adler, Nancy, & Matthews, Karen. (1994). Health psychology: Why do some people get sick and some stay well? *Annual Review of Psychology, 45,* 229–259.

Adolphs, Ralph; Tranel, Daniel; & Damasio, Antonio R. (1998). The human amygdala in social judgment. *Nature, 393,* 470–474.

Affleck, Glenn; Tennen, Howard; Pfeiffer, Carol; & Fifield, Judith. (1987a). Appraisals of control and predictability in reacting to a chronic disease. *Journal of Personality and Social Psychology, 53,* 273–279.

Affleck, Glenn; Tennen, Howard; & Croog, Sydney. (1987b). Causal attribution, perceived control, and recovery from a heart attack. *Journal of Social and Clinical Psychology, 5,* 399–355.

Aggleton, John P. (Ed.). (1992). *The amygdala: Neurobiological aspects of emotion, memory, and mental dysfunction.* New York: Wiley-Liss.

Aghajanian, George K. (1994). Serotonin and the action of LSD in the brain. *Psychiatric Annals, 24*(3), 137–141.

Agosta, William C. (1992). *Chemical communication: The language of pheromones.* New York: Scientific American Library.

Agras, W. Steward, & Apple, Robin F. (1997). *Overcoming eating disorders: A cognitive-behavioral treatment for bulimia nervosa and binge-eating.* San Antonio, TX: Harcourt Brace.

Aiken, Lewis R. (1997). *Psychological testing and assessment* (9th ed.) Boston: Allyn & Bacon.

Ainslie, George. (1975). Specious reward: A behavioral theory of impulsiveness and impulse control. *Psychological Bulletin, 82,* 463–496.

Ainslie, George. (1992). *Picoeconomics: The strategic interaction of successive motivational states within the person.* Cambridge, MA: Cambridge University Press.

Ainsworth, Mary D. Salter. (1979). Attachment as related to mother-infant interaction. In J. G. Rosenblatt, R. A. Hinde, C. Beer, & M. Busnel (Eds.), *Advances in the study of behavior* (Vol. 9). New York: Academic Press.

Ainsworth, Mary D. Salter; Blehar, Mary C.; Waters, Everett; & Wall, Sally. (1978). *Patterns of attachment: A psychological study of the Strange Situation.* Hillsdale, NJ: Erlbaum.

Akins, Chana K., & Zentall, Thomas R. (1996). Imitative learning in Japanese quail (*Coturnix japonica*) using the two-action method. *Journal of Comparative Psychology, 110,* 316–320.

Albright, Thomas D.; Jessell, Thomas M.; Kandel, Eric R.; & Posner, Michael I. (2000, February). Neural science: A century of progress and the mysteries that remain. *Neuron, 25*(Suppl.), S1–S55.

Alcock, James E. (1978–1979). Psychology and near-death experiences. *Skeptical Inquirer, 3,* 25–41.

Alexander, Charles N.; Robinson, Pat; Orme-Johnson, David W.; & Schneider, Robert H. (1994). The effects of transcendental meditation compared to other methods of relaxation and meditation in reducing risk factors, morbidity, and mortality. *Homeostasis in Health and Disease, 35,* 243–263.

Alexander, James F.; Holtzworth-Munroe, Amy; & Jameson, Penny. (1994). The process and outcome of marital and family therapy: Research review and evaluation. In Allen E. Bergin & Sol L. Garfield (Eds.), *Handbook of psychotherapy and behavior change* (4th ed.). New York: Wiley.

Alford, Brad A., & Correia, Christopher J. (1994). Cognitive therapy of schizophrenia: Theory and empirical status. *Behavior Therapy 25,* 17–33.

Allen, Karen M.; Blascovich, Jim; Tomaka, Joe; & Kelsey, Robert M. (1991). Presence of human friends and pet dogs as moderators of autonomic responses to stress in women. *Journal of Personality and Social Psychology, 61,* 582–589.

Allen, Vernon L., & Levine, John M. (1969). Consensus and conformity. *Journal of Experimental Social Psychology, 5,* 389–399.

Allen, Vernon L., & Levine, John M. (1971). Social support and conformity: The role of independent assessment of reality. *Journal of Experimental Social Psychology, 7,* 48–58.

Allison, David B.; Fontaine, Kevin R.; & others. (1999, October 27). Annual deaths attributable to obesity in the United States. *Journal of the American Medical Association, 282,* 1530–1538.

Allman, John Morgan. (1999). *Evolving brains.* New York: Scientific American Library.

Allodi, Frederico A. (1994). Post-traumatic stress disorder in hostages and victims of torture. *Psychiatric Clinics of North America, 17,* 279–288.

Allport, Floyd H. (1920). The influence of the group upon association and thought. *Journal of Experimental Psychology, 3,* 159–182.

Allport, Floyd H. (1924). *Social psychology.* Boston: Houghton Mifflin.

Allport, Gordon W., & Odbert, Harold S. (1936). Trait-names: A psycho-lexical study. *Psychological Monographs, 47*(211).

Almeida, David M., & Kessler, Ronald C. (1998). Everyday stressors and gender differences in daily distress. *Journal of Personality and Social Psychology, 75,* 670–680.

Alonso, Anne, & Swiller, Hillel I. (Eds.). (1993a). *Group therapy in clinical practice.* Washington, DC: American Psychiatric Press.

Alonso, Anne, & Swiller, Hillel I. (1993b). Introduction: The case for group therapy. In Anne Alonso & Hillel I. Swiller (Eds.), *Group therapy in clinical practice.* Washington, DC: American Psychiatric Press.

Alvarez, A. (1995). *Night: Night life, night language, sleep and dreams.* New York: Norton.

Amabile, Teresa. (1996). *Creativity in context.* Boulder, CO: Westview Press.

Amabile, Teresa. (2001). Beyond talent: John Irving and the passionate craft of creativity. *American Psychologist, 56,* 333–336.

Amabile, Teresa M., & Tighe, Elizabeth. (1993). Questions of creativity. In John Brockman (Ed.), *Creativity.* New York: Simon & Schuster.

American Psychiatric Association. (1994). *Diagnostic and statistical manual of mental disorders* (4th ed.). Washington, DC: American Psychiatric Association.

American Psychiatric Association. (2000a). *Diagnostic and statistical manual of mental disorders* (4th ed., text revision: DSM-IV-TR). Washington, DC: American Psychiatric Association.

American Psychiatric Association. (2000b). Practice guidelines for the treatment of patients with eating disorders [Revision]. *American Journal of Psychiatry, 157*(Suppl.).

American Psychological Association (APA). (1986). *Animal Research Survey, 1985–1986.* Washington, DC: American Psychological Association.

American Psychological Association (APA). (1992a). *Ethical principles of psychologists and code of conduct.* Washington, DC: American Psychological Association.

American Psychological Association (APA). (1992b). *Guidelines for ethical conduct in the care and use of animals.* Washington, DC: American Psychological Assocation.

American Psychological Association (APA). (1993). Guidelines for practitioners of psychological services to ethnic, linguistic, and culturally diverse populations. *American Psychologist, 48,* 45–48.

American Psychological Association (APA). (1995). *Behavior research with animals.* Washington, DC: American Psychological Association.

American Psychological Association (APA). (2001). *Information on hypnosis: What is hypnosis? The Division 30 definition and description of hypnosis.* Retrieved January 9, 2002, from http://www.apa.org/divisions/div30/hypnosis.html

Amering, Michaela, & Katschnig, Heinz. (1990). Panic attacks and panic disorder in cross-cultural perspective. *Psychiatric Annals, 20,* 511–516.

Amir, Yehuda. (1994). The contact hypothesis in intergroup relations. In Walter J. Lonner & Roy Malpass (Eds.), *Psychology and culture.* Boston: Allyn & Bacon.

Anastasi, Anne. (1988). *Psychological testing* (6th ed.). New York: Macmillan.

Anastasi, Anne, & Urbina, Susana. (1997). *Psychological testing* (7th ed.). Upper Saddle River, NJ: Prentice Hall.

Anch, A. Michael; Browman, Carl P.; Mitler, Merrill M.; & Walsh, James K. (1988). *Sleep: A scientific perspective.* Englewood Cliffs, NJ: Prentice-Hall.

Ancoli-Israel, Sonia. (1997). The polysomnogram. In Mark R. Pressman & William C. Orr (Eds.), *Understanding sleep: The evaluation and treatment of sleep disorders.* Washington, DC: American Psychological Association.

Andersen, Arnold R. (1995). Eating disorders in males. In Kelly D. Brownell & Christopher G. Fairburn (Eds.), *Eating disorders and obesity: A comprehensive handbook.* New York: Guilford Press.

Anderson, Craig A., & Dill, Karen E. (2000). Video games and aggressive thoughts, feelings, and behavior in the laboratory and in life. *Journal of Personality and Social Psychology, 78,* 772–790.

Andersson, Bengt-Erik. (1989). Effects of day care: A longitudinal study. *Child Development, 60,* 857–866.

Andersson, Bengt-Erik. (1992). Effects of day care on cognitive and socioemotional competence of thirteen-year-old Swedish schoolchildren. *Child Development, 63,* 20–36.

Andreasen, Nancy C., & Flaum, Michael. (1991). Schizophrenia: The characteristic symptoms. *Schizophrenia Bulletin, 17,* 27–49.

Andresen, Jensine. (2000). Meditation meets behavioural medicine: The story of experimental research on meditation. *Journal of Consciousness Studies, 7,* 17–73.

Andrew, David, & Craig, Andrew D. (2001). Spinothalamic lamina I neurons selectively sensitive to histamine: A central neural pathway for itch. *Nature Neuroscience, 4,* 72–77.

Angermeyer, Matthias C., & Matschinger, Herbert. (1996). The effect of violent attacks by schizophrenic persons on the attitude of the public towards the mentally ill. *Social Science & Medicine, 43*(12), 1721–1728.

Angier, Natalie. (1995, February 14). Powerhouse of senses, smell, at last gets its due. *New York Times,* pp. C1, C6.

Anonymous. (1990). First person account: Birds of a psychic feather. *Schizophrenia Bulletin, 16,* 165–168.

Antony, Martin M.; Brown, Timothy A.; & Barlow, David H. (1992). Current perspectives on panic and panic disorder. *Current Directions in Psychological Science, 1,* 79–82.

APA Research Office. (2001). *2000 APA Directory Survey.* Washington, DC: American Psychological Association Research Office.

Arciero, Paul J.; Goran, Michael I.; & Poehlman, Eric T. (1993). Resting metabolic rate is lower in women than in men. *Journal of Applied Physiology, 75,* 2514–2520.

Arkin, Arthur M. (1981). *Sleep talking: Psychology and psychophysiology.* Hillsdale, NJ: Erlbaum.

Arkin, Arthur M., & Antrobus, John S. (1991). The effects of external stimuli applied prior to and during sleep on sleep experience. In Steven J. Ellman & John S. Antrobus (Eds.), *The mind in sleep: Psychology and psychophysiology* (2nd ed.). New York: Wiley.

Armstrong, G. Blake, & Sopory, Pradeep. (1997). Effects of background television on phonological and visuo-spatial working memory. *Communication Research, 24,* 459–480.

Arnkoff, Diane B., & Glass, Carol R. (1992). Cognitive therapy and psychotherapy integration. In Donald K. Freedheim (Ed.), *History of psychotherapy: A century of change.* Washington, DC: American Psychological Association.

Aron, Arthur; Aron, Elaine N.; & Smollan, Danny. (1992). Inclusion of other in the self scale and the structure of interpersonal closeness. *Journal of Personality and Social Psychology, 63,* 596–612.

Aronson, Elliot. (1987). Teaching students what they think they already know about prejudice and desegregation. In Vivian Parker Makosky (Ed.), *G. Stanley Hall Lecture Series* (Vol. 7). Washington, DC: American Psychological Association.

Aronson, Elliot. (1990). Applying social psychology to desegregation and energy conservation. *Personality and Social Psychology Bulletin, 16,* 118–132.

Aronson, Elliot. (1992). The return of the repressed: Dissonance theory makes a comeback. *Psychological Inquiry, 3,* 303–311.

Aronson, Elliot. (1995). *The social animal* (7th ed). New York: Freeman.

Aronson, Elliot. (1999). The power of self-persuasion. *American Psychologist, 54,* 875–883.

Aronson, Elliot, & Bridgeman, Diane. (1979). Jigsaw groups and the desegregated classroom: In pursuit of common goals. *Personality and Social Psychology Bulletin, 5,* 438–466.

Arvey, Richard D.; Bouchard, Thomas J.; Segal, Nancy L.; & Abraham, Lauren M. (1989). Job satisfaction: Environmental and genetic components. *Journal of Applied Psychology, 74,* 187–192.

Asay, Ted P., & Lambert, Michael J. (1999). The empirical case for the common factors in therapy: Quantitative findings. In Mark A.

Hubble, Barry L. Duncan, & Scott D. Miller (Eds.), *The heart and soul of change: What works in therapy*. Washington, DC: American Psychological Association.

Asay, Ted P., & Lambert, Michael J. (2002). Therapist relational variables. In David J. Cain & Julius Seeman (Eds.), *Humanistic psychotherapies: Handbook of research and practice*. Washington, DC: American Psychological Association.

Asch, Solomon E. (1951). Effects of group pressure upon the modification and distortion of judgments. In Harold S. Guetzkow (Ed.), *Groups, leadership, and men: Research in human relations. Reports on research sponsored by the Human Relations and Morale Branch of the Office of Naval Research, 1945–1950.* Pittsburgh, PA: Carnegie Press.

Asch, Solomon E. (1955, November). Opinions and social pressure. *Scientific American, 193,* 31–35.

Asch, Solomon E. (1956). Studies of independence and conformity: A minority of one against a unanimous majority. *Psychological Monographs, 70*(9, Whole No. 416).

Asch, Solomon E. (1957). An experimental investigation of group influence. In *Symposium on preventive and social psychiatry.* Washington, DC: U.S. Government Printing Office, Walter Reed Army Institute of Research.

Aschoff, Jurgen. (1993). On the passage of subjective time in temporal isolation. *Psychologica Belgica, 33,* 147–157.

Aschoff, Jurgen. (1994). The timing of defecation within the sleep-wake cycle of humans during temporal isolation. *Journal of Biological Rhythms, 9,* 43–50.

Aserinsky, Eugene, & Kleitman, Nathaniel. (1953). Regularly occurring periods of eye motility and concomitant phenomena during sleep. *Science, 118,* 273–274.

Aspinwall, Lisa G., & Taylor, Shelley E. (1992). Modeling cognitive adaptation: A longitudinal investigation of the impact of individual differences and coping on college adjustment and performance. *Journal of Personality and Social Psychology, 63,* 989–1003.

Astrup, Arne; Götzsche, Peter C.; & others. (1999). Meta-analysis of resting metabolic rate in formerly obese subjects. *American Journal of Clinical Nutrition, 69,* 1117–1122.

Atkinson, Richard C., & Shiffrin, Richard M. (1968). Human memory: A proposed system and its control processes. In Kenneth W. Spence & Janet T. Spence (Eds.), *The psychology of learning and motivation: Advances in research and theory* (Vol. 2). New York: Academic Press.

Austin, James H. (1998). *Zen and the brain.* Cambridge, MA: MIT Press.

Australian Institute of Health and Welfare (AIHW). (1999). *Heart, stroke and vascular diseases: Australian facts* (AIHW Cat. No. CVD 7). Canberra, Australia: AIHW and the Heart Foundation of Australia (Cardiovascular Disease Series No. 10).

Ax, Robert K., & Resnick, Robert J. (2001, March). Prescription privileges: An immodest proposal. *APA Monitor on Psychology, 32*(3), 53–54.

Axel, Richard. (1995, October). The molecular logic of smell. *Scientific Amerian, 273,* 154–159.

Axelrod, Saul, & Apsche, Jack. (1983). *The effects of punishment on human behavior.* New York: Academic Press.

Azuma, Hiroshi. (1984). Secondary control as a heterogeneous category. *American Psychologist, 39,* 970–971.

Bachelor, Alexandra, & Horvath, Adam. (1999). The therapeutic relationship. In Mark A. Hubble, Barry L. Duncan, & Scott D. Miller (Eds.), *The heart and soul of change: What works in therapy*. Washington, DC: American Psychological Association.

Baddeley, Alan D. (1995). Working memory. In Michael S. Gazzaniga (Ed.), *The cognitive neurosciences.* Cambridge, MA: MIT Press.

Baddeley, Alan D. (1998). *Human memory: Theory and practice* (2nd ed.). Boston: Allyn & Bacon.

Baenninger, Ronald. (1997). On yawning and its functions. *Psychonomic Bulletin and Review, 4,* 198–207.

Baer, John. (1993). *Creativity and divergent thinking: A task-specific approach.* Hillsdale, NJ: Erlbaum.

Baer, Paul E.; Garmezy, Lisa B.; McLaughlin, Robert J.; Pokorny, Alex D.; & Wernick, M. J. (1987). Stress, coping, family conflict, and adolescent alcohol use. *Journal of Behavioral Medicine, 10,* 449–466.

Bahrick, Harry P., & Hall, Lynda K. (1991). Lifetime maintenance of high school mathematics content. *Journal of Experimental Psychology: General, 120,* 20–33.

Bahrick, Harry P., & Phelps, Elizabeth. (1987). Retention of Spanish vocabulary over eight years. *Journal of Experimental Psychology: Learning, Memory, and Cognition, 13,* 344–349.

Bailey, J. Michael; Bobrow, David; Wolfe, Marilyn; & Mikach, Sarah. (1995). Sexual orientation of adult sons of gay fathers. *Developmental Psychology, 31,* 124–129.

Bailey, J. Michael; Dunne, Michael P.; & Martin, Nicholas G. (2000). Genetic and environmental influences on sexual orientation and its correlates in an Australian twin sample. *Journal of Personality and Social Psychology, 78,* 524–536.

Bailey, J. Michael, & Pillard, Richard C. (1991). A genetic study of male sexual orientation. *Archives of General Psychiatry, 48,* 1089–1096.

Bailey, J. Michael; Pillard, Richard C.; Neale, Michael C.; & Agyei, Yvonne. (1993). Heritable factors influence sexual orientation in women. *Archives of General Psychiatry, 50,* 217–223.

Bailey, J. Michael, & Shriver, Amy. (1999). Does childhood sexual abuse cause borderline personality disorder. *Journal of Sex and Marital Therapy, 25,* 45–57.

Bailey, J. Michael, & Zucker, Kenneth J. (1995). Childhood sex-typed behavior and sexual orientation: A conceptual analysis and quantitative review. *Developmental Psychology, 31,* 43–55.

Bailey, Marian Breland, & Bailey, Robert E. (1993). "Misbehavior": A case history. *American Psychologist, 48,* 1157–1158.

Baillargeon, Renée. (1987). Young infants' reasoning about the physical and spatial characteristics of a hidden object. *Cognitive Development, 2,* 179–200.

Baillargeon, Renée. (1994). How do infants learn about the physical world? *Current Directions in Psychological Science, 3,* 133–140.

Baillargeon, Renée, & De Vos, Julie. (1991). Object permanence in young infants: Further evidence. *Child Development, 62,* 1227–1246.

Bakaly, Charles J., Jr., & Grossman, Joel M. (1995). *The modern law of employment relationships.* Upper Saddle River, NJ: Prentice-Hall.

Baker, Robert A. (1992). *Hidden memories: Voices and visions from within.* Buffalo, NY: Prometheus Books.

Baker, Robert A. (1996). Hypnosis. In Gordon Stein (Ed.), *The encyclopedia of the paranormal.* Amherst, NY: Prometheus Books.

Baker, Robert A. (Ed.). (1998). *Child sexual abuse and false memory syndrome.* Amherst, NY: Prometheus Books.

Ballinger, Barbara, & Yalom, Irvin. (1995). Group therapy in practice. In Bruce Bongar & Larry E. Beutler (Eds.), *Comprehensive textbook of psychotherapy: Research and practice.* New York: Oxford University Press.

Baltes, Paul B., & Mayer, Karl Ulrich. (2001). *The Berlin aging study: Aging from 70 to 100.* New York: Cambridge University Press.

Bamer, Donald R. (1996). *Practical iridology and sclerology.* Pleasant Grove, UT: Woodland Publishing.

Banaji, Mahzarin R., & Prentice, Deborah A. (1994). The self in social contexts. *Annual Review of Psychology, 45,* 297–332.

Bandura, Albert. (1965). Influence of models' reinforcement contingencies on the acquisition of imitative behaviors. *Journal of Personality and Social Psychology, 1,* 589–595.

Bandura, Albert. (1974). Behavior theory and the models of man. *American Psychologist, 29,* 859–869.

Bandura, Albert. (1977). *Social learning theory.* Englewood Cliffs, NJ: Prentice-Hall.

Bandura, Albert. (1986). *Social foundations of thought and action: A social cognitive theory.* Englewood Cliffs, NJ: Prentice-Hall.

Bandura, Albert. (1989a). Human agency in social cognitive theory. *American Psychologist, 44,* 1175–1184.

Bandura, Albert. (1989b). Regulation of cognitive processes through perceived self-efficacy. *Developmental Psychology, 25,* 729–735.

Bandura, Albert. (1990). Conclusion: Reflections on nonability determinants of competence. In Robert J. Sternberg & John Kolligian, Jr. (Eds.), *Competence considered.* New Haven, CT: Yale University Press.

Bandura, Albert. (1991). Self-regulation of motivation through anticipatory and self-reactive mechanisms. In Richard Dienstbier (Ed.), *Nebraska Symposium on Motivation 1990* (Vol. 38). Lincoln: University of Nebraska Press.

Bandura, Albert. (1992). Exercise of personal agency through the self-efficacy mechanism. In Ralf Schwarzer (Ed.), *Self-efficacy: Thought control of action.* Washington, DC: Hemisphere.

Bandura, Albert. (1996). Failures in self-regulation: Energy depletion or selective disengagement? *Psychological Inquiry, 7,* 20–24.

Bandura, Albert. (1997). *Self-efficacy: The exercise of control.* New York: Freeman.

Bandura, Albert. (2001). Social cognitive theory: An agentic perspective. *Annual Review of Psychology, 52,* 1–26.

Bandura, Albert; Ross, Dorothea; & Ross, Sheila A. (1963). Imitation of film-mediated aggressive models. *Journal of Abnormal and Social Psychology, 66,* 3–11.

Banich, Marie T. (1998). Integration of information between the cerebral hemispheres. *Current Directions in Psychological Science, 7,* 32–37.

Banse, Rainer, & Scherer, Klaus R. (1996). Acoustic profiles in vocal emotion expression. *Journal of Personality and Social Psychology, 70,* 614–636.

Barch, Deanna M., & Berenbaum, Howard. (1996). Language production and thought disorder in schizophrenia. *Journal of Abnormal Psychology, 105,* 81–88.

Barclay, Deborah R., & Houts, Arthur C. (1995a). Childhood enuresis. In Charles E. Schaefer (Ed.), *Clinical handbook of sleep disorders in children.* Northvale, NJ: Aronson.

Barclay, Deborah R., & Houts, Arthur C. (1995b). Parenting skills: A review and developmental analysis of training content. In William O'Donohue & Leonard Krasner (Eds.), *Handbook of psychological skills training: Clinical techniques and applications.* Boston: Allyn & Bacon.

Barefoot, John C. (1992). Developments in the measurement of hostility. In Howard S. Friedman (Ed.), *Hostility, health, and coping.* Washington, DC: American Psychological Association.

Barefoot, John C.; Dahlstrom, W. Grant; & Williams, Redford B. (1983). Hostility, CHD incidence, and total mortality: A 25-year follow-up study of 255 physicians. *Psychosomatic Medicine, 45,* 59–63.

Bar-El, Yair; Durst, Rimona; Katz, Gregory; & others. (2000). Jerusalem syndrome. *British Journal of Psychiatry, 176,* 86–90.

Bargh, John A.; Chen, Mark; & Burrows, Lara. (1996). Automaticity of social behavior: Direct effects of trait construct and stereotype activation on action. *Journal of Personality and Social Psychology, 71,* 230–244.

Bargh, John A., & Churchland, Tanya L. (1999). The unbearable automaticity of being. *American Psychologist, 54,* 462–479.

Barlow, David Harrison. (1991). Disorders of emotion. *Psychological Inquiry, 2,* 58–71.

Barnett, Rosalind C.; Marshall, Nancy L.; & Singer, Judith D. (1992). Job experiences over time, multiple roles, and women's mental health: A longitudinal study. *Journal of Personality and Social Psychology, 62,* 634–644.

Barnier, Amanda J., & McConkey, Kevin M. (1998). Posthypnotic responding away from the hypnotic setting. *Psychological Science, 9,* 256–262.

Barnier, Amanda J.; & McConkey, Kevin M. (1999). Absorption, hypnotizability and context: Non-hypnotic contexts are not all the same. *Contemporary Hypnosis, 16,* 1–8.

Barondes, Samuel H. (1993). *Molecules and mental illness.* New York: Scientific American Library.

Barrett, Stephen. (1996). "Alternative" health practices and quackery. In Gordon Stein (Ed.), *The encyclopedia of the paranormal.* Amherst, NY: Prometheus Books.

Barrick, Murray R., & Mount, Michael K. (1991). The Big Five personality dimensions and job performance: A meta-analysis. *Personnel Psychology, 44,* 1–26.

Barrick, Murray R., & Mount, Michael K. (1993). Autonomy as a moderator of the relationship between the Big Five personality dimensions and job performance. *Journal of Applied Psychology, 78,* 111–118.

Barsh, Gregory S.; Farooqi, L. Sadaf; & O'Rahilly, Stephen. (2000, April 6). Genetics of body-weight regulation. *Nature, 404,* 644–651.

Bartecchi, Carl E.; MacKenzie, Thomas D.; & Schrier, Robert W. (1995, May). The global tobacco epidemic. *Scientific American, 272,* 44–51.

Bartels, Andreas, & Zeki, Semir. (2000, November 27). The neural basis of romantic love. *NeuroReport, 11,* 3829–3834. PDF of article retrieved on March 1, 2002 from http://www.vislab.ucl.ac.uk/pdf/NeuralBasisOfLove.pdf

Bartlett, Frederic C. (1932). *Remembering.* Cambridge, England: Cambridge University Press.

Bartoshuk, Linda M., & Beauchamp, Gary K. (1994). Chemical senses. *Annual Review of Psychology, 45,* 419–449.

Barzilai, Nir, & Gupta, Gaurav. (1999). Revisiting the role of fat mass in the life extension induced by caloric restriction. *Journal of Gerontology, Series A, 54,* B89–B97.

Bashore, Theodore R., & Rapp, Paul E. (1993). Are there alternatives to traditional polygraph procedures? *Psychological Bulletin, 113,* 3–22.

Basil, Robert. (1991). Graphology and personality: "Let the buyer beware." In Kendrick Frazier (Ed.), *The hundredth monkey and other paradigms of the paranormal.* Buffalo, NY: Prometheus Books.

Baskin, Denis G.; Lattemann, Dianne Figlewicz; Seeley, Randy J.; Woods, Stephen C.; Porte, Daniel, Jr.; & Schwartz, Michael W. (1999). Insulin and leptin: Dual adiposity signals to the brain for the regulation of food intake and body weight. *Brain Research, 848,* 114–123.

Bass, Bernard M. (1981). *Stogdill's handbook of leadership.* New York: Free Press.

Bass, Ellen, & Davis, Linda. (1994). *The courage to heal* (3rd ed.). New York: Harper-Perennial.

Baudry, Michel, & Davis, Joel L. (1992). Neurotransmitter systems and memory. In Larry R. Squire (Ed.), *Encyclopedia of learning and memory.* New York: Macmillan.

Bauer, Patricia J. (1996). What do infants recall of their lives? Memory for specific events by one- to two-year-olds. *American Psychologist, 51,* 29–41.

Baum, William, & Heath, Jennifer L. (1992). Behavioral explanations and intentional explanations in psychology. *American Psychologist, 47,* 1312–1317.

Baumeister, Roy F., & Leary, Mark R. (1995). The need to belong: Desire for interpersonal attachments as a fundamental human motivation. *Psychological Bulletin, 117,* 497–529.

Baumeister, Roy F.; Stillwell, Arlene M.; & Heatherton, Todd F. (1994). Guilt: An interpersonal approach. *Psychological Bulletin, 115,* 243–267.

Baumrind, Diana. (1964). Some thoughts on ethics of research: After reading Milgram's "Behavioral Study of Obedience." *American Psychologist, 19,* 421–423.

Baumrind, Diana. (1971). Current patterns of parental authority. *Developmental Psychology Monographs, 4,* 1–103.

Baumrind, Diana. (1991). The influence of parenting style on adolescent competence and substance abuse. *Journal of Early Adolescence, 11,* 56–95.

Baumrind, Diana. (1995). Commentary on sexual orientation: Research and social policy implications. *Developmental Psychology, 31,* 130–136.

Baylis, Gordon C., & Driver, Jon. (2001). Shape-coding in IT cells generalizes over contrast and mirror reversal, but not figure-ground reversal. *Nature Neuroscience, 4,* 937–942.

Beal, Carole R. (1994). *Boys and girls: The development of gender roles.* New York: McGraw-Hill.

Beaman, Arthur L.; Klentz, Bonnel; Diener, Edward; & Svanum, Soren (1979). Self-awareness and transgression in children: Two field studies. *Journal of Personality and Social Psychology, 37,* 1835–1846.

Beatty, Barbara. (1998). From laws of learning to a science of values: Efficiency and morality in Thorndike's educational psychology. *American Psychologist, 53,* 1145–1152.

Bechara, Antoine; Damasio, Hanna; Tranel, Daniel; & Damasio, Antonio. (1997). Deciding advantageously before knowing the advantageous strategy. *Science, 275,* 1293–1295.

Beck, Aaron T. (1991). Cognitive therapy: A 30-year retrospective. *American Psychologist, 46,* 368–375.

Beck, Aaron T. (1993). Cognitive therapy: Past, present, and future. *Journal of Consulting and Clinical Psychology, 61,* 194–198.

Beck, Aaron T.; Rush, A. John; Shaw, Brian F.; & Emery, Gary. (1979). *Cognitive therapy of depression.* New York: Guilford Press.

Beck, Aaron T.; Steer, Robert A.; Beck, Judith S.; & Newman, Cory F. (1993). Hopelessness, depression, suicidal ideation, and clinical diagnosis of depression. *Suicide and Life Threatening Behavior, 23,* 139–145.

Beck, Melinda, & Borger, Gloria. (1979, August 20). The polite bandit: A priest on trial. *Newsweek,* p. 26.

Beck, Melinda; Springen, Karen; & Foote, Donna. (1992, April 13). Sex and psychotherapy. *Newsweek,* pp. 52–57.

Bednar, Richard L., & Kaul, Theodore J. (1994). Experiential group research: Can the canon fire? In Allen E. Bergin & Sol L. Garfield (Eds.), *Handbook of psychotherapy and behavior change* (4th ed.). New York: Wiley.

Beecher, Michael D. (1988). Some comments on the adaptationist approach to learning. In Robert C. Bolles & Michael D. Beecher (Eds.), *Evolution and learning.* Hillsdale, NJ: Erlbaum.

Beeman, Mark Jung, & Chiarello, Christine. (1998). Complementary right- and left-hemisphere language comprehension. *Current Directions in Psychological Science, 7,* 2–8.

Begg, Ian M.; Needham, Douglas R.; & Bookbinder, Marc. (1993). Do backward messages unconsciously affect listeners? No. *Canadian Journal of Experimental Psychology, 47,* 1–14.

Beilin, Harry. (1994). Jean Piaget's enduring contribution to developmental psychology. In Ross D. Parke, Peter A. Ornstein, John J. Rieser, & Carolyn Zahn-Waxler (Eds.), *A century of developmental psychology.* Washington, DC: American Psychological Association.

Bekoff, Marc. (2000). Animal emotions: Exploring passionate natures. *BioScience, 50,* 861–870.

Bell, Alan; Weinberg, Martin; & Hammersmith, Sue. (1981). *Sexual preference: Its development in men and women.* Bloomington: Indiana University Press.

Bellak, Leopold. (1993). *The Thematic Apperception Test, the Children's Apperception Test, and the Senior Apperception Technique in clinical use* (5th ed.). Boston: Allyn & Bacon.

Belle, Deborah. (1991). Gender differences in the social moderators of stress. In Alan Monat & Richard S. Lazarus (Eds.), *Stress and coping: An anthology* (3rd ed.). New York: Columbia University Press.

Belsky, Jay. (1986). Infant day care: A cause for concern. *Zero to Three, 6,* 1–7.

Belsky, Jay. (1992). Consequences of child care for children's development: A deconstructionist view. In Alan Booth (Ed.), *Child care in the 1990s: Trends and consequences.* Hillsdale, NJ: Erlbaum.

Belsky, Jay. (2001). Emanuel Miller Lecture: Developmental risks (still) associated with early child care. *Journal of Child Psychology, Psychiatry and Allied Disciplines, 42,* 845–859.

Belsky, Jay, & Rovine, Michael J. (1988). Nonmaternal care in the first year of life and security of infant-parent attachment. *Child Development, 59,* 157–167.

Bem, Daryl J., & Honorton, Charles. (1994). Does psi exist? Replicable evidence for an anomalous process of information transfer. *Psychological Bulletin, 115,* 4–18.

Bem, Sandra L. (1981). Gender schema theory: A cognitive account of sex typing. *Psychological Review, 88,* 354–364.

Bem, Sandra L. (1987). Gender schema theory and the romantic tradition. In P. Shaver & C. Hendrick (Eds.), *Sex and gender.* Beverly Hills, CA: Sage.

Bem, Sandra L. (1989). Genital knowledge and gender constancy in preschool children. *Child Development, 60,* 649–662.

Benet-Martínez, Verónica, & John, Oliver P. (1998). *Los Cinco Grandes* across cultures and ethnic groups: Multitrait multimethod analyses of the Big Five in Spanish and English. *Journal of Personality and Social Psychology, 75,* 729–750.

Benjamin, Ludy T., Jr. (1997). Wilhelm Wundt: The American connection. In Wolfgang G. Bringmann, Helmut E. Lück, Rudolf Miller, & Charles E. Early (Eds.), *A pictorial history of psychology.* Chicago: Quintessence.

Bennett, George K. (1940). *Bennett Test of Mechanical Comprehension.* New York: Psychological Corporation.

Benson, Herbert. (1993). The relaxation response. In Daniel Goleman & Joel Gurin (Eds.), *Mind / body medicine: How to use your mind for better health.* Yonkers, NY: Consumer Reports Books.

Beratis, Stavroula; Gabriel, Joanna; & Holdas, Stavros. (1994). Age of onset in subtypes of schizophrenic disorders. *Schizophrenia Bulletin, 20,* 287–296.

Bergeman, Cindy S.; Chipuer, Heather M.; Plomin, Robert; Pedersen, Nancy L.; McClearn, Gerald E.; Nesselroade, John R.; & others. (1993). Genetic and environmental effects on openness to experience, agreeableness, and conscientiousness: An adoption/twin study. *Journal of Personality, 61,* 159–179.

Berkman, Lisa F. (1995). The role of social relations in health promotion. *Psychosomatic Medicine, 57,* 245–254.

Berkman, Lisa F.; Leo-Summers, Linda; & Horowitz, Ralph I. (1992). Emotional support and survival after myocardial infarction. *Annals of Internal Medicine, 117,* 1003–1009.

Berkman, Lisa F., & Syme, S. Leonard. (1979). Social networks, host resistance, and mortality: A nine-year follow-up study of Alameda County residents. *American Journal of Epidemiology, 109,* 186–204.

Berlyne, Daniel E. (1960). *Conflict, arousal, and curiosity.* New York: McGraw-Hill.

Berlyne, Daniel E. (1971). *Aesthetics and psychobiology.* New York: Appleton-Century-Crofts.

Bermond, Bob; Fasotti, L.; Nieuwenhuyse, B.; & Schuerman, J. (1991). Spinal cord lesions, peripheral feedback and intensities of emotional feelings. *Cognition & Emotion, 5,* 201–220.

Bernard, Luther L. (1924). *Instinct: A study in social psychology.* New York: Holt.

Berndt, Thomas J. (1992). Friendship and friends' influence in adolescence. *Current Directions in Psychological Science, 1,* 156–159.

Bernstein, David P.; Useda, David; & Siever, Larry J. (1995). Paranoid personality disorder. In W. John Livesley (Ed.), *The DSM-IV personality disorders: Diagnosis and treatment of mental disorders.* New York: Guilford Press.

Berrettini, Wade H. (2001). Images in neuroscience: The human genome: Susceptibility loci. *American Journal of Psychiatry, 158,* 865.

Berridge, Kent C., & Robinson, Terry E. (1995). The mind of an addicted brain: Neural sensitization of wanting versus liking. *Current Directions in Psychological Science, 4,* 71–76.

Berry, John W. (1994). Acculturative stress. In Walter J. Lonner & Roy Malpass (Eds.), *Psychology and culture.* Boston: Allyn & Bacon.

Berry, John W. (1997). Immigration, acculturation, and adaptation. *Applied Psychology: An International Journal, 46,* 5–68.

Berry, John W., & Kim, Uichol. (1988). Acculturation and mental health. In Pierre R. Dasen, John W. Berry, & Norman Sartorius (Eds.), *Health and cross-cultural psychology: Toward applications* (Cross-cultural Research and Methodology Series, Vol. 10). Newbury Park, CA: Sage.

Berry, Lilly M., & Houston, John P. (1993). *Psychology at work.* Madison, WI: Brown & Benchmark.

Best, Deborah L. (2001). Gender concepts: Convergence in cross-cultural research and methodology. *Cross-Cultural Research: The Journal of Comparative Social Science, 35,* 23–43.

Best, Deborah L., & Williams, John E. (1997). Sex, gender, and culture. In John W. Berry, Marshall H. Segall, & Cigdem Kagitçibasi (Eds.), *Handbook of cross-cultural psychology: Vol. 3, Social behavior and applications.* Boston: Allyn & Bacon.

Betancourt, Hector, & López, Steven Regeser. (1993). The study of culture, ethnicity, and race in American psychology. *American Psychologist, 48,* 629–637.

Beumont, Pierre J. V. (1995). The clinical presentation of anorexia and bulimia nervosa. In Kelly D. Brownell & Christopher G. Fairburn (Eds.), *Eating disorders and obesity: A comprehensive handbook.* New York: Guilford Press.

Beutler, Larry E. (2000). Empirically based decision making in clinical practice. *Prevention and Treatment, 3,* article 27. Available on the World Wide Web: http://journals.apa.org/prevention/volume3/pre0030027a.html

Beutler, Larry E.; Machado, Paulo P. P.; & Neufeldt, Susan Allstetter. (1994). Therapist variables. In Allen E. Bergin & Sol L. Garfield (Eds.), *Handbook of psychotherapy and behavior change* (4th ed.). New York: Wiley.

Beyerstein, Barry. (1996). Graphology. In Gordon Stein (Ed.), *The encyclopedia of the paranormal.* Amherst, NY: Prometheus Books.

Beyerstein, Barry, & Beyerstein, Dale (Eds.). (1992). *The write stuff: Evaluations of graphology—The study of handwriting analysis.* Amherst, NY: Prometheus Books.

Bhatara, Vinod S.; Sharma, J. N.; Gupta, Sanjay; & Gupta, Y. K. (1997). Rauwolfia serpentina: The first herbal antipsychotic. *American Journal of Psychiatry, 154,* 894.

Binder, Jeffrey L.; Strupp, Hans H.; & Henry, William P. (1995). Psychodynamic theories in practice: Time-limited dynamic psychotherapy. In Bruce Bongar & Larry E. Beutler (Eds.), *Comprehensive textbook of psychotherapy: Theory and practice.* New York: Oxford University Press.

Binet, Alfred, & Simon, Théodore. (1905). New methods for the diagnosis of the intellectual level of subnormals. *L'Année Psychologique, 11,* 191–244.

Bjork, Daniel W. (1997a). *B. F. Skinner: A life.* Washington, DC: American Psychological Association.

Bjork, Daniel W. (1997b). *William James: The center of his vision.* Washington, DC: American Psychological Association.

Bjork, Robert A. (2001, March). How to succeed in college: Learn how to learn. *APS Observer, 14,* 3, 9.

Bjorklund, Barbara R. (1995). Language development and cognition. In David F. Bjorklund (Ed.), *Children's thinking: Developmental function and individual differences* (2nd ed.). Pacific Grove, CA: Brooks/Cole.

Black, Donald W.; Monahan, Patrick; Baumgard, Connie H.; & Bell, Sue E. (1997). Predictors of long-term outcome in 45 men with antisocial personality disorder. *Annals of Clinical Psychiatry, 9,* 211–217.

Black, Stephen L., & Bevan, Susan. (1992). At the movies with Buss and Durkee: A natural experiment on film violence. *Aggressive Behavior, 18,* 37–45.

Blackmore, Susan. (1985). Belief in the paranormal: Probability judgements, illusory control, and the chance baseline shift. *British Journal of Psychology, 76,* 459–468.

Blackmore, Susan. (1998). Lucid dreams. In Kendrick Frazier (Ed.), *Encounters with the paranormal: Science, knowledge, and belief.* Amherst, NY: Prometheus Books.

Blair, Sampson Lee, & Lichter, Daniel T. (1991). Measuring the division of household labor: Gender segregation of housework among American couples. *Journal of Family Issues, 12,* 91–113.

Blascovich, Jim; Spencer, Steven J.; Quinn, Diane; & Steele, Claude. (2001). African Americans and high blood pressure: The role of stereotype threat. *Psychological Science, 12,* 225–229.

Blass, Thomas. (1991). Understanding behavior in the Milgram obedience experiment. *Journal of Personality and Social Psychology, 60,* 398–413.

Blass, Thomas. (1992). The social psychology of Stanley Milgram. In Mark P. Zanna (Ed.), *Advances in experimental social psychology* (Vol. 25). San Diego, CA: Academic Press.

Blass, Thomas. (2000). The Milgram Paradigm after 35 years. Some things we now know about obedience to authority. In Thomas Blass (Ed.), *Obedience to authority: Current perspectives on the Milgram paradigm.* Mahwah, NJ: Erlbaum.

Bliwise, Donald L. (1997). Sleep and aging. In Mark R. Pressman & William C. Orr (Eds.), *Understanding sleep: The evaluation and treatment of sleep disorders.* Washington, DC: American Psychological Association.

Block, Jack. (1995). A contrarian view of the five-factor approach to personality description. *Psychological Bulletin, 117,* 187–215.

Blumberg, Mark S., & Sokoloff, Greta. (2001). Do infant rats cry? *Psychological Review, 108,* 83–95.

Blumberg, Mark S.; Sokoloff, Greta; Kirby, Robert F.; & Kent, Kristen J. (2000). Distress vocalizations in infant rats: What's all the fuss about? *Psychological Science, 11,* 78–81.

Blumberg, Mark S., & Wasserman, Edward A. (1995). Animal mind and the argument from design. *American Psychologist, 50,* 133–144.

Blumenthal, Arthur L. (1998). Leipzig, Wilhelm Wundt, and psychology's gilded age. In Gregory A. Kimble & Michael Wertheimer (Eds.), *Portraits of pioneers in psychology* (Vol. 3). Washington, DC: American Psychological Association.

Bobo, Lawrence. (1988a). Attitudes toward the black political movement: Trends, meaning, and effects on racial policy preferences. *Social Psychology Quarterly, 51,* 287–302.

Bobo, Lawrence. (1988b). Group conflict, prejudice, and the paradox of contemporary racial attitudes. In Phyllis A. Katz & Dalmas A. Taylor (Eds.), *Eliminating racism: Profiles in controversy.* New York: Plenum Press.

Bolger, Niall, & Schilling, Elizabeth A. (1991). Personality and problems of everyday life: The role of neuroticism in exposure and reactivity to stress. *Journal of Personality, 59,* 355–386.

Bolger, Niall, & Zuckerman, Adam. (1995). A framework for studying personality in the stress process. *Journal of Personality and Social Psychology, 69,* 890–902.

Bolles, Robert C. (1972). Reinforcement, expectancy, and learning. *Psychological Review, 79,* 394–409.

Bolles, Robert C. (1985). The slaying of Goliath: What happened to reinforcement theory? In Timothy D. Johnston & Alexandra T. Pietrewicz (Eds.), *Issues in the ecological study of learning.* Hillsdale, NJ: Erlbaum.

Bond, Michael Harris. (1986). *The psychology of the Chinese people.* New York: Oxford University Press.

Bond, Michael Harris. (1994). Continuing encounters with Hong Kong. In Walter J. Lonner & Roy Malpass (Eds.), *Psychology and culture.* Boston: Allyn & Bacon.

Bond, Michael Harris, & Smith, Peter B. (1996). Cross-cultural social and organizational psychology. *Annual Review of Psychology, 47,* 205–235.

Bond, Rod, & Smith, Peter B. (1996). Culture and conformity: A meta-analysis of studies using Asch's (1952b, 1956) line judgment task. *Psychological Bulletin, 119,* 111–137.

Bond, Susan B., & Mosher, Donald L. (1986). Guided imagery of rape: Fantasy, reality, and the willing victim myth. *Journal of Sex Research, 22,* 162–183.

Bonin, Michel F.; Norton, G. Ron; & others. (2000). Drinking away the hurt: The nature and prevalence of PTSD in substance abuse patients attending a community-based treatment program. *Journal of Behavior Therapy and Experimental Psychiatry, 31,* 55–66.

Boon, Suzette, & Draijer, Nel. (1993). Multiple personality disorder in the Netherlands: A clinical investigation of 71 patients. *American Journal of Psychiatry, 150,* 489–494.

Bootzin, Richard R., & Rider, Steven P. (1997). Behavioral techniques and biofeedback for insomnia. In Mark R. Pressman & William C. Orr (Eds.), *Understanding sleep: The evaluation and treatment of sleep disorders.* Washington, DC: American Psychological Association.

Bornstein, Marc H., & Lamb, Michael E. (1992). *Development in infancy: An introduction* (3rd ed.). New York: McGraw-Hill.

Bornstein, Marc H., & Marks, Lawrence E. (1982, January). Color revisionism. *Psychology Today, 16,* 64–73.

Bornstein, Robert F. (1989). Subliminal techniques as propaganda tools: Review and critique. *Journal of Mind and Behavior, 10,* 231–262.

Bornstein, Robert F. (1993). Subliminal mere exposure effects. In Robert F. Bornstein &

Thane S. Pittman (Eds.), *Perception without awareness: Cognitive, clinical, and social perspectives.* New York: Guilford Press.

Botella, Cristina; Banos, Rosa M.; Villa, Helena; Perpina, Conxa; & Garcia-Palacios, Azucena. (2000). Virtual reality in the treatment of claustrophobic fear: A controlled, multiple-baseline design. *Behavior Therapy, 31,* 583–595.

Bouchard, Claude. (1997). Genetics of human obesity: Recent results from linkage studies. *Journal of Nutrition, 127,* 1887S–1890S.

Bouchard, Thomas J., Jr. (1994, June 17). Genes, environment, and personality. *Science, 264,* 1700–1701.

Bouchard, Thomas J., Jr.; Lykken, David T.; McGue, Matthew; Segal, Nancy L.; & Tellegen, Auke. (1990). Sources of human psychological differences: The Minnesota Study of Twins Reared Apart. *Science, 250,* 223–250.

Bouton, Mark E. (2000). A learning theory perspective on lapse, relapse, and the maintenance of behavior change. *Health Psychology, 19,* 57–63.

Bouton, Mark E.; Mineka, Susan; & Barlow, David H. (2001). A modern learning theory perspective on the etiology of panic disorder. *Psychological Review, 108,* 4–32.

Bower, Bruce. (1997, March 29). Forbidden flavors: Scientists consider how disgusting tastes can linger surreptitiously in memory. *Science News, 151,* 198–199.

Bower, Gordon H. (1993). The fragmentation of psychology? *American Psychologist, 48,* 905–907.

Bower, Thomas G. R. (1989). *The rational infant: Learning in infancy.* New York: Freeman.

Bowers, Kenneth S. (1976). *Hypnosis for the seriously curious.* Monterey, CA: Brooks/Cole.

Bowers, Kenneth S. (1992). Imagination and dissociation in hypnotic responding. *International Journal of Clinical and Experimental Hypnosis, 40,* 253–275.

Bowers, Kenneth S. (1995). Unconscious influences and hypnosis. In Jerome L. Singer, (Ed.). *Repression and dissociation: Implications for personality theory, psychopathology, and health.* Chicago: University of Chicago Press.

Bowers, Kenneth S., & Favolden, Peter. (1996). Revisiting a century-old Freudian slip—From suggestion disavowed to the truth repressed. *Psychological Bulletin, 119,* 355–380.

Bowers, Kenneth S.; Regehr, Glenn; Balthazard, Claude; & Parker, Kevin. (1990). Intuition in the context of discovery. *Cognitive Psychology, 22,* 72–110.

Boyce, Nell. (2001, January 15). Truth and consequences: Scientists are scanning the brain for traces of guilty knowledge. *U.S. News & World Report, 130,* 40–42.

Boynton, Robert M. (1988). Color vision. *Annual Review of Psychology, 39,* 69–100.

Boysen, Sally T., & Hines, G. T. (1999). Current issues and emerging theories in animal cognition. *Annual Review of Psychology, 50,* 683–705.

Bozarth, Jerold D.; Zimring, Fred M.; & Tausch, Reinhard. (2002). Client-centered therapy: The evolution of a revolution. In David J. Cain & Julius Seeman (Eds.), *Humanistic psychotherapies: Handbook of research and practice.* Washington, DC: American Psychological Association.

Bracha, H. Stefan; Wolkowitz, Owen M.; Lohr, James B.; Karson, Craig N.; & Bigelow, Llewellyn B. (1989). High prevalence of visual hallucinations in research subjects with chronic schizophrenia. *American Journal of Psychiatry, 146,* 526–528.

Bradbard, Marilyn R.; Martin, Carol L.; Endsley, Richard C.; & Halverson, Charles F. (1986). Influence of sex stereotypes on children's exploration and memory: A competence versus performance distinction. *Developmental Psychology, 22,* 481–486.

Braff, David L. (1993). Information processing and attention dysfunctions in schizophrenia. *Schizophrenia Bulletin, 19,* 233–259.

Braffman, Wayne; & Kirsch, Irving. (1999). Imaginative suggestibility and hypnotizability: An empirical analysis. *Journal of Personality and Social Psychology, 77,* 578–587.

Brainard, George C.; Hanifin, John P.; Rollag, Mark D.; & others. (2001a). Action spectrum for melatonin regulation in humans: Evidence for a novel circadian photoreceptor. *Journal of Neuroscience, 21,* 6405–6412.

Brainard, George C.; Hanifin, John P.; Rollag, Mark D.; & others. (2001b). Human melatonin regulation is not mediated by the three cone photopic visual system. *Journal of Clinical Endocrinology and Metabolism, 86,* 433–436.

Brainerd, Charles J. (1996). Piaget: A centennial celebration. *Psychological Science, 7,* 191–195.

Bransford, John D., & Stein, Barry S. (1993). *The IDEAL problem solver: A guide for improving thinking, learning, and creativity* (2nd ed.). New York: Freeman.

Braun, Allen R.; Balkin, Thomas J.; Wesensten, Nancy J.; Gwadry, Fuad; Carson, Richard E.; Varga, Mary; & others. (1998, January 2). Dissociated patterns of activity in visual cortices and their projections during human rapid eye movement during sleep. *Science, 279,* 91–95.

Braun, Stephen. (2001, Spring). Ecstasy on trial: Seeking insight by prescription. *Cerebrum, 3,* 10–21.

Bray, George A., & Tartaglia, Louis A. (2000, April 6). Medicinal strategies in the treatment of obesity. *Nature, 404,* 672–677.

Brecher, Edward M. (1984). *Love, sex, and aging.* Mount Vernon, NY: Consumers Union.

Breedlove, S. Marc. (1994). Sexual differentiation of the human nervous system. *Annual Review of Psychology, 45,* 389–418.

Breedlove, S. Marc. (1997, October 23). Sex on the brain. *Nature, 389,* 801.

Breggin, Peter R. (1979). *Electroshock: Its brain disabling effects.* New York: Springer.

Breggin, Peter R. (1991). *Toxic psychiatry.* New York: St. Martin's Press.

Bregman, Elsie O. (1934). An attempt to modify the emotional attitude of infants by the conditioned response technique. *Journal of Genetic Psychology, 45,* 169–198.

Brehm, Sharon S. (1992). *Intimate relationships* (2nd ed.). New York: McGraw-Hill.

Breland, Keller, & Breland, Marian. (1961). The misbehavior of organisms. *American Psychologist, 16,* 681–684.

Brenneis, C. Brooks. (2000). Evaluating the evidence: Can we find authenticated recovered memory? *Psychoanalytic Psychology, 17,* 61–77.

Breslau, Naomi; Kilbey, M. Marlyne; & Andreski, Patricia. (1993). Nicotine dependence and major depression: New evidence from a prospective investigation. *Archives of General Psychiatry, 50,* 31–35.

Breslau, Naomi; Peterson, Edward L.; Schultz, Lonni R.; & others. (1998). Major depression and stages of smoking: A longitudinal investigation. *Archives of General Psychiatry, 55,* 161–166.

Bretschneider, Judy G., & McCoy, Norma L. (1988). Sexual interest and behavior in healthy 80- to 102-year-olds. *Archives of Sexual Behavior, 17,* 109–129.

Breuer, Josef, & Freud, Sigmund. (1895/1957). *Studies on hysteria* (James Strachey, Ed. & Trans., in collaboration with Anna Freud). New York: Basic Books.

Brewer, Marilyn B. (1994). The social psychology of prejudice: Getting it all together. In Mark P. Zanna & James M. Olson (Eds.), *The psychology of prejudice: The Ontario Symposium* (Vol. 7). Hillsdale, NJ: Erlbaum.

Brewin, Chris R. (1996). Theoretical foundations of cognitive-behavior therapy for anxiety and depression. *Annual Review of Psychology, 47,* 33–57.

Brewin, Chris R.; Andrews, Bernice; & Gotlib, Ian H. (1993). Psychopathology and early experience: A reappraisal of retrospective reports. *Psychological Bulletin, 113,* 82–98.

Brice, Thomas S., & Waung, M. (2001). Web site recruitment characteristics: America's Best v. America's Biggest. *Society for the Advancement of Management Journal.*

Briere, John, & Conte, Jon. (1993). Self-reported amnesia for abuse in adults molested as children. *Journal of Traumatic Stress, 6*(1), 21–31.

Bringmann, Wolfgang G.; Voss, Ursula; & Ungerer, Gustav A. (1997). Wundt's laboratories. In Wolfgang G. Bringmann, Helmut E. Lück, Rudolf Miller, & Charles E. Early (Eds.), *A pictorial history of psychology.* Chicago: Quintessence.

Brock, Dwight B.; Lemke, Jon H.; & Berkman, Lisa F. (1994). Mortality and physical functioning in epidemiologic studies of three older populations. *Journal of Aging and Social Policy, 6*(3), 21–32.

Broder, Michael S. (1999). So you want to work in the media? 21 things I wish I had known when I first asked myself that question. In Lita Linzer Schwartz (Ed.), *Psychology and the media: A second look*. Washington, DC: American Psychological Association.

Brody, Arthur L.; Saxena, Sajaya; Stoessel, Paula; Gillies, Laurie; Fairbanks, Lynn A.; Alborzian, Shervin; & others. (2001, July). Regional brain metabolic changes in patients with major depression treated with either paroxetine or interpersonal therapy. *Archives of General Psychiatry, 58*, 631–640.

Brody, Leslie R. (2000). The socialization of gender differences in emotional expression: Display rules, infant temperament, and differentiation. In Agneta H. Fischer (Ed.), *Gender and emotion: Social psychological perspectives*. New York: Cambridge University Press.

Brody, Leslie R., & Hall, Judith A. (1993). In Michael Lewis & Jeannette M. Haviland (Eds.), *Handbook of emotions*. New York: Guilford Press.

Brody, Nathan. (1997). Intelligence, schooling, and society. *American Psychologist, 52*, 1046–1050.

Brooks-Gunn, Jeanne. (1988). Antecedents and consequences of variations of girls' maturational timing. In Melvin D. Levine & Elizabeth R. McAnarney (Eds.), *Early adolescent transitions*. Lexington, MA: Lexington Books.

Brooks-Gunn, Jeanne, & Furstenberg, Frank F., Jr. (1989). Adolescent sexual behavior. *American Psychologist, 44*, 249–257.

Brooks-Gunn, Jeanne, & Reiter, Edward O. (1990). The role of pubertal processes. In S. Shirley Feldman & Glen R. Elliott (Eds.), *At the threshold: The developing adolescent*. Cambridge, MA: Harvard University Press.

Broughton, Roger J. (1989). Chronobiological aspects and models of sleep and napping. In David F. Dinges & Roger J. Broughton (Eds.), *Sleep and alertness: Chronobiological, behavioral, and medical aspects of napping*. New York: Raven Press.

Brown, Alan S. (1991). A review of the tip-of-the-tongue experience. *Psychological Bulletin, 109*(2), 204–223.

Brown, Alan S.; Schaefer, Catherine A.; Wyatt, Richard J.; & others. (2000). Maternal exposure to respiratory infections and adult schizophrenia spectrum disorders: A prospective birth cohort study. *Schizophrenia Bulletin, 26*, 287–295.

Brown, Bernard. (1999, April). Optimizing expression of the common human genome for child development. *Current Directions in Psychological Science, 8*, 37–41.

Brown, Gary E.; Davis, Eric; & Johnson, Amanda. (1999). Forced exercise blocks learned helplessness in the cockroach (*Periplaneta americana*). *Psychological Reports, 84*, 155–156.

Brown, George William; Harris, Tirril Olivia; & Hepworth, Cathy. (1994). Life events and endogenous depression: A puzzle reexamined. *Archives of General Psychiatry, 51*, 525–534.

Brown, Gregory M. (1994). Light, melatonin, and the sleep-wake cycle. *Journal of Psychiatry and Neuroscience, 19*(5), 345–353.

Brown, Richard A.; Kahler, Christopher W.; Niaura, Raymond; Abrams, David B.; Sales, Suzanne D.; Ramsey, Susan E.; & others. (2001). Cognitive-behavioral treatment for depression in smoking cessation. *Journal of Consulting and Clinical Psychology, 69*, 471–480.

Brown, Roger, & Kulik, James. (1982). Flashbulb memories. In Ulric Neisser (Ed.), *Memory observed: Remembering in natural contexts*. San Francisco: Freeman.

Bruner, Jerome. (1992). Another look at New Look 1. *American Psychologist, 47*, 780–783.

Brüning, Jens C.; Gautam, Dinesh; & others. (2000, September 22). Role of brain insulin receptor in control of body weight and reproduction. *Science, 289*, 2122–2125.

Bryan, James H., & Test, Mary Ann. (1967). Models and helping: Naturalistic studies in aiding behavior. *Journal of Personality and Social Psychology, 6*, 400–407.

Buchanan, Christy Miller; Eccles, Jacquelynne S.; & Becker, Jill B. (1992). Are adolescents the victims of raging hormones? Evidence for activational effects of hormones on moods and behavior at adolescence. *Psychological Bulletin, 111*, 62–107.

Buck, Linda B. (2000). The molecular architecture of odor and pheromone sensing in mammals. *Cell, 100*, 611–618.

Buckley, Kerry W. (1982). The selling of a psychologist: John Broadus Watson and the application of behavioral techniques to advertising. *Journal of the History of the Behavioral Sciences, 18*, 207–221.

Buckley, Kerry W. (1989). *Mechanical man: John Broadus Watson and the beginnings of behaviorism*. New York: Guilford Press.

Buckley, Peter F. (1998). Structural brain imaging in schizophrenia. *Psychiatric Clinics of North America, 21*, 77–91.

Buckner, Randy L., & Wheeler, Mark E. (2001). The cognitive neuroscience of remembering. *Nature Reviews Neuroscience, 2*, 624–634.

Buhrmester, Duane, & Furman, Wyndol. (1987). The development of companionship and intimacy. *Child Development, 50*, 1101–1115.

Bulcroft, Richard A., & Bulcroft, Kris A. (1991). The nature and functions of dating in later life. *Research on Aging, 13*, 244–260.

Bulik, Cynthia M.; Sullivan, Patrick F.; & Kendler, Kenneth S. (2000). An empirical study of the classification of eating disorders. *American Journal of Psychiatry, 157*, 886–895.

Bureau of Labor Statistics. (2000). *Occupational outlook handbook*. Washington, DC: U.S. Department of Labor.

Burger, Jerry M. (1992). *Desire for control: Personality, social, and clinical perspectives*. New York: Plenum Press.

Burgess, Cheryl A., & Kirsch, Irving. (1999). Expectancy information as a moderator of the effects of hypnosis on memory. *Contemporary Hypnosis, 16*, 22–31.

Buri, John R.; Louiselle, Peggy A.; Misukanis, Thomas M.; & Mueller, Rebecca A. (1988). Effects of parental authoritarianism and authoritativeness on self-esteem. *Personality and Social Psychology Bulletin, 14*, 271–282.

Burke, Deborah M.; MacKay, Donald G.; Worthley, Joanna S.; & Wade, Elizabeth. (1991). On the tip of the tongue: What causes word finding failures in young and older adults? *Journal of Memory and Language, 30*, 542–579.

Burks, Nancy, & Martin, Barclay. (1985). Everyday problems and life change events: Ongoing versus acute sources of stress. *Journal of Human Stress, 11*, 27–35.

Burman, Bonnie, & Margolin, Gayla. (1992). Analysis of the association between marital relationships and health problems: An interactional perspective. *Psychological Bulletin, 112*, 39–63.

Burnfield, Jennifer L., & Medsker, Gina J. (1999). Income and employment of SIOP Members in 1997. *The Industrial-Organizational Psychologist, 36*, 19–30.

Burns, Melanie, & Seligman, Martin E. P. (1989). Explanatory style across the lifespan: Evidence for stability over 52 years. *Journal of Personality and Social Psychology, 56*, 471–477.

Burt, Diana Byrd; Zembar, Mary Jo; & Niederehe, George. (1995). Depression and memory impairment: A meta-analysis of the association, its pattern, and specificity. *Psychological Bulletin, 117*, 285–305.

Bush, R. (1989). Defining quality in dispute resolution: Taxonomies and anti-taxonomies of quality arguments. *Denver University Law Review, 66*, 335.

Bushman, Brad J. (1993). Human aggression while under the influence of alcohol and other drugs: An integrative research review. *Current Directions in Psychological Science, 2*, 148–152.

Bushman, Brad J. (1995). Moderating role of trait aggressiveness in the effects of violent media on aggression. *Journal of Personality and Social Psychology, 69*, 950–960.

Bushman, Brad J., & Anderson, Craig J. (2001). Media violence and the American public: Scientific facts versus media misinformation. *American Psychologist, 56*, 477–489.

Bushman, Brad J., & Huesmann, L. Rowell. (2001). Effects of televised violence on aggression. In Dorothy G. Singer & Jerome L. Singer (Eds.), *Handbook of children and the media*. Thousand Oaks, CA: Sage.

Bushman, Brad J., & Phillips, Colleen M. (2001). If the television program bleeds, memory for the advertisement recedes. *Current Directions in Psychological Science, 2,* 43–47.

Buss, Arnold H. (1989). Personality as traits. *American Psychologist, 44,* 1378–1388.

Buss, David M. (1989). Sex differences in human mate preferences: Evolutionary hypotheses tested in 37 cultures. *Behavioral and Brain Sciences, 12,* 1–49.

Buss, David M. (1991). Evolutionary personality psychology. *Annual Review of Psychology, 42,* 459–491.

Buss, David M. (1994). *The evolution of desire: Strategies of human mating.* New York: Basic Books.

Buss, David M. (1995a). Evolutionary psychology: A new paradigm for psychological science. *Psychological Inquiry, 6,* 1–31.

Buss, David M. (1995b). Psychological sex differences: Origins through sexual selection. *American Psychologist, 50,* 164–168.

Buss, David M. (1996). Sexual conflict: Evolutionary insights into feminism and the "Battle of the Sexes." In David M. Buss & Neil M. Malamuth (Eds.), *Sex, power, conflict: Evolutionary and feminist perspectives.* New York: Oxford University Press.

Buss, David M. (1999). *Evolutionary psychology: The new science of the mind.* Boston: Allyn & Bacon.

Butcher, James N. (1999). *A beginner's guide to the MMPI-2.* Washington, DC: American Psychological Association.

Butcher, James N., & Rouse, Steven V. (1996). Personality: Individual differences and clinical assessment. *Annual Review of Psychology, 47,* 87–111.

Butler, Robert A., & Harlow, Harry F. (1954). Persistence of visual exploration in monkeys. *Journal of Comparative and Physiological Psychology, 47,* 258–263.

Butters, Nelson, & Delis, Dean C. (1995). Clinical assessment of memory disorders in amnesia and dementia. *Annual Review of Psychology, 46,* 493–523.

Byne, William. (1994, May). The biological evidence challenged. *Scientific American, 270,* 50–55.

Byne, William, & Parsons, Bruce. (1993). Human sexual orientation: The biologic theories reappraised. *Archives of General Psychiatry, 50,* 228–239.

Cacioppo, John T., & Gardner, Wendi L. (1999). Emotion. *Annual Review of Psychology, 50,* 191–214.

Cain, David J. (2002). Defining characteristics, history, and evolution of humanistic psychotherapies. In David J. Cain & Julius Seeman (Eds.), *Humanistic psychotherapies: Handbook of research and practice.* Washington, DC: American Psychological Association.

Cain, David J., & Seeman, Julius (Eds.). (2002a). *Humanistic psychotherapies: Handbook of research and practice.* Washington, DC: American Psychological Association.

Cain, David J., & Seeman, Julius. (2002b). Preface. In David J. Cain & Julius Seeman (Eds.), *Humanistic psychotherapies: Handbook of research and practice.* Washington, DC: American Psychological Association.

Calignano, Antonio; La Rana, Giovanna; Giuffrida, Andrea; & Piomelli, Daniele. (1998, July 16). Control of pain initiation by endogenous cannabinoids. *Nature, 394,* 277.

Calkins, Mary W. (1893). Statistics of dreams. *American Journal of Psychology, 5,* 311–343.

Calkins, Susan D., & Fox, Nathan A. (1994). Individual differences in the biological aspects of temperament. In John E. Bates & Theodore D. Wachs (Eds.), *Temperament: Individual differences at the interface of biology and behavior.* Washington, DC: American Psychological Association.

Campbell, Jennifer D., & Fairey, Patricia J. (1989). Informational and normative routes to conformity: The effect of faction size as a function of norm extremity and attention to the stimulus. *Journal of Personality and Social Psychology, 57,* 457–458.

Campbell, John B., & Hawley, Charles W. (1982). Study habits and Eysenck's theory of extraversion-introversion. *Journal of Research in Personality, 16,* 139–146.

Campbell, Scott S. (1997). The basics of biological rhythms. In Mark R. Pressman & William C. Orr (Eds.), *Understanding sleep: The evaluation and treatment of sleep disorders.* Washington, DC: American Psychological Association.

Campbell, Scott S. (2000, May 19). Is there an intrinsic period of the circadian clock? *Science, 288,* 1174.

Campbell, Scott S., & Murphy, Patricia J. (1998, January 16). Extraocular circadian phototransduction in humans. *Science, 279,* 396–399.

Campfield, L. Arthur; Smith, Francoise J.; Rosenbaum, Michael; & Hirsch, Jules. (1996). Human eating: Evidence for a physiological basis using a modified paradigm. *Neuroscience and Biobehavioral Reviews, 20,* 133–137.

Campion, James E. (1972). Work sampling for personnel selection. *Journal of Applied Psychology, 56,* 40–44.

Campion, Michael A.; Pursell, Elliot D.; & Brown, Barbara K. (1988). Structured interviewing: Raising the psychometric properties of the employment interview. *Personnel Psychology, 41,* 25–42.

Canli, Turhan; Zhao, Zuo; Desmond, John E.; Kang, Eunjoo; Gross, James; & Gabrieli, John D. E. (2001). An fMRI study of personality influences on brain reactivity to emotional stimuli. *Behavioral Neuroscience, 115,* 33–42.

Cannon, Tyrone D., & Marco, Elysa. (1994). Structural brain abnormalities as indicators of vulnerability to schizophrenia. *Schizophrenia Bulletin, 20,* 89–102.

Cannon, Walter B. (1927). The James-Lange theory of emotion: A critical examination and an alternative theory. *American Journal of Psychology, 39,* 106–124.

Cannon, Walter B. (1932). *The wisdom of the body.* New York: Norton.

Cannon, Walter B.; Lewis, J. T.; & Britton, S. W. (1927). The dispensability of the sympathetic division of the autonomic nervous system. *Boston Medical and Surgical Journal, 197,* 514.

Cantor, Joanne. (1999). Review of the book *Children and media violence. Journal of International Communication, 6,* (1). Retrieved September 6, 2001 from http://www.mnstate.edu/gunarat/jicreviews6-1.htm

Cantor, Joanne. (2000, August 5). *Media violence and children's emotions: Beyond the "smoking gun."* Paper presented at the annual convention of the American Psychological Association, Washington, DC. Retrieved September 29, 2001 from http://www.joannecantor.com/EMOTIONS2_sgl.htm

Capaldi, Elizabeth D. (1996). Conditioned food preferences. In Elizabeth D. Capaldi (Ed.), *Why we eat, what we eat: The psychology of eating.* Washington, DC: American Psychological Association.

Caporael, Linnda R. (2001). Evolutionary psychology: Toward a unifying theory and a hybrid science. *Annual Review of Psychology, 52,* 607–628.

Caporael, Linda R., & Brewer, Marilynn B. (1995). Hierarchical evolutionary theory: There *is* an alternative, and it's not creationism. *Psychological Inquiry, 6,* 31–33.

Caraballo, Ralph S.; Giovino, Gary A.; Pechacek, Terry F.; Mowery, Paul D.; Richter, Patricia A.; Strauss, Warren J.; & others. (1998, July 8). Racial and ethnic differences in serum cotinine levels of cigarette smokers. *Journal of the American Medical Association, 280,* 135–139.

Cardeña, Etzel. (1992). Trance and possession as dissociative disorders. *Transcultural Psychiatric Research Review, 29,* 287–300.

Carli, Linda L., & Leonard, Jean B. (1989). The effect of hindsight on victim derogation. *Journal of Social and Clinical Psychology, 8,* 331–343.

Carlson, Eve Bernstein; Putnam, Frank W.; Ross, Colin A.; Torem, Moshe; Coons, Philip; Dill, Diana L.; & others. (1993). Validity of the Dissociative Experiences Scale in screening for multiple personality disorder: A multicenter study. *American Journal of Psychiatry, 150,* 1030–1036.

Carlson, Neil R. (1994). *Physiology of behavior* (5th ed.). Boston: Allyn & Bacon.

Carlson, Shawn. (1985, December 5). A double-blind test of astrology. *Nature, 318,* 419–425.

Caro, José F.; Kolaczynski, Jerzy W.; & others. (1996, July 20). Decreased cerebrospinal-fluid serum leptin ratio in obesity: A possible mechanism for leptin resistance. *Lancet, 348,* 159–161.

Carpenter, Ronda J. (1997). Margaret Floy Washburn. In Wolfgang G. Bringmann, Helmut E. Lück, Rudolf Miller, & Charles E. Early (Eds.), *A pictorial history of psychology.* Chicago: Quintessence.

Carroll, Kathleen Whiteman. (1993). Family support groups for medically ill patients and their families. In Anne Alonso & Hillel I. Swiller (Eds.), *Group therapy in clinical practice.* Washington, DC: American Psychiatric Press.

Carroll, Marilyn E., & Overmier, J. Bruce (Eds.). (2001). *Animal research and human health: Advancing human welfare through behavioral science.* Washington, DC: American Psychological Association.

Carskadon, Mary A., & Taylor, Jennifer F. (1997). Public policy and sleep disorders. In Mark R. Pressman & William C. Orr (Eds.), *Understanding sleep: The evaluation and treatment of sleep disorders.* Washington, DC: American Psychological Association.

Carter, C. Sue, & DeVries, A. Courtney. (1999). Stress and soothing: An endocrine perspective. In Michael Lewis & Douglas Ramsay (Eds.), *Soothing and stress.* Mahwah, NJ: Erlbaum.

Carter, Jerry L. (1992). Visual, somatosensory, olfactory, and gustatory hallucinations. *Psychiatric Clinics of North America, 15,* 347–358.

Cartwright, Rosalind Dymond, & Kaszniak, Alfred. (1991). The social psychology of dream reporting. In Steven J. Ellman & John S. Antrobus (Eds.), *The mind in sleep: Psychology and psychophysiology* (2nd ed.). New York: Wiley.

Casey, M. Beth; Nuttall, Ronald; Pezaris, Elizabeth; & Benbow, Camilla Persson. (1995). The influence of spatial ability on gender differences in mathematics college entrance test scores across diverse samples. *Developmental Psychology, 31,* 697–705.

Catania, A. Charles, & Laties, Victor G. (1999). Pavlov and Skinner: Two lives in science (an introduction to B. F. Skinner's "Some responses to the stimulus 'Pavlov'"). *Journal of the Experimental Analysis of Behavior, 72,* 455–461.

Cattell, Raymond B. (1973, July). Personality pinned down. *Psychology Today,* 40–46.

Cattell, Raymond B. (1994). A cross-validation of primary personality structure in the 16 P.F. by two parcelled factor analysis. *Multivariate Experimental Clinical Research, 10*(3), 181–191.

Cattell, Raymond B.; Cattell, A. Karen S.; & Cattell, Heather E. P. (1993). *16 PF questionnaire* (5th ed.). Champaign, IL: Institute for Personality and Ability Testing.

Ceci, Stephen J., & Loftus, Elizabeth F. (1994). "Memory work": A royal road to false memories? Special issue: Recovery of memories of childhood sexual abuse. *Applied Cognitive Psychology, 8,* 351–364.

Cecil, Joanne E.; Francis, John; & Read, Nicholas W. (1998). Relative contributions of intestinal, gastric, oro-sensory influences and information to changes in appetite induced by the same liquid meal. *Appetite, 31,* 377–390.

Cefalu, William T.; Wagner, Janice D.; & others. (1997). A study of caloric restriction and cardiovascular aging in cynomolgus monkeys (*Macaca fascicularis*): A potential model for aging research. *Journal of Gerontology, Series A, 52,* B10–B21.

Centers for Disease Control and Prevention. (1998a). Combating complacency: Geneva 1998: A closer look at trends by race and gender. *CDC Trends.* <http://www.cdcnpin.org/geneva98/trends/trends6.htm> (1999, February 18).

Centers for Disease Control and Prevention. (1998b, June). Basic statistics: AIDS cases by exposure category. *CDC Update: HIV & AIDS Prevention.* <http://www.cdc.gov/nchstp/hiv-aids/stats/exposure.htm> (1999, February 18).

Centers for Disease Control and Prevention. (1998c, July). Critical need to pay attention to HIV prevention for women: Minority and young women bear the greatest burden. *CDC Update: HIV & AIDS Prevention.* <http://www.cdc.gov/nchstp/hiv-aids/pubs/facts/women.htm> (1999, February 18).

Centers for Disease Control and Prevention. (1998d, July). Impact of HIV/AIDS on Hispanics in the United States. *CDC Update: HIV & AIDS Prevention.* <http://www.cdc.gov/nchstp/hiv-aids/pubs/facts/hispanic.htm> (1999, February 18).

Centers for Disease Control and Prevention. (1998e, July). Critical need to pay attention to HIV prevention for African Americans. *CDC Update: HIV & AIDS Prevention.* <http://www.cdc.gov/nchstp/hiv-aids/pubs/facts/afram.htm> (1999, February 18).

Centers for Disease Control and Prevention. (1998f, September). Young people at risk: Epidemic shifts further toward young women and minorities. *CDC Update: HIV & AIDS Prevention.* <http://www.cdc.gov/nchstp/od/news/youth98.htm> (1999, February 16).

Centers for Disease Control and Prevention. (1999). Increases in unsafe sex and rectal gonorrhea among men who have sex with men: San Francisco, California, 1994–1997. *Morbidity and Mortality Weekly Report, 48,* 45–48. <http://www.cdc.gov/epo/mmwr/preview/mmwrhtml/00056314.htm> (1999, February 16).

Centers for Diseases Control and Prevention. (2001, January 26). Diabetes rates rise another six percent in 1999. Office of Commication, Press release. <http://www.cdc.gov/od/oc/media/pressrel/r010126.htm> (May 25, 2001).

Centers for Disease Control and Prevention. (2001, October 12). Cigarette smoking among adults—United States, 1999. *Morbidity and Mortality Weekly Report, 50,* 869–873. Available as a PDF document and retrieved on October 14, 2001 at http://www.cdc.gov/tobacco/research_data/adults_prev/mm5040.htm

Cervone, Daniel. (1997). Social-cognitive mechanisms and personality coherence: Self-knowledge, situational beliefs, and cross-situational coherence in perceived self-efficacy. *Psychological Science, 8,* 43–50.

Chabris, Christopher F., & Kosslyn, Stephen M. (1998). How do the cerebral hemispheres contribute to encoding spatial relations? *Current Directions in Psychological Science, 7,* 8–14.

Chadwick, P. D. J.; Lowe, C. F.; Horne, P. J.; & Higson, P. J. (1994). Modifying delusions: The role of empirical testing. *Behavior Therapy, 25,* 35–49.

Chambless, Dianne L., & Gillis, Martha M. (1993). Cognitive therapy of anxiety disorders. *Journal of Consulting and Clinical Psychology, 61,* 248–260.

Chambless, Dianne L., & Ollendick, Thomas H. (2001). Empirically supported psychological interventions: Controversies and evidence. *Annual Review of Psychology, 52,* 685–716.

Chance, Paul. (1999). Thorndike's puzzle boxes and the origins of the experimental analysis of behavior. *Journal of the Experimental Analysis of Behavior, 72,* 433–440.

Chao, Dong M.; Shen, Lin L.; Tjen-A-Looi, Stephanie; Pitsillides, Koullis F.; Li, Peng; & Longhurst, John C. (1999). Naloxone reverses inhibitory effect of electroacupuncture on sympathetic cardiovascular reflex responses. *American Journal of Physiology: Heart and Circulatory Physiology, 276,* 2127–2134.

Chaudhari, Nirupa; Landin, Ana Marie; & Roper, Stephen D. (2000). A metabotropic glutamate receptor variant functions as a taste receptor. *Nature Neuroscience, 3,* 113–119.

Chemelli, Richard M.; Willie, Jon T.; Sinton, Christopher M.; & others. (1999, August 20). Narcolepsy in orexin knockout mice: Molecular genetics of sleep regulation. *Cell, 98,* 409–412.

Chen, Chuansheng; Greenberger, Ellen; Lester, Julia; Dong, Qi; & Guo, Miaw-Sheue. (1998). A cross-cultural study of family and peer correlates of adolescent misconduct. *Developmental Psychology, 34,* 770–781.

Chen, Eric Y. H.; Wilkins, A. J.; & McKenna, Peter J. (1994). Semantic memory is both impaired and anomalous in schizophrenia. *Psychological Medicine, 24,* 193–202.

Cheney, Dorothy L., & Seyfarth, Robert M. (1990). *How monkeys see the world.* Chicago: University of Chicago Press.

Chiba, Andrea A.; Kesner, Raymond P.; & Gibson, Chris J. (1997). Memory for temporal order of new and familiar spatial location sequences: Role of the medial prefrontal cortex. *Learning and Memory, 4,* 311–317.

Choi, Incheol; Nisbett, Richard E.; & Norenzayen, Ara. (1999). Causal attribution across cultures: Variation and universality. *Psychological Bulletin, 125,* 47–63.

Chomsky, Noam. (1965). *Aspects of a theory of syntax.* Cambridge, MA: MIT Press.

Christensen, Andrew, & Heavey, Christopher L. (1993). Gender differences in marital conflict: The demand/withdraw interaction pattern. In Stuart Oskamp & Mark Costanzo (Eds.), *Gender issues in contemporary society.* Newbury Park, CA: Sage.

Christensen, Andrew, & Heavey, Christopher L. (1999). Interventions for couples. *Annual Review of Psychology, 50,* 165–190.

Christensen, Andrew, & Jacobson, Neil S. (1994). Who (or what) can do psychotherapy: The status and challenge of nonprofessional therapies. *Psychological Science, 5,* 8–14.

Church, A. Timothy, & Katigbak, Marcia S. (1989). Internal, external, and self-report structure of personality in a non-Western culture: An investigation of cross-language and cross-cultural generalizability. *Journal of Personality and Social Psychology, 54,* 296–308.

Chusmir, L. H., & Mills, J. (1989). Gender differences in conflict resolution styles of managers: At work and at home. *Sex Roles, 20,* 149–163.

Chwalisz, Kathleen; Diener, Ed; & Gallagher, Dennis. (1988). Autonomic arousal feedback and emotional experience: Evidence from the spinal cord injured. *Journal of Personality and Social Psychology, 54,* 820–828.

Cialdini, Robert B. (2000). *Influence: Science and practice.* Boston: Allyn & Bacon.

Cialdini, Robert B.; Darby, Betty Lee; & Vincent, Joyce E. (1973). Transgression and altruism: A case for hedonism. *Journal of Experimental Social Psychology, 9,* 502–516.

Cialdini, Robert B., & Trost, Melanie R. (1998). Social influence, social norms, conformity, and compliance. In Daniel T. Gilbert, Susan T. Fiske, & Gardner Lindzey (Eds.), *The handbook of social psychology* (4th ed., Vol. 2). New York: McGraw-Hill.

Ciccocioppo, Roberto; Sanna, Pietro Paolo; & Weiss, Friedbert. (2001). Cocaine-predictive stimulus induces drug-seeking behavior and neural activation in limbic brain regions after multiple months of abstinence: Reversal by D1 antagonists. *Proceedings of the National Academy of Sciences, USA, 98,* 1976–1981.

Cioffi, Delia, & Holloway, James. (1993). Delayed costs of suppressed pain. *Journal of Personality and Social Psycyhology, 64,* 274–282.

Clark, Damon A.; Mitra, Partha P.; & Wang, Samuel S.-H. (2001). Scalable architecture in mammalian brains. *Nature, 411,* 189–193.

Clark, Robert E., & Squire, Larry R. (1998, April 3). Classical conditioning and brain systems: The role of awareness. *Science, 280,* 77–81.

Clark, Russell D., III, & Word, Larry E. (1974). Where is the apathetic bystander? Situational characteristics of the emergency. *Journal of Personality and Social Psychology, 29,* 279–287.

Clarke, Dave. (1991). Belief in the paranormal: A New Zealand survey. *Journal of the Society for Psychical Research, 57,* 412–425.

Clarke-Stewart, K. Alison. (1989). Infant day care: Maligned or malignant? *American Psychologist, 44,* 266–273.

Clarke-Stewart, K. Alison. (1992). Consequences of child care for children's develop-ment. In Alan Booth (Ed.), *Child care in the 1990s: Trends and consequences.* Hillsdale, NJ: Erlbaum.

Clay, Rebecca A. (1995, November). Working mothers: Happy or haggard? *APA Monitor, 26*(1), 37.

Cody, Michael J., & Seiter, John S. (2001). Compliance principles in retail sales in the United States. In Wihelmina Wosinska, Robert B. Cialdini, Daniel W. Barrett, & Janusz Reykowski (Eds.), *The practice of social influence in multiple cultures.* Mahwah, NJ: Erlbaum.

Cohen, Jonathan D., & Tong, Frank. (2001, September 28). Perspectives. Neuroscience: The face of controversy. *Science, 293,* 2405–2407.

Cohen, Sheldon; Frank, Ellen; Doyle, William J.; Skoner, David P.; Rabin, Bruce; & Gwaltney, Jack M., Jr. (1998). Types of stressors that increase susceptibility to the common cold in healthy adults. *Health Psychology, 17,* 214–223.

Cohen, Sheldon; Gottlieb, Benjamin H.; & Underwood, Lynn G. (2000). Social relationships and health. In Sheldon Cohen, Lynn Underwood, & Benjamin H. Gottlieb (Eds.), *Social support measurement and intervention: A guide for health and social scientists.* New York: Oxford University Press.

Cohen, Sheldon, & Herbert, Tracy B. (1996). Health psychology: Psychological factors and physical disease from the perspective of human psychoneuroimmunology. *Annual Review of Psychology, 47,* 113–142.

Cohen, Sheldon; Tyrrell, David A. J.; & Smith, Andrew P. (1991). Psychological stress and susceptibility to the common cold. *New England Journal of Medicine, 325,* 606–612.

Cohen, Sheldon; Tyrrell, David A. J.; & Smith, Andrew P. (1993). Negative life events, perceived stress, negative affect, and susceptibility to the common cold. *Journal of Personality and Social Psychology, 64,* 131–140.

Cohen, Sheldon, & Williamson, Gail M. (1988). Perceived stress in a probability sample of the United States. In Shirlynn Spacapan & Stuart Oskamp (Eds.), *The social psychology of health: The Claremont Symposium on Applied Social Psychology* (4th ed.). Newbury Park, CA: Sage.

Cohn, D'Vera. (2002, January 24). For zoo denizens, a taste of the wild. *Washington Post.* Retrieved January 25, 2002, from http://www.msnbc.com/news/693181.asp

Colby, Anne, & Kohlberg, Lawrence. (1984). Invariant sequence and internal consistency in moral judgment stages. In William M. Kurtines & Jacob L. Gewirtz (Eds.), *Morality, moral behavior, and moral development.* New York: Wiley.

Colby, Anne; Kohlberg, Lawrence; Gibbs, John; & Lieberman, Marcus. (1983). A longitudinal study of moral judgment. *Monographs of the Society for Research in Child Development, 48* (Nos. 1–2, 1–123).

Coles, Robert, & Stokes, Geoffrey. (1985). *Sex and the American teenager.* New York: Harper & Row.

Colicos, Michael A.; Collins, Boyce E.; Sailor, Michael J.; & Goda, Yukiko. (2001). Remodeling of synaptic actin induced by photoconductive stimulation. *Cell, 107,* 605–616.

Collaer, Marcia J., & Hines, Melissa. (1995). Human behavioral sex differences: A role for gonadal hormones during early development? *Psychological Bulletin, 118,* 55–107.

Collier, R. M. (1940). An experimental study of the effects of subliminal stimuli. *Psychological Monographs, 52*(2), 1–59.

Collins, Allan M., & Loftus, Elizabeth F. (1975). A spreading activation theory of semantic processing. *Psychological Review, 82,* 407–428.

Collins, W. Andrew, & Gunnar, Megan. (1990). Social and personality development. *Annual Review of Psychology, 41,* 387–416.

Comas-Diaz, Lilian. (1993). Hispanic/Latino communities: Psychological implications. In Donald R. Atkinson, George Morten, & Derald Wing Sue (Eds.), *Counseling American minorities: A cross-cultural perspective* (4th ed.). Madison, WI: Brown & Benchmark.

Comuzzie, Anthony G., & Allison, David B. (1998). The search for human obesity genes. *Science, 280,* 1374–1377.

Congressional Public Health Summit. (2000, July 26). *Joint statement on the impact of entertainment violence on children.* Retrieved September 29, 2001 from http://www.aap.org/advocacy/releases/jstmtevc.htm

Connor-Greene, Patricia A. (1993). From the laboratory to the headlines: Teaching critical evaluation of the press reports of research. *Teaching of Psychology, 20*(3), 167–169.

Contrada, Richard J.; Ashmore, Richard D.; Gary, Melvin L.; Coups, Elliot; Egeth, Jill D.; Sewell, Andrea; & others. (2000). Ethnicity-related sources of stress and their effects on well-being. *Current Directions of Psychological Science, 9,* 136–139.

Conway, Martin A.; Cohen, Gillian; & Stanhope, Nicola. (1991). On the very long-term retention of knowledge acquired through formal education: Twelve years of cognitive psychology. *Journal of Experimental Psychology: General, 120,* 395–409.

Cook, Michael, & Mineka, Susan. (1990). Selective associations in the observational conditioning of fear in rhesus monkeys. *Journal of Experimental Psychology: Animal Behavior Processes, 16,* 372–389.

Coons, Philip M. (1994). Confirmation of childhood abuse in child and adolescent cases of multiple personality disorder and dissociative disorder not otherwise specified. *Journal of Nervous and Mental Disease, 182,* 461–464.

Cooper, Rosemary. (1994). Normal sleep. In Rosemary Cooper (Ed.), *Sleep.* New York: Chapman & Hall.

Cooper, Rosemary, & Bradbury, Sue. (1994). Techniques in sleep recording. In Rosemary

Cooper (Ed.), *Sleep*. New York: Chapman & Hall.

Corballis, Michael C. (1997). The genetics and evolution of handedness. *Psychological Review, 104*, 714–727.

Corballis, Paul M.; Funnell, Margaret G.; & Gazzaniga, Michael S. (2002). Hemispheric asymmetries for simple visual judgments in the split brain. *Neuropsychologia, 40*, 401–410.

Coren, Stanley. (1992). *The left-hander syndrome: The causes and consequences of left-handedness*. New York: Free Press.

Coren, Stanley. (1994). Twinning is associated with an increased risk of left-handedness and inverted writing hand posture. *Early Human Development, 40*(1), 23–27.

Corkin, Suzanne; Amaral, David G.; González, R. Gilberto; Johnson, Keith A.; & Hyman, Bradley T. (1997). H. M.'s medial temporal lobe lesion: Findings from magnetic resonance imaging. *Journal of Neuroscience, 17*, 3964–3979.

Corrigan, Patrick W. (1998). The impact of stigma on severe mental illness. *Cognitive and Behavioral Practice, 5*, 201–222.

Corsini, Raymond J. (1957). *Non-verbal reasoning test*. Park Ridge, IL: London House Press.

Corvin, Aiden; O'Mahony, Ed; O'Regan, Myra; & others. (2001). Cigarette smoking and psychotic symptoms in bipolar affective disorder. *British Journal of Psychiatry, 179*, 35–38.

Coryell, William; Akiskal, Hagop S.; Leon, Andrew C.; Winokur, George; Maser, John D.; Mueller, Timothy I.; & Keller, Martin B. (1994a). The time course of nonchronic major depressive disorder: Uniformity across episodes and samples. *Archives of General Psychiatry, 51*, 405–410.

Coryell, William; Winokur, George; Shea, Tracie; Maser, Jack D.; Endicott, Jean; & Akiskal, Hagop S. (1994b). The long-term stability of depressive subtypes. *American Journal of Psychiatry, 151*, 199–204.

Cosmides, Leda; Tooby, John; & Barkow, Jerome H. (1992). Introduction: Evolutionary psychology and conceptual integration. In Jerome H. Barkow, Leda Cosmides, & John Tooby (Eds.), *The adapted mind: Evolutionary psychology and the role of culture*. New York: Oxford University Press.

Costa, Paul T., Jr., & McCrae, Robert R. (1989). Personality continuity and the changes of adult life. In Martha Storandt & Gary R. VandenBos (Eds.), *The adult years: Continuity and change*. Washington, DC: American Psychological Association.

Costa, Paul T., Jr., & McCrae, Robert R. (1994). "Set like plaster?" Evidence for the stability of adult personality. In Todd F. Hetherton & Joel L. Weinberger (Eds.), *Can personality change?* Washington, DC: American Psychological Association.

Costello, Charles G. (1996). The advantages of focusing on the personality characteristics of the personality disordered. In Charles G. Costello (Ed.), *Personality characteristics of the personality disordered*. New York: Wiley.

Council, James R. (1999). Measures of hypnotic responding. In Irving Kirsch, Antonio Capafons, Etzel Cardena-Buelna, & Salvador Amigo (Eds.), *Clinical hypnosis and self-regulation: Cognitive-behavior perspectives*. Washington, DC: American Psychological Association.

Cowan, Nelson. (1994). Mechanisms of verbal short-term memory. *Current Directions in Psychological Science, 6*, 185–189.

Cowan, Nelson; Wood, Noelle L.; & Borne, Dawn N. (1994). Reconfirmation of the short-term storage concept. *Psychological Science, 5*, 103–108.

Coyne, James C., & Downey, Geraldine. (1991). Social factors and psychopathology: Stress, social support, and coping processes. *Annual Review of Psychology, 42*, 401–425.

Coyne, James C.; Ellard, John H.; & Smith, David A. F. (1990). Social support, interdependence, and the dilemmas of helping. In Barbara R. Sarason, Irwin G. Sarason, & Gregory R. Pierce (Eds.), *Social support: An interactional view*. New York: Wiley.

Craik, Fergus I. M., & Lockhart, Robert S. (1972). Levels of processing: A framework for memory research. *Journal of Verbal Learning and Verbal Behavior, 11*, 671–684.

Craik, Fergus I. M., & Tulving, Endel. (1975). Depth of processing and the retention of words in episodic memory. *Journal of Experimental Psychology: General, 104*, 268–294.

Craske, Michelle G.; Miller, Patricia P.; Rotunda, Robert; & Barlow, David H. (1990). A descriptive report of initial unexpected panic attacks in minimal and extensive avoiders. *Behavior Research and Therapy, 28*, 395–400.

Crawley, Jacyntha. (1996). *The biorhythm kit: Plan for the ups and downs in your life*. Boston: Journey Editions.

Crews, Frederick. (1984/1986). The Freudian way of knowledge. In *Skeptical engagements*. New York: Oxford University Press.

Crews, Frederick. (1995). Confessions of a Freud basher. In Frederick Crews (Ed.), *The memory wars: Freud's legacy in dispute*. New York: New York Review of Books.

Crews, Frederick. (1996). The verdict on Freud. *Psychological Science, 7*, 63–68.

Croft, Rodney J.; Klugman, Anthony; Baldeweg, Torsten; & Gruzelier, John H. (2001). Electrophysiological evidence of serotonergic impairment in long-term MDMA ("Ecstasy") users. *American Journal of Psychiatry, 158*, 1687–1692.

Croizet, Jean-Claude, & Claire, Theresa. (1998). Extending the concept of stereotype and threat to social class: The intellectual underperformance of students from low socioeconomic backgrounds. *Personality and Social Psychology Bulletin, 24*, 588–654.

Crosscope-Happel, Cindy; Hutchins, David E.; & others. (2000). Male anorexia nervosa: A new focus. *Journal of Mental Health Counseling, 22*, 365–370.

Crowe, Richard A. (1990). Astrology and the scientific method. *Psychological Reports, 67*, 163–191.

Cumming, Elaine, & Henry, William. (1961). *Growing old: The process of disengagement*. New York: Basic Books.

Cunningham, Jacqueline L. (1997). Alfred Binet and the quest for testing higher mental functioning. In Wolfgang G. Bringmann, Helmut E. Lück, Rudolf Miller, & Charles E. Early (Eds.), *A pictorial history of psychology*. Chicago: Quintessence.

Czeisler, Charles A., & Dijk, Derk-Jan. (2001). Human circadian physiology and sleep-wake regulation. In Joseph Takahashi, Fred W. Turek, & Robert Y. Moore (Eds.), *Handbook of behavioral neurobiology: Circadian clocks* (Vol. 12). New York: Kluwer/Plenum.

Czeisler, Charles A.; Dijk, Derk-Jan; Kronauer, Richard E.; & others. (2000, May 19). Is there an intrinsic period of the circadian clock? Response to Campbell. *Science, 288*, 1174–1175.

Czeisler, Charles A.; Johnson, Michael P.; Duffy, Jeanne F.; Brown, E. N.; Ronda, J. M.; & Kronauer, Richard E. (1990). Exposure to bright light and darkness to treat physiologic maladaptions to night work. *New England Journal of Medicine, 322*(18), 1253–1259.

Czeisler, Charles A.; Shanahan, Theresa L.; Klerman, Elizabeth B.; Martens, Heinz; Brotman, Daniel J.; Emens, Jonathan S.; & others. (1995). Suppression of melatonin secretion in some blind patients by exposure to bright light. *New England Journal of Medicine, 332*(1), 6–11.

Czeisler, Charles A., & Wright, Kenneth P., Jr. (1999). Influence of light on circadian rhythmicity in humans. In Fred W. Turek & Phyllis C. Zee (Eds.), *Regulation of sleep and circadian rhythms*. New York: Dekker.

Dallery, Jesse; Silverman, Kenneth; Chutuape, Mary Ann; Bigelow, George E.; & Stitzer, Maxine L. (2001). Voucher-based reinforcement of opiate plus cocaine abstinence in treatment-resistant methadone patients: Effects of reinforcer magnitude. *Experimental and Clinical Psychopharmacology, 9*, 317–325.

Damasio, Antonio R. (1994). *Descartes' error: Emotion, reason, and the human brain*. New York: Putnam.

Damasio, Antonio R. (1999a, December). How the brain creates the mind. *Scientific American, 281*(6), 112–177.

Damasio, Antonio R. (1999b). *The feeling of what happens: Body and emotion in the making of consciousness*. New York: Harcourt Brace.

Damasio, Antonio R., & Damasio, Hanna. (1992, September). Brain and language. *Scientific American, 267*, 62–71.

Damasio, Antonio R.; Grabowski, Thomas J.; Bechara, Antoine; Damasio, Hanna; Ponto, Laura L. B.; Parvizi, Josef; & Hichwa, Richard D. (2000). Subcortical and cortical brain activity during the feeling of self-generated emotions. *Nature Neuroscience, 3,* 1049–1056.

Damasio, Hanna; Grabowski, Thomas; Frank, Randle; Galaburda, Albert M.; & Damasio, Antonio R. (1994, May 20). The return of Phineas Gage: Clues about the brain from the skull of a famous patient. *Science, 264,* 1102–1105.

Dansereau, Fred; Graen, George; & Haga, William. (1975). A vertical dyad linkage approach to leadership within formal organizations. *Organizational Behavior and Human Performance, 13,* 46–78.

Darley, John M. (1992). Social organization for the production of evil. Book Review Essay. *Psychological Inquiry, 3,* 199–218.

Darley, John M., & Shultz, Thomas R. (1990). Moral rules: Their content and acquisition. *Annual Review of Psychology, 41,* 525–556.

Darwin, Charles R. (1859/1998). *On the origin of species by means of natural selection.* New York: Modern Library.

Darwin, Charles R. (1871/1981). *The descent of man, and selection in relation to sex* (Introductions by John T. Bonner and Robert M. May). Princeton, NJ: Princeton University Press.

Darwin, Charles. (1872/1998). *The expression of emotions in man and animals* (3rd ed.) New York: Appleton.

Davey, Graham C. L. (1989). Dental phobias and anxieties: Evidence for conditioning processes in the acquisition and modulation of a learned fear. *Behavior Research and Therapy, 27,* 51–58.

Davey, Graham C. L. (1993). Factors influencing self-rated fear to a novel animal. *Cognition & Emotion, 7,* 461–471.

Davidson, Alec J.; Cappendijk, Susan L.; & Stephan, Friedrich K. (2000). Feeding-entrained circadian rhythms are attenuated by lesions of the parabrachial region in rats. *American Journal of Physiology, 278,* R1296–R1304.

Davidson, Jonathan R. T. (1993). Introduction: Social phobia in review: 1993. *Journal of Clinical Psychiatry, 54*(Suppl. 12), 3–4.

Davidson, Jonathan R. T. (2001). Recognition and treatment of posttraumatic stress disorder. *Journal of the American Medical Association, 286,* 584–588.

Davidson, Julian M., & Myers, L. S. (1988). Endocrine factors in sexual psychophysiology. In Raymond C. Rosen & J. Gayle Beck (Eds.), *Patterns of sexual arousal: Psychophysiological processes and clinical applications.* New York: Guilford Press.

Davidson, Paul R., & Parker, Kevin C. H. (2001). Eye movement desensitization and reprocessing (EMDR): A meta-analysis. *Journal of Consulting and Clinical Psychology, 69,* 305–316.

Davidson, Richard J.; Jackson, Daren C.; & Kalin, Ned H. (2000). Emotion, plasticity, context, and regulation: Perspectives from affective neuroscience. *Psychological Bulletin, 126,* 890–909.

Davidson, Terry L. (2000). Pavlovian occasion setting: A link between physiological change and appetitive behavior. *Appetite, 35,* 271–272.

Davis, Adrian, & Annett, Marian. (1994). Handedness as a function of twinning, age, and sex. *Cortex, 30*(1), 105–111.

Davis, Glenn Craig, & Breslau, Naomi. (1994). Post-traumatic stress disorder in victims of civilian and criminal violence. *Psychiatric Clinics of North America, 17,* 289–299.

Davis, Kenneth L.; Kahn, René S.; Ko, Grant; & Davidson, Michael. (1991). Dopamine in schizophrenia: A review and reconceptualization. *American Journal of Psychiatry, 148,* 1474–1486.

Davis, Mary Helen; Drogin, Eric Y.; & Wright, Jesse H. (1995). Therapist-patient sexual intimacy: A guide for the subsequent therapist. *Journal of Psychotherapy Practice and Research, 4,* 140–149.

Davis, Michael. (1992). The role of the amygdala in fear and anxiety. *Annual Review of Neuroscience, 15,* 353–375.

Davis, Michael, & Whalen, Paul J. (2001). The amygdala: Vigilance and emotion. *Molecular Psychiatry, 6,* 13–14.

Davis, Susan. (2000). Testosterone and sexual desire in women. *Journal of Sex Education and Therapy, 25,* 25–32.

Davison, Gerald C., & Neale, John M. (1998). *Abnormal psychology* (7th ed.). New York: Wiley.

Daw, Jennifer. (2001, November). APA's Disaster Response Network: Help on the scene. *APA Monitor on Psychology, 32.*

Dawson, Deborah A. (1991). Family structure and children's health and well-being: Data from the 1988 national health interview study on child health. *Journal of Marriage and the Family, 53,* 573–584.

Dawson, Drew. (1995). Improving adaptation to simulated night shift: Timed exposure to bright light versus daytime melatonin administration. *Sleep, 18,* 11–18.

Dawson, Drew, & Campbell, Scott S. (1991). Time exposure to bright light improves sleep and alertness during simulated night shifts. *Sleep, 14,* 511–516.

Dean, Geoffrey. (1992). The bottom line: Effect size. In Barry Beyerstein & Dale Beyerstein (Eds.), *The write stuff: Evaluations of graphology—The study of handwriting analysis.* Amherst, NY: Prometheus Books.

Dean, Geoffrey; Mather, Arthur; & Kelly, Ivan W. (1996). Astrology. In Gordon Stein (Ed.), *The encyclopedia of the paranormal.* Buffalo, NY: Prometheus Books.

DeAngelis, Tori. (1994, February). People's drug of choice offers potent side effects. *APA Monitor, 25,* 16.

DeAngelis, Tori. (1997, August). "Shock radio" is chasing away psychologists: In the era of "Dr. Laura," some psychologists opt out of radio programs. *APA Monitor, 28*(8), 10.

DeBell, Camille, & Jones, R. Deniece. (1997). As good as it seems? A review of EMDR experimental research. *Professional Psychology: Research and Practice, 28,* 153–163.

DeCasper, Anthony, & Fifer, William. (1980). Of human bonding: Newborns prefer their mothers' voices. *Science, 208,* 1174–1176.

de Castro, John M.; Bellisle, France; Dalix, Anne-Marie; & Pearcey, Sharon M. (2000). Palatability and intake relationships in free-living humans: Characterization and independence of influence in North Americans. *Physiology and Behavior, 70,* 343–350.

Deci, Edward L., & Ryan, Richard M. (1985). *Intrinsic motivation and self-determination in human behavior.* New York: Plenum Press.

Deci, Edward L., & Ryan, Richard M. (2000). The "what" and "why" of goal pursuits: Human needs and the self-determination of behavior. *Psychological Inquiry, 11,* 227–268.

de Fonseca, Fernando Rodriguez; Carrera, M.; Rocío A.; Navarro, Miguel; Koob, George F.; & Weiss, Friedbert. (1997, June 27). Activation of corticotropin-releasing factor in the limbic system during cannabinoid withdrawal. *Science, 276,* 2050–2054.

De Jongh, A.; Muris, P.; Ter Horst, G.; & Duyx, M. P. M. A. (1995). Acquisition and maintenance of dental anxiety: The role of conditioning experiences and cognitive factors. *Behavior Research and Therapy, 33,* 205–210.

DeLisi, Richard, & Staudt, Joanne. (1980). Individual differences in college students' performance on formal operations tasks. *Journal of Applied Developmental Psychology, 1,* 163–174.

Dell, Paul F. (2001). Why the diagnostic criteria for dissociative identity disorder should be changed. *Journal of Trauma and Dissociation, 2,* 7–37.

DeLoache, Judy S. (1995). Early symbol understanding and use. In Douglas L. Medin (Ed.), *The psychology of learning and motivation: Advances in research and theory* (Vol. 33). New York: Academic Press.

DeLongis, Anita; Coyne, James C.; Dakof, C.; Folkman, Susan; & Lazarus, Richard S. (1982). Relationship of daily hassles, uplifts, and major life events to health status. *Health Psychology, 1,* 119–136.

DeLongis, Anita; Folkman, Susan; & Lazarus, Richard S. (1988). The impact of stress on health and mood: Psychological and social resources as mediators. *Journal of Personality and Social Psychology, 54,* 486–495.

Delprato, Dennis J., & Midgley, Bryan D. (1992). Some fundamentals of B. F. Skinner's behaviorism. *American Psychologist, 47,* 1507–1520.

Dement, William C. (1992). The proper use of sleeping pills in the primary care setting. *Journal of Clinical Psychiatry, 53,* 50–58.

Dement, William C., & Pelayo, Rafael. (1997). Public health impact and treatment of insomnia. *European Psychiatry, 12,* 31s–39s.

DeNelsky, Garland Y. (1996). The case against prescription privileges for psychologists. *American Psychologist, 51,* 207–212.

DePaulo, Bella. (1992). Nonverbal behavior and self-presentation. *Psychological Bulletin, 111,* 203–243.

de Rivera, Joseph. (2000). Understanding persons who repudiate memories recovered in therapy. *Professional Psychology: Research and Practice, 31,* 378–386.

Desforges, Donna M.; Lord, Charles G.; Ramsey, Shawna L.; Mason, Julie A.; Van Leeuwen, Marilyn D.; West, Sylvia C.; & Lepper, Mark R. (1991). Effects of structured cooperative contact on changing negative attitudes toward stigmatized social groups. *Journal of Personality and Social Psychology, 60,* 531–544.

De Silva, Padmal, & Rachman, Stanley. (1992). *Obsessive-compulsive disorder: The facts.* Oxford, England: Oxford University Press.

Deutsch, Morton, & Gerard, Harold B. (1955). A study of normative and informational social influence upon individual judgment. *Journal of Abnormal and Social Psychology, 51,* 629–636.

DeValois, Russell L., & DeValois, Karen K. (1975). Neural coding of color. In E. C. Carterette & M. P. Friedman (Eds.), *Handbook of perception* (Vol. 5). New York: Academic Press.

Devanand, Davangere P.; Dwork, Andrew J.; Hutchinson, Edward R.; Bolwig, Tom G.; & Sackeim, Harold A. (1994). Does ECT alter brain structure? *American Journal of Psychiatry, 151,* 957–970.

Devanand, Davangere P.; Michaels-Marston, Kristin S.; Liu, Xinhua; Pelton, Gregory H.; Padilla, Margarita; & others. (2000). Olfactory deficits in patients with mild cognitive impairment predict Alzheimer's disease at follow-up. *American Journal of Psychiatry, 157,* 1399–1405.

Devine, Patricia G., & Monteith, Margo J. (1993). The role of discrepancy-associated affect in prejudice reduction. In Diane M. Mackie & David L. Hamilton (Eds.), *Affect, cognition, and stereotyping: Interactive processes in group perception.* San Diego, CA: Academic Press.

Devine, Patricia G.; Monteith, Margo J.; Zuwerink, Julia R.; & Elliot, Andrew J. (1991). Prejudice with and without compunction. *Journal of Personality and Social Psychology, 60,* 817–830.

Devine, Patricia A.; Plant, E. Ashby; & Buswell, Brenda N. (2000). Breaking the prejudice habit. In Stuart Oskamp (Ed.), *Reducing prejudice and discrimination.* Mahwah, NJ: Erlbaum.

De Vos, George Alphonse. (1992). *Social cohesion and alienation: Minorities in the United States and Japan.* Boulder, CO: Westview Press.

De Vos, George Alphonse, & Wagatsuma, Hiroshi. (1967). *Japan's invisible race: Caste in culture and personality.* Berkeley and Los Angeles: University of California Press.

De Vries, J.; Strubbe, J.H.; Wildering, W.C.; Gorter J. A.; & Prins A. J. (1993). Patterns of body temperature during feeding in rats under varying ambient temperatures. *Physiology and Behavior, 53,* 229–235.

de Waal, Frans B. M. (1995, March). Bonobo sex and society. *Scientific American, 271,* 82–88.

de Waal, Frans B. M., & Lanting, Frans. (1998). *Bonobo: The forgotten ape.* Berkeley: University of California Press.

Dewsbury, Donald A. (1998). Celebrating E. L. Thorndike a century after *Animal Intelligence. American Psychologist, 53,* 1121–1124.

Diamond, Lisa M. (1998). Development of sexual orientation among adolescent and young adult women. *Developmental Psychology, 34,* 1085–1095.

Diamond, Marian Cleeves. (1988). *Enriching heredity: The impact of environment on the anatomy of the brain.* New York: Free Press.

Diamond, Marian Cleeves; Scheibel, Arnold B.; Murphy, Greer M.; & Harvey, Thomas. (1985). On the brain of a scientist: Albert Einstein. *Experimental Neurology, 88,* 198–204.

Dickinson, Anthony. (1997). Bolles's psychological syllogism. In Mark E. Bouton & Michael S. Fanselow (Eds.), *Learning, motivation, and cognition: The functional behaviorism of Robert C. Bolles.* Washington, DC: American Psychological Association.

Dickinson, Anthony, & Balleine, Bernard W. (2000). Causal cognition and goal-directed action. In Cecilia Heyes & Ludwig Huber (Eds.), *The evolution of cognition.* Cambridge, MA: MIT Press.

Dictionary of occupational titles. (1991). Washington, DC: U.S. Government Printing Office.

Diener, Ed. (1980). Deindividuation: The absence of self-awareness and self-regulation in group members. In Paul B. Paulus (Ed.), *Psychology of group influence.* Hillsdale, NJ: Erlbaum.

Diener, Ed; Larsen, Randy J.; Levine, Steven; & Emmons, Robert A. (1985). Intensity and frequency: Dimensions underlying positive and negative affect. *Journal of Personality and Social Psychology, 48,* 1253–1265.

Dies, Robert R. (1993). Research on group psychotherapy: Overview and clinical applications. In Anne Alonso & Hillel I. Swiller (Eds.), *Group therapy in clinical practice.* Washington, DC: American Psychiatric Press.

Dillard, James Price. (1991). The current status of research on sequential-request compliance techniques. *Personality and Social Psychology Bulletin, 17,* 283–288.

Dillbeck, Michael C., & Orme-Johnson, David W. (1987). Physiological differences between transcendental meditation and rest. *American Psychologist, 42,* 879–881.

Dinges, David F. (1989). Napping patterns and effects in human adults. In David F. Dinges & Roger J. Broughton (Eds.), *Sleep and alertness: Chronobiological, behavioral, and medical aspects of napping.* New York: Raven Press.

Dinges, David F. (1990). Are you awake? Cognitive performance and reverie during the hypnopompic state. In Richard R. Bootzin, John F. Kihlstrom, & Daniel L. Schacter (Eds.), *Sleep and cognition.* Washington, DC: American Psychological Association.

Dinsmoor, James A. (1992). Setting the record straight: The social views of B. F. Skinner. *American Psychologist, 47,* 1454–1463.

Dixon, John F., & Hokin, Lowell E. (1998, July 7). Lithium acutely inhibits and chronically up-regulates and stabilizes glutamate by presynaptic nerve endings in mouse cerebral cortex. *Proceedings of the National Academy of Sciences, USA, 95,* 8363–8368.

Dohrenwend, Bruce P.; Raphael, Karen G.; Schwartz, Sharon; Stueve, Ann; & Skodol, Andrew. (1993). The structured event probe and narrative rating method for measuring stressful life events. In Leo Goldberger & Shlomo Breznitz (Eds.), *Handbook of stress: Theoretical and clinical aspects* (2nd ed.). New York: Free Press.

Domhoff, G. William. (1993). The repetition of dreams and dream elements: A possible clue to a function of dreams. In Alan Moffitt, Milton Kramer, & Robert Hoffman (Eds.), *The functions of dreaming.* Albany: State University of New York Press.

Domhoff, G. William. (1996). *Finding meaning in dreams: A quantitative approach.* New York and London: Plenum Press.

Domhoff, G. William. (1999). Drawing theoretical implications from descriptive empirical findings on dream content. *Dreaming, 9,* 201–210.

Domjan, Michael, & Purdy, Jesse E. (1995). Animal research in psychology: More than meets the eye of the general psychology student. *American Psychologist, 50,* 496–503.

Dornbusch, Sanford M.; Glasgow, Kristan L.; & Lin, I-Chun. (1996). The social structure of schooling. *Annual Review of Psychology, 47,* 401–429.

Dornbusch, Sanford M.; Ritter, Philip L.; Leiderman, P. Herbert; Roberts, Donald F.; & Fraleigh, Michael J. (1987). The relation of parenting style to adolescent school performance. *Child Development, 58,* 1244–1257.

Doty, Richard L. (2001). Olfaction. *Annual Review of Psychology, 52,* 423–452.

Dovidio, John F. (1984). Helping behavior and altruism: An empirical and conceptual overview. *Advances in Experimental Social Psychology, 17,* 361–427.

Dovidio, John F.; Piliavin, Jane A.; Gaertner, Samuel L.; Schroeder, David A.; & Clark, Russell D., III. (1991). The arousal: Cost-reward model and the process of intervention: A review of the evidence. In Margaret S. Clark

(Ed.), *Prosocial behavior: Vol. 12. Review of personality and social psychology.* Newbury Park, CA: Sage.

Downing, Paul E.; Jiang, Yuhong; Shuman, Miles; & Kanwisher, Nancy. (2001, September 28). A cortical area selective for visual processing of the human body. *Science, 293,* 2470–2473.

DSM-IV-TR. (2000). *Diagnostic and Statistical Manual of Mental Disorders* (4th ed., Text Revision). Washington, DC: American Psychiatric Association.

Duclos, Sandra E.; Laird, James D.; Schneider, Eric; Sexter, Melissa; Stern, Lisa; & Van Lighten, Lisa. (1989) Emotion-specific effects of facial expressions and postures on emotional experience. *Journal of Personality and Social Psychology, 51,* 100–108.

Duncan, David F.; Donnelly, William J.; & Nicholson, Thomas. (1992). Belief in the paranormal and religious belief among American college students. *Psychological Reports, 70,* 15–18.

Duncker, Karl. (1929/1967). Induced motion. In Willis D. Ellis (Ed.), *Source book of Gestalt psychology.* New York: Humanities Press.

Duncker, Karl. (1945). On problem solving. *Psychological Monographs, 58*(Whole No. 270).

Dunkel-Schetter, Christine; Feinstein, Lawrence G.; Taylor, Shelley E.; & Falke, Roberta L. (1992). Patterns of coping with cancer. *Health Psychology, 11,* 79–87.

Dunning, David; Leuenberger, Ann; & Sherman, David A. (1995). A new look at motivated inference: Are self-serving theories of success a product of motivational forces? *Journal of Personality and Social Psychology, 69,* 58–68.

Dura, Jason R.; Stukenberg, Karl W.; & Kiecolt-Glaser, Janice K. (1990). Chronic stress and depressive disorders in older adults. *Journal of Abnormal Psychology, 99,* 284–290.

Dusenberry, David B. (1992). *Sensory ecology: How organisms acquire and respond to information.* New York: Freeman.

Eagle, Morris N. (1959). The effects of subliminal stimuli of aggressive content upon conscious cognition. *Journal of Personality, 23,* 48–52.

Eagle, Morris N., & Wolitzky, David L. (1992). Psychoanalytic theories of psychotherapy. In Donald K. Freedheim (Ed.), *History of psychotherapy: A century of change.* Washington, DC: American Psychological Association.

Eagly, Alice H. (1992). Uneven progress: Social psychology and the study of attitudes. *Journal of Personality and Social Psychology, 63,* 693–710.

Eagly, Alice H. (1995a). The science and politics of comparing women and men. *American Psychologist, 50,* 145–158.

Eagly, Alice H. (1995b). Reflections on the commenters' views. *American Psychologist, 50,* 169–171.

Eagly, Alice H.; Ashmore, Richard. D.; Makhijani, Mona G.; & Longo, Laura C. (1991). What is beautiful is good, but . . . : A meta-analytic review of research on the physical attractiveness stereotype. *Psychological Bulletin, 110,* 109–128.

Eagly, Alice H., & Chaiken, Shelly. (1993). *The psychology of attitudes.* Fort Worth, TX: Harcourt Brace.

Eagly, Alice H., & Chaiken, Shelly. (1998). Attitude structure and function. In Daniel T. Gilbert, Susan T. Fiske, & Gardner Lindzey (Eds.), *The handbook of social psychology* (4th ed., Vol. 1). New York: McGraw-Hill.

Early, Charles E.; Bringmann, Wolfgang G.; & Bringmann, Michael W. (1997). G. Stanley Hall and American psychology. In Wolfgang G. Bringmann, Helmut E. Lück, Rudolf Miller, & Charles E. Early (Eds.), *A pictorial history of psychology.* Chicago: Quintessence.

Eastman, Kenneth K. (1994). In the eyes of the beholder: An attributional approach to ingratiation and organizational citizenship behavior. *Academy of Management Journal, 37,* 1379–1391.

Ebbinghaus, Hermann. (1885/1987). *Memory: A contribution to experimental psychology* (Henry A. Ruger & Clara E. Bussenius, Trans.). New York: Dover.

Eckensberger, Lutz H. (1994). Moral development and its measurement across cultures. In Walter J. Lonner & Roy Malpass (Eds.), *Psychology and culture.* Boston: Allyn & Bacon.

Edelman, Lauren B., Erlanger, Howard S., & Lande, John. (1993). Informal dispute resolution: The transformation of civil rights in the workplace. *Law & Society Review, 27,* 497–534.

Edwards, Anthony G. P., & Armitage, Peter. (1992). An experiment to test the discriminating ability of graphologists. *Personality and Individual Differences, 13,* 69–74.

Edwards, Randall. (1995a, February). Future demands culturally diverse education. *APA Monitor,* 43.

Edwards, Randall. (1995b, September). Psychologists foster the new definition of family. *APA Monitor, 26,* 38.

Egan, Gerard. (1994). *The skilled helper: A problem-management approach to helping* (5th ed.). Pacific Grove, CA: Brooks/Cole.

Egan, Susan K., & Perry, David G. (2001). Gender identity: A multidimensional analysis with implications for psychosocial adjustment. *Developmental Psychology, 37,* 451–463.

Ehlers, Anke, & Breuer, Peter. (1992). Increased cardiac awareness in panic disorder. *Journal of Abnormal Psychology, 101,* 371–382.

Eibl-Eibesfeldt, Irenäus. (1973). The expressive behavior of the deaf-and-blind-born. In M. von Cranach & I. Vine (Eds.), *Social communication and movement.* New York: Academic Press.

Eich, Eric. (1980). The cue-dependent nature of state-dependent retrieval. *Memory & Cognition, 8,* 157–173.

Eich, Eric. (1989). Theoretical issues in state-dependent memory. In Henry L. Roediger, III & Fergus I. M. Craik (Eds.), *Varieties of memory and consciousness: Essays in honor of Endel Tulving.* Hillsdale, NJ: Erlbaum.

Eich, Eric. (1995). Searching for mood dependent memory. *Psychological Science, 6,* 67–75.

Eich, Eric, & Macaulay, Dawn. (2000). Fundamental factors in mood-dependent memory. In Joseph P. Forgas (Ed.), *Feeling and thinking: The role of affect in social cognition.* New York: Cambridge University Press.

Eich, Eric; Macaulay, Dawn; & Lam, Raymond W. (1997). Mania, depression, and mood dependent memory. *Cognition & Emotion, 11,* 607–618.

Eisenberg, Nancy. (1991). Meta-analytic contributions to the literature on prosocial behavior. *Personality and Social Psychology Bulletin, 17,* 273–284.

Eisenberger, Robert; Armeli, Stephen; & Pretz, Jean. (1998). Can the promise of reward increase creativity? *Journal of Personality and Social Psychology, 74,* 704–714.

Eisenberger, Robert, & Cameron, Judy. (1996). Detrimental effects of reward: Reality or myth? *American Psychologist, 51,* 1153–1166.

Ekman, Paul. (1980). *The face of man.* New York: Garland.

Ekman, Paul. (1982). *Emotion in the human face* (2nd ed.). New York: Cambridge University Press.

Ekman, Paul. (1992a). Are there basic emotions? *Psychological Review, 99,* 550–553.

Ekman, Paul. (1992b). Facial expressions of emotion: New findings, new questions. *Psychological Science, 3,* 34–38.

Ekman, Paul. (1993). Facial expression and emotion. *American Psychologist, 48,* 384–392.

Ekman, Paul. (1994a). Are there basic emotions? In Paul Ekman & Richard J. Davidson (Eds.), *The nature of emotion: Fundamental questions.* New York: Oxford University Press.

Ekman, Paul. (1994b). Strong evidence for universals in facial expressions: A reply to Russell's mistaken critique. *Psychological Bulletin, 115,* 268–287.

Ekman, Paul. (1998). Afterword. In Darwin, Charles (1872/1998), *The expression of the emotions in man and animals.* New York: Oxford University Press.

Ekman, Paul, & Davidson, Richard J. (1993). Voluntary smiling changes regional brain activity. *Psychological Science, 4,* 342–345.

Ekman, Paul, & Friesen, Wallace V. (1978). *Facial action coding system: A technique for the measurement of facial movement.* Palo Alto, CA: Consulting Psychologists Press.

Ekman, Paul; Friesen, Wallace V.; O'Sullivan, Maureen; Chan, Anthony; Diacoyanni-Tarlatzis, Irene; Heider, Karl; & others. (1987). Universals and cultural differences in the judgments of facial expressions of emotion. *Journal of Personality and Social Psychology, 53,* 712–717.

Ekman, Paul; O'Sullivan, Maureen; & Frank, Mark G. (1999). A few can catch a liar. *Psychological Science, 10,* 263–266.

Elkin, Irene; Shea, M. Tracie; Watkins, John T.; Imber, Stanley D.; Sotsky, Stuart M.; Collins, Joseph F.; & others. (1989). National Institute of Mental Health Treatment of Depression Collaborative Research Program: General effectiveness of treatments. *Archives of General Psychiatry, 46,* 971–982.

Elliott, Robert, & Greenberg, Leslie S. (2002). Process—experiential psychotherapy. In David J. Cain & Julius Seeman (Eds.), *Humanistic psychotherapies: Handbook of research and practice.* Washington, DC: American Psychological Association.

Ellis, Albert. (1991). *Reason and emotion in psychotherapy.* New York: Carol.

Ellis, Albert. (1993). Reflections on rational-emotive therapy. *Journal of Consulting and Clinical Psychology, 61,* 199–201.

Ellis, Albert, & Bernard, Michael E. (1985). What is rational-emotive therapy (RET)? In Albert Ellis & Michael E. Bernard (Eds.), *Clinical applications of rational-emotive therapy.* New York: Plenum Press.

Ellis, Albert, & Harper, Robert A. (1975). *A new guide to rational living.* Hollywood, CA: Wilshire Book Company.

Ellman, Steven J.; Spielman, Arthur J.; Luck, Dana; Steiner, Solomon S.; & Halperin, Ronnie. (1991). REM deprivation: A review. In Steven J. Ellman & John S. Antrobus (Eds.), *The mind in sleep: Psychology and psychophysiology* (2nd ed.). New York: Wiley.

Elmquist, Joel K.; Maratos-Flier, Eleftheria; Saper, Clifford B.; & Flier, Jeffrey S. (1998). Unraveling the central nervous system pathways underlying responses to leptin. *Nature Neuroscience, 1*(6), 445–450.

EMDR Institute. (2001). Overview and general description of EMDR. Retrieved October 15, 2001, from http://www.emdr.com/general.htm

Emmelkamp, Paul M. G. (1994). Behavior therapy with adults. In Allen E. Bergin & Sol L. Garfield (Eds.), *Handbook of psychotherapy and behavior change* (4th ed.). New York: Wiley.

Emmons, Robert, & King, Laura. (1988). Conflict among personal strivings: Immediate and long-term implications for psychological and physical well-being. *Journal of Personality and Social Psychology, 54,* 1040–1048.

Empson, Jacob. (1993). *Sleep and dreaming* (2nd ed.). New York: Harvester Wheatsheaf.

Engel, Stephen A. (1999). Using neuroimaging to measure mental representations: Finding color-opponent neurons in visual cortex. *Current Directions in Psychological Science, 8,* 23–27.

English, Horace B. (1929). Three cases of the "conditioned fear response." *Journal of Abnormal and Social Psychology, 24,* 221–225.

Epley, Nicholas; Savitsky, Kenneth; & Kachelski, Robert A. (1999, September/October). What every skeptic should know about subliminal persuasion. *Skeptical Inquirer, 23*(5), 40–45, 58.

Epstein, Leonard H., & Jennings, J. Richard. (1985). Smoking, stress, cardiovascular reactivity, and coronary heart disease. In Karen A. Matthews & others (Eds.), *Handbook of stress, reactivity, and cardiovascular disease.* New York: Wiley.

Epstein, Mark. (1995). *Thoughts without a thinker: Psychotherapy from a Buddhist perspective.* New York: Basic Books.

Epstein, Russell, & Kanwisher, Nancy. (1998). A cortical representation of the local visual environment. *Nature, 392,* 598–601.

Epstein, Seymour. (1982). Conflict and stress. In Leo Goldberger & Shlomo Breznitz (Eds.), *Handbook of stress: Theoretical and clinical aspects.* New York: Free Press.

Erdelyi, Matthew Hugh. (1993). Repression: The mechanism and the defense. In Daniel M. Wegner & James W. Pennebaker (Eds.), *Handbook of mental control.* Englewood Cliffs, NJ: Prentice-Hall.

Ericsson, K. Anders, & Kintsch, Walter. (1995). Long-term working memory. *Psychological Review, 102,* 211–245.

Erikson, Erik H. (1964a). *Childhood and society* (Rev. ed.). New York: Norton.

Erikson, Erik H. (1964b). *Insight and responsibility.* New York: Norton.

Erikson, Erik H. (1968). *Identity: Youth and crisis.* New York: Norton.

Erikson, Erik H. (1982). *The life cycle completed: A review.* New York: Norton.

Erikson, Erik H.; Erikson, Joan M.; & Kivnick, Helen Q. (1986). *Vital involvement in old age: The experience of old age in our time.* New York: Norton.

Eriksson, Cynthia B.; Vande Kemp, Hendrika; & others. (2001). Trauma exposure and PTSD symptoms in international relief and development personnel. *Journal of Traumatic Stress, 14,* 205–219.

Eriksson, Peter S.; Perfilieva, Ekaterina; Björk-Eriksson, Thomas; Alborn, Ann-Marie; Nordborg, Claes; Peterson, Daniel A.; & Gage, Fred A. (1998). Neurogenesis in the adult hippocampus. *Nature Medicine, 4,* 1313–1317.

Eronen, Markku; Angermeyer, Matthias C.; & Schulze, Beate. (1998). The psychiatric epidemiology of violent behaviour. *Social Psychiatry and Psychiatric Epidemiology, 33* (Suppl. 1), S13–S23.

Esch, Harald E.; Zhang, Shaowu; Srinivasan, Mandyan V.; & Tautz, Juergen. (2001). Honeybee dances communicate distances measured by optic flow. *Nature, 411,* 581–583.

Esses, Victoria M.; Haddock, Geoffrey; & Zanna, Mark P. (1993). Values, stereotypes, and emotions as determinants of intergroup attitudes. In Diane M. Mackie & David L. Hamilton (Eds.), *Affect, cognition, and stereotyping: Interactive processes in group perception.* San Diego, CA: Academic Press.

Estes, William K., & Skinner, B. F. (1941). Some quantitative properties of anxiety. *Journal of Experimental Psychology, 29,* 390–400.

Etscorn, Frank, & Stephens, Ronald. (1973). Establishment of conditioned taste aversions with a 24-hour CS-US interval. *Physiological Psychology, 1,* 251–253.

Evans, Frederick J., & Orne, Martin T. (1971). The disappearing hypnotist: The use of simulating subjects to evaluate how subjects perceive experimental procedures. *International Journal of Clinical and Experimental Hypnosis, 19,* 277–296.

Evans, Gary W.; Bullinger, Monika; & Hygge, Staffan. (1998). Chronic noise exposure and physiological response: A prospective study of children living under environmental stress. *Psychological Science, 9,* 75–77.

Evans, Rand B. (1991). E. B. Titchener on scientific psychology and technology. In Gregory A. Kimble, Michael Wertheimer, & Charlotte White (Eds.), *Portraits of pioneers in psychology* (Vol. 1). Washington, DC: American Psychological Association.

Evans, Rand B. (1999a, December). Psychology continues to redefine itself. *APA Monitor, 30*(11), 15.

Evans, Rand B. (1999b, December). Behaviorism: The rise and fall of a discipline. *APA Monitor, 30*(11), 19.

Evans, Rand B. (1999c, December). Cognitive psychology sees a return to power. *APA Monitor, 30*(11), 20.

Evans, Rand B., & Rilling, Mark. (2000). How the challenge of explaining learning influenced the origins and development of John B. Watson's behaviorism. *American Journal of Psychology, 113,* 275–301.

Exner, John E., Jr. (1993). *The Rorschach: A comprehensive system* (3rd ed., Vol. 1). New York: Wiley.

Eysenck, Hans J. (1952). The effects of psychotherapy: An evaluation. *Journal of Consulting Psychology, 16,* 319–324.

Eysenck, Hans J. (1982). *Personality, genetics, and behavior.* New York: Praeger.

Eysenck, Hans J. (1985). *Decline and fall of the Freudian empire.* New York: Penguin.

Eysenck, Hans J. (1990). Biological dimensions of personality. In Lawrence A. Pervin (Ed.), *Handbook of personality: Theory and research.* New York: Guilford Press.

Eysenck, Hans J. (1994). The outcome problem in psychotherapy: What have we learned? *Behavior Research and Therapy, 32,* 447–495.

Eysenck, Hans J., & Eysenck, Sybil B. G. (1975). *Psychoticism as a dimension of personality.* London: Hodder & Stoughton.

Faedda, Gianni L.; Tondo, Leonardo; Teicher, Martin H.; Baldessarini, Ross J.; Gelbard, Harris A.; & Floris, Gianfranco F. (1993). Seasonal mood disorders: Patterns of seasonal recurrence in mania and depression. *Archives of General Psychiatry, 50,* 17–23.

Fagot, Beverly I., & Hagan, Richard. (1991). Observations of parent reactions to sex-stereotyped behaviors: Age and sex effects. *Child Development, 62,* 617–628.

Fagot, Beverly I.; Leinbach, Mary D.; & O'Boyle, Cherie. (1992). Gender labeling, gender stereotyping, and parenting behaviors. *Developmental Psychology, 28,* 225–230.

Fairburn, Christopher G. (1995). Physiology of anorexia nervosa. In Kelly D. Brownell & Christopher G. Fairburn (Eds.), *Eating disorders and obesity: A comprehensive handbook.* New York: Guilford Press.

Fancher, Raymond E. (1973). *Psychoanalytic psychology: The development of Freud's thought.* New York: Norton.

Fancher, Raymond E. (1996). *Pioneers of psychology* (3rd ed.). New York: Norton.

Fantz, Robert L. (1963). Pattern vision in newborn infants. *Science, 140,* 296–297.

Farah, Martha J. (1995). The neural bases of mental imagery. In Michael S. Gazzaniga (Ed.), *The cognitive neurosciences.* Cambridge, MA: MIT Press.

Farber, Ilya B., & Churchland, Patricia S. (1995). Consciousness and the neurosciences: Philosophical and theoretical issues. In Michael S. Gazzaniga (Ed.), *The cognitive neurosciences.* Cambridge, MA: MIT Press.

Farberman, Rhea S. (1999). What the media needs from news sources. In Lita Linzer Schwartz (Ed.), *Psychology and the media: A second look.* Washington, DC: American Psychological Association.

Farwell, Lawrence A., & Donchin, Emanuel. (1991). The truth will out: Interrogative polygraphy ("lie detection") with event-related brain potentials. *Psychophysiology, 28,* 531–547.

Farwell, Lawrence A.; & Smith, Sharon S. (2001). Using Brain MERMER testing to detect concealed knowledge despite efforts to conceal. *Journal of Forensic Sciences, 46,* 1–9.

Fastovsky, Natasha; Teitelbaum, Alexander; & others. (2000). The Jerusalem syndrome. *Psychiatric Services, 51,* 1052.

Fava, Maurizio, & Kaji, Junko. (1994). Continuation and maintenance treatments of major depressive disorder. *Psychiatric Annals, 24,* 281–290.

Fawcett, Jan. (1994). Antidepressants: Partial response in chronic depression. *British Journal of Psychiatry, 165*(Suppl. 26), 37–41.

Feeney, Brooke C., & Kirkpatrick, Lee A. (1996). Effects of adult attachment and presence of romantic partners on physiological responses to stress. *Journal of Personality and Social Psychology, 70,* 255–270.

Feingold, Alan. (1992). Good-looking people are not what we think. *Psychological Bulletin, 111,* 304–341.

Feingold, Alan. (1994). Gender differences in personality: A meta-analysis. *Psychological Bulletin, 116,* 429–456.

Feldman, Larry B., & Powell, Sandra L. (1992). Integrating therapeutic modalities. In John C. Norcross & Marvin R. Goldfried (Eds.), *Handbook of psychotherapy integration.* New York: Basic Books.

Feldman Barrett, Lisa; Lane, Richard D.; Sechrest, Lee; & Schwartz, Gary E. (2000). Sex differences in emotional awareness. *Personality and Social Psychology Bulletin, 26,* 1027–1035.

Feldman Barrett, Lisa, & Russell, James A. (1999). The structure of current affect: Controversies and emerging consensus. *Current Directions in Psychological Science, 8,* 10–14.

Fenwick, Peter. (1987). Meditation and the EEG. In Michael A. West (Ed.), *The psychology of meditation.* New York: Oxford University Press.

Fernald, Ann. (1985). Four-month-old infants prefer to listen to motherese. *Infant Behavior and Development, 8,* 181–182.

Fernandez, E. (1986). A classification system of cognitive coping strategies for pain. *Pain, 26,* 141–151.

Feske, Ulrike, & Goldstein, Alan J. (1997). Eye movement desensitization and reprocessing treatment for panic disorder: A controlled outcome and partial dismantling study. *Journal of Clinical and Consulting Psychology, 65,* 1026–1035.

Festinger, Leon. (1957). *A theory of cognitive dissonance.* Stanford, CA: Stanford University Press.

Festinger, Leon. (1962). Cognitive dissonance. *Scientific American, 207,* 93–99. (Reprinted in *Contemporary psychology: Readings from Scientific American,* 1971, San Francisco: Freeman).

Field, Tiffany. (1991). Quality infant day-care and grade school behavior and performance. *Child Development, 62,* 863–870.

Field, Tiffany. (1996). Attachment and separation in young children. *Annual Review of Psychology, 47,* 541–561.

Field, Tiffany; Masi, Wendy; Goldstein, Sheri.; Perry, Susan; & Parl, Silke. (1988). Infant day-care facilitates preschool behavior. *Early Childhood Research Quarterly, 3,* 341–359.

Field, Tiffany M.; Woodson, Robert; Greenberg, Reena; & Cohen, Debra. (1982). Discrimination and imitation of facial expressions by neonates. *Science, 218,* 179–182.

Fieldhouse, Paul. (1986). *Food and nutrition: Customs and culture.* London: Croom Helm.

Fields, Howard L., & Levine, Jon D. (1984). Placebo analgesia: A role for endorphins. *Trends in Neuroscience, 7,* 271–273.

Fields, Jason. (2001). *American's families and living arrangements: March 2000* (Current Population Reports, P20–537). Washington, DC: U.S. Government Printing Office. PDF of report retrieved February 13, 2002, from http://www.census.gov/prod/2001pubs/p20-537.pdf

Fischer, Kurt W., & Hencke, Rebecca W. (1996). Infants' construction of actions in context: Piaget's contribution to research on early development. *Psychological Science, 7,* 204–210.

Fisher, Carrie. (2001). In her own words: Carrie Fisher interviewed by Robert Epstein, Ph.D. *Psychology Today, 34,* 36–37.

Fisher, Celia B., & Fyrberg, Denise. (1994). Participant partners: College students weigh the costs and benefits of deceptive research. *American Psychologist, 49,* 417–427.

Fisher, Kathleen. (1986, March). Animal research: Few alternatives seen for behavioral studies. *APA Monitor,* 16–17.

Fisher, Seymour, & Greenberg, Roger. (1996). *Freud scientifically appraised.* New York: Wiley.

Fisher, William A.; Fisher, Jeffrey D.; & Rye, Barbara J. (1995). Understanding and promoting AIDS-preventative behavior: Insights from the theory of reasoned action. *Health Psychology, 14*(3), 255–264.

Fishman, C. (2000). Moving toward a balanced work life. *Workforce, 79,* 38–42.

Fishman, Joshua A. (1960/1974). A systematization of the Whorfian hypothesis. In John W. Berry & P. R. Dasen (Eds.), *Culture and cognition: Readings in cross-cultural psychology.* London: Methuen.

Fiske, Susan T. (1993). Social cognition and perception. *Annual Review of Psychology, 44,* 155–194.

Fiske, Susan T. (1998). Stereotyping, prejudice, and discrimination. In Daniel T. Gilbert, Susan T. Fiske, & Gardner Lindzey (Eds.), *The handbook of social psychology* (4th ed., Vol. 2). New York: McGraw-Hill.

Fiske, Susan T., & Neuberg, Steven L. (1990). A continuum of impression formation, from category-based to individuating processes: Influences of information and motivation on attention and interpretation. In Mark P. Zanna (Ed.), *Advances in experimental social psychology* (Vol. 23). San Diego, CA: Academic Press/Harcourt.

Fiske, Susan T., & Ruscher, Janet B. (1993). Negative interdependence and prejudice: Whence the affect? In Diane M. Mackie & David L. Hamilton (Eds.), *Affect, cognition, and stereotyping: Interactive processes in group perception.* San Diego, CA: Academic Press.

Fiske, Susan T., & Taylor, Shelley E. (1991). *Social cognition* (2nd ed.). New York: McGraw-Hill.

Fivush, Robyn; Brotman, Melissa A.; Buckner, Janine P.; & Goodman, Sherryl H. (2000). Gender differences in parent-child emotion narratives. *Sex Roles, 42,* 233–253.

Flack, William F.; Laird, James D.; & Cavallaro, Lorraine A. (1999). Separate and combined effects of facial expressions and bodily postures on emotional feelings. *European Journal of Social Psychology, 29,* 203–217.

Flaks, David K.; Ficher, Ilda; Masterpasqua, Frank; & Joseph, Gregory. (1995). Lesbians choosing motherhood: A comparative study of lesbian and heterosexual parents and their children. *Developmental Psychology, 31,* 105–114.

Flaten, Magne Arve. (2001). Personal Communication, August 24, 2001.

Flaten, Magne Arve, & Blumenthal, Terry D. (1999). Caffeine-associated stimuli elicit conditioned responses: An experimental model of the placebo effect. *Psychopharmacology, 145,* 105–112.

Flavell, John H. (1996). Piaget's legacy. *Psychological Science, 7,* 200–203.

Fleishman, Edwin A., & Harris, Edwin F. (1962). Patterns of leadership behavior related to employee grievances and turnover. *Personnel Psychology, 15,* 43–56.

Flynn, James R. (1994). IQ gains over time. In Robert J. Sternberg (Ed.), *Encyclopedia of human intelligence.* New York: Macmillan.

Flynn, James R. (1999). Searching for justice: The discovery of IQ gains over time. *American Psychologist, 54,* 5–20.

Foa, Edna B., & Meadows, Elizabeth A. (1997). Psychosocial treatments for posttraumatic stress disorder: A critical review. *Annual Review of Psychology, 48,* 449–480.

Foertsch, Julie, & Gernsbacher, Morton Ann. (1997). In search of gender neutrality: Is singular *they* a cognitively efficient substitute for generic *he? Psychological Science, 8,* 106–111.

Folkard, Simon; Arendt, Josephine; & Clark, Mark. (1993). Can melatonin improve shift workers' tolerance of the night shift? Some preliminary findings. *Chronobiology International, 10,* 315–320.

Folkman, Susan, & Lazarus, Richard S. (1991). Coping and emotion. In Alan Monat & Richard S. Lazarus (Eds.), *Stress and coping: An anthology* (3rd ed.). New York: Columbia University Press.

"Forensic neuroscience on trial." (2001). *Nature Neuroscience, 4,* 1.

Foulkes, David. (1993). Data constraints on theorizing about dream function. In Alan Moffitt, Milton Kramer, & Robert Hoffman (Eds.), *The functions of dreaming.* Albany: State University of New York Press.

Foulkes, David. (1997). A contemporary neurobiology of dreaming? *Sleep Research Society Bulletin, 3*(1), 2–4.

Foulks, Edward F. (1991). Transcultural psychiatry and normal behavior. In Daniel Offer & Melvin Sabshin (Eds.), *The diversity of normal behavior: Further contributions to normatology.* New York: Basic Books.

Fowles, Don C. (1992). Schizophrenia: Diathesis-stress revisited. *Annual Review of Psychology, 43,* 303–336.

Fox, Michael J. (1998, December 2). Interview with Todd Gold, *People Magazine.* <http://www.pathfinder.com/people/weekly/ features/interview.html>

Fox, Nathan A.; Kimmerly, Nancy L.; & Schafer, William D. (1991). Attachment to mother/Attachment to father: A meta-analysis. *Child Development, 62,* 210–225.

Fox, William M. (1982). Why we should abandon Maslow's need hierarchy theory. *Journal of Humanistic Education and Development, 21,* 29–32.

Foxhall, Kathryn. (2000, January). Suddenly, a big impact on criminal justice. *APA Monitor on Psychology, 31,* 36–37.

Foxhall, Kathryn. (2001a, March). How psychopharmacology training is enhancing some psychology practices. *APA Monitor on Psychology, 32*(3), 50–52.

Foxhall, Kathryn. (2001b, May). New Mexico comes up on the inside. *APA Monitor on Psychology, 32*(5), 22–23.

Francis, Darlene; Diorio, Josie; Liu, Dong; & Meaney, Michael J. (1999). Nongenomic transmission across generations of maternal behavior and stress responses in the rat. *Science, 286,* 1155–1158.

Frank, Barney. (1996, February 4). Quoted in Claudia Dreifus: And then there was Frank. *New York Times Magazine,* pp. 22–25.

Frank, Ellen; Anderson, Barbara; Reynolds, Charles F., III; Ritenour, Angela; & Kupfer, David J. (1994). Life events and the research diagnostic criteria endogenous subtype: A confirmation of the distinction using the Bedford College methods. *Archives of General Psychiatry, 51,* 519–524.

Frank, Mark G., & Ekman, Paul. (1997). The ability to detect deceit generalizes across different types of high-stake lies. *Journal of Personality and Social Psychology, 72,* 1429–1439.

Frank, Mark G., & Stennett, Janine. (2001). The forced-choice paradigm and the perception of facial expressions of emotion. *Journal of Personality and Social Psychology, 80,* 75–85.

Frankel, Fred H. (1993). Adult reconstruction of childhood events in the multiple personality literature. *American Journal of Psychiatry, 150,* 954–958.

Frankenburg, Frances R. (1994). History of the development of antipsychotic medication. *Psychiatric Clinics of North America, 17,* 531–540.

Franz, Carol E.; McClelland, David C.; & Weinberger, Joel. (1991). Childhood antecedents of conventional social accomplishment in midlife adults: A 36-year prospective study. *Journal of Personality and Social Psychology, 60,* 586–595.

Frederickson, N. (1968). *Organization climates and administrative performance.* Princeton, NJ: Educational Testing Service.

Freeman, Lucy, & Strean, Herbert S. (1987). *Freud and women.* New York: Continuum.

Freeston, Mark H.; Ladouceur, Robert; Rhéaume, Josée; Letarte, Hélène; Gagnon, Fabien; & Thibodeau, Nicole. (1994). Self-report of obsessions and worry. *Behavior Research and Therapy, 32,* 29–36.

Freiberg, Peter. (1996, February). Answers are often closer than we think. *APA Monitor, 27,* 24–26.

French, Christopher C.; Fowler, Mandy; McCarthy, Katy; & Peers, Debbie. (1991, Winter). Belief in astrology: A test of the Barnum effect. *Skeptical Inquirer, 15,* 166–172.

Frenkel, Oded J., & Doob, Anthony N. (1976). Post-decision dissonance at the polling booth. *Canadian Journal of Behavioral Science, 8,* 347–350.

Freud, Anna. (1946). *The ego and mechanisms of defence* (Cecil Baines, Trans.). New York: International Universities Press.

Freud, Sigmund. (1900/1974). *The interpretation of dreams.* In James Strachey (Ed.), *The standard edition of the complete psychological works of Sigmund Freud* (Vols. 4 & 5). London: Hogarth Press.

Freud, Sigmund. (1904/1965). *The psychopathology of everyday life* (Alan Tyson, Trans. & James Strachey, Ed.). New York: Norton.

Freud, Sigmund. (1905/1975). *Three essays on the theory of sexuality* (James Strachey, Ed.). New York: Basic Books.

Freud, Sigmund. (1911/1989). *On dreams.* In Peter Gay (Ed.), *The Freud reader.* New York: Norton.

Freud, Sigmund. (1914/1948). On narcissism: An introduction. In Joan Riviere (Trans.), *Collected papers: Vol. 4. Papers on metapsychology and applied psychoanalysis.* London: Hogarth Press.

Freud, Sigmund. (1915a/1948). Repression. In Joan Riviere (Trans.), *Collected papers: Vol. 4. Papers on metapsychology and applied psychoanalysis.* London: Hogarth Press.

Freud, Sigmund. (1915b/1959). Analysis, terminable and interminable. In Joan Riviere (Trans.), *Collected papers: Vol. 5. Miscellaneous papers* (2nd ed.). London: Hogarth Press.

Freud, Sigmund. (1915c/1959). Libido theory. In Joan Riviere (Trans.), *Collected papers: Vol. 5. Miscellaneous papers* (2nd ed.). London: Hogarth Press.

Freud, Sigmund. (1916/1964). *Leonardo da Vinci and a memory of his childhood.* (James Strachey, Trans., in collaboration with Anna Freud). New York: Norton.

Freud, Sigmund. (1919/1989). *Totem and taboo: Some points of agreement between the mental lives of savages and neurotics* (James Strachey, Ed. & Trans., with a biographical introduction by Peter Gay). New York: Norton.

Freud, Sigmund. (1920/1961). *Beyond the pleasure principle* (James Strachey, Ed.). New York: Norton.

Freud, Sigmund. (1923/1962). *The ego and the id* (Joan Riviere, Trans., & James Strachey, Ed.). New York: Norton.

Freud, Sigmund. (1925/1989). Some psychical consequences of the anatomical distinction between the sexes. In Peter Gay (Ed.), *The Freud reader*. New York: Norton.

Freud, Sigmund. (1926/1947). *The question of lay analysis: An introduction to psychoanalysis* (Nancy Proctor-Gregg, Trans.). London: Imago.

Freud, Sigmund. (1930/1961). *Civilization and its discontents* (James Strachey, Ed. & Trans.). New York: Norton.

Freud, Sigmund. (1933). *New introductory lectures on psychoanalysis* (W. J. H. Sprott, Trans.). New York: Norton.

Freud, Sigmund. (1936). *The problem of anxiety* (Henry Alden Bunker, Trans.). New York: The Psychoanalytic Quarterly Press and Norton.

Freud, Sigmund. (1939/1967). *Moses and monotheism* (Katherine Jones, Trans.). New York: Vintage Books.

Freud, Sigmund. (1940/1949). *An outline of psychoanalysis* (James Strachey, Trans.). New York: Norton.

Friedland, Robert P.; Fritsch, Thomas; Smyth, Kathleen A.; Koss, Elisabeth; Lerner, Alan J.; Chen, Chien Hsiun; & others. (2001). Patients with Alzheimer's disease have reduced activities in mid-life compared with healthy control-group members. *Proceedings of the National Academy of Sciences, USA, 98*, 3440–3445.

Friedman, Howard S., & Booth-Kewley, Stephanie. (1987). The "disease-prone personality": A meta-analytic view of the construct. *American Psychologist, 42*, 539–555.

Friedman, Jeffrey M. (2000, April 6). Obesity in the new millenium. *Nature, 404*, 632–634.

Friedman, Jeffrey M.; & Halaas, Jeffrey L. (1998, October 22). Leptin and the regulation of body weight in mammals. *Nature, 395*, 763–770.

Friedman, Meyer, & Rosenman, Ray H. (1974). *Type A behavior and your heart*. New York: Knopf.

Friedrich, Frances J.; Egly, Robert; Rafal, Robert D.; & Beck, Diane. (1998). Spatial attention deficits in humans: A comparison of superior parietal and temporal-parietal junction lesions. *Neuropsychology, 12*, 193–207.

Friedrich, William N.; Fisher, Jennifer; Broughton, Daniel; Houston, Margaret; & Shafran, Constance R. (1998). Normative sexual behavior in children: A contemporary sample. *Pediatrics, 101*, 9–22.

Friend, Ronald; Rafferty, Yvonne; & Bramel, Dana. (1990). A puzzling misinterpretation of the Asch "conformity" study. *European Journal of Social Psychology, 20*, 29–44.

Friesen, Wallace V. (1972). *Cultural differences in facial expressions in a social situation: An experimental test of the concept of display rules.* Unpublished doctoral dissertation, University of California, San Francisco.

Frijda, Nico H. (1994). Varieties of affect: Emotions and episodes, moods, and sentiments. In Paul Ekman & Richard J. Davidson (Eds.), *The nature of emotion: Fundamental questions.* New York: Oxford University Press.

Fritz, Curtis L.; Farver, Thomas B.; Hart, Lynette A.; & Kass, Philip H. (1996). Companion animals and the psychological health of Alzheimer patients' caregivers. *Psychological Reports, 78*(2), 467–481.

Fuente-Fernández, Raúl de la; Ruth, Thomas J.; Sossi, Vesna; & others. (2001, August 10). Expectation and dopamine release: Mechanism of the placebo effect in Parkinson's disease. *Science, 293*, 1164–1166.

Fuligni, Andrew J. (1998). Authority, autonomy, and parent-adolescent conflict and cohesion: A study of adolescents from Mexican, Chinese, Filipino, and European backgrounds. *Developmental Psychology, 34*, 782–792.

Fullerton, Carol S.; Ursano, Robert J.; Epstein, Richard S.; & others. (2001). Gender differences in posttraumatic stress disorder after motor vehicle accidents. *American Journal of Psychiatry, 158*, 1486–1491.

Fumeron F.; Betoulle D.; Aubert R.; & others. (2001). Association of a functional 5-HT transporter gene polymorphism with anorexia nervosa and food intake. *Molecular Psychiatry, 6*, 9–10.

Funder, David C. (2001). Personality. *Annual Review of Psychology, 52*, 197–221.

Furness, John B.; Kunze, Wolfgang A. A.; & Clerc, Nadine. (1999). Nutrient tasting and signaling mechanisms in the gut II. The intestine as a sensory organ: Neural, endocrine, and immune responses. *American Journal of Physiology, 277*, G922–G928.

Furnham, Adrian. (1991). Write and wrong: The validity of graphological analysis. In Kendrick Frazier (Ed.), *The hundredth monkey and other paradigms of the paranormal.* Buffalo, NY: Prometheus Books.

Gabrieli, John D. E. (1998). Cognitive neuroscience of human memory. *Annual Review of Psychology, 49*, 87–115.

Gabrieli, John D. E. (2001, February 4). Quoted in APA news release: Personality influences the brain's responses to emotional situations more than thought, according to new research. Retreived November 9, 2001, from http://www.apa.org/releases/brain.html

Gagne, Gerard G., Jr.; Furman, Martin J.; Carpenter, Linda L.; & Price, Lawrence H. (2000). Efficacy of continuation ECT and antidepressant drugs compared to long-term antidepressants alone in depressed patients. *American Journal of Psychiatry, 157*, 1960–1965.

Galaburda, Albert M. (1999). Albert Einstein's brain. *Lancet, 354*, 1821.

Galanter, Eugene. (1962). Contemporary psychophysics. In R. Brown, E. Galanter, E. H. Hess, & G. Mandler (Eds.), *New directions in psychology.* New York: Holt, Rinehart & Winston.

Galati, Dario; Scherer, Klaus B.; & Ricci-Bitti, Pio E. (1997). Voluntary facial expression of emotion: Comparing congenitally blind with normally sighted encoders. *Journal of Personality and Social Psychology, 73*, 1363–1379.

Galef, Bennett G., & Whiskin, Elaine E. (1995). Learning socially to eat more of one food than another. *Journal of Comparative Psychology, 109*, 99–101.

Gallo, Linda C., & Eastman, Charmane I. (1993). Circadian rhythms during gradually delaying and advancing sleep and light schedules. *Physiology and Behavior, 53*, 119–126.

Gallup, George H., Jr., & Newport, Frank. (1991). Belief in paranormal phenomena among adult Americans. *Skeptical Inquirer, 15*, 137–146.

Gambrill, Eileen. (1995a). Assertion skills training. In William O'Donohue & Leonard Krasner (Eds.), *Handbook of psychological skills training: Clinical techniques and applications.* Boston: Allyn & Bacon.

Gambrill, Eileen. (1995b). Helping shy, socially anxious, and lonely adults: A skill-based contextual approach. In William O'Donohue & Leonard Krasner (Eds.), *Handbook of psychological skills training: Clinical techniques and applications.* Boston: Allyn & Bacon.

Gansberg, Martin. (1964, March 27). 37 who saw murder didn't call the police. *New York Times,* pp. 1, 38.

Garcia, John. (1981). Tilting at the paper mills of academe. *American Psychologist, 36,* 149–158.

Garcia, John. (1997). Foreword: Robert C. Bolles: From mathematics to motivation. In Mark E. Bouton & Michael S. Fanselow (Eds.), *Learning, motivation, and cognition: The functional behaviorism of Robert C. Bolles.* Washington, DC: American Psychological Association.

Garcia, John; Ervin, Frank R.; & Koelling, Robert A. (1966). Learning with prolonged delay of reinforcement. *Psychonomic Science, 5,* 121–122.

Garcia, John, & Gustavson, Andrew R. (1997, January). Carl R. Gustavson (1946–1996): Pioneering wildlife psychologist. *APS Observer, 10*(1), 34–35.

Garcia, John, & Koelling, Robert A. (1966). Relation of cue to consequence in avoidance learning. *Psychonomic Science, 4,* 123–124.

Garcia-Palacios, Azucena; Hoffman, Hunter G.; See, Sheer Kong; Tsai, Amy; & Botella, Cristina. (2001). Redefining therapeutic success with virtual reality exposure therapy. *CyberPsychology and Behavior, 4,* 341–348.

Gardner, Gary; & Halwell, Brain. (2000). *Overfed and underfed: The global epidemic of malnutrition* (Worldwatch Paper 150). Washington, DC: Worldwatch Institute.

Gardner, Howard. (1985). *Frames of mind: The theory of multiple intelligences.* New York: Basic Books.

Gardner, Howard. (1993). *Frames of mind: The theory of multiple intelligences* (2nd ed.). New York: Basic Books.

Gardner, Howard. (1995). Cracking open the IQ box. In Steven Fraser (Ed.), *The Bell Curve wars: Race, intelligence, and the future of America.* New York: Basic Books.

Gardner, Howard. (1998a). Are there additional intelligences? The case for naturalist, spiritual, and existential intelligences. In J. Kane (Ed.), *Education, information, and transformation.* Upper Saddle River, NJ: Prentice Hall.

Gardner, Howard. (1998b, Winter). A multiplicity of intelligences. *Scientific American Presents: Exploring Intelligence, 9,* 18–23.

Gardner, Howard, & Taub, James. (1999, Fall). Debating "Multiple Intelligences." *Cerebrum, 1,* 13–36.

Garfield, Sol L. (1992). Eclectic psychotherapy: A common factors approach. In John C. Norcross & Marvin R. Goldfried (Eds.), *Handbook of psychotherapy integration.* New York: Basic Books.

Garfield, Sol L., & Bergin, Allen E. (1994). Introduction and historical overview. In Allen E. Bergin & Sol L. Garfield (Eds.), *Handbook of psychotherapy and behavior change* (4th ed.). New York: Wiley.

Garguilo, J.; Attie, I.; Brooks-Gunn, Jeanne; & Warren, M. P. (1987). Dating in middle school girls: Effects of social context, maturation, and grade. *Developmental Psychology, 23,* 730–737.

Garry, Maryanne, & Loftus, Elizabeth F. (1994). Pseudomemories without hypnosis. *International Journal of Clinical and Experimental Hypnosis, 42*(4), 363–373.

Gastil, John. (1990). Generic pronouns and sexist language: The oxymoronic character of masculine generics. *Sex Roles, 23,* 629–642.

Gauld, Alan. (1995). *A history of hypnotism.* Cambridge, England: Cambridge University Press.

Gay, Peter. (1988). *Freud: A life for our time.* New York: Norton.

Gay, Peter (Ed.). (1989). *The Freud reader.* New York: Norton.

Gay, Peter. (1999, March 29). Psychoanalyst: Sigmund Freud. *Time 100 Special Issue: Scientists and Thinkers of the 20th Century, 153*(12), 66–69.

Gazzaniga, Michael S. (1995). Consciousness and the cerebral hemispheres. In Michael S. Gazzaniga (Ed.), *The cognitive neurosciences.* Cambridge, MA: MIT Press.

Gazzaniga, Michael S. (1998, July). The split brain revisited. *Scientific American, 279,* 50–55.

Geen, Russell G. (1991). Social motivation. *Annual Review of Psychology, 42,* 377–399.

Geen, Russell G. (1995). *Human motivation: A social psychological approach.* Pacific Grove, CA: Brooks/Cole.

Geldard, Frank A. (1972). *The human senses* (2nd ed.). New York: Wiley.

Gendolla, Guido H. E. (2000). On the impact of mood on behavior: An integrative theory and a review. *Review of General Psychology, 4,* 378–408.

Gerard, Harold B.; Wilhelmy, Roland A.; & Conolley, Edward S. (1968). Conformity and group size. *Journal of Personality and Social Psychology, 8,* 79–82.

Gerbner, George. (1993). Images that hurt: Mental illness in the mass media. *Journal of the California Alliance for the Mentally Ill, 4*(1), 17–20.

Gerlach, Jes, & Peacock, Linda. (1994). Motor and mental side effects of clozapine. *Journal of Clinical Psychiatry, 55*(9, Suppl. B), 107–109.

Getka, Eric J., & Glass, Carol R. (1992). Behavioral and cognitive-behavioral approaches to the reduction of dental anxiety. *Behavior Therapy, 23,* 433–448.

Gibbons, Vincent P., & Kotagal, Suresh. (1995). Narcolepsy in children. In Charles E. Schaefer (Ed.), *Clinical handbook of sleep disorders in children.* Northvale, NJ: Aronson.

Gieser, Marlon T. (1993). The first behavior therapist as I knew her. *Journal of Behavior Therapy and Experimental Psychiatry, 24,* 321–324.

Gilbert, Lucia Albino. (1993). *Two careers/one family: The promise of gender equality.* Beverly Hills, CA: Sage.

Gilbert, Lucia Albino. (1994). Current perspectives on dual-career families. *Current Directions in Psychological Science, 3,* 101–105.

Gillberg, Mats; Kecklund, Goeran; Axelsson, John; & Akerstedt, Torbjoern. (1996). The effects of a short daytime nap after restricted night sleep. *Sleep, 19,* 570–575.

Gillham, Jane E.; Shatte, Andrew J.; Reivich, Karen J.; & Seligman, Martin E. P. (2001). Optimism, pessimism, and explanatory style. In Edward C. Chang (Ed.), *Optimism and pessimism: Implications for theory, research, and practice.* Washington, DC: American Psychological Association.

Gilligan, Carol. (1982). *In a different voice: Psychological theory and women's development.* Cambridge, MA: Harvard University Press.

Gilligan, Carol, & Attanucci, Jane. (1988). Two moral orientations. In Carol Gilligan, Janie Victoria Ward, & Jill McLean Taylor (Eds.), *Mapping the moral domain: A contribution of women's thinking to psychological theory and education.* Cambridge, MA: Harvard University Press.

Gilman, Sander L. (2001). Images in psychiatry: Karen Horney, M.D., 1885–1952. *American Journal of Psychiatry, 158,* 1205.

Gilovich, Thomas. (1997, March/April). Some systematic biases of everyday judgment. *Skeptical Inquirer, 21,* 31–35.

Gitlin, Michael J.; Swendsen, Joel; Heller, Tracy L.; & Hammen, Constance. (1995). Relapse and impairment in bipolar disorder. *American Journal of Psychiatry, 152,* 1635–1640.

Gladue, Brian A. (1994). The biopsychology of sexual orientation. *Current Directions in Psychological Science, 3,* 150–154.

Glass, Richard M. (2001). Electro convulsive therapy: Time to bring it out of the shadows. *Journal of the American Medical Association, 285,* 1346–1348.

Gleaves, David H. (1996). The sociocognitive model of dissociative identity disorder: A reexamination of the evidence. *Psychological Bulletin, 120,* 42–59.

Gleitman, Henry. (1991). Edward Chace Tolman: A life of scientific and social purpose. In Gregory A. Kimble, Michael Wertheimer, & Charlotte White (Eds.), *Portraits of pioneers in psychology.* Washington, DC & Hillsdale, NJ: American Psychological Association & Erlbaum.

Glenn, S. M. (1990). Token economy approaches for psychiatric patients. *Behavior Modification, 14,* 383–407.

Glick, Peter, & Fiske, Susan T. (2001). An ambivalent alliance: Hostile and benevolent sexism as complementary justifications for gender inequality. *American Psychologist, 56,* 109–118.

Glick, Peter; Gottesman, Deborah; & Jolton, Jeffrey. (1989). The fault is not in the stars: Susceptibility of skeptics and believers in astrology to the Barnum effect. *Personality and Social Psychology Bulletin, 15,* 572–583.

Glynn, Laura M.; Christenfeld, Nicholas; & Gerin, William. (1999). Gender, social support, and cardiovascular responses to stress. *Psychosomatic Medicine, 61,* 234–242.

Godden, Duncan R., & Baddeley, Alan D. (1975). Context-dependent memory in two natural environments: On land and underwater. *British Journal of Psychology, 66,* 325–331.

Goff, Donald C., & Simms, Claudia A. (1993). Has multiple personality remained consistent over time? A comparison of past and recent cases. *Journal of Nervous and Mental Disease, 181,* 595–600.

Gökcebay, Nilgün; Cooper, Rosemary; Williams, Robert L.; Hirshkowitz, Max; & Moore, Constance A. (1994). Function of sleep. In Rosemary Cooper (Ed.), *Sleep.* New York: Chapman & Hall.

Goldberg, Lewis R. (1993). The structure of phenotypic personality traits. *American Psychologist, 48,* 26–34.

Golden, Robert N., & Gilmore, John H. (1990). Serotonin and mood disorders. *Psychiatric Annals, 20,* 580–586.

Goldman, Ronald, & Goldman, Juliette. (1982). *Children's sexual thinking: A comparative study of children aged 5 to 15 years in Australia, North America, Britain, and Sweden.* Boston: Routledge & Kegan Paul.

Goldman-Rakic, Patricia S. (1992, September). Working memory and the mind. *Scientific American, 267,* 110–117.

Goldsmith, H. Hill; Buss, Arnold H.; Plomin, Robert; Rothbart, Mary Klevjord; Thomas, Alexander; Chess, Stella; & others. (1987). Roundtable: What is temperament? Four approaches. *Child Development, 58,* 505–529.

Goldsmith, H. Hill, & Harman, Catherine. (1994). Temperament and attachment; individuals and relationships. *Current Directions in Psychological Science, 3,* 53–61.

Goldstein, Alan J.; de Beurs, Edwin; Chambless, Dianne L.; & Wilson, Kimberly A. (2000). EMDR for panic disorder with agoraphobia: Comparison with waiting list and credible attention-placebo control condition. *Journal of Consulting and Clinical Psychology, 68,* 947–956.

Goleman, Daniel. (1980, February). 1,528 little geniuses and how they grew. *Psychology Today,* pp. 28–53.

Goleman, Daniel. (1995). *Emotional intelligence.* New York: Bantam Books.

Gollwitzer, Peter M. (1999). Implementation intentions: Strong effects of simple plans. *American Psychologist, 54,* 493–503.

Gollwitzer, Peter M., & Brandstätter, Veronika. (1997). Implementation intentions and effective goal pursuit. *Journal of Personality and Social Psychology, 73,* 186–199.

Golomb, Claire, & Galasso, Lisa. (1995). Make-believe and reality: Explorations of the imaginary realm. *Developmental Psychology, 31,* 800–810.

Golombok, Susan, & Tasker, Fiona. (1996). Do parents influence the sexual orientation of their children? Findings from a longitudinal study of lesbian families. *Developmental Psychology, 32,* 3–11.

Goodenough, Donald R. (1991). Dream recall: History and current status of the field. In Steven J. Ellman & John S. Antrobus (Eds.), *The mind in sleep: Psychology and psychophysiology* (2nd ed.). New York: Wiley.

Goodenough, Florence. (1932). The expression of emotion in a blind-deaf child. *Journal of Abnormal Social Psychology, 27,* 328–333.

Goodman, Elizabeth, & Capitman, John. (2000). Depressive symptoms and cigarette smoking among teens. *Pediatrics, 106,* 748–755.

Gopnik, Alison. (1996). The post-Piaget era. *Psychological Science, 7,* 221–225.

Gorassini, Donald R., & Olson, James M. (1995). Does self-perception change explain the foot-in-the-door effect? *Journal of Personality and Social Psychology, 69,* 91–105.

Gorski, Roger. (1995, February 28). Man's world, woman's world? Brain studies point to differences. *New York Times,* pp. C1, C7.

Gotlib, Ian H. (1992). Interpersonal and cognitive aspects of depression. *Current Directions in Psychological Science, 1,* 149–154.

Gottesman, Irving I. (1991). *Schizophrenia genesis: The origins of madness.* New York: Freeman.

Gottesman, Irving I. (1997). Twins: En route to QTLs for cognition. *Science, 276,* 1522–1523.

Gottfredson, Linda S. (1998, Winter). The general intelligence factor. *Scientific American Presents: Exploring Intelligence, 9,* 24–29.

Gottman, John M. (1994). *Why marriages succeed or fail: What you can learn from the breakthrough research to make your marriage last.* New York: Simon & Schuster.

Gottman, John M., & Levenson, Robert W. (1992). Marital processes predictive of later dissolution: Behavior, physiology, and health. *Journal of Personality and Social Psychology, 63,* 221–233.

Gough, Harrison G. (1989). The California Personality Inventory. In Charles S. Newmark (Ed.), *Major psychological assessment instruments* (Vol. 2). Boston: Allyn & Bacon.

Gould, Elizabeth; Beylin, Anna; Tanapat, Patima; Reeves, Alison; & Shors, Tracey J. (1999a, March). Learning enhances adult neurogenesis in the hippocampal formation. *Nature Neuroscience, 2*(3), 260–265.

Gould, Elizabeth; Reeves, Alison J.; Graziano, Michael S. A.; & Gross, Charles G. (1999b, October 15). Neurogenesis in the neocortex of adult primates. *Science, 286,* 548–552.

Gould, Elizabeth; Tanapat, Patima; McEwen, Bruce S.; Flügge; & Fuchs, Eberhard. (1998, March 17). Proliferation of granule cell precursors in the dentate gyrus of adult monkeys is diminished by stress. *Proceedings of the National Academy of Sciences, USA, 95,* 3168–3171.

Gould, James L., & Gould, Carol Grant. (1994). *The animal mind.* New York: Freeman.

Gould, Stephen Jay. (1993). *The mismeasure of man* (2nd ed.). New York: Norton.

Graen, George, & Cashman, James F. (1975). A role making model of leadership in formal organizations: A developmental approach. In J. G. Hunt & L. L. Larson (Eds.), *Leadership frontiers.* Kent, OH: Kent State University Press.

Graham, John R. (1993). *MMPI-2: Assessing personality and psychopathology* (2nd ed.). New York: Oxford University Press.

Graham, William K.; & Balloun, Joe. (1973). An empirical test of Maslow's need hierarchy theory. *Journal of Humanistic Psychology, 13,* 97–108.

Graig, Eric. (1993). Stress as a consequence of the urban physical environment. In Leo Goldberger & Shlomo Breznitz (Eds.), *Handbook of stress: Theoretical and clinical aspects* (2nd ed.). New York: Free Press.

Gray, John. (1992). *Men are from Mars, women are from Venus: A practical guide for improving communication and getting what you want in your relationships.* New York: HarperCollins.

Greasley, Peter. (2000). Handwriting analysis and personality assessment: The creative use of analogy, symbolism, and metaphor. *European Psychologist, 5,* 44–51.

Green, Joseph P. (1999a). Hypnosis and the treatment of smoking cessation and weight loss. In Irving Kirsch, Antonio Capafons, Etzel Cardena-Buelna, & Salvador Amigo (Eds.), *Clinical hypnosis and self-regulation: cognitive-behavior perspectives.* Washington, DC: American Psychological Association.

Green, Joseph P. (1999b). Hypnosis, context effects, and the recall of early autobiographical memories. *International Journal of Clinical and Experimental Hypnosis, 47,* 284–300.

Green, Joseph P., & Lynn, Steven Jay. (2000). Hypnosis and suggestion-based approaches to smoking cessation: An examination of the evidence. *International Journal of Clinical and Experimental Hypnosis, 48,* 195–224.

Green, Leonard, & Rachlin, Howard. (1996). Commitment using punishment. *Journal of the Experimental Analysis of Behavior, 65,* 593–601.

Green, Richard. (1985). Gender identity in childhood and later sexual orientation: Follow-up of 78 males. *American Journal of Psychiatry, 142,* 339–341.

Green, Richard. (1987). *The "sissy boy syndrome" and the development of homosexuality.* New Haven, CT: Yale University Press.

Greenberg, Leslie S.; Elliott, Robert K.; & Lietaer, Germain. (1994). Research on experiential psychotherapies. In Allen E. Bergin & Sol L. Garfield (Eds.), *Handbook of psychotherapy and behavior change* (4th ed.). New York: Wiley.

Greenfield, Patricia M. (1997). You can't take it with you: Why ability assessments don't cross cultures. *American Psychologist, 52,* 1115–1124.

Greengard, Paul. (2001). The neurobiology of slow synaptic transmission. *Science, 294,* 1024–1030.

Greeno, Catherine G., & Wing, Rena R. (1994). Stress-induced eating. *Psychological Bulletin, 115,* 444–464.

Greenwald, Anthony G. (1992). New Look 3: Unconscious cognition reclaimed. *American Psychologist, 47,* 766–779.

Greenwald, Anthony G.; Spangenberg, Eric R.; Pratkanis, Anthony R.; & Eskenazi, Jay. (1991). Double-blind tests of subliminal self-help audiotapes. *Psychological Science, 2,* 119–122.

Gregory, Richard L. (1968, November). Visual illusions. *Scientific American, 212,* 66–76.

Griffin, Donald R. (2001). *Animal minds: Beyond cognition to consciousness* (2nd ed.). Chicago: University of Chicago Press.

Gross, Charles G. (2000). Neurogenesis in the adult brain: Death of a dogma. *Nature Reviews Neuroscience, 1,* 67–73.

Gross, James J., & John, Oliver P. (1998). Mapping the domain of expressivity: Multi-method evidence for a hierarchical model. *Journal of Personality and Social Psychology, 74,* 170–191.

Gross, James J.; John, Oliver P.; & Richards, Jane M. (2000). The dissociation of emotion expression from emotion experience: A personality perspective. *Personality and Social Psychology Bulletin, 26,* 712–726.

Grossman, Michele, & Wood, Wendy. (1993). Sex differences in intensity of emotional experience: A social role interpretation. *Journal of Personality and Social Psychology, 65,* 1010–1022.

Grossman, Randi Priluck, & Till, Brian D. (1998). The persistence of classically conditioned brand attitudes. *Journal of Advertising, 27,* 23–31.

Grossmann, Klaus E., & Grossmann, Karin. (1990). The wider concept of attachment in cross-cultural research. *Human Development, 33,* 31–47.

Grotevant, Harold D. (1987). Toward a process model of identity formation. *Journal of Adolescent Research, 2,* 203–222.

Grotevant, Harold D. (1992). Assigned and chosen identity components: A process perspective on their integration. In Gerald R. Adams, Thomas P. Gullotta, & Raymond Montemayor (Eds.), *Adolescent identity formation.* Newbury Park, CA: Sage.

Grunberg, Leon; Moore, Sarah; Anderson-Connolly, Richard; & Greenberg, Edward. (1999). Work stress and self-reported alcohol use: The moderating role of escapist reasons for drinking. *Journal of Occupational Health Psychology, 4,* 29–36.

Guarnaccia, Peter J. (1993). *Ataques de nervios* in Puerto Rico: Culture-bound syndrome or popular illness? *Medical Anthropology, 15,* 157–170.

Guarnaccia, Peter J. (1997). A cross-cultural perspective on anxiety disorders. In Steven Friedman (Ed.), *Cultural issues in the treatment of anxiety.* New York: Guilford Press.

Gudykunst, William B., & Bond, Michael Harris. (1997). Intergroup relations across cultures. In John W. Berry, Cigdem Kagitcibasi, & Marshall H. Segall (Eds.), *Handbook of cross-cultural psychology* (2nd ed., Vol. 3). Boston: Allyn & Bacon.

Guérin, Bernard (1986). Mere presence effects in humans: A review. *Journal of Experimental Social Psychology, 22,* 38–77.

Guinard, Jean-Xavier; & Brun, Patrice. (1998). Sensory-specific satiety: Comparison of taste and texture effects. *Appetite, 31,* 141–157.

Gunderson, John G. (1997). The borderline patient's intolerance of aloneness: Insecure attachments and therapist availability. *American Journal of Psychiatry, 153,* 752–758.

Gunnar, Megan R. (1994). Psychoendocrine studies of temperament and stress in early childhood: Expanding current models. In John E. Bates & Theodore D. Wachs (Eds.), *Temperament: Individual differences at the interface of biology and behavior.* Washington, DC: American Psychological Association.

Gusnard, Debra A., & Raichle, Marcus E. (2001). Searching for a baseline: Functional imaging and the resting human brain. *Nature Reviews Neuroscience, 2,* 685–694.

Gustavson, Carl R.; Kelly, Daniel J.; Sweeney, Michael; & Garcia, John. (1976). Prey-lithium aversions: I. Coyotes and wolves. *Behavioral Biology, 17,* 61–72.

Guzzo, Richard A., & Dickson, Marcus W. (1996). Teams in organizations: Recent research on performance and effectiveness. *Annual Review of Psychology, 47,* 307–338.

Haaga, David A. F., & Davison, Gerald C. (1991). Cognitive change methods. In Frederick H. Kanfer & Arnold P. Goldstein (Eds.), *Helping people change: A textbook of methods* (4th ed.). New York: Pergamon Press.

Haaga, David A. F., & Davison, Gerald C. (1993). An appraisal of rational-emotive therapy. *Journal of Consulting and Clinical Psychology, 61,* 215–220.

Habermas, Tilmann, & Bluck, Susan. (2000). Getting a life: The emergence of the life story in adolescence. *Psychological Bulletin, 126,* 748–769.

Habib, Michel; Gayraud, D.; Oliva, A.; Regis, J.; Salamon, G.; & Khalil, R. (1991). Effects of handedness and sex on the morphology of the corpus callosum: A study with brain magnetic resonance imaging. *Brain & Cognition, 16,* 41–61.

Hackel, Lisa S., & Ruble, Diane N. (1992). Changes in the marital relationship after the first baby is born: Predicting the impact of expectancy disconfirmation. *Journal of Personality and Social Psychology, 62,* 944–957.

Haddock, Geoffrey; Zanna, Mark P.; & Esses, Victoria M. (1993). Assessing the structure of prejudicial attitudes: The case of attitudes toward homosexuals. *Journal of Personality and Social Psychology, 65,* 1105–1118.

Hagerty, Michael R. (1999). Testing Maslow's hierarchy of needs: National quality-of-life across time. *Social Indicators Research, 46,* 249–271.

Haidt, Jonathan; Koller, Silvia Helena; & Dias, Maria G. (1993). Affect, culture, and morality, or is it wrong to eat your dog? *Journal of Personality and Social Psychology, 65,* 613–628.

Haight, Barbara Kavanagh. (1992). Long-term effects of a structured life review process. *Journal of Gerontology, 47*(5), 312–315.

Halaas, Jeffrey L.; Gajiwala, Ketan S.; Friedman, Jeffrey M.; & others. (1995, July 28). Weight-reducing effects of the plasma protein encoded by the *obese* gene. *Science, 269,* 543–546.

Hall, Calvin S., & Van de Castle, R. L. (1966). *Content analysis of dreams.* New York: Appleton-Century-Crofts.

Hall, Christine C. Iijima. (1997). Cultural malpractice: The growing obsolescence of psychology with the changing U.S. population. *American Psychologist, 52,* 642–651.

Hall, Gordon C. Nagayama. (2001). Psychotherapy research with ethnic minorities: Empirical, ethical, and conceptual issues. *Journal of Consulting and Clinical Psychology, 69,* 502–510.

Halliday, Gordon. (1995). Treating nightmares in children. In Charles E. Schaefer (Ed.), *Clinical handbook of sleep disorders in children.* Northvale, NJ: Aronson.

Halmi, Katherine A., Sunday, Suzanne R.; Strober, Michael; & others. (2000). Perfectionism in anorexia nervosa: Variation by clinical subtype, obsessionality, and pathological eating behavior. *American Journal of Psychiatry, 157,* 1799–1805.

Halonen, Jane S. (1995). Demystifying critical thinking. In Diane F. Halpern & Susan G. Nummedal (Eds.), Psychologists teach critical thinking [Special issue]. *Teaching of Psychology, 22*(1).

Halpern, Diane F. (1998). Teaching critical thinking for transfer across domains: Dispositions, skills, structure training, and metacognitive monitoring. *American Psychologist, 53,* 449–455.

Halpern, Diane F., & Nummedal, Susan G. (Eds.). (1995). Psychologists teach critical thinking [Special issue]. *Teaching of Psychology, 22,* No 1.

Hamburg, David A., & Takanishi, Ruby. (1989). Preparing for life: The critical transition of adolescence. *American Psychologist, 44,* 825–827.

Hamilton, Mykol C. (1988). Using masculine generics: Does generic *he* increase male bias in the user's imagery? *Sex Roles, 19,* 785–799.

Hamilton, Mykol C. (1991). Masculine bias in the attribution of personhood. *Psychology of Women Quarterly, 15,* 393–402.

Harlow, Harry F. (1953a). Learning by Rhesus monkeys on the basis of manipulation-exploration motives. *Science, 117,* 466–467.

Harlow, Harry F. (1953b). Mice, monkeys, men, and motives. *Psychological Review, 60,* 23–32.

Harlow, Harry F. (1953c). Motivation as a factor in new responses. In *Current theory and research in motivation: A symposium*. Lincoln: University of Nebraska Press.

Harlow, John M. (1848, December 13). Passage of an iron rod through the head. *Boston Medical and Surgical Journal, 39*(20), 389–393.

Harlow, John M. (1868). Recovery from the passage of an iron bar through the head. *Publications of the Massachusetts Medical Society, 2*, 327–347.

Harrington, David M.; Block, Jeanne H.; & Block, Jack (1987). Testing aspects of Carl Rogers' theory of creative environments: Child-rearing antecedents of creative potential in young adolescents. *Journal of Personality and Social Psychology, 52*, 851–856.

Harris, Ben. (1979). What ever happened to Little Albert? *American Psychologist, 34*, 151–160.

Harter, Susan. (1990). Self and identity development. In S. Shirley Feldman & Glen R. Elliott (Eds.), *At the threshold: The developing adolescent*. Cambridge, MA: Harvard University Press.

Hartshorn, Kristin; Rovee-Collier, Carolyn; Gerhardstein, Peter; Bhatt, Ramesh S.; Klein, Pamela J.; Aaron, Fiamma; & others. (1998). Developmental changes in the specificity of memory over the first year of life. *Developmental Psychobiology, 33*, 61–78.

Hauser, Marc D. (2000). *Wild minds: What animals really think*. New York: Holt.

Havighurst, Robert J.; Neugarten, Bernice L.; & Tobin, Sheldon S. (1968). Disengagement and patterns of aging. In Bernice L. Neugarten (Ed.), *Middle age and aging*. Chicago: University of Chicago Press.

Hawkins, J. David; Catalano, Richard F.; & Miller, Janet Y. (1992). Risk and protective factors for alcohol and other drug problems in adolescence and early adulthood: Implications for substance abuse prevention. *Psychological Bulletin, 112*, 64–105.

Hawkins, John N. (1994). Issues of motivation in Asian education. In Harold F. O'Neil, Jr. & Michael Drillings (Eds.), *Motivation: Theory and research*. Hillsdale, NJ: Erlbaum.

Haxby, James V.; Gobbini, M. Ida; Furey, Maura L.; & others. (2001, September 28). Distributed and overlapping representations of faces and objects in ventral temporal cortex. *Science, 293*, 2425–2430.

Hayes, Jeffrey A., & Mitchell, Jeffrey C. (1994). Mental health professionals' skepticism about multiple personality disorder. *Professional Psychology: Research and Practice, 25*, 410–415.

Hearst, Eliot. (1999). After the puzzle boxes: Thorndike in the 20th century. *Journal of the Experimental Analysis of Behavior, 72*, 441–446.

Heart and Stroke Foundation of Canada. (1999). *The Changing Face of Heart Disease and Stroke in Canada: 2000*. Ottawa, Ontario, Canada: Heart & Stroke Foundation of Canada.

Hebb, Donald O. (1955). Drives and the C. N. S. (central nervous system). *Psychological Review, 62*, 243–254.

Hedge, Alan, & Yousif, Yousif H. (1992). Effects of urban size, urgency, and cost of helpfulness: A cross-cultural comparison between the United Kingdom and the Sudan. *Journal of Cross-Cultural Psychology, 23*, 107–115.

Hedges, Larry V., & Nowell, Amy. (1995, July 7). Sex differences in mental test scores, variability, and numbers of high-scoring individuals. *Science, 269*, 41–45.

Heider, Eleanor Rosch, & Olivier, Donald C. (1972). The structure of the color space in naming and memory for two languages. *Cognitive Psychology, 3*, 337–354.

Heinrichs, R. Walter. (1993). Schizophrenia and the brain: Conditions for a neuropsychology of madness. *American Psychologist, 48*, 221–233.

Helgeson, Vicki S. (1992). Moderators of the relation between perceived control and adjustment to chronic illness. *Journal of Personality and Social Psychology, 63*, 656–666.

Helgeson, Vicki S. (1994). Relation of agency and communion to well-being: Evidence and potential explanations. *Psychological Bulletin, 116*, 412–428.

Heller, Wendy; Nitschke, Jack B.; & Miller, Gregory A. (1998). Lateralization in emotion and emotional disorders. *Current Directions in Psychological Science, 7*, 26–32.

Hendrix, Mary Lynn. (1993). *Bipolar disorder* (NIMH Publication No. 93–3679). Rockville, MD: National Institute of Mental Health.

Henley, Nancy M. (1989). Molehill or mountain? What we know and don't know about sex bias in language. In M. Crawford & M. Gentry (Eds.), *Gender and thought: Psychological perspectives*. New York: Springer-Verlag.

Henninger, Polly. (1992). Conditional handedness: Handedness changes in multiple personality disordered subject reflects shift in hemispheric dominance. *Consciousness & Cognition, 1*, 265–287.

Henry, William P.; Strupp, Hans H.; Shacht, Thomas E.; & Gaston, Louise. (1994). Psychodynamic approaches. In Allen E. Bergin & Sol L. Garfield (Eds.), *Handbook of psychotherapy and behavior change* (4th ed.). New York: Wiley.

Hepper, Peter G.; Shahidullah, Sara; & White, Raymond. (1990, October 4). Origins of fetal handedness. *Nature, 347*, 431.

Herbert, James D.; Lilienfeld, Scott O.; Lohr, Jeffrey M.; Montgomery, Robert W.; O'Donohue, William T.; Rosen, Gerald M.; & Tolin, David F. (2000). Science and pseudoscience in the development of Eye Movement Desensitization and Reprocessing: Implications for clinical psychology. *Clinical Psychology Review, 20*, 945–971.

Herbert, Tracy Bennett, & Cohen, Sheldon. (1993). Depression and immunity: A meta-analytic review. *Psychological Bulletin, 113*, 472–486.

Herkenham, Miles A. (1992). Cannabinoid receptor localization in brain: Relationship to motor and reward systems. *Annals of the New York Academy of Sciences, 654*, 19–32.

Herman, Louis M.; Kuczaj, Stan A., II; & Holder, Mark D. (1993). Responses to anomalous gestural sequences by a language-trained dolphin: Evidence for processing of semantic relations and syntactic information. *Journal of Experimental Psychology: General, 122*, 184–194.

Hermans, Hubert J. M. (1996). Voicing the self: From information processing to dialogical interchange. *Psychological Bulletin, 119*, 31–50.

Hertel, Paula T., & Rude, Stephanie S. (1991). Depressive deficits in memory: Focusing attention improves subsequent recall. *Journal of Experimental Psychology: General, 120*, 301–309.

Hertz, Marguerite R. (1992). Rorschach-bound: A 50-year memoir. *Professional Psychology: Research and Practice, 23*, 168–171.

Herzog, D. B.; Nussbaum, K. M.; & Marmar, A. K. (1996). Comorbidity and outcome in eating disorders. *Psychiatric Clinics of North America, 19*, 843–859.

Hess, Ursula; Senecal, Sacha; Kirouac, Gilles; Herrera, Pedro; Philippot, Pierre; & Kleck, Robert E. (2000). Emotional expressivity in men and women: Stereotypes and self-perceptions. *Cognition & Emotion, 14*, 609–642.

Hetherington, Marion M.; & Rolls, Barbara J. (1996). Sensory-specific satiety: Theoretical frameworks and central characteristics. In Elizabeth D. Capaldi (Ed.), *Why we eat what we eat: The psychology of eating*. Washington, DC: American Psychological Association.

Hettema, John M.; Neale, Michael C.; & Kendler, Kenneth S. (2001). A review and meta-analysis of the genetic epidemiology of anxiety disorders. *American Journal of Psychiatry, 158*, 1568–1578.

Hetzel, Lisa; & Smith, Annetta. (2001). *The 65 years and over population: Census 2000 brief* (Series C2KBR/01–10). Washington, DC: U.S. Census Bureau. PDF of document retrieved February 20, 2002, from http://www.census.gov/prod/2001pubs/c2kbr01-10.pdf

Hewstone, Miles; Rubin, Mark; & Willis, Hazel. (2002). Intergroup bias. *Annual Review of Psychology, 53*, 575–604.

Hilgard, Ernest R. (1982). Hypnotic susceptibility and implications for measurement. *International Journal of Clinical and Experimental Hypnosis, 30*, 394–403.

Hilgard, Ernest R. (1986a). *Divided consciousness: Multiple controls in human thought and action*. New York: Wiley.

Hilgard, Ernest R. (1986b, January). A study in hypnosis. *Psychology Today, 20*, 23–27.

Hilgard, Ernest R. (1991). A neodissociation interpretation of hypnosis. In Steven J. Lynn & J. Rhue (Eds.), *Theories of hypnosis: Current models and perspectives.* New York: Guilford Press.

Hilgard, Ernest R. (1992). Divided consciousness and dissociation. *Consciousness & Cognition, 1,* 16–32.

Hilgard, Ernest R. (1994). Neodissociation theory. In Steven Jay Lynn & Judith W. Rhue, (Eds.), *Dissociation: Clinical and theoretical perspectives.* New York: Guilford Press.

Hilgard, Ernest R.; Hilgard, Josephine R.; & Barber, Joseph. (1994). *Hypnosis in the relief of pain* (Rev. ed.). New York: Brunner/Mazel.

Hilgard, Ernest R., & Marquis, D. G. (1940). *Conditioning and learning.* New York: Appleton-Century-Crofts.

Hilton, James L., & Darley, John M. (1991). The effects of interaction goals on person perception. In Mark P. Zanna (Ed.), *Advances in experimental social psychology* (Vol. 24). San Diego, CA: Academic Press/Harcourt.

Hilton, James L., & von Hippel, William. (1996). Stereotypes. *Annual Review of Psychology, 47,* 237–271.

Hines, Terence. (1988). *Pseudoscience and the paranormal: A critical examination of the evidence.* Buffalo, NY: Prometheus Books.

Hines, Terence. (1996). Biorhythms. In Gordon Stein (Ed.), *The encyclopedia of the paranormal.* Amherst, NY: Prometheus Books.

Hines, Terence M. (1998). Comprehensive review of biorhythm theory. *Psychological Reports, 83,* 19–64.

Hines, Terence. (1998). Further on Einstein's brain. *Experimental Neurology, 150,* 343–344.

Hingson, Ralph; Heeran, Timothy; Zakoc, Ronda C.; Kopstein, Andrea; & Wechsler, Henry. (2002). Magnitude of alcohol-related mortality and morbidity among U.S. college students ages 18–24. *Journal of Studies on Alcohol, 63,* 136–144.

Hinshaw, Stephen P., & Cicchetti, Dante. (2000). Stigma and mental disorder: Conceptions of illness, public attitudes, personal disclosure, and social policy. *Developmental Psychopathology, 12,* 555–598.

Hirshkowitz, Max; Moore, Constance A.; & Minhoto, Gisele. (1997). The basics of sleep. In Mark R. Pressman & William C. Orr (Eds.), *Understanding sleep: The evaluation and treatment of sleep disorders.* Washington, DC: American Psychological Association.

Hobfoll, Stevan E.; Lilly, Roy S.; & Jackson, Anita P. (1992). Conservation of social resources and the self. In Hans O. F. Veiel & Urs Baumann (Eds.), *The meaning and measurement of social support.* New York: Hemisphere.

Hobfoll, Stevan E., & Stephens, Mary Ann Parris. (1990). Social support during extreme stress: Consequences and intervention. In Barbara R. Sarason, Irwin G. Sarason, &

Gregory R. Pierce (Eds.), *Social support: An interactional view.* New York: Wiley.

Hobfoll, Stevan E., & Vaux, Alex. (1993). Social support: Resources and context. In Leo Goldberger & Shlomo Breznitz (Eds.), *Handbook of stress: Theoretical and clinical aspects* (2nd ed.). New York: Free Press.

Hobson, Charles J.; Kamen, Joseph; Szostek, Jana; & Nethercut, Carol M. (1998). Stressful life events: A revision and update of the Social Readjustment Rating Scale. *International Journal of Stress Management, 5*(1), 1–23.

Hobson, J. Allan. (1988). *The dreaming brain.* New York: Basic Books.

Hobson, J. Allan. (1995). *Sleep.* New York: Scientific American Library.

Hobson, J. Allan. (1999). *Consciousness.* New York: Scientific American Library.

Hobson, J. Allan, & McCarley, Robert W. (1977). The brain as a dream state generator: An activation-synthesis hypothesis of the dream process. *American Journal of Psychiatry, 134,* 1335–1348.

Hobson, J. Allan, & Stickgold, Robert. (1995). The conscious state paradigm: A neurological approach to waking, sleeping, and dreaming. In Michael S. Gazzaniga (Ed.), *The cognitive neurosciences.* Cambridge, MA: MIT Press.

Hobson, J. Allan; Stickgold, Robert; & Pace-Schott, Edward F. (1998). The neuropsychology of REM sleep dreaming. *NeuroReport, 9*(3), R1–R14.

Hoffman, Martin L. (1977). Moral internalization: Current theory and research. In Leonard Berkowitz (Ed.), *Advances in experimental social psychology* (Vol. 10). New York: Academic Press.

Hoffman, Martin L. (1988). Moral development. In Marc H. Bornstein & Michael E. Lamb (Eds.), *Developmental psychology: An advanced textbook.* Hillsdale, NJ: Erlbaum.

Hoffman, Martin L. (1994). Discipline and internalization. *Developmental Psychology, 30,* 26–28.

Holahan, Carole K., & Sears, Robert R. (1995). *The gifted group in later maturity* (in association with Lee J. Cronbach). Stanford, CA: Stanford University Press.

Holden, Constance. (2001). Polygraph screening: Panel seeks truth in lie detector debate. *Science, 291,* 967.

Hollander, Edwin P., & Julian, James W. (1970). Studies in leader legitimacy, influence, and innovation. In L. Berkowitz (Ed.), *Advances in experimental social psychology* (Vol. 5). New York: Academic Press.

Hollon, Steven D., & Beck, Aaron T. (1994). Cognitive and cognitive-behavioral therapies. In Allen E. Bergin & Sol L. Garfield (Eds.), *Handbook of psychotherapy and behavior change* (4th ed.). New York: Wiley.

Holmes, David. (1990). The evidence for repression: An examination of sixty years of research. In Jerome Singer (Ed.), *Repression*

and dissociation: Implications for personality theory, psychopathology, and health. Chicago: University of Chicago Press.

Holmes, Stanley. (1994, April 25). The tortuous tale of a serial killer. *Newsweek,* p. 30.

Holmes, Thomas H., & Masuda, Minoru. (1974). Life change and illness susceptibility. In Barbara Snell Dohrenwend & Bruce P. Dohrenwend (Eds.), *Stressful life events: Their nature and effects.* New York: Wiley.

Holmes, Thomas H., & Rahe, Richard H. (1967). The Social Readjustment Rating Scale. *Journal of Psychosomatic Research, 11,* 213–218.

Holt, Robert R. (1993). Occupational stress. In Leo Goldberger & Shlomo Breznitz (Eds.), *Handbook of stress: Theoretical and clinical aspects* (2nd ed.). New York: Free Press.

Holyoak, Keith J., & Spellman, Barbara A. (1993). Thinking. *Annual Review of Psychology, 44,* 265–315.

Hopkins, William D. (1995). Hand preference for a coordinated bimanual task in 110 chimpanzees (*Pan troglodytes*). *Journal of Comparative Psychology, 109*(3), 291–297.

Hoptman, Matthew J., & Davidson, Richard J. (1994). How and why do the two cerebral hemispheres interact? *Psychological Bulletin, 116,* 195–219.

Horgan, John. (1994, July). Can science explain consciousness? *Scientific American, 271,* 88–94.

Horney, Karen. (1926/1967). The flight from womanhood. In Harold Kelman (Ed.), *Feminine psychology.* New York: Norton.

Horney, Karen. (1945/1972). *Our inner conflicts: A constructive theory of neurosis.* New York: Norton.

Hornig-Rohan, Mädy, & Amsterdam, Jay D. (1994). Clinical and biological correlates of treatment-resistant depression: An overview. *Psychiatric Annals, 24,* 220–227.

Horton, David L., & Mills, Carol B. (1984). Human learning and memory. *Annual Review of Psychology, 35,* 361–394.

House, Robert J. (1977). A 1976 theory of charismatic leadership. In J. G. Hunt & L. L. Larsen (Eds.), *Leadership: The cutting edge* (pp. 189–207). Carbondale: Southern Illinois University Press.

House, Robert J.; Spangler, William D.; & Woycke, James. (1991). Personality and charisma in the U.S. presidency: A psychological theory of leader effectiveness. *Administrative Science Quarterly, 36,* 364–396.

Howard, Ann. (1986). College experiences and managerial performance. *Journal of Applied Psychology, 71,* 530–552.

Howard, J. C. (2000). At-home work spurs risk management concerns. *National Underwriter, 18,* 6.

Howard, Kenneth I.; Kopta, S. Mark; Krause, Merton S.; & Orlinsky, David E. (1986). The dose-effect relationship in psychotherapy. *American Psychologist, 41,* 159–164.

Howard, William, & Crano, William D. (1974). Effects of sex, conversation, location, and size of observer group on bystander intervention in a high risk situation. *Sociometry, 37,* 491–507.

Howe, Mark L., & Courage, Mary L. (1993). On resolving the enigma of infantile amnesia. *Psychological Bulletin, 113,* 305–326.

Howes, Carollee. (1991). Caregiving environments and their consequences for children: The experience in the United States. In E. C. Melhuish & P. Moss (Eds.), *Day-care for young children.* London: Routledge.

Hoyert, Donna L.; Arias, Elizabeth; Smith, Betty L.; Murphy, Sherry L.; & Kochanek, Kenneth D. (2001, September 21). Deaths: final data for 1999. *National Vital Statistics Reports, 49,* No. 8. Hyattsville, MD: National Center for Health Statistics. Document PDF retrieved on October 30, 2001, from http://www.cdc.gov/nchs/data/nvsr/nvsr49/nvsr49_08.pdf

HRFocus News Briefs. (2000, June). *HRFocus, 77,* 8–9.

Hubble, Mark A.; Duncan, Barry L.; & Miller, Scott D. (Eds.). (1999). *The heart and soul of change: What works in therapy.* Washington, DC: American Psychological Association.

Hubel, David H. (1995). *Eye, brain, and vision.* New York: Scientific American Library.

Hull, Clark L. (1943). *Principles of behavior: An introduction to behavior theory.* New York: Appleton-Century-Crofts.

Hull, Clark L. (1952). *A behavior system: An introduction to behavior theory concerning the individual organism.* New Haven, CT: Yale University Press.

Hume, K. Michelle, & Crossman, Jane. (1992). Musical reinforcement of practice behaviors among competitive swimmers. *Journal of Applied Behavior Analysis, 25,* 665–670.

Hunt, Earl, & Agnoli, Franca. (1991). The Whorfian hypothesis: A cognitive psychology perspective. *Psychological Review, 98,* 377–389.

Hunt, Stephen P., & Mantyh, Patrick W. (2001). The molecular dynamics of pain control. *Nature Reviews Neuroscience, 2,* 83–91.

Hunter, John E., & Hunter, Ronda F. (1984). Validity and utility of alternative predictors of job performance. *Psychological Bulletin, 96,* 72–98.

Hurovitz, Craig S.; Dunn, Sarah; Domhoff, G. William; & Fiss, Harry. (1999). The dreams of blind men and women: A replication and extension of previous findings. *Dreaming, 9,* 183–193.

Hurvich, Leo M. (1981). *Color vision.* Sunderland, MA: Sinauer.

Huston, Ted L.; Ruggiero, Mary; Conner, Ross; & Geis, Gilbert. (1981). Bystander intervention into crime: A study based on naturally-occurring episodes. *Social Psychology Quarterly, 44,* 14–23.

Huttunen, Matti O.; Machon, Ricardo A.; & Mednick, Sarnoff A. (1994). Prenatal factors in the pathogenesis of schizophrenia. *British Journal of Psychiatry, 164*(Suppl. 23), 15–19.

Hyde, Janet Shibley. (1996). Where are the gender differences? Where are the gender similarities? In David M. Buss & Neil M. Malamuth (Eds.), *Sex, power, conflict: Evolutionary and feminist perspectives.* New York: Oxford University Press.

Hyde, Janet Shibley, & Plant, Elizabeth Ashby. (1995). Magnitude of psychological gender differences. *American Psychologist, 50,* 159–161.

Hyman, Ira E., Jr.; Gilstrap, Livia L.; Decker, Kevin; & Wilkinson, Carol. (1998). Manipulating remember and know judgments of autobiographical memories: An investigation of false memory creation. *Applied Cognitive Psychology, 12,* 371–386.

Hyman, Ray. (1994). Anomaly or artifact? Comments on Bem and Honorton. *Psychological Bulletin, 115,* 19–24.

Iacono, William G., & Lykken, David T. (1997). The validity of the lie detector: Two surveys of scientific opinion. *Journal of Applied Psychology, 82,* 426–433.

Inouye, Sharon L.; Albert, Marilyn S.; & Mohs, Richard. (1993). Cognitive performance in a high-functioning community-dwelling elderly population. *Journal of Gerontology, 48,* 146–157.

Irwin, Harvey J. (1994). Proneness to dissociation and traumatic childhood events. *Journal of Nervous and Mental Disease, 182,* 456–460.

Isabella, Russell A.; Belsky, Jay; & von Eye, Alexander. (1989). Origins of infant-mother attachment: An examination of interactional synchrony during the infant's first year. *Developmental Psychology, 25,* 12–21.

Iversen, Iver H. (1992). Skinner's early research: From reflexology to operant conditioning. *American Psychologist, 47,* 1318–1328.

Iwamasa, Gayle Y. (1997). Asian Americans. In Steven Friedman (Ed.), *Cultural issues in the treatment of anxiety.* New York: Guilford Press.

Izard, Carroll E. (1989). The structure and function of emotions: Implications for cognition, motivation, and personality. In Ira S. Cohen (Ed.), *The G. Stanley Hall Lecture Series* (Vol. 9) (1988 lectures). Washington, DC: American Psychological Association.

Izard, Carroll E. (1990a). Facial expressions and the regulation of emotions. *Journal of Personality and Social Psychology, 58,* 487–498.

Izard, Carroll E. (1990b). The substrates and functions of emotion feelings: William James and current emotion theories. *Personality and Social Psychology Bulletin, 16,* 626–635.

Izard, Carroll E. (1994). Innate and universal facial expressions: Evidence from developmental and cross-cultural research. *Psychological Bulletin, 115,* 288–299.

Jackson, Adam J. (1995). *Eye signs: What your eyes reveal about your health, emotions, personality, and love life.* London: Thorsons.

Jackson, Jeffrey M., & Harkins, Stephen G. (1985). Equity in effort: An explanation of the social loafing effect. *Journal of Personality and Social Psychology, 49,* 1199–1206.

Jacob, Suma; Kinnunen, Leann H.; Metz, John; Cooper, Malcolm; & McClintock, Martha K. (2001). Sustained human chemosignal unconsciously alters brain function. *NeuroReport, 12,* 2391–2394.

Jacob, Suma, & McClintock, Martha K. (2000). Psychological state and mood effects of steroidal chemosignals in women and men. *Hormones & Behavior, 37,* 57–78.

Jacobs, Bob. (1993, April 12). Quoted in Ronald Kotulak, Mental workouts pump up brain power. *Chicago Tribune,* p. 12.

Jacobs, Bob; Schall, Matthew; & Scheibel, Arnold B. (1993). A quantitative dendritic analysis of Wernicke's area in humans: II. Gender, hemispheric, and environmental factors. *Journal of Comparative Neurology, 327,* 97–106.

Jacobs, Marion K., & Goodman, Gerald. (1989). Psychology and self-help groups: Predictions on a partnership. *American Psychologist, 44,* 536–545.

Jacox, Ada; Carr, D. B.; & Payne, Richard. (1994, March 3). New clinical-practice guidelines for the management of pain in patients with cancer. *New England Journal of Medicine, 330,* 651–655.

Jaffee, Sara, & Hyde, Janet Shibley. (2000). Gender differences in moral orientation: A meta-analysis. *Psychological Bulletin, 126,* 703–726.

James, William. (1884). What is an emotion? *Mind, 9,* 188–205.

James, William. (1890). *Principles of psychology.* New York: Holt.

James, William. (1892). *Psychology, briefer course.* New York: Holt.

James, William. (1899/1958). *Talks to teachers.* New York: Norton.

Jameson, Dorothea, & Hurvich, Leo M. (1989). Essay concerning color constancy. *Annual Review of Psychology, 40,* 1–22.

Jamison, Kay Redfield. (1993). *Touched with fire: Manic-depressive illness and the artistic temperament.* New York: Free Press.

Janisse, Michel Pierre, & Dyck, Dennis G. (1988). The Type A behavior pattern and coronary heart disease: Physiological and psychological dimensions. In Michel Pierre Janisse (Ed.), *Individual differences, stress, and health psychology.* New York: Springer-Verlag.

Jarrett, Robin B.; Kraft, Dolores; Doyle, Jeanette; Foster, Barbara M.; Eaves, G. Greg; & Silver, Paul C. (2001). Preventing recurrent depression using cognitive therapy with and without a continuation phase: A randomized clinical trial. *Archives of General Psychiatry, 58,* 381–388.

Jefferson, James W. (1995). Lithium: The present and the future. *Journal of Clinical Psychiatry, 56,* 41–48.

Jewett, Megan E.; Wyatt, James K.; Ritz-De Cecco, Angela; Khalsa, Sat Bir; Dijk, Derk-Jan; & Czeisler, Charles A. (1999). Time course of sleep inertia dissipation in human performance and alertness. *Journal of Sleep Research, 8,* 1–8.

Jilek, Wolfgang G. (1993). Traditional medicine relevant to psychiatry. In Norman Sartorius, Giovanni de Girolamo, Gavin Andrews, G. Allen German, & Leon Eisenberg (Eds.), *Treatment of mental disorders: A review of effectiveness.* Washington, DC: World Health Organization/American Psychiatric Press.

John, Oliver P. (1990). The "Big Five" factor taxonomy: Dimensions of personality in the natural language and in questionnaires. In Lawrence A. Pervin (Ed.), *Handbook of personality: Theory and research.* New York: Guilford Press.

Johnson, Hollyn M. (1994). Processes of successful intentional forgetting. *Psychological Bulletin, 116,* 274–292.

Johnson, Jeffrey G.; Cohen, Patricia; & others. (2001). Association of maladaptive parental behavior with psychiatric disorder among parents and their offspring. *Archives of General Psychiatry, 58,* 453–460.

Johnson, John A., & Ostendorf, Fritz. (1993). Clarification of the five-factor model with the abridged Big Five dimensional circumplex. *Journal of Personality and Social Psychology, 65,* 563–576.

Johnson, Katrina W.; Anderson, Norman B.; Bastida, Elena; Kramer, B. Josea; Williams, David; & Wong, Morrison. (1995). Panel II: Macrosocial and environmental influences on minority health. *Health Psychology, 14,* 601–612.

Johnson, Mark H.; Dziurawiec, Suzanne; Ellis, Hadyn; & Morton, John. (1991). Newborns' preferential tracking of face-like stimuli and its subsequent decline. *Cognition, 40,* 1–19.

Johnson, Sheri L., & Roberts, John E. (1995). Life events and bipolar disorder: Implications from three biological theories. *Psychological Bulletin, 117,* 434–449.

Johnston, Daniel; Magee, Jeffrey C.; Colbert, Costa M.; & Christie, Brian R. (1996). Active properties of neuronal dendrites. *Annual Review of Neuroscience, 19,* 165–186.

Jones, Edward E. (1990). *Interpersonal perception.* New York: Freeman.

Jones, Edward E., & Nisbett, Richard E. (1971). *The actor and the observer: Divergent perceptions of the causes of behavior.* Morristown, NJ: General Learning Press.

Jones, Ernest. (1953). *The life and work of Sigmund Freud: Vol. 1. The formative years and the great discoveries: 1856–1900.* New York: Basic Books.

Jones, Ernest. (1955). *The life and work of Sigmund Freud: Years of maturity, 1901–1919.* New York: Basic Books.

Jones, James M. (1991). Psychological models of race: What have they been and what should they be? In Jacqueline D. Goodchilds (Ed.), *Psychological perspectives on human diversity in America.* Washington, DC: American Psychological Association.

Jones, Mary Cover. (1924a). The elimination of children's fears. *Journal of Experimental Psychology, 7,* 382–390.

Jones, Mary Cover. (1924b). A laboratory study of fear: The case of Peter. *Pedagogical Seminary and Journal of Genetic Psychology, 31,* 308–315.

Jones, Mary Cover. (1974). Albert, Peter, and John B. Watson. *American Psychologist, 29,* 581–583.

Jones, Mary Cover. (1975). A 1924 pioneer looks at behavior therapy. *Journal of Behavior Therapy and Experimental Psychiatry, 6,* 181–187.

Jones, Rachel. (2001). Mapping grey matter. *Nature Reviews Neuroscience, 2,* 759.

Jones, Warren H., & Russell, Dan W. (1980). The selective processing of belief-discrepant information. *European Journal of Social Psychology, 10,* 309–312.

Jonnes, Jill. (1999). *Hep-cats, narcs, and pipe dreams: A history of America's romance with illegal drugs.* Baltimore: Johns Hopkins University Press.

Joyner, Kara, & Laumann, Edward O. (2001). Teenage sex and the sexual revolution. In Edward O. Laumann & Robert T. Michael (Eds.), *Sex, love, and health in America: Private choices and public policies.* Chicago: University of Chicago Press.

Judd, Charles M., & Park, Bernadette. (1993). Definition and assessment of accuracy in social stereotypes. *Psychological Review, 100,* 109–128.

Judge, Timothy A., & Watanabe, Shinichiro. (1993). Another look at the job satisfaction–life satisfaction relationship. *Journal of Applied Psychology, 78,* 939–948.

Julien, Robert M. (2001). *A primer of drug action: A concise nontechnical guide to the actions, uses, and side effects of psychoactive drugs.* (9th ed.). New York: Worth.

Jung, Carl G. (1923/1976). Psychological types. In Joseph Campbell (Ed.), *The portable Jung.* New York: Penguin.

Jung, Carl G. (1931/1976). The structure of the psyche. In Joseph Campbell (Ed.), *The portable Jung.* New York: Penguin.

Jung, Carl G. (1936/1976). The concept of the collective unconscious. In Joseph Campbell (Ed.), *The portable Jung.* New York: Penguin.

Jung, Carl G. (1951/1976). Aion: Phenomenology of the self. In Joseph Campbell (Ed.), *The portable Jung.* New York: Penguin.

Jung, Carl G. (1963). *Memories, dreams, reflections* (Richard and Clara Winston, Trans.). New York: Random House.

Jung, Carl G. (1964). *Man and his symbols.* New York: Dell.

Jung, Carl G. (1974). *Dreams* (R. F. C. Hull, Trans.). New York: MJF Books.

Kaas, Jon H., & Collins, Christine E. (2001). Evolving ideas of brain evolution. *Nature, 411,* 141–142.

Kagitçibasi, Cigdem. (1997). Individualism and collectivism. In John W. Berry, Cigdem Kagitçibasi, & Marshall H. Segall (Eds.), *Handbook of cross-cultural psychology* (2nd ed., Vol. 3). Boston: Allyn & Bacon.

Kahn, Edwin; Fisher, Charles; & Edwards, Adele. (1991). Night terrors and anxiety dreams. In Steven J. Ellman & John S. Antrobus (Eds.), *The mind in sleep: Psychology and psychophysiology* (2nd ed.). New York: Wiley.

Kahneman, Daniel, & Tversky, Amos. (1982). On the psychology of prediction. In Daniel Kahneman, Paul Slovic, & Amos Tversky (Eds.), *Judgment under uncertainty: Heuristics and biases.* New York: Cambridge University Press.

Kail, Robert. (1991). Developmental change in speed of processing during childhood and adolescence. *Psychological Bulletin, 109,* 490–501.

Kaiser, Daren H.; Zentall, Thomas R.; & Galef, Bennett G., Jr. (1997). Can imitation in pigeons be explained by local enhancement together with trial-and-error learning? *Psychological Science, 8,* 459–460.

Kaitz, Marsha; Lapidot, Pnina; Bronner, Ruth; & Eidelman, Arthur I. (1992). Parturient women can recognize their infants by touch. *Developmental Psychology, 28,* 35–39.

Kalat, James W. (1985). Taste-aversion learning in ecological perspective. In Timothy D. Johnston & Alexandra T. Pietrewicz (Eds.), *Issues in the ecological study of learning.* Hillsdale, NJ: Erlbaum.

Kalawsky, Roy. S. (1993). *The science of virtual reality and virtual environments.* Reading, MA: Addison-Wesley.

Kalbfleisch, Pamela J., & Cody, Michael J. (Eds.). (1995). *Gender, power, and communication in human relationships.* Hillsdale, NJ: Erlbaum.

Kalichman, Seth C. (1998). *Understanding AIDS: A guide for mental health professionals* (2nd ed.). Washington, DC: American Psychological Association.

Kamin, Leon J. (1995). The pioneers of IQ testing. In Russell Jacoby & Naomi Glauberman (Eds.), *The Bell Curve debate: History, documents, opinions.* New York: Times Books.

Kampe, Knut K. W. (2001, October 10). Quoted in MSNBC Science News, "When eyes meet, the brain soars." Retrieved on February 27, 2002 from: http://stacks.msnbc.com/news/641208.asp

Kampe, Knut K. W.; Frith, Chris D.; Dolan, Raymond J.; & Frith, Uta. (2001, October 11).

Reward value of attractiveness and gaze. *Nature, 413,* 589.

Kamps, Debra M.; Leonard, Betsy R.; Vernon, Sue; Dugan, Erin P.; & Delquadri, Joseph C. (1992). Teaching social skills to students with autism to increase peer interactions in an integrated first-grade classroom. *Journal of Applied Behavior Analysis, 25,* 281–288.

Kandel, Eric A. (2001). The molecular biology of memory storage: A dialogue between genes and synapses. *Science, 294,* 1030–1038.

Kane, John M. (1994). Editorial: Risperidone. *American Journal of Psychiatry, 151,* 802–803.

Kanin, Eugene J. (1982). Female rape fantasies: A victimization study. *Victimology, 7,* 114–121.

Kanner, Allen D.; Coyne, James C.; Schaefer, Catherine; & Lazarus, Richard S. (1981). Comparison of two modes of stress management: Daily hassles and uplifts versus major life events. *Journal of Behavioral Medicine, 4,* 1–39.

Kanwisher, Nancy. (2001). Faces and places: Of central (and peripheral) interest. *Nature Neuroscience, 4,* 455–456.

Kaplan, Craig A., & Simon, Herbert A. (1990). In search of insight. *Cognitive Psychology, 22,* 374–419.

Kaplan, Steve. (1990). Capturing your creativity. In Michael G. Walraven & Hiram E. Fitzgerald (Eds.), *Annual editions: Psychology: 1990/91.* Guilford, CT: Dushkin.

Kaplan, Stuart L., & Busner, Joan. (1993). Treatment of nocturnal enuresis. In Thomas R. Giles (Ed.), *Handbook of effective psychotherapy.* New York: Plenum Press.

Karau, Steven J., & Williams, Kipling D. (1993). Social loafing: A meta-analytic review and theoretical integration. *Journal of Personality and Social Psychology, 65,* 681–706.

Karney, Benjamin R., & Bradbury, Thomas N. (1995). The longitudinal course of marital quality and stability: A review of theory, method, and research. *Psychological Bulletin, 118*(1), 3–34.

Karni, Avi; Tanne, David; Rubenstein, Barton S.; Askenasy, Jean J. M.; & Sagi, Dov. (1994, July 29). Dependence on REM sleep of overnight improvement of a perceptual skill. *Science, 265,* 679–682.

Karson, Samuel, & O'Dell, Jerry W. (1989). The 16 PF. In Charles S. Newmark (Ed.), *Major psychological assessment instruments* (Vol. 2). Boston: Allyn & Bacon.

Kasl, Charlotte Davis. (1992). *Many roads, one journey: Moving beyond the twelve steps.* New York: HarperPerennial.

Kasser, Tim, & Sharma, Yadika S. (1999). Reproductive freedom, educational equality, and females' preference for resource-acquisition characteristics in mates. *Psychological Science, 10,* 374–377.

Kastenbaum, Robert. (1986). *Death, society, and the human experience.* Columbus, OH: Merrill.

Kastenbaum, Robert. (1992). *The psychology of death.* New York: Springer-Verlag.

Katchadourian, Herant A. (1990). Sexuality. In S. Shirley Feldman & Glen R. Elliott (Eds.), *At the threshold: The developing adolescent.* Cambridge, MA: Harvard University Press.

Katkin, Edward S.; Wiens, Stefan; & Ohman, Arne. (2001). Nonconscious fear conditioning, visceral perception, and the development of gut feelings. *Psychological Science, 12,* 366–370.

Katkowski, David A., & Medsker, Gina J. (2001). SIOP income and employment: Income and employment of SIOP members in 2000. *The Industrial-Organizational Psychologist, 39,* 21–36.

Katz, David M. (1999). Caution urged on e-mail probes. *National Underwriter, 17,* 3.

Katz, Donald B.; Nicolelis, Miguel A. L.; & Simon, S. A. (2000). Nutrient tasting and signaling mechanisms in the gut IV. There is more to taste than meets the tongue. *American Journal of Physiology, 278,* G6–G9.

Katzman, Robert. (1993). Education and the prevalence of dementia and Alzheimer's disease. *Neurology, 43,* 13–18.

Kaufman, Alan S. (1990). *Assessing adolescent and adult intelligence.* Boston: Allyn & Bacon.

Kaufman, Lloyd, & Kaufman, James H. (2000). Explaining the moon illusion. *Proceedings of the National Academy of Sciences, USA, 97,* 500–505.

Kaufmann, Dagmar; Gesten, Ellis; Santa Lucia, Raymond C.; & others. (2000). The relationship between parenting style and children's adjustment: The parents' perspective. *Journal of Child and Family Studies, 9,* 231–245.

Kawamura, Kathleen Y.; Frost, Randy O.; & Harmatz, Morton G. (2002). The relationship of perceived parenting styles to perfectionism. *Personality and Individual Differences, 32,* 317–327.

Kaye, Walter H.; Klump, K. L.; Frank, G. K. W.; & Strober, Michael. (2000). Anorexia and bulimia nervosa. *Annual Review of Medicine, 51,* 299–313.

Kazdin, Alan E. (1982). The token economy: A decade later. *Journal of Applied Behavior Analysis, 15,* 431–445.

Kazdin, Alan E. (1994a). Methodology, design, and evaluation in psychotherapy research. In Allen E. Bergin & Sol L. Garfield (Eds.), *Handbook of psychotherapy and behavior change* (4th ed.). New York: Wiley.

Kazdin, Alan E. (1994b). Psychotherapy for children and adolescents. In Allen E. Bergin & Sol L. Garfield (Eds.), *Handbook of psychotherapy and behavior change* (4th ed.). New York: Wiley.

Kazdin, Alan E. (2001). *Behavior modification in applied settings* (6th ed.). Belmont, CA: Wadsworth.

Keating, Daniel P. (1990). Adolescent thinking. In Glen R. Elliott & S. Shirley Feldman (Eds.), *At the threshold: The developing adolescent.* Cambridge, MA: Harvard University Press.

Keck, Paul E., & McElroy, Susan L. (1993). Current perspectives on treatment of bipolar disorder with lithium. *Psychiatric Annals, 23,* 64–69.

Keefe, Richard S., & Harvey, Philip D. (1994). *Understanding schizophrenia: A guide to the new research on causes and treatment.* New York: Free Press.

Keesey, Richard E., & Hirvonen, Matt D. (1997). Body weight set-points: determination and adjustment. *Journal of Nutrition, 127,* 1875S–1883S.

Keesey, Richard E., & Powley, Terry L. (1986). The regulation of body weight. *Annual Review of Psychology, 37,* 109–133.

Keller, Martin B.; McCullough, J. P.; Klein, D. N.; Arnow, B.; Dunner, D. L.; Gelenberg, A. J.; & others. (2000). A comparison of nefazodone, the cognitive-behavioral analysis system of psychotherapy, and their combination for the treatment of chronic depression. *New England Journal of Medicine, 342,* 1462–1470.

Kelly, Ciara, & McCreadie, Robin. (1999). Smoking habits, current symptoms, and premorbid characteristics of schizophrenic patients in Nithsdale, Scotland. *American Journal of Psychiatry, 156,* 1751–1757.

Keltner, Dacher, & Anderson, Cameron. (2000). Saving face for Darwin: The functions and uses of embarrassment. *Current Directions in Psychological Science, 9,* 187–192.

Keltner, Dacher, & Buswell, Brenda N. (1997). Embarrassment: Its distinct form and appeasement functions. *Psychological Bulletin, 122,* 250–270.

Kempermann, Gerd, & Gage, Fred H. (1999, May). New nerve cells for the adult brain. *Scientific American, 280,* 48–53.

Kempermann, Gerd; Kuhn, H. Georg; & Gage, Fred H. (1998, May 1). Experience-induced neurogenesis in the senescent dentate gyrus. *Journal of Neuroscience, 18,* 3206–3212.

Kendler, Kenneth S., & Diehl, Scott R. (1993). The genetics of schizophrenia: A current genetic-epidemiologic perspective. *Schizophrenia Bulletin, 19,* 261–285.

Kendler, Kenneth S.; Kessler, Ronald C.; Neale, Michael C.; Heath, Andrew C.; & Eaves, Lindon J. (1993a). The prediction of major depression in women: Toward an integrated etiologic model. *American Journal of Psychiatry, 150,* 1139–1148.

Kendler, Kenneth S.; Neale, Michael C.; MacLean, Charles J.; & others. (1993b). Smoking and major depression: A causal analysis. *Archives of General Psychiatry, 50,* 36–43.

Kendler, Kenneth S.; Neale, Michael C.; Kessler, Ronald C.; Heath, Andrew C.; & Eaves, Lindon J. (1993c). A longitudinal twin study of personality and major depression in women. *Archives of General Psychiatry, 50,* 853–862.

Kendler, Kenneth S.; Neale, Michael C.; Kessler, Ronald C.; Heath, Andrew C.; & Eaves, Lindon J. (1993d). The lifetime history of major depression in women: Reliability of diagnosis and heritability. *Archives of General Psychiatry, 50,* 863–870.

Kenrick, Douglas T.; Trost, Melanie R.; & Sheets, Virgil L. (1996). Power, harassment, and trophy mates: The feminist advantages of an evolutionary perspective. In David M. Buss & Neil M. Malumuth (Eds.), *Sex, power, conflict: Evolutionary and feminist perspectives.* New York: Oxford University Press.

Kessen, William. (1996). American psychology just before Piaget. *Psychological Science, 7,* 196–199.

Kessler, Ronald C. (1994, January 22). "Really serious conditions. . . ." Quoted in *Science News, 145,* 55.

Kessler, Ronald C.; McGonagle, Katherine A.; Zhao, Shanyang; Nelson, Christopher B.; Hughes, Michael; Eshleman, Suzann; & others. (1994). Lifetime and 12-month prevalence of DSM-III-R psychiatric disorders in the United States: Results from the National Comorbidity Survey (NCS). *Archives of General Psychiatry, 51,* 8–19.

Kessler, Ronald C.; Price, Richard H.; & Wortman, Camille B. (1985). Social factors in psychopathology: Stress, social support, and coping processes. *Annual Review of Psychology, 36,* 531–572.

Kibel, Howard D. (1993). Inpatient group psychotherapy. In Anne Alonso & Hillel I. Swiller (Eds.), *Group therapy in clinical practice.* Washington, DC: American Psychiatric Press.

Kiecolt-Glaser, Janice K. (1999). Stress, personal relationships, and immune function: Health implications. *Brain, Behavior and Immunity, 13*(1), 61–72.

Kiecolt-Glaser, Janice K., & Glaser, Ronald. (1991). Stress and immune function in humans. In Robert Ader, David L. Felten, & Nicholas Cohen (Eds.), *Psychoneuroimmunology.* San Diego, CA: Academic Press.

Kiecolt-Glaser, Janice K., & Glaser, Ronald. (1993). Mind and immunity. In Daniel Goleman & Joel Gurin (Eds.), *Mind / body medicine: How to use your mind for better health.* Yonkers, NY: Consumer Reports Books.

Kiecolt-Glaser, Janice K., & Glaser, Ronald. (2001, Winter). Psychological stress and wound healing. *Advances in Mind-Body Medicine, 17,* 15–17.

Kiecolt-Glaser, Janice K.; McGuire, Lynanne; Robles, Theodore, F.; & Glaser, Ronald. (2002). Emotions, morbidity, and mortality: New perspectives from psychoneuroimmunology. *Annual Review of Psychology, 53,* 83–107.

Kiecolt-Glaser, Janice K., & Newton, Tamara L. (2001). Marriage and health: His and hers. *Psychological Bulletin, 127,* 472–503.

Kiecolt-Glaser, Janice K.; Page, Gayle G.; Marucha, Phillip T.; MacCallum, Robert C.; & Glaser, Ronald. (1998). Psychological influences on surgical recovery: Perspectives from

psychoneuroimmunology. *American Psychologist, 53,* 1209–1218.

Kiesler, Charles A., & Kiesler, Sara B. (1969). *Conformity.* Reading, MA: Addison-Wesley.

Kihlstrom, John F. (1992). Dissociation and dissociations: A comment on consciousness and cognition. *Consciousness & Cognition, 1,* 47–53.

Kihlstrom, John F. (1993). The continuum of consciousness. *Consciousness & Cognition, 2,* 334–354.

Kihlstrom, John F. (1995, September). On the validity of psychology experiments. *APS Observer, 8*(5), 10–11.

Kihlstrom, John F. (2001). Hypnosis and the psychological unconscious. In Howard S. Friedman (Ed.), *Assessment and therapy: Specialty articles from the Encyclopedia of Mental Health.* San Diego, CA: Academic Press.

Kihlstrom, John F., & Barnhardt, Terrence M. (1993). The self-regulation of memory: For better and for worse, with and without hypnosis. In Daniel M. Wegner & James W. Pennebaker (Eds.), *Handbook of mental control.* Englewood Cliffs, NJ: Prentice-Hall.

Kihlstrom, John F.; Barnhardt, Terrence M.; & Tataryn, Douglas J. (1992). The psychological unconscious: Found, lost, and regained. *American Psychologist, 47,* 788–791.

Kihlstrom, John F.; Glisky, Martha L.; & Angiulo, Michael J. (1994). Dissociative tendencies and dissociative disorders. *Journal of Abnormal Psychology, 103,* 117–124.

Kihlstrom, John F.; Mulvaney, Shelagh; Tobias, Betsy A.; & Tobis, Irene P. (2000). In Eric Eich, John F. Kihlstrom, Gordon H. Bower, Joseph P. Forgas, & Paula M. Niedenthal (Eds.), *Cognition and emotion.* New York: Oxford University Press.

Kimura, Doreen. (1992, September). Sex differences in the brain. *Scientific American, 267,* 80–87.

Kimura, Doreen. (1999). *Sex and cognition.* Cambridge, MA: MIT Press.

Kimzey, Stephen L. (1975). The effects of extended spaceflight on hematologic and immunologic systems. *Journal of the American Medical Women's Association, 30,* 218–232.

King, D. Brett; Cox, Michaella; & Wertheimer, Michael. (1998). Karl Duncker: Productive problems with beautiful solutions. In George A. Kimble & Michael Wertheimer (Eds.), *Portraits of pioneers in psychology* (Vol. 3). Washington, DC: American Psychological Association.

Kinsella, Kevin, & Velkoff, Victoria A. (2001). *An Aging World: 2001* (International Population Report, Series P95/01–1). Washington, DC: U.S. Government Printing Office, U.S. Census Bureau.

Kirchgessner, Annette L., & Liu, Min-tsai. (1999). Orexin synthesis and response in the gut. *Neuron, 24,* 941–51.

Kirsch, Irving. (1996). Hypnotic enhancement of cognitive-behavioral weight loss treatments:

Another meta-reanalysis. *Journal of Consulting and Clinical Psychology, 64,* 517–519.

Kirsch, Irving, & Braffman, Wayne. (2001). Imaginative suggestibility and hypnotizability. *Current Directions in Psychological Science, 10,* 57–61.

Kirsch, Irving; Montgomery, Guy; & Sapirstein, Guy. (1995). Hypnosis as an adjunct to cognitive-behavioral psychotherapy: A meta-analysis. *Journal of Consulting and Clinical Psychology, 63,* 214–220.

Kitayama, Shinobu; Markus, Hazel Rose; & Kurokawa, Masaru. (2000). Culture, emotion, and well-being: Good feelings in Japan and the United States. *Cognition & Emotion, 14,* 93–124.

Kitayama, Shinobu; Markus, Hazel Rose; Matsumoto, Hisaya; & Norasakkunkit, Vinai. (1997). Individual and collective processes in the construction of the self: Self-enhancement in the United States and self-criticism in Japan. *Journal of Personality and Social Psychology, 72,* 1245–1267.

Kivlighan, Dennis M., Jr.; Multon, Karen D.; & Patton, Michael J. (2000). Insight and symptom reduction in time-limited psychoanalytic counseling. *Journal of Counseling Psychology, 47,* 50–58.

Klahr, David. (1992). Information-processing approaches. In Ross Vasta (Ed.), *Six theories of child development: Revised formulations and current issues.* London: Jessica Kingsley.

Klein, Donald F., & Wender, Paul H. (1993). *Understanding depression: A complete guide to its diagnosis and treatment.* New York: Oxford University Press.

Klein, Stephen B., & Mowrer, Robert R. (1989). *Contemporary learning theories: Instrumental conditioning theory and the impact of biological constraints on learning.* Hillsdale, NJ: Erlbaum.

Klerman, Elizabeth B.; Rimmer, David W.; Czeisler, Charles A.; & others. (1998). Nonphotic entrainment of the human circadian pacemaker. *American Journal of Physiology, 274,* R991–R996.

Klerman, Gerald L., & Weissman, Myrna M. (Eds.). (1993). *New applications of interpersonal psychotherapy.* Washington, DC: American Psychiatric Association.

Klerman, Gerald L.; Weissman, Myrna M.; Markowitz, John; Glick, Ira; Wilner, Philip J.; Mason, Barbara; & Shear, M. Katherine. (1994). Medication and psychotherapy. In Sol L. Garfield & Allen E. Bergin (Eds.), *Handbook of psychotherapy and behavior change* (4th ed.). New York: Wiley.

Klerman, Gerald L.; Weissman, Myrna M.; Rounsaville, Bruce J.; & Chevron, Eve S. (1984). *Interpersonal psychotherapy of depression.* New York: Basic Books.

Klinger, Eric. (1993). Clinical approaches to mood control. In Daniel M. Wegner & James W. Pennebaker (Eds.), *Handbook of mental control.* Englewood Cliffs, NJ: Prentice-Hall.

Kluft, Richard P. (1993). Multiple personality disorders. In David Spiegel (Ed.), *Dissociative disorders: A clinical review*. Lutherville, MD: Sidran.

Knowles, John B. (1963). Conditioning and the placebo effect: The effects of decaffeinated coffee on simple reaction time in habitual coffee drinkers. *Behavior Research and Therapy, 1,* 151–157.

Koffka, Kurt. (1935). *Principles of Gestalt psychology*. New York: Harcourt, Brace.

Kohen, Daniel P., & Olness, Karen. (1993). Hypnotherapy with children. In Judith W. Rhue, Steven J. Lynn, & Irving Kirsch (Eds.), *Handbook of clinical hypnosis*. Washington, DC: American Psychological Association.

Kohlberg, Lawrence. (1976). Moral stages and moralization: The cognitive-developmental approach. In T. Lickona (Ed.), *Moral development and behavior: Theory, research, and social issues*. New York: Holt, Rinehart & Winston.

Kohlberg, Lawrence. (1981). *The philosophy of moral development: Moral stages and the idea of justice: Vol. 1. Essays on moral development*. New York: Harper & Row.

Kohlberg, Lawrence. (1984). *The psychology of moral development*. New York: Harper & Row.

Kolb, Bryan, & Whishaw, Ian Q. (1998). Brain plasticity and behavior. *Annual Review of Neuroscience, 49,* 43–64.

Konishi, Masakazu. (1993, April). Listening with two ears. *Scientific American, 268,* 66–73.

Kopelman, Peter G. (2000, April 6). Obesity as a medical problem. *Nature, 404,* 635–643.

Koplan, Jeffrey P., & Dietz, William H. (1999, October 27). Caloric imbalance and public health policy. *Journal of the American Medical Association, 282,* 1579–1581.

Kopta, S. Mark; Lueger, Robert J.; Saunders, Stephen M.; & Howard, Kenneth I. (1999). Individual psychotherapy outcome and process research: Challenges leading to greater turmoil or a positive transition? *Annual Review of Psychology, 50,* 441–469.

Korabik, Karen; Baril, Galen L.; & Watson, Carol. (1993). Managers; conflict management style and leadership effectiveness: The moderating effects of gender. *Sex Roles, 29,* 405–420.

Koriat, Asher. (1993). How do we know that we know? The accessibility model of the feeling of knowing. *Psychological Review, 100,* 609–639.

Koriat, Asher; Goldsmith, Morris; & Pansky, Ainat. (2000). Toward a psychology of memory accuracy. *Annual Review of Psychology, 51,* 481–537.

Kornfeld, Alfred D. (1989). Mary Cover Jones and the Peter case: Social learning versus conditioning. *Journal of Anxiety Disorders, 3,* 187–195.

Koss, Mary P., & Shiang, Julia. (1994). Research on brief psychotherapy. In Allen E. Bergin & Sol L. Garfield (Eds.), *Handbook of psychotherapy and behavior change* (4th ed.). New York: Wiley.

Kosslyn, Stephen M. (2001, May-June). Quoted in Andrew Cocke, "The science behind hypnosis." *BrainWork: The Neuroscience Newsletter, 11,* 7.

Kosslyn, Stephen M.; Ball, Thomas M.; & Reiser, Brian J. (1978). Visual images preserve metric spatial information: Evidence from studies of image scanning. *Journal of Experimental Psychology: Human Perception and Performance, 4,* 47–60.

Kosslyn, Stephen M.; Ganis, Giorgio; & Thompson, William L. (2001). Neural foundations of imagery. *Nature Reviews Neuroscience, 2,* 635–642.

Kosslyn, Stephen M., & Thompson, William L. (2000). Shared mechanisms in visual imagery and visual perception: Insights from cognitive neuroscience. In Michael S. Gazzaniga (Ed.), *The new cognitive neurosciences* (2nd ed.). Cambridge, MA: MIT Press.

Kosslyn, Stephen M.; Thompson, William L.; Costantini-Ferrando, Maria F.; Alpert, Nathaniel M.; & Spiegel, David. (2000). Hypnotic visual illusion alters color processing in the brain. *American Journal of Psychiatry, 157,* 1279–1284.

Kramer, Jack L., & Conoley, Jane Close (Eds.). (1992). *The eleventh mental measurements yearbook*. Lincoln: Buros Institute of Mental Measurements/University of Nebraska Press.

Kramer, Peter D. (1993). *Listening to Prozac: A psychiatrist explores antidepressant drugs and the remaking of the self*. New York: Viking.

Krantz, David S., & McCeney, Melissa K. (2002). Effects of psychological and social factors on organic disease: A critical assessment of research on coronary heart disease. *Annual Review of Psychology, 53,* 341–369.

Krauss, Robert M., & Chiu, Chi-Yue. (1998). Language and social behavior. In Daniel T. Gilbert, Susan T. Fiske, & Gardner Lindzey (Eds.), *The handbook of social psychology* (4th ed.). New York: McGraw-Hill.

Krausz, Michael, & Müller-Thomsen, Tomas. (1993). Schizophrenia with onset in adolescence: An 11-year followup. *Schizophrenia Bulletin, 19,* 831–841.

Kreisman, Jerold J., & Straus, Hal. (1991). *I hate you—don't leave me: Understanding the borderline personality*. New York: Avon.

Kring, Ann M., & Gordon, Albert H. (1998). Sex differences in emotion: Expression, experience, and physiology. *Journal of Personality and Social Psychology, 74,* 686–703.

Krippner, Stanley. (1994). Cross-cultural treatment perspectives of dissociative disorders. In Steven Jay Lynn & Judith W. Rhue (Eds.), *Dissociation: Clinical and theoretical perspectives*. New York: Guilford Press.

Kronauer, Richard E. (1994). Circadian rhythms. In Rosemary Cooper (Ed.), *Sleep*. New York: Chapman & Hall.

Krosnick, Jon A.; Betz, Andrew L.; Jussim, Lee J.; & Lynn, Ann R. (1992). Subliminal conditioning of attitudes. *Personality and Social Psychology Bulletin, 18,* 152–162.

Kübler-Ross, Elisabeth. (1969). *On death and dying*. New York: Macmillan.

Kuhl, Patricia K.; Andruski, Jean E.; Chistovich, Inna A.; Chistovich, Ludmilla A.; Kozhevnikova, Elena V.; Ryskina, Viktoria L.; & others. (1997, August 1). Cross-language analysis of phonetic units in language addressed to infants. *Science, 277,* 684–686.

Kuhl, Patricia K.; Williams, Karen A.; Lacerda, Francisco; Stevens, Kenneth N.; & Lindblom, Bjorn. (1992, January 31). Linguistic experience alters phonetic perception in infants by 6 months of age. *Science, 255,* 606–608.

Kuhn, Cynthia M., & Wilson, Wilkie A. (2001, Spring). Ecstasy on trial: Our dangerous love affair with Ecstasy. *Cerebrum, 3,* 22–33.

Kunoh, Hiroshi, & Takaoki, Eiji. (1994). *3-D planet: The world as seen through stereograms*. San Francisco: Cadence Books.

Kupfer, David J., & Frank, Ellen. (2001). The interaction of drug- and psychotherapy in the long-term treatment of depression. *Journal of Affective Disorders, 62,* 131–137.

Kurdek, Lawrence A. (1995). Developmental changes in relationship quality in gay and lesbian cohabiting couples. *Developmental Psychology, 31,* 86–94.

Kurtz, Paul, & Fraknoi, Andrew. (1986). Scientific tests of astrology do not support its claims. In Kendrick Frazier (Ed.), *Science confronts the paranormal*. Buffalo, NY: Prometheus Books.

LaFrance, Marianne. (2000, January 26). *The psychological, interpersonal, and social effects of bad hair*. Unpublished manuscript. CNN.com: The psychology of bad hair days. <http://cnn.com/2000/STYLE/fashion/01/26/bad.hair.ap/index.html> (February 17, 2000).

LaFromboise, Teresa D.; Coleman, Hardin L. K.; & Gerton, Jennifer. (1993a). Psychological impact of biculturalism: Evidence and theory. *Psychological Bulletin, 114,* 395–412.

LaFromboise, Teresa D.; Trimble, Joseph E.; & Mohatt, Gerald V. (1993b). Counseling intervention and American Indian tradition: An integrative approach. In Donald R. Atkinson, George Morten, & Derald Wing Sue (Eds.), *Counseling American minorities: A cross-cultural perspective* (4th ed.). Madison, WI: Brown & Benchmark.

Lamb, Michael E.; Sternberg, Kathleen J.; & Prodromidis, Margarita. (1992). Nonmaternal care and the security of infant-mother attachment: A reanalysis of the data. *Infant Behavior and Development, 15,* 71–83.

Lamb, Michael E.; Thompson, Ross A.; Gardner, William; & Charnov, Eric L. (1985). *Infant–mother attachment: The origins and developmental significance of individual differences in Strange Situation behavior*. Hillsdale, NJ: Erlbaum.

Lambert, Michael J., & Bergin, Allen E. (1994). The effectiveness of psychotherapy. In Allen E. Bergin & Sol L. Garfield (Eds.), *Handbook of psychotherapy and behavior change* (4th ed.). New York: Wiley.

Lamson, Ralph. (1994, November). Quoted in Virtual therapy. *Psychology Today, 27,* 21.

Lance, Charles E.; Lautenschlager, Gary J.; Sloan, Christopher E.; & Varcar, Philip E. (1989). A comparison between bottom-up, top-down, and bidirectional models of relationships between global and life facet satisfaction. *Journal of Personality, 57,* 601–624.

Landau, Barbara. (1994). Where's what and what's where: The language of objects in space [Special issue]. *Lingua, 92,* 259–296.

Landau, Barbara, & Jackendoff, Ray. (1993). "What" and "where" in spatial language and spatial cognition. *Behavioral and Brain Sciences, 16,* 217–265.

Lander, Hans Jürgen. (1997). Hermann Ebbinghaus. In Wolfgang G. Bringmann, Helmut E. Lück, Rudolf Miller, & Charles E. Early (Eds.), *A pictorial history of psychology.* Chicago: Quintessence.

Lane, Richard D.; Reiman, Eric M.; Ahern, Geoffrey L.; Schwartz, Gary E.; & Davidson, Richard J. (1997). Neuroanatomical correlates of happiness, sadness, and disgust. *American Journal of Psychiatry, 154,* 926–933.

Lange, Carl G., & James, William. (1922). *The emotions* (I. A. Haupt, Trans.). Baltimore: Williams & Wilkins.

Langer, Ellen, & Rodin, Judith. (1976). The effects of choice and enhanced personal responsibility for the aged: A field experiment in an institutional setting. *Journal of Personality and Social Psychology, 34,* 191–198.

Lashley, Karl S. (1929). *Brain mechanisms and intelligence.* Chicago: University of Chicago Press.

Lashley, Karl S. (1950). In search of the engram. *Symposia of the Society for Experimental Biology, 4,* 454–482.

Lask, Bryan. (1995). Night terrors. In Charles E. Schaefer (Ed.), *Clinical handbook of sleep disorders in children.* Northvale, NJ: Aronson.

Lasser, Karen; Boyd, J. Wesley; Woolhandler, Steffie; & others. (2000). Smoking and mental illness: A population-based prevalence study. *Journal of the American Medical Association, 284,* 2606–2610.

Latané, Bibb. (1981). The psychology of social impact. *American Psychologist, 36,* 343–356.

Latané, Bibb, & Darley, John M. (1970). *The unresponsive bystander: Why doesn't he help?* New York: Appleton-Century-Crofts.

Latané, Bibb, & Nida, Steve A. (1981). Ten years of research on group size and helping. *Psychological Bulletin, 89,* 308–324.

Laumann, Edward O.; Gagnon, John H.; Michael, Robert T.; & Michaels, Stuart. (1994). *The social organization of sexuality: Sexual practices in the United States.* Chicago: University of Chicago Press.

Laumann, Edward O., & Michael, Robert T. (Eds.). (2001). *Sex, love, and health in America: Private choices and public policies.* Chicago: University of Chicago Press.

Laumann, Edward O.; Paik, Anthony; & Rosen, Raymond C. (1999, February 10). Sexual dysfunction in the United States: Prevalence and predictors. *Journal of the American Medical Association, 281,* 537–544.

Laumann, Edward O.; Paik, Anthony; & Rosen, Raymond C. (2001). Sexual dysfunction in the United States: Prevalence and predictors. In Edward O. Laumann & Robert T. Michael (Eds.), *Sex, love, and health in America: Private choices and public policies.* Chicago: University of Chicago Press.

Laumann, Edward O., & Youm, Yoosik. (2001). Sexual expression in America. In Edward O. Laumann & Robert T. Michael (Eds.), *Sex, love, and health in America: Private choices and public policies.* Chicago: University of Chicago Press.

Laurence, Jean-Roth, & Perry, Cambell. (1983). Hypnotically created memory among highly hypnotizable subjects. *Science, 222,* 523–524.

Laursen, Brett, & Collins, W. Andrew. (1994). Interpersonal conflict during adolescence. *Psychological Bulletin, 115*(2), 197–209.

Lavie, Peretz. (1989). To nap, perchance to sleep—ultradian aspects of napping. In David F. Dinges & Roger J. Broughton (Eds.), *Sleep and alertness: Chronobiological, behavioral, and medical aspects of napping.* New York: Raven Press.

Lavie, Peretz. (2001). Sleep-wake as a biological rhythm. *Annual Review of Psychology, 52,* 277–303.

Lawler, Edward E., III. (1973). *Motivation in work organizations.* Pacific Grove, CA: Brooks/Cole.

Lawrence, D. H. (1928/1960). *Lady Chatterley's lover.* Hammondsworth, UK: Penguin.

Lazar, Sara W.; Bush, George; Gollub, Randy L.; Fricchione, Gregory L.; Khalsa, Gurucharan; & Benson, Herbert. (2000). Functional brain mapping of the relaxation response and meditation. *Neuroreport: For Rapid Communication of Neuroscience Research, 11,* 1581–1585.

Lazarus, Arnold A. (2000). Will reason prevail? From classic psychoanalysis to New Age therapy. *American Journal of Psychotherapy, 54,* 152–155.

Lazarus, Richard S. (1991). Cognition and motivation in emotion. *American Psychologist, 46,* 352–367.

Lazarus, Richard S. (1993). From psychological stress to the emotions. A history of changing outlooks. *Annual Review of Psychology, 44,* 1–21.

Lazarus, Richard S. (1995). Vexing research problems inherent in cognitive-mediational theories of emotion—and some solutions. *Psychological Inquiry, 6,* 183–197.

Lazarus, Richard S. (1999). *Stress and emotion: A new synthesis.* New York: Springer.

Lazarus, Richard S. (2000). Toward better research on stress and coping. *American Psychologist, 55,* 556–773.

Lazarus, Richard S., & Folkman, Susan. (1984). *Stress, appraisal, and coping.* New York: Springer.

Leach, Carolyn S., & Rambaut, Paul C. (1974). Biochemical responses of the *Skylab* crewmen. *Proceedings of the Skylab Life Sciences Symposium, 2,* 427–454.

LeBlanc, Jacques. (2000). Nutritional implications of cephalic phase thermogenic responses. *Appetite, 34,* 214–216.

Lebow, Jay L., & Gurman, Alan S. (1995). Research assessing couple and family therapy. *Annual Review of Psychology, 46,* 27–57.

LeDoux, Joseph E. (1994a, June). Emotion, memory, and the brain. *Scientific American, 270,* 50–57.

LeDoux, Joseph E. (1994b). Memory versus emotional memory in the brain. In Paul Ekman & Richard J. Davisdon (Eds.), *The nature of emotion: Fundamental questions.* New York: Oxford University Press.

LeDoux, Joseph E. (1995). Emotion: Clues from the brain. *Annual Review of Psychology, 46,* 209–235.

LeDoux, Joseph. (1996). *The emotional brain: The mysterious underpinnings of emotional life.* New York: Simon & Schuster.

LeDoux, Joseph E. (2000). Emotion circuits in the brain. *Annual Review of Neuroscience, 23,* 155–184.

Lee, Kimberly L.; Vaillant, George T.; Torrey, William C.; & Elder, Glen H. (1995). A 50-year prospective study of the psychological sequelae of World War II combat. *American Journal of Psychiatry, 152,* 516–522.

Lees, G. J. (1993). The possible contributions of microglia and macrophages to delayed neuronal death after ischemia. *Journal of the Neurological Sciences, 114,* 119–122.

Lefebvre, Louis; Templeton, Jennifer; Brown, Kathleen; & Koelle, Michelle. (1997). Carib grackles imitate conspecific and Zenaida dove tutors. *Behaviour, 134,* 1003–1017.

Leger, Damien; Guilleminault, Christian; Defrance, Remy; Domont, Alain; & Paillard, Michel. (1999). Prevalence of sleep/wake disorders in persons with blindness. *Clinical Science, 97,* 193–199.

Leibel, Rudolph L.; Rosenbaum, Michael; & Hirsch, Jules. (1995, March 9). Changes in energy expenditure resulting from altered body weight. *New England Journal of Medicine, 332,* 621–628.

Leibenluft, Ellen. (1996). Women with bipolar illness: Clinical and research issues. *American Journal of Psychiatry, 153,* 163–173.

Leitenberg, Harold, & Henning, Kris. (1995). Sexual fantasy. *Psychological Bulletin, 117*(3), 469–496.

Lemish, Dafna. (1998). Fighting against television violence: An Israeli case study. In Ulla Carlsson & Cecilia von Feilitzen (Eds.), *Children and media violence*. Göteborg, Sweden: The UNESCO International Clearinghouse on Children and Media Violence.

Leon, Scott C.; Kopta, S. Mark; Howard, Kenneth I.; & Lutz, Wolfgang. (1999). Predicting patients' responses to psychotherapy: Are some more predictable than others? *Journal of Consulting and Clinical Psychology, 67,* 698–704.

Lepore, Frederick E. (2001, Winter). Dissecting genius: Einstein's brain and the search for the neural basis of intellect. *Cerebrum, 3,* 11–26.

Lepore, Stephen J. (1993). Social conflict, social support, and psychological distress: Evidence of cross-domain buffering effects. *Journal of Personality and Social Psychology, 63,* 857–867.

Lepore, Stephen J.; Silver, Roxane Cohen; Wortman, Camille B.; & Wayment, Heidi A. (1996). Social constraints, intrusive thoughts, and depressive symptoms among bereaved mothers. *Journal of Personality and Social Psychology, 70,* 271–282.

Lerner, M. R.; Gyorgyi, T. K.; Reagan, J.; Roby-Shemkovitz, A.; Rybczynski, R.; & Vogt, R. (1990). Peripheral events in moth olfaction. *Chemical Senses, 15,* 191–198.

Lerner, Melvin J. (1980). *The belief in a just world: A fundamental delusion.* New York: Plenum Press.

Leshner, Alan I. (1997, October 3). Addiction is a brain disease, and it matters. *Science, 278,* 45–47.

Lester, David. (1990, Summer). Biorhythms and the timing of death. *Skeptical Inquirer, 14,* 410–412.

Lester, David. (1997). *Making sense of suicide: An in-depth look at why people kill themselves.* Philadelphia: Charles Press.

Lester, Gregory W. (2000, November/December). Why bad beliefs don't die. *Skeptical Inquirer, 24,* 40–43.

Leuchter, Andrew F.; Cook, Ian A.; Witte, Elise A.; & others. (2002). Changes in brain function of depressed subjects during treatment with placebo. *American Journal of Psychiatry, 159,* 122–129.

LeVay, Simon. (1991, August 30). A difference in hypothalamic structure between heterosexual and homosexual men. *Science, 253,* 1034–1037.

LeVay, Simon, & Hamer, Dean H. (1994, May). Evidence for a biological influence in male homosexuality. *Scientific American, 270,* 44–49.

Levenson, Robert W. (1992). Autonomic nervous system differences among emotions. *Psychological Science, 3,* 23–27.

Levenson, Robert W.; Carstensen, Laura L.; & Gottman, John M. (1994). The influence of age and gender on affect, physiology, and their interrelations: A study of long-term marriages. *Journal of Personality and Social Psychology, 67,* 56–68.

Levenson, Robert W.; Ekman, Paul; & Friesen, Wallace V. (1990). Voluntary facial action generates emotion-specific autonomic nervous system activity. *Psychophysiology, 27,* 363–384.

Levenson, Robert W.; Ekman, Paul; Heider, Karl; & Friesen, Wallace V. (1992). Emotion and autonomic nervous system activity in the Minangkabau of west Sumatra. *Journal of Personality and Social Psychology, 62,* 972–988.

Levin, William C. (1988). Age stereotyping: College student evaluations. *Research on Aging, 10,* 134–148.

Levine, Allen S., & Billington, Charles J. (1997). Why do we eat? A neural systems approach. *Annual Review of Nutrition, 17,* 597–619.

Levine, James A.; Eberhardt, Norman L.; & Jensen, Michael D. (1999, January 8). Role of nonexercise activity thermogenesis in resistence to fat gain in humans. *Science, 283,* 212–214.

Levine, Robert V. (1997). *A geography of time: The temporal misadventures of a social psychologist, or how every culture keeps time just a little bit differently.* New York: Basic Books.

Levine, Robert V., & Norenzayan, Ara. (1999). The pace of life in 31 countries. *Journal of Cross-Cultural Psychology, 30,* 178–205.

Levy, Becca. (1996). Improving memory in old age through implicit self-stereotyping. *Journal of Personality and Social Psychology, 71,* 1092–1107.

Levy, Becca, & Langer, Ellen. (1994). Aging free from negative stereotypes: Successful memory in China and among the American Deaf. *Journal of Personality and Social Psychology, 66,* 989–997.

Levy-Shiff, Rachel. (1994). Individual and contextual correlates of marital change across the transition to parenthood. *Developmental Psychology, 30,* 591–601.

Lewis, Robin J., & Janda, Louis H. (1988). The relationship between adult sexual adjustment and childhood experiences regarding exposure to nudity, sleeping in the parental bed, and parental attitudes toward sexuality. *Archives of Sexual Behavior, 17,* 349–362.

Lewontin, Richard. (1970, March). Race and intelligence. *Bulletin of the Atomic Scientists,* pp. 2–8.

Lewy, Alfred J., & Sack, Robert L. (1987). Phase typing and bright light therapy of chronobiological sleep and mood disorders. In Angelos Halaris (Ed.), *Chronobiology and psychiatric disorders.* New York: Elsevier.

Lickey, Marvin E., & Gordon, Barbara. (1991). *Medicine and mental illness: The use of drugs in psychiatry.* New York: Freeman.

Liddle, Rodger A. (1997). Cholecystokinin cells. *Annual Review of Physiology, 59,* 221–242.

Lieberman, Matthew D. (2000). Intuition: A social cognitive neuroscience approach. *Psychological Bulletin, 126,* 109–137.

Lieberman, Robert Paul. (2000). The token economy. *American Journal of Psychiatry, 157,* 1398.

Liebowitz, Michael R.; Salmán, Ester; Jusino, Carlos M.; Garfinkel, Robin; Street, Linda; Cárdenas, Dora L.; & others. (1994). *Ataque de nervios* and panic disorder. *American Journal of Psychiatry, 151,* 871–875.

Liff, Zanvel A. (1992). Psychoanalysis and dynamic techniques. In Donald K. Freedheim (Ed.), *History of psychotherapy: A century of change.* Washington, DC: American Psychological Association.

Light, Kathleen C.; Smith, Tara E.; Johns, Josephine M.; Brownley, Kimberly A.; Hofheimer, Julie A.; & Amico, Janet. (2000). Oxytocin responsivity in mothers of infants: A preliminary study of relationships with blood pressure during laboratory stress and normal ambulatory activity. *Health Psychology, 19,* 560–567.

Lilie, Jamie K., & Rosenberg, Russell P. (1990). Behavioral treatment of insomnia. In Michel Hersen, Richard M. Eisler, & Peter M. Miller (Eds.), *Progress in behavior modification* (Vol. 25). Newbury Park, CA: Sage.

Lilienfeld, Scott O. (1998, Fall). Pseudoscience in contemporary clinical psychology: What it is and what we can do about it. *Clinical Psychologist, 51,* 3–9.

Lilienfeld, Scott O.; Wood, James M.; & Garb, Howard N. (2000). The scientific status of projective techniques. *Psychological Science in the Public Interest, 1,* 27–66.

Lilienfeld, Scott O.; Wood, James M.; & Garb, Howard N. (2001). What's wrong with this picture? *Scientific American, 284,* 80–87. Retrieved on November 13, 2001, from http://www.psychologicalscience.org/newsresearch/publications/journals/sa1_2.pdf

Lillard, Angeline. (1998). Ethnopsychologies: Cultural variations in theories of mind. *Psychological Bulletin, 123,* 3–32.

Lin, Ling; Faraco, Juliette; Kadotani, Hiroshi; Rogers, William; Lin, Xiaoyan; Qui, Xiaohong; & others. (1999, August 20). The sleep disorder canine narcolepsy is caused by a mutation in the hypocretin (orexin) receptor 2 gene. *Cell, 98,* 365–376.

Lindsay, D. Stephen, & Read, J. Don. (1994). Psychotherapy and memories of childhood and sexual abuse: A cognitive perspective. *Applied Cognitive Psychology 8,* 281–338.

Link, Bruce G.; Andrews, Howard; & Cullen, Francis T. (1992). The violent and illegal behavior of mental patients reconsidered. *American Sociological Review, 57,* 275–292.

Link, Bruce G., & Stueve, Ann. (1998). Commentary: New evidence on the violence risk posed by people with mental illness. *Archives of General Psychiatry, 55,* 403–404.

Links, Paul S. (1996). *Clinical assessment and management of severe personality disorders* (Clinical Practice No. 35). Washington, DC: American Psychiatric Press.

Lipsey, Mark W., & Wilson, David B. (1993). The efficacy of psychological, educational, and behavioral treatment: Confirmation from meta-analysis. *American Psychologist, 48,* 1181–1209.

Liu, Dong; Diorio, Josie; Tannenbaum, Beth; Caldji, Christian; Francis, Darlene; Freedman, Alison; & others. (1997). Maternal care, hippocampal glucocorticoid receptors, and hypo-thalamic-pituitary-adrenal responses to stress. *Science, 277,* 1659–1662.

Livingstone, Margaret, & Hubel, David. (1988, May 6). Segregation of form, color, movement and depth: Anatomy, physiology, and perception. *Science, 240,* 740–749.

Lockard, Robert B. (1971). Reflections on the fall of comparative psychology: Is there a message for us all? *American Psychologist, 26,* 168–179.

Locke, Edwin A. (1976). The nature and causes of job satisfaction. In M. D. Dunnette (Ed.), *Handbook of industrial and organizational psychology.* Chicago: Rand McNally.

Locke, Edwin A., & Schweiger, David M. (1979). Participation in decision-making: One more look. In B. M. Staw (Ed.), *Research in organizational behavior* (Vol. 1). Greenwich, CT: JAI Press.

Lockhart, Robert S., & Craik, Fergus I. M. (1990). Levels of processing: A retrospective commentary on a framework for memory research. *Canadian Journal of Psychology, 44*(1), 87–112.

Loewenstein, George F.; Weber, Elke U.; Hsee, Christopher K., & Welch, Ned. (2001). Risk as feelings. *Psychological Bulletin, 127,* 267–286.

Loewenstein, Richard J. (1993). Psychogenic amnesia and psychogenic fugue: A comprehensive review. In David Spiegel (Ed.), *Dissociative disorders: A clinical review.* Lutherville, MD: Sidran.

Loftus, Elizabeth F. (1992). When a lie becomes memory's truth: Memory distortion after exposure to misinformation. *Current Directions in Psychological Science, 1,* 121–123.

Loftus, Elizabeth F. (1993). The reality of repressed memories. *American Psychologist, 48,* 518–537.

Loftus, Elizabeth F. (1997). Memory for a past that never was. *Current Directions in Psychological Science, 6,* 60–65.

Loftus, Elizabeth F.; Donders, Karen; Hoffman, Hunter G.; & Schooler, Jonathan W. (1989). Creating new memories that are quickly accessed and confidently held. *Memory & Cognition, 17,* 607–616.

Loftus, Elizabeth F.; Garry, Maryanne; Brown, Scott W.; Rader, Marcella. (1994). Near-natal memories, past-life memories, and other memory myths. *American Journal of Clinical Hypnosis, 36,* 176–179.

Loftus, Elizabeth F., & Ketcham, Katherine. (1991). *Witness for the defense: The accused, the eyewitness, and the expert who puts memory on trial.* New York: St. Martin's Press.

Loftus, Elizabeth F., & Ketcham, Katherine. (1994). *The myth of repressed memory: False memories and allegations of sexual abuse.* New York: St. Martin's Press.

Loftus, Elizabeth F.; Nucci, Michele; & Hoffman, Hunter. (1998). Manufacturing memory. *American Journal of Forensic Psychology, 16,* 63–75.

Loftus, Elizabeth F., & Palmer, J. C. (1974). Reconstruction of automobile destruction: An example of the interaction between language and memory. *Journal of Verbal Learning and Verbal Behavior, 13,* 585–589.

Logothetis, Nikos K., & Sheinberg, David L. (1996). Visual object recognition. *Annual Review of Neuroscience, 19,* 577–621.

LoLordo, Vincent M. (2001). Learned helplessness and depression. In Marilyn E. Carroll & J. Bruce Overmier, *Animal research and human health: Advancing human welfare through behavioral science.* Washington, DC: American Psychological Association.

Lonetto, Richard, & Templer, Donald I. (1986). *Death anxiety.* Washington, DC: Hemisphere.

Lord, Charles G.; Ross, Lee; & Lepper, Mark R. (1979). Biased assimilation and attitude polarization: The effects of prior theories on subsequently considered evidence. *Journal of Personality and Social Psychology, 37,* 2098–2109.

Lord, Robert G.; DeVader, Christy L.; & Alliger, George M. (1986). A meta-analysis of the relation between personality traits and leadership perceptions: An application of validity generalization procedures. *Journal of Applied Psychology, 71,* 402–410.

Louie, Kenway, & Wilson, Matthew. (2001). Temporally structured replay of awake hippocampal ensemble activity during rapid eye movement sleep. *Neuron, 29,* 145–156.

Lovallo, William R.; al'Absi, Mustafa; Pincomb, Gwen A.; Everson, Susan A.; Sung, Bong Hee; Passey, Richard B.; & Wilson, Michael F. (1996). Caffeine and behavioral stress effects on blood pressure in borderline hypertensive Caucasian men. *Health Psychology, 15,* 11–17.

Lumer, Erik D.; Friston, Karl J.; & Rees, Geraint. (1998, June 19). Neural correlates of perceptual rivalry in the human brain. *Science, 280,* 1930–1934.

Lykken, David. (1983, April). Polygraph prejudice. *APA Monitor,* p. 4.

Lykken, David T. (1995). *The antisocial personalities.* Hillsdale, NJ: Erlbaum.

Lykken, David T. (1998). *A tremor in the blood* (2nd ed.) New York: Perseus Books.

Lykken, David T.; McGue, Matthew; Tellegen, Auke; & Bouchard, Thomas J., Jr. (1992). Emergenesis: Genetic traits that may not run

in families. *American Psychologist, 47,* 1565–1577.

Lyles, Jeanne N.; Burish, Thomas G.; Krozely, Mary G.; & Oldham, Robert K. (1982). Efficacy of relaxation training and guided imagery in reducing the aversiveness of cancer chemotherapy. *Journal of Consulting and Clinical Psychology, 50,* 509–524.

Lyness, Scott A. (1993). Predictors of differences between Type A and B individuals in heart rate and blood pressure reactivity. *Psychological Bulletin, 114,* 266–295.

Lynn, Richard. (1987). The intelligence of the Mongoloids: A psychometric evolutionary and neurological theory. *Personality and Individual Differences, 8,* 813–844.

Lynn, Steven Jay; Lock, Timothy G.; Myers, Bryan; & Payne, David G. (1997). Recalling the unrecallable: Should hypnosis be used to recover memories in psychotherapy? *Current Directions in Psychological Science, 6,* 79–83.

Lynn, Steven Jay, & Nash, Michael R. (1994). Truth in memory: Ramifications for psychotherapy and hypnotherapy. *American Journal of Clinical Hypnosis, 36,* 194–208.

Lytton, Hugh, & Romney, David M. (1991). Parents' differential socialization of boys and girls: A meta-analysis. *Psychological Bulletin, 109,* 267–296.

Maccoby, Eleanor E., & Martin, John A. (1983). Socialization in the context of the family: Parent-child interaction. In Paul H. Mussen (Ed.), *Handbook of child psychology: Vol. IV. Socialization, personality, and social development.* New York: Wiley.

MacKenzie, Brian. (1984). Explaining race differences in IQ: The logic, the methodology, and the evidence. *American Psychologist, 39,* 1214–1233.

Mackie, Diane M., & Hamilton, David L. (1993). Affect, cognition, and stereotyping: Concluding comments. In Diane M. Mackie & David L. Hamilton (Eds.), *Affect, cognition, and stereotyping: Interactive processes in group perception.* San Diego, CA: Academic Press.

Macmillan, Malcolm. (2000). *An odd kind of fame: Stories of Phineas Gage.* Cambridge, MA: MIT Press.

Macmillan, Malcolm. (2001). Limitations to free association and interpretation. *Psychological Inquiry, 12,* 113–128.

Macrae, C. Neil; Milne, Alan B.; & Bodenhausen, Galen V. (1994). Stereotypes as energy-saving devices: A peek inside the cognitive toolbox. *Journal of Personality and Social Psychology, 66,* 37–47.

Maes, Hermine H.; Neale, Michael C.; & Eaves, Lindon J. (1997). Genetic and environmental factors in relative body weight and human adiposity. *Behavior Genetics, 27,* 325–351.

Magherini, Graziella. (1992). *The Stendhal syndrome.* Milan: Fettrinelli.

Magnavita, Jeffrey J. (1993). The evolution of short-term dynamic psychotherapy: Treatment of the future? *Professional Psychology: Research and Practice, 24,* 360–365.

Maguire, Eleanor A.; Gadian, David G.; Johnsrude, Ingrid S.; Good, Catriona D.; Ashburner, John; Frackowiak, Richard S. J.; & Frith, Christopher D. (2000). Navigation-related structural change in the hippocampi of taxi drivers. *Proceedings of the National Academy of Sciences, USA, 97,* 4398–4403.

Mahler, D. A.; Cunningham, L. N.; Skrinar, G. S.; Kraemer, W. J.; & Colice, G. L. (1989). Beta-endorphin activity and hypercapnic ventilatory responsiveness after marathon running. *Journal of Applied Physiology, 66,* 2431–2436.

Mahmood, Iftekhar, & Sahajwalla, Chandrahas. (1999). Clinical pharmacokinetics and pharmacodynamics of buspirone, an anxiolytic drug. *Clinical Pharmacokinetics, 36,* 277–287.

Mahowald, Mark W., & Schenck, Carlos H. (1990). REM-sleep behavior disorder. In Michael J. Thorpy (Ed.), *Handbook of sleep disorders.* New York: Dekker.

Maier, Steven F.; Seligman, Martin E.; & Solomon, Richard L. (1969). Pavlovian fear conditioning and learned helplessness: Effects of escape and avoidance behavior of (a) the CS=UCS contingency, and (b) the independence of the US and voluntary responding. In B. A. Campbell & R. M. Church (Eds.), *Punishment and aversive behavior.* New York: Appleton-Century-Crofts.

Maier, Steven F., & Watkins, Linda R. (2000). The neurobiology of stressor controllability. In Jane E. Gilham (Ed.), *The science of optimism and hope: Research essays in honor of Martin E. P. Seligman.* Philadelphia: Templeton Foundation Press.

Maj, Mario; Magliano, Lorena; Pirozzi, Raffaele; Marasco, Cecilia; & Guarneri, Manuela. (1994). Validity of rapid cycling as a course specifier for bipolar disorder. *American Journal of Psychiatry, 151,* 1015–1019.

Major, Brenda; Carrington, Patricia I.; & Carnevale, Peter J. (1984). Physical attractiveness and self-esteem: Attribution for praise from an other-sex evaluator. *Personality and Social Psychology Bulletin, 10,* 43–50.

Makin, Jennifer W. (1989). Attractiveness of lactating females' breast odors to neonates. *Child Development, 60,* 803–810.

Malaspina, Dolores; Harlap, Susan; & others. (2001). Advancing paternal age and the risk of schizophrenia. *Archives of General Psychiatry, 58,* 361–367.

Malenka, Robert C., & Nicoll, Roger A. (1999). Long-term potentiation: A decade of progress? *Science, 285,* 1870–1874.

Mallinckrodt, Brent. (2001) Interpersonal processes, attachment, and development of social competencies in individual and group psychotherapy. In Barbara R. Sarason & Steve Duck (Eds.), *Personal relationships: Implications for clinical and community psychology.* Chichester, England: Wiley.

Malnic, Bettina; Hirono, Junzo; Sato, Takaaki; & Buck, Linda B. (1999). Combinatorial receptor codes for odors. *Cell, 96,* 713–723.

Mandler, George. (1993). Thought, memory, and learning: Effects of emotional stress. In Leo Goldberger & Shlomo Breznitz (Eds.), *Handbook of stress: Theoretical and clinical aspects* (2nd ed.). New York: Free Press.

Mandler, Jean. (1990). A new perspective on cognitive development in infancy. *American Scientist, 78,* 236–243.

Mangina, Constantine A., & Beuzeron-Mangina, J. Helen. (1996). Direct electrical stimulation of specific human brain structures and bilateral electrodermal activity. *International Journal of Psychophysiology, 22,* 1–8.

Mann, J. John; Waternaux, Christine; Haas, Gretchen L.; & Malone, Kevin M. (1999). Toward a clinical model of suicidal behavior in psychiatric patients. *American Journal of Psychiatry, 156,* 181–189.

Mann, Leon. (1981). The baiting crowd in episodes of threatened suicide. *Journal of Personality and Social Psychology, 41,* 703–709.

Maquet, Pierre. (2001). The role of sleep in learning and memory. *Science, 294,* 1048–1052.

Maquet, Pierre; Faymonville, Elisabeth; Degueldre, Christian; & others. (1999). Functional neuroanatomy of hypnotic state. *Biological Psychiatry, 45,* 327–333.

Maquet, Pierre; Laureys, Steven; Peigneux, Phillippe; Fuchs, Sonia; Petiau, Christophe; Phillips, Christophe; & others. (2000). Experience-dependent changes in cerebral activation during human REM sleep. *Nature Neuroscience, 3,* 831–836.

Marañon, Gregorio. (1924). Contribution à l'etude de l'action emotive de l'adrenaline. *Revue Francaise d'Endocrinologie, 2,* 301–325.

Marcelino, A.S.; Adam, A.S.; & others. (2001). Internal and external determinants of eating initiation in humans. *Appetite, 36,* 9–14.

Marcia, James E. (1991). Identity and self-development. In R. M. Lerner, A. C. Petersen, & Jeanne Brooks-Gunn (Eds.), *Encyclopedia of adolescence* (Vol. 1). New York: Garland.

Marco, Christine A., & Suls, Jerry. (1993). Daily stress and the trajectory of mood: Spillover, response assimilation, contrast, and chronic negative affectivity. *Journal of Personality and Social Psychology, 64,* 1053–1063.

Marder, Stephen R.; Ames, Donna; Wirshing, William C.; & Van Putten, Theodore. (1993). Schizophrenia. *Psychiatric Clinics of North America, 16,* 567–587.

Marder, Stephen R., & Meibach, Richard C. (1994). Risperidone in the treatment of schizophrenia. *American Journal of Psychiatry, 151,* 825–835.

Margolin, Gayla, & Gordis, Elana B. (2000). The effects of family and community violence on children. *Annual Review of Psychology, 51,* 445–479.

Margraf, Jürgen, & Ehlers, Anke. (1989). Etiological models of panic: a) Medical and biological aspects; b) Psychophysiological and cognitive aspects. In Roger Baker (Ed.), *Panic disorder: Theory, research and therapy.* Chichester, England: Wiley.

Markman, Arthur B., & Gentner, Dedre. (2001). Thinking. *Annual Review of Psychology, 52,* 223–247.

Markowitz, John C. (Ed.). (1998). *Interpersonal psychotherapy: Vol. 17. Review of psychiatry.* Washington, DC: American Psychiatric Association.

Markus, Hazel Rose, & Cross, Susan. (1990). The interpersonal self. In Lawrence A. Pervin (Ed.), *Handbook of personality: Theory and research.* New York: Guilford Press.

Markus, Hazel Rose, & Kitayama, Shinobu. (1991). Culture and the self: Implications for cognition, emotion, and motivation. *Psychological Review, 98,* 224–253.

Markus, Hazel Rose, & Kitayama, Shinobu. (1994). The cultural construction of self and emotion: Implications for social behavior. In Shinobu Kitayama & Hazel Rose Markus (Eds.), *Emotion and culture: Empirical studies of mutual influence.* Washington, DC: American Psychological Association.

Markus, Hazel Rose, & Kitayama, Shinobu. (1998). The cultural psychology of personality. *Journal of Cross-Cultural Psychology, 29,* 63–87.

Markus, Hazel Rose, & Kunda, Ziva. (1986). Stability and malleability of the self-concept. *Journal of Personality and Social Psychology, 51,* 858–866.

Markus, Hazel Rose, & Nurius, Paula. (1986). Possible selves. *American Psychologist, 41,* 954–969.

Markus, Hazel Rose, & Wurf, Elissa. (1987). The dynamic self-concept: A social psychological perspective. *Annual Review of Psychology, 38,* 299–337.

Marlatt, G. Alan; Baer, John S.; Donovan, Dennis M.; & Kivlahan, Daniel R. (1988). Addictive behaviors: Etiology and treatment. *Annual Review of Psychology, 39,* 223–252.

Marler, Peter. (1967). Animal communication symbols. *Science, 35,* 63–78.

Marmonier, Corinne; Chapelot, Didier; & Louis-Sylvestre, Jeanine. (1999). Metabolic and behavioral consequences of a snack consumed in a satiety state. *American Journal of Clinical Nutrition, 70,* 854–866.

Marsella, Anthony J., & Dash-Scheuer, Alice. (1988). Coping, culture, and healthy human development: A research and conceptual overview. In Pierre R. Dasen, John W. Berry, & Norman Sartorius (Eds.), *Health and cross-cultural psychology: Toward applications* (Vol. 10, Cross-cultural Research and Methodology Series.). Newbury Park, CA: Sage.

Marshall, Grant N.; Wortman, Camille B.; Kusulas, Jeffrey W.; Hervig, Linda K.; & Vickers, Ross R., Jr. (1992). Distinguishing optimism from pessimism: Relations to fundamental dimensions of mood and personality. *Journal of Personality and Social Psychology, 62,* 1067–1074.

Martens, Brian K.; Lochner, David G.; & Kelly, Susan Q. (1992). The effects of variable-interval reinforcement on academic engagement: A demonstration of matching theory. *Journal of Applied Behavior Analysis, 25,* 143–151.

Martin, Bruce. (1998, May). Coincidences: Remarkable or random? *Skeptical Inquirer, 22,* 23–28.

Martin, Carol L., & Halverson, Charles F., Jr. (1981). A schematic processing model of sex typing and stereotyping in children. *Child Development, 52,* 1119–1134.

Martin, Carol L., & Halverson, Charles F., Jr. (1983). The effects of sex-typing schemas on young children's memory. *Child Development, 54,* 563–574.

Martin, Laura. (1986). "Eskimo words for snow": A case study in the genesis and decay of an anthropological example. *American Anthropologist, 88,* 418–423.

Martin, Stephen J.; Grimwood, Paul D.; & Morris, Richard G. M. (2000). Synaptic plasticity and memory: An evaluation of the hypothesis. *Annual Review of Neuroscience, 23,* 649–711.

Martin, Stephen D.; Martin, Elizabeth; Santoch, S. Rai; Richardson, Mark A.; & Royall, Robert. (2001). Brain blood flow changes in depressed patients treated with interpersonal psychotherapy or venlafaxine hydrochloride. *Archives of General Psychiatry, 58,* 641–648.

Martinez-Taboas, Alfonso. (1991). Multiple personality in Puerto Rico: Analysis of fifteen cases. *Dissociation, 4,* 189–192.

Marucha, Phillip T.; Kiecolt-Glaser, Janice K.; & Favagehi, Mehrdad. (1998). Mucosal wound healing is impaired by examination stress. *Psychosomatic Medicine, 60,* 362–365.

Masland, Richard H. (2001). The fundamental plan of the retina. *Nature Neuroscience, 4,* 877–886.

Maslow, Abraham H. (1943). A theory of human motivation. *Psychological Review, 50,* 370–396.

Maslow, Abraham H. (1954). *Motivation and personality.* New York: Harper.

Maslow, Abraham H. (1968). *Toward a psychology of being* (2nd ed.). Princeton, NJ: Van Nostrand.

Maslow, Abraham H. (1970). *Motivation and personality* (2nd ed.). New York: Harper & Row.

Mason, Paul T., & Kreger, Randi. (1998). *Stop walking on eggshells: Taking your life back when someone you care about has borderline personality disorder.* New York: New Harbinger.

Masson, Jeffrey M. (1984a). *The assault on truth: Freud's suppression of the seduction theory.* New York: Farrar, Straus & Giroux.

Masson, Jeffrey M. (1984b, February). Freud and the seduction theory: A challenge to the foundations of psychoanalysis. *The Atlantic, 253,* 33–60.

Masters, William H., & Johnson, Virginia E. (1966). *Human sexual response.* Boston: Little, Brown.

Masters, William H.; Johnson, Virginia E.; & Kolodny, Robert C. (1995). *Human sexuality* (5th ed.). New York: HarperCollins.

Matarazzo, Joseph D. (1981). Obituary: David Wechsler (1896–1981). *American Psychologist, 36,* 1542–1543.

Mathews, Judith R.; Hodson, Gary D.; Crist, William B.; & LaRoche, G. Robert. (1992). Teaching young children to use contact lens. *Journal of Applied Behavior Analysis, 25,* 229–235.

Matlin, Margaret W. (1985). Current issues in psycholinguistics. In Theodore M. Shlechter & Michael P. Toglia (Eds.), *New directions in cognitive science.* Norwood, NJ: Ablex.

Matson, Claire A.; Reid, Dana F.; Cannon, Todd A.; & Ritter, Robert C. (2000). Cholecystokinin and leptin act synergistically to reduce body weight. *American Journal of Physiology, 278,* R882–R890.

Matsuda, Lisa A.; Lolait, Stephen J.; Brownstein, Michael J.; Young, Alice C.; & Bonner, Tom. (1990, August 9). Structure of a cannabinoid receptor and functional expression of the cloned CDNA. *Nature, 346,* 561–564.

Matsumoto, David. (1994). *People: Psychology from a cultural perspective.* Pacific Grove, CA: Brooks/Cole.

Matsumoto, David. (2000). *Culture and psychology: People around the world* (2nd ed.). Belmont, CA: Wadsworth/Thomson Learning.

Matsumoto, David. (2001). Cross-cultural psychology in the 21st century. In Jane S. Halonen & Stephen F. Davis (Eds.), *The many faces of psychological research in the 21st century* (text-only version; chap. 5). Retrieved February 9, 2002 from http://teachpsych.lemoyne.edu/teachpsych/faces/text/ch05.htm

Matsumoto, David; Kitayama, Shinobu; & Markus, Hazel. (1994). Culture and self: How cultures influence the way we view ourselves. In David Matsumoto (Ed.), *People: Psychology from a cultural perspective.* Pacific Grove, CA: Brooks/Cole.

Mavromatis, Andreas. (1987). *Hypnagogia: The unique state of consciousness between wakefulness and sleep.* New York: Routledge & Kegan Paul.

Maxmen, Jerrold S., & Ward, Nicholas G. (1995). *Essential psychopathology and its treatment* (2nd ed.). New York: Norton.

Mayer, John D., & Salovey, Peter. (1993). The intelligence of emotional intelligence. *Intelligence, 17,* 433–442.

Mayer, John D., & Salovey, Peter. (1997). What is emotional intelligence? In Peter

Salovey & David J. Sluyter (Eds.), *Emotional development and emotional intelligence: Educational implications.* New York: Basic Books.

McAdams, Dan P. (1992). The five-factor model in personality: A critical appraisal. *Journal of Personality, 60,* 329–362.

McAndrew, Francis T.; Akande, Adebowale; Turner, Saskia; & Sharma, Yadika. (1998). A cross-cultural ranking of stressful life events in Germany, India, South Africa, and the United States. *Journal of Cross-Cultural Psychology, 29,* 717–727.

McCall, Robert B. (1988). Science and the press: Like oil and water. *American Psychologist, 43,* 87–91.

McCartney, Kathleen; Harris, Monica J.; & Bernieri, Frank. (1990). Growing up and growing apart: A developmental meta-analysis of twin studies. *Psychological Bulletin, 107,* 226–237.

McCaul, Kevin D., & Malott, James M. (1984). Distraction and coping with pain. *Psychological Bulletin, 95,* 516–533.

McClearn, Gerald E.; Johansson, Boo; Berg, Stig; Pederson, Nancy L.; Ahern, Frank; Petrill, Stephen A.; & Plomin, Robert. (1997, June 6). Substantial genetic influence on cognitive abilities in twins 80 or more years old. *Science, 276,* 1560–1563.

McClelland, David C. (1961). *The achieving society.* Princeton, NJ: Van Nostrand.

McClelland, David C. (1975). *Power: The inner experience.* New York: Irvington.

McClelland, David C. (1985a). How motives, skills, and values determine what people do. *American Psychologist, 40,* 812–825.

McClelland, David C. (1985b). *Human motivation.* Glenview, IL: Scott, Foresman.

McClelland, David C. (1987). Characteristics of successful entrepreneurs. *Journal of Creative Behavior, 21,* 219–233.

McClelland, David C. (1989). Motivational factors in health and disease. *American Psychologist, 44,* 675–683.

McClelland, David C.; Atkinson, John W.; Clark, Russell A.; & Lowell, Edgar L. (1953). *The achievement motive.* New York: Appleton-Century-Crofts.

McClelland, David C.; & Winter, David G. (1971). *Motivating economic achievement.* New York: Free Press.

McClintock, Martha K. (1971). Menstrual synchrony and suppression. *Nature, 229,* 244–245.

McClintock, Martha K. (1992, October). Quoted in John Easton, Sex, rats, and videotapes: From the outside in. *The University of Chicago Magazine, 85*(1), 32–36.

McClintock, Martha K. (2001, July 25). Quoted in Marcella S. Kreiter, "Neurology: Brain smells out signals," *MedServ Medical News.* Retrieved from the World Wide Web on November 8, 2001: http://www.medserv.no/article/php?sid=666

McCoy, Robert. (1996). Phrenology. In Gordon Stein (Ed.), *The encyclopedia of the paranormal.* Amherst, NY: Prometheus Books.

McCrae, Robert R. (1993). Moderated analyses of longitudinal personality stability. *Journal of Personality and Social Psychology, 65,* 577–585.

McCrae, Robert R., & Costa, Paul T., Jr. (1990). *Personality in adulthood.* New York: Guilford Press.

McCrae, Robert R., & Costa, Paul T., Jr. (1996). Toward a new generation of personality theories: Theoretical contexts for the five-factor model. In Jerry S. Wiggins (Ed.), *The five-factor model of personality: Theoretical perspectives.* New York: Guilford Press.

McCrae, Robert R., & Costa, Paul T., Jr. (1997). Personality trait structure as a human universal. *American Psychologist, 52,* 509–516.

McDougall, William. (1908). *Introduction to social psychology.* London: Methuen.

McDowell, David J., & Parke, Ross D. (2000). Differential knowledge of display rules for positive and negative emotions: Influences from parents, influences on peers. *Social Development, 9,* 415–432.

McFadden, Lisa; Seidman, Edward; & Rappaport, Julian. (1992). A comparison of espoused theories of self- and mutual help: Implications for mental health professionals. *Professional Psychology: Research and Practice, 23,* 515–520.

McGue, Matt, Bouchard, Thomas J., Jr.; Iacono, William G.; & Lykken, David T. (1993). Behavioral genetics of cognitive ability: A life-span perspective. In Robert Plomin & Gerald E. McClearn (Eds.), *Nature, nurture, and psychology.* Washington, DC: American Psychological Association.

McGuire, Anne M. (1994). Helping behaviors in the natural environment: Dimensions and correlates of helping. *Personality and Social Psychology Bulletin, 20,* 45–56.

McKean, Keith Joseph. (1994). Academic helplessness: Applying learned helplessness theory to undergraduates who give up when faced with academic setbacks. *College Student Journal, 28,* 456–462.

McKellar, Peter. (1972). Imagery from the standpoint of introspection. In Peter W. Sheehan (Ed.), *The function and nature of imagery.* New York: Academic Press.

McKernan, Margaret G., & Shinnick-Gallagher, Patricia. (1997, December 11). Fear conditioning induces a lasting potentiation of synaptic currents *in vitro. Nature, 390,* 607–611.

McManus, I. Chris, & Bryden, M. Philip. (1992). The genetics of handedness, cerebral dominance, and lateralization. In Isabelle Rapin & Sidney J. Segalowitz (Eds.), *Handbook of neuropsychology: Vol. 6. Developmental neuropsychology* (Pt. 1). New York: Elsevier.

McNally, Richard J. (1987). Preparedness and phobias: A review. *Psychological Bulletin, 101,* 283–303.

McNally, Richard J. (1994). Cognitive bias in panic disorder. *Current Directions in Psychological Science, 3,* 129–132.

McNally, Richard J. (1998, September 14). Quoted in Judy Foreman, "New therapy for trauma is doubted." *The Boston Globe Online.* Retrieved from the World Wide Web on October 10, 2001: http://www.globe.com/globe/ search/stories/health/health_sense/091498.htm

McNally, Richard J., & Louro, Christine E. (1992). Fear of flying in agoraphobia and simple phobia: Distinguishing features. *Journal of Anxiety Disorders, 6,* 319–324.

McNeilly, Cheryl L., & Howard, Kenneth I. (1991). The effects of psychotherapy: A reevaluation based on dosage. *Psychotherapy Research, 1,* 74–78.

Mebert, Carolyn J. (1991). Variability in the transition to parenthood experience. In Karl Pillemer & Kathleen McCartney (Eds.), *Parent-child relations throughout life.* Hillsdale, NJ: Erlbaum.

Meichenbaum, Donald H. (1995). Cognitive-behavioral therapy in historical perspective. In Bruce Bongar & Larry E. Beutler (Eds.), *Comprehensive textbook of psychotherapy: Theory and practice.* New York: Oxford University Press.

Meichenbaum, Donald H., & Fitzpatrick, Deborah. (1993). A constructivist narrative perspective on stress and coping: Stress inoculation applications. In Leo Goldberger & Shlomo Breznitz (Eds.), *Handbook of stress: Theoretical and clinical aspects* (2nd ed.). New York: Free Press.

Melanson, Kathleen J.; Smith, Françoise J.; Campfield, L. Arthur; & others. (1999). Blood glucose patterns and appetite in time-blinded humans: Carbohydrate versus fat. *American Journal of Physiology, 277,* R337–R345.

Mellers, Barbara A. (2000). Choice and the relative pleasure of consequences. *Psychological Bulletin, 126,* 910–924.

Meltzer, Herbert Y. (1994). Clozapine and other atypical neuroleptics: Efficacy, side effects, optimal utilization. *Journal of Clinical Psychiatry Monograph, 12*(2), 38–42.

Meltzer, Herbert Y. (1995). The role of serotonin in schizophrenia and the place of serotonin-dopamine antagonist antipsychotics. *Journal of Clinical Psychopharmacology, 15*(Suppl. 1), 2S–3S.

Meltzoff, Andrew N., & Moore, M. Keith. (1977). Imitation of facial and manual gestures by human neonates. *Science, 198,* 75–78.

Meltzoff, Andrew N., & Moore, M. Keith. (1983). Newborn infants imitate adult facial gestures. *Child Development, 54,* 702–709.

Melzack, Ronald, & Wall, Patrick D. (1965). Pain mechanisms: A new theory. *Science, 150,* 971–980.

Melzack, Ronald, & Wall, Patrick D. (1996). *The challenge of pain* (2nd ed.). Harmondsworth, UK: Penguin.

Mendlowicz, Mauro V., & Stein, Murray B. (2000). Quality of life in individuals with anxiety disorders. *American Journal of Psychiatry, 157,* 669–682.

Mennella, Julie A., & Beauchamp, Gary K. (1996). The early development of human flavor preferences. In Elizabeth D. Capaldi (Ed.), *Why we eat, what we eat: The psychology of eating.* Washington, DC: American Psychological Association.

Merckelbach, Harald; Arntz, Arnoud; Arrindell, Willem A.; & De Jong, Peter J. (1992). Pathways to spider phobia. *Behavior Research and Therapy, 30,* 543–546.

Merikle, Philip M., & Daneman, Meredyth. (1998). Psychological investigations of unconscious perception. *Journal of Consciousness Studies, 5,* 5–18.

Merikle, Philip M.; & Skanes, Heather E. (1992). Subliminal self-help audiotapes: A search for placebo effects. *Journal of Applied Psychology, 77,* 772–776.

Merskey, Harold. (1992). The manufacture of personalities: The production of multiple personality disorder. *British Journal of Psychiatry, 160,* 327–340.

Mervis, Carolyn B., & Rosch, Eleanor. (1981). Categorization of natural objects. *Annual Review of Psychology, 32,* 89–115.

Metcalfe, Janet, & Mischel, Walter. (1999). A hot/cool-system analysis of delay of gratification: Dynamics of willpower. *Psychological Review, 106,* 3–19.

Miceli, Maria, & Castelfranchi, Cristiano. (2000). Nature and mechanisms of loss of motivation. *Review of General Psychology, 4,* 238–263.

Michael, Robert T.; Gagnon, John H.; Laumann, Edward O.; & Kolata, Gina. (1994). *Sex in America: A definitive survey.* New York: Warner Books.

Mikalsen, Anita; Bertelsen, Bård; & Flaten, Magne Arve. (2001). Effects of caffeine, caffeine-associated stimuli, and caffeine-related information on physiological and psychological arousal. *Psychopharmacology, 157,* 373–380.

Miklowitz, David J. (1994). Family risk indicators in schizophrenia. *Schizophrenia Bulletin, 20,* 137–149.

Milgram, Stanley. (1960). *Conformity in Norway and France: An experimental study of national characteristics.* Doctoral dissertation, Harvard University, Cambridge, MA.

Milgram, Stanley. (1961, December). Nationality and conformity. *Scientific American, 205,* 45–51.

Milgram, Stanley. (1963). Behavioral study of obedience. *Journal of Abnormal Psychology, 67,* 371–378.

Milgram, Stanley. (1964). Issues in the study of obedience: A reply to Baumrind. *American Psychologist, 19,* 848–852.

Milgram, Stanley. (1965/1992). Some conditions of obedience and disobedience to authority. In John Sabini & Maury Silver (Eds.), *The individual in a social world: Essays and experiments* (2nd ed.). New York: McGraw-Hill.

Milgram, Stanley. (1974a). *Obedience to authority: An experimental view.* New York: Harper & Row.

Milgram, Stanley. (1974b, June). Interview by Carol Tavris: The frozen world of the familiar stranger: An interview with Stanley Milgram. *Psychology Today,* 71–80.

Milgram, Stanley. (1980). Interview by Richard I. Evans. In Richard I. Evans (Ed.), *The making of social psychology: Discussions with creative contributors.* New York: Gardner Press.

Milgram, Stanley. (1992). On maintaining social norms: A field experiment in the subway. In John Sabini & Maury Silver (Eds.), *The individual in a social world: Essays and experiments* (2nd ed.). New York: McGraw-Hill.

Milgrom, Peter; Mancl, Lloyd; King, Barbara; & Weinstein, Philip. (1995). Origins of childhood dental fear. *Behavior Research and Therapy, 33,* 313–319.

Miller, Arthur G. (1986). *The obedience experiments: A case study of controversy in social science.* New York: Praeger.

Miller, George A. (1956/1994). The magical number seven, plus or minus two: Some limits on our capacity for processing information [Special centennial issue]. *Psychological Review, 101,* 343–352.

Miller, Gregory A., & Keller, Jennifer. (2000). Psychology and neuroscience: Making peace. *Current Directions in Psychological Science, 9,* 212–215.

Miller, Kevin F.; Smith, Catherine M.; Zhu, Jianjun; & Zhang, Houcan. (1995). Preschool origins of cross-national differences in mathematical competence: The role of number-naming systems. *Psychological Science, 6,* 56–60.

Miller, Mark A., & Rahe, Richard H. (1997). Life changes scaling for the 1990s. *Journal of Psychosomatic Research, 43*(3), 279–292.

Miller, Neal E. (1985, April). The value of behavioral research on animals. *American Psychologist, 40,* 423–440.

Miller, Patricia H. (1993). *Theories of developmental psychology* (3rd ed.). New York: Freeman.

Miller, Richard E., & Sarat, Austin. (1981). Grievances, claims, and disputes: Assessing the adversary culture. *Law & Society Review, 15,* 525.

Miller, Scott D.; Blackburn, Terrell; Scholes, Gary; White, George L.; & Mamalis, Nick. (1991). Optical differences in multiple personality disorder: A second look. *Journal of Nervous and Mental Disease, 179,* 132–135.

Miller, Scott D., & Triggiano, Patrick J. (1992). The psychophysiological investigation of multiple personality disorder: Review and update. *American Journal of Clinical Hypnosis, 35,* 47–61.

Miller, Todd Q.; Smith, Timothy W.; Turner, Charles W.; Guijarro, Margarita L.; & Hallet, Amanda J. (1996). A meta-analytic review of research on hostility and physical health. *Psychological Bulletin, 119,* 322–348.

Miller-Jones, Dalton. (1989). Culture and testing. *American Psychologist 44,* 360–366.

Milne, Sarah; Sheeran, Paschal; & Orbell, Sheina. (2000). Prediction and intervention in health-related behavior: A meta-analytic review of protection motivation theory. *Journal of Applied Social Psychology, 30,* 106–143.

Milner, Brenda. (1965). Memory disturbance after bilateral hippocampal lesions. In Peter M. Milner & Steven E. Glickman (Eds.), *Cognitive processes and the brain: An enduring problem in psychology: Selected readings.* Princeton, NJ: Van Nostrand.

Milner, Brenda. (1970). Memory and the medial temporal regions of the brain. In Karl H. Pribram & Donald E. Broadbent (Eds.), *Biology of memory.* New York: Academic Press.

Milton, Julie, & Wiseman, Richard. (1999). Does psi exist? Lack of replication of an anomalous process of information transfer. *Psychological Bulletin, 125,* 387–391.

Milton, Julie, & Wiseman, Richard. (2001). Does psi exist? Reply to Storm and Ertel (2001). *Psychological Bulletin, 127,* 434–438.

Mindell, Jodi A. (1993). Sleep disorders in children. *Health Psychology, 12,* 152–163.

Mindell, Jodi A. (1997). Children and sleep. In Mark R. Pressman & William C. Orr (Eds.), *Understanding sleep: The evaluation and treatment of sleep disorders.* Washington, DC: American Psychological Association.

Mineka, Susan, & Cook, Michael. (1988). Social learning and the acquisition of snake fear in monkeys. In Thomas R. Zentall & Bennett G. Galef (Eds.), *Social learning: Psychological and biological perspectives.* Hillsdale, NJ: Erlbaum.

Mineka, Susan, & Cook, Michael. (1993). Mechanisms involved in the observational conditioning of fear. *Journal of Experimental Psychology: General, 122,* 23–38.

Mineka, Susan, & Nugent, Kathleen. (1995). Mood-congruent memory biases in anxiety and depression. In Daniel L. Schacter (Ed.), *Memory distortion: How minds, brains, and societies reconstruct the past.* Cambridge, MA: Harvard University Press.

Minino, Arialdi M., & Smith, Betty L. (2001, October 9). Deaths: Preliminary data for 2000. *National Vital Statistics Report, 49,* No. 12. Hyattsville, MD: National Center for Health Statistics. Document PDF retrieved on October 30, 2001, from http://www.cdc.gov/nchs/data/nvsr/nvsr49/nvsr49_12.pdf

Mintzberg, H. (1973). *The nature of managerial work.* New York: Harper & Row.

Mischel, Walter. (1966). Theory and research on the antecedents of self-imposed delay of reward. *Progress in Experimental Personality Research, 3,* 85–132.

Mischel, Walter. (1990). Personality dispositions revisited and revised: A view after three decades. In Lawrence Pervin (Ed.), *Handbook of personality: Theory and research.* New York: Guilford Press.

Mischel, Walter. (1996). From good intentions to willpower. In Peter M. Gollwitzer & John A. Bargh (Eds.), *The psychology of action: Linking cognition and motivation to behavior.* New York: Guilford Press.

Mischel, Walter, & Shoda, Yuichi. (1995). A cognitive-affective system theory of personality: Reconceptualizing situations, dispositions, dynamics, and invariance in personality structure. *Psychological Review, 102,* 246–268.

Mischel, Walter; Shoda, Yuichi; & Rodriguez, Monica L. (1989, May 26). Delay of gratification in children. *Science, 244,* 933–938.

Mitchell, Clifton W. (1995). Effects of subliminally presented auditory suggestions of itching on scratching behavior. *Perceptual and Motor Skills, 80,* 87–96.

Mitler, Merrill M. (1994). Sleep and catastrophes. In Rosemary Cooper (Ed.), *Sleep.* New York: Chapman & Hall.

Modgil, Sohan, & Modgil, Celia. (1986). Lawrence Kohlberg: Consensus and controversy. In Sohan Modgil & Celia Modgil (Eds.), *Lawrence Kohlberg: Consensus and controversy.* Philadelphia: Falmer Press.

Moghaddam, Fathali M.; Taylor, Donald M.; & Wright, Stephen C. (1993). *Social psychology in cross-cultural perspective.* New York: Freeman.

Mohr, Charles. (1964, March 28). Apathy is puzzle in Queens killing: Behavioral specialists hard put to explain witnesses' failure to call police. *New York Times,* pp. 21, 40.

Mombaerts, Peter. (1999). Molecular biology of odorant receptors in vertebrates. *Annual Review of Neuroscience, 22,* 487–509.

Monahan, John. (1992). Mental disorder and violent behavior: Attitudes and evidence. *American Psychologist, 47,* 511–521.

Mondimore, Francis Mark. (1993). *Depression: The mood disease* (Rev. ed.). Baltimore: Johns Hopkins University Press.

Monk, Timothy H. (1997). Shift work. In Mark R. Pressman & William C. Orr (Eds.), *Understanding sleep: The evaluation and treatment of sleep disorders.* Washington, DC: American Psychological Association.

Monteith, Margo J.; Devine, Patricia G.; & Zuwerink, Julia R. (1993). Self-directed versus other-directed affect as a consequence of prejudice-related discrepancies. *Journal of Personality and Social Psychology, 64,* 198–210.

Montgomery, Guy H.; DuHamel, Katherine N.; & Redd, William H. (2000). A meta-analysis of hypnotically induced analgesia: How effective is hypnosis? *International Journal of Clinical and Experimental Hypnosis, 48,* 138–153.

Moore, Timothy E. (1988). The case against subliminal manipulation. *Psychology and Marketing, 46,* 297–316.

Moore-Ede, Martin C. (1993). *The twenty-four hour society: Understanding human limits in a world that never stops.* Reading, MA: Addison-Wesley.

Morelli, Gilda A.; Rogoff, Barbara; Oppenheim, David; & Goldsmith, Denise. (1992). Cultural variation in infants' sleeping arrangements: Questions of independence. *Developmental Psychology, 28,* 604–613.

Morgan, Christiana, & Murray, Henry A. (1935). A method of investigating fantasies: The Thematic Apperception Test. *Archives of Neurology and Psychiatry, 4,* 310–329.

Morgan, William P. (1993). Hypnosis and sport psychology. In Judith W. Rhue, Steven J. Lynn, & Irving Kirsch (Eds.), *Handbook of clinical hypnosis.* Washington, D.C.: American Psychological Association.

Morgenstern, Jon; Langenbucher, James; Labouvie, Erich; & Miller, Kevin J. (1997). The comorbidity of alcoholism and personality disorders in a clinical population: Prevalence rates and relation to alcohol typology variables. *Journal of Abnormal Psychology, 106,* 74–84.

Morris, John S.; Öhman, Arne; & Dolan, Raymond J. (1998, June 4). Conscious and unconscious emotional learning in the human amygdala. *Nature, 393,* 467.

Morris, John S.; Scott, Sophie K.; & Dolan, Raymond J. (1999). Saying it with feeling: Neural responses to emotional vocalizations. *Neuropsychologia, 37,* 1155–1163.

Morris, Michael W., & Peng, Kaiping. (1994). Culture and cause: American and Chinese attributions for social and physical events. *Journal of Personality and Social Psychology, 67,* 949–971.

Morris, Richard J. (1991). Fear reduction methods. In Frederick H. Kanfer & Arnold P. Goldstein (Eds.), *Helping people change: A textbook of methods* (4th ed.). New York: Pergamon Press.

Mortensen, Preben B.; Pedersen, Carsten B.; & Westergaard, Tine. (1999, February 25). Effects of family history and place and season of birth on the risk of schizophrenia. *New England Journal of Medicine, 340,* 603–608.

Moscovitch, Morris. (1985). Memory from infancy to old age: Implications for theories of normal and pathological memory. *Annals of the New York Academy of Sciences, 444,* 78–96.

Moss, Cynthia. (2000). *Elephant memories: Thirteen years in the life of an elephant family.* Chicago: University of Chicago Press.

Motowidlo, Stephen J., Hanson, Mary A.; & Crafts, Jennifer L. (1997). Low-fidelity simulations. In D. L. Whetzel & G. R. Wheaton (Eds.), *Applied measurement methods in industrial psychology* (pp. 241–260). Palo Alto, CA: Consulting Psychologists Press.

Mounts, Nina S., & Steinberg, Laurence. (1995). An ecological analysis of peer influence on adolescent grade point average and drug use. *Developmental Psychology, 31,* 915–922.

Muchinsky, Paul M. (2000). *Psychology applied to work: An introduction to industrial and organizational psychology* (6th ed.). Belmont, CA: Wadsworth.

Mueser, Kim T.; Bellack, Alan S.; & Brady, E. U. (1990). Hallucinations in schizophrenia. *Acta Psychiatrica Scandinavica, 82,* 26–29.

Mueser, Kim T., & Glynn, Shirley M. (1993). Efficacy of psychotherapy for schizophrenia. In Thomas R. Giles (Ed.), *Handbook of effective psychotherapy.* New York: Plenum Press.

Mukerjee, Madhusree. (1997, February). Trends in animal research. *Scientific American, 276*(2), 86–93.

Mulhern, Sherrill. (1991). Embodied alternative identities: Bearing witness to a world that might have been. *Psychiatric Clinics of North America, 14,* 769–786.

Mullen, Mary K. (1994). Earliest recollections of childhood: A demographic analysis. *Cognition, 52,* 55–79.

Mulrine, Anna. (1998, July 20). Take a nap: It's on the house: When sacking out is a company benefit. *U.S. News and World Report, 125,* 61.

Murphy, Sheila T.; Monahan, Jennifer L.; & Zajonc, Robert B. (1995). Additivity of nonconscious affect: Combined effects of priming and exposure. *Journal of Personality and Social Psychology, 69,* 589–602.

Murray, Bridget. (1995, November). Gender gap in math scores is closing. *APA Monitor, 26*(11), 43.

Murray, Henry A. (1938). *Explorations in personality.* New York: Oxford University Press.

Murray, Henry A. (1943). *Thematic Apperception Test Manual.* Cambridge, MA: Harvard University Press.

Murray, John B. (1995). Evidence for acupuncture's analgesic effectiveness and proposals for the physiological mechanisms involved. *Journal of Psychology, 129,* 443–461.

Murtagh, Douglas R. R., & Greenwood, Kenneth M. (1995). Identifying effective psychological treatments for insomnia: A meta-analysis. *Journal of Consulting and Clinical Psychology, 63,* 79–89.

Musto, David F. (1991, July). Opium, cocaine and marijuana in American history. *Scientific American, 265,* 40–47.

Muth, Denise K.; Glynn, Shawn M.; Britton, Bruce K.; & Graves, Michael F. (1988). Thinking out loud while studying text: Rehearsing key ideas. *Journal of Educational Psychology, 80,* 315–318.

Myers, David G. (1999). *Social psychology* (6th ed.). Boston: McGraw-Hill.

Myers, David G., & Diener, Ed. (1995). Who is happy? *Psychological Science, 6*(1), 10–19.

Myers, Mark G.; Steward, David G.; & Brown, Sandra A. (1998). Progression from conduct disorder to antisocial personality disorder following treatment for adolescent substance abuse. *American Journal of Psychiatry, 155,* 479–485.

Nader, Karim; Bechara, Antione; & van der Kooy, Derek. (1997). Neurobiological constraints of behavioral models of motivation. *Annual Review of Psychology, 48,* 85–114.

Narrow, William E.; Regier, Darrel A.; Rae, Donald S.; Manderscheid, Ronald W.; & Locke, Ben Z. (1993). Use of services by persons with mental and addictive disorders: Findings from the National Institute of Mental Health Epidemiologic Catchment Area Program. *Archives of General Psychiatry, 50,* 95–107.

Nash, Michael. (1987). What, if anything, is regressed about hypnotic age regression? A review of the empirical literature. *Psychological Bulletin, 102*(1), 42–52.

Nash, Michael R. (1997). Why scientific hypnosis needs psychoanalysis (or something like it). *International Journal of Clinical and Experimental Hypnosis, 45,* 291–300.

Nash, Michael R. (2001, July). The truth and the hype of hypnosis. *Scientific American, 285,* 46–49, 52–55. HTML version of article retrieved January 14, 2002, from http://www.sciam.com/2001/0701issue/0701nash.html

Nathan, Peter E.; Stuart, Scott P.; & Dolan, Sara L. (2000). Research on psychotherapy efficacy and effectiveness: Between Scylla and Charybdis? *Psychological Bulletin, 126,* 964–981.

National Association for the Education of Young Children. (1998). *Choosing a good early childhood program.* Washington, DC: National Association for the Education of Young Children.

National Center for Health Statistics. (2000a). *Health, United States, 2000, with adolescent health chartbook* (DHHS Pub. No. (PHS) 2000-1232-1). Hyattsville, MD: U.S. Department of Health and Human Services, Centers for Disease Control and Prevention, National Center for Health Statistics.

National Center for Health Statistics. (2000b). *Prevalence of overweight and obesity among adults: United States, 1999.* Centers for Disease Control and Prevention, National Center for Health Statistics, Health E-Stats. <http://www.cdc.gov/nchs/products/pubs/pubd/hestats/3and4/sedentary.htm> (May 25, 2001)

National Center for Health Statistics. (2000c). *Prevalence of sedentary leisure-time behavior among adults in the United States.* Centers for Disease Control and Prevention, National Center for Health Statistics, Health E-Stats. <http://www.cdc.gov/nchs/products/pubs/pubd/hestats/obese/obse99.htm> (May 25, 2001)

National Center for Health Statistics. (2001). *Prevalence of overweight and obesity among children and adolescents: United States, 1999.* Centers for Disease Control and Prevention, National Center for Health Statistics, Health E-Stats. <http://www.cdc.gov/nchs/products/pubs/pubd/hestats/overwght99.htm> (May 25, 2001)

National Conference of Christians and Jews. (1994). *Taking America's pulse: The National Conference Survey on Intergroup Relations.* New York: National Conference of Christians and Jews.

National Council on Aging. (1998, September 28). News: Half of older Americans report they are sexually active and 4 in 10 want more sex, says new survey. <http://www.ncoa.org/news/archives/sexsurvey.htm> (1999, April 12)

National Institutes of Health. (2000). *Statistics related to overweight and obesity* (NIH Publication No. 96-4158). Bethesda, MD: National Institutes of Health: National Institute of Diabetes & Digestive & Kidney Diseases. <http://www.niddk.nih.gov/health/nutrit/pubs/statobes.htm> (May 25, 2001)

National Institute of Neurological Disorders and Stroke. (2001). *Restless legs syndrome fact sheet* (NIH Publication No.01-4847). Bethesda, MD: National Institutes of Health. Retrieved January 12, 2002, from http://www.ninds.nih.gov/health_and_medical/pubs/restless_legs.htm

National Opinion Research Center. (2001). *Doctoral recipients from United States universities: Summary report 2000.* Chicago: University of Chicago National Opinion Research Center.

National Science Foundation. (2000). *Characteristics of Doctoral Scientists and Engineers: 1999 [Early Release Tables].* Arlington, VA: National Science Foundation, Division of Science Resources Studies. Retrieved February 10, 2002 from http://www.nsf.gov/sbe/srs/srs01406/start.htm

National Sleep Foundation (2002, April 2). *2002 "Sleep in America" Poll.* Washington, DC: National Sleep Foundation. PDF of report retrieved on May 5, 2002 from: http://www.sleepfoundation.org/img/2002SleepInAmericaPoll.pdf

National Stigma Clearinghouse. (1993, July/August). *Prime-time TV portrayals of mentally ill as villains perpetuate stigma, advocates charge* [Press release]. Albany, NY: National Stigma Clearinghouse.

National Television Violence Study (Vol. 1). (1996). Thousand Oaks, CA: Sage.

National Television Violence Study (Vol. 2). (1997). Thousand Oaks, CA: Sage.

National Television Violence Study (Vol. 3). (1998). Thousand Oaks, CA: Sage.

Naveilhan, Philippe; Hassani, Hessameh; & others. (1999). Normal feeding behavior, body weight and leptin response require the neuropeptide Y Y2 receptor. *Nature Medicine, 5,* 1188–1193.

Nederkoorn, Chantal; Smulders, Fren T.Y.; & Jansen, Anita. (2000). Cephalic phase responses, craving and food intake in normal subjects. *Appetite, 35,* 45–55.

Neher, Andrew. (1991). Maslow's theory of motivation: A critique. *Journal of Humanistic Psychology, 31,* 89–112.

Neisser, Ulric (Chair); Boodoo, Gwyneth; Bouchard, Thomas J., Jr.; Boykin, A. Wade; Brody, Nathan; Ceci, Stephen J.; & others. (1996). Intelligence: Knowns and unknowns. *American Psychologist, 51,* 77–101.

Nelson, Charles A. (1995). The ontogeny of human memory: A cognitive neuroscience perspective. *Developmental Psychology, 31,* 723–738.

Nelson, Charles A. (1998). The nature of early memory. *Preventive Medicine: An International Journal Devoted to Practice and Theory, 27,* 172–179.

Nelson, Katherine. (1993). The psychological and social origins of autobiographical memory. *Psychological Science, 4,* 7–14.

Nelson, Marcia Z. (2001). *Come and sit: A week inside meditation centers.* Woodstock, VT: Skylight Paths.

Nemeroff, Charles B. (1998, June). The neurobiology of depression. *Scientific American, 278,* 42–49.

Nestler, Eric J. (2001a). Molecular basis of long-term plasticity underlying addiction. *Nature Reviews Neuroscience, 2,* 119–128.

Nestler, Eric J. (2001b, June 22). Total recall—the memory of addiction. *Science, 292,* 2266–2267.

Neter, Efrat, & Ben-Shakhar, Gershon. (1989). The predictive validity of graphological inferences: A meta-analytic approach. *Personality and Individual Differences, 10,* 737–745.

Nevid, Jeffrey S.; Fichner-Rathus, Lois; & Rathus, Spencer A. (1995). *Human sexuality in a world of diversity* (2nd ed.). Boston: Allyn & Bacon.

New prairie dog vacuum catching on in Southwest. (1992, January 24). *Tulsa World,* p. C-7.

Newberg, Andrew B., & d'Aquili, Eugene G. (2000). The neuropsychology of religious and spiritual experience. *Journal of Consciousness Studies, 7,* 251–266.

Newberg, Andrew B.; d'Aquili, Eugene G.; & Rause, Vince. (2001). *Why God won't go away: Brain science and the biology of belief.* New York: Ballantine Books.

Newcombe, Nora S.; Drummey, Anna Bullock; Fox, Nathan A.; Lie, Eunhui; & Ottinger-Alberts, Wendy. (2000). Remembering early childhood: How much, how, and why (or why not). *Current Directions in Psychological Science, 9,* 55–58.

Nichols, M. James, & Newsome, William T. (1999, December 2). The neurobiology of cognition. Impacts of foreseeable science. *Nature, 402*(Suppl.), C35–C38.

Nickerson, Raymond S., & Adams, Marilyn J. (1982). Long-term memory for a common object. In Ulric Neisser (Ed.), *Memory observed: Remembering in natural contexts.* San Francisco: Freeman.

Nikles, Charles D.; Brecht, David L.; Klinger, Eric; & Bursell, Amy L. (1998). The effects of current-concern- and nonconcern-related waking suggestions on nocturnal dream content. *Journal of Personality and Social Psychology, 75,* 242–255.

Nisbet, Matthew. (1998, May/June). Psychic telephone networks profit on yearning, gullibility. *Skeptical Inquirer, 22,* 5–6.

Nishio, Kazumi, & Bilmes, Murray. (1993). Psychotherapy with Southeast Asian American clients. In Donald R. Atkinson, George Morten, & Derald Wing Sue (Eds.), *Counseling American minorities: A cross-cultural perspective* (4th ed.). Madison, WI: Brown & Benchmark.

Nobler, Mitchell S.; Oquendo, Maria A.; Kegeles, Lawrence S.; Malone, Kevin M.; Sackeim, Harold A.; & Mann, J. John. (2001). Decreased regional brain metabolism after ECT. *American Journal of Psychiatry, 158,* 305–308.

Nolen-Hoeksema, Susan. (2001). Gender differences in depression. *Current Directions in Psychological Science, 10,* 173–176.

Nolen-Hoeksema, Susan; Larson, Judith; & Grayson, Carla. (1999). Explaining the gender difference in depressive symptoms. *Journal of Personality and Social Psychology, 77,* 1061–1072.

Norris, Joan E., & Tindale, Joseph A. (1994). *Among generations: The cycle of adult relationships.* New York: Freeman.

North, Carol S.; Nixon, Sara Jo.; Shariat, Sheryll; Mallonee, Sue; McMillen, J. Curtis; Spitznagel, Edward L.; & Smith, Elizabeth M. (1999). The psychiatric impact of the Oklahoma City bombing on survivors of the direct blast. *Journal of the American Medical Association, 282,* 755–762.

North, Carol S.; Smith, Elizabeth M.; & Spitznagel, Edward L. (1994). Posttraumatic stress disorder in survivors of a mass shooting. *American Journal of Psychiatry, 151,* 82–88.

Noseworthy, John H. (1999, June 24). Progress in determining the causes and treatment of multiple sclerosis. *Nature, 399*(Suppl.), A40–A47.

Noyes Russell, Jr.; & Hoehn-Saric, Rudolf. (1998). *The anxiety disorders.* New York: Cambridge University Press.

Nyberg, Lars; Habib, Reza; McIntosh, Anthony R.; & Tulving, Endel. (2000). Reactivation of encoding-related brain activity during memory retrieval. *Proceedings of the National Academy of Sciences, USA, 97,* 11120–11124.

Oakley, Bruce. (1986). Basic taste physiology: Human perspectives. In H. L. Meiselman & R. S. Rivlin (Eds.), *Clinical measurement of taste and smell.* New York: Macmillan.

O'Brien, Charles P. (1997, October 3). A range of research-based pharmacotherapies for addiction. *Science, 278,* 66–70.

Ochse, R. (1990). *Before the gates of excellence: The determinants of creative genius.* New York: Cambridge University Press.

O'Craven, Kathleen M., & Kanwisher, Nancy. (2000). Mental imagery of faces and places activates corresponding stimulus-specific brain regions. *Journal of Cognitive Neuroscience, 12,* 1013–1023.

O'Doherty, John; Kringelbach, Morten L.; Rolls, Edmund T.; Hornak, Julia; & Andrews, Caroline. (2001a, January). Abstract reward and punishment representations in the human orbitofrontal cortex. *Nature Neuroscience, 4,* 95–102.

O'Doherty, John; Rolls, E. T.; Francis, S.; Bowtell, R.; & McGlone, F. (2001b). Representation of pleasant and aversive taste in the humn brain. *Journal of Neurophysiology, 85,* 1315–1321.

Oettingen, Gabriele, & Gollwitzer, Peter M. (2001). Goal setting and goal striving. In A. Tesser & N. Schwarz (Vol. Eds.), & M. Hewstone & M. Brewer (Series Eds.), *Intraindividual processes. Vol. 1 of the Blackwell handbook in social psychology.* Oxford, England: Blackwell.

Ogbu, John U. (1986). The consequences of the American caste system. In Ulric Neisser (Ed.), *The school achievement of minority children: New perspectives.* Hillsdale, NJ: Erlbaum.

Ogden, Jenni A., & Corkin, Suzanne. (1991). Memories of H. M. In Wickliffe C. Abraham, Michael Corballis, & K. Geoffrey White (Eds.), *Memory mechanisms: A tribute to G. V. Goddard.* Hillsdale, NJ: Erlbaum.

Öhman, Arne; Flykt, Anders; & Esteves, Francisco. (2001a). Emotion drives attention: Detecting the snake in the grass. *Journal of Experimental Psychology: General, 130,* 466–478.

Öhman, Arne; Lundqvist, Daniel; & Esteves, Francisco. (2001b). The face in the crowd revisited: A threat advantage with schematic stimuli. *Journal of Personality and Social Psychology, 80,* 381–396.

Öhman, Arne, & Mineka, Susan. (2001). Fears, phobias, and preparedness: Toward an evolved module of fear and fear learning. *Psychological Review, 108,* 483–522.

Öhman, Arne, & Soares, Joaquim J. F. (1994). "Unconscious anxiety": Phobic responses to masked stimuli. *Journal of Abnormal Psychology, 103,* 231–240.

Olds, James. (1958). Self-stimulation of the brain. *Science, 127,* 315–324.

Olds, James. (1962). Hypothalamic substrates of reward. *Physiological Reviews, 42,* 554–604.

Olds, M. E., & Fobes, James L. (1981). The central basis of motivation: Intracranial self-stimulation studies. *Annual Review of Psychology, 32,* 523–574.

O'Leary, K. Daniel, & Wilson, G. Terence. (1987). *Behavior therapy: Application and outcome* (2nd ed.). Englewood Cliffs, NJ: Prentice-Hall.

Oliver, Mary Beth, & Hyde, Janet Shibley. (1993). Gender differences in sexuality: A meta-analysis. *Psychological Bulletin, 114,* 29–51.

Olson, James M., & Zanna, Mark P. (1993). Attitudes and attitude change. *Annual Review of Psychology, 44,* 117–154.

Olson, Michael A., & Fazio, Russell H. (2001). Implicit attitude formation through classical conditioning. *Psychological Science, 12,* 413–417.

Olton, David S. (1992). Tolman's cognitive analysis: Predecessors of current approaches in psychology. *Journal of Experimental Psychology: General, 121,* 427–428.

Ones, Deniz S.; Viswesvaren, Chockalingam; & Schmidt, Frank I. (1993). Comprehensive meta-analysis of integrity test validities: Findings for personnel selection and theories of job performance. *Journal of Applied Psychology, 78,* 679–703.

Orne, Martin T., & Holland, Charles H. (1968). On the ecological validity of laboratory deceptions. *International Journal of Psychiatry, 6,* 282–293.

Orr, William C. (1997). Obstructive sleep apnea: Natural history and varieties of the clinical presentation. In Mark R. Pressman & William C. Orr (Eds.), *Understanding sleep: The evaluation and treatment of sleep disorders.* Washington, DC: American Psychological Association.

Osborne, Jason W. (2001). Testing stereotype threat: Does anxiety explain race and sex differences in achievement? *Contemporary Educational Psychology, 26,* 291–310.

Ottati, Victor, & Lee, Yueh-Ting. (1995). Accuracy: A neglected component of stereotype research. In Yueh-Ting Lee, Lee J. Jussim, & Clark R. McCauley (Eds.), *Stereotype accuracy: Toward appreciating group differences.* Washington, DC: American Psychological Association.

Overmier, J. Bruce, & Carroll, Marilyn E. (2001). Basic issues in the use of animals in health research. In Marilyn E. Carroll & J. Bruce Overmier (Eds.), *Animal research and human health: Advancing human welfare through behavioral science.* Washington, DC: American Psychological Association.

Oyserman, Daphna; Grant, Larry; & Ager, Joel. (1995). A socially contextualized model of African American identity: Possible selves and school persistence. *Journal of Personality and Social Psychology, 69,* 1216–1232.

Ozbayrak, Kaan R., & Berlin, Richard M. (1995). Sleepwalking in children and adolescents. In Charles E. Schaefer (Ed.), *Clinical handbook of sleep disorders in children.* Northvale, NJ: Aronson.

Ozer, Elizabeth M., & Bandura, Albert. (1990). Mechanisms governing empowerment effects: A self-efficacy analysis. *Journal of Personality and Social Psychology, 58,* 472–486.

Paik, Haejung, & Comstock, George. (1994). The effects of television on antisocial behavior: A meta-analysis. *Communication Research, 21,* 516–546.

Paillère-Martinot, M. L.; Caclin, A.; Artiges, E.; Poline, J. B.; Joliot, M.; & others. (2001). Cerebral gray and white matter reductions and clinical correlates in patients with early onset schizophrenia. *Schizophrenia Research, 50,* 19–26.

Paivio, Allan. (1986). *Mental representations: A dual coding approach.* New York: Oxford University Press.

Palm, Kathleen M., & Gibson, Pamela. (1998). Recovered memories of childhood sexual abuse: Clinicians' practices and beliefs. *Professional Psychology: Research and Practice, 29,* 257–261.

Palmblad, J.; Petrini, B.; Wasserman, J.; & Akerstedt, T. (1979). Lymphocyte and granulocyte reactions during sleep deprivation. *Psychosomatic Medicine, 41,* 273–278.

Palmer, Emma J., & Hollin, Clive R. (2001). Sociomoral reasoning, perceptions of parenting and self-reported delinquency in adolescents. *Applied Cognitive Psychology, 15,* 85–100.

Panksepp, Jaak. (1998). *Affective neuroscience.* New York: Oxford University Press.

Panksepp, Jaak. (2000). The riddle of laughter: Neural and psychoevolutionary underpinnings of joy. *Psychological Science, 9,* 183–186.

Pannemans, D. L., & Westerterp, K. R. (1995). Energy expenditure, physical activity and basal metabolic rate of elderly subjects. *British Journal of Nutrition, 73,* 571–581.

Papini, Mauricio R. (2002). Pattern and process in the evolution of learning. *Psychological Review, 109,* 186–201.

Papoušek, Mechthild; Papoušek, Hanus; & Bornstein, Marc H. (1985). The naturalistic vocal environment of young infants: On the significance of homogeneity and variability in parental speech. In Tiffany M. Field & N. Fox (Eds.), *Social perception in infants.* Norwood, NJ: Ablex.

Paris, Joel. (1997). Antisocial and borderline personality disorders: Two separate diagnoses or two aspects of the same psychopathology? *Comprehensive Psychiatry, 38,* 237–242.

Park, Bernadette; Ryan, Carey S.; & Judd, Charles M. (1992). Role of meaningful subgroups in explaining differences in perceived variability for in-groups and out-groups. *Journal of Personality and Social Psychology, 63*(4), 553–567.

Parkin, Alan J.; Walter, Brenda M.; & Hunkin, Nicola M. (1995). Relationships between normal aging, frontal lobe function, and memory for temporal and spatial information. *Neuropsychology, 9,* 304–312.

Patrick, Gentry N.; Zukerberg, Lawrence; Nikolic, Margareta; de la Monte, Suzanne; Dikkes, Pieter; & Tsai, Li-Huei. (1999, December 9). Conversion of p35 to p25 deregulates Cdk5 activity and promotes neurodegeneration. *Nature, 402,* 615–622.

Patterson, Charlotte J. (1992). Children of lesbian and gay parents. *Child Development, 63,* 1025–1042.

Patterson, Charlotte J. (1995a). Sexual orientation and human development: An overview. *Developmental Psychology, 31,* 3–11.

Patterson, Charlotte J. (1995b). Families of the lesbian baby boom: Parents' division of labor and children's adjustment. *Developmental Psychology, 31,* 115–123.

Patterson, Charlotte J. (1995c). Lesbian mothers, gay fathers, and their children. In Anthony R. D'Augelli & Charlotte J. Patterson (Eds.), *Lesbian, gay and bisexual identities across the lifespan: Psychological perspectives.* New York: Oxford University Press.

Paul, Diane B., & Blumenthal, Arthur L. (1989). On the trail of Little Albert. *The Psychological Record, 39,* 547–553.

Paul, Gordon L., & Menditto, Anthony A. (1992). Effectiveness of inpatient treatment programs for mentally ill adults in public psychiatric facilities. *Applied and Preventive Psychology, 1,* 41–63.

Paunonen, Sampo V.; Jackson, Douglas N.; Trzebinski, Jerry; & Fosterling, Friedrich. (1992). Personality structure across cultures: A multimethod evaluation. *Journal of Personality and Social Psychology, 62,* 447–456.

Pavlov, Ivan. (1904/1965). On conditioned reflexes. In Richard J. Herrnstein & Edwin G. Boring (Eds.), *A source book in the history of psychology.* Cambridge, MA: Harvard University Press.

Pavlov, Ivan. (1927/1960). *Conditioned reflexes: An investigation of the physiological activity of the cerebral cortex* (G. V. Anrep, Trans.). New York: Dover Books. <http://psychclassics.yorku.ca/Pavlov/index.htm> (May 25, 2001)

Pavlov, Ivan. (1928). *Lectures on conditioned reflexes.* New York: International Publishers.

Payne, David G.; Neuschatz, Jeffrey S.; Lampinen, James M.; & Lynn, Steven Jay. (1997). Compelling memory illusions: The qualitative characteristics of false memories. *Current Directions in Psychological Science, 6,* 56–60.

Payne, John W.; Bettman, James R.; & Johnson, Eric J. (1993). *The adaptive decision maker.* Cambridge, England: Cambridge University Press.

Payton, Jack R. (1992, May 16). The sad legacy of Japan's outcasts. *Chicago Tribune,* Sect. 1, p. 21.

Pearce, John M., & Bouton, Mark E. (2001). Theories of associative learning in animals. *Annual Review of Psychology, 52,* 111–139.

Pearlin, Leonard I. (1993). The social contexts of stress. In Leo Goldberger & Shlomo Breznitz (Eds.), *Handbook of stress: Theoretical and clinical aspects* (2nd ed.). New York: Free Press.

Peirce, Robert S.; Frone, Michael R.; Russell, Marcia; & Cooper, M. Lynne. (1996). Financial stress, social support, and alcohol involvement: A longitudinal test of the buffering hypothesis in a general population study. *Health Psychology, 15,* 38–47.

Pekala, Ronald J. (1987). The phenomenology of meditation. In Michael A. West (Ed.), *The psychology of meditation.* New York: Oxford University Press.

Peltin, Steven R., & Crowder, J. Lane. (2000). Reducing telecommuting management risks. *National Underwriter, 18,* 14.

Pendergrast, Mark. (1996). *Victims of memory: Sex abuse accusations and shattered lives* (2nd ed.). Hinesburg, VT: Upper Access.

Pepler, Debra J., & Craig, Wendy M. (1995). A peek behind the fence: Naturalistic observations of aggressive children with remote audiovisual recording. *Developmental Psychology, 31*(4), 548–553.

Pepperberg, Irene. (1993). Cognition and communication in an African gray parrot (*Psittacus erithacus*): Studies on a nonhuman, nonprimate, nonmammalian subject. In Herbert L. Roitblat, Louis M. Herman, & Paul E. Nachtigall (Eds.), *Language and communication: Comparative perspectives.* Hillsdale, NJ: Erlbaum.

Pepperberg, Irene M. (2000). *The Alex studies: Cognitive and communicative abilities of gray parrots.* Cambridge, MA: Harvard University Press.

Pepperberg, Irene M. (2001). Avian cognitive abilities. *Bird Behavior, 14,* 51–70.

Pérez-Stable, Eliseo J.; Herrera, Brenda; Peyton, Jacob, III; & Bonowitz, Neal L. (1998, July 8). Nicotine metabolism and intake in black and white smokers. *Journal of the American Medical Association, 280,* 152–156.

Perloff, Richard M. (1993). *The dynamics of persuasion.* Hillsdale, NJ: Erlbaum.

Pert, Candace B., & Snyder, Solomon H. (1973). Opiate receptor: Demonstration in the nervous tissue. *Science, 179,* 1011–1014.

Perugini, Eve Marie; Kirsch, Irving; Allen, Sarah T.; Coldwell, Eleanor; Meredith, Janelle; Montgomery, Guy H.; & Sheehan, Julia. (1998). Surreptitious observation of responses to hypnotically suggested hallucinations: A test of the compliance hypothesis. *International Journal of Clinical and Experimental Hypnosis, 46,* 191–203.

Pervin, Lawrence A. (1994). A critical analysis of current trait theory. *Psychological Inquiry, 5,* 103–113.

Peters, Roger, & McGee, Rob. (1982). Cigarette smoking and state-dependent memory. *Psychopharmacology, 76*(3), 232–235.

Peterson, Christopher. (2000). Optimistic explanatory style and health. In Jane E. Gillham (Ed.), *The science of optimism and hope: Research essays in honor of Martin E. P. Seligman.* Philadelphia: Templeton Foundation Press.

Peterson, Christopher, & Bossio, Lisa M. (1993). Healthy attitudes: Optimism, hope, and control. In Daniel Goleman & Joel Gurin (Eds.), *Mind/body medicine: How to use your mind for better health.* Yonkers, NY: Consumer Reports Books.

Peterson, Christopher, & Bossio, Lisa M. (2001). Optimism and physical well-being. In Edward C. Chang (Ed.), *Optimism and pessimism: Implications for theory, research, and practice.* Washington, DC: American Psychological Association.

Peterson, Christopher; Maier, Steven F.; & Seligman, Martin E. P. (1993). *Learned helplessness: A theory for the age of personal control.* New York: Oxford University Press.

Peterson, Christopher; Seligman, Martin E. P.; & Vaillant, George E. (1988). Pessimistic explanatory style as a risk factor for physical illness: A thirty-five-year longitudinal study. *Journal of Personality and Social Psychology, 55,* 23–27.

Petraitis, John; Flay, Brian R.; & Miller, Todd Q. (1995). Reviewing theories of adolescent substance abuse: Organizing pieces of the puzzle. *Psychological Bulletin, 117,* 67–86.

Petrovic, Predrag; Kalso, Eija; Petersson, Karl Magnus; & Ingvar, Martin. (2002, March 1). Placebo and opioid analgesia—Imaging a shared neuronal network. *Science, 295,* 1737–1740.

Petry, Nancy M.; Martin, Bonnie; Cooney, Judith L.; & Kranzler, Henry R. (2000). Give them prizes and they will come: Contingency management for treatment of alcohol dependence. *Journal of Consulting and Clinical Psychology, 68,* 250–257.

Petry, Nancy M.; Petrakis, Ismene; Trevisan, Louis; Wiredu, George; Boutros, Nashaat N.; Martin, Bonnie; & Kosten, Thomas R. (2001). Contingency management interventions: From research to practice. *American Journal of Psychiatry, 158,* 694–702.

Pham, Lien B., & Taylor, Shelley E. (1999). From thought to action: Effects of process-versus outcome-based mental simulations on performance. *Personality and Social Psychology Bulletin, 25,* 250–260.

Phelps, Elizabeth A.; O'Connor, Kevin J.; Gatenby, J. Christopher; Gore, John C.; Grillon, Christian; & Davis, Michael. (2001). Activation of the left amygdala to a cognitive representation of fear. *Nature Neuroscience, 4,* 237–441.

Phillips, Antoinette S., & Bedeian, Arthur G. (1994). Leader-follower exchange quality: The role of personal and interpersonal attributes. *Academy of Management Journal, 37,* 990–1001.

Phillips, David P., & Brugge, John F. (1985). Progress in neurophysiology of sound localization. *Annual Review of Psychology, 36,* 245–274.

Phillips, Deborah. (1991). Day care for young children in the United States. In E. C. Melhuish & Peter Moss (Eds.), *Day care for young children.* London: Routledge.

Phillips, Deborah A., & Howes, Carollee. (1987). Indicators of quality in child care: Review of research. In Deborah A. Phillips (Ed.), *Quality in child care: What does research tell us?* (Research monograph of the National Association for the Education of Young Children, Vol. 1). Washington, DC: National Association for the Education of Young Children.

Phillips, Jean M. (1998). Effects of realistic job previews on multiple organizational outcomes: A meta-analysis. *Academy of Management Journal, 41,* 673–690.

Phillips, Michael. (1999). Problems with the polygraph. *Science, 286,* 411.

Phillips, Susan D., & Blustein, David L. (1994). Readiness for career choices: Planning, exploring, and deciding. *The Career Development Quarterly, 43,* 63–75.

Phillips-Bute, Barbara G., & Lane, James D. (1997). Caffeine withdrawal symptoms following brief caffeine deprivation. *Physiology and Behavior, 63,* 35–39.

Piaget, Jean. (1952). *The origins of intelligence in children* (Margaret Cook, Trans.). New York: International Universities Press.

Piaget, Jean. (1972). Intellectual evolution from adolescence to adulthood. *Human Development, 15,* 1–12.

Piaget, Jean. (1973). The stages of cognitive development: Interview with Richard I. Evans. In Richard I. Evans (Ed.), *Jean Piaget: The man and his ideas.* New York: Dutton.

Piaget, Jean, & Inhelder, Bärbel. (1958). *The growth of logical thinking from childhood to adolescence: An essay on the construction of formal operational structures* (Anne Parsons and Stanley Milgram, Trans.). New York: Basic Books.

Piaget, Jean, & Inhelder, Bärbel. (1974). *The child's construction of quantities: Conservation and atomism.* London: Routledge & Kegan Paul.

Piliavin, Jane Allyn, & Charng, Hong-Wen. (1990). Altruism: A review of recent theory and research. *Annual Review of Sociology, 16,* 27–65.

Piliavin, Jane Allyn; Dovidio, John F.; Gaertner, Samuel L.; & Clark, Russell D., III. (1981). *Emergency intervention.* New York: Academic Press.

Pillemer, David B. (1998). *Momentous events, vivid memories.* Cambridge, MA: Harvard University Press.

Pillow, David R.; Zautra, Alex J.; & Sandler, Irwin. (1996). Major life events and minor stressors: Identifying mediational links in the stress process. *Journal of Personality and Social Psychology, 70,* 381–394.

Pinel, John P. J.; Assanand, Sunaina; & Lehman, Darrin R. (2000). Hunger, eating, and ill health. *American Psychologist, 55,* 1105–1116.

Pinker, Steven. (1994). *The language instinct: How the mind creates language.* New York: Morrow.

Pinker, Steven. (1995). Introduction: Language. In Michael S. Gazzaniga (Ed.), *The cognitive neurosciences.* Cambridge, MA: MIT Press.

Pinker, Steven. (1997). *How the mind works.* New York: Norton.

Pirke, Karl M. (1995). Physiology of bulimia nervosa. (1995). In Kelly D. Brownell & Christopher G. Fairburn (Eds.), *Eating disorders and obesity: A comprehensive handbook.* New York: Guilford Press.

Pitschel-Walz, Gabi; Leucht, Stefan; Bauml, Josef; Kissling, Werner; & Engel, Rolf. (2001). The effect of family interventions on relapse and rehospitalization in schizophrenia—A meta-analysis. *Schizophrenia Bulletin, 27,* 73–92.

Plake, Barbara S., & Impara, James C. (2001). *The mental measurements yearbook* (14th ed.). Lincoln: Buros Institute of Mental Measurements/University of Nebraska Press.

Plant, E. Ashby; Hyde, Janet Shibley; Keltner, Dacher; & Devine, Patricia G. (2000). The gender stereotyping of emotions. *Psychology of Women Quarterly, 24,* 81–92.

Plomin, Robert. (1990). The role of inheritance in behavior. *Science, 248,* 183–188.

Plomin, Robert, & DeFries, John C. (1998, May). The genetics of cognitive abilities and disabilities. *Scientific American, 278,* 62–69.

Plomin, Robert; Owen, Michael J.; & McGuffin, Peter. (1994, June 17). The genetic basis of complex human behaviors. *Science, 264,* 1733–1739.

Plomin, Robert, & Rende, Richard. (1991). Human behavioral genetics. *Annual Review of Psychology, 42,* 161–190.

Plous, Scott. (1996). Attitudes toward the use of animals in psychological research and education: Results from a national survey of psychologists. *American Psychologist, 51*(11), 1167–1180.

Poehlman, Eric T., & Horton, Edward S. (1995). Measurement of energy expenditure. In Kelly D. Brownell & Christopher G. Fairburn (Eds.), *Eating disorders and obesity: A comprehensive handbook.* New York: Guilford Press.

Polk, Thad A., & Newell, Allen. (1995). Deduction as verbal reasoning. *Psychological Review, 102,* 533–566.

Poole, Joyce. (2000). Family reunions. In Marc Bekoff (Ed.), *The smile of a dolphin: Remarkable accounts of animal emotions.* New York: Discovery Books/Random House.

Pope, Harrison G., Jr.; Gruber, Amanda J.; Hudson, James I.; Huestis, Marilyn A.; & Yurgelun-Todd, Deborah. (2001). Neuropsychological performance in long-term cannabis users. *Archives of General Psychiatry, 58,* 909–915.

Pope, Kenneth S. (1990). Therapist–patient sexual involvement: A review of the research. *Clinical Psychology Review, 10,* 477–490.

Pope, Kenneth S., & Bouhoutsos, Jacqueline C. (1986). *Sexual intimacy between therapists and patients.* New York: Praeger.

Pope, Kenneth S., & Brown, Laura S. (1996). *Recovered memories of abuse: Assessment, therapy, forensics.* Washington, DC: American Psychological Association.

Pope, Kenneth S., & Tabachnick, Barbara G. (1993). Therapists' anger, hate, fear, and sexual feelings: National survey of therapist responses, client characteristics, critical events, formal complaints, and training. *Professional Psychology: Research and Practice, 24,* 142–152.

Pope, Victoria. (1997, August 4). Day-care dangers. *U.S. News & World Report, 123,* 30–37.

Pope-Davis, Donald B.; Liu, William M.; Toporek, Rebecca L.; & Brittan-Powell,

Christopher S. (2001). What's missing from multicultural competency research: Review, introspection, and recommendations. *Cultural Diversity and Ethnic Minority Psychology, 7,* 121–138.

Porkka-Heiskanen, Tarja; Strecker, Robert E.; Thakkar, Mahesh; Bjørkum, Alvhild A.; Greene, Robert W.; & McCarley, Robert W. (1997, May 23). Adenosine: A mediator of the sleep-inducing effects of prolonged wakefulness. *Science, 276,* 1265–1268.

Portas, C. M.; Thakkar, Mahesh; Rainnie, D. G.; Greene, Robert W.; & McCarley, Robert W. (1997). Role of adenosine in behavioral state modulation: A microdialysis study in the freely moving cat. *Neuroscience, 79,* 225–235.

Porter, Kenneth. (1993). Combined individual and group psychotherapy. In Anne Alonso & Hillel I. Swiller (Eds.), *Group therapy in clinical practice.* Washington, DC: American Psychiatric Press.

Porter, Richard H., & Moore, John D. (1981). Human kin recognition by olfactory cues. *Physiology and Behavior, 27,* 493–495.

Posner, Michael I. & DiGirolamo, Gregory J. (2000). Attention in cognitive neuroscience: An overview. In Michael S. Gazzaniga (ed.), *The New Cognitive Neurosciences,* 2e: MIT Press, 621–632.

Poulin-Dubois, Diane; Serbin, Lisa A.; Kenyon, Brenda; & Derbyshire, Alison. (1994). Infants' intermodal knowledge about gender. *Developmental Psychology, 30,* 436–442.

Powlishta, Kimberly K. (1995a). Gender bias in children's perceptions of personality traits. *Sex Roles, 32,* 223-240.

Powlishta, Kimberly K. (1995b). Intergroup processes in childhood: Social categorization and sex role development. *Developmental Psychology, 31,* 781–788.

Pratkanis, Anthony R. (1992). The cargo-cult science of subliminal persuasion. *Skeptical Inquirer, 16,* 260–273.

Pratkanis, Anthony R., & Aronson, Elliot. (1992). *Age of propaganda: The everyday use and abuse of persuasion.* New York: Freeman.

Pratkanis, Anthony R.; Eskenazi, Jay; & Greenwald, Anthony G. (1994). What you expect is what you believe (but not necessarily what you get): A test of the effectiveness of subliminal self-help audiotapes. *Basic and Applied Social Psychology, 15,* 251–276.

Pratto, Felicia. (1996). Sexual politics: The gender gap in the bedroom, the cupboard, and the Cabinet. In David M. Buss & Neil M. Malumuth (Eds.), *Sex, power, conflict: Evolutionary and feminist perspectives.* New York: Oxford University Press.

Premack, Steven L., & Wanous, John P. (1985). A meta-analysis of realistic job preview experiments. *Journal of Applied Psychology, 70,* 706–719.

Prescott, Carol A., & Gottesman, Irving I. (1993). Genetically mediated vulnerability to schizophrenia. *Psychiatric Clinics of North America, 16,* 245–268.

Preti, George; Cutler, Winnifred B.; Garcia, C. R.; Huggins, G. R.; & Lawley, H. J. (1986). Human axillary secretions influence women's menstrual cycles: The role of donor extract of females. *Hormones and Behavior, 20,* 474–482.

Previde, Emanuela Prato, & Poli, Marco D. (1996). Social learning in the golden hamster (*Mesocricetus auratus*). *Journal of Comparative Psychology, 110,* 203–208.

Prinzmetal, William. (1995). Visual feature integration in a world of objects. *Current Directions in Psychological Science, 4,* 90–94.

Pryzgoda, Jayde, & Chrisler, Joan C. (2000). Definitions of gender and sex: The subtleties of meaning. *Sex Roles, 43,* 553–569.

Pujol, Jesus; Deus, Joan; Losilla, Josep M.; & Capdevila, Antoni. (1999). Cerebral lateralization in normal left-handed people: Studies by functional MRI. *Neurology, 52,* 1038–1043.

Pulakos, Elaine D., & Schmitt, Neal. (1995). Experience-based and structured interview questions: Studies of validity. *Personnel Psychology, 48,* 289–308.

Pullum, Geoffrey K. (1991). *The great Eskimo vocabulary hoax and other irreverent essays on the study of language.* Chicago: University of Chicago Press.

Punamäki, Raija-Leena, & Joustie, Marja. (1998). The role of culture, violence, and personal factors affecting dream content. *Journal of Cross-Cultural Psychology, 29,* 320–342.

Purkey, William Watson, & Stanley, Paula Helen. (2002). The self in psychotherapy. In David J. Cain & Julius Seeman (Eds.), *Humanistic psychotherapies: Handbook of research and practice.* Washington, DC: American Psychological Association.

Putnam, Frank W. (1993). Dissociative phenomena. In David Spiegel (Ed.), *Dissociative disorders: A clinical review.* Lutherville, MD: Sidran.

Quattrocki, Elizabeth; Baird, Adigail; & Yurgelun-Todd, Deborah. (2000). Biological aspects of the link between smoking and depression. *Harvard Review of Psychiatry, 8,* 99–110.

Quinn, Diane M., & Spencer, Steven J. (2001). The interference of stereotype threat with women's generation of mathematical problem-solving strategies. *Journal of Social Issues, 57,* 55–71.

Rabinowitz, Jonathan; Lichtenberg, Pesach; Kaplan, Zeev; Mark, Mordechai; Nahon, Danielle; & Davidson, Michael. (2001). Rehospitalization rates of chronically ill schizophrenic patients discharged on a regimen of risperidone, olanzipine, or conventional antipsychotics. *American Journal of Psychiatry, 158,* 266–269.

Rachlin, Howard. (1974). Self-control. *Behaviorism, 2,* 94–107.

Rachlin, Howard. (1995). The value of temporal patterns in behavior. *Current Directions in Psychological Science, 4,* 188–192.

Rachlin, Howard. (2000). *The science of self-control.* Cambridge, MA: Harvard University Press.

Rahe, Richard H. (1972). Subjects' recent life changes and their near-future illness reports. *Annals of Clinical Research, 4,* 250–265.

Rainville, Pierre; Duncan, Gary H.; Price, Donald D.; Carrier, Benoît; & Bushnell, M. Catherine. (1997, August 15). Pain affect encoded in human anterior cingulate but not somatosensory cortex. *Science, 277,* 968–971.

Rainville, Pierre; Hofbauer, Robert K.; Paus, Toma; Duncan, Gary H.; Bushnell, M. Catherine; & Price, Donald D. (1999). Cerebral mechanisms of hypnotic induction and suggestion. *Journal of Cognitive Neuroscience, 11,* 110–125.

Rakic, Pasko. (1995). Corticogenesis in human and nonhuman primates. In Michael S. Gazzaniga (Ed.), *The cognitive neurosciences.* Cambridge, MA: MIT Press.

Ramachandran, Vilayanur S. (1992a, May). Blind spots. *Scientific American, 266,* 86–91.

Ramachandran, Vilayanur S. (1992b). Filling in gaps in perception: Part 1. *Current Directions in Psychological Science, 1,* 199–205.

Randi, James. (1980). *Flim-flam!* New York: Lippincott & Crowell.

Randi, James. (1982). *The truth about Uri Geller.* Buffalo, NY: Prometheus Books.

Rapee, Ronald M.; Brown, Timothy A.; Antony, Martin M.; & Barlow, David H. (1992). Response to hyperventilation and inhalation of 5.5% carbon dioxide-enriched air across the *DSM-III-R* anxiety disorders. *Journal of Abnormal Psychology, 101,* 538–552.

Rapoport, Judith L. (1989). *The boy who couldn't stop washing: The experience and treatment of obsessive-compulsive disorder.* New York: Dutton.

Rapoport, Judith L. (1991). Basal ganglia dysfunction as a proposed cause of obsessive-compulsive disorder. In Bernard J. Carroll & James E. Barrett (Eds.), *Psychopathology and the brain.* New York: Raven Press.

Rasmussen, Steven A., & Eisen, Jane L. (1992). The epidemiology and clinical features of obsessive-compulsive disorder. *Psychiatric Clinics of North America, 15,* 743–758.

Rasmussen, Theodore, & Milner, Brenda. (1977). The role of early left brain injury in determining lateralization of cerebral speech functions. *Annals of the New York Academy of Sciences, 299,* 355–369.

Ratcliff, Roger, & McKoon, Gail. (1994). Retrieving information from memory: Spreading-activation theories versus compound-cue theories. *Psychological Review, 101,* 177–184.

Ravussin, Eric. (1995). Energy expenditure and body weight. In Kelly D. Brownell & Christopher G. Fairburn (Eds.), *Eating disorders and obesity: A comprehensive handbook.* New York: Guilford Press.

Ravussin, Eric, & Danforth, Elliot, Jr. (1999, January 8). Beyond sloth—physical activity and weight gain. *Science, 283,* 184–185.

Rawlings, Steve W., & Saluter, Arlene F. (1995). *Household and family characteristics: March 1994* (U.S. Bureau of the Census, Current population reports, Series P20–483). Washington, DC: U.S. Government Printing Office.

Rawlins, William K. (1992). *Friendship matters: Communication, dialectics, and the life course.* Hawthorne, NY: de Gruyter.

Raynor, Hollie A.; & Epstein, Leonard H. (2001). Dietary variety, energy regulation, and obesity. *Psychological Bulletin, 127,* 325–341.

Refinetti, Roberto. (2000). *Circadian physiology.* Boca Raton, FL: CRC Press.

Regan, Dennis T., & Kilduff, Martin. (1988). Optimism about elections: Dissonance reduction at the ballot box. *Political Psychology, 9,* 101–107.

Regan, Dennis T.; Williams, Margo; & Sparling, Sondra. (1972). Voluntary expiation of guilt: A field experiment. *Journal of Personality and Social Psychology, 24,* 42–45.

Regier, Darrel A.; Narrow, William E.; Rae, Donald S.; Manderscheid, Ronald W.; Locke, Ben Z.; & Goodwin, Fredrick K. (1993). The de facto U.S. mental and addictive disorders service system: Epidemiologic catchment area prospective one-year prevalence rates of disorders and services. *Archives of General Psychiatry, 50,* 85–94.

Register, Patricia A., & Kihlstrom, John F. (1986). Finding the hypnotic virtuoso. *International Journal of Clinical and Experimental Hypnosis, 34,* 84–97.

Register, Patricia A., & Kihlstrom, John F. (1987). Hypnotic effects on hypermnesia. *International Journal of Clinical and Experimental Hypnosis, 35,* 155–170.

Reiman, Eric M.; Lane, Richard D.; Ahern, Geoffrey L.; Schwartz, Gary E.; Davidson, Richard J.; Friston, Karl J.; & others. (1997). Neuroanatomical correlates of externally and internally generated human emotion. *American Journal of Psychiatry, 154,* 918–925.

Reis, Harry T.; Collins, W. Andrew; & Berscheid, Ellen. (2000). The relationship context of human behavior and development. *Psychological Bulletin, 126,* 844–872.

Reisberg, Daniel, & Chambers, Deborah. (1991). Neither pictures nor propositions: What can we learn from a mental image? *Canadian Journal of Psychology, 45,* 336–348.

Reisel, William D., & Kopelman, Richard E. (1995). The effects of failure on subsequent group performance in a professional sports setting. *Journal of Psychology, 129,* 103–113.

Reisenzein, Rainer. (1983). The Schachter theory of emotion: Two decades later. *Psychological Bulletin, 94,* 239–264.

Reiss, B. K. (1990). *A biography of Mary Cover Jones*. Berkeley, CA: Wright Institute.

Reiss, Diana, & Marino, Lori. (2001, May 7). Mirror self-recognition in the bottlenose dolphin: A case of cognitive convergence. *Proceedings of the National Academy of Sciences, 98,* 5937.

Rejeski, W. Jack; Gregg, Edward; Thompson, Amy; & Berry, Michael. (1991). The effects of varying doses of acute aerobic exercise on psychophysiological stress responses in highly trained cyclists. *Journal of Sport and Exercise Psychology, 13,* 188–199.

Rejeski, W. Jack; Thompson, Amy; Brubaker, Peter H.; & Miller, Henry S. (1992). Acute exercise: Buffering psychosocial responses in women. *Health Psychology, 11,* 355–362.

Reneman, Liesbeth; Booij, Jan; de Bruin, Kora; & others. (2001a). Effects of dose, sex, and long-term abstention from use on toxic effects of MDMA (Ecstasy) on brain serotonin neurons. *Lancet, 358,* 1864–1869.

Reneman, Liesbeth; Lavalaye, Jules; Schmand, Ben; deWolff, Frederik A.; & others. (2001b). Cortical serotonin transporter density and verbal memory in individuals who stopped using 3,4-methylenedioxy-methamphetamine (MDMA or "Ecstasy"). *Archives of General Psychiatry, 58,* 901–906.

Renzulli, Joseph S. (1986). The three-ring conception of giftedness: A developmental model for creative productivity. In Robert J. Sternberg & Janet E. Davidson (Eds.), *Conceptions of giftedness.* New York: Cambridge University Press.

Repetti, Rena L. (1989). Effects of daily workload on subsequent behavior during marital interaction: The roles of withdrawal and spouse support. *Journal of Personality and Social Psychology, 57,* 651–659.

Repetti, Rena L. (1993). Short-term effects of occupational stressors on daily mood and health complaints. *Health Psychology, 12,* 125–131.

Repetti, Rena L., & Wood, Jenifer. (1997). The effects of daily stress at work on mothers' interactions with preschoolers. *Journal of Family Psychology, 11,* 90–108.

Rescorla, Robert A. (1968). Probability of shock in the presence and absence of CS in fear conditioning. *Journal of Comparative and Physiological Psychology, 66,* 1–5.

Rescorla, Robert A. (1980). *Pavlovian second-order conditioning: Studies in associative learning.* Hillsdale, NJ: Erlbaum.

Rescorla, Robert A. (1988). Pavlovian conditioning: It's not what you think it is. *American Psychologist, 43,* 151–160.

Rescorla, Robert A. (1997). Quoted in James E. Freeman, Pavlov in the classroom: An interview with Robert A. Rescorla. *Teaching of Psychology, 24,* 283–286.

Rescorla, Robert A. (2001). Retraining of extinguished Pavlovian stimuli. *Journal of Experimental Psychology: Animal Behavior Processes, 27,* 115–124.

Rest, James R. (1983). Morality. In Paul H. Mussen, John H. Flavell, & Ellen M. Markman (Eds.), *Handbook of child psychology* (4th ed., Vol. 3). New York: Wiley.

Restless Legs Syndrome Foundation. (2001). *Living with restless legs.* Rochester, MN: RLS Foundation, Inc. PDF of document retrieved January 12, 2002, from http://www.rls.org/frames/home_frame.htm

Reuter-Lorenz, Patricia A., & Miller, Andrea C. (1998). The cognitive neuroscience of human laterality: Lessons from the bisected brain. *Current Directions in Psychological Science, 7,* 15–20.

Revelle, William. (1995). Personality processes. *Annual Review of Psychology, 46,* 295–328.

Reynolds, David K. (1990). *A thousand waves: A sensible life-style for sensitive people.* New York: Morrow.

Rhodes, Richard. (2000, September 17). Hollow claims about fantasy violence. *New York Times,* Sect. 4, p. 19.

Ricaurte, George A., & McCann, Una D. (2001). Assessing long-term effects of MDMA (Ecstasy). *Lancet, 358,* 1831–1832.

Riccio, David C.; Rabinowitz, Vita C.; & Axelrod, Shari. (1994). Memory: When less is more. *American Psychologist, 49,* 917–926.

Rice, Laura N., & Greenberg, Leslie S. (1992). Humanistic approaches to psychotherapy. In Donald K. Freedheim (Ed.), *History of psychotherapy: A century of change.* Washington, DC: American Psychological Association.

Rice, Robert W.; McFarlin, Dean B.; & Bennett, Debbie E. (1989). Standards of comparison and job satisfaction. *Journal of Applied Psychology, 74,* 591–598.

Richelson, Elliott. (1993). Treatment of acute depression. *Psychiatric Clinics of North America, 16,* 461–478.

Riefer, David M.; Keveri, Mary K.; & Kramer, Daniel L. F. (1995). Name that tune: Eliciting the tip-of-the-tongue experience using auditory stimuli. *Psychological Reports, 77,* 1379–1390.

Riegel, B.; Simon D.; Weaver, J.; Carlson, B.; Clapton, P.; & Gocka, I. (1996). *Ayurvedic medicine demonstration project* (1R21 RR09726–01). Bethesda, MD: Report submitted to the National Institutes of Health, Institute for Alternative Medicine.

Rilling, Mark. (2000). John Watson's paradoxical struggle to explain Freud. *American Psychologist, 55,* 301–312.

Rimm, Eric B.; Giovannucci, Edward L.; Willett, Walter C.; Colditz, Graham A.; Ascherio, Alberto; Rosner, Bernard; & Stampfer, Meir J. (1991, August 24). Prospective study of alcohol consumption and risk of coronary disease in men. *Lancet, 338,* 464–468.

Rioult-Pedotti, Mengia-S.; Friedman, Daniel; & Donoghue, John P. (2000). Learning-induced LTP in neocortex. *Science, 290,* 533–536.

Rissman, Emilie F. (1995). An alternative animal model for the study of female sexual behavior. *Current Directions in Psychological Science, 4,* 6–10.

Rivkin, Inna D.; & Taylor, Shelley E. (1999). The effects of mental simulation on coping with controllable stressful events. *Personality and Social Psychology Bulletin, 25,* 1451–1462.

Roazen, Paul. (1999). *Freud: political and social thought.* Piscataway, NJ: Transaction.

Roazen, Paul. (2000). *The historiography of psychoanalysis.* Piscataway, NJ: Transaction.

Robbins, Ann S.; Spence, Janet T.; & Clark, Heather. (1991). Psychological determinants of health and performance: The tangled web of desirable and undesirable characteristics. *Journal of Personality and Social Psychology, 61,* 755–765.

Roberts, Elizabeth J. (Ed.). (1980). *Childhood sexual learning: The unwritten curriculum.* Cambridge, MA: Ballinger.

Robin, Nina, & Holyoak, Keith J. (1995). Relational complexity and the functions of the prefrontal cortex. In Michael S. Gazzaniga (Ed.), *The cognitive neurosciences.* Cambridge, MA: MIT Press.

Robins, Clive J., & Hayes, Adele M. (1993). An appraisal of cognitive therapy. *Journal of Consulting and Clinical Psychology, 61,* 205–214.

Robins, Lee N. (1998). The intimate connection between antisocial personality and substance abuse. *Social Psychiatry and Psychiatric Epidemiology, 33,* 393–399.

Robinson, Daniel N. (1993). Is there a Jamesian tradition in psychology? *American Psychologist, 48,* 638–643.

Robinson, Daniel N. (1997). Aristotle and psychology. In Wolfgang G. Bringmann, Helmut E. Lück, Rudolf Miller, & Charles E. Early (Eds.), *A pictorial history of psychology.* Chicago: Quintessence.

Robinson, John P., & Godbey, Geoffrey. (1998, February). No sex, please . . . we're college students. *American Demographics, 20*(2), 18–23.

Robinson, Paul. (1993). *Freud and his critics.* Berkeley: University of California Press.

Robinson, Thomas N.; Wilde, Marta L.; Navracruz, Lisa C.; Haydel, K. Farish; & Varady, Ann. (2001). Effects of reducing children's television and video game use on aggressive behavior. *Archives of Pediatric and Adolescent Medicine, 155,* 17–23.

Rochat, François; Maggioni, Olivier; & Modigliani, Andre. (2000). Captain Paul Grueninger: The Chief of Police who saved Jewish refugees by refusing to do his duty. In Thomas Blass (Ed.), *Obedience to authority: Current perspectives on the Milgram paradigm.* Mahwah, NJ: Erlbaum.

Rock, Irvin. (1995). *Perception.* New York: Scientific American Library.

Rodin, Judith. (1986, September 19). Aging and health: Effects of the sense of control. *Science, 233,* 1271–1275.

Rodin, Judith, & Langer, Ellen. (1977). Long-term effects of a control-relevant intervention with the institutionalized aged. *Journal of Personality and Social Psychology, 35,* 897–902.

Roediger, Henry L., III. (1990). Implicit memory: Retention without remembering. *American Psychologist, 45,* 1043–1056.

Rogers, Carl R. (1951). *Client-centered psychotherapy.* Boston: Houghton-Mifflin.

Rogers, Carl R. (1957a/1989). A note on "The Nature of Man." In Howard Kirschenbaum & Valerie Land Henderson (Eds.), *The Carl Rogers Reader.* Boston: Houghton Mifflin.

Rogers, Carl R. (1957b/1989). A therapist's view of the good life: The fully functioning person. In Howard Kirschenbaum & Valerie Land Henderson (Eds.), *The Carl Rogers reader.* Boston: Houghton Mifflin.

Rogers, Carl R. (1957c). The necessary and sufficient conditions of therapeutic personality change. *Journal of Consulting Psychology, 21,* 95–103.

Rogers, Carl R. (1959). A theory of therapy, personality, and interpersonal relationships, as developed in the client-centered framework. In S. Koch (Ed.), *Psychology: A study of a science: Vol. 3. Formulations of the person and the social context.* New York: McGraw-Hill.

Rogers, Carl R. (1961). *On becoming a person.* Boston: Houghton Mifflin.

Rogers, Carl R. (1964/1989). Toward a modern approach to values: The valuing process in the mature person. In Howard Kirschenbaum & Valerie Land Henderson (Eds.), *The Carl Rogers reader.* Boston: Houghton Mifflin.

Rogers, Carl R. (1977). *Carl Rogers on personal power: Inner strength and its revolutionary impact.* New York: Delacorte Press.

Rogers, Carl R. (1980). *A way of being.* Boston: Houghton Mifflin.

Rogers, Carl R. (1981/1989). Notes on Rollo May. In Howard Kirschenbaum & Valerie Land Henderson (Eds.), *Carl Rogers: Dialogues.* Boston: Houghton Mifflin.

Rogers, Carl R., & Skinner, B. F. (1956, November 30). Some issues concerning the control of human behavior: A symposium. *Science, 124,* 1057–1066.

Rogers, Susan M., & Turner, Charles F. (1991). Male-male sexual contact in the U.S.A.: Findings from five sample surveys, 1970–1990. *Journal of Sex Research, 28,* 491–519.

Rogers, Timothy B.; Kuiper, N. A.; & Kirker, W. S. (1977). Self-reference and the encoding of personal information. *Journal of Personality and Social Psychology, 35,* 677–688.

Rogo, D. Scott. (1985). *The search for yesterday: A critical examination of the evidence for reincarnation.* Englewood Cliffs, NJ: Prentice-Hall.

Rogoff, Barbara, & Chavajay, Pablo. (1995). What's become of research on the cultural basis of cognitive development? *American Psychologist, 50,* 859–877.

Rolls, Edmund T. (2000). Memory systems in the brain. *Annual Review of Psychology, 51,* 599–630.

Ronen, Tammie. (1991). Intervention package for treating sleep disorders in a four-year-old girl. *Journal of Behavior Therapy and Experimental Psychiatry, 22,* 141–148.

Rook, Karen S. (1992). Detrimental aspects of social relationships: Taking stock of an emerging literature. In Hans O. F. Veiel & Urs Baumann (Eds.), *The meaning and measurement of social support.* New York: Hemisphere.

Rosch, Eleanor H. (1973). Natural categories. *Cognitive Psychology, 4,* 328–350.

Rosch, Eleanor H. (1978). Principles of categorization. In Eleanor H. Rosch & Barbara B. Lloyd (Eds.), *Cognition and categorization.* Hillsdale, NJ: Erlbaum.

Rosch, Eleanor H. (1987). Linguistic relativity. *Et Cetera, 44,* 254–279.

Rosch, Eleanor H., & Mervis, Carolyn B. (1975). Family resemblances: Studies in the internal structure of categories. *Cognitive Psychology, 7,* 573–605.

Rose, Richard J. (1995). Genes and human behavior. *Annual Review of Psychology, 46,* 625–654.

Rose, Susan A., & Feldman, Judith F. (1995). Prediction of IQ and specific cognitive abilities at 11 years from infancy measures. *Developmental Psychology, 31,* 685–696.

Rosen, Gerald M., & Lohr, Jeffrey. (1997, January/February.) Can eye movements cure mental ailments? *NCAHF Newsletter.* Retrieved from the World Wide Web on October 15, 2001: http://www.pseudoscience.org/rosen-and-lohr.htm

Rosen, Gerald M.; McNally, Richard J.; & Lilienfeld, Scott O. (1999). Eye movement magic: Eye movement desensitization and reprocessing a decade later. *Skeptic, 7*(4), 66–69.

Rosenbaum, David A.; Carlson, Richard A.; & Gilmore, Rick O. (2001). Acquisition of intellectual and perceptual-motor skills. *Annual Review of Psychology, 52,* 453–470.

Rosenberg, Harold. (1993). Prediction of controlled drinking by alcoholics and problem drinkers. *Psychological Bulletin, 113,* 129–139.

Rosenberg, Joan I. (1999). Suicide prevention: An integrated training model using affective and action-based interventions. *Professional Psychology: Research and Practice, 30,* 83–87.

Rosenfeld, J. Peter. (1995). Alternative views of Bashore and Rapp's (1993) alternatives to traditional polygraphy: A critique. *Psychological Bulletin, 117,* 159–166.

Rosenlicht, Nicholas, & Feinberg, Irving. (1997). REM sleep = dreaming: Only a dream. *Sleep Research Society Bulletin, 3*(1), 2–4.

Rosenman, Ray H., & Chesney, Margaret A. (1982). Stress, Type A behavior, and coronary disease. In Leo Goldberger & Shlomo Breznitz (Eds.), *Handbook of stress: Theoretical and clinical aspects.* New York: Free Press.

Rosenthal, Abraham M. (1964a, May 3). Study of the sickness called apathy. *The New York Times Magazine,* Sect. VI, pp. 24, 66, 69–72.

Rosenthal, Abraham M. (1964b). *Thirty-eight witnesses.* New York: McGraw-Hill.

Rosenthal, Norman E. (1998). *Winter blues: Seasonal affective disorder: What it is and how to overcome it* (Rev. ed.). New York: Guilford Press.

Rosenzweig, Mark R. (1996). Aspects of the search for neural mechanisms of memory. *Annual Review of Psychology, 47,* 1–32.

Rosenzweig, Saul. (1997). Freud's only visit to America. In Wolfgang G. Bringmann, Helmut E. Lück, Rudolf Miller, & Charles E. Early (Eds.), *A pictorial history of psychology.* Chicago: Quintessence.

Ross, Barbara. (1991). William James: Spoiled child of American psychology. In Gregory A. Kimble, Michael Wertheimer, & Charlotte White (Eds.), *Portraits of pioneers in psychology.* Washington, DC: American Psychological Association.

Ross, Jerilyn. (1993). Social phobia: The consumer's perspective. *Journal of Clinical Psychiatry, 54*(12, Suppl.), 5–9.

Ross, Lee. (1977). The intuitive psychologist and his shortcomings: Distortions in the attribution process. In Leonard Berkowitz (Ed.), *Advances in experimental social psychology* (Vol. 10). New York: Academic Press.

Ross, Lee, & Anderson, Craig A. (1982). Shortcomings in the attribution process: On the origins and maintenance of erroneous social assessments. In Daniel Kahneman, Paul Slovic, & Amos Tversky (Eds.), *Judgment under uncertainty: Heuristics and biases.* New York: Cambridge University Press.

Rossman, Martin L. (1993). Imagery: Learning to use the mind's eye. In Daniel Goleman & Joel Gurin (Eds.), *Mind / body medicine: How to use your mind for better health.* Yonkers, NY: Consumer Reports Books.

Rothbart, Mary K.; Derryberry, Douglas; & Posner, Michael I. (1994). A psychobiological approach to the development of temperament. In John E. Bates & Theodore D. Wachs (Eds.), *Temperament: Individual differences at the interface of biology and behavior.* Washington, DC: American Psychological Association.

Rothbaum, Barbara Olasov; Hodges, Larry; Smith, Samantha; Lee, Jeong Hwan; & Price, Larry. (2000). A controlled study of virtual reality exposure therapy for the fear of flying. *Journal of Consulting and Clinical Psychology, 68,* 1020–1026.

Rothenberg, Saul A. (1997). Introduction to sleep disorders. In Mark R. Pressman & William C. Orr (Eds.), *Understanding sleep: The evaluation and treatment of sleep disorders.* Washington, DC: American Psychological Association.

Rovee-Collier, Carolyn. (1997). Dissociations in infant memory: Rethinking the development of implicit and explicit memory. *Psychological Review, 104,* 467–498.

Rovee-Collier, Carolyn. (1999). The development of infant memory. *Current Directions in Psychological Science, 8,* 80–85.

Rowan, Andrew N. (1997, February). The benefits and ethics of animal research. *Scientific American, 276*(2), 79.

Rozin, Paul. (1996). The socio-cultural context of eating and food choice. In H.L. Meiselman & H.J.H. MacFie (Eds.), *Food choice, acceptance and consumption.* London: Blackie Academic and Professional.

Rozin, Paul; Dow, Sara; Moscovitch, Morris; & Rajaram, Suparna. (1998). What causes humans to begin and end a meal? A role for memory for what has been eaten, as evidenced by a study of multiple meal eating in amnesic patients. *Psychological Science, 9,* 392–396.

Rubin, Edgar. (1921/2001). Readings in perception. In Steven Yantis (Ed.), *Visual perception: Essential readings.* Philadelphia: Psychology Press.

Rubin, Nava. (2001). Figure and ground in the brain. *Nature Neuroscience, 4,* 857–858.

Rugg, Michael D.; Mark, Ruth E.; Walla, Peter; Schloerscheidt, Astrid, M.; Birch, Claire S.; & Allan, Kevin. (1998, April 9). Dissociation of the neural correlates of implicit and explicit memory. *Nature, 392,* 595–598.

Ruiz-Miranda, Carlos R.; Kleiman, Devra G.; Dietz, James M.; Moraes, Ezequiel; Grativol, Adriana D.; Baker, Andrew J.; & Beck, Benjamin B. (1999). Food transfers in wild and reintroduced golden lion tamarins, *Leontopithecus rosalia. American Journal of Primatology, 48*(4), 305–320.

Ruscio, John. (1998, November/December). The perils of post-hockery. *Skeptical Inquirer, 22,* 44–48.

Russek, Linda G., & Schwartz, Gary E. (1997). Perceptions of parental caring predict health status in midlife: A 35-year follow-up to the Harvard Mastery of Stress Study. *Psychosomatic Medicine, 59,* 144–149.

Russell, James A. (1980). A circumplex model of affect. *Journal of Personality and Social Psychology, 39,* 1161–1178.

Russell, James A. (1991). Culture and the categorization of emotions. *Psychological Bulletin, 110,* 426–450.

Russell, Tanya G.; Rowe, Wayne; & Smouse, Albert E. (1991). Subliminal self-help tapes and academic achievement: An evaluation. *Journal of Counseling and Development, 69,* 359–362.

Russon, Anne E., & Galdikas, Birute M. F. (1995). Constraints on great apes' imitation: Model and action selectivity in rehabilitant orangutan (*Pongo pygmaeus*) imitation. *Journal of Comparative Psychology, 109,* 5–17.

Rutherford, Alexandra. (2000). Radical behaviorism and psychology's public: B. F. Skinner in the popular press, 1934–1990. *History of Psychology, 3,* 371–395.

Rutherford, F. James, & Ahlgren, Andrew. (1991). *Science for all Americans.* New York: Oxford University Press.

Rutowski, Ronald L. (1998, July). Mating strategies in butterflies. *Scientific American, 279,* 64–69.

Rutter, Michael L. (1997). Nature-nurture integration: The example of antisocial behavior. *American Psychologist, 52,* 390–398.

Ruvolo, Ann Patrice, & Markus, Hazel Rose. (1992). Possible selves and performance: The power of self-relevant imagery. *Social Cognition, 10,* 95–124.

Ryan, Ellen B. (1992). Beliefs about memory across the life span. *Journal of Gerontology: Psychological Sciences, 47,* 41–47.

Ryan, Richard M., & Deci, Edward L. (2000). Self-determination theory and the facilitation of intrinsic motivation, social development, and well-being. *American Psychologist, 55,* 68–78.

Ryan, Richard M., & Deci, Edward L. (2001). On happiness and human potentials: A review of research on hedonic and eudaimonic well-being. *Annual Review of Psychology, 52,* 141–166.

Ryan, Richard M., & La Guardia, Jennifer G. (2000). What is being optimized over development? A self-determination theory and basic psychological needs. In Sara Honn Qualls & Norman Abeles (Eds.), *Psychology and the aging revolution: How we adapt to longer life.* Washington, DC: American Psychological Association.

Sabbatini, Renato M.E. (1997, March–May). Phrenology: The history of brain localization. *Brain and Mind: Electronic Magazine on Neuroscience,* No. 1. <http://www.epub.org.br/cm/n01/frenolog/frenologia.htm> (January 20, 2000).

Sachs, Gary S.; Lafer, Beny; Truman, Christine J.; Noeth, Mary; & Thibault, Amy B. (1994). Lithium monotherapy: Miracle, myth and misunderstanding. *Psychiatric Annuals, 24,* 299–306.

Sachse, Rainer, & Elliott, Robert. (2002). Process—Outcome research on humanistic therapy variables. In David J. Cain & Julius Seeman (Eds.), *Humanistic psychotherapies: Handbook of research and practice.* Washington, DC: American Psychological Association.

Sack, Robert L.; Lewy, Alfred J.; Blood, Mary L.; Keith, L. D.; & Nakagawa, Hiroki. (1992). Circadian rhythm abnormalities in totally blind people: Incidence and clinical significance. *Journal of Clinical Endocrinology and Metabolism, 75,* 127–134.

Sackeim, Harold A. (2001). Functional brain circuits in major depression and remission. *Archives of General Psychiatry, 58,* 649–650.

Sackeim, Harold A.; Haskett, Roger F.; Mulsant, Benoit H.; Thase, Michael E.; Mann, J. John; Pettinati, Helen M.; & others. (2001). Continuation psychotherapy in the prevention of relapse following electroconvulsive therapy: A randomized controlled trial. *Journal of the American Medical Association, 285,* 1299–1307.

Sacks, Michael H. (1993). Exercise for stress control. In Daniel Goleman & Joel Gurin (Eds.), *Mind/body medicine: How to use your mind for better health.* Yonkers, NY: Consumer Reports Books.

Sakheim, David K., & Devine, Susan E. (Eds.). (1992). *Out of darkness: Exploring Satanism and ritual abuse.* New York: Lexington Books.

Salancik, G. R., & Pfeffer, J. (1977). An examination of needs satisfaction models of job satisfaction. *Administrative Science Quarterly, 22,* 427–456.

Salmán, Ester; Diamond, Kimberly; Jusino, Carlos; & others. (1997). Hispanic Americans. In Steven Friedman (Ed.), *Cultural issues in the treatment of anxiety.* New York: Guilford Press.

Salokangas, Raimo K.R.; Vilkman, Harry; Ilonen, Tuula; & others. (2000). High levels of dopamine activity in the basal ganglia of cigarette smokers. *American Journal of Psychiatry, 157,* 632–634.

Salovey, Peter; Mayer, John D.; & Rosenhan, David L. (1991). Mood and helping: Mood as a motivator of helping and helping as a regulator of mood. In Margaret S. Clark (Ed.), *Prosocial behavior: Vol. 12. Review of personality and social psychology.* Newbury Park, CA: Sage.

Salthouse, Timothy. (1993). Speed mediation of adult age differences in cognition. *Developmental Psychology, 29,* 722–738.

Saltzman, Ann L. (2000). The role of the obedience experiments in Holocaust studies: The case for renewed visibility. In Thomas Blass (Ed.), *Obedience to authority: Current perspectives on the Milgram paradigm.* Mahwah, NJ: Erlbaum.

Sanbonmatsu, David M.; Akimoto, Sharon A.; & Gibson, Bryan D. (1994). Stereotype-based blocking in social explanation. *Personality and Social Psychology Bulletin, 20,* 71–81.

Sánchez, Heriberto G. (2001). Risk factor model for suicide assessment and intervention. *Professional Psychology: Research and Practice, 32,* 351–358.

Sandelowski, Margarete; Holditch-Davis, Diane; & Harris, Betty G. (1992). Using qualitative and quantitative methods: The transition to parenthood among infertile couples. In Jane F. Gilgun, Kerry Daly, & Gerald Handel (Eds.), *Qualitative methods in family research.* Newbury Park, CA: Sage.

Sandler, Jack, & Steele, Holly Villareal. (1991). Aversion methods. In Frederick H. Kanfer & Arnold P. Goldstein (Eds.), *Helping people change: A textbook of methods* (4th ed.). New York: Pergamon Press.

Sanna, Lawrence J. (1999). Mental simulations, affect, and subjective confidence: Timing is everything. *Psychological Science, 10,* 339–345.

Sanna, Lawrence J. (2000). Mental simulation, affect, and personality: A conceptual framework. *Current Directions in Psychological Science, 9,* 168–173.

Sarason, Irwin G.; Sarason, Barbara R.; Pierce, Gregory R.; Shearin, Edward N.; & Sayers, Merlin H. (1991). A social learning approach to increasing blood donations. *Journal of Applied Social Psychology, 21,* 896–918.

Sarbin, Theodore R. (1999). Whither hypnosis? A rhetorical analysis. In Irving Kirsch, Antonio Capafons, Etzel Cardena-Buelna, & Salvador Amigo (Eds.), *Clinical hypnosis and self-regulation: Cognitive-behavior perspectives.* Washington, DC: American Psychological Association.

Sargent, Marilyn. (1993). *Depressive illnesses: Treatments bring new hope* (NIH Publication No. 93-3612). Rockville, MD: National Institute of Mental Health.

Saskin, Paul. (1997). Obstructive sleep apnea: Treatment options, efficacy, and effects. In Mark R. Pressman & William C. Orr (Eds.), *Understanding sleep: The evaluation and treatment of sleep disorders.* Washington, DC: American Psychological Association.

Saufley, William H.; Otaka, Sandra R.; & Bavaresco, Joseph L. (1985). Context effects: Classroom tests and context independence. *Memory & Cognition, 13,* 522–528.

Savage-Rumbaugh, E. Sue. (1993). Language learnability in man, ape, and dolphin. In Herbert L. Roitblat, Louis M. Herman, & Paul E. Nachtigall (Eds.), *Language and communication: Comparative perspectives.* Hillsdale, NJ: Erlbaum.

Savage-Rumbaugh, E. Sue, & Lewin, Roger. (1994, September). Ape at the brink. *Discover, 15,* 91–98.

Savage-Rumbaugh, E. Sue; Shanker, Stuart G.; & Taylor, Talbot J. (1998). *Apes, language, and the human mind.* New York: Oxford University Press.

Savin-Williams, Ritch C., & Berndt, Thomas J. (1990). Friendship and peer relations. In S. Shirley Feldman & Glen R. Elliott (Eds.), *At the threshold: The developing adolescent.* Cambridge, MA: Harvard University Press.

Saxe, Glenn N.; Chinman, Gary; Berkowitz, Robert; Hall, Kathryn; Lieberg, Gabriele; Schwartz, Jane; & van der Kolk, Bessel A. (1994). Somatization in patients with dissociative disorders. *American Journal of Psychiatry, 151,* 1329–1334.

Saxe, Glenn N.; van der Kolk, Bessel A.; Berkowitz, Robert; Chinman, Gary; Hall, Kathryn; Lieberg, Gabriele; & Schwartz, Jane. (1993). Dissociative disorders in psychiatric inpatients. *American Journal of Psychiatry, 150,* 1037–1042.

Scanlon, Matthew, & Mauro, James. (1992, November/December). The lowdown on handwriting analysis: Is it for real? *Psychology Today, 25,* 46–53.

Scarr, Sandra, & Eisenberg, Marlene. (1993). Child care research: Issues, perspectives, and results. *Annual Review of Psychology, 44,* 613–644.

Scarr, Sandra, & Weinberg, Richard A. (1976). IQ test performance of black children adopted by white families. *American Psychologist, 31,* 726–739.

Schachter, Stanley, & Singer, Jerome E. (1962). Cognitive, social, and physiological determinants of emotional state. *Psychological Review, 69,* 379–399.

Schacter, Daniel L. (1995a). Consciousness: Introduction. In Michael S. Gazzaniga (Ed.), *The cognitive neurosciences.* Cambridge, MA: MIT Press.

Schacter, Daniel L. (1995b). Implicit memory: A new frontier for neuroscience. In Michael S. Gazzaniga (Ed.), *The cognitive neurosciences.* Cambridge, MA: MIT Press.

Schacter, Daniel L. (1995c, April). Memory wars. *Scientific American, 272,* 135–139.

Schacter, Daniel L. (1998, April 3). Memory and awareness. *Science, 280,* 59–60.

Schacter, Daniel L.; Chiu, Peter C.-Y.; & Ochsner, Kevin N. (1993). Implicit memory: A selective review. *Annual Review of Neuroscience, 16,* 159–182.

Schacter, Daniel L., & Moscovitch, Morris. (1984). Infants, amnesics, and dissociable memory systems. In Morris Moscovitch (Ed.), *Infant memory.* New York: Plenum Press.

Schacter, Daniel L.; Norman, Kenneth A.; & Koutstaal, Wilma. (1998). The cognitive neuroscience of constructive memory. *Annual Review of Psychology, 49,* 289–318.

Schaie, K. Warner. (1994). The course of adult intellectual development. *American Psychologist, 49,* 304–313.

Schaie, K. Warner. (1995). *Intellectual development in adulthood: The Seattle Longitudinal Study.* New York: Cambridge University Press.

Schaie, K. Warner, & Willis, Sherry L. (1986). Can decline in adult intellectual functioning be reversed? *Developmental Psychology, 22,* 223–232.

Schaie, K. Warner, & Willis, Sherry L. (1996). *Adult development and aging* (4th ed.). New York: HarperCollins.

Schaller, Mark, & Cialdini, Robert B. (1990). Happiness, sadness, and helping: A motivational integration. In Richard M. Sorrentino & E. Tory Higgins (Eds.), *Handbook of motivation and cognition: Vol. 2. Foundations of social behavior.* New York: Guilford Press.

Schattschneider, Doris. (1990). *Visions of symmetry: Notebooks, periodic drawings, and related work of M. C. Escher* (p. 169, notes on p. 301). New York: Freeman.

Schatzman, Morton, & Fenwick, Peter. (1994). Dreams and dreaming. In Rosemary Cooper (Ed.), *Sleep.* New York: Chapman & Hall.

Scheibel, Arnold B. (1994, July). Quoted in Daniel Golden, Building a better brain. *Life,* p. 66.

Scherer, Klaus R.; Banse, Rainer; & Wallbott, Harald G. (2001). Emotion inferences from vocal expression correlate across languages and cultures. *Journal of Cross-Cultural Psychology, 32,* 76–92.

Scherer, Klaus R., & Wallbott, Harald G. (1994). Evidence for universality and cultural variation of differential emotion response patterning. *Journal of Personality and Social Psychology, 66,* 310–328.

Schiffman, Susan S. (1983). Taste and smell in disease. *New England Journal of Medicine, 308,* 1275–1279, 1337–1343.

Schiffman, Susan S.; Graham, Brevick G.; Sattely-Miller, Elizabeth A.; & Warwick, Zoe S. (1998). Orosensory perception of dietary fat. *Current Directions in Psychological Science, 7,* 137–143.

Schilling, Stephen L. (1999). The basics of a successful telework network. *HRFocus, 76,* 9–10.

Schlenker, Barry R., & Weigold, Michael F. (1992). Interpersonal processes involving impression regulation and management. *Annual Review of Psychology, 43,* 133–168.

Schlenker, Barry R.; Weigold, Michael F.; & Hallam, J. R. (1990). Self-serving attributions in social context: Effects of self-esteem and social pressure. *Journal of Personality and Social Psychology, 58,* 855–863.

Schmelz, Martin. (2001). A neural pathway for itch. *Nature Neuroscience, 4,* 9–10.

Schmolck, Heike; Buffalo, Elizabeth A.; & Squire, Larry R. (2000). Memory distortions develop over time: Recollections of the O. J. Simpson trial verdict after 15 and 32 months. *Psychological Science, 11,* 39–45.

Schneider, Barry H. (1998). Cross-cultural comparison as doorkeeper in research on the social and emotional adjustment of children and adolescents. *Developmental Psychology, 34,* 793–797.

Schneider, David J. (1993). Mental control: Lessons from our past. In Daniel M. Wegner & James W. Pennebaker (Eds.), *Handbook of mental control.* Englewood Cliffs, NJ: Prentice-Hall.

Schneider, Kirk. (1998). Toward a science of the heart: Romanticism and the revival of psychology. *American Psychologist, 53,* 277–289.

Schooler, Jonathan W.; Ohlsson, Stellan; & Brooks, Kevin. (1993). Thoughts beyond words: When language overshadows insight. *Journal of Experimental Psychology: General, 122,* 166–183.

Schrater, Paul; Knill, David C.; & Simoncelli, Eero P. (2001). Perceiving visual expansion without optic flow. *Nature, 410,* 616–619.

Schredl, Michael; Frauscher, Saskia; & Shendi, Acram. (1995). Dream recall and visual memory. *Perceptual and Motor Skills, 81,* 256–258.

Schredl, Michael, & Montasser, Alyaa. (1997). Dream recall: State or trait variable? Part II. State factors, investigations, and final conclusions. *Imagination, Cognition and Personality, 16,* 239–261.

Schroth, Marvin L., & McCormack, William A. (2000) Current problems and resolutions— Sensation seeking and need for achievement among study-abroad students. *The Journal of Social Psychology, 140,* 533.

Schuckit, Marc A.; Smith, Tom L.; Daeppen, Jean-Bernard; Eng, Mimy; Li, T.-K.; Hesselbrock, Victor M.; & others. (1998). Clinical relevance of the distinction between alcohol dependence with and without a physiological component. *American Journal of Psychiatry, 155,* 733–740.

Schulman, Michael, & Mekler, Eva. (1985). *Bringing up a moral child: A new approach for teaching your child to be kind, just, and responsible.* Reading, MA: Addison-Wesley.

Schultz, Wolfram; Dayan, Peter; & Montague, P. Read. (1997, March 14). A neural substrate of prediction and reward. *Science, 275,* 1593–1599.

Schulz, Richard, & Schlarb, Janet. (1987–1988). Two decades of research on dying: What do we know about the patient? *Omega, 18,* 299–317.

Schuster, Mark A.; Stein, Bradley D.; Jaycox, Lisa H.; & others. (2001, November 15). A national survey of stress reactions after the September 11, 2001, terrorist attacks. *New England Journal of Medicine, 354,* 1507–1512. PDF of article retrieved on March 7, 2002 from: http://content.nejm.org/cgi/reprint/345/20/1507.pdf

Schwartz, Arthur, & Schwartz, Ruth M. (1993). *Depression: Theories and treatments: Psychological, biological, and social perspectives.* New York: Columbia University Press.

Schwartz, Jeffrey M.; Stoessel, Paula W.; & Phelps, Michael E. (1996). Systematic changes in cerebral glucose metabolic rate after successful behavior modification treatment of obsessive-compulsive disorder. *Archives of General Psychiatry, 53,* 109–117.

Schwartz, Mark S., & Schwartz, Nancy M. (1993). Biofeedback: Using the body's signals. In Daniel Goleman & Joel Gurin (Eds.), *Mind/body medicine: How to use your mind for better health.* Yonkers, NY: Consumer Reports Books.

Schwartz Michael W.; Baskin, Denis G.; Kaiyala, Karl J.; & Woods, Stephen C. (1999). Model for the regulation of energy balance and adiposity by the central nervous system. *American Journal of Clinical Nutrition, 69,* 584–596.

Schwartz, Michael W.; Woods, Stephen C.; Porte, Daniel, Jr.; Seeley, Randy J.; & Baskin, Denis G. (2000, April 6). Central nervous system control of food intake. *Nature, 404,* 661–671.

Seeley, Randy J.; Matson, Claire A.; Chavez, M.; & Woods, Stephen C. (1996). Behavioral, endocrine, and hypothalamic responses to involuntary overfeeding. *American Journal of Physiology, 271,* R819–R823.

Seeman, Mary V. (Ed.). (1995). *Gender and psychopathology.* Washington, DC: American Psychiatric Press.

Seeman, Philip. (1999). Brain development, X: Pruning during development. *American Journal of Psychiatry, 156,* 168.

Seeman, Philip, & others (1987). Human brain dopamine receptors in children and aging adults. *Synapse, 1,* 399–404.

Segall, Marshall H. (1994). A cross-cultural research contribution to unraveling the nativist/empiricist controversy. In Walter J. Lonner & Roy Malpass (Eds.), *Psychology and culture.* Boston: Allyn & Bacon.

Segall, Marshall H.; Campbell, Donald T.; & Herskovits, Melville J. (1963). Cultural differences in the perception of geometric illusions. *Science, 193,* 769–771.

Segall, Marshall H.; Campbell, Donald T.; & Herskovits, Melville J. (1966). *The influence of culture on visual perception.* Indianapolis, IN: Bobbs-Merrill.

Segall, Marshall H.; Lonner, Walter J.; & Berry, John W. (1998). Cross-cultural psychology as a scholarly discipline: On the flowering of culture in behavioral research. *American Psychologist, 53,* 1101–1110.

Segerstrom, Suzanne C.; Taylor, Shelley E.; Kemeny, Margaret E.; & Fahey, John L. (1998). Optimism is associated with mood, coping, and immune change in response to stress. *Journal of Personality and Social Psychology, 74,* 1646–1655.

Seidman, Stuart N., & Rieder, Ronald O. (1994). A review of sexual behavior in the United States. *American Journal of Psychiatry, 151,* 330–341.

Seligman, Martin E. P. (1970). On the generality of the laws of learning. *Psychological Review, 77,* 406–418.

Seligman, Martin E. P. (1971). Phobias and preparedness. *Behavior Therapy, 2,* 307–320.

Seligman, Martin E. P. (1990). *Learned optimism.* New York: Knopf.

Seligman, Martin E. P. (1992). *Helplessness: On development, depression, and death.* New York: Freeman.

Seligman, Martin E. P., & Maier, Steven F. (1967). Failure to escape traumatic shock. *Journal of Experimental Psychology, 37B,* 1–21.

Selye, Hans. (1956). *The stress of life.* New York: McGraw-Hill.

Selye, Hans. (1976). *The stress of life* (Rev. ed.). New York: McGraw-Hill.

Seta, John J., & Seta, Catherine E. (1993). Stereotypes and the generation of compensatory and noncompensatory expectancies of group members. *Personality and Social Psychology Bulletin, 19,* 722–731.

Shanahan, Theresa L., & Czeisler, Charles A. (1991). Light exposure induces equivalent phase shifts of the endogenous circadian rhythms of circulating plasma melatonin and core body temperature in men. *Journal of Clinical Endocrinology and Metabolism, 73*(2), 227–234.

Shapiro, Francine. (1989a). Efficacy of the eye movement desensitization procedure in the treatment of traumatic memories. *Journal of Traumatic Stress, 2,* 199–223.

Shapiro, Francine. (1989b). Eye movement desensitization: A new treatment for post-traumatic stress disorder. *Journal of Behavior Therapy and Experimental Psychiatry, 20,* 211–217.

Shapiro, Francine. (1995). *Eye movement desensitization and reprocessing: Basic principles, protocols, and procedures.* New York: Guilford Press.

Shapiro, Francine, & Forrest, Margot Silk. (1997). *EMDR: The breakthrough therapy for overcoming anxiety, stress, and trauma.* New York: Basic Books.

Shapiro, Johnna K. (1995). Dr. Kohlberg goes to Washington: Using congressional debates to teach moral development. *Teaching of Psychology, 22*(4), 245–247.

Shapiro, K. L. (1991, July). Use morality as basis for animal treatment. *APA Monitor,* p. 5.

Sharan, Pratap; Chaudhary, Geeta; Kavathekar, Surabhi A.; & Saxena, Shekhar. (1996). Preliminary report of psychiatric disorders in survivors of a severe earthquake. *American Journal of Psychiatry, 153,* 556–558.

Shatz, Carla J. (1992, September). The developing brain. *Scientific American, 267,* 34–41.

Shaywitz, Bennett A.; Shaywitz, Sally E.; & Gore, J. C. (1995, February 16). Sex differences in the functional organization of the brain for language. *Nature, 373,* 607–615.

Shedler, Jonathan; Mayman, Martin; & Manis, Melvin. (1993). The *illusion* of mental health. *American Psychologist, 48,* 1117–1131.

Sheldon, Kennon M.; Elliot, Andrew J.; Kim, Youngmee; & Kasser, Tim. (2001). What is satisfying about satisfying events? Testing 10 candidate psychological needs. *Journal of Personality and Social Psychology, 80,* 325–339.

Shepard, Roger N. (1990). *Mind sights: Original visual illusions, ambiguities, and other anomalies, with a commentary on the play of mind in perception and art.* New York: Freeman.

Sherif, Muzafer. (1956, November). Experiments in group conflict. *Scientific American, 195,* 33–47.

Sherif, Muzafer. (1966). *In common predicament: Social psychology of intergroup conflict and cooperation.* Boston: Houghton Mifflin.

Sherif, Muzafer; Harvey, O. J.; White, B. Jack; Hood, William R.; & Sherif, Carolyn W. (1961/1988). *The Robbers Cave experiment: Intergroup conflict and cooperation.* Middletown, CT: Wesleyan University Press.

Shermer, Michael. (1997). *Why people believe weird things: Pseudoscience, superstition, and other confusions of our time.* New York: Freeman.

Shields, Stephanie A. (1987). Women, men, and the dilemma of emotion. In Phillip Shaver

& Clyde Hendrick (Eds.), *Sex and gender: Review of personality and social psychology*. Newbury Park, CA: Sage.

Shiffman, Saul; Paty, Jean A.; Gnys, Maryann; Kassel, John D.; & Elash, Celeste. (1995). Nicotine withdrawal in chippers and regular smokers: Subjective and cognitive effects. *Health Psychology, 14,* 301–309.

Shiffrin, Richard M., & Nosofsky, Robert M. (1994). Seven plus or minus two: A commentary on capacity limitations. *Psychological Review, 101,* 357–361.

Shih, Margaret; Pittinsky, Todd L.; & Ambady, Nalini. (1999). Stereotype susceptibility: Identity salience and shifts in quantitative performance. *Psychological Science, 10,* 80–83.

Shneidman, Edwin S. (1998). *The suicidal mind.* New York: Oxford University Press.

Shors, Tracey J.; Miesegaes, George; Beylin, Anna; Zhao, Mingrui; Rydel, Tracy; & Gould, Elizabeth. (2001). Neurogenesis in the adult is involved in the formation of trace memories. *Nature, 410,* 372–376.

Shotland, R. Lance, & Straw, Margret K. (1976). Bystander response to an assault: When a man attacks a woman. *Journal of Personality and Social Psychology, 34,* 990–999.

Shou, Mogens. (1993). *Lithium treatment of manic-depressive illness: A practical guide* (5th ed.). Basel, Switzerland: Karger.

Shulman, Ian D.; Cox, Brian J.; Swinson, Richard P.; Kuch, Klaus; & Reichman, Jaak T. (1994). Precipitating events, locations and reactions associated with initial unexpected panic attacks. *Behavior Research and Therapy, 32,* 17–20.

Shumaker, Sally A., & Hill, D. Robin. (1991). Gender differences in social support and physical health. *Health Psychology, 10,* 102–111.

Shuval, Judith T. (1993). Migration and stress. In Leo Goldberger & Shlomo Breznitz (Eds.), *Handbook of stress: Theoretical and clinical aspects* (2nd ed.). New York: Free Press.

Shweder, Richard A., & Haidt, Jonathan. (1993). The future of moral psychology: Truth, intuition, and the pluralist way. *Psychological Science, 4,* 360–365.

Shweder, Richard A.; Mahapatra, Manamohan; & Miller, Joan G. (1990a). Culture and moral development. In James W. Stigler, Richard A. Shweder, & Gilbert Herdt (Eds.), *Cultural psychology.* New York: Cambridge University Press.

Shweder, Richard A.; Mahapatra, Manamohan; & Miller, Joan G. (1990b). Culture and moral development. In Jerome Kagan & Sharon Lamb (Eds.), *The emergence of morality in young children.* Chicago: University of Chicago Press.

Siegel, Jerome M. (2000, January). Narcolepsy. *Scientific American, 282,* 77–81.

Siegel, Jerome M. (2001). The REM sleep–memory consolidation hypothesis. *Science, 294,* 1058–1063.

Siegel, Judith M. (1990). Stressful life events and use of physician services among the elderly. *Journal of Personality and Social Psychology, 58,* 1081–1086.

Siegel, Shepard. (1984). Pavlovian conditioning and heroin overdose: reports of overdose victims. *Bulletin of the Psychonomic Society, 22,* 428–430.

Siegel, Shepard. (1999). Drug anticipation and drug addiction. *Addiction, 94,* 1113–1124.

Siegel, Shepard, & Allan, Lorraine G. (1998). Learning and homeostasis: Drug addiction and the McCullough Effect. *Psychological Bulletin, 124,* 230–239.

Siegel, Shepard; Baptista, Marco A. S.; Kim, Joseph A.; McDonald, Robert V.; & Weise-Kelly, Lorraine. (2000). Pavlovian psychopharmacology: The associative basis of tolerance. *Experimental and Clinical Psychopharmacology, 8,* 276–293.

Siegel, Shepard; Hinson, Riley E.; Krank, Marvin D.; & McCully, Jane. (1982, April 23). Heroin "overdose" death: Contribution of drug-associated environmental cues. *Science, 216,* 436–437.

Siegler, Robert S. (1991). *Children's thinking* (2nd ed.). Englewood Cliffs, NJ: Prentice-Hall.

Siegler, Robert S. (1992). The other Alfred Binet. *Developmental Psychology, 28,* 179–190.

Siegler, Robert S., & Ellis, Shari. (1996). Piaget on childhood. *Psychological Science, 7,* 211–215.

Silbersweig, David A.; Stern, Emily; & Frackowaik, R. S. J. (1995, November 9). A functional neuroanatomy of hallucinations in schizophrenia. *Nature, 387,* 176–184.

Silver, Eric; Mulvey, Edward P.; & Monahan, John. (1999). Assessing violence risk among discharged psychiatric patients: Toward an ecological approach. *Law and Human Behavior, 23*(2), 237–255.

Silverman, Irwin, & Eals, Marion. (1996, August). Quoted in Beth Azar "Why men lose keys—and women find them." *APA Monitor, 27*(8), 32.

Silverstein, Steven M.; Menditto, Anthony A.; & Stuve, Paul. (2001). Shaping attention span: An operant conditioning procedure to improve neurocognition and functioning in schizophrenia. *Schizophrenia Bulletin, 27,* 247–257.

Simon, Allie; Worthen, David M.; & Mitas, John A. (1979). An evaluation of iridology. *Journal of the American Medical Association, 242*(13), 1385–1389.

Simon, Bernd; Pantaleo, Giuseppe; & Mummendey, Amelie. (1995). Unique individual or interchangeable group member? The accentuation of intragroup differences versus similarities as an indicator of the individual self versus the collective self. *Journal of Personality and Social Psychology, 69,* 106–119.

Sirey, Jo Anne; Bruce, Martha L.; Alexopoulos, George S.; & others. (2001). Perceived stigma as a predictor of treatment discontinuation in young and older outpatients with depression. *American Journal of Psychiatry, 158,* 479–481.

Skinner, B. F. (1938). *The behavior of organisms: An experimental analysis.* New York: Appleton-Century-Crofts.

Skinner, B. F. (1948a/1976). *Walden two.* Englewood Cliffs, NJ: Prentice-Hall.

Skinner, B. F. (1948b/1992). Superstition in the pigeon. *Journal of Experimental Psychology: General, 121,* 273–274.

Skinner, B. F. (1953). *Science and human behavior.* New York: Macmillan.

Skinner, B. F. (1954). A critique of psychoanalytic concepts and theories. *Scientific Monthly, 79,* 300–305.

Skinner, B. F. (1956). A case history in scientific method. *American Psychologist, 11,* 221–233.

Skinner, B. F. (1961, November). Teaching machines. *Scientific American, 205,* 90–102.

Skinner, B. F. (1966). Some responses to the stimulus "Pavlov." *Conditional Reflex, 1,* 74–78. (Reprinted in 1999 in the *Journal of the Experimental Analysis of Behavior, 72,* 463–465.)

Skinner, B. F. (1967). B. F. Skinner . . . an autobiography. In E. G. Boring & G. Lindzey (Eds.), *A history of psychology in autobiography* (Vol. 5). New York: Appleton-Century-Crofts.

Skinner, B. F. (1971). *Beyond freedom and dignity.* New York: Bantam.

Skinner, B. F. (1974). *About behaviorism.* New York: Knopf.

Skinner, B. F. (1979). *The shaping of a behaviorist.* New York: Knopf.

Slabbert, J. M., & Rasa, O. Anne E. (1997). Observational learning of an acquired maternal behaviour pattern by working dog pups: An alternative training method? *Applied Animal Behavior Science, 53,* 309–316.

Slamecka, Norman J. (1992). Forgetting. In Larry R. Squire (Ed.), *Encyclopedia of learning and memory.* New York: Macmillan.

Sleek, Scott. (1994, April). Could Prozac replace demand for therapy? *APA Monitor,* p. 28.

Smith, Andrew W.; Whitney, Helen; Thomas, Marie; Perry, Kate; & Brockman, Pip. (1997). Effects of caffeine and noise on mood, performance and cardiovascular functioning. *Human Psychopharmacology: Clinical and Experimental, 12,* 27–33.

Smith, Carlyle, & Lapp, Lorelei. (1991). Increases in numbers of REMs and REM density in humans following an intensive learning period. *Sleep, 14*(4), 325–330.

Smith, David E., & Seymour, Richard B. (1994). LSD: History and toxicity. *Psychiatric Annals, 24,* 145–147.

Smith, Eliot R. (1993). Social identity and social emotions: Toward new conceptualizations of prejudice. In Diane M. Mackie & David L. Hamilton (Eds.), *Affect, cognition, and stereotyping: Interactive processes in group perception.* San Diego, CA: Academic Press.

Smith, Gerard P., & Gibbs, James. (1998). The satiating effects of cholecystokinin and bombesin-like peptides In Gerard P. Smith (Ed.), *Satiation: From gut to brain.* New York: Oxford University Press.

Smith, Kirk H., & Rogers, Martha. (1994). Effectiveness of subliminal messages in television commercials: Two experiments. *Journal of Applied Psychology, 79,* 866–874.

Smith, Marilyn C. (1983). Hypnotic memory enhancement of witnesses: Does it work? *Psychological Bulletin, 94*(3), 387–407.

Smith, Michael T.; Perlis, Michael L.; Park, Amy; & others. (2002). Comparative meta-analysis of pharmacotherapy and behavior therapy for persistent insomnia. *American Journal of Psychiatry, 159,* 5–11.

Smith, Steven M.; Glenberg, Arthur M.; & Bjork, Robert A. (1978). Environmental context and human memory. *Memory & Cognition, 6,* 342–355.

Smith, Timothy W. (1992). Hostility and health: Current status of a psychosomatic hypothesis. *Health Psychology, 11,* 139–150.

Smuts, Barbara. (1996). Male aggression against women: An evolutionary perspective. In David M. Buss & Neil M. Malumuth (Eds.), *Sex, power, conflict: Evolutionary and feminist perspectives.* New York: Oxford University Press.

Snaith, Philip. (1998). Meditation and psychotherapy. *British Journal of Psychiatry, 173,* 193–195.

Snyder, Solomon H. (1984). Drug and neurotransmitter receptors in the brain. *Science, 224,* 22–31.

Snyder, Solomon H. (1986). *Drugs and the brain.* New York: Scientific American Books.

Snyder, Solomon H. (1990, August 9). Planning for serendipity. *Nature, 346,* 508.

Snyderman, Mark, & Rothman, Stanley. (1987). Survey of expert opinion on intelligence and aptitude testing. *American Psychologist, 42,* 137–144.

Snyderman, Mark, & Rothman, Stanley. (1988). *The IQ controversy, the media, and public policy.* New Brunswick, NJ: Transaction Books.

Snyman, J.; Aamodt, M. G.; Johnson, D. L.; & Frantzve, J. (1991). Pre-employment paper-and-pencil testing: A quantitative review. *Journal of Police and Criminal Psychology, 7,* 11–25.

Soares, Joaquim J. F., & Öhman, Arne. (1993). Preattentive processing, preparedness and phobias: Effects of instruction on conditioned electrodermal responses to masked and non-masked fear-relevant stimuli. *Behavior Research and Therapy, 31,* 87–95.

Solomon, Henry; Solomon, Linda Zener; Arnone, Maria M.; Maur, Bonnie J.; Reda, Rosina M.; & Roth, Esther O. (1981). Anonymity and helping. *Journal of Social Psychology, 113,* 37–43.

Solomon, Linda Zener; Solomon, Henry; & Stone, Ronald. (1978). Helping as a function of number of bystanders and ambiguity of emergency. *Personality and Social Psychology Bulletin, 4,* 318–321.

Soukup, James E. (1996). *Alzheimer's disease: A guide to diagnosis, treatment, and management.* New York: Praeger.

Spangler, William D. (1992). Validity of questionnaire and TAT measures of need for achievement: Two meta-analyses. *Psychological Bulletin, 112,* 140–154.

Spanos, Nicholas P. (1986). Hypnotic behavior: A social-psychological interpretation of amnesia, analgesia, and "trance logic." *Behavioral and Brain Sciences, 9,* 449–502.

Spanos, Nicholas P. (1987–1988, Winter). Past-life hypnotic regression: A critical view. *Skeptical Inquirer, 12,* 174–180.

Spanos, Nicholas P. (1989). Hypnosis, demonic possession, and multiple personality: Strategic enactments and disavowals of responsibility for actions. In Colleen A. Ward (Ed.), *Altered states of consciousness and mental health: A cross-cultural perspective.* Newbury Park, CA: Sage.

Spanos, Nicholas P. (1991). A sociocognitive approach to hypnosis. In Steven Jay Lynn & Judith W. Rhue (Eds.), *Theories of hypnosis: Current models and perspectives.* New York: Guilford Press.

Spanos, Nicholas P. (1994). Multiple identity enactments and multiple personality disorder: A sociocognitive perspective. *Psychological Bulletin, 116,* 143–165.

Spanos, Nicholas P. (1996). *Multiple identities & false memories: A sociocognitive perspective.* Washington, DC: American Psychological Association.

Spanos, Nicholas P.; Burnley, Caroline E.; & Cross, Patricia A. (1993). Response expectancies and interpretations as determinants of hypnotic responding. *Journal of Personality and Social Psychology, 65,* 1237–1242.

Spanos, Nicholas P.; McNulty, Stacey A.; DuBreuil, Susan C.; & Pires, Martha. (1995a). The frequency and correlates of sleep paralysis in a university sample. *Journal of Research in Personality, 29,* 285–305.

Spanos, Nicholas P.; Mondoux, Thomas J.; & Burgess, Cheryl A. (1995b). Comparison of multi-component hypnotic and non-hypnotic treatments for smoking. *Contemporary Hypnosis, 12,* 12–19.

Spearman, Charles E. (1904). "General intelligence" objectively determined and measured. *American Journal of Psychology, 15,* 201–293.

Spence, Janet T., & Buckner, Camille. (1995). Masculinity and femininity: Defining the undefinable. In Pamela J. Kalbfleisch & Michael J. Cody (Eds.), *Gender, power, and communication in human relationships.* Hillsdale, NJ: Erlbaum.

Spencer, Steven J.; Steele, Claude M.; & Quinn, Diane M. (1999). Stereotype threat and women's math performance. *Journal of Experimental Social Psychology, 35,* 1–28.

Sperling, George. (1960). The information available in brief visual presentations. *Psychological Monographs, 74*(Whole No. 48).

Sperry, Roger W. (1982). Some effects of disconnecting the cerebral hemispheres. *Science, 217,* 1223–1226.

Spiegel, David. (1993a). Dissociation and trauma. In David Spiegel (Ed.), *Dissociative disorders: A clinical review.* Lutherville, MD: Sidran.

Spiegel, David. (1993b). Social support: How friends, family, and groups can help. In Daniel Goleman & Joel Gurin (Eds.), *Mind/body medicine: How to use your mind for better health.* Yonkers, NY: Consumer Reports Books.

Spiegel, David. (1998a). Hypnosis and implicit memory: Automatic processing of explicit content. *American Journal of Clinical Hypnosis, 40,* 231–240.

Spiegel, David. (1998b). Social psychological theories cannot fully account for hypnosis: The record was never crooked. *American Journal of Clinical Hypnosis, 41,* 158–161.

Spiegel, David; Bloom, J. R.; Kraemer, H. C.; & Gottheil, E. (1989). Effect of psychosocial treatment on survival of patients with metastatic breast cancer. *Lancet, 2,* 888–891.

Spiegel, David, & Cardeña, Etzel. (1991). Disintegrated experience: The dissociative disorders revisited. *Journal of Abnormal Psychology, 100,* 366–378.

Spiegel, Karine; Leproult, Rachel; & Van Cauter, Eve. (1999, Oct. 23). Impact of sleep debt on metabolic and endocrine function. *Lancet, 354,* 1435–1439.

Springer, Sally P., & Deutsch, Georg. (1998). *Left brain, right brain: Perspectives from cognitive neuroscience* (5th ed.). New York: Freeman.

Squire, Larry R., & Butters, Nelson. (1992). *Neuropsychology of memory.* New York: Guilford Press.

Squire, Larry R., & Kandel, Eric R. (1999). *Memory: From mind to molecules.* New York: Scientific American Library.

Squire, Larry R., & Knowlton, Barbara J. (1995). Memory, hippocampus, and brain systems. In Michael S. Gazzaniga (Ed.), *The cognitive neurosciences.* Cambridge, MA: MIT Press.

Squire, Larry R.; Ojemann, Jeffrey G.; Miezin, Frances M.; Petersen, Steven E.; Videen, Thomas O.; & Raichle, Marcus E. (1992). Activation of the hippocampus in normal humans: A functional anatomical study of memory. *Proceedings of the National Academy of Sciences, USA, 89,* 1837–1841.

Sroufe, Alan. (1995, September). Quoted in Beth Azar, The bond between mother and child. *APA Monitor, 26*(9), 28.

Stacy, Alan W.; Widaman, Keith F.; & Marlatt, G. Alan. (1990). Expectancy models of alcohol use. *Journal of Personality and Social Psychology, 58,* 918–928.

Staddon, John E. R. (1988). Learning as inference. In Robert C. Bolles & Michael D. Beecher (Eds.), *Evolution and learning.* Hillsdale, NJ: Erlbaum.

Stafford, Laura, & Dainton, Marianne. (1994). The dark side of "normal" family interaction. In William R. Cupach & Brian H. Spitzberg (Eds.), *The dark side of interpersonal communication.* Hillside, NJ: Erlbaum.

Stajkovic, Alexander D., & Luthans, Fred. (1997). A meta-analysis of the effects of organizational behavior modification on task performance, 1975–1995. *Academy of Management Journal, 40,* 1122–1149.

Stake, Jayne E., & Oliver, Joan. (1991). Sexual contact and touching between therapist and client: A survey of psychologists' attitudes and behavior. *Professional Psychology: Research and Practice, 22,* 297–307.

Stangor, Charles. (1995). Content and application inaccuracy in social stereotyping. In Yueh-Ting Lee, Lee J. Jussim, & Clark R. McCauley (Eds.), *Stereotype accuracy: Toward appreciating group differences.* Washington, DC: American Psychological Association.

Stangor, Charles, & Lange, James E. (1994). Mental representations of social groups: Advances in understanding stereotypes and stereotyping. In Mark P. Zanna (Ed.), *Advances in experimental social psychology* (Vol. 26). San Diego, CA: Academic Press.

Stanne, Mary Beth; Johnson, David W.; & Johnson, Roger T. (1999). Does competition enhance or inhibit motor performance: A meta-analysis. *Psychological Bulletin, 125,* 133–154.

Stanton, Annette L., & Snider, Pamela R. (1993). Coping with a breast cancer diagnosis: A prospective study. *Health Psychology, 12,* 16–23.

Statham, Anne. (1987). The gender model revisited: Differences in the management styles of men and women. *Sex Roles, 16,* 409–429.

Staub, Ervin. (1978). *Positive social behavior and morality: Social and personal influences* (Vol. 1). New York: Academic Press.

Staub, Ervin. (1996). Cultural-societal roots of violence: The examples of genocidal violence and of contemporary youth violence in the United States. *American Psychologist, 51,* 117–132.

Staw, Barry M., & Ross, Jerry. (1985). Stability in the midst of change: A dispositional approach to job attitudes. *Journal of Applied Psychology, 70,* 469–480.

Steadman, Henry J.; Mulvey, Edward P.; Monahan, John; Robbins, Pamela Clark; Appelbaum, Paul S.; Grisso, Thomas; & others. (1998). Violence by people discharged from acute psychiatric inpatient facilities and by others in the same neighborhoods. *Archives of General Psychiatry, 55,* 393–401.

Steblay, Nancy Mehrkens. (1987). Helping behavior in urban and rural environments:

A meta-analysis. *Psychological Bulletin, 102,* 346–356.

Steele, Claude M. (1997). A threat in the air: How stereotypes shape intellectual identity and performance. *American Psychologist, 52,* 613–629.

Steele, Claude M., & Aronson, Joshua. (1995). Stereotype threat and the intellectual performance of African Americans. *Journal of Personality and Social Psychology, 69,* 797–811.

Steele, Claude M., & Josephs, Robert A. (1990). Alcohol myopia: Its prized and dangerous effects. *American Psychologist, 45,* 921–933.

Stein, Elliot A.; Pankiewicz, John; Harsch, Harold H.; Cho, Jung-Ki; Fuller, Scott A.; Hoffmann, Raymond G.; & others. (1998). Nicotine-induced limbic cortical activation in the human brain: A functional MRI study. *American Journal of Psychiatry, 155,* 1009–1015.

Stein, Marvin, & Miller, Andrew H. (1993). Stress, the immune system, and health and illness. In Leo Goldberger & Shlomo Breznitz (Eds.), *Handbook of stress: Theoretical and clinical aspects.* New York: Free Press.

Stein, Richard, & Nemeroff, Carol. (1995). Moral overtones of food: Judging others by what they eat. *Personality and Social Psychology Bulletin, 21,* 480–490.

Steinberg, Laurence. (1990). Autonomy, conflict, and harmony in the family relationship. In S. Shirley Feldman & Glen R. Elliott (Eds.), *At the threshold: The developing adolescent.* Cambridge, MA: Harvard University Press.

Steinberg, Laurence; Darling, Nancy E.; Fletcher, Anne C.; Brown, B. Bradford; & Dornbusch, Sanford M. (1995). Authoritative parenting and adolescent adjustment: An ecological journey. In Phyllis Moen, Glen H. Elder, Jr., & Kurt Luscher (Eds.), *Examining lives in context: Perspectives on the ecology of human development.* Washington, DC: American Psychological Association.

Stern, Kathleen, & McClintock, Martha K. (1998, March 12). Regulation of ovulation by human hormones. *Nature, 392,* 177.

Stern, Marilyn, & Karraker, Katherine Hildebrandt. (1989). Sex stereotyping of infants: A review of gender labelling studies. *Sex Roles, 20,* 501–522.

Stern, Peter. (2001). Sweet dreams are made of this. *Science, 294,* 1047.

Stern, Yaakov; Alexander, Gene E.; & Prohovnik, Isak. (1992). Inverse relationship between education and parietotemporal perfusion deficit in Alzheimer's disease. *Annals of Neurology, 32,* 371–377.

Stern, Yaakov; Gurland, B.; & Tatemichi, T. K. (1994, April 6). Influence of education and occupation on the incidence of Alzheimer's disease. *Journal of the American Medical Association, 271*(13), 1004–1007.

Sternberg, Robert J. (1982). Lies we live by: Misapplication of tests in identifying the gifted. *Gifted Child Quarterly, 26,* 157–161.

Sternberg, Robert J. (1985). *Beyond IQ: A triarchic theory of human intelligence.* New York: Cambridge University Press.

Sternberg, Robert J. (1988). A three-facet model of creativity. In Robert J. Sternberg (Ed.), *The nature of creativity.* New York: Cambridge University Press.

Sternberg, Robert J. (1990). *Metaphors of mind: Conceptions of the nature of intelligence.* New York: Cambridge University Press.

Sternberg, Robert J. (1995). For whom the bell curve tolls: A review of *The Bell Curve. Psychological Science, 6,* 257–261.

Sternberg, Robert J. (1997). The concept of intelligence and its role in lifelong learning and success. *American Psychologist, 52,* 1030–1037.

Stevens, Gwendolyn, & Gardner, Sheldon. (1982). *The women of psychology: Vol. I. Pioneers and innovators.* Cambridge, MA: Schenkman.

Stevenson, Harold L., & Stigler, James. (1992). *The learning gap: Why our schools are failing and what we can learn from Japanese and Chinese education.* New York: Summit Books.

Stevenson, Harold W., & Lee, Shin-Ying. (1990). Contexts of achievement: A study of American, Chinese, and Japanese children. *Monographs of the Society for Research in Child Development, 55* (Serial No. 221, Nos. 1–2).

Stevenson, Harold W.; Lee, Shin-Ying; & Stigler, James W. (1986). Mathematics achievements of Chinese, Japanese, and American children. *Science, 236,* 693–698.

Steward, Barbara. (2000). Changing times: The meaning, measurement and use of time in teleworking. *Time & Society, 9,* 57–74.

Stewart, Sherry H. (1996). Alcohol abuse in individuals exposed to trauma: A critical review. *Psychological Bulletin, 120,* 83–112.

Stewart, V. Mary. (1973). Tests of the "carpentered world" hypothesis by race and environment in America and Zambia. *International Journal of Psychology, 8,* 83–94.

Stickgold, Robert; Hobson, J. Allan; Fosse, Roar; & Fosse, M. (2001). Sleep, learning, and dreams: Off-line memory reprocessing. *Science, 294,* 1052–1057.

Stipek, Deborah. (1998). Differences between Americans and Chinese in the circumstances evoking pride, shame, and guilt. *Journal of Cross-Cultural Psychology, 29,* 616–629.

Stogdill, Ralph M. (1948). Personal factors associated with leadership: A survey of the literature. *Journal of Psychology, 25,* 35–71.

Stone, Arthur A.; Cox, Donald S.; Valdimarsdottir, Heiddis; Jandorf, Lina; & Neale, John M. (1987). Evidence that secretory IgA antibody is associated with daily mood. *Journal of Personality and Social Psychology, 52,* 988–993.

Stone, Arthur A.; Neale, John M.; Cox, Donald S.; Napoli, Anthony; Valdimarsdottir, Heiddis;

& Kennedy-Moore, Eileen. (1994). Daily events are associated with a secretory immune response to an oral antigen in men. *Health Psychology, 13,* 440–446.

Stone, Jeff; Lynch, Christian I.; Sjomeling, Mike; & Darley, John M. (1999). Stereotype effects on Black and White athletic performance. *Journal of Personality and Social Psychology, 77,* 1213–1227.

Storm, Lance, & Ertel, Suitbert. (2001). Does psi exist? Comments on Milton and Wiseman's (1999) meta-analysis of Ganzfield research. *Psychological Bulletin, 127,* 424–435.

Strack, Fritz; Martin, Leonard L.; & Stepper, Sabine. (1988). Inhibiting and facilitating conditions of the human smile: A non-obtrusive test of the facial-feedback hypothesis. *Journal of Personality and Social Psychology, 54,* 768–777.

Straus, Joshua L., & von Ammon Cavanaugh, Stephanie. (1996). Placebo effects: Issues for clinical practice in psychiatry and medicine. *Psychosomatics, 37*(4), 315–326.

Strickland, Bonnie R. (1995). Research on sexual orientation and human development: A commentary. *Developmental Psychology, 31,* 137–140.

Striegel-Moore, Ruth H.; Wilson, G. Terrence; Wilfrey, Denise E.; Elder, Katherine A.; & Brownell, Kelly D. (1998). Binge eating in an obese community sample. *International Journal of Eating Disorders, 23,* 27–37.

Strober, Michael; Freeman, Roberta; Kaye, Walter; & others. (2001). Males with anorexia nervosa: a controlled study of eating disorders in first-degree relatives. *International Journal of Eating Disorders, 29,* 262–269.

Strober, Michael; Kaye, Walter; & others. (2000). Controlled family study of anorexia nervosa and bulimia nervosa: evidence of shared liability and transmission of partial syndromes. *American Journal of Psychiatry, 157,* 393–401.

Strupp, Hans H. (1996). The tripartite model and the *Consumer Reports* study. *American Psychologist, 51,* 1017–1024.

Stryker, Susan. (1996, July/August). Portrait of a new man. *Utne Reader, 76,* 76–79.

Stuart, Richard B., & Davis, Barbara. (1972). *Slim chance in a fat world.* Champaign, IL: Research Press.

Styron, William. (1990). *Darkness visible: A memoir of madness.* New York: Vintage.

Subkov, A. A., & Zilov, G. N. (1937). The role of conditioned reflex adaptation in the origin of hyperergic reactions. *Bulletin de Biologie et de Médecine Expérimentale, 4,* 294–296.

Substance Abuse and Mental Health Services Administration. (1994). *National Household Survey on Drug Abuse: Population Estimates 1993* (DHHS Publication No. (SMA) 94–3017). Rockville, MD: U.S. Department of Health and Human Services.

Suchman, Anthony L., & Ader, Robert. (1992). Classic conditioning and placebo effects in crossover studies. *Clinical Pharmacology and Therapeutics, 52,* 372–377.

Sue, David; Sue, Derald; & Sue, Stanley. (1994). *Understanding abnormal behavior* (4th ed.). Boston: Houghton Mifflin.

Sue, David; Sue, Derald; & Sue, Stanley. (1997). *Understanding abnormal behavior* (5th ed.). Boston: Houghton Mifflin.

Sue, Stanley; Zane, Nolan; & Young, Kathleen. (1994). Research on psychotherapy with culturally diverse populations. In Allen E. Bergin & Sol L. Garfield (Eds.), *Handbook of psychotherapy and behavior change* (4th ed.). New York: Wiley.

Suess, Gerhard J.; Grossmann, Klaus E.; & Sroufe, L. Alan. (1992). Effects of infant attachment to mother and father on quality of adaptation in preschool: From dyadic to individual organisation of self. *International Journal of Behavioral Development, 15*(1), 43–65.

Sullivan, Cath, & Lewis, Suzan. (2001). Home-based telework, gender, and the synchronization of work and family: Perspectives of teleworkers and their co-residents. *Gender, Work & Organization, 8,* 123–145.

Sumerlin, John R., & Bundrick, Charles M. (1996). Brief Index of Self-Actualization: A measure of Maslow's model. *Journal of Social Behavior and Personality, 11,* 253–271.

Super, Donald E. (1990). Career and life development. In Duane Brown, Linda Brooks, & Associates (Eds.), *Career choice and development: Applying contemporary theories to practice.* San Francisco: Jossey-Bass.

Sutker, Patricia B.; Uddo, Madeline; Brailey, Kevin; Vasterling, Jennifer J.; & Errara, Paul. (1994). Psychopathology in war-zone deployed and nondeployed Operation Desert Storm troops assigned graves registration duties. *Journal of Abnormal Psychology, 103,* 383–390.

Swain, Sharon Ann; Polkey, C. E.; Bullock, P.; & Morris, Robin G. (1998). Recognition memory and memory for order in script-based stories following frontal lobe excisions. *Cortex, 34,* 24–45.

Swan, Daniel C., & Big Bow, Harding. (1995, Fall). Symbols of faith and belief—Art of the Native American Church. *Gilcrease Journal, 3,* 22–43.

Swann, William B. (1984). Quest for accuracy in person perception: A matter of pragmatics. *Psychological Review, 91,* 457–477.

Swart, Lyle C., & Morgan, Cynthia L. (1992). Effects of subliminal backward-recorded messages on attitudes. *Perceptual and Motor Skills, 75*(3, Pt. 2), 1107–1113.

Swim, Janet K. (1994). Perceived versus meta-analytic effect sizes: An assessment of the accuracy of gender stereotypes. *Journal of Personality and Social Psychology, 66,* 21–36.

Syvälahti, Erkka K. G. (1994). Biological factors in schizophrenia: Structural and functional aspects. *British Journal of Psychiatry, 164*(Suppl. 23), 9–14.

Taft, Lois B., & Nehrke, Milton F. (1990). Reminiscence, life review, and ego integrity in nursing home residents. *International Journal of Aging and Human Development, 30,* 189–196.

Takahashi, Joseph S. (1999, Sept. 24). Narcolepsy genes wake up the sleep field. *Science, 285,* 2076–2077.

Takei, Noriyoshi; Sham, Pak; O'Callaghan, Eadbhard; Murray, Graham K.; Glover, Gyles; & Murray, Robin M. (1994). Prenatal exposure to influenza and the development of schizophrenia: Is the effect confined to females? *American Journal of Psychiatry, 151,* 117–119.

Tallman, Karen, & Bohart, Arthur C. (1999). The client as a common factor: Clients as self-healers. In Mark A. Hubble, Barry L. Duncan, & Scott D. Miller (Eds.), *The heart and soul of change: What works in therapy.* Washington, DC: American Psychological Association.

Tanaka-Matsumi, Junko, & Draguns, Juris G. (1997). Culture and psychopathology. In John W. Berry, Marshall H. Segall, & Cigdem Kagitçibasi (Eds.), *Handbook of cross-cultural psychology: Vol. 3. Social behavior and applications.* Boston: Allyn & Bacon.

Tanford, Sarah, & Penrod, Steven. (1984). Social influence model: A formal integration of research on majority and minority influence processes. *Psychological Bulletin, 95,* 189–225.

Tankova, Iren; Adan, Ana; & Buela-Casal, Gualberto. (1994). Circadian typology and individual differences: A review. *Personality and Individual Differences, 16,* 671–684.

Tannen, Deborah. (1990). *You just don't understand: Women and men in conversation.* New York: Ballantine.

Tart, Charles T. (Ed.). (1990). *Altered states of consciousness* (3rd ed.). San Francisco: HarperCollins.

Tart, Charles T. (1994). *Living the mindful life: A handbook for living in the present moment.* Boston: Shambhala.

Taylor, Donald M., & Porter, Lana E. (1994). A multicultural view of stereotyping. In Walter J. Lonner & Roy Malpass (Eds.), *Psychology and culture.* Boston: Allyn & Bacon.

Taylor, Shelley E. (2000, July/August). Quoted in Beth Azar, A new stress paradigm for women. *APA Monitor on Psychology, 31,* 42–43.

Taylor, Shelley E., & Aspinwall, Lisa G. (1993). Coping with chronic illness. In Leo Goldberger & Shlomo Breznitz (Eds.), *Handbook of stress: Theoretical and clinical aspects* (2nd ed.). New York: Free Press.

Taylor, Shelley E.; Helgeson, Vicki S.; Reed, Geoffrey M.; & Skokan, Laurie A. (1991). Self-generated feelings of control and adjustment to physical illness. *Journal of Social Issues, 47,* 91–109.

Taylor, Shelley E.; Klein, Laura Cousino; Lewis, Brian P.; Guenewald, Tara L.; Gurung, Regan A.; & Updegraff, John A. (2000). Biobehavioral responses to stress in females: Tend-and-befriend, not fight-or-flight. *Psychological Review, 107,* 411–429.

Taylor, Susan M., & Sackheim, Kathryn K. (1988). Graphology. *Personnel Administrator, 33,* 71–76.

Templeton, Jennifer J. (1998). Learning from others' mistakes: A paradox revisited. *Animal Behaviour, 55,* 79–85.

Terman, Lewis M. (1916). *Measurement of intelligence.* Boston: Houghton Mifflin.

Terman, Lewis M. (1926). *Genetic studies of genius* (2nd ed., Vol. I). Stanford, CA: Stanford University Press.

Terman, Lewis M., & Oden, Melita H. (1947). *Genetic studies of genius: Vol. IV. The gifted child grows up: Twenty-five years' follow-up of a superior group.* Stanford, CA: Stanford University Press.

Terman, Lewis M., & Oden, Melita H. (1959). *Genetic studies of genius: Vol. V. The gifted at mid-life: Thirty-five years' follow-up of the superior child.* Stanford, CA: Stanford University Press.

Terrace, Herbert S. (1985). In the beginning was the "name." *American Psychologist, 40,* 1011–1028.

Tett, Robert P.; Jackson, Douglas N.; & Rothstein, Mitchell. (1991). Personality measures as predictors of job performance: A meta-analytic review. *Personnel Psychology, 44,* 703–742.

Thacker, Rebecca A., & Wayne, Sandy J. (1995). An examination of the relationship between upward influence tactics and assessments of promotability. *Journal of Management, 21,* 739–757.

Thase, Michael E. (2001). Neuroimaging profiles and the differential therapies of depression. *Archives of General Psychiatry, 58,* 651–653.

Thase, Michael E.; Entsuah, A. R.; & Rudolph, R. L. (2001). Remission rates during treatment with venlafaxine or selective serotonin reuptake inhibitors. *British Journal of Psychiatry, 178,* 234–241.

Thomas, Alexander, & Chess, Stella. (1977). *Temperament and development.* New York: Brunner/Mazel.

Thomas, Alexander, & Chess, Stella. (1986). The New York Longitudinal Study: From infancy to early adult life. In Robert Plomin & Judith Dunn (Eds.), *The study of temperament: Changes, continuities, and challenges.* Hillsdale, NJ: Erlbaum.

Thompson, Clara. (1950/1973). Some effects of the derogatory attitude toward female sexuality. In Jean Baker Miller (Ed.), *Psychoanalysis and women.* Baltimore, MD: Penguin Books.

Thompson, Paul M.; Giedd, Jay N.; Woods, Roger P.; MacDonald, David; Evans, Alan C.; & Toga, Arthur W. (2000, March 9). Growth patterns in the developing human brain detected by using continuum-mechanical tensor maps. *Nature, 404,* 190–193.

Thompson, Paul M.; Vidal, Christine; Gledd, Jay N.; Gochman, Peter; Blumenthal, Jonathan; Nicolson, Robert; & others. (2001).

Mapping adolescent brain change reveals dynamic wave of accelerated gray matter loss in very early-onset schizophrenia. *Proceedings of the National Academy of Sciences, USA, 98,* 11650–11655.

Thompson, Richard F. (1994). Behaviorism and neuroscience. *Psychological Review, 101,* 259–265.

Thompson, Richard F. (1997). Will the mind become the brain in the 21st century? In Robert L. Solso (Ed.), *Mind and brain sciences in the 21st century.* Cambridge, MA: MIT Press.

Thompson, Richard F. (2000). *The brain: A neuroscience primer* (3rd ed.). New York: Freeman.

Thompson, Suzanne C.; Nanni, Christopher; & Levine, Alexandra. (1994). Primary versus secondary and central versus consequence-related control in HIV-positive men. *Journal of Personality and Social Psychology, 67,* 540–547.

Thompson, Suzanne C.; Sobolew-Shubin, Alexandria; Galbraith, Michael E.; Schwankovsky, Lenore; & Cruzen, Dana. (1993). Maintaining perceptions of control: Finding perceived control in low-control circumstances. *Journal of Personality and Social Psychology, 64,* 293–304.

Thompson, Suzanne C., & Spacapan, Shirlynn. (1991). Perceptions of control in vulnerable populations. *Journal of Social Issues, 47,* 1–21.

Thompson-Pope, Susan K., & Turkat, Ira D. (1993). Schizotypal, schizoid, paranoid, and avoidant personality disorders. In Patricia B. Sutker & Henry E. Adams (Eds.), *Comprehensive handbook of psychopathology* (2nd ed.). New York: Plenum Press.

Thorndike, Edward L. (1898). Animal intelligence: An experimental study of the associative processes in animals. *Psychological Review Monograph Supplement, 2*(Serial No. 8).

Thorndike, Edward L. (1911). *Animal intelligence.* New York: Macmillan.

Thorndike, Robert L. (1991). Edward L. Thorndike: A professional and personal appreciation. In Gregory A. Kimble, Michael Wertheimer, & Charlotte L. White (Eds.), *Portraits of pioneers in psychology.* Washington, DC: American Psychological Association.

Thorne, Barrie. (1993). *Gender play: girls and boys in school.* New Brunswick, NJ: Rutgers University Press.

Thornton, Bill. (1992). Repression and its mediating influence on the defensive attribution of responsibility. *Journal of Research in Personality, 26,* 44–57.

Thunberg, Monika, & Dimberg, Ulf. (2000). Gender differences in facial reactions to fear-relevant stimuli. *Journal of Nonverbal Behavior, 24,* 45–51.

Thurstone, Louis L. (1937). *Primary mental abilities.* Chicago: University of Chicago Press.

Tienari, Pekka; Sorri, Anneli; Lahti, Ilpo; Naarala, Mikko; Wahlberg, Karl-Erik; Moring,

Juha; & others. (1987). Genetic and psychosocial factors in schizophrenia: The Finnish Adoptive Family Study. *Schizophrenia Bulletin, 13,* 477–484.

Tienari, Pekka; Wynne, Lyman C.; Moring, Juha; Lahti, Ilpo; Naarala, Mikko; Sorri, Anneli; & others. (1994). The Finnish Adoptive Family Study of Schizophrenia: Implications for family research. *British Journal of Psychiatry, 164*(Suppl.), 20–26.

Tindall-Ford, Sharon; Chandler, Paul; & Sweller, John. (1997). When two sensory modes are better than one. *Journal of Experimental Psychology: Applied, 3,* 257–287.

Todd, James T., & Morris, Edward K. (1992). Case histories in the great power of steady misrepresentation. *American Psychologist, 47,* 1441–1453.

Toews, John A.; Lockyer, Jocelyn M.; Dobson, Deborah J. G.; & Simpson, Elizabeth (1997). Analysis of stress levels among medical students, resident, and graduate students at four Canadian schools of medicine. *Academic Medicine, 72*(11), 997–1002.

Tolman, Edward C. (1932). *Purposive behavior in animals and men.* New York: Appleton-Century-Crofts.

Tolman, Edward C. (1948). Cognitive maps in rats and men. *Psychological Review, 55,* 189–208.

Tolman, Edward C., & Honzik, Charles H. (1930a). "Insight" in rats. *University of California, Berkeley, Publications in Psychology, 4,* 215–232.

Tolman, Edward C., & Honzik, Charles H. (1930b). Introduction and removal of reward, and maze performance in rats. *University of California, Berkeley, Publications in Psychology, 4,* 257–275.

Tolman, Edward C.; Ritchie, B. F.; & Kalish, D. (1946/1992). Studies in spatial learning. I. Orientation and the short-cut. *Journal of Experimental Psychology: General, 121,* 429–434.

Tomaka, Joe; Blascovich, Jim; Kelsey, Robert M.; & Leitten, Christopher L. (1993). Subjective, physiological, and behavioral effects of threat and challenge appraisal. *Journal of Personality and Social Psychology, 65,* 248–260.

Tomb, David A. (1994). The phenomenology of post-traumatic stress disorder. *Psychiatric Clinics of North America, 17,* 237–250.

Tononi, Giulio, & Edelman, Gerald M. (1998, December 4). Consciousness and complexity. *Science, 282,* 1846–1851.

Tooby, John, & Cosmides, Leda. (2000). Evolutionary psychology and the emotions. In Michael Lewis & Jeanette M. Haviland-Jones (Eds.), *Handbook of emotions* (2nd ed.). New York: Guilford Press.

Torrey, E. Fuller. (1992). Are we overestimating the genetic contribution to schizophrenia? *Schizophrenia Bulletin, 18,* 159–170.

Torrey, E. Fuller. (1999, February 25). Quoted in CNN Interactive Health News Report, "Study: Schizophrenia linked to date, place of birth." <http://www.cnn.com/HEALTH/9902/25/schizophrenia.risk/> (March 8, 1999)

Torrey, E. Fuller; Bowler, Ann E.; Rawlings, Robert; & Terrazas, Alejandro. (1993). Seasonality of schizophrenia and stillbirths. *Schizophrenia Bulletin, 19,* 557–562.

Torrey, E. Fuller; Bowler, Ann E.; Taylor, Edward H.; & Gottesman, Irving I. (1994). *Schizophrenia and manic-depressive disorder: The biological roots of mental illness as revealed by the landmark study of identical twins.* New York: Basic Books.

Trappey, Charles. (1996). A meta-analysis of consumer choice and subliminal advertising. *Psychology and Marketing, 13,* 517–530.

Travis, L. E. (1925). The effect of a small audience upon eye-hand coordination. *Journal of Abnormal and Social Psychology, 20,* 142–146.

Triandis, Harry C. (1994). *Culture and social behavior.* New York: McGraw-Hill.

Triandis, Harry C. (1995). *Individualism and collectivism.* Boulder, CO: Westview Press.

Triandis, Harry C. (1996). The psychological measurement of cultural syndromes. *American Psychologist, 51,* 407–415.

Trimble, Joseph E. (1994). Cultural variations in the use of alcohol and drugs. In Walter J. Lonner & Roy Malpass (Eds.), *Psychology and culture.* Boston: Allyn & Bacon.

Trope, Yaacov, & Fishbach, Ayelet. (2000). Counteractive self-control in overcoming temptation. *Journal of Personality and Social Psychology, 79,* 493–506.

Trull, Timothy. J. (1995). Borderline personality disorder features in nonclinical young adults: I. Identification and validation. *Psychological Assessment, 7,* 33–41.

Tsien, Joe Z. (2000, April). Building a brainier mouse. *Scientific American, 282,* 62–68.

Tsuang, Ming T.; Stone, William S.; & Faraone, Stephen V. (2000). Toward reformulating the diagnosis of schizophrenia. *American Journal of Psychiatry, 157,* 1041–1050.

Tucker, Phebe; & Trautman, Richard. (2000). Understanding and treating PTSD: past, present, and future. *Bulletin of the Menninger Clinic, 64*(Suppl. A), A37–A51.

Tulving, Endel. (1983). *Elements of episodic memory.* Oxford, England: Clarendon Press/Oxford University Press.

Tulving, Endel. (1985). How many memory systems are there? *American Psychologist, 40,* 385–398.

Tulving, Endel. (1995). Organization of memory: *Quo vadis?* In Michael S. Gazzaniga (Ed.), *The cognitive neurosciences.* Cambridge, MA: MIT Press.

Tulving, Endel. (1997). Human memory. In Michael S. Gazzaniga (Ed.), *Conversations in the cognitive neurosciences.* Cambridge, MA: MIT Press.

Tuomisto, Terhi; Tuomisto, Martti T.; Hetherington, Marion; & Lappalainen, Raimo. (1998). Reasons for initiation and cessation of eating in obese men and women and the affective consequences of eating in everyday situations. *Appetite, 30,* 211–222.

Turek, Fred W.; & Czeisler, Charles A. (1999). Role of melatonin in the regulation of sleep. In Fred W. Turek & Phyllis C. Zee (Eds.), *Regulation of sleep and circadian rhythms.* New York: Dekker.

Turk, Dennis C. (1994, April). Perspectives on chronic pain: The role of psychological factors. *Current Directions in Psychological Science, 3*(2), 45–48.

Turk, Dennis C., & Nash, Justin M. (1993). Chronic pain: New ways to cope. In Daniel Goleman & Joel Gurin (Eds.), *Mind/body medicine: How to use your mind for better health.* Yonkers, NY: Consumer Reports Books.

Turk, Dennis C., & Rudy, Thomas E. (1992). Cognitive factors and persistent pain: A glimpse into Pandora's box. *Cognitive Therapy and Research, 16*(2), 99–122.

Turner, Patricia J., & Gervai, Judit. (1995). A multidimensional study of gender typing in preschool children and their parents: Personality, attitudes, preferences, behavior, and cultural differences. *Developmental Psychology, 31,* 759–772.

Tversky, Amos. (1972). Elimination by aspects: A theory of choice. *Psychological Review, 80,* 281–299.

Tversky, Amos, & Kahneman, Daniel. (1982). Judgment under uncertainty: Heuristics and biases. In Daniel Kahneman, Paul Slovic, & Amos Tversky (Eds.), *Judgment under uncertainty: Heuristics and biases.* New York: Cambridge University Press.

Tversky, Amos, & Shafir, Eldar. (1992). Choice under conflict: The dynamics of deferred decision. *Psychological Science, 3,* 358–361.

Tweney, Ryan D. (1997). Edward Bradford Titchener (1867–1927). In Wolfgang G. Bringmann, Helmut E. Lück, Rudolf Miller, & Charles E. Early (Eds.), *A pictorial history of psychology.* Chicago: Quintessence.

Uchino, Bert N.; Cacioppo, John T.; & Kiecolt-Glaser, Janice K. (1996). The relationship between social support and physiological processes: A review with emphasis on underlying mechanisms and implications for health. *Psychological Bulletin, 119,* 488–531.

Ulett, George A.; Han, Songping; & Han, Ji-sheng. (1998). Electroacupuncture: Mechanisms and clinical application. *Biological Psychiatry, 44,* 129–138.

Underwood, Geoffrey (Ed.). (1996). *Implicit cognition.* New York: Oxford University Press.

Unger, Rhoda K., & Crawford, Mary. (1993). Commentary: Sex and gender: The troubled relationship between terms and concepts. *Psychological Science, 4,* 122–124.

U.S. Census Bureau. (2001). *Census 2000: Profile of general demographic characteristics for the United States: 2000* (Table DP-1). Washington, DC: U.S. Census Bureau. PDF of document retrieved February 13, 2002 from: http://www.census.gov/Press-Release/www/2001/tables/dp_us_2000.PDF

U.S. Census Bureau. (2002a). *Population profile of the United States: 2000* (Internet release). PDF of document retrieved February 21, 2002 from: http://www.census.gov/population/pop-profile/2000/profile2000.pdf

U.S. Census Bureau. (2002b). *Statistical abstract of the United States: 2001* (121st ed.). Washington, DC: U.S. Government Printing Office.

U.S. Department of Health and Human Services. (1999). *Mental health: A report of the Surgeon General.* Rockville, MD: U.S. Department of Health and Human Services, Center for Mental Health Services, National Institute of Mental Health. <http://www.nimh.nih.gov/mhsgrpt/home.html> (February 22, 2000).

U.S. Department of Justice Technical Working Group for Eyewitness Evidence. (1999). *Eyewitness evidence: A guide for law enforcement* (NCJ 178240). Washington, DC: U.S. Department of Justice, National Institute of Justice. Also posted at: http://www.ojp.usdoj.gov/nij/pubs-sum/178240.htm (January 21, 2000).

U.S. National Center for Health Statistics. (1990). *Vital and health statistics* (Series 10). Washington, DC: U.S. Government Printing Office.

U.S. Public Health Service. (1999). *The surgeon general's call to action to prevent suicide.* Washington, DC: U.S. Government Printing Office. Document PDF retrieved on October 30, 2001, from http://www.surgeongeneral.gov/library/calltoaction/calltoaction.pdf

Uttal, William R. (2001). *The new phrenology: The limits of localizing cognitive processes in the brain.* Cambridge, MA: MIT Press.

Vallee, Bert L. (1998, June). Alcohol in the western world. *Scientific American, 278,* 80–85.

Van Boven, Leaf; Kamada, Akiko; & Gilovich, Thomas. (1999). The perceiver as perceived: Everyday intuitions about the correspondence bias. *Journal of Personality and Social Psychology, 77,* 1188–1199.

Van Cauter, Eve. (1999, October 21). Quoted in "Lack of sleep ages body's systems." <http://www.psycport.com/news/1999/10/21/tbl-z/4265-0775-SLEEP-DEBT-MED.html> (1999, November 22).

Vandell, Deborah Lowe, & Corasaniti, Mary Ann. (1990). Child care and the family: Complex contributors to child development. In Kathleen McCartney (Ed.), *Child care and maternal employment: A social ecology approach* (New Directions for Child Development Series, No. 49). San Francisco: Jossey-Bass.

van den Boom, Dymphna C., & Hoeksma, Jan B. (1994). The effect of infant irritability on mother-infant interaction: A growth-curve analysis. *Developmental Psychology, 30,* 581–590.

van der Helm, Peter A. (2000). Simplicity versus likelihood in visual perception: From surprisals to precisals. *Psychological Bulletin, 126,* 770–800.

Vanderlinden, Johan; Van Dyck, Richard; Vandereycken, Walter; & Vertommen, Hans. (1991). Dissociative experiences in the general population in the Netherlands and Belgium: A study with the Dissociative Questionnaire (DIS-Q). *Dissociation, 4,* 180–184.

Van Dijk, Gertjan; Seeley, Randy J.; Campfield, L. Arthur; Woods, Stephen C.; Schwartz, Michael W.; & others. (1999). Metabolic, gastrointestinal, and CNS neuropeptide effects of brain leptin administration in the rat. *American Journal of Physiology, 276,* R1425–R1433.

van Geert, Paul. (1998). A dynamic systems model of basic developmental mechanisms: Piaget, Vygotsky, and beyond. *Psychological Review, 105,* 634–677.

van Praag, Henriette; Schinder, Alejandro F.; Christie, Brian R.; Toni, Nicolas; Palmer, Theo D.; & Gage, Fred H. (2002, Feb. 28). Functional neurogenesis in the adult hippocampus. *Nature, 415,* 1030–1034.

van Wyhe, John. (2000). *The History of Phrenology on the Web.* <http://www.jmvanwyhe.freeserve.co.uk/> (January 17, 2000)

Venables, Peter H. (1996). Schizotypy and maternal exposure to influenza and to cold temperature: The Mauritius study. *Journal of Abnormal Psychology, 105,* 53–60.

Venditti, Elizabeth M.; Wing, Rena R.; Jakicic, John M.; Butler, Betsy A.; & Marcus, Marsha D. (1996). Weight cycling, psychological health, and binge eating in obese women. *Journal of Consulting and Clinical Psychology, 64,* 400–405.

Verplanken, Bas, & Faes, Suzanne. (1999). Good intentions, bad habits, and effects of forming implementation intentions on healthy eating. *European Journal of Social Psychology, 29,* 591–604.

Vingerhoets, Ad J. J. M.; Cornelius, Randolph R.; Van Heck, Guus L.; & Becht, Marleen C. (2000). Adult crying: A model and review of the literature. *Review of General Psychology, 4,* 354–377.

Vink, T.; Hinney, A.; & others. (2001). Association between an agouti-related protein gene polymorphism and anorexia nervosa. *Molecular Psychiatry, 6,* 325–328.

Vitkovic, Ljubisa. (1995). Neuroimmunology and neurovirology. In Stephen H. Koslow (Ed.), *The neuroscience of mental health II: A report on neuroscience research: Status and potential for mental health and mental illness* (NIMH Publication No. 95–4000). Rockville, MD: National Institute of Mental Health.

Vokey, John R., & Read, J. Don. (1985). Subliminal messages: Between the devil and the media. *American Psychologist, 40,* 1231–1239.

Volkow, Nora D.; Chang, Linda; Wang, Gene-Jack; Fowler, Joanna S.; Leonido-Yee, Maria; & others. (2001a). Association of dopamine transporter reduction with psychomotor impairment in methamphetamine abusers. *American Journal of Psychiatry, 158,* 377–382.

Volkow, Nora D.; Chang, Linda; Wang, Gene-Jack; Fowler, Joanna S.; Franceschi, Dinko; & others. (2001b). Higher cortical and lower subcortical metabolism in detoxified methamphetamine abusers. *American Journal of Psychiatry, 158,* 383–389.

Volkow, Nora D.; Chang, Linda; Wang, Gene-Jack; Fowler, Joanna S.; Ding, Yu-Sin; & others. (2001c). Low level of brain dopamine D2 receptors in methamphetamine abusers: Association with metabolism in the orbitofrontal cortex. *American Journal of Psychiatry, 158,* 2015–2021.

Volkow, Nora D.; Wang, Gene-Jack; Fischman, M. W.; Foltin, R. W.; Fowler, Joanna S.; Abumrad, N. N.; & others. (1997, April 24). Relationship between subjective effects of cocaine and dopamine transporter occupancy. *Nature, 386,* 827–830.

Volkow, Nora D.; Wang, Gene-Jack; Fowler, Joanna S.; & others. (1999a). Association of methylphenidate-induced craving with changes in right striato-orbitofrontal metabolism in cocaine abusers: Implications in addiction. *American Journal of Psychiatry, 156,* 19–26.

Volkow, Nora D.; Wang, Gene-Jack; Fowler, Joanna S.; & others. (1999b). Prediction of reinforcing responses to psychostimulants in humans by brain dopamine D$_2$ receptor levels. *American Journal of Psychiatry, 156,* 1440–1443.

Voyer, Daniel; Voyer, Susan; & Bryden, M. Philip. (1995). Magnitude of sex differences in spatial abilities: A meta-analysis and consideration of critical variables. *Psychological Bulletin, 117,* 250–270.

Vygotsky, Lev S. (1978). *Mind in society: The development of higher psychological processes.* (Michael Cole, Vera John-Steiner, Sylvia Scribner, & Ellen Souberman, Eds.). Cambridge, Mass.: Harvard University Press.

Vygotsky, Lev S. (1987). *Thinking and speech* (Norris Minick, Trans.). New York: Plenum Press.

Wadsworth, Barry J. (1996). *Piaget's theory of cognitive and affective development: Foundations of constructivism* (5th ed.). White Plains, NY: Longman.

Wagner, Shlomo; Castel, Mona; Gainer, Harold; & Yarom, Yosef. (1997, June 5). GABA in the mammalian suprachiasmatic nucleus and its role in diurnal rhythmicity. *Nature, 387,* 598–603.

Wagstaff, Graham F. (1996). Compliance and imagination in hypnosis. In Robert G. Kunzendorf, Nicholas P. Spanos, & Benjamin Wallace (Eds.), *Hypnosis and imagination.* Amityville, NY: Baywood.

Wagstaff, Graham F. (1999). Hypnosis. In Sergio Della Sala (Ed.), *Mind myths: Exploring popular assumptions about the mind and brain.* Chichester, England: Wiley.

Wahba, Mahmoud A., & Bridwell, Lawrence G. (1976). Maslow reconsidered: A review of research on the need hierarchy theory. *Organizational Behavior and Human Decision Processes, 15,* 212–240.

Waite, Linda J., & Joyner, Kara. (2001). Emotional and physical satisfaction with sex in married, cohabiting, and dating sexual unions: Do men and women differ? In Edward O. Laumann & Robert T. Michael (Eds.), *Sex, love, and health in America: Private choices and public policies.* Chicago: University of Chicago Press.

Waldman, Irwin D.; Weinberg, Richard A.; & Scarr, Sandra. (1994). Racial group differences in IQ in the Minnesota Transracial Adoption Study: A reply to Levin and Lynn. *Intelligence, 18,* 29–44.

Walker, J. Michael; Huang, Susan M.; Strangman, Nicole M.; Tsou, Kang; & Sanudo-Pena, M. Clara. (1999, October 12). Pain modulation by release of the endogenous cannabinoid anandamide. *Proceedings of the National Academy of Sciences, USA, 96,* 12198–12203.

Walker, Lawrence J. (1989). A longitudinal study of moral reasoning. *Child Development, 60,* 157–166.

Wallach, Hans. (1987). Perceiving a stable environment when one moves. *Annual Review of Psychology, 38,* 1–27.

Walters, Ellen E., & Kendler, Kenneth S. (1995). Anorexia nervosa and anorexic-like syndromes in a population-based female twin sample. *American Journal of Psychiatry, 152,* 64–71.

Walton, Richard E. (1973, Fall). Quality of work life: What is it? *Sloan Management Review,* pp. 11–21.

Wang, Gene-Jack; Volkow, Nora D.; Logan, Jean; & others. (2001). Brain dopamine and obesity. *Lancet, 357,* 354–357.

Wang, Qi. (2001). Culture effects on adults' earliest childhood recollection and self-description: Implications for the relation between memory and the self. *Journal of Personality and Social Psychology, 81,* 220–223.

Wang, Qi; Leichtman, Michelle D.; & Davies, Katherine I. (2000). Sharing memories and telling stories: American and Chinese mothers and their 3-year-olds. *Memory, 8,* 159–178.

Ward, Colleen, & Rana-Deuba, Arzu. (1999). Acculturation and adaptation revisited. *Journal of Cross-Cultural Psychology, 30*(4), 422–442.

Ware, Jacqueline; Jain, Kumud; Burgess, Ian; & Davey, Graham C. L. (1994). Disease-avoidance model: Factor analysis of common animal fears. *Behavior Research and Therapy, 32,* 57–63.

Washburn, D. (1997). Study shows rise in employee theft in 1996. *Home Improvement Market, 234,* 22.

Watson, David, & Pennebaker, James W. (1989). Health complaints, stress, and distress: Exploring the central role of negative affectivity. *Psychological Review, 96,* 234–254.

Watson, Jeanne C. (2002). Re-visioning empathy. In David J. Cain & Julius Seeman (Eds.), *Humanistic psychotherapies: Handbook of research and practice.* Washington, DC: American Psychological Association.

Watson, John B. (1913). Psychology as the behaviorist views it. *Psychological Review, 20,* 158–177.

Watson, John B. (1916). The place of the conditioned-reflex in psychology. *Psychological Review, 23,* 89–116.

Watson, John B. (1919). A schematic outline of the emotions. *Psychological Review, 26,* 165–196.

Watson, John B. (1924/1970). *Behaviorism.* New York: Norton.

Watson, John B. (1930). *Behaviorism* (Rev. ed.). Chicago: University of Chicago Press.

Watson, John B., & Rayner, Rosalie. (1920/2000). Conditioned emotional reactions. *Journal of Experimental Psychology, 3,* 1–14. (Reprinted March 2000: *American Psychologist, 55*(3) 313–317).

Weaver, Charles N. (1978). Job satisfaction as a component of happiness among males and females. *Personnel Psychology, 31,* 831–840.

Weaver, Charles A., III. (1993). Do you need a "flash" to form a flashbulb memory? *Journal of Experimental Psychology: General, 122,* 39–46.

Weaver, David R. (1998). The suprachiasmatic nucleus: A 25-year retrospective. *Journal of Biological Rhythms, 13,* 100–112.

Webb, Katie., & Davey, Graham C. L. (1993). Disgust sensitivity and fear of animals: Effect of exposure to violent or revulsive material. *Anxiety, Coping and Stress, 5,* 329–335.

Webb, Wilse B. (1975). *Sleep: The gentle tyrant.* Englewood Cliffs, NJ: Prentice-Hall.

Webb, Wilse B. (1994). Sleep as a biological rhythm: A historical review. *Sleep, 17,* 188–194.

Webb, Wilse B., & Dinges, David F. (1989). Cultural perspectives on napping and the siesta. In David F. Dinges & Roger J. Broughton (Eds.), *Sleep and alertness: Chronobiological, behavioral, and medical aspects of napping.* New York: Raven Press.

Wechsler, David. (1944). *The measurement of adult intelligence* (3rd ed.). Baltimore: Williams & Wilkins.

Wechsler, David. (1977). *Manual for the Wechsler Intelligence Scale for Children* (Rev.). New York: Psychological Corporation.

Wechsler, Henry; Dowdall, George W.; Maenner, Gretchen; Gledhill-Hoyt, Jeana; & Lee, Hang. (1998). Changes in binge drinking and related problems among American college students between 1993 and 1997: Results from the Harvard School of Public Health College Alcohol Study. *Journal of American College Health, 47,* 57–68.

Wechsler, Henry; Lee, Jae Eun; Kuo, Meichun; Seibring, Mark; Nelson, Toben F.; & Lee, Hang. (2002). Trends in college binge drinking during a period of increased prevention efforts: Findings for 4 Harvard Public School of Public Health College Alcohol Study Surveys: 1993–2001. *Journal of American College Health, 50,* 203–217.

Wegner, Daniel M. (1989). *White bears and other unwanted thoughts: Suppression, obsession, and the psychology of mental control.* New York: Viking Press.

Weinberg, Richard A. (1989). Intelligence and IQ: Landmark issues and great debates. *American Psychologist, 44,* 98–104.

Weinberg, Richard A.; Scarr, Sandra; & Waldman, Irwin D. (1992). The Minnesota Transracial Adoption Study: A follow-up of IQ test performance at adolescence. *Intelligence, 16,* 117–135.

Weinberger, Daniel R. (1995, June). Quoted in Joel L. Swerdlow, "Quiet miracles of the brain." *National Geographic, 187,* 2–41.

Weindruch, Richard. (1996). Caloric restriction and aging. *Scientific American, 274,* 46–52.

Weiner, Bernard. (1985). An attributional theory of achievement motivation and emotion. *Psychological Review, 92,* 548–573.

Weinstein, Lissa N.; Schwartz, David G.; & Arkin, Arthur M. (1991). Qualitative aspects of sleep mentation. In Steven J. Ellman & John S. Antrobus (Eds.), *The mind in sleep: Psychology and psychophysiology* (2nd ed.). New York: Wiley.

Weisberg, Robert W. (1988). Problem solving and creativity. In Robert J. Sternberg (Ed.), *The nature of creativity.* New York: Cambridge University Press.

Weisberg, Robert W. (1993). *Creativity: Beyond the myth of genius.* New York: Freeman.

Weiss, Howard M., & Shaw, James B. (1979). Social influences on judgments about tasks. *Organizational Behavior and Human Performance, 24,* 136–140.

Weisse, Carol Silvia. (1992). Depression and immunocompetence: A review of the literature. *Psychological Bulletin, 111,* 475–489.

Weissman, Myrna M.; Markowitz, John C.; & Klerman, Gerald L. (2000). *Comprehensive guide to interpersonal psychotherapy.* New York: Basic Books.

Weisz, Carolyn, & Jones, Edward E. (1993). Expectancy disconfirmation and dispositional inference: Latent strength of target-based and category-based expectancies. *Personality and Social Psychology Bulletin, 19,* 563–573.

Weisz, John R.; Rothbaum, Fred M.; & Blackburn, Thomas C. (1984). Standing out and standing in: The psychology of control in Japan and America. *American Psychologist, 39,* 955–969.

Wells, Gary L., & Bradfield, Amy L. (1999). Distortions in eyewitnesses' recollections: Can the postidentification-feedback effect be moderated? *Psychological Science, 10,* 138–144.

Wells, Gary L.; Malpass, Roy S.; Lindsay, R. C. L.; Fisher, Ronald P.; Turtle, John W.; & Fulero, Solomon M. (2000). From the lab to the police station: A successful application of eyewitness research. *American Psychologist, 55,* 581–598.

Wells, Kenneth B.; Burnam, M. Audrey; Rogers, Williams; Hayes, Ron; & Camp, Patti. (1992). The course of depression in adult outpatients: Results from the Medical Outcomes Study. *Archives of General Psychiatry, 49,* 788–794.

Wenar, Charles. (1994). *Developmental psychopathology: From infancy through adolescence* (3rd ed.). New York: McGraw-Hill.

Werker, Janet, & Desjardins, Renee. (1995). Listening to speech in the 1st year of life: Experiential influences on phoneme production. *Current Directions in Psychological Science, 4,* 76–81.

Wertheimer, Max. (1912/1965). Experimentelle Studien über das Sehen von Bewegung. *Zeitschrift für Psychologie, 61,* 162–163, 221–227. (Portions of original publication translated and reprinted in Richard J. Herrnstein & Edwin G. Boring (Eds.), *A source book in the history of psychology* (Don Cantor, Trans.). Cambridge, MA: Harvard University Press).

Wertsch, James V., & Tulviste, Peeter. (1992). L. S. Vygotsky and contemporary developmental psychology. *Developmental Psychology, 28,* 548–557.

Wertsch, James V., & Tulviste, Peeter. (1994). Lev Semyonovich Vygotsky and contemporary developmental psychology. In Ross D. Parke, Peter A. Ornstein, John J. Rieser, & Carolyn Zahn-Waxler (Eds.), *A century of developmental psychology.* Washington, DC: American Psychological Association.

West, Michael A. (1987). Traditional and psychological perspectives on meditation. In Michael A. West (Ed.), *The psychology of meditation.* New York: Oxford University Press.

Westen, Drew. (1990). Psychoanalytic approaches to personality. In Lawrence A. Pervin (Ed.), *Handbook of personality: Theory and research.* New York: Guilford Press.

Westen, Drew. (1998). The scientific legacy of Sigmund Freud: Toward a psychodynamically informed psychological science. *Psychological Bulletin, 124,* 333–371.

Westergaard, Charles Gregory; Kuhn, Heather E.; & Suomi, Stephen J. (1998). Bipedal posture and hand preference in humans and other primates. *Journal of Comparative Psychology, 112*(1), 55–64.

Wethington, Elaine; McLeod, Jane D.; & Kessler, Ronald C. (1987). The importance of life events for explaining sex differences in psychological distress. In Rosalind C. Barnett, Lois Biener, & Grace K. Baruch (Eds.), *Gender and stress.* New York: Free Press.

Wheeler, Mark E., Petersen, Steven E., & Buckner, Randy L. (2000). Memory's echo: Vivid remembering reactivates sensory-specific cortex. *Proceedings of the National Academy of Sciences, USA, 97,* 11125–11129.

Wheeler, S. Christian, & Petty, Richard E. (2001). The effects of stereotype activation and behavior: A review of possible mechanisms. *Psychological Bulletin, 127*, 797–826.

Whisman, Mark A. (2001). Marital adjustment and outcome following treatments for depression. *Journal of Consulting and Clinical Psychology, 69*, 125–129.

White, Geoffrey M. (1994). Affecting culture: Emotion and morality in everyday life. In Shinobu Kitayama & Hazel Rose Markus (Eds.), *Emotion and culture: Empirical studies of mutual influence.* Washington, DC: American Psychological Association.

White, Lon; Katzman, Robert; & Losonczy, Katalin. (1994). Association of education with incidence of cognitive impairment in three established populations for epidemiologic studies of the elderly. *Journal of Clinical Epidemiology, 47*, 363–371.

White, Robert W. (1959). Motivation reconsidered: The concepts of competence. *Psychological Review, 66*, 297–333.

Whiten, Andrew; Custance, Deborah M.; Gomez, Juan-Carlos; Teixidor, Patricia; & Bard, Kim A. (1996). Imitative learning of artificial fruit processing in children (*Homo sapiens*) and chimpanzees (*Pan troglodytes*). *Journal of Comparative Psychology, 110*, 3–14.

Whitley, Bernard E., & Frieze, Irene H. (1985). Children's causal attributions for success and failure in achievement settings: A meta-analysis. *Journal of Educational Psychology, 77*, 608–616.

Whorf, Benjamin L. (1956). Science and linguistics. In J. B. Carroll (Ed.), *Language, thought, and reality: Selected papers of Benjamin Lee Whorf.* Cambridge, MA: MIT Press.

Whyte, Jamie, & Schaefer, Charles E. (1995). Introduction to sleep and its disorders. In Charles E. Schaefer (Ed.), *Clinical handbook of sleep disorders in children.* Northvale, NJ: Aronson.

Widiger, Thomas A., & Clark, Lee Anna. (2000). Toward DSM-V and the classification of psychopathology. *Psychological Bulletin, 126*, 946–963.

Widom, Cathy Spatz. (1999). Posttraumatic stress disorder in abused and neglected children grown up. *American Journal of Psychiatry, 156*, 1223–1229.

Wiggins, Jerry S. (1996). *The five-factor model of personality: Theoretical perspectives.* New York: Guilford Press.

Wilcoxon, Hardy C.; Dragoin, William B.; & Kral, Paul A. (1971). Illness-induced aversions in rat and quail: Relative salience of visual and gustatory cues. *Science, 171*, 826–828.

Wilfley, Denise E., & Rodin, Judith. (1995). Cultural influences on eating disorders. In Kelly D. Brownell & Christopher G. Fairburn (Eds.), *Eating disorders and obesity: A comprehensive handbook.* New York: Guilford Press.

Wilkinson, R. T. (1992). How fast should the night shift rotate? *Ergonomics, 35*, 1425–1446.

Williams, A. C., Jr. (1938). Perception of subliminal visual stimuli. *Journal of Psychology, 6*, 187–199.

Williams, Carolyn L., & Berry, John W. (1991). Primary prevention of acculturative stress among refugees. *American Psychologist, 46*, 632–641.

Williams, John E.; Satterwhite, Robert C.; & Best, Deborah L. (1999). Pancultural gender stereotypes revisited: The five factor model. *Sex Roles, 40*, 513–525.

Williams, Martin H. (1992). Exploitation and inference: Mapping the damage from therapist-patient sexual involvement. *American Psychologist, 47*, 412–421.

Williams, Robert L.; Gökcebay, Nilgün; Hirshkowitz, Max; & Moore, Constance A. (1994). Ontogeny of sleep. In Rosemary Cooper (Ed.), *Sleep.* New York: Chapman & Hall.

Wilson, G. Terence, & Fairburn, Christopher G. (1993). Cognitive treatments for eating disorders. *Journal of Consulting and Clinical Psychology, 61*, 261–269.

Wilson, Wayne. (1999). *The psychopath in film.* Lanham, MD: University Press of America.

Wimbush, James C., & Dalton, Dan R. (1997). Base rate for employee theft: Convergence of multiple methods. *Journal of Applied Psychology, 82*, 756–763.

Windholz, George. (1990). Pavlov and the Pavlovians in the laboratory. *Journal of the History of the Behavioral Sciences, 26*, 64–73.

Windle, Michael, & Windle, Rebecca C. (2001). Depressive symptoms and cigarette smoking among middle adolescents: Prospective associations and intrapersonal and interpersonal influences. *Journal of Consulting and Clinical Psychology, 69*, 215–226.

Winner, Ellen. (1997). Exceptionally high intelligence and schooling. *American Psychologist, 52*, 1070–1081.

Winner, Ellen. (1998, Winter). Uncommon talents: Gifted children, prodigies, and savants. *Scientific American Presents: Exploring Intelligence, 9*, 32–37.

Winokur, George; Coryell, William; Endicott, Jean; & Akiskal, Hapog. (1993). Further distinctions between manic-depressive illness (bipolar disorder) and primary depressive disorder (unipolar depression). *American Journal of Psychiatry, 150*, 1176–1181.

Winstead, Barbara A. (1986). Sex differences in same-sex friendships. In Valerian J. Derlega & Barbara A. Winstead (Eds.), *Friendship and social interaction.* New York: Springer-Verlag.

Wise, Roy A. (1996). Addictive drugs and brain stimulation reward. *Annual Review of Neuroscience, 19*, 319–340.

Witelson, Sandra F. (1985). The brain connection: The corpus callosum is larger in left-handers. *Science, 229*, 665–668.

Witelson, Sandra F.; Kigar, Debra L.; & Harvey, Thomas. (1999). The exceptional brain of Albert Einstein. *Lancet, 353*, 2149–2153.

Wohlschläger, Andreas, & Wohlschläger, Astrid. (1998). Mental and manual rotation. *Journal of Experimental Psychology: Human Perception and Performance, 24*, 397–412.

Wolpe, Joseph. (1958). *Psychotherapy by reciprocal inhibition.* Stanford, CA: Stanford University Press.

Wolpe, Joseph. (1982). *The practice of behavior therapy.* New York: Pergamon Press.

Wonderlic, E. F. (1998). *Wonderlic personnel test manual.* Libertyville, IL: Wonderlic & Associates.

Wood, David. (1988). *How children think and learn.* New York: Blackwell.

Wood, James M., & Bootzin, Richard R. (1990). The prevalence of nightmares and their independence from anxiety. *Journal of Abnormal Psychology, 99*(1), 64–68.

Wood, Robert, & Bandura, Albert. (1991). Social cognitive theory of organizational management. In Richard M. Steers & Lyman W. Porter (Eds.), *Motivation and work behavior.* New York: McGraw-Hill.

Woods, Stephen C.; Schwartz, Michael W.; Baskin, Denis G.; & Seeley, Randy J. (2000). Food intake and the regulation of body weight. *Annual Review of Psychology, 51*, 255–277.

Woodward, Amanda L.; Markman, Ellen M.; & Fitzsimmons, Colleen M. (1994). Rapid word learning in 13- and 18-month-olds. *Developmental Psychology, 30*, 553–566.

Woodworth, Robert S. (1918). *Dynamic psychology.* New York: Columbia University Press.

Woodworth, Robert S. (1921). *Psychology: A study of mental life.* New York: Holt.

Woody, Shelia R. (1996). Effects of focus of attention on anxiety levels and social performance of individuals with social phobia. *Journal of Abnormal Psychology, 105*, 61–69.

World Health Organization. (1998, June). *Global HIV/AIDS and STD surveillance: Report on the global HIV/AIDS epidemic: June, 1998.* <http://www.unaids.org/highband/document/epidemio/june98/global_report/index.html> (1999, February 16, 1999)

World Health Organization. (2001, February 6). *Nutrition data banks: Global database on Obesity and body mass index (BMI) in adults.* <http://www.who.int/nut/db_bmi.htm> (May 25, 2001)

Worrall, Russell S. (1986). Iridology: Diagnosis or delusion? In Kendrick Frazier (Ed.), *Science confronts the paranormal.* Buffalo, NY: Prometheus Books.

Wortman, Camille B.; Sheedy, Collette; Gluhoski, Vicki; & Kessler, Ron. (1992). Stress, coping, and health: Conceptual issues and directions for future research. In Howard S. Friedman (Ed.), *Hostility, coping, and health.* Washington, DC: American Psychological Association.

Wright, Kenneth P., Jr.; Hughes, Rod J.; Kronauer, Richard E.; Dijk, Derk-Jan; & Czeisler, Charles A. (2001). Intrinsic near-24-h pacemaker period determines limits of circadian entrainment to a weak synchronizer in humans. *Proceedings of the National Academy of Sciences, USA, 98,* 4027–14032.

Wu, Li-Tzy, & Anthony, James C. (1999). Tobacco smoking and depressed mood in late childhood and early adolescence. *American Journal of Public Health, 89,* 1837–1840.

Wundt, Wilhelm. (1874). *Grundzüge der physiologischen Psychologie* [Principles of physiological psychology] (5th ed.). Leipzig, Germany: Engelmann. (English version published by Macmillan, New York, 1904)

Wyatt, Holly R.; Grunwald, Gary K.; & others. (1999). Resting energy expenditure in reduce-obese subjects in the National Control Registry. *American Journal of Clinical Nutrition, 69,* 1189–1193.

Wyatt, Joseph W.; Posey, Anne; Welker, William; & Seamonds, Carla. (1984). Natural levels of similarities between identical twins and between unrelated people. *Skeptical Inquirer, 9,* 62–66.

Yapko, Michael D. (1994a). Suggestibility and repressed memories of abuse: A survey of psychotherapists' beliefs. *American Journal of Clinical Hypnosis, 36,* 163–171.

Yapko, Michael D. (1994b). *Suggestions of abuse: True and false memories of childhood sexual trauma.* New York: Simon & Schuster.

Yarnell, Phillip R., & Lynch, Steve. (1970, April 25). Retrograde memory immediately after concussion. *Lancet, 1,* 863–865.

Yeomans, Martin R.; Gray, Richard W.; Mitchell, Carole J.; & True, Sarah. (1997). Independent effects of palatability and within-meal pauses on intake and appetite ratings in human volunteers. *Appetite, 29,* 61–76.

Yonkers, Kimberly A.; Dyck, Ingrid R.; & Keller, Martin B. (2001). An eight-year longitudinal comparison of clinical course and characteristics of social phobia among men and women. *Psychiatric Services, 52,* 637–643.

York, Janine; Nicholson, Thomas; Minors, Patricia; & Duncan, David F. (1998). Stressful life events and loss of hair among adult women: A case-control study. *Psychological Reports, 82,*(3, Pt. 1), 1044–1046.

Youdim, Moussa B. H., & Riederer, Peter. (1997, January). Understanding Parkinson's disease. *Scientific American, 276,* 52–59.

Young, Michael W. (2000, March). The tick-tock of the biological clock. *Scientific American, 282*(3), 64–71.

Yu, Bolin; Zhang, W.; Jing, Qicheng; Peng, R.; Zhang, G.; & Simon, Herbert A. (1985). STM capacity for Chinese and English language materials. *Memory & Cognition, 13,* 202–207.

Yukl, Gary. (1989). Managerial leadership: A review of theory and research. *Journal of Management, 15,* 251–289.

Yukl, Gary; Guinan, P. J.; & Sottolano, D. (1995). Influence tactics used for different objectives with subordinates, peers, and superiors. *Group and Organization Management, 20,* 272–296.

Zajonc, Robert B. (1984). On the primacy of affect. *American Psychologist, 39,* 117–123.

Zajonc, Robert B. (1998). Emotions. In Daniel T. Gilbert, Susan T. Fiske, & Gardner Lindzey (Eds.), *Handbook of social psychology* (4th ed.). New York: McGraw-Hill.

Zammit, Gary K. (1997). Delayed sleep phase syndrome and related conditions. In Mark R. Pressman & William C. Orr (Eds.), *Understanding sleep: The evaluation and treatment of sleep disorders.* Washington, DC: American Psychological Association.

Zanarini, Mary C., & Frankenburg, Frances R. (1997). Pathways to the development of borderline personality disorder. *Journal of Personality Disorders, 11,* 93–104.

Zanarini, Mary C.; Williams, Amy A.; Lewis, Ruth E.; Reich, R. Bradford; Vera, Soledad C.; Marino, Margaret F.; & others. (1997). Reported pathological childhood experiences associated with the development of borderline personality disorder. *American Journal of Psychiatry, 154,* 1101–1106.

Zandstra, Elizabeth H.; de Graaf, Cees; & van Trijp, Hans C.M. (2000). Effects of variety and repeated in-home consumption on product acceptance. *Appetite, 35,* 113–119.

Zeki, Semir. (2001). Localization and globalization in conscious vision. *Annual Review of Neuroscience, 24,* 57–86.

Zgourides, George. (1996). *Human sexuality: Contemporary perspectives.* New York: Harper-Collins.

Zhou, Jing, & George, Jennifer M. (2001). When job satisfaction leads to creativity: Encouraging the expression of voice. *Academy of Management Journal, 44,* 682–696.

Zickler, Patrick. (2001, May). *National Institute of Drug Abuse (NIDA) Research reports: Annual survey finds increasing teen use of ecstasy, steroids.* (NIDA Notes, 16, No. 2). Retrieved January 14, 2002, from http://www.nida.nih.gov/NIDA_Notes/NNVol16N2/Annual.html

Zimbardo, Philip G. (1992). Foreword. In Stanley Milgram (Ed.), *The individual in a social world: Essays and experiments* (2nd ed.). New York: McGraw-Hill.

Zimbardo, Philip G., & Leippe, Michael R. (1991). *The psychology of attitude change and social influence.* New York: McGraw-Hill.

Zimbardo, Philip G.; Weisenberg, Matisyohu; Firestone, Ira; & Levy, Burton. (1965). Communicator effectiveness in producing public conformity and private attitude change. *Journal of Personality, 33,* 233–256.

Zimmerman, Mark; McDermut, Wilson; & Mattia, Jill I. (2001). Frequency of anxiety disorders in psychiatric outpatients with major depressive disorder. *American Journal of Psychiatry, 157,* 1337–1340.

Zimring, Fred M., & Raskin, Nathaniel J. (1992). Carl Rogers and client/person-centered therapy. In Donald K. Freedheim (Ed.), *History of psychotherapy: A century of change.* Washington, DC: American Psychological Association.

Zinbarg, Richard E.; Barlow, David H.; Brown, Timothy; & Hertz, Robert M. (1992). Cognitive-behavioral approaches to the nature and treatment of anxiety disorders. *Annual Review of Psychology, 43,* 235–267.

Zisook, Sidney, & Shuchter, Stephen R. (1993). Uncomplicated bereavement. *Journal of Clinical Psychiatry, 54,* 365–372.

Zola-Morgan, Stuart. (1995). Localization of brain function: The legacy of Franz Joseph Gall (1758–1828). *Annual Review of Neuroscience, 18,* 359–383.

Zola-Morgan, Stuart, & Squire, Larry R. (1993). Neuroanatomy of memory. *Annual Review of Neuroscience, 16,* 547–563.

Zoltoski, Rebecca K., & Gillin, J. Christian. (1994). The neurochemistry of sleep. In Rosemary Cooper (Ed.), *Sleep.* New York: Chapman & Hall.

Zuckerman, Marvin (1979). *Sensation seeking: Beyond the optimal level of arousal.* Hillsdale, NJ: Erlbaum.

Zuckerman, Marvin. (1994). *Behavioral expression and biosocial bases of sensation seeking.* New York: Cambridge University Press.

Zuckerman, Marvin; Kuhlman, D. Michael; Joireman, Jeffrey; Teta, Paul; & Kraft, Michael. (1993). A comparison of three structural models for personality: The Big Three, the Big Five, and the Alternative Five. *Journal of Personality and Social Psychology, 65,* 757–768.

Zusne, Leonard, & Jones, Warren H. (1989). *Anomalistic psychology: A study of magical thinking* (2nd ed.). Hillsdale, NJ: Erlbaum.

Zweig, Richard A., & Hinrichsen, Gregory A. (1993). Factors associated with suicide attempts by depressed older adults: A prospective study. *American Journal of Psychiatry, 150,* 1687–1692.

illustration credits

CHAPTER 1

2 Richard Hutchings/PhotoEdit **3** A. Glauberman/Photo Researchers **4** Corbis **5** (*top*) Archives of the History of American Psychology, The University of Akron; (*bottom*) Corbis **6** (*top*) Corbis; (*bottom*) Wellesley College Archives **7** (*top*) Archives of the History of American Psychology, The University of Akron; (*bottom*) Clark University **8** (*top*) Culver Pictures; (*center*) Corbis; (*bottom*) Archives of the History of American Psychology, The University of Akron **9** (*top*) Courtesy of Carl Rogers Memorial Library; (*bottom*) Courtesy of Brandeis University **10** Charles Gupton/Stock Boston **11** Neville Elder/Corbis Sygma **13** Figaro Magahn/Photo Researchers **14** (*left*) Keren Su/Corbis; (*right*) Paul Souders/Corbis **15** (*top*) Tom and Deann McCarthy/The Stock Market; (*bottom*) Ralf-Finn Hestoff/Saba Press Images **16** John Neubauer/PhotoEdit/PictureQuest **18** Scott T. Baxter/PhotoDisc **22** Mark Stouffer/Animals Animals **26** (*top*) Telegraph Colour Library/FPG; (*bottom left*) Paul Almasy/Corbis; (*bottom right*) Jeremy Horner/Corbis **29** Rockstar Games **31** Courtesy of Dr. Craig Anderson, Department of Psychology, Iowa State University **32** National Aeronautics and Space Administration **36** Beate Rettberg-Beck

CHAPTER 2

44 Ted Kawalerski/The Image Bank **46** CNRI/Science Source/Photo Researchers **50** Courtesy Tim Murphy and Gil Wier, The University of British Columbia **53** (*top*) John Chiasson/The Gamma-Liaison Network; (*bottom*) AP/Wide World Photos **55** Biophoto Associates/Science Source/Photo Researchers **57** Frank Siteman/Stock Boston **62** Geoff Tompkinson/SPL/Photo Researchers **63** Reprinted with permission of S. Witelson, D. Kigar, T. Harvey, and *The Lancet,* June 19, 1999. **64** (*top right*) Hulton Getty/Liaison Agency; (*bottom*) M. James Nichols & William T. Newsome (1999, December 2). "The neurobiology of cognition." *Nature,* vol. 402, no. 6761 **65** (*top*) Richard Nowitz/Photo Researchers; (*bottom*) Nestle/Petit Format/Science Source/Photo Researchers **66** (*left*) Hank Morgan/Science Source/Photo Researchers; (*center*) Scott Camazine/Science Source/Photo Researchers; (*right*) *The American Journal of Psychiatry,* 155:8, 1009–1015, 1998. Copyright © 1998 the American Psychiatric Association **67** M. E. Raichle, Mallinckrodt Institute of Radiology, Washington University School of Medicine **68** Courtesy of Fred H. Gage, The Salk Institute, San Diego **72** Martin M. Rotker **74** Damasio, H., Grabowski, T., Frank, R., Galaburda, A. M., & Damasio, A. R. The return of Phineas Gage: Clues about the brain from the skull of a famous patient, *Science,* 264:1102–1105, 1994. **77** Courtesy of Terence Williams, University of Iowa **80** (*top*) Courtesy of the California Institute of Technology; (*bottom*) Dan McCoy/Rainbow **83** Bryn Alan **84** Courtesy T. A. Jones and W. T. Greenough **85** Barlettani-Sestini/The Gamma-Liaison Network

CHAPTER 3

90 Paul Conklin/Monkmeyer **93** AFP/Corbis **95** John Downer/Planet Earth Pictures **97** Lennart Nilsson/Bonnier Alba AB/*Behold Man*; Little, Brown & Company **100** NIMH/NIH **101** Patrick Collins/Monkmeyer **105** Lennart Nilsson/Bonnier Alba AB/*Behold Man*; Little, Brown &

Company **107** © 2002 Joseph Scafuro **108** Lennart Nilsson/Bonnier Alba AB/*Behold Man*; Little, Brown & Company **109** Roy Botterell/FPG **110** Science Source/Photo Researchers **112** W. Hill, Jr./The Image Works **116** (*top*) Courtesy of the authors; (*bottom*) Bettmann/Corbis **118** (*top*) © 1996 M. C. Escher/Cordon Art-Baarn-Holland. All rights reserved; (*bottom*) PhotoDisc **120** (*left*) Mike Caldwell/Tony Stone Images; (*center*) Superstock; (*right*) Steve McGurry/Magnum Photos **121** © Hiroshi Kunoh. Originally published in *3-D Planet,* Cadence Books, San Francisco. Reprinted by permission. **122** (*top*) Julie Houck/Stock Boston; (*bottom*) AP/Wide World Photos **123** Globus Brothers Studios/The Stock Market **124** Joel Meyerowitz **126** (*top left*) Sol Mednick; (*top right*) Sol Mednick; (*bottom*) Shay Stevens Photography **127** (*top*) From *Mind Sights* by Shepard. © 1990 by Roger N. Shepard. Used with permission of W. H. Freeman and Company. **128** Michael A. Dwyer/Stock Boston **129** (*top*) Dick Ruhl; (*bottom*) NASA/JPL/Malin Space Science Systems

CHAPTER 4

136 The Granger Collection **137** Colin Molyneux/The Image Bank **138** Robert Bennett/FPG **139** Scott S. Campbell, Cornell University Medical College, Laboratory of Human Chronobiology **140** (*top*) Barbara Alper/Stock Boston; (*bottom*) PhotoDisc **142** Hank Morgan/Rainbow **144** Estate of Ted Spagna **147** Lennart Nilsson/Bonnier Alba AB, *A Child Is Born,* Dell Publishing Company **148** Courtesy of Gould, Evans, Goodman Associates L.C. **149** Michio Hoshino/Minden Pictures **151** Carmen Tylor/AP **153** Joel Deutsch/Slim Films **154** (*top*) Robert Landau/Corbis; (*bottom left*) Courtesy of Dr. Allen R. Braun, Language Section, National Institute on Deafness and other Communication Disorders, NIH; (*bottom right*) Courtesy of Dr. Allen R. Braun, Language Section, National Institute on Deafness and other Communication Disorders, NIH **158** Courtesy of J. Allan Hobson **161** Kyoko Hamada **162** (*top*) Courtesy of the late Earnest Hilgard, Photo News and Publications Service, Stanford University; (*bottom*) Paul Avis/The Gamma-Liaison Network **164** Courtesy of Stephen Kosslyn, Ph.D., and William L. Thompson, Department of Psychology, Harvard University **166** (*left*) © Allison Wright/Stock Boston; (*right*) Andres Hernandez/The Gamma-Liaison Network **167** Andrew Newberg, Hospital at the University of Pennsylvania **169, 170** AP/Wide World Photos **172** Reuters/Charles Platiau/Archive Photos **173** Bob Daemmrich/Stock Boston **174** Corbis **175** Greg Meadors/Stock Boston **176** (*top*) The Granger Collection; (*bottom*) Brookhaven National Laboratories **177** Kal Muller/Woodfin Camp & Associates **178** Dr. Liesbeth Reneman, Academisch Medisch Centrum, Universiteit van Amsterdam, Amsterdam, Netherlands

CHAPTER 5

187 Kerbs/Monkmeyer **188** Stock Montage **190** (*top*) Sovfoto: (*bottom*) Michael Newman/PhotoEdit **192, 194** Archives of the History of American Psychology, The University of Akron **195** (*left*) Duke University, Special Collections Library; (*right*) Gaslight Advertising Archives **198** Courtesy of Shepard Siegel **199** (*top left*) Faye Norman/Science Photo Library/Photo Researchers; (*bottom*) Damian Dovarganes/AP Photo **200** Courtesy Robert A. Rescorla/University of Pennsylvania **201** Darren Bennett/Animals Animals **202** Courtesy of John Garcia **203** (*left*) Victoria McCormick/Animals Animals; (*right*) Joe McDonald/Animals Animals **204** Stuart Ellins, California State University **205** Courtesy of Columbia University **206** Yale University Library **207** Bettmann/Corbis **209** (*top*) Ed Malitsky/The Gamma-Liaison Network; (*bottom*) Matthew Stockman/Allsport **211** Courtesy of Morten

Kringelbach and Edmund T. Rolls/Department of Experimental Psychology, University of Oxford **215** TimePix **217** (*top*) Nina Leen, LIFE Magazine © Time Warner, Inc.; (*bottom*) Courtesy of the authors **218** Corbis **220** L. Marescot/The Gamma-Liaison Network **222** Archives of the History of American Psychology, The University of Akron **224** Ed Zurga/AP Photo **225** Robert and Marion Bailey/Animal Behavior Enterprises **227** (*top*) Courtesy of Albert Bandura; (*bottom*) Courtesy of Albert Bandura, Stanford University

CHAPTER 6

238 PBJ Pictures/The Gamma-Liaison Network **240** Wernher Krutein/The Gamma-Liaison Network **242** Travis Morisse/The Hutchinson News **246** Carol Halebeian/The Gamma-Liaison Network **247** A. Ramey/Stock Boston **252** Doug Pensinger/Allsport **254** Bob Schatz/The Gamma-Liaison Network **255** (*top*) Courtesy of the authors; (*bottom*) Brewer, W. F., and Treyens, J. C. (1981). Role of schemata in memory for place. *Cognitive Psychology,* 23, Figure 1, pp. 207–230. **258** Corbis **259** (*top*) Robbie McClaran; (*bottom*) Sylvie Chappaz/Vandy Stadt/Allsport **260** Corbis **266** Archives of the History of American Psychology, The University of Akron **267** Courtesy of Richard F. Thompson **268** Courtesy of Mark E. Wheeler, Randy L. Buckner, and Steven E. Petersen **269** (*top*) © Karen Kuehn/Matrix International; (*bottom*) Michael Colicos, UCSD **271** Jonathan Daniel/Allsport

CHAPTER 7

281 Willem Harinck/Holt Studios International/Photo Researchers **282** Courtesy of Kathleen O'Craven, Rotman Research Institute **283** (*center*) Merlin Tuttle/Photo Researchers; (*bottom*) Flip Nicklin/Minden Pictures **289** Beth A. Kaiser, Pool/AP Photo **292** Michael Newman/PhotoEdit **295** (*top*) Frans Lanting/Minden Pictures; (*bottom*) Photo by Anne Clopet, courtesy of Language Research Center, Georgia State University **296** Michael Goldman **297, 298** Archives of the History of American Psychology, The University of Akron **299** News Service, Stanford University **300** Laura Dwight/PhotoEdit **302, 303** Archives of the History of American Psychology, The University of Akron **304** (*left*) John Blaustein/The Gamma-Liaison Network; (*center*) Michael Tackett/Corbis; (*right*) Reuters NewMedia/Corbis **306** Mary Kate Denny/PhotoEdit **308** Robert A. Isaacs/Photo Researchers **310** Tom Wagner/Saba Press Images **311** Alexandra Avakian/Contact Press Images **312** Garry Conner/PhotoEdit **314** Jerry Cleveland/Denver Post

CHAPTER 8

320 Brandi Stafford **322** Peter Glass/Monkmeyer **324** (*top*) Tom Sanders/Adventure Photo & Film; (*bottom*) Harlow Primate Laboratory, University of Wisconsin **325** Natalie Behring/Reuters/Archive Photos **328** Don Mason/The Stock Market **329** Remi Banali/Liason **333** George D. Lepp/Corbis **335** Courtesy of Dr. Gene-Jack Wang, Brookhaven National Laboratory **336** Jill Greenberg © 1996 The Walt Disney Co. Reprinted by permission of *Discover* Magazine **339** Courtesy of Brandeis University **341** Agence France-Presse/Corbis **342** Worth Publishers **343** Reuters NewMedia/Corbis **344** Tony Freeman/PhotoEdit **345** (*top*) RNT Productions/Corbis; (*bottom*) From Charles Darwin, *The Expression of the Emotions in Man and Animals,* Definitive Edition. Paul Ekman (ed.). New York: Oxford University Press, 1998. **347** Catherine Karnow/Corbis **348** Deborah Cannon/AP Photo **349** Courtesy of Dr. Lawrence A. Farwell, Brain Wave Science **351** Courtesy of Antonio R. Damasio, Department of Neurology and PET Imaging Center, University of Iowa College of Medicine **352** (*top*) Louis Schakel/Michael Kausman/The New York Times Pictures; (*bottom*) From Eibl-Eibesfeldt, I. (1970). *Ethology: The Biology of Behavior.* New York: Holt. Photo courtesy of I. Eibl-Eibesfeldt **353** (*top*) From Matsumoto, D., & Ekman, P. (1989) Japanese and Caucasian facial expressions of emotion. *JACFEE.* Photographs courtesy of Paul Ekman; (*bottom*) Courtesy of Dacher Keltner, Department of Psychology, University of California, Berkeley **354** (*left*) Michael Dick/Animals Animals; (*right*) Alan and Sandy Carey **355** Art Wolfe/Photo Researchers **356** Corbis **358** Joel Gordon **359** Nancy Richmond/The Image Works

CHAPTER 9

369 (*top left*) Nancy Sheehan/PhotoEdit; (*top right*) D. Young-Wolf/PhotoEdit; (*bottom left*) Bill Lai/Index Stock Imagery; (*bottom right*) M. Ferguson/PhotoEdit **370** CNRI/Science Photo Library/Photo Researchers **372** Biophoto Associates/Photo Researchers **373** Petit Format/Nestle/Science Source/Photo Researchers **374** (*left*) Elizabeth Crews/The Image Works; (*right*) Petit Format/Science Source/Photo Researchers **375, 376** Courtesy of the authors **378** John Lei/Stock Boston **379** Stephen Agricola/ The Image Works **380** Romilly Lockyer/The Image Bank **382** Bill Anderson/Photo Researchers **383** Elizabeth Crews/The Image Works **384** (*top*) Laura Dwight; (*bottom*) Bill Armstrong **385** Mug Shots/The Stock Market **386** Courtesy of Renee Baillargeon, University of Illinois at Urbana-Champaign **387** Sovfoto/Eastfoto **388** Courtesy of Philip Seeman, M.D., Ph.D., Department of Pharmacology, University of Toronto **389** Bob Daemmrich/Stock Boston **390** Gary Connor/PhotoEdit **391** Sarah Putnam/The Picture Cube/Index Stock **396** David Young-Wolff/PhotoEdit **398** Michael Newman/PhotoEdit **399** Michelle Bridwell/PhotoEdit **400** Jonathan Nourok/PhotoEdit **401** Joel Gordon

CHAPTER 10

411 Jose L. Pelaez/The Stock Market **412** David Young-Wolff/PhotoEdit 12 (*top*) Jerry Koontz/The Picture Cube/Index Stock; (*bottom*) Bob Daemmrich/The Image Works **416** © 1995 Newsweek, Inc. All rights reserved. Reprinted with permission. Photo by Douglas Levere. **418** Myrleen Ferguson/PhotoEdit **419** (*left*) Tony Freeman/PhotoEdit; (*right*) Myrleen Ferguson/PhotoEdit **421** (*top*) Tom McCarthy/The Picture Cube/Index Stock; (*bottom*) From *Good Night, Sleep Tight! Shh . . .* by Gyo Fujikawa. Copyright © 1990 by Gyo Fujikawa. Reprinted by permission of Random House Inc. **423** (*top*) Jonathan Novak/PhotoEdit; (*bottom*) Jon Chiasson/The Gamma-Liaison Network **425** Frans Lanting/Minden Pictures **428** Burke Uzzle **429** Deborah Davis/PhotoEdit **434** Frank Wartenburg/Corbis/The Picture Press **435** (*left*) Tony Anderson/FPG; (*right*) A. Bartels and S. Zeki, University College London. Originally published in *NeuroReport,* Neural basis of romantic love, vol. 11, no. 17, pages 3829–3834 (2000) **436** Sotographs/The Gamma-Liaison Network **437** (*top*) Dennis Degnan/Corbis; (*bottom*) Pam Francis/The Gamma-Liaison Network **438** © Treë **442** © Loren Cameron, photograph originally published in *Body Alchemy;* Cleis Press, 1996. Reprinted by permission of Cleis Press. **443** AP/Wide World Photos

CHAPTER 11

452 Courtesy of Don Hockenbury **453** Steve Chenn/Corbis **454** Mary Evans/Sigmund Freud Copyrights/Photo Researchers **455** (*top*) Culver Pictures; (*bottom*) Corbis **457** Tony Freeman/PhotoEdit **458** Michael Newman/PhotoEdit **459** Eric Futran/The Gamma-Liaison Network **462** Paul Gish/Monkmeyer **464** Karsh/Woodfin Camp & Associates **465** (*top*) Photofest; (*bottom left*) Courtesy of Department of Library Services, American Museum of Natural History. Photo by P. Hollembeak; (*bottom right*) Courtesy of Dharma Publishing **466** (*top*) Corbis; (*bottom*) Corbis **467** TimePix **469** Corbis **470** Courtesy of Carl Rogers Memorial Library **471** Jean Michel Turpin/The Gamma-Liaison Network **472** Russell D. Curtis/Photo Researchers **474** Courtesy of Albert Bandura, Stanford University **475** Jean Hangarter/The Picture Cube/Index Stock **476** Corbis **478** Courtesy of Mary Cattell **480** Courtesy of Dr. Turhan Canali, Stanford University **481** Courtesy of Don Hockenbury **482** Myrleen Ferguson/PhotoEdit **483** Mike Derer/AP **486, 488** Lew Merrim/Monkmeyer

CHAPTER 12

499 Tony Freeman/PhotoEdit **500** © Alan Carey/The Image Works **501** (*top*) Chicago Tribune Photo; (*bottom*) Photofest **502** (*left*) Knut Kampe, University College London; (*right*) Knut Kampe, University College London **503** Anchorage Daily News/The Gamma-Liaison Network **509** Paul Warner/AP **510** Dean Dunson/Corbis **513, 514** From Sherif, M., Harvey, O. J., White, B. J., Hood, W. R., & Sherif, C. W. (1961/1988). *The Robbers Cave Experiment: Intergroup Conflict and Cooperation.* Middletown, CT: Wesleyan University Press. **517** David Young-Wolff/

PhotoEdit   **518** Courtesy of CUNY Graduate School and University Center   **519** (*top*) From the film *Obedience,* distributed by the New York University Film Library; (*bottom*) Courtesy of Alexandra Milgram   **523** From the film *Obedience,* distributed by the New York University Film Library   **524** (*top*) Corbis; (*bottom*) Adam Butler/AP Photo   **525** (*top*) The New York Times Pictures; (*bottom*) Edward Hausner/The New York Times Pictures   **526** (*top*) Skjold/The Image Works; (*bottom*) Dunn/Monkmeyer   **527** Michael Newman/PhotoEdit   **529** L. Kolvoord/The Image Works   **530** Hangarter/The Picture Cube/Index Stock   **531** Michael Grecco/Stock Boston

CHAPTER 13

538 (*top left and right*) Carmen Tylor/AP; (*bottom*) Paul Hawthorne/AP   **539** (*top*) Mario Tama/Getty Images; (*bottom*) Ed Bailey/AP   **540** Myrleen Ferguson/PhotoEdit   **542** (*top*) Tony Freeman/PhotoEdit; (*bottom*) Courtesy of Richard S. Lazarus/University of California, Berkeley   **543** (*top*) Billy E. Barnes/Stock Boston; (*bottom*) Bebeto Matthews/AP   **545** Steve Liss/The Gamma-Liaison Network   **546** Tina Fineberg/AP   **547** Edgar Fahs Smith Collection, University of Pennsylvania Library   **548** (*top*) © 1974 John Olson/People Weekly; (*bottom left and right*) Petrovic, P., Kalso, E., Petersson, K. M., and Ingvar, M. Placebo and opioid analgesia—Imaging shared neuronal network. *Science*, 295, 1737–1740.   **549** Omikron/Science Source/Photo Researchers   **550** (*left*) Courtesy of Robert Ader, photo by James Montanus, University of Rochester; (*right*) Courtesy of Nicholas Cohen, University of Rochester   **551** (*top*) Courtesy of Janice Kiecolt-Glaser, Ohio State University College of Medicine; (*bottom*) Gary A. Connor/PhotoEdit   **553** Shaul Schwarz/Getty Images   **554** David Lassman/Syracuse Newspapers/The Image Works   **556** Robert Brenner/PhotoEdit   **559** © Macduff Everton/The Image Works   **560** (*top*) Jim Vecchione/The Gamma-Liaison Network; (*bottom*) Joe Carini/The Image Works   **561** Tony Freeman/PhotoEdit   **562** © 2002 The New Yorker Collection from cartoon bank.com. All Rights Reserved.   **562** Lester Sloan/The Gamma-Liaison Network   **563** Joel Gordon   **565** (*top*) Marko Shark/Corbis; (*bottom*) Joshua Griffler   **567** Piers Cavendish/Zuma Press

CHAPTER 14

574 Photofest   **575** Reprinted with permission from *Diagnostic and Statistical Manual of Mental Disorders,* Fourth Edition, Text Revision. Copyright © 2000 by the American Psychiatric Association.   **576** Billy Barnes/PhotoEdit   **579** Treë   **581** Bernard Wolf/Monkmeyer   **582** (*top*) John Kaprielian/Photo Researchers; (*bottom*) Seth Resnick   **583** Suzanne

Plunkett/AP   **585** © 1996, American Medical Association from *Archives of General Psychiatry,* February 1996, Vol. 53. Courtesy of Jeffrey M. Schwartz.   **587** Eric Fenblatt/Sigma   **588** Corbis/S.I.N.   **589** The Everett Collection   **590** Courtesy of Dr. Lew Baxter and Dr. Michael Phelps, University of California, Los Angeles   **591** (*left and center*) Corbis; (*right*) Robert Capa/Magnum Photos   **592** Jeff Greenberg/PhotoEdit   **593** Courtesy of Dr. Elliot A. Stein, Department of Psychiatry, Medical College of Wisconsin   **597** AP/Wide World Photos   **599** © K. McGlynn/The Image Works   **602** Courtesy of Mental Health Clinical Research Center, University of Iowa   **603** Courtesy of David Silbersweig, M.D., Emily Stern, M.D., Cornell Medical Center   **604** (*top*) A. Ramey/PhotoEdit; (*bottom*) Barbara Alper/Stock Boston   **607** Courtesy of Dr. Wade Berrettini, Center for Neurobiology and Behavior, University of Pennsylvania School of Medicine   **609** Joe McNally/National Geographic Society Image Collection   **610** Courtesy of Dr. Paul Thompson, Department of Neurology, UCLA Lab of Neuro-Imaging & Brain Mapping Division   **613** Joel Gordon

CHAPTER 15

621 Bruce Ayres/Tony Stone Images   **622** Culver Pictures   **624** AP   **626** Michael Rougier, LIFE Magazine Inc.   **627** Richard Nowitz/Photo Researchers   **628** Innervisions   **630** Larson/Watson Papers, Archives of the History of American Psychology, The University of Akron   **631** Françoise Sauze/Science Photo Library/Photo Researchers   **632** Bob Mahoney/The Image Works   **633** Courtesy of Wayne Simpson/Simtek, Inc.   **636** Courtesy of Albert Ellis   **638** Courtesy of Aaron T. Beck, University of Pennsylvania Medical Center   **642** Hank Morgan/Science Source/Photo Researchers   **643** (*top*) F. Pedrick/The Image Works; (*bottom*) Michael Newman/PhotoEdit   **646** Worth Publishers   **648** Michael Newman/PhotoEdit   **649** Steve Liss/The Gamma-Liaison Network   **651 top** (*top left*) The Granger Collection; (*bottom left*) Corbis; (*right*) Culver Pictures   **651 bottom** Woodson, R. E., Jr., Youngken, H. W., Schlittler, E., and Schneider, J. A. (eds.). (1957). *Rauwolfia; Botany, Pharmacognosy, Chemistry and Pharmacology.* Boston: Little, Brown. Reprinted with permission.   **654** Corbis   **656** (*top*) Courtesy of Arthur Brody, M.D., UCLA; (*bottom*) Jonathan Nourok/Stone   **657** James Wilson/Woodfin Camp & Associates

APPENDIX B

B-2 Ralf Finn-Hestoft Saba   **B-8** James Schnepf/The Gamma-Liaison Network   **B-10** Forrest Anderson/The Gamma-Liaison Network   **B-12** Pictor International/PictureQuest